Library of
Davidson College

FROM
IMPERIUM TO *AUCTORITAS*

DEDICATED
TO
MY WIFE

FROM
IMPERIUM TO *AUCTORITAS*

A HISTORICAL STUDY OF
AES COINAGE IN THE ROMAN EMPIRE
49 B.C.—A.D. 14

by

MICHAEL GRANT

CAMBRIDGE
AT THE UNIVERSITY PRESS
1946
REPRINTED
1969

Published by the Syndics of the Cambridge University Press
Bentley House, 200 Euston Road, London N.W. 1
American Branch: 32 East 57th Street, New York, N.Y. 10022

PUBLISHER'S NOTE

Cambridge University Press Library Editions are re-issues of out-of-print standard works from the Cambridge catalogue. The texts are unrevised and, apart from minor corrections, reproduce the latest published edition.

Standard Book Number: 521 07457 6

First published 1946
Reprinted with corrections 1969

First printed in Great Britain at the University Press, Cambridge
Reprinted in Great Britain by John Dickens & Co. Ltd, Northampton

CONTENTS

PREFACE — PAGE ix
ADDENDA AND CORRIGENDA — xiii

PART I. THE OFFICIAL COINAGES

INTRODUCTION — 1

CHAPTER 1. Coinage by *imperium maius*, 49–28 B.C. — 3
  A. The Caesarians — 4
  B. The Pompeians — 20
  C. The Republicans — 33
  D. The Triumvirs — 37
  E. Octavian as sole ruler — 66

CHAPTER 2. Coinage by *auctoritas principis*, 27 B.C.—A.D. 14 — 80
  A. The transition: 27–23 B.C. — 80
  B. The need for reform — 85
  C. The bases of the reform — 91
  D. Provincial issues by *legati Augusti* — 119
  E. Provincial issues by equestrian governors — 131
  F. Provincial issues by 'senatorial' governors — 134

PART II. THE ROMAN CITIES

INTRODUCTION — 147

CHAPTER 1. The Roman *municipia* — 149

CHAPTER 2. The Roman colonies — 205

CHAPTER 3. The Roman cities and the State — 290
  A. The foundation coinages — 290
  B. The contribution to the Imperial monetary system — 295
  C. Colonisation policies of Julius and Augustus — 302
  D. Bureaucratic policy concerning the Roman cities — 308
  E. Administrative interference by provincial officials — 314
  F. Relation of the cities to Augustus — 317

PART III. THE PEREGRINE COMMUNITIES

INTRODUCTION PAGE 327

CHAPTER 1. The communities and the *princeps* 328

A. Augustus on posthumous coinages 328
B. Augustus as *constitutor* of Latin cities 335
C. Augustus as *liberator* of 'free' communities 338
D. Augustus as *constitutor* of 'stipendiary' communities 346
E. Augustus as κτίστης and θεὸς ἐπιφανής 356
F. Augustus as heir to the Hellenistic monarchs 368
G. Augustus as ἀρχιερεύς 376

CHAPTER 2. The communities and the Roman officials 379

A. Heads of officials on the coinages 379
B. Names of officials on the coinages 390
C. *Libertas* and *civitas* 401

PART IV. *IMPERIUM* AND *AUCTORITAS*

INTRODUCTION 407

CHAPTER 1. Rule by *imperium maius*, 49–28 B.C. 408

A. The revolutionary title of *Imperator*: earliest official documents 408
B. The *imperium maius* on which the title of *Imperator* was based 411

CHAPTER 2. Rule by *auctoritas principis*, 27 B.C.—A.D. 14 424

A. Abolition of government by *imperium* in 27 B.C. 424
B. Eclipse of the title *Imperator* from 27 B.C. 440
C. *Auctoritas* 443
D. The vehicle of *auctoritas*: *tribunicia potestas* 446

APPENDICES

1. Summary of the official *aes* coinages, 49–28 B.C. 455
2. Summary of the official *aes* coinages, 27 B.C.—A.D. 14 457
3. Proposed additions and alterations to lists of provincial governors 458

CONTENTS

		PAGE
4.	Summary of foundation coinages	459
5.	Proposed additions and alterations to lists of Roman foundations	461
6.	Proposed additions and alterations to lists of peregrine foundations	462
7.	Posthumous local issues with heads of Augustus	463
8.	Asian local issues with contemporary heads of Augustus	467
9.	Asian local issues of the principate of Augustus portraying members of his family	471
10.	The 'autonomous' series	472
11.	Art	477

ABBREVIATIONS	480
SOURCES	483
KEY TO SPECTROGRAMS	493
KEY TO MONOGRAMS AND LIGATURES	494
INDICES	495
KEY TO PLATES	509
PAGE REFERENCES FOR PLATES	511
PLATES	513

PREFACE

THIS book has two interdependent aims. The first is the correct attribution of the aes[1] coinage between 49 B.C. and A.D. 14—comprising the periods of *imperium* and *auctoritas*[2]—of all Roman officials and cities, and of those peregrine communities throughout the Empire whose money bears or implies a reference to Roman institutions.[3] The second aim is the reconsideration of the historical problems in the light of this evidence.

My subject-matter includes more than a thousand separate issues, which can be divided into approximately 340 series. It would seem that not more than 76 of these series have hitherto been correctly attributed and defined;[4] at least 120 major varieties have not even been published or catalogued. The first of the aims stated above may be justified by these statistics, although its complete fulfilment is much more than I could claim. Three peculiar features of the *aes* issues of this period enhance greatly the normal difficulties of classical research: the coins are usually of extreme rarity,[5] faultily executed, and in execrable preservation. The photographic Plates, in which preference has been given to coins previously unknown or not reproduced, illustrate only too clearly these disadvantages, which will, I hope, partially serve as my apology for the inadequacies of this book. Another obstacle has been the almost complete lack of information concerning the alloys of which the coins are composed, in spite of the vital importance, in the official currency at least, of their determination. This deficiency has been due to the expense, labour and rarity of chemical analyses. It has here been possible to make use of an analytical method not (as far as I can discover) hitherto applied to coins, effected by the spectrograph (pp. xii, 493).

The historical enquiry depending on the numismatic attributions perhaps needs no justification. But remarkably enough, no attempt has hitherto been made to collate for any one period the bulk of information to be derived from these coinages.[6]

---

[1] This word is used, as in the British Museum Catalogues, as a 'portmanteau' description for *orichalcum*, bronze and copper coins. These present contrasts to the gold and silver in many fields.

[2] The reasons for choosing 49 B.C. as a starting-point for the transitional epoch are given below, p. 412. Syme, *RR*. p. 374, rightly says that the year A.D. 14 'marks the legal termination of the Republic'.

[3] The Client Kingdoms have not been included, since they were not within the *limes*, and their institutions were irrelevant to the problems of provincial administration: cf. Sands, *The Client Princes of the Roman Empire*, Stevenson, *RPA*. pp. 36 ff.

[4] A correct attribution of a series may be held to be achieved when the date and place of all its component issues are determined as closely as possible, and when their scope and source are demonstrated to be identical.

[5] Milne, *JRS*. xxvi, 1936, p. 109, calculates that even of an important official issue of provincial origin (at Alexandria under Tiberius) only about 0·0625% survives. For the backwardness of current knowledge of coin-circulation cf. Rostovtzeff, *Anatolian Studies to Buckler* (1939), p. 277.

[6] Nicodemi, *Milan cat.* pp. xvi f., points out the advantage of this method.

PREFACE

They form a remarkable collection of contemporary, authoritative and variegated material. The *aes* issues of the followers of Caesar, the last Republicans, and Augustus are peculiarly rich in allusions of constitutional, administrative, and prosopographical significance: many (though by no means all) of these are intentional, since the ancients were not unsusceptible to numismatic propaganda.[1] In the hands of Caesar and his successors, coinage in *aes* was revived, in forms as novel and as mutable as almost all other institutions of the same epoch. It was a period of unparalleled evolution and transition. Yet, by an unfortunate contrast, the literary and epigraphic evidence hardly supplies even the framework for a reconstruction, as the existence of so many diametrically opposed views emphasises. Hence this attempt to supplement it by the material provided by the *aes* currencies. The information which they supply has led me to venture upon a new approach to the constitutional problems. In particular, it has appeared to me to necessitate the complete elimination of the supposed *imperium maius* of Augustus from 27 B.C. onwards, and so to warrant the title of this book. The dominant constitutional theme is the contrast between the military administration from 49 to 28 B.C. and the civilian government thereafter; recent research has removed many obstacles to the appreciation of the latter, but the coins alone reveal its principal executive activity. I hope that doubts regarding some of my conclusions, of whose controversial character I am aware, will not lead readers to disbelieve that in the hands of others, of greater experience than myself, the coins can yield important constitutional results.

A brief explanation of the arrangement of my material may be desirable. In dealing with 'Roman' *aes*, it has unfortunately not been customary to distinguish thoroughly between governmental and official series on the one hand, and on the other the currencies of cities throughout the Empire; the latter, in their turn, have not always been observed to fall naturally into two groups, comprising the issues of the citizen and non-citizen communities. Since the distinction between these three classes is essential to any historical investigation, one Part of this book is allotted to each of them. Parts I, II and III are thus concerned respectively with the coinages of Roman government officials,[2] of Roman cities, and of peregrine cities; the attribution of each series is accompanied by a discussion of its particular historical significance. Finally, in Part IV an effort is made to see the constitutional problems in the new light which the foregoing evidence has thrown upon them. Its first chapter is devoted to the *régime* of *imperium maius* which paralysed the Republic from 49 to 28 B.C., and its second to the system which followed it, based on the powers comprehended by the word *auctoritas*.

Responsibility is assumed by the writer for all numismatic attributions and historical deductions of which the sources are not acknowledged in the text and notes.

[1] Cf. Mattingly, *CAH*. XII, p. 716; Miss Toynbee, *JRS*. XXIX, 1939, p. 119, points out that there is no reason for Miss Newby's astonishment (p. xvi) at finding correspondences between coin-types and themes of the *Res Gestae*.

[2] Described henceforward as 'official coinages'.

PREFACE

But I have been very fortunate in my helpers. I hereby record, although an enumeration cannot adequately express it, my deepest gratitude to the following: Professor F. E. Adcock, for reading parts of the book and giving me on numerous occasions the benefit of his learning and judgment; Dr C. Bosch, for putting at my disposal his numismatic card-index of Asia Minor; the Rev. M. P. Charlesworth, for advice after studying the typescript; Professor P. W. Duff, for comments on points of Roman Law; Mr G. M. Fitzgerald, for reference to a find; Mr A. S. F. Gow, for several philological rulings; the late Mr E. Harrison, for many corrections and improvements; Mr R. P. Hinks, for iconographical assistance; Mr A. H. M. Jones, for fruitful discussions, and the loan, in typescript, of his book *The Greek Cities from Alexander to Justinian*; Mr H. Mattingly, for fifteen years of inspiration and help—the cause of my interest in the subject; Dr J. G. Milne, for answering several queries; Professor D. S. Robertson, for a number of helpful comments; Mr E. S. G. Robinson, for the continual and invaluable advantage of his experience and advice; Mr I. N. Scott-Kilvert, for the elucidation of my argument at many points; Mr A. N. Sherwin-White and Mr C. H. V. Sutherland, for allowing me to read the proofs of their books, *The Roman Citizenship* and *The Romans in Spain* respectively; the Rev. E. A. Sydenham, for sending me unpublished notes on official mints; Mr R. Syme, for introducing me to new aspects of history by his guidance and by the loan, in proof, of his book *The Roman Revolution*; Miss J. M. C. Toynbee, for putting at my disposal her lists of medallic issues and a privately published catalogue; Professor A. D. Trendall, for several contributions to my study of Paestum; and my father and mother, for indispensable assistance of many kinds.

I must acknowledge with many thanks the use of material from the following coin-collections, made accessible to me either personally, or by letter—and in both cases I am deeply indebted to directors and staffs for their invariable kindness—or through the medium of publications: Alcacer do Sal, Amman, Amsterdam University (Allard Pierson Stichting), Antakya (Committee for Excavation), Aquileia, Athens, Augsburg, Avignon, Basel, Beirut American College, Belgrade University, Berkeley (California University), Berlin, Berne, Besançon, Béziers, Bingen, Bolzano, Bonn, Brussels, Bucharest, Bucharest University, Budapest, Bursa, Cadiz, Cagliari, Cambridge University, Cambridge (Corpus Christi College, Lewis Collection), Canterbury, Catania University, Cefalù, Châtillon, Chester, Chur, Cologne, Constantine, Copenhagen, Copenhagen (Thorvaldsen Museum), Danzig Gymnasium, Donaueschingen, Dresden, Ehingen, el Escorial, Florence, Glasgow University (Hunterian Collection), Graz, Hague, Hague (Museum Meermanno-Westreenianum), Hamburg, Hanau, Hanover, Heidelberg University, Hofheim, Istanbul, Jerusalem, Karlsruhe, Klagenfurt, Kolin, Landshut, Leiden, Leiden University, Leipzig, Leningrad, Lewes, Lisbon, Lisbon University, London (British Museum), Luxembourg, Lyon, Madrid, Madrid (Instituto de Valencia de Don Juan), Magdeburg, Mainz, Mantua, Marseilles, Milan, Modena, Montivilliers, Moscow, Mulhouse, Munich,

PREFACE

Namur, Naples, Narbonne, Nemi, New York (American Numismatic Society), Nicosia, Nijmegen, Nîmes, Odessa, Oporto, Orange, Oxford University, Oxford (Christ Church), Palermo, Paris, Parma, Pesaro, Philadelphia University, Prague, Ptuj, Pujol, Ravenna, Rennes, Riedlingen, Rome (Museo Nazionale), Rome (Museo Capitolino), Rottweil, Saalburg, S. Bertrand de Comminges, St Florian, Saint Germain-en-Laye, Schotten Stift, Skoplje, Sofia, Stockholm, Strasbourg, Stuttgart, Tarragona, Tartù, Tomar, Tübingen University, Tunis (Bado), Turin, Utrecht, the Vatican, Vienna, Vienna (Römisches Museum), Vienna University, Vienne, Winchester, Winterthur, Xanten, Yale University, Zagreb, Zürich [see also Addenda].

I want, too, to express my thanks to the following private collectors who have generously shown me their coins: Signor A. Castoldi, Mr N. G. L. Hammond, Hauptmann L. Hollschek, Dr L. A. Lawrence, Mr R. C. Lockett, Monsieur A. Nier, Jonkheer F. Scharp. Professor T. O. Mabbott and the late Professor E. T. Newell kindly sent me descriptions of coins in their possession. I must also record the use of other private collections, past and present: MM. Adda, Arendt, Baeth, Berlichingen, Braun, Brenner, Caballero Infante, Carelli, Cavierzel, Coliez, Delagarde, Fischer, Gago, Garnier, Glanville, Guyon, Hall, Hengen, Hönisch, Hoffmann, Körperich, Kotschoubey, Landolina-Paterno, Louis, Mavromichalis, Michahelles, Grand Duke Mihailovitch, Odescalchi, Comte du Palin, Baron Pennisi di Floristella, Peter, Philbert, Prowe, Pujol y Santo, Quadras y Ramon, Rauch, Rothelin, Rubio, Sanahuja, Sanchez de la Cotera, Graf Schenk von Stauffenberg, Schreiber, Seripopoli, de Sousa Vilhena, Count Stroganoff, Urbano, Count Uwaroff, Vilá, Welter, and an unnamed collector in Minas de S. Domingos. Reference to other collections has been possible through sale-catalogues, and I am grateful to the dealers who produced these catalogues and who have given me a kind welcome.

I have a profound obligation to the Director of the British Non-Ferrous Metal Research Association, and to Mr D. M. Smith of its Research Department, for carrying out for me a large number of spectrographic analyses; also to the Chiswick Press for the difficult photographic undertaking represented by the Plates.

Finally, I owe a great debt of gratitude to the Syndics of the Cambridge University Press for accepting this work; and to the Master and Fellows of Trinity College, Cambridge, for a generous grant from the Rouse Ball Fund towards the cost of publication.

I had completed the manuscript of the book by July 1939; the postponement of its publication has been largely due to my subsequent lack of time for proof reading.

ANKARA, 1945   MICHAEL GRANT

NOTE ON THE C.U.P.L.E. REPRINT

In addition to a number of corrections, this reprint incorporates (on page 511) a list of page references to the plates. This was compiled by the late Dr Karl Pink and published in the *Numismatische Zeitschrift*, 1946-7, p. 138. It is included here by the kind permission of the Austrian Numismatic Society.

GATTAIOLA, 1969   MICHAEL GRANT

ADDENDA & CORRIGENDA

Under this heading will be grouped a few conclusions and observations reached as a result of the latest publications and (particularly) of the writer's recent travels in and near Anatolia. Lists of the numerous recent coin-finds in this area, and of relevant 1940–1945 publications (the bibliography on p. 486 only goes up to 1939), will not be set out here, since only those will be quoted which actually amplify, confirm or correct facts or views described in this book.

p. xi. Add Gotha to acknowledgments.

p. 15 n. 8. The attribution of the Q. coinage to this area is corroborated by the discovery of yet another specimen in Istanbul—five years later (own collection).

p. 22 n. 5. These comments regarding the Pompeian *asses* are underlined by the discovery of an isolated specimen of Cnaeus as far East as Lycaonia (Konya museum—found locally).

p. 45 l. 9, n. 2. Two specimens of the issue of Bibulus have also been found near Nicosia (acquired by the writer there). This evidence, added to the other, makes it advisable at least to keep open the possibility that Bibulus continued to coin after his return to the East.

p. 67 (cf. p. 383). An important contemporary parallel to Proculeius is provided by a certain C. Baebius T. f. Clu. tr. mi[l. leg. x]x. praef. ora[e marit. Hi]span. citer[ioris b]ello Actiens[i] (Barbieri, *Rivista di filologia*, 1942, p. 274, cf. Henzen, *Bull. Corr. Arch.* 1874, p. 119). For a similar title six years earlier, see p. 46. It would be interesting to know the official relationship between Baebius and C. Calvisius Sabinus (p. 160).

p. 85 n. 3. Under the Republic the maximum occurrence of zinc is actually about 4 % (Forbes, *Jaarboek van het Vooraziatisch-Egyptisch Gezelschap Ex Oriente Lux*, VIII, 1942, p. 753). Forbes, ibid., points out that, in spite of its high value under Caesar, *orichalcum* actually gained in value vis-à-vis copper during the Empire (p. 88 n. 8).

p. 92. The statistics of circulation given here and elsewhere (e.g. pp. 71, 101, 105, 116, etc.) do not of course prove that all the circulation in question occurred as early as the principate of Augustus. There is, on the other hand, a general presumption that a not inconsiderable proportion of circulation evidence regarding coins minted during any single period applies to the decades immediately following the date of mintage. A study of countermarks (e.g. those described on p. 94) may be considered to provide evidence corroborating this presumption. Those stamps are all of post-Augustan date, and it seems legitimate to suppose that, until they were affixed, the coinage circulated without let or hindrance. In the light of the inherent improbability that *all* of the extensive circulation statistics are post-Augustan, the opposite conclusion from the date of the countermarks—namely that the coins were not even introduced into the various provinces until they were thus stamped—seems less plausible.

pp. 97 f. Last, *JRS*. 1940, p. 201, ibid. 1944, pp. 51 ff., shows that the informal origins of the central *fiscus* date from Augustus. But the *aerarium* was still the sole official treasury. Sutherland, *AJP*. 1945, pp. 159 ff., 169, ascribes important developments regarding the *fiscus* to Tiberius.

ADDENDA AND CORRIGENDA

pp. 98 ff. *Eastern SC coinages*. The attribution of II (p. 99) to Cyprus (already certain by analogy) is confirmed by the occurrence of two examples at Nicosia (one acquired by the writer, and one in Nicosia museum—the former of considerable size and weight, but on this see p. 101). Additional specimens of IV (pp. 99 f.) have been found at or near Beirut (acquired by the writer), Adana (ditto), Antakya (Antakya museum—a very thick coin), and Ağlasun (Sagalassus in Pisidia—collection of Commander George C. Miles, U.S.N.R.): these finds do not contradict the assumption of Syrian origin, though they raise an alternative possibility of S.E. Anatolian mintage. Knowledge of the circulation of VIII (pp. 100 f.) is likewise enlarged by the discovery of examples in Mesopotamia (Urfa—in private collection at Aydın), Syria (acquired by writer, found at or near Antakya), and perhaps Pontus (specimen acquired by writer, believed to have been found at Samsun).

p. 102 n. 7: perhaps Gabala also (Seyrig, *Syria*, xx, 1939, pp. 39 ff.). A new group IX should perhaps be recorded, to include a specimen of un-Syrian (? Cilician) style in Antakya museum.

pp. 102 ff. *CA and AVGVSTVS coinages*. Possibly two or three additional mints should be added here: (i) it is tempting to add a Phrygian one, characterised by particularly thick flans, an unusual feature common to all three of the specimens in this category in Afyonkarahisar museum, found locally (two CA *sestertii* and one AVGVSTVS *as*); (ii) Nicosia museum contains a small CA coin with obverse inscription CAISAR (cf. p. 107), differing in style from other CA issues including the known Cypriot group (p. 106), and therefore suggesting a *second* Cyprus mint. If this exists, the two mints are likely to be Salamis and Paphos. Furthermore a *dupondius* of so-called 'European' group 'B' (p. 107) was apparently found near the latter city (Nicosia museum), and perhaps suggests the reallotment of part of this subdivision to Cyprus. (iii) Large thin pieces with very broad heads, in Adana and Antakya museums, indicate the possibility of a Cilician (?) mint.

Circulation statistics of the principal 'Asian' groups can now be added to as follows: Lydia (AVGVSTVS *as*, p. 105 n. 4, at Aydın—in private collection there), Lycaonia (CA *dupondius* near Konya—Konya museum), Cilicia (CA *dupondius* near Adana, acquired there by the writer; and AVGVSTVS *asses* at Adana—Adana museum; Antakya—writer's collection, found locally, of both "A" and "B" types; and Maraş—Ankara museum). It is probable that, as further material comes to light, various additional ramifications will appear. The two Afyonkarahisar *sestertii* mentioned above differ from each other in portraiture though not in style. This diversity appears to be a special feature of CA *sestertii* and not, in this particular case, to indicate difference of mint.

p. 111 n. 16. The presence of the central mint of the 'colonist' coins in Mysia-Troas is further indicated by the appearance of very large numbers of them, at all times, among finds brought to Istanbul. N. 20: also found in Cilicia (Tiberius at Adana—in Adana museum).

pp. 139 f. Another proconsul of Africa, shortly before or after Passienus, can now be identified in L. Caninius L. f. Gallus (Fahrmann, *AA*. 1940, pp. 551 f.).

pp. 154 ff. Henderson, *JRS*. 1942, p. 7, doubts whether Caesar gave any charter to Emporiae, whereas she considers Romula (p. 220) to be a *colonia* of Caesar restored by Augustus; she includes Sexi and Obulco (p. 473, nn. 5, 9) among Augustan *municipia*.

ADDENDA AND CORRIGENDA

p. 165. The writer now feels that the association of the bull type with T. Statilius Taurus by a *jeu de mots* is, though not impossible, rather a long shot.

p. 180 n. 12. On the alternative *lex Antonia de coloniis deducendis* (cf. pp. 246, 274) see Berger, *PW. Suppl.* VII, 416.

pp. 194 ff. (and pp. 235 ff.). Kahrstedt, *Klio*, N.F. XVII, 1942, p. 255, seems to over-simplify in concentrating Augustan enfranchisement in Sicily at two dates only, to which he assigns six and nine (?) charters respectively.

p. 215 n. 9 (cf. p. 212 n. 3). Cf. L. Porcius *III vir IIIIvir augur* on an Ilici inscription (*CIL.* II. *Suppl.* 5950).

p. 236. This coin must be attributed to Dyme in Achaia (p. 264 no. 2).

p. 244 n. 16. One was probably found in Cilicia (Adana museum): but so too was an equally rare contemporary coin of another north Anatolian city—see Addendum to p. 255.

p. 250. If Ramsay, *The Social Basis of Roman Power in Asia Minor*, p. 184, is right in ascribing a (re)foundation of Lystra to Cornutus Arruntius Aquila *legatus Augusti* in 6 B.C., then the continued use of the epithet *Iulia*—without *Augusta* yet, cf. Pl. VIII, 11—presumably bears witness to the influence of C. Caesar (cf. pp. 259 f., 239 n. 7). But the coin, though later than 6 B.C., commemorates the jubilee of the *first* foundation.

p. 255 (2) (n. 7). See Addendum to p. 244, above. The presence together of these two at Adana museum strongly suggests some special cause irrelevant to mintage.

p. 269 n. 4 (cf. p. 402 n. 3). 'Cistophoric' tetradachms of Augustus circulated equally widely, at least in the East: the writer has noted finds in Ionia (near Izmir—Commander George C. Miles's collection), Phrygia (Afyonkarahisar museum), Lydia (private collection at Aydın), Lycaonia (*BMC. Imp. Aug.* 691—see p. 424 n. 4—at Cihanbeyli, in private possession there; and another near Konya—seen in trade there), Pisidia (at Egridir—belonging to the local Kaimakam) and Melitene (near Malatya—Commander G. C. Miles's collection).

pp. 298 f. n. 22. Further finds of post-Augustan colonial pieces of Antioch in Pisidia have been noted near Antalya (Antalya museum), at Konya, Ankara and in N.W. Anatolia (own collection), at Adana (Adana museum), and at Ilgin and Niğde (Konya museum). Similar evidence could be collected of other colonies in Asia minor, etc.

p. 301. The citizen, as opposed to his city, probably still contributed rather than profited (cf. pp. 203, 367).

p. 312 n. 1. But no birth-certificates as early as Augustus are extant (Schulz, *JRS.* 1942, pp. 78 ff.).

p. 350 n. 6. Friedrich, *PW.* XX, 1, 828, appears to consider Fulvia as a separate foundation from Eumenia.

p. 361 (cf. pp. 75, 463 ff.). Further light is thrown by Schweitzer, *Röm. Mitt.* LVII, 1942, p. 97 (Dresden cameo), on the Claudian date of portraits hitherto considered as Augustan.

p. 401 n. 8. Phrygian Apamea may perhaps be added to the list of appreciable contributors: its Augustan coinage figures very largely in finds from that region (many in Afyonkarahisar museum).

p. 414. It is probable that most coinage of colonies and *municipia* before 27 B.C. emanated from this *imperium* (cf. pp. 10, 34, 274; but see p. 317 nn. 7, 8).

ADDENDA AND CORRIGENDA

p. 415 n. 1. On these preliminary steps see Last, *JRS*. 1945, p. 125, who also points out that Salmon, *History of the Roman World* (1944), p. 5, misleads by calling the *praenomen* 'permanent from c. 30 B.C.' (cf. p. 417 n. 11).

p. 417. Staedler, *Sav.Z.* 1942, p. 118, considers that the principate can be said to have started in 32 B.C. Kornemann, *Römische Geschichte*, II (1939), pp. 121 ff., stresses the autocratic character of the ensuing five years, *pace* Kolbe, *Klio*, 1943, p. 43.

p. 426 n. 1. The *provincia* could surely be confirmed with each new consulship, *pace* Salmon, l.c. p. 339, though it had been allotted for a longer period (p. 434; see Last, *JRS*. 1943, p. 104). Siber, *Abh. Leipzig*, XLIV, 2, 1940, still adhered to his reluctance to describe Augustus's *imperium* in either sort of province as 'proconsular', cf. Schwartz, *Revue de philologie*, 1945, p. 40, *pace* Wickert, *Klio*, N.F. XVI, 1942, p. 144. Siber's avoidance of the description 'proconsular' applies to the period after 23 B.C. also (*Sav.Z.* 1944, pp. 261 ff., cf. *Abh. Leipzig*, l.c. pp. 38 ff.).

p. 426 n. 9 (cf. pp. 452 f. n. 5). Staedler, *Sav.Z.* 1943, pp. 384 ff., restates with variations the theory of the legalised *auctoritas*, which is rejected by Strack, *Die alten Sprachen*, 1939, pp. 197 ff., Müller-Graupa, *Phil. Woch.* 1940, p. 93 n. 2, and again by Siber, *Abh. Leipzig*, 1940, p. 78, and Kübler, *Sav. Z.* 1940, p. 325.

p. 429 n. 12. Germanicus may not have received the *imperium* until 14 (Kroll, *PW*. X, 438, cf. Schwartz, l.c. p. 37 n. 1).

p. 431 n. 9. Wenger, *Sav. Z.* 1942, p. 428, sums up *Die Tatsache bleibt dass Augustus auch in Kyrene regierte*; Visscher, *Recueil des Travaux d'Histoire et de Philologie de l'Université de Louvain*, 1940, pp. 38 ff., Last, *JRS*. 1945, p. 93, pronounce for *imperium* as the basis. These three writers discuss the significance of *dico* (p. 432 n. 12).

p. 433 n. 14. The rudimentary *fiscus* however (see addendum to pp. 97 f.) was Augustus' property (Eliachevitch, *La Personnalité Juridique en Droit Privé Romain* [1942], cf. Kaden, *Sav. Z.* 1944, p. 442 n. 23), rather than a product of his *auctoritas* (as Bolla, *Die Entwicklung des Fiscus zum Privatsrechtssubject* [1939], p. 38).

p. 434 n. 4. Together with 27 and 23 B.C., Kornemann, *Römische Geschichte*, II (1939), p. 129, rightly considers 12 and 2 B.C. to be the decisive dates in the foundation of the principate.

p. 437 n. 1. Last, *JRS*. 1943, p. 104, still rejects Dio LIII, 32, 5.

p. 442 n. 8. Mention should have been made here (and on p. 91) of the inauguration of official Roman *aes* by the type of Numa Pompilius (*BMC. Imp.* p. 28, *NZ*. 1919, pp. 105 f.). Did a 'Numa period' follow the 'Romulus period' (on which see p. 424 and Borzsák, *Archivium Philologicum*, 1943, pp. 180 f.)?

p. 444. Instinsky, *Hermes*, 1942, p. 346, follows the erroneous view that *pater patriae* was a 'title of magistracy', cf. Staedler, *Sav. Z.* 1941, pp. 88 ff., 101 ff., 105, 119, for *princeps* and *Augustus*, of which he detects a conferment as *cognomen* in 19 B.C. or a little before (p. 120).

p. 449 n. 3. *Ius auxilii* and *intercessio* are still considered the essential features of the *tribunicia potestas* by Țopa, *Ephemeris Dacoromana*, 1940, p. 173, Kornemann, *Gestalten und Reiche* (1943), p. 465.

ADDENDA AND CORRIGENDA

p. 453, line 6. This reference to a 'committee' does not sufficiently stress Tiberius' chairmanship of it, cf. p. 430 above, Kornemann, *Grosse Frauen des Altertums* (1942), pp. 199 ff., id., *Gestalten und Reiche*, pp. 157 ff., etc. Volkmann, *Bursians Jahresberichte*, 276, 1942, pp. 78 ff., rightly criticises Staedler's view (*Sav. Z.* 1942, pp. 84 ff., cf. 1944, p. 368) of a formal *eiuratio* by Augustus accompanied by the publication of the *Res Gestae*.

p. 458. Groag, *PIR.*² III (1943), 15. 72, adds A. Didius Postumus to the *Fasti* of Cyprus (soon after 22 B.C.).

pp. 463 ff. (cf. pp. 75, 328 ff.). Appendix 7 comprises uninscribed portraits that have been attributed to Augustus as well as those inscribed as ΣΕΒΑΣΤΟΣ etc. Their classifications according to principates are necessarily very approximate and only intended as a general guide. But recent publications, including those of Poulsen, *Kongelige Danske Videnskabernes Selskab, Archaeologisk-Kunsthistorisk Middelelser*, II, 5, 1939, Goethert, *Röm. Mitt.* 1939, pp. 176 ff., Curtius, ibid. 1940, pp. 36 ff., Toynbee, *JRS.* 1941, pp. 188 f., Sutherland, *NC.* 1941, pp. 97 ff., Schweitzer, *Klio*, 1941, pp. 328 ff., id. *Röm. Mitt.* 1942, pp. 92 ff., Hohl, *Klio*, 1942, pp. 227 ff., 1943, p. 144, etc., seem to leave these classifications more or less unaffected.

p. 463 (1). A coin of Mallus (Berlin = Wellenheim 6213; another acquired by the writer at Adana) has the reverse of the piece here attributed to Caligula's principate (p. 464 n. 20, pl. XII, 18), but a head facing left with the features of Tiberius.

p. 476. Other possible additions are, in Asia, Midaeum (coin in private collection at Aydın) and Synnada (own collection, found near Konya); and, in Syria-Cilicia, Magydus (Antalya museum).

Pl. II, 8. The reverse of this coin is inadvertently represented sideways.

Part I
THE OFFICIAL COINAGES

INTRODUCTION

THE pieces whose significance is discussed in this Part are those struck in *aes* by the representatives of the Roman *res publica*, that is, by the officials who acted, or claimed to act, on its behalf. The differentiation of these series from local issues does not usually cause great difficulty, since most city-currencies bear the name, if not of their town, at least of one or more of its representatives or institutions. Except on a few insignificant local coins which are too small to show any of these signs, their absence entitles us to postulate official authority.[1]

The two Chapters which follow attempt a survey of these official issues and an estimation of the historical importance of each. The historical turning-point is the year 27 B.C., when *auctoritas principis* superseded *imperium* as the origin of coinage. Statistics reveal the remarkable extent to which even these official issues have been neglected. There are about 93 mint-groups, of which 39 are of the period treated by the *British Museum Catalogue of Republican Coins*, and the remaining 54 are in the sphere of its *Imperial* counterpart; yet the former of these publications only recognises the character of 17 out of the 39 groups—and, in the present writer's opinion, describes only three of them correctly—while the masterly *Imperial Catalogue* is permitted to rescue only about 10 groups (under five general headings) from the less appropriate catalogues of

---

[1] There are, however, some cases where the distinction is not clear. The following special conditions are considered to justify inclusion in the present Part. (1) The signature of a colonial founder from Rome, when the scope of his activity, and of his coinage, embraces more than one foundation; (2) The conjunction of an ethnic with the name of a Roman official, when (*a*) it can be established that the latter is mentioned as a responsible authority rather than by courtesy, (*b*) there is evidence of extended circulation, indicating that the ethnic is merely the mint-mark on an official issue; (3) The conditions of (2 *b*) are occasionally fulfilled when no name of an official, but only a mint-mark, appears. On the other hand, certain classes must be eliminated for addition to other categories. (1) Local coins whose only ethnic is in the form of a *type parlant* or local era; (2) Issues by small Asiatic, Gallic and Spanish tribes whose status is merely a substitute for municipal organisations; (3) Coinage in the name of Cleopatra or her children in the territories which nominally belonged to them, unless the name of a Roman provincial official indicates that no transference had in fact taken place.

Greek coins. Other works recognise the official character of 33 additional groups, of which, if all the contributions of heterogeneous and scattered publications be collected, no more than 17 have been even once correctly attributed. Thus, of the 93 discoverable groups, only 25 appear to have received acceptable interpretations, and these have been sporadic and often remote. As many as 36 different pieces appear to be unpublished. Yet this was the currency, not of local communities, but of the Roman government itself: it provides direct and official evidence, to an extent which mere statistics cannot reveal, for the administration and constitution of the Empire during this vital evolutionary period.

The coinages before and after 27 B.C. are summarised in Appendices 1 and 2 respectively.

Chapter 1

COINAGE BY *IMPERIUM MAIUS*, 49–28 B.C.

At the time of Caesar's dictatorship the Roman *aes* had not yet recovered from the crises which had caused its suppression in the eighties.[1] Official coinage in this medium only survived at Panormus, where quaestors issued a long series of quartuncial *asses* (p. 26). In the fifties, or thereabouts, a few pieces were struck by Roman magistrates in Crete[2] and Sicily (at Lilybaeum [p. 26], Agrigentum [p. 28], Syracuse[3]); at the end of the decade[4] A. Hirtius signs an issue in the country of the Treveri (Pl. IX, 25).[5] With the possible exception of the last, whose denomination is uncertain, these were fiduciary currency,[6] which was possible in Hellenised provinces since the principle had long been familiar to the Greek world.[7] But no attempt was made to introduce token coinage into Italy: as Mattingly says,[8] 'bimetallism was at last breaking down, but rather than avow the abandonment of the use of bronze as a true value-money, the Romans preferred to suspend its issue and to shelve the problem'.

[1] Cf. Mattingly, *RC.* p. 26; Lenormant, *La monnaie dans l'antiquité*, II, p. 204.
[2] Robinson, *BMC. Cyrenaica*, p. 131. 1, cf. pp. ccxi f.: types of head of Minerva and bee. These coins may possibly be as early as the sixties.
[3] Holm III, p. 707. 557.
[4] *BMCR.* I, p. 526; Babelon, *Monnaies de la République romaine*, I, p. 343; Blanchet, *Traité*, p. 427. The Roman name and type, and the lack of any ethnic or sign of local authority, make it necessary to assume that this was an official issue (*pace* Babelon, l.c.), though tribal imitations exist (cf. Babelon, l.c.). The word CARIN, which he finds on one of these and seeks to identify with C. Carrinas—cf. Blanchet, l.c. p. 356—is merely a blundered retrograde version of HIRTIVS (cf. Kremer, *Publications de la section des sciences historiques de l'Institut Grand-ducal de Luxembourg*, LXVII, 1938, p. 19. For variations of the same error vide Blanchet, l.c. p. 122). Hirtius was in Gaul (where these are found; vide next note) in 54–52, 51–50 and 45–44 B.C. (Münzer, *PW.* VIII, 1956 f.): since the types are imitated from (rather than prototypes of) official denarii, probably Gallic of 50–49 B.C., the issue may with the greatest probability be ascribed to 50, *pace* Maxe-Werly, *Rb.* 1888, p. 435. It is distinct from later tribal issues with the name of Hirtius (p. 391).
[5] Grueber, *BMCR.* I, p. 526; Lenormant, l.c. II, p. 315; Blanchet, l.c. p. 383; Kremer, l.c., show that Treveran provenance is most frequent: there are many at Trier mus., Luxembourg mus., and at local colls. of MM. Erpelding, Ehlinger, Brenner, Henger, Louis, Coliez, Philbert, Körperich, Arendt, Welter, Garnier, and Differd. Maxe-Werly, *État actuel de la numismatique rémoise*, p. 11, cites other but less extensive finds from the territory of the Remi. Decisive is the fact that Caesar's headquarters were transferred to Treveran territory in spring 50 (*BG.* VIII, 52).
[6] Cf. Milne, *The Development of Roman Coinage*, p. 21, for the quartuncial standard.
[7] Cf. Segrè, *Metrologia e circolazione degli antichi*, p. 251; Burns, *Money and Monetary Policy in Ancient Times*, pp. 288 f.
[8] *RC.* p. 28.

A. THE CAESARIANS

Under the *imperium maius* of Caesar there were several curious and sporadic attempts to revive this coinage. Of the four issues which can be identified, one is entirely unpublished, and the remainder have been gravely misunderstood. By way of introduction it may be pointed out that the issue under Caesar's Gallic command in Treveran territory in 50 had been made and signed, not by a military personage, but by Caesar's own private secretary, A. Hirtius.[1] As dictator also, as will be seen, the former did not hesitate to entrust coinage, like other functions, to unconstitutional *praefecti*.

1. CORDUBA

The earliest Caesarian issue under the dictatorship consists of bronze[2] pieces with the head of Venus, and the legend CN. IVLI. L. F. Q. On the reverse is a figure of Cupid with *cornucopiae* and *caduceus*; in the field, with three pellets, is CORDVBA[3] (Pl. I, 1), or CORDVBA BAL.[4] The conjunction of the names of Roman official and of township does not cause a real difficulty here. The city-name 'Corduba' was never used after the establishment of *colonia Patricia*. This colony was founded not earlier than 48,[5] but a later date than 45 is incompatible with its title; it must, therefore, have been carried out during the Pompeian occupation of c. 46–45.[6] To this conclusion the absence of the epithet *Iulia* is particularly appropriate.[7] Caesar punished the city severely,[8] but the survival of the title *Patricia* without addition indicates that he neither degraded nor refounded it. Exactly parallel is the retention by Salacia of the

---

[1] Strack, *BJ*. CXVIII, 1909, p. 190, notes that he held no military commission in Gaul, and rightly interprets his post as the directorship of Caesar's administrative bureau: Münzer, *PW*. VIII, 1957, plausibly suggests that he succeeded Pompeius Trogus, killed at Atuatuca, whose office is described by Justin (XLIII, 12) as *epistularumque ac legationum, simul et anuli cura*. Hirtius was high in Caesar's favour (Cic. *Att*. VII, 4. 2, etc.), but was not yet of praetorian rank (Münzer, l.c.). The coins bear no title, and his duties were not those of a quaestor.

[2] Spectrogram 54. Copper, lead and tin were all available locally: cf. Davies, *Roman Mines in Europe*, pp. 114, 115, 103 ff. respectively.

[3] BM, Madrid, Instituto de Valencia de Don Juan (variants). Delgado I, p. 125. 1; Vives III, p. 115; cf. Hübner, *PW*. IV, 1221.

[4] Instituto de Valencia de Don Juan, from Sanchez de la Cotera collection: Hübner, *MLI*. p. 112, no. 124 n.; Vives III, p. 115. 4. This coin unfortunately remained inaccessible to me (cf. pp. 145, 178 f., 192 n. 2, 208, etc.). Although Vives's photograph (pl. CXVIII, 4) is too dim for the reading to be confirmed, it can hardly be supposed that he and Hübner invented it. At least the photograph shows that the piece is genuine.

[5] Cf. Hübner, *CIL*. II, p. 306, correcting erroneous beliefs of an earlier colony (Hübner, *La Arqueología de España*, p. 176; Taberner, *QAS*. XVIII, 1939, p. 16).

[6] Cf. Blok, *Sextus Pompeius Magnus Gnaei Filius*, Diss. Leyden, 1879, p. 7; Hübner, *PW*. IV, 1222.

[7] Cf. Kornemann, *PW*. IV, 527. 82.

[8] Cf. Frank, *ES*. I, p. 317; Meyer, *Cäsars Monarchie*, p. 485.

title given it by Sextus, *Imperatoria* (p. 409). Octavian likewise was to refrain from interfering with the *patrocinium* of his enemy Antony at Bononia.[1]

This issue, then, must be prior to the date of colonisation, when Corduba was a peregrine town containing a *vicus* of Roman citizens.[2] But the types of Venus and Cupid indicate a connection with the dictator,[3] and so a date not earlier than 49. This conclusion is in accordance with the appearance on the coins of a relative of his, Cn. Julius L.f. No doubt this was a son of L. Julius Caesar—who was *legatus* to his distinguished relative in Gaul[4]—and so a younger brother of the other Lucius who declared for Pompey;[5] the noble families often resorted to such schisms in order to play for safety.[6] Cn. Julius L.f. can scarcely be the local Q(*uinquennalis*) of peregrine Corduba:[7] his connections and all available analogies refer him to a Roman provincial quaestorship.[8] Probably he succeeded M. Marcellus Aeserninus[9] in Farther Spain in c. 47, and was the quaestor either of Q. Fabius Maximus[10] or of Q. Trebonius.[11]

The coinage is therefore official in character, and the ethnic does not represent the source of issue, but is merely a mint-mark. Exact parallels to such usage are afforded, during this period, by official issues—in *aes* with VRSONE, PANOR., ΛΙΛ., ZA(κυνθος) and IΘΑΚ(η) (pp. 24, 26, 26, 39, 66), and in silver with SAL (p. 22), OSCA,[12] and EMERITA (p. 119). By the analogy of VRSONE it is quite possible that CORDVBA is also an Ablative. The circulation of such currency, in *aes* and silver alike, was not limited to the towns where they were struck. As a provincial quaestor signing this coinage, Cn. Julius follows the regular monetary tradition of the Republic,[13] which appears to have been maintained as late as c. 36–35 B.C. (p. 53).

It remains to attempt an explanation of the abbreviation BAL. Now it was customary for quaestors to mention on some or all of their coinage a superior authority, either in their province or at home. The former of these alternatives does not provide a suitable interpretation, since no known governor of Hispania Ulterior during this period had a name beginning BAL;[14] and, although the dates of some of these are controversial,[15] there is not room for any fresh importation into the Fasti. The other

---

[1] Suet. *Aug.* 17. 2; cf. Levi II, p. 181. But vide also Dio L, 6. 3.
[2] Cf. Hübner, *PW.* IV, 1221; Sutherland, *RIS.* p. 117.
[3] Eckhel, *DN.* I, p. 18; Syme, *RR.* p. 66 n. 3.
[4] Münzer, *PW.* X, 469 (143).
[5] Ibid. 471 (144); Syme, *RR.* pp. 64 n. 3, 192.
[6] Cf. Syme, *RR.* p. 64.
[7] As Delgado I, pp. 128 f.
[8] As Florez, *ap.* Delgado, l.c.; Bülz, *De Provinciarum Romanarum Quaestoribus*, Diss. Leipzig, 1893, p. 14.
[9] Cf. Dio XLII, 15; Bülz, l.c. p. 12.
[10] As Wilsdorf, *Fasti Hispaniarum provinciarum*, Diss. Leipzig, 1878, p. 131.
[11] As Letz, *Die Provinzialverwaltung Cäsars*, Diss. Strassburg, 1912, p. 31.
[12] *BMCR.* II, p. 373. 109.
[13] E.g. *BMCR.* II, p. 355. 32 (L. Fabius Hispaniensis), p. 356. 35 (C. Tarquitius), p. 463. 16 (A. Manlius); Babelon, *Monnaies de la république romaine*, I, p. 408. 32 (Q.), etc.
[14] The identification by Florez with L. Cornelius Balbus *minor* is unacceptable, since he did not arrive in Spain until c. 45 B.C. and was not even quaestor until 44/3 (Groag, *PW.* IV, 1269; Syme, *RR.* p. 80).
[15] Cf. Wilsdorf, Letz, Bülz, ll.cc.

possibility is exemplified by quaestorian issues reading L. TORQVA. Q. EX S. C.,[1] M. SERGIVS SILVS Q. EX S. C.,[2] CN. LEN. Q. EX S. C.[3] But the senatorial formula could scarcely be expected during the years 49–45, for the excellent reason that no State affairs of any kind were entrusted to the senate by the absent dictator. Caesar claimed that his offer to that body of a share in the government[4] had been rejected,[5] and entrusted all business to his two personal representatives[6]—with no rank in the government[7]—whose influence on provincial officials was precisely that previously maintained by the senate. The foremost of these two men[8] was the knight or ex-knight[9] L. Cornelius Balbus *maior*:[10] it must be more than a mere coincidence that BAL appears on the quaestorian coinage of this period where EX S. C. had stood before. Not only does the evidence of *denarii* and of the literary authorities confirm that he is the signatory of these coins, but the *aes* of the period provides twofold analogies. A precisely similar agent Hirtius—with whom, incidentally, Balbus was in the closest co-operation[11]—had been responsible for Caesar's Gallic *aes* (p. 3), and the next coinage will supply the signature of an equally unconstitutional *praefectus* (p. 7). The evidence of Balbus's omnipotence is overwhelming: in his hands were *condiciones pacis et arbitria belli*.[12] Included within this sweeping assertion are all the departments of finance which the enforced paralysis of the senate had deprived of the power to function:[13] we actually hear of the staff of Balbus's bureau[14] which took over their duties, at least until the appointment of eight *praefecti urbi* in 46.[15] The activities of Balbus were automatically ratified by the dictator.[16] Thus he, and not the senate, was in a position to grant the right of coinage to Cn. Julius, quaestor of Farther Spain. It is interesting to note that, like Hirtius and Pansa (p. 396), to whom also Caesar entrusted coinage, Balbus was himself, in his private capacity, an important financier;[17] very probably these men were permitted to make their concession profitable to themselves as well as to Caesar (p. 19). An additional reason for the appearance of Balbus's name may well have been his origin from the province.[18] In the same way his nephew, L. Balbus *minor*, is later commemorated on the coinage of Gades (p. 172).

[1] *BMCR.* II, p. 270. 518.
[2] Ibid. p. 269. 512.
[3] Ibid. p. 358. 52.
[4] Caesar, *Bell. Civ.* I, 32. 7.
[5] Cf. Wickert, *Klio*, 1937, p. 245; Oppermann, *Neue Wege zur Antike*, II, 2, 1933, pp. 27, 94.
[6] For collections of material, vide Münzer, *PW.* IX, 1264 ff.; Tyrrell and Purser, *Cicero's Letters*, IV, pp. lxvii ff.; Jullian, *De L. Cornelio Balbo maiore*, Diss. Paris, 1886.
[7] Münzer, l.c. 1265.
[8] Tyrrell and Purser, l.c. p. lxix.
[9] He was probably not a member of the senate;

cf. Syme, *RR.* p. 81; *pace* Tyrrell and Purser, l.c. p. lxvii. Münzer, l.c. 1266 reserves his judgment.
[10] Cf. Cic. *Att.* VIII, IX *passim*, X, 11, XI, 6. 7, XII, 12; *Fam.* IX, 19; Gellius, *NA.* XVII, 9. 1, etc.
[11] Cic. *Att.* XIV, 20. 4, 21. 2.
[12] Tac. *Ann.* XII, 60.
[13] Cf. Adcock, *CAH.* X, p. 694.
[14] Cic. *Att.* XI, 22.
[15] Dio XLIII, 28.
[16] Cic. *Fam.* VI, 8.
[17] For similar indications concerning moneyers of *orichalcum*, see p. 89.
[18] Münzer, l.c.

Here, then, is a sidelight on Caesar's revolutionary—or makeshift—administrative methods. The choice of Corduba for the mint, which this unusual executive machinery produced, is easily explicable by its position as a military centre. These bronze coins may well be composed of the famous *aes Marianum* or *Cordubense* (p. 87). By all precedents, the three pellets on the reverses should be a mark of value for *quadrans*: the heaviest of these coins approximate to the traditional uncial standard.[1]

2. MEDIOLANUM (?)

Another element in the revival of *aes* under new management in the lifetime of Julius has aroused a very extensive, but inaccurate, controversy. Coins of fine style[2] bear the draped bust, to right, of Winged Victory (sometimes with a star in the field), and CAESAR DIC. TER.; on the reverse, with the inscription C. CLOVI. PRAEF., is Minerva walking to left, carrying a shield with the head of Medusa on its face, and also a trophy and objects that Laffranchi,[3] following Cavedoni[4] and Dressel,[5] identifies as Thessalian arms, referring to Pharsalus.[6]

The fine workmanship led Cavedoni[7] to attribute the series to some Eastern province; but Roman *denarii*[8] offer many analogies, and why should a Greek not have been employed in the West? For similar reasons Laffranchi's[9] recent comparison of other heads of Winged Victory—not, incidentally, very like the present ones[10]—on local coins of Philomelium fails completely to prove their attribution to that town, or to any other in its neighbourhood. Such attempts to attribute official mints from local analogies are based on an entirely fallacious principle (p. 122). In his study of these coins Laffranchi, like others, has completely neglected provenance. Specimens have been found at Sinalungo (Florence),[11] Capua,[12] Este,[13] Xanten,[14] Kaiseraugst (Basel),[15] Rottenburg (Württemberg),[16] Rokytzan (Bohemia);[17] probably also at Painten (Oberpfalz),[18] Orlagau (Brandenburg),[19] in Aquitaine,[20] and in the Graubünden (Grisons).[21]

[1] *BM*. 108, 101 grains; 71, 51 grains.
[2] *BMCR*. I, p. 539. 4125.
[3] *Historia*, IX, 1935, p. 57.
[4] *Appendice al Saggio* (1835), p. 67 f.
[5] *ZfN*. 1910, pp. 365 ff.
[6] A specimen from the Leipzig collection (sale 1853, p. 182. 3673), with a reverse type of a warrior and a serpent, is undoubtedly a forgery.
[7] *Annali dell' Inst. di corr. arch.* 1850, p. 152.
[8] Pace de Saulcy, *Mémoires de la Société française de numismatique et d'archéologie*, 1873, p. 11.
[9] *Historia*, IX, 1935, p. 55.
[10] They resemble heads of Fulvia (p. 350), and are thus attributable to a later date: cf. particularly Pl. VII, 52.

[11] *Notizie degli scavi*, 1898, p. 276.
[12] Ruggiero, *Degli scavi di antichità nelle province di terraferma dell' antico regno di Napoli*, 1888, p. 287.
[13] *Notizie degli scavi*, 1883, p. 411.
[14] Steiner, *Cat. Xanten mus.* p. 84.
[15] Basel mus.
[16] Nestle, *Funde*, p. 64; in trade, Rottenburg.
[17] Bolin, *Fynden, Bilagor,* p. 112.
[18] *Verhandlung des historischen Vereins von Oberpfalz*, XXVI, p. 114.
[19] *Verhandlungen der Berliner Gesellschaft für Anthropologie usw.*, XII, 1880, p. 131.
[20] Bordeaux mus.
[21] *Mitteilungen der antiquarischen Gesellschaft in Zürich*, XXVI, 1903, p. 39.

COINAGE BY *IMPERIUM MAIUS*, 49–28 B.C.

The fact that no finds from the Eastern provinces can be set against these is as important as such evidence can ever be.[1] Willers[2] recants his previous assumption[3] of a Spanish find, and Laffranchi's corrections of Havercamp's[4] often accepted[5] (but in any case inconclusive) interpretation of Minerva's trappings as Spanish has removed all cause for attribution to that peninsula. Gnecchi[6] guessed that the issue was Sicilian merely on account of the Greek style; Grueber[7] and Milne[8] prefer Rome, owing to an unfortunate comparison with a bronze piece of Plancus *Praef(ectus) Vrb(is)*,[9] which is in fact a forgery.[10] In any case, Clovius cannot be a *praefectus urbis*, since genuine coins struck by these officials[11] do not omit the qualifying Genitive. Nor are other conjectures any more satisfactory: Cavedoni[12] considers him a *praefectus classis*, Willers[13] an extra-ordinary *praefectus aere flando feriundo*, Münzer[14] (following Mommsen's groundless attribution to Spain) a *praefectus fabrum*. Two courses of research can be combined to produce a more suitable identification. It will first be shown that literary and epigraphic sources contribute a member of the *gens* Clovia (Cluvia)[15] who held a prominent appointment when this coin was struck: then an unpublished numismatic inscription will be cited to show the peculiar applicability of the title and task of that official to the present coinage.

In the autumn of 45[16] Cicero[17] writes to a C.(?) Cluvius, who has already left for Gallia Cisalpina[18] to supervise land settlements. Borghesi,[19] followed by Bonazzi,[20] assigns these coins to him, but wrongly calls him 'governor'—C. Vibius Pansa Caetronianus held this post[21]—and makes no attempt to explain his title. However, the attribution of the coins to this personage is not stopped by Laffranchi's limitation of the issue to 46,[22] which is incorrect since Julius was DIC. TER. until December 45.[23] Similar emissaries in the same year are M. Rutilius, of unknown rank,[24] and Q. Valerius

---

[1] They also invalidate the suggestion of Milne, *Development of Roman Coinage*, p. 21, that the issues were medallic. (This view is intended to explain the supposed exceptional use of the Roman mint.)

[2] *Geschichte*, p. 107.

[3] *NZ*. XXXIV, 1902, p. 46.

[4] Morelli, *Familiarum Romanarum Numismata*, II, p. 97.

[5] E.g. by Mommsen, *Mẕw*. p. 654 n. 552; Ribbeck, *Senatores Romani etc.*, Diss. Berlin, 1899, p. 16, no. 57.

[6] Gnecchi, *R.it.* XV, 1902, p. 17.

[7] *NC*. 1904, pp. 235 ff.

[8] L.c. p. 21: cf. also Stella Maranca, *Memorie della R. Ac. dei Lincei (sc.-mor.)*, VI, 2, 1926, p. 336.

[9] *BMCR*. I, p. 538. 4124.

[10] Laffranchi, *Historia*, IX, 1935; Mattingly is of the same opinion.

[11] *BMCR*. I, p. 537. 4118 ff.

[12] *Appendice al Saggio*, p. 63; cf. Lenormant, *La monnaie dans l'antiquité*, II, pp. 312 f.

[13] *Geschichte*, p. 104.

[14] *PW*. IV, 120 (4).

[15] For orthographical identity, cf. Lewis and Short, p. 1231.

[16] Tyrrell and Purser, ad l.c. (DCLXXIV) n.

[17] *Fam.* XIII, 7.

[18] Münzer, Tyrrell and Purser, ll.cc.

[19] *Œuvres*, I, p. 148.

[20] *R.it.* 1920, p. 157.

[21] Cf. Sternkopf, *Hermes*, XLVII, 1912, p. 328.

[22] L.c. p. 52; cf. Stella Maranca, l.c.

[23] Mommsen, *CIL*. I, p. 451; cf. Schnabel, *Klio*, XIX, 1925, p. 354; Andersen, *Neue Deutsche Forschungen*, CXCVI, 1938, p. 24.

[24] Cic. *Fam.* XIII, 8; cf. Münzer, *PW*. (2R.), I, 1248; Zumpt, *Commenta Epigraphica*, I, p. 301.

Orca *legatus pro praetore*[1] in Italy, and Ti. Claudius Nero, an ex-quaestor in Gaul;[2] in 44 L. Plautius (originally C. Munatius) Plancus *praetor designatus* is similarly occupied in Epirus.[3] Nero was sent to found Narbo and Arelate,[4] and L. Plautius Plancus to superintend the allotments of a new colony at Buthrotum.[5] In Cisalpina, where Cluvius was employed, not only had lands to be found for the veterans, but it is unlikely that the Civil War had hitherto allowed time for the completion of the colonial and municipal foundations[6] resulting from the general enfranchisement of the *Lex Roscia* (49 B.C.),[7] and the supplementary law (probably not yet the *Lex Rubria*) of which the Atestine fragment is a part:[8] even at Caesar's death the process had not sufficiently developed for Gallia Cisalpina to be a part of Italy, and so without a governor.[9] Hence the special importance of Cluvius, which Cicero is at pains to underline.[10]

Thus, in 45–44, the dictator's representatives were busy allotting land and founding colonies on both sides of the frontier of Italy. Moreover, beyond it at least, each possessed independent control over the foundation which was entrusted to him. Münzer[11] considers that L. Plautius Plancus at Buthrotum was one of a body of *IIIviri agris dandis adsignandis*, in the Republican tradition. But *deductiones* had been carried out by all three of such officials in conjunction,[12] while Cicero makes it abundantly clear that Plancus alone was in control in Epirus: *praesertim cum tota potestas eius rei tua sit*[13]—*omnia posita putamus in Planci tui liberalitate*.[14] The latter sentiment is even included in a letter to one of the supposed colleagues of Plancus. There is no indication whatever that these, C. Ateius Capito and C. Cupiennius, were more than his subordinates, or perhaps merely people with a financial interest in the foundation. In writing to Rutilius and Orca Cicero dwells with no less emphasis on the unhampered initiative of both these commissioners.[15] Caesar had obtained the right to make colonies through his personal representatives as early as the *Lex Vatinia* of 59,[16] and he clung to it, unmoved by the condemnation of this practice by the consul M. Marcellus as *per ambitionem et ultra praescriptum*.[17] Indeed, the *IIIviri agris dandis adsignandis* and *coloniis deducendis* were not employed for the foundations of his

---

[1] *Fam.* XIII, 5.
[2] Münzer, *PW.* III, 2778.
[3] Cf. Münzer, *PW.* XVI, 542. Not Cnaeus (as Borghesi, *Œuvres*, I, p. 203).
[4] Suet. *Ti.* 4.   [5] Cic. *Att.* XVI, 16a–e.
[6] Hardy, *Some Problems in Roman History*, p. 290.
[7] A beginning had been made by the establishment of Novum Comum under the *Lex Vatinia* of 59 (cf. Cary, *CAH*. IX, p. 519 n. 2), but this was cancelled by the consul M. Marcellus (Suet. *Caes.* 28).
[8] Rudolph, *Stadt und Staat im römischen Italien*, p. 236; cf. Stuart Jones, *JRS.* 1936, p. 271; *pace* Hardy, *EHR.* XXXI, 1916, pp. 356, 359; Dio XLI, 36.
[9] Cf. Hardy, *EHR*. l.c. p. 357; Caland, *De nummis M. Antonii etc.*, Diss. Leyden, 1883, p. 97, App. 2; Jullian, *TP.* p. 1; cf. Donatus, *Vita Verg.* 19 [30]; see also below, p. 438.
[10] The Cluvii subsequently attained patrician rank; Pais, *Ricerche sulla storia ecc.*, ser. II, p. 408.
[11] *PW.* XVI, 542.
[12] Cf. Marquardt, *St. V.* I, p. 457; Rudorff, *Gromatische Institutionen*, pp. 229 ff.
[13] *Att.* XVI, 16e. 15.
[14] *Att.* XVI, 16f. 18.
[15] *Fam.* XIII, 8. 1 ff., 4. 4.
[16] Cf. Cary, *CAH*. IX, p. 519 n. 2. But he still often employed the *IIIviri*, e.g. *CIL.* X, 3861.
[17] Suet. *Caes.* 28.

dictatorship, and became entirely obsolete.¹ Men like Cluvius made the precedent for similar officials acting directly under the *imperium maius* of Brutus and the triumvirs² (pp. 34, 274)—manifestations of a return to the Hellenistic practice of personal κτίσμα (p. 356).³ The military ceremony and terminology still accompanying *deductio*⁴ only serve to emphasise the connection of these founders with the *imperium maius*. Indeed, the *deductores* themselves usually possessed a subordinate *imperium*,⁵ although this cannot be stated with certainty of the exceptional circumstances of the dictatorship: Cluvius certainly did not possess *imperium* as governor, since C. Vibius Pansa Caetronianus occupied this position (p. 12).

So far it has only been shown that Cluvius had a special appointment in Cisalpine Gaul, like other single officials elsewhere, in the year in which the coin of Clovius was issued in some Western province. Since there is no orthographical difficulty in their identification, it only remains to show that the title PRAEF. is applicable to Cluvius. Its complete relevance has been obscured by false deductions and a wrong reading.

The title of a similar commissioner under Brutus, Q. Hortensius (p. 33), hitherto wrongly restored from an imperfect specimen as *legatus*,⁶ is seen beyond all doubt from an example in the British Museum (Pl. II, 8) to be PRAEF. COLON. DEDV. The analogy with Clovius is complete. The discovery that such officials bore the title *praefectus* has been needed to explain the description of L. Memmius, who settled two legions, probably in 42 B.C.,⁷ as *PRAEF. legionum XXVI et XXVII*(?) *Lucae ad agros dividundos*.⁸ The terminology of Cicero and Servius is not, therefore, inexact when they say, to L. Plancus and of Pollio respectively, *ei negotio te PRAEFICERE*,⁹ and *agris PRAEERAT dividundis*.¹⁰ Zumpt,¹¹ observing that references by Cicero¹² point to a personal commission rather than a *potestas*, argued from the single title of Q. Valerius Orca (disregarding those of other commissioners) that all such officials were *legati pro praetore*; using this dubious analogy, Gaebler¹³ has found general acceptance for his discovery, on a coin of Philippi (p. 274), of a LEG(*atus*) C(*oloniae, -is*) D(*educendae,*

---

¹ Cf. Pais, *Memorie della R. Ac. dei Lincei* (*sc.-mor.*), VI, 1, 1925, pp. 360 ff.
² *iussu, arbitratu*—e.g. *Liber Coloniarum* (*Feldm.* p. 213); von Premerstein, *SavZ.* 1922, p. 120.
³ Cf. Skard, *Festskrift til Koht*, p. 58.
⁴ E.g. *Feldm.* p. 213; von Premerstein, l.c.; Marquardt, *St. V.* I, p. 448.
⁵ Cf. Jullian, *TP.* p. 28; Lauria, *Studi Bonfante*, II, p. 489.
⁶ Gaebler, *ZfN.* XXXVI, 1926, p. 137.
⁷ Honigmann, *PW.* XV, 1538; cf. Miltner, ibid. 621; Pais, *Museo italiano di antichità classica*, I, 1885, p. 38.
⁸ *CIL.* XIV, 2264; cf. Ritterling, *PW.* XII, 1820 f. Jullian, *TP.* p. 29, unaware of the coins, confuses

the post of Memmius with the local *praefectura iure dicundo* (see below, p. 323). The example which he cites from Venafrum (*Inscr. Reg. Neap.* 4627) belongs to the latter class. It is true that, in the Civil Wars, *praefecti* were appointed for emergencies without specific definitions (cf. Cagnat, *Rev. arch.* XXVII, 1895, p. 137 n. 69 for a Pompeian official at Curubis): but, legally speaking, a *praef.i.d.* was a city-magistrate, and a *praef.a.d.a.* a military representative of the *imperator*.
⁹ *Att.* XVI, 16a. 5.   ¹⁰ *Ad* Verg. *Ecl.* II, 1.
¹¹ *Commenta Epigraphica*, p. 301; cf. Meyer, *Cäsars Monarchie*, p. 414.
¹² *Fam.* XIII, 5. 1, 7. 1, etc.
¹³ *ZfN.* XXXIX, 1929, p. 261.

THE CAESARIANS

-is). It will be shown elsewhere (p. 275) that an unknown colonial coin of Dyrrhachium corrects this interpretation to C(*oloniam*) D(*eduxit*), so that the title *legatus* is due to the ordinary circumstances of a provincial governorship (p. 247). It is irrelevant to the land settlements, which were in the hands of *praefecti*.

The ascription of the coins to such an official is entirely in accord with the evidence already cited of Caesar's administrative methods, and with the frequency of coinages celebrating foundations (pp. 147 ff.).[1] It may be added that the attribution to Cisalpine Gaul agrees both with the evidence of provenance and with the metallic content of the coins, which are composed of the alloy of *orichalcum*[2] (containing zinc instead of the tin of Republican bronze[3]), of which a principal constituent, *cadmea*, was, at this date, chiefly supplied from the *ager Bergomatium* in this territory.[4] The cleverness of the metallic innovation lies in the fact that, although the coins weighed not much more than half an ounce, invidious comparisons were avoided since the metal had not been used for money before (p. 88): it is significant that Clovius, to whom the launching of the scheme was entrusted, came of a great banking family (p. 18).[5] But the idea may be referred to Julius himself, under whose dictatorial *imperium maius* this —the first of many 'foundation' issues—was made. The choice of Cisalpine Gaul for the inauguration of this custom was no doubt dictated by its reputation at this time as a land of promise and the bulwark of Italy and the State.[6] The coinage was probably issued at the capital and commercial centre, Mediolanum[7]—where a mint for *denarii* had possibly already been opened in 50–49.[8] Clovius, like all the other official moneyers in this alloy before Augustus, namely, M. Acilius, C. Sosius and Q. Oppius, came of a family of wealthy financiers:[9] no doubt the coinage was a profitable concern (p. 19).

3. AMISUS

An unpublished and apparently unique coin (Pl. II, 1)[10] (which may be of the same metal[11]) has the inscriptions P. SVLPICIVS RVFVS (with an owl facing, standing on a crab) and PRO PR. (a turreted female head to right). The only known specimen was found in Turkey. The appearance of an exactly similar owl on fourth-century coins of

---

[1] The suggestion of Milne, *Development of Roman Coinage*, p. 20, that the issue celebrated the triumph of Caesar in 46, is based on a parallel attribution (of Q. Oppius) to the triumph of 45: this will be shown to be incorrect (see below, p. 62).

[2] Bahrfeldt, *NZ*. XXXVII, 1905, p. 42 analysed.

[3] Beanlands, *NC*. 1918, pp. 187 ff.

[4] Pliny, *NH*. XXXIV, 2; cf. Mattingly, *BMC. Imp.* p. xlvii. Caesar did not contravene the mysterious veto on mining in Italy (Pliny, *NH*. III, 138; XXXIII, 78; XXXVII, 202; cf. Frank, *ES*. I, pp. 263 f.), since Cisalpine Gaul was still outside its borders.

[5] Cic. *Fam.* XIII, 56. 1–3; cf. Frank, *ES*. I, p. 388.

[6] Cic. *III Phil.* 13; cf. Syme, *RR*. p. 79.

[7] Suet. *De viris illustribus, De claris gram. et rhet.* 6.

[8] Cf. Grueber, *BMCR*. II, p. 391 n. 1.

[9] Cic. *Fam.* XIII, 56. 1–3; cf. Frank, *ES*. I, p. 388; Carettoni, *Civiltà Romana*, III, 1938, p. 15.

[10] Istanbul.

[11] The metal was soon adopted for coinage by the city of Obulco (Zobel de Zangroniz, *MNE*. V, 1880, p. 137): the style of that coinage suggests a date very close to that of the present issue.

COINAGE BY *IMPERIUM MAIUS*, 49–28 B.C.

Amisus,[1] in the company of a turreted female head of the type also found here, suggests strongly that Sulpicius was governor of Pontus and Bithynia; this is rendered certain by his appearance in that very capacity on an unknown coin of *colonia* Sinope (p. 251). The colony was founded in 45,[2] in a month that cannot be established since the era apparently followed the Roman calendar.[3] The title of Sulpicius eliminates the possibility of a date after 27 B.C. Between these limits there are three gaps in the Bithynian Fasti. Two of them immediately precede and succeed respectively the governorship of Ahenobarbus: there is a hiatus from the surrender of M. Appuleius after Philippi[4] until 40[5]—a period partly filled by Antony's personal administration[6]—and another from c. 35 to 33 until Actium.[7] But the Sinopitan piece of Sulpicius differs, by reason of its rough fabric and early appearance, from those coins of the colony which were struck in 31 and even as early as 38 (Pl. IX, 4) (p. 253). Moreover, it will be shown elsewhere to associate him with the city in a finite sentence to which the only parallels are issues commemorating *deductiones*, and which is to be reconstructed D[*eduxit*] or [DE]D(*uxit*) I(*ussu*) C(*aesaris*). Attribution to 45, when the *deductio* of Sinope occurred, is entirely in accordance not only with the style of both these unrecorded coins, but also with the provincial activity of Sulpicius, of which the latest known example is his governorship of Illyricum in 47–46.[8] The year 45 also coincides with a third blank in the list of governors of Pontus and Bithynia. After extensive controversy, it appears likely that C. Vibius Pansa Caetronianus[9] governed the province in 47–46[10] rather than in 48–47,[11] unless he was there during both periods.[12] His predecessor was probably either Cn. Domitius Calvinus[13] or M. Coelius M. f. Vinicianus;[14] his immediate successor, in the years 46–45—Pansa was back in Rome before the end of 46[15]—has not hitherto been identified.[16]

This official issue, whose types indicate Amisus as its mint, is not followed by a second Roman coinage of the province until c. A.D. 14 (p. 145). It provides a further

[1] E.g. *Rec.* I, p. 47. 5.
[2] Kubitschek, *NZ*. 1908, pp. 68 f., from numismatic evidence; cf. Reinach, *Rev. arch.* 1916, p. 339; Meyer, *Cäsars Monarchie*, p. 492; *pace* Adcock, *CAH.* IX, p. 708.
[3] Kubitschek, l.c.
[4] Appian, *BC.* IV, 195–7.
[5] Ibid. v, 63; cf. Ganter, p. 33; Raillard, p. 18; Craven, *University of Missouri Studies (Social Science)*, III, 2, 1920, p. 51.
[6] Josephus, *BJ.* I, 242: cf. Ganter (who exaggerates a short stay).
[7] Ganter, ibid. (?33 B.C.); cf. Münzer, *PW.* V, 1330; Raillard, p. 18.
[8] Cic. *Fam.* XIII; cf. Hölzl, *Fasti praetorii*, Diss. Leipzig, 1876, p. 82; Münzer, *PW.* IV, 849; Sternkopf, *Hermes*, XLVII, 1912, p. 329; Letz, *Die*

Provinzialverwaltung Cäsars, Diss. Strassburg, 1912, p. 67; *pace* Marquardt, *St. V.* I, p. 298 n. 6.
[9] Vide Syme, *RR.* p. 71 n. 4, for his name.
[10] As Hölzl, l.c. pp. 79, 81; Ruge, *PW.* XVII (1936), pp. 229, 472; Syme, *Anatolian Studies to Buckler* (1939), p. 322.
[11] As Borghesi, *Œuvres*, II, pp. 347 ff.; Wroth, *BMC. Pontus*, etc., p. xiv; Stella Maranca, *Memorie della R. Ac. dei Lincei*, V, 1926, p. 336.
[12] Sternkopf, *Hermes*, XLVII, 1912, p. 330.
[13] Münzer, *PW.* V, 1422: cf. Dio XLII, 49. 1.
[14] Münzer, *PW.* IV, 198 (26); cf. *Bell. Alex.* 77. 2; *ILS.* 883; Cavedoni, *Bull. dell' Inst. di corr. arch.* 1849, p. 125 to 47–46.
[15] Cic. *Fam.* VI, 12. 5; *Pro Lig.* 1. 7; cf. Syme, l.c.
[16] Cf. Sternkopf, l.c.; Q. Marcius Crispus arrived in 45; Levi I, p. 171 n. 2; Syme, l.c.; cf. Plutarch, *Brut.* 19.

THE CAESARIANS 13

example of Caesar's unrecognised provision of *aes* currency for the Empire. The owl of Amisus is accompanied by a crab: the implications of this include sea power, but, on coins of Cassius,[1] Alföldi[2] sees in it an example of the profound 'Messianic' feeling of the times, and an expression of the coming *Cosmocrator*, who will, according to astrological beliefs,[3] inaugurate the rebirth of Nature under the sign of the crab. This explanation may be equally applicable to the present coin. The immediate occasion for the issue is likely to have been the liberation of Amisus by Caesar.[4] The contemporary Sinopitan issue bearing the name of Sulpicius celebrated a similar promotion—though to Roman not Greek *libertas* (p. 402)—and such changes of status were regularly commemorated in this way, either by official or by local coinage (pp. 338 ff.). Sulpicius probably owed this rare (and often profitable) privilege of coining *aes* to kinship by marriage with the dictator.[5] Like most moneyers of the period, he was probably a financier: this is suggested by his election to the censorship in 41.[6]

4. THESSALONICA(?)

Julius Caesar's most important coinage—which has, however, not been attributed to him—was composed, like that of Clovius and perhaps that of Sulpicius, of the new alloy of *orichalcum*.[7] It comprises three values (p. 88). The two largest of these[8] have, on the reverse, a *fiscus*, *sella quaestoria*[9] and *hasta*[10] (Pl. II, 3); the third has a prow[11] (Pl. II, 2). All three have the letter Q,[12] and on the obverse particularly striking portrait-heads to right. Of these there is an exact copy (rather than a prototype), inscribed PRINCEPS[13] FELIX, on a coin of a COLONIA IVLIA whose ethnic, hitherto misread, is ALE., and whose attribution to a foundation of Alexandria Troas in c. 42–41 B.C. is confirmed by analogies and provenance (p. 244).

The pieces with Q are assigned by Friedländer[14] to Brutus. But a slight similarity of the portrait to him is due merely to contemporary workmanship. Moreover, the titles PRINCEPS FELIX, applied to the same portrait on the colonial coins, are singularly

[1] *BMCR*. II, p. 484. 84.
[2] *Röm. Mitt.* L, 1935, p. 146.
[3] Bouché-Leclercq, *L'Astrologie grecque*, p. 33 n. 1.
[4] Strabo XII, 547; Dio XLII, 48.
[5] For his wife, a Julia, see Syme, *RR.* p. 65.
[6] *CIL.* I², p. 64.
[7] Shown by spectrographic test: Spectrogram 12.
[8] Largest: Berlin, Istanbul; middle denomination: BM, Berlin, own collection, Cahn sale 60 (1928) 1315; Gaebler, *NG.* III, 1, p. 74, cf. p. 69.
[9] Cf. Kübler, *PW.* (2R.), II, 1314, *pace* Longpérier, *Recherches sur les insignes de la questure*, pp. 9 ff., 43 ff. (*subsellium*).
[10] Identified conclusively by Helbig, *Abhandlungen der königlichen Gesellschaft der Wissenschaften zu Göttingen, Philol.-hist. Kl.*, NF. X, 3, 1908, p. 36; *pace* Grueber, *BMCR*. II, p. 473. 47, who interprets it, for no clear reason, as the *virga* of a tribunician viator.
[11] Istanbul. Riggauer, *SB. München*, 1897, p. 533.
[12] Gaebler, l.c. p. 74 for the two largest: Riggauer, l.c., omits this from his description of the other.
[13] Misread by Friedländer, *BB.* 1868, p. 26; *Bull. dell' Inst. di corr. arch.* 1870, p. 193, etc.
[14] *BB.* 1865, p. 143; cf. *Bull. dell' Inst.* l.c.

unsuitable to Brutus, in view of the semi-monarchist ideas already associated with the title *Princeps*,[1] and of the special connection of *Felicitas* with the cult of Venus and with the Julian house.[2] It may be noted also that Brutus allotted to his provinces, not quaestors, but proquaestors.[3] Finally, it is unthinkable that Alexandria Troas, a colony in the provinces of Brutus, could flaunt, on coins with his head, the epithet IVLIA. In view of such considerations Imhoof-Blumer[4] suggests that the portraits on the quaestorian and colonial coins represent Augustus; but even Gaebler,[5] who takes the same view, must admit that their features (which have much individuality) do not resemble his in the slightest. Furthermore, not only does an inspection of the coins with Q give the general impression that they could hardly be so late as 31 B.C., but this conclusion is confirmed by a number of particular considerations. (1) Pieces of the largest denomination[6] have a curious concave flan found on coins of Q. Hortensius (44–42 B.C.) (p. 33), of Philippi (c. 42–41) (p. 274),[7] and Thessalonica (41–40).[8] (2) They closely resemble, in weight, diameter, and bevelled edge, pieces struck at Thessalonica in c. 42–41,[9] and contemporary issues of Pella.[10] (3) Another coin of Thessalonica,[11] of c. 50–40 B.C., has a similar prow as its type.

A date in the forties is thus indicated; but Brutus is excluded, and the features could not be Antony's. Now if it is taken into consideration that these coins with Q are of different workmanship from Roman issues, it will be seen that the portraits on the specimens illustrated by Gaebler[12] are not unlike those of Julius on two *denarii* of Sepullius Macer.[13] Other examples, too, of the *orichalcum* issue[14] have respectively the beard, and the sharp physiognomy, of two further *denarii* of the same moneyer.[15] Correspondingly the head as rendered on the colonial pieces of Alexandria Troas strongly resembles a fifth of these *denarii*.[16] There are minor differences in each case; but, in spite of the distinctive style of the quaestorian *orichalcum* coinage, they are no greater than those which separate even the portraits on the series of *denarii* from each other. With regard to PRINCEPS FELIX, the inscription of the colonial issue of Alexandria Troas, we may anticipate a later discussion (p. 244) by noting that Julius is called *princeps civitatis* by Suetonius.[17] Gwosdz[18] and Sprey[19] interpret the word as 'a

---

[1] Gwosdz, *Der Begriff des römischen 'Princeps'*, Diss. Breslau, 1933, pp. 29 ff., 48 etc.
[2] Berlinger, *Zur inoffiziellen Titulatur der römischen Kaiser*, Diss. Breslau, 1935, pp. 9 f.; cf. Levi, *Rendiconti del. R. Ist. lombardo*, LXXI, III, 2, 1938, p. 114.
[3] Cf. Gaebler, *ZfN*. XXIII, 1902, pp. 184 ff.; Bülz, l.c. p. 46, and below, p. 36.
[4] *MG*. p. 89; cf. Gardthausen II, 1, p. 70.
[5] *ZfN*. XXIII, 1902, p. 186.
[6] E.g. Berlin = Gaebler, *NG*. III, 1, p. 74, no. 226.
[7] *ZfN*. XXXIX, 1929, pl. I. 14.
[8] Gaebler, *NG*. III, 2, pp. 121–4.
[9] Gaebler, *NG*. II, p. 97.
[10] Ibid. p. 96. 19.
[11] Ibid. p. 121. 22.
[12] *NG*. III, 1, p. 74. 226, 228.
[13] *BMCR*. pl. LIV, 20, 19.
[14] BM, Berlin.
[15] *BMCR*. pl. LIV, 17, 23.
[16] Ibid. 16.
[17] *Caes*. 29.
[18] L.c. p. 39.
[19] *De M. Tullii Ciceronis politica doctrina*, Diss. Amsterdam, 1928; cf. *Tijdschrift voor Geschiedenis*, LXV, 1930, pp. 341 ff.

princeps', but Cicero calls Pompey *LONGE princeps civitatis*,[1] and speaks of autocrats like Demetrius of Phaleron as *princeps*;[2] it would be difficult to differentiate the reference of Suetonius from these.[3] *Felix* too is known to have been a favourite appellative of the dictator.[4] These considerations do not, therefore, invalidate the conclusion that the portrait is of Caesar himself.

Now the three comparisons, which have been cited to indicate a date in the forties for the quaestorian issue, serve also to reveal its extensive Macedonian affinities. Further and conclusive evidence in this connection is provided by the latest previous Roman coins of that province, struck by Aesillas *quaestor*[5] and Q. Sura *legatus pro praetore*,[6] which have (together with the national Macedonian club[7] instead of the Roman *hasta*) a precisely similar type of *fiscus* and *subsellium*. One of the present quaestorian pieces has been found in Thrace or Mysia,[8] but another probably in Greece.[9] It is true that the colonial issues with PRINCEPS FELIX are of Asiatic provenance[10] in accordance with their ascription to Alexandria Troas. But this does not at all affect the attribution of the quaestorian series to Macedonia, since in the time of Julius (though, perhaps, not in the Augustan epoch to which Gaebler attributes them) no official model existed in Asia itself to exclude the use of a prototype from Macedonia.

It remains to discover the date and occasion of the issue. An exact chronology is difficult to attain owing to erroneous assumptions which have been made concerning heads of the dictator on coins—based on a misinterpretation of a passage of Dio: ΠΑΤΕΡΑ τε αὐτὸν ΤΗΣ ΠΑΤΡΙΔΟΣ ἐπωνόμασαν καὶ ἐς τὰ νομίσματα ἐνεχάραξαν.[11] This has been understood to imply that a decree was passed in 44 permitting his portraiture on currency.[12] But ΠΑΤΕΡΑ ΤΗΣ ΠΑΤΡΙΔΟΣ, rather than αὐτόν, must be the object of ἐνεχάραξαν, and there is only one possible translation: 'they named him "Father of his Country" and engraved it on the coinage.'[13] This interpretation is reinforced by the presence of PARENS PATRIAE on *denarii* with his portrait.[14] But the modification does not assist precision, since a number of these *denarii* are certainly posthumous;[15] and Dio, who says vaguely of the honorary decrees to Julius καθ' ἓν γὰρ εἰ καὶ μὴ πάντα ἅμα μήτε ἐσηνέχθη μήτε ἐκυρώθη λελέξεται,[16] often confuses the periods of the dictator's worshipfulness in life, his worship in death, and tendencious

[1] *De Domo sua*, 66.
[2] *Fam.* XVI, 21. 5.
[3] This is the conclusion of Wagenvoort, *Philologus*, XCI, 1936, pp. 206 ff.; *QAS.* X, p. 16.
[4] Berlinger, l.c. pp. 9 f.
[5] Gaebler, *NG.* III, 1, p. 69.
[6] Ibid. p. 73.
[7] Ibid. p. 10; cf. *ZfN.* XXIII, 1902, pp. 184 ff.
[8] Own collection, acquired at Istanbul.
[9] Athens mus.
[10] Cf. Gaebler, *ZfN.* XXIII, 1902, p. 186.
[11] XLIV, 4.
[12] E.g. by Mattingly, *BMC. Imp.* p. xiv; Adcock, *CAH.* IX, p. 727; Ganter, *ZfN.* XIX, 1895, p. 183; Macdonald, *Coin Types*, pp. 193 f., etc.
[13] Thus interpreted by Grueber, *BMCR.* I, p. 547 n. 2. A. S. F. Gow confirms the correctness of this translation; cf. also McFayden, p. 20 n. 28.
[14] Grueber, l.c. pp. 549, 552.
[15] Ibid.; cf. Gabrici, *Augustus* (1938), p. 393 n. 1; H. Mattingly is of the same opinion.
[16] XLIV, 3.

interpretations of his policy.[1] Thus, even as evidence for the title *parens patriae*, the statement of Dio is of little use. Of indication concerning portraiture he gives no sign whatever. Even Ganter,[2] who accepts the misinterpretation, seeks to apply the reference not to 44 but to April 45, considering that the new quattuorvirate at the mint was not limited to a yearly tenure. There is no iconographic objection to this, since a numismatic portrait of Julius[3] has already appeared at Bithynian cities under C. Vibius Pansa Caetronianus, in 47–46 B.C. (p. 12). Thus 45 is preferable to 44 as a *terminus post quem* for the *denarii*. Since the *orichalcum* coins which are the subject of this discussion copy in many respects the portraits on these *denarii*, it may be supposed that they, too, were issued after April 45.

There is reason to think also that the issue was made before the death of Caesar whose portrait it bears.[4] Helbig[5] points out that the *hasta* which occurs here is found elsewhere, in conjunction with the same form of *sella*,[6] on the coinage of two officials of quaestorian rank, who lived within the same transitional epoch when *imperatores* held the power. Since the *hasta* was regularly an emblem of *imperium*,[7] and of these two officials one—A. Pupius Rufus (p. 69)—was certainly *pro praetore*, and the other— L. Sestius[8]—may well have been also,[9] he rightly deduces that the joint appearance of this form of *sella* and a *hasta* denotes a rank of *quaestor* (or *pro quaestore*) *pro praetore*, that is, with praetorian *imperium*. Since, at this time at least,[10] ordinary provincial quaestors did not possess this, it is necessary to conclude that our present moneyer, who signs with the letter Q, held some position in Macedonia exceptionally carrying with it an *imperium*: he must have been a commander or governor, owing obedience only to the supreme *imperium maius* of his war-lord (p. 33). It has been shown that the latter cannot have been Brutus. But it is in accordance with the early date of these coins that Antony's first governor in Macedonia-Achaia was a *legatus* (Q. Paquius Rufus [p. 274]), and that, by the analogy of other provinces, there is no likelihood of subsequent quaestorian governors in Macedonia.[11] On the other hand, at least one

[1] Cf. Adcock, *CAH*. IX, p. 728 n. 3.
[2] *ZfN*. XIX, 1895, pp. 199 f.
[3] Cf. Curtius, *Röm. Mitt.* XLVII, 1932, p. 230.
[4] This is necessary owing to the probability— which Ganter, l.c., fails to consider—that many of the *denarii* used as models were struck after the dictator's death. This is confirmed by H. Mattingly.
[5] *Abh. Göttingen, Ph.-h. Kl.*, NF. x, 3, 1908, p. 35.
[6] Following Longpérier, *Recherches sur les insignes de la quaesture*, ll.cc., he inaccurately calls it a *subsellium*.
[7] Ibid. p. 37; cf. Klingmüller, *PW*. VII, 2502; Fiebiger, ibid. 2506.
[8] *BMCR*. II, p. 473. 47. (43–42 B.C.).

[9] Cf. Helbig, l.c. p. 35. It is highly probable that Q. Hortensius, contemporary and governor of the whole Balkan region (see below, p. 33), was assisted by officials of praetorian or propraetorian rank: P. Spinther, *pro q.* in Asia at the same date, was of this standing (cf. Chapot, *La province romaine proconsulaire d'Asie*, p. 309), and, in Macedonia-Achaia itself, Atratinus appears to have held a similar assistant governorship (in Achaia) under Antony (*ILS*. 9461; cf. below, p. 382).
[10] For their status under Augustus, see below, pp. 136, 140 f.
[11] Cf. Ganter, Raillard, *passim*. It should be noted that the present issue must be attributed to Macedonia itself, not outlying parts of the large province.

quaestor pro praetore had governed a major province for Caesar in his dictatorship, namely his kinsman Sex. Julius Caesar.[1] Moreover, the head of the dictator on these coins bears little resemblance to the posthumous conceptions of Antony's *aes* (p. 264). Nor is it accidental that, on *denarii* of Brutus, Victory is seen trampling down and breaking just such a *hasta* as appears here:[2] the *hasta* of *imperium* (which is here substituted for the national Macedonian club of earlier issues) was a suitable symbol, for Republican propaganda, of the autocratic *régime* of the dictatorship[3]—and of the *regnum* which it threatened to become. Moreover, the extensive preparations at this time for the coming Eastern campaigns (which would hasten this development[4]) included, as Nicolaus of Damascus explicitly informs us,[5] the dispatch of an army to Macedonia—an exceptionally plausible occasion for a military issue of this unusual type. It may, then, be concluded that the dictator himself authorised this coinage.

The *quaestor pro praetore* who signs it will, in this case, have been his representative and governor in Macedonia during the last year of his life. No doubt he is the army-commander mentioned by Nicolaus as Μάρκος 'Ακίλιος[6] and by Cicero as Acilius.[7] He has been identified with Caesar's *legatus* in the Civil War, Acilius Caninus(?);[8] but coins reveal the *praenomen* of that officer to have been Manius (p. 26), as a number of MSS. render it,[9] and, in any case, he cannot have been *quaestor pro praetore* in 44 B.C., since he was proconsul of Sicily in 46–45.[10] Much more appropriate is the M. Acilius who was *consul suffectus* in 33[11]—perhaps the Aviola who miraculously survived when seemingly burnt to death.[12] He is likely to be the signatory of this coinage, and, as *quaestor pro praetore* like Sex. Julius Caesar in a precisely similar appointment, the

---

[1] Münzer, *PW*. x, 477; cf. *Bell. Alex*. 66. 1; Livy, *Ep*. cxiv; Josephus, *AJ*. xiv, 160.

[2] *BMCR*. ii, p. 478. 63; cf. Alföldi, *Röm. Mitt*. 1935, p. 110.

[3] Alföldi, l.c.; cf. Helbig, l.c. pp. 30 f. The fact that another issue of Brutus's government (that of L. Sestius) does not scruple to give honourable place to the *hasta* is irrelevant, since propaganda is notoriously shortsighted, and the associations of such a symbol could differ in accordance with the aspect to which it was applied. A parallel instance is provided by the *vexillum*, which is trampled under foot in the same manner on one coin of Brutus, but appears in the usual manner on another (pp. 272 ff.). The existence of two such examples merely bears witness to a somewhat unimaginative publicity department.

[4] Levi, *Annali dell' Ist. Superiore di Magistero del Piemonte*, vii, 1934, p. 10; id., *Athenaeum*, 1936, p. 210, shows that the consideration of kingship was postponed until the successful conclusion of the campaigns. Cf. also Rostovtzeff, *SEH*. p. 494 n. 23.

[5] *Vita* 16 (Hall, *Smith College Classical Studies*, iv, 1923, p. 19).

[6] As emended by Schwartz, *Hermes*, xxxiii, 1898, p. 182 (*Codex Escorialensis* reads Αἰμίλιος). But Hall, l.c. p. 81, points out that his further emendation of Μάνιος for Μάρκος is unjustifiable (it is also unnecessary).

[7] *Fam*. vii, 30. 3, *qui in Graeciam cum legionibus missus est*. Cf. Groag, *SB*. ix, 1939, p. 6.

[8] E.g. by Hall, l.c.; Klebs, *PW*. i, 252 (15).

[9] Caesar, *Bell. Civ*. iii, 39. 1.

[10] Hölzl, *Fasti praetorii*, Diss. Leipzig, 1876, p. 87.

[11] *Fasti Venusini* (*CIL*. x, 422).

[12] Val. Max. i, 8. 12; cf. Klebs, *PW*. i, 253 (19). Von Rohden's suggested identification of M. Acilius with Acilius Caninus(?) (ibid. 253 [16]) is invalidated by the difference of *praenomina*. M. Acilius Caninus, *quaestor urbanus* (*CIL*. xiv, 153), was too young at this date to be considered here.

army-commander and provincial governor. There are no other probable candidates for the governorship of Macedonia in 45–44,[1] or, for that matter, for its provincial quaestorship.[2]

It is reasonable to suppose that this issue, like that of the dictator's other quaestor, Cn. Julius, and like all financial enterprises of the period, was planned and supervised by the central bureau of Balbus, to which, no doubt, heavy profits accrued owing to the false values attached to *orichalcum* (p. 88). But Acilius himself, like all other moneyers in *orichalcum* before Augustus, came of a family with large financial interests; indeed, the Balkans were the special sphere of the Acilii,[3] and the calamine needed for the alloy may well be of Macedonian origin.[4] It is not surprising that the series, though as pretentious in type and range of denominations as in metal, is now of exceptional rarity: there was little time for the development of its circulation before the type became unacceptable to the government of Brutus and Cassius. Moreover, these obtained possession of the *fisci* (including the revenue of the last administrative year) not only of Macedonia, but of Asia and Syria also,[5] and were therefore in a position to suppress this unsuitably autocratic mintage not only at the source, but at the points to which its circulation naturally tended to flow. The coins may have been at once melted down; more probably they were overstruck by the Republican issues at Thessalonica, which followed almost immediately (p. 33). Overstrikings of Macedonian coinage of this period are by no means infrequent.[6]

The official Caesarian *aes* coinage, therefore, is complex in character. It can be classified according to objective, and also from administrative, economic and metallurgical standpoints. As regards objective, the mints in Spain and Macedonia were primarily strategic, but Clovius—like many later founders—commemorates the enfranchisement of cities, and the issue of Sulpicius Rufus may have had both *raisons d'être*. From an administrative point of view there are two groups: the governor of Pontus-Bithynia, quaestor of Farther Spain, and quaestor-governor of Macedonia were not inconsistent with Republican traditions, but Clovius (like Hirtius before him) was an extra-constitutional representative of the dictator; intermediate is the issue at Corduba, which appears to combine the signatures of a quaestor and of Caesar's financial secretary Balbus. Sulpicius Rufus possessed the *imperium*, and possibly Clovius also, but the rest did not: however, an essential and persistent feature of the issues is the ultimate responsibility of the dictator's *imperium maius*. Caesar is likely to have profited heavily from the *orichalcum* issues, and subsequent moneyers in this

---

[1] Cf. Letz, *Die Provinzialverwaltung Cäsars*, Diss. Strassburg, 1912, p. 60. R. Syme agrees that the reasons for assigning to Q. Hortensius a first tenure of 45–44 are inadequate.

[2] Cf. Bülz, *De Provinciarum Romanarum Quaestoribus*, Diss. Leipzig, 1893.

[3] *CIG.* 1793.

[4] Cf. Dioscorides, *De Materia Medica*, v, 74; von Lippmann, *Entstehung und Ausbreitung der Alchemie*, p. 592; Davies, *Roman Mines in Europe*, p. 227. Copper too was a local product, Davies, l.c. n. 4.

[5] Cf. Syme, *RR.* p. 171.

[6] E.g. Gaebler, *NG.* II, p. 96. 19.

metal are, significantly enough, wealthy magnates (p. 89): it is therefore interesting to note that Caesar's coiners, not only in this alloy but in bronze also, include some eminent financiers—namely, Hirtius, Balbus, C. Vibius Pansa,[1] and probably Q. Sulpicius Rufus also. It is difficult to resist the conclusion that coinage in bronze at a standard below the ounce was also not unprofitable to those privileged to provide it, although the percentages were perhaps not so high as those derived from the dictator's own perquisite, *orichalcum*.

[1] The last-named collaborates with cities for coinage: see below, p. 396.

B. THE POMPEIANS

1. UTICA(?)

The coinage of the dictatorship, like the forces of the dictator, did not hold the field alone: the regular magistrates of the Republic still functioned where they might, and at least survived the death of their principal enemy. Their earliest bronze issue, with a female head to right, and a male head to right[1] or left,[2] has fallen into oblivion after a single and entirely inaccurate description by Muller, who reads its legends as follows:[3] C. AL. POMP. M. F. VIC. Q. A. F. C. KAR.— ····· M. M··A. The ethnic leads him to assign the series to Carthage, and Kubitschek is rightly astonished by it.[4] But the true obverse reading is as follows:

A. POMP. M. F. VIC. Q. A. F. C. EXERC. (Pl. II, 4)

and the reverse legend is merely an inversion of this—obviously the work of an illiterate who was presented with an obverse die and told to produce a coin (Pl. II, 4, 5).[5]

F. C. is found very commonly on inscriptions for *faciundum curavit*.[6] Q. A. is so frequent an abbreviation for Q(*uaestor ad*) A(*erarium*) or A(*erarii*) or A(*rcae*)[7] that no

---

[1] Berlin, Copenhagen.
[2] Berlin, Paris ('uncertain' and too worn to supply assistance).
[3] *Suppl.* p. 55. 230 *a–c*.   [4] *Imp.* p. 147 n. 211.
[5] The three necessary corrections are these: (1) A Berlin example (Pl. II, 4) on which the male head faces left shows clearly that the reverse legend, if inverted, reads APOMPMI········. The execution on this side is much inferior to the obverse, whose inscription has merely been reproduced on the reverse die, where it appears from right to left; the O has been somewhat mangled by the barbarian die-cutter. (2) The engraver of the reverse has inserted a palm-branch round part of the edge, so that the inscription can clearly be seen to commence with the A which Muller places second. Neither on the reverse of this piece, nor on any of the obverses—all of which are legible at this point—is there any sign of the ligatured L imagined by Muller. Thus the name is A. POMP. M. F. VIC., and the C is not the first, but the last, letter of the inscription. (3) The better of the Berlin specimens shows that the ethnic KAR is the product of too powerful an imagination. In the first place, there are only two separate characters, not three. Muller does not mention a ligature here: but the first character is certainly composite. Nor does it include a K. There is only one stroke to the right from the centre of the main vertical line, and that is not only at right angles to it, but continued through to the left. Thus the basis is a cross: but at right angles to the vertical below the horizontal are two further horizontal lines, extending to the right only (Monogram 1). The monogram could conceivably include an I and T, but the horizontal stroke is so low as to make this combination very improbable. There only remains the possibility of an X, with which an E is certainly conjoined. The next letter is a P with distinct indications of a down-stroke to right: that is, an R. It has been shown that a C follows at the end. The interpretation seems to be XERC or EXRC. But there is no reason why the E of the ligature should not be repeated, like A in other numismatic monograms (e.g. below, p. 394). Its repetition gives us EXERC.
[6] E.g. coins (Muller II, pp. 159 ff., 364, 365) and many inscriptions.
[7] E.g. *Ephemeris Epigraphica*, III, p. 322; *CIL.* V, 6428; XI, 3009, 3215, 4389; IX, 4198; X, 5920; XIV, 298; cf. Mantey, *De gradu et statu quaestorum etc.*, Diss. Halle, 1882, pp. 32 ff.

alternative can be considered. Now in the place of an ethnic is $\overline{\text{EXERC}}$., which can represent the name of no known city, and appears to exclude all restorations but that of EXERCITVS in one of its cases. The present interpretation can be supported by no analogy, but the coins too are without a parallel; and the monogram appears to admit no alternative explanation. Muller has rightly seen that the fabric and style of these pieces is African. The lettering is particularly comparable to coins of Octavian attributed elsewhere to *colonia* Thapsus (p. 225), and it would be difficult to assign the series outside the *Provincia Vetus*.

The female heads are clearly not far from contemporary with very similar ones at *municipium* Simitthu, which will be attributed to 44 B.C. (p. 178). Moreover, one specimen of the present issue[1] shows a bust of a general design found on a colonial series of Celsa—also of c. 44 (p. 211). There can be little doubt, then, that the issue was made as early as the forties. The mention of the Roman *exercitus* makes it most unlikely that A. Pomponius M.f. Victor—for African epigraphic analogies justify this restoration of his name[2]—is a colonial or municipal *quaestor aerarii* or *ad aerarium*. Besides, the earliest known appearance of these officials in a colonial or municipal constitution is late Augustan (p. 270)—much too late for the fabric of these pieces. But the office had already existed at an earlier date in the government of Rome itself: until 45 B.C.[3] the director of the Roman treasury was known as *quaestor ad aerarium*.[4] When Julius conquered Italy at the beginning of 49 B.C., the majority of senators and officials preferred to leave for Pompeian territory, and these, headed by the consuls, one of whom had first rifled the treasury,[5] were made the nucleus of a Republican administration at the headquarters in Epirus.[6] After Pharsalus this was transferred to Africa, which had been secured for the Republic in the previous year[7] and was not lost to it until the battle of Thapsus (Feb. 46). The Pompeian administrative capital and military headquarters were combined at Utica,[8] and it is here that the present issue is most likely to have been struck. In any other situation but this it would be very difficult to explain the presence in Africa of the signatory of these coins: but the wandering *aerarium* of the Pompeian *régime*, which claimed to be the Roman government, was naturally in the hands of a regular *quaestor ad aerarium*, who may or may not, under the special circumstances, have been reappointed annually with the consuls. An exactly similar official is later found in the camp of Sextus (p. 24). Thus was bronze currency provided for the large Pompeian forces in Africa, in c. 48–46 B.C., by the head of the Roman Republican treasury.

[1] Copenhagen.
[2] E.g. *Recueil de la Soc. arch. du dép. de Constantine*, XXIX, 1894–5, p. 635, Pomponia L.f. Victorina; ibid. XXVIII, 1893–4, p. 176, Pomponia Victoria—probably from families freed by him.
[3] Dio XLIII, 48. 3.
[4] Polybius XXIII, 14. 5; cf. *Tabula Bantina* 24

(Bruns, *Fontes Iuris romani*[7] 8), *Lex Cornelia de XX quaestoribus* I. 10 (ibid. 12), *Lex Agraria* 46 (ibid. 11).
[5] Cf. Caesar, *Bell. Civ.* I, 14. 1; Fabre, *Revue des études anciennes*, XXXIII, 1931, p. 26.
[6] Cf. Adcock, *CAH*. IX, pp. 641 f.
[7] Ibid. pp. 653, 681 ff.
[8] Ibid. p. 684.

2. CORDUBA (?)

In 46 B.C. the Republic had to retire to yet another line of defences, in Spain. There M. Minatius Sabinus *pro quaestore* struck *denarii* for the younger Cnaeus Pompeius, describing him as CN. MAGNVS IMP. and CN. MAGNVS IMP. F.[1] There is also an *as* of traditional type[2] and heavy weight[3] (probably issued at Corduba) bearing the former of these titles. But Sextus, probably after Munda, coined *asses*—principally found in Spain[4] though of extensive circulation[5]—both through a *legatus* M. Eppius M.f.[6] as MAGNVS PIVS IMP. F.,[7] and without an additional signature as MAGNVS PIVS IMP.[8] Since, therefore, IMP. F. certainly remained in use in the Pompeian titulature after the introduction of plain IMP., Borghesi's[9] interpretation IMP(*erator*) F(*ilius*)—from the analogy of L. PROCILI. F., MESSAL. F., C. CVR. F., REGVLVS F.—is more probable than Visconti's IMP(*eratoris*) F(*ilius*).[10] It is not merely *Cn. Magnus filius, imperator*, that Cnaeus calls himself, but *Cn. Magnus, Imperator filius*. In the same way, since their father was not called Pius, the F. on Sextus's coin also must be limited to IMP.: his title is *Magnus Pius, Imperator filius*. Both of them are seen to have viewed the title *Imperator*, not as an ordinary personal distinction, but as the title to a special hereditary *imperium* (p. 409). The usage was, for Sextus, the prelude to an assumption of the titulature IMP. SEX. MAGNVS,[11] which appears on *denarii*

---

[1] Bahrfeldt, *NZ*. 1897, p. 47.

[2] Cf. Laffranchi, *Bollettino del Circolo Numismatico Napolitano*, 1917, pp. 21 ff.

[3] Bahrfeldt, *NZ*. 1909, p. 67.

[4] Cf. Mommsen, *Annali dell' Inst. di corr. arch.* 1863, p. 74, and del Rivero, *Madrid Cat.* p. 93.

[5] E.g. found at Pompeii (della Corte, *Not. d. Scavi*, 1929, p. 379), Nijmegen (mus.), Nîmes. Attribution of the issues to Nîmes by Goudard (*Monographie des monnaies frappées à Nîmes*, p. 36) is based merely on the discovery of a few coins there (as in countless other places) and on a double-bevelled edge (found at this period on issues from all regions). For these feeble reasons he calls them *un produit incontestable de l'atelier*. The wide circulation corrects the assumption of Milne, *Development of Roman Coinage*, p. 21, that these pieces did not find acceptance outside Sextus' own provinces.

[6] He also countermarks a *denarius* (Bordeaux). Served under Metellus Scipio; later pardoned by Caesar, Münzer, *PW*. VI, 259. Like so many moneyers of military *aes* at this period, the Eppii were eminent financiers; cf. Hatzfeld, p. 128.

[7] *BMCR*. II, p. 373. 104 ff.

[8] Ibid. p. 371. 95 ff.

[9] *Œuvres*, I, p. 158.

[10] *Iconografia romana*, pl. V, 7. F(*ecit*) is impossible, since the Pompeii were not their own moneyers.

[11] This reading is demanded by the following considerations. Two of the coins bear the head of Cnaeus *sen.* inscribed SEX. MAGN.—IMP. SAL. (PIETAS on reverse) (Laffranchi, *R.it.* 1912, p. 511. 2), and SEX. MAG.—PIVS IMP. SAL. (ibid. 3)—with legends reading outwards and upwards from low right. The third (ibid. 1) has a remarkable head that must be a portrait (cf. Hill, p. 87 n. 53), but is not of Cnaeus *sen.*: it must represent Sextus himself. On the first two coins the legend begins from low right, and the ethnic SAL. comes at the end: if both these reasonable conditions are applied to the third piece, its legend becomes IMP. SEX. MAGNVS SAL. Morelli's restoration SEX. MAGN. SAL. [PIVS] IMP. (*Familiarum Romanarum Numismata*, s.v. *Pompeia* 2, VI) is wrong.

THE POMPEIANS

struck at *Urbs Imperatoria* Salacia[1] late in 44.[2] Cnaeus the younger appears to have taken the title on his arrival in Spain,[3] but it is not clear whether his brother did likewise[4] or waited until his successes in 44.[5] The new *praenomen* of the latter, Magnus— inspired by Octavian's precedent (p. 415)—shows clearly that his aims were directed towards a greater *principatus* than his father's[6] rather than to the Republican tradition that was professed by his party. On the *as* with MAGNVS PIVS IMP. the loan of the features of Pompey himself[7] to the customary head of Janus shows an apt compromise between the ambitions of some, and the ideals of others, of the supporters of Sextus. *Pietas* was the slogan of the Pompeians at Munda:[8] the incorporation of PIVS in his name by Sextus expresses dutifulness to the Manes of the Cnaei[9]— including revenge.[10]

Burns[11] wrongly describes these bronze *asses*[12] as 'copper'. It cannot be determined whether Grueber[13] is right in considering their metal to be the Corduban *aes*

---

[1] *BMCR.* II, pp. 370 f. The generally accepted interpretation SAL (*dubia*) (Laffranchi, *R.it.* 1912, p. 511; cf. Charlesworth, *CAH.* x, p. 4 n. 1) is unacceptable, since, although after Munda Sextus took refuge among the northern tribe of the Lacetani (Dio XLV, 10), he did not begin to win cities over until his arrival in the *provincia ulterior* (ibid.; cf. Appian, *BC.* IV, 83; Blok, *Sextus Pompeius Magnus Gnaei Filius*, Diss. Leyden, 1879, p. 10), when he beat Carrinas (App. l.c.) and—*pace* the Augustan tradition in Velleius (II, 73. 2) (on whose unfairness vide Scott, *Memoirs of the American Academy in Rome*, XI, 1933, pp. 8 ff.)—Pollio, until finally πάντα ὀλίγου τὰ ταύτῃ κατέσχε (Dio, l.c.). The *denarii* must, then, have been issued in Farther Spain: about forty miles south-east of Olisipo lies the Latin city Salacia, which was striking pieces about now with the head of Neptune and IMP. SALAC. (Madrid: Vives III, p. 26. 11; cf. *Archeologo Portugues*, XVI, 1911, p. 103) and IMP. SAL. (Vives, l.c. 9. Provenance—20 at Alcacer do Sal mus., Leite de Vasconcellos, *Arquivos da Universidade de Lisboa*, IX [1923], p. 215. 20; also at Lisbon [*Academia das Sciencias*], ibid. p. 189). Pliny (*NH.* IV, 116) announces that it was called *Urbs Imperatoria*: this unexplained and unparalleled *cognomen* cannot have anything to do with the foundations of Julius or Augustus (called *Iulia, Augusta*), but is very relevant to the peculiar Pompeian adaptation of the title *Imperator*. Moreover, Neptune, who appears on the coins, was Sextus's tutelary deity (cf. Charlesworth, *CAH.* x, p. 67), and Salacia was Neptune's wife (cf. Witte, *PW.* [2R.] II, 1818). A Latin foundation of Salacia is (independently) attributed to Sextus by Wallrafen, *Die Einrichtung und kommunale Entwicklung der römischen Provinz Lusitanien*, p. 38 n. 4; cf. van Nostrand, *UCPH.* IV, 2, 1916, p. 101. Sestini's coin with COL. (Fontana, Sp. p. 16) cannot now be checked. The issues may well have commemorated the *constitutio* of the Latin city, since many mintages can be attributed to similar occasions (pp. 335 ff.).

[2] Dated by Ulrich, *Pietas (pius) als politischer Begriff*, Diss. Breslau, 1930, p. 12: Pietas holds an olive-branch marking the agreement reached by the mediation of Lepidus. For Sextus's claims at this time see below, p. 409.

[3] Grueber, *BMCR.* II, p. 371. [4] Ibid.

[5] As Hadas, *Sextus Pompey*, p. 58.

[6] Cf. Gwosdz, *Der Begriff des römischen Princeps*, Diss. Breslau, 1933, p. 48.

[7] Not Sextus's own, cf. Bahrfeldt, l.c.

[8] Appian, *BC.* II, 430; cf. Syme, *RR.* p. 157. For *Pietas* vide Ulrich, l.c.; Meister, *Heidelberger Universitätsreden*, XI, 1930, pp. 6 ff.

[9] Roscher, *Lexicon der Mythologie*, III, 1645.

[10] Drumann, *Grundriss der Kulturgeschichte*, III, pp. 567 f.

[11] *Money and Monetary Policy in Ancient Times*, p. 302 n. 1.

[12] Analysed *NZ.* 1909, pp. 67 ff.

[13] *BMCR.* II, p. 368.

Marianum[1] (p. 7): but Corduba is a probable choice of mint for these central issues, which would thus immediately succeed the Caesarian issue of Cn. Julius *quaestor*. A similarity in metal confirms this attribution.

3–5. URSO, MYRTILIS, BAELO

Further insight into the Pompeian cause can be obtained by an investigation of L. AP. DEC. Q., whose name is found on the coins of three other cities in Hispania Ulterior—accompanying the ethnics VRSONE, MVRT[IL.], and BAILO. At Urso (Pl. II, 6) it appears on three denominations, with different diademed heads,[2] weighing c. 512,[3] c. 303[4] and c. 286–147·5[5] grains respectively. Since *Colonia Genetiva Iulia Vrbanorum*, founded in c. 44, was a settlement of Romans[6] including all, or nearly all, the territory of Urso,[7] it is inconceivable that after that date the native community could have continued to have a nominal existence sufficient to justify the appearance of its name (rather than that of the colony) on coinage; even peregrine constitutions which survived combination with a colony were never favoured to this extent (p. 404). C. 44, then, is a *terminus ante quem* for the ethnic VRSONE. On some coins an F seems to appear after L. AP. DEC. Q.:[8] since there can be no question of *Quinti filius* following the *cognomen*, F(*ecit*)—as regularly on pottery[9]—must be supplied. At Myrtilis we find [L.] AP. DE.,[10] L. A. DEC.,[11] L. A. D.;[12] at Baelo—with the name of a local aedile FAT.[13]—L. AP. Q.[14] There are records of Appuleii Deciani of the first century B.C.,[15] with large commercial interests from which the present official, like the preceding moneyer M. Eppius, may well have derived monetary experience.[16] From the correspondence of these three issues there can be no doubt that he was a Roman, not a local, official; he must have been a Roman quaestor in Farther Spain.

It is therefore astonishing to meet the inscription L. $\overline{\text{AP}}$. $\overline{\text{DEC}}$. Q.,[17] and sometimes $\overline{\text{AP}}$.,[18] $\overline{\text{APVL}}$.,[19] on a series of coins which must inevitably be attributed to the mint of

---

[1] Pliny, *NH.* XXXIV, 4, says that this '*imitates* the goodness of *orichalcum*' (cf. below, p. 87); but it was apparently a variety of bronze: cf. Davies, *Roman Mines in Europe*, p. 114.
[2] Heiss, p. 319. 5, wrongly says one is laureate, and represents Octavian.
[3] BM, Milan, *Cat.* 144–5; cf. Vives III, p. 97.
[4] BM, Madrid.
[5] BM.
[6] Cf. Hardy, *Three Spanish Charters*, p. 10; Rice Holmes, *The Roman Republic*, III, p. 322 n., *pace* Zumpt, *Commenta Epigraphica*, pp. 317 f.
[7] Cf. Hardy, l.c. p. 7; Frank, *ES.* I, p. 317.
[8] BM (2); cf. Vives III, p. 97.
[9] Oswald, *Index of Potters' Stamps*, *passim*.
[10] Vives III, p. 91; cf. Heiss, p. 415, 1; BM, Madrid.
[11] Vives, l.c.; cf. Heiss, l.c. 2; BM.
[12] Madrid (del Rivero, *Cat.* p. 65).
[13] For the male name Fata, vide *Arch.-epigr. Mitt.* XVI, p. 42; for Fato, vide Schulze, p. 36. Both are Celtic.
[14] Vives, l.c. p. 45. 3. LAPO: Delgado I, 40 (Madrid; del Rivero, *Cat.* p. 9). L. AP.: BM cast.
[15] *PW.* XI, 259 f. For the family vide Syme, *Anatolian Studies to Buckler*, 1939. Hübner's suggestion 'Decimus' (*MLI.* p. 115) is less likely.
[16] Cic. *Pro Flacco* 70; cf. Frank, *ES.* I, p. 392; Hatzfeld, p. 120.
[17] Bahrfeldt, *RS.* XII, 1904, p. 363. 18 (Coll. Seripopoli, Trapani).
[18] Ibid. 19 *a*, 19 *b*; cf. Landolina-Paterno, *Ricerche numismatiche sull' antica Sicilia*, pp. 13–14.
[19] Bahrfeldt, l.c. p. 362, 17 *a*, 17 *b*; cf. Garrucci, *Le monete dell' Italia antica*, p. 137, 459 *b*.

THE POMPEIANS

Lilybaeum, on whose local issues both their types—Apollo head and lyre—occur with precisely similar execution (p. 26).[1] Baetica and Sicily never belonged to the same administrative unit, and there is no parallel for a second quaestorship in a different province. But in the last years of the Republic there was one occasion, and one only, to which the peculiar situation of L. Appuleius Decianus applies exactly. When Sextus Pompeius evacuated Baetica he was appointed *praefectus classis* by the senate; but, proscribed on 28 November 43, he sailed to Sicily, where he took Lilybaeum and gradually the rest of the island.[2] The fact that he struck there coins with HISPANORVM (p. 29) confirms the probability that he relied on supporters who had accompanied him from Spain; and since, outlawed by the triumvirate, he could derive no supply of administrative officials from Rome, it was entirely natural that men whom he or his brother had appointed to quaestorships in Baetica should serve him in the same capacity in Sicily. In particular, A. Pomp. Victor has provided an example of a similar coinage by a Pompeian *quaestor ad aerarium*. One of his successors was probably this L. Appuleius Decianus. It is not improbable that the extent of his coinage is partly due to a desire by Sextus to show that Octavian's kinsmen—among whom the Appuleii were[3]—were not all supporters of the triumvirate: a similar cause seems to prompt coinage for T. Octavius as proconsul for Antony (p. 373).

It is through this official, then, that Sextus issues *aes* at Lilybaeum, and earlier at three Baetican towns. In confirmation it may be added that Urso was noteworthy as his loyallest supporter.[4] Although Ablative ethnics occur elsewhere (p. 224), it may be significant of the undoubtedly official character of his coinage that the earliest coins of this city have VRSO,[5] while these (and a few unsigned[6]) have VRSONE. This may be a purely Local Ablative: it is possible, therefore, that CORDVBA on the official issue of Cn. Julius *quaestor* is an Ablative also.

L. Appuleius's choice of Spanish mints is interesting. The analogy of Roman officials' names at Vesci, Brutobriga and Antipolis within the next four years (pp. 379 ff.), and of Sextus's own issues at Salacia early in 44, makes it highly probable that the present group too commemorates the conferment of *Latinitas* or even Roman status. It is significant that the Caesarians found it desirable to eradicate completely the town of Urso in the same year; nor is the assumption that Baelo survived to obtain full *civitas* under Claudius[7] justified.[8] Myrtilis too was refounded as a Roman[9] or Latin town.[10]

The form of the ethnic VRSONE, and the lack of parallels for such signed issues among the Roman and Latin foundation-series, make it preferable to consider these coins official rather than local.

[1] Cf. Bahrfeldt, l.c. p. 362.
[2] Appian, *BC.* IV, 84; cf. Blok, l.c. p. 14.
[3] Cf. Syme, *RR.* p. 289.
[4] Cf. Meyer, *Cäsars Monarchie*, p. 485.
[5] Heiss, p. 319.   [6] Ibid.
[7] As Hübner, *PW.* II, 2759; Albertini, *Les divisions administratives de l'Espagne romaine*, pp. 61 f.

[8] Momigliano, *The Emperor Claudius and his Achievement*, pp. 64 f.; Sutherland, *RIS.* p. 176.
[9] Schulten, *PW.* XVI, 1151, suggests that it was one of the Julian *municipia*. For drafts of settlers at these see below, p. 155.
[10] As van Nostrand, *UCPH.* IV, 2, 1916, p. 101; Hübner, *La Arqueología de España*, p. 178.

6. LILYBAEUM

It is now necessary to return to the mint at which L. Appuleius Decianus issued coinage in c. 43–42 as quaestor of Western Sicily—Lilybaeum, its administrative capital.[1] Although Bahrfeldt never attempted the task, its *asses* and *semisses*[2] are easily distinguishable from those of Agrigentum (p. 28) and Panormus.[3] The latter often bear a mint-mark and the local types of Jupiter and warrior,[4] while at Lilybaeum reverse-types of lyre and wreath are linked by characteristic heads of Apollo:[5] the lyre is the city-type, and a specimen with wreath has the mint-mark ΛΙΛ.[6] Besides L. AP. DEC. Q. (AP., APVL.), the moneyers here are MAN. ACILI. Q.,[7] NASO,[8] Q. FAB.,[9] POR.,[10] Q. ANNI.[11] (AN.[12]), CRASSIPES[13] (variously abbreviated) (Pl. I, 2) and Q. B.[14] (Pl. I, 3).

These fall into two sharply defined groups. The quaestorship of M'. Acilius Caninus(?) was not later than the early fifties, since he was proconsul of Sicily in 46–45.[15] Q. Fabius will be of similar date, whether he is the Maximus who was *consul suffectus* in 45 [16] or the Vergilianus who was *legatus* in 51.[17] POR. too, if he was M. Cato, was quaestor not long after 60,[18] and it is as quaestor that all these officials coined.[19]

[1] Holm III, p. 75; cf. pseudo-Ascon. (ed. Orelli), p. 100; Halgan, *Essai sur l'administration des provinces sénatoriales*, p. 232.
[2] Av. c. 100 grains—occasionally heavier.
[3] A few *quadrantes* are border-line cases.
[4] Cf. Bahrfeldt, *RS*. XII, 1904, p. 385 n. 1.
[5] Ibid. pp. 362. 17*a*, 366. 22*a* (wreath); pp. 364. 19*b*, 371. 26 (lyre).
[6] Ibid. p. 346. 4 (Berlin). Vide Monogram 12; Bahrfeldt rightly accepts Garrucci's interpretation of this.
[7] Bahrfeldt, l.c. p. 346. 5 (Palermo, Gabrici, p. 156. 140).
[8] Bahrfeldt, l.c. p. 354. 12 (BM).
[9] Gabrici, p. 156. 133 (Palermo).
[10] Ibid. p. 344. 1 (*BMC*. p. 124. 29). Interpretation as POR(*tus*) (Poole, ibid.) is quite out of keeping with the series. A Hellenised P is used: vide Monogram 2.
[11] Bahrfeldt, l.c. p. 353. 10 (BM).
[12] Ibid. 11 (Colmar).
[13] Ibid. p. 368. 24 (BM).
[14] Ibid. p. 365. 20 (BM).
[15] Hölzl, *Fasti praetorii*, Diss. Leipzig, 1876, p. 87.
[16] Ibid. p. 66.   [17] Münzer, *PW*. VI, 1872 (154).
[18] Hölzl, l.c. p. 93.
[19] CAT. Q., not CATO, undoubtedly appears on Panormitan coins at Paris (Bahrfeldt, l.c. p. 397; cf. his pl. III, 53), Berlin and Palermo (Fraccia, *Antiche monete siciliane*, p. 32. 122). Since the issues are entirely uniform and the period was one of peace, it is probable that the other officials were also quaestors—who were the senior magistrates at Lilybaeum. This conclusion is confirmed by the probable identity of L. ME. (Bahrfeldt, l.c. p. 392. 45 [BM]) and L. CAEC. (Gabrici, p. 159. 200 [Palermo]) with L. Caecilius Metellus, who was quaestor of Sicily before his tribunate of 49 (Mommsen, *CIL*. X, 7258; cf. Münzer, *PW*. III, 75). Furthermore, CAT. Q. reveals a quaestorship of M. Porcius Cato in Sicily before his governorship of the same province in 49–48 (Hölzl, l.c. p. 93): exactly parallel is the case of MAN. ACILI. Q., since M'. Acilius governed Sicily in 46–45 (see n. 15). This evidence that men were sent as governors to the province of which they had gained experience as quaestors suggests that A. POM. also (Bahrfeldt, l.c. p. 399. 50 [Gotha]) indicates a quaestorship of the A. Pompeius Bithynicus who governed Sicily in 44–43/2 (Klein, *Die römischen Verwaltungsbeamten*, pp. 85 ff., Cichorius, *Römische Studien*, p. 245, Sternkopf, *Hermes*, XLVII, 1912, p. 328), and that either L. POS. (Bahrfeldt, l.c. p. 399. 51 [Capitoline]) or S. POS. (ibid. p. 400. 52 [Berlin, Palermo] = S.P. [Berlin]) recalls the quaestorship of the Postumius who was appointed, but not sent, as proconsul in 49 (Cic. *Att*. VII, 15. 2).

THE POMPEIANS

Naso's tenure will be only a few years later if he is the P. Naso who was praetor in 44.[1] Moreover, CAT. Q., NASO and Q. FAB. all coined also at Panormus,[2] and the other issues of that mint confirm c. 50 as its closing date.[3] It seems that Julius suppressed this long-standing Republican institution.

On the other hand, Q. B. (to whose issue that of Crassipes is markedly similar)[4] uses an individual form of B which is only found elsewhere on Antony's 'Fleet' currency of 37 B.C. (p. 43),[5] and, on the principle of the lesser copying the greater, must have been imitated from it. Since Caesar appears to have put an end to the coinage at Lilybaeum (as at Panormus) of the quaestors, who presumably supported Pompey the Great, it is highly significant that, when the mint at Lilybaeum reopens, L. Ap. Dec. falls at the beginning, and Q. B. at the end, of Sextus Pompeius's administration of the island in 43–36 B.C. They, Furius Crassipes, who may have been a friend of Cicero's,[6] and (as a later coinage will suggest [p. 29]) probably Q. Annius—perhaps the son of a Catilinarian of the same name[7]—represent a revival of the Republican coinage under Sextus, which terminated at his loss of Lilybaeum[8] and his fall. Possibly all are quaestors, but the exigencies of the period may well have caused deviations from this rule.[9] The choice of mint is interesting, since Lilybaeum, like other Sicilian cities, was enfranchised just before or during Sextus's occupation (p. 189).

---

[1] Hölzl, l.c. p. 98; cf. Ribbeck, *Senatores Romani*, Diss. Berlin, 1899, p. 23, no. 92.

[2] Bahrfeldt, l.c. pp. 397, 392, 393 respectively.

[3] Besides suggestions made on p. 26 it is possible to make conjectural identifications of Q. MALL (Bahrfeldt, l.c. p. 387 [Berlin]), P. AT. (Torremuzza, *Siciliae populorum et urbium, regum quoque et tyrannorum veteres nummi*, pl. LXI, 2; cf. Holm, III, p. 731. 773), M. MAR. (ll.cc. pl. LXI, 11; p. 773. 785), M. AVR. (ll.cc. pl. LXI, 4; p. 732. 775), P. RV. (Bahrfeldt, l.c. p. 400. 53 [Naples, Palermo = Gabrici, p. 158. 218]) to the quaestorships of Q. Poblicius, praetor in 69 (Cic. *Pro Cluentio*, 45; cf. Smith, *Dict. Biogr. and Mythol.* III, p. 600 [7]), Atilius the friend of Brutus (Cichorius, *Römische Studien*, p. 245), M. Marcellus consul in 51 (Hölzl, l.c. p. 69), M. Cotta *pro praetore* in Sardinia in 49 (ibid. p. 66), and P. Rutilius Lupus praetor in 49 (ibid. p. 76: Münzer, *PW*. [2R.] I, 1230 prefers attribution to a Rupilius) respectively. The issues can be divided according to the presence or absence of a monogrammed mint-mark. Some of the monogrammed issues seem to be of later fabric than the other group, since their flans are better but their execution less careful: however, a study of the styles makes it most probable that the two categories overlap in date. Coins with the head of Janus, signed P. TE. (Bahrfeldt, l.c. p. 378. 39 [BM]) and TRI. (ibid. p. 381. 41 [BM]), appear to precede the two main series, which include at least eight names on the monogrammed pieces, and fifteen (?) on the rest. Lenormant, *La monnaie dans l'antiquité*, II, p. 280, rightly sees that these groups precede the coinage here attributed to Lilybaeum.

[4] Cf. Bahrfeldt, l.c. p. 368.   [5] Ibid. p. 365.

[6] Cic. *Att.* IX, 11. 3; cf. Bahrfeldt, l.c.; Stein, *PW*, VII, 352 (54). No later member of the family is recorded.

[7] Cf. Klebs, *PW*. I, 2263.

[8] Cf. Levi II, p. 83.

[9] Coins also reveal several of his *legati* who coin (see below, pp. 30 ff.).

7. AGRIGENTUM

Bahrfeldt, who did not distinguish between the official issues of Panormus and Lilybaeum, failed also to discern several issues of a third mint. M'. Acilius Caninus(?), who has been met with at Lilybaeum, issued other coins with three distinctive types[1] all of which are found on the local series of Agrigentum, to which this issue must be ascribed. Early style and the analogy of his signature at Lilybaeum indicate attribution to his quaestorship,[2] which occurred in the early fifties.

But it appears that the official mint at Agrigentum also operated at a later date. A small piece with a Pharos as obverse-type, whose date could scarcely be much earlier than municipal coins under Sextus's administration (e.g. Pl. I, 6 [p. 191]), bears on the reverse the signature L. CN.[3] and a ligature[4] (wrongly reproduced by Torremuzza[5] and Bahrfeldt[6]) which must represent the letters ΑΓΡ (Pl. I, 5). This is best interpreted as the semi-Romanised mint-mark[7] of the city—*oppidum Agragas, quod Agrigentum nostri dixere*.[8] This conclusion is confirmed by the execution and fabric of the present piece, which show no kinship with the Panormus and Lilybaeum groups.[9] The moneyer is most likely to be a member of the rare *gens* Cnoria.[10] Very close to this issue in style are others with the signatures L. M. (Pl. I, 6)[11] and C. ALIO BALA,[12] whose mint can scarcely be different. The *cognomen* of the latter suggests oriental origin,[13] which the presence of Allii in business circles at Delos makes probable.[14]

Another group of *quadrantes*,[15] with the type of a club, is akin to these issues and may be ascribed with probability (though not with certainty) to the same mint: the style is not that of Panormus or Lilybaeum, but the names of West Sicilian officials occur. Among them are Q. FAB.,[16] who coined at both those mints in the fifties, and

---

[1] Bahrfeldt, l.c. p. 348.

[2] An attribution to his proconsulship by Capranesi, *Bull. dell' Inst. di corr. arch.* 1834, p. 74 (cf. 1835, p. 43), is based on a misreading of a coin of Tingis (p. 177).

[3] Berlin, Palermo (Gabrici, p. 156. 128).

[4] Monogram 3.

[5] L.c. pl. LX, 20; cf. p. 59.

[6] L.c. p. 420. 71. He makes it look like the monogram of Panormus which was to be expected; cf. also *BMC. Sicily*, p. 124. 41.

[7] Rather than ethnic.

[8] Pliny, *NH*. III, 89; cf. also, for the form, Verg. *Aen.* III, 703 (?); Silius Italicus XIV, 210; Mela II, 118.

[9] The fact that the same moneyers issued *asses* and *semisses* at Lilybaeum is by no means a reason for these *quadrantes* to be assigned to that mint as a complementary part of the same series. There are several examples of two mints co-operating to provide different denominations, e.g. Rome and Paestum; cf. also the Eastern official groups of Augustus (see below, pp. 98 ff.).

[10] Cf. Schulze, p. 182. Collart, *Philippes*, p. 262, wrongly reads *publice Gnatio* for *public. Egnatio* on an unpublished inscription from Philippi.

[11] Bahrfeldt, l.c. p. 422. 74 (Berlin); Friedländer, *BB*. V, 1870, pp. 53 f.

[12] Bahrfeldt, l.c. p. 424. 76 (Ravenna).

[13] Cf. Alexander Bala, from Smyrna (Justin XXXV, 1. 6. 9). I owe this suggestion to R. Syme.

[14] *CIL*. III, 14203; cf. Hatzfeld, *BCH*. XXXVI, 1912, p. 13.

[15] Av. c. 25 grains.

[16] Bahrfeldt, l.c. p. 394. 47.

four others who coined at Lilybaeum—$\overline{\text{AN}}$.[1] (= Q. Anni.), Q. B. (Pl. I, 4),[2] CRASIP.[3] (= Crassipes),[4] and $\overline{\text{AP}}$.[5] (= L. Ap. Dec.). It is necessary to ascribe the last three to the administration of Sextus, to which Q. Annius may therefore also be attributed.[6] This arrangement is strikingly corroborated by the strong resemblance to the whole series of a small piece signed by LIBO[7]—who is identifiable with Sextus's father-in-law L. Scribonius Libo, who was with him in Sicily.[8] The praetorian rank of L. Libo confirms doubts whether all or any of the Sextian moneyers were quaestors: similar variations are found at Octavian's military mint at Lipara (p. 52).

The issues probably to be ascribed to Agrigentum thus fall into the two chronological groups found also at Lilybaeum,[9] and it is possible to say that both mints functioned under Pompey, were suppressed by Caesar, revived by Sextus in c. 43/42, and suppressed by Octavian. Our prosopographical knowledge of the administration of Sextus is enlarged by the addition of a number of officers—L. Appuleius Decianus, Furius Crassipes, Q. Annius, Q. B., L. Cnorius and C. Allius Bala. Nor is this all the information which the coinages of Sextus provide.

8. PANORMUS

Equally interesting are bronze[10] pieces with the reverse legend HISPANORVM, most of which have the late Spanish type of a horseman. Some specimens have a head of Minerva (Pl. I, 11) imitated closely from *denarii* struck in Spain by M. Poblicius *legatus* for Cn. Pompeius *junior*.[11] Type and head combined establish a *terminus post quem* of c. 48 B.C.[12] But the Spanish analogies cannot alter the fact that the provenance of the series is entirely Sicilian.[13] This combination makes it very difficult to resist the conclusion that the occasion of issue was the influx of Spaniards into Sicily with Sextus in c. 43–42.[14] This deduction is corroborated by the strong resemblance of the rougher of the two stylistic groups, into which the series falls (Pl. I, 10), to a coin

---

[1] Bahrfeldt, l.c. p. 424; cf. *Rn.* 1869, p. 181. 35.
[2] Ibid. p. 367. 23 a, b (BM).
[3] Ibid. p. 370. 25 (BM).
[4] See note 13, p. 26.
[5] Bahrfeldt, l.c. p. 423. 75 e (Berlin).
[6] His issue here must be classed with that of Ap., etc., not M'. Acili.
[7] Landolina-Paterno, *Ricerche numismatiche sull' antica Sicilia*, p. 29 (his own coll.). The wreath on the reverse is not comparable to the Lilybaeum type; cf. also a QB *quadrans* (Bahrfeldt, l.c. p. 366. 22 a, b).
[8] Cf. Münzer, *PW*.(2R.) II, 883; Syme, *RR*. p. 228.
[9] But there M'. Acili. stands alone in the earlier period.
[10] Spectrogram 66.
[11] *BMCR.* II, p. 364. 72; cf. Heuten, *Rev. belge de la Philologie et d'Histoire*, XIV, 1935, p. 713.
[12] Pace Willers, *Geschichte*, p. 98; Gomez-Moreno, *Anuario del Cuerpo Facultativo de Archiveros*, II, 1934; Amorós, *Rassegna Monetaria*, XXXIII, 1936, p. 452.
[13] This was recognised as early as Paruta, *La Sicilia* (1612), and by all subsequent writers, e.g. Heiss, *Annuaire de la Soc. de numismatique*, III, 1868, p. 209. Some found at Agrigentum (own coll., acquired in Rome); others in Catania Univ. collection (De Agostino, *Archivio storico per la Sicilia orientale*, XXXI, 1935).
[14] Dio XLVIII, 17 etc.; cf. Heiss, l.c.; Scramuzza, *ES*. III, p. 309.

celebrating the foundation of *municipium* Panormus in c. 44–43 (Pl. VI, 2 [p. 190]). Attribution of the coinages with HISPANORVM to the same city is confirmed by the survival of specimens overstruck on Panormitan local coins.[1] The same group is often signed by L. IVNI. LEG(*atus*) SIC(*iliae*) (Pl. I, 10),[2] whose unusual title foreshadows the creation of the *legatus Augusti provinciae*.

At this time the local Sicilian coinage is limited to issues commemorating the municipalisation of the cities under the *Lex Iulia* of 44 (p. 189) and—as a foundation coinage of C. Caninius Rebilus at Cephaloedium proves (p. 192)—by Sextus after his occupation of the island in 43–42. The astonishing legend HISPANORVM is therefore best explained in connection with the establishment of Roman cities. It is in the highest degree probable that land at these was allotted with *civitas* to the Spanish immigrants, who were Sextus's loyalest partisans. They may have been established in colonies, but there are also many parallels for the drafting of settlers to *municipia* (p. 155); in either case L. Junius supervised the settlement and issued the coinage.[3] Since, as has been said, there are two stylistic varieties of this series, it must be considered an official inauguratory coinage from two mints: official issues with a similar purpose have been ascribed to C. Clovius (p. 7), were being made in Macedonia at about this very time by Q. Hortensius (p. 33), and occur a few years later in Crete and Mauretania (pp. 57, 59).

9. Syracuse

The other group of HISPANORVM coins (Pl. I, 11)[4] is much more artistic in execution. It is attributable to Syracuse on the grounds of a deliberate imitation of coins of Hiero II.[5] This is shown to be mere archaism, and thus evidence of mint rather than of date, by the appearance of the type and head whose lateness has been pointed out. Like Lilybaeum, Agrigentum and Panormus, Syracuse too had acted as an official mint earlier in the first century B.C.:[6] it was part of Sextus's policy to revive these Republican institutions, which had been abolished by Caesar. Like Panormus, Syracuse had presumably been enfranchised in 44, and these coins indicate that it too received a draft of Spanish settlers from Sextus. The unique nationalist legend HISPANORVM illustrates the political importance of the exiles among the more lukewarm Sicilians, and the two Spanish foundations recorded by these coinages may well not have been the only ones made. For example, it will be shown that some modification in the status of Messana is also probable (p. 194). The *deductor* (or, if it was a

[1] E.g. Palermo mus. (Gabrici, pl. X, 27, etc.). These affinities have led to mistaken interpretations of HISPANORVM as PANORM. (e.g. by Heiss, l.c.).

[2] Froehner, *Rn.* 1908, p. 15 (Naples, own coll.); correcting Sestini, *Fontana*, I, 11, Walcher sale 775, *Hu.* I, 258.

[3] Cf. Froehner, l.c.; he identifies him conjecturally with the Silanus who was refused a consulship in 21 B.C. (*PIR.* II, 245).

[4] Palermo (Gabrici, pl. X, 29), etc.

[5] Cf. Vives II, p. 31; *BMC. Sicily*, p. 215. 565 ff.

[6] Holm III, p. 707. 557; coins with Greek ethnic but signed Q(*uaestor*). See n. 1, p. 1.

municipium, constitutor [p. 180]) of the settlers at Syracuse is not explicitly stated to be L. Junius, who acted at Panormus, but it can well have been he. C. Caninius Rebilus, who performed the same function for Sextus at Cephaloedium (p. 192), is another possible founder. Wrong legends have been deduced from the appearance of several privy-marks,[1] as on Cretan issues of the next decade (p. 35).

Thus Sextus, on his arrival in Sicily, reopened all four of the Republican official mints,[2] or perhaps it is more accurate to say that he commandeered the local mints of the four cities for official coinage. To his brief rule at least, Scramuzza's denial of a regular official currency in Sicily[3] cannot be applied: the variegated coinage is in accordance with the intense industrial activity which the Civil Wars brought to the island.[4] Sextus's issues at Panormus and Syracuse are limited to commemoration of the military ceremony of *assignatio*; those at Lilybaeum and Agrigentum served more direct warlike purposes. The list of his officers is greatly lengthened, and it is possible to draw a less shadowy picture of the administration installed in 43-42.

10. A Sicilian Port

One of the last of the Pompeian issues is represented by an apparently unique coin[5] with a bearded Janiform head; on the reverse are two galleys with high prows and poops, accompanied by the legend ···N.[6] PISO FRVGI, ROMA(?).[7] Grueber and Willers[8] ascribe it to 91-89 B.C., comparing coins of Cn. Blasio.[9] It differs, however, almost totally from these in style, sharing with them only the commonplace and traditional Roman type of a bearded head of Janus. The view of Grueber and Willers was rejected by Bahrfeldt,[10] who adhered to his previous opinion[11] that analogies of weight and type suggest a comparison with the Spanish *asses* of Sex. Pompeius (p. 22). He therefore attributed the coin to the proquaestorship of Cn. Piso Frugi in Spain in 49 B.C.[12]

Both these theories neglect two facts. Not only is the entire galley as a type for bronze not known before the Tarentine (?) coinage of Antony in 37 B.C. (p. 43), but a second peculiarity first introduced by the latter is the appearance of three, two and one of these galleys on *tressis*, *dupondius*, and *as* respectively. Now this coin (357 grains) is only a little heavier than Antony's *dupondii*. That an obscure and exceptional issue like this could have inspired these two features in the important Tarentine (?) series fifty, or even twelve, years later is inconceivable. Furthermore, the present piece is markedly

---

[1] E.g. B (Naples), N (Milan), R (Heiss, l.c. pl. XVIII, 8).
[2] It is noteworthy that his issues of *aes* in Spain also had been distributed among four mints.
[3] *ES.* III, p. 308.   [4] Ibid. p. 309.
[5] Pesaro (mus. Olivieri).
[6] Read with probability by Bahrfeldt, *NZ.* 1909, p. 77; illustrated on his pl. I, 9.

[7] Doubted by Bahrfeldt, l.c., and Willers, *Geschichte*, p. 98 n. 2; accepted by Grueber, *BMCR.* II, p. 592 (engraved).
[8] Ll.cc. p. 592 n. 1, p. 59 n. 1.
[9] *BMCR.* pl. XLV, 5.
[10] *NZ.* 1918, p. 105.
[11] *NZ.* 1909, p. 78.
[12] *PIR.*² II, 57. 286.

distinguished from Pompey's Spanish *asses* by its fine and delicate lettering and careful execution. Its general style is reminiscent rather of an overstruck issue of Agrippa at Puteoli(?) in 37 B.C. (p. 46) than of any other. The doubts of Willers as to its genuineness are based only on its remarkable character, and have rightly not been accepted.[1] Cn. Piso Frugi fought for at least three Republican causes,[2] but after Philippi his career has hitherto been unknown until 23 B.C., the year of his consulship. Now that was his first post under Augustus.[3] Style precludes attribution to the dominions of Antony. Since, then, 37 B.C. is the *terminus post quem* for this coin, it can only be attributed to the last twelvemonth of Sextus's rule. Thus we can add at least one aristocratic figure to the plebeians and freedmen[4] who remained as his lieutenants after the treaty of Misenum.[5] His omission of any title recalls the silver coinage of another of Sextus's helpers, Q. Nasidius;[6] probably he and Piso held some extra-constitutional *praefectura*, like other moneyers who omitted their titles under Antony (p. 37) and Octavian (p. 66). The strictly Republican nature of the types is likely to be due to Piso's own principles, since the *aurei* and *denarii* of Sextus are often dynastic in character. No doubt the latter, like his opponents, claimed an *imperium maius*, and the coinage, like all others of the period, was ultimately the product of this. The probable appearance of the word ROMA on this piece shows the ultimate objective of such an *imperium*. The latest issues of his moneyers at Lilybaeum and Agrigentum are approximately contemporary with this isolated mintage, which seems to have been intended as a counterblast to the 'Fleet' series of Antony, Agrippa and Lepidus, to which this coin chronologically belongs.

[1] E.g. by *PIR*.² l.c.
[2] Cf. Syme, *RR*. p. 199.
[3] Tac. *Ann*. II, 43.
[4] Cf. Groag, *Klio*, XIV, 1914, pp. 51 ff.; Syme, *RR*. p. 201.
[5] Cf. Charlesworth, *CAH*. x, p. 56 n. 1; Syme, *RR*. p. 228.
[6] *BMCR*. II, p. 564. 21.

C. THE REPUBLICANS

1. MACEDONIA (THESSALONICA?)

Cn. Piso Frugi, whose coinage has just been discussed, was the remnant of a more genuine but briefer attempt to revive the moribund Republic, under Brutus and Cassius. This is represented, in *aes*, by coinages of Q. Hortensius and of P. Lepidus with P. Licinius. We have seen (p. 10) that, on the former, Gaebler's reverse reading ··· P.F. COLON. DED. L[EG].[1] should be altered to PRAEF. COLON. DEDV. (Pl. II, 8); there is also room for a few letters more. With regard to the obverse legend, faith and the knowledge that Q. Hortensius was proconsul cannot, unfortunately, confirm Gaebler's interpretation Q. HORTENSI. PRO [COS.]. On one of the two extant pieces (Pl. II, 7) (as on a specimen now undiscoverable[2]), the third letter of the title is undoubtedly a Q, and is followed by a pellet.[3] But Q. Hortensius Hortalus, whose head appears here, was not *pro quaestore*: in fact, he was empowered with the control of such officials.[4] However, his *proconsulare imperium* had the unusual limitation of subordination to that of his nephew Brutus,[5] officially Q. Caepio Brutus,[6] whose mention on the coin is therefore not improbable. As a conjecture, subject to the future discovery of a legible specimen, it is possible to hazard the readings Q. HORTENSI(*us*) PR(*o*) Q. [C[7](*aepione*) B(*ruto*)] PRAEF. COLON. DEDV. [PR(*o consule*)[8]]. A *praefectus* is by nature a substitute,[9] and a coin of Parium shows a municipal official actually described as PRAEF. PRO IIVIR. (p. 249). The novelty of the *imperium maius* might well justify such a phrase, and a second Republican issue will reveal a possible parallel (p. 36).

The policy in which Hortensius played a part is illustrated by several passages in Appian. He records that Brutus, in his speech to the people on 16 March 44 B.C., deplored Sulla's and Caesar's policy of military foundations,[10] but nevertheless dealt scrupulously with those whom the latter had promised an allotment (οἱ οἰκισθησόμενοι[11]). He promised the confirmation of all the dictator's grants of land, and, with Cassius, implemented his promise by praetorian edicts—διατάγμασιν οἷα στρατηγοὶ τοὺς κληρούχους ἐθεράπευον.[12] Thus the appointment as *praefectus* of Hortensius, whose

---

[1] *ZfN*. xxxvi, 1926, p. 137.
[2] Sestini, *Fontana*, I, pl. III, 10; Hedervar., II, p. 107. 23; cf. Cohen, *Description historique des monnaies frappées sous l'empire romain*, I, p. 47. 95.
[3] Berlin.
[4] Cic. *X Phil.* 26—e.g. L. Sestius.
[5] Ibid., cf. Gaebler, *NG*. III, 1, p. 7; Münzer, *PW*. VIII, 2. 2468 f.; see below, p. 414.
[6] Cf. Münzer, *PW*. x, 976; Hatzfeld, *BCH*. 1909, p. 467.
[7] The Wiczay piece (n. 2) is supposed to have the very similar letter S.
[8] The legitimacy of this abbreviation is shown by Cyrenaic coins; cf. below, p. 138.
[9] Cf. Zumpt, *Commenta Epigraphica*, I, pp. 54 ff.
[10] *BC*. II, 138–41.
[11] Ibid. 139.
[12] Ibid. III, 2.

provincia included Achaia, Macedonia and Illyria to the River Drilon,[1] coincided with the initiation of a conciliatory colonisation scheme by Brutus. On the obverse of one of our two specimens[2] there is a wand that may be a *pertica*, and the composition on the reverse (misinterpreted from the second specimen[3] by Gaebler) includes a plough, *vexillum*, and yoke[4]—all types connected with colonial foundation.

It will be shown in connection with the colonial coinage that both Dium and Cassandrea were established by Hortensius (p. 273). His plan, cut short by the Philippi campaign in which he met his end,[5] no doubt embraced the other foundations which remained for completion by a *legatus* of Antony (p. 274). Both Dium and Cassandrea strike small foundation issues with local ethnic or type; the style of the present coin suggests a different origin from either, and its scope—like that of similar mintages by Clovius and Appuleius Decianus—was clearly that of an official issue destined for the region comprised in the colonial scheme.

Clovius has inaugurated the custom of official foundation coinage; Appuleius provides an early example of *adsignatio* by regular provincial officials. The appointment of Hortensius signalises a new era by the identification of provincial founder with governor. His predecessors Ti. Nero and L. Plautius Plancus (p. 9) were, like Clovius, *praefecti* outside the provincial system; but his contemporary L. Munatius Plancus, *adsignator* in Gallia Comata, is already governor,[6] and so are all later provincial founders (p. 455). The *praefectura* at which Cicero had sneered (p. 9) had lost much of its offensiveness by being merged, and the title itself does not occur again.

The *Lex Coloniae Genetivae Iuliae*,[7] which announces Caesar's innovations of the forties with regard to Roman cities—from which Brutus, in his punctilious adhesion to the Caesarian scheme, did not deviate—defines the following as colonial *patroni*: (1) *qui eam colon(iam) deduxerit*—at *municipia* the word would be *constituerit*—(2) *cui c(olonis) a(grorum) d(andorum) a(dsignandorum) i(us) ex lege Iulia est*. Hortensius, like Clovius, is in the former category of *deductores-constitutores*, who drew up the colonial *leges datae*.[8] The second group consists of *adsignatores* (*curatores*),[9] perhaps sometimes dispensed with,[10] who were entrusted with a *locatio operis* in accordance with the general principles propounded by the *Lex Mamilia Roscia Peducaea Alliena Fabia* of 55 B.C.:[11] they, also, can be identified on a number of coins (p. 294). These two classes of official superseded the Republican *IIIviri agris dandis adsignandis* (p. 9). The significance of the new commissioners, of whom Clovius and

---

[1] Cic. *X Phil.* 26; cf. Ganter, p. 31.
[2] BM.
[3] Berlin.
[4] Identified by E. S. G. Robinson.
[5] Velleius II, 71; cf. Syme, *RR.* p. 205; pace Volkmann, *Münchener Beiträge z. Papyrusforschung*, XXI, 1935, p. 19.
[6] *ILS.* 886.
[7] *ILS.* 6087 (ch. 97).
[8] Cf. Hardy, *Three Spanish Charters*, p. 8.
[9] Rudorff, *Gromatische Institutionen*, p. 334; Marquardt, *St. V.* I, p. 458. For *curator* applied loosely to the founder, cf. Jullian, *TP.* p. 28.
[10] Hardy, l.c. p. 43 n. 88.
[11] Rudolph, *Stadt und Staat im römischen Italien*, pp. 126 ff.; cf. Stuart Jónes, *JRS.* 1936, p. 270; pace Fabricius, *SB. Heidelberg*, XV, 1924-5, p. 8.

L. Plancus were among the first, was their direct subordination to the orders of the *Imperator*:[1] and this significance remains when the governors combined such commissions with their own duties. Thus the numismatic and historical phenomenon of the unrecognised *praefectus coloniis deducendis* is closely connected with the new era of autocracy, and directly derived from the *imperium maius* of the autocrats. Hortensius no doubt owed the signal honours of *aes* coinage and portraiture (p. 33) to his kinship with Brutus,[2] for whose sake he had deserted the memory of favours from Julius.[3]

2. CNOSSUS (?)

It is possible to identify another issue of the Republicans from an unexpected source. It bears the heads of Libya and Creta-Artemis; the inscriptions have been restored by E. S. G. Robinson,[4] from the four specimens known to him, as follows: ΛIBYH, P. LICINIVS PRO Q.—KPHTA B, P. LICINIVS P. F. PRO Q. PR···. But a further example (Pl. II, 15)[5] makes it clear that the correct reverse reading is P. LEPID., etc. Thus P. Licinius was not *pro quaestore* of a joint province, but only of Cyrenaica;[6] Crete was in the hands of another officer, P. Lepidus.

The style of these little pieces suggests the years immediately following the dictatorship; in particular, the coiffure which Libya wears here was in fashion during the late forties,[7] and appears on Republican *aes* as well as silver[8] of c. 43. By an unusual stroke of fortune, it is possible to identify the newly discovered P. Lepidus from the historical records of this date. In the summer of 44 Crete was among the provinces assigned to Brutus.[9] A gesture by Antony, who decreed its *libertas et immunitas* for the future,[10] from an apparently fictitious Caesarian document,[11] caused a temporary wave of feeling in favour of his faction,[12] but it was not long before a lieutenant of Brutus gained possession of the island.[13] This officer was called Lepidus[14] and was perhaps a kinsman of the triumvir[15] (whose brother L. Paullus was likewise a Republican[16]). The identification of this Lepidus with our signatory is confirmed by stylistic suitability and by the explicit mention of KPHTA as the province of Publius. When Brutus was appointed

---

[1] Cf. Marquardt, *St. V.* I, p. 448.
[2] Cf. Syme, *RR.* p. 171.
[3] Ibid. p. 205.
[4] *BMC. Cyrenaica*, p. 113. 2 f.; cf. p. ccxii.
[5] Berlin ('uncertain').
[6] R. Syme informs me that he is likely to be a Lucullus or a Crassus. For Crassi Juniani in Republican camps vide Münzer, *PW.* XIII, 347.
[7] Cf. Stephan, *PW. Suppl.* VI, 91.
[8] E.g. *BMCR.* II, p. 396, cf. n. 2 (? Fulvia).
[9] Sternkopf, *Hermes*, XLVII, 1912, pp. 381 ff.; cf. Charlesworth, *CAH.* X, p. 9 n. 3.

[10] Cic. *II Phil.* 38. 97; not merely *immunitas*, as e.g. Ker, *ad loc.*; Romanelli, *CAH.* XI, p. 659.
[11] Cic. l.c.
[12] Dio XLVII, 21. 1; cf. Raven, *NC.* 1938, p. 146.
[13] An alternative account by Paribeni (*Dizionario epigrafico*, II, 2. 165), placing Lepidus's occupation before Antony's decree, does not take all the evidence into consideration; cf. also Borghesi, *Œuvres*, II, p. 400.
[14] Appian, *BC.* V, 2; cf. Raven, l.c.
[15] As conjectured by White (Loeb ed.), Appian, l.c.
[16] Appian, *BC.* IV, 2; cf. Klebs, *PW.* I, 564 (81).

to Crete, Cyrenaica was allotted to Cassius:[1] their joint leadership of the Republican cause amply suffices to explain the conjunction on the same coins of two Roman officers, explicitly apportioned to different regions. A second reason for their combination in this way may have been the temporary inability of P. Licinius to establish a separate mint in Cyrenaica owing to the difficulties of wresting that region from its anti-Republican neighbour Egypt.[2] This was, however, finally achieved, as an unknown and unique coin shows; and P. Licinius even planted an ephemeral colony at Cyrene (p. 261).

But these pieces are Cretan rather than Cyrenaican in style, and are therefore to be attributed to the Republican occupation of the island by P. Lepidus, which apparently preceded the Cyrenaican adventure. Lepidus's exact title is unrecoverable from the five extant specimens. Robinson conjectures PRO Q(*uaestore*) PR[O PR](*aetore*),[3] which is supported by the analogy of L. Lentulus at the same date;[4] but the other bronze issue of the Republicans, in Macedonia, has suggested the possibility, albeit conjectural, of another interpretation, PRO Q. BR(*uto*) PR(*o cos.*) (p. 33), a formula that might have been caused by the new phenomenon of the *imperium maius*. The seniority of P. Lepidus to his colleague would be entirely in accordance with the fact that there was a fleet-station in Crete[5] (where the capital of the joint province had been[6]), and that the Cassian expeditionary force to Cyrenaica may not yet have obtained a foothold; its advertisement was probably one of the aims of this coinage. But particularly significant is the fact that, on 28 November 43, Brutus and Cassius were officially deprived of these two provinces,[7] which they had at first, until their assumption of wider powers, refused to take over.[8] It is highly probable that the coins were struck on the receipt of the news of this deprivation, as a gesture of defiance and a demonstration that the territories were in the hands of Republicans. It may, therefore, be considered a military issue by the representative of Brutus in Crete, in the months immediately preceding Philippi and P. Lepidus's subsequent flight.[9] The coin may be attributed to Cnossus, since the ships were probably at its port, Heracleum.[10]

Thus the Republican coinages of the period, like those of the dictator, are directly derived from the *imperium maius* of their respective war-lords.

[1] Sternkopf, l.c. p. 384.
[2] Charlesworth, *CAH*. x, p. 18; cf. Tarn, ibid. p. 39.
[3] L.c., p. ccxii. He cites PRO Q. P. on coins; *BMCR*. II, p. 491.
[4] Cic. *Fam*. XII, 15 init.   [5] Appian, *BC*. v, 2.
[6] Cf. Romanelli, *CAH*. XI, p. 663.
[7] Cf. Syme, *RR*. p. 184 n. 1.
[8] Ibid. p. 166; Gelzer, *PW*. x, 1000; cf. Dio XLVII, 21. 1.
[9] Appian, l.c.
[10] Cf. Bürchner, *PW*. XI, 927.

D. THE TRIUMVIRS

1. ITALY (BRUNDUSIUM?)

The first bronze coins after the establishment of the triumvirate by the *Lex Titia* have the types of a prow and a beardless head of Janus, inscribed respectively ANTONIVS IMP. and ATRATINVS AVGVR (Pl. II, 9).[1] Willers attributes their lower limit to 36 B.C.[2] But L. Sempronius Atratinus was probably *legatus pro praetore* of Antony in Achaia in c. 39–37 (p. 382);[3] moreover, Antony invariably uses the *cognomen* with number, never alone, after his second salutation in the autumn of 39.[4] Accordingly, the *terminus ante quem* may be moved back to 39.[5] This eliminates the suggestion of De Salis[6] that these coins were struck in the East, since Antony did not leave Italy until a very short time before his second salutation.[7] Atratinus might conceivably have preceded him to the East to assume his governorship, but he could not then have omitted on his coinage the title *legatus pro praetore*, in favour of the unauthoritative *augur*. An upper limit for the issue is fixed at 40 B.C. by his election to the augurate.[8]

An even closer attribution is possible. In 40, Atratinus could hardly have collaborated with Antony until about September, and could not safely have coined in his interests in Italy during the troubled weeks immediately preceding the reconciliation: the coinage must follow this. On the other hand, Antony was saluted *imperator* a second time almost as soon as he reached Athens, and the break in his journey at Zacynthus will be seen to be celebrated by another commander, C. Sosius (p. 40). It is difficult, therefore, to see where Atratinus can have coined outside Italy. There are several considerations which make Borghesi's[9] attribution to Rome itself unacceptable. Antony could not well have ignored his colleague in this way at the capital; Atratinus is unlikely to have been a monetary *quattuorvir*—as the title apparently was at this time[10]—since the appellation which he uses is far more unplausible as a pretext for coinage; finally, on general grounds there is no probability of just a single isolated exception to the sixty years' lack of bronze coinage at Rome. But the attribution to Italy can be supported by historical evidence, numismatic parallels, and analogies of titulature. In the first place, Antony certainly possessed recruiting rights in the

---

[1] Milan, Capitoline, Bourgey sale, 1913. 712, Lawrence coll. (c. 221·5 grains).
[2] *Geschichte*, pp. 113 f.; cf. Borelli, *Numismatica e scienze affini*, IV, 1938, p. 55, who classes these with a later series.
[3] *ILS*. 9461; cf. Münzer, *PW*. II, 1367.
[4] *BMCR*. II, pp. 506 ff., IMP. TER. The only coin believed to read IMP. ITER. (ibid. p. 505) is very doubtful. Cf. Tarn, *CAH*. X, p. 50 n. 1, correcting Bahrfeldt, *JIAN*. XII, 1910, p. 89.
[5] This invalidates the suggestion of Syme, *RR*. p. 231 n. 2, that the issue is Sicilian.
[6] Cf. Grueber, *BMCR*. II, p. 50.
[7] Cf. Tarn, *CAH*. X, p. 51.
[8] *ILS*. 9398; cf. Münzer, *Hermes*, LII, 1917, pp. 152 ff.; id. *PW*. II, 1366 ff.
[9] *Œuvres*, II, p. 417; cf. Babelon, *Rn*. 1884, p. 413.
[10] Cf. *BMCR*. I, pp. 565. 4198, 593. 4313.

peninsula after October 40[1] and assigned lands to his veterans there:[2] hindrances in the way of his exercise of these rights were later a cause for indignant complaint.[3] Dio's omission of Italy from the new *provincia* of Octavian[4] shows that it was theoretically common ground.[5] Secondly, not only will the following pages provide several examples of Italian *aes* mintage (pp. 43, 46), but recent research on contemporary silver issues can be adduced to show that Antonian coinage was certainly being issued at this period within the peninsula. Liegle[6] has established with success that a group of *denarii* with PIETAS COS., and the head and title of Antony,[7] were struck in 41 by L. Antonius at Praeneste, not, as Grueber believed, in Gaul or the East. It is thus unreasonably arbitrary to emend[8] or reject[9] the explicit statement of Servius[10] that Antony coined at Anagnia also. Moreover, a second group with PIETAS COS.[11]—of different style from the others—is undoubtedly from a mint near, but not at, Praeneste—from which Anagnia is a mere twenty miles away! Furthermore, coins of Ventidius Bassus, again without any cause described by Grueber as 'provincial',[12] are convincingly reattributed to Italy,[13] where Ventidius was certainly employed at the time of the Perusine War;[14] Q. Salvius Salvidienus Rufus, who coined at the same time,[15] is known to have been before Perusia.[16] The attribution of the coin of Atratinus to Italy is therefore not only itself historically plausible, but supported by numerous parallels.

Furthermore, the titulature supplies evidence of a specific connection of our *aes* coin with some of these Italian issues. The heads on certain coins of Salvius[17] and of the second PIETAS COS. group[18] are precisely the same as those on two *denarii* which bear (in conjunction with CAESAR IMP.) the exceptional title of the *aes*—ANTONIVS IMP.[19] The *praenomen* is regularly omitted from about this time by Octavian, but never by Antony except on these silver and bronze issues: on the latter its absence is emphasised by the insertion of the *praenomen* of Atratinus. The co-incidence is not accidental. In anticipation of a fuller constitutional discussion (p. 408), it may be mentioned that Julius, omitting the salutation number, had also called himself CAESAR IMP.—which is on the way from C. CAESAR IMP. to IMP. CAESAR. Much more striking than the simple *cognomen* is the solitary gentile name 'Antonius'.

[1] Appian, *BC.* v, 65; Dio L, 1. 3.
[2] Cf. Jullian, *TP.* pp. 17 f.
[3] Cf. Syme, *RR.* p. 276; cf. p. 294.
[4] XLVIII, 28. 4.
[5] In any case, the second Edict of Octavian to Rhosus (c. 35 B.C.) shows that the triumvirs could act in each other's territories; vide Levi, *Rivista di filologia*, 1938, p. 116.
[6] *ZfN.* 1932, pp. 80 ff.
[7] *BMCR.* II, p. 400. 65 ff.
[8] Svoronos, *Ptolemies*, 1897–8; cf. Regling, *ZfN.* XXV, 1906, p. 397.
[9] Laffranchi, *Bollettino di numismatica*, 1911, p. 162.
[10] *ad* Verg. *Aen.* VI, 684.
[11] *BMCR.* II, p. 402. 69.
[12] Ibid. p. 403. 73.
[13] As Mattingly informs me.
[14] Cf. Charlesworth, *CAH.* x, p. 29; Syme, *RR.* p. 210.
[15] *BMCR.* II, p. 407. 86 ff.
[16] Cf. Charlesworth, l.c.; Syme, l.c. p. 209.
[17] *BMCR.* II, p. 407. 88.
[18] Ibid. p. 402. 69.
[19] Ibid. p. 409. 94 and 93 respectively. There are no grounds for Miss Newby's attribution of this to 43 (p. 9).

The triumvirs, like Sex. Pompeius, are testing the possibilities of titulature, which Octavian is to develop remarkably. Antony, however, not only does not use the *praenomen Imperatoris*, but after his second salutation always adds the number. He also returns to his personal *praenomen*. These *denarii* and *asses*, by their unique suppression of this, show a temporary uniformity to the constitutional programme of Octavian.

Correspondence of the *aes* and the *denarii* with each other and with historical circumstances cannot be fortuitous. It has been established that they are both Italian. They are also products of the same phase. It has been proved that the *aes* were struck between autumn 40 and autumn 39: it is thus significant that the silver show a *caduceus*, which is likely to symbolise the reconciliation of the triumvirs at the Pact of Brundusium,[1] in October 40.[2] Indeed, both *aes* and silver may well have been struck in that *municipium*;[3] the Pact of Tarentum may provide a parallel example of such commemorative types (p. 45) at the city where the agreement took place. But the *raison d'être* of the present *aes* coinage, as of the Tarentine and of nearly every other *aes* issue of the triumvirate, is likely to have been primarily military or naval: and the coinages which follow show that Antony's departure from Italy was coincident with a reorganisation of his fleet. Since Atratinus was one of the officers later sent with a naval detachment to assist Octavian in Sicily, it is reasonable to believe that he was appointed to a naval *praefectura* as early as the reorganisation in 39, in the same way as C. Sosius (p. 40) (who, like him, was soon afterwards, in c. 38, appointed to a governorship). Antony had arrived in Italy with a fleet, and left it with a fleet: it is certain that the work of reconstruction began before Antony left the valuable recruiting ground of Italy, and probable that Atratinus was in charge of it, perhaps at Brundusium itself. His omission of the title *praefectus*—if he held this—is explicable by reason of its unofficial and irregular character, to which attention has already been called. Caesar might have risked the sneers of constitutionalists, but the new rulers took greater pains to save appearances (p. 415). The official basis of the issue, as of its successors during this period, was the *imperium maius* of the triumvirs.[4]

2. Zacynthus

In 39 Antony left to take up his headquarters at Athens, where the news of Ventidius's victories probably reached him, and he was saluted *Imperator* for the second time. But his tranquillity on the journey from Italy was troubled by the knowledge that Sextus Pompeius had wrung large concessions from the triumvirs at Misenum: Antony himself had promised him the Peloponnese.[5] Sextus later complained that this was never fairly given up to him;[6] and a coinage at this time shows that Antony never seriously

---

[1] Cf. Grueber, *BMCR*. II, p. 408 n. 2.
[2] Cf. Carcopino, *Virgile et le Mystère de la IVe Églogue*[3], pp. 111 ff.; Charlesworth, *CAH*. x, p. 44.
[3] Cf. Hülsen, *PW*. III, 905.
[4] Cf. Gabrici, *Augustus* (1938), p. 379.
[5] Cf. Charlesworth, *CAH*. x, p. 46.
[6] Ibid. p. 56; cf. Larsen, *ES*. IV, p. 433.

intended to lose the territory. An *orichalcum*[1] piece in the British Museum has a head of Antony (Pl. I, 9) and an eagle on a thunderbolt, inscribed respectively IMP. and C. SOSIVS Q., ZA.[2] The attribution ZA to Zacynthus is confirmed by provenance.[3] The lack of a number with IMP. provides the reasonable supposition that C. Sosius was left with a detachment at Zacynthus when Antony passed it *en route* for Athens, where he was saluted for the second time. The quaestorian title of Sosius has been thought to cause difficulty only because of a groundless identification[4] with a praetor of 49 B.C.[5] It is difficult to see how Sextus could have occupied the Peloponnese effectively when Sosius was established at Zacynthus. Probably a detachment still remained there when the latter took up his Syrian governorship in 38.[6] His movements from 37 to 34 are unrecorded:[7] but it is likely that he remained in Syria for most or the whole of 37,[8] and his name on a local piece of Agrigentum (p. 392) shows that he was assisting Octavian in Sicily in the last months of 36. No doubt he called at Zacynthus earlier in the year on his way there from the East: and to this visit may be ascribed a second issue with ZA and C. SOSIVS IMP.,[9] accompanied respectively by Antony's head and by a trophy—celebrating the capture of Jerusalem which earned Sosius his salutation (Pl. I, 7).

But this fleet-station had not outlived its use when Sextus, the foe against whom it was originally directed, fell. On the contrary, its need was all the greater in view of the ever-widening gap between the two remaining masters of the Empire. Thus Sosius returned there when the Antonian reinforcements in Sicily were dismissed by Octavian. A third issue has ZA (head of Bacchus-Apollo) and C. SOSIVS COS. DESIG. (tripod).[10] Sosius had been *consul designatus* as early as 39;[11] but this coin may be placed third in his series owing to the omission of Antony's head, which is also absent on a fourth coin, but occurs on the two earliest. Gardner[12] has pointed out that this omission implies a greater independence on the part of Sosius, whose position at Zacynthus was exceptional by virtue of his repeated returns to the island, and its presumable continuance of subordination to him in his absence. His status recalls that of the various princelings established in other parts of Antony's dominions at this time.[13] The type of a tripod is unplausibly connected by Shipley[14] with a statue of Apollo brought to Rome by Sosius in 33 B.C.;[15] Wissowa's[16] reference to the quin-

[1] Grueber, *BMCR.* II, p. 504.
[2] Bahrfeldt, *JIAN.* VIII, 1911, pp. 215 ff., 1; id. *JIAN.* V, 1908, pp. 221 f.; *NZ.* 1918, pp. 159 ff.
[3] Gardner, *NC.* 1885, pp. 81 ff.
[4] As by Dessau, *PIR.* III, 253. 556.
[5] Cic. *Att.* VIII, 6. 1; IX, 2.
[6] Raillard, p. 35; cf. Levi II, p. 120.
[7] Cf. Fluss, *PW.* (2R.) III, 1178.
[8] Cf. Raillard, l.c.; Ganter, p. 42.
[9] BM; Bahrfeldt, *JIAN.* VIII, 1911, 2; cf. Mattingly, *RC.* pl. XX, 14.
[10] Venice; Bahrfeldt, l.c. 3; id. *NZ.* 1897, p. 76.
[11] Charlesworth, *CAH.* X, p. 46 n. 1.
[12] L.c.
[13] Tarn, *CAH.* X, pp. 69, 80.
[14] *Washington University Studies (Lang. Lit.)*, III, 1920, pp. 85 f.
[15] Pliny, *NH.* VIII, 53; cf. Glauning, *Die Anhängerschaft des M. Antonius und des Octavian*, Diss. Leipzig, 1935, p. 8.
[16] *Ephemeris epigraphica*, VIII, p. 241.

THE TRIUMVIRS

decemvirate is more probable, if any special allusion is thought to be necessary. The coin was struck after the Sicilian campaigns and before Sosius's triumph in 34 B.C.;[1] thereafter he probably stayed in Rome until his famous consulship of 32. The title COS. DESIG., preferred even to IMP. on this coin, informed those who saw it of Antony's claims in Rome and of an uncomfortable prospect for Octavian. But the speech with which Sosius inaugurated his consulship, and the imminence of war which it did nothing to dispel, necessitated his departure from Rome before January 32 was ended:[2] he is shown to have returned for the last time to Zacynthus—a vital point on Antony's strategic lines, which extended all down the west coast of Greece[3]—by a coin with ZA (head of Neptune) and C. SOSIVS COS. (dolphin and trident) (Pl. I, 8).[4] He and his coinage had played a considerable part in the history and numismatics of Antony's dominions; he was lucky to be spared by Octavian.[5]

As a moneyer in *orichalcum*, Sosius's only precedents were the agents of Caesar, whose financial acumen in this matter has been mentioned, and his only imitator in the triumvirate was Q. Oppius, whose family were bankers (p. 61). It is difficult to resist the conclusion that Sosius—who was also a wealthy man[6]—made an equally 'good thing' out of it.

3. NARBONESE GAUL (ARELATE?)

Parallel to these coinages of Antony are larger military issues by Octavian. The first of them[7] is of bronze,[8] with his bare head, inscribed only CAESAR;[9] on the reverse is a prow, with high poop and mast. Provenance is conclusive for Gallic mintage.[10] A beard on one variety[11] suggests a lower limit of c. 39–38:[12] anachronism is of course possible, but a similar date is indicated by the resemblance of some of the heads to so-called 'Gallic' *denarii* of c. 39,[13] and of another (diademed)[14] to *denarii* apparently issued by Agrippa in Gaul in c. 38.[15] Several other unpublished divergencies of type exist, which are more important to the study of ancient ships than to history. Some

[1] Cf. Fluss, *PW*. (2R.), III, 1176 ff.
[2] Dio L, 3; cf. *CAH*. X, p. 95.
[3] Cf. Syme, *RR*. p. 280.
[4] Milan, Oxford; Bahrfeldt, l.c. 4; cf. Lambros, Ἀναγραφὴ τῶν νομισμάτων τῆς κυρίας Ἑλλάδος, Πελοπόννησος, p. 73.
[5] Cf. Tarn, *CAH*. X, p. 105.
[6] Cf. Fluss, *PW*. (2R.), III, 1179.
[7] BM, Paris, etc.; cf. Sydenham, *NC*. 1917, no. 17 (270, 251 grains [BM]).
[8] Spectrogram 10.
[9] A Paris example with D. IVLIVS, described by de Saulcy, *Mémoires...de numismatique et d'archéologie*, 1873, p. 26, and cited by Mommsen,

Berichte über die Verhandlungen der k. sächs. Ges. der Wissenschaften zu Leipzig, ph.-h. Kl. III, 1851, p. 222, is a forgery.
[10] Vienne (3), Nîmes (2), Narbonne (2); cf. *Rn*. 1899, p. 175. A coin countermarked ΠΕΡ (in trade: Perga, Pergamum or Perperene) is a complete freak.
[11] Naples.
[12] Dio XLVIII, 34. 3; cf. Brendel, *Ikonographie des Kaisers Augustus*, Diss. Heidelberg, 1931, pp. 38 f.
[13] E.g. *BMCR*. II, p. 409. 92 (pl. CV, 1).
[14] Hall coll. (cast in BM).
[15] *BMCR*. II, pp. 410. 101, 411. 102, 412. 103 (pl. CV, 6–8); cf. Berve, *Hermes*, LXXI, 1936, p. 251 n. 3; *pace* Schulz, *ZfN*. 1935, p. 103.

specimens[1] show a small sail, others grapnels[2] and an unusual *acrostolium*,[3] while a fourth[4] has an extensive system of rigging; more remarkable is another[5] (Pl. II, 11), on which two standards are placed fore and aft of the mast respectively.

On a further coin—like most of these, apparently represented by only one extant example, but certainly genuine[6]—in addition to the standards (which here recall the ἐπισείων of Pollux[7]), there is a mast-box, and from the *acrostolium* to the mast-head is a conventional representation apparently of the mainsail straining in the wind. There are also remains of lettering, which, though not decipherable with certainty, seem to include the letters AR.[8] It is by no means improbable that they represent part of the mint-mark of Arelate, since this piece, like the rest, is of French provenance.[9] The hypothetical ethnic CV on other coins is rightly rejected by Willers:[10] it has been tooled or imagined from the various superstructures of the galley.

A large number of specimens with these types have a countermark which is not elsewhere found. De Saulcy[11] interprets this as the *protome* of a dog, Willers[12] as a dolphin. But it is clear from examples of the principal variety (Pl. II, 10),[13] and from that with AR.(?), that a bird is represented, facing right. The legs are clearly visible, and the general appearance strongly suggests a cock. Now even if the original meaning of *gallus* is not *gallicum animal*[14] and its popular national significance[15] is merely based on a play upon words,[16] the existence of this pun, combined with the known confusion of its meanings[17] and with the frequency of *types parlants* on ancient coins,[18] seems to justify the assumption that this countermark is intended to ensure Gallic circulation for these issues. But they do not appear with contemporary bronze of Gallia Comata in the extensive Neuss finds;[19] and there seems nothing in favour of E. A. Sydenham's[20] attribution to Lugdunum, whose contemporary colonial issues are wholly different in style (p. 206). Since the coins originate from the south of France,[21] and the mint-marks of a Narbonese city may appear, it may be justifiable to limit their validity, as defined by the 'Gallic' countermark, to the old *provincia*. Sosius has already placed Antony's

---

[1] Copenhagen, BM(?).
[2] Paris. [3] Paris.
[4] Seen in trade—from Vierordt collection (Schulman sale 1923. 661); it appears to have been cleaned, but has probably not been tooled.
[5] Cambridge.
[6] Own collection.
[7] I, 90; cf. Smith, *Dictionary of Antiquities*, II, p. 215.
[8] A photograph could not reproduce these traces.
[9] Acquired in Paris.
[10] *NZ.* XXXIV, 1902, p. 119. 27.
[11] *JIAN.* I, 1898, p. 191.
[12] L.c.
[13] Paris, Copenhagen.

[14] *Thesaurus Linguae Latinae*, VI, 1685, 1. 44, s.v. *Gallus*.
[15] Cf. Hatzfeld-Darmesteter, *Dictionnaire général de la langue française*, I, p. 538.
[16] Ducrocq, *Le coq prétendu gaulois*, 1908; cf. Chatelain, *Bibliothèque de l'École des hautes études*, CLXII, 1908, p. 71 n. 5.
[17] Shipp, *CR.* L, 1936, pp. 164 f.
[18] Cf. especially Eckhel, *DN.* V, pp. 90 f. and a collection at Utrecht (van Hoorn, *Gids*, p. 51).
[19] Strack, *BJ.* CXII, 1904, pp. 444 ff.
[20] *NC.* 1917, p. 58.
[21] Attributed to Narbo(?) in *Milan Cat.*, p. 23. 233, and to Vienna by Duchalais, *Description des médailles gauloises*, p. 20.

THE TRIUMVIRS

head on his coins, but this is the first official bronze issue to bear the effigy of Octavian. It is characteristic of his aims at this period to be plain CAESAR, while the beard on a Naples specimen (as on *denarii*) is further evidence of his claim to succeed Julius.[1]

The analogy of contemporary *aes* issues, and the varieties of naval type, suggest that, as often, provision was being made for the fleet. Points of comparison with *denarii* of c. 39–38 have been summarised: this was a period when Agrippa was active in Gaul,[2] and the river harbour[3] at Arelate may (if the conjectural reading AR. is correct) have been his Narbonese headquarters. It had been made a naval arsenal and a colony[4] by Julius,[5] and not long afterwards became the economic centre of its province.[6]

4. TARENTUM(?)

Antony now made a more elaborate attempt to create a coinage of small change in bronze.[7] His titulature on this famous but enigmatic 'Fleet' coinage is M. ANT. IMP. TER. COS. DES. ITER. ET TER. IIIVIR R. P. C.; Bahrfeldt establishes its outermost chronological limits as the autumn of 38 and the autumn of 35.[8] On the reverses of its three groups are the legends L. BIBVLVS M. F. PR. DESIG., L. ATRATINVS AVGVR COS. DESIG., and M. OPPIVS CAPITO PRO PR. PRAEF. CLASS. F. C.;[9] coins bearing the name of C. Fonteius Capito are tooled or false.[10] Complete uniformity of style and types decreases the possibility of more than a single mint.[11]

After the Treaty of Tarentum (spring 37[12]), Antony lent Octavian 120 or 130 ships (two squadrons[13]) for the war against Sextus; the types of these coins—hippocampquadriga, galleys, *acrostolium*, *triskeles*[14]—clearly refer to the prosecution of that campaign. Grueber sees in them 'an accomplished fact';[15] he therefore agrees with Münzer[16] in assigning the issue to a date after the battle of Naulochus (3 September 36). But there are numerous obstacles in the way of attribution to so late a date. It may be mentioned first that a *triskeles* will be seen to appear also on a coin which cannot be later than 37 (p. 46). Secondly, Grueber's theory is contradictory: he, like others,[17]

[1] Cf. Bernhart, *Handbuch zur Münzkunde*, p. 34; *AJA*. 1921, p. 261 n. 3.
[2] Cf. Charlesworth, *CAH*. x, p. 46; Levi II, p. 65.
[3] Ihm, *PW*. II, 643; Grenier, *ES*. III, p. 473.
[4] Cf. Rice Holmes, *The Roman Republic*, III, pp. 322 n., 321; Constant, *Arles*, p. 56.
[5] Caesar, *Bell. Civ.* I, 36; II, 5.
[6] Constant, l.c. p. 405.
[7] Not *orichalcum*, *pace* Grueber, *BMCR*. II, p. 412 n. 2. Analysed, *NC*. 1904, p. 244 n.; cf. *NC*. 1918, p. 181.
[8] Bahrfeldt, *NZ*. 1905, p. 31. For illustrations, see that article.

[9] Ibid. nos. 1–6, 7–13, 14–22 respectively.
[10] Ibid. p. 25, *pace* Caland, *De nummis M. Antonii etc.*, Diss. Leyden, 1883, pp. 66 ff.
[11] Bahrfeldt, l.c. p. 40, *pace* Cavedoni, *Numismatica Biblica*, p. 120 n. 197; Caland, l.c. pp. 73 ff.
[12] Tarn, *CAH*. x, p. 54, especially n. 3.
[13] Levi II, p. 73 n. 1.
[14] Emblem of Sicily; cf. Ziegler, *PW*. (2R.), II, 467 f. [15] *BMCR*. II, p. 410.
[16] *PW*. II, 1367. Accepted by Newby (p. 12); Levi, *Rivista di filologia*, 1938, p. 114; Milne, *Development of Roman Coinage*, p. 21.
[17] E.g. Babelon, *Monnaies de la république romaine*, I, p. 190; Caland, l.c. pp. 69 ff.; Milne, l.c.

assigns the issues to the East, although the appearance of the name of Atratinus on local Sicilian issues of Entella and Lilybaeum (p. 392) must be dated to the last months of 36—the very time to which he ascribes the present coinage.[1] Others who accept Grueber's dating less inconsistently attribute the present issues to Sicily.[2] But it is possible to show that the coins were struck before the end of the war. In the first place, it must have been for a fleet that such distinctive types were struck; whereas after Naulochus, although Atratinus at least was active in Sicily, he had no naval duties, since the Antonian fleet was in dock at Tarentum:[3] indeed, Entella, whose coins he signs, is far inland. Secondly, the issue was early enough for Cn. Piso, a lieutenant of Sextus, to imitate a reverse-type (p. 31). It is therefore necessary, contrary to Grueber and Münzer, to establish the battle of Naulochus as a *terminus ante quem*.

There are, however, additional reasons for believing that the coins could not have been issued even as late as 36. The head of Octavia appears with Antony on the *sestertii*, and with Octavian also on the *tresses*.[4] Now it was only a few months after the Treaty of Tarentum, in 37, that Antony finally abandoned Octavia in favour of Cleopatra.[5] Tarn,[6] unlike Levi,[7] believes that he married Cleopatra later in the same year, and it is at any rate certain that their joint regnal era commenced then.[8] It was no doubt discreet to omit Cleopatra's name and portrait from Roman issues for as long as possible, but it is almost inconceivable that Antony's intimate lieutenants could deliberately act such an unplausible and useless lie on their coinage after the *volte-face*. On the other hand, the obverse types—heads of Antony, Octavian,[9] and Octavia—are entirely suitable to the Treaty of Tarentum:[10] Octavia's latest portrait on gold and silver coins was in connection with this event.[11] Other considerations demonstrate the peculiar applicability of this date. We know that Antony sent only two squadrons to the Sicilian campaigns,[12] and the evidence of an official coinage of Lipara (p. 52) proves that Oppius, as well as Atratinus, held a command in the war zone: here, already, are two commanders. There is no evidence that Bibulus was there;[13] a passage of Appian suggests that he was already in the East late in 36.[14] Particularly significant in this

---

[1] For slightly earlier activity of Oppius in Sicily, see p. 53.
[2] Scramuzza, *ES*. III, p. 308; Babelon, l.c. II, pp. 277, 434; Holm III, p. 460; Gardthausen I, p. 28.
[3] Appian, *BC*. v, 129.
[4] Bahrfeldt, l.c. nos. 1, 2, 7, 8, 11, 14, 15, 19.
[5] Tarn, *CAH*. x, p. 55.
[6] Ibid. p. 66.   [7] II, p. 36.
[8] Porphyrius, *Fragmenta Historicorum Graecorum*, III, 724. 9; cf. Tarn, l.c. p. 81.
[9] Not Julius, *pace* Elsner, *MBNGW*. VIII, 1905, p. 43.
[10] Bahrfeldt, l.c. p. 37.
[11] *BMCR*. II, p. 507. 144.

[12] Levi II, p. 73 n. 2.
[13] Bahrfeldt's conjecture that Oppius was commander-in-chief, leaving the squadrons to Bibulus and Atratinus, is not supported by any evidence.
[14] *BC*. v, 132: ὁ δὲ (sc. Antony) καὶ Βύβλον ἀπιόντα πρὸς αὐτὸν (sc. Octavian) ἐντυχεῖν ἐδίδασκε. Viereck, in ed. 2 of the Teubner text, does not consider possible emendations, cited in ed. 1 by Mendelssohn, to be worthy of mention. White, in the Loeb Text, translates 'Antony gave instructions to Bibulus, who was going away from him, to confer with Octavian'; but A. S. F. Gow points out that this involves an unplausible translation of ἐδίδασκε, and considers the meaning obscure.

connection is the fact that his issues are never so light in weight as many with the signatures of Oppius and Atratinus. Bahrfeldt's distinction of two separate standards[1] is impossible to maintain owing to the very wide range of fluctuations in weight. On the other hand, it was very common for the weights of an issue gradually to decline. If the series is attributed to the time of the Treaty in 37, this phenomenon is perfectly explicable. Oppius and Atratinus remained in the West—as their coinage at Lipara, Entella and Lilybaeum proves—and continued the present issue, which gradually declined in weight, but Bibulus sailed back to the East with Antony, and his mintage ceased. Thus too is explained the Eastern origin of the few pieces whose provenance has been noted:[2] Antony and Bibulus took with them at least 170 out of the 300 ships,[3] so that much of the earlier part of this coinage naturally found its way to the East with the returning troops.

Thus many indications demonstrate that the issue commenced at the date of the Treaty of Tarentum (spring 37), when Antony and Bibulus were in the West. Sicily, to which many have ascribed the group, was inaccessible at this time. Bahrfeldt's suggestion that the series was struck on ship-board[4] is unnecessary, since previous issues have shown that the Italian harbour-towns were used as mints during the triumvirate, even by Antony. The occasion is the conference at Tarentum, and Tarentum was the headquarters of the Antonian contingent:[5] the coinage may be attributed to that colony.[6]

The denominations, specified by value-marks,[7] range from *sextans*[8] to *sestertius*. The novelty of this wide upward range, made necessary by the rise of prices,[9] is paralleled by a new debasement to an *as* whose upper limit is only ¼ oz.,[10] and which fluctuates extravagantly, in the later issues of Oppius and Atratinus, to less than half that weight.[11] Antony then freely admits a token standard,[12] *funeste doctrine, fille du despotisme*;[13] and Pliny informs us that he debased the silver also.[14]

This series, or the circumstances which had inspired it, led other authorities to issue bronze coinage of an equally unusual character.

However, he agrees that it does not warrant the interpretation (by Bahrfeldt, l.c.) that Antony, in the East, gave these instructions to Bibulus in Sicily. ἀπιόντα implies rather that Bibulus was on the point of leaving Antony; ἐντυχεῖν may be Consecutive.

[1] Cf. Mattingly, *BMC. Imp.* p. xlvi n. 2.

[2] Bahrfeldt, l.c.; cf. Edwards, *Corinth*, VI, 1933, p. 75; Woodward, *Transactions of the International Numismatic Congress* (1936), p. 128. Omitted, e.g., by Willers, *Geschichte*, p. 125.

[3] Levi II, p. 69; cf. n. 3.

[4] Cf. also Vittinghoff, *PW.* (2R.), VI, 2298 in oder um Sizilien.

[5] Appian, *BC.* V, 129.

[6] Kornemann, 28.

[7] Cf. Vittinghoff, l.c., *pace* Dattari, *R.it.* 1908, p. 547.

[8] Cf. Grueber, *BMCR.* II, p. 514.

[9] Mattingly, *BMC. Imp.* p. xlvi f.

[10] Sydenham, *NC.* 1918, pp. 172 ff., points out Grueber's mistakes in this respect.

[11] Cf. Burns, *Money and Monetary Policy in Ancient Times*, p. 301.

[12] Cf. Milne, *Development of Roman Coinage*, p. 21.

[13] Lenormant, *La monnaie dans l'antiquité*, III, p. 29.

[14] *NH.* XXXIII, 132; cf. Mommsen, *Berichte über die Verhandlungen der k. sächs. Ges. der Wissenschaften zu Leipzig, ph.-h. Kl.* III, 1851, p. 219.

5. PUTEOLI (?)

An extraordinary coin, accepted as genuine by Mattingly[1] and Bahrfeldt,[2] has on the obverse the legend M. AGRIPPA ORAE····· CLAS. PRAE. C., with Agrippa's bare head to left, and on the reverse CAESAR IIIVIR R. P. C., with *triskeles* and *gorgoneion*[3] (Pl. I, 13). By analogy with *denarii* of Sex. Pompeius,[4] Agrippa's naval title can be restored as *Orae maritimae et classis praefectus*. The final C most naturally, though not certainly, refers to his consulship of 37:[5] in any case, the type not only shows a general connection with the Sicilian campaigns, but in particular recalls the 'Fleet' issues of Antony, which have been attributed to the months following the Treaty of Tarentum (spring 37). Mattingly ascribes the present coin to the months preceding the treaty; but it can be shown that only a date subsequent to this is suitable to Agrippa's title, and that the same date is equally relevant to Octavian's.

The exceptional glorification of the self-effacing Agrippa is likely to commemorate some unusual distinction. Dio[6] states that in this year he succeeded Calvisius Sabinus in the office of high admiral—which is explicitly recorded on the coin—and Appian[7] clearly connects this appointment with events later than the Treaty of Tarentum.[8] It is therefore hard to see how the title could have appeared on coinage before the Treaty. A *terminus ante quem* is provided by the legend CAESAR IIIVIR R. P. C., which bears on a controversy concerning the renewal of the triumvirate.[9] It has been rightly noted that Octavian, unlike Antony, invariably places ITERVM on his coins during the second *quinquennium* (37–32).[10] However, this prolongation was not confirmed by law until some months after the informal agreement at Tarentum,[11] and, in the meanwhile, the triumvirs continued their administration (as, during the first months of 37, between the finish of the *Lex Titia* and the new agreement) 'on the ground that their powers could not lapse until they formally laid them down'.[12] Thus the present usage could be considered technically correct if, as is on other grounds probable, the issue was made between the Treaty and the date of its confirmation by law (summer 37).

The circumstances of the issue suggest a geographical attribution. A second specimen is reported, though not with certainty, from a collection at Acireale in

---

[1] *NC.* 1934, p. 48.
[2] *Numismatisches Literaturblatt*, 1934, p. 2781.
[3] BM.
[4] *BMCR.* II, pp. 560 ff., 7 ff.
[5] Mattingly, l.c.
[6] XLVIII, 49.
[7] *BC.* v, 96.
[8] Cf. Charlesworth, *CAH.* x, p. 59, correcting Gardthausen I, p. 25; Hadas, *Sextus Pompey*, p. 122, etc.
[9] Summarised (most recently) by Charlesworth, l.c. and p. 904; Levi I, pp. 71 f. n. 2.
[10] Charlesworth, l.c. p. 59 n. 1.
[11] Cf. Wilcken, *SB. Berlin*, 1925, pp. 70 f.; Glauning, *Die Anhängerschaft des Antonius und des Octavian*, p. 49.
[12] Charlesworth, l.c.; cf. Levi, *Rivista di filologia*, 1938, p. 115; Syme, *RR.* p. 225. This is the point of the distinction between Appian, *BC.* v, 95, and *Rom. Hist.* x, 28.

Sicily.[1] Furthermore, the first example (which weighs 424·4 grains) is so exceedingly thick that its reputed resemblance to coins of Caralis[2] is slight in comparison with its similarity to Sicilian issues of the fourth century B.C., on one of which it must have been overstruck.[3] But the piece cannot be Sicilian, since both legends and analogies eliminate the possibility of a date after 37: as on the Tarentine coinage, the *triskeles* must refer to the campaign, rather than to the mintage. The overstriking suggests a town within easy reach of the island—and our specimen comes from an Italian collection.[4] The unique emphasis on Agrippa makes attribution to his naval headquarters exceptionally probable. It is therefore significant that his appointment was at once signalised by a grandiose scheme of harbour construction, and a concentration of forces, at Puteoli.[5] Previous sections have provided precedents for mintage at military ports, and it is difficult to resist the conclusion that this coin, celebrating the high admiral's appointment, was struck at his new headquarters at that colony.[6]

This unorthodox issue was similar to the 'Fleet' coinage of Antony in type and in the circumstances which prompted it, but not in its circulation, which must have been exceedingly small; the expedient of overstriking suggests that the technical departments of the mint were rudimentary. There is, however, reason to believe that it was the inauguratory issue of a naval mint which fulfilled the same needs for Octavian as Tarentum (?) for Antony.

There are comparatively common bronze coins with DIVI F. (head of Octavian to right) and DIVOS IVLIVS (in wreath).[7] These are sometimes found in the south[8] and east[9] of Gaul; but Goudard's attribution to Nîmes is based on wholly fallacious reasoning[10] (p. 122), and their delicate yet somewhat unattractive workmanship differs greatly from the rough style of the official issues of Arelate(?) (p. 41). Even greater is their dissimilarity to contemporary colonial coinage at Lugdunum, and Sydenham's attribution to that mint[11] is unacceptable. Finds also are reported from Sardinia,[12] and probably occur in Africa;[13] provenance does not support attribution to Spain.[14] They occur particularly often in Italy.[15] The fact that Campania is

---

[1] Bahrfeldt, l.c.: Pennisi di Floristella coll.
[2] Mattingly, l.c.
[3] Ibid. L. A. Lawrence also holds this view.
[4] Larizza coll. (Santamaria sale 1928, 26).
[5] Dio XLVIII, 50; cf. Charlesworth, l.c. p. 58.
[6] Kornemann 14.
[7] BMCR. III, p. 413. 108 ff. Analysed NC. 1904, p. 244; see below, p. 89, for errors in this respect. The erratic striking makes it probable that a single denomination was intended, rather than four or two (Sydenham, NC. 1917, pp. 53 ff.; cf. M. & S. p. 43 n. 1).
[8] E.g. Sillingy (Boutkowski, DN. I, p. 75), Nîmes; cf. Eckhel, DN. VI, p. 138.
[9] E.g. Neuss (Strack, BJ. CXII, 1904, p. 452).
[10] He is followed by Lacroix, Les médailles de Nîmes au pied de sanglier, p. 8.
[11] NC. 1917, l.c. no. 20.
[12] Spano, Bullettino archeologico sardo, IV, 1858, p. 199.
[13] Constantine mus.; Hinglais, Recueil de la Soc. arch. du dép. de Constantine, XXXVIII, 1904, p. 21.
[14] de Saulcy, Mémoires de la société française de numismatique et d'archéologie, 1873, p. 26; pace Milan Cat. p. 12. 131–3; Laffranchi, R.it. 1912, p. 170.
[15] Many in trade at Milan and in Rome; noticeably more in all Italian museums than in those of other countries.

especially productive of them[1] recalls the attribution of the coin last discussed to Puteoli.

Chronological indications suggest a further connection with that piece. Laffranchi's ascription to c. 20 B.C.[2] is entirely groundless. Sydenham[3] establishes a *terminus ante quem* of 29 B.C., Bahrfeldt[4] narrows the limits to c. 39–38 B.C., and Grueber[5] prefers c. 38. Analogies of legend and style can be combined with historical considerations to show a probable occasion of issue. An upper limit is provided by two groups of *denarii* of c. 39–38:[5] the portraits of the one group[6] are closely imitated on some specimens of the *aes*,[7] and the other[8] displays the same otherwise unparalleled titulature DIVI F. Confirmation of these comparisons is provided by a third series of *denarii*[9] whose reverse plan shows a considerable technical similarity with the *aes* issues: in this case the titulature is in the form IMP. CAESAR DIVI F., COS. ITER. ET TER. DESIG. It is significant that these further resemble our *aes* in their lack of the triumviral title. By way of contrast, the immediate predecessors and successors of the *denarii* respectively bear the legends: IMP. CAESAR DIVI F. IIIVIR. R. P. C.;[10] IMP. CAESAR DIVI F. IIIVIR. *ITER*. R. P. C. COS. ITER. ET TERT. DESIG.[11] It has been pointed out (p. 46) that there were intervals between the expiration of the *Lex Titia* (December 38) and the decisions at Tarentum (spring 37), and between the latter and the formal ratification of the new *quinquennium* (summer 37). The omission of the triumviral title on our third series of *denarii* indicates attribution to one of those intervals, when the new appellation IMP(*erator*) was given a serious trial (p. 415). During the second of these intervals—as later—Antony quoted his triumviral rank without the addition of *iterum*, and Agrippa's 'Fleet' coin has borne witness to the same practice—during this interval only—by Octavian. It is unlikely that, if the last-named had already abandoned the triumviral title in January 37, he would have permitted its reintroduction without iteration—as on the *aes* of Agrippa—in the second interval; this is especially improbable in view of his subsequent emphasis on *iterum*. Our three series of *denarii* lacking the title cannot, therefore, be placed in the first interval, and must have been struck in the second—between the agreement and its formal ratification. The second of the *denarius* groups has DIVI F. alone: and the *aes*, with the same titulature, is likely to belong to the same period of constitutional suspense. Moreover, this must follow, rather than precede, the 'Fleet' coin of Agrippa which has not yet abandoned the titulature of the first *quinquennium*. It can therefore be approximately attributed to the summer of 37. The coin of Agrippa was probably

---

[1] Many in Naples mus.; a number found at Salerno, including imitations (some acquired by the writer in Naples).
[2] L.c.
[3] *NC*. 1917, l.c.
[4] *NZ*. 1918, p. 105; cf. Weickert, *Die Antike*, 1938, p. 211.
[5] *BMCR*. II, pp. 412 f.
[6] Especially Cahn sale 71. 1445 (Frankfurt, 1931).
[7] E.g. Ars Classica sale 13. 1116 (Geneva, 1928); Cahn sale 68. 156.
[8] *BMCR*. II, p. 410. 100.
[9] Ibid. p. 415. 115.
[10] Ibid. p. 414. 114.
[11] Berlin, ibid. p. 415.

THE TRIUMVIRS 49

struck at Puteoli, and that provenance suggests that the present *aes* coinage should be assigned to the same mint. The former was a makeshift inauguratory issue as a preliminary to the production of this extensive coinage. The attribution to a military port is supported by precedents at Brundusium(?), Zacynthus, Arelate(?) and Tarentum(?), and by the great activity of Octavian and Agrippa at this very time in shipbuilding and the training of crews.[1]

An issue with DIVOS IVLIVS and CAESAR DIVI F. and their heads[2] (Pl. I, 14) bears such a close resemblance to the last series that it must belong to the same mint, and may well have been engraved by the same hand.[3] Although it was imitated in Sicily,[4] Sardinia,[5] Gaul[6] and Spain,[7] and is found rarely as far as Germany,[8] this, like the other, occurs particularly often in Italy.[9] No attempt has hitherto been made to distinguish it in date from the issue just described—from which, indeed, it cannot be far removed.[10] The legend CAESAR DIVI F. follows plain DIVI F. on the *aes* as on *denarii*,[11] and it is natural to suppose that, just as DIVI F. occurs at the same date in both metals, so does CAESAR DIVI F.[12] But, contrary to the current view, there are many reasons for believing that the earliest *denarii* with the latter inscription (namely, those without a portrait of Octavian) are not as late as c. 31,[13] or even as 36.[14] The *aes*,

[1] Dio XLVIII, 49. 2; cf. Ganter, p. 11.

[2] *BMCR.* II, p. 412. 105. Many hybrids occur (Sydenham, *NC.* 1917, 21).

[3] A Milan piece of divergent style (Sacchi, *Historia*, IX, 1935, p. 485; *Milan Cat.* p. 12. 122) is false. An identical forgery has been shown me by a dealer, and another figured in the collections of Bachofen von Echt (sale 1903. 667) and Faure (sale 1923. 14).

[4] In trade, Rome.

[5] Hybrid in style of Atius Balbus (p. 150): in trade, London.

[6] Strack, *BJ.* CXII, 1904, p. 452.

[7] Overstruck on *as* of Sex. Pompeius (Capitoline, cf. Bahrfeldt, *NZ.* 1896, pp. 152 f.); portrait imitated at Calagurris (Hill, pl. XXXV, 10) and Tarraco (ibid. pl. IV, 16).

[8] E.g. at Öhringen (Nestle, *Funde*, p. 79): but none among many hundreds of coins collected in Bonn mus.

[9] Italian museums and dealers' stocks are especially prolific (e.g. *Milan Cat.* 123–30), and the coins are rated as very common. Some found at Salerno, in own collection (acquired in Naples). The Gutteridge gift to Cambridge, of South Italian provenance, includes three coins of this type, but no other contemporary *aes*.

[10] The occasional appearance of a beard is anachronistic. Cf. also p. 74.

[11] *BMC. Imp. Aug.* 590 ff.

[12] This conclusion is confirmed by their isolation among coins and inscriptions with the *praenomen imperatoris*: see below, p. 417.

[13] As Mattingly, *BMC. Imp.* p. cxx; cf. n. 3.

[14] As Grueber, *BMCR.* II, p. 8. De Salis preferred c. 39 as a starting-point, and in support of his view there are three categories of evidence: (1) *Hoards*. The Chantenay find contained one of these *denarii* with a figure of Mercury, *BMC. Imp. Aug.* 596, but no other coins later than c. 40–38 B.C. (*BMCR.* III, p. 29). Additional arguments will show that this does not warrant doubts of the hoard (as Mattingly, *BMC. Imp.* p. lxxvi). (2) *Types*. This Mercury type, which refers specially to the restoration of commerce (Six, *Rev. arch.* IV, 1916, pp. 247 ff.), is more apposite to the riddance of Sextus than to Actium (cf. Cesano, *QA.* III, p. 15). Venus Victrix(?) (*BMC. Imp. Aug.* 609) and Neptune (ibid. 615) are ambiguous; however, it may be significant that the latter deity was honoured conspicuously by Octavian before Mylae and Naulochus (Appian, *BC.* v, 96 and 98 respectively) whereas there is curiously little trace of his worship by the *princeps* after Actium (cf. Gagé, *Mélanges d'archéologie*

50   COINAGE BY *IMPERIUM MAIUS*, 49–28 B.C.

then, may be attributed to c. 37–36, and be considered a third issue of the mint ascribed to Puteoli. It is in accordance with this conclusion that the last stages of the Sicilian war were accompanied by extensive official currency from a more advanced base (p. 52), so that all the issues from the present mint may be ascribed with probability to the year 37.

Two further coinages of exceptional interest bear witness to the feverish military and naval preparations of the same year.

6. AFRICA (CARTHAGE?)

One of these (Pl. II, 12)[1] has suffered two entirely erroneous attributions. It reads DIVOS IVLIVS (diademed head of Julius to left; *lituus*) and DICTATOR PER····· (galley with sail; *sidus Iulium*). Sestini,[2] with his customary flair for *litterae evanidae*, discovered the ethnic [AC]HVLLA on an example known to him; this may well be the single specimen now extant, since oxidisation and portions of the type give an excuse, but no sort of justification, for this hypothetical reading. The fiction has been

et d'histoire, LIII, 1936, p. 85). Furthermore, in direct contrast to later-*denarii* with IMP. CAESAR and the type of Octavian on a quadriga (*BMC. Imp. Aug.* 617), referring to his triumph of 29, is the type of an empty quadriga (ibid. 590), which, as Mattingly (ibid. p. cxxii) infers from Cassiodorus (*Chronica s.* 19 B.C.), 'suggests a victory for which no formal triumph was celebrated'; thus it is inapplicable to Actium, but peculiarly relevant to the Illyrian successes of 35–34. (3) *Style.* A number of the CAESAR DIVI F. coins show Greek workmanship, which is even more noticeable on subsequent official issues: but the group without the heads of Octavian (with which the present series of *aes* is here held to be associated) lacks this refinement and is comparable to earlier pieces of 'Italian' style. Moreover, heads of Pax(?) (*BMC. Imp. Aug.* 611) and Venus(?) (ibid. 609) show striking affinities (especially in the ever-changing feature of coiffure) with a Roman coin (*BMCR.* pl. LVIII, 5) considered by Mattingly (as he informs me) to be no later than c. 42–39 B.C.; the *denarius* with Pax resembles the same series in having a beaded edge rather than the line-edge of other *denarii* with the same legend (except the distinctive *BMC. Imp. Aug.* 605 whose style suggests a separate mint—cf. *Milan Cat.* p. 45. 442). Thus stylistic considerations support the evidence of provenance and types, and strongly suggest that the CAESAR DIVI F. coinage was the immediate successor of the quattuorviral issues, which terminated apparently in about 37 B.C. Mattingly confirms that the exact date is quite uncertain, and that the whole group needs reconsideration. One or two issues may even be post-Actian (e.g. *BMCR.* I, p. 571), but a cessation in about 37 is certain. Groag (*PW.* IV, 104 f.; cf. Mommsen, *ZfN.* 1887, pp. 202 ff.) has rightly eliminated C. Clodius Vestalis from the series. On the new series *quattuorviri* are no longer mentioned, but senatorial feeling is characteristically respected by the omission of Octavian's portrait on the earliest coins. This omission accounts for the lack of parallels in other metals for the head of Octavian on our *aes*, since it is contemporary with these *denarii*. The early date accounts for the beard on the former. It is possible that the official mint at Puteoli(?), which has already issued *aes* (and perhaps *denarii*?), now took over the functions of the 'senatorial' officials and produced the first of the silver with CAESAR DIVI F. But Mattingly (*BMC. Imp.* p. cxx n. 4) has established a strong probability that the mint had a period of 'travel' before it settled at Asiatic cities after Actium. Between Naulochus and Actium it may well have been transferred to North Italy to serve the Illyrian campaigns. Regling's rejection of such interpretations (*Phil. Woch.* 1924, pp. 364 ff.) is quite unwarranted in view of Lucan's express testimony to *castrensis moneta* (I, 380).

[1] Copenhagen.
[2] *Hedervar.* III, cont. p. 79, no. 1, pl. XXXIII, 14.

copied from Sestini by Werlhof,[1] Mionnet,[2] Boutkowski,[3] and De Schodt.[4] Another error common to them all is that of TER[T]. for PER. on the reverse. A further example is quoted from Borghesi and Riccio[5] by Muller[6] as reading D. IVLIVS (laureate head) and CAES. (galley). E. Babelon[7] cites it too, and Cavedoni[8] is wrong (as the specimen here illustrated suggests) in doubting its existence. Grueber[9] is cautious, but paradoxical, in stating that it is probably not ancient, and in any case barbarous; the extant piece again shows the incorrectness of both these incompatible suppositions. Muller[10] attributes Riccio's piece, for no good reason, to Iol Caesarea. Charrier[11] arbitrarily considers the legend to be C. IVLIVS and assigns the coin to Juba.[12] These hypotheses are useless, but Riccio's example at least enables the restoration of the legends: DIVOS IVLIVS—CAES[AR] DICTATOR PERP. or PERPET. The execution is of the thirties B.C., and the galley on the reverse shows such kinship with the Tarentine (?) *asses* of Atratinus[13] (which our coin also resembles in weight[14]) that it is justifiable to assume a connection with the Sicilian War of 37–36.

However, differences of style preclude attribution to the mint of the principal 'Fleet' series. Muller, Charrier, and Sestini and his followers all agree that the fabric is African; this is clearly correct, and the patina of the coin is of a reddish brown colour frequent on African coins of the period.[15] The responsible authority must therefore have been Lepidus. His triumvirate was apparently renewed by the Treaty of Tarentum,[16] since he played a very prominent part in the subsequent campaign, conducting a huge armada to Sicily with ambitions that extended far beyond co-operation.[17] The mint is likely to have been at his principal colony of Carthage (pp. 227, 231). This issue must be almost contemporary with the corresponding coin of Agrippa, which was struck during the preparations of 37. The emphasis on Julius is significant, and its cause is not far to seek: Lepidus had owed the precarious maintenance of his position to his loyalty to the Caesarian party,[18] which had already, perhaps rightly, been called into question.[19] This issue exceeds those of the other triumvirs in piety to the common cause, at a time when Lepidus was preparing to vindicate his own private ambitions to the detriment of his colleagues: it provides a very rare instance of the propaganda with which this *homo ventosissimus*[20] forwarded his claims. This and the other programme 'Fleet' coinages of the triumvirs provoked the Pompeian Cn. Piso Frugi to imitation (p. 31).

[1] *Handbuch der griechischen Numismatik* (1850), p. 261.   [2] *S.* IX, 202. 1.   [3] *DN.* I, p. 145.
[4] *Rb.* 1887, p. 381.
[5] *Monete di famiglie romane*, s.v. *Julia*, suppl., pl. LVIII, 19.   [6] III, p. 139. 213.   [7] II, pp. 47–8. 100.
[8] *Numismatica Biblica*, p. 126.
[9] *BMCR.* II, pp. 412 f. n. 2.   [10] III, p. 139. 213.
[11] *Description des monnaies de la Numidie et de la Maurétanie*, 407.
[12] Following de la Blanchère, *Bulletin de correspondance africaine*, 1884, p. 470.

[13] E.g. Rome; Willers, *Geschichte*, pl. X, 11.
[14] 143 grains.
[15] E.g. *municipia* of Zama Regia, Simitthu (?) (pp. 182, 178).
[16] Cf. Charlesworth, *CAH.* x, p. 59; cf. n. 1.
[17] Ibid. p. 59; cf. n. 1.
[18] Ibid. p. 26.
[19] Cf. Brueggemann, *De Marci Aemili Lepidi vita et rebus gestis*, Diss. Münster, 1887, pp. 52 f.
[20] Dec. Brutus (*ap.* Cic. *Fam.* XI, 9. 1); cf. Syme, *RR.* p. 166 n. 1.

7. LIPARA

A move of Octavian's military mint southwards is announced by a variegated series with a curious and entirely homogeneous style: it has neither been attributed nor collected, since the coins are very rare, poorly preserved, and insignificant. But when they are seen as a whole, it is not difficult to deduce their time and place. Those with signatures fall into the following three groups:

I. (1) OPPI. (Pl. I, 15).[1] (2) SEX. ANN.[2] (3) P. CORNELI.[3]
II. (4) L. ANNI.[4] (5) AN. (Pl. I, 12).[5] (6) L. CAE.[6]
III. (7) STATI. TREBO7[NI[8]]. (8) IMP. (Pl. II, 13).[9] (9) D. POR(?).[10] (10) SACER.[11] (11) P. AL. (Pl. I, 17).[12] (12) CAP.[13] (13) P. CALP.[14] (14) M. AVFI. SCAEVA.[15]

The first of these three groups is distinct in types and in weight—c. 85 grains, nearly double that of the rest. The other two, bridged by (5), are separated by a slight evolution of type arrangement. The representations on these coins are manifold:[16] but the curious persistence of a single unusual type leads to a geographical attribution. All issues in Group II are accompanied by Vulcan: not only does his head appear, with tongs, on coins with each of the three signatures, but (5) shows his running figure. This is identical with a local type of Lipara,[17] on whose series Vulcan, significantly absent in Sicily,[18] is regularly portrayed. No less noteworthy is the recurrence of his head on (7) and of his running form on (9): both types are also found on pieces without a legend.[19] Since these associations with Lipara are unavoidable, the persistence of a highly individual style makes it inevitable that the whole series, whose uniformity escaped Bahrfeldt, should be assigned to this mint—to which only a single piece among all these issues has hitherto been attributed.[20]

[1] Bahrfeldt, *RS*. 1904, p. 408. 58, 61 (*BMC. Sicily*, p. 127. 10, var. Vienna).
[2] Ibid. p. 414. 62 (Glasgow).
[3] Ibid. p. 418. 69 (Berlin).
[4] Ibid. p. 416. 64 (Basel). P. ANNI. (ibid. 65, 66) (Berlin) is very doubtful.
[5] Ibid. p. 417. 68 (Paris), p. 434. 87 (Berlin). Wrongly attributed to Zacynthus by Gardner, *BMC. Peloponnese*, p. 102. 90.
[6] Bahrfeldt, l.c. p. 417. 67 (Basel).
[7] Id. *NZ*. 1918, p. 169 (Paris).
[8] Ibid. (Capitoline).
[9] Unpublished (Turin).
[10] Bahrfeldt, *RS*. 1904, p. 435 (Berlin).
[11] Misread, ibid. p. 433. 86. Cesano, *Fascicolo-omaggio per il primo Centenario del Gabinetto di Brera*; cf. *Rassegna numismatica*, VI, 1909, p. 15 (Rome).
[12] Unpublished (Copenhagen—attributed to Paestum).
[13] Bahrfeldt, l.c. p. 411; Imhoof-Blumer, *MG*. p. 36. 84.
[14] Not in Bahrfeldt, l.c. Misread by Boissevain, *Amsterdam Cat*. p. 222. 6 (now at Hague).
[15] Not in Bahrfeldt, l.c. Babelon, *Monnaies de la république romaine*, I, p. 234 (Capitoline); cf. Klebs, *PW*. II, 2296 (37).
[16] E.g. Janus, Jupiter, Mercury, Hercules, Cupid, Bacchus, Medusa, Victory, centaur, elephant, pig, panther, Ulysses(?), etc.
[17] *BMC. Sicily*, p. 263. 79 (etc.).
[18] Cf. Cesano, *R.it.* XXX, 1917, pp. 11 ff.
[19] Bahrfeldt, l.c. p. 442. 104 (Gotha), and unpublished (Berlin), respectively.
[20] By Babelon, l.c. I, p. 244. 21.

Lipara was a naval station of Octavian[1] and a *municipium* from 37 B.C. (p. 195): it was one of the principal bases for the campaigns of 36. A number of extraordinary overstruck pieces (Pl. I, 16),[2] and the careless striking of small flans on large dies on (7), (10) and unsigned coins[3]—in both cases the type is often Vulcan—strongly suggest that part of the series at least was a product of the war emergency. The signatories of (1) and (7) confirm that the coinage should be assigned to this occasion. OPPI. must be M. Oppius Capito, who coined at Tarentum in 37 and then fought in the Sicilian War (p. 45). STATI., of (7), is referred by Grueber[4] to Murcus, whose *gentilicium*, however, was not Statius but Staius.[5] STATI. TREBONI. is likely to represent two names, not one, owing to the absence of a *praenomen*: by the analogy of Oppius it is probable that the former of the two persons thus named is another commander. He may therefore confidently be identified with T. Statilius Taurus, the Lucanian *novus homo*,[6] who played a prominent part in the campaign of 36[7] and was then Octavian's first governor of Sicily.[8] Treboni[us], who is unidentifiable,[9] is likely to be his quaestor, coining with the counter-signature of his commander in accordance with Republican precedent.[10] Some of these pieces have a quadriga identical with one on (14). This has the legend IMP. and a remarkable head with heavy features which are not those of a triumvir (Pl. II, 13): Statilius Taurus was saluted *imperator* after Naulochus,[11] and this may well be his title and portrait. CAP., whose coins are overstruck on those of Oppius,[12] confirms the view that the issues persisted for some little time. A further chronological indication may perhaps be derived from pieces of the same distinctive style without a legend: these have the type of an elephant's head,[13] which is likely to refer either to Lepidus's African forces in Sicily or to Octavian's subsequent occupation of Africa.

Thus all detectable signs refer to the years 37–36 and to the circumstances of the war for which Lipara was an important base. Statilius (if it is he whose portrait appears) was not *imperator* until after Naulochus: the concentration of enormous forces in north-eastern Sicily,[14] just opposite Lipara, provides a reason for the continuation of the issues for a short time after the war. Thus the officers here named probably represent a period of a year or two, but not more. Lipara was a Roman community, and a convenient base for a mint to supply payment for a large force; many technical freaks bear witness to the rapidity of mintage which the huge numbers of the soldiery

[1] Orsi, *Notizie degli Scavi*, v, 1929, pp. 98 f.
[2] Berlin.
[3] Bahrfeldt, l.c. p. 435.
[4] *BMCR.* II, p. 485 n. 2.
[5] *Bull. dell' inst. di corr. arch.* 1879, p. 224; cf. *Wochenschrift für klassische Philologie*, XXXIII, 1916, pp. 791 f.; Kloevekorn, *De proscriptionibus a tribus viris factis*, Diss. Königsberg, 1891, p. 55.
[6] Cf. Syme, *RR.* p. 237.
[7] Cf. Charlesworth, *CAH.* X, pp. 59 f.
[8] Orosius VI, 18. 32.
[9] Caesar's *legatus* seems to have left no close relations (Cic. *Fam.* XII, 164).
[10] Cf. Longpérier, *Recherches sur les insignes de la questure*, p. 6.
[11] Cf. Stein, *PW.* (2R.), III, 2200.
[12] Bahrfeldt, *RS.* l.c. p. 411; cf. Imhoof-Blumer, *MG.* p. 36. 84.
[13] BM ('uncertain'); unpublished.
[14] Cf. Charlesworth, l.c. p. 63.

necessitated. The signatories of the coinage, with the exception of Oppius and Statilius, do not assist a closer attribution. L. CAE. may tentatively be identified with the Volaterran L. Caecina L.f., who was tribune, praetor and proconsul during the last years of the Republic:[1] he or a kinsman was a confidential ambassador of Octavian.[2] P. Cornelius is likely to be either the P. Scipio who was *consul suffectus* in 35[3] or the P. Dolabella (at one time praetor) who was one of Octavian's younger supporters.[4] The other names—all unknown—reveal the inadequacy of our prosopographical knowledge of the period, and the effectiveness of the coins in adding to existing lists. SACER(*dos*) was perhaps a kinsman of the Carsidius who became *praetor urbanus* in A.D. 27,[5] or of Licinius Sacerdos who had held the praetorship in 75 B.C.[6] P. AL. is just conceivably P. Alfenus Varus jun., the consul of A.D. 2.[7] P. CALP*urnii* and CALP*etani* are excessively rare, and no suitable one can be found. SEX. ANN*ius* was possibly a Celer[8] or a Gallus,[9] since these combinations occur. The partisanship of the Annii is strongly indicated by (2), (4), and (5), but Augustan Fasti do not suggest that it gained them much preferment—it was nearly half a century before an Annius Pollio became known.[10] CAP. is unidentifiable, and there are no signs of a suitable Dec. POR(cius) who, if not of freedman stock, is the last known member of his family.[11] M. SCAEVA, whether AVFI(dius) or not,[12] provides an unusual combination of *nomen* and *cognomen*.[13] The lofty *dignitas* of Oppius and Statilius makes it clear that this, like Sextus's rival establishments, was no regular quaestorian mint: probably the unknown names are mostly those of legionary commanders. These issues provide the basis, but not the material, for an extended prosopography of the triumvirate.

8. AGRIGENTUM (?)

A curious little coin with a head of Octavian, and a palm-branch and club inscribed VICTORIA (Pl. II, 14),[14] is stylistically distinct from the Liparitan group, and of Sicilian style. The club suggests a connection with Sextus's issues at Agrigentum (p. 28), and this piece, although differing somewhat from those in style, is likely to have been a final issue of the same mint after Octavian's occupation. No further Agrigentine

---

[1] *PIR*^{2}. II, 17. 96; cf. Schulze, p. 75.
[2] Cic. *Att.* XVI, 82.
[3] Cf. Syme, *RR*. p. 244.
[4] *PIR*^{2}. 13. 45. For other Cornelii in his service vide Syme, *RR*. p. 235 n. 6.
[5] Cf. Groag, *PW*. III, 1615.
[6] Cic. *Verr.* I, 27. 104; cf. Münzer, *PW*. XIII, 458.
[7] *PIR*^{2}. I, 89. 523.
[8] Cf. *CIL*. VI, 2263.
[9] Ibid. XI, 1953.
[10] Von Rohden, *PW*. I, 2277 (71–2). Perhaps of this family (cf. ibid. 73) was a C. Annius, *IVvir.a.a.a.f.f.* in c. 9 B.C. (Mattingly, *BMC. Imp.* p. xcvii).
[11] Cf. Syme, *RR*. p. 492.
[12] Possibly Auficius, Aufidatorius, Aufidenus, Aufidienus, Aufillenus, Aufillius, Aufincidius, Aufitius, Aufius: cf. Schulze, pp. 203, 348, 203, 203, 114, 114, 202, 203, 202 respectively.
[13] For the Aufidii vide Schulze, p. 203; for their Eastern business interests vide Hatzfeld, *BCH*. XXXVI, 1912, p. 19.
[14] Glasgow (*Hu*. III, p. 734. 24).

official issues can be traced, but the city struck a few municipal coins subsequently (p. 191). The present piece appears to be unique, and its legend too is unique at this period: in the *Aeneid*,[1] Victory is still hovering on the border-line between poetical personification and deity.[2]

9. CNOSSUS(?)

E. S. G. Robinson has identified a Cretan mint, which struck a Latin *dupondius* and *as* with the name CRAS(*sus*). The former shows a prow and a crocodile, and the latter head of Apollo and *fasces*.[3] These are found in Crete,[4] and the curious prow on the higher denomination is precisely similar to one on a tetradrachm of Gortyna.[5] The issue of Crassus may, therefore, be ascribed to the same island.

Chronological limits can be derived from the type of a crocodile, which refers to the nominal rule of the Ptolemaic house (c. 37–31). Robinson attributes it in particular to Cleopatra Selene: but Dio's[6] explicit account, which records the Donation to her of Cyrenaica in 34,[7] does not include Crete among her possessions.[8] The reference is rather to her mother Cleopatra, who, as Dio[9] informs us in an earlier passage, possessed Κρήτης τινα—that is, probably the whole island except for the proposed colony at Cnossus (p. 261)[10]—in 37–34.[11] It is entirely in accordance with this view that the name of Crassus appears also on coins of Cyrenaica (p. 57): Cleopatra was granted that territory also in 37 (p. 58), and so there was, in 37–34, a reason for the identity of its governor with that of Crete such as existed neither before nor after that period. Before it, since the brief interlude of P. Lepidus under Brutus (p. 35), Crete was *libera et immunis*;[12] after it, the two territories were separated. Conclusive in favour of the attribution of the coins to the administration of Cleopatra in 37–34 rather than to the following years is a piece showing that a *régime* of quite a different kind existed in 34–31, between the date of this issue and the reversion of Crete to a province after Actium.[13] This was the government of a Cretarch Cydas, one of whose bronze pieces[14] is found overstruck on a *dupondius* of Crassus.[15] Cydas has hitherto been tentatively ascribed to the period before or soon after Philippi:[16] but here is proof that he was later than Crassus. Here too is a revelation of the lost history of Crete between 34 and 31. When Cyrenaica passed to Selene in 34, the island also passed from the Romano-Egyptian administration of her mother and Crassus, and continued its career,

---

[1] XII, 187. [2] Cf. Stössl, *PW*. XIX, 1055.
[3] *BMC. Cyrenaica*, p. 119. For illustrations, ibid. pl. XLII, 8, 9. [4] Ibid. p. ccix n. 1.
[5] Ibid. p. ccxxi. [6] XLIX, 41. 5.
[7] Cf. Tarn, *CAH*. x, p. 80; Dobiáš, *Mélanges Bidez*, 1934, p. 287.
[8] *Pace* Shipley, *Res Gestae* (Loeb ed.), p. 393 n. 1.
[9] XLIX, 32. 5.
[10] Id. XLIX, 14; cf. Strabo X, 478.
[11] For the date, vide Tarn, l.c. p. 67.

[12] Cic. *II Phil*. 38. 97; cf. Romanelli, *CAH*. XI, p. 659; Syme, *RR*. p. 272; not merely *immunis*, as Ker, *ad loc*.
[13] Cf. *RG*. 27.
[14] Provenance assured by finds, e.g. Halbherr, *Museo italiano di antichità classica*, II, 1888, p. 766.
[15] BM; E. S. G. Robinson has pointed this out to me.
[16] Paribeni, *Dizionario epigrafico*, II, 2. 165; Raven, *NC*. 1938, p. 146.

started by Antony nine years earlier, of Greek *libertas et immunitas*—autonomy under a Cretarch. Cydas, who alone of a number of Greek coining officials strikes a silver piece, and on it exceptionally writes KPHTAIEΩN,[1] was similar in power, if not in title, to Cleopatra's governors of Cyprus, Demetrius and Serapion.[2] The annals of the island during the triumvirate now begin to take shape.

Crassus, then, must have been in the island between 37 and 34. All proposed chronologies are therefore unacceptable.[3] Robinson accepts Svoronos's identification with P. Canidius Crassus;[4] but this is fraught with insuperable difficulties. The literary authorities account for his movements during these years in such a way as to leave no room for a governorship, or official post, in Crete and Cyrenaica. He was in Armenia, Iberia and Parthia in 37–36,[5] and again in the Armenian campaign of 34;[6] he had the difficult task of effecting the retreat after the disasters of 36,[7] and—since he retained his command—was in charge of the reorganisation preceding the later campaign. Thus he could have held no regular governorship from May to May in any part of this period, and was, indeed, so preoccupied with more important concerns that it is difficult to see how he could have had any connection with Crete and Cyrenaica, and the present issue. There was, however, another distinguished Crassus who joined Antony's camp before c. 36,[8] M. Licinius.[9] His official career under the triumvir is unknown except for a possible proconsulship of Bithynia-Pontus.[10] But, when he went over to Octavian in c. 31,[11] his experience was deemed sufficient for a consulship and proconsulship, though he had never been praetor.[12] It is difficult to resist the conclusion that he was the Crassus who was present in Crete in c. 37–34 B.C. A closer definition of his office will be attempted in the next section.

A second Latin series was struck by a similar official, L. Lollius. Heads of Diana and of a youthful male deity[13] are accompanied by types of *sella curulis*[14] and stag[15] respectively; a smaller piece has a club and laurel-wreath.[16] The moneyer is con-

[1] Svoronos, *Crete*, p. 334; cf. Imhoof-Blumer, *MG*. p. 210. 1 (Naples, Paris). His predecessors often inscribe their coins KN[ΩΣIΩN] (Svoronos, l.c. pp. 82, 85): the office of Cretarch probably evolved from a Cnossian magistracy which ceased to exist, or, at any rate, to be important, when Cnossus became a colony in c. 36 B.C. (p. 261).

[2] Appian, *BC*. IV, 61. 9; cf. Syme, *Anatolian Studies to Buckler*, p. 324 n. 5.

[3] E.g. of Stähelin, *PW*. XI, 776, Gardthausen, *NZ*. XLIX, 1916, pp. 153 ff. (after Actium); Robinson, *BMC. Cyrenaica*, l.c. (just before Actium).

[4] Ll.cc.

[5] Plut. *Ant*. 34. 3; Dio XLIX, 24. 1; cf. Levi II, p. 120.

[6] Plut. *Ant*. 42. 3.

[7] Cf. Tarn, *CAH*. X, p. 75.

[8] Cf. Glauning, *Die Anhängerschaft des Antonius und des Octavian* (Diss. Leipzig, 1935), pp. 13, 16; Syme, *RR*. pp. 269, 296.

[9] Dio LI, 4. 3; cf. *PIR*. II, 275. 126.

[10] Cuntz, *Jahreshefte des öst. arch. Inst*. XXV, 1929, p. 79, conjectures that a L. Licinius from Sebastopolis in the Koptos inscription (Mommsen, *Ephemeris Epigraphica*, V, pp. 5 ff.) derived his *nomen* from M. Crassus. In this case the latter could have succeeded Cn. Ahenobarbus in the governorship of Bithynia-Pontus at some date after 35 (Appian, *BC*. V, 137).

[11] Dio, l.c.; cf. Groag, *PW*. XIII, 271.

[12] Dio, l.c.

[13] For discussion vide Robinson, l.c. pp. ccxiv f.

[14] Ibid. p. 114. 3.   [15] Ibid. 4 ff.

[16] Ibid. 16 *bis* ff.

jecturally identified by E. S. G. Robinson with Palikanus, *IIIvir a.a.a.f.f.* in c. 47 B.C.[1] Like Crassus, he too is recorded on Greek issues, and by analogy the two groups have been assigned to Crete and Cyrenaica respectively.[2] But the evidence of provenance adds complexity: his Greek coins are found in considerable numbers in Crete,[3] and the Latin group, though represented there,[4] also appears extensively in Cyrenaica.[5] The possibility must therefore be admitted—as the style does not exclude it—that the two categories were struck at a single mint and then distributed: but certainty is not obtainable.

The occasions of both these series can, however, be deduced with probability from the certain Cretan origin of the issue of Crassus. Far the most important event in the history of the island during the years 37–34 B.C. was the establishment of a colony at Cnossus in c. 36 (p. 261). We may assume with some plausibility that the coinage of Crassus commemorated this *deductio*, and thus followed in the tradition of the Roman officials C. Clovius and Q. Hortensius (pp. 7, 33)—who likewise struck money to inaugurate new foundations—and in that of numerous colonies and *municipia* whose issues served the same purpose (p. 290). Furthermore, this interpretation explains the isolated appearance of our two signatures: it will be shown elsewhere that the funds devoted to the establishment of a colony regularly enabled the inauguratory coinage to be followed by a second (p. 291). From this fund was probably derived the Latin issue of Lollius. It has already been noted that such 'foundation' series are no less the product of the autocrat's *imperium maius* than are all the contemporary coinages which supply some more direct military need.

10, 11. CYRENE AND PTOLEMAIS

In Cyrenaica, Lollius and Crassus employed different monetary methods. The former issued a coinage (probably at Cyrene) without any ethnic or mint-mark, inscribed ΛΟΛΛΙΟΥ, with additional "privy-marks"; the types include heads of Ammon, Apollo, Libya, and (reverses) *sella curulis*,[6] dromedary,[7] *caduceus* with poppy and corn-ear,[8] respectively. Crassus, however, acted in co-operation with the local authorities of Cyrene[9] and Ptolemais:[10]

    KPA. head of Libya r.—KY[PA.] silphium.[9]

    KPA[Σ?.] crocodile—ΠΤΟΛΕΜΑΙ. turreted head of Tyche r.[10]

---

[1] Ibid. p. ccxvi; cf. Grueber, *BMCR.* I, p. 518 n. For the banking interests of the Lollii in the East, vide Herzog, *PW*. XVII, 1442.

[2] Robinson, l.c.

[3] Ibid. p. ccix n. 1.

[4] Cf. Halbherr, *Museo italiano di antichità classica*, II, 1888, p. 765.

[5] Sestini, *Fontana*, I, pp. 124 ff.; cf. Robinson, l.c.

[6] *BMC. Cyrenaica*, 19 f.

[7] Ibid. 21 ff.

[8] Ibid. p. ccvi, 23 *a*, *b*; Berlin, Paris. For illustrations of these coins, ibid. pl. XLI f.

[9] Ibid. 26; cf. *Hu.* III, p. 571. 29, Leningrad.

[10] Vienna = *BMC. Cyrenaica*, p. ccvi, 25 *bis* (*a*).

These issues are on the border-line between official and local coins. Those of Lollius belong to the former category: since his name appears in Greek, they perhaps have the character of a truly provincial currency (p. 119)—that is, an official substitute for local issues such as those sponsored by Crassus—rather than of a military or 'foundation' coinage like the others of the epoch.

It has been pointed out that the union of Crete and Cyrenaica under the rule of Lollius and Crassus can be justified by no circumstances other than those of coalescence in the realm of Cleopatra from 37 to 34. This view is corroborated by the remarkable omission by both these officers, on all their issues, of any Roman titulature. This feature would have been entirely exceptional and incorrect in a regular province, but it was understandable, if not essential, in royal territory. The issues provide an excellent commentary on the anomalous situation created by the Donations. The Roman provincial government was not, indeed, superseded,[1] as the *fasces* on Crassus's Latin issue indicate:[2] Crete and Cyrene did not yet fall into the same category as Cyprus, a gift to Cleopatra by Julius,[3] where purely regal coins were minted[4] and Greeks were governors (p. 56). On the other hand, the administrations had lost their formal constitutional character, and were mere survivals, permitted from motives of strategy and convenience, in peregrine territory. The Donations were sufficiently real to warrant administrative and numismatic union,[5] the use of a Ptolemaic type by Crassus,[6] and the suppression of Roman titles. Later, however, during the crisis preceding Actium, this aspect of Antony's rule must have receded into the background (p. 370): L. Pinarius Scarpus, an officer in Cyrenaica—now part of the dominions of the *reine fainéante* Cleopatra Selene—inscribes his own title IMPERATOR on his coins, and mentions Antony to the exclusion of the women.[7] Since Antony gives place to Octavian on these pieces,[8] Scarpus is identifiable with the commander mentioned by Plutarch[9] after Actium: καὶ τὴν ἐν Λιβύῃ δύναμιν ὁ πεπιστευμένος ἀπέστησεν.[10] It is in accordance with the present interpretation of the coinages of Crassus and Lollius that the issues of Scarpus bear the head of Ammon, but show no connection with Crete; this had been separated from Cyrenaica by the changes of 34.

[1] Cf. Syme, *RR*. p. 276, *pace* Levi II, p. 19 n. 1.
[2] Cf. Mommsen, *St. R*. I³, p. 377.
[3] Giles, *CR*. 1935, p. 199.
[4] Svoronos, *Ptolemies*, 1874; Regling, *ZfN*. XXV, 1906, p. 395.
[5] Unrecognised by Ganter, p. 46.
[6] If, as seems probable, coins with this type were minted at Cnossus, its character was there honorary, since the colony was officially founded on Roman soil.
[7] Cf. *BMC. Cyrenaica*, p. ccx.
[8] *BMC. Imp. Aug.* 686 ff.
[9] *Ant.* 69. 1; cf. Dio LI, 59; *PIR*. III, 40. 311.
[10] A further moneyer of *denarii*, M. Silanus *q. pro cos.*, who is ascribed by Ganter (p. 46), followed by Syme, *RR*. p. 266 n. 3, to this province, should be reattributed to Achaia (Münzer, *PW*. X, 1096; Mommsen, *Gesammelte Schriften*, p. 204; Glauning, l.c. p. 28 n. 88; cf. *IG*. III, 568).

12. Melita

A small issue at this mint presents problems that are not wholly soluble. The legends are ΜΕΛΙΤΑΙΩΝ and C. ARRVNTANVS BALBVS PRO PR.; the types a veiled female head and *sella curulis*.[1] It is unique in possessing completely the features both of local and of official currency: the ethnic appears in its fullest form and in Greek, and yet there is the name of a Roman official, with the title of his rank, written in Latin. Technically, then, this is a perfect example of co-operation between the commander and the city to produce a coinage. The closest parallel—though there the ethnic is only monogrammatic—is the issue of Sosius at Zacynthus. Nor is the resemblance fortuitous. To the realms of Sex. Pompeius, and of Octavian after him, Melita had precisely the same strategic position as Zacynthus bore to the dominions of Antony; it was, as it is still, the key to Sicily and the Straits of Tunis. It is therefore very likely that the coins indicate the presence of a fleet-station and served its monetary needs. Probably, then, Arruntanus was not governor of Sicily, but held a position analogous to that of Sosius.

The upper limit for this issue is 36 B.C., when Octavian suppressed a colony at Melita which a unique coin shows to have been founded by Murcus in 42 B.C. (p. 234). The numismatic history of this period provides a further reason for the coinage of Arruntanus. Issues of Entella, Lilybaeum and Agrigentum (p. 392) indicate that the end of the Sicilian war was marked by the imposition on the Sextian communities of a vast indemnity,[2] for whose extortion a number of officers were sent the round of the island. Of these, Sosius and Atratinus, as will be shown, ordered the local authorities to pay in *aes* coinage, whose occasion is marked by the appearance of the extortioners' names in Greek characters. Arruntanus, however, who signs these pieces in Latin, apparently took over the control of his mint, but still permitted the Melitan authorities a share in its administration. It will be shown elsewhere that soon after his special commission the mint was transferred to the *quaestor* of eastern Sicily (p. 68).

13. Mauretania Caesariensis (Iol?)

The *praenomen imperatoris*, exceptionally omitted on the group of *aes* and *denarii* with CAESAR DIVI F. (p. 49), appears on inscriptions of c. 36–32 B.C.[3] It is also found on the last Octavianic coinage before Actium, which bears the legends IMP. CAESAR. DIVI F. This series creates a break in the succession of purely military groups, recalling the more indirect purpose of the 'foundation' currencies.

---

[1] Glasgow; *Hu.* III, p. 605. 30 f.; cf. *PIR.*[2] I, 220. 1122.

[2] A principal citizen of Melita, A. Licinius Aristo- teles, was a strong Republican; cf. Cic. *Fam.* XIII, 52.

[3] *ILS.* 77, 128, 8893; *CIL.* I, p. 28; cf. Schön, *PW.* VI, 2031 ff.

COINAGE BY *IMPERIUM MAIUS*, 49–28 B.C.

The types include a bull and a lion[1] (Pl. II, 16), a head of Ammon and an elephant,[2] and heads of Octavian and Africa.[3] These representations are decisively African in character: in particular, no less than three of them are also found on the coins of Bocchus III of Mauretania.[4] Berbruegger[5] sees in the head of Africa a portrait of Cleopatra Selene; but her husband did not succeed to the throne until 25 B.C.,[6] and the titulature is unsuitable to so late a date.[7] Muller[8] rightly assigns the series to the *interregnum* between Bocchus and Juba (33–25); but his classification with a local group (of Tingis [p. 175]) is refuted by the provenance of the present issues from Mauretania Caesariensis.[9] The close correspondence in type and style with issues of Bocchus suggests a date early in the *interregnum*.

There is no evidence of military activity (the cause of so many contemporary issues) in the region at this time. On the other hand, soon after 33, an extensive scheme of colonisation was carried out, such as had inspired earlier coinage by the *praefecti a.d.a. et coloniis deducendis*. At least nine colonies were founded at this time in eastern Mauretania (p. 223),[10] and the analogies of Clovius, Hortensius, and M. Crassus make it particularly probable that this coinage commemorated their *deductio*. Such functions were, as has been shown, delegated to a representative by the *imperium maius* of the autocrat. Hortensius was not only founder but governor, and an extensive array of later parallels from the local series will show that Octavian too, as was reasonable, regularly assigned *deductiones* to the governors of his provinces (p. 459). But Mauretania does not appear in the *Res Gestae* as a province in which he founded colonies, and Gsell[11] has drawn the conclusion that it was attached during the *interregnum* to the jurisdiction of Africa. But a coin of Babba (p. 222) shows that the *deductor* of that city in 32 was officially Octavian himself; and the same is probably true here also. Probably no one in Mauretania possessed high enough rank to be entrusted with this honour.

---

[1] Copenhagen; Charrier, *Description des monnaies de la Numidie et de la Maurétanie*, 165, corrects Muller, *Suppl.* p. 73. 176.

[2] Paris; Muller, l.c.

[3] BM; id. III, p. 101. 17; cf. Charrier, l.c. 164.

[4] Charrier, l.c. p. 28.

[5] *Revue africaine*, v, 1860, pp. 60 ff.

[6] Syme, *CAH*. x, p. 346; cf. Gsell VIII, p. 209; other views are incorrect.

[7] A group of *denarii* with the same legend (*BMC. Imp. Aug.* 309 ff.) is assigned by Mattingly to c. 22–19 B.C. and to the Emeritan series (from which, however, they differ extensively in style). But Sydenham, like Grueber (*BMCR*. II, p. 416), does not accept this view, and three considerations are in conjunction decisive in favour of c. 32. (1) The same legend occurs regularly on *denarii* of this time, but not later (cf. M. & S. I, p. 62 n. 2). (2) An identical head is found on pieces with LEG. XVI, which can be plausibly assigned to a date earlier than Actium from arguments by Willers (*NZ*. XXXIV, 1902, pp. 83, 80; cf. *ZfN*. 1875, p. 117; Ritterling, *PW*. XII, 1376). (3) A variant of *BMC*. 309 in the British Museum has a portrait that resembles very closely that of *BMC*. 602 which belongs to the pre-Actian mint operating first at Puteoli (?), vide p. 50 f. n. 14. Thus the *denarii* do not interfere with, but rather confirm, the present attribution.

[8] III, p. 101.

[9] Cagnat, *Recueil de la soc. arch. du dép. de Constantine*, XL, 1906, p. 97; cf. Charrier, l.c., and Gsell VIII, p. 201 n. 5.

[10] Carcopino, *Rev. hist.* CLXII, 1929, p. 90; cf. Gsell VIII, p. 202; Kornemann, 359 ff.

[11] VIII, p. 201.

It is likely to have been a non-provincial zone—like Galatia in similar circumstances after the death of Amyntas (p. 250). Thus the present issues were made, primarily for commemorative purposes, by an unidentifiable *adsignator* in c. 33–31 at an East Mauretanian city; this may have been one of the newly founded colonies, or more probably the ex-capital of Bocchus, Iol.[1]

Meanwhile the *imperium maius* of Antony was continuing to provide coinage for more direct military purposes.

14, 15. Antioch and Laodicea(?) (Syria)

The penultimate coinage of the period, of an unidentified Q. Oppius, can be ascribed to a region in which no official currency had hitherto appeared. It is of *orichalcum*, as analysis[2] proves; this contradicts Sydenham's[3] assumption that the metal is copper, and his subsequent hypotheses based on that view. The coins have the following types:

(1) Head to right of female goddess. Sometimes crescent, capricorn, or both,[4] behind neck.—Q. OPPIVS PR. Winged Victory walking to left, looking backwards, carrying a bowl of fruit and a palm-branch (Pl. I, 19).[5]

(2) Similar head to left. Sometimes a star(?)—as last.[6]

(3) Similar head to right.—Same inscription. Winged Victory facing.[7]

Grueber's[8] attribution of these to Rome (46–45 B.C.)[9] is invalidated by the falsity of the coin of Plancus which he uses as an analogy. Further, we have seen (p. 11) that the issue of Clovius which he also compares is not Roman at all; and even if it were, the divergency of title would indicate a difference of office.[10] It too can no longer be cited as a parallel. Nor is it necessary to assume, with Wehrmann,[11] that PR. must imply a Roman praetorship: it may equally refer to a proconsul's rank of PR(*aetor*) (rather than his office), and might even stand for PR(*o consule*) itself (pp. 33, 135, 197). Thus every positive reason that has been adduced in favour of Rome as a mint is based on a fallacy; on less evidence than is recorded here, Laffranchi[12] has already rightly celebrated *il definitivo seppellimento della tese urbana*.

His own attribution, however, is no more acceptable: he ascribes the issue to a Q. Oppius who was in Pontus in 88 B.C.[13] Apart from the startling anomaly of

---

[1] Solin Polyhistor, *Collectanea Rerum Memorabilium*, 25. 16 (Mommsen ed. p. 113).
[2] Bahrfeldt, *NZ*. XXXVII, 1905, p. 42, 15 per cent zinc; cf. Münzer, *PW*. XVIII, 741.
[3] *NC*. 1918, p. 176; cf. Beanlands, ibid. p. 188.
[4] Bahrfeldt, *NZ*. 1909, p. 80.
[5] Cambridge; cf. *BMCR*. I, p. 541. 4132 ff.
[6] Laffranchi, *Historia*, IX, 1935, p. 42, no. 1, *pace* Bahrfeldt, l.c. p. 81.
[7] Paris.
[8] *NC*. 1904, pp. 235 ff.
[9] For some reason Pais, *Ricerche sulla storia ecc.*, ser. II, p. 296, prefers 44.
[10] Ignored by Bahrfeldt, l.c. p. 29; Willers, *Geschichte*, p. 215.
[11] *Fasti praetorii*, Diss. Berlin, 1875, p. 80; cf. Willers, l.c. p. 106 n. 1.
[12] L.c. p. 42.
[13] Ibid. pp. 39 ff.

orichalcum at so early a date (p. 88), the busts from Pontus and elsewhere which he cites in comparison are inconclusive, first, since the principle of attributing the mints of official issues from portrait-resemblances to local series is entirely fallacious (p. 122), and, secondly, since the heads on the present issue, whether they are of Felicitas,[1] Venus,[2] or Diana,[3] are not one whit less like those on a large number of *denarii* of far later date than 88 B.C., among which may be mentioned those of Considius Paetus,[4] T. Carisius,[5] Arrius Secundus.[6] In fact their real resemblance in coiffure[7] is to the *denarii* with CAESAR DIVI F.[8] and *aes* of Crassus (Cyrene),[9] as Woigt perceived.[10] Such indications, though useless for a geographical attribution, are invaluable for chronology: Friedländer[11] rightly recognises, in accordance with these analogies, that the *aes* of Oppius was issued in c. 36–31 B.C. But he errs in seeing a particular resemblance to coins of Thessalonica. Bonazzi,[12] following an interpretation by Babelon[13] of *praefectus* [*classis*], divides the rule of Oppius between Corduba and Syracuse; Gabrici[14] prefers the former part of this curious province—for which there is no historical likelihood[15]—and explains unplausibly that Spain lay under the constellation of the capricorn which is found on some specimens. But Eckhel[16] rightly saw long ago that this symbol must refer to Octavian. It is not precisely true to say that its only numismatic references are to him,[17] since it appears once on *denarii* of L. Papius, c. 80 B.C.;[18] but on those coins it is one of a multitude of mint-marks, and so isolated an exception is negligible in comparison with the hundreds of other occurrences of the capricorn, which point inevitably to a connection with Octavian.

It has not been noticed that the reverse of (1) (Pl. I, 19), an unusual type (unlike the commonplace heads, which are worthless for comparison), shows, if reversed, remarkable similarities—notably in the arrangement of the wings, the flying robe, and the palm-branch—to little regal coins of Phoenicia[19] with the head of Cleopatra (Pl. I, 18).[20] The legends of the latter, ΒΑΣΙΛΙΣΣΗΣ ΚΛΕΟΠΑΤΡΑΣ—ΕΤΟΥΣ ΚΑ·ΤΟΥ,

[1] Ibid.
[2] Bahrfeldt, l.c.
[3] Woigt, *JIAN*. 1911, pp. 25–7.
[4] *BMCR*. I, p. 532. 4081, pl. LII, 12.
[5] Ibid. p. 527. 4056, pl. LII, 1.
[6] Ibid. p. 568. 4209, pl. LV, 17.
[7] Cf. Stephan, *PW. Suppl.* VI, 91 for hair-styles.
[8] *BMC. Imp. Aug.* 609, 612.
[9] Especially the Capitoline specimen.
[10] L.c.
[11] *BB*. II, 1865, p. 147.
[12] *R.it*. 1920, pp. 153 ff.
[13] *Monnaies de la république romaine*, II, p. 276; cf. Ribbeck, *Senatores Romani*, Diss. Berlin, 1899, p. 57. 302.
[14] *Studi e materiali di Archeologia e Numismatica*, II, 1902, p. 155 n. 18.
[15] Even Sextus Pompeius did not possess both regions contemporaneously.
[16] *DN*. v, pp. 264 f.; S. L. Cesano states that she is of the same opinion.
[17] As Heeley, *Transactions of the Yorkshire Numismatic Society*, III, 1, 1927, p. 18.
[18] *BMCR*. I, p. 374. 3014.
[19] A unique example of numismatic ingenuity is provided by the theory of Woerl, *Bericht über eine Anzahl im J. 1849 aufgefundener röm. Münzen*, that this or a kindred issue has such ugly portraits that it must have been struck by Octavian as part of his anti-Cleopatran propaganda!
[20] Svoronos, *Ptolemies*, no. 1887; Turin. Cf. Hill, *BMC. Phoenicia*, p. lv; Rouvier, *JIAN*. III, 1900, p. 265. 438.

ΚΑΙ C. ΘΕΑΣ ΝΕШΤΕΡΑΣ, date them to 32–31 B.C.[1] Their insignificance and inferior execution indicate that they are copies, rather than prototypes, of the currency of Oppius. His coins have come to light in two known finds. One was at Rome,[2] where, owing to the complete deficiency of *aes* coinage, all manner of small change was accepted and is found.[3] But it is significant that the other was found in Cilicia,[4] which adjoins Syria and at this time formed a single province with it.[5] Thus type and provenance in conjunction provide evidence, much stronger than that of mere portrait-resemblances, for attribution to that region.

Now L. Calpurnius Bibulus was appointed governor of Syria-Cilicia between c. 34[6] and c. 32,[7] and died in office at some time between c. 33[8] and c. 31.[9] Q. Didius held the same command from about the beginning of 30 or the end of 31;[10] there is no evidence that he was already there at the end of 32,[11] since all that is known of his governorship is that in the winter of 31/30 he detained Antony's gladiators.[12] He was succeeded by M. Valerius Messalla Corvinus.[13] It has been shown that the capricorn on our coins is likely to apply to Octavian. The assumption becomes irresistible that Q. Oppius became governor of Syria-Cilicia, in succession to Bibulus, in c. 33/32;[14] that, like Scarpus, he went over to Octavian after Actium; and that, also like him, he was soon superseded. He began by striking coins without a capricorn—imitated by Cleopatra's neighbouring currency of 32/31—and his last issues, of 31/30, show a capricorn just as those of Scarpus show the name of Octavian.

As Bonazzi[15] points out, type (3) is of a different style and weight from the others; it is probable, therefore, that Oppius used two mints. One of them is likely to have been at Antioch, the proconsular residence; the other was perhaps Laodicea or Apamea, the next cities of the straitened province. The thunderbolt and crescent, which appear on some of his coins, are applicable equally to the Antonian or to the new *régime*. The bolt is the symbol of Jupiter Optimus Maximus, with whom Cleopatra, as θεὰ νεωτέρα, may have claimed a connection;[16] and the crescent can be conveniently referred both to the oriental *Aion* conception of Helios-Selene,[17] and to Western and

---

[1] Tarn, *CAH*. x, p. 81; cf. Kahrstedt, *Klio*, x, 1910, p. 277.
[2] *R.it.* xv, 1902, p. 16.   [3] Rome collection.
[4] *Rn.* 1898, p. 629.
[5] Raillard, p. 28; Ganter, p. 40; Dio XLIX, 22. 3.
[6] Raillard, p. 35.   [7] Ganter, p. 44.
[8] *PIR.*² II, p. 50, c. 32 B.C.
[9] Ganter, l.c.; Blok, *Sextus Pompeius Magnus Gnaei Filius*, Diss. Leyden, 1879, p. 97, *Appendix* II.
[10] Groag, *PW*. v, 407. 4; cf. *PIR.* II, 9. 59; Ganter, l.c.
[11] As Charlesworth, *CAH*. x, p. 100; Cuntz, *Jahreshefte des öst. arch. Inst.* xxv, 1929, p. 80; Syme, *RR*. p. 266 n. 3.
[12] Dio LI, 7. 3.
[13] Dio LI, 7. 7; Tibullus I, 7. 16 ff.; cf. Syme, *RR*. p. 302.
[14] It is tempting to connect with this governorship the inscription of a C. Julius from Ninica—very near the borders of the province—who professes: *carus sum Opiorum* (sic) (*Bull. di archeologia dalmata*, XXXI, 1908, p. 79, no. 3959A). Cf. also Cuntz, l.c. pp. 71, 73, who provides analogies for the form, and points out the intimate connection of the Oppii with Antony.   [15] L.c. p. 153.
[16] Taylor, *Divinity of the Roman Emperor*, p. 126.
[17] Alföldi, *Röm. Mitt.* L, 1935, p. 124; cf. Tarn, *CAH*. x, p. 68.

Vergilian thoughts of the 'new era'.[1] It may also show a claim to supremacy over Phraates.[2] The inauguration of this series by Antony was no doubt connected with preparations for the imminent emergency: Caesar, too, had coined *orichalcum* in the East on the verge of his proposed campaigns (p. 13). In view of the inexpensive form of inflation which currency in this metal provided, it is interesting to note that Oppius, who benefited by Caesar's scheme, belonged, like similar moneyers before him, to a well-known family of bankers.[3]

Since Oppius, unlike Lollius and Crassus, bears the title PR(*oconsule* or praetor), it is improbable that Levi[4] is right in supposing that the Syrian *provincia* was part of the dominions of Ptolemy Philadelphus in the same way that Crete and Cyrenaica belonged to Cleopatra. A Greek silver tetradrachm of Antony and Cleopatra attributed to Antioch by Svoronos[5] is considered by Regling[6] and Graindor[7] to belong elsewhere, and so does not serve to prove suppression of the proconsulship, which is positively contradicted by the coinage of Oppius.

16. PATRAE (?)

The latest official issue before Actium has no types, but the names ANTω. ΥΠΑ. Γ. and ΒΑΣΙΛ. ΘΕΑ ΝΕ. (Pl. I, 20).[8] It provides absolutely no indication of its origin. The old attribution to Cyrene[9] is now generally denied,[10] and there is no good reason to assign it to Syria.[11] It might conceivably be a regal coinage of Egypt: Antony was overlord of that realm, though not a Ptolemaic King.[12] But the style is against this attribution, and it is no less true that, from the inauguration of their joint regnal era of 37, Cleopatra stood by the side of Antony in his Roman dominions (p. 372). Moreover, the present coin not only emphasises the universal aspect of her power by its title θεά νεωτέρα— assumed at the outset of the new era—but stresses Antony's Roman authority in a remarkable way. Gone is the accumulation of titles which appears on his other coinages: there remains only the chief magistracy of the Roman state, which Antony claimed to hold in 31 (p. 421). Its presence is a witness to Octavian's illegality—one of many—in refusing to recognise this claim, and to the place of the consulship in the forefront of the voluminous propaganda of the period.[13] The emergency of the year, a long line of previous analogies, and the makeshift aspect of the issue, combine to

---

[1] Taylor, l.c. p. 177; cf. coins of P. Clodius and Augustus.
[2] Tarn, l.c.
[3] Cf. Syme, *RR.* p. 72; Frank, *ES.* I, p. 351.
[4] II, p. 146; ignored by Tarn, *CAH.* x, p. 80.
[5] *Ptolemies*, 1897 f.; cf. Lederer, *NC.* 1938, p. 68.
[6] *ZfN.* 1906, p. 397; cf. Tarn, *CAH.* x, p. 82; vide Fink, *JRS.* XXII, 1932, p. 111, for our uncertainty regarding Antioch's position.
[7] *Recueil des Travaux publ. par la Faculté des Lettres de l'Université Égyptienne à Caire*, 1937, p. 40: but his attribution to Alexandria is improbable.
[8] BM; Svoronos, *Ptolemies*, 1899 f., pl. LXIII, 26; Levis coll. sale 185.
[9] Cf. Muller, *Suppl.* p. 30. 428 a.
[10] E.g. by Regling, *ZfN.* 1906, pp. 395 ff.
[11] As in Berlin collection; cf. Lederer, l.c. p. 70.
[12] Levi II, p. 144.
[13] Cf. Syme, l.c. pp. 271, 282 ff.

associate it with the military crisis. At the beginning of 31 and until Actium, Antony's headquarters were at Patrae; the local mint of this town—which was also active in honour of Cleopatra (p. 374)—may well have been commandeered for this coinage.[1] Its legends present in their sharpest form the claims of Antony and Cleopatra, and their essential incompatibility.

Thus the last coinage of the triumviral epoch,[2] like the first, reflects a military emergency. Those between them equally cater for the needs of the troops, with the exception of Cyrenaic provincial issues, and of a Mauretanian and a Cretan issue in the tradition of the *praefecti coloniis deducendis*. But even these are, like the rest, based on the military administration of the *imperium maius*. A conspicuous feature is the continued avoidance of *aes* coinage in Rome: the triumvirs avoid the embarrassment of a choice between imperfect control of an economic necessity and open infringement of senatorial prerogative. The unification of both realms after Actium pointed the way to a solution of many problems, but for eight years more this one was not touched; no attempt was made at centralisation, and sporadic coinages continued, still by virtue of the *imperium* of commanders and the *imperium maius* of their overlord.

[1] Greek legends were not infrequently permitted on official *aes* owing to its limited circulation (Mommsen, *Mzw.* pp. 733 f.; Hahn, *Rom und Romanismus*, p. 71).

[2] Technically, however, the triumvirate was ended (p. 417).

E. OCTAVIAN AS SOLE RULER

1. ITHACA

Among the first issues after Actium was one whose date, geographical attribution and historical significance have alike been misinterpreted. Three coins, united by the possession of the same monogram,[1] have the following different types:

(1)[2] Head of Jupiter Terminalis to right—C. PROCVLEI. L. F. Skate (Pl. I, 22).
(2)[3] Laureate head of Jupiter to right—same legend. Double axe.
(3)[4] Turreted female head to right—same legend. Column on plinth (Pl. I, 21).

Gardner,[5] followed by Grueber,[6] made the mistake of believing that (2) bore a different monogram from the rest; an examination of the British Museum specimen which led them to that conclusion shows that it is quite untenable. The confusion which it caused must therefore be eliminated, and with it the hypothetical KPA. and the consequent explanation as KPA(νιον), accepted by Head.[7] Yet the provenance of these coins is chiefly Cephallenian.[8] For this reason the monogram which was rightly read on (1) and (3) by Grueber—and actually appears also on (2)—is interpreted by him as K(ε)ΦΑΛΛ.[9] But such a view defeats its own object. Greeks did not leave out letters in their monograms, which could attain great complexity; the absence of an E is thus conclusive against this solution. The same objection eliminates Bahrfeldt's KΦΑΛΟ.,[10] which further perpetrates an anachronistic and non-Greek spelling. His recantation[11] in favour of Corcyra (the choice of Morelli[12] and Eckhel[13]) is based on countermarks which, if indeed Corcyrean at all, might equally well support the opposite deduction to his—namely, that the coins were imported to Corcyra, not struck there. Besides, neither KO. nor KOPKYPAI. are adequate interpretations of the monogram, which includes an A, but lacks P. Moreover, provenance suggests a more southerly island. Thus another attribution must be sought. It is at hand—IΘΑΚ(η). This is perfectly in accordance with the contents of the monogram, and peculiarly suitable to the finds of these coins across the narrow strait near Cranium.

It remains to determine their date. Gardthausen[14] and Tarn[15] compare C. Proculeius with C. Sosius, and consider that both were commanders of a fleet-station (attributed to Cephallenia) in c. 39 B.C. But all other naval officers of Antony who issued coinage

---

[1] Monogram 4.
[2] Bahrfeldt, *JIAN.* VIII, 1911, pp. 222 ff. 1; cf. *BMC. Peloponnese*, p. 83. 65; *BMCR.* II, p. 533. 232.
[3] Ibid. 2, 67, 234 respectively.
[4] Bahrfeldt, l.c. 4; BM, Athens.
[5] *BMC. Peloponnese*, p. 83.
[6] *BMCR.* II, p. 533 n. 1.
[7] *HN.* p. 427.
[8] Cf. Bahrfeldt, l.c.; Gardner, l.c. p. xlii: especially near Cranium.
[9] L.c.; cf. Syme, *RR.* pp. 266 n. 3, 299 n. 1.
[10] L.c.
[11] *NZ.* 1918, pp. 159 f.
[12] *Familiarum Romanarum Numismata*, II, p. 361.
[13] *DN.* v, p. 289.
[14] II, 1, p. 228 n. 3.
[15] *CAH.* x, p. 52.

were at least of senatorial status, whereas Proculeius was a knight.[1] Furthermore, an anecdote of Pliny the Elder[2] shows that at least as early as c. 37 B.C. he was in the employment of Octavian: there is no record of any activity under Antony. Nor did his connection with Octavian cease. Macdonald[3] assigns the coinage to the year of Actium. But it could not have been issued for Octavian at Ithaca before the battle, and thereafter Proculeius accompanied the victor to Egypt, where he succeeded in capturing Cleopatra.[4] On the other hand, the period 30 (August[5]) to 28 is very probable for the coinage: it explains both the absence of title and the occasion of the issue.[6] The coin of a peregrine city will provide evidence that Octavian governed Asia at this time through an equestrian procurator and personal friend, Vedius Pollio (p. 382). It is thus very likely that he entrusted the southern part of the Balkans to his *confidant* Proculeius, who was also a knight;[7] possibly, however, one of the governors of Macedonia, T. Statilius Taurus(?)[8] or M. Licinius Crassus,[9] was his titular superior.[10] Octavian still held an extraordinary commission based on an *imperium maius*, which, until the *restitutio rei publicae*, enabled him to govern as he wished by personal delegation (p. 417).[11]

It is the writer's guess that the unexplained type of a skate alludes, like similar puns elsewhere,[12] to a subordinate of Proculeius of the Volscian family *Raia*,[13] who was possibly responsible for the coinage.

2. CEPHALLENIA(?)

Another piece signed by Proculeius[14] lacks the monogram, and shows a head of Apollo and a totally different style.[15] Only the type of a double-axe suggests some connection with the others. This was probably the emission of a neighbouring mint, which may have been on the island of Cephallenia. Whether this is so or not, the curious situation of Ithaca combines with the evidence of previous analogies to permit the ascription of both issues to a military occasion. It is highly probable that a section of the Actian fleet was temporarily posted at Ithaca and Cephallenia(?) after the battle, and that this, together with the whole region, was entrusted to Proculeius on his return from Egypt; his headquarters were probably at one of the islands at which the ships were concentrated.

[1] *PIR*. III, 100. 736; cf. Dio LI, 4.
[2] *NH*. VII, 148.
[3] *Hu*. II, p. 138.   [4] Plut. *Ant*. 77 ff.
[5] Cf. Tarn, l.c. p. 112 n. 1.
[6] Cf. Syme, *RR*. p. 266 n. 3.
[7] Ibid. p. 236.   [8] Ibid. p. 302.
[9] Ibid. p. 303; cf. Charlesworth, *CAH*. x, p. 117.
[10] Cf. Dio XXIII, 2. For Achaia as part of *prov*. Macedonia vide Cardinali, *Studi storici per l' Antichità Classica*, III, 1910, pp. 37 f.

[11] For commands entrusted to knights cf. Syme, *RR*. p. 201.
[12] E.g. Sura at *colonia* Buthrotum, Hiberus at *municipium* Saguntum, 'Gallus' at Arelate(?), and many others.
[13] For the *gens* vide Schulze, p. 217. For *raia* vide Pliny, *NH*. IX, 78, 144.
[14] Munich.
[15] Cf. Bahrfeldt, *NZ*. 1918, pp. 159 f. (illustration).

3. Melita(?)

Another commentary on the transitional naval arrangements of this period may be provided by a series of little coins with Q,[1] whose half-Greek and half-African style is characteristic of the Libyan islands. It has been variously attributed to Gaulus,[2] Cossura[3] and Melita,[4] and seems, for stylistic and administrative reasons, to be most suitable to the last of these. Within the last years before the principate the exact date of the issue cannot be determined. It is clear, however, that, since the special commission of Arruntanus Balbus at the island in c. 36 (p. 59), the mint has reverted to an official with the lower rank of *quaestor*—no doubt the *quaestor* of eastern Sicily, to whose jurisdiction Melita fell.[5] Possibly this coinage was made before 31; but the analogy of C. Proculeius shows that the fleet-stations were not immediately abandoned after Actium. On the contrary, the huge flotillas employed in the campaign needed extensive repairs which, at Ithaca and Cephallenia(?), were even accompanied by coinage. It seems, on the whole, most consistent with historical and stylistic probabilities that these issues recall a similar concentration of forces at Melita under the supervision of the quaestor to whose sphere the island belonged.

4. Alexandria

At about the same time an equestrian official inaugurated Octavian's coinage in Egypt.[6] This is at first in no way constructive in character, but adheres to the monetary system of the last years of Ptolemaic rule. The first issue comprises two denominations, marked Λ and M, of 80 and 40 copper drachmas[7]—corresponding to an obol and half an obol of the silver standard—in direct continuation of the depreciated coinage of Cleopatra.[8] Both coins bear the head of the new ruler; on the reverse is an eagle on a thunderbolt—both Jovian types.[9] The legend ΚΑΙΣΑΡΟΣ ΑΥΤΟΚΡΑΤΟΡΟΣ—ΘΕΟΥ ΥΙΟΥ is couched in the Genitive customary to Hellenistic rulers.[10] It also shows that Octavian at once accepted the imperfect Greek translation of *Imperator* for official use in Egypt.

These coins were issued by the first *praefectus*, the great C. Cornelius Gallus, who, like his friend Proculeius,[11] was a knight in Octavian's closest confidence, until his fall and suicide in 27 or 26.[12] Now Alexandria had always been administratively separate

---

[1] Bahrfeldt, *RS.* XII, 1904, p. 439. 97 ff.; BM, etc.
[2] Mayr, *Die antiken Münzen der Inseln Malta*; Muller III, p. 140.
[3] Landolina-Paterno, *Cat. Fischer coll.* pp. 36 f.
[4] Bahrfeldt, l.c.
[5] Pliny, *NH.* III, 92.
[6] Milne, *JEA.* 1927, Group 1.
[7] Regling, *ZfN.* 1901, p. 115.
[8] Cf. Johnson, *AJA.* 1934, pp. 49 ff.
[9] Cf. Jacobsthal, *Der Blitz in der Kunst*, Diss. Bonn, 1906, p. 12.
[10] Vogt, *Alexandrinische Münzen*, p. 13.
[11] Dio LIII, 24. 2.
[12] Cf. Stuart Jones, *CAH.* x, p. 134; Syme, *RR.* pp. 300, 334; id., *Actes du Ve Congrès de Papyrologie*, p. 460.

OCTAVIAN AS SOLE RULER

from Egypt;[1] and the words in an inscription from Philae, *praefectus Alexandriae et Aegypti primus*,[2] indicate that Cornelius' post was not yet thought of as an equestrian governorship,[3] but as an extended *praefectura urbis Alexandriae*, no doubt primarily military and naval in character. Other commands which were practically, but not actually, governorships occur in Africa, Galatia, Noricum, and elsewhere.

5. CYRENE

From the same transitional period there is a tridenominational issue, based on an *as* of c. 95 grains, by A. Pupius Rufus *quaestor pro praetore*.[4] Greek legends, the letters L and Λ (for Libya), and African types—head of Ammon, ram and serpent[5]—bear witness to the restriction of the coinage to the Cyrenaic half of the former province Creta-Cyrenaica,[6] divided in c. 34 (p. 58). When, at an earlier date, Cyrenaica had thus stood alone, it had been ruled by a *quaestor*:[7] it is therefore noteworthy that, alongside of coins with the quaestorian *sacculus* and *sella*,[8] Pupius strikes others emphasising his substantive praetorian rank by the types of *sella castrensis*[9] reserved for curule magistrates,[10] and *hasta donatica*, denoting *imperium* (p. 16). Since, then, the ordinary quaestors were not yet entitled to *imperium* (p. 140), and their signatures do not any longer appear on coinage (p. 141), Pupius must have been acting-governor of the Cyrenaica. This had ceased to be an important military post, since the legions of L. Pinarius Scarpus had been taken over by the new prefect of Egypt.[11] The present issue appears to indicate that some provinces at least were not governed at this time by knights in the same way as Asia, Egypt and Greece; but it also shows that important senators were not yet readmitted to the Eastern promagistracies, except, with misgivings, in special circumstances such as warranted the command of M. Licinius Crassus.

6. APAMEA (BITHYNIA)(?)

A very rare piece[12] with DIVO IVLIO (his laureate head to right) and AEGIPTO (*sic*) CAPTA (crocodile to right) derives its reverse type from *denarii* of 28 and 27 B.C.[13] struck, in an individual style, at an Eastern mint. The portrait, on the other hand, bears a very close resemblance to those on colonial issues, which are attributed elsewhere to Apamea in Bithynia (p. 256) on the grounds of a distinctive type and a peculiar execution. It is probable that the *denarii* were struck in the same province,[14]

[1] *OGIS.* 193; *Pap. Oxy.* 35. 899; cf. Jones, *GC.* II, 1.
[2] *ILS.* 8995.
[3] Cf. Horovitz, *Revue de philologie*, 1939, pp. 47 ff.
[4] *BMC. Cyrenaica*, p. 117. 27 ff., pl. XLIII.
[5] Ibid. p. ccxxii.
[6] Robinson, ibid. p. ccxxiii.
[7] Cf. Jones, *CERP.* p. 360.
[8] *BMC.* l.c. 33 ff.: not *subsellium*, pace p. ccxv, cf. above, p. 13, n. 9.   [9] Ibid. 27 ff.
[10] Ibid. p. ccxii; cf. Longpérier, *Revue archéologique, NS.* XVIII, 1868, p. 106.
[11] Cf. Tarn, *CAH.* x, p. 106.
[12] Cast at Winterthur [genuineness doubtful].
[13] *BMC. Imp. Aug.* 650 ff.
[14] Cf. Laffranchi, *R.it.* 1916, pp. 209 ff.

like an official tetradrachm of 28 B.C.[1]—imitated at Nicomedia (p. 384)—with the legend IMP. CAESAR DIVI F. COS. VI. LIBERTATIS P. R. VINDEX.[2] Mommsen[3] first showed that the latter celebrated the restoration of 'senatorial' government as a preliminary stage of the *restituta respublica*; this view has lately been confirmed and emphasised by Berve[4] and Barwick[5] (p. 424), and it is possible to identify local coinage commemorating the first proconsuls of Bithynia-Pontus and Asia (pp. 384, 385). The present piece is likely to be a product of the mint of Apamea in honour of the same occasion.

7. NEMAUSUS

Meanwhile, in the West, Octavian initiated a coinage with an ambitious scope, a wide range of varieties, and a long life, all of which have been gravely underestimated. This is the famous series with COL. NEM. and a crocodile. On the obverse is IMP. DIVI F., accompanied by two heads, facing outwards; the left-hand one invariably has a rostral crown. These coins have usually been divided into three main groups:

on (1) the right-hand head is bare (this group is divided into [*a*] 'large bronze', [*b*] 'middle bronze'),
on (2) it is crowned with a laurel-wreath,
on (3), with a similar wreath, the letters P.P. are added.

Willers,[6] who makes this arrangement, assigns the three groups to the years c. 29–28, 27–25, and 25–20 B.C. respectively, and classes them as local issues of Nemausus. But an ordinary city-series they cannot be, since their circulation in the West was extensive to a degree unparalleled even by the official *aes* of Augustus or his immediate successors. A representative selection of the find evidence will make this clear. They were current to the borders of the Narbonese province,[7] though countermarks of Arelate[8] show that (like issues known to be official) they later needed confirmation before acceptance by some cities; stamps of D.D.,[9] S.D.,[10] C.I.C.,[11] and C.DD.AR. (p. 117)[12] show other

[1] *BMC. Imp. Aug.* 691.
[2] These attributions are made in the face of Gabrici's condemnation of ascriptions to Bithynia (*Augustus* [1938], p. 388 n. 1) as *frutto del dilettantismo numismatico*. But he merely reaffirms old views (1902), ignoring recent researches whose conclusions tend against a centralisation of the official mints.
[3] *RGDA.* p. 147.
[4] *Hermes*, LXXI, 1936, p. 253.
[5] *Philologus*, XCI, 1936–7, p. 352.
[6] *NZ.* XXXIV, 1902, pp. 122 ff.
[7] Found at Marseille (Strack, *BJ.* 1902, 20 in museum, 2 acquired), Vienne (81 in museum), Narbonne (66 in museum), Apt (*Rev. arch.* I, 1903, p. 283), Avignon (15 in museum), Orange (½ in museum), Arles (seen in trade), Toulouse (9 in museum, 2 seen in trade, 2 acquired), Geneva (Soret, *Mémoires de la société d'histoire de Genève*, I, p. 233), S. Bertrand de Comminges (Lavedon, *Mémoires de la Société archéologique du Midi*, XVII, 1930, pl. XXI: mus. de Comminges); 279 in Nîmes museum, and nearly 200 collected in the neighbourhood by M. André Nier.
[8] C(*onsensu*) D.D. (=*decurionum*) AR., and D.AR. (Scott, *NC.* 1852, p. 111).
[9] Berlin, Gotha, Marseille, Toulouse.
[10] Paris.   [11] Berlin.
[12] Cf. Scott, l.c.

OCTAVIAN AS SOLE RULER

limitations, also of a post-Augustan date (p. 299). Enormous numbers have also been found in every part of Gallia Comata,[1] including all the Rhine camps of the province;[2] beyond the river they circulated to a vast extent in free Germany.[3] They abound in the region later comprising the equestrian provinces of Rhaetia-Vindelicia,[4] Noricum,[5] and the Pennine Alps,[6] and are commonly discovered even in Pannonia[7] and Illyricum.[8] But even this is far from the whole tale. Numerous specimens have come to light in Italy[9] and Spain,[10] and even in Portugal,[11] Britain[12] and North Africa;[13] the obverse type

[1] Rheims, Paris, Autun, S. Blaise, Castagnet, Metz (Strack, l.c.), Mont S. Michel (*Rev. arch.* II, 1904, p. 286), near Besançon (mus. [4½]), S. Saens, Teutre, Guerbaville-la-Mailleraye, Verneuil, Pitres, Cahaignes, Breteuil (Coutil, *Inventaire des monnaies gauloises de la Seine-Inférieure*), near Montivilliers (mus.), Caudebec-lès-Elbeuf (*Bull. de la Comm. arch. de la Seine-Inférieure*, VIII, 1888–90, p. 227 [3]), Orival (ibid. pp. 458, 460), Elbeuf (Drouet, ibid. IX, 1892, p. 226), Preignan (*ZfN.* XXIV, 1904, *Jahresbericht*, p. 17), Rennes (Toulmouche, *Cat.* p. 47), S. Germain-en-Laye (Reinach, *Cat.* p. 319), Bordeaux (mus.), Poitiers (mus.), etc.

[2] E.g. Ubbergen (Breuer, *Oudheidk. Meded. uit's Rijksmus. te Leiden*, NR. XII, 1931, p. 95), Hees (Brunsting, *Archaeologisch-Historische Bijdragen*, IV, 1937, p. 166), Nijmegen (mus.), Neuss (155 44/2!) (Strack, *BJ.* CXII, 1904, p. 452 n. 2), Wiesbaden, Mannheim, Coblenz, Crefeld (id. CVIII, 1902), Basel-Kaiseraugst (Basel [3]), Baden in Aargau (Basel), Mulhouse (mus.), Windisch (Laur-Belart, *Römisch-Germanische Forschungen*, x, 1935; cf. Stückelberg, *ZfN.* XXII, 1900, pp. 40 ff. [12]; *Anzeiger für Schweizerische Altertumskunde*, XXXIV, 1932, p. 112 [27 1.8/2]; ibid. XXXV, 1933, p. 17 [3 8/2]; ibid. XXXVI, 1934, p. 94 [1 8/2]), Lenzburg (ibid. XXXVIII, 1936, p. 12), Berne, Lausanne (Strack, l.c.), Enge (Tschumi, *Jahrbuch des Bernischen historischen Museums*, 1922, p. 23), Winterthur (mus.), Courroux (many) (Basel), Strasbourg (Forrer, *Strasbourg-Argentorate*, I, p. 272; II, p. 579; many), Bingen (Behrens, *Cat.* p. 153), Andernach (Mainz mus.; Forrer, *Keltische Numismatik*, fig. 13), Pommern, Urmitz, Calcar (Bonn Mus.), Xanten (Steiner, *Cat.* p. 85).

[3] Frankfurt-am-Main, Darmstadt (Strack, *BJ.* CVIII, 1902, p. 10), Saalburg (*Saalburg Jahrbuch*, V, pp. 49, 55; VI, pp. 45, 49), Nauheim (*Verhandlungen der Berliner Gesellschaft für Anthropologie*, XVIII,

1886, p. 22), Hammeran (ibid.), Rottweil (mus.; Nestle, *Funde*, p. 69), Tübingen (Univ. Coll.; ibid. p. 72), Öhringen (Barth coll.; ibid. p. 79), Riegel (Bissinger, *Funde*, p. 15), Utrecht (mus.; van Hoorn, *Gids*, p. 47), Tangermunde (Hansen, *Abhandlungen und Berichte aus dem Museum für Heimatkunde zu Magdeburg*, V, 1928, p. 310), Hofheim (Ritterling, *Cat.* p. 103), Mannheim (Karlsruhe mus.; letter from Director).

[4] S. Gall (Simonett, *Anzeiger für Schweizerische Altertumskunde*, XXXVI, 1934, p. 94), Oberhausen (Augsburg mus.), Riedlingen (mus.; Nestle, l.c. p. 86), Andeer (*Mitteilungen der antiquarischen Gesellschaft in Zürich*, XXVI, 1903, p. 42).

[5] E.g. Zollfeld (Graz mus.), Pichler, *Repertorium der steierischen Münzkunde*, II, p. 3).

[6] E.g. S. Bernard (Strack, l.c.).

[7] Budapest mus. Prof. Alföldi informs me that he has seen a number of Hungarian provenance. Also found at Vienna (Römisches mus., Vienna), Petronel (Elmer, *NZ.* LXVI, 1933, p. 56), Ptuj (Pichler, l.c.).

[8] Sišak (many), Osijek (Zagreb mus.). Two in Belgrade mus. probably found locally (Elmer, *Cat.* 24, 25; cf. p. iv).

[9] Aquileia, Trieste (Strack, l.c. p. 12 n. 1); many in Italian museums.

[10] Numantia, Sagunto (Simancas, *MJSEA.* XCII [IV, 1925–6], p. 25, also own collection (acquired from lot of Spanish origin); 12, probably mostly of Peninsular provenance, at Madrid (Calvo y Sanchez, *Salón de Numismática*, p. 209).

[11] E.g. Serrazeda (Tomar mus.; Leite de Vasconcellos, *Archeologo Portugues*, XXII, 1917, p. 143).

[12] Tewkesbury, Winchester (Berlin); others in Chester mus. (Sutherland, *Coinage and Currency in Roman Britain*, p. 4 n. 2), Winchester mus.

[13] Berlin. Specimens at Constantine (Hinglais, *Recueil de la Soc. arch. du dép. de Constantine*, XXXVIII, 1904, p. 24) are probably of African provenance.

was imitated in Sardinia (p. 146). This can be no ordinary city-mintage—it was utterly unwarranted by the commercial rank of Nemausus, which was only one of a number of fairly prosperous towns.

The circulation of these issues is thus totally inconsistent with the view that they were a local currency. In finds they completely eclipse the Gallic local series. In seven museums[1] and one private collection[2] of the Narbonese province there are $64\frac{3}{4}$ Augustan coins of *colonia Latina* Vienna (p. 337) and 14 of *colonia Copia* (p. 207), whereas there are no less than $663\frac{18}{2}$ of the Nemausan pieces! If the earliest of Willers's groups is considered separately, the same conclusion as to scope must be inevitably derived from it, for two reasons. In the first place, these coins were thought worthy of extensive contemporary imitation,[3] which very rarely befell any but official issues.[4] Secondly, a number of the countermarks which they present are of official character and are only found elsewhere on official *aes*—IMP. with *lituus*,[5] P.P.,[6] EQ.,[7] CA.,[8] and a star,[9] which appear otherwise only on the 'Altar' series of Lugdunum[10] (p. 117); IMP. AVG.,[11] CAESAR,[12] which are limited to Roman coins of the moneyers[13] (p. 94); VAR.,[14] which occurs on both the Roman and Lugdunese groups but not elsewhere;[15] and IMP.,[16] which is found on a number of official series.[17]

There is, then, a decisive combination of reasons for believing that these issues are not local. Moreover, whether Nemausus was at this time Roman or Latin,[18] conclusions reached on previous pages show that the choice of this town as the mint of an official series was neither unprecedented nor irregular. Coinage by officials, who represent the *res publica* and strike for military purposes or for a regional circulation, still often bears the mint-mark of the place of issue. L. Ap. Dec. *q.* strikes official (not local) currency with the names of Urso, Myrtilis and Baelo (p. 24); Cn. Domitius Calvinus issues silver inscribed OSCA, and P. Carisius later silver and bronze with IMIRITA (p. 119); Sex. Pompeius coins at the Latin city of SAL(*acia*) (p. 23), and C. Proculeius issues *aes* with the monogram of Ithaca (p. 66)—just as Sicilian quaestors place

---

[1] Nîmes, Vienne, Narbonne, Toulouse, Orange, Avignon, Marseille.
[2] Mons. A. Nier.
[3] Especially notable are copies at Nîmes, Oxford, Nier coll., Cambridge, own collection (acquired at Marseille).
[4] Cf. Sutherland, l.c. pp. 12 ff.
[5] Gotha, Vienna, Bonn, etc.
[6] Nîmes.
[7] Own collection (acquired at Toulouse).
[8] Basel.
[9] Brussels, Berlin, Gotha, etc.
[10] Respectively *BMC. Imp.* pp. xxxiii (as G. IMP.), xxxiv; Vienna, *BMC. Imp.* pp. xxxix, xxxii.
[11] Willers, *NZ.* xxxiv, 1902, p. 125.
[12] Basel.
[13] *BMC. Imp.* p. xxxiii.
[14] Budapest, Mainz.
[15] *BMC. Imp.* p. xxxvii.
[16] Berlin, Gotha, Vienna, Mainz, Bonn. This is shown to have been affixed on a different occasion from 'IMP. with *lituus*' (see above) by the presence of both on the same face of a single coin at Vienna.
[17] 'Altar' (*BMC. Imp.* p. xxxiii), *Commune Asiae* (p. 377); Caligula *sestertius* (Utrecht; van Hoorn, *Gids, Abb.* 29. 14).
[18] Conflicting views are expressed by Hirschfeld, *Wiener Studien*, 1883, p. 321; Mommsen, *Mzw.* p. 675; Kornemann, p. 517. 57; and more recently Ritterling, *PW.* xii, 1241; Grenier, *ES.* iii, p. 487; id. *QAS.* ix, p. 11.

the monogram of Panormus on their coins (p. 217). Of wider scope than any of these is this series struck at Nemausus: the evidence of provenance and countermarks is confirmed by the types, which are purely Roman and official. The crocodile refers to the conquest of Egypt.[1] It is found, inscribed AEGYPTO CAPTA, on Eastern *denarii* of 28 and 27 B.C.,[2] as on an official *aes* issue at Apamea (p. 69). Considered as the type for a local issue it has naturally caused confusion;[3] this view must now be abandoned.

It remains to attack Willers's view that the three main groups are to be assigned to c. 29–28, 27–25, and 25–20 B.C. respectively. It may first be remarked that this arrangement is seriously inadequate, since there are at least nineteen major subdivisions, and hundreds of varieties. The iconographical scheme which this wealth of material makes it possible to construct produces results which are surprising, but appear to be incontestable. A survey of the principal variations will now be attempted, under the main headings of Willers's groups.

I *a*. Since the appearance of the crocodile on coinage of the precious metals is likely to precede its introduction on the *aes*, there is reason for thinking that Willers's upper limit, c. 29 B.C., is unnecessarily early by a year or two. His first group is divided into two sections by weight. The heavier of these ('I *a*') averages c. 270 grains,[4] and the metal is not *orichalcum* as Willers suggests,[5] but bronze.[6] Comparison with earlier official Gallic and north Italian issues, and the appearance of a single pellet on some specimens,[7] makes it inevitable that the coins are *asses*, not, as Willers believed, *tresses* 'of the Fleet system'.[8] This view will be confirmed by a study of subsequent issues from the same mint (p. 77). The conclusion that 'I *a*' was inaugurated c. 28–27 B.C., suggested by the reverse type, is corroborated by the right-hand portraits, which on many specimens are closely copied from the *denarii* with CAESAR DIVI F.[9] (e.g. Pl. II, 18) and IMP. CAESAR[10] (e.g. Pl. II, 17).

It has always been assumed that the other head is that of Agrippa;[11] but on this early series the features are not his, and on the two illustrated specimens there is clearly a beard.[12] On the colonial issue of Lugdunum which is the prototype of such two-

---

[1] Cf. *Catalogo della Mostra Augustea*, p. 113. 23 *i*, etc. *Pace* Lenormant, *La monnaie dans l'Antiquité*, II, p. 217, who accepts 36 B.C. as an upper limit.

[2] *BMC. Imp. Aug.* 650–655.

[3] Conjectures by Friedländer, *BB*. II, 1865, pp. 277 ff.; cf. Hirschfeld, l.c. The adoption of the crocodile as a civic symbol of Nîmes, illustrated by the representation of one in the museum courtyard, was derived from these coins but dates only from the reign of François I.

[4] Av. 13. [5] L.c. p. 124.

[6] Spectrogram 1; considerable percentage of tin, some lead, no zinc.

[7] Paris.

[8] L.c. p. 134.

[9] Nîmes (large pattern piece), cf. *BMC. Imp. Aug.* 602, Paris, do. (Pl. II, 18). BM, Berlin, cf. *BMC.* 594, etc. Berlin, cf. *BMC.* 599, etc. Barbarous of this type, Nîmes (4), Toulouse, Nier, Oxford, Hague.

[10] Own collection, cf. *BMC.* 634. Paris (Pl. II, 17), cf. *BMC.* 652, etc. These two classes sometimes merge.

[11] Willers, l.c. p. 134.

[12] Cf. Lacroix, *Les médailles de Nîmes au pied de sanglier*, p. 19.

headed coins (p. 207) Julius is represented, and, since no bearded portrait of Agrippa appears to be known, this also might be the dictator. But the rostral crown, though not entirely inapplicable, is not so suitable to him, and Agrippa's features are probably intended. Such confusions of the traits of more than one person are paralleled in Asia (p. 334), and are a frequent phenomenon later at Nemausus (p. 75).

Other coins of the same large denomination make Willers's lower limit of c. 28 B.C. for 'I a' wholly unacceptable. The right-hand portraits of these are imitated both from the so-called 'Caesaraugusta' classes of gold and silver,[1] which will be shown to have commenced not before 25 (p. 83), and from *denarii* minted in the East not earlier than c. 20[2] (p. 467).

The lower limit thereby suggested for 'I a' is confirmed by reference to 'I b', which, though of a later date, will here be discussed in anticipation, since a general survey of the Nemausus series is necessary to correct the existing misconceptions. Willers[3] states that these coins are contemporary with the larger pieces of 'I a', but the right-hand portraits are, on non-barbarous specimens, drawn from no models earlier than the *aurei* and *denarii* of Lugdunum (c. 15–8 B.C.):

(1) c. 15–12 B.C.[4] (Pl. II, 19, 23). (2) c. 11–9 B.C.[5] (Pl. II, 20–22). (3) From c. 8 B.C.[6] (4) Thin distinctive features and fine Greek style.[7] (5) Distinctive but effective style.[8]

In all of these subdivisions the left-hand heads provide fine portraits of Agrippa. The prototypes of the right-hand busts suggest that the series was soon superseded, as official currency, by the Lugdunese 'Altar' issues, which commenced after c. 12 B.C. (p. 115). The mint-mark COL. NEM., recalling an obsolete custom, could have been misunderstood at a date when many colonies already struck their own bronze. Moreover, it was convenient that Western *aes* should be issued in conjunction with the Lugdunese silver (ibid.).[9] But the vast quantities of local imitations[9] reveal that these

---

[1] Vienne, cf. *BMC*. 339 (nose distinctive). The same features are copied for the *left*-hand head of a coin belonging to M. Nier, of which the right-hand portrait is imitated from *BMC*. 625.

[2] Nier, cf. *BMC*. 660. Avignon, cf. *BMC*. 663 (a particularly careful copy).

[3] L.c.

[4] Berlin (Pl. II, 19), Cambridge, own collection: cf. *BMC*. 443. Berlin: cf. *BMC*. 449(?). Cambridge: cf. *BMC*. 452. Cambridge (Pl. II, 23): modified version of *BMC*. 457(?).

[5] BM (Pl. II, 20), Paris: cf. *BMC*. 471. Variants with smaller heads at Vienna and Vienne. Cambridge (Pl. II, 22), Berlin: cf. *BMC*. 484 (semibarbarous?). Paris (Pl. II, 21), cf. *BMC*. 487 (semibarbarous?).

[6] Vienne: cf. *BMC*. 502, etc.

[7] Toulouse. On a somewhat similar coin at Nîmes, lacking a border, the left-hand head is bearded as on 'I a'.

[8] S. Bertrand de Comminges (cf. *Mémoires de la Société archéologique du Midi de la France*, XVII, 1930, pl. XXI). Not barbarous.

[9] Noteworthy among these are local fabrications from Gaul (own collection, acquired in Marseille), Spain (own collection, from Spanish lot), Frisia (Leiden), free Germany (many at Gotha, Vienna), N. Rhineland (Hague). Especially curious in technique are examples at Cambridge (heads ligatured, hair cf. *BMC*. 601, truncation cf. *BMC*. 277, 288, etc.; another with heads suggesting Roman models, e.g. from *BMC*. pl. 2), in trade, Paris (pellets in field), Oxford (of exceptional thickness), Vienna (distinctive right-hand portrait), Helbing sale (1930)

OCTAVIAN AS SOLE RULER

issues enjoyed a longstanding popularity. Willers considers that the group 'Ib' are *dupondii* 'of the Fleet system':[1] but they weigh c. 188·8 grains,[2] and the spectrograph reveals that they are composed of bronze[3] like many local *asses* of the same period and weight (p. 300). Moreover, coins in this group,[4] as in later ones,[5] have a unitary pellet between the heads. Mommsen's[6] interpretation of them as *asses* is therefore correct, and Willers's metrology as wrong as his chronology.[7]

More important still is his next error, whose results affect the numismatics and history of more than half a century. This concerns group 'II', which Willers assigns to the years 27–25 B.C.[8] But Strack's[9] researches on circulation lead him to state that 'II' and 'III' at least remained current in Julio-Claudian times. This is, in fact, an understatement: there are no grounds for believing that 'II' was even inaugurated before the principate of Tiberius or rather Caligula, and many positive reasons for attributing it to that period. It was the custom of ancient die-engravers, either consciously or unconsciously, to model the portraits of dead personages on a contemporary type—usually the reigning *princeps* (p. 334)—rather than on the features of the man himself. Such syncretism, illustrated for example by the coins of Divus Augustus (p. 360), is particularly probable in the case of a series such as this, whose plan had been stereotyped (and exact purpose forgotten) long before its termination. The survival of obsolete types for sentimental and commercial reasons was not unknown in the Roman world.[10] It cannot, therefore, be fortuitous that heads in group 'II' reflect the iconographic peculiarities of known numismatic portraits of prominent Julio-Claudian personalities. The following scheme shows the iconographical development:

(1) Tiberius or probably later.[11] (2) Caligula[12] (Pl. II, 24). (3) Claudius: (*a*) transi-

---

672, Vierordt coll. sale 684, Larizza coll. sale (Santamaria, 1928), 27. At Bonn there is a 'half' which the position of the lettering shows to have been struck as such; at Nauheim is a hybrid with Roman reverse (Kunkel, *Oberhessens vorgeschichtliche Altertümer* [1926], p. 205). For the difficulty of distinguishing barbaric styles from the inferior technique of the Nemausus mint itself, see further below, p. 115.
[1] L.c.

[2] Average of 23. That the 'ham'-shaped pieces are non-monetary has been shown by Willers, l.c. They are discussed also by Goudard, *Monographie des monnaies frappées à Nîmes*, p. 100; Kubitschek, *SB. Wien*, CCIX, 1929, p. 176 (St Florian coll.).

[3] Spectrogram 2, tin and lead. Perhaps from this group is the Nemausan coin chemically analysed by Phillips, *Quarterly Journal of the Chemical Society of London*, IV, 1852, pp. 272, 288, with 78·45 per cent copper, 12·9 per cent tin, and 8·62 per cent lead.

[4] In trade, London; cf. Berlin(?).

[5] 'II': in trade, London; 'III': own collection.

[6] *M\u{z}w.* p. 677.

[7] Group 'Ib' is elsewhere (p. 114) discussed in relation to its contemporary issues.

[8] L.c. p. 124.

[9] *BJ.* CXII, 1904, p. 433.

[10] Cf. Pick, *Die Münzkunde in der Altertumswissenschaft*, pp. 30 ff.; Rostovtzeff, *SEH.* p. 513 n. 17.

[11] Willers, l.c. pl. VII, 9; left cf. Tiberius *BMC.* 33; right cf. ibid. 25 f. Berlin: l. cf. ibid. 46; r. cf. ibid. (Divus Augustus) 146. Vienne: l. cf. ibid. 107, etc.; r. cf. ibid. 36, etc. Vienna: l. do.; r. distinctive. Hague, r. cf. ibid. 27. Nier: r. cf. ibid. 49 (including truncation); l. recalls group 'Ia' (characteristic eclecticism). Oxford, Vienna, Gotha: similar truncation, distinctive heads apparently barbarous.

[12] Own collection (Pl. II, 24): l. has the long skull, square forehead and small features of portraits of Caligula (e.g. *BMC.* 1); r. resembles the 'Divus

tional,[1] (b) Drusus sen.[2] (Pl. III, 1, 2), (c) other Claudian[3] (Pl. III, 3). (4) Nero[4] (Pl. III, 4, 5).

The striking indications of a post-Augustan date provided by this iconographic evidence are corroborated by seven additional considerations:—

(1) The only ancient countermarks recorded on coins of this category are P.P. (p. 117), S.D.[5] and L.A.;[6] the last two are local.[7] Thus the official countermarks which appeared in such large number on group 'I' are entirely lacking. Most of the varieties of 'II' are here assigned to a Claudian date, and it is not accidental that nearly all the official countermarks were affixed early in the principate of Claudius (p. 94).

(2) In marked contrast to 'I', imitations of coins in this category are exceptionally rare. Out of about eight hundred examples of 'II' which the writer has seen, only two —identical specimens belonging to the Tiberian subdivision[8]—seemed to be of barbarous execution. The present chronological arrangement is confirmed by a comparison with the Roman series. There, also, barbaric coins frequently imitate issues of Augustus,[9] of Tiberius and Caligula in honour of Divus Augustus and Agrippa,[10] and of Claudius (the initial series without P.P.);[11] but thereafter they terminate abruptly. It is therefore in accordance with the plan here suggested that the imitations common in 'I' have completely ceased by the end of 'II'.

Augustus' type of the same reign (e.g. Paris = BMC. Imp. pl. XXX, 8). Variant at Toulouse, Gotha: r. do.; l. distinctive. Budapest: r. cf. BMC. Caligula 17 ff.; l. distinctive. Escorial (Garcia, Cat. 43), cf. Nîmes mus. 'ham': distinctive portraits with Caligulan affinities. Narbonne: busts of same shape, l. with features of Caligulan heads of Germanicus (BMC. 49, etc.). For the iconography of Divus Augustus, see below, pp. 334, 467.

[1] Marseille: l. cf. Caligulan, Pl. II, 24, in shape, but both like Pl. II, 4 in features. Vienne: l. cf. Tiberian in shape and features; r. cf. Drusus (Claudius, BMC. 95).

[2] Own collection (Pl. III, 1): l. cf. Drusus, BMC. (Claudius) 105; r. cf. Claudius, BMC. 50. Oxford: l. do.; r. heroic Augustan. Mulhouse, cf. own collection: l. more pronounced features. Besançon: l. do.; r. heroic, cf. Pl. II, 9. Berlin (Pl. III, 2), own collection (½): l. Dr. ibid. 108; r. Cl. 8. Own collection: l. Dr. 95; r. Cl. 57 (including truncation). L. A. Lawrence, cf. Cambridge: l. Dr. 97. Nîmes: r. Drusus; l. heroic. Vienne, Nîmes: l. = r., Dr. 95. Hague: l. Dr. 208.

[3] Berlin (Pl. III, 3) (½): r. Cl. BMC. 70. Cambridge: r. Cl. 51, etc. L. A. Lawrence: l. = r., Cl. 23–24. Also stereotyped and featureless heads (in trade, London); ideal heads (own collection); ugly, wrinkled features (Budapest, Bement [Naville] sale [1924] 568, var. Merzbacher sale [1910] 1345)—all of Claudian technique.

[4] Vienne: l. unmistakably resembles first portraits of Nero's reign (BMC. 3, 4); r. Claudian. Var. Paris (Pl. III, 4), Münzhandlung Basel sale 1, 530, own collection. Avignon, Vienne: l. cf. Pl. III, 4; r. sharper features. Var. Paris (Pl. III, 5) countermarked P.P. Nier: r. do.; l. Neronian traits of Divus Claudius (BMC. Nero 6, etc.). Conclusive are—Vierordt coll. sale [1923] 686, Hess sale [1912] 1256: cf. BMC. 14, etc.

[5] Paris, Gotha; cf. Goudard, Monographie des monnaies frappées à Nîmes, p. 67.

[6] Munich.

[7] An incised stamp at the Hague has a medieval appearance: it includes characters that might be Scandinavian.

[8] Oxford, Gotha.

[9] E.g. BMC. Imp. Aug. 152, 155, 156; Blanchet, Manuel de numismatique française, 1, pp. 151 ff.; many in own collection.

[10] Cf. Sutherland, Coinage and Currency in Roman Britain, p. 10.

[11] E.g. ibid. Pl. I, 1–7, Pl. II, 1–7, Pl. III, 1–7.

(3) The lettering has begun to exhibit Julio-Claudian tendencies which are visible in accentuated form in group 'III'.

(4) At least four specimens of 'II' have been found in England,[1] where discoveries of Augustan *aes* are practically unknown,[2] but those of Claudian date comparatively frequent.[3]

(5) In the Neuss find, out of $155\frac{44}{2}$ of the Nemausan coins, very few indeed are of 'III',[4] which is elsewhere no less common than the rest.[5] Since the hoard contained 1291 *aes* pieces struck before the death of Augustus, but only 202 of a later date,[6] the deficiency of 'III' can be best explained by the assumption that it is of post-Augustan date.

(6) Hybrids[7] join the Nemausan reverse-type to the obverse of issues with DIVVS AVGVSTVS S. C. struck under Caligula.[8]

(7) Finally, it is hard to see how the neat, flat fabric and peculiar execution of these pieces could ever have been thought consistent with the early date postulated by Willers.

The weight of 'II' remains constant at c. 188·8 grains, and the spectrograph reveals that bronze is still the metal in use:[9] it will be confirmed elsewhere that the metropolitan system of *orichalcum* and copper was generally ignored (p. 300). Though its main lines are clear, the exact chronological limits of 'II' cannot be established. It is useless to endeavour to fit it into gaps in the other Julio-Claudian official coinages until more about the ramifications of those is known; nor are these complex problems relevant to the present study.[10] With regard to the lower limit of 'II', it is at least probable that the latest coins are those on which P.P. is stamped in two separate countermarks (e.g. Pl. III, 5), exactly where the same letters appear as part of the original type in 'III'.

On this last group, with P.P., Willers[11] is right in dismissing as fantasy the date-sign LIΔ of which Friedländer[12] discovered minute traces within the wreath on the reverse. In other respects, however, the errors of Willers reach alarming proportions, since, like Hirschfeld[13] and Mommsen,[14] he assigns the inception of the group to c. 25 B.C.— a date still actually before the Augustan reorganisation of *aes*! But the now regular appearance of the letters P.P., in the field, where they were first introduced as a countermark on the early Neronian piece which concludes 'II', suggests that 'III' started in c. A.D. 54; and this supposition is entirely corroborated by strong and persistent

---

[1] At Tewkesbury and Winchester (Berlin mus.); others in Chester mus. (Sutherland, l.c. p. 4 n. 2) and Winchester mus.

[2] Sutherland, l.c. pp. 4, 154.

[3] Ibid. pp. 5, 11, 154.

[4] Strack, *BJ.* CXII, 1904, p. 452 n. 2.

[5] E.g. rather over 33 per cent of all Nemausan coins in museums of S. France.   [6] Strack, l.c.

[7] Ménard, *Histoire de Nîmes*, VII, pp. 164 f.; Goudard, l.c. p. 58.

[8] *BMC. Imp.* Caligula, 88.

[9] Spectrogram 3, similar to 2.

[10] The writer is now engaged in research on these issues.

[11] L.c. p. 122 n.

[12] *BB.* II, 1865, p. 277. Accepted by Hirschfeld, *Wiener Studien*, 1883, p. 319; Goudard, l.c. p. 68; von Sallet, *ZfN.* 1885, p. 376.

[13] L.c.

[14] *MZw.* pp. 677 ff.

resemblances to Nero in the left-hand portraits (Pl. III, 9, 10).[1] These resemblances have actually been recognised by two authorities, one in a seventy-year-old provincial history[2] and the other in an article whose circulation has been prevented by the Spanish Civil War.[3] Other pieces show heroic adaptations of the Julio-Claudian versions of Agrippa[4] and Divus Augustus,[5] or the features of Divus Claudius.[6] Not only the portraiture, but the technique too is unmistakably of the middle of the century.[7] The chronological thesis here adopted is confirmed in the most satisfactory way possible by the latest issues, which show, first, the curious iconographic traits of the Revolution of 68–69[8] (e.g. Pl. III, 7), and then the features and styles of Galba (Pl. III, 8, 11, 12).[9]

No later models have been noted: the only official *aes* of Otho was Antiochene,[10] and the failure to revive this ancient coinage was not the only break in historical and numismatic continuity made by Vitellius. The influence of the century-long operation of the official Nemausan mint on our appreciation of Julio-Claudian *aes* and economic history cannot be exaggerated.[11] Nor is this *résumé* a digression in a work on the coin-

---

[1] Paris (Pl. III, 10), Schwing coll. (sale 1932. 428): *BMC*. Nero, 228, etc. Var. own collection, Merzbacher sale, [1909] 1140 (less distinctive). Paris (countermarked FAT, see below, p. 95): *BMC*. Nero, 162, etc. Toulouse: ibid. 47, etc. Berlin (Pl. III, 9): 119 (note nose). Own collection cf. BM: 320, etc. BM: 330, etc. In trade (Paris): 336. BM, Gotha: 388. Own collection: 398. Vienne: 252. Nier coll.: 235, etc. (straight nostril). Gotha: var. 155. Cambridge: modified, 244, etc. Hague: 255, etc.

[2] C. Robert, *Histoire générale de la province de Languedoc*, II (1875), p. 49 n.

[3] Cálico, *Numismática* (Lérida), 1935–6. The author has informed me of this study.

[4] Developments of *BMC*. Ti. 161 ff.: Vienna, Gotha (2), Narbonne, Nier coll. (2), Budapest, Egger sale XLIII (1913) 343, Ratto sale (1934) 7, Rosenberg sale 64 (1928), Helbing sale (1927) 3379.

[5] Nîmes.

[6] Münzhandlung Basel sale, I (1934), 101.

[7] Cf. also characterless ideal heads at Paris (Pl. III, 6), Avignon, Vierordt coll. sale (1923) 687, Hess sale (1933) 319. These show an advance on similar portraiture in group 'II'.

[8] Oxford: l. Civil Wars cf. Paris = *BMC*. pl. 51. 8; r. Civil Wars cf. Paris = *BMC*. pl. 51. 11. Copenhagen (Pl. III, 7), own collection (2): l. similar but finer; r. suggests date of Galba, *BMC*. 230, etc. (note nose). Vienna: both cf. Civil Wars, *BMC*. 48, 49, Paris = *BMC*. pl. 51. 15. Bonn: r. cf. Paris = *BMC*. pl. 51. 16; l. var. do. Hague: influenced by same group.

[9] Own collection (Pl. III, 11): l. cf. Galba, *BMC*. 77; r. distinctive heroic. Glendining sale, 1 (1927), 112: head of Galban Roman type. Berlin (Pl. III, 8): l. combines features of latest Nero and of Galba; r. ideal Augustus. Own collection: var., more Galban. These last tend towards: Copenhagen (Pl. III, 12): l. cf. Galba, *BMC*. 72.

[10] A Roman issue claimed by Ricci, *Historia*, VI, 1932, p. 495, cannot be accepted.

[11] P.P., which has already appeared as a countermark on group II (p. 76), must have some special purpose. Hirschfeld's P(*ater*) P(*atriae*) (l.c. n. 2) is no more likely than Friedländer's P(*atroni*) P(*arentes*) (l.c.); Willers's P(*arens*) P(*atriae*) (l.c.) is equally irrelevant and purposeless. Lenormant's suggestion P(*ermissu*) P(*roconsulis*) (*La monnaie dans l'antiquité*, II, p. 217) cannot be supported by a parallel. The Claudian and later affinities of 'III' provide a more significant explanation. The principate of Claudius saw the final suppression of all but two very unimportant and distant colonial series in the West (Ebusus and Babba); the use of COL. NEM. as the mint-mark on an official issue, without as a colonial ethnic, was an archaism unknown to the present generation, which might well consider the coinage inadmissible unless it bore the mark of authority. This was therefore affixed in the form P(*ecunia*) P(*ublica*), for which the initials were a well-known equivalent (cf. *ILS*. 432, 637, 4024, 5526, 5772, 6876). Blanchet, *Mélanges Radet*, V, on this subject, has not been seen.

ages of Augustus, since it results in the expulsion from his principate of a huge bulk of currency which has hitherto been attributed to it; it also shows that, contrary to all current opinion, the years immediately following Actium witnessed the inauguration of an official mint which was of the highest importance and apparently attained enormous popularity. Gaul was no doubt selected for the initial issue, commencing c. 28–27, owing to the new exploitation of its copper-mines and the commercial boom that the region was experiencing.[1] The prominence of Agrippa (if it is he who appears on 'I a') was justified by his recent triumph at Actium and his special importance in Gaul.[2]

There is no reason to believe that the administration of this mint was, before 27 B.C., in any way different from that of the other official mints instituted hitherto by the late Republican war-lords. It was naturally, at this stage, under the direct control of the provincial governor's *imperium* on behalf of the *imperium maius* of Octavian (p. 422), who represented the Roman *aerarium* (p. 97).[3] The initial issues of this mint are the latest made under these administrative conditions, and represent the first attempt at providing *aes* coinage on a large scale.

---

[1] Grenier, *Revue des études latines*, 1931, p. 374.

[2] Gagé, *QAS*. I, p. 6.

[3] A discussion of the situation of the mint after the initial issue ('I a') must be postponed to its relevant place (p. 114).

Chapter 2
COINAGE BY *AUCTORITAS PRINCIPIS*, 27 B.C.—A.D. 14

A. THE TRANSITION, 27–23 B.C.

THE first Nemausan coins had not long been issued when a vital constitutional change took place, involving the abolition of the *imperium maius* of the *princeps*, which had been, in law, the basis of the currencies hitherto discussed (p. 411). This reform occurred in 27, but it was not accompanied by any immediate monetary change:[1] not until 23 was launched the currency-system of the new *régime* (p. 91). Numismatic evidence from the transitional four years is therefore inextensive, but the three *aes* coinages that can be attributed to them are of considerable importance for an estimate of the constitutional position.

1. PAPHOS(?)

One of these three issues invalidates the conjecture of Sydenham[2] that Augustus abandoned the rights of coinage at this time.

> IMP. CAESAR DIVI F. AVGVSTVS, his bare head to right.
> COS. OCTAVO DESIG. Victory.[3]

This piece, which the evidence of provenance decisively assigns to Cyprus,[4] bears the date of 27 B.C., whose political events it commemorates. Cyprus had been recovered from Cleopatra in 31: but it is hard to determine whether it was at once made a province[5] or was attached to Syria-Cilicia.[6] At all events, it was not restored to proconsular government in 27:[7] so that the official who issued these coins was a *legatus*, whether of Cyprus or Syria-Cilicia. Perhaps the former alternative is the more plausible, since it is unlikely that the governor of Syria—who was probably M. Tullius Cicero at this date[8]—would have coined for Cyprus but not for the bulk of his province. The mint is likely to have been **Paphos**, the metropolis of the island.[9]

The reverse legend is highly significant. Not only does it refer exclusively to the consulship—the basis of the new dispensation (p. 426)—but stress is laid on the con-

[1] Cf. Syme, *RR*. p. 324.
[2] *NC*. 1920, pp. 25 f.
[3] Hill, *BMC*. Cyprus 1 (pl. XIV, 1).
[4] Hill, l.c.; cf. Gjerstad, *The Swedish Cyprus Expedition*, II (1931), p. 797 (finds at Ajia Irini). Miss Newby (p. 22), ignoring the research which has led to this unquestionable attribution, rejects the accepted reverse-reading—which is, however, proved to be correct by a number of well-preserved examples.
[5] As Charlesworth, *CAH*. x, p. 114.
[6] As Syme, *RR*. p. 326.
[7] Cf. Cardinali, *Augustus* (1938), p. 161.
[8] Syme, *RR*. p. 303 n. 1.
[9] Cf. Jones, *CERP*. p. 489 n. 14.

THE TRANSITION, 27–23 B.C.

tinuity of office, which was planned for ten years:[1] the *designatio*, which assured the future, is therefore considered more worthy of mention than the seventh consulship which the *princeps* was actually holding. This inscription on an official issue is explained by the fact that, contrary to frequently expressed opinions, the *imperium* by which Augustus controlled the 'imperial' provinces was not proconsular—since a 'cumulation' of consular and proconsular *imperia* is an absurdity—nor was it 'nameless': it was consular (p. 426).

2. BYZACENIAN MINT(?)

Both the other official issues in this transitional period occur in 'senatorial' provinces, and provide evidence for different problems. One of these was made by a governor of Africa:[2]

> IMP. CAESAR DIVI F. AVGVST. COS. IX. his bare head r., crowned by Victory standing l.
> M. ACILIVS GLABRIO PRO COS. heads facing each other, of a young man and a woman (Pl. I, 23).

This official, striking in 25 B.C. apparently at a **Byzacenian mint**, is probably the *consul suffectus* of 33;[3] the uniqueness of the issue is in keeping with his superior post. From three untooled specimens[4] it is clear that the male head on the reverse is too youthful for Julius Caesar and quite unlike Agrippa. Attribution of the other to Octavia would make it impossible to find a suitable partner for her. But it was in this year that Marcellus married Julia;[5] and, since Tiberius cannot be considered at this date, it is necessary to assume that Glabrio represents the marriage pair (rather than Marcellus and Livia) on his coin, evidently interpreting the match as dynastic. Augustus never adopted his son-in-law,[6] and did not indeed adopt a son until c. 17 B.C.,[7] so that this, besides being unique as a numismatic representation of Marcellus,[8] provides important evidence that, at such an early date, the hereditary principle was tacitly accepted even by a senior proconsul.[9] But the obverse type alone disposes of the view that during the

---

[1] Dio LIII, 13. 1; cf. Riccobono, *Annali del Seminario giuridico della R. Univ. di Palermo*, xv, 1936, p. 374.
[2] Misread by Morelli, *Familiarum Romanarum Numismata*, s.v. *Acilia*, and Patin, *Thesaurus numismatum antiquorum et recentiorum*, p. 308; *Wad.* 7449, BM, and Vienna (*a*) badly tooled.
[3] *PIR.*² I, II. 71, *pace PIR.* I, 7. 49.
[4] Paris (2), Vienna.
[5] Stuart Jones, *CAH.* x, p. 135.
[6] Ibid. p. 137; cf. *L'Année épigraphique*, 1928, no. 88.
[7] Stuart Jones, l.c. p. 151.

[8] R. P. Hinks informs me that there is no positive iconographical evidence for Marcellus. A coin cited by Koehne (*Mém. de la Soc. d'arch. et de num. de S. Pétersbourg*, I, pp. 145 ff.) is shown to be false by Duchalais (*Rn.* 1848, pp. 72 ff.), and the attribution of statues and cameos by Mau (*Atti dell'Accademia di archeologia, lettere e belle arti di Napoli*, xv, 1890, *Estratto*, p. 12) and Koehne, l.c., are dubious in the extreme.
[9] Such evidence is neglected e.g. by Sprey, *De grondslagen van het principaat van Augustus* (Diss. Amsterdam, 1933), p. 11, who minimises the dynastic element.

years 27–23 the governors of the 'senatorial' provinces did not consider themselves subordinate to Augustus (p. 426). Glabrio saw the position as it was, not as theoretical argument has tried to make it. The problem whether the supremacy of the *princeps* was exercised, as von Premerstein[1] believed, by an *imperium maius* of 27, or, more simply, by the outstanding force of his *auctoritas*, is illustrated by the next, and last, coin.

3. MACEDONIAN MINT(?)

This has a bare head of Augustus, to right, and a prow, with no legends (Pl. III, 13, 14).[2] Sydenham,[3] following Duchalais,[4] assigns it to Gaul, and to a date of c. 40–38 B.C.; but both the geographical and the chronological attribution can be shown to be erroneous. It is significant that, out of 847 Augustan Gallic *aes* seen in the South of France by the present writer, this coin is entirely absent. Sydenham describes the Gallic series, to which he ascribes the piece, as 'clumsy, irregular, early, and of high relief': but these qualities are completely alien to the discreet Greco-Roman execution, mature style, careful die-setting, low relief, and double-bevelled edge of the present issue. These characteristics seem to exclude Western, African or Farther Eastern attribution. Thus it is not surprising that the only specimen whose provenance is discoverable was found within a few miles of Istanbul.[5] The type, style and lack of ethnic preclude the possibility that this was a local issue; such a city-coinage would be particularly anomalous in the Near East. It is, then, an official issue from some part of the Aegean area.

It remains to disprove the attribution to 40–38 B.C. This is not difficult, since the head on one specimen[6] is precisely similar to a distinctive portrait on a *denarius* of the so-called 'Caesaraugusta' class,[7] while the others that are extant are unmistakably connected with other *denarii* of the same category.[8] The 'Caesaraugusta' class is ascribed by Mattingly to 18–17 B.C.[9] But the metrological properties of the present coins make it necessary to question this attribution also. It can be considered certain that the portraits on the rare *aes* are imitated from the common and universal *denarii*: the converse is inconceivable. Now the former are uniform in weight, averaging c. 283 grains;[10] spectrographic analysis reveals that their composition is neither *orichalcum* nor copper, but bronze.[11] Such few official bronze coinages as survived after 23 B.C. were generally based on an *as* of c. 200–180 grains.[12] It is clear that the present series could not fit into any denomination of such a system. On the other hand, it corre-

[1] Pp. 225 f.
[2] Berlin, Paris, Escorial (Garcia, *Cat.* 354), Vienna, Rome, Walters coll., own coll.
[3] *NC.* 1917, p. 58; cf. M. & S. p. 43.
[4] *Description des médailles gauloises*, p. 141.
[5] Own collection, acquired at Istanbul.
[6] Cast in BM from Walters coll. (M. & S., l.c.).
[7] *BMC. Imp. Aug.* 338 (hooked nose); cf. p. cviii.
[8] Ibid. 330, etc. (straight nose).
[9] Ibid. p. cix.
[10] Five specimens weighed.
[11] Spectrogram 9.
[12] E.g. Nemausus (from 'I*b*', p. 114). Even most of the colonies and *municipia* adhere to the same standard (p. 300).

THE TRANSITION, 27–23 B.C.

sponds very closely in weight with a number of local *asses* struck soon after Actium, but more particularly with another official series which commenced in c. 28–27 B.C., group 'I*a*' of Nemausus. Module and fabric also point to a date not far removed from the issue of M. Acilius Glabrio in 25 B.C. These indications suggest that some of the 'Caesaraugusta' *denarii*, from which the present *aes* was imitated, were struck earlier than 23 B.C.—a conclusion supported by internal evidence from that series, which suggests that the year 25 is a more suitable *terminus post quem*.[1]

We may suppose, then, that the *aes* issue was made between 25 and 23. It remains to determine its geographical attribution. It has stylistic traits in common with official *aes*, also lacking an obverse inscription, which will be assigned to the Balkan area (p. 107), and with colonial coins of Dyrrhachium (p. 275); its somewhat unusual prow is imitated by issues of Thessalonica.[2] These indications are in accordance with the discovery of one specimen (the only one whose provenance is recorded) in the neighbourhood of Istanbul—where it was in the company of pieces of the κοινὸν Μακεδόνων. An issue from a mint in Macedonia, to which this evidence suggests attribution, would naturally circulate freely in Thrace.

Furthermore, a Macedonian coin would have especial reason to be there in c. 23 B.C. It was in 23[3] that M. Antonius Primus, proconsul[4] of that province, was impeached under the *Lex Iulia de maiestate* for invading Thrace.[5] The coincidence of date, combined with the evidence of style and provenance and the distinct likelihood that this exceptional issue had a military purpose, gives great plausibility to its attribution to this occasion. Like Glabrio, Primus, if it is he, places on his money the head of Augustus, thus furnishing a second proof of the effective supremacy of the *princeps*

---

[1] Sydenham has kindly pointed out to me that the title accorded to these *denarii* is not a good one, since they resemble *aes* of Celsa far more closely than that of Caesaraugusta. But elsewhere (p. 122) it will be shown that the arguments on which such attributions are based are fallacious. Here it will be suggested that the traditional chronology is equally false. Some types certainly refer to the Armenian diplomatic success of 20 B.C. (e.g. *BMC. Imp. Aug.* 315, 322, etc.), another, the *Sidus Iulium*, was well known to coinage long before the comet of 17 B.C., to the occasion of which Mattingly, *BMC. Imp.* p. cxi, ascribes it (e.g. *BMCR.* I, p. 548. 4165), while other reverses clearly refer to honours of 27 (ibid.). The other official mints attributed to Spain are discussed in another connection (see pp. 122, 222, 269). Some categories are clearly evolved from the official coinage at Emerita (Mattingly, l.c. p. cix), but stylistic dissimilarity makes it particularly improbable that this is true of the 'Caesar-

augusta' mint. Some of its portraits are closely allied to Eastern heads of c. 28 (ibid. Aug. 334, 628), and there is no reason why its commencement should not have been independent of Emerita but contemporary with it—in c. 25–24 (ibid. p. cix). Its operation thus continued until c. 19 B.C., when the 'Patricia' mints took over the coinage, imitating the topical types of SIGNIS RECEPTIS, etc., adding new ones (ibid. p. cxi), and reduplicating the general themes. A reconsideration of the whole group of *denarii* is suggested elsewhere (p. 468). At present it is only desired to show the early date of the 'Caesaraugusta' group, from which the present issue was imitated before the reorganisation of 23 B.C.

[2] Copenhagen; Gaebler, *NG.* III, 2, p. 121. 22.

[3] Stuart Jones, *CAH.* x, p. 136 n. 6.

[4] Cf. Volkmann, *Münchener Beitr. z. Papyrusforschung*, XXI, 1935, p. 55, for discussion of his title.

[5] Dio LIV, 3. 2.

84 COINAGE BY *AUCTORITAS PRINCIPIS*, 27 B.C.–A.D. 14

from 27 to 23. A passage from Dio[1] concerning the trial of Primus elucidates the new methods of his control: Μάρκου τέ τινος Πρίμου αἰτίαν ἔχοντος ὅτι τῆς Μακεδονίας ἄρχων 'Οδρύσαις ἐπολέμησε, καὶ λέγοντος τοτὲ μὲν τῇ τοῦ Αὐγούστου, τοτὲ δὲ τῇ Μαρκέλλου γνώμῃ τοῦτο πεποιηκέναι κτλ. McFayden[2] points out that the war began, and Stuart Jones[3] that the trial itself took place, while Augustus was still consul; the former adds rightly that Primus does not claim to have acted under an overriding consular *imperium* of Augustus, such as he would certainly have cited had it existed. Equally, the *imperium proconsulare maius* of 27–23 postulated by Kolbe[4] cannot have existed, or Primus must have invoked it (p. 425).[5] As it is, he states explicitly that the authority which inspired his action was of a character by which not only Augustus, but Marcellus also, possessed competence—merely γνώμη. In fact, he acted at the supposed bidding of a superior *auctoritas*: a word like γνώμη is the only possible Greek equivalent for so Roman a conception.[6] Marcellus possessed *auctoritas* as being of praetorian rank,[7] but much more so by reason of his marriage connection with the Julian house, which possessed it *par excellence* (p. 444).[8] In plain words, the opinion of Marcellus now carried authority. That is why Primus invokes him in the Senate, and Glabrio places his head on his coins. The authority of Augustus' opinion, however, was unique: in 27–23 that—emphasised by his renewed tenures of the consulship—is the basis of his supremacy, of which the proconsuls show their recognition by their coinage. The unusual absence of legend on the issues of Primus (?) may show his consciousness of the ambiguity, for which he was later to suffer; nor did he even try to shift his responsibility to any superior *imperium*. It is not possible adequately to analyse the principate in terms of component *potestates*. The issues of Glabrio and Primus (?) are the first of many mintages by *auctoritas*: they therefore constitute a prologue to the vast scheme of similar currencies which was now to develop, and an epilogue to the two preceding decades of coinage by *imperium*.

[1] LIV, 3. 2.
[2] *CP*. XVI, 1921, p. 38.
[3] L.c.
[4] *Das Erbe der Alten*, I, pp. 37 ff.
[5] Cf. Volkmann, l.c. p. 55.
[6] Cf. ἀξίωμα in *RG*. 34; inaccurate, vide Henze, *Hermes*, LX, 1925, pp. 348 ff.; elsewhere not even translated (e.g. Dio LVI, 3).
[7] Cf. Fürst, *Die Bedeutung der Auctoritas*, Diss. Marburg, 1934, pp. 13 ff.
[8] Cf. Stone, *CR*. LI, 1937, p. 29.

B. THE NEED FOR REFORM

The last of the official *aes* currencies before 23 has now been discussed. Their variety and extent refutes the common generalisation that 'practically no bronze coins were minted between 80 B.C. and 22 B.C.'[1] If this refers to products of the Roman workshop, then none were minted at all; but if, as is probable, it refers to official coinage in general, it neglects the issues of some sixty separate coining authorities between the years 49 and 23 alone. The only unity, besides that of subject-matter, which it has been practicable to observe, is that of approximate order in time: only a chronological way can be pursued through the historical and numismatic tangle which obstructs advance during the whole of this period.[2]

From a metrological point of view, however, it is possible to trace a certain evolution —or rather, degeneration—in the coinages of this quarter-century; and its correct interpretation is vital for an understanding of the reformed *aes* currency which was now to be inaugurated. From this aspect the bronze, and then the *orichalcum*, issues will now be briefly discussed.

1. Bronze Coinage

The metal used regularly during the Republic consisted of copper alloyed with from 5 to 40 per cent of both tin and lead.[3] Zinc, the important secondary element in *orichalcum*,[4] is present in no greater quantity than a number of other minute constituents.[5] The spectrograph has revealed that the colour of a coin is not an adequate criterion for the interpretation of its alloy as bronze or *orichalcum* (p. 88). This may, in part, account for a number of attributions to the latter metal which conflict with analytic results. Grueber strangely speaks both of the issues of Puteoli(?) with DIVOS IVLIVS and of Antony's Tarentine (?) series as *orichalcum*, and in the former case Sydenham[6] retains the error: but analyses quoted elsewhere by Grueber himself show clearly that both these series are of a lead and tin alloy,[7] and the chemical results have been confirmed by two spectrographic tests.[8] The analysis of the Tarentine (?) coinage has been misused in favour of further interpretation as *orichalcum* owing to a misprint of 'zinc' for 'tin'.[9]

The Spanish bronze of the Pompeys provide a fixed point for metrological research by their value-mark of one *as*. Their average weights of c. 332–c. 267 grains are in

---

[1] Stevenson, *CAH*. x, p. 197.
[2] Appendix I provides a summary of the coinages of 49–28.
[3] Cf. Beanlands, *NC*. 1918, p. 191, etc.
[4] Cf. Gowland, *Journal of Institute of Metals*, VII, 1912, p. 43.
[5] E.g. iron, nickel, manganese (*NZ*. 1909, p. 67), silver (spectrographic test).
[6] *NC*. 1917, p. 62.
[7] *NC*. 1904, p. 244 (81·20 per cent copper, 3·9 per cent tin, 14·5 per cent lead; and 76·5 per cent copper, 14 per cent tin, 8·3 per cent lead, respectively).
[8] Spectrogram 5, 5 a. In the latter of these (a barbaric piece) a minute fraction of zinc occurs.
[9] *BMC. Imp.* p. xlvii n. 2.

accordance with the bronze[1] Caesarian *quadrantes*(• • •) of the quaestor Cn. Julius L.f., which are based on an *as* of c. 300 grains. Such *asses* of c. ¾ oz. provide conclusive confirmation of Mattingly's[2] statement that the semuncial reduction was never considered permanent. It is possible, however, that even this higher weight left a margin of profit for the moneyers, as their frequent identity with distinguished financiers suggests. A similar standard, exceeding half an ounce, is attained by the issue of the quaestor L. Appuleius Decianus at Myrtilis and Urso (where this highest denomination [c. 512 grains] is much too heavy for an *as* and must be a *dupondius*), and by Octavian's earliest *asses*[3] at Puteoli(?) and in Narbonese Gaul, which average c. 280 and c. 250 grains respectively (pp. 46, 41).. In the same system are colonial issues of Lugdunum (c. 300) and Arausio(?) (c. 250) (pp. 207, 208), and official of Nemausus (c. 270); while Spanish colonies and *municipia* often strike at approximately half an ounce (c. 200) (p. 156 etc.). On these pieces denominations are not marked, but unitary coinage is always most frequent and its assumption here accords with the official analogies: in Spain at least it can hardly be doubted.

But the same period also provides many lighter coinages. In accordance with earlier practice,[4] the semuncial reduction at Rome produced a corresponding reduction to ¼ oz. in Sicily,[5] which was maintained by Sex. Pompeius: a fixed type for each value establishes clearly the denominations. Also during the last half-century of the Republic, *municipium* Paestum reduces its *as* from a weight fluctuating somewhat below the half-ounce (c. 153 grains) to the quartuncial standard (c. 105) (p. 202). The discussion of *orichalcum* will make it clear that Julius first utilised the possibilities of a fiduciary coinage. But it was Antony who first firmly applied the principle to bronze,[6] since the *asses* of his coinage at Tarentum began by adhering to a standard of c. 91·5 grains, and finally fell to little over half that weight. Perhaps the proximity of the Sicilian issues, which had been artificially valued for years, facilitated this step. A comparison of the denominations subsequently struck by Antony's officers L. Lollius and M. Licinius Crassus indicates that this basis was further reduced to c. 80 and even less —a natural economic development once the principle was accepted. An interesting result of the introduction of unreal values is a complete absence of *tesserae nummulariae* for more than a decade after 44 B.C.:[7] this bears witness to an official veto on the traditional initiative of private bankers in coin-testing (*spectatio*).

Octavian too issues a number of series at the reduced rate. His emergency coinage at Lipara—where the denomination of *as* is often indicated by a head of Janus—is very light. Near by M. Arruntanus Balbus strikes *asses* at c. 90·5 grains, and subsequent quaestors at the same naval base reach a lower level still. In Mauretania a *tressis* and

[1] Spectrogram 54.
[2] *RC*. p. 28.
[3] Contemporary analogies make it unlikely that these are *sestertii*, as Milne, *The Development of Roman Coinage*, p. 22.
[4] Mattingly, *RC*. p. 17.
[5] Bahrfeldt, *RS*. 1904, p. 342.
[6] Cf. Milne, *The Development of Roman Coinage*, p. 21.
[7] Cf. Herzog, *PW*. XVII, 1446.

THE NEED FOR REFORM 87

as—for such denominations are more probable than the obsolete grades of *as* and *triens*—reach a standard of c. 112 grains, and in another African province, Cyrenaica, A. Pupius Rufus continues at Antony's rate of c. 95. At Ithaca the *as* of C. Proculeius is only a little lighter; the Cypriot issue of 27 B.C. attains 104 grains. But it may be said in anticipation that a much higher standard of about ½ oz. is still achieved by the Spanish communities, and about ⅔ oz. by colonies in Gaul (p. 208). The official bronze coinage at Nemausus also begins at the latter weight, and the Macedonian(?) *as* of Primus(?) is based on a similar standard.¹ Such figures inspired sufficient confidence, after what had gone before, for a gradual slackening of the restrictions on banking.² But the market value of c. 250–270 grains of bronze must still have been lower than one *as*. Perhaps also such an unit was inconvenient to adjust to the currency of precious metals (p. 90). The moment had come to restore by a detailed scheme the dignity of the coinage in the eyes of a people not habituated to token issues, and no doubt resentful of an economic makeshift, or at least of coins which may not have found ready acceptance. But it would have been wasteful to strike heavier *asses*, and a more ingenious solution combined a scheme of Julius with an entirely new metal.

2. ORICHALCUM COINAGE

The terminology in these matters is unsatisfactory: the *orichalcum* (or *aurichalcum*) of Roman coinage is of course distinct from the alloy of gold and copper of the same name.³ It is the former of which, as Pliny⁴ states, *aes Cordubense*—apparently a variety of bronze of a misleading colour—imitates the goodness (*bonitatem*). This *orichalcum* was not itself a natural alloy,⁵ as Pollux,⁶ speaking in connection with γῆ ὑπόχαλκος, assures us: τὸ γὰρ τοῦ ὀρειχάλκου μέταλλον οὐδέπω καὶ νῦν εἰς πίστιν ἥκει βεβαίαν. Its distinguishing feature was zinc; but even this was not, in its metallic form, known to the Romans,⁷ who were only acquainted with *cadmea*. *Cadmea* is roughly described by Pliny⁸ as a *lapis aerosus*, but it is really zinc-ore⁹ of any kind,¹⁰ especially in the form of silicious carbonate of zinc (calamine).¹¹ For alloying purposes this was not mixed with copper-ore,¹² but heated with metallic copper.¹³ Although the presence of zinc

---

[1] Insufficient numbers of the coins of Glabrio are accessible for deductions to be drawn from them.
[2] Herzog, l.c. 1427, cf. 1446.
[3] Cf. Layard, *Nineveh and Babylon*, p. 285; Meissner, *Babylon und Assyrien*, I, p. 269.
[4] *NH.* xxxiv, 4.
[5] As Mattingly, *BMC. Imp.* p. xlvii. The nearest approach was *spodium* = *cadmea* + copper ore (Pliny, *NH.* xxxiv, 130).
[6] *Onomasticon*, vii, 98.
[7] Gowland, *Journal of Institute of Metals*, vii,

1912, p. 43; cf. Davies, *Roman Mines in Europe*, p. 60, who records a few accidental occurrences.
[8] *NH.* xxxiv, 2.
[9] Davies, *JRS.* 1937, p. 283.
[10] Cf. Partington, *Origins and Development of Applied Chemistry*, p. 368.
[11] Beanlands, *NC.* 1919, pp. 192 f.
[12] As Täckholm, *Studien über den Bergbau der römischen Kaiserzeit*, pace Davies, *JRS.* l.c.
[13] Dioscorides, *De Materia Medica*, v, 74; Festus III, 36; cf. Davies, *Roman Mines in Europe*, p. 62.

does not appear to us to enhance its value,[1] the virtual state monopoly of that constituent, and the novelty and pretentious appearance of the alloy, combined to make a success of *orichalcum*, as its long history shows. Cicero[2] seems to sneer at its popular qualities, but this, like similar comments, may be caused by an anti-Caesarian bias. Control of the *cadmea*-quarries,[3] which were few in number,[4] indicated to Julius a masterly solution to the monetary difficulties of the State. The first issue in the new alloy of *orichalcum* is that of Clovius in 45[5]—issued in the very district of the quarries. The spectrograph reveals that Caesar's tridenominational issue in 44, under the quaestor Acilius (?), is, contrary to its appearance, of the same metal.[6] This issue is divided into the three denominations of *tressis*, *as* and *semis*,[7] weighing respectively c. 347–319, c. 135–103·5, and c. 58 grains. It is therefore necessary to suppose either that the coin of Clovius, which weighs c. 232 grains, was a *dupondius*, or that the standard was arbitrarily reduced by half during the year 45–44. In view of the unusualness of a solitary double-unit coinage at this time, the latter alternative is the more probable.

Indeed, it is clear that Caesar could and did attach entirely fictitious values to this alloy,[8] of which he possessed considerable quantities and controlled the market. The fact that *orichalcum* was familiar from the earliest times[9] and still in the Hellenistic period[10] did not detract from its entire novelty for coinage:[11] the spectrograph reveals that all is not *orichalcum* which glitters with the colour of brass, but that yellow Greek coins of earlier date are in fact composed of a variety of the ordinary alloy with lead and tin.[12] Thus Caesar could and did strike coins in this metal as light as he pleased and satisfy everyone except Cicero. Grueber's dismissal of the innovation as 'evidently a failure'[13] does not take into consideration its persistence under the triumvirate and long-lived success in the Empire. There is every reason then to suppose that the

---

[1] Cf. Segrè, *Metrologia e circolazione degli antichi*, pp. 361 f.

[2] *De Officiis*, III, 23.

[3] Cf. Beanlands, *NC*. 1918, p. 187, etc.

[4] Ibid.; cf. Pliny, l.c. The principal quarries of the Empire were not yet discovered; cf. Davies, *Roman Mines in Europe*, p. 61.

[5] Analysed by Bahrfeldt, *NZ*. xxxvii, 1905, p. 42.

[6] Spectrogram 12: 10–15 per cent of zinc; not more than c. 1 per cent of lead; traces only of tin, iron, silver. Augustan *orichalcum* has from c. 15 per cent zinc (Beanlands, l.c. p. 203).

[7] The middle value (c. 135–103·5 grains) can neither be a *semis*—since the largest, which is just thrice as heavy (c. 347–319), would then be the impossible denomination of 1½ *asses*—nor a *quadrans*, since the smallest (c. 58) could under no circumstances represent 1½ *unciae*. Issues of *as*, *triens* and *sextans* would be both extremely unlikely at this period of elevated prices (cf. Mattingly, *BMC. Imp.* p. xlvii) and extravagantly unnecessary if struck, in this valuable and exceptional metal, at a standard no lower than that of the heaviest contemporary bronze.

[8] M. & S. i, p. 24, see that it was rated higher than bronze, *pace* Burns, *Money and Monetary Policy in Ancient Times*, p. 302; cf. below, p. 300.

[9] Cf. Macalister, *Excavations of Gezer*, ii, 1912, p. 265.

[10] Cf. Oberhummer, *Die Insel Cypern*, i, p. 182.

[11] Small percentages at Syracuse are accidental: Caley, *MAPS*. xi, 1939, p. 76.

[12] E.g. Spectrograms 15, 21, 33 (Amphipolis, Amisus, Smyrna); the first has no zinc, the other two only traces.

[13] *BMCR*. i, p. xxxiii.

THE NEED FOR REFORM

dictator derived a heavy profit from the coinages, which are therefore a relic of a characteristically brilliant and unethical financial policy.

This conclusion is strikingly confirmed by investigation of the moneyers who use this alloy. Not only was Clovius a member of a very wealthy banking family,[1] but M. Acilius(?), the quaestor who signs the Macedonian issue of 44—himself of a *gens* with Eastern business interests—is likely to have operated under the control of Balbus and C. Oppius, the most notorious figures in the same profession. The coincidence is seen not to be accidental when it is noted that, of the other two coiners of *orichalcum* before Actium,[2] Q. Oppius belonged to the same prominent house of bankers as the last named,[3] and C. Sosius too was a successful financier![4] Thus every one of the *orichalcum* issues was the work of a professional economist: the titles of Sosius and Oppius show that they operated under the guise of military commissions. These coinages provided an exceptionally easy means of inflation, a mine of easy wealth, made accessible by the economic genius of Caesar in collaboration with the financial experience of Clovius. No wonder that Cicero sneers at such schemes of revenue, and no wonder that the issues of Clovius are among the commonest of Republican coinages.

The issue of M. Acilius(?), had it not been suppressed by Brutus, was planned to increase the profits by one hundred per cent: that may be why the year 44 saw the suspension of private initiative in *spectatio*.[5] Sosius, the first to follow Caesar's lead, began with an *as* on the same standard, but finally reached a new low level with *semisses* based on an *as* of only c. 63 grains. These *semisses* were issued in 32 B.C., and in about the same year Q. Oppius is another convert to this tempting alloy (p. 61). Sydenham,[6] followed by Beanlands[7] and Burns,[8] describes his coins as 'almost pure copper', but chemical analysis conclusively reveals their metal to be *orichalcum*:[9] this error and an equally mistaken supposition by Burns,[10] that Sextus's Spanish *aes* was of copper, are balanced by even more frequent attributions of bronze issues to the *orichalcum* series (p. 85). Thus Sydenham's discovery of a Caesarian dual system of *orichalcum* and copper is a hypothesis whose metallurgical premises are as false as its chronological. There were no copper issues during the period before 23 B.C.; nor were the *orichalcum* currencies anything but fiduciary either then or later.[11] They did, however, make a favourable impression on the acute financial brain of Augustus, in whose

---

[1] Cic. *Fam.* XIII, 56. 1–3; cf. Frank, *ES.* I, p. 388.

[2] Owing to the rare facilities for the application of the spectrographic tests, and the regulations governing museum property, this statement must be qualified by the fact that there is, at present, no way of determining the constituents of the issues of P. Sulpicius Rufus *pro pr.*, L. Atratinus *augur*, and Q. Hortensius *pr. praef.* The last-named may perhaps have overstruck the *orichalcum* issues of M. Acilius(?), and the coin of Rufus resembles Clovius's pieces in date, weight and colour: but Atratinus's coinage is a precursor of the Tarentine(?) currency, which was of bronze.

[3] Cf. Syme, *RR.* p. 72; Frank, l.c. p. 351.

[4] Cf. Fluss, *PW.* (2R.) III, 1179.

[5] Herzog, *PW.* XVII (1937), 1446.

[6] *NC.* 1918, p. 176.

[7] Ibid. p. 188.

[8] L.c. p. 302 n. 1.

[9] Bahrfeldt, *NZ.* XXXVII, 1905, p. 42.

[10] Ibid.

[11] *Pace* Beanlands, l.c.

scheme, which was now to be inaugurated, they played an important part. A great lesson of the preceding period was the practicability of a token coinage and the special utility of *orichalcum* as its basis. This alloy revealed the way to a systematic reconstitution of *aes* coinage in the Empire, and to its reinstitution at Rome itself, where the various provincial military issues that have been discussed had probably made very little headway.[1] A reopening of the Roman *aes* mint must depend ultimately on a secure relationship with the silver *denarius*.[2] The entirely artificial value of *orichalcum* made it particularly suitable for this adjustment, but confidence would be best achieved if it were allied to a metal which the people knew. It is understandable that bronze was not selected, since this had never been formally employed for fiduciary currency: Augustus's choice of copper (almost pure) was a clever one, since although the metal was in everyday use, it was, like *orichalcum* twenty-two years earlier, new to coinage.[3] Its comparative cheapness also avoided an insignificant size for the *as*: this would have over-emphasised the definite adoption of token coinage, which now occurred.[4]

[1] Cf. Milne, *The Development of Roman Coinage*, p. 22.
[2] Ibid.
[3] Cf. Mattingly, *BMC. Imp.* p. xlvii.
[4] The copper *as* was struck at two-fifths of an ounce, but the *dupondius* of *orichalcum* was based on an *as* of only one-quarter: Willers, *Geschichte*, pp. 168 ff., and Mattingly, *BMC. Imp.* p. xlviii, explain that ten of the *asses* at $\frac{2}{5}$ oz. equalled sixteen of those at $\frac{1}{4}$ oz., so that the *as* of the soldier's pay ($\frac{1}{10}$ *denarius*) was ingeniously linked to the current rate of 16 *asses* to the *denarius*. This interpretation is doubted by Burns, l.c. p. 304.

C. THE BASES OF THE REFORM

1. ITALIAN MINTS

A numismatic aim of this and the following Chapter is the demonstration that, contrary to a frequently expressed view,[1] Augustus did not neglect a serious economic problem, but made a successful attempt to provide a universal currency of *aes*. At the centre of a complicated system, whose main lines were dictated by the considerations just discussed, was an extensive coinage at Italian mints in *orichalcum* and copper, first signed by *tresviri*,[2] then by *quattuorviri*,[3] and then without signature. Contrary to previous practice, the writer prefers to attribute the series to a number of other cities as well as Rome. This view is supported by stylistic considerations and by analogies from other series. It would be very difficult to believe that *asses* so varying in style and size as Pl. I, 27[4] and Pl. I, 28[5]—both of L. Naevius Surdinus—originated from the same mint; of the *asses* of Volusus Valerius Messalla (Pl. I, 24[6] and Pl. I, 25[7]), there is likewise every sign that this was not so. In each of these cases the distinction is not between an original and its barbarous imitation, but between two divergent styles of equal competence; and the differences are seemingly too great to be accounted for by a multiplicity of *officinae*. The *asses* provide other examples of similar discrepancies;[8] and the moneyers' *dupondii* also, equally without barbarity of execution, diverge startlingly from the norm (Pl. I, 26).[9] Equally strange is a stylistic variant of the late unsigned *asses*[10] which has a large crescent in the field beside the SC. Exact analogies for the distribution of large official coinages among a number of mints will be forthcoming from all the principal Eastern currencies—those with SC (p. 98), with CA and AVGVSTVS (p. 102), and with types of a colonist ploughing (p. 111). The anomaly of Roman mint-officials on coins struck at other Italian cities is not much greater than that of their appearances on coins circulating in those cities—or elsewhere outside Rome.

[1] E.g. Willers, *Geschichte*, p. 187; Rostovtzeff, *SEH*. p. 542 n. 47.
[2] For the sake of prosopographical completeness these may be listed: Cn. Calpurnius Piso, L. Naevius Surdinus, C. Plotius Rufus; C. Asinius Gallus, C. Cassius Celer, C. Gallius Lupercus; Q. Aelius Lamia, C. Marcius Censorinus, T. Quinctius Crispinus Sulpicianus; M. Sanquinius, P. Licinius Stolo, Ti. Sempronius Gracchus; [L. Aelius?] Lamia, [P.?] Silius, [C.?] Annius [Pollio?]; [Claudius] Pulcher, [Statilius?] Taurus, Regulus; P. Lurius Agrippa, M. Maecilius Tullus, M. Salvius Otho, A. Licinius Nerva Silianus, Sex. Nonius Quinctilianus, Vol. Valerius Messalla.
[3] [L.?] Apronius, [Sulpicius?] Galus, [Valerius] Messalla, [Cornelius?] Sisenna; P. Betilienus Bassus, C. Naevius Capella, C. Rubellius Blandus, L. Valerius Catullus.
[4] BM. [5] Berlin, Bordeaux.
[6] BM. [7] BM.
[8] E.g. Oxford:—Tiberius (cf. *NC*. 1939, p. 217); Bordeaux:—C. Plotius Rufus.
[9] Berlin: again of L. Naevius Surdinus. Oxford: C. Asinius Gallus.
[10] Cambridge. A specimen in the writer's collection has the same distinctive style, but no crescent.

92 COINAGE BY *AUCTORITAS PRINCIPIS*, 27 B.C.–A.D. 14

This is largely a numismatic matter;[1] but it is essential both to the main constitutional theme of this book, and for a correct estimate of Imperial finance, that three current and accepted opinions should be refuted. Issue will be joined with those who maintain the limitation of the coins to Italy,[2] their exclusively senatorial character,[3] and the existence of a large group of Augustan countermarks facilitating special circulation in the northern provinces.[4]

The first of these views can be contradicted in the most decisive manner by the evidence of provenance.[5] Extensive finds of uncountermarked Roman coins of the principate of Augustus are recorded not only from Cisalpine Gaul[6] (which was still occasionally under proconsular government [p. 38]), but from at least seven regular 'senatorial' provinces[7]—Sardinia,[8] Sicily,[9] Africa,[10] Narbonese Gaul,[11] Achaia,[12] Farther Spain,[13] and even Asia.[14] But especially significant, in view of the presence of the formula SC, is the large number of these pieces found—uncountermarked—in the 'imperial' provinces. The Roman *aes* was current from the very beginning in the new provinces of Rhaetia-Vindelicia,[15] Noricum,[16] Pannonia-

[1] Since the validity of SC throughout Italy should cause no constitutional difficulty.

[2] As Willers, l.c.; Mattingly, l.c. p. xvii.

[3] As Mattingly, ibid. p. ci.

[4] As Mattingly, ibid. pp. xxix f.

[5] The finds quoted, here and elsewhere, are not intended to attain completeness, but to provide a representative selection and to give a general view of the circulation of the issues discussed. For this reason, vague and indefinite descriptions such as '*Æ* Augustus'—which, unfortunately, predominate even in the most recent of the widely scattered publications which contribute this type of evidence—are ignored.

[6] E.g. at Migliadino S. Vitale (Urbano coll., cf. Prosdocimi, *Notizie degli Scavi*, III, 1906, p. 422), S. Polo di Piave (Gatti, ibid. p. 141), Serravalle Scrivia (Moretti, ibid. x, 1913, p. 123), Pavia (Patroni, ibid. IX, 1912, p. 5), Mologno (*Bull. dell' Inst. di corr. arch.* 1878, p. 171), Aquileia (Brusin, *Scavi di Aquileja*, p. 143).

[7] To simplify these lists fluctuations of status are ignored.

[8] Arbus (*Notizie degli Scavi*, 1927, p. 364; cf. Ricci, *Historia*, v, 1931, p. 109); cf. Spano, *Bullettino archeologico sardo*, III, 1857, p. 199; many in Cagliari mus., nearly all collected in Sardinia by Spano (as D. Levi informs me). Others of Sardinian origin acquired by a collector in Hamburg.

[9] Syracuse (Orsi, *Notizie degli Scavi*, II, 1905, p. 383); Sicilian finds seen in trade in Rome; also imitated (Mattingly, *BMC. Imp.* p. xxiii). Out of four coins at Magdeburg (Realgymnasium; Lilie, *Jahresbericht über das Realgymnasium in Magdeburg*, 1902–3, p. 19, nos. 142–5), most, or all, are of Sicilian provenance (ibid. p. 1).

[10] Soukh-Aras, ? Sousse, Carthage (Cagnat, *Klio*, IX, 1914, pp. 200 ff.).

[11] Vienne (6), Orange, Narbonne (3) (in local museums), Montans (*Mémoires de la Société archéologique du midi de la France*, IX, 1872, p. 228); the greater part of the large collections at Avignon, Nîmes and Marseille is also of local provenance.

[12] Corinth (Edwards, *Corinth*, VI, 1933, p. 76), Delos (Athens mus.), etc.

[13] Lisbon mus. (cf. Teixeira de Aragão, *Cat.* pp. 251 ff.), Oporto mus. (as Krusse Gomes informs me).

[14] Istanbul mus.

[15] Many from Oberhausen (Augsburg mus., cf. *Zeitschrift des historischen Vereins für Schwaben und Neuburg*, XL, 1914, p. 165; *Bayerische Vorgeschichtsblätter*, X, 1931, pp. 42, 52), Hegau (Bissinger, *Funde*, p. 7), Giubiasco (Zürich mus.), Hazzen (*Anzeiger für Schweizerische Altertumskunde*, 1903, p. 7), Chur (cf. *Mitteilungen der antiquarischen Gesellsch. in Zürich*, XXVI, 1903, p. 42; mus. Chur), Constance (Woerl, *Bericht über eine Anzahl im J. 1849 aufgefundener römischer Münzen*, p. 14).

[16] Enns, Wels (Pink, *Jahrbuch für Landeskunde von Niederösterreich*, XXV, 1932, pp. 62 ff.), Mönchsberg (Salzburg mus.; *Fundberichte aus Österreich*, II, 1937, p. 297).

THE BASES OF THE REFORM

Illyricum,[1] and Moesia,[2] besides Gallia Comata[3] and Nearer Spain.[4] Imitations are numerous and widespread;[5] the coinage was common far into 'free' Germany,[6] and is found from Britain[7] to Esthonia.[8] It was, indeed, only natural that the pieces of the earlier moneyers should circulate widely at a date when the Lugdunum *aes* mint had not yet been opened; but the finds show decisively that the Roman *aes* issues of the later part of Augustus's principate were no less thoroughly dispersed[9] without any additional stamp. Nor is it even true to say that the *quadrantes* were limited to Italy,[10] since they are scarcely less abundant in provincial finds.[11]

---

[1] Ptuj (Hönisch coll.: Pichler, *Repertorium der steierischen Münzkunde*, I, pp. 196 f., 203), Leibnitz (Braun coll.: ibid. pp. 196, 204), Petronel (Elmer, *NZ*. LXVI, 1933, pp. 56 ff.), Kašina (*Viestnik Hrvatskoga Arheologičkoga Društva*, XIII, 1891, p. 27), Selče (Skoplje mus., cf. Grbić, *Glasnik Skopskog Naučnog Društva*, XIII, 1891, p. 27: also Zagreb mus.), Novi Banovci, Sišak, Stankamen, Perušić, Prozor (Zagreb mus.); another at Belgrade mus. probably of local provenance. For a Sarmatian imitation from the Pannonian border vide Gohl, *Numizmatikai Közlöny*, IV, 1904, p. 78, Fig. 2; Cahn sale, 60. 2259.

[2] On Danube (Sofia mus., in trade).

[3] Trier, Bonn etc. (Strack, *BJ*. CVIII, 1902, p. 10), 130 ⅔ at Neuss (ibid. p. CXII, 1904, p. 419), Kaiseraugst (Basel mus.), many at Windisch (*Anzeiger für Schweizerische Altertumskunde*, XXXIV, 1932, p. 112; XXXV, 1933, p. 17; XXXVI, 1934, p. 94; XXXVIII, 1936, p. 176; cf. Laur-Belart, *Römisch-Germanische Forschungen*, X, 1935), Strasbourg (mus., cf. Forrer, *Strasbourg-Argentorate*, I, p. 580), three at Mulhouse (mus.), Köln (mus., in trade, cf. probably Fremersdorf, *Römisch-Germanische Forschungen*, VI, 1933, p. 85), Nijmegen (mus.; cf. Evelein, *Gids*, p. 61), Ubbergen (Leiden mus.; Breuer, *Oudheidkundige Meded.*, *NR*. XII, 1931, p. 95), Hees (Brunsting, *Archaeologisch-Historische Bijdragen*, IV, 1937, pp. 166, 170), Mainz (mus., cf. Klein, *Programm des Grossherzoglichen Gymnasiums zu Mainz*, 1868-9, p. 12), Bingen (Behrens, *Cat.* p. 152), Xanten (Steiner, *Cat.* p. 85), Pommern, Grimlinghausen, Urmitz, Remagen, Nettersheim etc. (Bonn mus.). Also in the centre of the province, e.g. Besançon (mus., several), S. André sur Cailly (coll. Glanville; Coutil, *Inventaire*, p. 13), Mont Jouer à S. Goussand (*Spink's Numismatic Circular*, 1902, 5216), Rennes (many; Toulmouche, *Cat.* pp. 43, 47), Bordeaux (mus.).

[4] Twelve at Numantia (Schulten, *Numantia*, II, p. 198), nine from Spanish source seen in trade in London.

[5] E.g. Gohl, *Numizmatikai Közlöny*, IV, 1904, p. 78; Elmer, *NZ*. LXVI, 1933, p. 56; Zagreb mus., Basel mus., Leiden mus.; in own collection from Salerno, Paris, London. This is a selection representing eight different regions.

[6] Found at Saalburg (*Saalburg Jahrbuch*, V, p. 41; VI, 1924, p. 45; cf., probably, VII, 1930, p. 23), Öhringen (Nestle, *Funde*, p. 79), Donaueschingen (mus.; Bissinger, *Funde*, p. 11), Mahlberg (Karlsruhe mus.; ibid. p. 17), Neidenstein (Karlsruhe mus.; *Jahresberichte an die Mitglieder der Sinsheimer Gesellschaft*, II, p. 13), Gschiess (Sércz) (Kubitschek, *Sonderschriften des öst. arch. Inst. in Wien*, XI, 1926, p. 47), Nova Ves (Kolin mus., Bolin, *Fynden*, p. 107), Vechten (Leiden mus.), Rossum (Utrecht mus., cf. van Hoorn, *Gids*, p. 51), Hofheim bei Taunus (Ritterling, *Cat.* p. 100), Hanau (Kutsch, *Cat.* p. 136).

[7] J. G. Milne informs me that the coins of this type are found at Woodeaton.

[8] Jerwen (Ebert, *Prähistorische Zeitschrift*, V, 1913, p. 531 etc.).

[9] One of the commonest in all finds is a member of the last college to issue *asses*, Sex. Nonius Quinctilianus (6 B.C.; Mattingly, *BMC. Imp.* p. xcviii); the issues at the end of the reign (ibid. p. 50) are also practically universal.

[10] As Mattingly, *BMC. Imp.* pp. xvi f. n. 4.

[11] E.g. at Straubenzell (Zürich mus.), Windisch (Basel mus.), Hofheim (Ritterling, *Cat.* p. 102), Petronel (Elmer, *NZ*. LXVI, 1933, p. 56), Ptuj (Hönisch coll.; Pichler, *Repertorium der steieri*

In every case a very large number of the coins found lack countermarks; particularly striking is the fact that out of 139 of these pieces seen in the collections of southern France not a single one is stamped. The evidence of provenance therefore decisively contradicts any theory that these countermarks were affixed in this period to make the Roman *aes* legal tender. It was already legal tender in every province in the West; the alleged limitation to Italy is quite unacceptable. Since this is the case, we cannot admit that a large group of countermarks is to be 'connected with the frontier wars on the Rhine, and perhaps also with the Rhaetian campaign and the Pannonian revolt':[1] in all these regions large numbers of uncountermarked specimens have been discovered,[2] and, on the other hand, the countermarks even occur in Italian finds.[3] Now the latest coin to which each countermark is affixed will provide its *terminus post quem*.[4] An examination of the countermarks on this basis conclusively corroborates the evidence of provenance, and assigns them to the post-Augustan period. Mattingly ascribes TIB., TIB. C., and TIB. IMP. to the wars of A.D. 5–6, 6–9, 9–12 respectively;[5] but such attributions are not valid in that or in any other order, since TIB. is found on coins of the principate of Tiberius,[6] and TIB. C. also,[7] whereas TIB. IMP.,[8] like T.C. IMP.,[9] is equally common under Caligula. IMP.[10] and TIB. CAESAR[11] likewise appear under Claudius, and TI. A̅V̅.[12] and TI. C. A.[13] are found on coins of the same reign. It is his name that the whole group undoubtedly represents. Equally unsuccessful is an attribution of IMP. and AVG. to the campaigns of 15 and 12–7 B.C.[14] Both IMP.[15] and I̅M̅P̅.[16] are found as late as Claudius; and AVG.[17] and A̅V̅.[18] as late as Caligula. CAESAR, found on coins of Tiberius,[19] is little, if at all, earlier.

---

schen *Münzkunde*, I, p. 203), Strasbourg (mus.), in Spain (seven from Spanish source seen in trade in London), Syracuse (Orsi, *Notizie degli Scavi*, II, 1905, p. 383); two at Cagliari, almost certainly of Sardinian provenance (as D. Levi informs me). Mme Christodoulopoulos states that a specimen at Athens is likely to be from a Greek source. Pieces at Constantine (Hinglais, *Recueil de la Soc. arch. du dép. de Constantine*, XXXVIII, 1904, pp. 16 f.) were very probably found in Africa.

[1] Mattingly, *BMC. Imp.* p. xxix.

[2] Even on the Rhine the average proportion of uncountermarked to countermarked specimens is approximately 5 : 3.

[3] E.g. at S. Appiano di Val d' Elsa (Milani, *Notizie degli Scavi*, 1938, p. 112).

[4] It may be confidently assumed that no single one of these stamps can have continued to be affixed over a period comprising more than one principate. There are many varieties, and each must have served for one special occasion: many of them have a distinctive shape or orthography which decisively confirms this conclusion (e.g. the stamp of TIB. is roughly circular).

[5] *BMC. Imp.* p. xxix n. 3.

[6] Roman *asses* (Leiden, found at Mook), Divus Augustus (*BMC. Imp.* p. xxxvi; BM, own collection).

[7] Roman *asses* (*BMC. Imp.* p. xxxvi; Mainz).

[8] *Sestertius* (Utrecht, van Hoorn, *Gids, Abb.* 29. 14), Germanicus (*BMC. Imp.* l.c.), Agrippa *as* (Berlin), Tiberius (Mainz).

[9] Germanicus (Berlin), Agrippa *as* (BM); T̅I̅B̅. C. IMP. on Germanicus (Cologne).

[10] Berlin, Bonn.   [11] Berlin, Rennes.

[12] Utrecht; also Caligula (Berlin), Agrippa (Berlin), Nero Drusus (Cologne).

[13] Berlin.   [14] Mattingly, l.c.

[15] Claudius (Leiden), Caligula (Bonn).

[16] Claudius (Rennes), Antonia (Berlin), Nero Drusus (Cologne).

[17] Caligula (Mainz), Germanicus (Bonn), Tiberius (*BMC. Imp.* p. xxxii), Drusus jun. (ibid.).

[18] Agrippa *as* (Bonn).   [19] Tiberius (Berlin).

THE BASES OF THE REFORM

Thus, contrary to the accepted view, the vast majority of extant countermarks are completely irrelevant to the principate of Augustus, and may therefore be ignored in its study. It will be shown elsewhere that the countermarking of official coinage by colonial ethnics (p. 299), legionary numbers (p. 117), and devaluation marks,[1] is equally alien to the period. A few Augustan categories remain, which suggest that, whereas there was no limit within the Empire to the circulation of the Roman *aes*, its introduction into a newly conquered territory, such as Germany, needed—probably only for a short time[2]—the governor's stamp of approval, since otherwise it would not be willingly accepted at more than its metal value by the inhabitants.[3] Countermarks of P. Varus in the new province[4] are almost certain: T.Q.F. (or R.?)[5] also suggests the name of a governor. CONST.[6] suggests one of the *constitutiones* by which an equestrian procurator, such as those of Rhaetia and Noricum,[7] could legislate even as early as this date.[8] IMP. AVG.,[9] which otherwise stands alone, may perhaps be referred to a similar occasion.

Another exceptional countermark, F*N*, which appears on an *as* of Volusus Valerius Messalla[10] (6 B.C.), and—misinterpreted as FAN.—not only on *asses* of Lugdunum[11] and Nemausus,[12] but also (a very unusual feature) on a *denarius* of Rome (16 B.C.),[13] can be elucidated by comparison with F·A·T, a countermark, apparently contemporary with issue, on Nemausan *asses* of Claudius (p. 78).[14] F is a rare initial letter, and the pellets on these *asses* suggest that *N* commences a new word: this monogram is used frequently for AV(*gustus, -i*).[15] Nothing appears to satisfy the conditions but F(*iscus*) AV(*gusti*). If this is accepted, the T can suitably stand for T(*arraconensis*), since there is every reason to believe that such 'clearing houses that balanced their accounts with the treasury (the *aerarium*)'[16] existed at this time in other central camps or provincial capitals, as they did at Lugdunum;[17] they had not yet been centralised in Rome as in Flavian times.[18] It only concerns our purpose here to say that the countermark F(*iscus*) AV(*gusti*) on the Augustan issues is probably not itself of Tarraconensis, but of some area where Roman silver is not yet current. Since the upper limit for its affixation is 6 B.C., it is tempting to assign it to a base for the Danubian or

---

[1] DVP(*ondius*) is found under Claudius (*BMC. Imp.* p. xxxvi), and AS under Caligula (ibid.). Also in this category is SE(*mis*), not earlier than Caligula (in trade, Brussels), which is wrongly attributed to 'Segovia or Segontia' by de Saulcy (*Mélanges de Numismatique*, I, pp. 113 ff.).

[2] Since many uncountermarked pieces are always found also.

[3] Cf. Bolin, *Deutsches Archäologisches Institut, Römisch-Germanische Kommission*, 19 *Bericht*, 1929, p. 134.

[4] Mattingly, *BMC. Imp.* p. xxix.

[5] Ibid. p. xxxvi.

[6] Ibid. p. xxxiii.

[7] Cf. Stevenson, *CAH.* x, p. 215.

[8] E.g. *CIL.* 7124, *pace* Jörs, *PW.* IV, 1106.

[9] *BMC. Imp.* pp. xxxiii, xxxvii.

[10] Ibid. *Aug.* 242 bis.

[11] Ibid. p. xxxiii.

[12] Ibid. p. xlii.

[13] Ibid. *Aug.* 94.

[14] Paris, own collection.

[15] E.g. *BMC. Imp.* p. xxxii.

[16] Frank, *JRS.* 1933, p. 144.

[17] Habel, *PW.* II, 425 ff.

[18] Rostovtzeff, *PW.* VI, 2385 f.

Rhenish campaigns of 6 B.C.–A.D. 6.[1] The unusual stamp on the *denarius* is thus explained by the Germans' known distrust of the new silver, and preference for that of the Republic.[2]

Countermarks of the *triskeles* and other symbols[3] must be allotted to Sicily on grounds of provenance.[4] It cannot, however, be maintained that they were necessary for the circulation of Roman coinage in this province,[5] since this is found without these stamps (p. 92) and was even imitated there.[6] A clue to the purpose of these countermarks can be derived from the fact that no coins are stamped except *sestertii* and *dupondii*.[7] The bronze *as*, which had been universally current in Sicily for more than half a century (p. 27), and which was not altered for the few Augustan local currencies (pp. 195, 237), weighed little more than half of the Roman copper *as* and the bronze *as* of the Western cities. The readjustments which this anomaly necessitated are hidden from us: but it is probable that, even if the light bronze *as* was decreed equal to the heavier copper *as* (p. 300), the higher denominations of the Roman series, in a metal reputed to be more valuable, acquired an enhanced value unless stamped to assure a relationship with the Sicilian *as*. The *denarius* was everywhere current: but since *orichalcum*, bronze, and copper coins were now all fiduciary, their relationship to it could be arranged arbitrarily, as convenience and the confidence or suspicions of the population dictated. Presumably such *sestertii* and *dupondii* as were not stamped could be exchanged with Sicilian *asses* at a favourable rate; but it is hardly possible, in this case, that only sixteen of the latter went to the *denarius*. The solution of such economic problems appears to be beyond reach.

The Roman *aes* coinage was primarily intended for the West. Specimens are rarely found as far as Asia,[8] but it appears that here certain limitations existed. For example, the countermark of a capricorn,[9] found also on official coins of Parium (p. 113) and local issues at Pitane, Apamea and Amisus,[10] may have regulated the relationship of the Roman *aes* to the currencies of north-western Asia Minor. In the western provinces, however, it circulated in Augustus's time without hindrance. Its adaptation to the coinage of Sicily necessitated countermarks, and likewise its introduction among peoples new to the Roman Empire and to its principle of token-coinage; elsewhere the Roman *aes* was the staple currency of the West, and was accepted uncountermarked in all parts of it.

The evidence from the 'imperial' provinces makes it quite clear that the S(*enatus*) C(*onsultum*) which sanctioned the coinage was valid for these also. The next section will describe another large series, with the same mark, which circulated chiefly in

---

[1] Syme, *CAH*. x, pp. 365 ff.
[2] Ullmann, *Philological Quarterly*, I, 1922, pp. 311 ff.
[3] Mattingly, *BMC. Imp.* p. xxx n. 4.
[4] Cf. Bahrfeldt, *Blätter für Münzfreunde*, 1926, p. 396.
[5] As Scramuzza, *ES*. III, p. 359.
[6] Mattingly, *BMC. Imp.* p. xxiii.
[7] Including a copper *dupondius* of Plotius; cf. Walters, *NC*. 1915, pp. 325 ff.
[8] E.g. Istanbul mus., and in trade.
[9] *BMC. Imp.* p. xxxviii.
[10] Vienna, Oxford (*NC*. 1935, p. 134) and Karlsruhe respectively.

THE BASES OF THE REFORM

Syria. The so-called 'senatorial' treasury, the *aerarium*, was certainly not limited in scope to Italy and the 'senatorial' provinces. Frank[1] has recently pointed out that it even received the Egyptian revenues[2] and paid the armies of the State,[3] besides officially providing for the upkeep of Augustus's own *curae*.[4] The coins weigh the balance heavily in favour of his view that its range was universal. No central *fiscus* yet existed,[5] since there was no dyarchy to necessitate it;[6] the *res privata* of the *princeps* was theoretically irrelevant for administration, though often used to contribute to the *aerarium*.[7] The provincial *fisci*, although used extensively as repositories,[8] were merely departments of the *aerarium*.[9] It is therefore inaccurate to say that this was exclusively 'senatorial'. It was the only Roman treasury. The senate had lost control of it first to Caesar,[10] and then in 44 to Antony,[11] and very shortly afterwards to Octavian;[12] Brutus and Cassius seized two of its provincial *fisci* early in 43,[13] and thereafter it was entirely dominated first by the triumvirs[14] and then by the *auctoritas* of Augustus.[15] In 23 he felt this to be strong enough for the abandonment of the consulship (p. 437). It is noteworthy that the headship of the *aerarium* was simultaneously transferred from *praefecti* chosen by the senate to two praetors,[16] whose appointment by lot indicated that the real control was exercised by another.[17] It was the *princeps* who supervised the central staff of accountants who managed it,[18] and it is highly significant that the output of the supposedly 'senatorial' Roman *aes*, otherwise regular, ceases during his absences from Rome.[19] Some pieces omit the symbol SC,[20] just as a few official *aurei* and *denarii*

---

[1] *JRS*. 1933, pp. 143 ff.; cf. also Stevenson, ibid. 1936, p. 511. [But see Last, *JRS*. 1944, pp. 58 f.]

[2] Velleius II, 39. 2; cf. P. W. Duff, *Personality in Roman Private Law*, p. 57; Grimm, *Zapiski S. Peterburgskago Univ.* LV, 1900, pp. 109 ff.

[3] Frank, l.c. p. 144 n. 1; Stevenson, *RPA*. p. 155.

[4] *BMC. Imp. Aug.* 79; cf. Stevenson, *CAH.* X, p. 205; Jullian, *TP.* p. 75.

[5] Cf. Humbert, *Finances chez les romains*, p. 195; Cardinali, *Augustus* (1938), pp. 177 f.

[6] Willers, *Geschichte*, p. 189, correcting Mommsen, *Mzw.* p. 745; id. *St.R.* II³, p. 1026.

[7] *RG.* 17. Duff (l.c. p. 59) points out that certain sections of the *res privata* were habitually devoted to public purposes, but only from a feeling of moral obligation. There was no confusion, as implied by Stevenson, *RPA.* p. 119.

[8] Cf. Last, *JRS.* XXVIII, 1938, p. 214, correcting Cardinali, l.c. pp. 176 f.

[9] Cf. Syme, *RR*. p. 410.

[10] Cf. Rice Holmes, *The Roman Republic*, III, p. 44.

[11] Cf. Frank, *ES.* I, p. 340.

[12] Cf. Motzo, *Ann. della Facoltà di filosofia e lettere della R. Univ. di Cagliari*, 1933; Syme, *RR.* p. 131.

[13] Cf. Syme, *RR.* p. 171.

[14] Cf. Siber, *Abh. Leipzig*, 42, III, 1934, p. 15.

[15] Cf. Strack, *BJ.* CXII, 1904, p. 437; von Premerstein, p. 192.

[16] Tac. *Ann.* XIII, 29; for *praefecti*, cf. Suet. *Aug.* 36, Dio LIII, 2. 1.

[17] Cf. Hammond, pp. 157 ff. etc.

[18] Last, *ap.* Rice Holmes, *Architect*, II, p. 178, and *JRS.* XXVIII, 1938, p. 214; cf. Siber, l.c. p. 14.

[19] Cf. Mattingly, *BMC. Imp.* p. xcvi: 20–19 and 15–14 B.C. The same is true of the even more jealously guarded gold and silver.

[20] Cf. Gnecchi, *R.it.* 1890, pp. 353 ff. for later examples. The omission of the formula on the first coins struck in 23 (*BMC. Imp.* p. 28) shows, not that Augustus 'probably first thought of partial control' (ibid. p. xvi)—since he already possessed complete control—but that an experimental issue was made which did not adequately represent the component elements of the *respublica*, or, alternatively, that the *senatus consultum* had not yet been formally passed.

include it:[1] Pink's description of that formula as 'a mere sign without legal importance'[2] is understandable in so far as SC does not make the *aes* issues any more 'senatorial' than the gold and silver.[3]

This financial situation is entirely in accordance with the new position of the senate in the State. It now preceded the people in the formula expressing the *res publica*;[4] it had received additional dignities and functions;[5] in particular, its advisory *senatus consulta* were now, in practice[6] if not in theory (p. 108), given the force of law, and, like the coinage which bore their sign, were valid in 'senatorial' and 'imperial' provinces alike.[7] The methods by which the *princeps* controlled the senate, no less than its treasury, will be exemplified by further official coinages (p. 110), and defined, in connection with further evidence, in a later chapter (p. 446). Meanwhile, the present interpretation of the functions of the senate can be corroborated by further SC coinages in 'imperial' provinces.

2. EASTERN COINAGE WITH SC

A number of official series, much misunderstood, obtained a wide circulation in the East during the principate of Augustus: they bear on the reverse the uniform type of a wreath, in which are the letters SC, AVGVSTVS or CA. The coinage with SC, a 'sort of Eastern counterpart'[8] of the 'senatorial' *aes* that has just been discussed, was the first to appear and will be dealt with first. It is traditionally associated with Antioch in Syria,[9] where the bulk of the coinage with this type, continuing until the third century, was undoubtedly struck;[10] but no notice has been taken of sharp distinctions of style, which occur in the early years of the principate. These suggest a new interpretation.

I. The earliest coin of the series is a *dupondius* (cf. p. 91) with the inscription ΚΑΙΣΑΡΟΣ ΣΕΒΑΣΤΟΥ, accompanied by a laureate head of Augustus to right (with *lituus*)[11] (Pl. III, 15). This recalls the portrait on an official tetradrachm,[12] attributed by Mattingly[13] to Syria or Pergamum, after 27 B.C., and by Sydenham[14] to Syria, after

[1] Cf. Mattingly, l.c. p. ci n. 5; also p. 106 no. 656, p. clxxxvii.
[2] *Transactions of the International Numismatic Congress of 1936*, p. 241; cf. *Klio*, XXIX, 1936, pp. 226 f.
[3] A reason for its general limitation to the *aes* will be suggested by an official Spanish issue (p. 120).
[4] Cf. Gardthausen II, 1. 2, p. 306; Mommsen, *Hermes*, II, 1867, p. 262.
[5] Cf. Stevenson, *CAH*. x, pp. 159 ff. etc.
[6] Cf. Syme, *RR*. p. 410; Arangio-Ruiz, *Augustus* (1938), p. 123, etc.
[7] It is particularly significant that the formula SC even appears on the coinage of Agrippa II

(*BMC.* 49), one of the client-kings who are explicitly assigned by Strabo (XVII, 840) to the administration of the *princeps*.
[8] Mattingly, *RC.* p. 197.
[9] Cf. Mommsen, *Mzw.* p. 718, etc. Rice Holmes's reference to Antioch in Caria (*Architect*, II, p. 64) is presumably a misprint.
[10] Cf. Wruck, *Die Syrische Provinzialprägung von Augustus bis Trajan*, p. 5.
[11] Milan (*Cat.* 457), Berlin, own coll. (Wruck, l.c. no. 13).
[12] *BMC. Imp. Aug.* 700.
[13] *BMC. Imp.* p. 113; cf. p. 112 n.
[14] *NC.* 1920, p. 33.

THE BASES OF THE REFORM

c. 23/22. Dismissal of the *aes* coin as a 'hybrid' is impracticable, since such a Greek legend does not appear on any coin with this head; there are no signs of barbarity in style. The portrait is not like those on the earliest silver coins attributed to Antioch, of c. 20–19 B.C.[1] The official tetradrachm, which it resembles, cannot be confidently assigned to any mint: even if it could, it would not be necessary for the *aes* issue to be a product of the same mint, although the likeness is very close. The style of the latter suggests the province of Asia rather than Syria. It may be added that it is considerably alloyed both with tin and with lead,[2] while pieces of known Antiochene origin only contain a trace of the latter component.[3] However, there is, of course, no reason why a mint should not alter its alloys. Wherever this initial issue was made, a suitable occasion for the inauguration of such an important series was the visit of Augustus to the East in 22–19 B.C., during the years immediately following the commencement of the reformed Roman *aes* coinage.[4]

II. Some pieces[5] with the legend IMP. AVGVST. TR. POT. (which is found on all the *dupondii* of SC issues) show a divergency of type: the wreath on the reverse appears to be of oak- instead of laurel-leaves. Moreover, this group exhibits a portrait (Pl. III, 17) which is identical with the highly distinctive heads on coins attributed beyond any doubt, for reasons of provenance, to Cyprus (e.g. Pl. IV, 8) (p. 143). The large flat die is another feature shared with these pieces, whose upper limit is the year 12 B.C. The portrait of the present coin, like those of the other Cypriot issues, somewhat resembles those of Roman *denarii* of 13 B.C.[6] It is interesting to note that provenance[7] likewise supports the attribution by Bosch of SC issues of Caracalla and his successors to Cyprus, rather than Antioch.[8]

III. A further issue (Pl. III, 18)[9] has an individual style, and a truncation and style of portraiture which may be derived from Lugdunese *denarii*.[10] A variant (Pl. III, 20) bears a countermark.[11] The general appearance of this group indicates Syrian workmanship, being particularly suggestive of coins of Damascus; there is, however, no resemblance to those of Antioch. Here, again, it is significant that Damascus is one of the very few mints whose third-century issues include pieces with SC.[12]

IV. A *dupondius* (IMP. AVGVST. TR. POT.)[13] and an *as* (AVGVST. TR. POT.)[14] (Pl. III, 19) combine with a truncation found on late Augustan silver of Antioch a peculiar style and lettering, whose distinctive features are exactly paralleled on certain

---

[1] Wruck, l.c. 1.
[2] Spectrogram 16.
[3] Ibid. 22, 37, 38.
[4] There seems no reason to adopt so late a *terminus post quem* as A.D. 5, as in *Milan Cat.* p. 47.
[5] BM, Milan.
[6] *BMC. Imp. Aug.* 100 ff.
[7] Westholm, *Temples of Soli*, p. 135.
[8] Of this class is probably a Cypriot find described in the *Antiquaries' Journal*, XIII, 1933, p. 107.
[9] Vatican, own coll. Spectrogram 36.
[10] E.g. *BMC. Imp. Aug.* 500.
[11] Paris, own coll. Spectrogram 22.
[12] Mommsen, *Berichte über die Verhandlungen der k. sächs. Ges. der Wissenschaften zu Leipzig, ph.-h. Kl.* III, 1851, pp. 209 f. Cf. also a coin at Amman mus., Bellinger, *NNM.* LXXXI, 1938, p. 32.
[13] Vienna.
[14] Vienna (Wruck, l.c. 10); Hess sale (1933), 305.

coins inscribed CA (p. 106) which have been found in Syria.[1] Thus, like III, this joint issue is probably **Syrian**, but again there is no stylistic similarity whatever to the known issues of Antioch.

V. The first of the latter is an *as*[2] (Pl. III, 21), whose portrait is modelled on Roman *denarii* of 18 B.C.;[3] the current attribution is confirmed by the recent discovery of a specimen on the site of **Antioch**.[4]

VI. A number of *asses* of less careful or semi-barbaric style[5] appear to be modelled on this. Among these are some with distinctive fabric and execution (Pl. III, 16),[6] and with a truncation found on Antiochene tetradrachms of c. 20–19 B.C.[7]

VII. A *dupondius*[8] has a portrait and truncation resembling those on Antiochene tetradrachms of 4–3 B.C.,[9] and also on local coins of the same mint with ΑΡΧΙΕΡΑΤΙΚΟΝ ΑΝΤΙΟΧΕΙΣ (p. 376). The attribution of this piece to Antioch is confirmed by the presence of monograms ΕΛ.,[10] ΕΛΕΥ. (Pl. III, 22),[11] representing ἐλευθέρα. Antioch was a free city,[12] even after the employment from c. A.D. 5 of the incompatible title μητρόπολις (p. 398).

VIII. Another *dupondius* (Pl. III, 23)[13] has a similar portrait, but lacks the monogram: its attribution to the same mint is probable. A variety of this type[14] appears to be influenced by the style of portraiture employed by *denarii* of Lugdunum after c. 2 B.C.[15]

Here, then, are issues from a number of mints, not only Antioch but at least one and probably two more in Syria (III, IV)—the pivot of the Eastern strategic system[16]— besides others in Cyprus (II), and perhaps Asia (I). The series is inaugurated in c. 22–19 B.C., and issues continue at intervals throughout the principate of Augustus. The corresponding issues of Tiberius show similar strong divergencies of style and fabric,[17] which confirm the view of a multiplicity of mints (e.g. Pl. III, 24, 25); moreover, it has been shown that even in the third century branches existed in Cyprus and Syria (p. 99). Thus the present interpretation of the Augustan issues is rich in analogies. But that they all contributed to a single general scheme is demonstrated by a regular distinction in weight between the pieces with AVGVST. TR. POT. (average c. 150–151 grains) and those with IMP. AVGVST. TR. POT. (average c. 240 grains).[18] Wruck points out that the four denominations postulated by Macdonald[19] would

---

[1] Istanbul mus.

[2] Wruck, l.c. 9: his illustration gives a somewhat incorrect impression of the coin, which is well preserved at Marseille and Vienna.

[3] *BMC. Imp. Aug.* 51 ff.

[4] Mrs F. Waagé, of the Committee for the Excavation of Antioch, has sent me a cast of this.

[5] E.g. BM.   [6] Gotha, Milan.

[7] Wruck, l.c. 1.   [8] Wruck, l.c. 12.

[9] Wruck, l.c. 4.

[10] Glasgow: *Hu.* III, p. 150. 69.

[11] Paris: Monogram 5, Spectrogram 37.

[12] Cf. Jones, *CERP.* p. 263.

[13] Wruck, l.c. 11: Cambridge, Santamaria sale (1926). 35; variety at Florence.

[14] Vatican, Ball sale 29. 1131.

[15] E.g. *BMC. Imp. Aug.* 519.

[16] Cf. Anderson, *CAH.* x, pp. 279 ff.

[17] E.g. BM, Vienna, Berlin show at least four principal varieties; cf. also *Annuaire de la Société française de numismatique*, 1884, p. 46.

[18] Wruck, l.c. p. 36 f.   [19] *NC.* 1904, pp. 105 ff.

THE BASES OF THE REFORM

have been in practice indistinguishable. The former are of bronze with much tin but very little lead,[1] and are clearly depreciated *asses*;[2] the others are not *sestertii*[3] but rather *dupondii*,[4] whose high weights are explained[5] by the inferiority to *orichalcum* of their metallic composition, which is, at Antioch, of a tin alloy indistinguishable from that of the *asses*.[6] These issues, like many others, appear to infringe the spirit of the *Lex Iulia peculatus*, which ordained *ne quis in aes publicum quid indet neve immisceat...quo id peius fiat*;[7] but this clause left the coining authorities much latitude.

The explanation given above of the imperial and national character of the formula SC (p. 97) removes what has been considered a serious difficulty, namely its occurrence on these issues in the 'imperial' province of Syria. It is not necessary to postulate special control by the Roman senate,[8] much less—on such coins as are Antiochene—by the senate of Antioch;[9] nor is a 'polite fiction'[10] the correct explanation for what was a natural emphasis on the senior partner of the *res publica* with which Augustus identified himself. The invariable TR. P. likewise illustrates both the *populus Romanus*, and the cooperation of the *princeps* whose portrait appears (p. 446). Thus two sides of a small coin compendiously expressed to the East the Roman commonwealth. The mints were indeed official,[11] and the Roman financial authorities in the provinces were responsible for their operation.

Mintage appears usually to have been irrelevant for the circulation of particular groups, though group II is likely to have been generally limited to Cyprus, and group IV seems to be Syrian in provenance.[12] The most widely current was VII, which has been found in Bithynia[13] and Phrygia,[14] and was imitated in Asia Minor.[15] Coins of one of the eight Augustan groups have appeared also in Galatia[16] and even in Rhaetia,[17] and were copied in Moesia,[18] Dacia,[19] and probably Germany.[20] Those of later rulers circulated occasionally as far as Cologne[21] and Basel[22] to the

---

[1] Spectrogram 38.
[2] For the variability of this denomination at all times, see below, p. 300.
[3] *Pace* Mommsen, *Mzw.* p. 718.
[4] Perhaps equal to only one Roman *as*: cf. *Bab. Kiddush.* 12*a*, *M. Maaser Scheni*, IV, 8 (Heichelheim, *ES.* IV, pp. 212, 216) at least for second century.
[5] Wruck, l.c.
[6] Spectrograms 37, 22.
[7] *Dig.* 48. 13; cf. Weiss, *PW.* XII, 2364; Mommsen, l.c. p. 221.
[8] Dieudonné, *Mélanges numismatiques*, 2e sér. II, (1919), p. 131.
[9] Bouchier, *A Short History of Antioch*, p. 311 n. 1, seems to suggest this.
[10] Wruck, l.c.
[11] It did not 'pose as a branch of the Roman mint' (Milne, *JRS.* 1938, p. 97).
[12] E.g. Istanbul; one or more(?) from Lebanon.
[13] In trade, Istanbul.
[14] Do.; possibly also in Pisidia (*NC.* 1914, pp. 312 ff.).
[15] Istanbul.
[16] Found at Adalia and Yalvaç (Istanbul mus.).
[17] Found at Giubiasco (Zürich mus.).
[18] Sofia.
[19] Zagreb (bought at Bucarest).
[20] Krosch, *BJ.* II, 1843, p. 75.
[21] Prinz Philipp von Sachsen-Coburg-Gotha coll. (Hamburger sale [1928] 420).
[22] Elagabalus found at Kaiseraugst (Basel mus.).

west, Tell Umar¹ and Dura² to the east, and Egypt to the south,³ and were copied by Parthian monarchs.⁴

There are a few countermarks on the SC issues of Augustus which, owing to their non-appearance on the coins of later rulers, may perhaps be assigned to the same principate. For example, a plough⁵ perhaps sets apart a *dupondius* of group VII for the use of the colony of Berytus, and a crescent,⁶ also on VII, either for one of the Greek cities that employs it as badge,⁷ or for circulation in Cilicia.⁸ Several obscure symbols⁹ and monograms¹⁰ are also affixed as countermarks. But in general this series has, in the East, the same wide circulation as thĕ Roman *aes* in the West.¹¹ Yet, in spite of the variety of mints, its quantity was insufficient for the economic needs of the numerous Eastern provinces, and it had to be supplemented by a number of other issues. On these a significant formula, hitherto unrecognised, supplies the key to the executive methods by which such coinages were produced.

3. AVGVSTVS, CA

The coins with either AVGVSTVS or CA, in a wreath, occupying the reverse field, show remarkable divergencies, which defy all attempts either to fit them into a single homogeneous series¹² or to divide them into two separate groups according to their reverse inscription.¹³ As, however, in the two series with SC that have been discussed, it is at least possible to distinguish a central series.

I. Asiatic groups

(A) This consists of *sestertii*¹⁴ with AVGVSTVS (bare head to right) and CA (in laurel-wreath); *dupondii*¹⁵ (Pl. III, 26) with the same legends but a *corona navalis*; and *asses*¹⁶ (Pl. III, 27) with CAESAR (same head) and AVGVSTVS (in laurel-wreath). The

---

¹ Trajan (McDowell, *Preliminary Report upon the Excavations at Tell Umar*, Iraq, p. 59).

² Claudius, Nero, Vespasian (Bellinger, *Dura*, IV, p. 268).

³ California Univ. Museum (Berkeley), found at Tebtunis (Milne, *JEA.* XXI, 1935, p. 213); this may be of the Cypriot branch-mint.

⁴ Berlin, own collection. It is interesting to note that a local series of Augustus at Antioch (p. 376) closely resembles group VII; no doubt in consequence of this resemblance, it had a very wide circulation, even bearing a countermark (L. XV—Zagreb) of a type otherwise found exclusively on official coins (Wruck, l.c., Claudius).

⁵ Istanbul.   ⁶ Athens.

⁷ E.g. Byzantium, Magnesia Ioniae, Magydus, Colbasa, Cydonia, Nicopolis, Marcianopolis use it as a type.

⁸ Unpublished provincial coins of Tiberius (Munich, Athens, Istanbul), which are found in this region and resemble issues of Aegeae, have the crescent as a type.

⁹ E.g. BM.   ¹⁰ E.g. Paris, Istanbul.

¹¹ S on a light *as* of (8) (Berlin) probably = SE(*mis*) at Rome and Lugdunum (*pace* de Saulcy, *Mélanges de Numismatique*, I, pp. 113 ff.) and is post-Augustan.

¹² E.g. Mattingly, *BMC. Imp.* pp. 115 ff.; Laffranchi, *R.it.* XXX, 1917, p. 255 n.

¹³ Grueber, *BMCR.* II, p. 546 n. 1—ignoring nine-tenths of the material.

¹⁴ *BMC. Imp. Aug.* 713; Copenhagen, Hamburger sale (1925) 518.

¹⁵ *BMC. Imp. Aug.* 721, Leningrad.

¹⁶ Paris, Stockholm, in trade (Paris), Prague, New York, Avignon, Nîmes.

THE BASES OF THE REFORM

asses are of copper, and the other two denominations of *orichalcum* (p. 104). In each case the portraits are closely imitated from an unusual series of *denarii* with a cow as reverse type (Pl. III, 28).[1] Several variants, also from this original, occur in the same three denominations.[2] They include a number of CA *sestertii*, practically all differing slightly;[3] the finest of these (Pl. III, 29)[4] is of beautiful workmanship. There is also an AVGVSTVS coin with the die of an *as* struck on a *sestertius* flan (Pl. III, 30).[5]

(B) A closely connected group[6] has portraits copied from a series of *denarii* with the types of wreath[7] and temple of Jupiter Olympius (IOVI OLV.).[8] The latest examples of the *aes*[9] (Pl. IV, 2) show a long line of brow and nose suggesting the influence of products of the mint at Lugdunum.[10]

Mattingly states that both the Eastern groups of *denarii* that have been cited as prototypes[11] should be reattributed from 27 B.C.[12] to c. 21–19 B.C., when Augustus visited the East; Gabrici[13] and Rostovtzeff[14] agree, and Graindor[15] disagrees. Sydenham[16] and Laffranchi[17] prefer a date of c. 17 B.C., which is particularly probable in view of Agrippa's return to the East in 17:[18] the *corona navalis* which appears on the *dupondii* was his special attribute.[19] Citing the cow of Myron[20] and the completion of the temple of Olympian Zeus,[21] Gabrici and Rostovtzeff attribute the *denarii* to Athens. Graindor does not accept this, and Laffranchi prefers Lycia as origin for the IOVI OLV., and Phrygia for the cow type.[22] But such attributions, based on portrait resemblances on

---

[1] *BMC. Imp. Aug.* 663. Some of the portraits are closely akin to the Munich and Prima Porta heads (cf. Gabrici, *Augustus* [1938], p. 384, pls. II, IV).

[2] E.g. *dupondius* :—Prague; cf. *as*:—Turin, Vatican = *BMC. Imp. Aug.* 734, also 735; Leningrad, Paris, Oxford (*NC.* 1939, p. 216).

[3] *sestertii*: Milan (Sacchi, *Historia*, IX, 1935, pl. p. 485, cat. 438), *BMC. Imp. Aug.* 716, Trau coll. sale 231, Hague, Leningrad, New York, Narbonne, Toulouse, Nier coll., Hamburger sale (1925) 517, Vierordt coll. sale 663, Schulmann sale 78 (1928) 115, Santamaria sale (1926) 61, Hess sale (1931) (Otto coll.), (1932) 242 (Walters coll.), Hirsch sale (1905) 4516 (Rhusopoulos coll.), Naville sale VIII (1924) 558 (Bement coll.), Cahn sale (1913) 986 (Oertel coll.), Ars Classica sale XVII (1934) 1185.

[4] Naples; Hess sale 211. 242 (retouched).

[5] Oxford.

[6] *sestertii*: Prague (pl. IV, 1); Münzhandlung Basel sale 8. 446 (? retouched), Naples, Budapest, Florence, Ars Classica sale XVI (1933) 1547, Santamaria sale (1928) 19 (Larizza coll.). *dupondius*: Berlin (modified). *assés*: *BMC. Imp. Aug.* 731, Vatican, own collection, Ball sale VI (1931) 975.

[7] *BMC. Imp. Aug.* 669.

[8] Ibid. 666. Miss Newby's reading IAN. CLV. (p. 48), instead of IOVI OLV., is an error copied from Cohen, *Description historique des monnaies frappées sous l'empire romain*, I, p. 79. 110; Boutkowski, *DN.* I, p. 327. 717.

[9] E.g. New York (3), Gotha, Marseille.

[10] E.g. *BMC. Imp. Aug.* 443 ff.

[11] Ibid. 663, 666–9.

[12] As *BMC. Imp.* p. 108.

[13] *Rendiconti della R. Acc. di Napoli*, 1900, pp. 59 ff.; id. *Studi e materiali di archeologia e numismatica*, II, 1902, pp. 163 ff.; id. *Augustus* (1938), p. 386.

[14] *Festschrift O. Hirschfelds* (1903), p. 303.

[15] *Athènes sous Auguste*, pp. 36 ff.

[16] *NC.* 1920, p. 40.

[17] *R.it.* 1916, p. 294.

[18] Cf. Stuart Jones, *CAH.* X, p. 142.

[19] Cf. Steiner, *BJ.* CXIV, 1906, pp. 36 f.

[20] Cf. E. Babelon, *Gazette archéologique*, VIII, 1883, pp. 91 ff.

[21] Cf. Wachsmuth, *Die Stadt Athen*, I, pp. 669 ff.

[22] Ibid.; cf. *Milan Cat.* p. 45. 437; Bahrfeldt, *Münzstudien* I, 1923, p. 125.

local coins, are particularly dangerous and inconclusive,[1] since the official silver was universally current (p. 122).

However, Asia must be the home of these silver coins, as Sydenham sees. A variant *denarius* of the IOVI OLV. class[2] has a portrait closely resembling those on the large series with ARMENIA CAPTA (c. 20–18 B.C.)[3] and on a dated official tetradrachm[4] of 19–18 B.C., which is connected with a series plausibly assigned by Mattingly,[5] on the grounds of an 'Altar' type,[6] to **Ephesus**. Probably, therefore, the IOVI OLV. series is Ephesian also. The *denarii* with the cow have portraits with a considerable similarity to these, but there is a distinct difference in technique: since this divergency is maintained on the *aes* groups, it is permissible to assume the existence of two mints, rather than merely two hands, for *aes* and silver alike. An investigation of the composition of the *aes* produces results in accordance with this view. The coins with the long brow, some examples of which are closely allied to the IOVI OLV. silver, are shown by the spectrograph[7] to be alloyed with a percentage of tin; the series modelled on the 'cow' *denarii* is divided between the correct official metals of *orichalcum*[8] and copper.[9] Here is a powerful argument in favour of the production of the *aes* by at least two mints. It must also influence attribution of the *denarii*. Since the IOVI OLV. *denarii* were probably issued at Ephesus, it is likely that those with the cow, and their corresponding *aes*, were **Pergamene**.

Nor is it probable that the *aes* mints in Asia Minor were two only:

(C) An *as* of variant style (Pl. IV, 3),[10] whose portrait is imitated from Ephesian (?) *denarii* of c. 20 B.C.,[11] is of copper alloyed with about 20 per cent of tin and not much less of lead.[12]

(D) Another[13] (Pl. IV, 4), of less competent execution, also contains these constituents, but in much smaller quantities.

It is not probable that such widely divergent metallic compositions were produced by the same workshop within the short period to which iconographic considerations assign these pieces. Nor are even the weights uniform: an AVGVSTVS[14] weighs as much as 213·5 grains, and may be a *dupondius*. Thus styles, alloys and weights alike all indicate that interpretations of CA as a local ethnic, *Colonia Augusta*[15] or Caesarea Augusta (Panias)[16] or Caesarea Arca[17] or Caesaraugusta (Tarraconensis),[18] are ex-

[1] Cf. Gabrici, *Augustus* (1938), p. 388 n. 1.
[2] *BMC. Imp. Aug.* 665.
[3] Ibid. 675, etc.
[4] Ibid. 703.
[5] *BMC. Imp.* p. cxix.
[6] Ibid. *Aug.* 694.
[7] Spectrogram 20.
[8] Ibid. 32 (*dupondius*); cf. chemical analysis (*sestertius*), *BMCR.* II, p. 546 n. 1.
[9] Spectrogram 19; no tin, minute traces of lead, iron, silver.
[10] Own collection, New York.
[11] E.g. *BMC. Imp. Aug.* 678, etc.
[12] Spectrogram 31.
[13] Own collection: Spectrogram 18.
[14] *BMC. Imp. Aug.* 731.
[15] Attribution to one or more of the *Coloniae Augustae* is ruled out by the absence of any such city in Ionia, which was one of the principal centres of the coinage.
[16] Pellerin, *Mélanges*, I, p. 36; Eckhel, *DN.* III, p. 339; Stevenson, *Dictionary of Roman Coins*, p. 162.
[17] de Saulcy, *Ann. de la Soc. de Num.* III, 1868, p. 259.
[18] First refuted by Akerman, *Numismatic Illustrations of the New Testament*, p. 15.

ceedingly improbable. The circulation of these issues gives a truer impression of their character. It disposes finally, by its magnitude, not only of interpretation as an ethnic, but also of attribution to the Lycian League,[1] of the current solution C(*ommune*) A(*siae*)[2] and of the alternative C(*ommune*) A(*chaiae*).[3] Furthermore, it shows that, as their joint presence in the two principal Asian mint-groups has suggested, the CA and AVGVSTVS series were intended for the same purposes. Coins of these two classes occur together in numerous finds in *provinciae* Asia,[4] Illyricum-Pannonia,[5] and Macedonia-Moesia;[6] they were both imitated in Pannonia.[7] The *as*, which might be expected, like nearly all *asses* elsewhere, to be far the most popular denomination,[8] has come to light also in Rhaetia-Vindelicia,[9] Achaia,[10] Bithynia,[11] Pamphylia,[12] Syria,[13] and perhaps Cappadocia,[14] and was imitated in Bohemia.[15] Moreover, a barbaric AVGVSTVS type found near Bucarest, beyond the borders of the Empire (Pl. IV, 5),[16] is overstruck over a contemporary imitation of one of the moneyers' coins. We have already seen that the Roman issues were current at first in the Lower Danube region: this counterstruck piece indicates clearly that the Eastern series were inaugurated to supersede them in those parts. Britain[17] and Gallia Narbonensis[18] have each revealed at least two CA specimens; but the limits of the normal circulation of the issues with CA and AVGVSTVS is fixed by their absence from Rhine finds.[19] *Asses* in poor condition or of barbaric fabric[20] bear the same Claudian stamps as the Roman *aes*; CA occasionally have these also.[21] A *sestertius* found in European Turkey[22] is counter-

---

[1] Cf. *Milan Cat.* p. 45. 438–441.

[2] Froehner, *Mélanges d'Épigraphie et d'Archéologie*, XXII, p. 77; cf. Sydenham, *NC.* 1920, pp. 41 ff.; Mattingly, *BMC. Imp.* p. cxxv; Gabrici, *Augustus* (1938), p. 388 n. 1.

[3] Laffranchi, *R.it.* 1916, p. 293, mentions that this would suit Gabrici's interpretation of the 'cow' *denarii*.

[4] AVGVSTVS: found at Sart (Bell, *Sardis*, XI, pp. 47, 427), Aezanis (Çavder H.) (BM), at Bergama (Regling, *Münzfunde aus Pergamon*, 1915), Lampsak, Bandirma (in trade, Istanbul). CA: at Sart (Bell, *Sardis*, l.c.), Priene, Manisa (Hill, *NC.* 1927, p. 381), Bergama (Regling, l.c.), Izmir (Head, *HN.* p. 786), Samos (Berlin).

[5] AVGVSTVS: found, without countermarks, at Novi Banovci and Mitrovica: one also at Belgrade, probably of local provenance (Elmer, *Cat.* p. 36, cf. p. iv); CA: *dupondii* at Banostor, Osijek (Zagreb mus.).

[6] AVGVSTVS: found in N. Bulgaria (Sofia mus.). CA: *sestertii* and *dupondii* at Aquae Calidae (Sofia, Berlin, and notice in latter coll. from Dr Pick).

[7] Found on Danube (Vienna). *Dupondius* of similar style at New York.

[8] Cf. Elmer, *NZ.* 1933, pp. 57, 61.

[9] Found at Oberhausen (Augsburg mus.); cf. *Zeitschrift des historischen Vereins für Schwaben und Neuburg*, XL, 1914, p. 165.

[10] Delos (Athens mus.); in trade (Athens).

[11] In trade, Istanbul.

[12] Found at Adalia (Istanbul mus.).

[13] Lebanon (Istanbul mus.).

[14] Derek Maden (Milne, *Annals of Archaeology and Anthropology*, III, 1910, p. 91). [15] Prague mus.

[16] Zagreb mus.; acquired at Bucarest.

[17] At Lewes (Lewes mus.) and Hayling Island (Head, *HN.* p. 786).

[18] Narbonne, Toulouse. Others at Avignon, Marseille, and Nîmes museums, and in the collection of M. Nier, may or may not have been found in the neighbourhood.

[19] E.g. none among 2718 copper at Neuss (Strack, *BJ.* CXII, 1904, pp. 419 f.).

[20] Many at Zagreb mus.

[21] E.g. at Vienna ($\overline{\text{AVG}}$.).

[22] Istanbul.

marked with the horseman of Thrace,[1] probably for circulation in that kingdom. A *dupondius* of Bulgarian provenance has the stamp ΤΟΝΣΟΥ:[2] Tonsus was a tributary of the Hebrus,[3] and the river-god of Hadrianopolis.[4] That this stamp, like most others, is post-Augustan is proved by its recurrence on coins of Trajan.[5]

II. Cypriot group

These ambitious central issues, emanating from Ephesus and other Asiatic mints, were supplemented by a number of others whose divergent style, fabric, weight, details and provenance indicate that they not only circulated, but were struck, in a number of different provinces. One of these varieties, an *as* with IMP. AVGVST. TR. POT. (laureate head to right) and AVGVST. (in wreath) (Pl. IV, 8),[6] was found in Cyprus, and is identical in style not only with pieces known to be of Cypriot provenance[7] (p. 143), but with the SC issue attributed to the same island (group II [p. 99], e.g. Pl. III, 17).

III. Syrian groups

With the aid of this certain analogy, it is possible to detect a Syrian group of mints, represented by three CA copper coins. (A) One of these (Pl. IV, 6),[8] an *as*, has the same legend AVGVST. TR. POT.—unusual on CA issues—and the same peculiar lettering and execution as group IV of the SC coinage (e.g. Pl. III, 19). (B) A heavier coin (probably a *dupondius*), with the same inscription (Pl. IV, 9),[9] has an equally close portrait resemblance to group V of the SC series (e.g. Pl. III, 21). These coincidences from Syria, as from Cyprus, show decisively that a number of the SC and AVGVSTVS-CA issues were made in conjunction by the same authorities. (C) A third CA piece with the characteristic Syrian reverse style[10] has no obverse legend (Pl. IV, 11), and a portrait imitated from an Eastern *denarius*.[11] An AVGVSTVS *as*, which may be barbaric (Pl. IV, 7),[12] also appears to be of Syrian workmanship.[13] These attributions are confirmed by provenance;[14] moreover, there are imitations of this group by a Phoenician city-issue, which will be discussed elsewhere (p. 344).

[1] For this vide Godisnik, *Annuaire des musées nationaux bulgares*, v, 1926–31, pp. 147 ff.; Cantacuzène, *Mélanges Glotz*, p. 105.
[2] Sofia.
[3] Oberhummer, *PW*. vi, 1714.
[4] Head, *HN*. p. 28.   [5] Sofia.
[6] BM. A second and finer specimen is illustrated in two sale catalogues: Merzbacher (1909) 1130, Hamburger (1925) 515.
[7] Hill, *NC*. 1924, p. 14.

[8] *BMC. Imp. Aug.* 740.
[9] Ibid. 739, Vatican, New York.
[10] Rome.
[11] *BMC. Imp. Aug.* 679.
[12] Gotha, Vatican.
[13] *Milan Cat.* p. 46. 443–6 generalises from pieces of Syrian appearance to attribute all AVGVSTVS pieces to Antioch.
[14] Boutkowski, *DN*. p. 684. 1286, Beirut, Jerusalem.

IV. European groups

Several European categories can also be recovered. (A) *Asses* with CAISAR (*sic*) on the obverse, and AVGVSTVS in two lines on the reverse[1] (Pl. IV, 13), have a distinctive portrait that is a modified form of the IOVI OLV. prototype[2]—not derived from earlier models, as Grueber[3] assumed from a bad specimen—and corresponds, in the Hellenised obverse spelling as in style, to *dupondii* of *orichalcum*[4] and copper *semisses* with CA[5] (Pl. IV, 12). Two of the latter are from Thrace or the Black Sea[6] (a third may be of Gallic provenance[7]). Since, moreover, a number of the *asses* have been found in Greece,[8] and the portrait is imitated at *colonia* Pella (p. 249), the issues can be allotted with great probability to an East European mint.[9]

(B) A very rare *sestertius* with the reverse legend AVGVSTVS[10] has on the obverse IMP. CAESAR with a rudimentary form of E; a kindred series, with IMP. CAISAR, includes CA *semisses*[11] and *dupondii*[12] (Pl. IV, 14), besides *sestertii*[13] which are unique in their denomination owing to the appearance of a *corona navalis* (Pl. IV, 16). One of the *dupondii* was found in Greece,[14] and the group is likely to be the product of a second Balkan mint.

(C) It seems possible to connect another issue with a mint even farther to the West: a CA *as*, which like others lacks an obverse legend, but whose style is distinctive (Pl. IV, 10),[15] is represented among finds at Aquileia.[16] In execution it recalls local issues of *colonia* Dyrrhachium (p. 276), and the use of a Roman portrait model[17]—very rare in the East (p. 470)—confirms attribution to the Adriatic region.

It is now clear that CA pieces circulated, and were issued, alongside both AVGVSTVS and SC. The formula which CA represents may be expected, then, to express the authority of *princeps* or senate. The latter's prestige obtained invariable and stereotyped expression by the *senatus consultum*, which cannot in any way be represented by the letters CA. As the *asses* with the bare inscriptions CAESAR-AVGVSTVS suggest, and as the wide provenance of that series and of CA and SC issues proves, the coinage is official. The interpretation of CA as C(*ommune*) A(*siae*) (p. 105) is clearly beside the point for a series of such enormous scope and circulation.

---

[1] New York, Paris, Athens, *BMC. Imp. Aug.* 730.
[2] *BMC. Imp. Aug.* 669.
[3] *BMCR.* II, p. 546.
[4] *BMC. Imp. Aug.* 724.
[5] Ibid. 708, 711, Leningrad (2), New York (3), Avignon.
[6] *BMC. Imp.* p. 115. Perhaps also the Leningrad specimens.
[7] Avignon.
[8] Athens mus., also in trade there.
[9] The *orichalcum* pieces may be composed of zinc ore from Laurium—cf. Landerer, *Neues Jahrbuch für Mineralogie*, 1849, p. 417; Davies, *Roman Mines in Europe*, p. 247. The famous 'Corinthian bronze' may also have contained zinc, ibid. p. 253.
[10] *BMC. Imp. Aug.* 729.
[11] Munich.
[12] *BMC. Imp. Aug.* 724, illegible; Berlin, Oxford, own coll.
[13] Hague.
[14] Own coll., acquired in Athens.
[15] BM, New York (2), Zagreb.
[16] Zagreb specimen, from Horvat coll.
[17] *BMC. Imp. Aug.* 74 (17 B.C.).

Laffranchi's *Certamina Actiaca*[1] did not possess any of the necessary qualities; yet his next version, *Classiarium Actium*,[2] is a change for the worse, being as hard to construe as to justify. Regling's[3] C(*onsensu*) A(*ugusti*) is in conformity with the official character of the coins, but is bad Latin[4] and inaccurate constitutional phraseology. His alternative C(*oncessu*) A(*ugusti*) would, like it, be unparalleled as a variant for *Permissu Augusti*,[5] which was in regular use at this very time (p. 220). Moreover, his version would require mention of the city, or man, to whom the permission is extended—which is invariably and naturally displayed on coins with such formulas. These suggestions, then, must all be regarded as unplausible. Augustus is not here conceding coin-rights to a local community, but licensing currency for the Empire. The appearance of CA on several copper issues of varying denomination, besides on those of *orichalcum*, shows that the significance of the formula cannot be limited to any value or metal. Again, the deliberate alternation, on the principal groups, of the legends CAESAR-AVGVSTVS and AVGVSTVS-CA, makes it most improbable that an entirely otiose AVGVSTVS-C(*aesar*) A(*ugustus*) can be intended, but likely, nevertheless, that the word *Caesar* should somehow appear;[6] while the (often exact) parallel afforded by the SC variants suggests that here is a similar constitutional formula.

All these requirements are fulfilled by interpretation as *CAESARIS AVCTORITATE*. The supreme *auctoritas* of Augustus was, needless to say, virtually binding (p. 443),[7] even if not officially recognised by the Senate in 27[8] or legally confirmed in 24 (p. 445).[9] There are additional reasons for its peculiar relevance here. It is especially significant that even the *senatus consultum*, though in practice binding (p. 98), was not yet a source of law: it was itself an *auctoritas*.[10] Thus there is point and accuracy in the parallelism, on otherwise identical coins, from identical mints, of SC and C(*aesaris*) A(*uctoritate*). Secondly, it has been established that it was precisely by his *auctoritas* that Augustus controlled the *aerarium*.[11] Thirdly, a large number of extant inscriptions conjoin the two formulas in phrases such as *Caesaris* or *principis auctoritate et ex s.c.*, *Ex s.c. auctore Caesare* or *principe*:[12] in a Cyrenian Edict is κατὰ...δόγμα τοῦ συνκλήτου...

[1] *R.it.* XXIX, 1916, p. 296.
[2] *R.it.* XXX, 1917, p. 255.
[3] *BMB.* 1907, p. 503.
[4] Cf. Hill, *NC.* 1927, p. 381.
[5] Mattingly, *BMC. Imp.* p. cxxv.
[6] CA(*esar*), however, is impossible, owing to the frequent interpolation of a dot.
[7] Cf. Gmelin, *Forschungen zur Kirchen- und Geistesgeschichte*, XI, 1937, p. 58; Wenger, *Deutsche Literaturzeitung*, 1939, p. 874, etc. Ovid is in no doubt about this: '*nec mea* damnasti *decreto facta senatus*' (*Tristia*, II, 131).
[8] von Premerstein, p. 218, corrected by Kahrstedt, *GGA.* 1938, p. 16.
[9] von Premerstein, p. 192; cf. Volkmann, *Münchener Beiträge zur Papyrusforschung*, XXI, 1935, pp. 218 ff.
[10] Cf. Fürst, *Die Bedeutung der Auctoritas*, Diss. Marburg, 1934, pp. 47 f.; Riccobono, *Annali del Seminario giuridico della R. Univ. di Palermo*, XV, 1936, p. 386; Siber, *SavZ.* LVII, 1937, p. 450, *pace* De Martino, *Lo Stato di Augusto*, p. 34.
[11] von Premerstein, p. 192; cf. Anderson, *JRS.* XXIX, 1939, p. 96.
[12] von Premerstein, pp. 222 f.; cf. Gmelin, *Römische Herrscheridee und päpstliche Autorität*, p. 74.

THE BASES OF THE REFORM 109

τῶι ἐμῶι ἐπικρίματι.¹ Even in the 'senatorial' province of Cyprus, P. Paquius Scaeva is reappointed to the proconsulate *auctoritate Caesaris Augusti et ex s.c.*² A remarkably similar collocation is found on the state-controlled coinage of *colonia* Paestum (p. 289). Similar measures without reference to the Senate³ need not be quoted, since here already are exact parallels to the joint coinages—sometimes at the same mint—with CA and SC. Both formulas refer to the same executive process: it was now customary for the *princeps*, when *auctor sententiae* of a *senatus consultum*, to be mentioned in that capacity in its official record.⁴ In this sense, of course, the *auctoritas principis* is valid in 'senatorial' provinces, just as the 'imperial' provinces are included in the scope of the *auctoritas senatus consulti* (pp. 434 ff.). This coinage, with its striking and extensive application of the *auctoritas principis*, shows, like so many other of his interventions, that, if Augustus was careful to maintain correct forms and strong enough for them to suffice, he was not afraid to govern his Empire. The main issue of CA was in a 'senatorial' province, and, conversely, the SC series was largely struck in 'imperial' Syria: these emphases on the components of the State which were least prominent in the different administrations of the two provinces bear witness to Augustus's desire to avoid a dyarchy, and to the full existence of the Republic in all parts of the Empire alike. For *princeps* and senate were only co-operating in the interests of the sovereign people.⁵ Egypt provides the best illustration of the triple combination: it belonged to the Roman people,⁶ its revenues fell to the senatorial *aerarium*, but it was governed by the personal representative of the *princeps* (p. 133). Thus CA and SC were alike universally valid, and the coinages so inscribed are part of a vast scheme of publicity whose ramifications will be discovered again and again throughout this book.⁷

The use of *Caesaris* rather than *Augusti* with *auctoritate* is given a meaning by the economical coin-legends which this propagandist aim required: C(*aesaris*) A(*uctoritate*) balances AVGVSTVS on the *dupondii* as AVGVSTVS balances CAESAR on the *asses*. This avoids *Augusti auctoritate*, a tautology of phrase and sense⁸ of which the Romans would have been conscious,⁹ and presents throughout two contrasted features¹⁰ of the compound political theory that constituted the principate. A second cause for

¹ III (*SEG*. IX, 1938, p. 14; cf. de Visscher, *Comptes-rendus de l'Académie des Inscriptions*, 1939, p. 112).
² *ILS*. 915. The same combination enabled Cassius Severus to be condemned: Suet. *Cal.* 16; Tac. *Ann.* I, 72, IV, 21, cf. Lengle, *Neue Wege zur Antike*, XI, 1934, p. 62; Ovid, *Tristia*, II, 131.
³ Cf. Gagé, *Revue historique*, CLXXVII, 1936, p. 341.
⁴ von Premerstein, p. 222.
⁵ Emphasised by Zmigryder-Konopka, *VIIIe Congrès international des sciences historiques*, II, 1938,

p. 23; cf. Riccobono, *Annali del Seminario giuridico della R. Univ. di Palermo*, XV, 1936, pp. 478, 506.
⁶ *RG*. 27.
⁷ The care with which the Romans studied their coins is emphasised by Mattingly, *CAH*. XII, p. 716.
⁸ Cf. Reiter, *Phil. Woch.* (1930) 1199, *Augeo, Augustus*; for full bibliography, see below, p. 444.
⁹ Cf. Ribezzo, *Rivista indo-greco-italica*, XXI, 1937, p. 19, etc.
¹⁰ Cf. distinction between the two titles by Mattingly, *BMC. Imp.* III, pp. xxiv f.; Toynbee, *NC*. LXIV, 1937, p. 325.

the preference of *Caesaris* to *Augusti* may have been the crystallisation of the formula —like a number of others[1]—before the invention of the name Augustus. The retention of plain *Caesaris* was all the easier since the *princeps* was, all his life, frequently known by this name alone.[2] The different legend of the *asses*, on whose reverses AVGVSTVS is substituted for CA, is merely a device—like the rostral wreath on the *dupondii*, and the varying titulatures on Eastern SC coins—to maintain a distinction between the two denominations: these were even more easily confused than at Rome, owing to the employment of impure copper (p. 104). On outlying issues, as we have seen, these devices were neglected and other divergencies also occur. Nevertheless, the coinage as a whole was a remarkable attempt to achieve an uniform official currency of *aes* for the East. Greater homogeneity was attained later, when issues with SC were made from a central mint, and became universal in East as in West. However, under Tiberius, as has been seen, the SC currency is still not uniform. His official issues include one of uncertain mintage, reading DIVVS AVG.,[3] which supports our interpretation of CA by its reverse legend—TA.[4] This cannot be T(ρία) A(σσάρια), as Grueber suggests:[5] Γ, not T, is the Greek numeral 3, and the ambiguity with T(έσσαρα) would be intolerable.[6] On the other hand, T(*iberii*) A(*uctoritate*) is entirely suitable, and is corroborated by our demonstration that *Augusti auctoritate* would have been a clumsy and pleonastic expression.

The striking parallelism of Eastern CA and SC coinages has been seen to confirm the hypothesis that *Caesaris auctoritas* and the *senatus consultum* are the two components in a single executive progress that produced coinage. The analogy of the Eastern SC issues must be extended to the Roman, whose problematical constitutional position is thus solved. These three currencies, like those of Glabrio, Primus(?), and a Cypriot *legatus*—their only predecessors since 27—have no connection whatever with the *imperium principis*: it will be shown that supplementary issues of the same date lack this equally (p. 130). These *orichalcum* and copper pieces reveal clearly the manner in which, throughout the Empire, the *princeps* could rule but the senatorial authority still be recorded. Nor was this a dyarchy, but collaboration for the welfare of the sovereign people by means of its single treasury.

The official coinages in the East are now seen not only to provide vital historical evidence, but to have attained, as currency, unrecognised dimensions and complexity. But they must be completed by the addition of several series whose insignificant module and non-informative design have enabled their participation in the official system to escape notice.

[1] E.g. ἔτος Καίσαρος, Wilcken, *Griechische Ostraka*, pp. 787 f.
[2] Cf. de Zulueta, *JRS*. 1932, p. 186; Nock, *CR*. 1938, p. 146 (*pace* Markowski, *Poznańskie Towarzystwo Przyjaciól Nauk* [*Pr. K. Fil.*], VIII, 2); Cumont, *Rev. hist.* CLXIII, 1930, p. 242; Eger, *SavZ*. 1938, p. 274; de Sanctis, *Riv. di filologia*, 1937, p. 337.
[3] BM (uncertain): not DIVI F. AVGVSTVS, as Grueber, *NC*. 1904, p. 210.
[4] Not to be confused with Augustan issues with ΛT, for which see below, p. 344.
[5] L.c.   [6] Cf. below, p. 344, for a similar error.

4. Types of Colonists and Capricorn

The frequent halving of *asses* in Gaul and elsewhere,[1] and their fabrication already in this form by natives,[2] shows that this denomination was not low enough to meet every provincial need.[3] The deficiency of subdivisions would be especially inconvenient in the Asiatic provinces, where the absence of large coins from the local series (p. 377) suggests that small pieces alone were universally acceptable. Yet the Eastern SC issues did not include *semisses* or lower values, and we have seen good reason to think that the few *semisses* with CA were only struck, and only regularly circulated, in Eastern Europe. According to Dio,[4] Maecenas urged the abolition of city-currencies: but if Dio's mention of this policy is not anachronistic,[5] and it was really proposed at this time, it could only be successful if official coins of equally diminutive size were substituted for the local pieces. The attempt which Augustus and his immediate successors made to provide such a currency of *semisses*[6] has not been recognised, since the type, two colonists ploughing, has invariably led to attribution to a Roman city, such as Parium[7] or Berytus.[8] Whether these two mints were employed or not, there are numerous indications that the whole series—including heads of Augustus[9] (Pl. IV, 29–31; V, 1, 2), Tiberius[10] and Caligula[11]—was official:—

(1) Such a vast circulation would be completely unparalleled and anomalous for a single colonial series. Specimens have been discovered in Illyricum,[12] Upper[13] and Lower Moesia,[14] and the Thracian Chersonese,[15] besides Mysia-Troas;[16] others have come to light in Bithynia,[17] and a countermark $\overline{\text{PHR}}$.[18] (Phrygia minor?) is only paralleled at Bithynian Apamea (p. 256). More finds are reported from Pisidia,[19] Syria,[20] and even Armenia.[21] Indeed, a countermark $\overline{\text{EMP}}$.[22] seems to indicate that these coins penetrated as far as Emporiae in Spain;[23] perhaps even more remarkable is the history of a specimen[24] which was twice countermarked by Cos[25] and finally went to ground in free Germany.[26]

[1] Strack, *BJ*. CVIII, 1902, pp. 1 ff.
[2] E.g. at Bonn, COL. NEM. struck as half.
[3] The same deficiency is pointed out by Forrer, *Strasbourg-Argentorate*, I, p. 273.   [4] LII, 30. 9.
[5] As Meyer, *De Maecenatis oratione a Dione ficta* (Diss. Berlin, 1891); Schwartz, *PW*. III, 1720.
[6] Av. 68 grains (14 specimens); cf. Mattingly, *BMC. Imp.* p. lvi.
[7] M. S. v, 395. 707, etc.   [8] Berlin.
[9] *BMC*. 86; Turin, Oxford, Paris; M. S. l.c.
[10] *BMC*. 89; M. S. v, 397. 716.
[11] Istanbul, ?BM (AVG.).
[12] Augustus at Sišak (Zagreb mus.).
[13] Augustus from Serbia (Zagreb).
[14] Augustus (Sofia).
[15] Augustus at Elaeus (Eski Hisarlik) (Istanbul mus.).
[16] Many at Istanbul and in trade (Istanbul-Pera).
[17] E.g. Tiberius at Ereğli (in trade, Istanbul-Pera), and near Bursa (seen by the writer in the Bursa bazaar).
[18] Augustus (Gotha); Tiberius (Istanbul).
[19] Tiberius at Eğridir (?) (in trade, Istanbul).
[20] Attribution to Berytus in the Berlin collection is based on provenance.
[21] Tiberius at Diyarbakir (Istanbul).
[22] Augustus (Turin).
[23] An example at Nîmes (from the de Villeperdrix coll.) may also have been found locally.
[24] Ehingen coll.; cf. Goessler, *Fundberichte aus Schwaben*, *NF*. IV, 1928, p. 105.
[25] Crab, NIKOMH(δης), rightly attributed by Bernhart, *Fundb.*, l.c.
[26] At Unterkirchberg in N. Württemberg, *Fundb.*, l.c.

112 COINAGE BY *AUCTORITAS PRINCIPIS*, 27 B.C.–A.D. 14

(2) A number of other countermarks appear which are peculiar to the official coinage: $\overline{\text{AV}}$.[1] is common on issues of the moneyers and on Lugdunese 'Altar' coins,[2] a wheel[3] is characteristic of Nemausus,[4] a prow[5] is found on the Roman series.[6] The first two at least are specifically official countermarks, which would be quite irregular on colonial pieces.

(3) It is therefore not surprising that these coins, unlike city-issues, have neither ethnic, nor local formula, nor magistrate's signature.

The type which they bear is no less significant to the propaganda of the new order than the duality of CA and SC on the larger denominations. Not only did Augustus establish many settlers in the East—and pay for the land they occupied (p. 305)—but one of the chief elements in the theory of the principate was his position as universal refounder, which is emphasised in numerous ways on the coinage of Roman and peregrine cities alike (pp. 290, 335 ff.): particularly important was his association with Romulus in the capacity of *conditor*.[7] The manifold influence of the conception cannot be exaggerated (p. 356); and the significance of the coin-type was not limited to the details of colonial foundation.

It has been shown that complete centralisation of mint was not attempted for the SC and CA-AVGVSTVS series: there was in each case a principal issue—for the former group in Syria and for the latter in Ionia—supplemented by the products of a number of lesser workshops. An examination of the present issues makes it clear that here also more than one mint was at work. There can be no doubt that the central point of the system was in Mysia or the Troad, where many are found. A number of countermarks on these coins indicate extensive circulation in that region: an owl[8] is stamped also at Miletopolis,[9] a capricorn[10] at Pitane,[11] a star[12] at Ilium,[13] Lampsacus,[14] Imbros[15] and *colonia* Alexandria Troas,[16] whose acceptance of this series is further indicated by another countermark $\overline{\text{TR}}$.[17] There is, however, good reason to think that the principal centre for the issue was at **Parium**,[18] since in the principate of Tiberius almost identical issues with the 'colonist' type (and the heads of Drusus[19] or Tiberius and Drusus[20]) have the letters C.G.I.P. The final closure of the official mint in favour of a colonial one is announced by two subsequent coinages of Caligula(?)[21]

[1] Tiberius (Copenhagen).
[2] Mattingly, *BMC. Imp.* p. xxxii.
[3] Augustus (Zagreb).   [4] Berlin, Paris, Brussels.
[5] Augustus (Istanbul).
[6] Mattingly, *BMC. Imp.* p. xxxix.
[7] Kornemann, *Klio*, 1938, pp. 81 f., 85.
[8] Augustus (Vienna).
[9] Winterthur, cf. Imhoof-Blumer, *RS.* XIII, 1905, p. 208.
[10] Tiberius (in trade, Istanbul-Pera).
[11] Vienna, cf. *Wad.* 991.
[12] Augustus (Vienna).
[13] Copenhagen, cf. *Wad.* 1154.
[14] Paris (M. *S.* v, 375. 593).
[15] Athens (Postolacca, *Cat.* p. 163).
[16] In trade (Paris).   [17] Augustus (Vienna).
[18] Such provincial mints as Parium and Antioch make Mattingly's description of Rome as 'the one great centre' of *aes* coinage in the Early Empire (*CAH.* XII, p. 714) seem scarcely applicable to the principate of Augustus.
[19] Berlin, Oxford; cf. M. *S.* v, 397. 719.
[20] *BMC.* 92, Berlin; cf. M. *S.* v, 413. 818.
[21] Ibid. 397. 720; not seen.

THE BASES OF THE REFORM

Claudius[1] with the same letters. This ethnic explicitly imposes a limitation shown by provenance, countermarks, and the lack of a reverse legend, to have been absent from the earlier series. Other official mints in the same region may have augmented the output of Parium; but the divergencies in style between the various coins of this class are so significant that it is impossible to resist the conclusion that many were struck much farther afield. Their circulation, and the analogy of other widespread Eastern official series, make this particularly probable. Several specimens both of Augustus[2] and Tiberius[3] have styles alien to Parium; the late Augustan piece which reached Emporiae[4] is again of quite different execution. Examples found in Armenia[5] and Syria[6] appear to originate from a mint in or near Syrian Antioch; the style of others[7] is very close to that of Antioch in Pisidia, where specimens have come to light. Perhaps a Bithynian town also contributed to the circulation of these coins in the province;[8] and the two countermarks of Cos which appear on one specimen (found in Germany) led Goessler[9] to the not improbable conclusion that that island was the place of its origin. Most significant of all is a rare issue[10] with a strongly individual portrait (Pl. V, 1), whose style and fabric recall coins of Pontus and Paphlagonia and certainly have no connection with the central Mysian mint. This conclusion is confirmed by the presence in this (but not the central) group of traces of zinc;[11] the Mysian coins also have much less lead than these.[12]

However, the Mysian mint was certainly the focal point of all these issues. A very young portrait of Augustus on one 'colonist' specimen[13] connects the series with a *quadrans* on which an identical head is accompanied by the type of a capricorn and *cornucopiae*:[14] the only inscription is still AVG., on the obverse (Pl. V, 3). There is also an *as*[15] of similar style and type, reading AVGVSTVS (here on the reverse) (Pl. IV, 32). Similar coins of Nero[16] prove, by their countermark C.G.I.P., the connection of this piece with the *semisses* of 'colonist' type. Moreover, the capricorn, the type of these *asses* and *quadrantes*, is affixed as a stamp on the 'colonist' coins. We have seen that the Julio-Claudian period witnessed a transformation of the 'colonist' coinage into a local currency: the *asses* with capricorn are shown to have undergone a similar alteration of scope by the appearance of D.D. on otherwise similar *asses* of Claudius(?)[17] and Nero.[18] Another issue with Nero's head bears the name of a local magistrate.[19] But in the principate of Augustus it is evident that the 'capricorn' *asses* were official issues, exhibiting a divergency of type from the much more frequent *asses* with the same inscrip-

[1] *BMC*. 93.
[2] E.g. BM.
[3] E.g. Paris, Nîmes, Ball sale 39 (1937) 1157.
[4] Turin.   [5] Istanbul.   [6] Berlin.
[7] Istanbul; in trade (Istanbul-Pera).
[8] In trade (Bursa).
[9] *Fundberichte aus Schwaben*, l.c.
[10] R. C. Lockett coll., Paris, own coll.
[11] Spectrogram 39.
[12] Spectrograms 40, 41, 42.   [13] Munich.
[14] Vienna, Berlin, Cahn sale, 60. (1928) 1401.
[15] Paris, Simon coll. (Cahn sale 68 [1930] 150); cf. M. S. v, 395. 710; Cohen, *Description historique des monnaies frappées sous l'empire romain*, Aug. 781.
[16] Munich.   [17] Glasgow (*Hu*. III, p. 67).
[18] Sofia; cf. M. II, 579. 430 and S. v, 595. 706 (both misread).
[19] Paris.

tion, AVGVSTVS, in a wreath (p. 102). The curious portrait of the 'capricorn' *asses* is imitated at Cyzicus;[1] the young head on the 'colonist' *semisses* and 'capricorn' *quadrantes* is very similar to that on a famous group of *aurei* and *denarii* inscribed CAESAR AVGVST.,[2] which have, moreover, the type of a candelabrum whose arrangement is copied on Cyzicene bronze.[3] It is probable that these too were struck at Parium, if not at Cyzicus itself. An explanation of the portraits will be derived from the local issues (p. 357). Finds establish an upper limit of c. 11 B.C. for the *aurei* and *denarii*;[4] the 'colonist' *semisses* employ portrait-models which suggest that they also, like the principal CA-AVGVSTVS groups which supplied the higher denominations, were of about that date. The coins with the capricorn illustrate a brief phase in which the official mint at Parium supplied the surrounding region with *asses*, and imitated Rome by issuing *quadrantes*, which were absent from the main Eastern series. But Parium was most important as the focal point of the widely current and much reduplicated series of 'colonist' *semisses*: these are an essential constituent of the elaborate *aes* system which formed the nucleus of all official and local currencies in the East.[5] It is characteristic of Rome, and of Augustus, to have sacrificed the uniformity of a bureaucracy in favour of the thoroughness which means good government.[6]

The analogies of other official currencies indicate that these groups, centred as they were in 'senatorial' provinces and designed as supplementary to the higher denominations, were likewise a product of *senatus consulta Caesaris auctoritate*.

5. NEMAUSUS 'I*b*'

The second major issue at Nemausus (I*b*) started not long after 15, and ended after 8 B.C. (p. 74) (Pl. II, 19–23). After consideration of the complicated network of official currencies in the East, it should not cause surprise that the mint of Rome, with its few supplementary mints in Italy, soon proved inadequate for the needs of the West; it was, in particular, somewhat inaccessible to the principal military centres on the Rhine. An indication has already been given of the enormous bulk and scope of 'Nemausus I*b*'. If the present chronological and administrative reattribution is accepted, it necessitates an entirely new view of Augustan mint policy in the West. This, not the 'Altar' series, was the first official token coinage to be issued in co-operation with the mint for gold and silver at Lugdunum (15 B.C.).[7] The new system was perhaps connected with a financial revision following the expulsion of the procurator Licinus.[8]

---

[1] Paris.
[2] *BMC. Imp. Aug.* 683 f.; cf. Bahrfeldt, *Münzstudien*, I, 1923, pp. 136 f.
[3] Weber Cat. 5055, Vienna, Berlin.
[4] Mattingly, *BMC. Imp.* pp. cxxvi f.
[5] Broughton's statement (*ES.* IV, p. 882, cf. 886) that there was 'hardly any imperial small change' in Asia is inapplicable to this period.
[6] For the diversity of imperial arrangements cf. Larsen, *CP.* XXXIV, 1939, p. 162; Last, *CAH.* XI, p. 475; Cary, *History*, XXII, 1938, p. 59.
[7] Strabo IV, 192; Boissieu, *Inscriptions antiques de Lyon*, pp. 126, 181; Mattingly, *BMC. Imp.* p. cxiii.
[8] Cf. Stevenson, *CAH.* X, pp. 189, 193.

THE BASES OF THE REFORM

The analogy of the groups previously described in this chapter—especially those from the 'senatorial provinces', of which Gallia Narbonensis was now one[1]—indicates that the mint of Nemausus was no longer governed in the same way as at its institution in c. 28. Indeed, it will be shown that Augustus no longer possessed in this period an *imperium maius* such as he had exercised at that date (p. 428). There is, then, no reason to doubt that the present issues, like their immediate predecessors in the official coinages elsewhere, were based on the co-operation of *auctoritas principis* and the *senatus consultum*.

'Nemausus I*b*' did not, however, provide a permanent solution. One reason for its abandonment is shown by the spectrograph, which reveals that the new metals of *orichalcum* and copper were not here employed.[2] The retention of the old alloy of bronze, and of an *as* weighing c. 188·8 grains,[3] was no doubt intended to assist exchange with the previous official and local currencies of Gaul and elsewhere which were still in circulation; but, in view of the Imperial importance of the Gallic monetary centre, it is not surprising that this defection from the new system proved unsatisfactory. Furthermore, in view of their distance from each other and their different administrative position, Nemausus and Lugdunum were ill-suited for collaboration.[4] At about the beginning of the last decade B.C., therefore, a new solution was envisaged.

6. LUGDUNUM (AND AUXILIARY MINTS?)

Both the principal disadvantages of the Nemausan coinage were abolished by the institution of a series consisting chiefly of copper *asses*[5] (but including a *sestertius* of *orichalcum*[6]) whose famous 'Altar' type demands attribution to Lugdunum:[7] an altar, probably with the inscription of the coins ROM. ET AVG.,[8] was dedicated at this city in 12 B.C.[9] The somewhat rough style of these pieces (Pl. V, 4, 5) is no evidence for 'provincial' origin under the *Concilium Galliarum*,[10] since the technical departments no doubt employed local labour. Moreover, a second and larger issue of four denominations with precisely the same types[11] is of superior workmanship. It marks a recovery from the irregular fabric and execution of previous Nemausan and Lugdunese issues, and served an additional purpose since native imitations, no longer being so easy, become much rarer.

Strabo's[12] reference to a coinage of 'gold and silver by the *principes*' at Lugdunum does not imply[13] that the *aes*, which he ignores, was the concern of the *Concilium*, since

---

[1] Ibid. p. 211. [2] Spectrogram 2.
[3] Average of 23.
[4] I hope to deal at a later date with Tiberius's reasons for resuming the Nemausan coinage (p. 75).
[5] *BMC. Imp. Aug.* 549 ff.
[6] Ibid. 548 (analysed). [7] Mattingly, ibid. p. cxvii.
[8] *CIL.* XIII, 1664. For this cf., most recently, Dragendorff, *Jahrbuch des deutschen archäologischen Instituts*, 1937, p. 111.

[9] Livy, *Epit.* 137; Dio LIV, 321; cf. Rice Holmes, *Architect*, II, p. 158, *pace* Suet. *Claudius*, 2. 1 (10 B.C.); *Catalogo della Mostra Augustea di Romanità*, p. 146. 6 (13 B.C.).
[10] As Sydenham, *NC.* 1917, p. 75; Sutherland, *RIS.* p. 243 n. 19.
[11] *BMC. Imp. Aug.* 565 ff.
[12] IV, 192.
[13] As Sydenham, *NC.* 1917, p. 75.

at the date at which Strabo wrote[1] the *aes* issues had either ceased or were limited to an occasional *quadrans*.[2] The provincial allusion of the 'Altar' has no autonomous significance whatsoever:[3] on the contrary, it refers to the ruler-worship of which Lugdunum was the centre—and of which, indeed, the *Concilium Galliarum* was the prime mover—in the area for which these coins were primarily intended, namely, the vital and complex province of Gallia Comata.[4]

However, as might be expected from the study of other official issues, their scope was by no means limited to this region. They circulated widely without countermarks in the ring of surrounding territories, Gallia Narbonensis,[5] Rhaetia-Vindelicia,[6] and free Germany.[7] Occasionally, too, they are found much farther afield, in Hispania Ulterior,[8] Italy,[9] Sicily,[10] Sardinia,[11] Illyricum-Pannonia[12] and Epirus.[13] Imitations

---

[1] Cf. Aly, *PW.* IV, 77 f.

[2] E.g. Mattingly, *BMC. Imp.* p. cxxx; cf. *Ti.* 62.

[3] As Mowat, *Rn.* 1895, p. 160.

[4] The circulation and countermarks of the earlier and later groups do not warrant any distinction between the two. Many in all museums, e.g. Lyon (about 60), Besançon (8), Dijon, Châtillon (Daguin, *Bulletin de la Soc. nat. des antiquaires de France*, 1901, p. 216), S. Germain-en-Laye (Reinach, *Cat.* II, p. 320), Rennes (Toulmouche, *Cat.* p. 41). Found at the frontier-posts of Neuss (222$\frac{18}{2}$; Strack, *BJ.* CXII, 1904, pp. 419 ff.), Courroux, Kaiseraugst (Basel mus.), Windisch (*Anzeiger für Schweizerische Altertumskunde*, XXXIV, 1932, p. 112; XXXVIII, 1936, p. 176; Stückelberg, *ZfN.* XXII [1900], pp. 40 ff., 100), Ehl (Colmar mus.), Mulhouse (mus.), Hees (Brunsting, *Archaeologisch-Historische Bijdragen*, IV, 1937, p. 170), Nijmegen, Helden, Valkenburg, Heerewaarden (Leiden mus.), Pommern, Urmitz, Andernach (Bonn mus.), Strasbourg (Forrer, *Strasb.* I, p. 273), Xanten (Steiner, *Cat.* p. 85), Ubbergen (*Oudheidk. Med. Leiden, NR.* XII, 1931, p. 95), Bingen (Behrens, *Cat.* p. 153) etc.

[5] Found at Vienne (3), Orange (2), Narbonne (24) (in local museums), Montans (*Mémoires de la Société archéologique du midi de la France*, IX, 1872, p. 228); seen in trade at Arles. Most of those in museums at Nîmes (31), Marseille (20) and Avignon (12) are also of local provenance.

[6] Found at Giubiasco (Basel mus.), Hegau (Bissinger, *Funde*, p. 27), Winterthur (mus.), Wangen (Nestle, *Funde*, p. 90), Risstissen (ibid. p. 82; Schenk von Stauffenberg coll.), Constance

(Woerl, *Bericht über eine Anzahl im J. 1849 aufgefundener röm. Münzen*, p. 13), Neustadt a. D. (Landshut mus.; *Verhandlungen des historischen Vereins für Niederbayern*, IX, 1863, p. 40).

[7] E.g. Saalburg (mus.; *Saalburg Jahrbuch*, V, 1924, pp. 41, 49, 54; VI, p. 46), Jagsthausen (Nestle, *Funde*, p. 57; Berlichingen coll.), Obernau (ibid. p. 69), Lorch (Goessler, *Fundberichte aus Schwaben, NF.* I, 1922, p. 104; Peter coll.), Rottweil (ibid. *NF.* V, 1930, p. 94), Badenweiler (Bissinger, *Funde*, p. 13; Karlsruhe mus.), Riegel (ibid. p. 15; Schreiber coll.), Baden (ibid. p. 19; Karlsruhe), Pforzheim (ibid. p. 23), Daxlanden (ibid. p. 24), Wiesloch (ibid. p. 26), Walldorf (ibid.; Heidelberg Univ. mus.), Prague (*Verhandlungen der Berliner Gesellschaft für Anthropologie*, X, 1878, p. 45), Vechten (Leiden mus.), Karlsruhe (mus.).

[8] Cf. Correia de Fonseca, *Archeologo Portugues*, XVII, 1912, pp. 113, 116.

[9] E.g. found at Naples: Sgobbo, *Notizie degli Scavi*, 1926, p. 77.

[10] Now at Magdeburg (Realgymnasium): for provenance cf. Lilie, *Jahresbericht über das Realgymnasium in Magdeburg*, 1902–3, p. 18, cf. p. 1.

[11] Cavedoni, *Bullettino archeologico sardo*, IV, 1858, p. 156; also one at Cagliari mus., as D. Levi informs me.

[12] E.g. Petronel (Elmer, *NZ.* LXVI, 1933, p. 66), Sotin, Novi Banovci, Sišak, and on coast (Zagreb mus.); two in Belgrade (Elmer, *Cat.* pp. 36 f.), probably of Serbian provenance.

[13] Found in Albania (Zagreb mus.).

THE BASES OF THE REFORM

abound,[1] but varieties in style (e.g. Pl. V, 4, 5) make it by no means inconceivable that a few auxiliary mints assisted Lugdunum in the production of the issues. Their mint superseded the Italian mints of Rome as the chief source of supply for the West, although, as we have seen, no effort whatever was made to remove the Roman issues from circulation. As in other 'imperial' provinces, the *princeps* no doubt preferred to coin by *auctoritas* through a *senatus consultum* rather than by his *imperium*.

Various categories of countermark occur. It has been shown that the stamps with the names and titles of members of the ruling house are post-Augustan (p. 94), and elsewhere a discussion of Spanish ethnics similarly affixed will lead to the same result (p. 299). It is therefore significant that most of the other countermarks also which appear on these coins demand a *terminus post quem* considerably later than A.D. 14. Thus C.A.[2] is found also on Antiochene *aes* of Otho,[3] P.R.[4] on Commagenian of Tiberius[5] and on Antiochene of Tiberius,[6] Claudius and Nero,[7] R.[8] on Lugdunensian of Nero.[9] VAL(*eat*),[10] which appears elsewhere variously abbreviated VA. and VALE.,[11] is stamped on Tiberian issues of Cascantum.[12] It is hardly possible that each of these had more than one period of affixation. RE.[13] and REP.[14] perhaps stand for *rependatur*[15] and belong to the same time. EQ.[16] may probably be assigned to an equestrian *ala*, in unknown circumstances, and III[17] to the third legion; such legionary stamps are also post-Augustan.[18]

Another series of stamps may conjecturally be attributed to Gallia Narbonensis, on the grounds that no other interpretations permit such a homogeneous solution for a homogeneous group. C.A.A.,[19] C.I.A.,[20] (IMP. AV.)C.N.[21] seem to indicate *coloniae Augusta* Arelate and *Iuliae* Arausio and Narbo respectively;[22] VIGI.[23] and VIGIN.[24] suggest the *Vigintiviri* who still governed Vocontio,[25] and P.P. recalls the formula of Claudian date on the coins of Nemausus. Similarly, on that series itself (p. 70), C.DD.AR. may perhaps be interpreted as C(*onsensu*) DD(= *decurionum*) AR(*elatensium*), and C.I.C. might represent C(*olonia*) I(*ulia*) C(*arcaso*).[26] These restorations are individually unimpressive, but gain some plausibility by their number and uniformity. Since these 'Altar' coins demonstrably circulated with the greatest freedom throughout

---

[1] Among the more unusual is one found at Novi Banovci (Zagreb mus.). Large collection at Bonn.
[2] *BMC. Imp.* p. xxxii.
[3] Wruck, *Die Syrische Provinzialprägung von Augustus bis Trajan*, p. 184. 64*b*.
[4] *BMC. Imp.* p. xxxiv.
[5] Vienna. [6] Istanbul.
[7] Wruck, l.c. p. 120. 18*d*, p. 183. 53*a*.
[8] In trade (Brussels); BM, incised.
[9] *BMC. Imp.* p. xxxv. [10] Ibid. p. xxxvi.
[11] Cf. de Saulcy, *Mélanges de Numismatique*, I, pp. 113 ff.
[12] Hill, p. 170. [13] Basel.
[14] Vienna. [15] Cf. *valeat*.
[16] Vienna. [17] In trade, Brussels.
[18] Cf. Wruck, l.c. p. 180. 28*b*, *e*; p. 183. 53*c*.
[19] Mattingly, *BMC. Imp.* p. xxxii, prefers Colonia Augusta Agrippina.
[20] Brussels.
[21] de Saulcy, l.c. pp. 421 ff.
[22] Kornemann 93, 95, 31.
[23] *BMC. Imp.* p. 395. 587 bis.
[24] Ibid. p. xxxvii.
[25] Rushforth, *Latin Historical Inscriptions*, p. 12. 11 = *CIL*. XII, 1376.
[26] Kornemann 54.

Gallia Narbonensis at this time, these countermarks, like most of the other principal groups, could not be as early as the principate of Augustus. C.A.B.,[1] if not of Babba or Banasa, represents the name of one of the Spanish colonies, Barcino or Bilbilis; GR.[2] (Graccurris) is also found at Graccurris itself and at *colonia* Celsa (p. 212). These countermarks are also of a date well outside the present period (p. 299).

There are, however, several stamps that may be Augustan. A capricorn[3] possibly assures validity outside the general sphere of circulation, in north-west Asia Minor; APX(οντες)[4] perhaps serves for a single Greek community. The 'Altar' series, like others, is also confirmed by Varus[5] for circulation in a new province (p. 95); other governors may perhaps be seen in L.C.[6] and TER(*entius?*) A(*fer??*).[7] Since P.S.P.[8] and P.S.T.[9] are uniform, they may be traced to the only province with suitable neighbouring colonies or *municipia*, namely, Sicily: the formula P(*ermissu*) S(*enatus*) is paralleled elsewhere, and the cities are probably *coloniae* Panormus and Tyndaris (or Tauromenium or Thermae) (p. 237 f.). The difficulty which necessitated the stamping of Roman *orichalcum* coins in Sicily (p. 96) must have extended, sooner or later, to copper *asses*, such as these. Finally, a large countermark, including some letters and an animal, interpreted dubiously by Blanchet as A.AT.C. and a bull, occurs on coins found near Mayenne.[10] It is probably assignable to some tribal community which marked it for circulation alongside its own issues. This stamp, together with the persistence of Gallic 'autonomous' coinage at least until the death of Augustus,[11] makes it doubtful whether, as yet, the tribes of the North freely accepted Roman coin. The day of centralised bureaucracy had not yet come, but the Imperial range of Augustus's currency heralds the decline of particularism.

The mint at Lugdunum, guarded by a cohort,[12] was operated by freedmen and slaves of the *res publica*;[13] owing to special circumstances by which the headquarters of the *legatus*—at least from c. 12 to 9 B.C.[14] if not from c. 38[15]—were distant from the capital, the mint can safely be attributed to the control of the provincial procurator,[16] who was also in charge of the provincial *arca fisci*.[17] In the other 'imperial' provinces the situation will be shown to have been somewhat different (p. 130).

[1] Paris.
[2] Cf. *BMC. Imp.* p. xxxiii (C.R.).
[3] Berlin.   [4] Basel.
[5] *BMC. Imp.* p. xxix.
[6] Ibid. p. xxxiii.
[7] Ibid. p. xxxv. Unidentifiable.
[8] Paris.   [9] *BMC. Imp.* p. xli.
[10] Blanchet, *Traité*, p. 252; own collection.
[11] Strack, *BJ*. cxii, 1904, p. 426; cf. Neuss finds, *pace* Willers, *NZ*. xxxii, 1900, p. 136.

[12] *ILS.* 2130.   [13] *ILS.* 5197, etc.
[14] Ritterling, *BJ*. cxiv, 1906; Syme, *CAH.* x, p. 359.
[15] Jullian, *Histoire de la Gaule*, iv, p. 103 n. 6; Rice Holmes, *Architect*, ii, pp. 145 f.
[16] Hirschfeld, *Die kaiserlichen Verwaltungsbeamten*, p. 181 n. 4; cf. *ILS.* 1514.
[17] Boissieu, *Inscriptions antiques de Lyon*, pp. 277 ff., 260, 265 ff.; Habel, *PW.* ii, 425 ff., misleadingly distinguishes *arca* from *fiscus*.

D. PROVINCIAL ISSUES BY *LEGATI AUGUSTI*

It was part of the plan of Augustus that the complex system of official *aes* series should be supplemented by other official issues of smaller scope. It is possible to recognise such coinages in most of the provinces. They differ from the currencies already described only by reason of their approximate limitation to a single province or territory: the administrative officers who provided them are the same.[1] They are, in fact, official, but owing to an unreasonable convention—and the failure to recognise the character of most of them—they are habitually excluded from studies of the so-called 'Imperial' coinage.[2] In contrast to the general constitutional implications of the principal issues, these 'provincial' or 'regional' ones supply much detailed information concerning the administration of the Empire. A chronological survey of their occurrence in the 'imperial' provinces will first be attempted.

1. Hispania Ulterior: Emerita, uncertain Mint

Some bronze *asses*[3] bear the head of Augustus to right, with the variously abbreviated inscription CAESAR AVGVSTVS TRIBVNICIA POTESTATE, and on the reverse, without a type, P. CARISIVS LEG(*atus*) AVG(*usti*). A *dupondius*[4] has the head to left. Other *asses* indicate an attribution for the whole group by the addition of the mint-mark EMERITA, and the type of a bird's-eye view of the town[5]—as on *denarii* of the same *legatus*.[6] P. Carisius[7] commanded the legions of Farther Spain in the Cantabrian and Asturian wars of 26–25 B.C.,[8] founded Emerita not long afterwards,[9] and remained as provincial *legatus*, to the discomfiture of the inhabitants, until at least 22 B.C.[10] A discrepancy regarding his *praenomen* between manuscripts of Dio[11] and the coins does not warrant Gardthausen's[12] unacceptable hypothesis that a later P. Carisius struck the issue in commemoration of his father's exploits. The coinage of Carisius, composed of products of the newly organised mines,[13] is called by Sydenham[14] 'one of the turning points in the monetary history of the period'; but the theory of Augustus's

---

[1] The distinction of Lenormant, *La monnaie dans l'antiquité*, II, p. 149, is unsound.
[2] Only two of them are cited in the British Museum Catalogue devoted to this subject.
[3] *BMC. Imp. Aug.* 298 ff., weighing 176·0–137·0 grains. Spectrogram 35.
[4] Ibid. 302, weighing 253·0 grains.
[5] Cf. Cohen, *Description historique des monnaies frappées sous l'Empire romain*, I, pp. 117 f., no. 395.
[6] *BMC. Imp. Aug.* 288; cf. Bahrfeldt, *NZ.* XXVIII, 1896, p. 80.
[7] *PIR.*² II, p. 99. 422.
[8] Syme, *AJP.* LV, 1934, pp. 293 ff.; cf. Orosius VI, 21. 10; Florus II, 33. 56; Dio LIII, 25. 8.
[9] Syme, l.c. p. 307.
[10] Ibid. p. 302; cf. Dio LIV, 5. 1; unjustifiably doubted by Faucci, *Historia*, IX, 1935, p. 139.
[11] LIII, 25. 8, Τίτος.
[12] II, 2. p. 375; vide Syme, l.c. p. 316; Groag, *PW.* III, 1592.
[13] Richmond, *AJA*, LXXXVII, 1930, pp. 98 ff.
[14] *NC.* 1920, p. 44.

complete surrender of moneying-rights in 28 which warranted this statement has been shown by a Cypriot mintage to be baseless (p. 80). However, these issues possess features of great importance to our constitutional theme.

The silver coinage of Carisius is relevant to the present study by reason of two contrasts it presents to his *aes*. In the first place, the latter invariably mentions the tribunician power of the *princeps*, while the *denarii*, except for one hybrid,[1] always employ his *praenomen imperatoris* instead. Thus the *aes* and silver cite powers distinct in content and origin [2] It is uncertain whether any of the silver was struck after his assumption, or reassumption, of the *tribunicia potestas* in 23 B.C. (p. 452). But that, in any case, the distinction between the two titles is due primarily to different metal and scope rather than to difference of date can be inferred from a second consideration. Carisius is LEG. PRO PR(*aetore*) on the silver,[3] and LEG. AVGVSTI on the *aes*.[4]

The first of these contrasts is explained by the administrative machinery of the *aes* as revealed by the primary official coinages. Carisius coins *denarii* as the last of a line of officers who sign the so-called 'imperatorial' silver.[5] His *imperium* is subordinate to that of Augustus,[6] which is accordingly emphasised by the *praenomen* (p. 442): this was one of the military provinces, in which it had for years been part of the function of the *Imperator* to provide coinage in the precious metals. On the other hand, as has been shown, the *aes* coinages, which often bear the formula SC, were issued *Caesaris auctoritate*: on them, therefore, the *praenomen imperatoris* is omitted, as irrelevant to their mintage. It is reasonable to infer that the formula which instead occurs, *tribunicia potestate*, is, like it, closely connected with the executive functions which produced the coinage on which it appears so significantly. It will be shown in a later chapter that the *potestas* was, indeed, actually the vehicle of the *auctoritas* in its most potent aspect (p. 446): it supplied the *ius senatus consulendi*. It was this which enabled co-operation with the senate by the *senatus consulta auctore Caesare*, whose existence has already been pointed out. Besides this coinage, there is evidence to show that, even in the 'imperial' provinces, this method was preferred to the *imperium* for administrative purposes (p. 435). Thus the substitution of TR. P. for IMP. on the *aes* has much point.

This particular contrast between *aes* and silver bears on a more general contrast—the frequent appearance of SC on the former coinages, and its rarity on the latter. Under Augustus, of course, that formula is far from indispensable to the official *aes*:[7] it occurs chiefly as a reminder of the co-operative process by which the coinage was produced, and is absent, for example, on the issues of Carisius. Again, SC occurs

---

[1] Copenhagen; *BMC. Imp.* p. 52 n.
[2] Cf. Groh, *Studi Riccobono*, II, p. 3.
[3] Except on a *quinarius* (*BMC. Imp. Aug.* 293), which has no room for more than LEG.
[4] Except on an *as* (ibid. 303) (Pl. V, 10), which has LEG. alone: possibly the earliest.
[5] Cf. Mattingly, *RC.* p. 34. Described as *castrenses nummi* by Lenormant, *Daremberg and Saglio*, I, 2. 120.
[6] Cf. Cardinali, *Augustus* (1938), p. 162.
[7] It is limited to Rome (where it is not invariable) and to the Eastern group described above, p. 98.

occasionally—in special circumstances—even on the gold and silver, now[1] as later.[2] The complete distinction in this respect between official *aes* on the one hand, and gold and silver on the other, has not yet appeared. Yet even at this date the formula appears to have some special relevance to the *aes* alone, and the coinage of Carisius may provide a clue to the character of this. TR.P. on the *aes* indicates the warrant of a *senatus consultum*; but IMP. on the silver demonstrates its absence. Carisius's issues follow very closely on the reform of the coinage: they will therefore illustrate better than any other series phenomena making their appearance at that time, such as the general limitation of SC to the *aes* pieces. The *aes* were the product of the executive process TR.P.—C.A.—S.C., but the *denarii* were not; it cannot, however, be ascertained whether this distinction remained valid throughout Augustus's principate, since the mints of his subsequent gold and silver issues are very imperfectly known (p. 122). If they can all be attributed to 'imperial' provinces, there is no reason to believe that the distinction lapsed: but if, as seems more probable, some of the mints were in 'senatorial' territory—where, as will be shown, Augustus possessed no *imperium* whatsoever (pp. 427 ff.)—then the process TR.P.—C.A.—S.C. was no doubt used, but the formula S.C. omitted merely in accordance with precedent. The question whether the coinage itself was 'senatorial' or 'imperial'—in any case meaningless as regards the *aes*—will in that case become irrelevant to the gold and silver also.

The second contrast—between LEG. PRO PR. and LEG. AVGVSTI—is less important, but seems equally deliberate. The former title is in the tradition of the 'imperatorial' silver, coined by officials with *imperium* subordinated to an *imperium maius*, like P. Carisius in the war-emergency. The auspices, of course, remained with the *princeps*, and this aspect is emphasised by Carisius's title on the *aes*. This coinage was provided by civilian machinery: thus, avoiding the title *pro praetore*, Carisius expresses the source of the *auctoritas* which produced his coinage, just as it produced the SC issues in another 'imperial' province, Syria.

On another bronze series,[3] including *dupondii*[4] and *asses*,[5] appears the bare head of Augustus to left, with the inscription IMP. AVG. DIVI F., and, on the reverse— accompanied on the *dupondii* by other symbols—a round object which has been variously explained (cf. Pl. V, 6). Haym[6] thought it was the Cretan labyrinth, and allots the issue to Cnossus; du Mersan's[7] imagination discovered the circus of Saguntum.[8] Delgado propounded the view of an alliance of Saguntum and Segobriga. This may be rejected like other similar alliances, African and Spanish;[9] but his interpretation of the type as a shield is correct. A similar shield appears on Emeritan

---

[1] E.g. *BMC. Imp. Aug.* 1 ff., 656; cf. pp. ci n. 5.
[2] Ibid. p. clxxxvii.
[3] BM, Levis sale 247 (illustrated): Spectrogram 30.
[4] 296 grains (BM).
[5] Av. c. 171 grains.
[6] *Trésor Britannique*, II, p. 117.
[7] *Rn.* 1846, p. 10.
[8] Cf. Palosy, *Discertacion sobra el theatro y circo de Sagunto* (1793).
[9] Cf. below, pp. 185 n. 6, 188 n. 12, 339.

denarii of P. Carisius,[1] together with a Spanish knife and spear-head,[2] with which the two symbols on the *dupondii* are clearly identifiable. Attribution to Spain is confirmed by style and provenance, and by the occurrence of countermarks of Saguntum;[3] but ascription to a local series is rendered impossible by the absence both of ethnic and of local magistrate's name. The issue must, then, be official. An attempt at a closer definition raises problems of general significance. Besides the Emeritan analogies, the style is akin to *aes* of Patricia in Baetica, and the heads to a group of *denarii*,[4] which have—since their portraits resemble that *aes*—been attributed by Laffranchi[5] to the same mint.

But there is a second subdivision of the present series. *Asses* of a totally different style (Pl. IV, 18)[6] have heads closely imitated from several *denarii*[7] which belong to the 'Caesaraugusta' group discussed in connection with the Macedonian *aes* of Primus (?) (p. 82). Moreover, all specimens in this subdivision have a shield only, without spear- and knife-head (Pl. V, 6), and a similar shield appears unaccompanied on the same group of *denarii*.[8]

Thus, in accordance with the current attribution of their models (the 'Patricia' and 'Caesaraugusta' *denarii*), the two categories of *aes* which have been described would be attributed to Farther and Nearer Spain respectively. But it appears necessary to conclude that such a view is based on a complete fallacy. Currency in the precious metals circulated everywhere: it is therefore wholly incorrect to assign it to mints on the grounds of portrait-similarities to local *aes*, since the latter merely imitated the ubiquitous *denarii*, not vice versa.[9] Thus the mints of 'Caesaraugusta' and 'Patricia', whose value even as generic appellations has been rightly doubted by Hill[10] and Regling,[11] must be eliminated.

[1] *BMC. Imp. Aug.* 277.
[2] Mattingly, *BMC. Imp.* p. cx; cf. Sanders, *Archaeologia*, LXIV, 1912, pp. 205 ff. [3] Hill, p. 127.
[4] *BMC. Imp. Aug.* 344 ff. Note especially the resemblance of Levis sale, 247.
[5] *R.it.* XXV, 1912, pp. 155 f.; id. *La monetazione di Augusto*, pp. 23–5. The generic appellations are retained by Mattingly, l.c. pp. cviii f.
[6] BM, Vatican, Naples, Turin, av. c. 181 grains.
[7] BM; cf. *BMC. Imp. Aug.* 339; others, cf. 335.
[8] *BMC. Imp. Aug.* 334.
[9] The present study has afforded the writer abundant proofs of this. For example, Laffranchi (*R.it.* 1916, p. 294; vide Bahrfeldt, *Münzstudien* I, 1923, p. 125) erred in allotting the principal CA issues to Lycia: both the Lycian League and the CA mints naturally used the same official models in widely separated regions. Similarly, the 'Caesaraugusta' group is copied on the issue of Primus(?), which is of Balkan provenance. The Roman colonies and *municipia* will supply further evidence of the incorrectness of Laffranchi's principle: the 'Patricia' group, supposedly of Baetican affinities, is imitated —in preference to the 'Caesaraugusta' group—on the *aes* of at least seven cities of Tarraconensis. Thus too even some of the *aes* coins of Carisius copy models from the 'Caesaraugusta' group rather than from Emerita itself. Nor were these prototypes imitated solely by the Spanish cities. For example, Corinth utilises each of them, in the same way as Gallic local and official *aes*—e.g. of Arausio(?) and Nemausus—imitate the portraits of Eastern *denarii*: presumably, but for their mint-mark, Laffranchi would attribute the Corinthian issues to Spain, and those of Nemausus to the East. Finally, it will be shown (p. 351) that the peregrine cities of Asia choose their models with especial frequency from the *denarii* assigned by Laffranchi to Patricia (p. 467). See also pp. 222, 269, 83, 470. [10] P. 98; cf. n. 73.
[11] *Phil. Woch.* 1924, pp. 364 ff.

PROVINCIAL ISSUES BY *LEGATI AUGUSTI* 123

It is, however, possible to find a use for the *denarii* in connection with the present issues: but this is of a chronological rather than a geographical order. It has been shown, in connection with the mintage of Primus(?) (p. 83), that the 'Caesaraugusta' group was not, as has been thought, contemporary with the 'Patricia' series, but was its predecessor, giving way to it in c. 19 B.C. Thus the use of prototypes from both groups for this Spanish *aes* with the type of a shield signifies the order in which the two subdivisions were issued.[1] The general principle that one of the latest models from the official series was copied by the *aes* of provincial cities and governors can be substituted for the false geographical arguments initiated by Laffranchi. When a new portrait of Augustus came into fashion, it was likely to be used for *aes* by officials and by communities throughout the Empire—having first been popularised by the *denarii*.[2] Thus portrait-resemblances, which have been used to such ill effect, can in general only be employed to establish a *terminus post quem*. If, as on these *asses* with the shield and on the issues of Primus (?), more than one model from the same group is employed, it is probable that the time-lag is negligible; and if, as is again the case with the present issue, a prototype from a subsequent group follows, there is a strong presumption that the two categories of *aes* correspond approximately in date with the two groups of *denarii*.[3]

Style (rather than the dangerous criterion of portraiture) suggests that the later subdivision of this series, which uses the 'Patricia' model, originated from **Farther Spain**, which was probably still one province. Specimens are found in the northwestern area:[4] and the prototype of the earlier group (c. 25–23 B.C.) confirms that they too, like the *denarii*, were issued for the needs of the war, and so in the *provincia Ulterior*. The mint or mints cannot be identified. The abandonment of these short-lived military issues in favour of a system of city-coinages was no doubt necessitated by the difficulties of communication and distribution in the peninsula,[5] and facilitated by the aptitude of the cities for the responsibility and privilege (p. 297).

2. GALLIA COMATA: Tribal Mint, Lugdunum(?)

A number of unsigned issues can be traced to this country also. One of these,[6] of rough fabric, has AVGVSTVS · · · ·, with his bare head to right, and on the reverse IMP X · · · · · and a horse (Pl. IV, 19). The style is Gallic: the type is the symbol of 'free' Gaul, and occurs on coinage of all parts of the *provincia Comata*.[7] The coin can be safely

---

[1] The eclecticism of peregrine cities is also of interest in this respect (pp. 349 ff.).
[2] Naturally, however, allowance must be made for arbitrary circumstances, such as time-lag, or the individual preference of a die-engraver for an obsolete portrait, or of a Greek for Hellenistic styles.
[3] An attempt to reconstruct the history of parallel silver issues is beyond the bounds of the present study: but see suggestions on p. 468.

[4] E.g. at Citania de Troña, Pontevedra (Garcia and Cuevillas, *MJSEA*. CXV [IV, 1930], p. 37). The definition as *pequeño bronce* could scarcely refer to the other variety of *as*, which is flatter and so larger.
[5] Cf. Syme, *CAH*. X, p. 343.
[6] Paris = M. *S*. IX, 247. 41.
[7] E.g. De La Tour, *Atlas des monnaies gauloises*, 4561, etc.

attributed to a Gallic tribe, though its legends suggest the co-operation or command of a Roman authority. A. Hirtius had previously utilised a tribal mint in the same way (p. 3). His issue and this are interruptions in the 'autonomous' coinage of the tribes, which were otherwise permitted to use their own money and their own types at least until the principate of Tiberius,[1] by whom the order for withdrawal was probably given.[2] The coin appears to be dated to 15–13 B.C., the time of Augustus's visit; this provides an explanation for the unusual introduction of the head and title of the *princeps* at a tribal centre.[3]

A second piece,[4] reading IMP. CAESAR (his bare head to right) (Pl. V, 9) and AVGVSTVS DIVI F. (bull to left), is reattributed by Mattingly from c. 27–25 B.C.[5] to c. 10 B.C., since the bull is clearly imitated from *denarii* of about the later date.[6] But its distinctive style, metal (*orichalcum*[7]), and titulature speak strongly against attribution to the official mint which struck the contemporary and entirely different 'Altar' money. The type of a bull is found,[8] and widely imitated by tribal moneyers, in Gallia Comata[9] and Narbonensis[10] and even in Britain[11] and perhaps Spain;[12] it perhaps refers to Augustus's sobriquet *Thurinus*.[13] The existence (if true) of a similar coin inscribed COPIA (p. 208) perhaps indicates that a special mint for small *aes* (whose deficiency in Gaul is underlined by the frequency of half-coins in the early 'Altar' series[14]) existed at Lugdunum itself, by the side of, but separately from, the official mint.

Another *orichalcum*[15] piece, with the type of an eagle,[16] has a laureate portrait (Pl. V, 8) whose truncation and general appearance are imitated from late *denarii* from Lugdunum[17] (A.D. 2–14), not from earlier *denarii* (15–11 B.C.)[18] or *asses* (c. 10 B.C.).[19] Its

---

[1] Strack, *BJ.* CXII, 1904, p. 426; cf. Neuss find, correcting Willers, *NZ.* XXXII, 1900, p. 136.

[2] *Annalen des Vereins für Nassauische Altertumskunde*, XXXIV, pp. 38 f.

[3] In the same way British tribal gold and silver (BM) represent Tiberius and perhaps Augustus.

[4] *BMC. Imp. Aug.* p. 93, 564.

[5] Grueber, *NC.* 1904, pp. 221 ff.

[6] E.g. *BMC. Imp. Aug.* 464 ff.

[7] Spectrogram 25. It is possible, though not probable, that a small Gallic *orichalcum* quarry was used (Forrer, *Zeitschrift für Ethnologie*, 1909, p. 458; cf. Davies, *Roman Mines in Europe*, p. 61 n. 6).

[8] E.g. Blanchet, *Traité*, p. 254 n., etc. Found throughout Gaul.

[9] E.g. Ambactus, ibid. p. 254 n. 7; Germanus, ibid. p. 255 n. 8; cf. Coutil, *Inventaire*, pp. 18, 39. Kremer, *Publications de la section des sciences historiques de l'Inst. Gd.-ducal de Luxembourg*, LXVII, 1938, p. 13, suggests that this was the issue of a native revolt. It is not Caesarian, *pace* Huber, *Jahrb. der Ges. f. lothringische Geschichte*, XI, 1896.

[10] E.g. T. Pom. Sex. f., ibid. p. 256 n. Senckler, *Jahrbücher des Vereins von Alterthumsfreunden im Rheinlande*, XXI, 1854, p. 84, plausibly considers him the grandson of Caesar's secretary Cn. Pompeius Trogus, the brother of the historian of that name, and so the kinsman of a *praefectus Vocontiorum*— no doubt the position of T. Pom. Sex. f. also. Vide, also, Justin XLV, 521.

[11] E.g. Cunobeline; Evans, *Coins of the Ancient Britons*, pl. XII, 15; *Hu.* III, p. 725. 37.

[12] Cf. Lorichs, *Recherches numismatiques*, p. 80. 403.

[13] Blanchet, *Comptes rendus des séances de l'Académie des Inscriptions*, 1919, p. 134.

[14] Strack, *BJ.* CVIII, 1902, pp. 1 ff.

[15] Spectrogram 24.   [16] *BMC. Imp. Aug.* 561 ff.

[17] E.g. ibid. 534, 511, 515.

[18] As Mattingly, ibid. p. cxviii n. 3.

[19] As Sydenham, *NC.* 1917, p. 76.

provenance is Gallic,[1] and the individual technique and lettering, coarser than those of contemporary 'Altar' coins, suggest that it too should not be allotted to the larger official mint. That these *orichalcum* pieces, though not lighter than Roman copper *quadrantes*,[2] are actually *semisses* is suggested by the much greater weight of a copper *semis*[3] at the end of the reign, which combines an obverse adapted from the 'Altar' pieces with the familiar reverse type of C. L. Caesares. This change of metal creates uniformity with the official mint; a similar *semis* of Tiberius is found later.[4] The separate existence of some workshop for small denominations with a limited circulation is confirmed by the persistence of little 'Altar' coins of poor style and varying metal with the heads not only of Tiberius[5] and Claudius,[6] when the larger mint had closed, but even of Nero[7] when it was reopening in another form.[8]

3. SYRIA: Sidon(?), Berytus, Laodicea(?)

Of the next coins to be signed by an official in an 'Imperial' province two specimens have been published, none attributed. Rauch[9] described a coin in his collection reading ΣΕΒΑΣΤ. ΑΥ····· (bare head r. of Augustus) and ΡΗΓΛΟΣ ΣΤΡΑΤ·····. The reverse legends end, in his version, with a number of incomprehensible signs. But he read them upside down. They are actually the letters ΗΓΟΣ, and the whole legend, as an extant piece[10] shows, is ΡΗΓΛΟΣ ΣΤΡΑΤΗΓΟΣ (Pl. IV, 21). The obverse reading is uncertain. Another[11] has ΣΕΒΑΣΤΟ····; on the reverse it reads ΡΗΓΛΟΣ only, like a smaller coin,[12] which has a star for type and apparently lacks an obverse legend (Pl. IV, 20). The heads of all but the last show a striking resemblance in features and style—if allowance is made for wear—to local coins of Balanea (Pl. XII, 20) (p. 331) and Berytus (Pl. IX, 10) (p. 260), towns on the Phoenician coast. On general grounds, and because they are of inferior style, both these local pieces are likely to imitate the issues of Regulus rather than to be their prototype. The Phoenician origin of Regulus's series, which the local analogies suggest, is confirmed by a similarity of reverse plan to coins of Berytus[13] and Damascus,[14] and by a line-beading that is peculiar to this region.[15] A *terminus post quem* is supplied for Regulus's coinage by his smallest piece, which has a head closely copied from Eastern silver coins of c. 20–18 B.C.[16] The issue, then, is Phoenician or Syrian,[17] and was made not long after c. 20 B.C.

The lack of ethnic would be unparalleled on a Greek local coin; Regulus is a Roman,

---

[1] E.g. Strack, *BJ*. CXII, 1904, pp. 419 ff., also *Rn.* 1894, pp. 24 f. (latter doubtful; cf. Blanchet, *Traité*, p. 216).
[2] E.g. eagle type 48·5 grains (*BMC. Imp. Aug.* 564); bull type 50·0–36·0 grains (*BMC. Imp. Aug.* 561 ff.).
[3] 77·0–66·2 grains (*BMC. Imp. Aug.* 589, etc.).
[4] Own collection.
[5] *BMC. Imp.* p. 127, no. 62 (*orichalcum*—Milan).
[6] Ibid. p. 196, no. 227.
[7] Ibid. p. 279 n.; Paris (copper), Copenhagen.
[8] Mattingly, *BMC. Imp.* pp. clxiii f.
[9] *BB*. v, 1870, p. 30; cf. Boutkowski, *DN*. 2631.
[10] *Wad.* 7451.   [11] Vienna.   [12] *Wad.* 7452.
[13] Berlin, Gotha.   [14] E.g. Paris.
[15] Mommsen, *ZfN*. XI, 1884, p. 187.
[16] Especially *BMC. Imp. Aug.* 682.
[17] This argument does not seem to contain the flaw in Laffranchi's similar deductions (p. 122), since here style, reverse plan, and beaded edge

and a Roman provincial official. But στρατηγός means *praetor*, or might naturally be used by a praetorian proconsul or *legatus*[1] emphasising rank rather than office; the *legati* of Syria-Cilicia,[2] on the other hand, were never of praetorian rank but always consular. Although it is true that Greek authors often used στρατηγός inaccurately[3] and even added it to ὕπατος, etc., to express *imperium*,[4] there is no reason to suppose that a governor's coin should be lax in such technicalities: similar Greek official issues at Cyrene, etc. (p. 69), show that no less care in this respect was exercised than on governmental coins with Latin inscriptions. An explanation for Regulus's title ΣΤΡΑΤΗΓΟΣ can be found in the history of the East during the period. Agrippa could not have held an Eastern command continually from 23 B.C., but it is generally agreed that at least after his return to the Orient in 17 B.C. he held some superior command in that half of the Empire (p. 428). Dio[5] expressly states that, even during his first visit to the East, in Syria at least Agrippa governed *in absentia* by his own ὑποστρατηγοί: the analogy can be extended to his second visit also. Now both ὑποστρατηγός, the word used by Dio, and στρατηγός, which is found on the present coins, appear elsewhere as the titles of praetorian *legati* (other than governors), in 'imperial' provinces.[6] The suggested attribution of these coins to Phoenicia, and their chronological limits, seem to necessitate the interpretation that Regulus was Agrippa's representative with that rank. He was probably Q. Articuleius Regulus,[7] who is celebrated by an inscription[8] of 14 B.C. as *praetor*, proconsul, and *legatus*.

The proof by these coins of the official validity of the title στρατηγός has repercussions on the administrative history of the period (p. 428). It remains here to discuss the location of the issues of Regulus within Phoenicia or its neighbourhood. Subsequent coins of Syro-Cilician *legati* have Latin inscriptions and military types: but these are Greek, and therefore probably for circulation in Greek cities. Now the 'enslavement' of Tyre and Sidon in 20 B.C.—that is, loss of ἐλευθερία[9]—did not affect the silver and bronze coinage of the former town,[10] but caused a gap of some years in the Sidonian issues (p. 345).[11] In view of their previous plentifulness,[12] this hiatus is unlikely to be accidental, especially since the recommencement of the coinage is signalised by

---

support the iconographic analogy: moreover, even though Regulus's coins were official, their circulation was infinitesimal compared to that of the 'Patricia' and 'Caesaraugusta' silver.

[1] Cf. Magie, *De Romanorum vocabulis, etc.*, p. 84, praetorian proconsul (cf. Waddington and Lebas, *Voyage archéologique*, III, 409); p. 87, praetorian *legatus pro praetore* (*BCH*. XXIII, 1899, p. 589).

[2] Still joined, Anderson, *CR*. XLV, 1931, pp. 189 f., pace Gwatkin, *Univ. of Missouri Studies*, V, 1930.

[3] E.g. Appian, *BC*. V, 10; Lydus, *De mag.* II, 2; cf. Chapot, *La province romaine proconsulaire d'Asie*, p. 282 n. 1; Magie, l.c. pp. 62, 96.

[4] Chapot, l.c. p. 284.   [5] LIII, 32. 1.

[6] Magie, l.c. II, p. 123, Vrind, *De Cassii Dionis vocabulis*, p. 94 n. 220.

[7] *PIR*.² I, 236. 1178; cf. Liebenam, *Legaten*, p. 398.

[8] *CIL*. IX, 331.

[9] Dio LIV, 7. 6; Suet. *Aug.* 47; cf. Honigmann, *PW*. (2R.), II, 2226.

[10] E.g. *BMC*. 183 ff., silver, 20/19 B.C.; 186 f. 17/16 B.C.; bronze 18/17 B.C.

[11] None known between Rouvier, *JIAN*. IV, 1901, 1391 (yr. 89 = 23/22 B.C.), and ibid. 1388 (yr. 101 = 11/10 B.C.).

[12] Rouvier, ibid.; previously not more than four years pass without coinage.

the appearance for the first time of the Imperial head on many of the bronze,[1] and of the word ΚΑΙ(σαρ) on the silver.[2] It seems possible that the gap was filled, and the humiliation emphasised, by the expedient of this official issue at Sidon, struck by the praetorian *legatus* who was acting as governor. This interpretation is also in accordance with the penetration of the coinage—shown by the local portraits—to not far distant Berytus and Balanea. Why Tyre was not equally deprived of coining rights is obscure, but in numismatic research uniformity should never be expected and is seldom found. It is at least consistent with this guess that, after Sidon's recovery of coining privileges, the *legati* coin in Latin—and elsewhere.

The first of these is P. Quinctilius Varus,[3] who was *legatus* in c. 7 to 3 B.C. (p. 396). He issued—probably, to judge from his record,[4] with a heavy margin of profit—two or three denominations[5] with the following types:

IMP. CAESAR AVGVSTVS: bare head of Augustus to right.
P. QVINCTILIVS VARVS (blundered in various forms[6]): two legionary eagles and standards.

There is no ethnic on these issues, which are clearly official. The same type occurs on later colonial pieces of Berytus[7] (a veteran colony since c. 14 B.C. [p. 259]), to which Mommsen[8] reattributes them from Ruscino in Gaul.[9] These coins, which lack the name of the city or its representatives, must have been struck at the colony by the *legatus*. They have the appearance of a hasty issue for some special occasion or emergency, and were possibly, therefore, issued in connection either with the punitive expedition to Palestine[10] after Herod's death, or with the legionary movements in the governorship of Varus, on the occasion of the Homanadensian War.[11]

The next issue, however, which cannot be similarly explained, shows that Varus's coins may equally have been ordinary peace-time currency for the legions. Q. Caecilius Metellus Creticus Silanus, who was *legatus* of the same province at least from A.D. 12/13 until his deposition in A.D. 17,[12] is recorded on a number of issues before and after the death of Augustus. A number of these can be shown to be colonial (p. 260); but there are a few small coins which are apparently official—though style,[13] type[14] and provenance[15] again require attribution to Berytus. Some of these have as their type an eagle, and on the obverse SILANVS AVG.,[16] SILAN. AVG.,[17] or SILANVS P. AVG.[18]

[1] Ibid. no. 1444, yr. 102 = 10/9 B.C.
[2] *BMC.* 113, yr. 106 = 6/5 B.C.
[3] *PIR.* III, p. 118. 27.
[4] Velleius II, 117.
[5] Macdonald, *NC.* 1904, p. 107.
[6] E.g. *BMC.* 56, P. QVINCTILLVS VVRS; Berlin, P. QVIHVLILLL·····RVS; Gotha, QVIIIVCTI·····; ibid. ·····TILVVVRVS.
[7] E.g. *BMC.* 58, 61, etc.
[8] *ZfN.* XI, 1884, p. 187.
[9] As e.g. Boutkowski, *DN.* II, p. 1395. 2380.
The error is repeated faithfully by Miss Newby (p. 87) despite warnings by Newell (ibid. n. 46).
[10] Momigliano, *CAH.* x, p. 338.
[11] Syme, *JRS.* XXIII, 1933, pp. 24, 29 ff.; Anderson, l.c. pp. 271 ff., 280.
[12] *PIR.*² II, 10. 64; cf. Liebenam, *Legaten*, p. 369 n. 11.
[13] Coins of Berytus similarly blundered (in trade, Milan). [14] von Weckbecker, l.c.
[15] Cf. Mommsen, *ZfN.* XI, 1884, p. 187.
[16] Gotha. [17] *BMC.* 54 (39 grains). [18] Berlin.

COINAGE BY *AUCTORITAS PRINCIPIS*, 27 B.C.–A.D. 14

That these were struck in Augustus's lifetime is suggested by a piece seen by Rouvier[1] with the first of these legends, and the head and name of that *princeps*. There can be little doubt that von Weckbecker[2] is right in interpreting P. AVG. as the common formula *Permissu Augusti*, rather than as the unparalleled and hypothetical *Pontifex Augusti*, or as *Pontifex* with the Nominative AVG(*ustus*) independently in the field.[3] If P(*ermissu*) AVG(*usti*) is accepted, the coins will provide confirmation of the *auctoritas principis*[4] by which, as has been already indicated, official *aes* was issued in 'imperial' and 'senatorial' provinces alike. The same interpretation establishes that, although *colonia* Berytus can coin PERMISSV SILANI (p. 260), the governor's own coinage there needs the sanction of Augustus's *auctoritas*. It is clear that the executive activity of the *princeps* has been modified since the coinage of P. Carisius (p. 119). Then the emphasis was on the *tribunicia potestas*, which, as will be shown, was exercised through the senate (p. 448); now the mediation of that body is dispensed with. This accords with the gradual crystallisation of the *auctoritas* of Augustus, but more particularly with the aggrandisement of his *consilium* in A.D. 13. Thenceforward its decrees had the validity of *senatus consulta*,[5] but did not, no doubt, bear that name, since its advice was tendered to the *princeps*, not the senate (p. 453). Thus the governors of A.D. 13–14, like Silanus, could obtain the right to coin, no longer from the senate, but from the *consilium*, now the medium of the *princeps*' executive activity. The relevant formula is correctly simplified from *ex s.c., auctoritate Caesaris, tribunicia potestate* to *permissu Augusti*.

Yet the colonial coinage of Berytus, where Silanus's official issue was struck, was minted, not *permissu Augusti*, but *permissu Silani*. This distinction of formulae bears witness to a natural precaution exercised by Augustus against the uncontrolled commandeering of city-mints and the infringement of local privilege by his subordinates. He was willing for such mints to strike their own coinage without reference to Rome itself, so long as his own cognisance of the more important official issues was maintained.

The type of an eagle on a similar small coin only inscribed AVG.[6] links the issues of Silanus with a further group—likewise unsigned by a *legatus*—whose types include *simpulum*[7] and *lituus*.[8] These are all ascribed by Rouvier to Berytus. So is another series which has the inscription CAESAR but a late laureate head of Augustus(?), and on the reverse a dolphin and trident in wreath (Pl. V, 13).[9] The type seems to indicate an official character, but the style is not that of the official series of Berytus or of any other of the issues which proceeded from that mint. The coins are, however, Syro-Phoenician in appearance, and must have originated either from a commandeered

---

[1] *JIAN*. III, 1900, p. 278, no. 494.
[2] L.c.
[3] Cf. Bahrfeldt, *BMB*. 1902, p. 6.
[4] Cf. *CIL*. x, 5393, *ex auctoritate Ti. Caesaris Augusti et permissu eius*.
[5] Dio LVI, 28. 2; cf. Hammond, p. 168; Dessau, *Geschichte der römischen Kaiser*, I, p. 134.
[6] *BMC. Phoenicia*, p. 53, Rome (36 grains).
[7] Rouvier, *JIAN*. III, 1900, no. 489.
[8] Not 'S' (von Weckbecker, l.c. p. 399. 3).
[9] Rouvier, l.c. nos. 486 f.; Paris, *BMC*. p. 58. 48 (52·8, 37·0 grains).

PROVINCIAL ISSUES BY *LEGATI AUGUSTI*   129

city-mint or a legionary station in that area. Laodicea is a probable choice,[1] since the sites of other camps would not warrant the marine type.[2]

The omission of all names but theirs indicates that Q. Silanus and P. Carisius were the responsible agents for the various coins that they sign. Their signatures provide valuable evidence for the superiority at this date, even in financial matters, of *legatus* to *procurator*. But there are other ways also of proving that at this period the procurators did not yet possess independent control over provincial finances.[3] Official coinages already discussed have indicated that the *senatus consultum*, and coinages bearing its mark, were current throughout the whole Empire, including the 'imperial' provinces; the 'senatorial' treasury on which this money was based was the *aerarium*. This view accords with Frank's demonstration that no central 'imperial' *fiscus* yet existed (p. 97): the *aerarium* was sufficiently controlled by the *auctoritas principis*. Just as official *aes* in Italy depended upon the *aerarium*, so, outside the peninsula, it depended upon the provincial departments of the *aerarium*, namely the *arcae* or *fisci*, where the funds accruing from taxes, etc., were stored to meet provincial expenses, and periodically were handed to the central treasury. This task was no doubt performed by the governors' representatives, whose presence in the *aerarium* is attested by inscriptions.[4]

It is therefore only to be expected that the officials superintending the departmental *bureaux* of the 'senatorial' *aerarium* should have been in the senatorial, and not the equestrian, service. This conclusion is corroborated by evidence concerning those important financial operations, the censuses. These were still invariably conducted by senators. Special *legati* (often *pro praetore*[5]) for this purpose are known to have been sent to Lugdunensis,[6] Spain,[7] etc. (even as late as Trajan[8]), but often also the provincial *legatus* himself presided: Quirinius is a famous example.[9] Conclusive against the control, in our period, of such financial activity by procurators is an inscription from the second or third century[10] with *primus umquam eq[ues] R[omanus] a censibus accipiendis*.[11] Provincial *legati* and senatorial officials were bound as much as procurators to the unique *auctoritas* of Augustus: there was no reason yet for the distrust which was to make the latter into influential spies, instead of co-operative lieutenants and subordinate economic advisers.[12] Even a single case of recalcitrance, by Volumnius in Syria,[13] may not be relevant, since his position is uncertain.[14] There was no 'dyarchy'.

[1] Tac. *Ann.* II, 79. 3; cf. Anderson, *CAH.* X, p. 283, for the camp.
[2] Anderson, l.c. pp. 282 f.
[3] *Pace* Waddington, *Fastes des provinces asiatiques*, p. 661.
[4] Delamare, *Rev. de phil.* 1895, p. 131 = *OGIS.* II, 494. [But see Last, *JRS.* 1944, pp. 58 f.]
[5] For the *imperium* of *legati*, see below, p. 136 n. 1.
[6] *CIL.* XIII, 6558.
[7] *CIL.* X, 680, etc.; cf. van Nostrand, *ES.* III, p. 145.

[8] Mommsen, *Inscriptiones Confoederationis Helveticae Latinae*, 175.
[9] Josephus, *AJ.* XVII, 13. 5; Luke ii, 2.
[10] Kubitschek, *PW.* III, 1920.
[11] Orelli, *Inscriptiones Latinae Selectae*, 6944; cf. Boissieu, *Inscriptions antiques de Lyon*, p. 269.
[12] The comprehensive commission of Licinus was an isolated experiment; cf. Stevenson, *RPA.* p. 119.
[13] Josephus, *AJ.* XVI, 369; cf. 277, 283, 344.
[14] Volkmann, *Münchener Beiträge z. Papyrusforschung*, XXI, 1935, p. 157 n. 5, calls him pro-

E

Thus there is evidence of many kinds to show that the procurators did not yet play an independent part in the conduct of provincial finances. In the 'imperial' provinces the *legati* themselves controlled the normal financial operations: the signatures of Spanish and Syrian governors appear on the coinage which they organised. It is to Creticus Silanus *legatus* himself that permission to coin was extended from Rome; he was the responsible financial official in his province. It has been pointed out that the *consilium Augusti*, which granted him permission, could decree with the validity of a *senatus consultum*, and so could govern the *aerarium*. The expression *Permissu Augusti* in no way alludes to Augustus's *patrimonium*: its relevance is to the national treasury, controlled by the *auctoritas principis* which this formula represents (p. 438). Nor does it justify the assumption that the *patrimonium* and the treasury were indistinguishable. Their distinction is attested by Dio[1] and confirmed by Augustus's own record of gifts from one to the other,[2] although the very size of these donations made the distinction sometimes seem merely formal.[3] But it was more than that; and, with all his constitutional discretion, Augustus never tried to dissemble the fact that he was *princeps*. Many coinages combine to show that the authority of *princeps* and senate was valid in every part of the Empire alike (p. 435). Thus the governors of 'imperial' provinces were both *legati Augusti* and representatives of the only national treasury, the senatorial *aerarium*. In 'imperial', as in 'senatorial' provinces (p. 428), the permission of Augustus is a product of his *auctoritas*—not of his *imperium*, which would not justify such a phrase (p. 439).

curator; but Bleckmann, *Klio*, XVII, 1921, p. 111, believes that he was a Jew of Herod's court, and distinct from the Roman official of that name, and ascribes moreover to the latter a military office.

[1] LIII, 16. 1; cf. Rice Holmes, *Architect*, II, p. 177.

[2] *RG*. 17.

[3] Cf. Duff, *Personality in Roman Private Law*, p. 59. This aspect is emphasised by Nilsson, *Eranos*, XII (1912), pp. 95 ff.

E. PROVINCIAL ISSUES BY EQUESTRIAN GOVERNORS

It was natural that knights who were acting *vice praesidis*[1] should superintend coinage for their own provinces, where this was needed, just as they appear to have countermarked it (p. 95). Two such series, each fulfilling a special requirement, are known.

1. JUDAEA: Caesarea Samariae(?)

The conversion of the Judaean ethnarchy of Archelaus into a Roman province in A.D. 6[2] was the occasion for a series of little coins, of pitiful style.[3] The legend is KAICAPOC,[4] but there is a discreet avoidance of Roman portraits or types[5] which might cause offence to the Jews' sensitive religious susceptibilities. The earliest coins bear the date 36[6] by the Actian era, that is, A.D. 6;[7] the province was not important enough for a new era.[8] However, the procurators had troops under their command, and possessed the *ius gladii*:[9] according to the latest view they owed no allegiance to the governors of Syria.[10] The coins were probably struck at Caesarea, which was the official Residence.[11] Their wide diffusion[12] bears witness to their official character. Both Coponius (6–9) and M. Ambibulus (9–12) struck two issues, but, like the equestrian officials whose coins we have next to discuss, they refrained from competing with 'senatorial' governors by placing their names on their money.

2. EGYPT: Alexandria

Throughout Augustus's principate the prefects of Egypt issued coinage at Alexandria, no doubt by virtue of their characteristic decree or διάταγμα[13] and under the immediate control of the ἰδιόλογος.[14] This currency could maintain itself at purely nominal values,[15] since Egypt was a land commercially self-contained and relied on its

---

[1] Hirschfeld, *Die kaiserlichen Verwaltungsbeamten*, p. 181 n. 4; cf. Mattingly, *BMC. Imp.* p. lix.
[2] Cf. Stevenson, *RPA*. p. 215.
[3] Cf. Schiffer, *Aréthuse*, 1930, p. 9.
[4] Hill, *BMC. Judaea*, pp. ci ff.
[5] Cf. Pick, *ZfN*. XIV, 1887, p. 306.
[6] Pick, l.c.; cf. Hill, l.c. p. ci: not ΛΓ (Madden, *Coins of the Jews*, p. 174; cf. Head, *HN*, p. 809).
[7] Pick, l.c., *pace* de Saulcy, *Numismatique de la Terre Sainte*, p. 70, Mommsen, *St.R*. III, p. 307 n. 1, based on wrong coin.
[8] Pick, l.c.
[9] Momigliano, *CAH*. X, p. 339; cf. Josephus, *AJ*. XVIII, 3.
[10] Horovitz, *Rev. de phil*. 1939, p. 51; id., *Revue belge de philologie et d'histoire*, XVII, 1938, p. 781.
[11] Schürer, *Geschichte des jüdischen Volkes*, II⁴, pp. 209 ff.; cf. Hill, *BMC. Judaea*, p. ci.
[12] E.g. found in Gallia Narbonensis and Aquitania, Blanchet, *NZ*. 1913, p. 195; in Epirus (Feniki), Ugolini, *Albania antica*, II, p. 167; etc.
[13] Vide Wilcken, *Hermes*, LV, 1920, pp. 27 ff.; Cuq, *Rev. hist. de droit français et étranger*, IV sér. XI, 1932, p. 112.
[14] Milne, *Catalogue of the Alexandrian coins in the Ashmolean Museum*, p. xviii.
[15] Id. *JEA*. 1927, pp. 135 ff.

export trade.[1] Augustus made no initial attempt to restore the standard that had depreciated under Cleopatra.[2] But his principate is notable for a series of fluctuations and experiments, chiefly to test Egyptian feeling.[3] The conservatism of the first coinage after Actium has already been noted (p. 68). Subsequent issues, still including pieces of 80, 40, 20 and ?5 copper *drachmae*,[4] diminish in weight[5] until c. 8–7 B.C., when there is a reorganisation on the standard of the *denarius*.[6] On this new basis begins a more plentiful output[7] of diobols, obols and *dichalca*:[8] but Milne[9] points out that the problem of the debased Ptolemaic silver tetradrachm was not solved.[10] Coins of Augustus's Egyptian series, being official, are occasionally found even in the West,[11] in spite of their high fiduciary value.

The Ptolemaic type of the first series (p. 68) gives way to imitations of official *cistophori* (c. 15 B.C.).[12] Later we find the Egyptian deity Euthenia (c. ?A.D. 1),[13] and the Greek Athena and Nike (c. ?A.D. 12).[14] To complete the hotch-potch, the capricorn symbol occurs after 2 B.C.[15] Earlier in the principate, a feature unique on the official coinage is introduced by the portrayal of Livia (Pl. V, 12), sometimes as ΛΙΟΥΙΑ ΣΕΒΑΣΤΟΥ.[16] This development was unknown to Hellenism;[17] the succession claimed by Augustus and shown by his use of the regnal era[18] was Pharaonic,[19] and made its appeal to the Egyptian nation itself. In this sense it is not untrue to say with Vogt: *Die Kaiserin hat...in Ägypten an der Herrschergewalt ihres Gemahls...teilgenommen*;[20] indeed, Livia's *auctoritas* in her own right was enormous.[21] But his additional statement

---

[1] Johnson, *AJA*. XXXVIII, 1934, p. 54; cf. Cahn, *RS*. XXVI, 1936, p. 173.

[2] Johnson, l.c. p. 49; cf. Segrè, *Studi italiani di filologia classica*, IV, 1926, fasc. IV. Thus no other official *aes* is admitted to Egypt (Johnson, *ES*. II, p. 432, cf. Milne, *JEA*. VIII, 1922, p. 159); but official gold and silver were current here as elsewhere (Mommsen, *Archiv für Papyrusforschung*, I, 1900, pp. 274 ff.).

[3] Milne, *Cat. Ashmolean*, p. xxxv.

[4] Regling, *ZfN*. 1901, p. 115; cf. Milne, *Cat. Ashmolean*, p. xvi.

[5] Milne, *JEA*. 1927, p. 139.

[6] Ibid.   [7] Id. *Cat. Ashmolean*, p. xviii.

[8] Id. *Annals of Archaeology and Anthropology*, VII, 1916, p. 59.

[9] *JEA*. 1927, p. 177.

[10] The fact that one issue contains 10 per cent of silver (cf. Dattari, *R.it.* 1902, p. 407), if of any significance at all, can be best interpreted merely as an attempt to gain confidence, like the high weight at which the *as* was struck at home.

[11] E.g. Gaul (Blanchet, *NZ*. 1913, pp. 194 ff., and on Rhine [Mulhouse, Colmar mus.]), Britain (Hill, *NC*. 1930, p. 335, Sutherland, *NC*. 1938, p. 311), Rhaetia (at Zillis: Caviezel coll., *Mitt. der antiquarischen Ges. in Zürich*, XXVI, 1903, p. 42), Lusitania (Lisbon mus.: Bayer, *Diario das primeiras viagens que fez pelas terras de Portugal*; cf. *Archeologo Portugues*, XXIV, 1920, p. 157, ibid. XXV, 1921, p. 132) and free Germany (Stuttgart mus., found at Cannstatt: Goessler, *Fundberichte aus Schwaben*, *NF*. I, 1922, p. 97. At Dreimannsdorf bei Salis: *Verhandl. der Berliner Ges. für Anthropologie*, XXIII, 1891, p. 225; cf. *Acta Dorpat*. III, 6, p. 112).

[12] Milne, *Cat. Ashmolean*, p. xxxv.

[13] Ibid. 23.   [14] Ibid. 25, 27.

[15] Ibid. 22.

[16] Vogt, *Alexandrinische Münzen*, p. 14.

[17] Ibid.

[18] Wilcken, *JRS*. 1937, p. 144; or era of κράτησις, Bell, *CAH*. x, p. 285 n.

[19] Cf. Bell, l.c. p. 285.   [20] Vogt, l.c.

[21] A striking manifestation of this is provided by her vast financial interests (cf. Hirschfeld, *Die kaiserlichen Verwaltungsbeamten*, pp. 26 f.)—including actually a private bank (cf. Herzog, *PW*. XVII, 1447).

that she had *Münzrecht* is based on an untenable view of portrait-rights (p. 228). In a country where Augustus was virtually king,[1] he could emphasise with freedom the 'royal family' and his dynastic intentions: after 8 B.C. we find also the portrait of Caius.[2] The imperialistic character of these coins is paralleled by a unique system of personal government.[3] And yet not only are the revenues of the region—it is never called *provincia*[4]—sent, like all other moneys, into the *aerarium*,[5] but Augustus can even say *Aegyptum imperio populi Romani adieci*.[6] Administrative peculiarities (caused by unwillingness to disturb an existing system) and precautions against their exploitation[7] make no difference to the essential unity of the Empire. Augustus was head of it and yet outside its structure, so that he could identify his interests equally with the *populus Romanus* and the senatorial *aerarium*: all parts of the Empire were the domain of *princeps*, senate and people alike.

[1] Cf. Reinmuth, *Klio Beih.* XXXIV, 1935, p. 2. Insufficiently known proof of this fact is supplied by two Egyptian inscriptions (*Annales du Service des Antiquités de l'Égypte*, IX [1909], p. 188, and *Recueil*, XXVI, 1904, p. 52), which, as rightly interpreted by Spiegelberg (*Zeitschr. für ägyptische Sprache und Altertumskunde*, XLIX, 1911, p. 85), reveal that Augustus was known as 'the Roman', i.e., according to local usage, 'the founder of the Roman dynasty'.

[2] *BMC.* 34. But probably not of Tiberius: Vogt, l.c. p. 15, *pace* Dattari, *R.it.* 1900, pp. 280 ff.

[3] Bell, *CAH.* X, pp. 284 ff.; p. 284 n. 2, differences from other provinces underestimated by van Groningen, *Aegyptus*, VII, 1926, pp. 189 ff.

[4] Cf. Horovitz, *Rev. de phil.* 1939, p. 47.

[5] Velleius II, 39. 2.

[6] *RG.* 27; cf. Reinmuth, *Klio Beih.* XXXIV, 1935, p. 2; Zmigryder-Konopka, *VIIIe Congrès int. des sciences hist.* II, 1938, p. 23.

[7] Cf. Bell, *CAH.* X, pp. 284 ff.; Mitteis-Wilcken, *Grundzüge und Chrestomathie der Papyruskunde*, I, 1, p. 28 n. 2; Levi, *Aegyptus*, V, 1924, pp. 231 ff.

F. PROVINCIAL ISSUES BY 'SENATORIAL' GOVERNORS

1. HISPANIA BAETICA: Castulonian mines

Baetica is likely to have been part of the 'imperial' province of Farther Spain at the date of the war coinage with a shield (p. 121); but it was probably transferred to the senate during Augustus's visit in 15–14 B.C.[1] From within its borders comes a coin of exceptional character and rarity, with the legend SC on both sides. It has a fairly late portrait of Augustus (with *lituus*), and the type of a horse.[2] The only known specimen (Pl. V, 7)[3] was found near el Centenillo, in the district of Castulo;[4] the issue has been rightly attributed to the **Castulonian mines**[5]—still within the borders of Baetica at this date.[6] This mintage stands alone in the period: coinage of mines does not reappear until the second century.[7] Hill writes that the letters SC 'can hardly represent anything but the usual formula *senatus consulto*, and it must be merely a coincidence that they are also the initials of the company which worked the mine'[8]—since they are stamped on coins, buckets, seals, etc., from the same site.[9] However, it should be noted that the repetition of the formula on the coin is entirely unusual; it strongly suggests that both the senatorial decree and the company's signature are represented.[10] Hill suggests S(*ocietas*) C(*astulonensis*). The identity of the abbreviations would not cause difficulty; formality was satisfied by the appearance of both. At all events, the senatorial formula occurs at least once.[11] It indicates that these mines at least had already passed into state control: although many were still privately owned,[12] a number had belonged to the government even under the Republic.[13] But since Castulo and its mines were still at this time within the borders of Baetica, it is difficult to generalise from a later period[14] to postulate ownership by Augustus. Control by his *auctoritas*, however, is scarcely questionable: since the mines were naturally of importance to him, there is every reason to suppose that the *senatus consultum* here recorded was, like those enabling other coinages with the same formula, moved *Caesaris auctoritate*. This was the regular means of interference in the 'senatorial' sphere. There is not enough evidence to de-

---

[1] Cf. Wallrafen, *Die Einrichtung und kommunale Entwicklung der römischen Provinz Lusitanien*; van Nostrand, *UCPH*. IV, 2, 1916, p. 96; Syme, *RR*. p. 395 n. 1. Mommsen, *RGDA*.[2] p. 222, recants his attribution of the change to Tiberius in ed. I, v, p. 25.

[2] Hill and Sandars, *JRS*. I, 1911, p. 100; Mattingly, *BMC. Imp. Aug.* 304.

[3] BM.

[4] *JRS*. l.c. p. 103.

[5] Ibid.; cf. Mattingly, l.c., n.

[6] Sutherland, *JRS*. XXIV, 1934, p. 38. See also pp. 37, 39.

[7] *BMC. Imp*. III, p. 234. 1106 ff.

[8] L.c. p. 100.

[9] Ibid. p. 102.

[10] Cf. Davies, *Roman Mines in Europe*, p. 13.

[11] It appears also on a mine-coin of Trajan (Egger sale (1913) 753; cf. M. and S. II, p. 295. 769).

[12] Cf. van Nostrand, *ES*. III, p. 166; Albertini, *CAH*. XI, p. 493.

[13] Cf. Stevenson, *RPA*. p. 153.

[14] Hirschfeld, *Die kaiserlichen Verwaltungsbeamten*, pp. 153 ff.; Rickard, *JRS*. XVIII, 1928, pp. 136 f.

PROVINCIAL ISSUES BY 'SENATORIAL' GOVERNORS 135

termine whether his procurators already shared supervision of the mines with the senatorial quaestors who were still the regular financial officers in these provinces (p. 136); but, at this stage, it is likely that the role of the procurators was largely advisory, like that of the *princeps* their master.

2-3. CYRENE, CNOSSUS(?)

A. Pupius Rufus, *quaestor pro praetore* of Cyrenaica, issued coinage for this region shortly after Actium with Greek inscriptions and types of local interest (p. 69). In 27 the joint province of Crete and Cyrenaica was revived,[1] and the reorganisation of the *aes* in 23 brought a renewal of coinage of Cyrenaican style and provenance,[2] but with Latin legends and Roman types. IMP. AVG. TR. POT. appears, in a laurel-wreath on *dupondii*—in imitation of the Roman *sestertii*[3]—and in a circle on *asses*;[4] the former show a *sella castrensis* on the reverse, while the *asses* have no type. These coins are signed by PALIK. PR.[5] and CAPITO Q.[6] The issues of Lollius(?) Palikanus[7] are shown to be the earlier by their higher weight and closer imitation of the Roman models: both of these considerations suggest a date very soon after 23. There are several parallels for the use of PR. as an abbreviation for PR(*aetor*), expressing the rank of a proconsul, or even perhaps for PR(*o consule*) (pp. 33, 61, 138, 197).

The issues of Capito, like those of Palikanus, have a *sella castrensis*. This was a variant of the *sella curulis*, intended for camp use:[8] it was reserved for commanders,[9] and its presence decisively shows that Capito possessed the *imperium* and was *quaestor pro praetore*.[10] Even in the Republic quaestors of double provinces had held this rank.[11] So, under Octavian, had P. Cornelius Scipio in Achaia[12] and A. Pupius Rufus in Creta-Cyrenaica itself. Pupius and Capito also recall the Republican custom that, in the event of a governor's absence or inaccessibility, the *locum tenens* had regularly been his quaestor[13]—whereas at a later date the deputies of proconsuls were their

---

[1] Cf. Strabo XVII, 840.
[2] Cf. attribution of Robinson, *BMC. Cyrenaica*, p. ccviii.
[3] *BMC. Imp. Aug.* 134, etc.
[4] *BMC. Cyrenaica*, p. cxxxvii.
[5] Ibid. p. 120. 44.
[6] Paris, Munich: ibid. p. ccviii.
[7] Perhaps a son of the *IIIvir monetalis* of c. 47 B.C.; ibid. p. ccxxiv.
[8] Ibid. p. ccxii; cf. Chapot, *Daremberg and Saglio*, IV, 1180, s.v., Helbig, *Abh. Göttingen, Philol.-hist. Kl. NF.* X, 3, 1908, p. 37.
[9] Cf. Longpérier, *Rev. arch. NS.* XVIII, 1868, p. 107; Chapot, l.c.
[10] Cf. Kübler, *PW.* (2R.), II, 1312: also Robinson,

l.c. p. ccxxiii, for Pupius Rufus; inexplicably contradicted for Capito, ibid. p. ccxxv.
[11] E.g. Spain (*CIL.* VI, 1276), Cn. Piso, cf. Borghesi, *Œuvres*, I, p. 484; Macedonia-Achaia (L. Sestius, see p. 16; for L. Atratinus *pro pr.*, p. 393); for quaestors of Cyrene, vide Jones, *CERP.* p. 360; cf. P. Licinius *pro q.* [*pro pr.*?] (p. 35). For the double quaestorship of Sicily, see p. 68.
[12] *IG.* 3580, cf. *PIR.*[2] I, 355. 1438, whose date 25 B.C. is unnecessarily late. P. Scipio is exactly paralleled by A. Pupius Rufus.
[13] Cic. *Div.* 2. 15. 4; *Att.* VI, 4, etc.; cf. Mommsen, *St.R.* II[3], p. 566. It is noteworthy that camp-construction was based on the duality of *praetorium* and *quaestorium*.

legati.[1] Even under Tiberius the quaestor still had pride of place:[2] in 'senatorial' as in 'imperial' provinces (p. 129), the procurators were as yet comparatively obscure,[3] the proconsul's liaison with Rome being maintained by a representative at the *aerarium*.[4] It is not therefore surprising that when—in double provinces or in other special circumstances (p. 141)—the task of a proconsul's chief lieutenant warranted the *imperium*, the quaestor was still selected for this distinction.

It is likely, then, that Capito held the rank of *quaestor pro praetore* as deputy in Cyrene for the proconsul of Creta-Cyrenaica. These proconsuls generally resided at Gortyna:[5] but there are special reasons for thinking that Capito's superior officer was stationed elsewhere. A third issue at Cyrene bears the name of Scato *pro cos.* (p. 137):[6] this emphasises the peculiar position of Capito, since his coinage is thus both preceded and followed, at brief intervals, by pieces with the names of proconsuls of Creta-Cyrenaica.[7] The contrast between their titles and Capito's is striking. Elsewhere, too, issues by governors are regular, but no Augustan quaestor signs coinage by himself: this was one of the Republican customs which the *princeps* did not revive. It is necessary to investigate the exceptional circumstances which must have caused Capito's interruption of normal routine. The fragmentary historical tradition is fortunately adequate for their reconstruction. The inclusion of the Syrtis Minor in Cyrenaica by the Agrippan source used by Pliny[8] makes it clear that for some time between 27 and 12 B.C. the province was enlarged.[9] This deduction is confirmed by the record of a war

---

[1] Mommsen, l.c. n. 4; cf. Liebenam, *PW*. IV. 920. Hence the gradual attainment by these officials also of a propraetorian *imperium* (cf. von Premerstein, *PW*. XII, 1143), which they had not necessarily had during the Republic. In the time of Augustus they still were junior to the quaestors (see pp. 140 f.), and are therefore unlikely to have regularly possessed *imperium* (p. 435). An inscription, cited by Borghesi (l.c. 1, p. 484), of C. Plautius C.f. Rufus *leg. pro pr.* of Sicily (*CIL*. IX, 5834) does not contradict this conclusion, since (1) there is no reason to identify him with Augustus's *IIIvir a.a.a.f.f.* of that name (p. 91 n. 2; Holm III, p. 530, *PIR*. III, 46. 360), since the *leg. pro pr.* was C.f. and perhaps also €.n. (cf. *CIL*. IX, 6384). (2) The inscription ends with the phrase *provincia defensa*. This suggests a special commission such as warranted, even under Augustus, the title of *legatus pro praetore* in 'senatorial' provinces—cf. the tax-collectors. Vide also Kubitschek, *PW*. III, 1920.

[2] Cf. Dio LVII, 14.

[3] The collection of *stipendia* was in Africa still contracted to *publicani* (Stevenson, *CAH*. x, p. 196 n. 3; Rostovtzeff, *PW*. VI. 2385; cf. *ILS*. 901), and was in all 'senatorial' provinces superintended by the governor (Mommsen, St.R. II³, p. 267). Even under Tiberius the procurators of Asia are only those who τὰ αὐτοκρατορικὰ χρήματα διοικοῦσι (Dio LVII, 23: cf. Jackson, ed. Tac. *Ann.* IV, 15 n. 4). The only procurator of a 'senatorial' province honoured with a coin-portrait under Augustus, M. Pompeius Macer, owes this distinction to his prestige as *amicus principis* (see below, p. 389). The quaestors were still the chief financial officials. On them vide Lauria, *Annali della R. Univ. di Macerata*, III, 1928, pp. 92 ff.

[4] *OGIS*. II, 494; cf. Delamare, *Rev. de philologie*, 1895, p. 131. The consuls maintained the same practice, *IGRR*. III, 83.

[5] Cf. Romanelli, *CAH*. XI, p. 663.

[6] *BMC*. 39 ff.

[7] Scato cannot have been proconsul of Africa, since there is no record or likelihood of his consulship.

[8] *NH*. V, 38; VI, 209.

[9] Cf. Romanelli, *CAH*. XI, p. 668; Gsell VIII, pp. 164 f.

PROVINCIAL ISSUES BY 'SENATORIAL' GOVERNORS 137

against the Marmaridae[1] and Garamantes[2]—far south of the Greater and Lesser Syrtis respectively—conducted by P. Sulpicius Quirinius, apparently in c. 15 B.C.[3] Quirinius is now generally recognised to have been at this time governor of Creta-Cyrenaica[4] (not Africa[5] or Syria[6]). The inclusion of the Garamantes in his sphere of operations corroborates Pliny's evidence for the enlargement of *provincia* Creta-Cyrenaica.[7] This extension was suggested by experience: L. Cornelius Balbus, whose African *provincia* in c. 21–20[8] had included the Garamantes but not the Marmaridae, had, as the renewed outbreak of revolt indicates, been unable permanently to subjugate either of these powerful nations. Quirinius aimed particularly at the Marmaridae, as yet untouched, but his command was planned for the simultaneous suppression of their ally. Now while he was in the deserts to the distant south of his province, someone must have remained to conduct its civil government—probably Capito. It is not so significant that he is called *pro praetore*, since the quaestor who resided at Cyrene is likely to have always borne this title: but only the warlike circumstances of Quirinius's governorship could have warranted the transference of the ordinary administration of the province from the proconsul to this *quaestor pro praetore*—and to this transference the coinage of Capito, interrupting the normal proconsular issues, bears witness. Quirinius bore the same relation to his quaestor Capito as Augustus bore to his *legati*, who often, like Capito, possessed *imperium*: but neither Capito nor the *legati* held the *auspicia*, being subordinate to an *imperium maius* (p. 435).

Capito, then, may be attributed to c. 15 B.C.,[9] and Palikanus to the years between 23 and c. 15. The enlargement of the province can only have lasted a very short time,[10] so that it is not surprising to find a return to proconsular coinage—under Scato.[11] His issues include four denominations. A coin of c. 92·5 grains has a ram on the obverse,[12] and SCATO (monogrammed) in a wreath on the reverse; another averaging c. 35 grains has the head of Libya, and the same monogram, abbreviated, beside a serpent.[13] A more pretentious group includes a piece of c. 246 grains with the heads of Augustus

---

[1] For these vide Kees, *PW*. XIV, 1883.

[2] Vide Dessau, *PW*. VII, 751.

[3] This is the most recent conclusion, of Syme, *RR*. p. 399 n. 1. An earlier date was preferred by Cagnat, *L'armée romaine d'Afrique*, p. 6; Mommsen, *RGDA*. pp. 170 f.; Ritterling, *PW*. XII, 1224; and a later one by Zumpt, *Commenta Epigraphica*, II, p. 92. Quirinius's successor may perhaps have been C. Sentius Saturninus (cf. Tissot, *Fastes de la province romaine d'Afrique*, p. 40 no. 41).

[4] Syme, Cagnat, Mommsen, Ritterling, ll.cc.; Anderson, *CAH*. X, p. 271; Groag, *PW*. (2R.), IV, 825.

[5] As Zumpt, l.c.

[6] As von Domaszewski, *Philologus*, LXVII (*NF*. XXI), 1908, pp. 4 f., corrected by Groag, l.c.

[7] Pliny's testimony makes it unnecessary to explain away the Garamantes as a 'collateral branch' of that race to the East, as Cagnat, l.c.; cf. Groag, l.c. 826.

[8] Cf. Groag, *PW*. IV, 1270; Pallu de Lessert, *Fastes des provinces africaines*, p. 70.

[9] An Augustan Capito at Cyrene (*IGRR*. I, 1026) was perhaps his freedman: his daughter's name is Irene.

[10] Cf. Romanelli, *CAH*. XI, p. 668.

[11] Probably a Vettius or a Magulnius: cf. *PIR*. III, 181; Robinson, *BMC. Cyrenaica*, p. ccxxiv. For the Marsian Vettii Scatones, vide Syme, *RR*. p. 91 n. 5.

[12] *BMC*. 42.

[13] Ibid. 43.

and Agrippa (CAESAR TR. POT. AGRIPPA), and SCATO PRO COS. in wreath,[1] and another of c. 170 grains with Augustus's head (CAESAR TR. POT.) and a *sella castrensis* (SCATO PR.).[2] Robinson[3] suggests that the differences in type between the two larger and two smaller denominations may be due to separate governorships of c. 27 and c. 18–12 B.C. But there are several obstacles to acceptance of the earlier date. In the first place, the resemblance in type of the smaller denominations to the issues of A. Pupius Rufus (c. 29–27 B.C.) (p. 69) is not in any way remarkable. The types in question are a serpent and a ram—it is difficult to think of any more natural choice for an Augustan moneyer in this province. The serpent appears on the smallest denomination: the only piece of similar size since Actium was that of Pupius, which was therefore an obvious model. The community of types, then, is not evidence for a close correspondence in date. A serpent was a national badge,[4] and was considered the regular device for these small coins whenever they were struck. Moreover, Scato's type is by no means similar to Pupius's in execution. Again, why should the ram of Ammon[5] not be repeated, as Pupius himself was repeating it from earlier issues?[6] Here, too, there are signs of stylistic evolution between Pupius and Scato. Both these types of Scato, then, ram and serpent, are perfectly suitable to c. 18–12 B.C. A second objection to Robinson's division can be derived from the untitled name SCATO on these smaller pieces. Under Augustus no one except those of equestrian rank issued coinage which totally omitted their title of office: Scato was clearly not a knight, but the omission on the smaller pieces is easily comprehensible if they were part of a series including the larger ones specifying the title PRO COS. Indeed, the even gradation of weights strongly suggests that the four denominations were contemporary, and part of the same system. Palikanus and Capito strike *asses* of rather more than 100 grains;[7] Scato's pieces are probably *sestertius*, *dupondius*, *as* and *semis* (or *quadrans*), all based on a very slightly lower standard. The stylistic divergency between the two larger and two smaller of these coins may be explained, not by differences of date, but by the dual character of the *provincia*, which had already caused double coinage at an earlier period (p. 35). The small pieces were clearly intended for Cyrenaica, but the larger ones are of a general character, and probably did service for both parts of the province. They are not dissimilar in style from the colonial series of Cnossus (p. 261)—near the proconsular residency—where they are likely to have been struck.[8]

The slight reduction in weights suggests that these contemporary issues of Scato were a little later than those of Palikanus and Capito. This conclusion is confirmed

---

[1] *BMC.* 39. [2] Ibid. 40.
[3] Ibid. p. ccxxiv.
[4] Vide Robinson, l.c. p. ccxxiii. See below, p. 141, for an explanation of the type.
[5] Ibid. p. clxviii.
[6] Ibid. pp. liv, 105.
[7] Robinson, l.c. p. ccxxvii.

[8] Sestini's reference to Cyrenaican provenance (*Fontana*, I, p. 126) must be understood to refer only to the issues of L. Lollius, *pace* Robinson, l.c. p. ccix. But, even if Cyrenaican finds occurred, they would not contradict the present view since intercirculation is to be expected between two parts of a joint province.

PROVINCIAL ISSUES BY 'SENATORIAL' GOVERNORS 139

by changes in execution and fabric, and by the head of Agrippa which occurs on the *sestertii*. The gold and silver—and, for that matter, other official coinages also—do not portray him before 18 B.C.:[1] this, too, is official currency, and no tenure of the province by Agrippa had warranted his earlier appearance.[2] Scato's governorship is therefore most likely to belong to the proconsular year 13–12. The subsequent fate of the province will be seen to be intimately bound up with that of Africa.

4. AFRICA: Hadrumetum, uncertain Byzacenian mint

M. Acilius Glabrio has already struck an official coin, at an unknown mint, before the reorganisation of the *aes*, in 25 B.C. (p. 81). There are five other types whose lack of ethnic makes it impossible to consider them purely local.

(1)[3] ········STVS TR. POT. XVII. IM····· head of Augustus to right.—O.C.S. in wreath; laurel-branches. 7–6 B.C.; *sestertius*.

(2)[4] CAESAR AVGVSTVS head to right—C. CAESAR AVGVST. F., L. CAESAR AVGVST. F. bare heads of Caius and Lucius facing one another. *Sestertius*.

(3)[5] AFR. FA. MAX. COS. PRO COS. VIIVIR EPVLO head to right of Africanus Fabius Maximus, proconsul c. 6–5 B.C.[6]—C. LIVIN. GALLVS Q. PRO PR. elephant crushing serpent. *As* (Pl. IV, 28).

(4)[7] IMP. CAES·····DIVI F. P. P. head of Augustus to right, *lituus*.—L. PASS-[IENVS] RVFVS IMP. head to right of L. Passienus Rufus, proconsul and *imperator* c. A.D. 3.[8] *Sestertius* (Pl. IV, 26).

(5)[9] IMP. CAESAR DIVI F. AVGVS[TVS P. P.] head of Augustus to right—TI. CAESAR AVG. F. IMP····· head of Tiberius to right, *lituus*. *Sestertius*.

The reverse inscription of the last piece should be restored IMP[V., VI. or VII.], c. A.D. 8–14. A coin on which Borghesi[10] professed to decipher the name C[N]. P[IS]ONE,

---

[1] *BMC. Imp. Aug.* 110 ff.

[2] It will be shown elsewhere (p. 428) that Agrippa was *legatus* of the Asiatic provinces from 18 to 13: but Josephus explicitly limits his command to these (*AJ*. XVI, 86). Creta-Cyrenaica was not included among the *transmarinae provinciae*—those 'beyond the Ionian Sea' (ibid. XV, 350; cf. Stuart Jones, *CAH*. X, p. 142)—any more than Sicily or Africa.

[3] Paris; Cohen, *Description historique des monnaies frappées sous l'empire romain*, I, p. 827—misreading, repeated by Newby (p. 31).

[4] Hague, Paris; Muller II, p. 62. 39; *BMC. Imp.* p. 119.

[5] Hague, etc.; Muller II, p. 61. 37, Marchese coll. sale (Santamaria, 1924) 51.

[6] As Renault, *Bulletin archéologique du comité des travaux historiques et scientifiques*, 1897, p. 250, correcting Muller, l.c. (5–4 B.C.) and Tissot, *Fastes de la province romaine d'Afrique* (4–3 B.C.); *PIR*. II, 48. 37.

[7] Paris; Muller, *Suppl.* p. 43. 39 a.

[8] Velleius II, 216. 2; cf. *CIL*. VIII, 16456; *PIR*. III, 15. 111.

[9] Paris, BM, Hague (each contributing part of legend).

[10] Cf. Cavedoni, *Bullettino archeologico italiano*, I, 1862, p. 174.

although cited even by Groag and Stein,[1] is clearly seen by a Paris specimen[2] to be a colonial issue of Hippo, reading HIPPONE LIBERA (p. 224).

It is possible to assign (3) with certainty to Hadrumetum, since a coin bearing the ethnic of that city has the same individual style, portrait, titulature and fabric (p. 228), and is clearly struck by the same mint.[3] That the omission of the ethnic on (3) is not accidental is shown by an extremely close stylistic resemblance to (1) and (2), where it is equally lacking, and which can hardly be from another mint. (4) and (5) are also clearly from the same region, though not necessarily from Hadrumetum itself. The whole series, on each coin of which the ethnic is absent, seems to have an official and commemorative character. It presents a number of other unusual features. The tribunician power with a number on (1) (followed probably by a numbered imperatorship) is exceptional on official Augustan *aes* from provincial mints (p. 446); Passienus's *cognomen imperatoris* is unparalleled at so late a date; the conjoined portraits of Caius and Lucius are unique on official *aes* (but see pp. 144 f.).

Furthermore, these are the only official coins of Augustus's principate which include the portraits of proconsuls. It should be noted that both the governors who thus exceptionally allow their heads to be placed on their *aes* were full-fledged *amici principis*—a class already virtually defined,[4] to whose exaltation much publicity was devoted in the period to which these coins fall. Agrippa and Drusus were dead, Tiberius was in eclipse, and steps were taken to encourage loyal helpers.[5] The synchronisation of numismatic propaganda to this end in the great 'senatorial' provinces is discussed elsewhere (p. 228). The outstanding repute of Passienus is indicated by his now exceptional *cognomen imperatoris*:[6] he was the first man with this Italian name-formation to reach the consulship.[7] Africanus Maximus—like his brother Paullus in Asia (p. 387)—was portrayed also on city-coinages in his province (p. 228): he was a relation by marriage to Augustus,[8] and the *Lex Pompeia* seems to have been neglected for his early appointment as proconsul.[9]

Africanus's issues reveal another respect in which Augustus's lack of support within his family caused him to enhance the dignity of the senior proconsuls. The coins bear on the reverse the name of C. Livineius Gallus *quaestor pro praetore*. There are two reasons for thinking that this title is exceptional. First, the supposition that all provincial quaestors—not only quaestors of double provinces—already bore this title from 27 B.C.[10] is wholly unsupported by evidence from the principate of

---

[1] *PIR.*² II, 59. 287.
[2] Cf. Cohen, l.c. I, p. 185; Boutkowski, *DN.* p. 225; also Constantine mus.
[3] Cf. Muller II, p. 61. 37. The British Museum specimen is of Tunisian provenance.
[4] von Premerstein, pp. 223 f.; Syme, *RR.* p. 385, etc.
[5] Syme, *RR.* pp. 420 ff.
[6] Cf. Velleius II, 116. 2; *ILS.* 120; Syme, *CAH.* x, p. 347. See below, p. 430 n. 2.
[7] Syme, *JRS.* XXVIII, 1938, p. 123 n. 70.
[8] *PIR.* II, 48. 37, 38.
[9] Cf. Renault, *Bull. arch. du com.* 1897, p. 250.
[10] Borghesi, *Œuvres*, I, pp. 482 ff.; Dittenberger, *IG.* III, p. 120; Mommsen, *St.R.* II³, p. 246 n. 4.

PROVINCIAL ISSUES BY 'SENATORIAL' GOVERNORS 141

Augustus.[1] In the Republic this had not been the case,[2] and such a view is very inappropriate to so cautious a dispenser of *imperium* and so strong a traditionalist as the first *princeps*. Borghesi must admit that many quaestors show no signs of being *pro praetore*.[3] Secondly, the fact that only one other quaestor places his name on Augustan issues suggests that coinage cannot any longer be considered the prerogative of the quaestors even of double provinces: indeed, the official in question, Capito, owed his mintage to the inaccessibility of his proconsul for purposes of civil administration (p. 137). From these considerations it must be inferred that the propraetorian *imperium* of Livineius, and his name on official coinage, are due to exceptional circumstances.

Such a probability is strengthened by the type of the coin. This is derived from the coinage of Caesar,[4] whose name (in Punic[5]) and whose dignity[6] the elephant represented: it was *Caesaris armentum*.[7] Its action in crushing the serpent denotes the conclusion of a successful campaign.[8] Africanus's imitation of the type is peculiarly apt by reason of the special relevance of the serpent to Africa. It appears throttling the Turdetanian bull on coinage of Bogud's supporters at Lascuta;[9] but it was particularly the symbol of Ammon[10] and thus the national emblem of Cyrenaica,[11] on whose earlier coinage under Augustus it has twice been noted together with the head of Ammon and his ram (pp. 69, 137). Now Ammon was the emblem of Cyrenaica because of his great shrine to the south of the province, at Ammonium (Siwa).[12] This was in the middle of the territory of the Marmaridae, to whom therefore the god bore a special relation. The symbolism of this coin takes on a new importance when it is recollected that there was a recrudescence of hostilities against this nation near the beginning of the last decade B.C.,[13] and that war was still raging during the tenure of Maximus in Africa.[14] It has been shown that an earlier campaign necessitated the junction of part of Africa with Cyrenaica (p. 136): it is tempting to suppose that this coin, with a type so significantly referring to suppression of the people of Ammon by Caesar, bears

---

[1] The inscriptions Borghesi quotes are much later: the list can be checked by reference to *PIR*.² I, 13. 78; II, 34. 1403; *PIR*. II, 11. 64, 17. 107, 200. 274; III, 46. 360, 208. 326; and *CIL*. II, 1282, 1371; III, 14387*d*; V, 864; VIII, 2747, 2754; IX, 4194; X, 525, 1122, 4864, 6659, 7192, 7228, 7235–6, 7258, 7266, 7344, 8291; XII, 3164, 3169, 3171*b*, 3173; XIV, 4464–6; Klein, *Die römischen Verwaltungsbeamten*, p. 287. 3.

[2] Mommsen, l.c. p. 651; Borghesi, l.c. II, p. 405. Exceptions had only been due to double provinces and to war-emergencies; cf. Stevenson, *RPA*. p. 86.

[3] L.c. I, p. 485—*un amore di brevità* is a poor reason for failure to allude in any way to the vital part of a title.

[4] *BMCR*. II, p. 391.

[5] Spartian, *Vita Aelii*, 2; cf. Eckhel, *DN*. VI, p. 5; Clermont-Ganneau, *Recueil d'archéologie orientale*, I, 1888, p. 233.

[6] Artemidorus, *Onirocr*. II, 12; cf. Eckhel, l.c.

[7] Juvenal XII, 106.

[8] Suidas, s.v. Σημεῖα Σκυθικά; cf. Babelon, *Rn*. 1902, p. 7.

[9] Heiss, p. 358; Delgado I, p. clxvii; cf. II, pp. 168 f.; and below, p. 473.

[10] Robinson, *BMC. Cyrenaica*, p. ccxxiii; cf. Cook, *Zeus*, I, pp. 358 ff. (from Hesychius), *pace* Muller I, p. 163; Thrige, *Res Cyrenensium*, pp. 289 f.

[11] Synesius IV, 167; cf. Riess, *PW*. I, 1856.

[12] Cf. Pietschmann, *PW*. I, 1858.

[13] Cf. Romanelli, *CAH*. XI, p. 669; cf. p. 667 n. 1.

[14] Ibid. p. 669.

witness to a temporary fusion of the provinces, such as Romanelli, for other reasons, believes to have occurred.[1]

This hypothesis is confirmed by further considerations. It explains the special rank and dignity of Livineius, who was probably, like Capito, left by his proconsul in charge of the civil administration of Cyrenaica (and no doubt Crete also). It is noteworthy that an inscription from Berenice[2] describes M. Tittius Sex. f.,[3] the Resident in Cyrenaica in c. 9–8 B.C.,[4] as παραγενηθεὶς εἰς τὴν ἐπαρχείαν ἐπὶ δημοσίων πραγμάτων. This descriptive *détour* is quite unsuitable to a proconsul, although the inscription speaks of Tittius's εὔχρηστος προστασία; but it is peculiarly applicable to the position of *quaestor pro praetore* which, it is here argued, Livineius held in c. 6–5 B.C., as 'subgovernor' of Crete and Cyrenaica under the *imperium maius* of the proconsul of Africa. In the same way, the first 'Edict' of Cyrene[5] withholds—otherwise inexplicably—the proconsular title from the Resident of c. 7–6 B.C., P. Sextius Scaeva: he is evidently to be classed with Tittius and Capito. These 'Edicts' provide for possible administrative changes by referring to future Residents only in the most indefinite terms.[6] The inscription of Tittius indicates that the transference to the proconsul of Africa should be placed before c. 9 B.C.: it might have occurred a year or two earlier, but not more, since Scato (c. 13–12) was not the last of the proconsuls of Crete and Cyrenaica before the transfer, a successor called Q. Lucanius Proculus possessing the same title.[7] Lucanius's fortification of Cyrene implies that hostilities were already threatening.[8] The year 9 B.C., it may be noted, is for two reasons a particularly appropriate one for official aggrandisement of the governors of Africa. Augustus had extended the *imperium maius* in his own province in that year, so that it was tactful to allow the same power to the senior proconsul; and the death of Drusus in the same year was one of the chief causes contributing to the development of the *amici principis*, who included a succession of these proconsuls (p. 229). A fragmentary passage of Dio[9] relating to c. 1 B.C. suggests that there was still no proconsul in Cyrenaica at that date, when the decision was taken to transfer its Eastern half to the more accessible governor of Egypt and so to 'imperial' rule.[10] A Cyrenean inscription of A.D. 2[11] celebrates the conclusion of hostilities in that region, but the coin of Passienus in A.D. 3 shows that the African command—whether still inclusive of Crete and Western Cyrenaica or not—could not say the same: it was reserved for Cossus Lentulus in 6[12] to bring peace for a

[1] *CAH.* XI, p. 659.
[2] *IGRR.* I, 1024.
[3] Not = Tittius, Münzer, *PW.* VI, 1573 correcting Cagnat, *IGRR.* l.c.
[4] Cagnat, l.c., *pace* Münzer, l.c.; cf. Cary, *CAH.* IX, p. 292.
[5] Vide *JRS.* 1927, p. 34; *SEG.* IX, 1938, p. 118.
[6] E.g. *Ed.* I, l. 14, οἱ τὴν Κρητικὴν καὶ Κυρηναϊκὴν ἐπαρχῆαν καθέξοντες; l. 37, ὅσοι Κρήτης καὶ Κυρήνης στρατηγήσουσιν; IV, l. 65 ὃς ἂν τὴν ἐπαρχῆαν διακατέχῃ.
[7] *Documenti antichi dell' Africa italiana*, II; *Cirenaica, fasc.* I, p. 101 = *L'Année épigraphique*, 1934, no. 256; correcting Cagnat's restoration, *IGRR.* I, 1032.
[8] Cf. Romanelli, l.c. p. 667 n. 1.   [9] LV, 10a. 1.
[10] Cf. Syme, *RR.* p. 357. Groag, *PW.* (2R.), IV, 827 reserves his judgment on this point.
[11] *Documenti antichi ecc., Cirenaica, fasc.* II, no. 67: cf. Romanelli, l.c. p. 668.
[12] Cf. Syme, *CAH.* X, p. 347.

PROVINCIAL ISSUES BY 'SENATORIAL' GOVERNORS

decade, and it is very probable that his appointment brought another administrative change—a temporary conversion of Africa (and so perhaps of the other regions also) to an 'imperial' province.[1] The history of these territories bears witness to the extreme elasticity of Augustus's provincial system.[2]

5. CYPRUS: Paphos, Salamis(?)

The return of this island to the senate in 22 B.C.[3] is closely followed by a bronze[4] series of A. PLAVTIVS PRO COS.[5] Like the issues of proconsuls in 29 B.C. (p. 385), his coinage—which is as isolated as theirs—probably commemorates the reinauguration of proconsular government. The fact that his diminutive *semisses* show, with slightly varying styles, the figure of Zeus of Salamis[6] and the temple of Aphrodite of Paphos[7] may possibly indicate the existence of two mints;[8] but if this was so, they were combined under Tiberius, in whose principate both types appear on a single coin.[9]

The more pretentious issues of official AVGVST. and SC types (pp. 106, 99) are very likely to have commemorated the bestowal on Paphos of the title Σεβαστή in c. 15 B.C.[10] Of exactly similar style and of Cypriot provenance[11] are a number of *asses*[12] which stress the honours to Caius Caesar: his bare head appears, inscribed C. CAESAR AVG. F. PRINC. IVVENT.[13] (from 5 B.C.) or C. CAESAR AVG. F. PONT. COS.[14] (from A.D. 1), with the laureate portrait of Augustus as AVGVST. TRIB. POT. PONT. MAX. On a third issue the *princeps* is CAESAR AVG. PAT. PATR.[15] Cyprus also has at this period a currency of small uninscribed *semisses*, presumably official, with types of capricorn and star, and scorpion and star.[16]

An issue of some historical importance can be reconstructed from its two extant examples.[17] On the reverse are two figures seated facing (Pl. IV, 25). The obverse shows a head of Augustus to right (Pl. IV, 24), which on one specimen is practically identical, in features, truncation, hair arrangement, and execution, with the portraits of Cypriot

---

[1] Argued plausibly by Cantarelli, *Studi romani*, II, 1914, p. 54.
[2] Emphasised by Sutherland, *RIS*. p. 208.
[3] Dio LIV, 4; cf. Jones, *CERP*. p. 488 n. 8; Cardinali, *Augustus*, p. 161.
[4] Spectrograms 26, 27. Zinc in very small quantities.
[5] Hill, *BMC. Cyprus*, p. cxx.
[6] Ibid. p. 73. 4 (67 grains) (pl. XIV, 4).
[7] Ibid. 2 (av. 67 grains) (pl. XIV, 2).
[8] Spectrographic tests (Spectrograms 26, 27) are inconclusive on this point.
[9] Ibid. 10.
[10] Halgan, *Essai sur l'administration des provinces sénatoriales*, p. 175.

[11] Hill, *NC*. 1924, p. 14. Their occasional discovery elsewhere (e.g. at Risstissen; Schenk von Stauffenberg coll., cf. Nestle, *Funde*, p. 82) is principally due to their official character.
[12] Av. c. 139·5 grains.
[13] Hill, l.c. no. 25.
[14] Ibid. no. 26, Hess sale (1933) 322.
[15] Ibid. no. 27; variants at Vienna and in Dupriez sale (1934) 85, with head to left; the latter coin is wrongly stated in its catalogue to have a head of Lucius.
[16] Hamburger sale (1925) 495; cf. Hill, *NC*. 1917, p. 24; found in Cyprus (BM label) (av. c. 48 grains).
[17] BM, Berlin (both 'uncertain').

coins with AVGVST. and SC (Pl. III, 17; IV, 8); it also resembles the series of Augustus and Caius Caesar from the same island. Further, the obverse legend is IMP. CAESAR DIVI F. AVGV·····,[1] a form of which the only known appearance on official issues in the East (to which these coins must, for stylistic reasons, be attributed) is at Cyprus (p. 80). The fabric of these pieces indicates a later date than the issue of A. Plautius *pro cos.* (on which this form of titulature occurs); they must be not far from contemporary with the series of Augustus and Caius Caesar. Imhoof-Blumer[2] not only wrongly describes the figures on the reverse as standing, thus inviting an entirely false analogy with much later coins of Selinus,[3] but reads (upside down) the Greek ethnic ΑΝΕΜΟΥΡΙΕШΝ, of Cilicia, whereas the inscription is actually in Latin:

··LVCAV················ QAMQVIN[4][TI][5]········

Both figures wear veils which are very like those worn by the Caesars Caius and Lucius, as priests, on the reverse of the famous Lugdunese *aurei* and *denarii*;[6] moreover, on one of the two specimens one figure is distinctly larger than the other, as on a number of the coins of Lugdunum.[7] On those the inscription is C. L. CAESARES AVGVSTI F. COS. DESIG. PRINC. IVVENT.; on colonial *aes* pieces of Tarraco and Traducta the Caesars are described as C. L. CAES. AVG. F. and C. CAESAR L. CAESAR AVG. F. (pp. 219, 221). These analogies necessitate the restoration of the first half of the present legend as [C]. LV. C(*aesares*) AV[G. F., PRINC. IVV. or COS. DESIG.]. The *praenomen* of Lucius is found likewise irregularly abbreviated as LVC. at Traducta (p. 221). Caius and Lucius are not here seated upon a *bisellium*, like Augustus and Agrippa on a Roman *denarius* which perhaps inspired the type,[8] but on an oriental high-backed throne with footstools (or pedestal), probably as *cultus*-statues. Greek cities are known to have worshipped the grandsons of Augustus;[9] it is possible that they were enshrined among the Lares at the colony[10] of Acerrae during their lifetime,[11] and they possessed a temple at the Roman or Latin colony of Nemausus.[12] But there were no colonies or *municipia* in Cyprus, so these cannot be local pieces. By analogy with other Cypriot issues Q. AM. QVINTI. should be a proconsul Quintianus, Quintillus, or Quintilianus, who might belong to one of several *gentes*.[13] He is the responsible authority for this issue, since, like the others of the island, it must be official. It may, therefore, provide a unique piece of evidence for the worship of Caius and Lucius in the provincial cult of a κοινόν, such as was here established at Paphos, henceforward called *Sebaste*, in 15 B.C.[14] The priestly veils indicate a date not

[1] BM.
[2] *Ant. GM.* p. 267.
[3] Id. *MG.* p. 364. 48 (Philip); *GM.* p. 714. 581 (Domna).
[4] Berlin.   [5] BM.
[6] *BMC. Imp.* p. cxvi; *Aug.* 513 ff.
[7] E.g. ibid. 534, 539.
[8] *BMC. Imp.* p. cvii; *Aug.* 115.

[9] E.g. *IGRR.* IV, 67 (Mytilene); IV, 468 (Pergamum), etc.
[10] *Liber Coloniarum* (*Feldm.*, p. 229).
[11] Cf. *ILS.* 137.   [12] *CIL.* XII, 3156.
[13] E.g. Ammia, Ampeia, Ampudia, Ampelia, Amullia, Amminia, etc.
[14] Dio LIV, 23; cf. Spyridaki, Κυπριακαὶ Σπουδαί, II, 1938, p. 37. Cf. above, p. 140.

PROVINCIAL ISSUES BY 'SENATORIAL' GOVERNORS 145

before 2 B.C. for these coins,[1] but it cannot be ascertained whether the issue was made after the Caesars' deaths. It is possible that the [C. L.] CAES. GEMINI on a colonial coin of Tarraco (p. 219) provides a parallel, and that they were worshipped as the twin Dioscuri[2] by the κοινὸν Κυπρίων as by the *Commune* which met at that town.[3]

6. ASIA: Ionian mint

This province was one of the principal centres of the large official mintages whose range and content have been discussed (pp. 102 ff.): they are supplemented by an issue of very rare *sestertii*[4] and *dupondii*(?)[5] which resemble some of them in manner:

IMP. AVGVST. TR. POT. Head of Augustus to right.
OB CIVIS SERVATOS. Oak-wreath between two laurel-branches (Pl. V, 11).

The type is that of Roman *sestertii*:[6] the reverse style recalls the CA issues attributed to Ephesus (p. 104). With these the portrait on one specimen[7] shows further kinship; on another[8] it imitates a 'cistophoric' tetradrachm.[9] The head on the third extant example[10] is perhaps tooled and therefore unreliable. Style and fabric indicate an Ionian mint. The occasion for so rare and special an issue cannot now be identified; it may conjecturally be attributed to the period of Agrippa's rule in c. 18–13 B.C.

7. BITHYNIA: Apamea

A proconsul of Bithynia-Pontus[11] also strikes one Latin coin:[12]

IMP. CAESAR AVGVSTVS PONTIF. MAX. TR. P. busts to left, jugate, of Augustus and Livia.
M. GRANIVS MARCELLVS PRO COS.[13] Livia seated to right (Pl. IV, 33, 34).

Bosch[14] shows that, of the two dates A.D. 13–14 and 14–15 suggested by Muret,[15] only the latter is probable; this issue was therefore made in the last few months of Augustus's life—or even just after his death, but before the news arrived. But there is no strength in the argument of Bosch that, since official coins of Bithynia have Greek inscriptions, this must be colonial: the Greek issues which he cites are silver of Hadrianic date, and provide no parallel for the present coinage, which cannot be other than official. Nevertheless, style[16] appears to warrant attribution to **Apamea**, in which Bosch, for

---

[1] Cf. Stuart Jones, *CAH*. x, p. 154.
[2] Cf. Hill, p. 48.
[3] Ibid. p. 47; cf. Quintilian VI, 3. 77.
[4] *BMC. Imp. Aug.* 737 f.
[5] Herpin, *Rn.* 1857, pp. 205 f.: not seen.
[6] *BMC. Imp.* p. cxix.
[7] *BMC. Imp. Aug.* 738.
[8] New York.   [9] *BMC. Imp. Aug.* 700.
[10] Ibid. 737.
[11] Tac. *Ann.* 1. 74, *pace* Grose, *McLean coll.* 3028.
[12] *Rec.* Apamea 38, Cambridge (*McLean* l.c.).
[13] The Granii were business men of Puteolan origin (Syme, *RR.* p. 90 n. 7).
[14] *KM.* p. 79.
[15] *BCH.* v, 1881, p. 120.
[16] Cf. coins of Vespasian (Muret, l.c.).

less cogent reasons, concurs.[1] The colonial mint of this city must, therefore, have been commandeered for an official issue (p. 314). The seated figure of Livia, so common a type under Tiberius, is already found, as Ceres,[2] on the latest *aurei* and *denarii* of Augustus,[3] and Juno-Livia appears on a Latin inscription of A.D. 3.[4] On the present piece her double role shows her importance, while not yet Augusta, in the honours of the *Gens Augusta*. It is natural for this coinage, like others of the same category, to be the product of the *auctoritas principis*; owing to its late date, however, it may, unlike them, resemble the Syrian issue of Silanus (p. 127) in being derived from the executive of the *consilium* rather than from a *senatus consultum*.[5]

Section C described the framework of the numismatic plan, and the last three sections have illustrated the methods by which the *princeps* filled in the gaps. The structure was complex and colossal; but initiative in details was left to those communities for which it was devised. The following two Parts will show their contribution to the monetary system.

[1] His argument that *Sinope kommt hierfür nicht in Betracht, weil im Osten der Provinz Proconsulnamen auf den Münzen nie genannt werden* is false, since (1) coins struck at Amisus and Sinope, unknown to him, bear the name of a governor (see pp. 11 f.); (2) even if they did not, this coin is in any case exceptional and Sinope was as much a part of the province as Apamea. Moreover, Eastern official *aes*, like that of P. Sulpicius Rufus, was struck in towns of peregrine right. But his attribution to Apamea is correct.
[2] Mattingly, *BMC. Imp.* p. cxvii.
[3] *BMC. Imp. Aug.* 544 ff.
[4] *ILS.* 1, 120, etc., etc.
[5] A bronze coin at Milan (*Cat.* p. 23. 232, attributed to Narbo[?]) (pl. IV, 27) has a prow with superstructure and I (mark of value), and on the obverse two heads which are imitated, in a style which is not Gallic, from the later issues of Nemausus with P.P. (cf. above, p. 75). This coin corresponds exactly with the description by Signor Baranowsky of one which was found at Sant' Antioco, an island off South Sardinia, near Cagliari, and was at one time in his possession; he did not know of the Milan specimen. It seems that this is an isolated provincial issue from the Sardinian capital at Caralis; it has been shown, however, that the issue of Nemausus which it copies is not Augustan, as is generally held.

Part II
THE ROMAN CITIES

⋘⋙

INTRODUCTION

It is not necessary to emphasise the importance of the colonies and *municipia*[1] as centres of Italian influence and institutions, and as conscious or unconscious[2] agents of the Romanisation of an Empire *créé et supporté par la bourgeoisie citadine*.[3] But, in view of the fragmentary treatment hitherto accorded it, it may be well to point out that the coinage of these cities is so numerous and varied as to provide an entirely unrivalled corpus of information: it can even be called the principal category of evidence for this vital topic. The significance of the coinage is particularly great in the present period, during which most of the Roman cities were founded or refounded. It gives a detailed picture of the transition from Republic to principate, from self-government to bureaucracy, and provides remarkable contributions to the central theme of this book, the beginning and development of rule by *auctoritas principis*. Furthermore, it provides ample documentation for prosopographical study of the local magistrates at this date, and for the dispersion of Italians throughout the Empire.

It is therefore surprising to find that, of the 78 Roman cities (32 *municipia* and 46 colonies)[4] which coined in this period, only about 31 series (those of 17 *municipia* and 14 colonies) have ever received a reasonably complete local attribution. In particular, the currencies of 10 *municipia* and 13 colonies have not been recognised at all, and some 35 principal varieties have not been published. These figures are necessarily based on reattributions in the following pages, although the writer is well aware that his own conclusions may be upset by greater knowledge or by new material. It is, however, at least possible to suggest that a dominant theme has escaped notice: the mintages are nearly all commemorative, a few celebrating the jubilee of their city, but the great majority its establishment or re-establishment. It is clear, therefore, that the coins

---

[1] These will here be considered to include the *oppida civium Romanorum* (*praefecturae, fora*, etc.), which were in law *municipia* (Sherwin-White, p. 87 n. 1) but still presented variations from that class at the date of Pliny's source (cf. Kornemann, *PW*. XVI, 597; Taberner, *QAS*. XVIII, 1939, p. 17), except in Italy and Baetica (Sherwin-White, pp. 141, 171). However, the divergencies were principally in administrative details, and no real distinction can be drawn now, or was then. Cf. below, p. 171, on Gades.

[2] Largely the latter according to Jones, *GC*. p. 70 etc.

[3] Rostovtzeff, *Mélanges Pirenne*, p. 425.

[4] For the purpose of this calculation *municipia* Simitthu and Panormus are considered different from the later colonies at the same cities.

will provide substantial assistance to the chronology of city-foundation.[1] It will be argued that the dates currently assigned to these are in many cases incorrect, and that, in particular, the main lines of the policies of Caesar and Augustus have been inadequately distinguished. This and other historical subjects are the concern of the third Chapter; the first two will attempt to establish the identities of the municipal and colonial mints, and the occasions of their issues.

[1] See Appendices 4 and 5.

Chapter 1
THE ROMAN *MUNICIPIA*

1. SARDINIA: Caralis, Uselis

THERE is a bronze[1] coin of unusual character whose Sardinian provenance has frequently been demonstrated,[2] but equally often ignored in favour of Muller's wrong attribution to Carthage:[3]
ARISTO MVTVMBAL RICOCE SVF.; two male busts, jugate, to right, one with *toga*—KAR. VENERIS tetrastyle temple (Pl. V, 14).[4]

The suffetes (*shophetim*) are inconsistent with the status of Carthage as a colony but much more in accordance with the original character of *municipia* as converted towns (p. 325). Caralis, in whose neighbourhood these coins are found, became a Roman *municipium* under either Augustus or Julius,[5] who visited Sardinia after Thapsus.[6] Already before the death of Augustus[7] *quattuorviri* are found: the appearance here of suffetes (as earlier at Tharros)[8] probably represents a transitional stage—already under the Roman right, as the Latin inscription suggests[9] and the togate bust of one of the suffetes proves. The survival of these magistrates confirms the view that enfranchisement did not cause a sudden break in tradition.[10] The curious omission of their *gentilicia* (which were perhaps in both cases 'Julius') is characteristic of this period when the theory of dual citizenship formulated by Cicero—*unam naturae alteram civitatis*[11]—had not yet taken root.[12] The portraits are quite unlike those of Octavian and Agrippa, to whom they have been attributed:[13] it seems that they must join the select and unknown gallery of municipal officials thus honoured (p. 290). In accordance with this view is the known existence in earlier times of pairs of eponymous suffetes.[14] The third name

---

[1] Spectrogram 23. Strong tin and lead alloy. The tin may have been imported from Tuscany, but both copper and lead were still worked locally (Davies, *Roman Mines in Europe*, pp. 69–72).

[2] Spano, *Scoperte archeologiche nell' isola*, 1865; ibid. 1870; cf. Bornemann, *Blätter für Münzfreunde*, 1900, pp. 156 f.; Albizzati, *Annali della Facoltà di Lettere della R. Univ. di Cagliari*, I, 1928, p. 7; Poinssot, *Bulletin de la Société nationale des antiquaires de France*, 1928, p. 266; Ricci, *Historia*, IV, 1930, p. 366; Milan Cat. p. 27. 285 n.

[3] II, p. 149. 319–320; cf. Cimino, *Libya*, III, 1927, p. 209; Ehrenberg, *PW*. (2R.), IV (1932), 651.

[4] BM, Cambridge (*McLean*, 9999), Castoldi coll., own coll.

[5] Kornemann, *PW*. XVI, 595; cf. *ILS*. 5350; Pliny, *NH*. III, 85; Kubitschek, *Imp.* p. 126; Hülsen, *PW*. III, 1568; Pais, *Storia della Sardegna e della Corsica*, p. 354.

[6] Gsell VIII, p. 154.

[7] Bouchier, *Sardinia in Ancient Times*, p. 90.

[8] *Comptes rendus de l'Académie des inscriptions*, 1901, p. 579.   [9] Albizzati, l.c.

[10] Cf. Sherwin-White, p. 139, following Mommsen, *St.R.* III, pp. 812 f.; *pace* Rudolph, *Stadt und Staat im römischen Italien*, pp. 225 f.

[11] *De Legibus*, II, 2. 5.

[12] Cf. Sherwin-White, pp. 133, 189.

[13] E.g. Grose, *McLean*, 9999.

[14] *Répertoire d'épigraphie sémitique*, I, 17. 183.

found here might be that of a third member of the college of suffetes (who in Sardinia,[1] as in Sicily,[2] occasionally exceeded two in number), but, in view of the two portraits, is more likely to be a patronymic of the second magistrate, whose name will then be Mutumbal Ricoce f. (*ben* Ricoce).[3] His colleague was perhaps a Greek.

The native characteristics of this issue are symbolic of the new period in which Latin culture was not an essential prerequisite of *civitas*.[4] Moreover, they suggest a contrast between *municipia* and colonies (p. 324). The coinage also provides an introduction to another topic of paramount importance. Its early date, and entirely isolated character, suggest strongly that the only suitable occasion for issue could have been the *constitutio* of the *municipium*: portraits of local magistrates at Roman cities—and perhaps at some classes of peregrine city—are entirely restricted to foundation-coinages, on which they occur at *municipia* Saguntum and Zama Regia (pp. 163, 183). Moreover, isolated colonial and municipal issues are almost invariably inauguratory (p. 290), and it is a remarkable fact that every single municipal mint in the provinces which is active at any time during our period issues a coinage of this type. The two suffetes, then, were the first magistrates of the new *municipium*, in whose establishment they may have taken a hand as founder and *adsignator*—like similar pairs of officials at *colonia* Paestum (p. 286)—or, since it is more in accordance with regular practice outside Italy for the founder to have been a governor, as a pair of *adsignatores*. Whoever the founder was, Caralis is likely to have been an Octavianic foundation, since the only remaining Roman city in Sardinia is of that date also.

This is represented by the principal coinage of the island, on which much time and labour have been expended, but in vain, since a vital part of the legends has remained undiscovered. The inscriptions appear to be M. ATIVS BALBVS PR., and SARD. PATER. On the one side is a head to left of Atius Balbus—not that of any triumvir or *princeps*—and on the other a helmed head of Sardus *pater* to right, spear at shoulder (Pl. VI, 4). These pieces are found in large quantities in the south-west of Sardinia,[5] where Sardopator was worshipped.[6] E. Babelon,[7] Albizzati,[8] and Pietrangeli[9] assign the issue to an imagined propraetorship of Atius, who was praetor before 59,[10] and must have died soon after.[11] Klebs[12] rightly agrees with Cavedoni[13] that such a coin, and

---

[1] *Corpus inscriptionum semiticarum*, I, 175; cf. Mommsen, *RGDA*. v, 645. 2.
[2] *Corpus inscriptionum semiticarum*, I, 135; cf. Ehrenberg, *PW*. (2R.), IV, 650.
[3] For the name cf. Mathanbaal (Levy, *Phönizisches Wörterbuch*, p. 32); ···tumbal (*Africa italiana*, VI, 1935, p. 28), Mutum (*CIL*. VIII, 8716), Musthumbal (ibid. 4922). Probably he was a 'C. Julius'.
[4] Cf. Sherwin-White, p. 168.
[5] Bouchier, *Sardinia in Ancient Times*, p. 165; cf. Spano, *Bullettino archeologico sardo*, I, 1855, p. 9; and Castoldi coll.
[6] Philipp, *PW*. [2R.], I, 2496; cf. Ptolemy III, 3. 2; Geogr. Ravenn. p. 411; Pausanias X, 17. 1.
[7] *Aréthuse*, I, 1923, p. 10 n. 4.
[8] *Annali della Facoltà di Lettere della R. Univ. di Cagliari*, I.
[9] *Civiltà Romana*, VII, 1938, p. 10.
[10] Cic. *III Phil*. 15 ff.; id. *Att*. II, 12. 1; cf. Klein, *Die römischen Verwaltungsbeamten*, I, II. Abt. p. 240. 54.
[11] Cf. Dio XLV, 1. 1, etc.
[12] *PW*. XI, 2253.
[13] *Bullettino archeologico sardo*, III, 1857, p. 90.

THE ROMAN *MUNICIPIA*

such a portrait, would be anomalous as early as c. 59, or, indeed, before 44;[1] nor does Albizzati's[2] citation of T. Quinctius Flamininus—who appears on an isolated Greek issue (p. 241)—in any way dispose of this objection. On the other hand, Eckhel's[3] attribution to the actual principate of Augustus, the kinsman of the Atii,[4] is invalidated by the early style and lettering;[5] moreover, it is known that in his final *statio principis* he was not flattered by his Arician origin.[6] There remains the second triumvirate. In this period portraits of the living and dead were not rare (p. 379). Moreover, in the first years after Octavian's occupation of Sardinia in 38,[7] it was very natural, not only for a city to be municipalised, but for its inhabitants to stress any connection with the new ruler's family that they could claim. New light is thrown on the nature of this connection by two unusually clear specimens (e.g. Pl. VI, 4),[8] on both of which the reading is clearly M. ATIVS BALBVS P.R.; on a third example[9] is P–R., like the C–G–I–L on a coin of *colonia* Lampsacus (p. 246). P(*raetor*) R(*omanus*) would be unparalleled, P(*opulus*, -*o*) R(*omanus*, -*o*) is inapplicable, and there is no suitable town whose name begins with R. There is nothing left but R(*es publica*), which, for purposes of epigraphic abbreviation, is sometimes considered as one word,[10] and which is commonly employed by Roman cities.[11] *Patronus Rei publicae* is a frequent phrase in inscriptions,[12] and P(*atronus*),[13] sometimes C(*oloniae*)[14] and M(*unicipii*),[15] is a regular abbreviation. Such a *patrocinium* is more suitable to the Atii than a local *praefectura* or praetorship—to which, moreover, no application of the letter R is discoverable.

The appearance of a Roman's head and name, with a title of this character, would be unparalleled at a peregrine community. By the *Lex Genetivae Iuliae* (p. 34), the *deductor* and *adsignator* of a colony are assigned its *patrocinium*.[16] The coinage of *municipium* Gades (p. 171) will be seen to confirm the natural conclusion that the *constitutores* of *municipia*, who supervised the installation of the new constitution until the first magistrates were ready,[17] became their *patroni* in the same way.[18] Very probably,

---

[1] But his refusal to accept PR. as an abbreviation of *pro praetore* is unjustifiable (cf. above, p. 61).
[2] L.c.
[3] *DN.* v, 145.
[4] Suet. *Aug.* 4.
[5] Albizzati, l.c.
[6] Suet. l.c.; cf. Syme, *RR.* p. 127; Heinze, *Vom Geist des Römertums*, p. 171.
[7] Cf. Ganter, p. 26.
[8] Both at Rome—from de Sanctis (photograph enlarged, *Catalogo della Mostra Augustea della Romanità*, p. 98. 19, and by Pietrangeli, l.c.), and Gnecchi collections.
[9] Castoldi coll.
[10] E.g. *CIL.* XII, 5572*a*, II, 353.
[11] E.g. *CIL.* X, p. 2.
[12] E.g. *CIL.* V, 3342, 6691, XIV, 2806; cf. VIII, 1548.
[13] E.g. *CIL.* III, 4537*a*, 5838, V, 135.

[14] E.g. *CIL.* X, 483, 524, 3723, 4737, 4750, 4860.
[15] E.g. *CIL.* X, 5654, 5919.
[16] Cf. Sebastian, *De patronis etc.*, Diss. Halle, 1884, p. 45; von Premerstein, p. 19; Adcock, *CAH.* IX, p. 709 n. 4, Kornemann, *PW.* XVI, 626, point out that this is a tralatician section later superseded by Ch. 130. But that chapter, which restricts the *patrocinium*, in the case of senators and their sons, to private persons in Italy without the *imperium*, cannot be as early as this period. Cf. also Syme, *RR.* p. 405 n. 4.
[17] Such officials had only been exceptionally appointed under the Republic (cf. Sherwin-White, p. 135) but were now regular: cf. below, p. 160.
[18] Cf. Sebastian, l.c. pp. 16 ff. for *patroni* of *municipia*.

therefore, this isolated issue served to commemorate its city's founder, like the coinage of Caralis, which also exceptionally honoured non-imperial personages with portraiture. Single portraits of founders occur in Sardinia at *colonia* Turris Libisonis (p. 205), and elsewhere at the colonies of Apamea and Lystra (pp. 238, 255). The founder of Turris Libisonis is not Atius Balbus but another; nor does the inauguratory coinage of Caralis permit collocation with the present pieces. There remains, in Sardinia, only Uselis. Pliny does not mention this city, but an inscription describes it as *colonia Iulia Augusta*.[1] This is inconsistent with Kornemann's inference[2] that the *municipium*, whose earlier existence he realises this inscription to imply, was not founded until after the compilation of the list used by Pliny. The title *Iulia* indicates that this foundation took place before 27 B.C.: and it will be shown that Pliny's list frequently omits to mention foundations which occurred before that date (p. 226). Uselis, as a *municipium Iulium*, is entirely appropriate for the attribution of these coins—especially since it is of precisely the same latitude as Sulci, where they are most often found.[3] *Pater*, the appellation of Sardus, is especially connected with foundations (p. 319), and it is clear that he and Atius are compared, as first and second founder—like Romulus and Octavian at Rome (p. 424).

This unknown M. Atius Balbus is almost certainly a son of the praetor of 59, and so a brother of Atia and uncle of Octavian. This conclusion is confirmed by the preponderance of the *princeps'* kinsmen in the select gallery of local coin-portraits (p. 229). The fact that the Atii were ignored in the post-Actian period suggests that M. Balbus *jun.* was founder and patron of Uselis very soon after the reconquest of Sardinia in 38. By the analogy of other municipal *constitutores* of the period 43–29 (p. 292), he is almost certain to have been the provincial governor. The compliment to Octavian is perhaps responsible for the popularity of this coinage, of which many barbarous specimens are known.[4]

A later stage in the history of the same *municipium* is demonstrated by an unpublished and apparently unique coin (Pl. VI, 5).[5] On the reverse, with the legend M. VEHIL. TVS ··· TVRPIL.[6] PRIS. IIV. Q.[7] round D. D., is a plough, of a curious kind found also on coins of *colonia* Turris Libisonis (p. 205). The obscure *gens* Vehilia provided a praetor to Caesar[8] and a praetorian proconsul of Cyprus to Augustus:[9] its only other discoverable appearance within the radius of a century is on an inscription—

[1] *ILS.* 6107.   [2] *PW.* XVI, 595.
[3] Bouchier, l.c. p. 166.
[4] E.g. Gotha, Castoldi coll., own coll.
[5] Berlin. It lies among the coins of *colonia* Buthrotum, from which, however, it exhibits considerable differences of style.
[6] For the Etruscan *gens* Turpilia, vide Schulze, *Abh. Göttingen, NF.* v, 5, 1904, p. 246.
[7] See below, pp. 154, 169 n. 3, 276.
[8] Cic. *III Phil.* pp. 24 ff.; cf. Sternkopf, *Hermes,*

XLVII, 1912, p. 387; Syme, *RR.* p. 91 n. 3; id. *Papers of the British School at Rome*, XIV (NS. I), 1938, p. 17.
[9] *BCH.* LI, 1927, p. 143: I owe to R. Syme the certain emendation of the reading MVPHILIO to M. VEHILIO. The existence of this governor proves that the Caesarian praetor is not the only senator from this family, as Ribbeck, *Senatores Romani,* p. 24. 96. The present *duovir* (Tuscus?) is almost certainly the freedman of one or the other.

THE ROMAN *MUNICIPIA*

likewise, by a coincidence which is unlikely to be accidental, from Turris Libisonis.[1] These two suggestions of Sardinian origin are shown in their true light by investigation of the unusual obverse legend, which is couched in the Possessive Genitive,[2] and accompanies a late head of Augustus to left. It is decipherable as: IMP. CAESARIS A. TR. P. MVPIVS. Given the two Sardinian analogies and our conclusion that Uselis was a Julian *municipium*, there can be little doubt that the correct interpretation is MV(*nicipium*) P(*ium*) I(*ulium*) VS(*elis*). The epithet P(*ium*), which occurs also elsewhere,[3] is particularly appropriate to a Julian foundation undertaken by Octavian.[4] The type of a plough is naturally as applicable to land allotments, such as might accompany all kinds of grants of *civitas*,[5] as to colonial foundations: it appears at Obulco,[6] and even on the inauguratory issue of the peregrine Caesarea at Tralles (p. 383). The foundation of *municipium* Emporiae by Caesar is, as will be shown, a certain example of a *constitutio* which was accompanied by allotments to veterans (p. 155), and similar settlements attended the foundation of *municipia* established by Vespasian[7] and probably by Tiberius.[8] This weakening of the practical distinction between *coloniae* and *municipia* is characteristic of the period (p. 324).

This is one of the few isolated issues in the colonial and municipal series which cannot be considered to celebrate a foundation. Uselis is still the *municipium Iulium* founded by Atius Balbus; the *deductio* must have been left to Tiberius or a successor, since *coloniae Augustae* are often post-Augustan (p. 198), and the portrait on this coin is from the very latest Augustan models. However, the *raison d'être* of so exceptional an issue is manifestly commemorative: and an occasion is identifiable with something like certainty. Practically the only other Roman city-issues of Augustus's last years (outside Spain) are equally isolated ones of Carthage, Cirta (?) and Lystra: and each of these commemorates the half-centenary of its city (pp. 231, 232, 250). Exactly the same phenomenon occurs at *civitas libera* Leptis Minor (p. 338). The date here ascribed to M. Atius Balbus's foundation (38 B.C.) makes the same conclusion particularly applicable to the present issue, whose existence cannot otherwise be explained. (See also p. 295.)

[1] *CIL.* x, 7967.
[2] This is found under Augustus at one other Roman city, *colonia* Lystra (p. 250), and on a number of his Greek coins; it is common in the Republic but not revived in Rome until 68–69 (Mattingly, *BMC. Imp.* pp. lxix, lxxiv. See also p. 271).
[3] E.g. Kornemann 201, 282; 72 *Pietas*.
[4] Cf. Wagenvoort, *QAS.* x, p. 12.
[5] Cf. Fabricius, *SB. Heidelberg*, xv, 1924–5, p. 23; Rudolph, *Stadt und Staat im römischen Italien*, pp. 186 ff.
[6] Cf. Delgado II, p. 230; Vives III, p. 59. 45 ff.
[7] Cf. Kornemann, *PW*. xvi, 599.
[8] Cf. Ritterling, *PW*. xii, 1243.

2. Hispania Tarraconensis: Emporiae, Dertosa, Saguntum, Calagurris, Osca, Turiaso, Bilbilis, Ilerda

The most extensive and one of the most significant of the coinages of Roman *municipia* is that of **Emporiae**. Hill[1] arranges the Roman *asses*, all of which have a Pegasus as reverse type, in the following chronological order:

A. EMPORIA head of Diana—MVNICIPI. (Pl. V, 18).
B. Head of Minerva, often with stylised helmet of two lobes (Pl. V, 16)—EMPOR.
C. (*a*) Head of Minerva as last: usually four initials, consisting of names of two magistrates, with Q.—EMPOR[IT.].
   (*b*) Do., usually with six initials. (Pl. V, 15 is transitional between C [*a*] and C [*b*]).

He classes smaller coins (D) partly with B and partly with C. This order is preferable to Delgado's arrangement A–C–B–D,[2] or to the distribution of B, by Pujol y Camps,[3] among the earliest and latest of the series. But a piece bearing the names Q. V., A. I., C(*ensores*),[4] classed by Hill with C (*a*), is distinct from that class in style; it is actually the earliest of the whole series, and belongs to the eighties B.C.[5] All other coins belong to our period. Hill concludes that 'an exact dating of the various Groups seems to be beyond reach',[6] but a very close approximation is possible.

The only issue in (A) (Pl. V, 18)[7] shows a head of Diana whose shape and style require comparison with coins of 49–44[8] rather than the *denarii* of 81–73[9] or the Massaliote pieces[10] quoted by Hill and Vives respectively. A portrait of the same curious form appears on coins of *colonia Lepida* Celsa, very soon after its foundation in

---

[1] Pp. 10 ff.   [2] III, p. 130.
[3] *MNE*. III, 1873, p. 10.
[4] Madrid, Pujol y Santo coll.; Hill, pl. III, 3; cf. Vives, pl. CXXXI, 2; Pujol y Camps, *MNE*. III, 1873, p. 154.
[5] Delgado's reverse reading MVNICIPI. is erroneous. Hill says of (C) (*a*): 'on the obverse is a string of initials usually accompanied by Q.' (p. 33) =*quinquennalis* (see below, p. 156). But Q. at the beginning, as here, can bear no such meaning. Moreover, the head is of a type quite foreign to all other coins of group (C) (as recognised by Delgado III, p. 224; Vives, p. 8), and strongly reminiscent of Roman *denarii* from c. 124 to c. 89 B.C. (e.g. *BMCR*. pl. XXVII ff.). In execution the coin most resembles heavy *asses* with similar groups of initials from Saguntum (e.g. Inst. de Valencia de Don Juan, Madrid, Hill, pl. XXIII, 4, etc.). These are asserted by Zobel de Zangroniz (*Commentationes philologicae in honorem Th. Mommsen*, p. 820) to have ceased by 133 B.C.; but they continued later (see p. 162 n. 5). The weight of the present piece, and its close resemblance to the Saguntine issues, indicate that it should be assigned to the brief period of semuncial coinage after 89 B.C. (Mattingly, *RC*. p. 17). Q.V., A.I., C. is parallel to P.L., L.L., Q., etc. of group (C): Q.V. and A.I. were C(*ensores*), local officials who were gradually superseded by Q(*uinquennales*) after the Lex Julia of 90 B.C. (cf. Marquardt, *St. V.* 1, pp. 485 f.; Sherwin-White, p. 85). The isolation of this coin is explained by the almost immediate general cessation of *aes* after that date (p. 3), from which this mint was not excepted.
[6] P. 37.   [7] BM, Berlin.
[8] E.g. *BMCR*. pl. LIII, 13–19; LIV, 1; LV, 8. E. S. G. Robinson confirms this.
[9] *BMCR*. pl. XLI, 16.
[10] Cf. Vives IV, p. 6.

THE ROMAN MUNICIPIA

44 B.C. (p. 211), and the style suggests a close parallel to inauguratory issues of *municipium* Simitthu (?) at the same date (p. 178). The new title of MVNICIPI. is explained by Livy,[1] who speaks of the previous existence at Emporiae of separate Spanish and Greek communities, which were enfranchised in turn, in 45–44, to become a citizen community with a core of *coloni ab divo Caesare post devictos Pompeii liberos adiecti*. This inexact use of *coloni* is paralleled at *municipium* Agrigentum[2] etc. (p. 324). A similar draft has already been noted at another Julian *municipium*, Uselis (p. 153), and occurred also at others of later date. The unique occurrence of MVNICIPI., and the stylistic analogies from c. 44, indicate that this coin commemorates the *constitutio* by Caesar:[3] it has been mentioned that there is not a single municipal mint outside Italy at which foundation-coinage does not open the series. The survival of Iberian letter-forms, rightly cited by Hill[4] as an argument in favour of earliness, is understandable at a time shortly after the amalgamation of the Iberian population, a member of which no doubt cut these dies.[5] Hill, who argues for a date earlier than the forties, remarks: 'the form of the P is not clear on specimens accessible to me';[6] but on the example of which he provides a photograph,[7] as on others,[8] it is clearly closed. That this, however, is not enough to justify the postponement of this issue by Botet y Siso[9] is shown by the following group:—

Hill's group (B), which (contrary to his statement)[10] exhibits every shape of the letter from square[11] to closed.[12] Even as early as c. 65 B.C. the same variation is visible on *denarii*,[13] so that the prolonged subsequent preference for the open form at Rome cannot be considered to exclude contemporary appearances of the closed form elsewhere. The earliest of the *asses*[14] in group (B) has a head of similar appearance to the semuncial piece of Q.V., A.I., C., though of later style; the likeness is not due to contemporaneity, but to a natural imitation of local models. A number of smaller denominations (D)[15] seem attributable (though without certainty) to this period. Its lower limit can be defined with some exactness by the following group, to which the *asses* of this class are closely linked, by style and by the common possession of a countermark[16] that may be intended to represent a palm-branch.

[1] XXXIV, 9.
[2] Cf. Kubitschek, *SB. Wien*, CLXXVII, Abh. 4. 1916, p. 104.
[3] Livy's silence regarding earlier *civitas* or *Latinitas* in no way invalidates the present attribution of Q.V., A.I., C., since at Saguntum, where, as has been mentioned, similar early Latin issues were struck, there is likewise no record of a Roman or Latin community before our period. In both cases it is unlikely that the cities possessed more than Latin rights before Julius.
[4] P. 36; cf. Sutherland, *RIS.* p. 113; Pujol y Camps, *MNE.* III, 1873, pp. 94, 135.
[5] The citation by Pujol y Camps, l.c. p. 156, of a trilingual piece from the Sanatuja collection (Tarragona) is very dubious.
[6] P. 32.
[7] Béziers (Hill, pl. III, 1).
[8] Vives, pl. CXXI, 1.
[9] *Noticia historica y arqueologica de la antiga ciudad de Emporion*, p. lxxiii.
[10] P. 33.
[11] BM.
[12] Leningrad.
[13] *BMCR.* pl. XLVI, 6, cf. 9: pl. XLVII, 4, cf. 6.
[14] BM.
[15] Hill, p. 34.
[16] Hague (Hill, pl. III, 2); cf. BM (P.L., L.L., Q.).

Hill's group (C) includes, if none are lost, sixteen sets of initials, each certainly including *praenomen, nomen* and sometimes *cognomen* of two men,[1] and each followed by Q. Hill's[2] interpretation as *quinquennalis* is clearly preferable to Hübner's[3] *quaestor*: the evidence of the early coin with Q. V., A. I., C[*ensores*] is supported by an analogy from Carteia,[4] where a similar series with Q. is preceded by issues of L. Rai. L. Agri. CE(*n*)S(*ores*).[5] The single letter Q. is a regular abbreviation for *quinquennalis*,[6] the name of the officials who were earlier called *censores* (p. 154). Without here entering into the difficult question of the exact incidence of these municipal officials,[7] it is clear that the sixteen quinquennial years represented by this group must be extended at least over a period varying only slightly from the theoretical figure of seventy-six years. Now it is unlikely that any of the series are pre-Caesarian, since a piece whose style indicates a date earlier than most of the rest bears the names of C. I. NICOM., P. FL., Q. (Pl. V, 15):[8] the first of these men is almost certainly a C. Julius with a Greek *cognomen*. Even if we could reckon the commencement of this group from the actual granting of municipal status in c. 45–44 B.C., its termination would leave a margin of not more than a decade before the general cessation of Spanish *aes* after the reign of Caligula.[9] But groups (A) and (B) are to be assigned to the first years of the *municipium*: it is therefore highly probable that the issues by *quinquennales* began in c. 40–39 or 35–34 B.C. and continued until the very last Spanish *aes* was suppressed. It is also noteworthy that an example with C. I. NICOM., P. FL., Q. (the name of P. FL. is repeated on the reverse, perhaps to indicate that he, as junior *duovir*,[10] was responsible for the issue) demonstrates a transitional fluctuation from the square open[11] to the closed form of P.[12] But three coins with four initials each (including one with a countermark found also on group [B]) have an exclusively open form,[13] and an early style; while on three other varieties, each including at least one magistrate with the *tria nomina*,[14] an exclusively closed form is accompanied by a debased style with a ridiculously formalised double-lobed helmet, and dots scattered even between the C and N of a *praenomen*.[15] The attribution of these two main varieties—without and with *cognomina* respectively—to the beginning and end of the series respectively is confirmed by the regular weights of the later group, approximating closely to those of the Roman *asses*,[16] by the wildly fluctuating standards of the earlier one,[17] recalling official coinage in the thirties and early twenties, and by the fact that Spanish citizens did not

[1] Hill, p. 33. [2] Ibid.
[3] *CIL.* II, p. 615. [4] Vives IV, p. 15.
[5] Stockholm; cf. Delgado I, p. 98; Lorichs, *Recherches numismatiques*, p. 111; cf. Zaccaria, *Instituciones antiquario-lapidarias*, p. 400.
[6] Cf. Neumann, *De quinquennalibus coloniarum et municipiorum*, Diss. Leipzig, 1892, p. 25.
[7] Ibid. pp. 30 ff.; see below, p. 159.
[8] BM; cf. Vives, pl. CXXI, 9 (but not two Q.'s).
[9] Cf. Mattingly, *BMC. Imp.* p. xix.
[10] I.e. not *comitialis* (p. 196).
[11] Berlin. [12] BM (or nearly closed?).
[13] L. C., C. R., Q.; C. I., L. C., Q.; P. L., L. L., Q. (BM: cf. Vives IV, pp. 8 f.; Hill, p. 35).
[14] C. C. AT., C. O. CAR., Q.; CN. C. GR., L. C. F., Q.; L. M. RVF., P. C., Q. (BM, ibid.).
[15] Copenhagen; cf. Vives IV, p. 8. 12.
[16] Average of fifteen specimens in BM: c. 166 grains.
[17] E.g. 206, 201, 186, 119, 93 grains (BM).

regularly use a *cognomen* until the middle of our period.¹ Transitional in style is a college which signs both as M. O. H., L. A. F., Q.² and as M. O., L. A., Q.,³ and others, after the introduction of the *tria nomina*, on which the letter P still fluctuates in form.⁴ Near, or at, the very end are C. T. C., Q. C. CAR., Q.,⁵ attempting a less peculiar kind of helmet, and M. A. B., M. F. M., Q.,⁶ with a much neater execution and a closed P with long upper stroke.

It is thus possible to make a fairly exact arrangement of the series. This arrangement permits the important conclusion that a Roman *municipium* still preserved semblance enough of its autonomy to continue, for three-quarters of a century, to issue coins differing only in *minutiae*, and identical in that they make no mention whatsoever of the *princeps* or any other central authority: they retain the early form of ethnic (probably in the Genitive Plural as on coins of Panormus⁷) which varies from EMPOR. to EMPORIT. Moreover, this coinage, although conservative in character, must have formed an important part of the monetary system, since its circulation was enormous.⁸ Such an extensive series is valuable evidence for comparison and contrast with the colonies (p. 324).

The magistrates who sign this coinage are impossible to identify, owing to the abbreviation of their signatures. But the names P. C., P. C. Pu., Cn. C. P., seem to bear witness to a dominant *clientela* of the Claudii Pulchri—possibly Emporitans figured largely in the suite of the tribune Clodius.⁹ If this is the case, these *quinquennales* enabled the conjunction of names to survive when the real Pulchri were nearly extinct.¹⁰ C. O. C(ar). is probably a kinsman of the North Spanish *libertus* M. Octavius Sabini f. Caricus,¹¹ who may have taken his name from the triumvir.¹² C. O. C(ar). is twice in office: so are a number of others, including C. Julius Nicomedes, if C. I. is the same man. His colleague P. Fl. is likely to be a relative of the renegade Caesarian from Hasta, C. Flavius.¹³ Elsewhere there is even less certainty. Q. C. C(ar). recalls the Cornelii Carpi,¹⁴ Cn. C. Gr. the Cornelii Gratiani,¹⁵ both Spanish families which perhaps owed their *gentilicia* to *legati* of Pompey.¹⁶ L. M. Ruf. may possibly be the Baetican L. Marcius Rufus,¹⁷ but might equally be a Spanish Magnius¹⁸ or a Memmius Rufus.¹⁹

---

¹ Cf. the earliest issues of *colonia* Celsa, in contrast to the rest; and, for elsewhere, Ramsay, *Anatolian Studies to Buckler*, 1939, p. 207.

² BM; cf. Vives IV, p. 9. 21.

³ BM; ibid. p. 8. 16.

⁴ E.g. CN. C. P., C. M. A., Q.; C. O. C., C. M. A., Q.; P. C. PV., Q. C. C., Q.

⁵ Instituto de Valencia de Don Juan; cf. Vives IV, p. 8. 4.

⁶ BM; cf. Vives IV, p. 8. 5.

⁷ BM, Paris (Tiberius).

⁸ Very large quantities not only in Spain (especially Pujol mus.; Engel, *Bulletin mensuel de Numismatique et d'Archéologie*, VI, 1890, p. 20), but also in Gallia Narbonensis and Comata (for statistics, see below, p. 297).

⁹ They seem established before the proconsulship of Ap. Pulcher in 33 B.C. (*CIL.* I², p. 77).

¹⁰ Cf. Syme, *RR.* p. 493.   ¹¹ *CIL.* II, 2928.

¹² On the choice of names by *liberti* vide Syme, *Actes du Ve Congrès de Papyrologie*, 1937, p. 466.

¹³ *Bell. Hisp.* 26. 2.

¹⁴ *CIL.* II, 3573, 4008.   ¹⁵ Ibid. 4143.

¹⁶ Cf. Syme, *JRS.* 1938, p. 118 n. 34.

¹⁷ *CIL.* II, 985.

¹⁸ Ibid. 2029.   ¹⁹ Ibid. 1460.

A second period of Julian enfranchisement in Tarraconensis is introduced by a single issue of **Dertosa** of the Ilercavones. This includes an *as*[1] and a *semis*,[2] whose types of a light galley, accompanying respectively a larger ship and a dolphin and anchor, indicate, as at Ilici (p. 213), the nautical preoccupations of the town. It is described, without any additional legend, as M(*unicipium*) H(*ibera*) IVLIA DERT(*osa*) IL(*ercavonia*)—the epithets being in apposition, not to the word *municipium*, but to the ethnic, just as at Bilbilis (p. 170) and Zama Regia (p. 182). Such completely isolated coinages within this period are scarcely found outside the category of foundation-issues,[3] of which a large number (including no less than eleven not explicitly referring to their occasion) stand equally alone at their city (p. 290). Nor is this at all likely to be a single exception to the invariable inauguration of municipal mints by coinage of this kind (p. 290). It is also significant that three other Tarraconensian *municipia* place their secondary names—like *Ilercavonia* here[4]—on their foundation-pieces, but none of them on issues of other kinds (pp. 165, 168, 170). This coinage must be considered to belong to the same category. Now the city, being *Iulia*, must have been established as a Roman *municipium* before 27:[5] but the style of these pieces is inconsistent with a date much earlier than the twenties.[6]

The inference of a municipalisation policy in the years immediately following Actium[7] is confirmed by the coinage of four other cities of this status which were founded by C. Calvisius Sabinus in c. 30–29 or T. Statilius Taurus in c. 29–28.

One of these can be deduced from pieces which have always been wrongly attributed to *colonia* Carthago Nova. These comprise the issues of six colleges:[8]

1. Helvius Pollio, Albinus *IIvir quinq.*—Sabinus *imp. C. M.* (Pl. VI, 6).[9]
2. Cn. Stati. Libo *praef. sacerdos* (Pl. VI, 9).[10]

---

[1] Berlin: Hill, pl. XI, 1.
[2] Vidal Quadras y Ramon coll.: Hill, pl. XI, 2 (illustrated).
[3] The coins are too early in appearance to belong to the series of jubilee issues (p. 153).
[4] It is explained by the local tribe of the Ilercavones (Schulten, *PW*. IX, 1092; cf. Hill, p. 74 nn. 18, 19), so that there is no reason to adopt the hypothesis of a double community—supposed to consist of two Roman *municipia*—put forward by Kubitschek, *Imp.* p. 193; Zobel de Zangroniz, *MNE.* v, 1880, p. 129.
[5] It remained of that rank throughout the present period, and attributions of colonial coinage and status are equally false: see Hill, p. 75 n. 20, correcting Hübner, *MLI.* p. 38, who is followed in the former assumption by Imhoof-Blumer, *MG*. pp. 162, 166, 252, and in the latter by Albertini, *Les divisions administratives de l'Espagne romaine*, p. 63. Albertini relies partly on Strabo's word κατοικία (III, p. 195), but Hill points out the elasticity of this term.
[6] Tiberius repeats the type (Hill, pl. XI, 3), but the execution is of a different character and does not warrant the attribution of the present pieces to the end of Augustus's principate, *pace* Vives IV, p. 18.
[7] Sutherland, *RIS.* p. 123, attributes the colonisation of Dertosa and other cities to Caesar, solely because 'the names *Iulius* or *Caesar*, unsupplemented by *Augustus*, are not characteristic of the foundations of the first *princeps*'. But he thereby entirely neglects the period before 27 B.C.: what else but *Iulia* could Octavian have called his colonies at this time? Similar attributions are made by van Nostrand, *UCPH.* IV, 2, 1916, p. 103, presumably for the same reason.
[8] In this list relevant details omitted on the coins are restored as far as possible.
[9] Vives IV, p. 34. 12 f.   [10] Delgado I, p. 126.

3. Hibero *praef.* M. Agrippae *IIviri quinq.*, Q. Vario *praef.* (Pl. VI, 8).[1]
4. L. Bennio *praef.* Imp. Caesaris *IIviri quinq.*, Q. Vario *praef.*[2]
5. L. Bennio *praef.* Imp. Caesaris *IIviri quinq.*, Hibero *praef.* M. Agrippae *IIviri quinq.*[3]
6. Hibero *praef.*, Helvio Pollione *praef.* Ti. Neronis *IIviri quinq.*[4]

It is necessary to demonstrate, first, that these constitute a homogeneous series, and secondly, that their attribution to Carthago Nova is groundless.

The first of these problems can be solved without much difficulty, although evidence concerning provenance is almost valueless.[5] Style and community of names indicate the conjunction of 1, 3, 4, 5 and 6;[6] 2 shows the same style, provenance,[7] and portraiture as 3 and 4,[8] which it also resembles significantly in metal.[9] Not one of these types has any connection with Carthago Nova: it is very difficult to find any reason at all for their inclusion among the series attributed to this town, which, together with Panormus, has succeeded Corinth among numismatists as a general repository for uncertain colonial pieces. Moreover, the present series presents a marked divergency from the certain coins of *colonia* Carthago Nova, whose style is distinct and whose honorary *duoviri quinquennales* are never accompanied by their *praefecti* (p. 215). Finally, although a few quinquennalian colleges have been rightly reattributed from Carthago Nova to Cnossus (p. 261),[10] there remain, by the current arrangement, at least seventeen (of most heterogeneous appearance), which must be crammed between the foundation in c. 45 B.C.—or even later[11]—and the death of Augustus. *Quinquennales* held office for one year,[12] every five (not four) years;[13] under exceptional circumstances longer gaps might occur (p. 164 n. 4), but nothing could necessitate their abbreviation. At least eighty-one years would be necessary for the inclusion of these seventeen colleges at one city; but less than sixty years are available, and even if two

[1] Hübner, *MLI.* p. 89; Paris.
[2] Vives, l.c. 21.   [3] Ibid. 18–20.
[4] Ibid. 17.   [5] E.g. Heiss, pp. 271 ff.
[6] And a coin with the names of Hiberus and C. Luci. P.f. (Vives 16, pl. VI, 7), which will be shown to belong to the earlier coinage of the city's Latin period (see below, p. 162). Another piece of the same category, signed by C. Caedi. and T. Popili. *IIvir. quinq.* (Vives 2), has a palm-branch of a characteristic type bound also on (5). A variant of 1 (BM) has a coiled snake which recalls a similar piece of L. Fabric. P. Atelli. (pl. VII, 17): attribution of the latter to Cyrenaica by Muller, l.c., Borghesi, *Œuvres*, II, pp. 403, 406 f. is rejected by Robinson, *BMC. Cyrenaica*, p. ccx; and an argument based on the occurrence of Atellii (Heiss, p. 273) fails completely to confirm its attribution to Carthago

Nova, since the same *gens* occurs on published inscriptions of at least three other towns in Tarraconensis, e.g. *CIL.* II, 6256 (Emporiae), 5834 (Osca), 3603 (Gandia). It is a common Etruscan name; cf. Schulze, p. 151.
[7] Cf. del Rivero, *Madrid Cat.* p. 24.
[8] Unrecognised by Babelon, *Rn.* 1889, p. 511; Eckhel, *DN.* v, p. 316; Delgado I, p. 126.
[9] Spectrogram 52; cf. 51. Both have traces of nickel, not a common constituent.
[10] Heiss, p. 275.
[11] Hübner, *PW.* III, 1624.
[12] Neumann, *De quinquennalibus coloniarum et municipiorum*, Diss. Leipzig, 1892, p. 35; cf. *CIL.* x, 5670, etc.
[13] Festus (Teubner ed. p. 316); cf. Neumann, ibid. p. 30; Mommsen, *St.R.* II, p. 344.

of the colleges could be believed to belong to the same year owing to resignation or death, the collective attribution to Carthago Nova remains impossible.[1]

A clue is fortunately obtainable from (1), which bears a veiled female head to right, and a trophy with the words SABINVS and IMP. in the upper and lower parts of the field respectively, on either side of the letters C. M. There can be little doubt that here is the name of C. Calvisius Sabinus,[2] who obtained the title of *imperator*[3] and a triumph during his governorship of Spain in c. 31–29 B.C.[4] For C. M., Sestini's[5] suggestion C(*naeus*) M(*agnus*) need only be mentioned to be refuted, since it accords neither with orthographical practice nor with the hitherto unrecognised identification with Calvisius. Nor does a suitable C(*olonia*) M · · · · exist.[6] A solution is provided by an examination of numismatic custom elsewhere. In this period the eponymous mention of governors is doubtful even on Eastern coinage (p. 399), and certainly does not occur in the West. Nor is there any reason to suppose that Calvisius's signature records his permission to coin, since even in 'senatorial' Baetica this is reserved for Augustus (p. 174);[7] moreover, Calvisius's title of proconsul—which would have been introduced to warrant such a permission—is here omitted. Indeed, at this time the name of a governor appears on the coinage of Roman cities in one connection only—when he was its founder or refounder. Not only are numerous colonial *deductores* and *adsignatores* recorded in this fashion, but several coinages commemorate the commissioners who supervised the enfranchisement of *municipia*.[8] Under the Republic such commissioners had been the exception rather than the rule,[9] but Julius's schemes necessitated them, and thereafter municipal foundations in the provinces were invariably placed in the hands of governors. These, like colonial founders,[10] are loosely described as *conditores*,[11] but, more exactly—as the terminology of Cicero[12] and of the *Lex Agraria*[13] shows—as *constitutores*. Sabinus, then, is C(*onstitutor*) M(*unicipi*), just as M. Lurius at colonia Turris Libisonis is D(*eductor*) C(*oloniae*) (p. 206). It is characteristic of a *municipium*, as opposed to a colony, that Augustus is honoured on these coins, not in his *statio principis*, but rather as an honorary local magistrate.[14] The view that this is a foundation-issue is not affected by the presence of *quinquennales*, who were entirely

---

[1] There is no record or probability of *suffectio*.
[2] *PIR.*² II, p. 83. 352.
[3] *ILS.* 889.
[4] Cf. Syme, *RR.* p. 302, correcting *CIL.* I², p. 77. Like Ganter, p. 17, he regards him as governor of the whole peninsula.
[5] *Mus. Fontana, Spain*, p. 220.
[6] Metellinum (in Lusitania) does not accord with style, provenance or probability.
[7] Permission by governors only occurs, several decades later, in the first-class consular provinces of Africa and Syria (*coloniae* Simitthu [?] and Berytus).
[8] Listed in Appendix 4.

[9] Cf. Sherwin-White, p. 135.
[10] Cf. Gauckler, *Bulletin de la Société nationale des antiquaires de France*, 1898, p. 114.
[11] E.g. *CIL.* VIII, 79.
[12] *Fam.* XIII, 11. 3: *constituendi municipii causa*.
[13] Fabricius, *SB. Heidelberg*, 1924–5, 1. *Abh.*, pp. 16 ff.: *quae colonia hac lege deducta quodve municipium praefectura forum conciliabulum constitutum erit*.
[14] This peculiarity of the coinage eliminates the possibility of the alternative interpretation *Coloniam munivit*; cf. the character of Spanish colonial coinages (pp. 211 ff.).

THE ROMAN MUNICIPIA

appropriate to cities which had already possessed *Latinitas*: the occurrence of a *lustrum* within Calvisius's governorship confirms the possibility of this at the present city, since it suggests a grant of *Latinitas* in c. 45–44 by Caesar, who was generous in this respect.[1]

The activity of Sabinus as a founder is confirmed by inscriptions. These record Spanish natives—of the tribe Galeria to which new citizens in Spain were at this time regularly assigned[2]—who are called Calvisius Sabinus, but are the sons of men with peregrine names. One of these, the son of Aiion, is commemorated at Uxama[3] and Clunia.[4] These towns are both unsuitable for the present coins, since they were not of Roman status.[5] Nevertheless, Spaniards are often found in cities other than those of their birth,[6] and this Calvisius Aiionis f. Sabinus may be considered to owe his name to the activity of the governor Calvisius as C(*onstitutor*) or C(*onditor*).[7]

Possibly Dertosa was one of his foundations, but the present coinage is incompatible in style and type with the issues of that city. Various indications combine to suggest that the town to which these six colleges belong was Saguntum. In the first place, the dolphin on the earlier coin of C. Caedi. and T. Popili. at the same mint (p. 159 n. 6)—a rare enough type in Spain to warrant comparisons—occurs in a similar form on a coin of Saguntum.[8] Further, for what such prosopographical indications are worth, the Popilii—spice magnates[9]—are found with especial frequency at that town,[10] and the C. Luci. P. f. on another early piece of the pre-municipal series[11] is very plausibly identifiable with a Saguntine *duovir* C. Lucilius who appears on an inscription of the last years of the Republic.[12] Thirdly, these pre-municipal coinages suggest the possession of *Latinitas*, which, as at *coloniae* Ilici and Carthago Nova (pp. 214, 217), explains the *quinquennales* on the foundation-issue. Many *foederati*, such as Saguntum had originally been,[13] were 'promoted' to *Latinitas* by Caesar;[14] but Saguntum may have received this much earlier. At all events, it was still lacking full *civitas* in the late Republic,[15] but had certainly attained municipal status by c. 8 B.C.;[16] and this coinage must be attributed to

---

[1] Cf. McElderry, *JRS.* VIII, 1918, pp. 70 ff.; Sherwin-White, pp. 176 f.

[2] Cf. Kubitschek, *Imp.* p. 167.

[3] *CIL.* II, 2822.   [4] Ibid. 2782.

[5] For Clunia, cf. Hübner, *PW.* IV, 113.

[6] Cf. Hübner, ibid.; West, *Imperial Roman Spain, The Objects of Trade*, pp. 80 ff.

[7] New citizens were already in the habit of taking the *nomen* (and often the *cognomen* also) of their enfranchiser; cf. Cuntz, *Jahreshefte des öst. arch. Inst.* XXV, 1929, p. 70.

[8] BM; cf. Hill, pl. XXIII, 13. At Carteia it is differently represented (Delgado I, pp. 98 ff.).

[9] Cf. Loane, *Johns Hopkins University Studies in History and Political Science*, LVI, 2, 1938, p. 142.

[10] *CIL.* II, 6026, etc.; cf. Hill, p. 124. His col-league is a Caedius or Caedicius (cf. Schulze, pp. 137, 522 n. 3). A Caedicius was a Roman banker under Augustus (cf. Herzog, *PW.* XVII, 1430).

[11] It occurs only at Carthago Nova—where, as has been mentioned, a different usage prevails, the *praefecti* being recorded together with the *quinquennales* whom they represent.

[12] *CIL.* II, p. 126. 6021 a, correcting 3861. *Duoviri* were quite frequent at provincial *municipia*; cf. Stevenson, *RPA.* p. 172 and below, p. 169 n. 3.

[13] Cf. Horn, *Foederati*, Diss. Frankfurt, 1930, p. 44 n. 26.

[14] Cf. McElderry, *JRS.* VIII, 1918, p. 70.

[15] Cf. Sutherland, *RIS.* p. 116.

[16] *CIL.* II, 3827; cf. Pliny, *NH.* III, 20; Kubitschek, *Imp.* p. 198.

one of the few *municipia* of which a series is not already known. Hill[1] particularly notes that 'the absence of coins of Augustus at Saguntum is puzzling'. An objection which this attribution might suggest is the division of Tiberius's coinage at that city between *duoviri* (for the *asses*) and *aediles* (for the *semisses*). But elsewhere also this division of labour does not begin before Tiberius:[2] in his principate, coinage by *quinquennales* is exceptional, but under Augustus it is regular. It may be added that Hübner's belief that the chief magistrates at Saguntum were aediles[3] cannot be maintained except perhaps for a much earlier period, since inscriptions of the early principate[4] show the usual *cursus honorum*, including the aedileship before the duovirate. As far, then, as the magistracies are concerned, there is a free range of choice; other available evidence tends to the view that Saguntum is the city which C. Calvisius Sabinus constituted as a *municipium* in 31–29 B.C., and is our mint.

It has been mentioned that at least three *collegia* generally attributed to Carthago Nova must be attributed to the pre-municipal period of the present city, when it was of Latin status.[5] The earliest coin after the *constitutio* appears to be that of Cn. Stati.

[1] P. 126.
[2] E.g. Turiaso (ibid. pl. XXXIV, 3–5), etc.
[3] *CIL.* II, 3853; cf. Hill, p. 123.
[4] *CIL.* II, 3864, 3865.
[5] See above, p. 159 n. 6—(*a*) L. Fabric. P. Atelli. (*b*) C. Caedi. T. Popili. *IIvir quinq.* (*c*) Hiberus C. Luci. P.f. *IIvir quinq.* (Pl. VI, 7). There is no reason why the issue with Sabinus's name should be earlier than these series, since Saguntum had an extensive (bilingual) Republican coinage. Hill points out that the assumption of Zobel de Zangroniz that this ceased as early as 133 B.C. is unacceptable (cf. Sutherland, *RIS.* p. 111): and weights make it likely that the Republican *asses* and *quadrantes* belong to successive periods. The former average c. 318 grains (six specimens), and were probably issued before the semuncial reduction, but the latter—which often bear a mark of value (Hill, p. 124)—are based on an *as* averaging only c. 198 grains (three specimens), just like the Julian (and many Augustan) *asses* of other cities (*semisses* usually weigh rather *more* than half their contemporary *asses*). These *quadrantes*, of which the earliest look only a little later than the heavy *asses*, fall most plausibly into the four decades between the semuncial reduction and the dictatorship. One of the latest of them (BM, cf. Hill, pl. XXIII, 13)—the only one with a Latin ethnic—has a dolphin type closely resembling that of C. Caedi. and T. Popili.:

the latter is also the earliest coin to state the transition from an aedilician to a duoviral *régime*. The two pieces therefore partly serve to bridge the gap between the bilingual and municipal coinages. Possibly slightly earlier are other small pieces with signatures unqualified by titles of office (Hill, p. 125), like the issue of L. Fabric. P. Atelli., whose fabric suggests a date earlier than 28 B.C. These attributions are supported by the general unlikelihood that the important Saguntine mint remained inactive in the years after c. 45 B.C., while many Spanish cities of all classes were coining (see Appendix 10). The last of the pre-municipal issues appears to be that of Hiberus and C. Luci. P.f. The inscription on which the Saguntine *duovir* C. Lucilius appears (*CIL.* II, 6021 *a*) is late Republican, and the style of the head on this coin suggests a similar date: but it is not Octavian or Antony, as has been suggested to the writer, and its manner induces doubts whether it represents a portrait at all. Some specimens (Paris, etc.) show clearly that the object in front of the face, sometimes described as a prow, is a stream pouring from the mouth of the head, as on coins showing the river-god of Emerita (p. 221): the type is thus clearly a play upon the name of the *quinquennalis* Hiberus. Similar *jeux de mots* accompany the names Malleolus and Sura in a similar office (at *coloniae* Carthago Nova and Buthrotum [pp. 217, 271]), and are common on official coins (e.g. *gallus* at Arelate,

Libo *praef. sacerdos*.[1] The execution of the portrait requires a date not more than a few years later than Actium, and Libo's exceptional non-quinquennalian rank suggests a date prior to the stereotyped formulae of issues (3)–(4). It has been pointed out that style, provenance and metal demand attribution with the present series; and *sacerdos* is a local rather than a Roman title. Libo's rank as *praefectus* without colleague is appropriate to personages representing the *princeps*, when the latter had accepted the honorary office of *duovir* or *quinquennalis*.[2] But this *praefectus* must have been of unusual significance, as his exceptional coinage and portrayal[3] show. The clue to his importance is provided by the close proximity in date of his pieces to the foundation-issue of Calvisius Sabinus. Sabinus was the *constitutor*, and in this capacity would naturally have appointed an *adsignator* for the actual task of installing municipal institutions (p. 151).[4] Since this was a lengthy operation, the *adsignator* was often elected to the first duovirate *iure dicundo* of the newly enfranchised city[5] in order to be able to see for himself, at first hand, the workings of his new constitution. Indeed, at *colonia* Venafrum, L. Aclutius T. f. Gallus completed his *adsignatio* and still stayed on for several years, at first as *praefectus i. d.* for Augustus (p. 285). This interpretation, as analogies will show, explains the very extraordinary issue of Cn. Stati. Libo. In 31, 30, or 29 he was *adsignator* to Calvisius, and, when the *quinquennales* of that year— who owe their title to the previous existence of a Latin community which observed the *lustra* (pp. 214, 217)—had retired from office, he continued in office as *praefectus iure dicundo*, acting for the *princeps* who had accepted the duovirate for the year. Thus Libo's coinage, like that of Calvisius, comes within the category of foundation-issues, and was no doubt provided from the fund allotted to that purpose (p. 291). This interpretation is confirmed by the discovery that, at *municipium* Cephaloedium also, separate coins were issued in honour both of *constitutor* and of *adsignator* (p. 192). At *municipium* Zama Regia an *adsignator* actually of 29 B.C. is honoured with portraiture (p. 184). This coincidence suggests that the foundation of Saguntum occurred in c. 29 (rather than 31), a conclusion confirmed by other evidence of an active enfranchisement policy at this date in Spain as in Italy (pp. 306 ff.). Thus we may attribute the *praefectura* of Cn. Stati. Libo to a year or so later (c. 28). He is unknown to history: no doubt he was a good party-man, like Bennius and Hiberus after him—both of whom belonged to families in the service of the *princeps*.[6] They too were honoured by

raia at Ithaca(?) [pp. 42, 67]). Hiberus appears later in the position of *praefectus*, but the quinquennalian duovirate could be held as young as the age of twenty (*CIL*. IX, 1156; cf. Neumann, *De quinquennalibus, etc.* p. 29). If (c) is placed later than Sabinus, it will be difficult to fit in the other colleges; it may, instead, be considered the last issue of the long series in the Latin right, and the immediate predecessor of the foundation-issue of Calvisius.

[1] Not of Julius, as del Rivero, *Madrid Cat.* p. 24.

[2] Liebenam, *St.V.* p. 263; Kornemann, *PW.* XVI, 623.

[3] The portrait cannot possibly represent any member of the *princeps*' house.

[4] The two of them were sometimes called, in conjunction, *duoviri urbis moeniundae* (p. 285).

[5] Cf. Jullian, *TP.* pp. 28 f.

[6] *PIR.*² I, 363. 107, *PIR.* II, 143. 118 respectively. The Bennii are a Messapian family (Schulze, p. 519), and Hiberus was presumably a Spaniard.

praefecturae for Augustus, in successive quinquennalian years. They do not venture, like Libo, to permit their own portrayal on their coins, but depict the honorary *duovir* Augustus, imitating the heads on his Emeritan *denarii*.[1] (5) provides an exception to the custom by which the *praefectus* of the *princeps* had no colleague: here this official is not alone, but accompanied by a *praefectus* of Agrippa. This is a striking demonstration of the importance of the latter during the last decade of his life (p. 429).

Even if this *municipium* was founded a year or two earlier than 29, the local *lustrum* did not coincide with that of Rome.[2] Apparently in defiance of a clause in the Table of Heraclea,[3] colonies and *municipia* generally preferred to observe their own *lustra* without co-ordination with Rome[4] (cf. pp. 310 ff.)—whose observances were indeed irregular even under Augustus,[5] who viewed the census as an exceptional rather than a regular measure.[6] The quinquennalian years of Saguntum probably fall in 29, 24, 19, 14, 9, 4 B.C., and A.D. 2, 7, 12. None of the issues is attributable to the last four of these dates; a curtailment of the independence of some, if not all, *municipia* is not improbable, since the revived Saguntine coinage under Tiberius is of the regular 'imperial' type.[7] The name of Ti. Nero on (6) suggests that c. 9 B.C. is the most appropriate of the quinquennalian years; but the order of (3)–(5) cannot be established with certainty. Unless—as is hard to believe—two *praefecti* could jointly represent Augustus, the legend of (4) makes it impossible to accept Hill's[8] conjecture that, when the *duovir* whom a *praefectus* represents is not specified, the absentee is the *princeps*. No answer can be given to the question whether Q. Varius could hold the inferior position of *praefectus* of Agrippa after he had already represented Augustus at a previous *lustrum*. But it is fairly certain that the five colleges fill the first five quinquennalian years.

The coinages of four other *municipia* in the same province are in many ways homogeneous. Each mint is inaugurated with a foundation-issue honouring the *princeps* with a portrait but not by name, and proceeds with a series on which his name appears in conjunction with portraits of the 'Caesaraugusta' and 'Patricia' models (or one of

---

[1] E.g. *BMC. Imp. Aug.* 291.
[2] Cf. de Boor, *Fasti Censorii*, Diss. Berlin, 1873, p. 29.
[3] *ILS*. 6085; cf. also Abbott and Johnson, pp. 294 f.
[4] E.g. Pompeii (cf. Mommsen, *CIL*. x, p. 92), Pella (30 and 25 B.C.: see below, p. 282); cf. Neumann, l.c. p. 34, who shows that a *lustrum* was never considered elastic. However, it might, in the transitional years of the late Republic, be omitted altogether, as at Venusia, which appointed *quinquennales* in 29–28 B.C., but none in 34–33 (*Fasti Venusini*, cf. Neumann, l.c. p. 31). Perhaps this was due to the non-observance of the *lustrum* in the same year at Rome (cf. de Boor, l.c. pp. 29 f.). The failure of Pompeii, Pella, etc., to adjust their *lustra* to Rome is curious, in view of Augustus's inclusion even of provincial citizens in his censorial operations (cf. Schulz, *Mnemosyne*, 1937, pp. 173 ff.). It must be concluded that the cities merely sent their latest available results for inclusion in the statistics quoted by Augustus (*RG*. 8).
[5] Cf. Stuart Jones, *CAH*. x, p. 148.
[6] Cf. Schmähling, *Würzburger Studien zur Altertumswissenschaft*, XII, 1938, p. 165.
[7] For the decline of the *municipia*, see below, p. 324.
[8] P. 91; cf. p. 81.

them) and finally with heads of the Lugdunese type. These cities also provide valuable prosopographical information, since nearly all the pieces are signed. Three of the four series bear witness to Octavian's enfranchisement policy in the period immediately following the governorship of Calvisius Sabinus. The first issue of *municipium* Calagurris[1] consists of *asses* (Pl. V, 20)[2] and *semisses*[3] on which the secondary name NASSICA is combined with CALAGVRRI IVLIA and C.VAL.C.SEX.AED. respectively. *Nassica* is to be compared with *Ilercavonia*, *Silbis*, and *Italica* on other initial coinages in the Tarraconensian municipal series:[4] all of these are programme issues requiring attribution to the *constitutio municipi*—an invariable occasion for production by municipal mints. The present coinage demands the same interpretation. Now since Calagurris is a Julian city, but the portraits on its first *semisses* and *asses* are copied from *denarii* of c. 30[5] and c. 29–27[6] respectively, the date of its *constitutio* can be narrowed down to the years 29–28. In c. May 29 Calvisius Sabinus was succeeded as governor of Spain by T. Statilius Taurus,[7] who is therefore most likely to have played some part in the foundation of Calagurris. This conclusion is confirmed in a remarkable way by the fact that all the foundation-pieces have the type of a bull, *taurus*—of which a head appears on the *semisses*, and a full-length representation on the *asses*. At this date the bull was a very rare type on Roman issues in Spain, having occurred hitherto only on the foundation-coinages of Celsa and Carthago Nova: and it will be argued that the former of these was likewise issued during a former residence of Statilius in the province, as *legatus pro praetore* (p. 212), and that the issue of Carthago Nova was, like the present piece, issued in 29–28 (p. 217). Such *jeux de mots* are characteristic of Roman coinage of this period: for example, a leg denotes Sura *IIvir* at *colonia* Buthrotum, a cock stands for Gallia at Arelate (?), a skate for a member of the *gens* Raia at Ithaca(?), a hammer for Malleolus at *colonia* Carthago Nova, and a river-god for Hiberus at *municipium* Saguntum (cf. p. 162 n. 5). The present pun had point owing to the religious importance of the bull not only in Spain,[8] but also in Lucania,[9] the land of Statilius's origin.[10] Thus Statilius was concerned in the foundation of Calagurris. But he does not appear to have been the *constitutor*. The head of the *princeps* is a novelty on the foundation-series, and suggests that the *constitutio* took place not in 29 but in 28, when, as an issue of Apamea demonstrates, he initiated the rule that foundations should be vested in his own hands, and reduced his governors to the role of *adsignatores* (pp. 293 ff.). It is in this capacity that T. Statilius Taurus supervises the enfranchisement of Calagurris

[1] Kubitschek, *Imp.* p. 190; cf. Hübner, *CIL.* II, p. 404. Attributions to Calagurris Fibularia are false; vide Lorichs, *Recherches numismatiques*, p. 87.
[2] BM; Hill, pl. XXXV, 10.
[3] Hague; Hill, pl. XXXV, 11.
[4] Dertosa, Turiaso, Bilbilis (pp. 158, 168, 170).
[5] *BMC. Imp. Aug.* 604, etc. (commemorating Actium).
[6] Ibid. 624, etc.
[7] Syme, *RR.* p. 302; Nagl, *PW.* (2R.), III, 2201; cf. Dio LI, 20.
[8] Cf. Lenzi, *Rassegna numismatica*, V, 1908, p. 33.
[9] I owe this information to R. Syme; cf. also Schulze, p. 418.
[10] Syme, *RR.* p. 237.

for the *constitutor* Octavian. *Municipium* Zama Regia (p. 182) provides a parallel for the signatures of aediles on foundation-coinages. Probably C. Valerius—who belongs to the local aristocracy (see below)—and his colleague C. Sextius were the chief local magistrates on the spot, owing to the honorary appointment of Octavian and Statilius Taurus to the senior college of *duoviri i.d.* At Paestum and Venafrum too the founders were elected to the first regular magistracy (p. 285).

The mint remained active to produce a series with obverse-legends MVN. CAL. IIVIRI[1] and MVN. CAL. IVL.,[2] with inferior portraits, first from early models,[3] and then, apparently, from the 'Caesaraugusta',[4] 'Patricia'[5] and 'Lugdunum' classes.[6] The title of the *princeps*, here in the form [IMP.] AVGVSTVS, is first introduced with a portrait modelled on Roman *denarii* of 18 B.C.[7] After a few other duoviral coinages with similar titles,[8] the Augustan series is terminated, as at other Tarraconensian cities, by a group on which the *princeps*, laureate and PATER PATRIAE occupies the whole of the obverse.[9] At about the same date a pair of aediles honours Ti. Caesar Augusti f. on a *semis*.[10] The dominant families of Calagurris were the Valerii, Baebii and Granii, who are represented by four (or five), two (or three) and two magistrates respectively. The occurrence of a Baebius Priscus at Ariminum[11] suggests Umbrian origin; but such deductions can never be certain;[12] a knight A. Baebius from Hasta had deserted to Julius in 45,[13] and Baebii are found at Saguntum under Augustus.[14] The Granii were certainly Italians, business-men from Puteoli,[15] and C. Mar. Cap. may be a Marius Capreolus from Beneventum.[16] On the other hand the Valerii Flavi, who occur at several Tarraconensian cities,[17] have a *cognomen* which suggests Spanish origin: a freedman of Tiberius or Germanicus bears the same name at Caesaraugusta (p. 218). Valentini too are not uncommon in the province.[18] But Novus is a very rare *cognomen*,[19]

---

[1] Hill, p. 176: Q. Aem., C. Post. Mil.; Q. Antoni., L. Fabi.; M'. Memmi., L. Juni.

[2] Ibid. p. 177: Q. Aemili., C. Post. Mil.; L. Granio, C. Valerio; C. Mar. Cap., Q. Vrso; M. Plae. Tran., Q. Vrso *iterum*.

[3] E.g. Q. Antoni., L. Fabi. (Hill, pl. XXXVI, 2—BM); cf. *BMC. Imp. Aug.* 597. Possibly L. Granio, C. Valerio (Hill, l.c. 3—in trade), M. Plae. Tran., Q. Vrso *iterum* (Hill, l.c. 4—BM) are in the same class, but they may be later.

[4] E.g. BM (M'. Memmi., L. Juni.) [in shape], ?? L. Granio, C. Valerio.

[5] E.g. BM (M'. Memmi., L. Juni.), ?? M. Plae. Tran., Q. Vrso *iterum*.

[6] E.g. BM (Q. Aem., C. Post. Mil.); cf. *BMC. Imp. Aug.* 455–7.

[7] *BMC. Imp. Aug.* 63 ff.

[8] Hill, p. 177: L. Baebio, P. Antestio; C. Mari., M. Val. *praef.*; L. Baeb. Prisco, C. Granio Broccho.

[9] Hill, p. 178: M. Lic. Capel., C. Ful. Rutil.; C. Semp. Barb., Q. Baeb. Flavo; L. Valentino, L. Novo.

[10] Hill, p. 179 (BM): L. Val. Flavo, T. Val. Merula. Cf. p. 436.

[11] *CIL.* XI, 447.

[12] Cf. Scharf, *Neue Deutsche Forschungen*, CLXXXV, 1938, p. 114 n. 129.

[13] *Bell. Hisp.* 26. 2.

[14] Cf. Simancas, *MJSEA.* CXXIV [III, 1932], p. 13.

[15] Cf. Syme, *RR.* p. 90 n. 7.

[16] Cf. *CIL.* IX, 1874.

[17] *CIL.* II, 2774, 2890, etc.

[18] *CIL.* II, 882, 2446, 3276, 4208.

[19] *CIL.* XI, 488, 7349.

THE ROMAN MUNICIPIA

and Ursus almost equally so:[1] the appearance, in Flavian times, of a P. Plaetorius Ursus at Potentia[2] suggests that Q. Ursus here was connected by marriage with his colleague M. Plaetorius Tranquillus.

The coinage of Osca follows an analogous process of development, and its enfranchisement appears to have been contemporary. Its inaugural *asses*,[3] inscribed only VRB. VIC.—OSCA, closely resemble in style, module and weight[4] the foundation-pieces of Calagurris, and its portrait of the *princeps* is an inferior version of the same type and date.[5] Again, there is, as at Calagurris, an accompanying *semis*[6] (with V.V.—OSCA).[7] Although in the earliest times *urbs* had signified a colony, and could still so be used (p. 215), it was later employed much more loosely:[8] Osca belonged to the class of Roman *municipia*,[9] whose new emergence from the category of *oppida* made of the more flattering *urbs*[10] a title worth using.[11] It is necessary to conclude that Osca was founded as a *municipium* at the same date as *municipium* Calagurris—in c. 28 B.C.—and that T. Statilius Taurus was its *adsignator* and Octavian its *constitutor*. In accordance with this chronological attribution is the peculiar applicability of Osca's epithet *Victrix* to the government of Statilius, who was apparently hailed *imperator* for the third time in Spain.[12]

The next issues from this mint[13] have magistrates' names[14] and AVGVSTVS DIVI F.; their portraits are imitated from *denarii* of the 'Patricia' class.[15] Two more colleges[16] strike in the usual late style incorporating the title PATER PATRIAE (Pl. V, 25) and a few *semisses* of about the same date are not signed.[17] It is interesting to note that at Osca, as at other Roman cities of the province and elsewhere,[18] a *gens* predominates in the chief magistracy—here the Aelii, of whom a second and a third, Q. Proculus and M. Maximus, appear as colleagues under Tiberius.[19] Another Aelius Proculus is found in the early Empire at Asturica.[20] The family no doubt owed its importance to a P. Aelius Proculus who was an imperial freedman.[21] An indication that the Aelii who settled at Osca were originally from central Italy may be provided by Aelii Maximi from Ostia[22]

---

[1] *CIL*. XI, 1777, XIV, 4054; cf. Schulze, p. 115 n. 2.
[2] *CIL*. X, 137.
[3] Milan, *Cat*. 137; cf. Hill, pl. XXVII, 4 (horseman). [4] 178 to 180 grains.
[5] Cf. *BMC. Imp. Aug*. 624 ff. [6] Madrid.
[7] Rather than MV. OSCA, as Heiss, p. 157 (reconstructed in this way on his pl. XIII, 8) and Hill, p. 141.
[8] Varro, *De Lingua Latina*, 143; Kornemann, *PW*. XVI, 570.
[9] Hübner, *CIL*. II, p. 407; cf. Pliny, *NH*. III, 24, by implication.
[10] Cf. Perin, *Lexicon Totius Latinitatis*, III, p. 873.
[11] Cf. Zobel de Zangroniz, *MNE*. v, 1880, p. 129: *distinción honorífica extraordinaria*.

[12] *ILS*. 893; cf. Hübner, l.c. p. 480.
[13] Hill, pl. XXVI, 11, 12; XXVII, 3.
[14] M. Quinctio, C. Aelio.
[15] Berlin (Hill, pl. XXVI, 11): cf. *BMC. Imp. Aug*. 378 ff. See Sutherland, *RIS*. pl. II, 6.
[16] Sparso *et* Caeciliano; Composto *et* Marullo.
[17] E.g. Hill, pl. XXVII, 1 (BM).
[18] E.g. the Caristanii at Pisidian Antioch: Ramsay, *Anatolian Studies to Buckler* (1939), p. 207.
[19] Vives IV, p. 51. 15.
[20] *CIL*. II, 2649.
[21] Gatti, *Notizie degli Scavi*, 1893, p. 30.
[22] *CIL*. XIV, 1591. But these might all be Spanish immigrants to Italy.

and Iguvium[1] and an Aelius Proculus from Tarquinii;[2] perhaps they were connected with the forebears of Hadrian, who migrated from Hadria to Italica in the Scipionic age.[3] Baeticans often moved to Tarraconensis.[4] The four moneyers who sign with their *cognomina* were probably all Spaniards: Caecilianus[5] is a common name in Spain, and the otherwise unknown name Compostus[6] is manifestly of native origin. Epigraphic records suggest that Marullus was a Spaniard[7] from Baetica;[8] a Marullus was Seneca's teacher.[9] A wealthy Sparsus was among the friends of the poet from Bilbilis, Martial,[10] and the same name is found on inscriptions from this province.[11]

In the same category is *municipium* Turiaso.[12] The earliest coins of this city are *asses* with TVRIASO accompanying an equestrian figure of Augustus (instead of a head) to right[13] or left;[14] on the reverse is a laureate female head to right, inscribed SILBIS (Pl. V, 22). Hill[15] compares the head with the Tiberian *Iustitia* and *Salus Augusta*; but there is a much greater resemblance, in general appearance and execution, to *denarii* with CAESAR DIVI F., struck in the thirties B.C.[16] (pp. 50 f. n. 14). These *asses* are of a distinctly earlier fabric and style than the late Augustan issues of Turiaso, and are clearly not far from contemporary with the foundation-coinages of Osca and Câlagurris. A further point of resemblance to coinages of this date is provided by the occurrence of the city's secondary appellation *Silbis*,[17] which presents a close parallel to *Ilercavonia* at Dertosa and *Nassica* at Calagurris. The initial issues of those two cities and of Osca inaugurate in each case not only the municipal mint but the *municipium* itself—and are all to be attributed to the same period, c. 31–28 B.C. Since the issue of Turiaso has exactly similar characteristics, it too must be considered a foundation-coinage of that time. The reverse type of a horseman is very closely paralleled on the Oscan foundation-coin, and suggests that the two issues, exactly similar in module as they are, were part of the same plan: the foundation of Turiaso is therefore to be ascribed to T. Statilius Taurus (29–28)—probably again as *adsignator* to the *princeps*—rather than to C. Calvisius Sabinus (31–29).

Turiaso misses out the usual stage of portraiture from 'Spanish' models, and does not coin again until near the end of Augustus's lifetime,[18] when it issues a series with his

[1] *CIL.* XI, 5840.
[2] Ibid. 3396.
[3] Spartian, *Vita Hadriani*, 1, 7; cf. Syme, *Historische Zeitschrift*, 1938, p. 558.
[4] Cf. West, *Imperial Roman Spain, The Objects of Trade*, p. 80.
[5] Cf. *CIL.* II, index cognominum, s.v.
[6] Cf. *Thes. Ling. Lat.*, *Onom.* I, s.v.
[7] Cf. Carpullus in Gaul, *CIL.* XIII, 5430; Scharf, *Neue Deutsche Forschungen*, CLXXXV, 1938, p. 40.
[8] *CIL.* II, 1995, 2144, 2150. For the name, vide Schulze, p. 461.
[9] Seneca, *Controversiae*, I, *praef.* etc. For a pro-curator of Judaea of the same name under Caligula, vide *PIR.* II, 351. 262.
[10] Martial XII, 57.   [11] *CIL.* II, 2648, 4198.
[12] Pliny, *NH.* III, 24; cf. *CIL.* II, p. 405.
[13] Vienna (Hill, pl. XXXII, 5).
[14] BM (ibid. 6).   [15] P. 166.
[16] E.g. *BMC. Imp. Aug.* 612, etc.
[17] Cf. Zobel de Zangroniz, *MNE.* v, 1880, p. 129. Hill, pp. 165 f., points out that this is not equivalent to the Iberian name for Turiaso, and conjectures that Silbis was a local goddess.
[18] An earlier coin cited by Morelli, *Thesaurus*, pl. XXXVII, 26, is probably false; cf. Hill, p. 165.

laureate head and a titulature including P(*ater*) P(*atriae*).[1] Some of these coins have on the reverse a distinctive head of Livia,[2] which anticipates her common appearance under Tiberius. The rest are signed by three pairs of *duoviri*[3] (not *quattuorviri*)[4]: at this town, as elsewhere, it was not until the principate of Tiberius that the aediles took over the coinage of *semisses*.[5] The dominant clan at Turiaso seems to have been the Caecilii, who are represented on three of the seven recorded Augustan and Tiberian colleges.[6] A certain D. Caecilius Severus was residing in Rome at about this period;[7] the present M. Severus was perhaps related to a M. Caecilius who was *duovir* at Celsa (p. 212), but the name is not uncommon in Spain.[8] A large number of Ser(r)ani[9] also in the peninsula probably bears witness to an extensive *patrocinium* of the *gens* Atilia.[10] The *duovir* L. Fenestella may well be the historian,[11] whose wife was certainly Spanish;[12] a C. Valerius Fen. is found at Caesaraugusta (p. 218). A further Aquinus coined at Pella at about this time (p. 283).

We now have five cities whose *constitutiones* can, with great probability, be divided between C. Calvisius Sabinus and T. Statilius Taurus. The foundation-policy which the *princeps* carried out by these intermediaries is comparable in extent to the commission which had earned Q. Hortensius the title of *praefectus coloniis deducendis* (p. 33). Calvisius and Statilius are not *praefecti municipiis constituendis*, since the title of governor now comprehended such activities. But the former of them is at least *constitutor* by the right of his own *imperium*, like a contemporary founder at Zama Regia (p. 184): they are the last of their kind, since already in 28 the *princeps* had vested such powers in his own hands (p. 293), and Statilius, like Ap. Pulcher *pro cos.* at Apamea (p. 255), is merely his *adsignator*. The change was already foreshadowed by the wide powers and high prestige of Calvisius's *adsignator* at Saguntum, who stole much of the governor's limelight (p. 163). But Calvisius too was a particularly staunch party-man[13] with a brain which Cicero had respected:[14] he and the formidable Lucanian Statilius (a man with a private bodyguard[15]) were spear-points of the new order, typical instruments for the policy of Romanisation with which they have been identified. Probably, so soon after Actium, there were allotments to veterans at his five foundations, as at other *municipia* (pp. 155, 324); but the persistence of this status in each case suggests that the

---

[1] Paris: Hill, p. 166. 7.
[2] Cf. Hill, l.c., *pace* Delgado III, p. 142.
[3] The coins of *municipia* will be seen to provide ample evidence that the statement by Manutius, *ap. Cic. pro Sest.* 8 (accepted by Rudolph, *Stadt und Staat im römischen Italien*, p. 87), that these cities always possessed *quattuorviri* is totally false; cf. Mantey, *De gradu et statu quaestorum*, etc., Diss. Halle, 1882, pp. 11, 25, 32; Jullian, *TP.* p. 32; and pp. 177, 190f., 195ff., 200, 324; cf. pp. 226 n. 7, 248 n. 7.
[4] L. Mario, L. Novio; L. Feneste., L. Serano; M. Caecil. Severo, C. Val. Aquino.
[5] Ibid. p. 167, cf. pl. XXXIV, 3–5.
[6] Under Tiberius: C. Caec. Sere., L. Caec. Aquin. (Vives IV, pp. 95. 25, 94. 24).
[7] *CIL.* VI, 9864.
[8] Cf. *Thes. Ling. Lat., Onomasticon*, I, p. 13.
[9] *CIL.* II, index cognominum, s.v.
[10] For this, vide *PW.* II, 2094 f.
[11] Cf. Hill, l.c.
[12] Cf. Wissowa, *PW.* VI, 2177.
[13] Cf. Plut. *Ant.* 58–59 (but vide Münzer, *PW.* III, 1412).
[14] *Fam.* x, 26. 3.
[15] Cf. Syme, *RR.* p. 372.

emphasis was rather on loyal Spaniards. It is significant that the promoted cities are distributed throughout the province: Calagurris and Turiaso are both in the Ebro Valley, but Osca, Saguntum and Dertosa represent different peoples and regions. No doubt the benefaction was a reward for Spain's share in the *coniuratio* of 32 B.C.:[1] it is closely connected with a contemporary foundation-scheme on a large scale in Italy.[2]

The fourth *municipium* whose coinage develops in a similar way is Bilbilis.[3] Here, however, although Bilbilis appears in Pliny as a *municipium*,[4] the commencement is later: Bilbilis was called *Augusta*,[5] and its initial issue, inscribed BILBILI[S]-ITALICA, portrays the *princeps* in the manner introduced by the 'Caesaraugusta' class not before 25 B.C.[6] A variant stylises the head in an archaising native manner (Pl. V, 19).[7] In other respects this issue resembles the rest of the Tarraconensian inaugural coinages: its type and legend are similar, and the town's secondary name again exceptionally appears.[8] The analogy is too close for this to be considered anything but a foundation-issue like the rest. The *constitutor* was Augustus himself, who—until a few delegations to his grandsons (p. 259)—was officially the founder of all new cities after 27 B.C. The most likely occasion for the establishment of Bilbilis is provided by his visit to Spain in 15–14, in which other cities also were promoted to Roman status.[9] The *adsignator* was no doubt the *legatus Augusti* of Tarraconensis.

The foundation-issue is soon followed by others, with the ethnic BILBILIS, and Augustus's name as DIVI F. and PATER PATRIAE.[10] Then, as at Turiaso at about the same date, a duoviral coinage commences: under Augustus two colleges coin with the ethnic MV. AVGVSTA BILBILIS.[11] One of the moneyers, L. Sempronius Rutilus, takes his names from a Caesarian soldier who held an ephemeral governorship of Asia (p. 238); the presence of a second Sempronius here suggests that the family possessed an important *clientela* at Bilbilis. The latter honours the *princeps*' heir by his unusual *cognomen* Tiberi(anus).[12] Other Calidi are found in the province,[13] but not, as here, with the gentile name of Cornelius.

Bilbilis was not the only *municipium* founded during Augustus's visit to Spain. The same is clearly true of Ilerda. This town restricted itself to a single issue—with [MVN.]ILERDA[14] and wolf (Pl. V, 21)—which, by the analogy of equally isolated mintages elsewhere, could scarcely be anything but a jubilee- or, more probably, foundation-coinage. It is therefore significant that the portrait-model—like the legend

---

[1] *RG*. 25.
[2] See pp. 284 f., 306.
[3] van Nostrand, *ES*. III, p. 204.
[4] *NH*. III, 24.
[5] *CIL*. II, p. 410.
[6] *BMC. Imp. Aug.* 321, etc.
[7] BM.
[8] It appears, in the lack of further evidence, rash to deny, with Hübner (*CIL*. II, l.c.), that *Italica* denotes what was later called *ius italicum*—probably a regular concomitant of *civitas* at this time (p. 315).
[9] Cf. Dio LIV, 23. 7, 25. 1.
[10] Hübner, *MLI*. p. 79; Delgado III, p. 34; Vives IV, p. 55. 10 ff.; Sutherland, *RIS*. pl. II, 5.
[11] L. Cor. Calido, L. Semp. Rutilo; M. Semp. Tiberi., L. Lici. Varo.
[12] Cf. *CIL*. X, 3728, 8072.
[13] E.g. *CIL*. II, 2817 (Valerius).
[14] BM; *Hu*. III, p. 650. 1; Hill, p. 72.

IMP. AVGVST. DIVI F.[1]—is exceptional on local issues: it is derived from Roman denarii of c. 16 B.C.[2] The assumption of a *constitutio* at this date accords with the appearance of the *municipium* in Pliny's list,[3] and its lack of the Julian *cognomen*. So Augustus, during his visit, may have varied his foundation-policy by the establishment of at least two *municipia* as well as colonies (p. 215).

The Tarraconensian *municipia*, like the rest, invariably inaugurate their mints with a foundation-coinage: but unlike most cities of the same status elsewhere in the West, none except Dertosa and Ilerda restricts its production to this single issue. The economic part played by their mintages will be reviewed elsewhere (p. 297). Another topic which must be left for later discussion is the comparative infrequency with which many of the *municipia*, as opposed to the colonies, place the *princeps*' name and head on their coins (p. 325). In the Farther province this distinction is again evident.

3. HISPANIA BAETICA: Gades, Italica

Although Gades obtained the full Roman *civitas* from Julius,[4] its later title was not *municipium Iulium Augustum*, but *municipium Augustum*:[5] Pliny curiously describes it as *oppidum civium Romanorum qui appellantur Augustani urbe Iulia Gaditana*.[6] In dealing with other towns, Kornemann[7] and Sherwin-White[8] point out that, at the time of the Agrippan statistics, there still existed various categories of *oppida civium Romanorum*—enfranchised *praefecturae, fora* etc.—which did not possess the full organisation of *municipia*, although they might be classed with these and usurp their title. The titulature of Gades indicates that it belonged to one of these classes until it obtained full municipal rank from Augustus[9]—a conclusion confirmed by Sherwin-White's note that the *princeps* was responsible for their assimilation in Baetica.[10]

The date of the transformation[11] can be determined from an exceptional series of very large bronze pieces in honour of Agrippa. His portrait appears, inscribed AGRIPPA (Pl. V, 29): on the reverse is MVNICIPI PATRONVS,[12] MVNICIPI PARENS,[13] MVNICIPI PATRONVS PARENS.[14] Others with the last of these legends[15] or M. AGRIPPA COS. III. MVNICIPI PARENS[16] have the head of Gaditan Hercules; also with the latter inscription is a type of Agrippa seated in a curule chair.[17] All have the naval device of an *acrostolium*: the attribution to Gades of these and the

---

[1] Misread by Cohen, *Description historique des monnaies frappées sous l'empire romain, Auguste*, 708.
[2] E.g. *BMC. Imp. Aug.* 88, etc.
[3] *NH.* III, 24.
[4] Dio XLI, 24. 1; Livy, *Epit.* CXI; cf. Horn, *Foederati*, Diss. Frankfurt, 1930, p. 44.
[5] *CIL.* II, p. 229.   [6] *NH.* IV, 119.
[7] *PW.* XVI, 597; cf. Taberner, *QAS.* XVIII, 1939, p. 17.
[8] Pp. 87 n. 1, 141 f.
[9] van Nostrand, *UCPH.* IV, 2, 1916, p. 116, suggests a refoundation.   [10] P. 171.
[11] For the principle involved in re-establishing Roman communities see below, p. 265.
[12] Vives III, p. 11. 35.   [13] Ibid. 36; cf. 41.
[14] Ibid. 39.   [15] Ibid. p. 11. 26.   [16] Ibid. 25. 27.
[17] Ibid. p. 12. 42; Madrid (del Rivero, *Cat.* pl. XI, 2).

other bronze coins here described is certain because of style, provenance,[1] and type.[2] The *Lex Coloniae Genetivae Iuliae* and the coins of Uselis (p. 151) have illustrated the frequent identity of municipal *patroni* with *constitutores*: and the assumption that Agrippa was a founder of the present *municipium*[3] is corroborated by the use of the words *parens* and *pater*, which, with or without the addition of *patriae*, were regularly and readily substituted by the Romans for *creator*, κτίστης, *conditor* (p. 319). These coins, then, probably belong to the category of foundation-issues, whose unrecognised extent and importance will be seen throughout the present survey. However, no early activity of Agrippa in Spain can warrant the supposition that he was the Julian founder. Moreover, some of the coins entitle him COS. III, establishing a *terminus post quem* of 27 B.C.;[4] and the homogeneous appearance of the whole group in his honour precludes extension over more than a very short time. Now Agrippa was proconsul of Spain in 19 B.C.;[5] the attribution to this date of his *constitutio* of *municipium* Gades accords with Sherwin-White's conclusion that the process of eliminating lesser *oppida civium Romanorum* was terminated in Baetica within the same decade.

The mint of Gades struck a few more commemorative pieces on the same large module—bronze *sestertii* of c. 630 grains[6] and *dupondii* of c. 319 grains.[7] These are all somewhat later than the inauguratory issue. Some honour TI. CLAVDIVS [NERO],[8] referring to his pontificate by a *simpulum*:[9] these can scarcely be earlier than his praetorship in 16 B.C.[10] A close correspondence with these coins in style and type contradicts the general assumption of a much earlier date for a similar series celebrating by name BALBVS PONT.[11] The unusual numismatic recognition of the Gaditan L. Cornelius Balbus is well warranted by his distinction of being the first provincial to reach the consulship.[12] These coins were struck in his honour or at his expense between c. 19 and c. 13 B.C.[13] Some equally rare pieces honour the *princeps* as AVGVSTVS D[IVI] F.: their upper limit is fixed by the use of a 'Patricia' portrait-model, and by the appearance of Caius and Lucius[14]—who do not occur on Spanish inscriptions until

---

[1] E.g. Atauri, *MJSEA*. (*Tr. en.* 1919, II), p. 5.
[2] But a variant quoted by Florez (*Medallas de las colonias*, etc., pl. XXVI, 7; cf. Delgado II, p. 67. 109) with MVNICI. GA. cannot be confirmed.
[3] Cf. perhaps his other *patrocinia*, e.g. *CIL*. IX, 262, 4677, *Inscr. Reg. Neap.* 3938.
[4] Cf. Dio LIII, *init.*
[5] Cf. Syme, *CAH*. x, p. 344.
[6] BM (average of three well struck). Since no larger bronze denomination than the *sestertius* is known at this time, the existence of these large pieces confirms the general (but unproved) assumption that the common Spanish coin of c. 160–200 grains is an *as* and not a *dupondius*. These, then, are *sestertii*.
[7] BM (2).
[8] Vives III, p. 11. 28, 29, p. 12. 43; Madrid (del Rivero, *Cat.* pl. XII, 4).
[9] Cf. Mattingly, *BMC. Imp.* p. cvi; *CIL*. VI, 385, 30751.
[10] *CIL*. II, 6080.
[11] Vives III, p. 10. 15 ff.; Madrid (del Rivero, *Cat.* pl. XI, 1).
[12] *PIR*.² II, 310. 1331; Sherwin-White, p. 183.
[13] Vide Dio LIV, 25. 2 for his last known public appearance.
[14] Madrid (del Rivero, *Cat.* pl. XII, 3); Caballero Infante coll. The correct reading is AVGVSTVS D(*ivi*) F(*ilius*) (cf. Delgado II, p. 65. 97), not D. D. (Vives, l.c. 34) or D. B. (*PIR*.² II, p. 310).

c. 6 B.C.¹ Other types with the same portraits show, on the reverse, the head² or temple³ of Gaditan Hercules. Of about the same date is a piece on which the *princeps* is described as PONTIFEX MAXIMVS.⁴

This unusually comprehensive series of commemorative coins is spread over the first two decades of the existence of the Augustan *municipium*. It is noteworthy that all of them are of denominations higher than the unit. This is significant in view of the existence of a much greater bulk of currency with the head of Hercules, two tunnies, and neo-Punic ethnic of Gades.⁵ Not only can many of these pieces, on grounds of style, be scarcely, if at all, earlier than the Latin issues, but their weight (c. 160 grains) is precisely half that of the Latin *dupondii*.⁶ The coinage of Lipara and Tingis (where the same Punic word for *civitas* appears), and inscriptions from Sicily, show that municipal status did not yet prevent the official retention of the native language (pp. 195, 178): in any case the latest *asses* of Gades cannot be earlier than the grant of *civitas* by Julius, and stylistic analogies suggest that they were contemporary with, or even later than, the commemorative issues. Such 'autonomy' of type is characteristic of the greater *municipia*, as is the avoidance of 'monarchic' portraits (p. 325): the *princeps* here shares the honour with four members of his house. But the growing significance of such portraiture is suggested by the omission of Balbus's head on the coins which bear his name.

The only other Roman *municipium* in Farther Spain of which coinage can be identified is Italica. Reverse legends include GEN(*ius*) POP(*uli*) ROM(*ani*) (Pl. V, 26)⁷— an invention of the late Republic⁸—MVNIC. ITALIC.,⁹ and ROMA, with the type of an armed warrior.¹⁰ These have portraits imitating respectively the Emeritan,¹¹ 'Patricia', and Roman *denarii*, the last of c. 18 B.C.:¹² no earlier models appear. When it is recollected that other municipal mints, probably without exception, begin their coinage with a foundation-issue, there is a strong presumption that a part of the series of Italica fulfils the same function. This is confirmed by the absence of evidence for a *municipium* before this coinage,¹³ though a *vicus civium Romanorum* had existed from c. 205 B.C.¹⁴ It is far more probable that the *constitutio* took place during Augustus's visit to Spain in 15–14, at a time when the portrait-models here used were fashionable, and when other Spanish *municipia*, such as Bilbilis and Ilerda, are likely to have been established (pp. 170, 171).¹⁵ As at other towns founded after 27 (p. 293), Augustus

---

¹ Sutherland, *JRS.* 1934, pp. 31 ff.
² Vives, l.c. 21 ff.   ³ Ibid. 31.
⁴ Heiss, p. 350. 39.
⁵ Vives, l.c. pp. 9 f.
⁶ BM (average of seven).   ⁷ Vives IV, p. 2.
⁸ Cf. Rink, *Die bildlichen Darstellungen des römischen Genius*, Diss. Giessen, 1933, pp. 41 ff.
⁹ Vives IV, p. 126.   ¹⁰ Ibid. 1.
¹¹ E.g. *BMC. Imp. Aug.* 277 ff.
¹² Ibid. 45, 47.

¹³ Hübner, *CIL.* II, p. 146, points out, *pace* Kubitschek, *Imp.* p. 177, Schulten, *PW.* IX, 2284, that the word *municeps* in *Bell. Alex.* 52. 4 merely means 'townsman'—as commonly elsewhere. Cf. Sutherland, *RIS.* p. 237 n. 30.
¹⁴ Cf. Mommsen, *ap. CIL.* II, 1119.
¹⁵ van Nostrand, *UCPH.* IV, 2, 1916, p. 114, considers that the foundation was Roman rather than Latin. Hübner, *La Arqueología de España*, p. 177, curiously omits mention of this stage.

himself was the *constitutor*—a conclusion entirely in accordance with the formula PER(*missu*) AVG(*usti*) on some of these coins. His *auctoritas*—to which this formula refers (p. 130)—was sufficient not only to found *municipia* in 'senatorial' provinces, but to sanction their coinage for as long as was desirable; it was only to governors of exceptional dignity, a consular *legatus* of Syria (p. 260) and a proconsul of Africa (p. 232), that he transferred the latter prerogative.

The psychological progress of the principate—for which, in Spain, Augustus's travels did more than constitutional changes at Rome[1]—is clearly to be seen from the issues of Italica. The types bear witness to the intense Romanisation of the province:[2] even the smallest coins, which omit verbal allusion to Rome, never forgo the Roman types, such as the wolf and twins,[3] *cornucopiae* and globe,[4] and, besides the *princeps*' head, his natal capricorn.[5] These representations, occurring even on the foundation-coinage, are in the strongest contrast to the strictly local references on inauguratory coinages of the early twenties. They show that the distinction between *municipia* and colonies was vanishing (p. 324), and that propaganda for the new *régime* had made great headway in the intervening period. However, the bronze unit remains at the earlier Spanish figure of c. 200 grains,[6] which is higher than the weight of official copper *asses*.

4. PATROCINIUM BOCCHI: Lix, Tingis

On the other side of the Mediterranean is Lix: of this city only a colonisation by Claudius is recorded,[7] but its coins of an earlier period already have distinguishing features of Roman *municipia*. They have the Punic word for township found also at *municipia* Gades and Tingis;[8] secondly, like no town in Mauretania but Tingis, their latest coins have partly Latin inscriptions—including the ethnic LIXS[9] or LIX,[10] substituted for the earlier neo-Punic ethnic.[11] The later pieces look about contemporary with those of Bocchus III.[12] It therefore appears very likely that Lix obtained promotion to the rank of a *municipium civium Romanorum* either in 38 B.C., with Tingis, or when the Mauretanian colonial grants were made in c. 33–25 B.C. (p. 60),[13] and that the few bilingual coins celebrate the *constitutio*. Pliny's earlier source is here superseded, as often,[14] by later information recording the Claudian colony.

[1] Cf. Sutherland, *JRS.* XXIV, 1934, p. 31; Syme, *RR.* p. 324.
[2] Sutherland, l.c. pp. 31 ff.
[3] Vives, l.c. 3.   [4] Ibid. 5.
[5] Ibid. 6 (Berlin).
[6] 221, 195 grains (BM).
[7] Pliny, *NH.* v, 2.
[8] Hübner, *PW.* (2R.), II, 2028. It appears also at the Latin town of Sexi: but *Latinitas* is unlikely for a town in Mauretania, since it is exceedingly rare in Africa, Last, *CAH.* XI, p. 452,

cf. Broughton, Gsell, etc. At the present period only one example is known—Uzalis, Pliny, *NH.* V, 29.
[9] Copenhagen; Muller II, p. 156. 239.
[10] Vienna, Copenhagen; Muller, l.c. 240 f.
[11] Muller II, p. 155.
[12] Cf. chronological observations of Muller III, p. 161 n. 7.
[13] Cf. Gsell VIII, p. 202; cf. Carcopino, *Rev. hist.* CLXII, 1929, p. 91.
[14] E.g. Jones, *CERP.* pp. 495 f.

THE ROMAN *MUNICIPIA*

In view of a statement of Pliny concerning *colonia Augusti* Zulil, believed to be Zilis[1] (*regum dicioni exempta et iura in Baeticam petere iussa*[2]), it has generally been considered that all the Mauretanian citizen communities were attached to the jurisdiction of the proconsul of Farther Spain and, later, Baetica.[3] But it may be noted that Icosium was attributed to Ilici in Tarraconensis;[4] and additional qualifications are invited by the coinage of Tingis. In 38 B.C.[5]—rather than 40[6]—Bocchus III seized this town together with the rest of the dominions of Bogud (who had invaded Spain); he was confirmed by Octavian in his possession of Bogud's kingdom, and Tingis was given Roman citizenship.[7] Its coins reveal its status to have been municipal: Pliny's attribution to this town of *Colonia Iulia* Traducta[8] has been shown to be misplaced.[9] Two strange issues are relevant to its position:

(1) neo-Punic inscription interpretable as *Bqs Hamamleket* (= *Bocchus*[10] *Rex*[11]). Head of Africa to right, with usual elephant-hide head-dress—·······SOS. L.[12] F., D. D. Janiform head, and corn-ear (?) (Pl. V, 27).[13]

(2) REX BOCCHVS SOS. L. F. (partly blundered and inverted). Bare-headed bearded portrait to right (Pl. V, 28)—Indecipherable neo-Punic legend. Elephant to right; palm-branch.[14]

Although it was possible for non-Roman communities to imitate Roman institutions and have decurions (p. 346), only one peregrine city is known to have struck coins with D. D.,[15] and among those of Mauretania Latin was not the language in use.[16] Nor do these pieces resemble in style the issues of Bocchus III from Siga;[17] but the wiry and linear execution of the former of them is precisely that of coins of Augustus and Agrippa struck at *municipium* Tingis (p. 177). This was, moreover, the only Roman community ever in Bocchus's occupation, since after its capture in 46 Cirta passed at once to Sittius.[18] *Rex Bocchus Sosi f(ilius)*[19] must be a wrong interpretation, since on (1) *Rex Bocchus* is written in the native language, but the rest is not. For the same reason Bocchus cannot here be merely one of the honorary *duoviri*, like Juba and

---

[1] Gsell VIII, p. 201, etc. [2] *NH*. v, 2.
[3] Gsell, l.c. p. 204; cf. Albertini, *Les divisions administratives de l'Espagne romaine*, p. 41 n. 2, also Reid, Broughton, etc.
[4] *NH*. III, 19; cf. Sutherland, *RIS*. p. 178.
[5] Gsell VIII, p. 200; cf. Dio XLVIII, 45. 3.
[6] Windberg, *PW*. (2R.), VI, 2517.
[7] Gsell, l.c.; cf. Dio, l.c.
[8] *NH*. v, 1.
[9] Windberg, l.c.; cf. Strabo III, 140; *CIL*. II, p. 241.
[10] Levy, *Zeitschrift der deutschen morgenländischen Gesellschaft*, XVIII, 1864, pp. 580 f.
[11] Berger, *Revue d'Assyriologie*, II, 1888, p. 44 n.3.
[12] On both these coins the L is a mere stroke—as frequently on coins of N.W. Africa (cf. p. 478). This interpretation is more probable than SOSI F(*ilius*), where the absence of a preceding name would be inexplicable, or SOSI(*us*) F(*ilius*), an unparalleled title for a local official. L. Sos(s)ii occur in Africa (p. 176 n. 3).
[13] Paris, BM; cf. Judas, *Rn*. 1856, p. 115; Muller II, p. 100. 15; Charrier, *Description des monnaies de la Numidie et de la Maurétanie*, p. 68. 128.
[14] BM; cf. coins published by Muller III, p. 100. 16; Judas, l.c.
[15] Abdera, Vives III, p. 12.
[16] Muller II, pp. 138 ff.   [17] Muller III, p. 97.
[18] Gsell VIII, p. 80; cf. *Bellum Africum*, XXV, 2. 3.
[19] Muller, Charrier, ll.cc.

Ptolomaeus at *colonia* Carthago Nova (p. 216). Muller's suggestion that the coins are posthumous is unplausible: why should a Roman community honour a dead king in this exceptional way? The Punic inscription on (1) eliminates any possibility of a governorship of Mauretania for Sosius; a king could not be mentioned with a governor. Nor, indeed, was Mauretania even a regular province at this time (p. 61). It is clear that the overlord is no other than Bocchus himself.

The head and effigy of Juba II are later found on city coins of Iol Caesarea,[1] but the remarkable feature here is the appearance of the king's portrait and inscription at a citizen community: the features of the Janiform head on (1) are those of the royal bust on (2). The town cannot, then, at this time have been in the jurisdiction of Baetica (that is, the proconsulship of Farther Spain); nor is it at all likely to have been in the same independent condition as the territory of Cirta: king Bocchus, since he appears on these coins, must have exercised some form of suzerainty. It is possible to define this with greater precision. In general, *municipia* prided themselves on their autonomy; but there was one occasion in their existence on which they, like the colonies, admitted on their coins the portraits of dignitaries who represented Rome (like M. Atius Balbus at Uselis [p. 150]), or who even enjoyed semi-princely rank, like P. Sittius at Simitthu (?) (p. 178). This occasion was the moment of their foundation, and the vast extent of such coinages is summarised elsewhere (p. 290). The present issues could not have been made more than a few years, at the most, after the establishment of Tingis: analogies from elsewhere point decisively to the occasion of its *constitutio*. The exceptional feature is the appearance of a king's portrait; only a foundation-coinage could bear such a type without offending the susceptibilities of Roman citizens, since *constitutores* alone were regularly honoured in this way. Here, too, is an explanation of the method by which Rome arranged for this *municipium* at least to receive a measure of supervision. *Constitutores* became *patroni*, to whom the states which they founded were bound in the relationship of a client (p. 151): when the *patronus* was a king who ruled the surrounding territory, the potential significance of this position is clear. It is not, however, possible to generalise from this case to those of later colonial enclaves in the territories of Juba (and Amyntas), since Pliny explicitly states that 'Zulil' and Icosium were detached from royal rule (p. 175). It was reasonable that, when the policy suggested by extensive colonisation in Mauretania had been reversed,[2] and a king re-established, the numerous Roman citizens in the province should be attached to the jurisdiction of a Roman official: but at first Tingis had stood alone, and these coins show a transitional period in which the king's supervision may have been more than nominal. Analogies from *coloniae* Paestum and Rhodus (pp. 286, 243) indicate that Sosius L. f. was the *adsignator* who regularly assisted the *conditor* in his task. Since the *constitutor* was a king, Sosius—whose father may have been a freedman of the eminent Antonian C. Sosius C. f.[3]—was no doubt in virtually independent control.

[1] Muller III, pp. 105 ff.   [2] Gsell VIII, p. 224.   For L. Sos(s)ii in N.W. Africa vide *CIL*. VIII, 6614,
[3] No son of his can be traced (Syme, *RR*. p. 498).   6619.

THE ROMAN *MUNICIPIA*

The subsequent coinage of the city, which is partly unpublished and has not been collected, does not illustrate further its external relations, but—in so far as it is decipherable—provides an unusual series of variations of municipal usage. The first group, whose attribution is certain by analogy with subsequent issues, has a female head in wreath, and two corn-ears; inscriptions include:

(1) EX D. D.—M? ·····L. AEMI., L. VAL., Q. FAB. FA. (Pl. VI, 10).[1]
(2) EX D. D.—······························· C. IVL. ATTIC.[2]
(3) ········ —··ALBIVS····························[3]

The last is shown not to be the same as (2) by the head, which is turned to the left, while the others face to the right. In each case it is clearly a college of *quattuorviri* which is described, in accordance with Republican usage.[4] A second group have the same reverse type—which is also found on neo-Punic coins of the same city[5]—and a bearded head of Baal, with the legends:

(4) AEM. POL. AED.—TING., MAIOR., SIMINT. IIVIR (Pl. VII, 1).[6]
(5) IVL. TING. EX D. D. IV VIR IVR. D.—Q. FABIVS FABVLLVS, L····· IVS SENECA.[7]

The appearance of Q. Fabius Fabullus on (5) as well as on (1) shows that the whole series probably only occupies a short period: Fabii Fabulli are common in Spain[8] like other names occurring on African issues, including that of another Tingitan moneyer, Seneca. The coinage exhibits a process of evolution which is paralleled by less complete evidence from other *municipia*. The quattuorviral college breaks up into pairs;[9] (4) represents a transitional stage when the only member of the *quattuorviri aedilicia potestate* who is mentioned is the official who, as elsewhere (p. 162), was responsible for the issue. On (5) the junior pair is already excluded: the others bear their full designation, *quattuorviri iure dicundo*, not found on coins of any other *municipium*.[10] The next step in the development is the alteration of their title to *duoviri*, whose frequent appearance on the coins of *municipia* shows how wrong it is to attempt their limitation to colonies (p. 169 n. 3).

It may be that this stage is represented by a coin with the head of Augustus and [·····?] AVGVS., all in wreath, and on the reverse, with a facing head of Baal, ········ A. ALLIENVS P. F. II[VIR??] (Pl. VI, 11).[11] II[II VIR] is equally possible in the context; but an earlier piece has shown that IV VIR is the form employed at

---

[1] Vatican.
[2] Gago, in Delgado II, p. 356. 19 (Gago coll.).
[3] Copenhagen.
[4] Cf. Rudolph, *Stadt und Staat im römischen Italien*, pp. 87 ff.   [5] Muller III, pp. 114 f.
[6] BM, misread in *Hu*. III, 675; M. *S*. I, 101, etc. The second *duovir*'s name may possibly be connected with the *gens* Siminia (cf. Schulze, p. 232).
[7] Newell, *American Journal of Numismatics*, XLVIII, 1914, p. 72.
[8] Groag, *PW*. VI, 1769 (75).
[9] For this tendency vide Sherwin-White, p. 137.
[10] At two colonies, Parium and Thapsus (pp. 248, 225).
[11] Copenhagen; incompletely read by Muller, *Suppl*. p. 73. 17c.

Tingis. However, there is no need to assume consistency. Charrier's[1] interpretation of Allienus as a governor was due to an incomplete reading, and to ignorance of the rest of the series of municipal magistrates at Tingis. The father of this Allienus was probably one of the extensive *familia* of the A. Allienus who had governed Sicily in 48.[2]

There remain three unsigned issues. A small piece[3] has one corn-ear and IVL. TINGI. inscribed on a shield; and two *asses*, with the same reverse type as the coin of Allienus, have the heads of Augustus and Agrippa, inscribed AVGVSTVS IVL. TIN.[4] and M. AGRIPPA IVL. TIN. respectively;[5] on the reverse, in neo-Punic characters, are the names of Baal and of the town.[6] It is usual for such imperial types to come at or near the end of the 'autonomous' series, and this piece is undoubtedly later than the other municipal coins, or the peregrine issues,[7] of the city. If this view is accepted, the latest issues show a revival of the neo-Punic language: this may perhaps be explained by its definite recognition as an official medium, after a period in which the citizen communities, lacking instructions, had considered it necessary to employ the Latin tongue.

5. Patrocinium Sittii: Simitthu(?)

A series with the name of P. Sittius stands in need of reinvestigation, which must begin with a more careful transcription than has hitherto been made. A specimen which is now lost[8] was thus described by Charrier[9] and Babelon:[10]—

(1) P. SITTIVS ········ VS IIII VIR male head to right—D. DICVR. (*sic*) head of Virtus to right (Æ 10).

On the only three extant pieces, hitherto wrongly described and restored, the visible lettering is as follows:

(2) P. SITTIVS MV ········ NVS IIII VIR DECR. DECVR. D. S. P. male head to right—HONOR VIRTVS jugate heads to right of Honos and Virtus (Æ 8) (Pl. VI, 15).[11]

(3) ················ NVS IIII VIR male head to right—········ RETO D. S. P. head of goddess to right.[12]

(4) ············ CONIANV. S ····· male head to right—D. CVR ·· CRET ····head of Jupiter to right (Æ 9) (Pl. VI, 16).[13]

---

[1] L.c. no. 135.

[2] Cf. *Thesaurus Ling. Lat.* I, 1688; Klebs, *PW.* I, 1585.

[3] Vilà coll. (Malaga); cf. Gago, Delgado II, p. 356. 17.

[4] Copenhagen; cf. Muller III, p. 146. 231; Charrier, l.c. no. 132.

[5] BM; cf. Muller III, p. 146. 232; Charrier, l.c. no. 133.

[6] One of these pieces is falsely attributed to M. Acilius, *pro cos.* of Sicily, by Capranesi, *Bull. dell' Inst. di corr. arch.* 1834, p. 74; cf. 1835, p. 43.

[7] Muller II, p. 144. 216 ff.

[8] The Director informs me that it is no longer in the Florence collection, where Charrier stated it to be.

[9] *Description des monnaies de la Numidie et de la Maurétanie*, p. 26. 73.

[10] *Rn.* 1889, p. 505, no. 3.

[11] Paris: Charrier, l.c. no. 75; Babelon, l.c. no. 1; *Recherche des antiquités dans le Nord de l'Afrique*, p. 182.

[12] Paris.

[13] Paris: Charrier, l.c. no. 75 A; Babelon, l.c. no. 2.

THE ROMAN *MUNICIPIA* 179

These legends have given rise to a number of conjectural interpretations and self-corrections. From (1) only, Muller attempted to read first CO(*lonia*) I(*ulia*)CIR(*ta*),[1] and then COI(= *colonia* [*sic*]) CVR(*ubis*);[2] both interpretations maltreat grievously the actual inscription visible on the coin. Mommsen's[3] C(*olonia*) I(*ulia*) C(*irta*) VIR(*tutis*) is no better. His alternative[4] D. I(*ulio* or *Iunio* etc.) CVR. (a *cognomen*) is belied by (2) and (3), which show clearly the usual formula *decreto decurionum* (inverted in the latter case). On (1) there is the same phrase: the substitution of I for E is paralleled exactly on a Numidian inscription.[5] D.CVR. on (4) cannot be similarly explained: but the use, later common,[6] of *curia* for *senatus*[7] provides the interpretation D[*e*] CVR(*iae*) [DE]CRET(*o*).[8] For D. S. P. on (2), Babelon's[9] conjecture *De Senatus Permissu* is invalidated by the impossibility of such a tautology after DECR. DECVR. His other guess, *De sententia publica*, is unacceptable owing to the overwhelming epigraphic evidence in favour of D(*e*) S(*ua*) P(*ecunia*),[10] or D(*e*) S(*uo*) P(*osuit*),[11] one or the other of which these initials universally represent. This makes it necessary to conclude that the person or persons here described presented the coinage; the possibility of a posthumous issue for the famous P. Sittius under Augustus is therefore excluded.

Charrier's comparison of the coins (1)–(4) leads him to produce a P. Sittius with the unknown *cognomen* of Mugonianus, by the analogy of other Numidian[12] and Mauretanian[13] citizens who took the same gentile name. In so doing he ignores a further coin, found at Constantine, which he himself quotes and illustrates:[14]

(5) [?·]SIT. | IIIIVIR | MVC.DI.[15] [D.] no type—boar to right (Æ 4).

The obverse legend is not written in a circle, but in three straight lines: thus, in the first place, IIIIVIR cannot be common to both SIT. and MVC., if these are considered to represent separate persons, and secondly, its position destroys the possibility of 'P. Sittius Mugonianus' as a single name. The latter conclusion is confirmed, if confirmation is necessary, by the presence on (4) (visible on Pl. VI, 16) of a pellet between the second V and the final S of the imagined *cognomen*: the reading is CONIANV.S. The coin appears to have been cleaned but not tooled; the spacing and the dot are secure pieces of evidence to support the testimony of (5). It is therefore clear that, on this, MVC. must represent either the name of a city or an explanatory addition to the quattuorviral title. The former possibility is excluded by the absence of a suitable MV(*nicipium*) C········ or M(*unicipium*) VC······.

[1] III, p. 65.
[2] *Suppl.* p. 73.
[3] *Gesammelte Schriften*, v, p. 476.
[4] Ibid.
[5] *CIL.* VIII, *add.* 10525 (Curubis).
[6] Kübler, *PW.* IV, 2319.
[7] Cf. *CIL.* VIII, 1828, etc.
[8] For similar divergencies of formula at a single city, see p. 263.
[9] *Rn.* 1889, p. 502.
[10] E.g. *CIL.* VIII, 4636; cf. 1648, XIV, 3540, etc.; either this or the next are V, 912, 1830, 3351, 4376, 6478, 7510, etc.
[11] E.g. VIII, 271, 1548, 2637; ? XIV, 3448, etc.
[12] E.g. ibid. VIII, 717, etc.
[13] E.g. ibid. 9259 (Icosium), etc.
[14] P. 26, no. 74; id. *Recueil de la Soc. arch. du dép. de Constantine*, XXX, 1895, pp. 310 f.
[15] Cf. (1) above.

Now that the imaginary *cognomen* 'Mugonianus' is eliminated, the plain legend P. SITTIVS and the distinctive portrait which is certainly not that of Julius or Octavian —as even Muller,[1] who endeavours to assign it to one of them, must confess—combine to indicate that it is the well-known adventurer himself who is portrayed, and who, as *quattuorvir*, strikes the coin himself D(*e*) S(*ua*) P(*ecunia*). After the successful termination of hostilities against the Pompeians, and the establishment of the curious territorial unit under his rule,[2] one of the latest roles assigned to Sittius was that of city-founder. Many local coinages exist in honour of colonial *deductores* (p. 290): others have shown the functions of Atius Balbus and C. Calvisius Sabinus as founders of *municipia*. It has been pointed out that the founder of a Republican *municipium* is *Municipii conditor* or *constitutor* (p. 160). Here, then, is a very likely explanation of MV. C. on (5), as of MV. CON. on (1)–(4).

It remains to interpret the last letters of the exploded *cognomen* of Sittius. These, IANV.S—now seen to be one of those combinations of initials so dear to the Romans and so tempting for conjecture—are inapplicable to Sittius's most famous foundation, Cirta, even if (as is very improbable) it was first enfranchised as a *municipium*.[3] But in Africa there were other Julian foundations,[4] which Julius is unlikely to have been able to superintend in person: some of these were outside the old province. Far the most influential Roman citizen in the neighbourhood, until his assassination in 44,[5] was P. Sittius. Although most of the known Julian foundations in Africa were colonial, one, **Simitthu**, clearly did not receive that dignity until Augustus.[6] Kubitschek[7] and Broughton[8] logically assume from its style, *Colonia Iulia Augusta Numidica*,[9] that it had first been a Julian *municipium*. Not only was Simitthu outside Africa Vetus—and within the range of Sittius's activity—but its unique epithet *Numidica* and the initial of its ethnic perfectly explain NV.S on these coins. Moreover, Simitthu sprang into particular importance at this time owing to the export of its marble.[10]

There is, also, a very probable interpretation for the remaining letters I. A. Simitthu is likely to have been founded, not in the dictator's lifetime, but, like so many other cities,[11] by a *Lex Antonia* in the months immediately after his death.[12] Now several Julian foundations carried out by Antony appear to have been called *Iulia Antonia* until Augustus removed the latter epithet:[13] Simitthu may well, owing to the circum-

---

[1] *Suppl.* p. 73.
[2] Cf. Appian, *BC.* IV, 54, etc.
[3] Cf. Mommsen, *Gesammelte Schriften*, V, p. 476; Wilmanns, *CIL.* VIII, p. 618; Kubitschek, *Imp.* p. 141.
[4] Cf. Carcopino, *Rev. hist.* CLXII, 1929, p. 91.
[5] Cic. *Att.* XV, 17. 1.   [6] Kornemann, 298.
[7] *Imp.* p. 154; cf. Pliny, *NH.* V, 29.
[8] P. 53 n. 1; cf. Haywood, *ES.* IV, p. 105.
[9] *CIL.* VIII, 14712; cf. 14559.
[10] Cf. Haywood, *ES.* IV, pp. 53; cf. p. 24, used at Rome as early as 78 B.C. (Pliny, *NH.* XXXVI, 49).

[11] Cf. Hardy, *Three Spanish Charters*, p. 9.
[12] Cf. von Premerstein, *Sav.Z.* XLIII, 1922, p. 117 n. 1.
[13] Cf. Mommsen, *Hermes*, XVIII, 1883, p. 188; Kornemann, p. 563; Lange, *De Legibus Antoniis*, etc., Diss. Leipzig, 1871 (II), p. 11 ff.; e.g. Dyme (p. 264), Pisaurum (Plut. *Ant.* 60, pace Pais, *Museo italiano di antichità classica*, I, 1885, p. 43). Cf. also C. Julius Antonius, *duovir* at Cnossus (p. 263), and Iullus Antonius, the son of Antony (*PIR*[2]. I, 153. 800). See p. 302.

stances of its foundation, provide another example of the conjunction.[1] The true interpretation of MVCONIANVS will, according to this theory, be MV(*nicipi*) CON(*stitutor*) I(*ulii*) A(*ntonii*) NV(*midici*) S(*imitthensium*). Thus the coins, whose responsible authority has been shown to be P. Sittius, can be ascribed to the last few months of his life, in 44 B.C.: he struck them, at his own expense—and in one case portraying his tutelary deities Honos and Virtus[2]—as founder and honorary *quattuorvir* of *municipium Iulium* Simitthu. He is a local magistrate like other founders at Saguntum, Zama Regia and Paestum (pp. 160, 183, 286): he is, nevertheless, a sort of dynast— like another founder, Bocchus at Tingis (p. 176). With the exception of that ruler, all founders whom cities outside Italy commemorate on their coinage were also governors of their provinces. It is therefore probable that, like Bocchus, Sittius exercised some form of supervision over Simitthu: he could scarcely have founded a *municipium* within the jurisdiction of the proconsul of Africa Nova.[3] There are no reasons to believe that Sittius's sphere of government, which included Cirta and its three subsidiary colonies,[4] was limited to these: Appian, who provides the evidence, emphasises the importance of his share—ἔλαβε παρὰ Καίσαρος τὴν Μασανάσσου γῆν, οὐχ ἅπασαν ἀλλὰ τὸ κράτιστον αὐτῆς.[5] The coins suggest that he controlled the north coast, and a strip of hinterland, at least as far as Simitthu, and thus to the borders of Africa Vetus. Sittiani abound in the inscriptions of the region. Furthermore, the new province of Africa Nova is known to have been centred elsewhere: Carcopino[6] and Gsell[7] assign the headquarters of the proconsul[8] to Zama Regia—a Julian *municipium* (p. 183)—or Thugga.[9] Appian adds: [τὴν γῆν] τοῖς ὑπ' αὐτὸν ἀνδράσιν ἐπιδιεῖλεν. Emporiae and Uselis have shown that *constitutio* was sometimes accompanied by land-allotment (pp. 155, 153); this was evidently the case at Simitthu, as elsewhere in Africa[10] and especially in the Bagradas valley, whose riches encouraged immigration.[11]

---

[1] *Iussu Antonii* is unlikely, since the full formula for posthumous Julian foundations is in a different form: *iussu C. Caesaris dictatoris imperatoris et lege Antonia* (*Lex Coloniae Genetivae*, ch. 104). *Iuli auctoritate* or *arbitratu* is not particularly probable, since it was only as *divus Iulius* that the dictator's gentile name regularly supplanted the *cognomen*. In view of his peculiar use of the title *Imperator* (p. 409), I(*mperatoris*) A(*uctoritate*) or A(*rbitratu*) is perhaps just possible, but not plausible.

[2] *PIR.*² I, 153. 800.

[3] On the province cf. Romanelli, *Atti del III Congresso di studi romani* (1933), I, p. 556.

[4] Gsell VIII, p. 184.

[5] IV, 54.

[6] *Rev. hist.* 1929, p. 90.

[7] Whose identity is unknown: cf. Sternkopf, *Hermes*, 1912, p. 379.   [8] L.c. p. 166 n. 1.

[9] If the *provincia nova* did not extend to the north coast, it probably stretched south as far as the Tripolitana. This was a period when provinces—except the highly populated Africa Vetus and Sicily—were large; and the military purpose of Africa Nova demanded the inclusion of the southern area. This province did not survive the early part of this period.

[10] Cf. Frank, *CR.* XL, 1926, pp. 15 f.; Broughton, pp. 78 ff.; Sherwin-White, p. 172; Haywood, *ES.* IV, p. 105, modifying Rostovtzeff, *SEH.* pp. 33 ff., and Heitland who opposed him in *JRS.* VIII, 1918, pp. 34 ff.

[11] Haywood, l.c. pp. 100 f.

6. AFRICA: Zama Regia, Thuburnica (?), Zitha

No issues by *municipia* in *provincia* Africa during this period have been rightly recognised.¹ But this deficiency is due, not to any ancient ban on issues by *municipia* in Africa, but to modern errors: besides Simitthu, it is possible to identify no less than three cities of this category as the producers of misread and neglected coinages. A specimen misread by E. Babelon² can be restored as follows from the second extant example:³

CAESAR AVGVS[TVS⁴] head of Augustus to right (Pl. VI, 12).
A. $\overline{\text{AM}}$BATVS⁵ PRAEF. ITER., IVLIA $\overline{\text{SAMA}}$ $\overline{\text{RE}}$.⁶ slightly bearded head to right, with distinctive features that clearly indicate a portrait⁷ (Pl. VI, 13).

In the ethnic, which has not been previously read, the S is perfectly clear: what looks at first sight like an I following it is merely part of an exaggerated twirl on its upper section. A similar ligature of $\overline{\text{RE}}$. is found on a countermark (p. 117). The letter Z did not reappear in the Latin alphabet until Cicero's time, and then only for the transcription of a few Greek names:⁸ otherwise initial Z 3 was still represented, as formerly, by S.⁹ We have then the name of one of the two cities of Zama:¹⁰ and $\overline{\text{RE}}$. is explained by the fact that one of these, **Zama Regia**, did not abandon its royal epithet even as a colony under Hadrian.¹¹

Confirmation of this attribution is obtained, in an unusual way, from a second piece of smaller module.¹² This is wrongly described by E. Babelon¹³ as follows: $\overline{\text{VAGAXA}}$ ET TIRO AED. female (?) head to right, two corn-ears—M. BATVS PRAEF. head of Bacchus to right. The correct description seems to be this:

$\overline{\text{VAGAX}}$. A. $\overline{\text{TE}}$. TIRO $\overline{\text{AED}}$. (the stop between X and A being clearly visible) young male head to right, two corn-ears.
··MBATVS PRAEF···········young male head to right (Pl. VI, 14).

---

¹ A small coin of Utica with the head of Livia (Naples: Muller II, p. 159. 344) should be classed on grounds of type and style among the issues of the reign of Tiberius. It is one of the numismatic curiosities of the period that this important *municipium* (since 36 B.C.) (Dio XLIX, 16; cf. Broughton, p. 77; Carcopino, *Bulletin de la Société nationale des Antiquaires de France*, 1931, p. 115) appears to coin only after his accession.
² *Rn.* 1889, p. 508. 1; Paris.
³ BM ('uncertain').
⁴ Paris specimen.
⁵ Correcting Mowat, *Bulletin épigraphique*, VI, 1886, p. 40 (Abbatus, etc.).
⁶ See Monogram 6.
⁷ Cf. Babelon, l.c.
⁸ Cf. Kent, *Sounds of Latin*, ch. 24; Lewis and Short, s.v. Z.
⁹ Cf. Perin, *Lexicon Totius Latinitatis*, III, p. 1049.
¹⁰ Mommsen, *Hermes*, XX, 1885, p. 144.
¹¹ *CIL*. VI, 1686; VIII, p. 211, *Tab. Peut.* The town is variously identified with Sra Uartan (Partsch, *Africae veteris itineraria*, p. 67), Sebar Biar (Veith, *Antike Schlachtfelder*, pp. 622 ff.), and Jama (Rice Holmes, *The Roman Republic*, III, p. 539).
¹² Paris.
¹³ *Rn.* 1889, p. 508. 2.

THE ROMAN *MUNICIPIA* 183

The latter bust may or may not represent Bacchus, but the head on the obverse can be assigned, from the legend VAGAX, to the god who is described on third-century inscriptions as Bacax.¹ There are many African examples of the use of V for B,² and the converse tendency was later frequent.³ This and the other consonantal change found here—from G to C—are both illustrated by the Mauretanian place-name Bagaza.⁴ But the centre of the cult of Bacax was Mt. Thaya, near Aquae Thibilitanae, in Numidia:⁵ no town was geographically better suited to do him honour than Zama Regia.

The appearance of Zama Regia as *libera* in Pliny's list⁶ causes no difficulty, since his 30 (?) 'free' cities include at least 4 which were certainly Julian *coloniae* or *municipia*, a class of community on which his information was peculiarly scrappy (p. 226). His list is rendered especially untrustworthy by his frequent description of these cities merely as *liberae*, since he understood *libertas* to be a characteristic of Roman communities (p. 225). The promotion of Zama Regia to *civitas* is not unlikely, since it had perhaps been the capital of Julius's temporary province Africa Nova (p. 181) (now united to the old province). Even if this city had been destroyed in the civil wars,⁷ Thaena and Achulla, whose fate was similar, already both coin under Augustus (pp. 346, 230), the latter as a Roman colony. Zama Regia became a colony under Hadrian as *colonia Aelia Hadriana Augusta*;⁸ it may perhaps have been even earlier a *colonia Augusta*.⁹ But this further promotion had certainly not taken place when the present coinage was struck with the Julian epithet. This, then, is an issue by the *municipium* Julia Zama Regia—the epithet being correctly in agreement with the ethnic, as at Dertosa and Bilbilis (pp. 158, 170).

The *cognomen Iulium* indicates that the foundation took place during the years 49–28 B.C. A closer attribution is obtainable from the singular appearance of A. Ambatus, who receives the unusual distinction of a repeated *praefectura i. d.*—without colleague, as representative of the *princeps* who is *duovir* (p. 323)—and of portraiture. Now within the whole of this period the only other *praefectus i. d.* who is honoured with a portrait at a Roman city is Cn. Stati. Libo at Saguntum (p. 163). This personage has been identified with the *adsignator* of the *municipium*, who stayed on in office as *praefectus* for Augustus, the first *duovir*. L. Aclutius L. f. Gallus, who fulfilled the same roles at Venafrum, actually remained for two years as *praefectus*.¹⁰ It is significant

¹ E.g. *Rev. arch.* VIII (3e sér.), 1886, 64–76.
² E.g. *CIL.* VIII, 828, 5352, 10640.
³ E.g. ibid. 10548; cf. p. 1109.
⁴ Ptol. IV, 6. 6; cf. Dessau, *PW.* II, 2767.
⁵ Cf. Wissowa, *PW.* II, 2720.
⁶ *NH.* v, 30.
⁷ Strabo XVII, 829 ff., records the destruction either of this or of the other Zama—this one, according to Rice Holmes, l.c. p. 538; Veith, l.c. pp. 622 ff.

⁸ *ILS.* 6111c.
⁹ One or the other of the Zamas is commemorated by an inscription (*Ephemeris Epigraphica*, v, p. 649, no. 1473; cf. ibid. p. 280, no. 289; and Mommsen, *Hermes*, XX, 1885, p. 144) as [COLONIA] AVG. ZAM(a) M[AI]O[R] or M[IN]O[R]. Veith's supposition that there were three Zamas (l.c. p. 627) is corrected by Rice Holmes (l.c. p. 539).
¹⁰ *CIL.* x, 4876 (= *Inscr. Reg. Neap.* 4627).

that Ambatus also is PRAEF(*ectus*) ITER(*um*). Only the duties of *adsignator* could warrant his double *praefectura* and exceptional portrait. This conclusion is confirmed by several considerations. First, his coinage is the only issue of Zama, and such isolated coinages are, except for a few jubilee issues in the last years of Augustus's life, foundation-issues (p. 290). Secondly, these are frequently postponed for one year or more (p. 291). Thirdly, Ambatus's second *praefectura* cannot have been earlier than 27, since the *princeps* is already Augustus; but it cannot have been later than 26, since the new foundation (completed before the first *praefectura*) is still *Iulia*. This provides the remarkably satisfactory conclusion that the issues of Ambatus and Libo —which are associated by the exceptional appearance of local magistrates' portraits— were precisely contemporary. This deduction is entirely suited by the portrait of Augustus on Ambatus's coins, which imitates a model fashionable immediately after Actium.[1]

Thus Saguntum and Zama Regia were both founded in c. 29–28 B.C. At this date the *princeps* had not yet concentrated all foundations in his own hands (p. 293). Just as C. Calvisius Sabinus was the *constitutor* of Saguntum, so, in all probability, L. Autronius Paetus, governor of Africa at this date,[2] played the same part at Zama Regia. His *adsignator* was A. Ambatus—a Berber with a Celtic name,[3] like many of his race[4]— who, in the same way as Cn. Statius Libo and L. Aclutius Gallus, remained in charge of the constitution inaugurated by himself, as representative of the first *duovir i. d.*, the *princeps*. The portraits of the *adsignatores* prove that they attained unusual importance in the years immediately following Actium. This was due to a limitation of the governors' powers at foundations. From 27 onwards they were no longer entrusted with *deductiones* and *constitutiones*, and undertook foundations in the subordinate capacity of *adsignatores* for Augustus (p. 293). Probably, in the years before 27 also, the real power in the important new Roman cities in the Western provinces—part of a huge plan in which Italian foundations were also prominent—was vested in the hands of special agents like Libo and Ambatus, who represented the *princeps* in deed as well as in name (p. 294). However, the coin-portraiture of *adsignatores* is extended to one proconsul before it ceases: Ap. Pulcher *pro cos*. is honoured in this role at Apamea (p. 255) at the very date at which Libo and Ambatus are similarly celebrated, and so bridges the transition between special plenipotentiary *adsignatores* and governors entrusted with those tasks. Ambatus, Libo and Pulcher close the list of portraits commemorating founders of Roman cities who do not belong to the *princeps*' house.

The aedile A. Terentius (?) Tiro, who, as at Tingis (p. 177), is named without a colleague, was no doubt immediately responsible for the issue.

[1] *BMC. Imp. Aug.* 625, etc.
[2] Charlesworth, *CAH.* x, p. 116; cf. *PIR.*[2] I, 342. 1680.
[3] The name appears in Spain (*CIL.* II, 623, 907, 2709, etc.) and on the Rhine (*Corpus Inscriptionum Rhenanarum*, 782; Schürmanns, *Sigles figulins*, 267). For a *gens* Ambasia, vide Schulze, p. 345. For another Celtic name in Numidia see below, p. 185.
[4] Cf. Schulten, *PW.* VII, 1721.

THE ROMAN *MUNICIPIA* 185

The obscure numismatics of Numidia, to which Simitthu(?) and Zama Regia contribute, are also illustrated by the totally unknown coinage of a neighbouring *municipium*:

(1)[1] $\overline{\text{VIR}}$[2]RES bearded head of Hercules-Melkart to left, with club behind neck—$\overline{\text{IIIIVIR}}$. $\overline{\text{AV}}$. head of Minerva to left, with helmet and sceptre (Pl. VII, 2).
(2)[3] Youthful male head to left—VIR.[4] IIIIV. round star (Pl. VII, 3).

The style of these pieces indicates this neighbourhood.[5] The same obverse type, similarly executed, is found on some of the coins of an unknown peregrine city of the same region,[6] and the head of Minerva recalls the coins of Simitthu(?) (p. 178). The slovenly epigraphy is characteristic of Numidia. Moreover, Virres has a Celtic name[7] like Ambatus, who was *praefectus* at Zama Regia (p. 182).

The title *IIIIvir. Au(gusti)* is paralleled by *IIvir. Aug. Des.* at Halaesa and *IIvir. quinq. Aug.* at Thermae Himeraeae (?) (pp. 195, 237). As Cuntz points out,[8] these formulae describe the first magistrates of a new enfranchised city: at Halaesa the first *duovir* has not yet even taken office. Thus the present issue also joins the ranks of the Roman foundation-coinages. The foundation in question must have occurred after the *princeps'* assumption of the name Augustus in 27: since it is not possible to find *quattuorviri* at any *colonia Augusta*,[9] it must be supposed that the city was a *municipium Augustum*. Style indicates a date very shortly after 27: there is therefore a strong presumption that the community will appear among Pliny's fifteen so-called *oppida civium Romanorum* of *provincia Africa*,[10] which include every known *municipium Augustum*.[11] His list, as it stands, raises considerable difficulties. *Absuritanum* and *Thibidrumense*[12] are probably Assuras[13] and Thub····,[14] both Julian colonies: Pliny

---

[1] BM (2), Paris. [2] Monogram 7 (*a*).
[3] Copenhagen.
[4] The V is misshapen (Monogram 7 (*b*)).
[5] This is confirmed by E. S. G. Robinson.
[6] BM, Copenhagen. Muller III, p. 53. 63 ff. attributes this to Hippo Regius and Tipasa in alliance: but such alliance-coins are generally discredited in Africa and Spain (p. 339), and id., *Suppl.* p. 66. 64*a*, sees that the supposed ethnic of Tipasa is not this at all. E. S. G. Robinson points out that the ethnic attributed to Hippo was read by Muller upside-down. The same applies to Charrier's interpretation of an ethnic of Icosium (*Description des monnaies de la Numidie et la Maurétanie*, p. 48, 100 ff.), so that there is no ground for the attribution of the present coins to that mint. The actual neo-Punic ethnic, however, entirely defies interpretation: and, in any case, its solution would not necessarily assist attribution of the present issue, whose style, though akin, is not identical.

[7] Cf. Holder, *Altceltischer Sprachschatz*, s.v.; Blanchet, *Traité*, p. 145 (VIRRE. COM. F.).
[8] *Klio*, VI, 1906, p. 471.
[9] They occur at two Julian colonies, e.g. Thapsus and Parium (pp. 225, 248).
[10] *NH.* v, 29, 22, 24.
[11] His misleading description of Roman towns as *liberae* (p. 183) applies only to Julian communities—regarding which his information was inadequate—and, as far as can be seen, only to colonies.
[12] For the textual variations vide Mayhoff, Teubner ed., l.c.
[13] Broughton, pp. 49 n. 14, 80; cf. Haywood, *ES.* IV, p. 106 for the identification.
[14] Identified by Kornemann, *PW.* XVI, 595; Haywood, l.c.; Treidler, *PW.* (2R.), VI, 282.

often confuses this class of city with other 'free' communities[1] (p. 226). Secondly, Broughton has convincingly established that this list includes a number of peregrine *oppida* which contained a *pagus* or *conventus civium Romanorum* (p. 403):[2] these are loosely classed with the true Roman communities whose organisations they tended to imitate (p. 404). In this category are Uchi Maius,[3] Thibica,[4] Chiniava[5] and Vaga.[6] *A minori*, Uchi Minus should join them. This city is entirely unrecorded except by Pliny: the same is true of *Abutucense*, *Aboriense* and *Canopicum*.[7] It is highly improbable that towns whose very names are unknown were ever of Roman status, and these communities may confidently be added to the *oppida peregrina* which included a paganal organisation of Romans. As for the rest of Pliny's list, Simitthu is unsuitable for the present issue since it was a *municipium Iulium*, and therefore founded before 27 B.C. (p. 180); so was Utica,[8] whose geographical position is incompatible with the execution of the pieces. Thabraca[9] also is a very unlikely choice for coins of such pronounced Numidian character:[10] the productions of coastal cities usually attain more civilised standards, and the cosmopolitan harbour-town of Thabraca[11] is too easterly for the attribution to be possible.

The only cities which remain eligible are Thuburnica and Thunusuda. Both of these are shown by Broughton[12] to be very likely *municipia Augusta*: both are in the Bagradas region, to which the style of these coins is entirely suitable. Both are, in particular, only six miles distant from Simitthu,[13] to whose coinage, and central position in the commerce of the area, allusion has been made. But foundation-coinages in Africa are highly infrequent, and were only permitted to Roman communities whose economic or political importance distinguished them from the rest. It is difficult to attribute the insignificant *municipium* at Thunusuda (Hr. Sidi Meskine) to this category; but Thuburnica (Sidi Ali bel-Kassem) was a large city. Its importance had already been recognised by Caesar, who had planted a *pagus* there. It is also, perhaps, more suitable for the attribution of these coins, with their pronounced native traits, by reason of its position in the foot-hills some way north of the Bagradas, whereas Thunusuda bordered the river some ten miles farther to the East. At this latitude those miles are

[1] For the *libertas* of colonies and *municipia*, see pp. 314, 324.
[2] P. 77.
[3] Ibid. pp. 50 n. 23, 82 n. 209.
[4] Ibid. p. 50 n. 22. Pliny's *Tibigense* refers to this town (Broughton, p. 81 n. 204; Windberg, *PW*. [2R.], VI, 812) rather than to Thigibba (as suggested by Haywood, *ES*. IV, p. 106).
[5] Broughton, pp. 50 n. 22, 82 n. 206. For the town vide *Atlas archéologique de la Tunisie*, XII, correcting Dessau, *PW*. III, 2545.
[6] Broughton, pp. 50 n. 22, 82 n. 207.
[7] Dessau's attribution of Canopicum (*PW*. III, 1491; cf. Ptol. IV, 3. 31) should probably be transferred to Canopitanum (Pliny, *NH*. v, 30). The two towns are distinguished, as according to Pliny, by Broughton, pp. 50 n. 24, 51 n. 31.
[8] Pliny, *NH*. v, 24.   [9] Ibid. 22.
[10] This is confirmed by E. S. G. Robinson.
[11] Cf. Haywood, *ES*. IV, p. 305, etc.
[12] Pp. 49 n. 14, 55 n. 64, 79 (Thuburnica)—unnecessarily queried by Treidler, *PW*. (2R.), VI, 620 —pp. 50 n. 18, 79 (Thunusuda).
[13] For the geographical position of Thuburnica, vide *Atlas archéologique de la Tunisie*, XXXI, no. 7; for Thunusuda, ibid. 113.

a region of transition from the Numidian cultural zone to the Zeugitanian. This is a conjectural argument, but, in a subject where a dearth of facts requires conjectures, it may possibly serve for the tentative attribution of these coins to *municipium Augustum Thuburnica*, whose establishment in the Roman right—perhaps accompanied by immigration—they will have commemorated at some date between 27 and 12 B.C. Here, at all events, is a third unrecognised municipal issue from the Eastern Numidian zone of Africa.

Another coin of mysterious character supplies information about an equally obscure *municipium Augustum* at the other end of the province:

SITVMCAESARIC turreted female head to left—capricorn, *cornucopiae*, rudder and globe (Pl. XII, 29).[1]

Muller[2] and Cavedoni[3] attribute this to Iol-Caesarea: the former is obliged to justify this view by remarking that the legend *doit se lire* SITVMCAESARIS. The epigraphical improbability is slight beside the fantastic unlikelihood of his interpretation: *Situm Caesaris* is translated '*l'établissement de César*' ou '*consacré à César*'.[4] It is difficult to see how *ara Druso sita*,[5] which he quotes, is parallel; moreover, the Latinity is intolerable,[6] especially for a cultural centre like Caesarea.[7] Muller's alternative suggestion[8]—S. II.V(*ir*) M(*unicipii*) CAESARIS—is invalidated by the unparalleled and improbable character of the phrase *Municipium Caesaris*, by its inapplicability to Caesarea, and more particularly by the clear appearance of SITVM on one of the extant specimens. Charrier rightly omits the coin from his work on Numidia and Mauretania, and thenceforward it has been discreetly ignored.

The fabric is certainly African; the unique and isolated character of the issue suggests a commemorative occasion such as a foundation, and Calvisius and Sittius have provided precedents for interpretation of the legend as CAESARI C(*onditori*) or C(*onstitutori*) (pp. 160, 181). SITVM CAESARI C(*onditori*) suggests a parallel to THAPSVM IVN(*oni*) AVG(*ustae*).[9] SITVM, then, is likely to be an ethnic like THAPSVM. A town which fulfils all the necessary conditions, orthographical, numismatic and historical alike, is Zitha. In the first place, it has been shown in connection with Zama Regia that initial Z 3 was represented at this time by S (p. 182). Secondly, the omission of the aspirate causes no difficulty in Africa: the *Itinerarium Antonini*[10] actually speaks of 'Zita'. Thirdly, the issues of Thapsus bear witness to the fluctuation of case-terminations in Africa: almost exact parallels for SITVM, where SITA might be expected, are provided by Sullechthi and Thubursicum, where we find Sublecte[11] and Σύλλεκτον,[12]

[1] The Berlin specimen illustrated shows the initial S; a second coin in the same collection and another at Copenhagen suggest that the last letter is C. The Copenhagen example makes it clear that the third letter, which on other pieces resembles an I, is a T.
[2] III, p. 138. 211 f.; cf. *Suppl.* p. 78.
[3] *Annali dell' Inst. di corr. arch.* XXXVII, 1865, p. 261.
[4] III, p. 141.
[5] Tac. *Ann.* II, 7.
[6] As suggested by Gsell VIII, p. 224 n. 2.
[7] Cf. Dessau, *PW.* III, 1294.
[8] L.c. n. 4.
[9] Hague; Muller II, p. 47. 12 (Tiberius).
[10] Ed. d'Urban, p. 19; Parthey-Pinder, p. 371.
[11] *Geogr. Raven.* 3. 5, 5. 5.
[12] Procopius, *De Bello Vandalico*, I, 16.

Θουβουρσίκα[1] and T(h)ubursicu(m).[2] Thus SITVM is an entirely regular transcription of the Punic ethnic of Zitha, which is seen, on an 'autonomous' coin rightly reascribed here by E. S. G. Robinson,[3] to be ST. Further numismatic considerations confirm the attribution of our Latin coin. Its types are peculiar to Tripolitana, in which Zitha lay.[4] A capricorn, with similar attributes, occurs nowhere else in Africa but at Leptis Magna[5] and Sabrata[6]—and Leptis Magna also portrays a turreted goddess precisely like ours,[7] while Sabrata also shares a bearded head of unusual appearance with the 'autonomous' coin of Zitha (n. 3). The historical aptness of Zitha is no less complete. The C(*onstitutio*) postulates Roman or Latin status; the latter may be excluded, since *Latinitas* was so rare at this time that it could not have escaped comment (p. 174 n. 8). The *Itinerarium*[8] describes Zitha as *municipium*, and so does the *Tabula Peutingeriana*.[9] Both these works obtained their information concerning city-statuses from an official document not later than the Antonine period.[10] Now Zitha cannot have been an Augustan *municipium* before c. 16–12 B.C., since it is absent from the list used by Pliny.[11] We have no more official lists before those of the geographers: any information that has survived concerning the intervening period is entirely fortuitous, as a study of Sicily will show (p. 189). There is, therefore, nothing to prevent an attribution of the *constitutio* of Zitha to any date after c. 16–12.[12] Pliny habitually omits foundations by Caesar (p. 226); but the capricorn type, as it appears here, indicates an Augustan date for this coin,[13] and, since Augustus continued to be known as plain 'Caesar' all his life (p. 110), it seems less likely that this was a belated commemoration of a Julian or Julio-Octavianic *constitutio* than that it was a normal contemporary foundation-issue after c. 16–12 B.C.

---

[1] Ptolemy IV, 3. 29.
[2] Vide Treidler, *PW*. (2R.), VI, 621 for material.
[3] BM. Muller (*Suppl*. p. 66) had already tentatively corrected his false attribution to Suthul (III, p. 59). The head shows a close resemblance to coins of Sabrata (II, p. 28). Particularly striking is the type of an olive-branch on the 'autonomous' piece—the Punic for this is the same as the ethnic of Zitha (cf. Levy, *Phönizisches Wörterbuch*, p. 34).
[4] Its exact site, however, is no less obscure than its history; but since it lay between Gigthis ('XXV *mpm*') and Villa Magna ('XXXV *mpm*'), and is further qualified in the *Itinerarium* by the word *Ponte*, it cannot have been far from the straits separating Meninx from the mainland. The only possible site, according to the present state of knowledge, is Hr. Zian. (This is the view of Reinach and Babelon, *Bull. du com.* 1886, pp. 64 f.; cf. Smith, *Atlas of Ancient Geography*, pl. 32; but Muller II, p. 20, thinks that it was at the bridgehead, and Parthey and Pinder, *Itin. Ant.* p. 371, identify it with Kaliat or Kelah. Cagnat and Schmidt, *CIL*. VIII, *Suppl*. I, p. 1145, do not accept any of these attributions.) Latin inscriptions of the early principate have been found at Hr. Zian (*CIL*. VIII, 11002, 22690), and one (ibid. 11016a) even bears the letters D.D.
[5] Muller II, p. 6. 17 ff.
[6] Ibid. p. 28. 61 ff.
[7] Ibid. p. 4. 6 f.
[8] L.c.
[9] Miller, *Itineraria Romana*, p. 899.
[10] Kubitschek, *Jahreshefte des öst. arch. Inst.* V, 1902, pp. 73 ff.
[11] Cf. Cuntz, *Jahrbücher für classische Philologie*, Suppl. XVII, 1890, pp. 489 ff.
[12] The attribution of 'alliance' peregrine coinage to Oea, Zitha and Zuchis by Muller (II, p. 20. 38 ff.) is based on a complete misunderstanding (p. 339).
[13] It could not be earlier than *denarii* after 27 B.C.; vide *BMCR*. II, p. 418 (Paris) for the earliest.

THE ROMAN *MUNICIPIA* 189

The coin is of too early appearance to join the African jubilee issues of c. A.D. 8 (p. 338). The exact date of the *constitutio* is perhaps shown to be 7 B.C. by gifts of *libertas* to the cities of the neighbouring Tripolis—Oea, Sabrata and Leptis Magna—as part of a general scheme at that date (p. 341). Their *libertas* is peregrine, but Zitha's is Roman: probably it was acquired at the same time. The *adsignator* may well have been P. Sextius Scaeva, *quaestor pro praetore* in Cyrene in c. 7–6—the proconsul of Africa being away in Marmarice fighting a war which had caused the amalgamation of Cyrenaica-Creta with Africa (p. 142). Here, at all events, is a second Augustan *municipium*, and a third *municipium* in all, which coins within the province of Africa.

It will be shown in the next Chapter (p. 223) that *aes* coinage throws no less light upon the African colonies than upon its *municipia*. The former coin for various commemorative purposes, but the issues of African *municipia* that have been discussed are limited to celebration of their city's *constitutio*. The same is true of the coinage of the next province to be examined.

7. SICILY: Panormus, Henna, Halaesa, Assorus, Agrigentum, Cossura, Melita, Cephaloedium, Messana, Tyndaris, Lipara, Lilybaeum, Haluntium

The administrative history of this province is complicated. It received *Latinitas* from Caesar in c. 44,[1] *civitas* from Antony by a *Lex Iulia* (of doubtful Caesarian inspiration) in April of that year:[2] after rescinding all Antony's enactments in the next winter,[3] Octavian was probably induced to recognise this one at least in autumn 43.[4] But Sex. Pompeius conquered the island a month or two later,[5] and so the Julian plan was suspended (pp. 25 ff.): Octavian definitely revoked it in 36,[6] retaining citizen communities only at Lipara (p. 195). Thus it appears that all other Julian communities must be limited to the years 44–43. Because of many misinterpretations due to chaotic execution, the coinage which falls in this brief period has hitherto been misleading rather than helpful. Quite wrong, for example, is Holm's[7] quotation from Imhoof-Blumer of the reading on a coin with the heads of Dioscuri to right, and a dolphin—MVSANO ATHEN····or MVIPSANO ATHEN····—C.IVLIO DIONVSIO IIVIRIS EX D. D. Holm assigns this to Tyndaris—presumably owing to the heads of the Tyndaridae, since no other grounds are discoverable. More significant than this common type is the close resemblance in style and obverse design to the pieces of Sex. Pompeius with HISPANORVM, which are found overstruck on

---

[1] Cic. *Att.* XIV, 12. 1.
[2] Ibid. *II Phil.* 92, *III Phil.* 10; cf. Syme, *RR.* p. 272; Charlesworth, *CAH.* x, p. 4; Sherwin-White, p. 175, denies Caesar's authorship.
[3] Cic. *XII Phil.* 12, *XIII Phil.* 5; cf. Scramuzza, *ES.* III, p. 343.
[4] Scramuzza, l.c.; cf. Mommsen, *CIL.* x, p. 713.
[5] Appian, *BC.* IV, 84; Dio XLVIII, 17. 16. The cities did not all fall at once. After a brief struggle A. Pompeius Bithynicus *pro cos.* made an agreement with him, and can scarcely have encouraged Julian foundations thereafter.
[6] Cf. Frank, *JRS.* 1927, p. 154.
[7] 757.

Panormitan *aes* (p. 29). Moreover, an examination of the half-dozen extant specimens of the present issue[1] indicates that the true obverse reading is this:

S.[2] AN̄TO.[3] ATHĒNI. [IIVIR] MV. I. P.[4] (Pl. VI, 1, 2).

The ethnic is MV(*nicipium*) I(*ulium*) P(*anormus*)—and the cult of the Dioscuri was honoured at **Panormus**[5] as well as Tyndaris. With these coins must be classed an issue, of similar style and equal rarity,[6] with C. IVLIVS [C(?).] F. LONGVS IIV̄IR (caps of Dioscuri) and EX. D. D. (dolphin) (Pl. VI, 3). The appearance of two Julii and an Antonius makes it certain that these coins (which are in the style of the forties) were produced during the brief period of Julio-Antonian enfranchisement in 44–43: never afterwards was Panormus a *municipium* or a Julian community (p. 198). There can be no doubt that C. Julius Dionysius and Sex. Antonius Athenio[7] (whose issue is of the more ambitious and 'programme' character) were the first magistrates of the Roman community: it is unlikely that they, or a previous pair, had taken office during the month or two of the *Latinitas* before the *constitutio municipi* under Antony's law. Their issue is a clear example of the foundation-coinage which plays so predominant a role at *municipia*. The coin of C. Julius C. f. Longus belongs to the interesting category, represented by no less than eight examples, of second issues from the foundation-fund (p. 291): it was probably struck after Octavian's recognition of the enfranchisement in autumn 43. The governor who must have constituted this *municipium* was A. Pompeius Bithynicus:[8] the coinage shows that his timid reliance on Cicero[9] did not prevent prompt compliance with Antony's enactments, and apparently the appointment of loyal Caesarians. It also resolves the doubts of Rostovtzeff[10] and Scramuzza[11] whether the Julio-Antonian enfranchisement was ever commenced.

To the same phase must be attributed an issue by **Henna**, of early fabric and denominations,[12] with MVN. HENNAE and L. MVNATIVS M. CESTIVS IIVIR (Pl. VII, 4).[13] Pliny's citation of the city as *stipendiaria*[14] bears witness to its subsequent loss of Roman status. This, too, is a foundation-issue of the new *municipium*. M. Cestius P. f. Primus was a *tribunus militum* who also found time to be *duovir* at another newly enfranchised city, Thermae Himeraeae;[15] soldiers are regularly found in leading local magistracies at this time.[16] The appearance of a freedman of L. Munatius Plancus sug-

---

[1] Berlin (3), Copenhagen, Palermo (2).
[2] Palermo (Gabrici, p. 194. 57).
[3] Berlin—cf. Pl. VI, 1.
[4] Palermo, Berlin—cf. Pl. VI, 2.
[5] Cf. *BMC*. 23; Kékulé, *Terrakotten von Sicilien*, p. 40, fig. 82, etc.
[6] Palermo (4) (Gabrici, p. 194. 53–56), Berlin (Holm 756).
[7] The *cognomen* is well known in Sicily—cf. Cic. *Verr*. III, 136.
[8] Klein, *Römische Verwaltungsbeamten*, pp. 85 ff.;

Cichorius, *Römische Studien*, p. 245; Sternkopf, *Hermes*, XLVII, 1912, p. 328.
[9] Bithynicus, *ad* Cic. *Fam*. VI, 16.
[10] *SEH*. p. 546 n. 19.   [11] *ES*. III, p. 343.
[12] E.g. *quincunx* (Cefalù; cf. Tropea, *Numismatica siceliota del Museo Mandralisca*, p. 28. 2).
[13] *BMC*. 9–11; Mommsen, *CIL*. x, p. 736.
[14] *NH*. III, 91; cf. Kornemann, *PW*. XVI, 593.
[15] *CIL*. x, 7348. For the family's business-connections, vide Hatzfeld, p. 128.
[16] Cf. Sherwin-White, p. 178.

THE ROMAN *MUNICIPIA*

gests appointment not before 43, when Plancus, previously a Republican,[1] had deserted to Antony and Octavian.[2] If this is so, the coin—and probably the *constitutio*—will belong (like the second issue of Panormus) to the last months of that year, when the cities prematurely believed that their Julian *civitas* was an established fact. The fact that both Henna and Panormus are *municipia*, not colonies, points to a generalisation: we have no record of Sicilian colonies at this date, and a similar mass enfranchisement of Cisalpine Gaul had been primarily municipal.[3]

The coinages of two other cities have a close connection with the issues described and with each other. Pieces of Halaesa with HALAESA ARCHONIDA and M. CASSIVS M. ANT.[4] or CAEC. RVF. IIVIR[5] do not resemble the Augustan municipal mintages of the same town (p. 195). On the other hand, style and fabric recall the inauguratory coins of Henna, which, like Halaesa,[6] became stipendiary under Octavian; and at Panormus, in just the same way, a foundation-issue signed by two *duoviri* is followed at a short interval by a single coinage only—signed by one. M. Cassius and M. Antonius are to be considered the first magistrates of Roman Halaesa, and probably —by the analogy of other issues on which the duoviral titles are omitted (p. 235)—its *adsignatores*. The fact that there is time for a second issue from the foundation-fund, with a different signature, suggests that the inauguration and inaugural coinage can be placed as early as 44. The moneyer of the second coin was probably a freedman of L. Caecilius Rufus, *praetor urbanus* in 57 B.C.[7]

Assorus, too, is stipendiary in Pliny,[8] but has a Latin issue which suggests a municipal foundation in 44–43. This includes a head of Apollo[9] which is exactly duplicated on the inaugural coinage of Halaesa,[10] and a reverse type (CRVSAS[11]) which strongly recalls that of Henna.[12] Another type at Assorus is a yoke of oxen:[13] this does not invalidate attribution to a *municipium*, but indicates that, as at many others (p. 324), allotments were made. No doubt some of the numerous Caesarian veterans were accommodated in this way at more than one of the new Sicilian *municipia*.

Other isolated Latin issues of similar appearance were made at Agrigentum,[14] and the island communities of Cossura[15] and Melita.[16] The whole group is clearly to be

[1] Cf. Plut. *Brut.* 19; Cic. *II Phil.* 78; Hanslik, *PW.* XVI, 546.
[2] Cf. Charlesworth, *CAH.* x, p. 17. For negotiations of c. Dec. 44, vide Cic. *XIII Phil.* 44; Bardt, *Hermes,* XLIV, 1909, pp. 576 f.
[3] Cic. *Att.* V, 2–3; cf. Rudolph, *Stadt und Staat im römischen Italien,* p. 97.
[4] Holm 729.
[5] Ibid. 752; Palermo (Gabrici, p. 136. 16).
[6] Pliny, *NH.* III, 91.
[7] Asconius, *ap.* Cic. *pro Milone*; cf. Stella Maranca, *Memorie della R. Ac. dei Lincei (sc.-mor.),* V, 1926, p. 330.

[8] L.c.
[9] *BMC.* 1. [10] E.g. BM.
[11] Head, *HN.* p. 127; cf. Cic. *Verr.* IV, 44.
[12] *BMC.* 11. [13] *BMC.* 2; Holm 759.
[14] Holm 735a; Mommsen, *Mzw.* p. 664. Torremuzza, *Siciliae populorum, etc., veteres nummi,* p. 7, pl. VI, 19, cites from Lucca mus. a very dubious silver coin of the same type. But cf. Hadrumetum (p. 227).
[15] Holm 733; Mommsen, *CIL.* x, p. 776.
[16] BM; cf. Mayr, *Die Insel Malta,* p. 106. 6. This city was enfranchised as a *municipium* (ibid. p. 106; cf. Kubitschek, *Imp.* p. 132, *pace* Mommsen, *CIL.* x, p. 773) like other cities of the province.

attributed to the brief period of universal Julian municipalisation, and shows that at least some cities completed their transformation before the forcible installation of a new order by Sex. Pompeius.

An important feature of Sextus's reorganisation was the settlement of Spanish refugees at Syracuse and Panormus, the latter by L. Junius *legatus Siciliae* (p. 30). These cities thereupon ceased to be called *Iulia*, but continued to have Roman constitutions: Sextus was naturally not disposed to cancel the technical processes of transformation which the previous government had laboriously undertaken. It is not, therefore, surprising that we find, at other cities also, completion by Sextus's agents of Julian enfranchisement plans. The most important coinage in this connection has, when not ignored, been misread. Its true description appears to be this:

(1)[1] C. CANIN. RE[BIL]VS········ his portrait to right—ΚΕΦΑ. Hercules standing with club and lionskin (Pl. XII, 28).

(2)[2] C. L. DOMINVS bearded head of Hercules to right—as last.

The reverse-type is well known on the issues of **Cephaloedium**. A chronological attribution is obtainable from comparison with the heads of Roman officials which appear on the coinage of Roman cities from the death of Caesar onwards. The style suggests a date very early in this period: and P. Sittius, M. Rutilus, Q. Hortensius, and M. Lurius, are all portrayed in this manner before 40 (pp. 240 etc.). The four portraits mentioned all occur on foundation-coinages: and no Roman city-issues in Sicily throughout the entire period covered by this book belong to any category but this. It is necessary to conclude that this, too, is a foundation-issue, as, indeed, the history of Cephaloedium, comprised as it was in the *Lex Iulia* of Antony, confirms. The Latin legend on the coin bears witness to citizenship—no peregrine town in Sicily uses Latin—and a Greek ethnic at a Roman *municipium* is paralleled in this province on coins of Lipara (p. 195) and on inscriptions of three Sicilian cities.[3] There can be little doubt, then, that this is a foundation-issue of the Roman *municipium* at Cephaloedium.

To the Julio-Antonian period of enfranchisement, however, it cannot belong. Provincial founder-portraits in the forties are invariably of governors: and the governor of Sicily in 44–43 was not C. Rebilus, but A. Pompeius Bithynicus. Our search for an attribution, therefore, is narrowed down to the period of Sextus's rule. Here attempts to identify C. Caninius Rebilus are rewarded. One of the proscribed in 43, who joined Sextus in Sicily, was called Rebilus:[4] he must be the man here represented, *constitutor* of

---

[1] Berlin (2), Paris, Cefalù, Palermo (Gabrici, p. 128. 27). Not as Holm 750, Cuntz, *Klio*, vi, 1906, p. 474, Hill, *Coins of Sicily*, p. 217.

[2] Cefalù (Tropea, *Numismatica siceliota del Museo Mandralisca*, p. 17. 28; Head, *HN*. p. 136).

[3] *IG*. xiv, 954 (μουνικίπιον τῶν 'Ακραγαντίνων);

ibid. 367 (μουνικίπιο, at Haluntium; cf. Jenison, *The History of the Province of Sicily*, p. 104); *CIL*. x, 7240 (δεκορίωνες, at Lilybaeum).

[4] Appian, *BC*. iv. 48; cf. Münzer, *PW*. iii, 1478 (6).

Cephaloedium and no doubt a successor of L. Junius as *legatus Siciliae*. He may have been a renegade Caesarian called C. Caninius Rebilus:[1] in this case he will have owed his promotion by Sextus to previous experience of the island.[2] Caninii found in Sicily[3] are likely to owe their *gentilicia* to enfranchisement by the founder of Cephaloedium (and probably of other cities also).

The same interpretation of this coinage supplies an explanation for the enigmatical C. L. DOMINVS. There can be little doubt that his coin is closely connected with (1): their type and style are similar, both are bilingual, and the pair of them stand together in complete isolation. *Dominus* would be exceptionally unusual as a *cognomen* at this early date;[4] moreover, the lack of any other title suggests a different interpretation. Although the two words were officially contrasted by the Caesarians,[5] *dominus* is well attested as an equivalent for *patronus*.[6] The supposition that C. L··· was *patronus* of the *municipium* of Cephaloedium is confirmed by our knowledge of current practice. As has been mentioned in connection with M. Atius Balbus *patronus reipublicae* at Uselis (p. 151), the *patroni* of a Roman city included its *constitutor* or *deductor* and his subordinate *adsignator* or *curator* (p. 34). The issues of Paestum provide an example of their combination, as *IIviri col. ded.*, for foundation and the coinage which celebrated it (p. 284),[7] and at Saguntum we actually find them commemorated on separate pieces (p. 163)—the two issues for which a foundation fund was often sufficient (p. 291). Moreover, these two coins suggest that Rebilus and C. L. were contemporary and connected; Rebilus appears to have been a founder; the omission, by contrast, of the latter's head indicates subordinate office. It is impossible to resist the conclusion that, just as Rebilus was the *constitutor* of *municipium* Cephaloedium (perhaps MV. CON. is missing) so C. L··· was its *adsignator*. Such appointments by Sextus in agreement with Caesarian practice are in accord with his completion and adaptation of the Julio-Antonian enfranchisement scheme: he often took special pains to avoid breaches of constitutional form and continuity.[8] We may compare the activity of Brutus in establishing colonies planned by the dictator (p. 33).

---

[1] *PIR.* II, p. 94; C. Caninius Rebilus, *legatus* of Caesar. Drumann-Groebe, *Geschichte Roms*, II, 109. 39, etc. do not identify him with the proscribed: but the *praenomen* on these coins suggests that identification is possible. They might also have been cousins.

[2] Adcock, *CAH.* IX, p. 652, suggests that Caesar's *legatus* was in charge of Sicily for a brief period in 49–48. In any case the coins cannot belong to so early a tenure, as the occurrence of Rebilus's portrait at that date would be out of the question. We may dismiss also the possibility that the portrait exceptionally refers, posthumously, to the C. Rebilus who governed Sicily in 171 B.C. (Münzer, *PW.* III, 1478 [8]).

[3] E.g. *CIL.* X, 7398 a.

[4] Its contracted form only becomes known after the accession of Julia Domna in A.D. 193 (cf. Wellmann, *PW.* V 1526), the uncontracted form only in Christian times (cf. *CIL.* XII, 3020, II, 3045, etc.).

[5] Serv. *ap.* Verg. *Aen.* VI, 612; cf. Suet. *Caes.* 27. 1; Tac. *Hist.* I, 2.

[6] E.g. *Notizie degli Scavi*, 1920, p. 229: *libertus domino suo*; cf. Martial I, 112. 1, II, 68. 2, X, 10. 5, etc.

[7] The two officials often remained in control of the civil administration of their city for a considerable time (Jullian, *TP.* p. 29).

[8] Cf. Volkmann, *Münchener Beiträge zur Papyrusforschung*, XXI, 1935, p. 41 n. 1.

It is possible to deduce other foundations of Sextus from the group of insignificant coinages. One issue has been attributed, without a shadow of justification, to the clearing-house favoured by puzzled numismatists, Panormus.[1] This is inscribed D.D., sometimes with L. Q.[2] The type is a Pharos, found also on *denarii* of Sextus,[3] where it is crowned by a statue of himself[4]—presumably erected after these *aes* pieces were struck. *Aes* and *denarii* alike may perhaps be supposed to represent the well-known lighthouse at **Messana**,[5] still recalled by the village of Faro.[6] Such *types parlants* occur not infrequently as ethnics,[7] but can only be considered as such when the ethnic itself is lacking.[8] There can be little doubt that these meagre bronze coins were issued on the capture of Messana by Sextus early in 42,[9] and that they bear witness to a garrison-settlement planted to enforce the heavy penalties inflicted on the city. It is unlikely that this is a solitary exception to the limitation of Sicilian city-coinage to foundation-issues: by the analogy of Cephaloedium it may be assumed that L. Q. was the *constitutor* or *adsignator*.

It is not improbable that a similar small piece, with no mint-mark but the caps of the Dioscuri (Pl. VII, 7),[10] refers, likewise by a city-badge, to **Tyndaris**, which was one of Sextus's first captures,[11] and may well have been treated in the same way as Messana. This attribution, again, is not invalidated by the occurrence, on other pieces with the same type, of the ethnic of Panormus: here the type itself must serve as ethnic.

On the whole, the foundation-policy of Sextus as illustrated by these unknown coinages does not suggest much consideration for the Sicilians. Panormus and Syracuse were devoted to refugee Spaniards, Messana and probably Tyndaris to Roman garrisons. But this may not be a fair cross-section of Sextus's policy: apart from his observance of constitutional forms, we learn that he was generally benevolent to the Sicilian people,[12] and that the emergencies of his rule stimulated an unparalleled industrial activity in the island.[13] Perhaps the foundation of Cephaloedium illustrates this more favourable aspect of his dominion, for which Augustan historians have naturally spared little sympathy.[14]

When Octavian, in 36, revoked not only the Pompeian settlements, but also the Julio-Antonian enfranchisement scheme, only two communities retained their *civitas*. In both of these, Lipara and Tauromenium, wholesale deportations of Pompeian supporters warranted fresh drafts of *cives* and so refoundations; and one celebrated

---

[1] E.g. *BMC. Sicily*, p. 124. 13.
[2] Palermo; cf. Gabrici, p. 156. 132. Pl. V, 24.
[3] *BMCR*. pl. CXX, 14, 15.
[4] Liegle, *Transactions of International Numismatic Congress of 1936*, p. 211.
[5] Cf. Baumeister, *Denkmäler des klassischen Altertums, usw.* p. 957.
[6] Philipp, *PW*. xv, 1230.
[7] Cf. Netzhammer, *VIIIe Congrès international des sciences historiques*, 1938, pp. 73 ff., and below, p. 259.
[8] I.e. the appearance of a Pharos *with* the ethnic of Agrigentum (p. 191) may be irrelevant to the present attribution.
[9] Dio XLVIII, 17. 6; cf. XLIX, 11. 2; Scramuzza, *ES*. III, p. 252.
[10] Berlin.
[11] Dio XLVIII, 17. 6.
[12] Ibid. 17. 2; cf. Scramuzza, l.c. p. 251.
[13] Scramuzza, l.c. pp. 251, 287, 309, 345, 372.
[14] Velleius II, 73. 3; cf. Scramuzza, l.c. p. 251.

its compulsory revolution with coinage. This issue of Lipara,[1] with a head of Vulcan and the type of his tongs, shows various forms of the legend Γ. MĀPKIOC ΛEY. Γ. AYC²ωNEYΣ[3] ΔYO[4] ĀNΔP. (Pl. V, 23). Rudolph's assumption of the invariability of *duoviri* at colonies and *quattuorviri* at *municipia* is unacceptable (p. 169): but Jenison's ruling,[5] that colonies must use Latin officially but *municipia* need not, is in general correct. Pliny[6] records the establishment—no doubt after the mass deportations by Octavian[7]—of a citizen community, which we may assume with Münzer[8] and Kornemann[9] to have been a *municipium*.[10] *Municipia*, like colonies, often consisted of drafts of settlers, and Orsi's[11] conjecture of a colony at Lipara is unplausible. With the exception of Tauromenium, Lipara was very soon the only citizen community in the province:[12] this may account for the choice of its mint for an extensive official coinage just before and after Naulochus (p. 52). There is every probability that C. Marcius L. f. and L. Ausonius (?)[13] were the first magistrates of the new foundation, which so isolated an issue inevitably commemorates; so this single coinage of Lipara appears to record the first stage of the disciplinary inflictions on the unfortunate province[14] (cf. pp. 395 ff.).

Subsequent phases of the gradual and partial re-enfranchisement and Romanisation[15] are strikingly illuminated by an obscure group of municipal coins which have been entirely misunderstood. They can be divided into two series according to the absence or presence of a proconsul's name. In the former category there are only three issues, of which one may be attributed to *colonia* Thermae Himeraeae (p. 238). Of the two municipal coinages, one was struck at Halaesa, which is shown to have exchanged stipendiary for municipal rank—after the compilation of Pliny's list—by an inscription IMP. CAESAREI (*sic*) DIVI F. AVGVSTO P. [P.] MVNICIPIVM.[16] The coins have a laureate head of Augustus to right[17] or to left,[18] with the legend HALAESA ARCHONIDA; on the reverse is M. PACCIVS MACXV. (*sic*)[19] FLAME. or M. PAC. MAX. IIVI[R A]VG. DES.[20] round A̅V̅G̅. in wreath (Pl. VII, 6). The formula *IIvir*

---

[1] Tropea, *Archivio storico per la Sicilia orientale*, I, 1901, p. 32.
[2] Friedländer, *Ann. dell' Inst. di corr. arch.* 1852, p. 156; Hill, *Coins of Sicily*, p. 216, read AC.
[3] As Muensterberg, *Beamtennamen*, s.v.; Friedländer, l.c.
[4] BM; not ΔYωN, as Holm 715.
[5] L.c. pp. 104 ff.; cf. *IG*. XIV, 367, 954; *CIL*. X, 7240. For exceptions vide Kubitschek, *SB. Wien*, CLXXVII, *Abh*. 4, 1916, p. 104 n. 1.
[6] *NH*. III, 93.
[7] Dio XLVIII, 48. 6—to be sent back later.
[8] *PW*. XIV, 1544. [9] *PW*. XVI, 593.
[10] It is impossible to verify a coin with the Latin legend LIPAR., quoted from the Carelli collection

(*Documenti inediti per servire alla storia dei Musei d'Italia*, III, 1880, p. 383. 156).
[11] *Notizie degli Scavi*, 1929, p. 99.
[12] Chilver, *JRS*. XXVIII, 1938, p. 246, points out that, *pace* Scramuzza, l.c., it is very unlikely that even *Latinitas* survived in Sicily.
[13] For this *gentilicium*—hitherto only known at a later date—see *Thesaurus Linguae Latinae*, II, 1540.
[14] Dio XLIX, 11. 5; cf. Scramuzza, l.c. p. 345.
[15] Cf. Mommsen, *CIL*. X, p. 772; Stevenson, *CAH*. X, p. 207. [16] *CIL*. X, 7458.
[17] Berlin; cf. Holm 754. [18] Paris.
[19] Berlin: not MAXSV. (as Holm).
[20] Berlin, Palermo (Gabrici, p. 136. 19). For the Etruscan *gens* Paccia vide Schulze, p. 204; for a

Aug(ustī) des(ignatus) is clearly of an exceptional character. Augustus would not have overridden ordinary municipal elections, and commendations *iudiciis Augusti*[1] are a later phenomenon which would not in any case justify the present phrase. Cuntz[2] rightly concludes that the only occasion which could warrant this was the foundation of the *municipium*: the *Lex Coloniae Genetivae Iuliae* expressly informs us that Caesar had appointed the first magistrates of Urso,[3] and similar titles occur on foundation-issues of *municipium* Thuburnica (?) (p. 185) and *colonia* Thermae Himeraeae (?). Strongly in favour of this view is the fact that the *duovir* is only *designatus*: he does not yet hold office, since the control of new Roman cities was for a time in the hands of the *adsignator* to whom the founder entrusted the work.[4] Here then is an issue similar to those of the *constitutores* of Simitthu (?) and Saguntum (pp. 178, 158). Since at this time Augustus can say *mea auctoritate deductas*,[5] or even baldly *deduxi*,[6] of foundations undertaken by his representatives, it is not surprising that the emphasis is laid on him alone (p. 293).

The second piece in this category bears the ethnic of **Lilybaeum**, and the name AVGV.:[7] this too is a kind of inauguratory issue, since the foundation-fund often enabled the initial coinage—with which, at Lilybaeum, this cannot be identified (p. 197)—to be repeated (p. 291).[8]

The remaining issues of Roman *municipia* include three *asses*,[9] with heads of Augustus, and a *semis*[10] with *triskeles*:

Asses

(1)[11] AVGVSTO P. P. AGRIGENTIN.—L. CLODIO RVFO PRO COS. in wreath round SALASSO[12] COMITIALE,[13] SEX. RVFO IIVIR. (Pl. VII, 5).
(2)[14] CAESAR AVGVSTVS—Q. TERENTIO CVLLEONE PRO COS. LILYB. head of Apollo.
(3)[15] AVGVSTVS—SISENNA PRO COS. in wreath round L. STATIVS FLACC... [P. COTTA BAL.[16]] IIVIR.

Pacius at Syracuse, vide *Notizie degli Scavi*, 1895, no. 174; for a Baggius, see below, p. 213. No Paccius Maximus is otherwise known until the second century A.D. (*CIL*. VI, 32638a. 26).

[1] Cf. Mommsen, *St.R.* II, 1082.
[2] *Klio*, VI, 1906, p. 471.
[3] Ch. 125.
[4] Rudorff, *Gromatische Institutionen*, p. 334; cf. Marquardt, *St.V.* V, 1, p. 458; Jullian, *TP.* p. 29, shows that he was actually sometimes one of the first *duoviri*.
[5] *RG*. 28, as restored by Weber, *Princeps*, I, p. 252* n. 672, etc.
[6] *RG*. 3.   [7] Palermo (Gabrici, p. 144).
[8] Panormitan issues with the head of Augustus and a Latin inscription are posthumous, as seen by Gabrici, p. 206, in correction of p. 98.
[9] Av. c. 110–125 grains.   [10] Av. c. 82 grains.
[11] *BMC*. 162, Munich; AVGVS. (BM); PR. (Munich); AGRIGETIN. (*BMC*. 160); CLDIO (Palermo: Gabrici, p. 119); RFO (own collection).
[12] The Salassi owed their position to support of Caesar (Cic. *Fam.* VI, 18. 2, Q. Salassus).
[13] I.e. senior *duovir*; cf. Hardy, *Roman Laws and Charters*, p. 69. Misread by Mommsen, *Mzw.* p. 663.
[14] BM, Florence, Paris, Athens, Palermo (2), own collection (2); LIL. (Glasgow).
[15] Paris ('Panormus'), Athens (uncertain); SISIINNA (Gotha), SISENA (Paris).
[16] Omitted on a Paris coin.

Semis

(4)¹ SEPT. ET BALB. II.VIR.—L. SEIO PRO COS. round D. D. (Pl. VII, 8).

(3) and (4), like the rest, are of Sicilian provenance.² Chronology is not assisted by portraiture, epigraphy or style, since these are of the poorest, and do not develop: they warrant the gloomiest descriptions of Sicilian civilisation at this time.³

(1) and (2) bear the ethnics of **Agrigentum** and **Lilybaeum**, both of which became *municipia* after the compilation of the list on which Pliny depends.⁴ By comparison with coinage of the Augustan and Tiberian colonies, it is possible not only to achieve attributions for (3) and (4)—which are often attributed without the slightest plausibility to the general 'dump' Panormus—but to establish the fact that (1), (2), (3) and (4) all belong to the 'foundation' category. The only colonial piece of Augustus—an *as* with the ethnic of Tyndaris and the signature of L. Mussidius *pro cos.* (p. 237)—resembles this series. Another colonial piece is a *semis* with the signatures of a college of *duoviri* and of P. F. Silva *pr*[aetor] or *pr*[*o cos.*]:⁵ it must be attributed to the principate of Tiberius and to *colonia* Panormus.⁶ A close similarity of types, size, and weight, indicates that

---

¹ BM, Berlin, Palermo, own coll.; misread by *BMC.* p. 128. 13, Holm III, p. 526, Bahrfeldt, l.c. p. 428. 79, etc. Borghesi's invention SESSTIO (*Bullettino archeologico napolitano*, *NS.* VI, 1858, pp. 31 f.) has been rightly rejected by Holm, l.c., and Imhoof-Blumer, *MG.* p. 37. Even Borghesi (l.c. p. 31) saw that Sestini's L. VIBIO was wrong. D'Ailly's APPVL. is expelled with justice by Klein (*Die römischen Verwaltungsbeamten*, I, 1, p. 100), while Sestini's L. SEXTI. PROCOS. (*Descrizione di molte medaglie*, p. 16; cf. Holm, l.c.) is tooled from a common coin of Panormus (Munich, etc., var. *BMC.* 47). These imaginative flights are due to the crudity of style and lettering.

² E.g. specimens of each, found in West Sicily, acquired by the writer in Rome. (3) is misattributed by Scott, *NC.* XIV, 1852, p. 123.

³ E.g. Holm III, pp. 232 f.—*Die Cultur eines Grenzlandes.*

⁴ For the former vide Kubitschek, *SB. Wien*, CLXXVII, *Abh.* 4, 1916, p. 104, *pace* Mommsen, *Mzw.* p. 663; for the latter, *ILS.* 6768; cf. Kornemann, p. 540; Pais, *Museo italiano di antichità classica*, I, 1885, p. 48 n. 1, correcting *Liber Coloniarum*, p. 236.

⁵ BM, Berlin, Naples, Palermo, own coll.; cf. Bahrfeldt, *RS.* XII, 1904, p. 426. 78: misread by Imhoof-Blumer, *MG.* p. 37, etc. Cuntz, *Klio*, VI, 1906, p. 471, does not know that PR. is found as an abbreviation for *pro consule*, or *praetor* as applied to proconsuls (pp. 61, 135).

⁶ Bahrfeldt, *RS.* XII, 1904, pl. IV, 92. 93 notes a striking similarity to a peregrine coin of the city. The issue of Silva (if that is his name: vide Borghesi, *Œuvres*, VIII, 397; *PW.* VI, 2617 [180]) may therefore be supposed to have been made, at the latest, not long after its 'refoundation'. But a late Augustan or Tiberian date for this piece is suggested by Kornemann (169), and indicated by the career of L. Seius, whose name appears on the parallel issue (see p. 198). There are, moreover, particular reasons for supposing that the *deductio* did not occur until after the mutiny of A.D. 14. The *aerarium militare*, founded in A.D. 6, did not quickly collect enough funds to make the demobilisation of veterans punctual (Parker, *The Roman Legions*, p. 212): indeed, after the German disaster of A.D. 9, none at all were discharged for the rest of the reign, and the mutineers of A.D. 14 made it very clear that it was this circumstance which had become particularly intolerable (Tac. *Ann.* I, 17, 35). Thereafter, however, their discharge was—for some time at least—prompt (ibid. I, 37, 52). Now the foundation of the colonies of Augustus, which were of a military character, was the result of a policy which gave allotments of land as partial substitute for the statutory donative of 12,000 sesterces (Parker, l.c. p. 246: Dio LV, 23. 1): thus the establishment of

this issue is not far from contemporary with (4), the *semis* of L. Seius. This probability is confirmed by his identification with Seius Tubero, *consul suffectus* as late as A.D. 18,[1] and by the spectrograph: his coin contains a certain proportion of zinc,[2] which is not found in the pieces with Augustus's head,[3] but appears in Tiberian peregrine mintages of the island,[4] to which the issue signed by Seius also approximates in weight. However, good specimens show that the resemblance to Silva's coin is one of category only, not of execution: Seius's piece is very unlikely to be of the same mint as Silva's, and, indeed, it cannot be classified at all satisfactorily with any of the coins of the Augustan period. (3) is likewise stylistically isolated. Thus, of the seven Augustan and Tiberian issues of Roman cities that have been discussed—five *asses* and two *semisses*—not only are five demonstrably from different mints, but stylistic considerations require that to the other two also should be attributed an origin different from the rest and from each other. A second curious feature is that the proconsuls are never the same: why should seven different cities all commemorate—on their only issue—a different governor? The difference of dates, which these names require, makes it clear that the whole group of issues cannot spring from a single general warrant; however, their uniformity of type and their variety of mint postulate a special commemorative occasion, shared by all, but at different times. Moreover, not only does each of these pieces appear to be of a different city, but the only other coins issued in Sicily during the same period are of three mints that are again separate from each other and from the rest.[5] Those are all foundation-issues: these must belong to the same category. Only in this way can be explained the uniformity of type, but the surprising variety of proconsuls and of mints: only in this way the commemorative character which the isolation of each issue at its city indicates.[6] Furthermore, not only will it be seen throughout this survey that coinages commemorating *deductio* or *constitutio* are far more common than has been believed—and have a monopoly of Roman city-currency in other provinces besides Sicily—but it is on such issues that the names of proconsuls regularly are found: in fact, apart from these their appearance at Roman cities is limited to a few honorary portraits in Africa (p. 229). The honorary insertion of their names on a regular colonial series would be pointless; on these seven foundation-issues, as on all the rest of the same category, its purpose is clear. When Augustus orders a foundation, a coin of Apamea (p. 255) shows that, as in Republican times, it is the governor who carries it out; but now the *auctoritas* springs from the *princeps* (p. 424) and it is no longer the governor himself who is *constitutor* (or *deductor*) and *patronus*, but Augustus. The governor is now merely in the position of *adsignator* (*curator operis*) (p. 293). It is

---

Panormus is very unlikely to have fallen in a period when no veterans were being discharged, but is most probable for the ensuing years of rapid demobilisation. There is no evidence for the attribution of *colonia* Panormus to Augustus, as by Paribeni, *Augustus* (1938), p. 413: Pais, l.c. p. 44, points out that the epithet 'Augusta' may well refer to post-Augustan foundations.

[1] *PIR.* III, 192, 248.
[2] Spectrogram 47. [3] Ibid. 45, 46. [4] Ibid. 44.
[5] Halaesa, Tauromenium, Segesta (pp. 195, 236, 335).
[6] The special circumstances which accompanied the Lilybaeum issue with AVGV. (p. 196) do not invalidate the present thesis.

for this reason that, like Ap. Pulcher at Apamea, the proconsuls of the present group have no explanatory title to add to their proconsular rank. The legend of (1) indicates that the coinage is by 'the Agrigentines to Augustus'; the proconsul's name (in the Ablative Absolute) serves both to date the foundation of the *municipium* and to honour with eponymy the governor who undertook it for the *princeps*. In this way is explained the bewildering variety of proconsuls commemorated, since there is no reason to believe that any foundations (after those of 21 B.C.) were simultaneous.

It remains to identify the mints of (3) and (4). Besides Tauromenium, whose *deductio* occurred too early for either (p. 236), there are four cities[1] of Roman rank under Augustus of whom no Augustan coin has yet been identified. *Coloniae* Catana and Syracuse, in Pliny's list,[2] were probably founded (by Mussidius) in 21 B.C.;[3] *municipium* Messana is likewise included in the list,[4] but need not be of that date;[5] another *municipium* was established at Haluntium shortly before the end of the reign.[6] Now the head on Sisenna's coin (3) is certainly not late enough for Haluntium: since, therefore, Catana and Syracuse were apparently founded by Mussidius, Sisenna must have been the *constitutor* of **Messana**, whose foundation-issue his coin thus represents.[7] It is now clear that (4), of Seius, similarly commemorates the *constitutio* of **Haluntium**, which must have occurred not more than a year or two before Augustus's death and the subsequent *deductio* of Panormus recorded by Silva's parallel issue (p. 197, n. 6). No veterans were being settled at this time, but the *constitutio* was facilitated by the presence of a large Roman *conventus*.[8]

The Augustan municipal currencies of Sicily—as of Africa—are therefore restricted to foundation-coinages: these occur at Messana (before 12 B.C.), Halaesa and Lilybaeum (after 12 B.C.), Agrigentum (after 2 B.C.[9]) and Haluntium (c. A.D. 12-14). These issues, like many others, show that it was customary for such foundations, each representing a fresh step in the Romanisation of the Empire, to be commemorated by this most enduring form of publicity. It was for a record rather than for a currency that such rare issues were intended: the *aes* coinage which supplied economic needs in Sicily consisted of specially counter marked official Roman pieces (p. 96), to which the foundation-series—sometimes similarly countermarked[10]—merely constituted a scanty addition. Apart from these, the veto on coinage of Roman cities by the *Lex Plautia Papiria* (cf. pp. 1, 154) remained in force on the island.

---

[1] It cannot entirely be excluded from possibility that one or two more existed (cf. Kornemann, *PW*. XVI, p. 593). But Scramuzza, *ES*. III, p. 347, has no authority for the Roman status of his nos. 21–25, and in nearly all cases inscriptions indicate or imply a later date for the enfranchisements.

[2] *NH*. III, 88, 93.

[3] Kornemann 166; Scramuzza, l.c. p. 346.

[4] Pliny, l.c. 88.

[5] Kornemann, *PW*. XVI, p. 593.

[6] Ibid.; cf. Cuntz, *Klio*, VI, 1906, p. 467. A *ter-minus ante quem* within the principate of Augustus is provided by *ILS*. 119.

[7] For conjectures as to his identity, vide *PIR*.[2] II, 362. 1455 (Cornelius).

[8] Cf. Sherwin-White, pp. 171 f.

[9] Probably L. Clodius Rufus is the *consul suffectus* of A.D. 7 (*PIR*.[2] II, 280. 1183).

[10] Own coll., found in Sicily; cf. Torremuzza, *Siciliae populorum, etc., veteres nummi*, pl. VIII, 9, 11, p. 9.

8. ITALY: Paestum

In Italy, only **Paestum**, a *municipium* since 90 B.C.,[1] was remarkably excepted from this veto.[2] A few words must be spared for its coinage before our period, since it has led to the gravest delusions concerning the status of the city. Mommsen[3] and Rudolph[4] deduce that a transition from *quattuorviri* to *duoviri* occurred in the time of Sulla; but an examination of the coins makes it clear that the last magistrate to bear the title of *quattuorvir*, M. Octavius (Pl. VII, 9, 10), is at least as late as c. 60–55 B.C.[5] Nor does he, as Mommsen believes,[6] issue some pieces as *duovir*.[7] A third mistake is the acceptance of Manutius's ruling[8] that the transition in question automatically indicates a change from Roman municipal to colonial rank: coins and inscriptions show that there are numerous exceptions both in the provinces[9] and in Italy.[10] Actually, the last years of

---

[1] Cf. Kubitschek, *Imp.* p. 46, etc.

[2] Cf. Nicodemi, *Milan Cat.* p. xvi.

[3] *CIL.* x, p. 53; *Hermes*, XVIII, 1882, p. 167.

[4] *Stadt und Staat im römischen Italien*, pp. 89 n. 3, 93 n. 3.

[5] The weakness of Mommsen's case is suggested by his self-contradictory query elsewhere (*Mzw.* p. 338) as to whether Paestum coined at all before Augustus. It did coin during the Republic—and extensively. A study of the types in use makes it evident that, as at Rome, the uncial standard was halved soon after the Social War. It is, for example, significant that uncial *semisses* have the types of a club (Garrucci, *Le monete dell' Italia antica*, pl. CXXII, 27) and Macedonian shield (ibid. 20), both found on Roman issues before c. 92 B.C. (*BMCR.* pl. XXIX, 15, 19) and that on subsequent semuncial issues (Garrucci, l.c. pl. CXXIII, 7, CXXII, 34; *BMC.* 67; Garrucci, l.c. pl. CXXIII, 2, respectively) are represented the Dioscuri heads of M'. Fonteius (c. 91 B.C., *BMCR.* pl. XXX, 16), the *fasces* and *securis* of C. Norbanus (c. 82 B.C., ibid. pl. XL, 13), and the elephant of Q. C. M. P. (c. 79–77, ibid. pl. C, 10). It is clear that Mommsen's query was unjustified. The coinages which follow indicate that his theory of a Sullan change from *quattuorviri* to *duoviri* was equally false. Later in style and lighter in weight than the issues with Dioscuri heads, *fasces* and *securis*, and elephant (the last not before c. 77), are pieces on which the names and titles of *quattuorviri* are clearly to be read. The standard gradually changes from semuncial to quartuncial: near the beginning of the change is C. As. Vi. *IIIIvir* (Garrucci, l.c. pl. CXXII, 6; cf. Leake, *Numismatica Hellenica*, p. 138) and at the end C. Ax. *IIIIvir* (Garrucci, l.c. 32)—perhaps a banker who issued *tesserae* in 68 (Herzog, *PW.* XVII, 1426)—and M. Oct. *IIIIvir* (Garrucci, l.c. 29; *BMC.* 48 f., Berlin). The former of these is late enough to borrow a type (boar pierced by javelin) from the Roman issues of C. Hosidius (c. 55 B.C.: *BMCR.* pl. XLIII, 14, corrected to this date by Mattingly, *RC.* pls. VIII, 15, XIII, 2).

[6] *CIL.* x, p. 53 n. 1.

[7] This conclusion is based on an examination of all six pieces known. These include four *semisses* (*BMC.* 48, 49, two at Berlin) (Pl. VII, 9, 10)—the type is a rudder, of which the handle becomes entangled in the lettering: but the four strokes of the numeral are clear—and two *trientes* (Berlin), with type of *caduceus*. All are poorly preserved and executed.

[8] *Ap.* Cic. *pro Sest.* 8: cf. Rudolph, l.c. p. 87.

[9] Coins of *municipia* Tingis, Henna and Panormus (pp. 177, 190 f.) and inscriptions of Gades, Asido, etc. (cf. McElderry, *JRS.* 1918, p. 81) with *duoviri*; coins of *coloniae* Thapsus, Parium with *quattuorviri* (pp. 225, 248). Cf. above, p. 169 n. 3.

[10] Rudolph admits a long list of exceptions, and, like Beloch (*Römische Geschichte*, pp. 497 ff.) and Degrassi (*Rivista di filologia*, 1938, pp. 129 ff.), tries to explain them *singulatim*. But the very existence of so many special cases shows the fallibility of his rule; and more exceptions have recently been added by Parker (*CR.* 1938, p. 8), Brusin (*Aquileia nostra*, pp. vii f.), and Banti (*PW.* XIX, 1083).

THE ROMAN *MUNICIPIA* 201

the Republic brought a general tendency for the colleges of four in both classes of community to divide into their constituent pairs (p. 177).

Sambon's assumption of a pre-Caesarian *colonia civium Romanorum* at Paestum[1] is based on a confusion with Tarentum,[2] and is equally erroneous. Finally, Marzullo[3] advances the extraordinary view that the original *colonia Latina* of 273 B.C.[4] continued in a kind of fusion with the *municipium* of 90: but his definition of this *mélange* fluctuates[5] and the parallels which he cites are largely irrelevant.[6] Also he is unaware[7] that the *quattuorviri* on the coins precede the *duoviri* (p. 202), and dismisses the former airily as numerically negligible;[8] he uses an admittedly undatable statue for his chronological argument,[9] wrongly regards its attribution to Marsyas as certain,[10] and then proceeds to interpret it, thus attributed, according to an obsolete view;[11] he seems, unless the present writer's understanding of Italian is at fault, to regard *ius Latinum* and *ius Italicum* as interchangeable,[12] and to confuse *coloniae Latinae* and *coloniae civium Romanorum*;[13] and he believes that colonies of one kind or the other were the only cities which coined under Augustus.[14]

However, Marzullo contributes two important inscriptions from the Augustan period, with PATR(*onus mun*)ICIPI and (*mu*)NICEPS respectively.[15] To the time of Augustus, too, he believes, should be assigned an inscription with PATRONO COL.[16]

---

[1] *Recherches sur les monnaies de la presqu'île italique*, p. 274.

[2] As seen by Marzullo, *Estratto degli Atti della Società Italiana per il Progresso delle Scienze*, v, 1932, p. 18 n. 4; cf. pp. 16 n. 5, 20 n. 8.

[3] Ibid. pp. 14 ff., 18.

[4] Not 293, as Besques, *Rev. arch.* 1935, p. 177.

[5] He says that the 'attributes and denomination' of the former continued alongside (*accanto a*) the latter. It might be imagined that he is thinking of a geographically divided double community: some of the parallels which he cites (pp. 18 ff.) suggest that this is his meaning, e.g. Tarentum-Neptunia, but he goes on to speak of 'interference' *di titoli, e spesso, di condizione giuridica*—and of *l' incertezza delle città che mal sapevano lasciare le lore prerogative per essere colle leges municipales incorporate nello stato romano* (*sic*) (p. 19).

[6] E.g. Croton, p. 19; Tarentum-Neptunia (ibid.) was at first not *municipium* + *colonia* as he states, but *foederata* + *colonia* (Rudolph, l.c. p. 125); Thurii and Vibo (ibid.) were also joined not to *municipia* but to peregrine communities (Kubitschek, *Imp.* p. 47; Philipp, *PW.* [2R.], IV, 1010).

[7] L.c. p. 16.   [8] Ibid. pp. 16, 18.

[9] Ibid. p. 26; cf. p. 1, pls. I–IV. The uncertainty of its date is confirmed by A. S. F. Gow and A. D. Trendall.

[10] Cf. Besques, l.c. The statue is omitted by Paoli, *Mélanges d'archéologie et d'histoire*, LV, 1938, p. 116 n. 1.

[11] It will be shown below, p. 315, that Marsyas was the attribute, not of *ius italicum*, etc., but, as Servius states, of *libertas*: that is, *libertas et civitas*. Cf. below, p. 225, for the coinage of Hippo.

[12] Ibid. p. 23.

[13] Ibid.—Augustus confirmed privileges 'that had never really been abandoned'. Cf. also p. 3, where Latin colonies are considered *simulacra* of Rome by Gellius's definition (*NA.* XVI, 3)—which is, however, as an after-thought (p. 4) rightly referred to Roman colonies (*pars civium* as opposed to *pars sociorum*—cf. Serv. *ad Aen.* I, 12).

[14] Ibid. p. 23—'colonies in the provinces were allowed to coin by Augustus: Paestum coined under Augustus: therefore Paestum was a colony at the time'. But over a hundred and thirty communities that were not Roman or Latin colonies (which does he mean?) coined under Augustus in the provinces: in Italy no colony except Paestum (p. 284) coined at all!   [15] Ibid. p. 17.

[16] von Duhn, *Notizie degli Scavi*, 1890–1, p. 92.

Criteria for an exact dating of these are wanting;[1] but they enable us to approach the coins of the Caesarian epoch with at least a little chance of avoiding the prodigality of error which has been lavished on the history of this city. So far, then, it is possible to say that Paestum became a *colonia Latina* in 273, a Roman *municipium* in 90, and remained in this latter condition until its Roman colonisation some time within or near the period to which this book is devoted. It is, then, to be assumed that the earliest colleges who coined in this period will be municipal—a conclusion confirmed by the discovery that the sixth of them founded the colony, in c. 36–28 B.C. (p. 284).

All the 'autonomous' issues after M. Oct. *IIIIvir* and C. Ax. *IIIIvir* fall within this period, and from the welter of blundered, ill-preserved and insignificant little pieces it is possible to attempt a reconstruction. Five colleges coined while the city was still a *municipium*:

(1) L. Fad., L. Sta.[2]
(2) L. Sei(?)., Q. Eq. (Pl. VII, 12).[3]
(3) L. Art. Ve., C. Comin. *IIvir*.[4]
(4) M. Sat., C. Hel. *quin*.[5]
(5) M. Marci., N. Gavi. *IIvir*.[6]

Various criteria can be combined to place these colleges in their present order. (3) still bears the 'boar' type of C. Hosidius (c. 55) used by the later *quattuorviri*. But (1) and (2) probably precede it by reason of their omission of a title, which is paralleled at other Roman cities in the forties (pp. 234, 243) and here suggests the period of transition from *quattuorviri* to *duoviri*. These two colleges are further connected by the type of clasped hands, which first appears on *denarii* of c. 49.[7] (1) and (3) are closely linked to each other and to the latest *quattuorviri* (and separated from *duoviri* who follow) by their uniform weight-standard, based on an *as* of c. 220–240 grains.[8] On (1), (2) and (4) only, there still appears the helmeted head of Minerva in the form and style used by the *quattuorviri*.[9] (4) and (5) are each based on an *as* of 90–100 grains,[10] but all succeeding issues on one of c. 73–77 grains (p. 284). This gradual decrease decisively indicates for (4) and (5) a date soon after 37, when the same decline was first manifested on the

---

[1] The last-named of them mentions a Q. Ceppius Q. f. Maximus of the *tribus Maecia*: but this tribe is in any case more likely to refer to the *constitutio* of 90 B.C. than to an Augustan *deductio*; cf. early appearances at Brundusium, Hadria and Neapolis (Kubitschek, *Imp.* pp. 39, 65, 25). For Ceppii at Paestum, vide Mommsen, *Inscr. Reg. Neap.* p. 8, no. 92.

[2] *BMC.* 50; Danzig (*Wissenschaftliche Beilage zum Programm des städtischen Gymnasiums zu Danzig*, 1893, p. 4). Garrucci, l.c. pl. CXXII, 23 is incomplete.

[3] Berlin. Unpublished.
[4] *BMC.* 58 f., Parma; Garrucci, l.c. 22.
[5] BM, etc.; Garrucci, l.c. 30.
[6] *BMC.* 56; Garrucci, l.c. 36.
[7] *BMCR.* pl. XLIX, 18.
[8] (1) c. 116; (2) 108 (one only, worn); (3) c. 117.
[9] The quinquennalian title of (4) does not assist chronology, since this office is often found in the late Republic before the dictatorship of Caesar (Rudolph, l.c. p. 214).
[10] (4) c. 93; (5) c. 96.

THE ROMAN *MUNICIPIA*   203

official coinage, but the lowest figure had not yet been attained (p. 45). (4) and (5) are distinct from later coinages in type as well as in weight: they are distinct also administratively, since their first successor, as will be shown elsewhere, was the inauguratory issue of a *colonia civium Romanorum* (p. 284).

These five coinages, then, are to be considered issues of the Roman *municipium* which existed until the establishment of that colony. Among the magistrates are several from families of recent eminence. A T. Cominius was *duovir* at Narbo at about the same date,[1] and both Articuleii (p. 126) and Artorii[2] rose socially under Augustus, like the Seii (p. 198); Q. Eq. is a member of one of the rare *gentes* Equilia[3] and Equitia;[4] Gavius has wrongly been considered a German name.[5] These issues are somewhat uninformative, and recourse must be had for their explanation to earlier issues of the same mint. One of those indicates State-control by its formula S(*ententia*) S(*enatus*) (Pl. VII, 16):[6] no doubt in our period the control was exercised, no longer by the Roman senate, but by the *imperium* of the successive war-lords (p. 411). But S.S. is amplified by S.P.D.D.—*suffragio populi*[7] (? *sumptu publico*,[8] *succlamante populo*[9]) *decreto decurionum*, referring to the local people and senate. The same piece alludes to a tax of $1\frac{1}{5}$ %,[10] and, like others of pre-Caesarian date recording $2\frac{1}{2}$ %[11] and 4% taxes,[12] indicates that the expenses of each coinage were defrayed by a special impost of local, not Roman, origin.[13] We may compare the variety of special sources from which cities always defrayed public works.[14] The conclusion that the Paestan issues were, in the last resort, municipal rather than official is corroborated, not only by the appearance of *quattuorviri*, *duoviri* and *decuriones*, but also by metrological con-

[1] *CIL*. XII, 4389. [2] Vide *CIL*. VI, 90.
[3] *CIL*. XI, 7772. [4] *CIL*. XI, 3648 f.
[5] Scharf, *Neue Deutsche Forschungen*, CLXXXV, 1938, p. 59, corrected by E.B., *JRS*. XXIX, 1939, p. 135.
[6] Garrucci, l.c. pl. CXXIII, 5; Hill, *Handbook of Roman Coins*, p. 148. This formula is regular at a date when SC was not yet common: the decree of the Roman senate was advisory, and called *sententia* (cf. Abbott and Johnson, pp. 279. 19, 284. 21) or *auctoritas* (cf. Fürst, *Die Bedeutung der Auctoritas*, Diss. Marburg, 1934, pp. 47 ff.). See p. 288.
[7] Cf. *CIL*. VIII, 14.   [8] Ibid. 309, 1412.
[9] Cf. Liebenam, *St.V.* p. 248 n. 1.
[10] MIL(*lesima*), cf. Seneca, *De Ira*, III, 33.
[11] *BMC*. 72, cf. Garrucci, l.c. pl. CXXIII (rightly *battuto col metallo raccolto per una imposta*): LL. EX. XXXX. = *lati* (sc. *nummi*) *ex quadragesima*; cf. Tac. *Ann.* XIII, 51, Symmachus, *Ep.* v, 65, Orelli, *Inscriptiones Latinae Selectae*, 3344. For *lati*, cf. next note. Garrucci sees that the ligature represents double L

(cf., from the neighbourhood, *CIL*. IV, 1604, 1645), but for that very reason his interpretation L(*ex*) L(*ata*) (accepted by Marzullo, l.c. p. 23 n. 3) is untenable: the ligature cannot include the initial letters of two separate words.
[12] Vienna (corrected by Imhoof-Blumer, *NZ*. XVIII, 1886, p. 235 from Garrucci, l.c. pl. CXXII, 27): Q. CEP(*pius*) DE $\overline{\text{III}}$. TOL. For the *triens* tax cf. *Dig*. 35. 2. 3. TOL. = TVL(*it*), an archaic form, *CIL*. I[2], 595. 11 (*Lex incerta*). For its meaning, *CIL*. IV. 429: *Polybius aedilis panem bonum fert*. Q. Ceppius produced the issue from the proceeds of the tax.
[13] For such taxes on water, fisheries, etc., cf. Reid, *Municipalities of the Roman Empire*, pp. 453 f. It is not accidental that it was under Tiberius, who diverted most local *vectigalia* into the Roman treasury (Suet. *Ti*. 49), that most coinage of Paestum and of most other Roman cities in the West ceased (cf. Mattingly, *BMC. Imp*. p. xxiv).
[14] Cf. Jones, *GC*. p. 236.

siderations. The *semisses* of the triumviral period make no pretence to tally in weight with the official military *asses* struck at the same date very near by in South Italy (probably at Puteoli [p. 46]), which are based on a far higher standard; it is true that *asses* of c. 250 and c. 80 persisted side by side during this period (p. 300), but this is a particularly curious example of their juxtaposition. Furthermore, the military mint used an alloy with a high percentage of lead and a smaller one of tin,[1] whereas the Paestan issues of the period contain more tin but very little lead[2]—approximately the alloy to be used after c. 28 B.C. at Nemausus (p. 73).[3]

It is clear, then, that the pre-Augustan issues of Paestum, although their character cannot be exactly paralleled elsewhere, must, in the last resort, be considered as municipal. The formula S(*enatus*) S(*ententia*) merely bears witness to a stricter form of the State-control which was later, when local issues developed, exercised also in the provinces. The names of the local magistrates corroborate the economic evidence to show that, subject to this control, the Paestan mint so functioned as to deserve the name of a city-mint, and inclusion in this Chapter.

[1] Spectrograms 5, 5 a.   [2] Ibid. 67.   [3] Ibid. 1.

Chapter 2

THE ROMAN COLONIES

1. SARDINIA: Turris Libisonis

Two closely connected Sardinian issues can be ascribed to this category. One of them (Pl. VI, 20) is found exclusively in Northern Sardinia, where specimens have come to light at Ploaghe,[1] Padria,[2] Sassari[3] and Truvine.[4] A helmeted head to right (resembling that of Sardus Pater at *municipium* Uselis [p. 150]) accompanies the inscription Q.A.M., L.C.Æ. IIV., misread by Spano;[5] on the reverse is D.D., and a plough, again recalling a type at Uselis (p. 152). But a second series clearly from the same mint as the first (with a bareheaded portrait to right, plough, and M. L. D. C. P.—hexastyle temple with Q. A. M., P. C. IIV. [Pl. VI, 19][6]) again emphasises, by its circulation, that its origin lay northwards of Uselis:[7] examples have been found at Antas,[8] Sassari (two),[9] Truvine,[10] and Masala.[11]

It is clear that on the reverses of the two varieties the first *duovir* is the same. The second name on the first coin may perhaps, by comparison with an inscription from Turris Libisonis, be restored as L. Cerdonius Veratus.[12] Attributions to Uselis[13] and Metalla[14] are based on conjectures derived from wrong readings. Plubium, which Bornemann suggests,[15] was not in any way privileged at the late Republican date which the style of these coins indicates, whereas the Latin inscription, and the institution of *duoviri*, both point to a citizen community. It is this, then, whose foundation is symbolised by the plough. In Northern Sardinia, which the provenance of these coins indicates, the only *oppidum civium Romanorum* was *colonia Iulia*—not *municipium*[16] —Turris Libisonis,[17] which was enfranchised before 27 B.C.[18]

[1] Bornemann, *Blätter für Münzfreunde*, 1900, pp. 97 ff.
[2] Turin (Lavy, *Cat.* 4719); cf. ibid.
[3] Gotha.
[4] Spano, *Scoperte arch. fattesi nell' isola Sardegna*, 1853, p. 17.
[5] Id., *Bullettino archeologico sardo*, IV, 1858, p. 199.
[6] Rome and Castoldi coll., correcting numerous misreadings of clumsily executed pieces (e.g. BM, Paris, Hunter, Castoldi) as by Albizzati, *Annali della Facoltà di Lett. della R. Univ. di Cagliari*, I, 1928, p. 1; cf. Ratto sale (1923) no. 1013.
[7] Correcting Muensterberg's attribution to Carthage, *Beamtennamen*, s.v.
[8] della Marmora, *Voyage en Sardaigne*, I, p. 391; cf. de Retz, *Bull. arch. sardo*, I, 1855, p. 71.
[9] Bornemann, l.c.
[10] Spano, *Bull. arch. sardo*, IV, l.c.
[11] BM.
[12] *CIL.* x, 7956.
[13] Cited by Mommsen, *CIL.* x, p. 810.
[14] Spano, *Bull. arch. sardo*, IV, l.c.
[15] L.c.
[16] Mommsen, *CIL.* x, 7951.
[17] Pliny, *NH.* III, 85; Geogr. Raven., 5. 26.
[18] Kornemann, *PW.* IV, 1. 81; cf. Kubitschek, *Imp.* p. 127. Colonies were founded by a *lex dicta*, Biondi, *CA.* p. 143 n. 1.

The distinctive portrait on the second coin is not that of dictator, triumvir, or *princeps*. By the analogies of M. Atius Balbus at Uselis, Q. Hortensius in Macedonia, Ap. Pulcher at Apamea, and M. Rutilus at Lystra (pp. 150, 33, 255, 238), it almost certainly represents a governor and colonial founder. The legend should naturally be read in the order M. L. D. C. P. D(*eductor*) C(*oloniae*) is peculiarly suitable to follow a founder's name. The last letter is unlikely to stand for *praefectus* or *proconsul*, as both should precede *deductor coloniae* (pp. 252, 274); since *municipium* Uselis, in the same island, probably honours its founder as P(*atronus*) (p. 151), this is also the most plausible restoration here. It remains to identify the personage whose name is abbreviated to M. L. A Julian colony could have been founded in Sardinia in c. 46–40 or c. 38–27:[1] but the earlier period is much more probable, since the omission of Sardinia from Augustus's colonised provinces in the *Res Gestae*[2] suggests a plan of the dictator.[3] We shall find that many other cities issued *deductio*-coinage very soon after the death of Brutus and Cassius:[4] by their analogy it is tempting to discover the name of M. L(urius), who was Octavian's governor in Sardinia from c. 42 until his defeat by Sextus Pompey in 40.[5] The restoration of an inscription consisting of initials only can seldom be certain; but the present interpretation is at least consistent both with the internal evidence and with parallels from elsewhere. Whereas the *constitutio* of Uselis by Atius Balbus was as late as c. 38–36, the *deductio* of Turris Libisonis by M. Lurius, for which published evidence has been equally lacking, took place during his governorship in c. 42–40, when Antony's lieutenants were employed in similar duties in the other half of the Empire. The foundation of Caralis, also of the triumvirate, may be ascribed to either of these dates. Thus there are foundation-issues of all three of the Roman cities of Sardinia; and no other coinage occurs, with the single exception of a piece celebrating the half-centenary of Uselis (p. 153). Here, then, as in other provinces, coinage is purely commemorative.

2. GALLIA COMATA: Lugdunum

Lugdunum also produced a foundation-issue, of which only one specimen of uncertain denomination is recorded.[6] The legends are COPIA FELIX and MVNATIA; on the obverse, with *cornucopiae*, is a turreted bust of the city goddess, and on the reverse a galloping bull, checked by Hercules (Pl. VII, 24). *Colonia Copia* at Lugdunum was founded in 43 B.C. by L. Munatius Plancus,[7] governor of Gallia Ulterior.[8] As Willers[9]

[1] Ganter, p. 26; cf. Klein, *Die römischen Verwaltungsbeamten*, Bd. I, Abt. 2, pp. 60 ff.
[2] 28.   [3] Cf. Mommsen, *RGDA*.² p. 120.
[4] E.g. Alexandria Troas, Parium, Lampsacus, Dyrrhachium, Philippi.
[5] Klein, l.c. p. 62; Syme, *RR*. p. 213, cf. p. 235 n. 6; id. *Papers of the British School at Rome*, XIV (NS. I), 1938, p. 17 n. 82 adds that his origin is unknown. A *tessera* of 51 B.C. (Herzog, *PW*. XVII [1937], 1427) shows banking interests.
[6] Paris, 46·5 grains.
[7] Dio XLVI, 50; *CIL*. X, 6087.
[8] Nicolaus Damascenus, *Vita* 28 (*Smith College Classical Studies*, IV, 1923, pp. 58, 94); cf. *PIR*. II, 390. 534.
[9] *NZ*. XXXIV, 1902, p. 68.

points out, the title of this coin indicates that he carried out the *deductio* without the supposed co-operation of Lepidus, who was governing the Narbonese province.[1] Hirschfeld's opinion[2] that the epithets *Felix Munatia* were only added by Augustus long after the foundation is unnecessary, since the style of this coin is early; later pieces have COPIA without those epithets; and a similar initial display of the first founder's name, followed shortly by its total omission from coinage, is to be seen at *colonia Lepida* Celsa (p. 211).[3] De la Tour[4] plausibly suggests that the Herculean type of the present piece is connected with Tibur, of which Plancus was probably a native.[5] Thus Grenier[6] rightly attributes the issue to the year of his governorship of Gallia Comata; and it joins the large category of foundation-issues, of which the majority occur at precisely the same period (p. 459).

A far more ambitious bronze[7] series bears the inscriptions DIVI IVLI, IMP. CAESAR DIVI F. and COPIA. On the obverse are heads of Julius to left, laureate, and Octavian to right bareheaded; on the reverse a prow, with the device of an eye,[8] and with oars. About half of these coins[9] have a palm-branch between the heads, and on the reverse a mast, a lofty deck-structure, and a star—no doubt the *sidus Iulium*[10]— superimposed on a globe (Pl. VII, 23).[11] A rare variety[12] has a star above the head of Julius on the obverse (Pl. VII, 22). On the rest[13] all these symbols are absent. The busts on the coins on which symbols appear are original; on the plainer varieties some heads are modelled on the Gallic *denarii* of c. 39, and others resemble those of L. Livineius Regulus at the same date.[14] The titulature of Octavian recalls Gallic silver of c. 38 B.C.[15] Thus three indications combine to associate the commencement of the issues with Agrippa's governorship at that time.[16]

This coinage, whose circulation within Gaul was very wide, appears quite distinct from the usual commemorative issues of colonies at this period, and provides a clear example of the requisitioning of a colonial mint to provide a province with currency. It is noteworthy that the Narbonese province was supplied with *aes*, at precisely the same date, from an official mint at Arelate (?) (p. 41). However, the Lugdunese series lacks countermarks, and does not compete in inter-provincial circulation with the issues of Nemausus (p. 72): unlike those, it cannot be considered more than semi-official. Imitations abound, especially of the plainer variety;[17] but certain pieces[18] invalidate

---

[1] *PIR.*² I, 59. 367.
[2] *CIL.* XIII, p. 250.
[3] It is true that Plancus did not fall into disgrace like Lepidus: but Octavian did not allow even his friends to name colonies, which were invariably *Iulia* (and later *Augusta*).
[4] Cf. Willers, l.c. p. 75.
[5] Acro, *ap.* Hor. *Carm.* I, 7.   [6] *ES.* III, p. 480.
[7] Probably this is the analysis quoted by Willers, l.c. p. 135 n. 78.
[8] Cf. Svoronos, *JIAN.* XX, 1920, 2, p. 65.

[9] Willers, l.c. 4, BM, etc.
[10] Cf. De Schodt, *Rb.* 1887.
[11] Undeciphered by Willers, l.c.
[12] Berlin.
[13] Willers, l.c. 5, BM, etc.
[14] E.g. Levis sale (1925), 165; cf. *BMCR.* pl. LVII, 9.
[15] *BMCR.* II, pp. 410 ff.
[16] Charlesworth, *CAH.* x, p. 46.
[17] E.g. Poncet, *Rn.* 1899, p. 173, Paris.
[18] E.g. Levis sale (1925), 165.

Willers's suggestion[1] that this was entirely barbaric. All varieties weigh c. 300 grains. It is necessary to consider them *asses* of the standard used by the Pompeys in Spain and Octavian at Puteoli (?) (pp. 22, 47); Willers's interpretation[2] as '*tresses* of the "Fleet" system' is anachronistic and unsuited to a unidenominational issue such as this.

The last issue of the colony has the inscriptions CAESAR····· and COPIA, accompanied by the bare head of Augustus and a bull respectively. Its rejection by Willers[3] is unacceptable, since at least two specimens have been recorded, from the Rothelin[4] and Récamier[5] collections. Their independent description makes it highly probable that both are authentic. They are connected in type with official *semisses*, probably from an auxiliary mint at Lugdunum (p. 124), issued in c. 10 B.C. Owing to the disappearance of both known specimens, the present issue cannot be dated with any certainty; but it is clearly commemorative—like all such isolated and uncommon colonial mintages—and the most probable occasion (owing to numerous analogies[6]) is the half-centenary of the colony in 7 A.D.[7]

3. GALLIA NARBONENSIS: Arausio (?)

The only colonial issue in this province (Pl. VI, 21)[8] has fallen between the two stools of the descriptions, by Willers[9] and Sydenham,[10] of the Gallic local and official currencies respectively. On the obverse, with the legend IMP. DIVI F., are two bare heads; on the reverse is a prow, with the 'eye' found also at Lugdunum; above it is a medallion enclosing a ram's head.[11] It is agreed that one of the heads is that of Augustus; the other is variously ascribed to Julius,[12] Agrippa,[13] and Caius Caesar.[14] These attempts are the more remarkable in view of the complete similarity of the two heads on the obverse: both of them are very closely modelled on Eastern *denarii* of Octavian struck later than c. 38 B.C.[15] An explanation for this exceptional duplication is forthcoming from Strack's[16] theory—based on other series—that all Gallic colonial coins with two

[1] L.c. p. 87.
[2] Ibid. p. 134.
[3] Willers, l.c.
[4] Ibid. p. 89.
[5] Cf. Panel, *Mémoires pour l'histoire des sciences*, 1738, p. 1263, fig. 82; Boutkowski, *DN*. 1, 1881; M. S. 1, 148, 152; seen by M. Dissard; Blanchet, *Traité*, p. 430.
[6] E.g. Uselis, Carthage, Cirta, Lystra (p. 295).
[7] Sutherland, *RIS*. p. 164, ignores this mint and the next—not to speak of Sicily and Sardinia—when he restricts true local coinages in the West to Spain and Africa.

[8] BM, Paris; De la Tour, *Atlas des monnaies gauloises*, pl. VII, 4660 ff.
[9] *NZ*. XXXIV, 1902, pp. 79 ff.
[10] *NC*. 1917, pp. 53 ff.
[11] Cohen, *Description historique des monnaies frappées sous l'empire romain*, I, p. 182, describes it as *disque au milieu d'un cercle*.
[12] Strack, *BJ*. CVIII, 1902, p. 16 n. 1.
[13] Duchalais, *Description des médailles gauloises*, p. 19.
[14] Cohen, l.c.
[15] *BMC. Imp. Aug.* 590 ff. (cf. even fringe and whiskers).
[16] *BJ*. CVIII, 1902, pp. 20 f.

heads were planned for the division into halves which they so frequently underwent. The fact that halves of these present pieces are extremely rare[1] is immaterial in view of the rarity of the coins even as wholes: only one, and that a very doubtful, identification can be made from the whole of the Neuss find.[2] Such specimens as are found come from the South of France,[3] and the style and two-headed plan confirm ascription to the Narbonese province. There is no reason to select Lugdunum[4] or Vienna,[5] since the styles do not in the least agree. The average weight of these coins—which, though yellow, are not of *orichalcum*[6]—is c. 270 grains,[7] like the *asses* at Puteoli (?) and, at first, at Nemausus (pp. 47, 73). These comparisons, confirmed by the portraiture, indicate a date in the middle or later thirties. The occurrence of one pellet[8] probably signifies the unitary denomination.

A conjectural attribution can be derived from the ram's head on the reverse. Similar types on Roman *denarii*[9] are irrelevant, since they appear to represent a family crest of the Rustii:[10] this is a badge of another sort. Now a *denarius* struck in c. 33 B.C. (p. 60), apparently at Lugdunum, has the inscription LEG. XVI., accompanied by a lion, which also occurs on an *aureus* of Antony;[11] Willers[12] and Ritterling[13] interpret this as a legionary device. The legionary title on the *denarius* indicates clearly that this is indeed the character of the type. Such crests were chiefly derived from the signs of the zodiac.[14] Those of Republican times are largely unknown, but a ram's head, as found on the present series, was later adopted by auxiliary cohorts[15] and by a legion founded by Domitian:[16] it represented the goddess Minerva.[17] Moreover, badges of this nature regularly appear in circular medallions such as the present coin displays.[18] Now the Julian *coloniae civium Romanorum* of the Narbonese province were invariably founded for the veterans of legions,[19] whose numbers they embodied in their titulature: Narbo is *Decimanorum*, Baeterrae *Septimanorum*, Forum Julii *Octavanorum*, Arelate *Sextanorum*, Arausio *Secundanorum*.[20] The veterans who composed the first three of these

---

[1] One at Nîmes.
[2] *BJ*. CXII, 1904, p. 451(?).
[3] 4 found at Toulouse (mus.), 2 at Narbonne (mus.), 2 at Vienne; specimens in the collections of Marseille (2), Nîmes (2½) and M. Nier (1) are also from the neighbourhood.
[4] As Blanchet, *Traité*, p. 434.
[5] As De la Tour, Duchalais, ll.cc.
[6] Spectrogram 6.
[7] Av. 7 (BM, Paris, own coll.).
[8] Between the heads (BM), or to their right (Naples) or left (Turin).
[9] *BMCR*. I, p. 398. 73; *BMC. Imp. Aug.* 2.
[10] Cf. *BMC. Imp.* p. ci.
[11] Grueber, *BMCR*. II, p. 505; cf. Morelli, *Familiarum Romanarum Numismata*, pl. II, 1.

[12] *NZ*. XXXIV, 1902, p. 83.
[13] *PW*. XII, 1376.
[14] Ibid. 1372.
[15] von Domaszewski, *Abhandlungen des archäologisch-epigraphischen Seminares der Universität Wien*, V, 1885, p. 74, fig. 89.
[16] Schilling, *De legionibus Romanis I Minervia et XXX Vlpiana*, Diss. Leipzig, 1893.
[17] Ritterling, l.c. 1420 f.
[18] von Domaszewski, l.c. p. 43, fig. 29; cf. p. 73, fig. 89.
[19] Cf. Digonnet, *Orange antique*, p. 5 n. 1, and Chatelain, *Bibliothèque de l'École des Hautes Études*, CLXII, 1908, p. 11, correcting Herzog, *Gallia Narbonensis*, pp. 81 f.
[20] Jullian, *Histoire de la Gaule*, IV, pp. 31 f.

colonies were all from legions established by the dictator, whose device was accordingly a bull, the badge of Venus.[1] VI *Ferrata*, which shared Arelate with VI *Victrix*, was represented by the Apolline symbol of the wolf and twins.[2] Arausio, however, must be classed apart: the second legion is not found in the Gallic campaigns.[3] Moreover, II *Adiutrix* was not established until Vespasian,[4] and the other second legion is entitled *Augusta*, and so can hardly have been founded before 27 B.C.[5] Only the older Pompeian *legio secunda*[6] can be considered in connection with the colony. The last-known appearance of this was at the battle of Forum Gallorum;[7] it has not been recorded what subsequent arrangement was made for its veterans. The foundation of Arausio is unlikely to have occurred before the death of Julius,[8] and may be as late as c. 33.[9] Minerva appears on the coins of Pompey,[10] and might conceivably be his natal deity; but legions also sometimes derived their crests from the time of year at which they were established.[11] However this may be, if the interpretation of the ram's head on these coins as a legionary symbol is accepted—and no alternative suggestion has been offered—then, with the possible exception of the insignificant Narbonese *colonia Valentia*,[12] whose foundation and titulature are alike uncertain, the only colony to which the device is not unsuitable is *colonia Firma Iulia Secundanorum* **Arausio**.[13] The possibility cannot be excluded that these are official coins issued for an unknown legion; but such an issue in *aes* would be unparalleled. On the other hand veteran colonies frequently specify on their coinage the legions from which they are sprung; moreover, city-badges occur frequently in the place of ethnics, and this isolated mintage is most naturally considered the foundation-issue of a new settlement. It may, moreover, be important that the arch at Orange bears numerous representations of prows[14] very like those which appear on these coins. It is, however, unfortunately impossible to corroborate this attribution, which must therefore remain conjectural.

[1] Ritterling, l.c. 1376, etc.; cf. von Domaszewski, l.c. p. 75, fig. 90.
[2] Ritterling, l.c.
[3] Jullian, l.c. p. 32 n. 2, correcting Reinach, *Comptes-rendus de l'Académie des Inscriptions*, 1909, pp. 513 f.
[4] Ritterling, l.c. 1439.
[5] Ibid. 1457.   [6] Ibid. 1437.
[7] Cic. *Fam.* x, 30.
[8] Carcopino, *Histoire Romaine*, II, p. 986 n. 332; cf. Meyer, *Cäsars Monarchie*, p. 488 n.; Rice Holmes, *The Roman Republic*, III, p. 322 n.; pace Kromayer, *Hermes*, XXX, 1896, pp. 1 ff.; Jullian, l.c. p. 31; Grenier, *ES.* III, p. 486.
[9] Kornemann 95; cf. Chatelain, l.c. pp. 10 ff.
[10] E.g. *BMCR*. pl. CI, 1.
[11] Ritterling, l.c. 1375.
[12] Jullian, l.c. p. 32 n. 4(??).
[13] The boar on a *vexillum* represented on the Orange arch has nothing to do with the colony, but is part of a captive trophy (Chatelain, l.c. pp. 52, 71).
[14] Not those of river craft: Desjardins, *Bulletin de la Société Centrale des Architectes*, 1883, p. 11.

4. HISPANIA TARRACONENSIS: Celsa, Ilici, Carthago Nova, Caesaraugusta, Tarraco

The coinage of this province, as the section concerning its *municipia* has suggested (p. 154), stands in need of a number of reattributions. The only pre-Augustan coinage of a Tarraconensian colony was made by COL(*onia*) VIC(*trix*) IVL(*ia*) LEP(*ida*), whose attribution to Celsa by Lorichs and Grotefend[1] is convincingly defended by Hill.[2] M. Aemilius Lepidus twice governed Nearer Spain, in 48–47 and 44–42 B.C.[3] Hill finds a number of models of the years 46–44[4] for the heads of Minerva[5] and Victory;[6] and a head of Venus (?) (Pl. VII, 21)[7] is particularly similar in arrangement to the bust of Diana on the foundation-issue of *municipium* Emporiae in 45–44 (p. 154).[8] Like Sutherland,[9] Hill nevertheless prefers the first governorship of Lepidus for the foundation of Celsa.[10] But its attribution by Adcock[11] to 44 at the earliest is confirmed, not only by the numismatic comparisons, but also by the absence of other Julian foundations (p. 461) and other Roman city-issues that can be ascribed to 47; both, however, occurred in 45 and 44. The use of portrait-models of this same period strongly suggests that one of the issues celebrates the *deductio*, though it is difficult to say which of the three colleges of PR(*aefecti pro*) IIVIR(*is*)[12] should be selected for this distinction. L. Nep. and L. Sura[13]—who coin with the head of Venus (Pl. VII, 21)—are the most probable choice, since their pieces are much the heaviest.[14] In the Republic there is only one well-known Sura, namely P. Cornelius Lentulus the Catilinarian.[15] The only *quadrans* of the group,[16] signed by the aediles L. Cal(purnius) and Sex. Nig(er)—whose names also appear on one of the two *semisses*[17]—is probably part of the foundation-issue, to judge from equally isolated bi- and tri-denominational coinages elsewhere (pp. 216, 165). It is interesting to note that Sex. Niger omits his *nomen*—because this, as an Augustan piece shows, was Pompeius (p. 213). But the family was staunchly Caesarian, a Q. Pompeius Niger from Italica having fought with distinction under Julius in 45.[18]

The type of a bull here makes its *début* on Roman city-issues. Now its second appearance was on a foundation-issue of Calagurris in 28, as a play on the name of the *adsignator* and governor T. Statilius Taurus (p. 165). It is not impossible that the same

---

[1] *Blätter für Münzfreunde*, IV, 1844, pp. 2 ff.
[2] P. 79; *pace* Vives IV, p. 102.
[3] Cf. von Rohden, *PW*. I, 556 f.
[4] E.g. *BMCR*. pl. CI, 1, 9–10, LIII, 13–14.
[5] Hill, pl. XII, 7.
[6] Ibid. 6.   [7] Ibid. 8.
[8] For a fourth bust, of Pax, vide Pl. VII, 20.
[9] *RIS*. p. 128.   [10] P. 79.
[11] *CAH*. IX, p. 708; cf. n. 3.
[12] Hill (p. 81 n. 4) successfully overcomes the objections of Lenormant (*La monnaie dans l'antiquité*, III, pp. 227 f.) to the interpretation as *praefectus*.
[13] BM: Hill, pl. XII, 8.
[14] Cf. Hill, p. 186.
[15] Cf. Münzer, *PW*. (2R.), IV, 963. L. Naevius Sura coins at Buthrotum (p. 269).
[16] Instituto de Valencia de Don Juan; Hill, pl. XII, 10, cf. p. 80 n. 32.
[17] Berlin: Hill, pl. XII, 9.
[18] *Bell. Hisp.* 25. 4.

man was *legatus pro praetore* of Tarraconensis under Lepidus, and his *adsignator* at Celsa, in 44–42: we have no record of Taurus's activity before his consulship in 37, and the *Fasti* of the province show an appropriate gap.[1] The undoubted play upon his name at Calagurris makes this guess not unplausible; nor is it contradicted by numerous later appearances of bulls, since the type was in any case appropriate to Roman foundations, and alluded, moreover, to Caesar's tutelary goddess Venus and to Augustus's nickname *Thurinus*.[2]

There remain—before 36, the *terminus ante quem* for coinage with *Lepida*—two colleges of PR(*aefecti pro*) IIVIR(*is*),[3] one of aediles,[4] and one of PR(*aefecti pro*) QVIN(*quennalibus*).[5] Saguntum has provided an example of a city where *praefecti* were regularly appointed to represent distinguished *duoviri* (p. 159); the present issues indicate that this kind of *praefectura* was already instituted in the forties. The Otacilii owed the revival of their repute to the social upheavals of the period;[6] P. Sal. Pa. may be a relative of T. Salvius Parianus who was *duovir* of Nola in A.D. 29.[7]

These coins are slightly heavier than semuncial;[8] subsequent issues, on the other hand, are based on the lighter standard used also at *municipium* Emporiae. These do not occur until c. 25 B.C. or later, since no models earlier than the 'Caesaraugusta'[9] and 'Patricia'[10] groups occur. Characteristic of colonies is the invariable appearance of the *princeps*' portrait, and no less instructive the gradual transition of the obverse legend from COL. V. I. CELSA, IIVIR[11] through $\overline{\text{AV}}$GVS., C. V. I. CELS.[12] to the orthodox AVGVSTVS DIVI F.[13] The *semisses* have no type; *asses* represent, with one exception, the usual bull—imitated from the earlier issues, since it was as applicable to a *deductio*, and to the Julian house, as to T. Taurus. The single exception is provided by a coin with pontifical emblems: this is usually ascribed to Carthago Nova,[14] but has obverse dies that are similar to,[15] if not the same as,[16] those of Celsan *asses*.[17] It was struck by the *quinquennales* C. Varius Rufus and Sex. Julius Pollio. In view of the ubiquity of officials of this rank, who actually appear on the earlier coins of Celsa itself besides on many other colonial coinages, it is strange that the arrangement of Heiss,[18] who could speak of *quinquennaux, magistrats spéciaux à Carthago Nova*, has not been finally

---

[1] Cf. Wilsdorf, *Fasti Hispaniarum Provinciarum*, Diss. Leipzig, 1878, pp. 133 f.; see below, p. 379, for the division of Spain at this date into two *legationes*. See also p. 381.

[2] Cf. Blanchet, *Comptes-rendus de l'Académie des Inscriptions*, 1919, p. 134; Mattingly, *BMC. Imp.* p. cxv.

[3] P. Sal. Pa., M. Fulvi.; C. Balbo, L. Porcio.

[4] L. Semp. Max., M. Caec.   [5] M. Ful., C. Otac.

[6] Syme, *RR*. p. 84 n. 6.   [7] *CIL*. XI, 1233.

[8] 280·5, 257·5, 203·5 grains (BM).

[9] Hill, pl. XIII, 1 f. For Sydenham's attribution of the *denarii* to Celsa, see pp. 122, 222.

[10] Hill, pl. XIII, 4.   [11] Ibid. pl. XIII, 1.

[12] Ibid. 2.   [13] Ibid. 4.

[14] Vives IV, pp. 34 ff., no. 28.

[15] Hill, p. 84.

[16] Lorichs, *Stockholm Cat.* p. 3.

[17] It must be admitted that its chemical content is different from that of a Celsan coin analysed (Spectrogram 49, cf. 14): but there is no reason to believe that the two specimens tested were contemporary. Finds are extensive but not helpful: cf. Visedo Moltó, *MJSEA*. XLI [VI, 1920–1], p. 10.

[18] P. 273. They appear also at many other cities; see references on p. 508.

THE ROMAN COLONIES   213

abandoned. Besides this pair of *quinquennales*, five colleges of *duoviri*[1] and one of aediles[2] strike for Augustus. Their chronology is beyond reach, since the only dated coin (5–3 B.C.) still uses the 'Patricia' models for its portraits; but there are no *asses* from the latest 'Lugdunese' models.

Some of the magistrates' names call for note. The clemency of the *régime*—or the treachery of men like the Nigri—is well illustrated by the presence of four Pompeii, who owe their citizenship either to Pompey[3] or to his father:[4] they are the leading family of Celsa. A governor of Octavian, Cn. Domitius Calvinus (39–36),[5] is recalled by the *duovir* Cn. Domitius; and a number of obscure names no doubt also indicate the reward for loyalty to the Caesarian party, and the rise of the lower classes to the surface of the muddy waters of the revolution.[6] L. Baggius may well be the L. Baggius Methodicus of a Roman inscription at about the same date;[7] the gentile name of L. Cor. Terrenus is paralleled by a single epigraphic record from Genava.[8] The *cognomen* of L. Pompeius Bucco, which recurs with the *gentilicium* Vetilius on a Tiberian issue,[9] is the same as a word usually employed to describe half-wits on the stage;[10] but the name may be a distinct Celtic formation.[11] There is record of a late Republican (perhaps Caesarian) senator called Licinius Bucco.[12] The Junii Hispani were well known in Spain,[13] like the Titii Hispani;[14] the name Secundinus was also common there.[15] Flavii Festi appear in Italy in the third century.[16]

The city of **Ilici** should be credited with a group of three misread and unrecognised issues, made during the fourteen years of its existence as a *colonia Iulia*:[17]

(1) C. Maeci. *quinq.*, L. Appul[ei]. *quinq.*[18]
(2) C. Maeci. *quinq.*, L. Appul. *quin.* II.[19]
(3) C. Maeci. *IIvir quinq.*, Q. Acilius *IIvir quin.*[20]

---

[1] Hill, p. 83; L. Sura, L. Pompei. Bucco; L. Cor. Terren., M. Jun. Hisp.; Sex. Cethego, Q. Pomp. Secundino; L. Baggio, M'. Flavio Festo; Cn. Domiti., C. Pompeio.
[2] L. Aufid. Pansa, Sex. Pomp. Nigro.
[3] Cf. Cic. *Pro Balbo* 9. 24, 18. 41; Stevenson, *RPA*. p. 92; Sutherland, *RIS*. pp. 96, 233 n. 23.
[4] Stevenson, l.c.; Sherwin-White, p. 130.
[5] Cf. Charlesworth, *CAH*. x, p. 46.
[6] Cf. Rostovtzeff, *Mélanges Pirenne*, 1926, p. 421.
[7] *CIL*. VI, 12819; cf. Schulze, p. 204.
[8] *CIL*. XII, 2632; cf. Schulze, p. 278 n. 1.
[9] Hill, p. 83.
[10] Cf. Milchöfer, *PW*. II, 1918.
[11] *Thes. Ling. Lat.* II, p. 2229.
[12] Valerius Maximus, VIII, 3. 2; cf. Münzer, *PW*. XIII, 232; *Thes. Ling. Lat.* II, l.c.

[13] *CIL*. II, 5924 (Acci: *trib.* Pupinia), 1166 (Hispalis: *trib.* Quirina).
[14] Cf. Syme, *Papers of the British School at Rome*, XIV (NS. I), 1938, p. 14 n. 71. The *cognomen* of Varius Hispanus (van Nostrand, *ES*. III, p. 144) was originally derogatory (cf. Sherwin-White, p. 179).
[15] *CIL*. II, 2534, 2877, 2933, 4569, 4970, 5366.
[16] *CIL*. XI, 1354.
[17] For the colony, vide Kornemann 182.
[18] Vives IV, p. 30 ('Carthago Nova').
[19] BM. This cannot represent *II*[*vir*] *quin.*, which is never found inverted.
[20] Vives IV, p. 34. 7. The accepted reading ACILIVS IIVIR QVINQ. is incorrect, since the omission of the *praenomen* here would be very curious, whereas QVIN. is a frequent abbreviation: it occurs with QVINQ. on (2).

These have been usually ascribed, together with so many heterogeneous and incongruous pieces, to Carthago Nova: but there is a total lack of evidence for such an attribution. The identification of this Acilius with one at that city is worthless for three reasons: first, the coins on which the latter appears belong, not to Carthago Nova, but to a Sicilian town, probably Thermae Himeraeae (p. 237); secondly, that personage is called Lucius, and the *praenomen* Quintus on these coins has escaped notice; thirdly, Acilius is a very frequent name, especially in Spain.[1] On the other hand, Maecii are very rare: and the existence of an inscription from Ilici with AVGVSTO DIVI F. C. MAECIVS C. F. CELER DEDIT DEDICAVIT[2] is strong evidence in favour of attribution to that town. Moreover, the type of (3), a single legionary eagle, reappears on the later issues of Ilici, and the galley of (1) suits its proximity to the sea. Now a very similar galley appears on the foundation-coinage of *municipium* Dertosa in c. 30–28 B.C. (p. 158): and not only is such a date entirely consistent with the style of the present pieces, but an inscription records that T. Statilius Taurus, governor c. 29–28, was the *patronus* of Ilici,[3] and therefore, in accordance with the *Lex Coloniae Genetivae Iuliae* (p. 34), in all likelihood one of its founders. It is in the highest degree probable that the first coin of C. Maecius and L. Appuleius celebrates the *deductio* of Ilici as *colonia Iulia* at that date, and so belongs to the category of foundation-issues. The appearance of *quinquennales* presents no obstacle to this view, since these officials naturally occur on the foundation-issues of cities which had received *Latinitas* five, or a multiple of five, years earlier—like Saguntum and Carthago Nova (pp. 163, 217). Moreover, if a *lustrum* occurred in 28, the promotion to the *ius Latinum* can be ascribed with great probability to 48, a plausible year for bestowal by Caesar. *Municipia* Calagurris and Osca, too, were enfranchised in the latter half of Statilius's governorship (pp. 165, 167), and, by their analogy, it may be supposed that he was, at Ilici also, technically *adsignator* to the founder and possessor of *imperium maius*, Octavian.

The leading citizen of the new foundation was clearly C. Maecius C. f. Celer. A M. Maecius became a senator early in this period,[4] and M. Maecius Celer was to give the family its first consulate in A.D. 101[5]—a L. Roscius Aelianus Maecius Celer having reached the same distinction in the previous year.[6] Statius describes M. Maecius Celer as *nobilis Ausoniae...armipotentis alumnus*[7]—which the probably servile origin of the earlier M. Maecius[8] renders suspiciously unplausible. Whether they were members of the ancient Latin clan of the Maecii[9] or not, it is clear that the family owed its emergence to its financial activities at Delos at the beginning of the first century B.C.[10] The move to Rome is characteristic of the early years of the principate.[11] It is interesting to note the predominance of Maecius at Ilici, which is paralleled

---

[1] Vide *CIL.* II, index, s.v.
[2] *CIL.* II. 3555.   [3] *ILS.* 893.
[4] Cf. Syme, *Papers of the British School at Rome*, XIV, 1938, p. 14 n. 65.
[5] Cf. Fluss, *PW.* XIV, 234.
[6] Cf. Groag, *PW.* I, 1116.   [7] *Silvae* III, 2. 20.
[8] Plutarch, *Cicero* 27; cf. Syme, l.c.
[9] Cf. Münzer, *PW.* XIV, 232.   [10] Ibid.
[11] Cf. West, *Imperial Roman Spain, The Objects of Trade*, p. 79, etc.

by hegemonies of the Pompeii at Celsa, Valerii at Calagurris, Aelii at Osca, Caecilii at Turiaso, and Sempronii at Bilbilis. L. Maecius's colleague L. Appuleius was probably a *cliens* of L. Appuleius Decianus, who was quaestor to Sex. Pompeius in Spain in 45–44 (p. 24).

The next stage in the history of Ilici is illustrated by *semisses* with Augustus's portrait:

(4)[1] AVGVSTVS DIVI F.—L. MANLIO T. PETRON(*io*) IIVIR(*is*), C(*oloni*) C(*oloniae*)[2] IL(*icis*) A(*ugustae*). *Aquila* and *vexillum*.

(5) The same,[3] or IMP. CAESARI DIVI F. AVGVSTO[4]—Q. PAPIR. CAR. Q. TERE. MONT. IIVIR. Q., C(*olonia*) I(*ulia*) IL(*ici*) A(*ugusta*). Tetrastyle temple inscribed on architrave IVNONI.

The heads are in the 'Patricia' style,[5] which suggests that Ilici, like *municipia* Bilbilis and Ilerda (pp. 170, 306), was refounded as *Augusta*[6] during the *princeps'* visit to Spain in c. 15–14. This conclusion is corroborated by the termination of the coinage of the Julian colony in the quinquennalian year 18–17, to which (3) must be assigned. It is also noteworthy that (4), alone of these five issues, is signed, not by *quinquennales*, but by *duoviri*. This suggests a special occasion in a year when no *lustrum* was due: and this is suitably supplied by a *restitutio* by Augustus in 15–14. L. Manlius and T. Petronius, then, coin to commemorate this refoundation, and so Ilici, like Dyme and Panormus (pp. 265, 190), has more than one inaugurative issue. Indeed, it has a third: (5) should almost certainly be attributed to the quinquennalian year 14–13 immediately following the refoundation, and so belongs to the curious category of second issues from the foundation-fund (p. 291). Here, as at eight other cities, a coinage of this type terminates the activity of the mint under Augustus. One of the *quinquennales* of (5) recalls by name the decayed family of the Papirii Carbones (cf. p. 244).[7]

The coinage of **Carthago Nova** now assumes a more homogeneous appearance, more manageable proportions, and a chronological arrangement more uniform with neighbouring colonies. It includes *asses*, without an ethnic and with portraits modelled on late Lugdunese *denarii*,[8] of M. Postum. Albin., L. Porci. Capit. *quinq*.[9] M. Postumius Albinus reappears, in a second tenure, with P. Turullius as his colleague,[10] on *semisses* which bear the ethnic V[R](*bs*) I(*ulia*) N(*ova*) K(*arthago*).[11] The two remaining

[1] Vives IV, p. 41. 1–3.
[2] Cf. *Thesaurus Ling. Lat.* III, p. 1705.
[3] Vives, l.c. 4.   [4] Ibid. 5.
[5] Cf. *BMC. Imp. Aug.* 378, etc.
[6] For the principles involved by *restitutio* (i.e. usually a second *deductio*) see below, p. 265.
[7] For the epithet, acknowledgments to R. Syme.
[8] *BMC. Imp. Aug.* 517, 519.
[9] Vives IV, pp. 34 ff. 26.

[10] It is interesting to note the appearance of a name only known to us in the person of Caesar's assassin, whose origin is obscure (cf. Syme, *RR*. p. 95).
[11] Vives 31. VRBS is found also on municipal coins of Osca (p. 167). An unusual variety of the ethnic exists here on a series of Tiberius with IN V(*rbe*) I(*ulia*) N(*ova*) K(*arthagine*); cf. Lorichs. *Recherches numismatiques*, p. 111.

Augustan quinquennalian pairs are Juba Rex Jubae f., Cn. Atellius Ponti.,[1] and Rex Ptol., C. Laetilius Apalus.[2] The absence of the names of the *praefecti* who represented the Mauretanian princes is a distinguishing feature from the series attributed above to *municipium* Saguntum. It is known from an inscription[3] that Juba II held the quinquennalian duovirate at Carthago Nova, and the coin of his son Ptolemy—whose royal blood already entitled him to be called *rex* by Roman usage[4]—must be assigned here owing to its similarity of style and *genre*. The latter issue is approximately datable by its use of no less than three different portrait-models of Augustus, namely *denarii* of the 'Caesaraugusta'[5] and 'Patricia'[6] types, and another from the Roman mint of c. 13 B.C.[7] The colleagues of the two princes are recorded by inscriptions. The fishermen and small tradesmen of Carthago Nova dedicated a shrine of the Lares Augustales and Mercury to C. Laetilius M. f. Apalus,[8] and freedmen of Cn. Atellius appear elsewhere in Tarraconensis:[9] he was perhaps the Cn. Atellius Cn. f. Pal. Longus who visited or resided at Smyrna.[10]

An earlier series includes two denominations:

CONDVC. (or CONTVC.[11]) MALLEOL., hand (Pl. VII, 18)—IIVIR QVINQ. bull;
COND. MAL. hammer—IIVIR. QVINQ shield.[12]

The shield is imitated from a Spanish (?) silver group of c. 33 B.C. (p. 60 n. 7). The present *aes* coins do not provide any positive evidence for attribution to Carthago Nova: it can only be said that style and—apparently—provenance[13] seem to favour this, and that the name Malleolus[14] suggests the *gens* Poblicia,[15] of which a member, C. Poplicius C. f., is recorded on a pre-Augustan inscription of that town.[16] Perhaps this family owed their name to a Cn. Poblicius Malleolus who coined in Spain as quaestor to Cn. Pompeius jun.[17] As for the other name, the single specimen with CONTVC. appears to rule out the possibility of reference to a *conductor*.[18] CONTVC. must represent a Celtiberian name such as Contuccius,[19] Contucius,[20] Contuciancus,[21] Contouca[22] and Contoutos.[23] Possibly the hand may be a pun on CONTVC., in the same way as the hammer is a

[1] Vives, l.c. 15.
[2] Vives, l.c. 24.
[3] *CIL.* II, 3417; cf. Sebastian, *De patronis etc.*, Diss. Halle, 1884, p. 12.
[4] Cf. Livy II, 2. 11, 3. 5, XLV, 48. 9; de la Blanchère, *Description de l'Afrique du Nord, mus. Oran*, p. 30.
[5] *BMC. Imp. Aug.* 343.
[6] Ibid. 440.   [7] Ibid. 106.
[8] *CIL.* II, 5929.
[9] Ibid. 3449–3451.
[10] *CIL.* III, 415; cf. Hatzfeld, p. 110 n. 10.
[11] Berlin.
[12] Vives IV, pp. 34 ff.

[13] Heiss, Delgado, Hübner and Vives are unanimous.
[14] Cf. *CIL.* II, 174 (Olisipo).
[15] Cf. Heiss, p. 274 n. 3.
[16] *CIL.* II, 3433.
[17] *BMCR.* II, 364. 72.
[18] *Conductor* could not be considered as a parallel to the Spanish forms *atlectus* (*CIL.* II, 4514), *atnati* (ibid. 4332), etc.
[19] *CIL.* VI, 555; cf. Fronto, *Ad amicos*, II, 4.
[20] *CIL.* VI, 1706.   [21] *CIL.* II, 3120.
[22] Holder, *Altceltischer Sprachschatz*, I, *Nachträge*, 1277.
[23] Ibid. I, 1109.

play upon the name of his colleague Malleolus. At all events the native name suggests a recently enfranchised town, just as the shield and style indicate a date not long after 36. These considerations, too, are suitable to Carthago Nova, which was a *colonia Iulia* as likely to have been founded by Octavian as by Caesar.[1] The coinage is not repeated for nearly twenty years and is thus a very likely candidate for inclusion among the foundation-issues. It has been shown that the presence of *quinquennales* is no obstacle, since Carthago Nova, like Ilici and many other cities, had probably attained Latinity under Caesar in c. 48 or c. 45–44. We therefore have the choice of c. 35–34, c. 33, or c. 30–29 for the foundation: the type of a bull suggests that T. Statilius Taurus was the founder in 29—the year before his foundation of Calagurris (p. 165). If he was the *deductor* in that year, this inaugural issue will precede by some fifteen years the next coinages from the mint. These include four colleges only, since the majority of the coins that appear at Carthago Nova in all current lists must be ejected—to Saguntum, Celsa, Ilici, Thermae Himeraeae (?) and Pella: other writers have already correctly reascribed coins to Carteia[2] and Cnossus,[3] and have rightly dismissed (but wrongly assigned) an official series with the type of a shield, and an issue of *colonia Latina* Nabrissa (pp. 121, 473).

The most extensive Augustan colonial series in the province is that of **Caesaraugusta** (Saldubia). It includes four denominations in 'bronze', namely *asses*—weighing less than at Ilici and elsewhere[4]—*dupondii,[5] semisses* and *quadrantes*. By the analogy of all other Augustan foundations in the province, the earliest issue probably commemorates the *deductio*: this distinction is likely, for iconographical reasons, to fall to the coins of Q. Lutatius and M. Fabius.[6] These use as portrait-models the *denarii* which have consequently also been ascribed to Caesaraugusta:[7] but the falsity of the attribution, and of the principle on which it is based, has been sufficiently demonstrated (p. 122). However, the use of these models, which gave way to the 'Patricia' class in c. 19 B.C., makes it probable that Caesaraugusta was founded in about that year[8] rather than 15–14.[9] The settlers were veterans from the Spanish garrisons.[10] By the analogy of Gades, enfranchised at the same date (p. 171), it may be assumed that Augustus was the *deductor*, and Agrippa the *adsignator* who installed the first *duoviri* Q. Lutatius and M. Fabius. The name of the former suggests a *clientela* of the Q. Catuli during the late Republic:[11]

[1] Hübner, *PW*. III, 1624 (correcting himself in *La Arqueología de España*, p. 174, and Kornemann 89, Taberner, *QAS*. XVIII, 1939, p. 16, Sutherland, *RIS*. p. 123).
[2] Vives IV, p. 26. 50 (Instituto de Valencia de Don Juan), correcting Lorichs, *Recherches numismatiques*, p. 121.
[3] Heiss, p. 275.
[4] 209·5 grains (av. 5).
[5] 413 grains (av. 3); unlikely therefore to be *sestertii, pace* Hill, p. 188.
[6] Madrid; Hill, pl. XIV, 2.
[7] *BMC. Imp. Aug.* 334, 336, 342, etc.
[8] Cf. Hübner, *PW*. III, 1287.
[9] As Ritterling, *PW*. XII, 1240.
[10] The standards of the fourth, sixth and ninth legions on some pieces (Hill, p. 95) should, as numerous analogies suggest, be interpreted in this way, rather than as indicative of an actual garrison from these legions, as Sutherland, *RIS*. p. 150 seems to imply.
[11] For these vide Münzer, *PW*. XII, 2082 ff.

M. Fabius may belong to a family whose enfranchisement dates back to the third or second century B.C.

Subsequent *denarius*-portraits attributed to Patricia or Lugdunum are copied on the undated issues, with usual types, of seven further duoviral colleges.[1] Heads of the same classes appear on dated coins of 6 B.C.[2] and 8–1 B.C.,[3] the latter of which has a titulature, IMP. AVGVSTVS XIV., that is of some interest for constitutional history (pp. 415, 440). A *dupondius* of 4–3 B.C. of another college represents Augustus standing with his grandsons;[4] a later one, with AVGVSTVS DIVI F. and the standards and titles of three legions instead of a portrait, is struck by a *duovir* L. Juventius Lupercus acting with Ti. Clodius Flavus, *praef. Germanici*.[5] The colonists in Spain looked well ahead in their flattery of the *domus principis*.[6] Ti. Clodius Flavus was no doubt a Spanish freedman and client of Tiberius[7]—rather than of Germanicus, whose original *praenomen* was probably Nero.[8] Other Clodii Flavi appear at several towns in the same province;[9] and Flavus is a common designation for Spaniards. A man of the same name as this *praefectus* appears at Rome within the next century.[10] The *duoviri* include some old Italian names. Amiturnum was probably the home of the Alliarii,[11] Tusculum of the noble Juventii:[12] the moneyer of the latter name is no doubt a relative of the Spanish mine-owner T. Juventius.[13] A T. Cervius appears with other members of his clan at Aufinum;[14] other Cervii include a Sabine neighbour of Horace[15] and a resident at Carthago Nova.[16] The Verrii[17] and Ampii,[18] too, were ancient Italian clans. M. Porcius no doubt recalls the large Spanish *clientela* of Cato.[19] Also remarkable are two *cognomina*. Alsanus[20] is derived from the Venetian river-name Alsa,[21] and Lancia recalls, in the same province, personal signatures LANCIQ.[22] and LANC.[23]—all are derived from the name of the Asturian town Lancia,[24] of which they were probably the freedmen.[25]

Alone of the Roman city-mints in the province, **Tarraco** does not appear to have a foundation-coinage. This deficiency is due to its establishment, as a civilian *colonia*

---

[1] Hill, p. 88: C. Alsano, T. Cervio; L. Cassio; C. Valerio Fen.; M'. Kan., L. Titio; M'. Kaninio, L. Titio *iter.*; Q. Maximo *iter.*, C. Valentino; C. Sabino, P. Varo; Q. Statio, M. Fabricio.
[2] Ibid. p. 89: C. Alliario, T. Verrio.
[3] Ibid.: M. Porci., Cn. Fad.
[4] Ibid.: Cn. Dom. Ampian., C. Vet. Lancia.
[5] Ibid. p. 90.
[6] Tiberius is also honoured on a *semis*, which, like a *quadrans*, lacks the signature of magistrates.
[7] Originally Ti. Claudius Nero: *ILS*. 95, 144–7.
[8] Mommsen, *Gesammelte Schriften*, IV, 287.
[9] *CIL*. II, 2486, 3626 (a man of Segontia at Saetabis).
[10] *CIL*. VI, 15067; cf. also 15066.

[11] *CIL*. IX, 4500. For the name, cf. Schulze, p. 416.
[12] Cic. *Pro Planc*. 19: cf. Afzelius, *Classica et Mediaevalia*, I, 1938, p. 71.
[13] *CIL*. II, 3280a; cf. van Nostrand, *ES*. III, p. 140.
[14] *CIL*. IX, 3392; cf. Schulze, p. 234.
[15] Hor. *Sat*. II, 6. 77. [16] *CIL*. II, 3433.
[17] Cf. Schulze, p. 278. [18] Ibid. p. 257.
[19] Cf. Stevenson, *RPA*. pp. 69 f.
[20] Cf. Hübner, *MLI*. p. 42.
[21] Pliny, *NH*. III, 126; cf. Hülsen, *PW*. I, 1638.
[22] *CIL*. II, 3088.
[23] Ibid. 4970. 258a.
[24] Schulten, *PW*. XII, 621.
[25] Cf. Mommsen, *Zeitschrift für geschichtliche Rechtswissenschaft*, XV, 1848, p. 297.

Iulia Victrix Triumphalis, as early as the lifetime of Caesar,[1] when Spanish communities had not yet been permitted to commemorate their foundation in this way.[2] The mint does not open until after 2 B.C., when it honours Caius and Lucius on light *asses*[3] and *semisses*,[4] on the former with Augustus, on the latter (with a type imitated from the *denarii*[5]) as GEMINI (Pl. VII, 19)—perhaps with reference to the Dioscuri,[6] as on an unpublished official series of Cyprus (p. 144). The next issue portrays Tiberius before his accession.[7] The attribution of the ethnic C.V.T. is confirmed by provenance.[8] This coinage has an unusually 'imperial' character appropriate to this new and impressive capital-city.[9] It is noteworthy that the share of the colony in its coinage is limited to the ethnic, which itself commemorates the triumphs of Julius; moreover, TR. POT. on the *asses*—extremely rare in the local series—is a further sign of liaison with authority (p. 446).

Thus the Tarraconensian colonies offer no parallel to the long early Augustan series of at least three *municipia* in the province. With the exceptions of the inaugural issue attributed to Carthago Nova and a few colleges at *colonia* Lepida, they produce no coinage at all during the triumvirate, and probably none until at least c. 25. Even then there can be no question of a general authorisation, since no coins are known of a considerable number of Julian and Augustan colonies (p. 297). Tarraco, established in Julius's lifetime, alone does not begin its coinage with a foundation-issue. But it is paralleled in this respect by a number of the dictator's colonies in Baetica.

5. HISPANIA BAETICA: Acci, Romula, Patricia, Traducta

This province has coinage from four Julian colonies,[10] but, as at Tarraco but no other city in Nearer Spain, there are no foundation-issues among them. Tarraco was established by Julius (p. 219), and the first foundation-coinage in Spain (at Celsa) does not occur until after his death (p. 211). The five colonies in Baetica could therefore be attributed to his lifetime; but they may also have been posthumous. At all events they are likely to have been founded within the forties.

---

[1] Dio XLIII, 39; cf. Schulten, *PW*. (2R.), IV, 2399; Hübner, *MLI*. p. 539; Meyer, *Cäsars Monarchie*, p. 486.
[2] The Caesarian foundation could possibly be Latin (cf. Sherwin-White, p. 177): but if this had been the case, the *deductio* would have to be attributed to 16–13 B.C., when the absence of a foundation-coinage would be inexplicable.
[3] BM: Hill, p. 48, pl. V, 5.
[4] BM: Hill, p. 48, pl. V, 4.
[5] *BMC. Imp. Aug.* 513 ff.
[6] Eckhel, *DN*. I, p. 58.
[7] Hill, p. 48.

[8] Cf. Vilaró, *MJSEA*. CXVI [V, 1930], p. 115; Oliva, ibid. LXXXVIII [VI, 1924–5], pp. 77 f.
[9] Cf. Hübner, Hill, ll.cc.
[10] An attribution to Hasta Regia by Florez and Eckhel (*DN*. I, p. 15; cf. Delgado III, p. 84. 36) is accepted by Miss Newby (p. 83), who ignores Hübner's demonstration of its falsity (*CIL*. II, p. 175). Miss Newby (p. 84) also cites from Eckhel (*DN*. I, p. 25) an obviously non-existent colonial coin of Munda, in the face of protest from E. T. Newell. Lorichs (*Recherches numismatiques*, p. 112) has an equally disastrous attribution to *col.* Onuba.

An issue of **Acci**,[1] which appears to have been at this time in the *provincia Vlterior*,[2] is probably the earliest colonial issue of the province, since its portrait—inscribed CAESAR AVG.—seems to be modelled on Emeritan *denarii*;[3] a second *as*[4] (AVGVSTVS DIVI F.) uses the regular 'Patricia' head. Except for one *semis* of the latter category with the type of pontifical emblems,[5] every coin of Augustus emphasises, by legionary eagles and standards, the *deductio* of the colony; the conjunction for this purpose of L(*egiones*) II. I., specified on the coins, accounts for the title *Gemina* found in the ethnic C. I. G. ACCI.[6] The Julian epithet[7] indicates that these pieces are not inauguratory. They are somewhat heavier than semuncial.[8]

The remaining three colonies do not coin before c. 19 B.C., since in each case the earliest portrait-model is of the 'Patricia' class. This *terminus post quem* is relevant to the point made by Sutherland,[9] that the beginning of the principate for the Spaniards was the visit of Augustus in 15–14 B.C. rather than the constitutional changes of 27 or 23. The occasion of the *princeps*' presence is further suggested by the appearance on each series of the formula PERM(*issu*) AVG(*usti*). When Augustus founded *municipium* Italica—where this also occurs (p. 173)—he presumably took the opportunity to permit coinage at a few older foundations also. This sanction, if attributed to the time of his visit, corresponds with the most probable date for the transference of Baetica to the senate (p. 134). It gives a striking demonstration of the activity of the *auctoritas principis* (p. 435)—which, incidentally, was not exercised in so downright a fashion in consular provinces, where the governors' own permission is recorded (p. 232). The three colonies accorded the privilege of celebrating his visit in this way (but of little or no subsequent coinage while Augustus still lived) were Romula, Patricia and Traducta—as the cities of Hispalis, Corduba and Ioza were now called. **Romula**[10] only strikes under Augustus one *semis*, with *cornucopiae* and globe;[11] **Patricia** issues all five of the Roman denominations and includes the common types of legionary eagle and standards,[12] and pontifical emblems.[13] (No confirmation is, or is likely to be, obtainable for Cohen's[14] citation of a piece bearing the name of the fifth and tenth legions.) On the same standard is the coinage of **Traducta**[15] which is based on a bronze *as* somewhat heavier than the copper one at Rome.[16] The ethnic IVLIA TRAD(*ucta*) testifies to the confusing practice of omitting the status of cities in their titulature.

---

[1] Pliny, *NH*. III, 1; Kornemann 91; Ritterling, *PW*. XII, 1215.
[2] Albertini, *Les divisions administratives de l'Espagne romaine*; Sutherland, *JRS*. XXIV, 1934, p. 38; id. *RIS*. p. 239 n. 15, attributes the change to the last few years B.C.—after the date of these coins.
[3] Berlin, Hall colls.: Vives IV, p. 120. 1.
[4] Ibid. 4.   [5] Ibid. 5.
[6] Kornemann, p. 528.
[7] van Nostrand, *UCPH*. IV, 2, 1916, p. 103, attributes Acci to Caesar; cf. Meyer, p. 484, for Romula.
[8] 277, 241, 221, 198 grains (BM).
[9] *JRS*. XXIV, 1934, p. 31; cf. Syme, *RR*. p. 324.
[10] Kornemann 83.
[11] Vives, p. 220, pl. CLXVII, 1.
[12] Vives IV, p. 118. 2.   [13] Ibid. 4.
[14] *Description historique des monnaies frappées sous l'empire romain, Auguste*, 605.
[15] Strabo III, 140.   [16] 172·7 grains (av. 6).

Caius[1] and Lucius Caesar[2] are honoured with portraits both separately and in conjunction;[3] on the reverse the usual priestly emblems alternate with local types, including a bunch of grapes, corn-ear, and tunny-fish.[4] Pliny[5] wrongly states that this colony was at Tingis: it was, in fact, composed of settlers from Tingis and Zilis, but situated on the coast of Baetica.[6] Its character suggests *civitas* rather than *Latinitas*.[7]

6. HISPANIA LUSITANA: Emerita, Pax

Hispania Lusitana, which was probably separated from Baetica in c. 15–14 B.C. (p. 134), is represented by an extensive coinage of its capital,[8] *colonia Augusta* Emerita, founded in 25 B.C.[9] This is in succession to the official issues of P. Carisius (p. 119), and, like them but unlike most colonial mintages, fulfils a certain economic role. It maintains an average standard of c. 191 grains,[10] which exceeds that used by the *legatus*, whose *as*, though of bronze,[11] was only equal in weight to the Roman copper *as* (p. 300). Emerita strikes for a longer period than other Spanish colonies, but every coin either bears the titles of Augustus or records his permission. On some pieces his portrait is omitted in favour of the head of a bearded male[12] or a female,[13] both river-deities.[14] The fifth and tenth legions, whose veterans composed the colony, are recorded with the usual military type,[15] and the *deductio* is further commemorated by the representation of a priest ploughing.[16] A type of Carisius, showing the walls and gate of the city, is repeated on what is very likely to be a belated foundation-issue of the colony in c. 23. But the same type appears on a coin[17] whose title (P.P.) and head, modelled on the latest Lugdunese *denarii*,[18] show that the issues, which seem to have started earlier than those of the Baetican colonies (except perhaps Acci), also outlasted them by continuing regularly until the death of the *princeps*.

Another colony in the province which coins is Pax. This, like the Baetican colonies, was a Julian foundation,[19] but nevertheless does not coin—as its 'Patricia' portrait shows—until after c. 19 B.C. No doubt, by the analogy of the same colonies, the single issue[20] commemorates the visit of Augustus to Spain. The type is a figure of Mercury(?),

---

[1] Vives IV, p. 115. 5; *var.* Delgado II, 308.
[2] Vives, l.c. 8, 9; *var.* BM. Abbreviated as LVC.
[3] Ibid. 12; *var.* Heiss, p. 337. 6.
[4] Vives, l.c. 10, 7, 11.
[5] *NH*. V, 1.
[6] Strabo III, 140; Mela II, 96; cf. Schulten, *PW*. (2R.), VI, 1892; Windberg, ibid. 2518.
[7] As Taberner, *QAS*. XVIII, 1939, p. 16.
[8] Ibid. p. 13.
[9] Kornemann 177; Sutherland, *RIS*. p. 135.
[10] Av. 9.   [11] Spectrogram 35.
[12] Vives IV, p. 63. 21.   [13] Ibid. 31.

[14] On the former coin there is a jar pouring forth water, and on the second a stream of water pours from the mouth of the divinity, as at Saguntum (p. 162 n. 5).
[15] Vives IV, p. 63. 23 ff.
[16] Ibid. 22.   [17] Ibid. 19.
[18] *BMC. Imp. Aug.* 533, etc.
[19] Kornemann 180; Hübner, *La Arqueología de España*, p. 174; van Nostrand, *UCPH*. IV, 2, 1916, p. 101; and Sutherland, *RIS*. p. 125, attribute it to Caesar, but on the inadequate grounds of its Julian epithet.   [20] Vives IV, p. 124.

and the only legend is PAX IVLIA. The epithet *Augusta*[1] must have been added not long after, but it was not in invariable use before the principate of Hadrian.[2] Other colonies in Lusitania do not appear to have coined.[3]

7. MAURETANIA: Babba

Far away in the interior of this territory was *colonia Campestris Iulia* **Babba**. Cagnat[4] stated that all issues of Augustus attributed to this mint were false or erroneously described;[5] but he ignores a coin unmistakably of this date and mint, cited by E. Babelon[6] [reattribute to Buthrotum—M.G. 1969]:

CAESAR AVGVSTVS[7] bare head to right
L. POMPON[I]. L. IVLI. IIVIR. Q., [C. C.] I. B.[8] Three-arched bridge (Pl. VI, 22).

The reverse-type occurs on later coins of Babba, whose ethnic is visible on one of the specimens. The portrait is imitated from Eastern *denarii* of 28 B.C.;[9] these are too early to have been used as models for posthumous coinage, and the unique appearance of *quinquennales* further distinguishes the issue from post-Augustan ones. Since Babba remained a *colonia Iulia*,[10] its foundation must be assigned to the years 33–28—between the death of Bocchus and the creation of the title *Augustus*. Its date can be even more closely fixed by the consideration of a Neronian piece—never attributed here but, for stylistic and iconographic reasons, clearly belonging to the series—with AVGVSTVS (radiate head to left with traits of Nero) and DEDVCTOR (curule chair).[11] This is distinguished sharply by its types from the remaining Neronian coinage of Babba, and is certainly commemorative: by the analogy of similar issues celebrating the half-centenary of Cirta, Carthage, Tarraco and Lystra, and the quarter-centenary of Dyrrhachium (p. 295), it is impossible to resist the conclusion that it celebrates the centenary of

---

[1] Strabo III, 151. But possibly not until Tiberius (p. 197 f. n. 6).
[2] *CIL.* II, 47.
[3] A survey of the portrait-models used by the Spanish cities, whose review is now complete, shows convincingly the fallacy of the arguments by which two groups of *aurei* and *denarii* are attributed to Hispania Tarraconensis and Baetica: (1) the 'Baetican' ('Patricia') group is imitated in Tarraconensis at Carthago Nova, Osca, Caesaraugusta, Calagurris, Celsa, Acci, Ilici; (2) even the Emeritan group is copied both in Baetica (at Italica) and in Tarraconensis (at Saguntum and Acci); (3) non-Spanish models are freely used: e.g. Eastern and Roman at Calagurris and Ilerda respectively; (4) both the 'Patricia' and 'Caesaraugusta' portraits appear on variants of the same coin (with *Rex Ptol.*) of Carthago Nova. This last example illustrates the time-lag sometimes caused by an eclectic choice of models, which can, as has been shown, only be employed to establish a *terminus post quem*. The same models are utilised with equal freedom in other provinces. See pp. 122, 269, 83, 470.
[4] *Klio*, IX, 1914, p. 196.
[5] E.g. Morelli, *Thesaurus*, p. 472.
[6] *Rn.* 1889, p. 506; Paris, own collection.
[7] Clear on Paris specimen.
[8] Clear on specimen in own collection.
[9] *BMC. Imp. Aug.* 650.
[10] Kornemann 352.
[11] Berlin, Vienna, Turin (Lavy, *Cat.* 4742)—'uncertain'.

THE ROMAN COLONIES 223

Babba's *deductio*. For this occasion to have fallen within Nero's principate, the colony must have been founded in 33–32 B.C.: it has been suggested that a group of colonies in Eastern Mauretania is to be attributed to the same date (p. 60). Heraclea Pontica will provide an example of foundation-coinage postponed until the first *decennium* of the colony (p. 295): the earliness of the present portrait-model[1] suggests that here the first *quinquennium* is celebrated. If this is the case, the appearance of the name Augustus indicates a year not before 27, and the foundation must have occurred within the year 32.

The extensive colonisation of Mauretania at this time bears witness to Octavian's desire to safeguard his southern flank before hostilities began: there had been serious trouble only a few years earlier.[2] It is not surprising that the hasty *deductio* for military purposes at Babba did not provide the opportunity for the regular commemorative coinage, which was, instead, struck by the first *quinquennales*. A secondary motive for the coinage may well be commemoration of the new order of 27. But, until the accession of Juba in 25, there was no change in the status of Mauretania. It does not appear in the *Res Gestae* as a province in which colonies were founded, and the assumption has been made that it was, for eight years after the death of Bocchus in 33, attached to Africa (p. 60): but the fact that the *deductor* of Babba was not the proconsul of that province, but, as the Neronian coin shows, Octavian—in anticipation of the regular practice after 27—suggests that it was a non-provincial zone (like Galatia after Amyntas's death) controlled by a comparatively junior officer directly under Octavian's orders. In 25 Babba became an *enclave* in the territory of Juba.[3]

8. AFRICA: Hippo Diarrhytus, Thapsus, Hadrumetum, Achulla, Carthage, Cirta (?), Simitthu (?)

The coinage of this province provides much evidence for a class of community, the *coloniae Iuliae*, with which fate, and Pliny, have dealt hardly. The basic work of Muller scarcely refers to constitutional questions; moreover, it omits a great many of the coins, and misinterprets others.[4] A series which he has partly collected is that of

[1] It has been shown (p. 83) that the 'Caesaraugusta' portraits came into use well before 23–22, when the present rather unusual model would almost certainly have been superseded.

[2] Cf. Gsell VIII, p. 201.

[3] He probably exercised *patrocinium* in the colony, which was quite inaccessible to the capital of any *conventus* and the jurisdiction of any governor. It is interesting to note that the general ban under Claudius on Roman city-coinage in the West is remitted only in the case of Babba (Charrier, *Description des monnaies de la Numidie et de la Maurétanie*, p. 150) and probably the equally remote town of Ebusus (vide Campaner y Fuertès, *Numismática Balear*; Vives IV, p. 14—doubted by Sutherland, *RIS*. p. 245)—both of which, it must be assumed, existed without the customary supervision of governors. The coastal colonies, like Zilis, could be attached to Baetica, but Babba was much too distant.

[4] A remarkable piece of *colonia* Diana quoted by Boutkowski (*DN*. p. 214 f.: IVBA REX diademed head r., countermarked, laurel-wreath—COL. I. F. DIAN. VET. in wreath, within P. LAEL.

Hippo Diarrhytus. Like those of Hadrumetum, the earliest issues bear no reference, by type or legend, to Rome, and like them they cannot have been struck much, if at all, before the final establishment of the principate. They have the inscription HIPPONE LIBERA, heads of Astarte, Juno (?) and Ceres; figures of Ceres, Thuso-Chusartis, and a warrior with a dog.[1] An unusual coin[2] (Pl. VI, 24) reads CLAVDIO NERONI HIPPONE LIBERA and FABIO AFRIKANO, accompanied by the heads respectively of Tiberius and Africanus Fabius Maximus, proconsul c. 6–5 B.C. (p. 139). Pansa[3] rightly points out that the Dative case is never eponymous; but his assumption that such inscriptions in honour of proconsuls refer to a period later than that of their governorships is inapplicable here, where both sides of the coin show ordinary honorary dedications. Another piece bears the same ethnic (misread by Borghesi[4] to produce the name of a proconsul [CN]. P[IS]ONE), and the heads of Caius and Lucius, inscribed C. L.; on the obverse is the head of Augustus to right, with CAESAR AVG.[5]

Since Hippo is shown by inscriptions to have been a Julian colony,[6] the epithet *libera* on these coins has been used as an argument for a double community.[7] Wilmanns[8] and Kubitschek,[9] however, maintain that a comparison of the Masculine Gender of the other Hippo—*Regius*[10]—demonstrates that here the word *colonia* is understood: but they are refuted by the examples of *municipium Hibera Iulia* Dertosa Ilercavonia and *municipium Augusta* Bilbilis (pp. 158, 170) which show that in these cases the epithets were thought of in connection with the name of the city rather than with the title of the rank. It is necessary, therefore, to believe that the two Hippos were originally of different Genders. Thus the deduction by Kubitschek[11] that *libera* here survived as a meaningless archaism applied to a colony is not acceptable. Nor is it now possible to consider the obsolete view[12] that there were separate classes of *coloniae liberae* and

ARRVNT. PONT. IIVIR LEG. A. DI. S. F.) must be rejected as false for a number of reasons: (1) Diana (Zama in the plain) was certainly not a Roman city until the second century, when it became a *municipium* (Dessau, *PW.* v, 339; cf. Broughton, p. 134 n. 75; *CIL.* VIII, p. 462; Renier, *Rev. arch.* IX, 1852, p. 38); (2) LEG(*ati*) A(*gris*) DI(*vidundis*) will be shown elsewhere (p. 11) to be a false invention of Zumpt; (3) Juba II can have had no liaison of any kind with Zama in the plain: his supposed brief period of rule in Numidia has been shown to be fictitious (Gsell VIII, p. 205; Syme, *CAH.* X, p. 346); (4) A coin of Juba II exists with an almost (or precisely) identical obverse and denomination (Muller III, p. 107. 73), supplying a basis for the tooler's vivid, but unhistorical, imagination. Boutkowski announces that despite every effort he was unable to persuade an Arab farmer to sell him this specimen. The Arab missed an unusually good bargain.

[1] Muller II, p. 167, *Suppl.* p. 58. 375 *a*.
[2] Paris; *Bull. arch. du com.* 1897, p. 250; ibid. 1901, p. cxciii.
[3] *R.it.* 1909, p. 365; Muensterberg, *MBNGW.* IX, 1913, p. 161. Cf. p. 399 n. 5.
[4] Cf. Cavedoni, *Bullettino archeologico italiano*, I, 1862, p. 174.
[5] Paris, Constantine (not seen by writer); cf. Muller, *Suppl.* p. 44.
[6] *ILS.* 6782; cf. *Catalogo della Mostra Augustea di Romanità*, p. 567. 11.
[7] E.g. Broughton, pp. 210 ff.; Rostovtzeff, *SEH.* p. 580 n. 59; Dessau, *Klio*, VIII, 1908, pp. 459 ff.
[8] *CIL.* VIII, p. 152.
[9] *SB. Wien*, CLXXVII, 4. *Abh.* 1916, p. 105.
[10] Cf. *Bell. Afr.* 96, etc.
[11] L.c. p. 110.
[12] Marquardt, *St.V.* I, p. 89, etc.; disregarded by Last, *CAH.* XI, p. 455, etc.; cf. Mommsen, *St.R.* III, pp. 810 f.

municipia libera. However, Kubitschek sees that there is no evidence for a double community. The truth is that *libertas* and colonial status were not mutually exclusive, but coincident. Cicero[1] shows that the truest *libertas* was actually that of Roman citizens, who possessed it even more distinctively than peregrine *liberae civitates*;[2] thus it is completely consistent with a Roman colony,[3] and the omission of the word *colonia* is frequent on colonial coinages of this period. In the same way as Bilbilis seems to have proclaimed its *civitas* by the word *Italica* (p. 170), the *ius Italicum* being a concomitant of citizenship at this time (p. 316), so Hippo commemorates it by the equally relevant word *libera*: but here there is special point in such advertisement—the epithet served to differentiate the privileged Hippo Diarrhytus from the peregrine and stipendiary Hippo Regius.

Relevant to *libertas* is another series which has been misattributed. This includes a large piece[4] with AVGVSTVS IMP. (his head to left, *simpulum*), whose reverse type is a figure of Mercury, with *caduceus*, seated on a rock, accompanied by the inscription C. I. P. IIIIVIR (Pl. VIII, 1). This, with a number of Tiberian issues with the same ethnic, has been ascribed, for no good reason, by Perizoni to Sabrata,[5] by Ramus to Utica,[6] by Havercamp to Carthage,[7] by Pellerin to Parada,[8] by Cavedoni to Pulput,[9] and by Eckhel to Clypea.[10] Although Eckhel, supported by Muller, makes out a case for the connection of Mercury with the promontory near Clypea, his theory, generally accepted though it is, does violence to the principles governing ethnics, by which C. I. regularly represents *colonia Iulia*.

Such doubts are shown to be justified by a piece, bought at Bir-Bou-Rekba (near Nabeul),[11] with CAESAR DIVI F. (his head to left, *simpulum* or *lituus*) and the same type of Mercury seated. On this the reverse legend is COLONIAE IVLIAE: two monograms follow, of which the former is $\overline{\text{PI}}$; the latter is corrected by E. S. G. Robinson (who has seen the coin) to a version of $\overline{\text{THAP}}$.,[12] and **Thapsus** may accordingly be considered a probable choice for the mint. The objection might be advanced that later Thapsitan coins, under Tiberius, omit the colonial title, and that legends from his principate, such as THAPSVM IVN. AVG.[13] and CERERI AVGVSTAE THAMPSITANI (*sic*),[14] are inconsistent with a previous use of this title. But the absence of the word *colonia* is very frequent in the colonial series at this time, many cities omitting it

[1] *II Verr.* 1. 7, 1. 13, 3. 66.
[2] Cf. Riccobono, *Annali del Seminario giuridico della R. Univ. di Palermo*, XV, 1936, p. 453; Kloesel, *Libertas*, Diss. Breslau, 1935, p. 44; von Premerstein, *PW*. x, 1248; Tellenbach, *Forschungen zur Kirchen- und Geistesgeschichte*, VII, 1936, p. 18; see below, p. 401, for a general discussion.
[3] Not only Pliny, but Pausanias also (VII, 18. 7), describes colonies merely as 'free cities'.
[4] Copenhagen, Leningrad; cf. Muller II, p. 155. 330, Suppl. p. 56.
[5] Cf. Muller, l.c.
[6] Copenhagen Cat. I, 391.
[7] *Méd. de la reine Christine*, pl. 48. 32.
[8] *Lettres*, II, pp. 152 f.
[9] *Bull. arch. italiano*, I, 1862, pp. 175 f.
[10] *DN.* IV, p. 14. The present list omits attributions so fanciful as to ignore the obvious African fabric.
[11] *Bull. arch. com.* 1915, p. cxciv.
[12] Monogram 8—*pace Bull. arch. du com.*, l.c.
[13] Muller II, p. 47. 12.
[14] Tunis (Bado mus.), Vatican; cf. BM.

long after their colonisation[1]—many too, as here, specifying it on an early programme issue but not thereafter. At Buthrotum, for example, the ethnic C. I. BVT. is earlier than BVTHR. (p. 270); at Emporiae MVNICIPI. is absent from all but the earliest coin in its Latin series (p. 154).[2] Indeed, on such commemorative pieces the title is more appropriate than on later issues. There remain two reasons for attribution to a Byzacenian mint, and two in support of the claims of Thapsus in particular. The title CAESAR DIVI F., indicating a date before 27 B.C., is only found elsewhere in Africa at Achulla, Thaena and Leptis minor (pp. 230, 346, 338), all in Byzacene; Mercury only occurs in Africa at Leptis minor and Thysdrus (pp. 338, 347). These general arguments in favour of the most natural interpretation of the monogram are augmented by particular resemblances to known Thapsitan issues. A seated figure on coins of Tiberius with C. I. P.[3] is remarkably like that on his issues with THAMPSITANI, while his peculiar portraits on the series with C. I. P. and THAPSVM are practically identical.

Thus *colonia Iulia P(ia?)* may confidently be assigned to Thapsus. Pliny[4] describes this as an *oppidum liberum*: but, on the one hand, of the other African cities in his list of *liberae*, at least four are certainly *coloniae Iuliae*; on the other, he only defines correctly six out of a probable nineteen of the latter category.[5] The explanations for this ambiguity are two. First, *libertas* is, as has been shown, a characteristic that can apply equally to Roman and peregrine communities; secondly, it has been established beyond all doubt that the Agrippan list, used by Pliny,[6] sometimes omits foundations which occurred before 27 B.C.[7] The present isolated issue celebrates the *deductio* of the new colony[8] just as all African pieces with similar obverse legends commemorate some such promotion of their city.

It is now clear that many Julian colonies may have lapsed into oblivion, from which they can only be recovered by numismatic study. For example, there is another for which dubious epigraphic evidence is supplemented by coinage. This includes issues by two colleges of *duoviri*, whose names have been frequently misread from the rare and ill-struck pieces:

(1)[9] C. FABIVS CATVLVS IIVIR head of Neptune to right with trident.
D.(?)SEXTILIVS CORNVTVS IIVIR facing head of Sun, with radiate crown.

[1] E.g. Corinth (*BMC.* 505, 509, 514, etc.).
[2] Cf. Corinth, which places an unusually full titulature on early pieces, e.g. *BMC.* 485.
[3] Paris; Muller II, p. 155.
[4] *NH.* v, 25.   [5] Broughton, p. 49.
[6] Cf. most recently Jones, *CERP.* p. 492.
[7] Cf. Broughton, p. 53 n. 40 for Africa—confirmed by the coins of Zama Regia, Hippo, Hadrumetum, Achulla. Pliny likewise completely omits *mun. Iulium* Uselis and *col. Iulia* Cnossus, attributes *col. Iulia* Traducta to the wrong shore of the Mediterranean, and ignores the *civitas* of *Iulia* Lystra and pre-Julian Italica. Sexi and Lix are other probable omissions (p. 174). His 24 *municipia* in Spain defy discovery: cf. van Nostrand, *UCPH.* IV, 2, 1916, pp. 114 ff. Julian communities are often ignored by him when they had been suppressed by a later foundation.

[8] For *quattuorviri* at colonies, cf. Parium (p. 248).
[9] Boissevain, *ZfN.* XXIX, 1912, p. 107; cf. Hague, Copenhagen, Pesaro, etc.; misread by Muller II, p. 51, Borghesi, Caronni, von Falbe, etc. A piece lacking legends, with the same reverse type and a horse on the obverse, is in the BM.

(2)[1] L. FLĀMIN. CAPIT. [IIVIR] obverse type of (1).
··LEIV. PERT. [IIVIR] radiate head of Sun to right.

Muller's[2] attribution to a governor of c. 94 B.C. is based on a completely erroneous reading: Mommsen[3] pointed out that the style is of a later period. Now the radiate head on (2) is precisely like a head of the same deity on coins of Augustan date with the ethnic of **Hadrumetum**:[4] the same mint also provides a head of Neptune practically identical with those on (1) and (2). There can be no doubt that this was the city to which the two colleges belong. The duoviral titles suggest Roman rank, and epigraphic and literary evidence can be quoted in favour of the interpretation of Hadrumetum as a *colonia Iulia*. First, there are tiles with C. I. H.[5] whose provenance suggests attribution here; secondly, Hadrumetum, like so many other Julian colonies, is described by Pliny as *oppidum liberum*.[6] Finally, on a Trajanic inscription it is entitled *colonia Concordia Vlpia Traiana Frugifera*:[7] abstract titles such as *Concordia* invariably date from the end of the Republic,[8] and this particular example has been shown by Carcopino to apply in the case of Carthage (as at Beneventum[9] and Brundusium[10]) to the circumstances of 42–40 B.C.[11] This is, moreover, one of the four possible periods for the foundation of *colonia* Hadrumetum deduced by Gsell[12] from the evidence known to him. An Augustan coin of the colony—nearly contemporary with a representation of Caius and Lucius[13]—bearing the head of Julius inscribed CAESAR[14] is confirmative, since it suggests that the dictator planned some advancement for the community, which, as so often, is very likely to have been achieved after his death. Similar heads appear at many other Julian colonies and at cities freed by him,[15] but not elsewhere. It is therefore certain that he planned the colony at Hadrumetum, and highly probable that this was carried out—like a foundation at Carthage (p. 231)—by Lepidus in 42–40. The isolated duoviral issues undoubtedly represent the foundation-issues of the new colony: the appearance of two colleges recalls the not infrequent custom of a second coinage, immediately after the first, defrayed from the surviving balance of a foundation-fund (p. 291). The interpretation of these as inauguratory issues is confirmed by the fact that C. Fabius Catulus and D. (?) Sextilius Cornutus also strike a very rare silver piece[16]—whose only certain parallel is on coinage celebrating the *liberatio* of Leptis Magna (p. 340). A Q. Fabius Ca... was a procurator of Augustus.[17]

[1] BM, Berlin, misread by *ZfN*. x, 1883, p. 84.
[2] II, p. 51; cf. Münzer, *PW*. VI, 1763.
[3] *Mzw.* p. 671.
[4] Muller II, p. 52. 27, p. 51.
[5] *CIL*. VI, p. 2319; cf. Broughton, p. 49.
[6] *NH*. v, 25.   [7] *CIL*. VI, 1687, etc.
[8] Cagnat, *Revue épigraphique*, 1913, pp. 4 ff.
[9] Pais, *Rend. della R. Ac. dei Lincei (sc.-mor.)*, VI, I, 1925, p. 363.
[10] *ILS*. 3784; cf. Syme, *RR*. p. 217 n. 4.
[11] *Rev. hist.* CLXII, 1929, p. 91; *pace* Gsell, ibid. CLVI, 1927, pp. 228 ff.; Markowski, *Eos*, XXXIV, 1933, p. 440; Frank, *ES*. I, p. 318.
[12] VIII, p. 171.
[13] BM, Paris: C. CAE. F., L. CAE. F. Misread by Muller II, p. 52. 32 f.
[14] BM, Paris; cf. Muller II, 52. 30 f.
[15] As late as the second century A.D., e.g. Apamea.
[16] Bahrfeldt, *NZ*. XXVII, 1896, pp. 118 f.
[17] *CIL*. III, 7071, cf. Groag, *SB*. IX, 1939, p. 139.

A later commemorative group shows the names and portraits of three proconsuls. Two coins, with heads of the Sun and an ethnic, have P. QVINCTILI. VARVS[1] and L. VOLVSIVS SATVRN.,[2] accompanied by busts—found also at Achulla (p. 230) (Pl. VII, 30, 29)—which, in spite of suppositions to the contrary,[3] certainly represent those governors. The third piece,[4] with the head of a bearded deity and an ethnic on the obverse, has a reverse precisely similar to that of an official coin which has been ascribed to the mint (p. 139): it reads AFRIC. FABIVS MAX. COS. PRO COS. VIIVIR[5] EPVL., and shows his portrait to right (Pl. VII, 28). These proconsuls, of whom the first two also appear at Achulla and the third at Hippo (p. 224) and on official coinage (p. 139), cannot be dated with certainty: Fabius is most likely to have governed from 6 to 5 B.C.,[6] to have been preceded by Volusius[7] and succeeded—probably at one remove—by Quinctilius.[8] These issues deserve further discussion, since they have been erroneously construed by Mommsen as proof of a proconsular *Prägerecht*,[9] and by Regling[10] and Kruse[11] as evidence of *Anteil am kaiserlichen Bildnisrechte*. These legalistic theories are invalidated not only by the local character of the coinages—which Mommsen does not distinguish from the official series of the province—but by the Dative inflection of Fabius's name at Hippo: this shows that the issues commemorated the proconsuls,[12] and that no *Recht* on their part is in question.[13] Mommsen and his followers failed to consider that this was a time when numerous cities engraved the portraits even of contemporary private citizens upon their coins,[14] and when colonies and *municipia* celebrate city-magistrates in the same way (pp. 163, 184). The attribution of any 'Rights' to those portrayed is wholly inadmissible: the procedure was still honorary,[15] and Mommsen's theory of their conferment on the senior proconsuls as a

---

[1] Muller II, p. 52. 26; du Palin coll., etc.

[2] Ibid. 27; BM, Vienna.

[3] E.g. Cavedoni, *Bullettino archeologico italiano*, I, 1862, pp. 171 f.; Borghesi, *Œuvres*, I, p. 312.

[4] Muller, l.c. 29; Hague, Paris, Copenhagen.

[5] Cf. Mommsen, *ZfN*. 1875, p. 72.

[6] Cf. Renault, *Bull. arch. du com.* 1897, p. 256, correcting de Lessert, *Fastes des provinces africaines*, p. 83, and Tissot, *Fastes de la province romaine d'Afrique*, p. 43.

[7] Dessau, *PIR*. III, 482. 660; cf. de Lessert, l.c. p. 81; but Renault disagrees.

[8] Dessau, *PIR*. III, 118. 27, de Lessert, l.c. p. 80 (7–6 B.C.), ignore coins (*BMC. Galatia*, etc., p. 158. 57) showing his presence in Syria: Waddington (*Rn*. 1867, p. 123) attributes his proconsulship to 4–3 B.C. Cf. also Momigliano, *CAH*. X, p. 338.

[9] *ZfN*. 1875, pp. 69 ff.

[10] *WMK*. p. 534.

[11] *Studien zur Geschichte und Kultur des Altertums*, 1934, *Kaiserbild*, p. 19 n. 1.

[12] Cf. Pansa, *R.it.* 1909, p. 365.

[13] This is also implied by Pippidi, *Revue des études latines*, 1935, p. 427; Arangio-Ruiz, *Studia et documenta historiae et iuris*, IV, 1938, pp. 235 f. A Genitive at Achulla is an archaism (cf. Mattingly, *BMC. Imp.* pp. lxix f.) often found on local issues.

[14] E.g. Pythes (*BMC*. 55, Pl. XI, 61) and Sitalcas (*BMC*. 54) at Laodicea, Antiochus at Miletopolis (Winterthur; Imhoof-Blumer, *RS*. XIII, p. 48), Attalus at Hypaepa, Papion at Dioshieron (pp. 349, 468), Charidamus on issues of the κοινὸν 'Ασίας (p. 377), Theophanes and Archedamis at the beginning of a long series at Mytilene (*ZfN*. IX, 1882, p. 131), Amnessus at Alabanda (p. 373).

[15] It may be noted that a similar 'decree' of portraiture to Julius has been shown to be false (p. 15).

THE ROMAN COLONIES   229

consolation at the time of Caius's designation as consul, and of their removal at his death, is based on unacceptable hypotheses.[1]

Yet it is impossible to believe, with Muller[2] and Waddington,[3] that these issues have no special historical significance. A coincidence too striking to be accidental makes it clear that they have. In the first place, the group is geographically and chronologically isolated and homogeneous: but in the other consular 'senatorial' province, Asia, three cities (Temnus, Hierapolis, Pitane) exceptionally honour three proconsuls whose tenures appear to be exactly or very nearly contemporary with those in the African group—Paullus Fabius Maximus, C. Asinius Gallus and L. Cornelius Scipio (pp. 387 f.). These contemporary phenomena are explained by a decisive link between the six governors. Five of them were relatives by marriage to the *princeps*,[4] and the sixth, Gallus, is explicitly stated by him to be his φίλος.[5] Syme points out that the inner circle of Augustus's associates were bound to him by marriage,[6] and he[7] and von Premerstein[8] have established that *amici principis* on the Hellenistic model[9] were already recognised, with gradations and ceremonial conferment. These six were of the *amici*—members of the *cohors primae admissionis*:[10] and the same can be established of the few other Romans whom cities henceforward honour with portraits. M. Plautius Silvanus, named and represented on a Pergamene coin probably of A.D. 4–5 (p. 388), was the son of a friend of Livia and the father of a wife of Claudius;[11] M. Pompeius Macer (at Priene, p. 388) was Augustus's librarian and one of Tiberius's intimates;[12] L. Passienus Rufus (on the official coinage of Africa, p. 139) was a close friend of Augustus, signally honoured by the last *cognomen imperatoris* awarded outside the imperial family; C. Poppaeus Sabinus (at Aegina under Tiberius[13]) is called by Tacitus *amicus principum*.[14] Thus portraiture on city coinage was, from c. 7 B.C., the prerogative of the select band of the *amici*. It remains to be seen why the first few years after this date saw an efflorescence of this phenomenon at Hadrumetum,[15]

---

[1] Criticism can also be levelled against its chronological bases: L. Apronius is honoured in precisely the same way at Hippo even under Tiberius (Berlin: Muller II, p. 167. 378); Caius was designated consul not in 6 B.C. but in 5 (cf. Stuart Jones, *CAH*. X, p. 154); and the proconsular *Fasti* are far from certain.

[2] *ZfN*. 1875, pp. 295 ff.

[3] *Rn*. 1867, pp. 102 f.

[4] For Volusius vide Syme, *RR*. p. 424; Quinctilius, ibid. p. 434; cf. Tac. *Ann*. IV, 52. 66. Afr. Maximus (*PIR*. II, 48. 37) was the brother of Paullus Maximus, for whom vide *PIR*. II, 48. 38; ibid. 340. 184; Syme, *RR*. p. 433. For Scipio, ibid. p. 379; *PIR*². II, 355. 1438.

[5] Dittenberger, *SIG*.³ I, p. 780. 11; cf. von Premerstein, pp. 223 f. Cf. also *CIG*. 3499 f.; Magie, *De Romanorum vocabulis, etc.*, p. 70.

[6] *RR*. pp. 373, 379.

[7] Ibid. p. 385.   [8] P. 224.

[9] Cf. Wilhelm, *SB. Wien*, CLXXXIII, 3. *Abh*. pp. 37 f. For the Greek Imperial counterpart, φιλοκαίσαρες, see p. 365, and Muensterberg, *MBNGW*. IX, 1913, p. 159.

[10] Seneca, *De Clementia*, I, 10. 1.

[11] Cf. Syme, *RR*. p. 422.

[12] Dessau, *PIR*. III, 67. 472, 473.

[13] Berlin: I hope to study such coins in a later work.

[14] *Ann*. VI, 39; cf. *PIR*. II, 86. 627.

[15] Including the official series issued at this city (p. 139).

Achulla, Hippo, and three cities of Asia. The reason is inherent in the deaths of Agrippa in 12 and of Drusus in 9, and in the growing desire of the *princeps*' other henchman, Tiberius, for retirement. These successive blows meant that the consulships and consular appointments had to be filled by *novi homines*,[1] who were necessary for the efficient administration of the enlarged Empire. Since this phenomenon was dangerously likely to alienate the most influential sections of society, Augustus made a counterblast in the institution of formal *amicitia principis*, a *cachet* of the Augustan aristocracy in which old and new nobility alike found a place. His *auctoritas* was sufficient to substitute this criterion for the different canons of snobbery which had hitherto been employed. The change was assisted by a series of appointments of his *amici* to the plums of the proconsular career, Africa and Asia, and was given publicity by directions to a few cities of those provinces to honour their governors in a signal way. Thus the coins establish the chronology of one of the decisive social institutions of the early principate, and the interpretation of the much misunderstood phenomenon of proconsular coin-portraiture.

One of the series on which this interpretation is based is that of **Achulla**. Its coins, all exceedingly rare, are the following:

(1) CAESAR DIVI F., ACHVLLA head of Octavian to right—DIVOS IVLIVS head of Julius to left; wreath round edge. Punic countermark.[2]

(2) ACHVLLA head of Astarte to right—L. VOLVSIVS SATVRN. head of the proconsul to right (Pl. VII, 29).[3]

(3) AVG. PONT. MAX., C. L. heads of Augustus, Caius and Lucius—same reverse with ACHVLLA; varieties of abbreviation.[4]

(4) Same obverse—P. QVINCTILI VARI, ACHVLLA head of the proconsul to right (Pl. VII, 31, 30).[5]

Also [TI.] CAESAR AVGV···· head of Tiberius to right—[ACH]VLLA radiate head of Augustus to left, bolt.[6]

Achulla was free before the reorganisation of Julius;[7] it is recorded by Pliny as still an *oppidum liberum*.[8] It is clear, however, from the cities that have already been discussed that, as far as Pliny's statement is concerned, it may well have been a Julian colony; and there are five positive reasons for considering this to have been the case:—

(1) Since Achulla was already free before Julius, its mention as free by Pliny implies, as Gsell[9] points out, that it probably underwent some change of status in the interim period, to warrant its appearance in the Agrippan list.

---

[1] Cf. Marsh, *The Founding of the Roman Empire*, p. 248.
[2] Milan, Levis coll. Muller II, p. 43. 6.
[3] Milan, Paris. Muller II, p. 44. 9–10.
[4] BM, Stockholm, Paris. Muller, l.c.
[5] BM, Glasgow, Berlin. Muller, l.c. 7; cf. von Sallet, *ZfN*. XVIII, 1892, p. 200.
[6] Paris: not in Muller.
[7] *Bell. Afr.* 33; *Lex Agraria* 79.
[8] *NH.* v, 30.   [9] VIII, p. 171.

THE ROMAN COLONIES

(2) The posthumous commemoration of Julius by name and portrait strongly suggests that he was responsible for that change of status (p. 318).

(3) There is not a single peregrine community in Africa which employs wholly Latin inscriptions; in fact, even its *municipia* often use the native tongue (p. 174).

(4) These issues show a striking general uniformity with the series of the Julian colony at Hadrumetum.

(5) There are similar commemorations of proconsuls at the Julian colonies of Hadrumetum and Hippo, but at no peregrine town in Africa.

This is the fifth indication of an unrecorded Julian foundation in Africa; the recurrence of the dictator's head and name demonstrates that they were planned by him, although their completion was the work of a triumvir. The isolated Octavianic coins of Thapsus and Achulla—like similar sporadic mintages elsewhere, and particularly at the peregrine towns of Leptis minor and Thaena (pp. 338, 346)—have the character of inauguratory issues, and indicate that these *deductiones* were postponed by the inefficient government of Lepidus and reserved for his successor.

However, Lepidus had founded Hadrumetum, and apparently **Carthage** (pp. 51, 227). It has been shown that the supposed suffetes of Carthage are in fact of Caralis (p. 149), and that the ethnic KAR. described by Muller on a Pompeian military issue was misread (p. 20). There remains, however, one pair of *duoviri* who can be attributed to the second foundation of this colony (28 B.C.),[1] on whose site the halves of two specimens may have been found.[2] This college can be dated to A.D. 8–10 by the obverse inscription TI. C(*aesar*) A(*ugusti*) F. IMP. V., accompanied by the bare head of Tiberius.[3] Other coins have the portrait of Augustus (Pl. VI, 25),[4] inscribed IMP. C(*aesar*) D(*ivi*) F. A(*ugustus*) P. M. P. P. All have on the reverse P. I. SP., D. V. SP. IIVIR. C. I. C. round P. P. D. D. For the *duoviri* Borghesi's[5] suggestion 'P. Junius Spendo, D. Valerius Speratus' is as good as any other. Interpretations of P. P. on the reverse as P(*ermissu*) P(*roconsulis*)[6] are invalidated by the stereotyped regularity of the formula *Pecunia Publica Decreto Decurionum*,[7] which must be intended here. It is very unusual for such issues not to be inauguratory: but the present coinage illustrates a kindred custom, namely the commemoration of the fiftieth anniversary of the foundation. Identical in purpose was an equally isolated issue at Uselis (p. 153), and further parallels will be afforded by Cirta (?)—whose issues will next be discussed—by another colony at Lystra (p. 249), and by the peregrine *civitas libera* of Leptis minor (p. 338), which remarkably provides exact duplicates for both the obverse legends found here.

---

[1] Cf. Poinssot, *Bulletin de la Société nationale des antiquaires de France*, 1928, p. 266, etc.

[2] Cagnat, *Klio*, IX, 1914, pp. 200 ff.

[3] To right: BM, cf. Muller II, p. 150. 325; to left: BM, cf. ibid. 326.

[4] To right: own coll., cf. ibid. 324; to left: Hague, cf. ibid. 323.   [5] *Œuvres* II, p. 480.

[6] Cf. Borghesi, l.c. p. 430, etc.

[7] *ILS*. 5668, etc.; cf. Kübler, *PW*. IV, 2338; Muller II, pp. 159 ff.

Carthage, being a *colonia Concordia* (p. 227), is particularly likely to have been founded in c. 42–40—exactly half a century before this coinage (cf. p. 295).

To Cirta will tentatively be attributed an issue generally assigned to Carthage, of which both denominations were gravely misread and misdescribed by Muller.[1] However, the preservation of the only three extant specimens does not permit more than a fragmentary description:

(1) ·········· R$\overline{TA}$ AVG. D. P. Q. C. bare head of Augustus to left.
TI. CAES., M. T. F., M. M. A. IIVIR. bare head of Tiberius to right (Pl. VIII, 3).[2]

A second issue, of which there is now only one example, was made by the same college:

(2) ········ ON., $\overline{MAN}$. T. F., M. M. [A. IIVIR]. laureate portrait to left.
············· C. I. C. D. D. P. P. bare head of Augustus (?) to right (Pl. VIII, 4).[3]

The formula of (1), D(*ecurionum*) P(*opuli*) Q(*ue*) C(*onsensu*), shows an interesting divergency from the usual phrase. Owing to the poor state of the legends, certainty regarding these coins cannot at present be attained: but, subject to the discovery of better specimens, some conjectures may be hazarded. It is possible, or probable, that the lost legend of (2), ····ON. represents [C]ON(*ditor*)—the title of yet another of the large but much neglected category of founders. Lepidus, who probably founded Carthage in c. 42–40 (p. 227), could not thus have been commemorated on such an issue of the last years of Augustus's principate. Nor is the style of these coins that of Carthage or Zeugitana. It is reasonable to deduce from (2) that the missing inscription of (1) included the name and title of the colony C. I. C. The laureate head on (2) has a skull with a strange protrusion, a feature of the portraits of P. Sittius on his foundation-issue of Simitthu (Pl. VI, 15). Since his most important foundation was *colonia Iulia* Cirta (p. 180), and the hiatus on our specimen of (1) ends with an R followed by $\overline{AT}$ or $\overline{TA}$, the following restorations may at least be considered possible:

(1) [COL. IVL. CI]R$\overline{TA}$, AVG. D. P. Q. C.
(2) [P. SIT. C]ON., $\overline{MAN}$. T. F. M. M. [A. IIVIR].

Here then is another isolated issue which, like that of Carthage, may celebrate not the foundation of its city but its fiftieth year (p. 153).

Another problematical issue (Pl. VIII, 2) is represented by only three specimens[4] whose style is certainly African.[5] It has a bare head of Augustus, accompanied by a *lituus* and IMP. CAESAR DIVI F. AVGVSTVS; on the reverse is a head of Minerva to right, a crab, and PERM. L. VOLVSI. PRO COS., followed by four letters—

---

[1] II, 149. 321.
[2] Paris, Berlin: lower part of TI. visible on Paris specimen.
[3] Paris: Muller, l.c. 322, $\overline{MAN}$. wrongly as M.
[4] BM, Paris, also an unpublished specimen at Avignon.
[5] Cavedoni, *Bull. arch. ital.* I, 1862, pp. 171 f.; cf. Muller, *Suppl.* p. 38.

variously read as GERG.,[1] CERC.,[2] CENE,[3] and CEN. P.[4] The last of these suggestions, referring to a supposed CEN(*soria*) P(*otestas*) of the proconsul, need not now be taken seriously. The town of Cene is a practically unknown *mal trovato* from Byzacene, GERG(*is*) a very obscure stipendiary town in Zeugitana. We know of no community of that rank in Africa which coins with the head of Augustus and with the Latin tongue. Nor do we know of any peregrine city in the whole Empire which records a proconsular permission to issue coinage: for this reason, attribution to the free city of CERC(*ina*)[5]—which would, moreover, like its peers, be expected to produce bilingual coinage (p. 346)—is also very unlikely.

However, the fourth letter is seen from one of our specimens[6] to be a C or G. But as to the third, the presence of a long diagonal stroke downwards, from left to right, shows that the eyes of Borghesi and Cavedoni, who saw an N, were better than those of Muller, who professed to discern an R. This he needed to accord with his view that the mention of the proconsular permission necessitated the presence of an ethnic:[7] for no CENC is discoverable in Africa, where the issue must be attributed on grounds of style. For these letters a preferable explanation is obtainable from another source. At this period Roman towns frequently sign their issues, not with an ethnic, but with a formula stating the sanction of the local senate. D. D., EX D. D., EX S. C., etc. are well known; and the municipalities also use phrases such as *universus pop. Aquinatium p. p. censuerunt*.[8] More correct still is the executive formula *senatus censuit populusque iussit*.[9] The verb *censeo* particularly refers to the decrees of the senate at Rome and of all *senatus civium Romanorum* throughout the Empire. Now the foundation-series of Sittius at Simitthu (?) has given a numismatic example of the common inscriptional use of *curia* for *senatus* (p. 179): thus the present formula may be restored as CEN(*sente*) C(*uria*). A strong likeness in style and size to the largest issue of Sittius, which has a helmeted bust of particularly similar execution (Pl. VI, 15), suggests that the resemblance of formula is not fortuitous, and that this coin too should be assigned to Simitthu—probably commemorating its exchange of municipal rank for the status of colony, already attributed to Augustus[10] (p. 180). This interpretation accounts for the mention of the proconsul: governors are similarly recorded on the Sicilian foundation-coinages, but not elsewhere, and it was natural for the *curator-adsignator* of a colony to sanction its inauguratory coinage—especially when (like Volusius) he was an *amicus principis*.

[1] Muller II, p. 35. 65.
[2] Ibid. (as an alternative).
[3] Borghesi, in letter to Cavedoni; cf. Muller, *Suppl.* p. 38 n. 3.
[4] Cavedoni, l.c.; cf. Muller, *Suppl.* p. 38.
[5] Pliny, *NH.* v, 27.
[6] BM.
[7] L.c.
[8] *CIL.* x, 5395.
[9] Cic. *Pro Plancio*, 17. 42; cf. Stevenson, *CAH.* x, p. 349.
[10] *CIL.* VIII, 14712; cf. 14559.

9. PROVINCIA MARITIMA: Melita(?)

There is reason to believe that **Melita**, a community usually within the jurisdiction of Sicily,[1] received a colony while attached to a special maritime province during the Civil Wars. This conclusion is derived from the following unpublished and apparently unique coin:—

TADI. veiled female head to right.
MARI. *sella quaestoria* (p. 13) and staff (Pl. VII, 25).[2]

The style is unmistakably that of the Maltese group of islands, and the type of the head recalls coinage of Melita itself during the last century B.C.:[3] the issue may confidently be ascribed to the city on that island. The stylistic probability of an early date is confirmed by the close imitation of the reverse type from a *quinarius* of L. Sestius,[4] who was *pro quaestore* of Macedonia-Achaia under Brutus and Q. Hortensius in 44–42 (p. 33). This resemblance is proved not to be fortuitous by the treatment of the head on the obverse, which is derived from a second coin of the same official.[5]

These similarities make it necessary to conclude that the authorities who issued these coins were of Republican sympathies. Now Melita was not omitted from the general enfranchisement of Sicily which, begun in 44, was continued under Sex. Pompeius (p. 193). But it is unlikely that Sextus himself was responsible for the present issue, since, although he professed to be an ally of the Republicans,[6] he failed to cooperate with them;[7] he could scarcely have desired the implication of subordination to Brutus carried by these types. But, early in 42, the Republican leaders could lay claim to more active supporters on their Western flank: Q. Cornuficius had won independent control of Africa,[8] and L. Staius Murcus had his headquarters at the south point of the Peloponnese.[9] The latter of these is the more likely to have been the agent for this coinage. It is very doubtful whether Cornuficius considered himself subordinate to Brutus's *imperium maius*[10]—and the types of our coin indicate some such allegiance— and, in any case, we hear nothing of his conquests outside Africa. Murcus, on the other hand, was in complete control of the seas.[11] He blockaded Brundusium,[12] and, collaborating with Ahenobarbus, dominated the Adriatic and Ionian seas:[13] yet his base was as far south as the Laconian Gulf. His ships were everywhere:[14] Cassius could

---

[1] Pliny, *NH.* III, 92.
[2] BM.
[3] E.g. Glasgow (*Hu.* III, 605. 15), Cambridge (*McLean* 10,015).
[4] *BMCR.* II, p. 473. 47. This composition is not found elsewhere, though the types occasionally occur (e.g. *BMC. Cyrenaica*, pl. XLIII, 4, and above, p. 13).
[5] *BMCR.* II, pp. 472 f.; Bahrfeldt, *NZ.* 1896, pl. VII, 166.
[6] Cf. Ganter, *Philologus*, LIII, 1894, pp. 144 f.
[7] Cf. Charlesworth, *CAH.* x, p. 23.
[8] Ganter, l.c. pp. 141 ff.
[9] Appian, *BC.* IV, 74.
[10] Cf. Ganter, l.c. p. 142, and Cicero's tact in *Fam.* XII, 22, 28, 30.
[11] Cf. Münzer, *PW.* (2R.), III, 2138.
[12] Appian, *BC.* IV, 82; Dio XLVII, 47.
[13] Appian, *BC.* IV, 100, 108, V, 2.
[14] Cf. ibid. IV, 86.

rightly claim that the Eastern Mediterranean was a Republican lake.[1] It is in the highest degree probable that Murcus occupied Melita—of which a principal citizen, A. Licinius Aristoteles, is described by Cicero as a man who outdid all in loyalty to the Republic.[2] Murcus was subordinate to the *imperium maius* of Brutus and Cassius,[3] but retained his *imperium* as *praefectus classis*.[4]

The names Tadi. Mari. could either be the signatures, on official coinage, of a commander and his lieutenant—like Stati. Trebo. at Lipara (p. 53)—or those of a pair of *duoviri*. Similar pairs of names without qualifying titles appear on the coinages of a contemporary Republican colony at Rhodes (p. 243), on issues at Paestum from the forties and thirties (pp. 202, 284) and at a triumviral settlement at Tingis (p. 175): in all these cases it is necessary to interpret the signatures as those of *duoviri*. At another transient Republican colony, at Cyrene, a single name appears, again unqualified (p. 240). These analogies make it necessary to conclude that the present coinage is likewise colonial: Melita was an ephemeral garrison-colony of Brutus and Cassius like Cyrene and Rhodes. It is possible to go farther, and to guess that this issue commemorated its foundation. At Rhodes, Tingis and Paestum alike the undefined pairs of magistrates are *duoviri coloniae deducendae* (*urbis moeniundae*), while at Cyrene—as at Venafrum (p. 285)—only the senior member of the college, the *deductor*, is mentioned.

Tadius and Marius, then—neither of whom are identifiable—collaborated in the *deductio* of Melita, previously of municipal rank, near the beginning of 42 B.C. When Murcus, after Philippi, transferred his allegiance to Sex. Pompeius[5] (who soon killed him[6]), the island no doubt passed, with the command of the seas[7] and of the rest of *provincia* Sicilia, to the latter; and there is no reason to suppose that Sextus suppressed so valuable a colony as well as its originator. A coin with Greek ethnic and the name, in Latin, of C. Arruntanus Balbus *pro pr.* (p. 59) indicates that it was Octavian who degraded the city to peregrine status; he installed an officer to superintend its subjugation, collect an indemnity, and fortify the island against the new public menace, Antony.

10. SICILY: [Tauromenium], Tyndaris, Thermae Himeraeae (?)

No colonies can be attributed to the period of general enfranchisement which came to an end in 36 B.C. (p. 193). To the rest of our period can be ascribed only three colonial issues, and, as in the municipal series, each of these commemorates a foundation.

The first issue recalls the degradation and punishment of the island which followed

---

[1] Appian, *BC.* IV, 100, 108.   [2] *Fam.* XIII, 52.   [5] Appian, *BC.* V, 2.
[3] Appian, *BC.* IV, 59.   [6] Dio XLVIII, 19.
[4] *BMCR.* II, 485 (IMP.); cf. Dio XLVII, 28. 4; Münzer, l.c.   [7] Ibid.; cf. Kromayer, *Philologus*, LVI, 1897, pp. 426 ff.

Naulochus in 36. It is represented by a single unpublished and unattributed specimen in poor condition:[1]

‥[C]ERD (?). A. F., C. A‥‥‥‥‥head of Minerva to right in crested Corinthian helmet.

IIV[IR. Q]VIN. EX D. D. *sella curulis* between bundles of *fasces* (Pl. VII, 27).

The first of the *quinquennales* here recorded apparently belongs to the obscure family of the Cerdonii.[2] The style of this piece may perhaps be Sicilian and demands attribution to the pre-Actian period. But it is unlikely to belong to the administration of Sex. Pompeius. Both types are closely imitated from Octavianic *denarii*—the reverse from an issue of L. Livineius Regulus,[3] *praefectus urbis* and *IVvir a. p. f.* in c. 43–42,[4] and the obverse from one of C. Vibius Varus[5] a few years later.[6] It must be concluded that this issue belonged to the early years of Octavian's government. It is unlikely to form a single exception to his limitation of Roman city-coinage in Sicily to foundation-issues: and the occurrence of *quinquennales* can be shown not to contravene this canon. The first magistrates of a refounded city might well bear this title when it had previously possessed *civitas* or *Latinitas*, and Roman institutions (p. 161).[7] The only city which fulfils these conditions, and, indeed, the only Roman city which still existed in Sicily itself,[8] was **Tauromenium**, to which this coin possibly belongs. In 36 its inhabitants were expropriated for their Pompeian sympathies;[9] however, the community, consisting of a new draft of Italian settlers, exceptionally retained the franchise, exchanging municipal for colonial status.[10] The fact that the first magistrates of the new *régime* in 36 were *quinquennales* indicates that, as elsewhere,[11] the municipalisation planned by the *Lex Iulia*, and taken over by the rival administration of Sextus, was not completed until a year or two later—in this case in c. 41: inauguratory *quinquennales* occur for similar reasons at three other cities (n. 7). It is noteworthy that some of the latest peregrine issues of Tauromenium before 41 have heads of Minerva closely resembling the present one in attributes and execution.[12]

[1] Paris ('uncertain') [this attribution is cancelled in the Corrigenda].
[2] Not in Schulze. A member of this *gens* can be conjecturally identified on coins of Turris Libisonis (p. 205); cf. *CIL*. x, 7956 (ibid.), vi, 34809 (Rome).
[3] *BMCR*. I, p. 580. 4261, pl. LVII, 12.
[4] The controversy regarding his date is summed up by Münzer, *PW*. XIII, 808 (3); *pace* Mommsen, *Mzw*. pp. 653, 741 f., Grueber, l.c.
[5] E.g. *BMCR*. pl. LVIII, 12.
[6] Grueber's dating to c. 38 B.C. is thought by H. Mattingly to be rather too late.
[7] Cf. Thermae Himeraeae(?), Saguntum, Carthago Nova.
[8] For the island of Lipara see p. 195: this retained its municipal rank, with a new population, and also issued 'refoundation' coinage (whose style excludes the possibility that the present issue formed part of it).
[9] Diodorus Siculus XVI, 7. 1; cf. Scramuzza, *ES*. III, p. 252.
[10] Diodorus, l.c.; Pliny, *NH*. III, 88. The words of Diodorus indicate attribution of the colony to this date; cf. Scramuzza, l.c. p. 345, Cuntz, *Klio*, VI, 1906, p. 467, Kornemann 80, Beloch, *Die Bevölkerung der griechisch-römischen Welt*, p. 337; *pace* Mommsen, *CIL*. x, p. 718, Ziegler, *PW*. (2R.), v, 30.
[11] E.g. different provincial *legati* (probably governors) are the founders of Cephaloedium and Panormus (pp. 192, 189).
[12] *BMC. Sicily*, pp. 233. 40, 43 and 234. 53. [*Note*. The writer now considers the present attribution erroneous. See n. 1 above.]

Thus *colonia* Tauromenium and *municipium* Lipara, the only communities of the province which emerge with *civitas* from Octavian's drastic inflictions, both commemorate their new pre-eminence. It will be shown elsewhere that three other cities of less happy fate were forced to perpetuate the record of their degradation by *aes* coinage struck for an indemnity (pp. 392 ff.).

The remaining colonial issues include an *as* and a *semis* of the same standard as Augustus's municipal series:

As.
AVGVSTVS [TV]NDAR. head to right—L. MVSSIDI. PRO COS. in wreath.[1]

Semis.
L. IVNIVS IIVIR QVIN. AVG. eagle, *aspergillum*—L. ACILIVS IIVIR QVINQ. AVG. *lituus, praefericulum, patera* (Pl. VI, 18).[2]

The issue of **Tyndaris** is a foundation-coinage (p. 306): the colony was established by L. Mussidius, in the capacity of Augustus's *adsignator*, probably in the year 21 B.C.[3] This *as* started the tradition continued by the uniform inauguratory issues of *municipia* Agrigentum, Lilybaeum, and Haluntium (pp. 196 ff.). Mussidius is recorded on Sicilian inscriptions:[4] his title is important to constitutional history as a proof that Augustus, on his travels to 'senatorial' provinces, did not take over their government from the proconsuls (p. 428).

The *semis* is one of the many coins that have been classed, in desperation, among the series of Carthago Nova, on the feeble analogy of an Acilius on the issues of that city. But the latter was called Quintus, not Lucius, and his coin, too, is wrongly attributed (p. 213). Thus the attribution of the present coin to Carthago Nova is wholly untenable; it is, indeed, sharply differentiated from that or any other Spanish series by style and formula. The style recalls Panormitan issues of C. Julius Longus (p. 190), and later Sicilian pieces of L. Seius (p. 197); a similar eagle is found at Panormus.[5] Thus a Sicilian origin is probable.[6] Moreover, a close parallel to the formula *quin(quennalis) Aug(usti)*[7] is *IIvir Aug. Des.* at Halaesa (p. 195). Here then is a second case of designation by Augustus of the first magistrates of a re-enfranchised city: here too is independent proof that this issue, like all contemporary coinages in Sicily, owes its existence to a foundation. In Sicily, moreover, inauguratory *quinquennales* are not unexpected, since all cities in the island had earlier possessed the *civitas* and the normal structure of Roman communities: for example, a peregrine coin of Panormus still has—

---

[1] BM, Paris, Turin, Copenhagen, own coll. Rightly restored by Borghesi, *Memorie numismatiche*², 1853, p. 91 = *Œuvres* II, p. 451; cf. Holm 726; Hill, *Coins of Sicily*, p. 215.

[2] BM, Cambridge, etc.; Heiss, p. 274. 9 ('Carthago Nova').

[3] Dio LIV, 7—ἑτέρας τινὰς πόλεις; cf. Pliny, *NH*. III, 90; Kornemann 167; Scramuzza, *ES*. III, p. 346.

[4] *Notizie degli Scavi*, 1887, p. 293.

[5] Cambridge (*McLean* 2522), Gotha, Munich.

[6] This conclusion may be refuted if, in the future, evidence is forthcoming of Spanish provenance. But the style suggests that this is unlikely.

[7] The suggestion AVG(*ustalis*) of Florez (*Medallas de las colonias, etc.*, p. 652) is impossible.

together with a Greek ethnic—the formula C(*onsensu*) D(*ecurionum*).[1] A possible interpretation of the present issue is provided by the appearance on an inscription of a L. ACILIVS L. F. RVFVS IIVIR COL. T[H]ER[MITANORVM],[2] and of another L. Acilius at the same city, *colonia* **Thermae Himeraeae**.[3] Given the Sicilian origin of our coin, the persistence at that town of Acilii with the *praenomen* Lucius provides an attribution more convincing than coincidences of a gentile name alone. Thermae Himeraeae was colonised by Augustus early enough to be included in the Plinian list;[4] its date and the name of the proconsul who acted as Augustus's *adsignator coloniae deducendae* cannot be determined. At all events, it is certain that the colonial series of Sicily under Augustus was, like the municipal, entirely limited to the foundation-issues which play such a great and unrecognised part in the coinage of the whole period.

11. ASIA: Lystra, Rhodes, Alexandria Troas, Lampsacus, Parium

The province of Asia provides four unrecognised examples of pre-Augustan colonisation, and six of inauguratory coinage. The earliest of these is an issue represented by two extant specimens:[5]

    M. RVTILVS PRO COS. COL. IVL.·······male head to right, with distinctive features.
    A. FERIDIVS IIVIR EX D. D. colonist ploughing to left with humped oxen (Pl. VIII, 8, 9).

The humped bull is commonly found in Asia Minor only in Caria, Lycaonia, and intervening territories,[6] and it was actually in this part of the peninsula that one of the two known examples was acquired.[7] The execution of these pieces is strongly in favour of attribution to Pisidia or Lycaonia—the southern half of the Augustan province of Galatia (pp. 249 ff.)—but stylistic considerations also indicate that they could hardly be as late as the principate of Augustus.[8] The history of these parts enables a definite *terminus ante quem* to be established. In 62 B.C. Pompey annexed inland Lycaonia, Pisidia and Southern Phrygia.[9] The territory indicated for these coins remained thereafter in Roman hands until c. 38. Then Iconium became the capital of a new kingdom of Cilicia Tracheia ruled by Polemo:[10] but in c. 36 he was sent to Pontus, and Galatia, together with Λυκαονίας Παμφυλίας τέ τινα,[11] was granted to Amyntas.[12]

[1] Bahrfeldt, *RS.* XII, 1904, p. 306 (illustrated on his pl. IV, 92).
[2] *CIL.* X, 7210, as rightly restored by Hülsen.
[3] *CIL.* X, 7344; cf. *PIR.*[2] I, 13. 78.
[4] Pliny, *NH.* III, 90.
[5] BM (E. S. G. Robinson, *JHS.* 1914, p. 46); Berlin (Imhoof-Blumer, *Ant. GM.* p. 302).
[6] Robinson, l.c.; cf. Imhoof-Blumer and Keller, *Tier- und Pflanzenbilder auf Münzen*, p. 23.
[7] BM (Robinson, l.c.); the provenance of the other is unknown.
[8] E. S. G. Robinson confirms this.
[9] Cary, *CAH.* IX, p. 392.
[10] Strabo XII, 568; cf. Jones, *CERP.* p. 392 n. 55.
[11] Dio XLIX, 32.
[12] Cf. Jones, *CERP.* p. 133; Syme, *Anatolian Studies to Buckler*, 1939, pp. 302 ff.

C. 38–36 must, then, be the lower limit not only for a proconsul such as Rutilus, but also for the foundation of a colony, which never took place on non-Roman soil.[1] Now an examination of the *deductiones* attributed to Augustus in his province of Galatia reveals a significant fact. Apart from Antioch in Pisidia—whose *cognomen* Caesarea is due to special circumstances and whose foundation is certainly Augustan (p. 250)—the colonies have the epithet *Iulia Augusta*[2] except one, which has *Iulia* alone.[3] This is Lystra.

Here the contrast with the known Augustan *deductiones* in the province is so arresting that Ramsay cannot be right in dismissing the distinction as 'probably accidental'.[4] Nearer the mark is Kubitschek,[5] who admits the possibility of an original Julian foundation. Kornemann[6] suggests that Augustus carried out a *deductio* based on an earlier design—*vielleicht projectiert (nach cäsarischem Plan?)*. But the fulfilment by Augustus of a Julian plan should be deduced for Lystra least of all the colonies in his province of Galatia: it is much more probable in the case of the others, which have both epithets together, *Iulia* and *Augusta* (the dictator may well have made such unfulfilled plans to defend his rear during his forthcoming campaigns).[7] Lystra is clearly distinguished from the other colonies by the possession of *Iulia* only: it must have been established before c. 38–36. Thus the puzzling existence of such an early Roman city-issue in that region is explained: conclusive is the reverse type of the coin, which is closely copied, feature by feature, especially in the treatment of the characteristic humped bulls, by a later specimen with the ethnic of Lystra (Pl. VIII, 10) (p. 250). This attribution is remarkably confirmed by the presence in c. 51 B.C.— only a few years before this coin must have been struck—of another member of the extremely rare *gens* Feridia[8] somewhere in the province of Cilicia,[9] in which Lystra had then been for a decade. Romans cannot have been common in Cilicia, and A. Feridius on the coin must be a freedman of this young knight and business man M. Feridius. That Pliny merely records *Lystreni*,[10] omitting to mention the colony, is readily understandable, not on the grounds that this was founded later than his list,[11] but because the document which he employs frequently neglects or misrepresents pre-Augustan foundations (p. 226). In the province of Galatia, in particular, the mention

[1] Ramsay, *JRS*. VI, 1916, p. 83. The problematical *colonia Caesaris dictatoris Pharos* (Pliny, *NH*. v, 128) cannot be taken as an exception to this rule, since it is not known (1) whether the island was ceded by Cleopatra for strategic purposes; (2) whether, as elsewhere (see below, p. 383), *colonia* is a loose expression for a garrison or a *conventus* of *negotiatores* (cf. Rice Holmes, *The Roman Republic*, III, p. 322 n.; Meyer, *Cäsars Monarchie*, p. 495 n. 2).

[2] Kornemann 256 ff.

[3] Ibid. 260; cf. Hahn, *Rom und Romanismus*, p. 93.

[4] L.c.

[5] *Imp*. p. 252.

[6] P. 550.

[7] The fact, therefore, that no Julian settlement can actually have taken place at Ninica and Germa need not (as Broughton sees, *ES*. IV, p. 703) lead to the conclusion that these were Domitianic and named after Julia Titi, as Jones, *CERP*. pp. 123, 213. It is, however, just possible that they were named after Caius Caesar Aug. n., like Berytus (p. 259). Cf. also p. 302.

[8] Cf. Schulze, p. 166.

[9] Cic. *Fam*. VIII, 9; cf. Hatzfeld, p. 139.

[10] *NH*. v, 147.

[11] As Jones, *CERP*. p. 496.

of *Sebasteni*[1] affords proof that his source was later than 27 B.C. (and probably than 25), while his attribution of the *Lystreni* to the same province affords additional evidence that documents before the rule of Amyntas (when Lystra had nothing to do with Galatia) were not used for this passage.[2]

The governorship and identity of M. Rutilus raise a number of difficult problems. There is no lack of analogies, in this transitional period, for the occurrence of a proconsul's name in conjunction with the name of a colony: thus coins honour P. Sulpicius Rufus at Sinope under Caesar (p. 11), Q. Hortensius Hortalus at Cassandrea under Brutus (p. 33), and M. Lurius at Turris Libisonis during the triumvirate (p. 205). The *raison d'être* of each of these three issues is commemoration of the colonial founder. The likelihood that Rutilus was also the *deductor* of Lystra is confirmed by the juxtaposition on these coins of the names of proconsul and colony—as in finite clauses at Sinope and Dyrrhachium (with DEDVX[*it*]) (pp. 252, 275)—and by the hiatus after COL. IVL., where the remains of three letters permit the restoration of DED. The legend then becomes M. RVTILVS PRO COS. COL(*oniam*) IVL(*iam*) DED(*uxit*).

Fortunately this fat proconsul of the forties or early thirties B.C. can be identified. He must be the Caesarian officer M. Sempronius Rutilus, who was second-in-command to T. Labienus in his campaign against the Sequani in 52 B.C.[3] This branch of the Sempronii had attained curule rank in the second century;[4] the existence of a *duovir* called L. Sempronius Rutilus at Turiaso under Augustus (p. 170) suggests that the present officer included a Spanish command in his *cursus honorum*. But, for his present governorship, we must search the Fasti of Asiatic provinces.

The *deductio* of *Iulia* Lystra must fall within the years 47–38. It might be ascribed to the competence of a governor from no less than three provinces. At the beginning of this period *provincia* Cilicia, in which Lystra had hitherto been, still existed: but Caesar detached Cyprus to give to Egypt,[5] three διοικήσεις of Phrygia returned to Asia,[6] and in 43 Side had joined them;[7] moreover, Cilicia is omitted from the list of Cassius's provinces.[8] The remaining territories of the old province of Cilicia cannot have warranted a separate governorship, and must have passed, at this date or earlier, to *provincia* Syria.[9] The Fasti of Cilicia, Syria and Asia must therefore be examined to

---

[1] L.c.
[2] Cf. Cuntz, *Jahrbücher für classische Philologie*, Suppl. XVII, 1890, pp. 489, 523.
[3] Caesar, *BG*. VII, 90. 4. I owe this identification to R. Syme.
[4] Livy XXXVII, 57, XXXIX, 9; cf. Münzer, *PW*. (2R.), II, 1437; Groebe, in Drumann, *Grundriss der Kulturgeschichte*, III, p. 699.
[5] Dio XLII, 35. 5; cf. Jones, *CERP*. p. 488 n. 8; Syme, *Anatolian Studies to Buckler*, p. 324.
[6] Cic. *Fam*. XIII, 67; cf. Marquardt, *St.V.* I, pp. 335 f.; Jones, *CERP*. pp. 61, 391; Syme, l.c.
[7] P. Lentulus Spinther, *ad Cic. Fam.* XII, 15. 5; cf. Syme, l.c. p. 325.
[8] Cic. *XI Phil*. 12.
[9] Syme, l.c. pp. 324 ff.; cf. Ganter, p. 40; Sternkopf, *Hermes*, XLVII, 1912, p. 352; Raillard, p. 35. The possibility, mentioned by Syme (l.c. p. 325), that the province lingered on in diminished form until c. 40 is very slight; in any case, it could scarcely have continued to support a separate proconsul at this time when incompletely Romanised provinces were very large.

find room for M. Rutilus. Syria provides no place:[1] the only uncertain year, 45–44, must be allotted either to C. Antistius Vetus[2] or to L. Volcacius Tullus.[3] In the Cilician lists there are probable or possible candidates for 47–46,[4] 46–45,[5] and 44[6] (if the province still existed [p. 240]), but 45–44 is less satisfactory: Sternkopf's attribution of Volcacius to this post,[7] rather than to Syria[8] or to no governorship at all,[9] is purely conjectural. Here then is one possible date for Rutilus. But the presence of his head necessitates reservations. No governor is so honoured under Caesar or earlier:[10] even P. Sittius, whose status was practically that of a client-prince, does not thus appear at *municipium* Simitthu (?) until the months after the dictator's death (p. 178). M. Rutilus, then, could—as governor of Cilicia—only have figured on this coin between March 44 and his recall not much later in the same year. But it must be admitted that even this is very unlikely. In the first place, *provincia* Cilicia had almost certainly disappeared by 43, and there is no reason to believe that it survived after 45, if as long. Secondly, if it did survive, and if Q. Marcius Crispus was its governor in 44, Rutilus could scarcely have had time to learn of the death of Caesar (of which the placing of the proconsul's head on this coin implies cognisance) before his supersession: news travelled slowly,[11] and the governors for 44 had already left Rome early in April.[12] Two or three weeks is scarcely enough for a *deductio* and its commemorative coinage.

There remains the province of Asia. Here, in the regular Fasti between 46 and 38, the only possible vacancy for a Caesarian—such as the epithet *Iulia* proves Rutilus still to have been—occurs in 39–38.[13] Yet even this year may be occupied by a continuation of Plancus's tenure, or by a governorship of M. Cocceius Nerva. There is no obvious reason why Lystra should have been colonised at this date, especially when Antony was on the verge of disposing of Lycaonia to a king—an indication of a policy opposed to colonisation (p. 250). Moreover, all other known Julio-Antonian

---

[1] Cf. Ganter, pp. 40 ff.; Raillard, p. 35; Sternkopf, l.c. p. 332; Syme, l.c. It is most improbable that L. Decidius Saxa (41) had a predecessor under Antony with the title of proconsul: cf. also in 42–41 *legati* in Asia and Macedonia (see pp. 247, 274).

[2] As Sternkopf, Syme, ll.cc.

[3] As Ganter, *Philologus*, LIII, 1894, pp. 134 ff.

[4] Syme, l.c., shows conclusively that Q. Marcius Philippus held this post (*pace* Constans, *Rev. phil.* LVI (3 ser. V), 1931, pp. 247 ff.; Springer, *Bursians Jahresbericht*, CCLX, 1938, p. 55, etc.).

[5] Q. Cornuficius; cf. Syme, l.c. pp. 318 ff.

[6] Q. Marcius Crispus; cf. Schwartz, *Hermes*, XXXIII, 1898, p. 186; Letz, *Die Provinzialverwaltung Cäsars*, Diss. Strassburg, 1912, p. 84.

[7] L.c., discussed without final acceptance by Syme, l.c.   [8] Ganter (Diss.), l.c.

[9] Vaglieri, *Dizionario epigrafico*, II, 1, pp. 227 f.

[10] It has been shown above that Pietrangeli, *Civiltà Romana*, VII, 1938, p. 10, is wrong in citing an instance of 59 B.C. (pp. 150 ff.); and that T. Quinctius Flamininus appears on a coin of quite different character (p. 151).

[11] Cf. Stevenson, *The Legacy of Rome*, p. 163.

[12] Cf. Charlesworth, *CAH*. X, p. 4.

[13] P. Servilius Isauricus, 46–44 (cf. Münzer, *PW*. [2R.], II, 1799); C. Trebonius, 44 (cf. Stein, *PW*. [2R.], VI, 2279); M. Turius *leg*. 42–41 (cf. coins, p. 246); L. Munatius Plancus, 41–c. 39/38 (left by Antony in Asia in 41, Dio XLVIII, 24. 2; cf. Hanslik, *PW*. XVI, 549, *pace* Ganter [Diss.], l.c.; retreats to islands before Labienus, Münzer, *PW*. XII, 259, and probably does not return, Tarn, *CAH*. p. 49, *pace* Hanslik, l.c.); M. Cocceius Nerva, between c. 39/38 and 36 (cf. Syme, *RR*. p. 266 n. 3). On the subsequent Fasti, see pp. 373, 383, 385, 395.

foundations in Asia Minor had been completed at an earlier date (p. 461); none of them warranted a governor's coin-portrait, and the known activity of M. Sempronius Rutilus was as long ago as the fifties. However, the history of the year 44–43—which accords much better with these considerations—provides a special opportunity for a proconsulship of Rutilus. P. Cornelius Dolabella, the Caesarian, murdered C. Trebonius and was recognised proconsul of Asia at least by 24 January 43, and probably rather earlier.[1] But he had left Asia and was marching on Syria by March 7th[2]—with a view to taking the governorship of that province. He must have left a governor behind him to deal with a serious threat from the Republican P. Cornelius Lentulus Spinther, who subsequently gained possession of Asia by the end of May.[3] Spinther's unsuccessful opponent has not hitherto been identified. It was, in all probability, M. Rutilus whom Dolabella left behind, on his way to Syria, and he who had the task of garrisoning Lystra, on the borders of the province. We know that *provincia* Asia stretched as far as the city of Side in this year,[4] and Western Lycaonia is therefore most likely to fall within its borders.[5] Perhaps the foundation had, like so many others, already been planned by Caesar. It was clearly intended to guard the vital road from Asia to Syria against attack by Antipater, a tyrant of Republican sympathies who held the neighbouring strongholds of Derbe and Laranda.[6] The record of Rutilus's tenure will have vanished owing to his complete failure to contend the province with P. Cornelius Lentulus Spinther, and the breakdown of communications.

Lystra, then, is likely to have been colonised with a garrison of veterans (like Augustan foundations in the middle of Anatolia[7]) by M. Sempronius Rutilus, named governor of Asia by P. Dolabella—perhaps on the strength of a faked *Lex Curiata*[8]— in the first months of 43. Much farther westwards Rutilus can scarcely have advanced; in view of the rapid failure and death of Dolabella at the hands of Cassius in Syria he was lucky if he escaped with his life. This coin bears witness to the ephemeral claim to fame of one of Caesar's most sinister lieutenants, Dolabella. Lystra was planned as his strategic link between the two provinces of Asia and Syria, at a time when the latter of these was a Republican stronghold and the former already falling into Republican hands. Lystra cannot have escaped the same fate; but its retention even after Augustus of the single epithet *Iulia* suggests restoration by Antony after Philippi. In c. 38–36 Lystra became an enclave in royal territories, like the colonies in Mauretania (p. 223): whether it was under some form of supervision from the king himself, like Tingis, or depended upon a proconsul like Zilis (?) (pp. 176, 175), cannot

---

[1] Cf. Groag, *PW*. IV, 1306.
[2] C. Cassius *ap*. Cic. *Fam*. XII, 12. 5.
[3] P. Lentulus Spinther, ibid. XII, 15; Chapot, *La province romaine proconsulaire d'Asie*, p. 309
[4] Spinther, l.c.
[5] This is confirmed by A. H. M. Jones.
[6] I owe this suggestion to R. Syme. For Antipater, vide Klebs, *PW*. I, 2513 (20); Jones, *CERP*. p. 413 n. 20; Syme, l.c. pp. 309 ff.
[7] Cf. Münzer, *PW*. IV, 1308.
[8] For this as the basis of *imperium* see Cic. *De lege agraria*, II, 12. 30; Stevenson, *RPA*, p. 73. In troubled periods it was often dispensed with; Stevenson, ibid. p. 74.

be determined. When it returned within the frontiers of the Empire, it was in a new province, Galatia (p. 249).

It is possible to deduce the transient existence of an equally unrecognised colony, founded by the forces that suppressed Rutilus, from an unattributed issue of which less than half-a-dozen specimens have survived. This shows a female head to right, and a rose, inscribed C. CAR., C. COS. (Pl. VII, 32).[1] It bears no resemblance to any known colonial series. But the type of a rose is characteristic of the coinage of Rhodes, on which it appears continually and exclusively.[2] Moreover, the present piece is distinctly similar to specimens from the Greek series of that city,[3] both in style and in a coiffure typical of the forties. It is therefore not surprising to find that the literary authorities bear witness to a period of Roman occupation during this decade. Early in 42, C. Cassius, with his lieutenant P. Cornelius Lentulus Spinther, attacked and took the city, treating it with great severity;[4] it was then left to the tender mercy of a succession of lieutenants, Cassius of Parma, L. Varus[5] and finally a certain Clodius.[6] After the battle of Philippi, the last-named extricated the garrison from the revolting Rhodians, and the occupation was at an end: Antony restored its peregrine freedom to the community.[7] This episode cannot but be connected with the Roman currency at Rhodes. It is interesting and relevant that a similar rose on a *denarius* of C. Cassius records the occupation of the island.[8]

Now the names C. Car. and C. Cos. could be explained in two different ways. They could appear on an official coinage, like Stati. Trebo. at Lipara (p. 52): Stati. has been identified as Statilius Taurus, and Trebo., by Republican usage, can only be his *quaestor* or *legatus*. But the commanders at Rhodes are all known: 'Car.' is suitable for the *cognomen* neither of the Cassii nor of Clodius. There remains only one possibility; the names must be those of *duoviri*, like Tadi. Mari. at Melita, and M. Cassius M. Ant. at Halaesa (pp. 234, 191), where the qualifying titles are omitted in the same way, and at about the same date. The number of Romans evacuated by Clodius was as high as three thousand,[9] and many executions and deportations by the Republicans must have left extensive property vacant for their colonists. These facts, combined with the existence of the present coin, enable the deduction to be drawn that the ownerless lands had been allotted to the soldiery, who were granted a colonial organisation. Precisely similar Republican garrison-colonies can be identified at Melita and Cyrene (pp. 234, 260). The analogy of magistrates' names, likewise without titles, on coins of those cities, and of Halaesa, Paestum (L. Vene. D. Fad. Epul.) and Tingis (*Rex*

---

[1] Glasgow (*Hu.* III, p. 45), Paris.
[2] Head, *BMC. Caria*, p. cii.
[3] E.g. ibid. p. 265. 384.
[4] Appian, *BC.* IV, 65 ff.; cf. Syme, *RR.* p. 203.
[5] Appian, *BC.* IV, 74.
[6] Ibid. v, 2. *Pace* von Gaertringen, *PW. Suppl.*
v, 807, the passage does not imply the arrival of Turullius at Rhodes.
[7] Cf. von Gaertringen, l.c.
[8] Hill, *Historical Roman Coins*, p. 122. The explanation of Alföldi, *Röm. Mitt.* L, 1935, p. 147 n. 6, does not supersede his interpretation, though it may supplement it.
[9] Appian, *BC.* v, 2.

244   THE ROMAN COLONIES

Bocchus and Sosius *Filius*) (pp. 191, 175), suggests that C. Car. and C. Cos. were *deductor* and *adsignator* respectively, combining—like L. Aclutius Gallus and his colleague at Venafrum[1]—to form a college of *duoviri coloniae deducendae* or *urbis moeniundae*. It may be conjectured that the *deductor* is a C. Papirius Carbo: a tribune of that name in 90 B.C. (murdered in 82) was of pronounced Republican tendencies,[2] but no record has survived of the next generation. Possibly his assistant was C. Cosconius Calidianus (?), aedile in 57, who was a friend of Cicero;[3] a Cosconius who held a praetorship a few years later was probably the same man.[4] The task of these *duoviri* was the settlement of veterans whose community was called a *colonia*, but whose duties, like those of colonists in Lycaonia and Pisidia, were virtually those of a garrison. Literary evidence is silent: but the coins are explicit, since peregrine city-coinage in the East never bears a Latin legend. It is not surprising that so transient and troubled a colony has escaped notice.[5]

The Republican *régime* collapsed a few months after this issue was made: to the first year of the ensuing government of Antony is to be referred another inauguratory coinage, at **Alexandria Troas**. The coinage of this town has already been mentioned in connection with the *orichalcum* issues by M. Acilius(?) *quaestor pro praetore* in 44 B.C., whose portraits of the dictator it imitates (p. 13). Accompanying the head is the inscription PRINCEPS[6] FELIX, whose peculiar applicability to Julius has been discussed. The reverses of the two denominations (c. 205·5, 127·5 grains) show a figure of Athena holding a small Nike (Pl. VIII, 5),[7] and two yoked oxen seen in perspective.[8] On both varieties the legend is COLONIA IVLIA, with IIV$\overline{\text{IR}}$ in the field. There are also two monograms: one is $\overline{\text{PE}}$. or $\overline{\text{EP}}$., no doubt one of the *duoviri*, who are often mentioned singly on early colonial coins.[9] The second monogram has always been interpreted as $\overline{\text{VE}}$.,[10] but $\overline{\text{ALE}}$.[11] is certainly the correct version:[12] it is conclusive that a variant[13] actually has $\overline{\text{ALEX}}$.[14] The non-recognition of these ethnics has been due to a confusion of the lettering with the beaded edge. Gaebler[15] sees that the style is not Macedonian: the evidence of provenance points conclusively to Asia Minor.[16] In

---

[1] *CIL.* x, 4876: cf. below, p. 285.
[2] Cic. *Brut.* 62; *Fam.* IX, 21. Cf. above, p. 215.
[3] Cic. *Vatin.* 16; cf. Münzer, *PW.* IV, 1668, 1670.
[4] Cf. Stella Maranca, *Mem. della R. Ac. dei Lincei (sc.-mor.)*, VI, 2, 1926, p. 334; cf. Plutarch, *Caes.* 51.
[5] It is possible that other short-lived and obscure colonies were founded on the islands off Asia Minor, e.g. at Samos:—Broughton, *ES.* IV (1938), pp. 703 f.; Gardthausen I, p. 831; Fabricius, *Ath. Mitt.* IX, 1884, p. 260; Hatzfeld, p. 98 n. 1.
[6] Not PRINCIPI: Imhoof-Blumer, *GM.* p. 772.
[7] BM, Berlin, Istanbul, Athens, Gotha.
[8] Berlin, Munich.
[9] E.g. Panormus, Halaesa, Thapsus.
[10] *NG.* III, p. 99; cf. Imhoof-Blumer, *MG.* p. 89. 107c; von Sallet, *ZfN.* XXIII, 1902, p. 186.
[11] Monogram 9 *a*.
[12] Clearly legible at Berlin: perceptible at BM, Athens, Istanbul.
[13] Berlin.
[14] Monogram 9 *b*.
[15] *NG.*, l.c., *pace* Imhoof-Blumer, l.c.
[16] Found in Cappadocia (Riggauer, *SB. München*, II, 1897, pp. 530, 533; cf. Gaebler, *ZfN.* XXIII, 1902, p. 186; Munich); another from central district (Oberhummer and Zimmerer, *Durch Syrien und Kappadokien*, 1899); from Izmir (Friedländer, *BB.* 1868, p. 27; Berlin).

particular, specimens have been found in the North-Western area[1] to which the countermark of a capricorn[2] is also peculiar.[3] There existed a suitable colony in this region. Colonia Alexandria Troas—which commonly employs either of these names alone[4]—bore the title *Augusta*,[5] perhaps from 20 B.C.[6] But its tribe (Aniensis) is extremely rare for original Augustan foundations.[7] Kornemann[8] remarks: *alle augustische Colonien, soweit sie bei Plinius vorkommen, gehen auf den agrippischen Teil der Reichsstatistik zurück und müssen daher vor 742 = 12...gegründet sein.* But, lacking knowledge of these coins, he ignores the possibility that, like so many other towns, Alexandria Troas was first a *colonia Iulia*, and then, not *Iulia Augusta*, but *Augusta*. When Suetonius records that Julius planned *migraturum Alexandream vel Ilium*,[9] the sense of the passage, and the distant position and alien status of the Egyptian Alexandria, make it by no means impossible that the neighbour of Ilium, Alexandria Troas, was the object of this belief: it was certainly in great favour with the dictator,[10] and could supply a cause for Horace's[11] and Vergil's[12] insistence that Troy must never be rebuilt.[13] These coins, with their monograms, at least show conclusively that Alexandria Troas was a *colonia Iulia*. The countermark ALE.[14] affixed to a coin of the neighbouring Julian colony of Lampsacus (p. 246)—with a similar portrait of the dictator—confirms the early date suggested by style and type.

The issue must have been made either shortly before, or shortly after, the administration of Brutus and Cassius. The later date is the more probable, since the *denarii* from which the portraits on the *orichalcum* issue were derived did not appear, at the earliest, until a very short time before the dictator's death (p. 4). Moreover, the present coinage, being imitated from the *orichalcum* series, is twice removed from the *denarii*, so that a considerable time-lag is probable. A similar portrait appears at Dyme (p. 264), for whose colonisation Kornemann[15] suggests a *terminus post quem* of 44 B.C.—and there is always a presumption that the dictator's colonisation plans were left for Antony to accomplish.[16] By the analogy of many other isolated Roman city-

---

[1] Found in Mysia (BM; acquired by Montague).
[2] Athens. Other countermarks on this group include a palm-branch (Gotha) and a bird (Istanbul).
[3] E.g. at Pitane (Vienna; cf. *Wad.* 991) and on 'colonist' series (p. 112) (in trade, Istanbul-Pera).
[4] Name Alexandria used by Strabo, XIII, 593; Ptol. V, 2. 4, VIII, 17. 9; cf. Head, *HN.* p. 931, COL. ALEXAND. AVG.
[5] *CIL.* III, 391.
[6] Weber, *Princeps*, I, p. 252* n. 672; cf. Gardthausen II, pp. 478 ff.; Paoli, *Mél. d'arch. et d'hist.* LV, 1938, p. 101.
[7] Kubitschek, *Imp.* p. 190; only one other (Caesaraugusta).

[8] 254.
[9] *Caes.* 79; cf. Barbagallo, *Nuova Rivista storica*, VI, 1922, pp. 141 ff.
[10] *PW.* I, 1396; cf. Livy XXXV, 42, XXXVII, 35.
[11] *Carm.* III, 3. 57 ff. etc.; cf. Syme, *RR.* p. 305.
[12] *Aen.* XII, 828, etc.
[13] This issue and the existence of the colony show that Broughton (*ES.* IV, p. 713) need not have been surprised to find no Greek coinage of Alexandria Troas at this time.
[14] Cast at Winterthur. Monogram 9c (*NZ.* 1884, p. 296).
[15] 107.
[16] Cf. Hill, *Historical Roman Coins*, p. 111; Rice Holmes, *The Roman Republic*, III, p. 321 n. 3.

issues, it is necessary to conclude that this is the foundation-coinage of the new colony. The *duovir* Pe. or Ep. is probably the *adsignator*, like similar officials mentioned without a colleague at Saguntum and Venafrum (pp. 158, 285).

An identification of the *deductor* of Alexandria Troas can be attempted from examination of the coinage of another Julian colony in the same region:

(1) C. G. I. L. diademed head of Julius to right—Q. LVCRETI[O] L. PONTI[O] IIVIR., M. TVRIO LEG. priest ploughing with oxen (Pl. VIII, 7).[1]
(2) same as last—Q. LVCRETI[O] L. PONTI[O] IIVIR. COL. DED. P. same as last (Pl. VIII, 6).[2]
(3) C. G. I. L. head of Janus—inscription of (1), abbreviated. Female figure wearing *polos*, with *cornucopiae* and *amphora*.[3]
(4) same as last—inscription as last. Prow.[4]
(5) same as last—inscription of (2), but COL. DED. PR. Prow.[5]
(6) C. G. I. L. female head to right, with wreath of corn-ears and ear-ring—same inscription as last: type of (3).[6] Variant with COL. DEDVC. PR.[7]

These coins are found on the Propontis,[8] and are countermarked with a capricorn and C. G.[9] (a Parian stamp[10]), $\overline{\text{ALE}}$.,[11] and a *cornucopiae*,[12] the last two both found also at Alexandria Troas.[13] Furthermore, the head on (6) closely recalls the earliest issues from Parium. But the general attribution to that mint is directly contradicted by the ethnic. There is no L(*aus*, etc.) in the title of Parium, which is C. G. I. P. C. G. I. L. must represent a different town, and the L., parallel to the P., is likely to be the initial of its ethnic. We must look for a Julian colony, with the initial L, near Parium. It has escaped notice that just such a colony existed, albeit for a very short time, at **Lampsacus**. Appian,[14] relating the Asiatic adventure of Sex. Pompeius in 35 B.C., says Λάμψακον ἐκ προδοσίας κατέλαβεν, ἣ πολλοὺς εἶχεν Ἰταλοὺς ἐξ ἐποικίσεως Γαΐου Καίσαρος. Here there is no need, or reason, to assume the existence of non-colonial *coloni* such as occur at Tralles (p. 383). ἐποικίζειν and ἔποικος are used by Strabo,[15] and probably in other passages of Appian,[16] to describe a formal *deductio coloniae*,[17] and this is its

---

[1] Imhoof-Blumer, *MG.* p. 252. 129 (Paris), BM, own collection.
[2] Ibid. 130 (Munich), 128 (Munich), BM. Misread by Hübner, *MLI.* p. 38, to include the ethnic of Dertosa.
[3] Imhoof-Blumer, *NZ.* 1884, p. 296 (Klagenfurt).
[4] Ibid. (Paris).
[5] Robinson, *NC.* 1921, p. 8. 6 (BM).
[6] Ibid. 7 (BM).   [7] Berlin.
[8] Robinson, l.c.
[9] Imhoof-Blumer, *MG.* p. 252.
[10] Similar countermark at Parium: in trade (Istanbul-Pera).
[11] Imhoof-Blumer, *NZ.* 1884, p. 296 (cast at Winterthur); cf. above, p. 245, Monogram 9c.
[12] Berlin.
[13] Cast at Winterthur (p. 245 n. 14); Athens.
[14] *BC.* v, 137.
[15] VIII, 381.
[16] *BC.* II, 135; I, 96.
[17] The implied definition by Menander Rhetor (p. 83, Heeren), ἢ γὰρ ἀπῳκίσθη—ἢ ἐπηυξήθη ἢ ὅλως οὐκ οὖσα πρότερον ἐπῳκίσθη, is irrelevant, since here there was in any case no question of founding a city where none had existed before.

regular meaning.¹ The same may be concluded of Lampsacus.² It is not surprising that, after its occupation by Sextus and his death, no more was heard of the colony. Pliny, whose source is not earlier than Actium,³ omits all mention of it; Strabo's similar neglect is even less significant, since he even omits Parium.⁴ The G. in the style of both these cities is G(*emina*) or G(*emella*). The latter word is correctly understood (in the case of Acci and Tucci) to refer to cities colonised by two legions—*coloniae a legionibus gemellis conditae*;⁵ but either epithet might well refer to twin foundations,⁶ such as Lampsacus and Parium. The two cities may have shared a legion (cf. p. 251). Mommsen,⁷ supported by inscriptions, rightly interprets the *duoviri* as IIVIR(*i*) COL(*onia*) DEDVC(*ta*) PR(*imi*)—yet another pair of inauguratory magistrates. One of these, L. Pontius, is probably a relative of the business man A. Pontius A. f. who resided at about this date at Mytilene.⁸

The portrait of Julius is modelled on *denarii* of P. Sepullius Macer,⁹ and is therefore less likely to date from the lifetime of Julius than from the first years of the *régime* of Antony (p. 245). This is in accordance with conclusions reached concerning Alexandria Troas, and is especially probable in view of the existence of an analogous *deductio* coinage at Philippi (p. 274). The latter, of similar style and portraiture, has the name of Q. Paquius Rufus *legatus*, who invites comparison with M. Turius here. Turius—whose daughter is likely to have been the heroine of the *Laudatio Turiae*¹⁰— was probably in charge of Asia from the battle of Philippi until the arrival of L. Munatius Plancus, probably late in 41 (p. 241). The title *legatus* for governors was frequent in the forties: in particular, it was much more appropriate than that of proconsul when, as at this time, the triumvir, who held a superior *imperium*, was himself in the same district.¹¹ Pompeian governors in Spain and Sicily, M. Eppius and L. Junius, used the same title in similar circumstances (pp. 22, 30). P. Sulpicius Rufus, at Sinope, gives an indication of the extent to which the use of titulature fluctuated in this transitional period (p. 252): but the coinage and status of Q. Paquius Rufus, who founded Philippi, will confirm that at least one title never existed—*legatus coloniae deducendae*. Before the triumvirate, governors and others were entrusted with schemes of settlement which warranted the honorific title of *praefectus* and the sneers of Cicero (p. 9); the title lapsed after Philippi, when it became customary for governors to monopolise the founding of new colonies in their provinces. Thus M. Turius, governor

---

¹ E.g. by Dindorf, *Thes. Graecae linguae* (*Stephanus*), s.v.; Liddell and Scott, s.v.; Magie, *De Romanorum vocabulis*, p. 60.
² Broughton, *ES.* IV, 1938, pp. 582, 703, reserves his judgment about Lampsacus, offering several conjectures, but ignoring these coins. Hahn, *Rom und Romanismus*, p. 61, rightly accepts the colony.
³ Jones, *CERP.* pp. 491 ff.
⁴ Ibid. p. 401 n. 98.

⁵ *Thesaurus Ling. Lat.*, s.v.; cf. Hübner, *PW.* I, 140. ⁶ Cf. Broughton, *ES.* IV, p. 582.
⁷ Cf. Robinson, *NC.* 1921, p. 8.
⁸ *IG.* XII, 88; cf. Hatzfeld, p. 92 n. 4.
⁹ E.g. *BMCR.* pl. LIV, 17, etc.
¹⁰ *ILS.* 8393; cf. (most recently) Giglioli, *Bollettino dell' Associazione Archeologica Romana*, I, 1937, pp. 2 ff.
¹¹ Cf. Dio XLVIII, 24; Raillard, l.c.

and *deductor* in Asia, is commemorated by the short-lived and unknown colony of Lampsacus, whose colonists were among the οἰκισθησόμενοι at Caesar's death whom Brutus had not had time to settle (p. 33).

The colony which was Lampsacus's twin, **Parium**, is also commemorated by an isolated issue. It has the ethnic C(*olonia*) G(*emina*) I(*ulia*) P(*ariana*), types of a female head and *praefericulum*, and usually two pairs of signatures:[1]

(1) MVC., PIC. IIII(*viri*) I(*ure*) D(*icundo*) D(*ecurionum*) D(*ecreto*).[2]
(2) C. MATVINVS, T. ANICIVS AED.[3] (or the same in the Ablative[4]).

Since no other quattuorviral coinage is found at Parium, and there is a close resemblance in type and denomination to the foundation-pieces of Lampsacus, it is necessary to conclude that the present issues commemorate the contemporary *deductio* of the sister-colony at Parium.[5] This conclusion is confirmed by a coin-portrait of Julius here in the second century,[6] which bears witness to a Julian plan (p. 318).[7] The foundation-coinage of Calagurris (p. 165) provides a parallel for the appearance of the aediles in addition to the senior college; with the former, probably, was the responsibility for the coinage (p. 177). It has been shown that M. Turius *legatus* is likely to have been the *deductor* of Parium in 42–41: the four personages here recorded were the first magistrates of the colony. The *duovir comitialis* is a Mucius, probably from the *clientela* of the Scaevolae: his colleague may belong to any one of a number of obscure *gentes*.[8] The Anicii were a Praenestine family which provided an Emperor five centuries later,[9] and a L. Anicius Paetinas in the time of Augustus.[10] Matuinus is an entirely unknown Italian *gentilicium*,[11] which may also be represented by MAT. on a Republican *denarius*.[12]

Unlike other colonies in the region, Parium produces a second coinage of an equally isolated character, probably including a *dupondius* and an *as*:

[1] A few pieces have no signature (Imhoof-Blumer, *MG*. p. 251. 120–1), and a few no ethnic either (Istanbul: found in Dardanelles region).
[2] Imhoof-Blumer, l.c. 118; variants.
[3] Ibid. 123.
[4] Ibid. 122.
[5] This view, explaining *Gemina* or *Gemella*, seems to the present writer to have more to recommend it than Broughton's conjecture (*ES*. IV, p. 702) that the colony was founded in c. 35 B.C.
[6] Berlin.
[7] The appearance of *quattuorviri*, as at *colonia* Thapsus, provides yet another piece of evidence against the limitation of these to *municipia* (showing that, for a time, they were equally appropriate to provincial colonies). For similar instances see Spehr, *De summis magistratibus etc.*, pp. 31 f., and Mantey, *De gradu et statu quaestorum*, p. 32. Possibly this is the solution of the difficulty concerning Narona, which is a colony in Pliny's list (*NH*. III, 142; cf. Kornemann, p. 530), but has *quattuorviri* (cf. Sherwin-White, p. 170 n. 3).
[8] Picarius (Schulze, pp. 366, 415, 483), Picatius (ibid. pp. 235, 366), Picentius (ibid. p. 523), Picidius (ibid. pp. 234, 428), Pictorius (ibid. pp. 333, 587).
[9] Seeck, *PW*. I, 2198 (Olybrius).
[10] *CIL*. III, 14712 f.; cf. Schulze, p. 130 n. 1.
[11] Schulze, p. 190.
[12] *BMCR*. II, p. 236. MAT(*ienus*) is the conjecture of Pais, *Ricerche sulla storia*, ser. II, p. 296.

THE ROMAN COLONIES

(1) IMP. CAESAR DIVI F., C. G. I. P. head of Octavian to right—M. AGRIPPA head of Agrippa to right (Pl. IX, 2).[1]

(2) M. BARBATIO, MAN. ACILIO IIVIR., C. G. I. P. as last (Pl. IX, 1)—P. VIBIO SAC. CAES., Q. BARBA. PRAEF. PRO IIVIR. Priest ploughing with two oxen.[2] A variant[3] has the names of the *duoviri* only, one on each side.

It is noteworthy that a change has occurred from *quattuorviri* to *duoviri*. A similar phenomenon is found at Tingis, Gades and Asido:[4] it is characteristic of the period. But the appearance of a second isolated coinage of this sort strongly suggests a special commemorative occasion. The portraiture of Octavian is of the period immediately after Actium, to which his titulature is also suitable; but this issue cannot be considered to celebrate the first *decennium* of the colony—which might fall in 31—since the magistrates are not *quinquennales* but *duoviri*. On the other hand there are, at this time, many examples of a second draft of colonists, involving the *restitutio* of the colony (p. 257); and there is evidence that P. Vedius Pollio, Octavian's *procurator et praeses* of Asia in 30-29, concerned himself with *adsignatio* (p. 383). It is highly probable that he was *adsignator* at Parium, and that the *deductor* was the *princeps* himself, who spent much of these two years in Asia.[5] The colony naturally, at this date, remains *Iulia*.[6] The unusual honour to Agrippa suggests that, as at Apamea in 28-27 (p. 255), he was, being consul, associated in the *patrocinium* of the city. The *duoviri* however (who were probably elected at the beginning of the year, before the *restitutio* was announced) are not Octavian and Agrippa, but two other senators. M. Barbatius, who had coined as quaestor of Antony in 41 B.C.,[7] is represented by a freedman; M'. Acilius—known to us from Cicero's *Pro Scauro*[8]—is represented by the local priest of Divus Julius. The fact that the worship of Julius by Roman citizens was officially organised in Asia in 29[9] suggests that the present coinage, and the refoundation of the colony, should be attributed to that year rather than to 30.

Thereafter the mint passed into the employment of the *aerarium* (p. 111). The colonies of Asia, then, like those of Sicily and Sardinia, do not coin except to commemorate foundations or refoundations.

12. GALATIA: Lystra, Antioch in Pisidia

The foundation-issue of Lystra as a *colonia Iulia* was made by a transient proconsul of Asia in 43 (p. 238). It fell to the Republicans, but its subsequent retention of the epithet *Iulia* without the addition of *Augusta* suggests restoration after Philippi. However, its next issue occurred after the interlude of royal rule in Lycaonia, and the subsequent

[1] *BMC.* 85. [2] *BMC.* 84. [3] Berlin. [6] Cf. Kornemann 110.
[4] Cf. McElderry, *JRS.* 1918, p. 81. [7] *PIR.*[2] 1, 352. 50.
[5] Cf. Waddington, *Fastes des provinces asiatiques*, [8] Cf. *PIR.*[2] 1, 11.
49. [9] Cf. Nock, *CAH.* x, p. 485.

formation of the province of Galatia. It includes two pieces, probably *dupondius* and *as*, with portraits of Augustus which proclaim a date at the end of his principate:[1]

(1) IMPE. AVGVSTI[2] laureate head to left; *cornucopiae*—COL. IVL. FEI (*sic*). GEM. LVSTRA priest ploughing with two humped oxen (Pl. VIII, 10).[3]

(2) IMP. AVG ········ laureate head to right— ······CERERIS Ceres seated to left (Pl. VIII, 11).[4]

The reappearance of Ceres on later coins of Lystra[5] confirms the attribution of (2) to this mint, as its style suggests. Now an altar to Ceres was inaugurated in Rome in A.D. 7[6]—a date appropriate to the portrait-models used for these coins. When it is recollected that this was the fiftieth year of the colony's existence, and that Uselis, Carthage and Cirta—beside peregrine cities—celebrate their half-centenary by equally isolated coinage (p. 153), it is impossible to resist the conclusion that these which, by every analogy, are likely to be commemorative issues served the same purpose.

The only other Roman city in *provincia* Galatia which issued money under Augustus is **Pisidian Antioch**. The colony there was of a singular character: it was not *Iulia* or *Augusta*, but *Caesarea*. It was founded at an early enough date for Drusus senior, who died in 9 B.C., to be twice *duovir*;[7] and it is the only colony in Galatia of which Pliny's source knows.[8] Moreover, a certain Caristanius, who was *praefectus pro duoviro* in c. 10–7 B.C., was already not a veteran of the first establishment.[9] But Suetonius[10] points out that the title *Caesarea* implies a regal origin: *reges in suo quisque regno Caesareas urbes condiderunt*. It is very probable that Amyntas initiated this habit,[11] and that on his death the distinctive epithet was maintained without change.[12] But the colony itself cannot have been founded during the government of Amyntas.[13] Coins of Vespasian found there commemorate LEG. V. and LEG. VI(··),[14] the latter probably the seventh legion[15] commanded by M. Lollius, the first Resident in Galatia. Veterans from these legions were probably settled at Antioch not long after the death of Amyntas—probably when the provincial era was inaugurated in 20–19 B.C.[16]

This attribution is confirmed by the 'Patricia' portrait-model of the inauguratory

---

[1] Late Lugdunum.

[2] The form of the *princeps*' titulature is strange, since the Possessive Genitive is a Republicanism not revived on official coinage until the Civil Wars of A.D. 68–69 (cf. Mattingly, *BMC. Imp.* pp. lxixf.).

[3] *BMC. Lystra* 1; cf. *Wad.* 4790; *NC.* 1893, p. 17; *ZfN.* 1890, p. 14; *Rn.* 1883, p. 57.

[4] Berlin ('uncertain').

[5] Head, *HN.* p. 714.

[6] Wilhelm, *Das römische Sakralwesen*, Diss. Strassburg, 1915, p. 84.

[7] Cf. Calder, *JRS.* 1913, p. 100.

[8] Pliny, *NH.* v, 94.

[9] *JRS.* 1914, pp. 253 f.

[10] *Aug.* 60.

[11] Broughton, *CJ.* 1935, p. 44.

[12] Ramsay, *JRS.* 1916, p. 83, more accurately than Cuntz, *Jahreshefte des öst. arch. Inst.* xxv, 1929, p. 77.

[13] Not as early as 29 B.C.; cf. last section, Ramsay, l.c. p. 111.

[14] Ritterling, *ZfN.* xxxviii, 1928, p. 56.

[15] Cf. *CIL.* III, 6826.

[16] Cf. Ramsay, *Anatolian Studies to Buckler* (1939), p. 203, repeating the conclusion (apparently unknown to him) of Bosch, *Kaiserdaten auf kleinasiatischen Münzen*, s.v. *Tavium*. This is also ignored by Ruge, *PW.* xix, 1107.

THE ROMAN COLONIES 251

issue. This includes a piece[1] whose attribution here is indicated by its inscription and Pisidian provenance:[2]

    CAESAR head of Augustus to right—AVGVSTVS,[3] COL. CAES. two legionary eagles (those of the two legions mentioned above) and two *vexilla* (Pl. IX, 5).

Hill also cites a second piece of larger denomination found in the same district:[4] it reads IMP. A·······TR. POT., accompanied by a head of the *princeps*, and has on the reverse a priest ploughing with two humped oxen, and an illegible inscription. There is a second and unpublished example of this coin,[5] revealing an unusual legend which confirms the evidence of provenance—PARENS CAESAREA COL. (Pl. VIII, 12). The word *parens* might refer to Augustus (who is described as IMP. AVGVST. TR. POT. on the obverse), but is more likely to be connected with the title of the colony: since the other Pisidian foundations were not made until the construction of the *Via Sebaste* in c. 6 B.C.,[6] Antioch might well consider itself their parent-city or μητρόπολις. Relevant to this title is an inscription describing Antioch and Lystra as sister-towns: τὴν λαμπροτάτην Ἀντιοχέων κολωνίαν ἡ λαμπροτάτη Λυστρέων κολωνία τὴν ἀδελφὴν τῷ τῆς ὁμονοίας ἀγάλματι ἐτείμησεν.[7] It is clear that the two colonies considered themselves senior by a generation to the other foundations in the province. The two coins of Antioch both imitate heads of c. 19–17 B.C.[8] and manifestly have the character of a single bidenominational foundation-issue. Their dates confirm Ramsay's attribution of the *deductio* to c. 20–19 B.C.

13. PONTUS ET BITHYNIA: Sinope, Heraclea, Apamea

One of the governors of this province,[9] P. Sulpicius Rufus, has already been ascribed to the years 46–45, in the latter of which a colony was founded at Sinope (p. 12). The unknown coin struck there with his name bears witness to this date by its style, which is considerably earlier than that of Sinopitan coins of 38 B.C. It appears to associate governor and town in a finite sentence, which by all analogies must refer to his *deductio* of the colony (p. 240)—especially as, unlike nearly all its subsequent coinage, it bears no date by the colonial era. The only extant specimen[10] reads as follows:

    COLON. FEL. SIN., P. SVLP. turreted head to right of the city-goddess
    —··F. RVF. PRO COS. PONTIFE·········· *apex, securis, simpulum*
    and *aspergillum* (Pl. VIII, 13).

[1] Hill, *NC*. 1914, p. 299. 10.
[2] Ibid. 11 (BM, Berlin, Vienna); *pace* Imhoof-Blumer, *KM*. 9.
[3] AVAVCTVS (*sic*) on BM specimen.
[4] *NC*. 1914, p. 299. 40.
[5] Berlin: it lies unaccountably among the coins of Caesarea Panias (which was not a colony).
[6] Ramsay, l.c. p. 216.
[7] Sterrett, *Wolfe Expedition*, 352.
[8] 'Patricia' and cistophoric tetradrachm.
[9] For the Fasti of Pontus and Bithynia at this time see p. 12.
[10] Paris.

There are about ten letters missing: a number of these can be restored from a description, by E. Babelon, of a now inaccessible example (the only one hitherto published):[1]

DICQFRVFR············

The last of the letters deciphered by him is seen from the extant piece to be not an R but a P. Since the governor's name was P. Sulpicius Rufus, it is certain that the inscription continues from obverse to reverse: the missing coin enables the interpretation Q(*uinti*) F(*ilius*), supplying the hitherto unknown *praenomen* of his father. Thus we have COLON. FEL. SIN., P. SVLP.—Q. F. RVF. PRO COS. PONTIFE······ DIC., with about six missing characters. An X may be supplied.[2] Since Sulpicius is unlikely to have omitted his *cognomen imperatoris* recently won in Illyricum,[3] and since also, for the reasons already given, he seems to have founded Sinope, the rest of the gap is satisfactorily filled by [IMP. DE]D. Such foundations were made by the orders of the dictator, and later by those of the triumvirs or *princeps* (p. 292):[4] the formula is *Iussu C. Caesaris*,[5] *Iussu Caesaris Augusti*,[6] *Iussu Aug.* (p. 289). The final letters IC, placed second and third in Babelon's description, are therefore very likely to represent I(*ussu*) C(*aesaris*). The whole inscription will then be:

COLON(*iam*) FEL(*icem*) SIN(*open*) P. SVLP(*icius*) Q(*uinti*) F(*ilius*) RVF(*us*)
PRO CO(*n*)S(*ule*) PONTIFE[X IMP(*erator*) DE]D(*uxit*) I(*ussu*) C(*aesaris*).

On his official coinage struck at Amisus, Rufus is only entitled PRO PR. Originally only governors with armies had been entitled to the proconsular title, but towards the end of the Republic this rule became abrogated,[7] and in addition proconsuls of praetorian rank became common;[8] so that Ganter's[9] attribution of this title to all governors of the triumvirs applies at least to the more important provinces.[10] Sulpicius's elevation in rank during his governorship is to be explained by the suddenly enhanced importance of certain Eastern governorships, especially this one,[11] owing to Caesar's preparations for world-conquest: the titulature of the contemporary governor of Asia, the consular P. Servilius Isauricus,[12] underwent a precisely similar change.[13]

Issues by the same colony continue for many years. Almost every specimen

---

[1] *Rec.* 75 a: Grand Duke Mihailovitch coll.
[2] The pontificate of Sulpicius is unknown to *Fasti* (p. 287).   [3] Cic. *Fam.* XIII, 77. 1.
[4] The tribe of Sinope is unfortunately uncertain: Reinach, *Rev. arch.* 1916, p. 341, pace Kubitschek, *Imp.* p. 252. For DEDVXIT see p. 275.
[5] *Lex Coloniae Genetivae Iuliae*, ch. 104.
[6] *Liber Coloniarum* (Feldm. p. 237): cf. also Pais, *Memorie della R. Ac. dei Lincei* (sc.-mor.), VI, 2, 1926, p. 394 on Feldm. p. 220 l. 1.

[7] Marquardt, *St.V.* p. 381 n. 3.
[8] Cf. Mommsen, *St.R.*³ II, 1, p. 244 n. 2.
[9] P. 45.
[10] *Pace* Marquardt, *St.V.* p. 193, of Pontus-Bithynia.
[11] Syme, *Anatolian Studies to Buckler* (1939), p. 322; cf. Mommsen, *Gesammelte Schriften*, IV, pp. 162 f.
[12] Cf. Münzer, *PW.* (2R.), II, 1799.
[13] Cic. *Fam.* XIII, 67 init.; cf. 68 init.

THE ROMAN COLONIES

is dated; calculations by Kubitschek[1] show that the era in use followed the Roman calendar. Though he is wrong in stating that no other Roman city ever dates its coinage,[2] this chronological system is the distinctive feature of an important but much neglected and misquoted series.[3] A number of the coins repay individual attention. It has often been said that *colonia Iulia* Sinope bore the *cognomen* of *Caesarea*;[4] but Babelon's reading of [C.I.]C. F. AN. XIX.[5] is denied not only by a variant of the same date and type with C. F. I. SI. AN. XIX.,[6] and by the lack of analogy, but by his own illustration. He misreads C. F. I. $\overline{AN}$. XV. (31 B.C.) (Pl. IX, 4) as [C $\cdots$ I.]F.-I(?)$\overline{AN}$. XI.[7] (Forrer[8] reads C. I. F. S. $\overline{AN}$. XV.). On no coin in the whole series is there a sign of the epithet Caesarea. The last-named coin possesses the pontifical type of the foundation-issue, but its style is so much more developed that it must be considerably later. The ethnics on the issues of 38 B.C. are also of the form C. F. I., but on all dated issues after 31 appears C. I. F.; however, the latter form was already permissible before Actium, since it is found on an undated coin with DIVO IVLIO and the features of Antony.[9] Another undated piece, probably later, bears the portrait and name of Diogenes.[10]

[1] *NZ.* 1908, p. 68.
[2] A later coin with ANN. CXXX. (Paris) has as ethnic not C. I. F. (as *Rec.* 1, p. 200) but C. G. I. P. (= Parium).

3	Date		Types
(1)	VIII	38 B.C.	head r. of Julius—*cornucopiae* and clasped hands (Milne, *NC.* 1935, p. 194: Oxford, Berlin, Vienna)
(2)	VIII	38	do.—head r. of Antony (Vienna)
(3)	XV	31	turreted female head r.—*apex, securis, simpulum, aspergillum* (Paris, misread by *Rec.* 75) (Pl. IX, 4)
(4)	XIX	27	female head r.—plough (Stroganoff coll., misread by *Rec.* 76)
(5)	XX(?)	26(?)	bull's head—*simpulum* (Berlin: *KM.* 5)
(6)	XXII	24	head r. of Augustus—*cornucopiae* and globe (BM: *KM.* 6, *Weber* 4835)
(7)	XXIII	23	do.—diademed head r. of Julius (Berlin)
(8)	XXIII	23	do., l.—star (Naples, cf. prob. BM: *Rec.* 83)
(9)	XXXII	14	do., r.—heads (facing outwards) of Caius and Lucius (Vienna)
(10)	XXXV	11	do. (Glasgow: *Hu.* 14)
(11)	XXXVI	10	do. (Berlin, Cahn sale, 66, pl. 9: *Rec.* 85)
(12)	XXXVII	9	do. (*Rec.* 86)
(13)	XXXIX	7	do. (Berlin: *Rec.* 87)
(14)	XLII	4	do. (Berlin: *Rec.* 89)
(15)	XLII	4	do.—heads (facing inwards) of Caius and Lucius (Istanbul: *Rec.* 88)
(16)	L(?)	A.D. 5(?)	do., l.—head l. of Tiberius (Berlin: misquoted by *Rec.* 90)
(17)	LI	6	do.—vase (Paris: *Rec.* 90a)
(18)	LI	6	do.—altar, wreath (Rome)
(19)	LIX	14	do. r.—turreted head r. of city-goddess (in trade: *Rec.* 90b)

[4] E.g. Smith, *Dictionary of Greek and Roman Geography*, p. 1007. [5] *Rec.* 76.
[6] *Rec.* 76a.   [7] *Rec.* 75.   [8] *Rb.* 1900, p. 288.
[9] Vienna: *Rec.* 74.   [10] Paris: *Rec.* 73a; cf. *Rn.* 1914, p. 14.

It is noteworthy that here the head of Augustus appears as early as 24 B.C., and is not again omitted; that Antony, and at first Augustus, honour the dictator, whose appearances at colonies are regularly restricted to his own foundations; that the grandsons of the *princeps* receive continual prominence, to the exclusion of all other types, from a date as early as 15 B.C.; and finally that, contrary to the opinion of Babelon, Tiberius is once honoured under Augustus. Eastern colonies, unlike those in the West, often persistently omit all mention of their duoviral colleges: here, instead, is the formula EX D. D. The coinage is sporadic, and was no doubt not struck at regular intervals, but, as at Corinth (p. 296), when needed.

It has escaped notice that coinage exists of another Julian colony in the same province. Unattributed hitherto has been the following piece, apparently unique:

T. VOMANIVS IIVIR QVINQ. head of Hercules to right.
MAN(?). FLAM(?). QVINQ. ITER. head of Mercury to right with *caduceus* (Pl. IX, 3).[1]

The style and fabric of this coin suggest the triumviral period, and indicate attribution to Northern Anatolia, beyond the boundaries of *provincia* Asia.[2] The double tenure of M'. Flaminius (if that is his name) bears witness to the survival of the colony[3] for at least ten years. Yet the appearance of the piece at once gives the impression that any known colonial series[4] is out of the question. The only other eligible foundation is **Heraclea Pontica**; and the eliminative argument is supported by positive considerations. Hercules was the tutelary deity of that city,[5] and on its earliest known currency of imperial date[6] his head shows striking affinities with the same type on the present issue: similarities of fabric strengthen the resemblance. Mercury, too, appears on other coins of the town.[7] Moreover, Heraclea is known to have held a colony, planned by Julius and completed in his lifetime or soon after,[8] which survived until its suppression in the late thirties by Adiatorix, tyrant of the peregrine portion of the double community.[9] Adiatorix claimed the connivance of Antony, but whether this was false or the triumvir was dissatisfied with the loyalty of the colony is not known. At all events this disappeared after a career long enough to include the two *quinquennia* to which the present coin refers, but short enough to account for the isolated character of the issue. Thus style, type and historical considerations combine to require attribution to Heraclea. The issue commemorates the first (and only) *decennium* of the ephemeral colony: a coin of Babba, which equally lacks foundation-coinage, commemorates a similar

---

[1] Paris.
[2] For general considerations see below, Appendix II, p. 478.
[3] *Municipia* do not occur in Asian provinces: cf. Jones, *GC*. p. 132.
[4] Of these Apamea is still to be discussed, p. 255.
[5] Cf. *BMC. Pontus*, pp. 139 ff.
[6] Own collection, not in *Rec.*, with the name of a proconsul.
[7] E.g. *Rec.* 158, 169, 178.
[8] Kornemann 112; Jones, *CERP*. pp. 163, 425 n. 30.
[9] Strabo XII, 542. Ruge, *PW*. VIII, 43, entirely ignores this incident and the whole colonial episode.

THE ROMAN COLONIES 255

occasion (p. 222). A single insignificant piece testifies to Heraclea's part in Caesar's colonial scheme. If the foundation was completed by the dictator,[1] the issue is to be dated to 35–34 B.C.; if it was left to Antony, the date is 32–31, not more than a few weeks before the *coup* of Adiatorix. One of the magistrates, T. Vomanius, is a member of a rare but authentic Etruscan *gens*.[2]

An ambitious series in three denominations recalls a more successful colony in the same province. The city has, however, never been rightly identified, owing to the invariable misreading and so misunderstanding of all the coins of which it is composed. These should be described as follows:

(1) AVGVSTVS DIV. F. COS. VII. IMP.············C.[3] RF̄V. (or V̄F.) laureate head of Augustus to right; corn-ear—DIVOS IVLIVS, C. CASSIVS C. F. IIVIR C. I. C. F. C. Diademed head of Julius to right (Pl. VIII, 15).[4]

(2) IMP. CAESAR. DIVI F. AVGVSTO COS. VII. bare head of Augustus to right—AGRIPPA COS. III., IMP.[5] C.[6] DI. F. S. C. C. R., C. CASSIVS C. F. IIVIR C. I. C. F. C. bare head of Agrippa to right (Pl. VIII, 16).[7]

(3) AP. PVLCHER PRO COS. head of Ap. Claudius Pulcher to right—C. CASSIVS C. F. IIVIR F. C., ĀVG. DI. F. S. C. C. R. wolf and twins[8] (Pl. VIII, 14).[9]

In these three rare coins is a mine of colonial history and procedure. It is first necessary to obtain a correct geographical attribution. E. Babelon[10] assigns them to Sinope: not only, however, are they, in style, type, and arrangement, completely alien to the homogeneous series of that city,[11] but there is no C······ among its *cognomina* (p. 253). Ascriptions to Carthage and Corinth by Groag[12] and de Saulcy[13] respectively are totally out of harmony with style and fabric. Klebs,[14] too, is wrong in attempting to locate a non-existent colony with the style C. I. C. F. C. or G.: F. C. is an extremely common formula for F(*aciundum*) C(*uravit* etc.), being found with this significance on innumerable inscriptions,[15] and a number of coins. Among the latter is the following piece:

(4) AGRIPPA, T. R. Q. (?), C. T. C. (?), F. C. head of Agrippa to right— AGRIPPA AVG. NEPOS head of Agrippa Postumus to right (Pl. VIII, 17).[16]

---

[1] As Meyer, *Cäsars Monarchie*, p. 492.
[2] Vide Schulze, p. 117—derived from the river Vomanus, ibid. p. 481.
[3] BM.
[4] BM, Berlin, Paris; a letter omitted by Imhoof-Blumer, *MG*. p. 15; wrongly described in *Rec*. 80.
[5] Berlin.   [6] BM.
[7] BM, Berlin, Paris, Munich, Schotten; wrongly described by Imhoof-Blumer, l.c. 16; *Rec*. 78; and Boutkowski, *DN*. II, p. 1747. 2866. The misquotation is renewed by Miss Newby (p. 41).
[8] For this colonial type vide Paoli, *Mél. d'arch. et d'hist*. LV, 1938, p. 128; cf. Eckhel, *DN*. IV, p. 492.
[9] Paris: wrongly described by *Wad*. 196, Imhoof-Blumer, l.c. 17, and *Rec*. 77.
[10] *Rec*. 77 ff.
[11] As recognised by von Sallet; cf. *PIR*. I, 394. 778.   [12] *PIR*.² II, 984.
[13] *Mémoires de la Société française de numismatique et d'archéologie*, 1873, p. 29.
[14] Ibid.   [15] E.g. *CIL*. VIII (index).
[16] BM (attributed to Sinope).

In style—and especially in portraiture of Agrippa—this bears a very close resemblance to (1)–(3) above, and the mint must be the same. As on those pieces, F. C. must be eliminated from the ethnic, which is therefore merely C. I. C. This solution is confirmed by a further unpublished issue of equally great rarity, whose portraits, style and types are closely modelled on (1) and (2), and indicate identity of mint:

(5) AVGVSTVS IMP. C. I. C. head of Augustus to right—DIVOS IVLIVS C. I. C. diademed head of Caesar to right.[1]

The fabric of all these pieces suggests the north-west regions of Asia Minor. Thus the countermarks, ABR.[2] and P̄H̄R.,[3] found on specimens of (1) and (2), are likely to represent the neighbouring districts of ABR(*ettene*)—the kingdom of Cleon under Bithynian Olympus[4]—and PHR(*ygia minor*). Furthermore, a specimen of a very rare coin of Caligula,[5] of similar style and with the same ethnic, was acquired by the writer at the very foot of Bithynian Olympus.[6] In the whole of Asia Minor there were few colonies, and we know of only one C(*olonia*) I. C.: that was precisely in the region to which these indications point—less than twenty miles from the mountain, at **Apamea**. Here was a *colonia Iulia*,[7] whose *cognomen, Concordia*,[8] points to a foundation in c. 42–40 B.C. by Antony (p. 227).

The elucidation of the formulae of (1)–(3) presents a number of difficulties. The self-contained clause C. CASSIVS C. F. IIVIR C(*oloniae*) I(*uliae*) C(*oncordiae*) F(*aciundum*) C(*uravit*) is in each case clear, but the reverse legends are otherwise of an unparalleled character. On (3), AVG(*ustus*) DI(*vi*) F(*ilius*) appears in an unexpected position; on (2), IMP(*erator*) C(*aesar*) DI(*vi*) F(*ilius*) is even more curious, since it shares a face of the coin with Agrippa and the *duovir*, while the title of the *princeps* has already occurred (in identical form except for the addition of AVGVSTVS) on the obverse. This cannot be fortuitous, nor can it be the ordinary *Nominativus Pendens* of a coin-legend; it is clear that in each case the name of Augustus plays a special part, probably in connection with the subsequent unusual formula S. C. C. R. This last is not adequately explained by Imhoof-Blumer's[9] S(*enatus*) C(*onsulto*) C(*ivium*) R(*omanorum*), which is less appropriate to a Roman than to a Latin city. It is most likely that a special action of the *princeps* is depicted on the reverses of (2) and (3), and also on the partially lost obverse of (1). Finite sentences occur on other colonial issues—at Cassandrea, Dyrrhachium, Philippi and probably Lystra: in each case the occasion is the *deductio*. Here a first foundation was not in question, but in view of the disgrace of the Antonian colonies after Actium and the known colonial activity of Octavian at that date (p. 305), nothing is more probable than a refoundation. Moreover, the agency

---

[1] Berlin ('uncertain').
[2] On (1); Paris. See Monogram 10.
[3] On (1) and (2); Paris. See Monogram 11.
[4] Tarn, *CAH*. x, p. 114.
[5] *Rec.* p. 252.
[6] At Bursa (Brusa).
[7] Pliny, *NH*. v, 149; cf. Strabo XII, 563; Pliny, *Ep.* x, 56; Ulp. *Dig.* L, 15. 1; *CIL.* III, 335; ibid. *Suppl.* 6992.
[8] Cf. Kornemann 113.
[9] *MG.* l.c.

THE ROMAN COLONIES 257

of the proconsul in this new establishment would align him with the many others who are honoured on colonial coins in a similar capacity. Since the only alternative on such issues—commemoration of *amici principis*—is a later phenomenon (p. 229), it is necessary to conclude that Ap. Pulcher is concerned with the foundation, like others who are portrayed at the same date elsewhere (p. 152). The colonial epithet *Iulia* would be correct for a colony founded in the first half of the governorship of 28–27 B.C. (May–May[1]), to which the date COS. VII. is appropriate[2] (pp. 293 n. 1, 422).

Now S. C., which appears on these coins, is much more likely to refer to the Roman senate than to local bodies, which generally use the formula [EX] D. D.[3] The following letters, C. R., recall that second founders are regularly entitled *coloniae restitutores*[4] —and Augustus appears in this capacity at Ilici, Parium, Pella, Dyrrhachium and Philippi. Thus a number of indications combine to restore the legends of (2) as follows:

IMP(*eratore*) CAESAR(*e*) DIVI F(*ilio*) AVGVSTO COS. VII. AGRIPPA COS. III., IMP(*erator*) C(*aesar*) DIVI F(*ilius*) S(*enatus*) C(*onsulto*) C(*oloniam*) R(*estituit*); C. CASSIVS C. F. IIVIR C(*oloniae*) I(*uliae*) C(*oncordiae*) F(*aciundum*) C(*uravit*).

The apparent redundance of the *princeps'* titles is due to the formal eponymous mention of the names of both consuls in the Ablative Absolute. In the same way (3) reads: AVG(*ustus*) DI(*vi*) F(*ilius*) S(*enatus*) C(*onsulto*) C(*oloniam*) R(*estituit*). A similar formula might well be expected to occur on (1): and it is most probable that the letters C. R., which follow the hiatus on all our specimens, were preceded by S. C., and that the *Imperator* title, not being prenominal as on the other coins, bore a number. The lettering of (1) may, then, be restored as follows: AVGVSTVS DIV. F. COS. VII. IMP. [VII. S. C.] C. R. F̄V̄. or V̄F̄. With regard to the final ligature it may be noted, first, that it must be an inorganic part of the formula, since this occurs on (2) and (3) without it; secondly, that VF. is a highly unplausible commencement for a word, so that it must begin with FV. Some additional explanatory verb like FV(*lsit*) or FV(*ndavit*) is indicated (cf. p. 425).

Ap. Claudius Pulcher, who was entrusted with this task of refoundation, had been consul in 38 B.C.,[5] and had triumphed from Spain in c. 33–32 B.C.,[6] receiving the title *imperator*.[7] It is significant of the administrative change in 27 that, on this 'programme' coinage, he bears neither this title nor those earlier applied to colonial founders—such as *praefectus, deductor* or *conditor*—but only shows his constitutional proconsular office (p. 292). His consular rank is in accordance with Syme's demonstration[8] that the

[1] Cf. Cic. *Fam.* XII, 16.
[2] The slight postponement of the foundation-issue, to 27 (COS. VII.), is quite understandable.
[3] EX S. C., as at Carteia and Toletum, is extremely rare (cf. Lenormant, *La monnaie dans l'antiquité*, III, p. 215); P. S. S. C. at *colonia* Paestum refers to the Roman senate (p. 287). Cf. p. 424.
[4] E.g. *CIL.* III, 7282, etc.
[5] Asconius, *ap.* Cic. *Pro Milone*, p. 29; cf. *PIR.* I, 394. 77.
[6] *CIL.* I², p. 176.
[7] *CIL.* X, 1423–4.
[8] *RR.* p. 393; *Anatolian Studies to Buckler* (1939), p. 331.

boundary between consular and praetorian provinces was not yet firmly fixed. The signal honour of portraiture is Pulcher's due as one of the first aristocrats to have supported the young Octavian.[1] Elsewhere mention will be made of Pulcher's predecessor Thorius Flaccus (p. 384). That governor imitates a tetradrachm of 28 which already announces the *restituta res publica*:[2] no doubt the order for the refoundation of the colony accompanied the general restoration of rights (p. 445).

The subsequent coinage of Apamea under Augustus only comprises (4) and (5).[3] Agrippa must have been held in special honour, since his portrait here appears after his death, together with that of his posthumous son, whose head appears elsewhere only at Corinth and Pella (pp. 268, 283); perhaps all three were occasioned by a visit to the East (p. 363). Tarraco too shows a sporadic output of coins in honour of members of the *domus principis* (p. 219). At the end of Augustus's lifetime Apamea is used for an official issue of M. Granius Marcellus (p. 145).

14. SYRIA: Berytus

The colonial history of this province has been recently enlightened by the demonstration by A. H. M. Jones[4] that Heliopolis was not raised to colonial rank until the time of Severus: in the Augustan period it was part of the territory of **Berytus**. The titles of this colony raise a problem to which the following coin is relevant:

C. VIBI. L. PONTI. IIVIR. C. F. I. bust of Ceres to right, with corn-ear crown, veil, ear-rings and necklace.

L. PONTI. C. VIBI. IIVIR. C. F. I. crescent with spikes indicating radiation; plough, locust.[5]

The attribution of this by Froehner[6] to the uniform issues of Sinope is completely out of harmony with its distinctive style and arrangement. Imhoof-Blumer's[7] statement that he 'obtained' (*erhielt*) the only known specimen 'together with Pontic and Paphlagonian coins' is worthless as evidence, since it is unknown what other coins

---

[1] Syme, *RR*. p. 368.

[2] *BMC. Imp. Aug.* 691; cf. Stuart Jones, *CAH.* x, p. 127. Miss Newby (p. 2) ignores the relevance of the coin.

[3] There is also a homogeneous series in honour of Divus Julius: since one coin has C. I. C. (*BMC.* 20, Munich) and others (BM, Berlin) the wolf and twins, which appear also on our number (3), the rest, inscribed D.D., may be assigned to the same mint. But none of these should be placed at the beginning of the series (as by Imhoof-Blumer, *JIAN.* I, 1898, p. 11): of the two already mentioned, the former is Domitianic in style, and the portraits on the coins with wolf and twins recall both Vespasian (BM) and an ideal type of second-century date (Berlin); another, with the type of *cornucopiae* (BM, Milan, *Cat.* 251), may be even later. This is an exceptional case of long-lived honours to the dictator, who planned the Julio-Antonian foundation.

[4] *CERP.* p. 465 n. 85; cf. p. 272; *pace* Sherwin-White, p. 174. Cf. Ulpian, *Dig.* L, xv, 1. 2; Strabo XVI, 276; *CIL.* III, 14387, do. *a* and *b*.

[5] Berlin; illustrated by Bosch, *Archäologischer Anzeiger, Beiblatt* 2, *Jahrb.* XLVI, 1931, *Abbildung* 15, p. 454.

[6] *Rn.* 1907, p. 168.   [7] *KM.* p. 74.

were in the same 'lot', and also whether this was the product of a find or merely of a fortuitous collocation. Moreover, the style and execution are alien to the northern region of Asia Minor. The crescent is essentially a Phoenician type,[1] and the large letters and oriental fabric are characteristic of the same region, being found on Augustan issues of Berytus (e.g. Pl. IX, 10). Moreover, the rare clan of the Pontii actually appears on inscriptions from the site of that city.[2] The remarkable main reverse type is either a radiate diadem or a conventional representation of the sun's disc and rays. Such an unusual solar type must have some special significance. By the analogy of other *types parlants* (p. 194) it is natural to think of the world-famous centre of the worship of Baal-Helios,[3] which is shown by Jones to have been within the territory of the colony of Berytus. The crescent is, moreover, an especially common type on coins and sculpture of Heliopolis,[4] and its radiate form was the especial prerogative of Helios.[5] If this attribution is accepted, the coin cannot be pre-Augustan, since Heliopolis was regal property until c. 20 B.C.;[6] thus it lends no support to the view of Ritterling[7] that the epithets *Iulia Augusta* at Berytus indicate an earlier Julian foundation. If there was such a foundation, it was cancelled by Cleopatra, since there are Greek local issues of the city with her head[8] (and others are dated to 28–27 B.C.[9]). Furthermore, coins later in the principate of Augustus, whose style, provenance and type demand attribution here, still have only COL. IVL. (p. 260), and the epithet *Augusta* does not appear until after his death.[10] This necessitates the conclusion that, whether there had been a Julian plan or not, the colony founded in c. 16–15 or 14–13 B.C.[11] exceptionally bore as its own the epithet *Iulia*: even if the theory of an early Julian foundation were acceptable, late Augustan coins could hardly have neglected the epithet *Augusta*, had it ever been assumed, in favour of *Iulia*. Only one explanation appears to be possible. It has been suggested by coins of *municipium* Gades, on which Agrippa is *parens patronus* (p. 171), that Augustus sometimes permitted his distinguished relatives to play a considerable part in foundations. It was again Agrippa who, during his governorship of the East, was responsible for the foundation of Berytus: the epithet seems to indicate that the titular founder—who must have been a Julius, but cannot have been Augustus—was one of Agrippa's sons who had recently been adopted by the *princeps*,[12] probably the eldest, Caius Caesar.[13] This view is given

---

[1] Cf. Ronzevalle, *Mélanges de l'Université S. Joseph*, XVIII, 1934, pp. 109 f., pls. II, III.
[2] *CIL.* III, 157.
[3] Beer, *PW.* VIII, 47; Ronzevalle, l.c. XXI, 1937–8, pp. 129 ff.
[4] Ronzevalle, l.c. XVIII, 1934, pp. 127 ff.
[5] Stephani, *Mémoires de l'Académie des sciences de S. Pétersbourg*, VI e sér., sc.-pol.-hist.-phil. cl., IX, 1859, p. 387.
[6] Jones, *CERP.* p. 271; cf. Head, *HN.* pp. 783 f.
[7] *PW.* XII, 1215; cf. Kornemann 115; Pliny, *NH.* v, 78.
[8] Athens; Svoronos, *Ptolemies*, 1886.
[9] *BMC.* 16.
[10] *BMC.* 57, etc.
[11] Anderson, *CAH.* x, p. 281 n. 3, gives bibliography.
[12] Stuart Jones, *CAH.* x, p. 151.
[13] Cf. other *patrocinia* of Caius, e.g. *CIL.* II, 1525 f., and Lucius, ibid. 3914, etc.

plausibility by Augustus's dedication of other new foundations, such as the Basilica Iulia, *sub titulo nominis filiorum*;[1] and *colonia Iulia Obsequens* Pisae, whose *patronus* was Lucius Caesar,[2] may well be in the same category. The analogy of many isolated issues elsewhere confirms the probability that the coinage of Vibius and Pontius commemorated this *deductio*.

Not much later is a little piece, imitated from the official series with CA which circulated here (p. 106), with CAISAR and COL. IVL. in wreath (Pl. IX, 9).[3] Later in the reign are found issues bearing the same ethnic but CAESAR AVGVSTVS, and a type of colonist ploughing (Pl. IX, 10):[4] the portrait is imitated from an official issue at Sidon by Q. Articuleius (?) Regulus (p. 125). The last coinage before Augustus's death is inscribed PERM(*issu*) SIL(*ani*): Q. Caecilius Metellus Creticus Silanus governed from c. A.D. 12 to 15,[5] and issued official coins at the same mint (p. 127). The distinction between the present formula and P(*ermissu*) AVG., which appears on his official pieces, is a natural one: small local issues could be left to the governors' discretion, but official coinages were co-ordinated by a central department. The colonial pieces with PERM. SIL. have the heads of Augustus and Tiberius, described respectively as IMP. AVG.[6] and TI. CAESAR AVGVST. F. IMPERAT. [VII?].[7] They are shown to be of this mint by the style, and by the characteristic Berytan type of two eagles and two standards. This is the only colonial mint which records the permission of a *legatus Augusti*; the only contemporary parallel of any kind is provided by a single coinage sanctioned by a proconsul of Africa (p. 232). Since cities in the praetorian 'senatorial' provinces of Baetica and Achaia display instead the formula *Permissu Augusti* (p. 174), it must be concluded that no differentiation in this respect existed between the two types of province, but that greater latitude was extended to important *consulares* than to those of lesser *dignitas*.

15. CYRENAICA ET CRETA: Cyrene, Cnossus

The fleeting existence of a colony in Cyrenaica, at a time when this was temporarily separated from Crete, is revealed by an unpublished and apparently unique coin:

> Head of goddess to right—P. COSCON. silphium-plant, with leaves and roots (Pl. IX, 6).[8]

The reverse type alludes beyond all doubt to Cyrene, on whose coinage it regularly

---

[1] *RG.* 20; cf. Kolbe, *GGA.* 1939, p. 166.
[2] *CIL.* XI, 1420–1; cf. Pais, *Memorie della R. Ac. dei Lincei* (*sc.-mor.*), VI, 2, 1926, p. 393.
[3] Not CAESAR, *pace* Rouvier, *JIAN.* III, 1900, no. 488; Berlin, BM.
[4] Rouvier, l.c. 491; *BMC.* 68. Seen in trade
(Bucharest) with many coins of Sidon and Aradus.
[5] *PIR.*² II, 10. 64.
[6] Rouvier, l.c. 495.
[7] Ibid. 504; *BMC.* 67.
[8] Paris ('uncertain').

THE ROMAN COLONIES 261

and exclusively appears,[1] sometimes without umbels as here.[2] This attribution is confirmed by African stylistic traits.

The date of this piece is indicated by striking similarities of type to the foundation-issue of Cassius's ephemeral colony at Rhodes (p. 243). The heads differ in style but their design is virtually the same: on both coins appears the appropriate city-badge, accompanied by a Latin signature without qualifying titles. Moreover, the two pieces are of identical weight and dimensions: it seems impossible to dissociate them. Indeed, the early months of the year 42, to which the Rhodian *deductio* and coinage must be attributed, provide a highly suitable occasion for a similar issue at Cyrene.[3] Brutus's governor in Crete, P. Lepidus, shares an official series with P. Licinius, *pro quaestore* of Cyrenaica (p. 35): Lepidus established himself in Crete in 43–42, and P. Licinius apparently occupied Cyrenaica a few months later. Thus at Cyrene, as at Rhodes, the signatory of the coinage is not the governor. At the latter city, C. Car. and C. Cos. were the *deductor* and *adsignator* respectively of a garrison-colony established by the Republicans, like Tadius and Marius (likewise bearing no titles) at Melita (p. 235). P. Cosconius at Cyrene must fulfil a similar function. Indeed, it is the exception rather than the rule that both founders should be mentioned: far more frequently only the *deductor* is recorded.

Brutus and Cassius founded several colonies in Macedonia (p. 272), and it is now becoming possible to assess their activity as founders in other parts of their short-lived empire. Melita, Rhodes and Cyrene were all at strategic points in the Mediterranean; their unrecognised coinage reveals *deductiones* of veterans who possessed the rights of a Roman community, but were scarcely distinguishable from a garrison. Many of Augustus's settlements were of similar character (p. 306).

P. Cosconius was perhaps a brother of C. Cos., who assisted C. Car. in the contemporary foundation at Rhodes.[4] The Cosconii were a distinguished family whose evident Republicanism did not prevent them from providing the mother of Sejanus.[5]

In Crete there is a rather insignificant though extensive coinage at Cnossus, which became *colonia Iulia Nobilis*, under the *patrocinium* of Capua,[6] in c. 36 B.C.[7] M. Licinius Crassus appears to have issued an official coinage to celebrate its foundation

[1] Cf. Robinson, *BMC. Cyrenaica*, pp. ccli ff.; *Intermédiaire des chercheurs et des curieux*, 1936, pp. 832 f.
[2] E.g. Robinson, l.c. pl. XXII, 16 (Paris), XLII, 11 (Glasgow)—the latter of c. 36 B.C., p. 57.
[3] The silphium trade was still flourishing at this date, though it soon died in the principate: cf. Jones, *CERP.* p. 363.
[4] P. Cosconius Chius (*CIL.* VI, 4742) may possibly have been his freedman.
[5] Velleius II, 127. 3; *PIR.*² II, 376. 1528.

[6] Dio XLIX, 14. This unusual liaison persisted: cf. *CIL.* X, 3938; Paribeni, *Dizionario epigrafico*, II, 2. 1265.
[7] Dio XLIX, 12. 4; Strabo X, 478; Appian, *BC.* V, 131; cf. Levi II, p. 86 n. 5. Romanelli, *CAH.* XI, p. 661, has no grounds for placing the foundation later—especially as the province is omitted from Augustus's list in *RG.* 28: cf. Mommsen, *RGDA.*² p. 120—nor Kornemann for ignoring it altogether. Pliny's omission of it is entirely in accordance with the imperfection of his sources for pre-Augustan colonies (p. 226).

(p. 55): he was Antony's representative in Crete and Cyrenaica at this time, when the whole of the latter, and all but Cnossus in the former, were nominally in Cleopatra's possession (p. 58).[1] The local mint soon reopens to produce a few unsigned pieces[2]—including one with the name of Augustus[3] and another with his head[4]—and a duoviral series in which eleven colleges are represented before the death of the *princeps*:

(1) M. Aimilius (sic) T. Fufius *IIvir*.[5] (or in Ablative[6]) (C. I. N. C. EX D. D.,[7] C. N. C. EX D. D.[8]) (Pl. IX, 7).

(2) C. Petronios M. Antonios (sic) *IIvir*.[9] (or in Ablative) (C. I. N. CN. EX D. D.).

(3) [C. Iulio] Aeschino *Caes. L.* [*IIvir.*] *iter.*, L. Plotio Pleb. *IIvir.* (C. N. I. GNO[S]. EX D. D.[10]).

(4) M. Acu. D. Acu. Tam. (??) *IIvir.* (C. I. N. C.).[11]

(5) uncertain *IIviri* (C. I. N. C.) (Pl. IX, 8).[12]

(6) M. Petronio C. Iulio Antonio *IIvir*. (C. I. N. C.).[13]

(7) Pollione *iter*. Labeone[14] [*IIvir*.[15]] (D. D.).

(8) Labeone Pollione *IIvir. q. iter.*[16]

(9) M. Aemilio Labeone, Ti. Caesare *IIv*. (Δ Δ,[17] or omitted[18]).

(10) [Augu]stus, ········ *iter.*[19]

(11) M. Aemili. *praef.* ······· *IIvir. iter.* (D. D.) (Pl. VIII, 18).[20]

Several somewhat unimportant points of colonial procedure are involved. (1) appears to have been struck soon after the *deductio*, and apparently has the heads of the two masters of the world,[21] who had ceased to appear together on official coinage at an earlier date. A labyrinth appears in the field, as on (2). M. Aemilius belongs to a dominant Cnossian family, and his colleague recalls the names, probably contemporary, of a T. Fufius at Veii[22] and a T. Fufius T. l. Hermocrates at Rome.[23] (3), with the name and

---

[1] Dio's statement (XLIX, 32. 5) that she only received part of the island (p. 55) is in accordance with the fact that colonies could not be founded on peregrine soil.
[2] Svoronos, *Crete*, 184–7.
[3] Ibid. 185 (Athens).
[4] Ibid. 184 (*BMC*. 77).
[5] Svoronos 180.
[6] *BMC*. 72.
[7] Ll.cc.
[8] Svoronos 183, Vienna.
[9] Svoronos 188 f.; *BMC*. 74; Milan, *Cat*. 426, Vienna. Miss Newby supports her citation of a non-existent Greek coin (p. 78) by showing a photograph of this.
[10] Svoronos 190 f.; cf. Imhoof-Blumer, *MG*. p. 214. 10; Friedländer, *ZfN*. VI, 1879, p. 13; Milan, *Cat*. 429.
[11] Svoronos 193 f.; cf. Friedländer, l.c.; Berlin, Vienna. Probably two members of the *gens* Acutia (Schulze, p. 68; Groag, *SB*. IX, 1939, p. 46) or Acutilia (Schulze, l.c. p. 403). A Tamudi(? anus) was a Republican banker (cf. Herzog, *PW*. XVII, 1426), and an Acuti(? us) also had banking interests at some date (ibid. 1434).
[12] BM.
[13] Svoronos 192; cf. Borrell, *Rn*. 1845, p. 340. 5.
[14] Svoronos 201.
[15] BM; attributed to Corinth, *BMC*. 513.
[16] Svoronos 199, Athens.
[17] Paris, Vienna.   [18] Paris (AIMILIO).
[19] Paris ('uncertain').   [20] Berlin.
[21] For Octavian, cf. *BMCR*. pl. CXIII, 15, etc. Robinson, *BMC. Cyrenaica*, p. ccix n. 2, thinks that the other head represents Agrippa.
[22] *CIL*. XI, 3828.   [23] *CIL*. VI, 7208.

figure of ROMA, is struck by a college one of whose members, Aeschinus, is a freedman of the *princeps*;[1] his appearance contrasts with the later election of Tiberius to the same office. The inscriptions of (4) and (5), which—like (6)—have the heads of Caius and Lucius, are invariably blundered and cannot be certainly restored; but their differentiation seems probable. The magistrates of (6) are curiously comparable to those of (2); they are to be assigned to this mint owing to their resemblance to (4), whose attribution is based on style and ethnic.[2] The double gentile name of C. Julius Antonius confirms the supposition that Julio-Antonian colonies bore both epithets (p. 180).[3] Earle Fox[4] is responsible for the convincing attribution of (7), which is supported by finds of (8):[5] the former of these reinforces the demonstration by Simitthu(?) (p. 232) and Carteia[6] that changes of colonial formula may well occur at the same mint, unaccompanied by any administrative change. The long and otherwise unknown career of M. Aemilius Labeo is noteworthy. He was at least once *duovir*— like another M. Aemilius before him—and at least twice *quinquennalis*: (8) is the only Cnossian issue (with the possible exception of [10]) to be signed by holders of the latter office, and may, like similar issues at *coloniae* Dyrrhachium and Patrae (?) and *civitas libera* Leptis Magna (pp. 275, 265, 340), celebrate the quarter-centenary of the foundation. The head of Tiberius appears not only on (9) but also on (10) and (11): the magistrate, whose second tenure is recorded on these two coins but whose name has not survived, is therefore probably Ti. Caesar *IIvir iterum*. On the obverses also of (9)–(11) the portraits are the same: the legend of (10) indicates that Augustus is represented. Indeed, the relegation of Tiberius to the second place is inexplicable except on the supposition that Labeo, whose name precedes his, was the *praefectus* deputising for the *princeps*. This conclusion is confirmed by the interchangeability of the names of Augustus and Labeo on otherwise similar obverses. Thus (9)–(11) represent two tenures of the duovirate by Augustus and Tiberius. As a general rule the *princeps* held honorary magistracies without a colleague: but a Saguntine issue has shown that he accepted Agrippa in that capacity (p. 159), and the powers of Tiberius in the last years before his accession were more extensive than those of the earlier 'co-regent' (p. 430). Tiberius owes his several appearances on these issues to a *patrocinium* of the city.[7]

---

[1] Possibly he was the son or kinsman of an Aeschinus who was prominent in Roman banking concerns in 69 B.C. (Herzog, *PW*. XVII, 1425; cf. Babelon, *Aréthuse*, XVIII, 1928, p. 21). See p. 322.

[2] Borrell, *Rn*. 1845, p. 340. 6, quotes an unplausible variety.

[3] For a similar double *gentilicium* at this time cf. C. Julius Calpurnius (Ramsay, *Anatolian Studies to Buckler* [1939], p. 210).

[4] *JIAN*. II, 1899, p. 90.

[5] Athens mus.

[6] Delgado I, p. 92; Vives IV, p. 26.

[7] For other *patrocinia* of Tiberius under Augustus, cf. *Eph. Epigr*. III, 53 and, according to Hübner, *CIL*. II, 1113.

16. MACEDONIA ET ACHAIA

(a) ACHAIA: Dyme, Patrae, Corinth

Three early coins can be assigned to a mint in the southern section of the province, united until 27 B.C., of Macedonia-Achaia (p. 67 n. 10):

(1) C. I. D., C. IVL. TANG. C. ARRI. A. F. laureate head of Julius to right—IIVIR. QVINQ. EX D. D. Plough.[1]
(2) same inscription. Head of Minerva in helmet to right—same inscription. Fasces and subsellium.[2]
(3) CN. OCTA. M. A̅N̅T. ARIS̅T̅A̅ ········ same head of Minerva—C. I. A. DVM. in wreath.[3]

The last has the name of **Dyme**; its similarity to (2) makes it inevitable that both colleges are of the same city, and that attributions to Dertosa[4] and Parium[5] are wrong. Imhoof-Blumer[6] also notes a bevelled edge and peculiar fabric found on contemporary coins of the Achaian region; the neighbouring mint of Corinth, whose Antonian issues exhibit similar features (p. 267), confirms the attribution.

In connection with Lampsacus and Alexandria Troas (p. 245) it has been pointed out that heads of Julius, especially those—like the present one—which are imitated from *denarii* of Sepullius Macer, are likely to date from the first years of Antony's government; this view is supported by Kornemann,[7] who fixes 44 as the upper limit for the foundation of Dyme. Furthermore, the gentile name of M. Antonius Arista(? rchus) indicates that at least one of the citizens was enfranchised by the triumvirs;[8] Cn. Octavius may equally have been a *libertus* of Octavian, but perhaps was an older man, a bore of that name whom Cicero avoided.[9] The coin signed by these two is shown to be early by its close stylistic resemblance to (2), which could scarcely be later than the forties. The ethnic of (3) cannot therefore represent C(*olonia*) I(*ulia*) A(*ugusta*). By the analogy of a number of *coloniae Antoniae* and *municipia Antonia* which existed until Octavian changed their epithet to *Iulia* (pp. 180, 302), the ethnic of Dyme on this piece may be interpreted as C(*olonia*) I(*ulia*) A(*ntonia*). It cannot, however, be determined whether Caesar, Q. Hortensius, or Antony was responsible for the foundation. The change from C. I. D. to C. I. A. D. suggests that Antony 'refounded'

---

[1] Berlin; Imhoof-Blumer, *MG*. p. 165. 42.
[2] Berlin; ibid. 43.
[3] Paris; ibid. 44 (part not read).
[4] Hübner, *MLI*. p. 38.
[5] de Saulcy, *Mémoires de la Société française de numismatique et d'archéologie*, 1873, p. 29.
[6] Ibid. But his argument based on a distinction between D. D. (at Dium) and EX D. D. (here) is groundless. Cf. p. 232 for similar changes of formula at single mints.
[7] 107. See also p. 4.
[8] Such arguments must, however, be treated with caution: e.g. Balbus, who was enfranchised by Pompey, took the name of Cornelius—cf. Syme, *Actes du Ve Congrès de Papyrologie*, 1937, pp. 466f.
[9] Cic. *Fam.* VII, 16. 2.

THE ROMAN COLONIES 265

an already existing (or planned) settlement of Julius by adding a draft of citizens. He had already accepted the principle of the refoundation of colonies, in the face of legalist protests from Cicero;[1] the practice later became common. In this case both coinages are probably foundation-issues.

There are two very rare issues with a portrait of Augustus, and types respectively of Victory on a prow,[2] and a prow alone (Pl. IX, 11).[3] On both the ethnic is C. I. A. D.: since A(*ntonia*) is no longer possible, this indicates a third foundation, with the epithet A(*ugusta*), at a date when Achaia was already a separate *provincia*. For no good reason Kornemann[4] rejects an explicit statement by Pausanias about Dyme: Αὔγουστος δὲ ὕστερον προσένειμεν αὐτὴν Πατρεῦσιν.[5] Not every colony could be successful, and it was remarkable that so many survived; but Dyme (like Pella, Heraclea Pontica, and Lampsacus) was not one of them, and it is **Patrae**, colonised in c. 16 B.C. as *colonia Aroe Augusta*,[6] which henceforward coins.[7] This colony was given a better chance by a synoecism of southern Aetolia to increase its population.[8] There is only one certain Augustan issue, after 2 B.C.:[9]

PATER bare head to right of Augustus.
PATRIAE, C. A. A. P. colonist and priest ploughing.[10]

Here exceptionally all other titles are excluded in favour of the climactic honour of *pater patriae*. This emphasises the aspect of the *princeps* as universal *conditor* (p. 318), and thus has a special relevance to the lengthening category of isolated coinages explicitly commemorating the possession of *civitas*. In view of its late date, this piece does not celebrate the foundation itself, but probably, like others at Dyrrhachium, Leptis Magna, and perhaps Cnossus, its quarter-centenary (pp. 263, 295).

With the exception of Buthrotum, **Corinth** is the only Eastern colony with an extensive coinage whose issues have been, on the whole, satisfactorily defined and arranged. Earle Fox[11] first expelled a large number of misread and misattributed duoviral colleges, so that numismatists had to look elsewhere for a colonial clearinghouse;[12] later Miss Edwards[13] completed and revised his list from material found in

[1] He recounts (*II Phil.* 102) that Antony asked him whether such a refoundation would be correct, and complains that, when he replied that a new *deductio* would not be, but that a new draft could—to avoid the difficulty—be called an *ascriptio*, Antony ignored this clever advice and proceeded with a complete military *deductio* at the old site of Casilinum!
[2] Athens; Imhoof-Blumer, *MG*. p. 165. 45.
[3] BM, Berlin, Athens; ibid. 46.
[4] 107. Hahn, *Rom und Romanismus*, p. 93, actually speaks of an enlargement of Dyme.
[5] VII, 17; cf. Dorsch, *De civitatis romanae apud Graecos propagatione*, Diss. Breslau, 1886, p. 19.

[6] Kornemann 248; Dorsch, l.c. pp. 25 f.; Ritterling, *PW*. XII, 1226 and 1241, are contradictory.
[7] Coins of Tiberius attributed here belong to Dyrrhachium (p. 278).
[8] Cf. Jones, *GC*. p. 65.
[9] Little coins of uninformative type (e.g. Paris) look post-Augustan.
[10] *BMC*. 18, Paris, Hollschek coll. Wrongly described by M. IV, 136. 916, etc.
[11] *JIAN*. II, 1899, pp. 98 ff.
[12] They chose *coloniae* Panormus and Carthago Nova (pp. 194, 217).
[13] *Corinth*, VI (Coins).

excavation on the site. Two neglected pieces, however, without the signature of magistrates, are relevant to the foundation of the colony:

(1) CREATOR vase—CORIN. in wreath.[1]
(2) CAESAR bare head of Julius to right—[C]OR. statue in hexastyle temple; amphora (Pl. VIII, 19).[2]

The former, whether contemporary or (as at Babba [p. 222]) later than the *deductio*, adds to the terminology of colonial foundation. The poetic phrase suggests the paternal relationship, by an extension of which the founder and *patronus* is compared with the *pater* himself (p. 319). The type of the unpublished second coin is based on a *denarius* of c. 50 B.C.,[3] but lacks the features which give that a special significance; the temple cannot be identified, but is not that of Vesta (as on the prototype) since it contains a statue.[4] The elderly features are skilfully and originally executed; the name CAESAR suggests that the coin was issued before his deification in January 42, and therefore before the *régime* of Brutus. The foundation of a commercial colony at Corinth was one of the most important of the dictator's plans,[5] but opinion has differed hitherto as to whether it was undertaken before his death. This coin appears to answer the question in the affirmative:[6] it is quite distinct in style from the group of posthumous colonial issues with laureate portraits of Julius imitated from *denarii*.

Of those, indeed, an example occurs on another coin of Corinth, signed by the *duoviri* L. Certus Aeficius and L. Julius.[7] Julii often occur at Antonian foundations from a Julian plan, and the portraiture, whose analogies we have seen (p. 264), demands attribution to the government of Antony. Its early date within this period is indicated by the exceptionally full ethnic LAVS IVLI CORINT (p. 226). Alterations in Miss Edwards's chronology seem to be necessary. She assigns only three duoviral colleges, besides L. Certus Aeficius and L. Julius, to a date earlier than Actium—P. Tadius Chilo and C. Julius Nicephorus[8] (Pl. IX, 12) (with CORINTHVM an Accusative ethnic as at Thapsus [p. 225]), Insteius (on some specimens HINST.[9]) and L. Cassius,[10] P. Aebutius and L. Pinnius.[11] But the unique piece of the uncertain college [NO]VIO (?) ····A··[12] closely resembles, in style and portraiture of the dictator, the issues of L. Aeficius and L. Julius, and must be ascribed to a date scarcely less early. Also not later than Actium are issues of a sixth college, Q. Caecilius Niger and C. Heius Pamphilus,[13] with the same early fabric and type, and a head of Aphrodite with the coiffure of the thirties. Again, the coins of P. Aebutius, as *quinquennalis* with M.

---

[1] *BMC*. 690. [2] Vienna.
[3] *BMCR*. I, 3871.
[4] Cf., for the absence of this at the Temple of Vesta, Plattner-Ashby, *Topographical Dictionary of Ancient Rome*, p. 557; Ovid, *Fasti*, VI, 295 ff.
[5] Adcock, *CAH*. IX, pp. 707 f.; cf. Larsen, *ES*. IV, p. 446.
[6] Cf. Dorsch, *De civitatis romanae...propagatione*, p. 20; *pace* Lenschau, *PW. Suppl.* IV, 1033.
[7] Edwards, l.c., p. 6. 1.
[8] Ibid. 2. [9] *BMC*. 526.
[10] Edwards, l.c. 3. [11] Ibid. 4.
[12] Paris; cf. Earle Fox, l.c. p. 101.
[13] Edwards, l.c. 6.

Antonius Theophilus,[1] cannot be much later than his issue with L. Pinnius, which bears the head of Antony. There is no reason to postpone their year of office to c. 24 or even as late as c. 29, since *quinquennales* already functioned during the triumvirate, and the piece is of early appearance. Nowhere else during the triumvirate do as many as seven colleges coin. The abundance of money shows how the colony flourished, since here *aes* currency was issued not at regular intervals, or only for commemorative occasions, but to need[2] (p. 296).

The names of some of the magistrates are interesting. M. Antonius Theophilus was Antony's procurator in this region,[3] and a certain rascally Insteius from Pisaurum was another of his satellites[4] whose freedmen occur not only here but at Mytilene[5] and perhaps Attaleia.[6] Later, in the same way, we find henchmen of Augustus represented at Saguntum and Cnossus (pp. 163, 263). C. Julius Nicephorus, like Theophilus, was a Greek who had profited by his association with the Caesarian party; it is clear that steps were taken to control the policy of important Roman cities (p. 314). The Pinnii, too, were a family—probably of Pannonian origin[7]—whose great riches and business interests in the East[8] must have made them useful to the triumvir. The importance of wealth in candidates for quinquennalian office at this commercial city (as, to a lesser degree, at all Roman communities[9]) is further shown by the position of the Heii too, of whom others are found at Sparta[10] among the foremost plutocrats.[11] Moreover, M. Antonius Theophilus was the father of a notorious profiteer,[12] and L. Aeficius Certus[13] is likely to be of the same *familia* as the contemporary M. Aeficius M. f. Apollonius at Cnidus[14]—both were probably connected with the millionaire knight Aeficius Calvinus.[15] The Novii too had large financial interests near by at Delos during the Republic;[16] and a Chilo represented the banking-house of the Murrii in the fifties B.C.[17] Q. Caecilius Niger recalls Verres's quaestor of the same names, who was probably a Sicilian[18] and

---

[1] Edwards, l.c. 5, rightly reattributes from Pella; *pace* Imhoof-Blumer, *MG*. pp. 88 f., 107 A; Gaebler, *ZfN*. XXXVI, 1926, p. 124.

[2] Cf. Edwards, l.c. p. 4.

[3] Strabo XVII, 840; cf. Magie, *De vocabulis sollemnibus, etc.*, II, p. 112.

[4] Cf. Syme, *RR*. p. 132.

[5] *IG*. XII, 361; cf. Hatzfeld, p. 95—Isteius (sic).

[6] *BCH*. XIV, 1890, p. 621. 20, restored by Hatzfeld, p. 140 n. 6, as Steius.

[7] Schulze, p. 31 n. 4; cf. *CIL*. III, 9275. For other Illyrian financiers—Genthius, Bato—vide Herzog, *PW*. XVII, 1441.

[8] Cic. *Fam.* XIII, 61; cf. Frank, *ES*. I, p. 388; Carettoni, *Civiltà Romana*, III, 1938, p. 15.

[9] Cf. Stevenson, *RPA*. p. 173.

[10] Cf. Box, *JRS*. XXII, 1932, p. 173.

[11] Cf. Münzer, *PW*. VII, 2646. Not in Schulze.

[12] Pliny, *NH*. XXXV, 200. I owe this reference to R. Syme.

[13] His *cognomen* and *nomen* are transposed on the coin in accordance with a custom first observed in Cicero's letters (e.g. *Fam.* VI, 12. 2): cf. Schulze, l.c. p. 491.

[14] Le Bas, *Voyage archéologique*, III, 1572; cf. Hatzfeld, p. 117.

[15] Suet. *De viris illustribus* (*de claris grammaticis et rhetoribus*), 3; cf. von Rohden, *PW*. I, 475.

[16] Cf. Hatzfeld, *BCH*. XXXVI, 1912, p. 55; Herzog, *PW*. XVII, 1439.

[17] *CIL*. I², 924; cf. Herzog, l.c. 1426.

[18] Cf. Syme, *Papers of the British School at Rome*, XIV, 1938, p. 14 n. 68.

was suspected of Judaism.[1] In this company of financiers and adventurers appears a *cliens* of an ancient family with a patrician branch, the Aebutii.[2] The whole group provides a curious illustration of the new society which was riding on the crest of the Revolution, and of the ruling classes in this great Eastern colony.

The principate of Augustus, and establishment of a separate proconsul in Achaia, did not interrupt the coinage of Corinth. There remain issues of four pairs of *duoviri*,[3] one pair of *praefecti*[4] and two of *quinquennales*;[5] each college has a distinctive type.[6] Their names bear witness to the unchanged persistence of the Caesarian faction dating from Antony's *régime*; authority was still concentrated in the hands of a few families.[7] Theophilus's son Hipparchus—a civil war profiteer (p. 267)—made his peace with the new *princeps*,[8] and coins as *duovir* on two separate occasions, retaining his names M. Antonius;-the frequent survival of this combination shows how soon its prohibition was forgotten.[9] The hereditary character of office is likewise shown by the election of C. Julius Hera., who is probably Heraclanus the relative of Eurycles:[10] we find also a second P. Aebutius and a second C. Heius Pamphilus, the type and style of whose coins distinguish them from their earlier relatives[11]—Aebutius also adds SP(*urii*) F. He and C. Heius Pamphilus *jun.* coin as *praefecti*, PRF. ITER.,[12] with a style late enough to suggest that the elder grandsons of Augustus were the *duoviri* whom they represent.[13] The head of the third grandson Agrippa Postumus (Pl. IX, 14),[14] who is similarly honoured by two other colonies (pp. 255, 283), appears on a coin of a third Heius (C. Pollio) and of C. Mussius—not Mussidius[15]—Priscus. The Mussii were a family with extensive Balkan business-connections dating back for a century;[16] they occur a little later at Miletus.[17] The same college commemorates Augustus, Tiberius, and—significantly in this principate—Germanicus (Pl. IX, 16) and Drusus *jun.* (Pl. IX, 15). This colony—like Caesaraugusta, which already in c. A.D. 4 elected Tiberius to the duovirate (p. 218)—did not miss any opportunity to improve its position for the future. Since the coin in honour of Agrippa Postumus is rarest, the college may well

---

[1] Cic. *Div. in Caec.* 4; Plut. *Cic.* 7. 3; cf. Münzer, *PW.* III, 1231. [2] Cf. Klebs, *PW.* I, 442.
[3] C. Servilius C. f. Primus, M. Antonius Hipparchus; M. Novius Bassus, M. Antonius Hipparchus; C. Heius Pollio, C. Heius Pamphilus; C. Heius Pollio, C. Mussius Priscus (Edwards, l.c. p. 6).
[4] P. Aebutius Sp. f., C. Heius Pamphilus *Prf. iter.* (ibid. p. 5).
[5] Cn. Publicius Regulus, M. Antonius Orestes; P. Aebutius Sp. f., C. Julius Hera(clanus) *quin. iter.* (ibid. p. 6).   [6] Cf. Edwards, l.c.
[7] Cf. at the peregrine cities—Jones, *GC.* pp. 170 ff.
[8] Plut. *Ant.* 73. 2.
[9] Cf. Charlesworth, *CAH.* x, p. 112.
[10] West, *AJA.* xxx, 1926, p. 391.

[11] Cf. Earle Fox, l.c. p. 95. For this family vide Box, *JRS.* XXII, 1932, p. 173.
[12] Edwards, l.c.; *pace* Earle Fox, l.c. p. 93.
[13] A small coin, without magistrates' names (BM, *Milan Cat.* 339), bears the heads of two young princes who are unidentifiable (pl. IX, 13): Laffranchi (*Milan Cat.* p. 34 n.) considers them to be Nero and Drusus, the brothers of Caligula.
[14] Shown, enlarged, by Pietrangeli, *Civiltà Romana*, VII, 1938, p. 21.
[15] Edwards, l.c. p. 6. 13. The correction is ignored by Miss Newby (p. 77).
[16] E.g. *CIL.* III, 609 (Dyrrhachium); Ἀθηνᾶ, XI, p. 271. 2 (Chalcis).
[17] *Revue des études grecques*, VI, 1893, pp. 179, 181, 188, 193; cf. Hatzfeld, p. 161.

be dated to the year of his disgrace.¹ A number of anonymous issues, with athletic types,² may or may not have been current; local bronze *tesserae* were also issued, with D. D. showing their official origin.³ The bulk of the coinage as a whole well illustrates the enormous commercial importance and success of this colony, which was not only planned but apparently founded in the dictator's own lifetime.⁴

(*b*) MACEDONIA—EPIRUS. Buthrotum, Cassandrea, Dium, Philippi, Dyrrhachium, Pella.

Owing to the ambiguity of a passage from Strabo,⁵ it is uncertain whether Epirus was attached in the Augustan period to Macedonia or Achaia; its southern region probably formed part of the latter province,⁶ but no conclusion can be reached about the north, in which lay **Buthrotum** (as also Dyrrhachium, p. 275). At all events this city belonged, in the earlier part of our period, to the combined proconsulship of Macedonia-Achaia. Its issues, like those of Cnossus, are perhaps of less general historical interest than the issues of Asia Minor and Macedonia; however, they raise a number of points connected with colonial procedure. The colleges of magistrates fall approximately into the following order:

(1)⁷ ······ et Sura [*IIvir.*⁸] *iter*.
(2)⁹ T. Pomponius, A. Cocceius¹⁰ *IIviri ter*.
(3)¹¹ P. Dastidius,¹² L. Cornelius *IIvir. Q. A.* (Pl. VIII, 20).
(4)¹³ P. Pomponius Graecinus [Milesius¹⁴], M. Pullienus¹⁵ *IIvir. quin*.
(5)¹⁶ Q. Naevius Sura, A. Hirtuleius¹⁷ *IIvir. B*.
(6)¹⁸ Graecinus *III* [et Sura] *quin*.

---

¹ Cf. Edwards, l.c. ² Ibid. p. 7.
³ Ibid. p. 9. Many other cities issued these tokens, which are not considered relevant to the present study, though their exact purpose is usually obscure: cf. Rostovtzeff, *Svintsoveya Tessere*, etc.
⁴ The variety of portrait-models used is particularly expressive of the futility of assigning *aurei* and *denarii* to the same area as any single group of cities which copies their heads on coins: if this method were permissible, it would be necessary to attribute the *denarii* of the East, of Lugdunum, and of the 'Caesaraugusta' group all to Corinth, since the heads of all three are imitated by the Corinthian die-engravers!—e.g. imitations of *BMC*. 316, 602 (BM), 666, etc. (Berlin), 500, etc. (Cambridge), 665? (Edwards). *Denarii* circulated widely, and the portrait-models were copied throughout the empire as each superseded the last: attribution of the *denarii* from the appearance of similar heads at this or that city is based on a false hypothesis. See pp. 122, 222, 83, 468.

⁵ XVII, 840; cf. Mommsen, *Provinces of the Roman Empire*, I, p. 256 n. 1.
⁶ Keil, *CAH*. XI, p. 557; but cf. p. 565; cf. Larsen, *ES*. IV, p. 437.
⁷ Imhoof-Blumer, *MG*. p. 138. 28; in trade.
⁸ Berlin.
⁹ Vienna; misread by Gardner, *BMC*. 1.
¹⁰ For the family, 'nobility of the revolution', vide Syme, *RR*. pp. 382, 385.
¹¹ Imhoof-Blumer, l.c. 30; BM, Naples.
¹² For the Messapian *gens* vide Schulze, p. 39 n. 1.
¹³ Ibid. 34; cf. Scholz, *NZ*. 1902, p. 26; Berlin.
¹⁴ Imhoof-Blumer, l.c. 36; Berlin, etc.
¹⁵ For the N. Italian name vide Schulze, p. 367.
¹⁶ Ibid. 27; Paris, Turin.
¹⁷ For the *gens* vide Schulze, p. 458. A L. Hirtuleius had been quaestor to Sertorius (Livy, *Ep*. XC, XCI).
¹⁸ Ibid. 37 ff.; cf. *BMC*. 2; Paris, Vienna.

The Sura of (1) must be earlier than the *duovir* of (5), since their coins have different ethnics, C. I. BVT. and C. A. BVT. respectively; we may assume a refoundation by Augustus (p. 305) who is portrayed on the latter coin. The other pieces, many of which, if not all, must be later than (1), have the plain ethnic BVT[HR].; such reversions to simplicity have been noted elsewhere (p. 266). A specimen of (1) reading ···ET SVRA ITER.[1] proves that the legend on the other variety is not ···ET SVRA IIVIRI TER. Contrarily, Gardner's[2] interpretation of (2) as IIVIRI EP., from an example on which the sixth letter resembles an (I),[3] is shown to be wrong by an example reading IIVIR. TER.[4] The same piece corrects the *praenomen* of Cocceius from Caius to Aulus. (3) lacks an ethnic, but must be placed here owing to its similarity in types and style to a coin of M. Pullienus.[5]

An interpretation of Q. A. on (3) is necessary. This is such a common abbreviation for Q(*uaestor*) A(*erarii*) that it could not have been understood if it represented any other title (p. 20).[6] Now it often happens that the municipal office of *quaestor aerarii* (*arcae*) is mentioned in inscriptions at the end of the *cursus honorum*.[7] Since such lists regularly include the successive posts in order of tenure,[8] Mommsen[9] and Spehr[10] consider that the *quaestura aerarii* was perhaps even superior to the duovirate, but Mantey[11] shows that lesser magistracies could be accepted after the duovirate. An alternative solution, which he offers, is corroborated by the present piece. The magistrates who place their names on colonial coins do not, as on inscriptions, record past distinctions and offices, but only their present office. The title of P. Dastidius and L. Cornelius therefore confirms his supposition[12] that the *quaestura aerarii* was in some cities at least coincidental with the chief magistracy.[13] At Buthrotum the later coinage is in general reserved for even higher financial officers, the *quinquennales*, who exercised a general supervision over the activity of the treasury;[14] however, the duoviral issue (5) may also be late, since it alone has C(*olonia*) A(*ugusta*).

[1] Berlin.
[2] *BMC.* 1.
[3] BM.
[4] Vienna.
[5] Imhoof-Blumer, l.c. 32; Berlin.
[6] Mantey, *De gradu et statu quaestorum, etc.*, Diss. Halle, 1882, p. 34, believes that this title is not pre-Trajanic. But even if Mommsen's supposition of an earlier appearance (*SB. Leipzig* 1849, p. 249; pace *Eph. epigr.* III, pp. 324, 327) is incorrect, the *argumentum ex silentio*, dubious in any case when the evidence is so slight, is shattered by this coin.
[7] *CIL.* v, 3938, 4459, 2785; cf. Orelli, *Inscriptiones Latinae Selectae*, 3966, etc.
[8] Mantey, l.c. p. 14.
[9] *CIL.* v, p. 240.
[10] *De summis magistratibus coloniarum atque municipiorum*, Diss. Halle, 1881, p. 38.
[11] L.c. p. 35.
[12] L.c. p. 49.
[13] Identity of the two offices is, by this analogy, likely to be the explanation of some of the inscriptions in which the quaestorship is omitted from the *cursus honorum*, e.g. Mantey, l.c. pp. 15, 49. It is possible also, though not considered by Mantey, that a number of appearances of plain *q*. at the end of a *cursus honorum* (e.g. *Inscr. Reg. Neap.* 3939, 4635, 4765, 5024) refer to the *quaestura aerarii*, since the ordinary quaestorship seems hardly important enough to warrant a tenure after the duovirate (cf. Last, *CAH.* XI, p. 461; *Dig.* L, 4. 18. 2). But the whole of this intricate problem needs a reconsideration based on the numismatic evidence which Mantey, Spehr, etc., ignore.
[14] Cf. Hardy, *Six Roman Laws*, p. 148.

THE ROMAN COLONIES 271

The same Sura who appears on (5) may be deciphered on a specimen of (6),[1] on which the single name of Graecinus is accompanied by the *type parlant* of a leg. 'B', in the reverse field of (5), suggests that the figure, who appears to be raising a cup for a toast, is the *genius* of Buthrotum; this issue is likely to commemorate the Augustan *restitutio* of the city, whose epithet it alone records. Since M. Pullienus *quin.* signs one coin by himself, another on which Graecinus *Milesius* (his colleague on [4]) appears in equal seclusion is no doubt parallel and contemporary. This Milesian must be a freedman of P. Pomponius Graecinus, known from the *Amores* of Ovid[2] (c. 15/14 B.C.), who became *consul suffectus* in A.D. 16.[3] T. Pomponius no doubt owes his *gentilicium* to a member of the same family, Atticus, who had possessed large estates at Buthrotum.[4]

The personifications SALVTIS[5] and CONCORDIA[6] which appear on coins of Graecinus and Pullienus are noteworthy for various reasons. The 'Possessive' Genitive Case is a Republicanism[7] not found on the Roman series until the Civil Wars of 68–70. It is remarkable to see on an *aureus*,[8] attributed to the revolt of Civilis (and excluded from an earlier date on grounds of style), the conjunction of the same personifications with the same difference of Case—SALVTIS CONCORDIA—suggesting that their connection is due to a special association and formula; the coincidence can hardly be accidental. Two writers confirm this conclusion. In 11 B.C., as Dio[9] announces, Augustus used a sum of money, subscribed for an effigy of himself, to erect instead statues of Salus Publica, Concordia and Pax. Ovid[10] records of March 30th: *Ianus adorandus, cumque hoc Concordia mitis, Et Romana Salus araque Pacis erit*. The word *Romana* is the key to the early manifestation, on these Buthrotan issues, of the kind of Imperial abstraction which became so prevalent and important in the propaganda of the years following the death of Nero.[11] The passages quoted make it significant that, at this early date when such ideas are still partly unformulated and coin-types on the whole somewhat feeble,[12] PACIS is found on a coin of Pella to complete the triad (p. 281). GEN. POP. ROM., ROMA, and SPES also occur colonial issues under Augustus (pp. 173, 263, 281); but on the official series the concrete is still preferred, and even under Tiberius abstractions are often presented in the form of a compliment to the ladies of the *domus principis* (p. 146). The PACIS type is as early as 25 B.C., but the coincidence at Buthrotum of Concordia and Salus is likely to refer (for some reason unknown) to the gesture of Augustus in 10 B.C. By calculation from the first foundation by L. Plautius Plancus (p. 9), a colonial *lustrum* fell due in

---

[1] Imhoof-Blumer, l.c. 38; Paris.
[2] II, 10; cf. *Ex Ponto* IV, 9.
[3] *CIL*. VI, 10399; cf. *PIR*. III, 76. 540.
[4] Cic. *Att*. I, 5, XII, 6, 16 A. I owe this suggestion to R. Syme.
[5] Imhoof-Blumer, l.c. 35; Vienna.
[6] Ibid. 36; Berlin.
[7] Mattingly, *BMC. Imp*. p. lxix. See also p. 153.
[8] Ibid. p. 308; Vienna.
[9] LIV, 35. 2.
[10] *Fasti* III, 881.
[11] Cf. Charlesworth, *The Virtues of a Roman Emperor*, pp. 12 ff.
[12] Cf. Syme, *RR*. pp. 469 f.

c. 10 B.C.; to this we may assign the quinquennalian college (4). By allotting the third quinquennalian tenure of Graecinus to c. A.D. 1, we see that, as at many other mints, the colonial series terminated some years before Augustus's death: discoveries of official *aes* in Epirus (p. 116) show that local issues were withdrawn in its favour.

Gaebler and Kubitschek have written the latest words about Macedonia, but not the last. Nor does the present writer aspire to do this. The coins are mostly very rare and very enigmatic; in no other part of the Empire, except perhaps Africa, were the die-engravers so lacking in forethought for future students of history. However, an investigation—taking into consideration certain new conclusions and unpublished pieces—necessitates drastic reattributions both of the coins and of colonial datings. It has, for example, escaped notice that the numismatic record of the period commences with two official Roman series, struck respectively by (?) M. Acilius, Caesarian *quaestor pro praetore*, and Q. Hortensius Hortalus, Republican *praefectus coloniis deducendis* (pp. 17, 33). The status of the second of these officials has been seen to suggest an extensive colonial programme: indeed, Brutus himself had promised, on the morrow of the dictator's assassination, that he would carry out all foundations that Caesar had planned (p. 33). Besides the official issue of Hortensius, two coins of the highest rarity survive as evidence of the fulfilment of this promise. The first of these is the following small piece (of different style from the larger proconsular coin of Hortensius):

HAMMON head of Jupiter Ammon to right—HORT. COL. D. two corn-ears (Pl. VIII, 21).[1]

Ammon was the tutelary deity of **Cassandrea**,[2] to which this coin is to be assigned. The reverse legend may represent *Hortensius coloniae deductor*[3] or *Hortensius coloniam deduxit*.[4] Here is a preliminary argument against Kornemann's[5] belief that Augustus was the originator of five Macedonian colonies—including Cassandrea. Like other cities that celebrate their *deductio* by such issues, Cassandrea does not strike again for many years.[6]

The foundation-coinage of another city is equally isolated:

COL. DIENSIS plough—DIANA BAPHVR. Diana Baphyras[7] running to right, with bow and arrow, and trampling on a *vexillum* lying horizontally with *taenia* waving upwards (Pl. IX, 18).[8]

[1] Gaebler, *ZfN*. XXXVI, 1926, p. 139; Berlin, Paris.
[2] Kubitschek, *Gnomon*, XIII, 1937, p. 24.
[3] Cf. Babba, and *creator* at Corinth (pp. 222, 266).
[4] Cf. Sinope, Dyrrhachium (pp. 252, 275).
[5] 242 ff.
[6] But, *pace* Gaebler, l.c., earlier than Claudius: there are coins of Tiberius (Dresden, ? Istanbul), and probably Caligula (Gotha).
[7] The local river is Baphyras; cf. Oberhummer, *PW*. II, 2850.
[8] Gaebler, *NG*. III, 2, p. 1; Vienna, BM; misread by Friedländer (*Bull. dell' Inst. di corr. arch.* 1870, p. 197), Imhoof-Blumer (*MG*. p. 74. 69), Head (*BMC*. 2). The type is clear on the Berlin specimen.

A number of coins attributed by Gaebler to Dium belong to Dyrrhachium (p. 275): on all that remain, with the exception of this alone, the colony is described as *colonia Iulia*.¹ Kubitschek interprets the reverse correctly, but with a protest that Diana, the tutelary goddess, can hardly be intended to trample down the *vexillum*,² of which use was commonly made in the foundation of colonies.³ However, a strangely similar type is pointed out by Alföldi⁴ on a *denarius* from the same part of the Empire, struck by Brutus: on that, Victory is trampling on the sceptre, which symbolised Caesar's illegal domination and was probably a type of his Macedonian *orichalcum* issue (p. 17). Now a *vexillum* could be made the object of hostile propaganda as well as a sceptre, especially on a colonial coin, and it is significant that, on 16 Mar. 44, Brutus explicitly alluded in public to the hateful military character of the dictator's colonial *deductiones*—he disliked the word *imperare*⁵—and announced his intention of avoiding such methods at his own foundations (p. 33). Although he failed entirely to live up to this civilian ideal,⁶ it is in accordance with his programme that Dium should, under his government, strike its inauguratory issue with a type adapted from his contemporary *denarii* and alluding to the same trend of his professed policy.⁷ There are two further reasons for attributing the foundation of Dium to the time of Brutus. First, the ethnic omits the epithet *Iulia* which rarely fails to accompany the word *colonia* at Julian foundations; secondly, an inscription,⁸ as rightly interpreted by Kubitschek,⁹ identifies its tribe as Papiria, which is found also at Cassandrea¹⁰—certainly established by Hortensius—but at no other Macedonian colony, and rarely elsewhere.¹¹

Thus two small Macedonian issues bear witness to the scope of the activity of Hortensius, the second *praefectus coloniis deducendis* of whom there is numismatic record. This title—probably reserved for comprehensive tasks and not held by contemporary founders of less importance such as Ti. Nero, Q. Orca and Cn. Plancus —became obsolete soon after Philippi. Hortensius is a proconsul to whom the title of *praefectus* was added; thereafter, the foundation of cities became a regular duty of

---

¹ Gaebler, *ZfN*. XXXVI, 1926, p. 127. The absence of the epithet here inspired Friedländer, l.c., with total lack of analogy or probability, to suppose that this is a pre-Caesarian colonial issue. An attribution to Balbinus (Head, *BMC*. l.c.) is based both on a misreading and on astonishing neglect of stylistic considerations.

² *Gnomon* XIII, 1937, p. 23 n. 2.

³ Gaebler, l.c. p. 126; cf. Cic. *II Phil*. 102.

⁴ *Röm. Mitt*. 1935, p. 110.

⁵ Quintilian IX, 3. 95; cf. Syme, *RR*. p. 320.

⁶ For his military colonies, vide Larsen, *ES*. IV, p. 448: for his levies in Macedonia, Appian, *BC*. III, 79; cf. Syme, *RR*. p. 295 n. 1.

⁷ That a *vexillum* occurs on the official issue of Hortensius need not seem contradictory to this interpretation: there it is accompanied by the other regular colonial emblems, the plough and the yoke, and the choice of the *vexillum* by the local mint at Dium as the symbol of an unpopular policy need have had no effect on a coin issued by different authority and perhaps far away, whose type merely includes the regular colonial features. No stigma attached to *vexilla* as such, but they were, on occasion, a convenient vehicle for symbolic propaganda; the apparent contradiction merely shows faulty co-ordination. See p. 34.

⁸ *CIL*. III, 592. ⁹ *Imp*. p. 241.

¹⁰ *Ephemeris Epigraphica* II, 1048.

¹¹ Kubitschek, l.c. p. 271.

governors, so that the special title was dropped (p. 206). The earliest Macedonian colonial issues of the Antonian *régime* illustrate this development:[1]

(1) A. I. C. V. P. head of Antony to right—Q. PAQVIVS RVF. LEG. C. D. colonist ploughing.[2]
(2) same—same inscription, man seated to left in curule chair: urn (Pl. VIII, 22).[3]
(3) same inscription, young head facing—same inscription and plough in wreath.[4]
(4) same—same inscription in wreath.[5]
(5) same inscription, urn—as (3).[6]

Coins of Sinope and Apamea suggest that Finite sentences are found on *deductio*-issues (p. 256); another of Dyrrhachium will demonstrate that these were in the form COLON(*iam*)··· DEDVX(*it*) (p. 275). The reverse of the present series should therefore be restored as Q. PAQVIVS RVF(*us*) LEG(*atus*) C(*oloniam*) D(*eduxit*). There is no evidence or analogy for the existence of any *legatus coloniae deducendae*: of the provincial *deductores* and *constitutores* (outside the imperial house) who coined in the triumvirate and principate, all who have been identified were also governors of provinces—thus the Oscan[7] Q. Paquius was Antony's governor in Macedonia-Achaia just as M. Turius, founder of Lampsacus, represented him in Asia (p. 246). We have seen that their title *legatus* is particularly applicable to the period of Antony's tour at the beginning of the triumvirate (p. 247); moreover, the predecessor of L. Marcius Censorinus (41 B.C.) in Macedonia is unknown,[8] just as there is a break in the Asiatic *Fasti* at the same time. The gaps are filled by Q. Paquius and M. Turius respectively. Ganter[9] describes these years as a period of provisional administration: this is true in so far as the governors, like those of Sextus Pompeius, did not use the regular proconsular title. Thus there is no reason to doubt the accepted interpretation A(*ntoni*) I(*ussu*),[10] which is paralleled at Paestum (p. 289). The ethnic C.V. P. has been rightly ascribed to *colonia victrix* Philippi[11]—founded just after the battle of that name. This attribution is confirmed by the appearance of that epithet (or a suitable allusion to the goddess Victoria) on later Augustan coins of the same colony:

COL. PHIL. plough—VIC. AVG. two *modii* (?).[12]
COHOR. PRAE. PHIL. three standards—VIC. AVG. Victory on *cippus*.[13]

---

[1] These are described in detail by Collart, *Philippes*, pp. 224 ff.
[2] Gaebler, *ZfN*. XXXIX, 1929, p. 261. 1; Berlin, Munich.   [3] Ibid. 2; BM, etc.
[4] Ibid. 3; Leningrad, Berlin.
[5] Ibid. 4; Berlin, Munich.
[6] Gotha. Others described (e.g. Gaebler, l.c. 5, 6) are false.
[7] Cf. Solmsen, *Studien zur lateinischen Lautgeschichte*, pp. 152, 171. For a somewhat later Paccius see Halaesa (p. 195).
[8] Gaebler, *NG*. III, 1, p. 7; cf. Ganter, p. 31.

[9] P. 35; cf. p. 39.
[10] Cf. *Lex Coloniae Genetivae Iuliae*, 104. Heuzey's suggestion *Augusta Iulia* (*Mission archéologique en Macédoine*, p. 18), improbable in itself, is eliminated by the presence of Antony's portrait.
[11] Gaebler, l.c.; cf. Imhoof-Blumer, *MG*. p. 253. Previously Eckhel's attribution to Gaul (*DN*. v, p. 265) had been maintained, e.g. by Ribbeck, *Senatores Romani*, p. 53. 280.
[12] Turin; Gaebler, *NG*. III, 2, p. 103. 16.
[13] BM, etc.; ibid. 14.

THE ROMAN COLONIES 275

A third coin of our period is the following:
 COL. AVG. IVL. PHIL. IVSSV AVG. laureate head of Augustus to right—
 AVG. DIVI F. DIVO IVL[IO] Augustus and Caesar, with outstretched hands,
 on a *cippus*; before it an altar[1] (Pl. IX, 22).

Probably these three pieces commemorate the refoundation. Antony had dedicated the first foundation to Julius—possibly as a *colonia Iulia Antonia* like Dyme (p. 264); the present group shows that Augustus ordered a second foundation,[2] for the benefit of ex-members of the praetorian cohorts, which had been reconstituted as an Imperial guard (p. 437). The last coin indicates that Julius and Augustus became the tutelary deities of the colony.[3]

It is noteworthy that Dio,[4] speaking of c. 30 B.C., links Philippi with Dyrrhachium: τοῖς μὲν πλείοσι τό τε Δυρράχιον καὶ τοὺς Φιλίππους ἄλλα τε ἐποικεῖν ἀντέδωκε. But this statement does not enable us confidently to attribute the colony to c. 30, since, first, the epithet *Augusta*, instead of *Iulia*, on the coins of Philippi shows that this allotment at least was not actually made (or completed) until after 27 B.C., and the portrait-model[5] of the last coin suggests c. 2 B.C. as a *terminus post quem*;[6] secondly, it must also be remembered that a number of pre-Augustan colonies have only been saved from total oblivion by coins. Such foundations are neglected by Pliny, and the Augustan tradition quickly swamped all record of beneficent activity by Antony. A number of coins of considerable obscurity will be used to show that both these reasons for scepticism are relevant to **Dyrrhachium** (pp. 276 ff.), which was founded by Antony, and refounded by Augustus, again not in 30 B.C., but shortly before our era. Dorsch[7] and Kubitschek[8] remark with surprise that there appears to be no coinage of this town. The latter suggests, first, that it was probably not in the Augustan *lex provinciae*, and, secondly, that in Macedonia coining-right was associated with the *ius Italicum*. Such conjectures cannot be supported by evidence, analogy or probability; an alternative solution is provided by two unattributed coins. Of the earlier of these only a single example appears to survive:[9]

 COLONIA··········· bust of Venus to right, with wing at shoulder.
 Q. PA. (?)········DEDVX. tripod (Pl. IX, 21).

This piece is of early style and fabric suggestive of the forties: the initial letters on the reverse leave little doubt that Sestini's[10] attribution to Q. Paquius Rufus was correct,

[1] BM, Cambridge (*McLean* 3269), Milan, *Cat.* 313; misread by M. I, p. 846. 280; Cohen, *Description historique des monnaies frappées sous l'empire romain*, Aug. 739 f., etc.
[2] It is noteworthy that *iussu Augusti* takes the place of the earlier phrase *iussu populi* (cf. Sherwin-White, p. 132: Sisenna 17. 119): *auctoritas* takes the place of *lex*.
[3] A similar type appears at the free city of Amphipolis (*BMC.* 77).
[4] 50. 4. Cf. Collart, *Philippes*, p. 229.
[5] *BMC. Imp. Aug.* 538.
[6] If, as seems probable, the issue was contemporary with the refoundation.
[7] *De civitatis romanae...propagatione*, Diss. Breslau, 1886, p. 11.
[8] *Gnomon* XIII, 1937, p. 24.
[9] Paris.
[10] *Lettere* VII, p. 39; cf. Pellerin, *Recueil de médailles de peuples et de villes*, III, pl. CXVI, 1.

and that we may read Q PA[QVI. RVF. COL.] DEDVX(*it*). This Gaebler[1] refuses to believe, since, owing to its incompatibility with any of his groups, he rejects the coin from the Macedonian series altogether. The style is, indeed, not that of the cities on or near the Thermaic Gulf; but it is certainly that of eastern Europe, where east and west meet to produce a style which decisively but indefinably distinguishes its issues from those of Asia or of regions west and south of Rome (p. 478). The reverse type occurs particularly on the east shores of the Adriatic—for example, at Zacynthus and Buthrotum (pp. 40, 269)—probably owing to the influence of the oracle in the hinterland at Dodona.[2] This coin cannot be of Buthrotum itself, since the first founder of this colony was L. Plancus (p. 9). Gaebler[3] points out the regularity with which Macedonian cities honour their tutelary deity: it is therefore significant that the head on the obverse of this coin is closely copied from winged busts of Venus such as appear on Roman *denarii* (p. 49 n. 14). Now Venus was the tutelary goddess of Dyrrhachium,[4] which is precisely in the region indicated by considerations of style and type: a very similar bust is found near by at Phoenice.[5]

The attribution to Dyrrhachium, tenuous in itself, is strongly reinforced by another very rare series. This is represented by only two known specimens, both unattributed;[6] it has been ignored by Gaebler and all other writers except Boutkowski,[7] who completely misreads it. On the obverse is a bare head of Augustus to right, and on the reverse of one example,[8] within a wreath, can be read: C. I.$\overline{\text{VE}}$.[9]| TI. TAR. | II$\overline{\text{VIR}}$. Q.| D. D. (Pl. VIII, 23). In style this piece is so closely akin to the foundation-coin just described that it could hardly originate from any other region. Since, by the analogy of other Balkan colonies (p. 282), Ti. Tar. may well be the name of a single unaccompanied *quinquennalis*,[10] it is probable that the first line of the legend, with its characteristic ethnic form C. I., contains the titulature of the city—C(*olonia*) I(*ulia*) VE(*neria*). Venus was the special protectress of no suitable city[11] except Dyrrhachium, whose Julio-Antonian establishment has been indicated by the cognate earlier coin with the head of Venus.[12] The attribution of the later piece is confirmed by a convenient prosopographical probability. There is good reason to believe that L. Tarius Rufus, the proletarian Picentine,[13] became *legatus pro praetore* in Macedonia—temporarily at least 'imperial'—not long before or after his suffect consulship of 16 B.C.[14] Nothing, then,

---

[1] *ZfN.* xxxix, 1929, p. 269.
[2] Cf. Reisch, *PW.* v, 1678.
[3] *ZfN.* xxxvi, 1926, p. 138.
[4] Catullus xxxiv, 11; cf. Philippson, *PW.* v, 1887.
[5] Ugolini, *Albania antica*, II, p. 160, fig. 95.
[6] BM, Gotha. [7] *DN.* 1338. [8] Gotha.
[9] On the London specimen VE is not ligatured.
[10] In view, however, of the conclusions reached in the last section, it cannot be considered entirely impossible that the present *duovir* was not rather *quaestor aerarii*; cf. for a similar official p. 152.

[11] Sicca, Nabrissa and Rusicade are excluded on grounds of style and fabric.
[12] Confirmative of this date is a letter of Brutus in 43 B.C. (Cic. *Brut.* I, 6. 4), mentioning Dyrrhachium without reference to enfranchisement.
[13] Syme, *RR.* p. 362.
[14] Ibid. pp. 330 n. 4, 373, 376; cf. Groag, *PW.* (2*R.*), III, 2321, *L'année épigraphique*, 1936. 18; Πρακτικὰ τῆς ἐν Ἀθήναις ἀρχαιολογικῆς ἑταιρίας, IX, 1934, p. 12.

THE ROMAN COLONIES 277

is more likely than that TI. TAR(*ius*), the *quinquennalis* of the coin, owed his *nomen* and enfranchisement to this man. *Gentilicia* beginning with Tar. are infrequent, and the Tarii at least were of such humble origin that a local magistrate of this name could scarcely owe it to any but L. Tarius Rufus. Both coins, then, must be attributed to an Antonian *colonia Iulia Veneria* at Dyrrhachium. The later one probably belongs to the category of isolated issues commemorating an anniversary of the colony, as at a number of other cities (p. 295): the portrait-model (of c. 20–18 B.C.)[1] suggests that the occasion was the quarter-centenary in c. 17 B.C.—a date in accordance with probabilities concerning Tarius's governorship and with the fact, shortly to be demonstrated, that Dyrrhachium was still *colonia Iulia* at that date.

The parallel between Dyrrhachium and Philippi is now seen to be a double one: not only were both, as Dio relates, refounded by Augustus, but the first foundations of both were Julio-Antonian. Kornemann's[2] assumption of a second tribe at Dyrrhachium, Quirina,[3] if it were justifiable—which is extremely doubtful[4]—would suggest successive Roman foundations far more readily than the double community, Dyrrhachium-Epidamnus, whose existence he groundlessly deduces. Augustus was chary of founding completely new colonies, but often adopted the more cautious policy of reinforcing those planned by his predecessors (p. 305), which then became *Iulia Augusta*. In particular, as Dio informs us of Bononia,[5] he was anxious to efface Antonian colonies by refoundation.

His refoundation of Dyrrhachium, explicitly recorded by Dio, is illustrated by an *as* and a *semis* of another college whose relevance and even existence have been ignored:

(1) CAESAR AVGVSTVS bare head to right—C. V. R., M. IVS., M. HERENN-IVS IIVIR. QVINQ.; C. I. A. D. in field. Rome standing with spear and globe (Pl. VIII, 25).[6]

(2) do.—C. V. R., M. I., M. H̅E̅R. IIVIR. QVINQ. C. I. A. D. plough (Pl. VIII, 24).[7]

The two coins cannot be rejected,[8] but they must be drastically reconsidered. Imhoof-

---

[1] *BMC. Imp. Aug.* 681, etc.
[2] P. 549; cf. *CIL.* VIII, 3079.
[3] Besides Aemilia, whose date cannot be determined (Kubitschek, *Imp.* p. 242).
[4] Kubitschek, *Imp.* l.c.; Praschniker and Schober, *Schriften der Balkankommission, Akademie der Wissenschaften in Wien*, VIII, p. 38 n. 46.
[5] Dio L, 6. 3.
[6] Berlin, Gotha; Gaebler, *ZfN.* XXXVI, 1926, pp. 127 f.
[7] Vatican.
[8] Gaebler, l.c. p. 127, considers that the known examples of (1) have been tooled, and Marchese Serafini (as he stated to the writer) holds the same opinion of the unique and unpublished specimen of (2). In view of their close correspondence to each other, their distinctive style and their complete difference from all other coins, it is most unlikely that the legend of either has been radically altered. In the first place, forgeries of obscure colonial issues are unusual. Secondly, it is improbable that a forger should have worked on coins now as far apart as Berlin, Gotha and the Vatican; thirdly, it would have been stupid and unprofitable to alter three

Blumer states Macedonian provenance,[1] and attributes the coin to Dium on the grounds of the figure of 'Pallas', which appears on much later issues of that mint.[2] But Minerva-Roma is an obvious colonial type: she is found, for example, in the present period, at Cnossus with ROMA (p. 263). Even if her appearance were rare, there was nothing to prevent third-century craftsmen at Dium from imitating a first-century model from another Macedonian city. Dium was indeed known, at the end of the first century, as *colonia Iulia Augusta*.[3] But the epithet *Augusta* is perfectly appropriate to post-Augustan foundations (p. 198); and it is significant that Dium's coins of Tiberius[4] still describe it merely as COLONIA IVL. DIENSIS, whereas the present pieces include A(*ugusta*) in the ethnic. The earliest issue, and tribe, of Dium have been shown to indicate a proposed Julian foundation, accomplished by Brutus: after the battle of Philippi this would naturally reassume the Julian epithet. Pliny's mention of the colony[5] does not prove an Augustan foundation: his evidence concerning Dium may not have been earlier than A.D. 14[6]—perhaps it was considerably later. But it might, equally, have been the Brutan foundation which he knew and recorded, or even a foundation by Octavian between 31 and 27, as in Spain. At any rate the ethnic COLONIA IVL. DIENSIS on the coinage of Tiberius disposes of the possibility of an Augustan draft after 27. Dium, like Pella, does not become *Augusta* until a later date, and our two coins must be ascribed elsewhere.

Their true origin is indicated by comparison with Tiberian issues, with the heads of the ruling *princeps* (TI. CA[E]. C. I. A. D.) and of Augustus (AVG[V]. C. I. A. D.,[7] AVG. P. P.[8]), radiate and laureate respectively (Pl. VIII, 26). These have been allotted, for no good reason, to Dium,[9] Dyme[10] and even Dertosa:[11] but a better attribution is suggested by a striking resemblance in portraiture to the smaller piece of M. Jus. and M. Herennius (with the same ethnic C. I. A. D.) and to the issue of Ti. Tarius with C. I. V̄E. Since C. I. VE. is a colony at Dyrrhachium, it is impossible to refrain from ascribing the issues of M. Jus. and M. Herennius, and those of Tiberius with

coins which were already of unparalleled character, and would not gain in value by the alteration. Fourthly, it is most unlikely of all that he would have been astute enough to retouch in such a seemingly unintelligent way: the general shape of the letters remains, but their exact interpretation can only be regained from a knowledge of (1). Such a forger would have expended much labour, originality and subtlety without the least recompense. It is more reasonable to infer that (2), if not blundered, is a genuine coin unskilfully cleaned or tooled without reference to (1). For the alteration of (1) there is no inherent probability, and no evidence: it was only urged by Gaebler because he found that Imhoof-Blumer's reading DVR̄MIVS (*MG.* p. 74.

58) was incorrect, and could find no parallel or likelihood for a name C. VRMIVS. The pellet after the C is clearly present on both (1) and (2). Miss Newby (p. 82), copying from Boutkowski, is not even *au fait* with Gaebler's correction.

[1] *MG.* p. 74.   [2] Cf. Gaebler, l.c. p. 128.
[3] *CIL.* III, 548 = *Suppl.* 7281.   [4] *BMC.* 3.
[5] *NH.* IV, 35.   [6] Cf. Jones, *CERP.* pp. 495 f.
[7] TI. CAE., AVG.: BM, Athens, Imhoof-Blumer, *MG.* p. 165. 47. TI. CA., AVGV.: Vienna, Paris. Inscriptions blundered: Berlin.
[8] Vienna.   [9] BM.
[10] BM (also!), Paris, Vienna.
[11] Eckhel, *DN.* I, 47; Hübner, *MLI.* p. 38; Newby, p. 83—entirely inappropriate to style.

THE ROMAN COLONIES 279

C. I. A. D., to the same mint.¹ C. I. VE. and C. I. A. D., then, are successive stages of the same town: Dyrrhachium, like Philippi, was first settled in 42–41 by Q. Paquius Rufus, and then, after c. 16 B.C., by Augustus.

It is now possible to attempt an interpretation of the curious legends of (1) and (2). An issue of Apamea (p. 257), supported by inscriptions, has documented the known fact that the second foundations of Augustus provided him with the title *Restitutor*—which has a long and noteworthy history.² Since, therefore, the new ethnic C. I. A. D. does not contain the old *cognomen* VE(*neria*), and C. V., the initial letters of the reverse inscriptions of both (1) and (2), are on both coins separated by a pellet, it is difficult to resist the interpretation:

C(*oloniae*) V(*eneriae*) R(*estitutori*) M. IVS(*tuleius?*³) [*et*] M. HERENNIVS IIVIR(*i*) QVINQ(*uennales*) C(*oloniae*) I(*uliae*) A(*ugustae*) D(*yrrhachensium*).⁴

The portrait-model⁵ establishes c. 17 B.C. as an upper limit for the *restitutio*: this limit can be further advanced by the consideration that Ti. Tarius, who coined before the restoration, took his name from the governorship of L. Tarius Rufus not long after 16 B.C. Reckoning, then, from the *deductio* by Paquius Rufus in c. 42–41, the quinquennalian year of M. Justuleius (?) and M. Herennius must fall, at the earliest, in 12–11 B.C.

Confirmation of such a formula, and yet another sign of the numismatic emphasis on such foundations and refoundations, is found at Pella. This was another *colonia Iulia Augusta*,⁶ for which, by analogy with the rest, there is a strong general probability of a first Julian settlement, carried out by Antony or Brutus. Here again the numismatic evidence corroborates this likelihood. The earliest coins of this important colony are the following two:

(1) IMP. DIVI F. ACTIO Augustus standing to left on prow—NONIVS SVLPICIVS IIVIR. QVINQ. wreath on curule chair.⁷
(2) SPES COLONIAE PELLENSIS Hope standing to left—CAES. A. R. FLARVNT N. S. IIVIR. QVIN. bare head of Augustus to right.⁸

Since some specimens of the latter (Pl. VIII, 27)⁹ certainly show a pellet between the A and R immediately following CAES., Gaebler¹⁰ has made an extraordinary interpretation of the legend, which has won the acceptance of Regling¹¹ and the applause of

---

¹ A countermark of P̄ĒL(*la*) on (1) (Gotha) is no more suitable to coins of Dium than to those of Dyrrhachium, at the head of the *Via Egnatia* (cf. Philippson, *PW*. v, 1883).
² Cf. Gagé, *Byzantion*, XI, 1936, p. 333.
³ Vide Schulze, p. 459. Or Justus, or Justius, ibid.: vide *CIL*. x, 2631, 5670, XI, 578*a, b*. It is fruitless to ask why the names are divided in this way: at this distance of time we cannot identify the fortuitous elements in numismatics.
⁴ For *quinquennales* at refoundations, when these occurred in the lustral year of a previous settlement, see p. 161.
⁵ *BMC. Imp. Aug.* 663–9 (Berlin).
⁶ Kornemann 243; cf. Imhoof-Blumer, *MG*. p. 86. 98 f.
⁷ BM; Gaebler, *NG*. III, 2, p. 21.
⁸ Berlin, BM, Vienna, etc.: ibid. 20.
⁹ E.g. Berlin.
¹⁰ *ZfN*. XXXVI, 1926, pp. 118, 137; cf. *NG*. III, 2, p. 97.
¹¹ *WMK*. p. 91.

Kubitschek[1] (*ein der reizendsten Wahrnehmungen*). Gaebler considers this to be the first issue of a new colony, and, presuming a lack of copper in the neighbourhood,[2] maintains that the inauguratory *quinquennales* had to sell local raw materials in order to procure the medium for coinage. This view he bases on the solution of the legend as CAESA R(*uta*)—citing the legal phrase *ruta caesa* denoting raw materials. He goes on to explain that CAESAR is here the vehicle for a *double entendre* (like T-Ερμησ-σεων with a type of Hermes at Termessus), and produces this restoration of the whole inscription:

CAESA R(*uta*) FLARVNT N(*onius*) S(*ulpicius*) IIVIR(*i*) QVIN(*quennales*).

To this arresting supposition a number of objections can be raised:

(i) The clause would be pregnant with meaning to an impossible degree. The *quinquennales* did not strike their coins from the raw material; far less did they strike the raw material itself! Even the most compressed numismatic Latin could not achieve such a compendium; if the sentence were perpetrated, nobody would have understood it, even in an unabbreviated form.

(ii) The set phrase was not *caesa ruta*, but *ruta caesa*;[3] no example of the inversion is extant.

(iii) *Quinquennales* could not have been appointed in the first year of a newly enfranchised city; for example at Lampsacus we have found IIVIRI COL(*onia*) DED(*ucta*) PR(*imi*). Exceptions to this rule could only occur when Roman institutions had already been established at an earlier date, as, for example, when the foundation in question was a *restitutio* (p. 277) or a conversion from *Latinitas* (p. 161). These coins, then, signed by a pair of *quinquennales*, cannot be the foundation-issue of a *new* colony.

(iv) Gaebler's interpretation is confirmed by no parallel of any kind, whereas a large number of analogies support another view:—

The coinages of Apamea and Dyrrhachium (pp. 257, 277) provide examples of *restitutio* issues comparable to those, almost equally unrecognised, which commemorate *deductiones* and *constitutiones*. Pella, which was first a *colonia Iulia*, is likely to have been refounded, rather than founded, by Augustus. The Apamean series shows the formula S(*enatus*) C(*onsulto*) C(*oloniam*) R(*estituit*). Now at this period administrative *senatus consulta*, when proposed (as they so frequently were) by Augustus, were recorded with the addition *auctore Caesare Augusto* or *Caesaris auctoritate* (p. 445). The important coinages with SC and CA, existing side by side at single mints, have illustrated this conjunction, and shown that the two formulas were complementary and interchangeable (p. 108). Other sources effectively corroborate this conclusion as regards the colonial settlements. Apamea is restored SC, but a passage of the *Res*

---

[1] *Gnomon*, XIII, 1937, p. 23.
[2] But there were Macedonian copper-mines: vide Davies, *The Roman Mines in Europe*, p. 227 n. 4.
[3] *Thesaurus Ling. Lat.* III, 56; cf. *Totius Latinitatis Lexicon*, v, p. 279.

THE ROMAN COLONIES

Gestae,[1] according to the best interpretation,[2] mentions *colonias mea auctoritate deductas*, and this formula is paralleled elsewhere.[3] The same will apply to refoundations, such as that of *colonia Iulia Augusta* Pella. Since, therefore, owing to the clear existence of a pellet between the A and R,[4] CAESAR cannot be read (except as a possible *sous-entendre*) the legends of (2) can be restored as follows:

SPES in the exergue. COLONIAE PELLENSIS—CAES(*aris*) A(*uctoritate*) R(*estitutae*), FLARVNT N(*onius*) S(*ulpicius*) IIVIR(*i*) QVIN(*quennales*).

Pella must have been founded after the government of Brutus, since a Greek series with ΠΕΛΛΑΙΩΝ[5] is contemporary with Thessalonican issues[6] struck after his death. As at *colonia* Philippi, the first foundation which these coins imply must have been the work of Antony after the battle of that name. *Colonia* Philippi, which commemorates the battle, is unlikely to have been planned by Julius, and was therefore probably a *colonia Antonia*; Pella may equally have been in this category, or may have been one of the Julian colonies which the *régime* of Brutus did not have time to carry out,[7] and so plain *Iulia*. The date of the foundation can be deduced from the subsequent coinage of the city.

This stands in no less need of a reconsideration. Imhoof-Blumer,[8] followed by Gaebler, rightly attributes here the tridenominational issues of two further Augustan colleges:

(1) *As.* IMP. CAESARI AVGVSTO IX. COS. his laureate head to right—M. FICTORI.[9] M. SEPTVMI. IIVIR. QVIN. in wreath.[10]

Semis. PACIS head of Peace to right—M. FICTORIVS M. SEPTVMIVS IIVIR. QVIN. colonist ploughing to right.[11]

Quadrans. M. FICTORIVS IIVIR QVI. town walls with six towers—M. SEPTIMIVS IIVIR QVIN. Amazon shield (Pl. IX, 19).[12]

Quadrans. same inscriptions. *Praefericulum—strigiles*.[13]

---

[1] 28. Cf. below, p. 293.
[2] First by Wölfflin, *SB. München*, 1886, p. 267; accepted by D. M. Robinson, *AJP.* XLVII, 1926, p. 17; and Weber, *Princeps*, I, p. 252* n. 672.
[3] Cf. Pais, *Museo italiano di antichità classica*, I, 1885, p. 39; *CIL.* III, 1443, etc.
[4] The omission of pellets between words is not unknown (it occurs even on this coin, between COLONIAE and PELLENSIS, and CAES(*aris*) and A(*uctoritate*)): but except at Emporiae, where a special ornamental custom inserts a dot between every letter (p. 154), there is no example of their random and otiose insertion, which would defeat the object of facilitating interpretation. This facilitation is particularly necessary on coins such as those of Sinope and the present city, where a Finite sentence extends from obverse to reverse.
[5] Gaebler, *NG.* III, 2, p. 96. 19.
[6] Ibid. p. 121.
[7] This is preferred by Dorsch, *De civitatis romanae... propagatione*, Diss. Breslau, 1886, p. 14.
[8] *MG.* p. 88.
[9] For the *gens* vide Schulze, pp. 108, 332. C. Fictorius C. L. Moschus appears at Tibur (*Ephemeris epigraphica*, IX, 1913, no. 915).
[10] Gaebler, l.c. p. 96. 23; BM, Berlin.
[11] Ibid. 24; BM.
[12] Ibid. 25; BM, Berlin.
[13] In trade.

(2) *As.* AVGVSTVS IMP. bare head to right—C. HERENNIVS L. TITVCIVS[1] IIVIR. QVIN. in wreath.[2]
Semis. same inscription; horseman to right—as last.[3]
Quadrans. C. HERENNIVS IIVIR QVIN. *praefericulum*—L. TITVCIVS IIVIR QVIN. *strigiles*.[4]

The close correspondence in types shows that these two colleges are of the same city. (1) is dated to 25 B.C.: its *quinquennales* are well suited therefore to follow the inaugural *quinquennales* of *col.* Pella *restituta*, Nonius and Sulpicius, to whose *asses* the present coins display a marked resemblance of style and fabric. Since, moreover, the view of the city on the *semis* is peculiarly apt to the highly fortified palace-town of Pella,[5] Imhoof-Blumer's attribution is very well attested.

It is therefore particularly hard to follow his and Gaebler's ascription to a different mint (Dium) of the coinage under Tiberius with C. BAEBIVS P. F., L. RVSTICELIVS BASTERNA IIVIR. QVINQ. D. D.[6] and L. RVSTICELIVS CORDVS IIVIR QVINQ. D. D.[7] These resemble the currency of Pella in the following respects: (i) style, thickness and fabric; (ii) both include *asses* with legend in several lines within a wreath, an arrangement strongly reminiscent of the *asses* of Fictorius and Septumius, and Herennius and Titucius; (iii) a *quadrans* of C. Baebius P. f. and L. Rusticelius Basterna shares a rare type of *praefericulum* and *strigiles*, referring to the quinquennalian games,[8] with the *quadrantes* of both Pellan magistrates. The coins of Baebius and Rusticelius are found in Bulgaria,[9] and are sometimes countermarked PEL(*la*):[10] such countermarks frequently include the ethnic of the coins to which they are affixed.[11] No reason for attribution to Dium can be discovered except the particularly feeble analogy of D. D. on other coins of that colony:[12] the formula is, in fact, frequent at many cities. These coins of Tiberius are certainly of Pella.

They permit two further coins of the principate of Augustus to be ascribed to the same mint. A coin whose patently Macedonian appearance escaped Gaebler's notice bears the head of the *princeps* (with AVGVSTVS) and on the reverse, round D. D., the legend P. BAEBIVS IIVIR QVINQ. (Pl. IX, 20).[13] Imhoof-Blumer attributed this also to Dium, rightly noting that P. Baebius is likely to be the father of C. Baebius P. f. who appears on the Tiberian issue just described. In view of our conclusion regarding the latter, this very argument supports attribution of the present coinage not to Dium but to Pella. Secondly, among the hotch-potch of coins habitually allotted to

---

[1] From a South Italian family: cf. Schulze, p. 405.
[2] Imhoof-Blumer, *MG.* p. 88. 104; Sofia. Omitted by Gaebler.
[3] Gaebler, l.c. 26; Berlin.
[4] Ibid. 27; Munich.   [5] Livy XLIV, 46.
[6] Imhoof-Blumer, *MG.* p. 74. 59 ff.; cf. Gaebler, l.c. Dium 3.
[7] Ibid. 62 ff.; cf. ibid. 4.
[8] Gaebler, l.c.   [9] Sofia mus.
[10] Gaebler, l.c.; BM, etc.
[11] E.g. C. G. I. P. at Parium (p. 246), and coinage of seven Spanish cities countermarked with their own ethnic (p. 299).
[12] Imhoof-Blumer, *MG.* p. 74.
[13] Copenhagen, BM, Berlin; Imhoof-Blumer, l.c. no. 57.

Carthago Nova (p. 215) lies one whose east European style particularly revolts against ascription to that city (which is based solely on the absurd imagination that *quinquennales* were peculiar to its coinage[1]), and whose types are closely connected with those of an Augustan coin of Philippi: Victory appears in the same guise on both, and on both reverses are standards—three at Philippi, two on the present coin (Pl. VIII, 28).[2] This, therefore, is likely to be Macedonian, but the different number of standards alludes to different circumstances of settlement, and confirms the indication of the spectrograph[3] that Philippi is not the mint. The magistrates are C. AQVINVS MELA IIVIR QVIN. and P. BAEBIVS POLLIO IIVIR QVIN. The latter of these is readily identifiable with P. Baebius, the father of Caius, of Pella, and this must be the mint of the coin. A fifth and last college of moneyers at Pella may be inferred from an unpublished piece whose figure of Victory is identical to that on the last-mentioned pieces.[4] The reverse legend is illegible, but on the obverse is AGRIPPA·····, with the head of Agrippa Postumus as a child (Pl. IX, 17).

The chronology of the mint can be deduced from the coins of M. Fictorius and M. Septumius, which are dated to 25 B.C. (COS. IX.). Thus the *restitutio* of the colony under Nonius and Sulpicius must be assigned to 30 B.C. From their quinquennalian title, it can be inferred that the first foundation took place in 40 or 35, probably the former; and their date proves that the title of *Augusta* subsequently borne by Pella[5] is the product of a later foundation—probably post-Augustan, following the economic collapse of the colony.[6] C. Herennius and L. Titucius, and C. Aquinus Mela and P. Baebius Pollio, are likely to belong to 20 and 15 B.C. respectively. Since the issue of P. Baebius (alone) derives its portrait-model from the principal series of CA—AVGVS-TVS *aes*, it falls readily into the next quinquennalian year, 10 B.C.: the unknown college honouring Agrippa Postumus—who is likewise portrayed at Corinth and Apamea—is plausibly attributable to 5 B.C. Thereafter the coinage ceased, no doubt in favour of the official *aes*, imitated by P. Baebius, which was designed for these regions. Even so, Pella, as the present survey has revealed its issues, stands alone as a mint of some importance among cities whose mintages were isolated and entirely commemorative.

[1] Heiss, p. 274.
[2] BM, etc., var. at Cambridge: Heiss, l.c. 8.
[3] Spectrogram 65; cf. Philippi, Spectrogram 64.
[4] Paris ('uncertain').
[5] Cf. Ulpian, *De Censibus*, 1.
[6] Vide Lucian, *Alex.* 6; Dorsch, *De civitatis romanae apud Graecos propagatione*, Diss. Breslau, 1886, p. 15.

17. ITALY: Paestum

There remains only **Paestum**, whose career as a *municipium* has been discussed (pp. 200 ff.). As a colony it coins under four colleges before the end of our period:

(6) L. Ve. Ne., D. Fad. *Epul. ded.* (Pl. VII, 14).[1]
(7) Q. Tre. *IIvir* (Pl. VII, 11).[2]
(8) L. Suei., M. Nun. *IIvir* (Pl. VII, 13).[3]
(9) M. I. Ne. *i. a. m. f.* (Pl. VII, 15).[4]

(6) and (7) are distinguished from their municipal predecessors by a sharp decline in weight, being based on *asses* of c. 73–77 grains only (p. 202). This decline demands attribution to the late thirties or early twenties—which is confirmed by the very close correspondence of Victory on (7), with her distinctive coiffure, to a bust on official *denarii* struck between c. 36 and 29 B.C.[5] (8) and (9) are decisively set apart from these by the absence both of $\overline{\text{PAE}}(sti)$ and of the large value-mark S(*emis*)—never omitted by previous colleges, but never to return on later issues—and by the first appearance of the formula P. S. S. C., likewise never again absent.[6]

(6) must, for several reasons, be considered the foundation-issue of the new colony, to whose origin in about this period an inscription bears witness (p. 201).[7] The last word of the legend cannot be other than DED(*uxerunt*): unlike DED(*erunt*)—for which no analogy can be offered—such a word and such an abbreviation are entirely regular.[8] Epigraphically speaking, then, reference to *deductio* is highly probable. Secondly, the *Liber Coloniarum* shows that, during the two decades of military government and later, certain of the colonial foundations in Italy (as opposed to the provinces) were not carried out in the usual way by the autocrats and *principes* themselves or by a single representative (pp. 8 f.), but, as in the earlier part of the century, by collegiate bodies. It is possible to cite, among several, Antium[9] and Anagnia[10] (*populus deduxit*),

[1] *BMC.* 63 ff., Berlin, Cambridge. The reading DED. of Garrucci (*Le monete dell' Italia antica*, pl. CXXIII, 39) is confirmed by several specimens at Berlin (*pace* Lenormant, *La monnaie dans l'Antiquité*, III, p. 229). *Trientes* have L. VE. NE. FAD. PONT. (Berlin) (see p. 287).

[2] *BMC.* 54, Berlin. Garrucci, l.c. 25.

[3] Berlin, Vienna; cf. Mommsen, *CIL.* x, p. 53. Wrongly ascribed by Muensterberg (*Beamtennamen*, ss.vv.) to Tiberius. Not in Garrucci, l.c.

[4] Garrucci, l.c. pl. CXXIII, 14. Misread by Poole, *BMC.* 77.

[5] *BMC. Imp. Aug.* 615. This style of hairdressing was only fashionable for a short time; cf. Stephan, *PW. Suppl.* VI, 91.

[6] Rarely altered to S.P.S.C. (Naples), $\overline{\text{PAE}}$ S.S.C. (Berlin, own collection), $\overline{\text{PAES}}$. S.S.C. (in trade, Naples).

[7] It is ignored by Hollaender, *Dissertationes philologicae. Halenses*, IV, 1880, pp. 353 ff.

[8] E.g. at Cassandrea is HORT(*ensius*) COL(*oniam*) DED(*uxit*), at Dyrrhachium Q. PA[QVIVS RVF(*us*)] DEDVX(*it*)—COLONIA[M], at Philippi Q. PAQVIVS RVF(*us*) LEG(*atus*) C(*oloniam*) D(*eduxit*), at Sinope almost certainly COL(*oniam*) ...P. SVLP(*icius*) Q. F. RVF(*us*) PROCOS. PONTIFE[X IMP(*erator*) DE]D(*uxit*), at Lystra very probably M. RVTILVS PRO COS. COL. IVL. [DED(*uxit*)].

[9] *Liber Coloniarum, Feldm.* p. 229.

[10] Ibid. p. 230.

and Sutrium[1] (*colonia...ab oppidanis est deducta*). Since such details are generally reliable in the *Liber Coloniarum*,[2] it is necessary to ask what sort of Boards actually performed the *deductio* in each case. Answers of more than one kind are provided by the same work. An Augustan *deductio* at Venafrum is by *quinqueviri*;[3] at Capua under Octavian[4] there are twenty—*iussu imperatoris Caesaris a vigintiviris est deducta*.[5]

It is clear, then, that, until the principate of Tiberius at least,[6] colonial foundations in Italy were carried out not only by individuals, but by committees of varying sizes. Also relevant to the present coinage is the *ritus deductionis*, whose most important feature was the demarcation of a wall.[7] It is, therefore, not surprising that, in the *Liber Coloniarum*, the word *deducta* is often not merely amplified but actually replaced by *muro ducta*[8] or *munita*.[9] In these contexts, in the official terminology employed in the work, *muro ducta* and *munita* are indiscriminately used as precise equivalents of *deducta*. In the light of this conclusion, it is necessary to study an inscription of Venafrum in honour of L. Aclutius L. f. Ter. Gallus, *duovir urbis moeniundae bis* (?), *praefectus iure deicundo bis* (?), *duovir iure deicundo, tr. mil. legionis primae, tr. militum legionis secundae Sabinae*.[10] Jullian,[11] although at fault in considering the *praefectura* here mentioned to be a Roman office rather than the local one to which the words *iure deicundo* clearly ascribe it,[12] correctly sees that the inscription refers to the period 43-27 B.C.[13]—there is no reason to attribute it, with Mommsen,[14] to 42 B.C.—and to a refoundation before the Augustan one. The connection between *duovir urbis moeniundae* and *colonia munita*, as the frequent substitute for *deducta*, is unmistakable. At Venafrum, then—which is known to have been *colonia Iulia Augusta*[15]—the Augustan *restitutio* was carried out by special *quinqueviri*, but the triumviral (Julian) one by special *duoviri*.

[1] Ibid. p. 217; cf. Pais, *Memorie della R. Ac. dei Lincei* (sc.-mor.), VI, 2, 1926, p. 369.
[2] Cf. Rostovtzeff, *SEH*. p. 587 n. 6.
[3] *Liber Coloniarum*, l.c. p. 239. Pais, l.c. p. 387, rightly attributes this to Augustus. *Quinqueviri* are also appointed for an *adsignatio* at Praeneste (*Liber Coloniarum*, l.c. p. 236).
[4] His titulature was correctly *Imp. Caesar*, whereas the dictator's had never been (p. 415). For an earlier foundation in 59 B.C. cf. Pais, l.c. p. 360; Zumpt, *Commenta Epigraphica*, I, p. 300.
[5] *Liber Coloniarum*, l.c. p. 231.
[6] Anagnia is of that date.
[7] Cf. Marquardt, *St.V.* I, pp. 457 f.; Rudorff, *Gromatische Institutionen* (*Feldm.* II), pp. 229 ff. Details in Hyginus, *De Limitibus Constituendis*, passim.
[8] *Liber Coloniarum*, l.c. p. 237 (Sinuessa), p. 239 (Verulae), p. 240 (Camerinum), p. 235 (Neapolis,

Liguris Baebianus et Cornelianus).
[9] Ibid. p. 233 (Castrimonium, Cadatia), p. 234 (Gabii).
[10] *CIL*. x, 4876 (= *Inscr. Reg. Neap.* 4627).
[11] *TP*. p. 29.
[12] He confuses the *praef. i. d.* with the *praef. col. ded.* owing to ignorance of the coins of Clovius and Hortensius, and misinterpretation of the inscription of Memmius (p. 10). He himself admits that it was not uncommon for a *deductor* to become the first *duovir i. d.* (p. 29, cf. Cic. *in Pisonem*, 11. 24, *pro Sestio*, 8. 19).
[13] By the analogy of similar 'city-governors' at Saguntum and Zama Regia (pp. 163, 184), Aclutius is most convincingly ascribed to the period between Actium and the *restitutio rei publicae*.
[14] *Zeitschrift für geschichtliche Rechtswissenschaft*, XV, 1848, p. 290.
[15] Cf. Pais, l.c. p. 387.

This too was the position of L. Ve. Ne. and D. Fad. *Epul.* at Paestum—a conclusion to which the letters DED. are most appropriate. The Venafrum inscription strongly suggests the identification of such *duoviri col. ded.* with the *deductor* and *curator-adsignator*, who were now habitually charged with such foundations, and whose names, indeed, appeared in c. 40 B.C. on two contemporary and parallel inauguratory issues at Cephaloedium (p. 193). The earlier BIS in this inscription—if correct[1]—recalls that these two officials were customarily responsible for the local government until the first *duoviri i. d.* were ready,[2] and, indeed, often acted in that capacity themselves.[3] When, as at Venafrum, the city had already been of Roman status previously, the *deductor* and *adsignator*—when these were two in number and not more or less[4]—simply became interlopers in the normal list of *duoviri i. d.*, from whom they were, *de facto* though not *de iure*, indistinguishable as regards matters of ordinary administration. If the tenure of Aclutius Gallus as *duovir col. ded.* was renewed, as the inscription may indicate, this merely shows that, as at Apamea (p. 257), the period between the *lex* of the colony and its final establishment overlapped the magisterial year. Even after this termination of his renewed commission *coloniae deducendae*, Aclutius was appointed as a member of the first real colonial *duoviri* (*i. d.*): the coins of Halaesa (p. 196) and Thermae (?) (p. 238) have shown that these were often chosen by Augustus himself, as by Julius before him.[5] At Saguntum the *curator mun. const.* Cn. Libo stayed on as *praefectus* Augusti, and at Zama Regia P. Sittius likewise remained in office as *quattuorvir* (pp. 163, 184).

L. Ve. Ne. and D. Fad. *Epul.*, at Paestum, now take shape as the *deductor* and *adsignator* respectively; that is, as foundation-officials who possessed the right to administer the new colony—as *duoviri urbis moeniundae* or *coloniae deducendae*—until their task of reorganisation was ended. Numismatic evidence has shown that they held this appointment at some date between 36 and 25: the feeble style of their coins and the Republican denomination of *triens*[6] suggest a date nearer to the earlier (municipal) group rather than to later categories, which possess other distinguishing features. Both personages are wholly unidentifiable. The *deductor*, if VENE. is part of his *nomen*, might belong to several *gentes*.[7] Of these perhaps Veneria is the least unlikely, since this family came from the neighbouring city of Pompeii.[8] But neither this nor any of the other clans whose names begin with these letters were, as far as we are acquainted with them, eminent enough to warrant the present official appointment: VENE. more probably

---

[1] Cf. *CIL.*, Jullian, l.c. for divergent interpretations.
[2] Marquardt, l.c. p. 458; Jullian, l.c.
[3] Jullian, l.c. pp. 28 f.; cf. Cic. *Pis.*, *Sest.*, ll.cc.
[4] For their possible occasional combination in one person cf. Hardy, *Three Spanish Charters*, p. 43 n. 88.
[5] *Lex Coloniae Genetivae Iuliae*, ch. 125; cf. Adcock, *CAH.* IX, p. 709.

[6] Berlin.
[7] E.g. Venecia (Schulze, p. 69), Venedia (ibid. p. 379), Veneia (ibid. p. 378), Veneilia (ibid. p. 445) = ? Venelia (ibid.), Veneria (ibid. p. 482), Veneteia (ibid. p. 434) = ? Venetia (ibid.).
[8] Schön, *ap.* Nissen, *Pompeianische Studien*, p. 218; Mommsen, *CIL.* X, p. 89.

includes parts both of *nomen* and of *cognomen*.¹ Equally unavailing is the attempt to find Dec. Fadius, whether among the *Septemviri Epulonum* or elsewhere. *Fasti* of the priestly college do not know him.² He may, as *adsignator*, have been one of the professional surveyors who were employed after the death of Julius³ for the first time.⁴ The situation is complicated by the legends on the *triens* (which must be struck by the same pair⁵), L. VE. NE.—FAD. PONT. Until the third century A.D. no man is known to have been simultaneously a member of two of the great priestly colleges.⁶ Fadius, then, can scarcely have held both *septemviratus* and *pontificatus* at the time of his *deductio*; even more improbable is a change from one to the other during his year or two as *duovir col. ded.* It is necessary to conclude that PONT(*ifex*) is here used loosely (and flatteringly) to denote membership of the septemviral college, which was a dependant of the pontificate.⁷ At all events, the two officials who collaborated in the *deductio* of Paestum at some date between c. 36 and 25 B.C. are unknown to history and to prosopography.

After this inauguratory issue only the three *collegia*, (7)–(9), strike before the accession of Tiberius.⁸ It has been mentioned that the first two of these are of low weights suggesting (like their styles) a date after the mid-thirties (p. 202); but (8) provides the first instance of the new formula P(*aesti*) S(*ignatum*) S(*enatus*) C(*onsulto*)—referring to the Roman senate⁹ like S(*enatus*) S(*ententia*) many years earlier (p. 203)—which appears on all subsequent issues. Chronological indications combine with general probability to suggest that the reappearance of the senatorial formula after so long an interval is due to the administrative reform of 28–27, which established the *senatus consultum* as the basis of the new executive system (p. 445). Elsewhere, indeed, the earliest known of its many occurrences on the *aes* coinage is provided by the *restitutio* coinage of Apamea in 27 (p. 257). The previous *régime* of *imperium maius* is unlikely to have warranted the formula P. S. S. C. (p. 203), which is a characteristic and invariable feature of the known Paestan issues in the principate. On general as on particular grounds, the constitutional reform of 28–27 must inevitably be considered as the

¹ This does not assist identification.
² Not in Bardt, *Jahresbericht des k. Wilhelms Gymnasium in Berlin*, XI, 1871, 1 ff.; Howe, *Fasti Sacerdotum, etc.* (1904); Klose, *Römische Priesterfasten* (Diss. Breslau, 1910).
³ Cic. *XI Phil.* 5; cf. Rudorff, *Feldm.* II, p. 321; Schulten, *PW.* VII, 1887, 1891.
⁴ Pseudo-Boethius, *Demonstratio Artis Geometricae, Feldm.* I, p. 395, attributes the institution to Julius: but for the uncertainty of the Gromatic ascriptions to him, see p. 252.
⁵ General probability, a close correspondence in style, the name of L. Ve. Ne., and the rare mention of any Roman priesthood on inauguratory issues—

the only other occurrence being at Sinope (see above, p. 252)—make this inevitable.
⁶ Howe, l.c. p. 20.
⁷ Cic. *Har. Resp.* 21, etc.; cf. Klotz, *PW.* (2R.), II, 1553.
⁸ The earliest coins to bear his head appear to be those signed by M. Egnatius Q. Octavius *IIviri*. There are at least five variants (Paris [2], Vienna, Berlin, Naples); many of these have late Augustan heads, but some (Berlin, etc.) unmistakably display the mature features of Tiberius. It is indicated elsewhere (pp. 328, 463) that a very large number of portraits of the late Augustan type are posthumous.
⁹ Milne, *The Development of Roman Coinage*, p. 22.

terminus post quem of this formula. (7), therefore, on which—as on no subsequent issue—it is still omitted, must be considered to be prior to this reform, but, as its style indicates, later than the *deductio* issue of L. Ve. Ne. and D. Fad. *Epul.*, whose chronological limits can accordingly be narrowed down from c. 36–27 to c. 36–28.

Q. Tre. *IIvir*, then, coined shortly before c. 28, and L. Suei. M. Nun. *IIviri* between that year and c. 23. Between the dates of the two issues, the senate regained the right to direct the Paestan coinage by 'decrees' (p. 293), which, although in law still advisory *senatus sententiae*, had exchanged that name for *senatus consulta*, and became *de facto* legislative (p. 98). As Mommsen[1] notes, the Paestan mint is still in the curious position of semi-independence which it had enjoyed in the Republic. Its coinage under Augustus is, however, sparse indeed. The only issue which can belong to his mature principate is that of M. I. $\overline{\text{NE}}$. I. A. M. F. (9). Its weight (c. 65 grains) shows a decided increase, which is subsequently maintained.[2] Official *quadrantes* weighed c. 48 grains[3] and were of copper:[4] since the present coin,[5] like later Paestan issues,[6] retains the Republican alloy of lead and tin, which was valued below copper (p. 300), it is probable that it—not (8), whose weight closely connects it with preceding issues —should be considered a *quadrans*, the first of a series.[7] Rome periodically issued this small denomination, but the large number of halved and quartered *asses* found in all regions[8] indicates that the supply of *semisses* and *quadrantes* was still far exceeded by the demand. Moreover, imitations of Roman *aes* which have come to light in Campania[9] reveal that the enormous circulation of that currency (pp. 92 f.) did not prevent a dearth of it quite near the capital. Industry was unusually extensive in Campania,[10] but it is difficult to see why a city so far south as Paestum was chosen to provide an auxiliary mint. At all events, it was chosen—and bears witness to the invariable readiness of the Roman government to sacrifice uniformity to expediency. The last half-decade B.C., when no *aes* seems to have been struck at Rome,[11] is particularly suitable for the present issue (9): the style of hairdressing is in accordance with this attribution.[12]

Parallels from the CA coinage (p. 108) suggest that the *senatus consultum*, which

---

[1] *Mzw.* p. 338: *aus Regierungsconcession und Delegation.*
[2] The average of twenty Tiberian pieces provides approximately the same figure.
[3] Cf. Mattingly, *BMC. Imp.* p. lvi.
[4] Ibid. p. xlix.
[5] Spectrogram 68.
[6] Spectrogram 69.
[7] Official *semisses* of Lugdunum (*BMC. Imp. Aug.* 568 f., 577 f., 588 f.) weighing c. 71 grains (ibid. p. vi) are too heavy, since their metal is *orichalcum*, which was rated far higher. On the other hand the weight of *orichalcum* Gallic *quadrantes* (see above, p. 124; Spectrograms 24, 25; weight from 36 grains, *BMC. Imp. Aug.* 561 ff.) is not far from appropriate to this interpretation. However, it is unlikely that the weights of these lowest token denominations are of much importance (cf. Mattingly, l.c. p. xlix).
[8] Cf. Strack, *BJ.* CVIII, 1902, pp. 1 ff. for details.
[9] Several of Augustus and Tiberius from finds at Salerno acquired by me.
[10] Cf. Rostovtzeff, *SEH.* pp. 69 ff.
[11] Cf. Mattingly, l.c. pp. xcviii, 50.
[12] *BMC. Imp. Aug.* 104 (13 B.C.) is close. For an enlargement vide Pietrangeli, *Civiltà Romana*, VII, 1938, p. 19. Unfortunately the official currency provides no female coiffure of the following twenty years: but a Hague cameo of Livia (Pietrangeli, l.c. p. 18) probably belongs to the period.

permitted the Paestan issue, was moved by the *auctoritas principis*. The mysterious obverse legend seems to confirm this conclusion. Poole's[1] interpretation of the legend as MONETAM. F. is, unfortunately, wishful thinking: the first stop is as clear as the second, and many specimens reveal clearly that MINEIA. M. F. is correct. The best interpretation requires a division of these letters into three groups—the last providing M(*onetam*) F(*lavit*) or F(*ecit*), and the first a proper name M. I. NE. There remains the formula I. A., which has been seen to occur, in reversed order, at Philippi (p. 274). There the solution A(*ntoni*) I(*ussu*) is recognised to be correct: here I(*ussu*) A(*ugusti*)—a more frequent order[2]—is the obvious choice. This interpretation is strikingly corroborated by analogies. C(*aesaris*) A(*uctoritate*) and S(*enatus*) C(*onsulto*) co-operate significantly in the production of official coinage, and were bound by a close constitutional tie (p. 445). In view, therefore, of the conjunction of IA and SC on this issue, it is interesting to note that colonial foundations by the authority of the *princeps* are indiscriminately described, from an early date, as *Caesaris auctoritate* (as at Pella) and *iussu Augusti* (as at Philippi) (pp. 280, 275). Thus *iussu Augusti*, like *permissu Augusti*, was viewed as the rough equivalent of *Caesaris auctoritate* (p. 445);[3] so that IA—SC here is similar to CA—SC; and, accordingly, I(*ussu*) A(*ugusti*)—S(*enatus*) C(*onsulto*) is a natural and correct combination which may confidently be read on these coins. It is, indeed, very probable that the Paestan mint, unique among Roman cities by explicitly recording its dependence on a senatorial decree, employed the Imperial counter-signature: the official issues with SC had done the same. Thus a further link is forged in the chain which connects the *senatus consulta* with the *auctoritas principis*. The psychological distinction between *iussu Augusti* here, and *permissu Augusti* at Baetican towns (p. 220), is entirely in accordance with the greater strictness of State-supervision at Paestum. The identity of M. I. Ne., who executed this unusual commission, is undiscoverable: he was probably M. Julius Nepos, related to a somewhat later Tiberius[4] and a much later Lucius[5] of the same names.

Throughout its career, both municipal and colonial, the Paestan mint occupies a class by itself. On the one hand it was 'official', since it produced coin by the same formula as the Roman *aes*: both series, too, are signed by city-magistrates. However, the Paestan signatures, unlike the Roman, are accompanied and emphasised by an ethnic; the circulation—though not confined to the city any more than in the case of other local currencies (p. 298)—was strictly limited; no countermarks appear; and there is not even the approximate conformity with metrological reforms at Rome which most official series attain. Moreover, the previous currency of the city (p. 203) shows that at an earlier date senatorial control, already in existence, had not prevented the operation of independent economic machinery: the dislocation of this under Tiberius coincided with the cessation of coinage. On the whole, then, the series may be defined as local.

[1] *BMC.* (Italy), p. 282, no. 77.
[2] E.g. *Liber Coloniarum, Feldm.* pp. 230 ff. etc.
[3] It is possible, however, that the *iussus Augusti* was exercised, *after* the SC, directly to M. I. Ne.; the commonest manifestation of CA was, of course, in the motion which produced the SC, although it was equally potent as a result of or apart from the SC (p. 443). [4] *CIL.* VI, 20149. [5] Ibid. 1057, 1058.

K

Chapter 3

THE ROMAN CITIES AND THE STATE

A. THE FOUNDATION COINAGES

THE numismatic history of the period is dominated by this institution. Nearly every city which coins does so first to celebrate its establishment in the Roman right: the same custom can be traced at Latin cities (pp. 335 ff.), and even many peregrine communities celebrate their liberation or reconstitution in this way (pp. 338 ff.). The arguments by which all the Roman issues of this type have been identified are largely based on fourteen coinages which explicitly refer to their inauguratory character.[1] With the assistance of these it is easy to multiply the list, since it is only as foundation coinages that the large number of isolated city-issues in this period can be explained. The various arguments that have contributed to their identification cannot be repeated here, but the conclusions are summarised in Appendix 4.

The Sicilian series with the names of proconsuls,[2] the special portrait-issues,[3] and the group with *IIviri Augusti*[4] are among those groups which demonstrate that this glorification might be implied rather than expressed. This indication makes it necessary to ask whether many issues, which are signed by magistrates or with an ethnic in the ordinary way, are not in fact of this same special character. The isolated issues of the colonies of Brutus and Cassius[5] are clear examples of such implicit foundation-coinages. Now a large proportion of the cities which explicitly celebrate this occasion do not coin again throughout our period: it is therefore significant that eleven cities, which lack explicit foundation-issues,[6] possess equally isolated coinages. Not one of these, moreover, can, at the latest, be more than a few years after the date of their city's Roman foundation; and special reasons have been adduced for supposing that most of them are actually foundation-issues. The same is probably true of all eleven.

Yet another sub-division of this category can be deduced from the consideration that some of the explicit foundation-coinages do not stand entirely alone at their mint, but are followed, before the death of Augustus, by other currency from the same mint. By

---

[1] *Mun.* Saguntum, Simitthu (?), Zitha, *col.* Turris Libisonis, Lystra, Sinope, Apamea, Cassandrea, Philippi, Dyrrhachium (two), Pella and Paestum, and Q. Hortensius *praef. col. ded.*

[2] *Mun.* Messana, Lilybaeum, Agrigentum, Haluntium, *col.* Tyndaris, Syracuse, Panormus.

[3] *Mun.* Cephaloedium, Saguntum, Zama Regia, Caralis, Tingis — besides explicit foundation-issues.

[4] *Mun.* Thuburnica (?), Halaesa, *col.* Thermae Himeraeae (?).

[5] Rhodes, Cyrene, Melita, Dium; Cassandrea is explicit.

[6] *Mun.* Dertosa, Ilerda, Lix, Henna, Agrigentum (first foundation), Lipara, *col.* Arausio (?), Simitthu (?) (second foundation), Thapsus, Alexandria Troas, Patrae. At Turiaso there is an interval of at least thirty years.

THE FOUNDATION-COINAGES

the analogy of these, it is highly probable that at many places, where no explicit foundation-issue occurs, the first issue of a more or less extensive colonial or municipal series may have served to commemorate the enfranchisement of its city. At twenty of such towns,[1] for example, there is good reason to believe that the initial coinages occurred only a very short time after the Roman foundation, and their attribution to that event is confirmed by the special nomenclature on eight of them.[2]

Four of these nineteen cities[3] share with five others[4] a curious feature which points to the existence of yet another branch of foundation-coinage. At these mints an initial issue, which is probably or certainly inauguratory, is succeeded by only one other, which was made very soon after the first, probably in the next year—then for the rest of the sixty years under review, and indeed in most cases for evermore,[5] there is no coinage whatever. The second issues, struck so soon after the first, could not possibly provide for the needs of the community for long: such meagre supplements to the official coinage must have been commemorative, and there is evidently some sort of connection in each case with the initial issues. This conclusion is corroborated by the coinage of Saguntum, where an issue commemorating the *constitutor* is followed a year later by another in honour of his *adsignator*; a similar pair of coins occurs at Cephaloedium. The economic reason for these double issues is provided by the Paestan series. This shows clearly that even a fairly prosperous city had no source of income by which it could regularly meet the expenses of coinage. It was necessary on each occasion specially to allocate a tax; and the record of no less than four different taxes at Paestum shows that there was no fund which could normally be spared for this purpose. On the other hand, there is evidence that foundation-coinages were not provided by the cities themselves: P. Sittius explicitly announces that he himself met the cost of the issue at *municipium* Simitthu (?) which bore his name and head. It is extremely probable that other pre-Augustan *deductores* and *constitutores* likewise produced enough money for the new city to have a fair start, and, in particular, to enable it to commemorate numismatically its foundation and its founder. The richer of the founders may, like Sittius, have raised this money from their own estate, and thus won additional glory; but since foundations were sanctioned by a *lex* and a *senatus consultum*, it is likely that most of the governors who were allotted these tasks—and all

---

[1] *Mun.* Emporiae, Panormus (first foundation), Assorus, Tingis, *col.* Lugdunum, Ilici (first and second foundations), Celsa, Calagurris, Osca, Turiaso, Bilbilis, Italica, Emerita, Hippo, Achulla, Parium, Antioch in Pisidia, Berytus, Corinth, Cnossus.

[2] Emporiae, Lugdunum, Celsa, Calagurris, Osca, Turiaso, Bilbilis, Antioch.

[3] Panormus, Assorus, Ilici (second foundation), Antioch.

[4] *Mun.* Cossura, Halaesa (first foundation), Lilybaeum (second foundation), *col.* Turris Libisonis, Dyme (the latter a special case). At the official mint of Cnossus (?) also, the inaugural issue of M. Licinius Crassus is very closely followed by another of L. Lollius (pp. 55 ff.), but then there are no more. A similar phenomenon occurs at the peregrine 'free' cities of Oea, Mylasa, etc. (pp. 339, 342 ff.).

[5] Assorus, Cossura, Lilybaeum, Turris Libisonis, Dyme. Halaesa only has another foundation-issue.

of them in the principate—were entrusted with a suitable sum by the *aerarium*. The large number of cases in which a *municipium* or colony contrives to make a second issue very shortly after the first, but then none ever again, shows that this sum was often large enough for the foundation coinage to be repeated by the second pair of magistrates. These issues, then, occupy a special place in the inauguratory branch of the colonial and municipal currency.

It is now possible to survey the ramifications of the foundation coinages. Their exceptional importance is suggested by the extreme rarity in all other contexts of the terms *constitutor* and *deductor*: indeed, the *Thesaurus* only knows one use of the latter word in this sense.[1] On the whole subject of colonial and municipal foundation there is very little evidence apart from the coins.[2] These provide a remarkable wealth of information. Nor are their quantity and interest accidental. The *princeps'* character as *conditor* plays a vital part in the publicity of the period (p. 319); he and his predecessors were always glad that their activity as founders should be advertised; and many examples have already been cited of the enlistment of *aes* coinage in this period as a powerful instrument of propaganda. It is astonishing that such an important aspect of the principate as the foundation-coinage has been so neglected, less than half a dozen of the sixty odd examples having been identified. Some of these issues were struck during the initial control of the *adsignator*, some even before the *deductor* enabled him to take charge: others evidently belong to the first, or even a later, year of regular local *collegia*. Despite these variations, a city-ethnic, or formula, or local magistrate's name, appears on every foundation-coinage; but the names of founder and *adsignator* are frequently omitted. It is clear, therefore, that although city revenues are not ultimately responsible for their production, these are city-issues no less than ordinary local currencies are.

It is possible to trace a distinct evolution in official policy concerning foundations. The decisive change occurs between the inauguratory issues of Saguntum in 29 (p. 158) and Apamea in 27 B.C. (p. 255). C. Calvisius Sabinus can still be called *conditor municipi* on the former. But at Apamea it is already Augustus who is *restitutor*, although absent: the proconsul Ap. Claudius Pulcher, who was in charge of the task, is already mentioned without any such title. So are all subsequent governors in a similar situation.[3] The change is not difficult to interpret, in view of the conclusions already reached concerning the new executive machinery of 27, embodying the *senatus consultum Caesaris auctoritate* (p. 445): the relevance of this reform is explicitly illustrated by the reference, on the second coin, to the *senatus consultum* which ordained the refoundation of Apamea. Since the days of Caesar, such measures had not generally been applied: the *deductores* had been the personal representatives of the various holders of

---

[1] Donatus, *ap*. Terent. *Adelph*. 583.
[2] Cf. Brugi, *Studi Bonfante*, I, p. 365.
[3] Even Agrippa is honoured at Gades (p. 171)

not explicitly as *constitutor*, but only as *patronus parens*—titles due even to a *curator-adsignator* (*Lex Coloniae Genetivae Iuliae*, ch. 97).

imperium maius and had carried out their military orders.¹ Henceforward, however, as Augustus himself—like the coins—informs us (n. 6), foundations in the provinces² were conducted by his own *auctoritas*; SC at Apamea and Paestum bears witness to the fact that, for inaugurations as for official coinage, this *auctoritas* was exercised through the senate.³ Here again, then, is evidence for the civilian administration of the new order: in the restored Republic, the senatorial proconsuls actually wielded less authority in this respect than their predecessors in the military autocracy! Calvisius and the like had been allowed the titles of *constitutor, deductor* etc., since, although subordinated by the *imperium maius*, they were nevertheless themselves in possession of an *imperium*.⁴ But Pulcher and other 'senatorial' governors are not permitted these titles, since Augustus is now the *deductor*: in his *Res Gestae* (which is never technically inaccurate⁵) he himself writes *deduxi*⁶ even of colonies, in 'senatorial' provinces, which he could not have founded in person.

But the *deductio*, too, has been altered in the great constitutional reform: it is no longer carried out by *imperium*, but is a product of *auctoritas*, and, as the Apamean issue shows, of *auctoritas* made manifest in a *senatus consultum*. The governors, therefore, who are in charge of the tasks, can clearly no longer act like their predecessors by *imperium*. They lack the titles hitherto considered appropriate to foundations in that capacity, and their part in the ceremony has diminished to the level of the Republican *curatores-adsignatores*. Those had been hirelings of the founder, paid from the sum allotted to the total expenses by the *aerarium*, who had—by a *locatio operis* without an *imperium*—superintended the details of the allotment and remained in charge of civil matters until local *duoviri* were ready to take charge (p. 34). In the provinces, then, this *locatio*, which survived for Augustus's *adsignationes* in Italy,⁷ was the task of his proconsuls, who did not use their *imperium* for these ceremonies. Thus further evidence is obtained of the abrupt administrative transition from *imperium maius* to *auctoritas*. It is clear, too, that the restoration of the Republic included a reform of city-foundation policy which contained a potent check on the alleged independence of the 'senatorial' governors.

An important feature of the same process is the evident repute attained by *adsignatores* of the period. Cn. Stati. Libo at Saguntum and A. Ambatus at Zama Regia (pp. 163, 182) are clearly personages of great distinction. It is significant that both of

---

¹ It is of importance to note that this reform was instituted in 28 rather than 27: the restored colony of Apamea still bears the title *Iulia*, not *Augusta*. But its actual refoundation is decisively dated by the titulature to 27. Thus we have a unique example of an administrative measure whose formalisation and execution fell respectively before and after the constitutional change of Jan. 27 (see also p. 424).

² For different circumstances in Italy, see p. 284.

³ From 31 to 23 Augustus possessed the *ius senatus consulendi* by virtue of the consulship (p. 450).

⁴ Cf. Jullian, *TP*. p. 28. Cf. pp. 79, 422, 424.

⁵ Cf. Hammond, *AJP*. 1938, p. 485: its inaccuracies are limited to implication.

⁶ *RG.* 5.

⁷ Hyginus, *De Limitibus Constituendis (Feldm.* p. 172).

them remained in office as local *praefecti i. d. pro Caesare IIviro* after the completion of their *adsignatio*: in the same way L. Aclutius Gallus stayed on at Venafrum for several years (p. 285). These extended tenures are evidence for a remarkable institution that amounts to prolonged 'city-governorship'. It is seen in its true light by reference to the new diminution of provincial governors' practical authority, which has just been discussed. Until he was ready (in 27) to vest foundations in his own hands, the *princeps* left them with these governors; but he denuded their authority of most of its meaning by appointing trusted agents as their assistant *adsignatores*, and elevating the prestige of these by plenary and prolonged powers at their respective cities. Thus, until the exaltation of his own *auctoritas* in 27 (p. 445), he had means of controlling the policy of the town-councils through his deputies. It is noteworthy that the coinages of Libo and Ambatus are later than the *restitutio rei publicae* of 28–27, whereas their foundations both preceded it: the same is true of the *adsignatio* of Apamea by Ap. Pulcher *pro cos*. (p. 255), who apes the 'city-governors' by numismatic portrayal in the same year as their own. Libo and Ambatus are the last of their ephemeral but important class, Pulcher, in the new era of the *auctoritas principis*, the first of the provincial governors whose relegation to *adsignatio* is recorded. The fact that Libo and Ambatus are commemorated by coinage at the outset of this era, which rendered impossible the great local powers which their commissions had entailed, is suggestive of the *princeps'* desire to commemorate his helpers who had made the new order possible. Pulcher, who, as proconsul, initiated the reformed foundation-system at the same date, is permitted to join his contemporaries on the coinage, but the same honour never again falls to founder-governors—although, as the foundation-piece *Permissu L. Volusi pro cos.* at *col.* Simitthu (?) (p. 232) suggests, the sanction of such coinages was left at the discretion of the senior proconsuls at least. The coinages in honour of C. Calvisius Sabinus, Ap. Pulcher, Cn. Stati. Libo and A. Ambatus are characteristic of the post-Actian preparations for the *restitutio rei publicae*, and indicative of the contributions made by the foundation-coinages to history.

B. THE CONTRIBUTION TO THE IMPERIAL MONETARY SYSTEM

However flattering the foundation-coinages may have been to the pride of those concerned, it is clear that they made none but the most ephemeral contribution to the currency of their respective regions. The same is true of a number of other mints whose activity is limited to jubilees—the fifth,[1] tenth,[2] twenty-fifth,[3] fiftieth,[4] or hundredth[5] anniversary of their *civitas*. Economically negligible also are isolated mintages commemorating a visit of Augustus,[6] the glorification of his house,[7] and of the *amici principis*.[8] Not one of these coinages could seriously compete with the official *aes*. Their appearance is explained by the formulas PERMISSV AVGVSTI and, on an equally isolated mintage of Patrae under Caligula, INDVLGENTIAE AVG. MONETA IMPETRATA.[9] Like the foundation-issues, these single coinages were privileges by which a *princeps* could gain the gratitude of provincial citizens—perquisites of *libertas* which did little harm to the Roman treasury. Since Patrae had already struck one commemorative piece at an earlier date, it is clear that such favours did not necessarily, or usually, comprise more than a single issue. There was, therefore, no danger of any of these cities dislocating the economic balance of its region, even if, as we may suppose, their commemorative pieces brought in a little profit by their variability in weight (p. 301). Moreover, such coinage is manifestly not related to commercial needs, since the issues of many cities of the first importance, such as Carthage and Tarraco, are negligible. Nor was there a 'general permission to coin' even in Tarraconensis[10] or among other Roman communities, since a large number of such cities—including many of the most prosperous, even in provinces where local issues were most frequent—appear to lack coinage throughout this period.[11] *Civitas* and monetary needs alike were irrelevant to the bestowal of this easily granted favour.

However, the official *aes*, though universally current, is shown to have been inadequate by the numerous occasions on which governors were called upon to augment

---

[1] *Col.* Babba.
[2] *Col.* Heraclea Pontica.
[3] *Col.* Dyrrhachium, Cnossus, Patrae(?); cf. *civitas libera* Leptis Magna.
[4] *Mun.* Uselis, *col.* Cirta, Carthage, Lugdunum(?), Lystra; cf. *civitas libera* Leptis Minor.
[5] *Col.* Babba (time of Nero).
[6] *Col.* Romula, Patricia, Traducta, Acci.
[7] *Col.* Tarraco, Apamea, Achulla, Hadrumetum, Hippo.
[8] *Col.* Achulla, Hadrumetum, Hippo. Special occasions are unidentifiable at Thapsus.

[9] Naples, cf. Regling, *WMK*. p. 282. Pace Gabrici, *Estratto del Corriere Numismatico*, p. 102, both types are imitated from coins of Caligula, not Augustus. Dieudonné, *Mélanges numismatiques*, 2e sér. II, p. 138 n. 1, rightly rejects the translation of *Moneta* as 'mint' by Mowat, *Rn.* 1909, p. 111.
[10] As Mattingly, *BMC. Imp.* p. xxiv n. 2.
[11] E.g. Utica and many colonies in Africa, Ucubi, Astigi, Tucci, Asido(?), Bracara—coins false, cf. Caetano de Bem, *Memorias historicas*, II, p. viii—Barcino, Libisosa, Salaria, Germe, Cremna, Byllis, etc. Vide Kornemann, *passim*.

it from near at hand (pp. 119 ff.). Augustus indeed rejected the decentralising policy of universal uncontrolled co-operation by Roman cities, with all its potentialities of abuse; but he was too wise not to see that the treasuries and mints of many provincial cities were as well equipped, situated and disposed to distribute coin as the *aerarium* or its regional *fisci*. There is, therefore, a great contrast in bulk between the various categories of commemorative coinage that have so far been summarised, and the output of some thirty other cities, whose mintages were extensive and regular.

Seven of these fall in the Eastern half of the Empire; it is impossible not to recognise a bureaucratic supervision extending beyond mere permission, when it is considered, first, that three of these series—those of *coloniae* Buthrotum, Pella and Parium—lapsed when it became possible to provide their regions with official *aes*; secondly, that all seven of them—the others are the colonies of Sinope, Berytus, Cnossus and Corinth—are spaced throughout the Eastern provinces in such a way as to obtain the maximum geographical advantage from each mintage. The network is completed by the utilisation of fourteen peregrine mints (pp. 336 f., 401). The chosen cities were sufficiently few in number for correlation with each other and with Rome to be a practical possibility.[1]

In the West circumstances are somewhat different. Pretentious early coinages at Tingis and Lugdunum[2] were no doubt not uncontrolled by the government, but their life was short. In Africa Vetus the issues of Hadrumetum and Hippo are only slightly more numerous than those of their Roman neighbours: the bulk of the coinage is still peregrine (p. 474). The mint of Paestum served a special purpose, and its state-control is proven. Otherwise there is only Spain: and in this peninsula alone there are as many prolonged series of Roman city-coinages as in the whole of the rest of the Empire. Evidently special considerations were involved. It is not that the currency of Spain was more extensive than of other provinces, such as Asia and Syria; the unusual feature is that it was principally entrusted to Roman citizen communities, and that a vast peregrine coinage stopped (p. 472). The change was no doubt part of the general policy of depressing *peregrini* in favour of Romans (p. 404): and Spain was the only region in which Augustus was lavish of colonisation (p. 306). The reasons for the multiplicity of the Roman mints thus installed in contrast to arrangements in the East are not only political but economic. We have seen that there can be no question of a general permission to the communities; those which coin must have been selected for special reasons. Nor can these reasons here have been geographical, as in the East: none of the Spanish mints, for example, is in the commercially important North-

---

[1] This is not the same as the 'financial autonomy' emphasised by Liebenam, *St.V.* p. 296; cf. Sherwin White, p. 139.

[2] The carefulness of the *princeps*' plan is indicated by the fact that, after this issue, South Gaul never had more than one *aes* currency of Roman city or official mint, but nearly always had one: this was not fortuitous. The succession was: Arausio? (*col.*), Nemausus (I A, official), Vienna (Latin; see p. 337), Nemausus (I B, official), Lugdunum (official), Nemausus (II, III).

CONTRIBUTION TO IMPERIAL MONETARY SYSTEM 297

Western region,[1] and others are very close to each other in the Ebro valley. Without regard, then, for geographical distribution, certain cities must have been chosen for reasons inherent in themselves. Now Paestum has shown us the complicated methods by which city-budgets had to be adapted to the problem of coinage. Even in the East, the geographical plan was guided in its details by considerations of local prosperity: no city coined which could not afford to coin. Spain was much more intensively Romanised; it was, moreover, at this time an unprecedentedly active field for commerce,[2] and contained more colonies and *municipia* which could show surpluses of revenue than any other part of the Empire.[3] In the East such cities were so irregularly distributed that it was simplest and most economical for only one central mint in each region to be permitted to coin on a large scale; in Spain, they were close neighbours, and their trade, when not with Rome, was principally with each other. Their coinages are extensively intermingled in finds:[4] it was not necessary to space the cities geographically, since circulation was so rapid. Here was an efficacious source of assistance to the *aerarium* in its task of providing *aes* for the provinces, especially as the most important mines of the Empire[5]—not yet all Imperial property[6]—were far more accessible to the Spanish cities than to Rome and Lugdunum. Thus several reasons combined to produce the customary Augustan sacrifice of uniformity to efficiency (p. 323).

It is now necessary to demonstrate that the principal colonial and municipal coinages actually circulated in such a way as to warrant the present explanation. This is abundantly confirmed by finds. Besides its wide circulation in Nearer Spain, the currency issued by Tarraconensian cities before A.D. 14[7] was regularly accepted in Lusitania,[8] Sardinia,[9] Gallia Narbonensis,[10] and Comata,[11] Rhaetia,[12] Germany,[13] and occasionally

---

[1] Cf. Charlesworth, *Trade Routes of the Roman Empire*, p. 154.
[2] Cf. Charlesworth, l.c. p. 150; Sutherland, *RIS*. p. 132.
[3] Cf. van Nostrand, *ES*. III, pp. 204, 208.
[4] E.g. found at Numantia (Schulten, *Numantia*, IV, pp. 246 ff.), Elche (Albertini, *Bulletin hispanique*, 1906, p. 343), Despeña Perros (Calvo and Cabre, *MJSEA*. IX [I, 1916], p. 40), Tarragona (Vilaró, ibid. CXVI [V, 1930], p. 115), Sagunto (Simancas, ibid. XCII [IV, 1925–6], p. 27).
[5] Cf. van Nostrand, *ES*. III, pp. 158, 162.
[6] Cf. Charlesworth, l.c. p. 158.
[7] The Latin cities also—see p. 335.
[8] Many at Lisbon (cf. Lenzi, *Rassegna numismatica*, V, 1908, p. 34) and Oporto mus.; de Sousa Vilhena coll. (Leite de Vasconcellos, *Arquivos da Universidade de Lisboa*, IX, 1923, p. 230), Minas de S. Domingos (id. *Archeologo Portugues*, XXII, 1917, p. 120; ibid. 1912, p. 113).

[9] E.g. of Saguntum, from near Sassari: in Castoldi coll.
[10] Many at all Provençal museums, especially of Emporiae (e.g. 50 at Narbonne, 7 at Marseille); finds at Montans (*Mémoires de la société archéologique du midi de la France*, IX, 1872, p. 228), S. Bertrand de Comminges (ibid. XVII, 1930).
[11] E.g. of Caesaraugusta, found at Preignan (*ZfN*. XXIV, 1904, *Jahresbericht*, p. 17); of Emporiae found in Franche-Comté (two at Besançon mus.). Nine of this class found at Neuss (Strack, *BJ*. CXII, 1904, p. 419); cf. also Windisch (Stückelberg, *ZfN*. XXII, 1900, pp. 40 ff.), and many at Rennes (Toulmouche, *Cat.* pp. 97 ff.); ½ at Vetera (Bonn mus.).
[12] E.g. at Oberhausen (Augsburg mus.).
[13] E.g. Hofheim bei Taunus (Ritterling, *Cat.* p. 100).

even in Numidia.[1] Lusitanian issues are found in Baetica,[2] and Baetican as far as free Germany;[3] the coins of Hippo circulated to the farthest borders of *provincia* Africa;[4] those of Paestum to Epirus.[5] Examples of the Lugdunese series—like those of a peregrine mint at Vienna (p. 337)—occur so frequently in finds from all parts of Gaul[6] (and even, probably, as far as Africa[7]) that for a short time it must have been almost comparable in scope to the official mint at Nemausus (p. 70). But the Lugdunese issues bear no official countermarks and were short-lived: there is no reason why they should not have been in the hands of local magistrates, like the equally extensive output of Corinth.[8] Coins of the latter city—of the principate of Augustus alone—have come to light not only at Argos,[9] Stratos in Acarnania,[10] Thrace[11] and Northern Asia minor,[12] but even in Gallia Narbonensis[13] and probably Italy;[14] while those of Berytus have come to light in Transjordan[15] and as far as Pamphylia.[16] Similarly, Augustan coins of Pella are discovered in Moesia or Northern Thrace.[17] Nor was there any reason why the lesser coinages, of an inauguratory or honorary character, should not add their slight weight to the bulk of currency in their province, and even outside it. Thus the coins of Ilerda are found on the site of Tarraco,[18] and those of Turris Libisonis, Uselis, and Caralis circulated freely in each other's areas in Sardinia (pp. 149, 205). At least five different foundation-issues were discovered together at Agrigentum;[19] Augustan coins of Philippi strayed as far as three sites in Illyricum,[20] and Antonian of Troas within the modern frontiers of Greece.[21] Evidence from later periods shows that colonial and municipal issues retained, throughout the next two centuries of the principate, this freedom of circulation based on the natural course of trade.[22]

[1] Probably of this category is a find at Ain-el-Hout (*Recueil de la Soc. arch. du dép. de Constantine*, XL, 1906, p. 97: cf. Constantine mus., ibid. XX, 1880, p. 147).
[2] E.g. Cadiz (Cervera and Jiménez-Alfaro, *MJSEA*. LVII [IV, 1922–3], p. 5).
[3] E.g. Riedlingen (Nestle, *Funde*, p. 87; cf. Bittel, *Römisch-germanische Forschungen*, VIII, 1934, p. 34).
[4] Found at Kef (*Bull. arch. du com.* 1897, p. 250).
[5] E.g. at Feniki (Ugolini, *Albania antica*, II, p. 162).
[6] E.g. at Paris, S. Blaise (Strack, *BJ*. CVIII, 1902, pp. 5, 10); in museums at Vienne (4), Nîmes (5), Narbonne, Toulouse; at Haltern, Neuss (Strack, l.c.), Windisch (*Anzeiger für schweizerische Altertumskunde*, XXXIV, 1932, p. 112, XXXV, 1933, p. 17), Nijmegen (mus.), Bourges (*Annuaire de la Société de Numismatique*, III, 1878, p. 377).
[7] Constantine mus. (Hinglais, *Rec. de la Soc. arch. du dép. de Constantine*, XXXVIII, 1904, p. 21).

[8] Their wide scope is seen by Mattingly (*BMC. Imp.* p. xxvii).
[9] Waldstein, *The Argive Heraeum*, p. 358.
[10] Courby and Picard, *Recherches archéologiques à Stratos d'Acarnanie*, p. 105.
[11] Sofia mus.
[12] Several from this region seen in trade at Istanbul and Istanbul-Pera.
[13] Marseille (Clerc and d'Agnel, *Découvertes archéologiques à Marseille*, 1904, p. 98).
[14] At Melendugno(?) (Bernardini, *Notizie degli Scavi*, 1934, p. 197).
[15] Jerash (Bellinger, *NNM*. LXXXI, 1938, p. 22).
[16] Istanbul mus.   [17] Sofia mus.
[18] Vilaró, *MJSEA*. CXVI [V, 1930], p. 115.
[19] Own collection.
[20] Sišak, Novi Banovci and Tulca (Zagreb mus.).
[21] Athens mus.
[22] E.g. coins of Utica found at Soukh-Aras (Cagnat, *Klio*, IX, 1914, pp. 200 ff.); of Paestum at Corinth (Edwards, *Corinth*, VI, 1933, pp. 54 ff.); of

CONTRIBUTION TO IMPERIAL MONETARY SYSTEM 299

Thus, conversely, it is not surprising to find an extensive variety of peregrine coinages still current with the rest on enfranchised territory in Italy[1] and on Roman sites in the provinces. This is demonstrated by finds at Tarraco,[2] Saguntum,[3] Gades,[4] Arelate,[5] Raurica,[6] Caralis,[7] Agrigentum,[8] Carthage[9] and Corinth.[10] Later evidence indicates that this, too, was not a transient phenomenon.[11]

Intercirculation, then, was regular and caused no difficulty. Countermarks of colonial and municipal ethnics on Spanish city-issues, as elsewhere, are post-Augustan.[12] The cessation of local *aes* in the West, and the growth of Roman bureaucracy, were to necessitate monetary restrictions that are demonstrably alien to the principate of Augustus. Not only the basic official *aes* but all other currencies also circulated with-

---

Tyre at Jerusalem (*Annual of the Palestine Exploration Fund*, 1927, p. 112) and Jerash (Bellinger, *NNM*. LXXXI, 1938, pp. 23 f.); of Viminacium at Rixdorf (*Verhandlungen der Berliner Gesellschaft für Anthropologie usw.* XVII, 1885, p. 26) and Eisenstadt (*Fundberichte aus Österreich*, II, 1937, p. 295); of Alexandria Troas at Corinth (Edwards, l.c.) and Cologne (Reusch, *Germania*, XXII, 1938, p. 169); of Patrae at Stratos (Courby and Picard, l.c. p. 106) and Pompeii (Gabrici, *Estratto del Corriere numismatico*, p. 102); of Berytus in Yugoslavia (Belgrade mus.; Elmer, *Cat.* 1468–1471; cf. p. iv); of Carthago Nova at Maresfield (Lewes mus.); of Dium in Spain (own collection); of Cremna at Rhodes (Maiuri and Jacopich, *Clara Rhodos*, I, p. 33); of Corinth at Tulle (Blanchet, *NZ*. 1913, p. 194).

[1] E.g. Massilian with Roman of Augustus and Tiberius at Como (*Rivista archeologica della provincia di Como*, 1904, pp. 48 f.), etc. Panormitan at Melendugno (?) (Bernardini, *Notizie degli Scavi*, 1934, p. 197), and Nemi (?) (Bosio, ibid. 1931, p. 293), etc.; many at Rome.

[2] Oliva, *MJSEA*. LXXXVIII [VI, 1924–5], pp. 77 f.

[3] Simancas, ibid. XCII [IV, 1925–6], p. 27.

[4] Atauri, ibid. [II, 1919], p. 5.

[5] Numidian collection.

[6] Coin of Athens in Augustan finds (Augsburg mus.).

[7] Spano, l.c. p. 181, confirmed by Castoldi collection.

[8] Find seen in Rome.

[9] Cagnat, l.c.

[10] Edwards, l.c.

[11] Peregrine coinage found at *coloniae* Poetovio (Ptuj mus.: Abramic, *Führer durch Poetovio*, p. 130),

Mursa (*Vjestnik Kt.-Hrvatsk.-slav.-dalm. Arkiva*, VII, 1903–4, p. 15), Agrippina (Reusch, *Germania*, XXII, 1938, p. 169; Krosch, *BJ*. II, 1843, p. 75), Viminacium (Belgrade mus.: Gren, *Skrifter utgivna av Kungl. humanistiska Vetenskapssamfundet i Uppsala*, XXIX, 2, p. 49). Countermarks of ILIC(i) and CAL(*agurris*) (see next note) occur on a coin of Segesta (Palermo; Gabrici, p. 166, 87).

[12] There are the following reasons for this conclusion: (1) Many countermarks are stamped by cities on their own coins: CA. I., CAS., CLV., TVR., GR., M. S., C. PA. (de Saulcy, *Mélanges de Numismatique*, I, p. 113 ff.; Hill, *passim*) and S. (Alcacer do Sal mus.; Leite de Vasconcellos, *Archeologo Portugues*, 1896) are found respectively at Calagurris (*Iulia*), Cascantum, Clunia, Turiaso, Graccurris, Saguntum, Patricia, and Salacia. It is difficult to see why this should have been done at a date when many of these issues were still being struck, and were accordingly current in the ordinary way. (2) This group has the appearance of uniformity, and thus of contemporaneity. Now the issues of Cascantum, Clunia, Graccurris do not even begin earlier than Tiberius; those of Saguntum thus countermarked are of him also; while TAR(*raco*) is stamped on Commagenian official issues of the same *princeps* (*BMC. Imp.* p. xliii). His reign therefore seems to establish a *terminus post quem*. (3) Many other similar stamps are demonstrably post-Augustan, such as those of BAN(*asa*) on Nero's coins of Babba, C. V. on his imperial issues, C. A. C. on Tiberian *aes* (*BMC. Imp.* pp. xxxii f.). (4) It has been shown elsewhere that most of the other principal categories of countermark also belong to the Julio-Claudian epoch (pp. 94, 117).

out restriction.[1] Those of certain colonies and *municipia* were specially encouraged. These issued money, within the limits of the general scheme, as they thought fit: at Carthago Nova, Saguntum, Pella, etc. coinage was at five-yearly intervals coinciding with the quinquennalian tenures, but elsewhere *quinquennales* or *duoviri* coined at irregular intervals according to local and regional needs.

It is, at first sight, somewhat astonishing to note that the cities as a general rule completely ignored the bimetallic reorganisation of Augustus: the spectrograph reveals that all types of colonial coin continued to be composed of bronze.[2] However, bronze also remained the medium for certain subsidiary official coinages, and even for the important and long-lived series at Nemausus. Stranger still is the complete failure to adhere to any common standard: the *as* fluctuates wildly from c. 350 to c. 80 grains, and even at neighbouring Spanish cities, or on consecutive issues of the same mint, there is no attempt at uniformity.[3] Nevertheless, the evidence of finds conclusively shows that all these bronze coinages circulated together with the official *orichalcum* and copper. Countermarks on the Sicilian series, and the appointment of exchange-controllers (ἀγορανόμοι) by Eastern cities,[4] show that this difficulty was felt. Owing to the extent of fluctuations, no attempt to estimate a relationship between bronze on the one hand, and copper and *orichalcum* on the other, can be conclusive: but since the bronze *asses* of Nemausus (c. 189 grains) (pp. 70, 114) were official and circulated widely, the weight of the Roman copper *as* (c. 167 grains) (p. 91) makes it probable that bronze was officially considered less valuable, not only than *orichalcum*,[5] but even than copper.[6] The relation of the three alloys as bullion cannot be assessed, and in any case has little bearing on a fiduciary currency. Augustus could not have grasped so firmly the principle of token coinage initiated by Caesar, and have extended it by such careful organisation throughout the Empire, if every *as* had to be assessed at a different value from the rest; in this case the task of ἀγορανόμοι would have been endless and intolerable. Nor could his careful provision of official coinage have been accepted as wholeheartedly as the finds indicate, if this had been given unfairly preferential treatment in relation to other currencies: moreover, the scale would have had to be different in every case, and the exchange so complicated as to cripple the circulation which caused trade. Although Sicilian distrust might cause difficulties, it is clear that the order went forth that, within the broadest limits, one *as* was as good as another:[7] this was perfectly logical, since all were of token value. In this way alone can the variations of standard be reconciled. Governors were perhaps expected to approach the Roman standard; the

---

[1] Strack, *Auf dem Wege zum nationalpolitischen Gymnasium*, VI, 1938, p. 20, notes this lack of economic control.

[2] Spectrograms 7, 14, 23, cf. Caley, *MAPS*. XI, 1939, pp. 63 f.—not 'copper', *pace* Burns, *Money and Monetary Policy in Ancient Times*, p. 305. Orichalcum comes in under Tiberius, cf. Zobel de Zangroniz, *MNE*. V, 1880, p. 123.

[3] Cf. Nicodemi, *Milan Cat*. p. xvi.

[4] Cf. Jones, *GC*. pp. 215 ff.

[5] As M. and S. I, p. 24; *pace* Burns, l.c. p. 302. Cf. p. 88.

[6] *Pace* Burns, l.c. p. 305.

[7] With the exception of Egypt (p. 131).

CONTRIBUTION TO IMPERIAL MONETARY SYSTEM 301

chosen colonies were probably allowed to make the profits which their considerable contribution to the money of the Empire warranted, so long as their coins remained heavy enough not to strike at the psychological basis of a fiduciary currency. Such is the most probable outline of a policy whose monetary results were considerable, but whose constitutional implications were as great. For an appreciation of the latter it is important to fix the precise point at which the network of colonial and municipal currencies was first planned.

C. COLONISATION POLICIES OF JULIUS AND AUGUSTUS

It is possible, by the aid of coins, not only to deduce a number of ephemeral Republican[1] and Pompeian[2] settlements, but to add considerably to the most recent lists of Julian foundations. Some of our additions to this category actually date from Caesar's lifetime:[3] and there is good reason to believe that the whole of this large group of communities was, in its general outline and in most of its details, his own. The Sicilian *municipia* were enfranchised according to his plan—although this had not openly gone beyond *Latinitas*[4]—and Octavian's extension of *civitas* in Sardinia[5] was no doubt part of the same policy. Here the plan was interrupted by Sextus; in the same way, Octavian's Julian colonies in Africa[6] were a heritage from Caesar which Lepidus had ignored—although Lepidus, too, had founded certain cities whose epithet *Iulia* (in contrast to *Munatia* at Lugdunum) bears witness to Caesarian origin.[7] The colonisation of Lystra, ultimately founded by a subordinate of Dolabella, had been part of Julius's strategic scheme for his Eastern campaigns: the Pisidian colonies and Ninica and Germa were left for Augustus to complete, but bear witness by their epithet *Iulia* to their inclusion in the dictator's far-reaching plan. Their establishment was postponed for a quarter of a century; but other Eastern colonies designed by Julius had only had to wait until after the battle of Philippi for their completion. Although Antony could invent *acta Caesaris*, there are reasons for thinking that all his Eastern colonies (except Philippi itself[8]) were planned by Caesar. In the first place, Appian[9] explicitly states this of Lampsacus, whose foundation-issue is uniform with those at the other cities. Secondly, Dyme may show, by a change from *Colonia Iulia* to *Iulia Antonia* —paralleled at Simitthu (?)—that *new* foundations of Antony bore the double epithet:[10] but the other colonies with which we are concerned are plain *Iuliae*. Thirdly, Caesar[11] himself testifies that there were many to whom he had extended the hope, but not the substance, of citizenship, and Appian[12] shows that at his death there were still many οἰκισθησόμενοι—whom Brutus, for all his colonisation programme, did not have the time to settle, or the inclination to spare from his army. Antony, too, did not

---

[1] Melita, Rhodes, Cyrene, Dium, Cassandrea. See p. 461.
[2] Panormus, Syracuse, Messana, Cephaloedium, Tyndaris.
[3] E.g. Corinth, Dyme (?), Sinope; cf. Buthrotum, Cirta (?).
[4] Cf. Cic. *Att.* xiv, 12. 1; Scramuzza, *ES.* III, p. 343.
[5] Caralis, Uselis, Turris Libisonis.
[6] Thapsus, Achulla, Lix, Babba.
[7] E.g. Celsa, Hadrumetum, Carthage.
[8] Commemorative of the victory; cf. Nicopolis after Actium.
[9] *BC.* v, 137.
[10] The retention of *Iulia* even at a *colonia Antonia* is probably due to confusion, officially encouraged, between genuine and fictitious *acta Caesaris* (cf. Cic. *Att.* l.c.; *II Phil.* 92, *III*, 10, 30, *V*, 12)—facilitated by the demonstrable unfulfilment of many of the dictator's plans. See pp. 180, 264.
[11] *Bell. Civ.* II, 21; cf. van Nostrand, *ES.* III, p. 143.
[12] *BC.* II, 139.

COLONISATION POLICIES OF JULIUS AND AUGUSTUS 303

disband many of his troops immediately after Philippi:[1] but claims of the civilian οἰκισθησόμενοι and of Caesar's veterans, many of whom, already discharged, had heard Brutus's speech after the Ides, could not safely be postponed. Even Brutus had not ventured to overlook their claims, and even his foundation-policy was merely a fulfilment of his murdered enemy's plan. Thus Brutan and Antonian colonies alike, no less than those of Octavian, Lepidus and Dolabella, must, to a very great extent, be considered as the elements of a vast scheme designed by Caesar himself. The new numismatic evidence gives credibility to Suetonius's figure of 80,000 from the urban proletariate alone[2]—besides twenty or thirty thousand veterans already due for discharge[3]—whom the dictator planned to settle overseas.

These unknown coinages heighten exceedingly the contrast between the inventor of this gigantic plan and all who precede and follow him. Republican theory and practice had viewed with disfavour the extension of the franchise to communities in the provinces.[4] It is well known that Caesar's wider sympathies (and over-population in Rome) led him to abandon this outlook; but the true proportion of his colonies in the provinces to those in Italy can only be discerned by a survey of the coinages. These have shown, furthermore, that many and perhaps most of the Julian *municipia*—of which, for example, the newly enfranchised province of Sicily was composed—must be included in this vast emigration plan.[5] The current view of a few isolated settlements must be abandoned in the face of such evidence: by the orders of Julius they were scattered in large numbers throughout the Empire. Probably many are still to be discovered.[6] Ex-soldiers were mingled with tradesmen and labourers[7]—following the precedent of Alexander[8]—and a real attempt was made to compose each community of the constituents which were best suited to its position. Each was, moreover, endowed with a real civic existence: for example, the year which witnessed the initiation of the settlements saw also their first local coinages (p. 308), and even local militias were permitted where necessary.[9] The portions of Charters which survive show, like many other indications, that the day of a single *Stadtstaat* was done.[10] It is indeed far from true to speak of a deposition of Rome from her pre-eminence, or of Italy from her place outside and above the provinces.[11] But it was not because these were Rome and Italy that Caesar maintained their privilege: it was because they contained the greatest

[1] Cf. Tarn, *CAH*. x, p. 42.
[2] Suet. *Caes*. 42. 1; cf. Adcock, *CAH*. IX, p. 710; Muttelsee, *Untersuchungen über die Lex Iulia municipalis*, Diss. Freiburg, 1913, p. 54.
[3] Adcock, l.c. pp. 706, 710.
[4] Cf. Stevenson, *CAH*. p. 463.
[5] For the other type of Julian *municipium*, by which the native community was enfranchised *en masse*, vide Sherwin-White, p. 170.
[6] For example, nothing whatever is known for or against Pliny's *colonia Caesaris dictatoris Pharos*

(*NH*. v, 128; cf. also p. 239) or *colonia Megara* (*NH*. IV, 11), or of Samos (cf. Broughton, *ES*. IV, pp. 703 f.).
[7] Adcock, l.c. p. 707; Rostovtzeff, *SEH*. p. 498 nn. 31, 32; Stevenson, *RPA*. p. 126.
[8] Cf. Jones, *GC*. p. 4.
[9] *Lex Coloniae Genetivae Iuliae*, ch. 103.
[10] Cf. Kornemann, *QAS*. IV, p. 14.
[11] Cf. Adcock, l.c.; Rostovtzeff, *SEH*. p. 494 n. 23; Strack, *Auf dem Wege zum nationalpolitischen Gymnasium*, VI, 1938, pp. 11, 12 n. 16.

number of Romans and Italians.¹ These, not the cities of their origin, were the basis of the Empire; and from their number came a large proportion of the settlers.² This was a policy even more Roman than that of the Republic. It envisaged the expansion of the Roman nucleus from the Italian peninsula to the provinces of the Empire; the cities were designed as bulwarks of Roman traditionalism.³ Caesar's outlook was not cosmopolitan;⁴ arbitrary and sometimes brutal confiscations of peregrine property marked his allotments.⁵ The intention of his policy, as illustrated by the sudden appearance everywhere of local coins with Latin legend, was to stamp the imprint of Rome upon the face of the Empire. But, for all the intense nationalism implied in this design, Caesar was no racial doctrinaire. The records of the colonies and *municipia*, and the prosopographical indications given by their coinages, show clearly that natives who conformed to the central tenets of Roman rule and Roman civilisation were admitted to the same privileges as Italians.⁶ The centuries which follow even suggest that he was not doctrinaire enough.⁷ Orontes flowed into Tiber,⁸ and distant colonies reverted to the Greek language which surrounds them:⁹ it was only on formal occasions that many *municipia* used the Latin tongue at all. But Caesar's scheme was of characteristic grandeur; he may have intended to devote a large part of the remainder of his life to the details of 'Romanisation' which were necessary to its successful fulfilment. His life was cut short, and, after a period in which his designs were not neglected but his Imperial purpose was not present to unify them, the more limited brain of Augustus was embarrassed by the gigantic remains of a policy which was too ambitious for him.

The bitter experiences brought to a conclusion by Actium did much to enhance this native caution, and in particular to inspire a distrust of the Orient. Thus a geographical viewpoint was substituted for the outlook of Caesar, which had known no such bounds. The sympathies of Augustus were Western and Italian:¹⁰ he had seen enough to believe that Rome could not associate, with dignity and integrity, with the East.¹¹ Thus, for

---

¹ The latter were now freely admitted to the senate: cf. Syme, *RR*. pp. 82, 93.

² The suggestion of Kornemann, *Philologus*, LX, 1901, pp. 417 f., that the colony of Carthage was composed of natives is unplausible: cf. Rice Holmes, *The Roman Republic*, III, p. 322 n.

³ Mitteis, *Reichsrecht und Volksrecht in den östlichen Provinzen*, p. 146.

⁴ Cf. Kornemann, *Gnomon*, 1938, p. 564.

⁵ E.g. Cic. *Att.* XVI, 16 ff.; cf. Adcock, l.c. p. 711; Jones, *GC*. p. 62.

⁶ Cf. especially Frank, *ES*. I, p. 317; also Syme, *RR*. p. 93, who discusses political appointments.

⁷ Cf. Nilsson, *Separat ur Hereditas*, II, 1921, pp. 372 ff.

⁸ Material collected by Rostovtzeff, *SEH*. p. 517 n. 31; cf. Volkmann, *Neue Jahrbücher für Antike und deutsche Bildung*, I, 1938, pp. 16 ff.

⁹ Cf. Hahn, *Rom und Romanismus*, p. 95; Scheffer-Boichorst, *Mitteilungen des Instituts für österreichische Geschichtsforschung*, VI, 1885, p. 527.

¹⁰ Cf. Stevenson, *CAH*. X, p. 207; Gordon, *JRS*. XXI, 1931, p. 66: repercussions on the arts shown by Snyder, *Tijdschrift voor Geschiedenis*, XLII, 1927, pp. 113 ff., etc.

¹¹ Cf. Strack, l.c. p. 16, who advances the singular theory that Augustus conquered the German and Galatian peoples rather than others because they were racially akin to the heterogeneous peoples of Italy! A strange deduction from a modern political grouping.

example, his attitude towards Greeks was one of suspicion,[1] and he abandoned the idea of commercial colonisation[2]—his civilian colonies are exceptional and apparently limited to Italy[3]—and founded no Eastern *municipia*.[4] But even if he was opposed to the spirit which had inspired the dictator's colonies, the claims of veterans—which could not be satisfied with cash alone[5]—presented him, throughout his principate, with problems which in magnitude and duration far exceeded those that had faced Julius. They could only be solved by colonisation, of which they, far more than 'Romanisation', were the cause.[6] The *Res Gestae*[7] give an outline of the method adopted, and coinage fills the gaps. It is necessary to add *municipium* Zitha, *colonia* Thapsus and many Spanish colonies to the current list of his own foundation projects, but to subtract from it numerous Eastern *coloniae* (p. 306). Except in the special area of Spain, the number of his settlements in half a century, though considerable, is small indeed in comparison with Caesar's plans, completed by him and his successors in less than a decade.[8] Moreover, some of Augustus's colonies were peopled with veterans who had deserted those of Julius to return to the colours.[9] This parsimony, imposed by conviction, was not lessened by a new principle of payment for land (after some confiscations following Naulochus[10] and Actium[11]). Of this Augustus—*id primus et solus omnium*—is rightly proud; but it cost his treasury two hundred and sixty million sesterces.[12] Thus, states Augustus,[13] was provision made, with land or money, for three hundred thousand veterans. But the soldiery themselves were not so pleased: as soon as the *princeps* was dead—after a period of exceptional inactivity in their interests (p. 197)[14]—they complained vociferously of the intolerable miserliness which had provided some of them with inferior plots of land, and failed to provide for the rest at all until they were grey with age.[15] The limitations of which they complain are strikingly illustrated by the hitherto unrecognised group of Eastern *restitutio*-coinages (p. 280). Augustus was unwilling, for political reasons, to increase unnecessarily the number of the Caesarian colonies; at the same time, their dissolution would merely add to his problems. So, by a characteristic compromise, he utilised them for his own settlements and so avoided too open a reversal of policy.[16] Each *restitutio* represents

---

[1] Cf. Sherwin-White, p. 175.

[2] Stevenson, l.c. Last, *JRS*. XXII, 1932, p. 60, shows that, contrary to the opinion of Carcopino, *Points de vue*, IV, no relaxation of Augustus's pro-Italian policy can be noted towards the end of his principate.

[3] E.g. Brixia, *colonia civica*; Kornemann, p. 536; Sherwin-White, p. 173.

[4] Cf. Jones, *GC*. p. 132.

[5] Cf. Parker, *The Roman Legions*, p. 246, etc.

[6] Cf. Jones, *GC*. p. 63.

[7] Chs. 3, 15, 16, 28.

[8] Cf. Cardinali, *Augustus* (1938), p. 193. It is misleading to speak, like Riccobono (*Capitolium*, XII, 1937, p. 578), of Augustus's 'intense policy of colonisation'.

[9] Siculus Flaccus, *De Condicionibus Agrorum* (Thulin, Teubner ed., p. 126, correcting text of *Feldm*. I, p. 162).

[10] Scramuzza, *ES*. III, p. 346; cf. Jullian, *TP*. p. 17.

[11] Syme, *CR*. 1938, p. 239; id. *RR*. p. 285, cf. n. 2.

[12] *RG*. 16.   [13] *RG*. 3.

[14] Cf. Sherwin-White, p. 181.

[15] Cf. Tac. *Ann*. I, 35 ff., 52, etc.

[16] Cf. Sherwin-White, pp. 174 ff.

a new draft of colonists; no wonder that, by the side of Julian settlements in each place, only the *uligines paludum* were left, or could be bought.[1]

The discovery that so many Eastern cities date from the forties leads to a remarkable redistribution of Augustus's foundations, and one which is entirely in accordance with his known views. Only one single newly planned foundation can now be attributed to him in established Eastern provinces;[2] and even that, Patrae, was merely a substitute for an unsuccessful pre-Augustan settlement at Dyme (p. 265)—and so practically another *restitutio*. Sherwin-White's surprise[3] at the length of current lists of Augustus's Eastern colonies is justified. On the other hand, a study of the coinage has revealed that his new foundations in the West were far more numerous than has been thought, and that, in particular, a huge scheme of colonisation and municipalisation was undertaken shortly after Actium, not only in Italy, but in Spain under Statilius and Calvisius (pp. 169, 214), and perhaps also in Africa under Autronius Paetus (p. 184). The inclusion of *municipia*—often with fresh drafts (p. 155)—in the Augustan plan for Spain and Sicily is in contrast to their complete absence from the East, and suggests a degree of conscious Romanisation.

But if this can be detected, it was slight. The commercial and cultural motives of Caesar were subordinated to the military needs of the Empire. The coins have demonstrated that, in the East, only the new province of Galatia contained new colonies. But, except for Antioch, these even lack the inauguratory coinages that were permitted to regular communities. Like Rhodes, Cyrene, and Melita under Brutus and Cassius, they cannot be considered civilian establishments so much as garrisons.[4] They were little more, but for their colonial status, than the *castella civium Romanorum* found in Africa.[5] Nor do the numerous Western foundations show a different spirit. In Spain the prime object of the numerous settlements was to guard a wild country.[6] Pseudo-Boethius[7] informs us that Augustus's colonies were often heavily fortified, and Lugdunum describes itself later as *coloniam Romanam et partem exercitus*.[8] In Sicily alone some attempt may have been made to Romanise a degraded civilisation: but all attempts to repopulate Magna Graecia failed.[9] In general, in the West, the first and only consideration was the protection of mistress Italy,[10] and the Italian colonies themselves were planned primarily for defence.[11] It is in this capacity that the military colonies receive the signal honour of triple mention in the *Res Gestae*.[12] It is not difficult to sympathise with the soldiers who complained, in A.D. 14, that they were not allowed

[1] Tac. *Ann.* I, 17.
[2] Berytus (p. 259) is uncertain.
[3] P. 174.
[4] Ibid.
[5] Cf. Rostovtzeff, *SEH.* p. 580 n. 60.
[6] Cf. Ritterling, *PW.* XII, 1239.
[7] *Demonstratio Artis Geometricae* (Feldm. I, p. 396).
[8] Tac. *Hist.* I, 65; cf. Syme, *RR.* p. 478 n. 1.
[9] Cf. Lécrivain, *Rev. hist.* CLV, 1927, p. 182.
[10] Ibid.; Syme, *RR.* pp. 323, 477.
[11] Cf. Säflund, *Skrifter utgivna av Svenska Institutet i Rom*, IV, 1, 1934, p. 68.
[12] Cf. Kolbe, *GGA.* 1939, p. 156, criticising Weber, *Princeps*, I, pp. 205 ff.

real retirement into civilian life after their discharge, or even after a subsequent reservist course with the *vexilla*.[1]

The contrast with Caesar is obvious. Brutus's attack in 44 B.C. on Caesarian colonisation studiously ignores the civilian projects. An immediate benefit of these was the relief of over-population in Rome,[2] but their more grandiose implications cannot be judged, since they had no time, before the death of their author, for the expansion and extension which they deserved.[3] Nor was it an unjustifiable experiment that the most vigorous of the Italian soldiers should be made to share ideas—and children—with peoples who were more civilised than themselves. The cultural viewpoint of Augustus may have been safer, and his problems greater; but the mutinies of A.D. 14 leave little doubt that his solution, as revealed by the coins, though suitable to the strategic needs of Rome, Italy and the Empire, was not satisfactory to the masses of population of whom those were composed and who toiled for their upkeep.

[1] Cf. Parker, *The Roman Legions*, p. 246, etc.
[2] Cf. Adcock, *CAH*. IX, p. 710.
[3] Cf. Rostovtzeff, *SEH*. p. 494 n. 23.

D. BUREAUCRATIC POLICY CONCERNING THE ROMAN CITIES

So much for the foundations; the next three sections will deal with the policy regarding the Roman cities once they were founded. The appearance of Roman city-coinage in the provinces, coinciding with the multiplication of the cities themselves, is a significant moment in the dawning era in which a degree of self-government was encouraged (p. 401). It has been shown that foundation-coinages, though paid for out of the Roman treasury or a benefactor's purse, were issued by local authority and local officials; certain of them provide clues which make it possible to determine with some exactness the date of the innovation. The issue of *municipium* Simitthu (?) was later than the battle of Thapsus; that of *colonia* Sinope was made in 45. Of the rest that seem to fall within the same category, *municipium* Emporiae struck soon after Munda, the colony at Corinth probably before the dictator's death; nor are these isolated, since thenceforward there is a rapid increase in the number of local coinages. It is not a coincidence that Roman communities as far apart as Spain and Achaia, Africa and Paphlagonia, all coin for the first time, initiating a new economic method, at least within the same eighteen months, and perhaps almost contemporaneously within the year 45; nor is it fortuitous that the same year sees a similar provision by Clovius for the new communities of Cisalpine Gaul (p. 7). These coincidences make it unlikely that Caesar's municipal reforms did not take the provinces into consideration,[1] and decisively indicate the existence of some sort of general enactment or declaration of policy—for which, indeed, political thought was prepared by Cicero's formulation, probably in this very year,[2] of the dual responsibilities of townsmen: *omnibus municipibus duas esse censeo patrias, unam naturae unam civitatis*.[3]

No subject is so controversial or obscure as the municipal reforms of Julius. Among the most recent writers, Adcock[4] and Cary[5] express doubts whether a single comprehensive reorganisation took place, rather than a gradual process of evolution. Rudolph,[6] indeed, exaggerates the activity of the dictator in this respect;[7] but still Stuart Jones[8] declares: 'That it was Caesar who took the decisive step which the Republic never faced, and which converted the city-state into empire, will not be denied', and Sherwin-White[9] concludes that he must have aimed at a 'reasonable uniformity of procedure', and that in this respect he was a pioneer. The group of early coins has the weight of

---

[1] As Sherwin-White, p. 178.
[2] Cf. Teuffel, *History of Roman Literature*, I, p. 292.
[3] *De Legibus*, II, 2. 5; cf. Sherwin-White, p. 133.
[4] *CAH*. IX, pp. 700 f.
[5] *JRS*. 1937, p. 53, doubting his own conclusions in *JRS*. 1929, pp. 116 ff.
[6] *Stadt und Staat im römischen Italien*, especially pp. 217 ff.
[7] Cf. Cary, Sherwin-White, ll.cc., Stuart Jones, *JRS*. 1936, p. 271.   [8] L.c.   [9] Pp. 144, 175.

concrete evidence, which is always exceptionally rare in a controversy of this sort: their narrow temporal and wide geographical limits strongly favour the probability at least of some co-ordination of policy regarding Roman cities, in the provinces as well as in Italy, at this time.[1] Moreover, the contemporary development of official *aes* currency illustrates a new recognition of the economic needs of the provinces in which the new Roman communities lay.

However, even the broadest features of enactments in their interests are undiscoverable amid the complications of the literary and epigraphic evidence. Adcock[2] shows the danger of assuming a general *lex municipalis* from a phrase in an inscription from Patavium,[3] which is likely to refer to a law of local application only: a general law is assumed by Rudolph,[4] but the date (47 B.C.) and clauses which he postulates are based on a single passage of Cicero[5] which cannot support a generalisation.[6] Again, von Premerstein[7] has convincingly shown that the Table of Heraclea[8] embodies a series of drafts prepared for Caesar in c. 45 and promulgated after his death (probably in a *lex satura*[9]): but the fourth law which it incorporates is not general as has been thought,[10] but refers to Fundi in particular.[11] The third item in the Table certainly concerns the tenure of city-magistracies, but Adcock points out that 'its position after one law and before another..... suggests that it is the whole of Caesar's draft legislation under this head', and deduces from its contents that Caesar had not passed a general law concerning colonies and *municipia*. In any case, the scope of this measure was Italian only:[12] even the general municipal laws postulated by Hardy[13] and Rudolph are not thought by them to include the Roman cities outside Italy.[14] Yet the evidence of the coinage strongly suggests the co-ordination of these.

The vexed question of general legislation for Roman cities throughout the Empire depends in the last resort on the wider problem of the progress under Caesar in the surveying and assessing of the entire Empire and its populations. If it could be shown that such bureaucratic statistics were highly developed by the dictator, it would follow that there existed at Rome—as later[15]—a 'corpus of normal municipal regulations'[16]— and with it the centralised policy of which the coins seem to indicate the beginning.

[1] Sutherland, *RIS*. p. 129, on other grounds remarks that this 'does not lie beyond the bounds of credibility'.
[2] *CAH*. IX, p. 700; cf. also Last, *JRS*. 1938, p. 214; Sherwin-White, p. 141. [3] *ILS*. 5406.
[4] L.c.; cf. (most recently) Cardinali, *Augustus* (1938), p. 167 (criticised by Last, l.c.).
[5] *Fam.* 13. 11. 3.
[6] Cf. Cary, Stuart Jones, ll.cc.; Strasburger, *Gnomon*, 1937, pp. 190 f.
[7] *SavZ*. XLII, 1922, pp. 45 ff.
[8] *ILS*. 6085; Hardy, *Six Roman Laws*, pp. 149 ff.; Peguero, *Mélanges Cornil*, II, pp. 385 ff.
[9] Cf. Sherwin-White, p. 144.
[10] E.g. by Rudolph, l.c. pp. 176 ff.
[11] Cf. Adcock, Stuart Jones, Cary, ll.cc.
[12] Cf. Adcock, l.c.
[13] *Some Problems in Roman History*, pp. 261 ff., etc.
[14] Cf. Mommsen, *Ephemeris Epigraphica*, IX, 1913, p. 5.
[15] Cf. Hyginus, *De Limitibus Constituendis* (Feldm. I, pp. 202 f.).
[16] Heitland, *Repetita*, p. 12; cf. Hirschfeld, *St.V.* p. 471 n. 1.

Unfortunately here the darkness does not lighten, but thickens. The early coinages of Emporiae (p. 156), etc., bear witness to the appointment of the censorial *quinquennales* already in the forties; but since such bodies do not coincide in date either with each other or, later, even with the *lustra* at Rome (p. 164), no central policy can be deduced. An 'Empire-census'[1] cannot conceivably have been completed at this early date. These failures to coincide show, incidentally, that even the third law on the Table of Heraclea—the only general enactment that has survived criticism—soon became a dead letter, since it enjoined a correspondence between Roman and municipal censuses.[2] Cassiodorus[3] and Isidorus[4] link with census operations their natural concomitant, land-surveying. Concerning Caesar's interest in this we have certain statements that are explicit but from lamentably untrustworthy authorities. Julius Honorius[5] records an 'Empire-survey', lasting several decades, dating from a *senatus consultum* in the consulships of Julius Caesar and Antony. He, or the authority from which his information is derived, is echoed by Diculus[6] and Felix Malleolus,[7] who speak of a *Cosmographia* of Caesar. Although the details of these accounts are wholly unplausible, certain modern authorities[8] are justified in refusing to view this persistent tradition with complete scepticism. Genuine reports may, for example, be reflected in the statement of Pseudo-Boethius[9] that an *epistula* of the dictator instituted the profession of official land-surveyor, and in the reference by Albertus Magnus[10] to pre-Augustan land-statistics in the West. These absurdly late authorities can scarcely be said to illuminate this most obscure of problems: but they are at least unanimous in referring the origins of the bureaucratic system back to Julius. Indeed, this was a logical necessity arising from the multiplication of communities, and in no sense a break with the past.[11] If the plan was still 'somewhat chaotic',[12] that was the fault not of Caesar but of his murderers.

One of the principal elements in any such centralisation must have been a co-ordinated policy concerning the Roman cities. The existence of this under Julius has been shown to be required by the numismatic evidence: a large number of Roman communities, and widespread local coinage, suddenly sprang into being in c. 45. Moreover,

---

[1] Luke ii, 1; Cedrenius, *Historia* (Bekker, p. 321); Syncellus (Dindorf, pp. 597 f.); Isidorus, *Origines*, v; Suidas, s.v. Αὔγουστος; Malalas (Dindorf, p. 226); cf. Orestano, *Bollettino dell' istituto di diritto romano*, 1937, p. 239 n. 2; Ritschl, *Rhein. Mus. NF.* I, 1842, p. 482.

[2] Abbott and Johnson, pp. 294 f.

[3] *Variae* III, 52 (emended by Huschke).

[4] *Origines* v (cf. Petersen, *Rhein. Mus. NF.* VIII, 1853, p. 188).

[5] *Cosmographia* (cf. Ritschl, *Rhein. Mus. NF.* I, 1842, p. 482). For the identification of this writer with 'Aethicus' or 'Ethnicus', cf. Cantor, *Die römischen Agrimensoren*, p. 83, etc.

[6] *De Mensura Orbis Terrae* (cf. Petersen, l.c. p. 163).

[7] *De Nobilitate et Rusticitate* (cf. Petersen, l.c. p. 164).

[8] E.g. Cantor, l.c. pp. 83, 85; Müllenhoff, *Schriften der Universität zu Kiel aus dem J. 1856*, VI, 1, p. 1; Humbert, *Daremberg and Saglio*, I, 1. 166.

[9] *Demonstratio Artis Geometricae* (Feldm. I, p. 395; cf. Schulten, *PW*. VII, 1889).

[10] Ed. Ven. p. 101.

[11] Sherwin-White, p. 145, emphasises that Caesar's reforms were in accordance with tradition.

[12] Ibid. p. 175.

BUREAUCRATIC POLICY CONCERNING ROMAN CITIES 311

early *IVviri* at Tingis, *praefecti* at Celsa, *quinquennales* at Emporiae, show that the provincial cities kept abreast with developments nearer home. On general grounds such a policy is in the highest degree probable: the influence of these communities was essential for 'Romanisation'; they were loaded with privileges (p. 404); and their vast extension, as revealed by the coinage, was one of the most progressive and characteristic of Caesar's projects. But, since even the broadest features of a central policy concerning them cannot now be reconstructed, it is only possible to say that this already existed.

Augustus's progress in the bureaucratic control of the Roman communities abroad is slightly better documented, although even this vital topic has been passed over in silence by most of the best-known authorities. Here again the coins are in the forefront of the evidence. In the first place, the Eastern colonies which coined were spaced in such a way that a maximum benefit was extracted from each mint (p. 297); this strategic arrangement must have originated from the central authority. The same conclusion must be derived from the formulas which refer so many issues to the permission of Augustus or his representative (pp. 314 ff.), and from the refoundation-coinage of Apamea which significantly refers to a senatorial decree (p. 255). This measure of centralisation indicates that the technical details were in the hands of a special secretary or committee. A financial staff of freedmen is recorded;[1] but those of them who dealt with matters of this kind must have been connected, not only with the *princeps*, but with the *aerarium*—since this was the only Roman treasury, and was concerned with every province alike (p. 97). Although the character of the bureau which supervised the finances of Roman cities is unknown, its existence can be safely deduced from the numismatic evidence.

The outlines of the policy by which this department was guided can be partially sketched by reference to other sources. The reforms of Augustus distinguish sharply between Roman communities and those of peregrine rank (p. 404). Provincial censuses[2] (which must be substituted for the fictitious 'Empire censuses' [p. 310 n. 1]) do not concern the former, whose members, as Meyer[3] rightly pointed out, are thenceforward included in the Roman censuses; Schulz[4] has recently demonstrated that the Roman returns were now to include, not only adults, but all the Roman population of the cities. Since the incidence of local *quinquennales* was (in apparent contravention to the third law in the Table of Heraclea) not generally adjusted to suit the date of Roman *lustra* (p. 164), it must be concluded that each city merely sent in its latest quinquennial returns to the statistical bureau which produced the figures of the *Res Gestae*.[5] There was no escape from the notice of this bureau: newborn children even of *peregrini*—and

---

[1] Suet. *Aug.* 101.
[2] E.g. Gaul (Livy, *Ep.* 134; cf. Kubitschek, *PW.* III, 1918), Spain (Dio LIII, 22. 5; *CIL.* VI, 332), Syria (Josephus, *AJ.* XVII, 13. 5; Luke ii, 2), Egypt (Calderini, *Rendiconti del R. Ist. Lombardo*, LXIV, 1931, pp. 551 ff.; Bell, *CAH.* x, p. 304), etc.
[3] *Conrad'sches Handwörterbuch der Staatswissenschaften*, II³, 1909, p. 908.
[4] *Mnemosyne*, 1937, p. 185.
[5] 8.

a fortiori of Romans—had to be recorded on birth-certificates,[1] and each new *adsignatio* was based on a carefully drawn-up list.[2] It is, therefore, not surprising that a land-survey including all the property of Roman (and probably peregrine[3]) communities was completed by Augustus. The evidence for its completion by him is unanimous,[4] although the initiator of the scheme is variously identified. The name of its technical director is equally unknown,[5] but there is reason to believe that his position in the State was now established on a new basis.[6] His achievement, at all events, is proved and illustrated by the resultant Commentarii and Map of Agrippa.[7]

The population and property, therefore, of the inhabitants of the Roman cities were now amply documented at Rome; and the record-office dealing with them, of which Hyginus[8] informs us, was in process of evolution. Various Gromatic writers, whose combined evidence there is no reason to doubt, indicate that this information was put to effect by special measures of Augustus for these communities as a whole. Frontinus[9] bears witness to an *oratio* by him *de statu municipiorum*, containing technical rulings about land-tenure: whether this *oratio* moved a *senatus consultum*—as terminological accuracy would demand[10]—or was merely one of the *dicta principis* whose *auctoritas* made it virtually binding (p. 433) cannot be determined. Equally significant is the reference of Hyginus[11] to a *lex et constitutio divi Augusti* concerning boundary-walls. *Constitutio* is an anachronistic expression for the informal *dicta principis* just mentioned (p. 432); here, as often, one of those expressions of *auctoritas* was

---

[1] Cf. Sanders, *AJA*. 1928, pp. 308 ff.; id. *Aegyptus*, 1937, pp. 233 ff.; Cuq, *Mélanges Fournier*, 1929, pp. 119 ff.

[2] Siculus Flaccus, *De Condicionibus Agrorum* (Thulin, Teubner ed. p. 101; cf. *Feldm.* I, p. 154): *agri...assignantur viritim nominibus*.

[3] Cf. Cumont, *JRS*. 1934, pp. 187 f., for Syria.

[4] E.g. Pliny, *NH.* III, 46 (Italy); *Fragm. Itin. Ant. ap.* Jul. Honorium (Simler ed., p. 295); Jul. Honorius, *Cosmographia* (Ritschl, *Rhein. Mus. NF.* I, 1842, p. 486); *anon. subscriptor ad Librum Coloniarum* (*MS. Arcerianus, Feldm.* I, p. 239); Agennius Urbicus, *ap.* Frontin. *De controversiis* (*Feldm.* I, p. 8); Suidas, s.v. ἀπογραφή; Albertus Magnus (ed. Ven. p. 101). Cf. Cantor, *Die römischen Agrimensoren*, p. 85; Schulten, *PW.* VII, 1887. For the *mensio* of Narbonensis, cf. Martianus Capella, *Encyclopaedia* VI (Cantor, l.c. p. 199 n. 163).

[5] Mommsen, *Die römischen Feldmesser*, p. 225; Gensel, *PW.* II, 2821; Schulten, ibid. VII, 1887; Cantor, l.c. p. 64, show that he cannot be identified with Balbus, as *anon. subscriptor ad Libr. Col.*, l.c.,

Pseudo-Boethius, *Demonstratio Artis Geometricae* (*Feldm.* I, p. 402), cf. Ritschl, l.c.: Balbus was a contemporary of Trajan.

[6] Schulten, *PW.* VII, 1889, believes that the professional *mensores* employed by the triumvirs (possibly Satrius Verus was one of these, *Liber Coloniarum* [*Feldm.* I, p. 244]) and perhaps created by Julius Caesar (cf. p. 9) were given a military standing by the army reforms of Augustus (cf. Neumann, *Klio*, XXVI, 1933, p. 362). But in view of the institution of civilian *deductio Caesaris auctoritate* (see above, p. 293) it is unlikely that all Augustan *adsignatores* were officers.

[7] Pliny, *NH.* III, 2; cf. Stevenson, *CAH.* X, p. 192; Jones, *CERP.* p. 495.

[8] *De Limitibus Constituendis* (*Feldm.* I, pp. 202, 203).

[9] *De Controversiis Agrorum* I (ibid. p. 18); cf. Pisani, *Annali della R. Scuola Normale Superiore di Pisa* (*lett.-st.-fil.*), ser. II, vol. VII, 1938, p. 224.

[10] Cf. Pisani, l.c.

[11] L.c. (*Feldm.* I, p. 194); cf. Orestano, *Bollettino dell' Istituto di diritto romano*, 1937, p. 246.

incorporated in a *lex* (p. 433). Hyginus's statement is supported by the allusion by Latinus and Mysrontius[1] to a *recensitio* by Augustus of all boundary-stones and the institution of a new kind called *termini Augustei*. A third passage of Hyginus[2] indicates that the general principles of *adsignatio* were also regulated by a *lex* under Augustus.

These are all measures whose scope is greater than a single community. Since the operations of the Roman census now included not only the Italian cities, but Roman cities abroad, it is unlikely that these reforms—especially the *oratio de statu municipiorum*—were limited to the peninsula: there was no legal distinction between Roman *civitates* in Italy and those abroad.[3] At all events, each of these enactments is a general ruling from the department at Rome. Other decrees were framed to comprise all the Roman citizen-bodies in a single province: Heitland's[4] suggestion that directions to these found their way into measures designed for whole provinces is confirmed by Buckland's demonstration that tralatician *edicta provinciarum* continued without a break under the early principate,[5] and were—like their counterparts at home, the *edicta urbana*—concerned solely with the citizens in the provinces to which they referred.[6] These provincial edicts, too, were manifestations of a central organisation, through its provincial representative; comparable, in the financial sphere, are the coinages and other operations of provincial branches of the *aerarium* (p. 97).

Comprehensive enactments of these kinds would not have been possible under the Republic, when the information on which they were based was not accessible. The coinage is the most important category of evidence which has enabled the evolutionary process to be faintly delineated. It leads to the conclusion that the bureaucratic organisation necessary for the unified control of the vital class of citizen-communities in the provinces was greatly developed by Augustus, but was begun by Caesar.

[1] *De Locis Suburbanis* (*Feldm.* I, p. 348).
[2] L.c. (ibid. p. 201).
[3] Cf. Sherwin-White, p. 180—although Roman snobbishness still made it difficult for citizens of the latter to 'get on' outside their cities, ibid.; cf. Sutherland, *RIS*. p. 169.
[4] *Repetita*, p. 7 n. 2.
[5] *Rev. hist. du droit français et étranger*, IV sér., XIII, 1934, p. 88; *pace* Velsen, *SavZ*. 1900, pp. 81 ff.
[6] Buckland, l.c. p. 91; *pace* Velsen, l.c.; Weiss, *Studien zu den römischen Rechtsquellen*, pp. 71 ff.; Walton, *Introduction to Roman Law*, p. 251.

E. ADMINISTRATIVE INTERFERENCE BY PROVINCIAL OFFICIALS

The control thus instituted was augmented by the establishment of various methods by which the policies of individual cities could be influenced and utilised. These methods can be divided into two groups, comprising their relationships to the provincial representatives of the central authority, and to that authority itself.

The first of these problems is rendered especially difficult by the discovery that very many of the numismatic appearances of governors are to be accounted for by the special circumstances of foundations. But evidence of an unusual kind can be derived from official coins discussed in the first Part (pp. 3 ff.). These were, very often, actually struck at the local mints of Roman cities. An enumeration will establish the value of such information. It is clear from the outset that *municipia* were not exempt from this requisition, since Lilybaeum, Panormus and Syracuse (?), where Sex. Pompeius issued coinage, were apparently cities of this class. The triumvirs coined at Italian cities, and Octavian's coinage at *municipium* Lipara indicates that, for a time at least, he maintained a similar practice. After Actium instances multiply, in East and West. Before the *restitutio rei publicae*, an official issue is struck at *colonia* Apamea celebrating the capture of Egypt (?): thereafter, even at the comparatively few mints that are certain, there are examples at every period from provinces both 'imperial' and 'senatorial', consular and praetorian. A part of the main official series was coined at Parium; the *legati* P. Carisius and P. Quinctilius Varus commandeer the mints at Emerita and Berytus respectively; Apamea is again requisitioned by the proconsul M. Granius Marcellus. Moreover, two distinct methods of encroachment can be traced. On the one hand, proconsular issues from Hadrumetum are shown by great similarities of die to originate from the same workshop as the local coinage; on the other, the *libertas* of Lugdunum was infringed by the establishment of a special official mint with a military guard. In both cases coinage was based on the permission and *auctoritas* of the *princeps*; supported by this, his subordinates were evidently permitted to make every use of the mints of colonies and *municipia*. Interventions by Pliny the Younger are not applicable to this period; more relevant is the practice of the Republic, when governors had already exercised a general authority over these cities.[1] The completeness of this control at the present period is made particularly clear by the coinage. Corroboration is obtainable from other sources. Utica and then Carthage, Corinth, Carthago Nova and then Tarraco, are among the proconsular residences of the period;[2] subordinates were established at other colonies such as Hippo.[3] A *legatus* of Syria was given

---

[1] Cf. Last, *CAH*. XI, p. 467; Halgan, *Essai sur l'administration des provinces sénatoriales*, p. 148.

[2] This encroachment was facilitated by its popularity in commercial circles in the cities: cf. Dio Chrysostom XXXV, 15; Jones, *GC*. p. 263.

[3] E.g. *CIL*. IX, 1592.

INTERFERENCE BY PROVINCIAL OFFICIALS

first hearing in the court of Berytus.[1] Both colonies and *municipia* paid taxes unless specially exempted.[2] It is difficult to reconcile these facts with a high degree of local independence. Furthermore, the higher jurisdiction of the *conventus*, in so far as these were yet established,[3] was in the hands of the governors, and colonies were included in these *conventus*.[4] The tenure of a governorship was now accompanied by eponymy throughout the province,[5] in the manner of the consuls at Rome; this is a sure sign of the general supremacy whose details are discovered from the coins. Consular governors in Africa and Syria are actually entitled to grant cities their *Permissus* to coin (pp. 232, 260).

The privilege later called *ius Italicum* comprised and exceeded *immunitas*;[6] yet von Premerstein cannot be right in including among its advantages complete autonomy (*Selbstverwaltung ohne Oberaufsicht des Statthalters*[7]), since Emerita, Parium, Apamea and Berytus[8] are among cities whom this title does not exempt from requisition for coinage by their respective governors.[9] Acci, also *iure Italico*, is even included in the *conventus* of Carthago Nova.[10] Nor does the badge of Marsyas (*Liber pater*) indicate freedom in this respect: it is found at the two requisitioned cities of Apamea and Parium.[11] Servius simply calls this *signum...liberae civitatis*;[12] the many complicated interpretations that have been given[13] ill accord with the heterogeneous list of colonies and *municipia*, some very unimportant, at which the badge is found.[14] Since it is now clear that each Roman community was *libera* (p. 225), each was entitled to this symbol, and the controversy is vain. Moreover, it is highly probable that at this time the *ius*

---

[1] Josephus, *AJ*. XVI, 368; cf. Volkmann, *Münchener Beitr. z. Papyrusforschung*, XXI, 1935, p. 157.

[2] Kornemann, *PW*. XVI, 633 f.

[3] Cf. Sutherland, *RIS*. p. 143.

[4] von Premerstein, *PW*. X, 1250; Kornemann, l.c. 634.

[5] Mommsen, *St.R*. II. 1, p. 261.

[6] von Premerstein, l.c. 1242 ff.

[7] Ibid.; cf. Marquardt, *St.V*. I, pp. 90 f.; Last, *CAH*. XI, p. 455.

[8] von Premerstein, l.c. 1240, for status.

[9] Marzullo, *Atti della Soc. Italiana per il Progresso delle Scienze*, V, 1932, Estr. p. 7 n. 1, points out similar limitations.

[10] Pliny, *NH*. III, 25; von Premerstein, l.c. 1250.

[11] von Premerstein, l.c. 1251.

[12] *ad Aen*. III, 20; cf. also ibid. IV, 58; Macrobius, *Sat*. III, 12.

[13] For various opinions vide Lenormant, Daremberg et Saglio, s.v. *colonia*, p. 1321; cf. Eckhel, *DN*. IV, p. 493; Toutain, *Mél. d'arch*. XVIII, 1898,

pp. 141 ff.; Heisterbergk, *Philologus*, L, 1892, pp. 648 f.; Kornemann, *PW*. IV, 580 ff.; Premerstein, l.c.; Burckhardt, *PW*. XIV, 1993; Jullian, *Rev. ét. anc*. 1913, p. 490; Seston, *Mél. de l'École française de Rome*, 1926–7, p. 167. The material has recently been carefully collected (with the omission of Marzullo's doubtful Paestan statue) by Paoli, *Mél. d'arch. et d'hist*. LV, 1938, pp. 98 ff. He admits that 'Marsyas' is linked with *civitas* (p. 114) and sees that most of the cities where he appears are not specified as possessors of *ius italicum* (p. 122), but nevertheless falls back on the old view. He has, however, neglected recent literature explaining the character of *libertas*. Furthermore, the worship of *Liber pater* was so widely diffused in the West (cf. Hoeppfner, *Bull. de la Fac. des lettres de Strasbourg*, X, 1931–2, pp. 135 f.) that it is very doubtful whether every 'Marsyas' can be used for the purpose of such arguments (p. 316). A complex theory of Marzullo, l.c., is based on several misconceptions (p. 201).

[14] von Premerstein, l.c. 1251.

Italicum was the exclusive and invariable concomitant of Roman status.[1] Servius says what he means. The rarity of 'Marsyas' in Italy, of which much is sometimes made, is due to the fact that, where all were of Roman status and all 'free', the distinctive symbol lacked purpose.[2] But this *libertas* depended upon acquiescence,[3] and the extent to which this was necessary is made abundantly clear by the numerous examples of requisitioning.

[1] Jones, *GC*. p. 133. Sherwin-White, p. 188 n. 3, Frank, *AJP*. XLVIII, 1927, p. 185, deny its conferment on peregrine cities at this date, *pace* Abbott and Johnson, p. 118; Marzullo, l.c. p. 24, cf. p. 9.

[2] Cf. Jordan, *Marsyas auf dem Forum in Rom*; Mommsen, *St.R.* III, pp. 808 ff.

[3] Cf. Kloesel, *Libertas*, Diss. Breslau, 1935, pp. 14 ff.

F. RELATION OF THE CITIES TO AUGUSTUS

Thus interference by provincial officials was frequent and universal. But every interference was in the last resort answerable to the *princeps* who represented the entire Roman state. Moreover, apart from his intermediaries, Augustus himself possessed a personal relationship with every community: and his position is vital to the thesis that the central government failed to solve the problem of its relationship to the cities.[1] As usual, the system of his supremacy is complex, and lacks the simple decisiveness which would have destroyed the intended illusion of independence.

One of the most important manifestations of this supremacy was the appearance on coins of his portrait. This was not yet, as later, a regular formality. The supposition of a special decree permitting this privilege to Caesar is based on a misinterpretation of Dio (p. 15), and phrases like *kaiserliches Bildnisrecht* are at this time meaningless (p. 228); while a vast array of exceptions denies the possibility even of a *Gesetzesstatt beobachtete Regel*.[2] Such bureaucratic institutions are alien to the lack of uniformity that is characteristic of Augustan policy, and the special significance of portraiture of the *princeps* lies beyond them. Yet it is true that, at the Roman cities, a few examples of portraiture under Antony swell to a multitude under Augustus.

It is worth noting that even the heads of the Ptolemies appear on coinage not from a royal right, but merely from feelings of respect—and thus even outside their realms.[3] Similar moral elements predominate here. All the Roman cities in the East, and most in the West, had a very special obligation to Augustus. Refoundations and foundations alike entitled him to their *patrocinium*,[4] which bound the cities to him in the relationship of *clientela*. The *officia* for which, in this capacity, they were morally responsible, were, in their origins, very comprehensive;[5] in particular, the clients were even within the *dicio* of their *patronus*.[6] In the last years of the Republic, indeed, the *clientela* of communities, as of individuals, had lost many of its implications; but Julius, by abolishing the *IIIviri coloniis deducendis* in favour of a more personal method (p. 9), had concentrated in his hands the *patrocinium* of many new foundations,[7] and strongly supported *clientela* as an institution.[8] Numismatic evidence shows that the lesson was not lost on the cities. For example, the appearance of Julius on coins during the princi-

[1] Cf. Heitland, *Repetita*, pp. 5 ff.; Reinhold, *CJ*. 1938, p. 369; Stuart Jones, *EHR*. 1931, p. 671.
[2] Kahrstedt, *Klio*, x, 1910, p. 289.
[3] Cf. Brett, *AJA*. 1937, pp. 453 ff.
[4] Cf. von Premerstein, p. 19. Hübner's denial (*CIL*. II, 5093) that any *princeps* was *patronus* of a city is shown not to apply to Augustus by Sebastian, *De patronis etc.*, Diss. Halle, 1884, p. 12, quoting *CIL*. x, 8305.
[5] Bernert, *De Vi atque Usu Vocabuli Officii*, Diss. Breslau, pp. 32 f.
[6] von Premerstein, *PW*. IV, 38. But Heinze, *Vom Geist des Römertums*, p. 171, shows that this was a question of *fides*, not of law.
[7] Cf. Skard, *Festskrift til Koht*, p. 58.
[8] *Pro Bithynis prooem*. (Gellius, *NA*. v, 13. 6).

pate is very rare—except at the cities which he founded or freed, where it is common: his head and image are engraved at Sinope, Apamea, Alexandria Troas, Lampsacus, Parium,[1] Achulla and Hadrumetum. Equally noteworthy is the appearance of Antony at his colony of Philippi, whereas Julius appears at the contemporary Julio-Antonian foundations at Lampsacus and Troas. Agrippa's effigy is, at peregrine cities, no less unusual, but at Gades he is found as PARENS PATRONVS, like M. Atius Balbus at Uselis. In the same way Augustus is described as PARENS COLONIAE on an inscription from Iader.[2] At communities where he planted settlements, his *patrocinium* bound the colonists to him in a perpetual cliental relationship. Where these had been Julian or Julio-Antonian before, he appeared, already in his lifetime, as colleague to the deified Caesar; a refoundation-issue of Philippi actually presents them together in this capacity. Thus the founder received special and scrupulous honour.

But, by an extension of the idea, every one of the Roman cities—like peregrine towns (p. 403), tribes[3] and client-kingdoms—was equally within the *patrocinium* of Augustus.[4] The *patrocinium orbis terrae*,[5] Scipio's ideal, was now a political entity. Proculus,[6] in defining the *libertas* which each possessed, explicitly states the cliental principle on which this relationship was based. Even such Roman settlements as were not *Augusta* owed their corporate existence to their cliental loyalty to Rome, and to the *princeps* who represented its senate and people. Augustus was universal *conditor*, just as he was universal κτίστης (p. 356).

Moreover, the significance of *clientela* in general was greatly enhanced just at this period. As an ancient institution of the Republic,[7] its implications in private life, sharply defended by Caesar, were further revived by Augustus. In the first place, all the personal procurators of the *princeps* were situated in this relationship to him.[8] Secondly, the new class of *Latini Iuniani*, and freedmen in general, were compelled to hold their *patroni* in profound respect:[9] Horace describes a *patronus* not as *pater* only, but as *rex*.[10] Indeed, the cliental idea played such a vital part in the politico-social thought of the period, that it can be considered the fundamental institution of the principate.[11] Carried away by this theme, von Premerstein has endeavoured not only to attribute a legal basis to the *tutela* which thus devolved upon Augustus (p. 452),[12] but also to apply the cliental principle to the conditions of many preceding decades.[13] At least four writers have voiced the widespread denial of the former of these

[1] BM, Vienna: second century A.D.
[2] *CIL*. III, 2907; cf. 13264.
[3] The Gallic tribes were first *clientes* of Caesar: cf. Syme, *RR*. p. 292.
[4] Cf. Syme, *RR*. p. 352. For the *coniuratio*, ibid. pp. 288 f.
[5] Cic. *Off*. II, 27; cf. Skard, l.c. p. 65.
[6] *Dig*. XLIX, 15. 7; cf. Kloesel, *Libertas*, Diss. Breslau, 1935, p. 87.
[7] In *XII Tabulae*, VIII, 21 (Girard); cf. Zmigryder-Konopka, *Studi italiani di filologia classica*, XIV, 1937, p. 94.
[8] Cf. Merkel, *Abhandlungen aus dem Gebiet des römischen Rechts*, III, pp. 42 f.
[9] Cf. Last, *CAH*. X, p. 431; Kaser, SavZ. 1938, p. 119; A. M. Duff, *Freedmen in the Early Roman Empire*, p. 37.
[10] *Ep*. I, 7. 37; cf. Friedländer, *Sittengeschichte*, pp. 385 ff.
[11] von Premerstein, *passim*; cf. Hammond, *AJP*. 1938, p. 483.
[12] Pp. 117 ff. [13] Pp. 13 ff.

hypotheses (p. 453 n.); Kahrstedt[1] has added that von Premerstein exaggerates its application to earlier periods. But its relevance to the *coniurationes* of the second triumvirate is unmistakable. The truth is that, like so much else, it was rescued by Caesar from the 'gangster' *régime* which he ended, but only given a permanent footing by Augustus. In his principate the influence of the *clientela* conception was manifold and widespread, and the veneration which it postulated was the basis of the Imperial structure. It was natural, then, for Roman cities to add the great *conditor et patronus* to the select gallery of founders' coin-portraits. But Pliny the elder actually shows that portraiture was a privilege specifically appropriate to *patroni*: *in atriis honos clientium instituit sic colere patronos*.[2] L. Abullius Dexter is honoured in this way by a *collegium clientium* at Aesernia.[3] This practice and this spirit played a decisive part in the inauguration of imperial coin-portraiture.

The conception of Augustus as universal founder underwent, in Roman communities, an obvious process of development. The first Roman founder, and the founder of Rome, was Romulus: the view that the new *princeps* was a second Romulus was not only everywhere current, but was politically stressed after Actium to such a degree that it became for a while the basis of official publicity.[4] This suggested an enlargement of the idea. Augustus, like Romulus, was not only the *conditor-patronus* of the State, he was thereby its *pater* also.[5] A *patronus* possessed a father's *auctoritas*, *dignitas* and *potestas*,[6] and Horace has already been cited to show that *patroni* could be hailed as *pater*. In another passage he calls Augustus *pater urbium*.[7] The *princeps* became the universal father; Dio[8] informs us of the moral responsibilities of both parties which this conception of the first *princeps* entailed. Such deductions from the *clientela* 'ideology' were formally recognised in 2 B.C. by the title of PATER PATRIAE[9]—the colony of Patrae relates its own establishment with that of the Empire by the simple description of the founder by this appellation (p. 265). It was the culmination of his honours, and the crystallisation of the *auctoritas* which was the moral and executive basis of the new *régime* (p. 444). Augustus was founder, patron and father to the whole Roman world.[10] It was, no doubt, owing to the rapid evolution of this idea that subsequent *principes* refused to become the *patroni* of individual cities,[11] since this position would have been supererogatory and invidious for the universal patron. Lesser *patrocinia* tended to die out as the *princeps* monopolised the idea.[12]

[1] *GGA*. 1938, pp. 5 f.
[2] *NH*. XXXIV, 17.
[3] *CIL*. X, 6094; cf. von Premerstein, p. 88.
[4] Kornemann, *Klio*, 1938, pp. 81 f., 85.
[5] Cf. Skard, l.c.; id. *QAS*. III, 1937, p. 29; Kornemann, *QAS* IV, 1938, p. 11; Berlinger, *Zur inoffiziellen Titulatur*, p. 77.
[6] Cf. Kaser, *SavZ*. 1938, pp. 62 ff.; Skard, l.c. p. 48.
[7] *Carm*. III, 24. 27; cf. Christ, *Tübinger Beiträge zur Altertumswissenschaft*, XXXI, 1938, p. 120.

[8] LIII, 18. 3.
[9] Unofficially bruited some years earlier: cf. Sutherland, *RIS*. p. 159.
[10] Cf. von Premerstein, p. 167; Skard, *QAS*. III, 1937, pp. 28 f.; Scott, *Archiv für Religionswissenschaft*, XXXV, 1938, p. 127.
[11] Sebastian, *De patronis*, etc., Diss. Halle, 1884, p. 11.
[12] Cf. von Premerstein, p. 113; Anderson, *JRS*. XXIX, 1939, p. 94.

It is, then, in this capacity—not as *Imperator*—that the Roman cities honoured Augustus with coin-portraiture.[1] However, like other institutions of the period, this portraiture had more than one origin, and was caused by a blend of interacting traditions. A large part was played in its development by the religious element—likewise a derivative of the 'charismatic' *auctoritas* (p. 444). Romulus was divine; it was easy to confuse the *imagines* of a *patronus* with those of a *genius*; and the *genius* (or *numen*) of Augustus[2] was given a place in the temples of Italian cities as early as 36 B.C.[3] In Roman cities outside the peninsula, the institution of *Augustales* in c. 13 B.C.[4] marks the standardisation of a process that had long been developing. Nock[5] reminds us that 'a municipality was free to show its loyalty in forms not always sanctioned for larger political units'. But even at Rome, where Augustus was not actually deified until his death,[6] the only other portraits besides his on the obverses of coins were those of gods. In other cities, the earliest occurrences of the triumvirs' heads suggest that a certain superhuman significance was attached to them. Antony follows closely upon Divus Julius at Corinth and Sinope—cities of whose restoration by the triumvir there is no record; but at that time he was being hailed as New Dionysus.[7] At Lugdunum, the first colony to employ a head of Octavian, it is actually equated with the portrait of the divine dictator. The colonists were already clearly aware of a new magnitude in the personalities of those who controlled them: later, the universal *patronus* of the re-founded Republic easily achieved a more than human status. Thus the sociological ideas of the principate began to take shape; the 'Imperial' portrait was a natural manifestation.

The development of these ideas soon caused a reflection of the glory to the dynastic house: a significant feature of the idea of *clientela* is its inheritability.[8] Sutherland[9] has shown the intense industry with which Caius, Lucius and Tiberius are honoured—not as local magistrates only—by the Spanish communities. The imagination of other cities was even more provident: Apamea, Corinth and Pella do not neglect the chances of Agrippa Postumus, and the financiers in power at Corinth look ahead two principates, doubt, and decide to omit neither Germanicus nor Drusus. These portraits of princes alternate with those of the *princeps*: a distinction made by Lampridius between heads of the Emperor and of his family[10] is the product of a later period. Augustus and his kinsmen were all alike possessors of a remarkable degree of *auctoritas*, and were all

---

[1] The ideas which contributed to this institution make it understandable that Gades, in commemorating Augustus and L. Cornelius Balbus, allows a portrait to the former but not to the latter (p. 172).

[2] Perhaps rather than he himself: von Premerstein, p. 170; cf. Taylor, *TAPA*. LI, 1920, pp. 116 ff.

[3] Cf. Nock, *CAH*. X, p. 482.

[4] Taylor, *TAPA*. XLV, 1914, pp. 234 ff.

[5] L.c. p. 487.

[6] Ibid. p. 488.

[7] Tarn, ibid. pp. 33, 53, 69.

[8] von Premerstein, p. 17; Anderson, *JRS*. 1939, p. 94; Stone, *CR*. LI, 1937, p. 29; Weber, *Princeps*, p. 221; pace Kübler, *Gnomon*, 1939, p. 325.

[9] *JRS*. 1934, pp. 31 ff.

[10] *Historia Augusta, Vita Antonini Diadumeni*, 2. 6: *statim apud Antiochiam moneta Antonini Diadumeni* (sic) *nomine percussa est, Macrini usque ad iussum senatus dilata est.*

alike portrayed. Yet there was never a formal assurance of the continuation of the principate,[1] and Augustus's predominance was not extended to his family.[2] Nothing could show more clearly than coins honouring the *domus Augusti* that the Roman citizenry of the Empire, like the Greeks,[3] were not deceived by the constitutional fictions.[4] Not that these fictions were neglected: they are seen embodied in the titulatures which accompany nearly every portrait of Augustus in the later part of his life.

So much for portraiture. Such a crystallisation of the sociological and constitutional elements of the principate shows an impressive blend of *auctoritas* and *potestas*, *dignitas* and divinity. But there was no apparent reason why it should have the least influence on the details of city policy. We must step from heaven to earth: Augustus had as large a stake in the latter as in the former, and neither godhead nor political theory sufficed for the successful control of his earthly property. It is necessary to examine the humbler practical methods employed for this purpose. The coinage has indicated that these included sheer administrative encroachment by his subordinates.[5] The mints of Roman cities are requisitioned and commandeered by his representatives; the African communities are instructed to publicise the institution of *amici principis*. Moreover, the formula PERMISSV AVGVSTI is openly recorded by cities even in the 'senatorial' province of Baetica; in Italy itself the Paestan mint, only operating on sufferance and under special conditions, appears to write I(*ussu*) A(*ugusti*) for the issue of its supervisor M. I. Ne. The patron and father of these cities was entitled to advise and influence their governing bodies as he thought fit, and this is only one of the many executive activities which were derived from his morally binding *auctoritas* (p. 433). It is significant that such intervention has no connection whatever with his *imperium*: without the assistance of this, the *auctoritas principis* was no less decisive than its frequent partner the *auctoritas senatus consulti*, though neither yet had theoretically the force of law.

Augustus's *auctoritas*, then, enabled him to interfere directly in the affairs of the cities. But, true to the indirect character of his policy, he preferred that these should seem to thrive without frequent and open application of pressure—for example, without his actually presiding in the colonial courts like Caesar.[6] Various subtler means of intervention can be discerned from extant material. For example, the construction of an aqueduct at Venafrum,[7] and of walls[8] elsewhere, shows that he made personal gifts to the colonies an excuse for legislation regarding their maintenance. A similar purpose

---

[1] Hohl, *GGA.* 1936, p. 137.
[2] Kahrstedt, *Klio*, x, 1910, p. 292.
[3] E.g. dedications εἴς τε τὸν αὐτοκράτορα καὶ τὸν οἶκον (*Monumenta Asiae Minoris Antiqua*, IV, 292). Cf. p. 471.
[4] Cf. Menadier, *ZfN.* XXXI, 1914, p. 17.
[5] Cf. Jones, *GC.* pp. 131 ff.
[6] E.g. at Carthago Nova: Nic. Dam. *De vita* XII

(*Smith College Classical Studies* IV, 1923, p. 12); cf. Volkmann, *Münchener Beitr. zur Papyrusforschung*, XXI, 1935, p. 205.
[7] *ILS.* 5743; cf. Mommsen, *Zeitschrift für geschichtliche Rechtswissenschaft*, XV, 1848, pp. 288 ff.; Abbott and Johnson, p. 33.
[8] Inscr. of Firmum, Fanum, Perusia, etc.; cf. Borghesi, *Œuvres*, v, p. 372; Jullian, *TP.* p. 74.

was no doubt served by his *cura viarum*[1]—at first unofficial and then official—and it is interesting to note that main roads often ran through a colonial *decumanus maximus*.[2] Such characteristic examples of the 'thin end of the wedge' may have been common. They were, moreover, encouraged by voluntary appeals to the *princeps* for legal interpretations.[3]

Yet, as at Rome and at the peregrine communities,[4] even this was less satisfactory than the more surreptitious regulation of local governing bodies by influencing their composition. Augustus found various ways of doing this, from the very beginning of a city's existence: and in so doing (as by his use of voluntary appeals) showed his careful study of the Hellenistic kingdoms.[5] At Saguntum and Zama Regia the *adsignatores* Libo and Ambatus are personages in high favour, who steal their respective governors' thunder in the years after Actium, when the *princeps* used his personal agents for administration and so lessened the proconsuls' initiative (pp. 421 f.). At Halaesa, as well, he designated the first college of magistrates, as Caesar had before him;[6] one of these was his *flamen* also, and such a combination became frequent at Paestum.[7] The eligibility of freedmen, established in the *Lex Coloniae Genetivae Iuliae*,[8] was also put to good use. Aeschinus, at Cnossus, is the *princeps*' own freedman,[9] and probably his *procurator*; Bennius and Hiberus, at Saguntum, are from similar families in his service. At Corinth, Insteius was a gangster of Antony, M. Antonius Theophilus his *procurator*. We find the names of many wealthy *gentes*, often with curiously non-Latin names, from the social stratum thrown to the top by the party politics of the revolutionary period. The son of Theophilus became *duovir* after him (p. 268): the continual reappearance of the kinsmen of past magistrates shows how closely the oligarchies were limited to those houses whose loyalty to the *régime* was proved.[10] Augustus inherited from the Republic[11] and from Caesar a close control over the methods of selection, and soon designations of colonial *patroni* occur by his *auctoritas*.[12]

Particularly significant was the innovation by which the *princeps* himself accepted the duovirate, an especially frequent practice in the early years of *civitas* (p. 163).

---

[1] Dio LIV, 8; cf. LIII, 22; Suet. *Aug.* 30; cf. Stevenson, *CAH.* x, p. 205; Jullian, *TP.* p. 75.

[2] E.g. at Axurna (Hyginus, *De Limitibus Constituendis*, *Feldm.* I, p. 179).

[3] As at Pompeii and Corfinium; cf. Jullian, *TP.* p. 88; Kornemann, *PW.* xvi, 634. These are distinct from utilisations of the *ius provocationis* (p. 450).

[4] Cf. Jones, *GC.* pp. 170 ff.

[5] Ibid. pp. 103 ff.

[6] *Lex Col. Genetivae Iuliae*, ch. 125.

[7] Berlin (Tiberius).

[8] Ch. 76; cf. Adcock, *CAH.* IX, pp. 709 f.

[9] His promotion shows that the exclusion of freedmen from municipal office by Augustus, alleged by Gordon, *JRS.* xxi, 1931, p. 66, Sutherland, *RIS.* p. 163, is incorrect. Mommsen, *RGDA.*[2] p. 121, does not dispose of this. It also apparently invalidates A. M. Duff's limitation of their honours to *ornamenta decurionatus* (*Freedmen in the Early Roman Empire*, p. 137).

[10] Cf. Jones, *GC.* pp. 170 ff.

[11] Cf. von Carolsfeld, *SavZ.* 1936, p. 302.

[12] E.g. at Aquinum, Pais, *Museo italiano di antichità classica*, I, 1885, p. 39.

When this occurred, he was represented on the spot by a single *praefectus iure dicundo*.[1] Abbott[2] remarks that the powers of these officials were such that they may be called the progenitors of the Trajanic *curatores reipublicae*. The coinage of Saguntum and Zama Regia reveals that certain occasions shortly after Actium endowed *praefecti* with an importance actually exceeding that of the *curatores*. Libo and Ambatus, after organising the *constitutio* of these cities, stay on—like L. Aclutius at Venafrum—as *praefecti* for the *princeps*, who, without a colleague, accepts the first (and often the second) duovirate of the newly founded towns. In a period when the powers of proconsuls were being limited, these *praefecti* were local dictators dependent only on Augustus: their portraits on the coins show that the local communities did not fail to hold them in due honour. Augustus's vicegerents also were occasionally allowed to accompany him: coins of Saguntum and Cnossus show that, contrary to the general view, Augustus permitted Agrippa and Tiberius to be his colleagues,[3] and each to be represented by his own *praefectus*. Two *praefecti* also regularly served when two members of the Augustan house (not including the *princeps*) were *duoviri*.[4] It was not long before other trusty servants of the *régime* were admitted to honorary duovirates: T. Statilius Taurus,[5] Sulpicius Quirinius,[6] and Man. Acilius (p. 249) are among those found in this capacity. Such honorary elections were utilised with the greatest freedom, and became a prominent feature in the competitive adulation of the cities. At Celsa, as early as the forties B.C., they were extended to the even more important quinquennalian magistracy, for which they are *de règle* at Saguntum. The custom was increased insidiously: it is understandable that, once commenced, its cessation might have caused offence, or invited unfavourable comparisons with a neighbour. Its value to Augustus was inestimable. His *praefecti* at least, and probably those of his regents, were chosen by himself, and for their year of office the government of their city was in their hands alone. The coinage shows that the citizens were sensible of the importance of these extraordinary magistrates.

Thus the methods of intervention used by Augustus were characteristically varied. At first sight they seem to present something of an anticlimax. Just as the official currencies were planned with insufficient completeness to exclude such a source of local pride as city-issues,[7] so the administrative interventions were not quite enough to ensure formal centralisation of policy: there is an apparent inconsistency between the loftiness of the Imperial dignity and the bathos of its application. The contrast was not accidental. Not one of the means of intervention, direct or indirect, which have been discussed, is traceable to the autocratic power of an *imperium*. On the contrary, they

---

[1] Kornemann, *PW*. XVI, 1623. It has been pointed out above, p. 10, that they must not be confused with *praefecti a. d. a.*, as by Jullian, *TP*. p. 29.
[2] Abbott and Johnson, p. 63.
[3] They owe their portraits to this office.
[4] Mommsen, *Gesammelte Schriften*, I, 308, etc.
[5] At Dyrrhachium (*CIL*. III, 605) and Ilici (*CIL*. II, 3556).
[6] At Pisidian Antioch (cf. Bleckmann, *Klio*, XVII, 1921, p. 111).
[7] Cf. Sutherland, *RIS*. p. 164.

belong to the nebulous realm of *auctoritas*, and to this all Roman city coinage must be assigned (p. 427). Such tact left room, not for freedom, but for *libertas*. It is not for nothing that the *duoviri* N. Gavius and M. Marcius at Paestum exalt the deity MENS BONA.[1] *Libertas* was often identified with political docility:[2] it had to be a *libertas plena pudoris*,[3] or it came to an end. The *Res Gestae* is divided into two sections, comprising *auctoritas* and *libertas* respectively—what the people gave to Augustus and what he gave to them.[4]

The extent and limitations of the latter are well illustrated by a comparison of the colonies and *municipia*. The original distinction between the two grades[5] was now, for all practical purposes, non-existent.[6] Even their governing bodies no longer observed the original restriction of *quattuorviri* to the *municipia*, and *duoviri* to the colonies (pp. 169, 200), and the former class was now as liable to drafts of settlers (pp. 155, 169), and often as exclusively Roman,[7] as the latter. The solid benefits of *immunitas*,[8] *iurisdictio*,[9] and *plena legis actio*,[10] were conferred on and withheld from both classes alike.[11] Siculus Flaccus emphasises the apparent arbitrariness of the grants to these cities—*casibus bellorum aut utilitatibus populi Romani aut ab iniustitia, ut dicunt, inaequales*.[12] The division was not between colonies and *municipia*. Yet the coinage provides several indications that the *municipia*—like the Latin cities (p. 336)—still cherished the out-

[1] For her shrine at Paestum vide *CIL*. x, 472. For her significance, vide Heinze, *Vom Geist des Römertums*, pp. 280 f.; Roloff, *GGA*. 1939, p. 98.

[2] Cf. Kloesel, *Libertas*, p. 15.

[3] *Laus Pisonis*, 106 ff. Cf. pp. 315 f.

[4] Ferrabino, *Augustus* (1938), pp. 50 ff.; cf. Last, *JRS*. XXVIII, 1938, p. 212; Kübler, *Gnomon*, 1939, p. 324. Cf. below, p. 403.

[5] Festus 126; Siculus Flaccus (*De Condicionibus Agrorum*, Thulin, Teubner ed. p. 98; *Feldm*. p. 134); Gellius XVI, 3, cf. Gelzer, *Frankfurter Universitätsreden*, XIX, 1924, p. 12 n. 29; Stevenson, *RPA*. p. 167; Bernardi, *Athenaeum*, 1938, pp. 240 ff.

[6] The views of Toutain, *Mél. d'arch*. 1896, pp. 315 ff., id. 1898, pp. 141 ff., Halgan, *Essai sur l'administration des provinces sénatoriales*, p. 118, Savigny, *Vermischte Schriften*, III, pp. 285 f., are corrected by Mommsen, *Hermes*, 1892, p. 112, id. *Abh. Göttingen* III, 18, p. 436 (modified in *Gesammelte Schriften*, pp. 113 ff.), Jullian, *TP*. pp. 31 ff., Beaudouin, *Revue générale du droit*, 1896, pp. 201 ff., M. Weber, *Römische Agrargeschichte*, pp. 64, 106 ff., Last, *CAH*. XI, p. 454, Rudolph, *Stadt und Staat im römischen Italien*, p. 176, Stuart Jones, *JRS*. 1936, p. 268, Sherwin-White, p. 86, Stevenson, *RPA*. p. 167.

[7] Cf. Sherwin-White, pp. 171 f., for the frequent limitation of the initial enfranchisement to resident Romans, as at Emporiae.

[8] Kornemann, *PW*. XVI, 634. It was no longer inseparable from *libertas*, either Roman or peregrine: cf. Stevenson, *RPA*. p. 151. *Ius italicum*, on the other hand, was probably still an invariable perquisite of *civitas* (p. 315).

[9] Hyginus, *De Condicionibus Agrorum* (*Feldm*. p. 120, l. 5, also p. 83, l. 5); cf. Frontinus, *De Controversiis Agrorum* (ibid. p. 19, l. 3, with *non* inserted, as by Thulin, Teubner ed. p. 8).

[10] *Dig*. 7. 1. 4, 26. 1. 6. 2; Paul. *Sent*. II, 25. 4; cf. Jullian, *TP*. pp. 32 f., correcting Mommsen, *Die Stadtrechte usw*. p. 436.

[11] Last, *JRS*. XXII, 1932, p. 59; Syme, *Papers of the British School at Rome*, XIV, 1938, p. 14, dispose of the view accepted by Schubart, *Bulletin de l'Institut français d'archéologie orientale*, XXX, 2, 1930, pp. 412 ff.; Homo, *Le Haut Empire*, pp. 270 f., and Carcopino, *Points de vue*, IV, pp. 170 f., that a fundamental difference still existed between cities which possessed and lacked the so-called *ius honorum*.

[12] Thulin, Teubner ed., p. 101, *Feldm*. p. 138: *inaequali*, according to *MS. Gudianum*. Not later than the first century: cf. Lange, *GGA*. 1853, pp. 530 f.

ward signs of their originally greater independence and seniority,[1] and that the colonies had not yet, as later,[2] attained higher prestige from their closer connection with the central government. Municipal coinage tends to avoid mention of Augustus,[3] or pointedly honours him as one of a series of benefactors or as local magistrate rather than as *princeps*:[4] it does not hesitate to portray local *adsignatores*.[5] These phenomena are profoundly in contrast with the regularity of colonial adulation. Augustus tried to foster loyalty to the Imperial idea by multiplying colonies, often in the place of *municipia* (p. 285); and he allowed colonial, but not apparently municipal, decurions to vote by proxy in the *comitia*.[6] But in the *Lex Iulia Vicesimaria*,[7] and the *Res Gestae* itself,[8] the *coloni* have not yet ousted the *municipes* from precedence;[9] and, after the triumvirate, Augustus does not seem to have ventured to requisition a *municipium* for official coinage. Indeed, even under Tiberius, *colonia* Praeneste petitioned for a return to municipal status.[10] The institutions of *municipia* were not yet reduced to an artificial uniformity;[11] they still valued the illusion of independence, and, as far as they could, ignored the concentration of power in the overwhelming *auctoritas* of one man. To the Roman cities—whose sympathy had been largely Republican in 44 B.C.[12]—this subordination still appeared humiliating: the day had not yet come when servility made it a privilege to stand closer to him in the position of a *colonus*.[13] *Auctoritas* lies heavier in the scales than its partner in the *Res Gestae*, *libertas*. The one was more than advice, and the other less than freedom.

[1] Kornemann, *PW*. IV, 513, 571. Apparent exceptions (e.g. *Lex Mamilia*) are due merely to groupings under the headings *deductio* and *constitutio*.

[2] Cf. Last, *CAH*. XI, p. 454; Jullian, *TP*. p. 35.

[3] E.g. Emporiae, Dertosa, Haluntium, Caralis.

[4] E.g. Saguntum, Gades; but not Italica.

[5] E.g. Saguntum, Caralis, Zama Regia.

[6] Suet. *Aug.* 46; cf. Jullian, *TP*. pp. 33 f.; Marzullo, l.c. p. 4. Suetonius is shown to be using *colonia* in its strict sense (i.e. not merely as 'Roman city') by his comment *Italiam...urbi quodam modo pro parte aliqua adaequavit*; that is, not all of Italy was involved. Translators usually take the two qualifying phrases as identical, which they cannot be: Philemon Holland renders 'after a sort, and in some part'. But the second phrase must be geographical in sense.

[7] Paul. *Sent.* IV, 6. 2.

[8] 21.

[9] As in Frontinus, *De Controversiis Agrorum* (*Feldm.* pp. 19. 4, 20. 8, 21. 4); *De Condicionibus Agrorum* (ibid. p. 35. 14); Hyginus, *De Condicionibus Agrorum* (ibid. p. 114. 2); Siculus Flaccus (ibid. pp. 135. 2, 163. 27). Cf. Jullian, *TP*. p. 35.

[10] Gellius, *NA*. XVI, 3; cf. Last, *CAH*. XI, p. 454.

[11] Cf. Sherwin-White, p. 215.

[12] Cf. Syme, *RR*. p. 101.

[13] Shuckburgh, ed. Suet. *Aug.* p. 102, antedates the change to this period.

Part III
THE PEREGRINE COMMUNITIES

INTRODUCTION

THE currency of the peregrine communities raises a new set of problems, which demand a different scheme of arrangement. Here local attributions should not in general cause great difficulty—although misreadings are as thick as flies—since it is customary for the ethnics to be written in full; on the other hand, the question of chronology is exceedingly complicated, owing to undescriptive titulatures and the long retention of Augustan portrait-types. The first Chapter is concerned with the coinages in honour of Augustus—a group whose link, his portrait, is the greatest unifying feature which had ever appeared in the coinages and loyalties of the Eastern cities. The coins which are the subject-matter of this Chapter number about 324 principal varieties, of which some 43 are unpublished. Half-a-dozen of these have been wrongly attributed to reigns; conversely, an important necessity is the expulsion of 151 issues from the Augustan series to a later period. The second Chapter deals with a topic of equal administrative importance, namely the relationship of the communities to the Roman governors and their administrations, as this is revealed by the coinage; the new evidence is then related to the much-disputed subject of local self-government. In this period occur the portraits or names of twenty-three officials, of whom five have been unrecognised.

Appendices 6–10 provide summaries connected with this Part.

Chapter 1
THE COMMUNITIES AND THE *PRINCEPS*
A. AUGUSTUS ON POSTHUMOUS COINAGES

THE current arrangement of peregrine issues bearing the head of Augustus gives a wholly false impression of their quantity and distribution, and is valueless as a basis of research. It has not been observed that a very large number of coins, generally attributed to his principate owing to the presence of his portrait and of the titles ΣΕΒΑΣΤΟΣ or ΚΑΙΣΑΡ ΣΕΒΑΣΤΟΣ, are actually of a later date.

Proofs of this contention are available from many sources. An arresting indication that it may well be the case is provided by a coin of **Aezanis** (?), on which ΑΥΤΟ. ΚΑΙ. ΣΕΒΑΣ. occurs without θεός and with a normal portrait of Augustus: but on the other side appear the head and title of Nero.[1] No less significant is the appearance of Augustus's own head, inscribed ΚΑΙΣΑΡ ΣΕΒΑΣΤΟΣ, on coins signed by the Galatian *legatus* T. Helvius T. f. Basila (Pl. IV, 23):[2] his tenure of the province must be attributed to the last years of the principate of Tiberius,[3] whose head elsewhere appears on his coins (Pl. IV, 22).[4]

It is, therefore, not surprising to find, at **Laodicea ad Lycum**, two pieces with different legends (ΣΕΒΑΣΤΟΣ[5] and ΚΛΑΥΔΙΟΣ ΚΑΙΣΑΡ[6]) whose identical portraits of Augustus (Pl. X, 20, 21), and identical reverse type and style (Pl. X, 23, 24), make it necessary to assume contemporaneous issue in the reign of Claudius. One of the signatories of these, Dioscurides β., issues coins in his first tenure (which can scarcely

---

[1] Mabbott collection; id. *Rassegna monetaria*, xxxiii, 1936, p. 548.

[2] Paris, Berlin; cf. *RS.* xxi, 1919, p. 47, completing *GR.M͡zk.* p. 228. 1.

[3] Decisively established by Ramsay, *Anatolian Studies to Buckler*, 1939, p. 219, who identifies him with a man named in the Ancyra Σεβαστεῖον inscription (*CIG.* 4039, *OGIS.* 533), following Rostovtzeff (*Mélanges Boissier*, 1903, pp. 418 ff.). R. Syme informs me that he withdraws the objections to this identification which he raised in *Klio*, xxvii, 1934, p. 134. On the strength of an inscription calling Basila *legatus Caesaris Augusti* (*ILS.* 977) he had (ibid.) attributed the commencement of his *legatio* to the lifetime of Augustus (and its termination to the following principate; cf. next note), but Calder (*JRS.* 1916, p. 134) and Ramsay (l.c. p. 210) have established that a certain Calpurnius (L. Piso Frugi?), recorded in an inscription, was *legatus* at the turn of the reign: *ILS.* 977 may easily refer to some less important *legatio* which Basila had held under Augustus. On him vide further *PIR.* ii, 131. 46. I hope at some later date to publish coins of Tiberius which further revise the *Fasti* of Galatia in his principate.

[4] BM, Berlin, own collection; cf. *GR.M͡zk.* p. 228. 2. A further unpublished specimen at Istanbul confirms his rank by the inscription ΕΠΙ ΒΑΣΙΛΑ ΠΡΕΣ. ΣΕΒ., and his province is confirmed by two coins in my collection found near Ankara.

[5] BM; *MG.* 404. 118 (Dioscurides β).

[6] BM; cf. *BMC.* 160 (Polemon Zenonos).

AUGUSTUS ON POSTHUMOUS COINAGES 329

have been thirty years earlier than his second) with a monogram KOP.,[1] which may represent Corbulo, proconsul c. A.D. 51.[2] A monogram $\overline{\text{NEP}}(\omega\nu)$ occurs on very similar coins of Trapezopolis.[3] The same portrait appears at Laodicea with the name Pythes Pythou β. (Pl. X, 22);[4] so that a different head with Pythes Pythou (Pl. X, 19)[5] must also be considered Claudian. It is not, therefore, an accidental coincidence that a series at Aphrodisias with ΣΕΒΑΣΤΟΣ, signed by Apollonius *jun.*, includes some portraits that recall Caligula[6] and others that suggest Claudius (Pl. X, 34);[7] and that Thaumastus, who strikes for ΣΕΒΑΣΤΟΣ at Mylasa,[8] also imitates a type of Caligula's *dupondii*.[9] In each case, as an examination of the fabric confirms, the issues are not of Augustus's principate.

Additions to this group are provided by a number of signatures which occur with ΣΕΒΑΣΤΟΣ and Augustus's head, and also with ΣΕΒΑΣΤΗ—a title of Livia only found after her assumption of the name Augusta after her husband's death.[10] This post-Augustan phenomenon is found with variant portraits at Apollonia Salbace (Pl. X, 27),[11] Tripolis (Pl. X, 30),[12] Eumenia (Pl. X, 16),[13] and Aezanis (Pl. X, 5, 9).[14] The first of these portrait-styles is found also at Dionysopolis (Pl. X, 28)[15] and Miletus,[16] and the second at Heraclea Salbace (Pl. X, 29).[17] The later date of the Aezanitan piece is confirmed by the appearance of Drusus *jun.* with the same moneyer.[18] Hieraticus, whose name occurs with ΣΕΒΑΣΤΟΣ and ΣΕΒΑΣΤΗ at Tripolis, is sometimes found with Tryphon,[19] who coins for ΣΕΒΑΣΤΟΣ and Caligula.[20] The same method necessitates the expulsion from the Augustan series of other ΣΕΒΑΣΤΟΣ portraits at Cidramus,[21] Philomelium (Pl. X, 40)[22] and Hierapolis[23] (cf. Pl. X, 35)[24] because each of the moneyers, on other coins, honours young Nero;[25] and at Lebedus (Pl. X, 4)[26] because a laureate head of Tiberius occurs.[27] Similarly Julius Callicles accompanies ΣΕΒΑΣΤΟΣ at Siblia (Pl. X, 71),[28] but Tiberius[29] and Germanicus[30] at Apamea; the curious post-

[1] *BMC.* 141.
[2] Waddington, *Fastes des provinces asiatiques*, 82.
[3] *BMC.* 8. [4] *BMC.* 138 ff.
[5] BM, Lockett coll., M. S. VII, 583. 441.
[6] *BMC.* 85—cf. *BMC. Imp. Caligula*, 2, etc.
[7] *BMC.* 88—cf. *BMC. Imp. Claudius*, 64, etc.
[8] *BMC.* 21, *KM.* 3.
[9] *BMC. Imp. Caligula*, 94.
[10] Never anticipated—Dittenberger, *OGIS*. p. 204 n. 15.
[11] Masc.: *BMC.* 17; fem.: *BMC.* 20 (Callippus Artemidorou).
[12] Masc.: *BMC.* 50; fem.: *Wad.* 2679, Copenhagen (Hieraticus).
[13] Masc.: *Wad.* 6026; fem.: *BMC.* 39 (Cleon Agapetus).
[14] Masc.: *BMC.* 53; fem.: *KM.* 5, Berlin (Menandrus).

[15] *Wad.* 5936.
[16] Paris = M. III, 167. 773.
[17] *BMC.* 15.
[18] Berlin.   [19] *BMC.* 52 (Pl. XI, 39).
[20] *BMC.* 52; *Lyd. S.* 39, 3.
[21] *Wad.* 4935 (Polemon Seleucou).
[22] Vienna = *GM.* 718a (Brocchi).
[23] *BMC.* 105; *Wad.* 6133 (Meniscus Diphilou γ.).
[24] Gotha (Charopides Sostratou); cf. *KM.* 24a (Diphilos Diphilou), *BMC.* 106 = *KM.* 22 (Matron Apolloniou); *BMC.* 107 (Iollas Iollou).
[25] Cidramus: *KM.* 6; Philomelium: *GM.* 721; Hierapolis: Cambridge (*McLean Cat.*, p. 312).
[26] *Wad.* 1706.
[27] *KM.* 13; variants at Athens, Istanbul.
[28] BM, cf. *GM.* 737.
[29] *BMC.* 142.
[30] *Wad.* 5705.

Augustan portraiture is repeated at **Metropolis** (Pl. X, 72),[1] **Prymnessus** (Pl. XI, 1),[2] **Amorium**,[3] and probably **Acmonia**[4] and **Synnada**.[5] Sosthenes, too, is common to ΣΕΒΑΣΤΟΣ (at Laodicea[6] and **Sebaste** [Pl. X, 33][7]) and Germanicus (at **Hypaepa**[8]); Muensterberg recognised one of the Laodicean pieces as Tiberian,[9] and a similar portrait style is found at Dionysopolis (Pl. X, 32)[10] and Eumenia (ibid. 31).[11] Yet another batch of coins with ΣΕΒΑΣΤΟΣ and similar heads is signed by magistrates called Claudius: these are found at **Pergamum** (Pl. X, 46),[12] Stratonicea (silver) (Pl. X, 47)[13] and Synnada (Pl. X, 25).[14] This *gentilicium* is very unlikely before the principate of Claudius.[15] Moreover, certain coins of the Synnadan official, Claudius Valerianus,[16] exactly resemble others signed by Claudius Andragathus,[17] who portrays on other pieces the Emperor Claudius[18] and young Nero;[19] a certain M. Claudius Valerianus was ἀρχιερεὺς 'Ασίας under Domitian.[20] With these pieces must be classed a Synnadan coin of precisely similar style signed by one Crassus (Pl. X, 26).[21]

All these pieces with ΣΕΒΑΣΤΟΣ, and the head of Augustus, are posthumous. Corroborative evidence is obtainable from the neglected coinages of Syria-Phoenicia. The only six stipendiary cities of this region which devote obverses to portraits of Augustus[22] portray him on a single coinage only.[23] This, in itself, suggests a special occasion shared by all of them. But this suggestion is confirmed in an arresting manner by the dates on these pieces: three of them (**Apamea**,[24] **Gabala**,[25] **Gadara**[26]) have '44';

[1] *Wad.* 1764.
[2] *GM.* 725.
[3] *BMC.* 24.
[4] *BMC.* 33 f.
[5] BM ('uncertain').
[6] *BMC.* 147; *Wad.* 6260.
[7] *BMC.* 21, Rome.
[8] *BMC.* 15.
[9] Walla sale, 1916.
[10] *BMC.* 14.
[11] *BMC.* 34.
[12] Cambridge, Paris, misread by M. II, 593. 339 (Claudius Cephalion).
[13] *BMC.* 33; cf. *KM.* 5.
[14] *BMC.* 34.
[15] Cf. Walton, *JRS.* XIX, 1929, pp. 38 ff.; Sherwin-White, p. 189.
[16] *BMC.* 8.
[17] *KM.* 11.
[18] *BMC.* 36, Naples. Scholz, *NZ.* 1910, p. 151; attribution of the Vienna University specimen to Caligula is wrong (as Elmer confirms).
[19] Oxford.
[20] Cf. Chapot, *La province romaine proconsulaire d'Asie*, p. 487.
[21] Paris.
[22] Publications and museum-cabinets provide a number of misleading false attributions. Among the necessary corrections are these: 'Caesarea Panias'

(Berlin) to Antioch in Pisidia, 'Damascus' (M. *S.* VIII, 11) to Tiberius (official series), 'Germanicia Caesarea' (Gotha) to official series of Augustus, Orthosia (M. III, 374. 416 f.; *S.* VI, 530. 460 ff.) to Carian Orthosia, Tripolis (Rouvier, *JIAN.* VI, 1903, 1681–3, and M. V, 397. 404 ff.) misreadings of later pieces e.g. *BMC.* 38, do. Caligula (Boutkowski, *DN.* 2617 ff.) to Lydian Tripolis.
[23] Aradus is the habitual exception which proves the rule: there (*BMC.* 356; Rouvier, *JIAN.* III, 1900, 386–7) the portrait of Augustus is merely a diminutive adjunct to the main type, a head of Astarte.
[24] Berlin (2) = M. *S.* VIII, 153. 145. Unknown to Jones, *CERP.* p. 263.
[25] *BMC.* 3, Paris (2), Berlin, Istanbul. The remaining symbols vary in each case—ΘΝΖΗ (*BMC.* 3), ΖΗΘΕ, ····Σ (Paris), ΘΕ··· (Berlin), ΘΝΖΚ (Istanbul)—and are therefore mint-marks as, e.g., at Laodicea ad Mare, Seleucia, Balanea. Part of the same issue (cf. style) is an undated piece at Munich (rev. eagle).
[26] Vienna = M. V, 323. 21 (misread), ibid. *S.* VIII, 227. 11.

one (Ace[1]) '43'; two (**Balanea** [Pl. XII, 20],[2] Gabala) have '59'; and one (**Orthosia** [Pl. XII, 21])[3] '60'. The fact that at least a dozen different eras were in use in Syria-Phoenicia at this period[4] makes the chances that these are accidental coincidences infinitesimal. The chances are made smaller still by the joint appearance of '44' and '59' on the same coin at Gabala. The conclusion that these six issues were struck on a single occasion is confirmed beyond any conceivable doubt by the blatant predominance of the year-sign '44' on 'autonomous' issues also: it appears on entirely isolated mintages at five cities. At the mints of **Tripolis**[5] and the 'free' cities **Seleucia**[6] and **Laodicea**[7] (at the latter on a large issue), it ends a period of inactivity lasting fifteen years or longer; at **Demetrias**[8] the 'autonomous' series had not produced a coin for more than a century, and at Ace[9] no other dated 'autonomous' issue whatever bears the same ethnic (AKH).[10]

There can therefore be no doubt whatever that the year '44' was an occasion for joint numismatic celebration. At Tripolis, Seleucia and Laodicea the era is demonstrably Actian. This is in accordance with evidence from one of our six portrait-issues, at Gabala: Jones's view[11] that '44' and '59' there refer to the Caesarian and Pompeian eras respectively is disproved by Lederer,[12] who shows that Caesar's era at Gabala began as late as 46–45 B.C.—considerably more than fifteen years after Pompey's. At Gabala also then, '44' must refer to the Actian era, with '59' alluding to the Caesarian. It is, accordingly, inevitable that the other coinages with '44' and '59' should be allocated to the same two eras. Thus all of them, at four cities with portraits and at five without, fall to the year A.D. 13 (September)–A.D. 14 (September).[13] Now Tiberius succeeded Augustus in Aug. 14, and an accession to the principate was

---

[1] Rouvier, *JIAN*. IV, 1901, p. 210, no. 985. Hill, *BMC. Phoenicia*, p. lxxxi, misattributed by de Saulcy, *Mélanges de Numismatique*, II, 1877, p. 143. To Claudius must be relegated coins with 'Antiochia' (Philadelphia University: reference owed to G. M. Fitzgerald. Cf. Rouvier, l.c. 995) and 'Germanicia' (Rauch, *BB*. 1870, p. 25, no. 37; Imhoof-Blumer, *NZ*. 1901, p. 11; Jones, *CERP*. p. 265).

[2] Paris, Berlin, Copenhagen, M. v, 226, misread by Sestini, *Hedervar*. pl. XXX, 12. This too has additional symbols which do not include a date, e.g. O Ƶ O (Paris, cf. Rollin et Feuardent sale [1864], 7106).

[3] Cast at Winterthur, Munich, Vienna; cf. M. v, 365. 184 (misread), ibid. *S*. VIII, 262. 105.

[4] Cf. Kubitschek, *PW*. I, 647 ff.; Jones, *CERP*. pp. 254 ff.

[5] Rouvier, *JIAN*. VI, 1903, no. 1677—previous one '29' (ibid. 1675).

[6] *BMC*. 27 (with symbol ΓΟ)—previous one '22' (*BMC*. 28).

[7] *BMC*. 16–18 (with various symbols)—previous one '24' (*BMC*. 15).

[8] Berlin = M. v, 359. 14—previous ones in c. 95–85 B.C. (*BMC*. 1 ff.). This coin appears to invalidate the assumption of Jones, *CERP*. p. 255 (cf. Wroth, *BMC. Galatia*, etc., p. lxxvi), that Demetrias was Damascus, since the latter maintains its own ethnic in the early principate: cf. also pp. 371 f.

[9] Rouvier, *JIAN*. IV, 1901, no. 983.

[10] The only other 'autonomous' coin of any kind with AKH is ibid. 984.

[11] *CERP*. p. 456 n. 46.

[12] *ZfN*. XXXIV, 1923, pp. 179 f.

[13] A supplementary date at Apamea, '28', must therefore refer to 15–14 B.C. This is highly appropriate in view of Agrippa's likely activity as a founder in Syria at this date: e.g. colonia Berytus (p. 259).

just the kind of occasion which such an isolated outburst of coinage must commemorate: certainly no other can be found within the year A.D. 13–14.

The presumption that this was the *raison d'être* of the six portrait-coinages is strikingly confirmed by another batch of issues. At Apamea, the only other portrait-piece for a quarter of a century[1] bears the Seleucid date '326', and so can be ascribed to A.D. 14–15:[2] and the resemblance between this and the Apamean issue with '44', which stand alone and together, is unmistakable. At **Damascus**, the only dated piece[3] of an issue which inaugurates the city's portrait-series[4] bears the Seleucid date 325, which can represent A.D. 13–14 or 14–15;[5] the next two portrait-mintages commemorate successive *decennia*—of Tiberius![6] The first portrait-coin at **Byblus**[7] bears the date '1': this is shown to be of Tiberius's regnal era by the appearance of his name (ΣΕΒΑΣΤΟΣ ΣΕΒΑΣΤΟΥ) on a second piece, of year '2'.[8] Here are three more cities which first engrave an Imperial portrait on their coins in the first year of Tiberius; and the same is undoubtedly true of the '44' and '59' groups. But if cities favoured by Caesar could reckon from 46–45 B.C., they could also reckon from 47–46:[9] Orthosia, then, with the date '60', might join this unrecognised category. So might two more cities whose first and only portrait is of Tiberius, **Epiphaneia**,[10] and Demetrias[11] whose precisely contemporary 'autonomous' issue has been mentioned (p. 331).

The only stipendiary portrait-coinage left is of Ace, with the date '43'. By the laws of averages, its isolated portrait-issue, dated only one year away from the rest, can scarcely but belong to the same category. In particular, it should be noted that the only other piece in existence with the same ethnic (ΑΚΗ) is actually of the autonomous '44' group. This coincidence is emphasised by the behaviour of the 'free' city of **Antioch**: Q. Metellus Creticus Silanus became governor in 12 (p. 127), but Antioch only begins coining under him (ΕΠΙ ΣΙΛΑΝΟΥ) with the dates '43' and '44'.[12] These pairs (like the others at Apamea and Byblus) recall the frequent habit, in

---

[1] Paris, Glasgow = M. S. VIII, 153. 144.
[2] Cf. Abel, *Revue biblique*, 1938, p. 213.
[3] Paris (2), Vienna = M. V, 285. 27.
[4] Undated piece: *BMC*. 5, Vienna, Berlin, Munich, Karlsruhe, with obscure symbols.
[5] Cf. Abel, l.c.: in some cities the era began in 311 instead of 312 B.C. The same date '325' appears on the 'autonomous' coin of Tripolis with '44' (see above, p. 331).
[6] Paris, Vienna = de Saulcy, *Numismatique de la Terre sainte*, p. 36. 2: '335'; Paris, Naples, Munich (barbarous): '345'.
[7] Hague = *Rn*. 1856, p. 394, misread by *BMC*. 19, Imhoof-Blumer, *MG*. 26.
[8] Berlin = Imhoof-Blumer, l.c. 26A, misread by M. S. VIII, p. 251. 67.
[9] Cf. Kubitschek, l.c.
[10] Vienna, '99'. In anticipation of a closer study of Tiberius's issues in a later work, it may be mentioned that Epiphaneia's nearest neighbour, Larissa, freed itself and began coining in 85 B.C. (cf. Jones, *CERP*. p. 255). Probably E. had the same era.
[11] Berlin = M. V, 359. 147; '100'—only one year later than Epiphaneia. The founder of Demetrias was probably Demetrius III Eucaerus (Wroth, *BMC. Galatia, etc.* p. lxxvi; Babelon, *Rois de Syrie*, p. clxxi; Jones, *CERP*. p. 255): if the establishment is attributed to the last year of his reign (88–87 B.C.), this coin will fall to A.D. 13–14. Indeed, the analogies of the 'foundation'-issues of Demetrias (*BMC*. 1 ff.) lie, as Sestini pointed out (cf. Wroth, l.c.; M. S. VIII, 207), with coins at least as late as 87.
[12] Macdonald, *NC*. 1904, p. 113, points out the falsity of earlier pieces.

AUGUSTUS ON POSTHUMOUS COINAGES

Roman cities, of saving some of their commemoration fund for a second issue also. Our acceptance of Ace as yet another city coining for Tiberius's accession depends on the answer to two questions. Could the Actian era here start—as would be necessary for '43' to be A.D. 13–14—as late as summer 30 B.C.? And, is an era from 157–156 or 156–155 B.C., required by the additional year-sign '170' which appears on this coin, probable? Both these questions can be answered in the affirmative. Syria was not definitely taken over by Octavian until winter 31–30 B.C., and, if Gabala could postpone its recognition of Caesar's activity in 47 until 46–45 B.C., then Ace's Actian era could begin a few months late: this is, in fact, peculiarly suitable, since Octavian visited Syria after the middle of 30.[1] With regard to the second question, Balanea had commenced to coin in 155 B.C., claiming freedom in a moment of anarchy:[2] and a similar assumption for Ace is far more plausible than the current and confused attribution to the seventies of that century.[3]

Ace, then, joins Apamea, Balanea, Byblus, Damascus, Gabala, Gadara and Orthosia, as commencing its portrait-coinage on the accession of Tiberius. Apart from the repercussions this conclusion has for the chronology of coinage[4] and of cities (p. 462), it adds very materially to the category of posthumous portraits of Augustus. At all these cities the features are more or less Augustan, and must represent the deified first *princeps*: at Damascus the legend is ΣΕΒΑΣΤΟΣ,[5] at Gabala (on the undated part of the issue) ΣΕ······;[6] at Byblus it is ΚΑΙΣΑΡ ΣΕΒΑΣΤΟΣ.

The recognition that so many pieces of different provinces with such inscriptions are posthumous makes it necessary to conclude that the survival of this titulature was frequent and regular; that its appearance is not enough, without further evidence, to warrant the attribution of any coin to his principate; and that deductions drawn from supposed iconographic resemblances to Augustus are equally unsafe. His features are accompanied by the title of Caligula at Corinth,[7] are overstruck, at Cragus, on coins of Tiberius (Pl. XII, 32);[8] and at Nicopolis share a reverse-die with a named portrait of Trajan.[9] In the same way, a medallion head of Augustus occurs on a sheath on which representations alluding to the principate of Tiberius also occur.[10] Montini has rightly recognised many busts of the first *princeps* as posthumous.[11]

[1] Cf. Tarn, *CAH*. x, p. 113.
[2] Cf. Jones, *CERP*. p. 254.
[3] Hill, *BMC. Phoenicia*, p. lxxxi, ascribes the date '43' here to the Caesarian era, but, in spite of his recognition (ibid.) that that era began in 48 B.C., assigns the accompanying date '170' to an era of 174–173 B.C. (his argument requires 176–175).
[4] All the issues (except the little-known mintage of Orthosia) have been regularly attributed to Augustus.
[5] A Paris specimen confirms M. v, 285. 27; but Mionnet's readings of titles are often products of a ready imagination.
[6] Munich.
[7] Earle Fox, *JIAN*. II, 1899, pp. 96 ff.
[8] Imhoof-Blumer, *ZfN*. v, 1878, p. 149.
[9] von Sallet, ibid. p. 331 n. 1 (ΣΕΒΑΣΤΟΥ ΚΤΙΣΜΑ). Wrongly attributed to Phina (presumably meaning Phinopolis, Strabo VII, 319) by Rauch, *Mittheilungen der numismatischen Gesellschaft in Berlin*, 1846, pp. 15 ff.
[10] BM; Franks, *Proceedings of the Society of Antiquaries, NS*. III, 1866, p. 358, has no justification for identifying the medallion portrait with Tiberius.
[11] *Civiltà Romana*, v, 1938, pp. 74 ff.

Thus the features of Augustus, like those of Alexander,[1] profoundly influenced the period after his death. But in many cases also, fortunately, Julio-Claudian iconography was influenced by the tendencies of the time and the physiognomy of the ruling *princeps*. Thus we find portraits which waver between the features of Julius and Augustus,[2] Claudius and Caligula,[3] or Claudius and Augustus:[4] in the same way, the Rhodians saved space and money by habitually adapting old statues to new faces![5] It is not surprising, therefore, that Augustus is represented with certain traits of his successors. These iconographic considerations and the demonstration that titulature hitherto held to be characteristic of Augustus may equally belong to a later date necessitate the transference of another huge group of Asian coins to the post-Augustan period. In this group no less than forty-five cities are concerned,[6] and perhaps a good many more.[7] It is therefore necessary to subtract, in all, at least a hundred issues from those generally attributed to Augustus: and evidence has been obtained from a posthumous coinage on a vast scale in honour of that *princeps*. This evidence will be used later for a general estimation of the local coinages.

[1] Cf. L'Orange, *Symbolae Osloenses*, VIII, 1929, p. 109.
[2] Berlin (Furtwängler, *Geschr. d. geschnittenen Steine im Antiquarium*, p. 349. 11210, pl. 68).
[3] Marlborough coll. (sale 1899, no. 407).
[4] The Veleia statue (Parma mus.) as interpreted by Stuart, *Portraiture of Claudius, Preliminary Studies*, p. 44.
[5] Dio Chrysostom XXXI; cf. Jones, *GC*. p. 243.
[6] Abydus (Pl. X, 1), Alabanda (ibid. 12), Aninetus, Antiochia ad Maeandrum (ibid. 36), Aphrodisias (ibid. 17), Apollonia Salbace (ibid. 13, 44), Apollonis (ibid. 49), Assus, Attaea, Cibyra (ibid. 41), Cidramus (ibid. 14, 48), Clazomenae (Pl. XI, 44), Cos (Pl. X, 37), Cotiaeum, Dardanus (?), Dionysopolis(?), Dioshieron (ibid. 10), Elaea, Ephesus, Euromus, Germe, Heraclea Salbace, Hypaepa, Lampsacus (ibid. 3), Laodicea (ibid. 18), Magnesia ad Maeandrum (ibid. 39, 42), Magnesia ad Sipylum(?) (ibid. 7), Methymna, Midaeum (ibid. 15), Miletus (ibid. 2), Mylasa (ibid. 38), Nysa, Orthosia, Pergamum, Philadelphia, Philomelium, Priene, Prymnessus (ibid.), Samos, Scepsis, Tabae (ibid. 45), Teos, Thyatira, Tiberiopolis, Trapezopolis(?), uncertain. An iconographic analysis of these issues is attempted in Appendix 7 (p. 463).
[7] Even issues with portraits closely imitated from Augustan originals, apparently, in the Augustan manner, are not above suspicion (p. 467).

B. AUGUSTUS AS *CONSTITUTOR*[1] OF LATIN CITIES

Since the monetary freedom of peregrine cities in the West was, at the beginning of the principate, demonstrably no greater than that of Roman communities (p. 476),[2] their issues—most of which are isolated—will almost certainly be commemorative; and since it is to be supposed that they will display the characteristics of Roman city-currencies in the same provinces as much as, or more than, the traits of Eastern peregrine series, civic promotions and 'foundations' supply likely occasions (pp. 290 ff.). A particularly close analogy to the Roman colonies and *municipia* is furnished by the important class of Latin towns. These, though peregrine,[3] came to be considered, in the first century B.C.,[4] as an intermediate class, since their magistrates, and their descendants, were Roman citizens:[5] Livy and the jurists tend to class them with Roman rather than peregrine communities.[6] Indeed, 'foundation'-issues celebrating the Latin *constitutio*[7] form the sole coinage of Salacia, Myrtilis and Baelo (pp. 23, 25), and, in a later section, it will be shown that the same applies to Vesci, Brutobriga and Antipolis (pp. 379, 381, 390). These foundations all belong to the forties, when the value of *Latinitas* in the provinces as a preliminary to *civitas* was first appreciated.[8] But Augustus maintained this policy,[9] and it is impossible to resist the conclusion that isolated mintages, with his head, of Latin cities are likewise foundation-issues. This is undoubtedly true of the single coinage of Segesta:[10] the town was Latin in Pliny's sources,[11] and the remaining Augustan local coinage of Sicily is entirely restricted to 'foundation'-issues (p. 238).[12] Segobriga, in Tarraconensis, obtained *Latinitas* after the compilation of Pliny's list, but, as the tribe Galeria indicates, before the death of Augustus:[13] it cannot be fortuitous that the only portrait on its single Augustan issue[14] is from a prototype introduced at Lugdunum not long before Agrippa's death. This too

---

[1] The word *promotor*, restored on a Flavian inscription (*CIL.* II, 1052) by Wilmanns, l.c., has a post-Augustan ring.
[2] Cf. Hirschfeld, *SB. Wien*, 1883, p. 295; pace Marquardt, *St.V.* I, p. 52.
[3] Last, *CAH.* XI, p. 452; cf. Gaius I, 79. Sherwin-White, p. 100, points out that the *Latini* possessed no right of appeal from a holder of *imperium*.
[4] Cf. Sherwin-White, p. 105.
[5] Steinwenter, *PW.* X, 1269; Cuq, *Les instituts juridiques des romains*, I, p. 708; cf. Asconius, *ap.* Cic. *In Pisonem*, p. 3. The doubts of Bersanetti, *Bollettino di filologia classica*, 1936, p. 71, are probably based on Mommsen's exclusion of the aediles from this privilege, shown to be false by McElderry, *JRS.* 1918, pp. 53 ff.; cf. Sutherland, *RIS.* p. 247 n. 9.
[6] Cf. Sherwin-White, pp. 93, 109.
[7] Probably not *Etrusco ritu*: cf. Säflund, *Skrifter utgivna av Svenska Institutet i Rom*, IV, 1, 1934, p. 69 n. 1.
[8] Cf. Sherwin-White, pp. 176 ff.
[9] Ibid. p. 177.
[10] *BMC.* 65, Cambridge (*McLean* 2569).
[11] *NH.* III, 14; cf. Scramuzza, *ES.* III, p. 346.
[12] The appearance of a Greek legend provides no obstacle: for parallels see p. 195. Peregrine issues of Augustus at Messana, cited by Torremuzza, *Siciliae populorum, etc., veteres nummi*, p. 49, pl. L, 14, 15, are gross forgeries.
[13] Cf. Kubitschek, *Imp.* p. 199.
[14] Vives IV, p. 47. 3.

commemorates the *constitutio*, and so, by analogy, does the only mintage of **Ercavica**[1] during this period. This obtained *Latinitas* in time for Pliny's list;[2] the modified 'Patricia' style suggests that the foundation (like that of Roman cities [p. 170]) should be attributed to Augustus's visit to Spain in c. 15–14. The title of *municipium*, which appears on the coins, had begun to supplant *colonia* as the honorary appellative of this class of city.[3] By these analogies, and owing to the lack of other stipendiary mints in Nearer Spain at this date, the isolated portrait-issue of **Segovia** (Pl. XII, 27)[4] may equally be ascribed to a Latin *constitutio*[5]—in this case, as the head is probably imitated from early Eastern *denarii*, perhaps by C. Calvisius Sabinus or T. Statilius Taurus (29–28). The legend CL. perhaps represents a native ethnic[6] such as is found on contemporary Roman foundation-issues (p. 170). At these Latin cities the coin-portraiture of Augustus is warranted by his *auctoritas* as *constitutor* and *patronus*. At another city his inscription, but not his portrait, occurs on a foundation-issue. A *quadrans* of **Cabellio** with COL. CABE. and IMP. CAESAR AVGVST. COS. XI. (accompanied by types of a turreted female head and *cornucopiae*)[7] is undoubtedly to be assigned to a similar occasion, since Augustus, not Julius, gave the city *Latinitas*,[8] no doubt during his visit to Gaul.

In provinces where the Roman city-coinage is not restricted to foundation-issues, there is no reason to suppose that the Latin towns either will observe such a limitation. In Baetica the Roman colonies were all founded at too early a date for numismatic commemoration, but coined to honour Augustus's visit in 15–14. The same is no doubt true of **Carteia** in Baetica, which had been Latin since 171–170 B.C.[9] It includes in its plentiful Augustan coinage—an important supplement to the monetary system (p. 296), worthy of this *doyen* of provincial *Latinitas*[10]—a single piece with the portrait of the *princeps*.[11] The reverse type is a rider on a hippocamp. Analogies of formula, style and provenance rightly induced Vives[12] to attribute this rare piece to Carteia, although he misread the legends. These are EX D. D.— · · AVFIDIVS RVFVS IIII[VIR][13] (Pl. IX, 27). Probably the *princeps* is again represented as *patronus*, though

---

[1] Vives IV, p. 109. 1 ff.
[2] *NH.* III, 24. Van Nostrand (*ES.* III, p. 204) ignores this in attributing Roman status to the city.
[3] Cf. Mommsen, *Gesammelte Schriften*, I, p. 293 n. 23; Steinwenter, l.c. [4] Vives IV, p. 46.
[5] It is not this, but the Baetican Segovia, which McElderry (*JRS.* 1918, pp. 69 ff.) points out to have been unprivileged. Pliny frequently omits to mention individual cases of *Latinitas* in Spain. Probably the Tarraconensian Segovia achieved Roman rank in Julio-Claudian times (*CIL.* III, 6419; cf. McElderry, l.c.). [6] Cf. Hübner, *MLI.* p. 97.
[7] Copenhagen, Berlin; cf. Willers, *NZ.* XXXIV, 1902, p. 119.
[8] Cf. Kubitschek, *Imp.* p. 207; Pliny, *NH.* III, 36.
[9] Kornemann, p. 516. 37.
[10] Cf. Sherwin-White, p. 95.
[11] Berlin, Madrid (del Rivero, *Cat.* p. 19), Rubio coll. (Cadiz). Misread by Muensterberg, *Beamtennamen* 'uncertain'.
[12] IV, p. 26. 56.
[13] For Roman magistrates' names on Latin city-issues cf. also Valentia (p. 472). The common generalisation that all Latin cities had *duoviri* (*CR.* 1938, p. 9; cf. Rudolph, *Stadt und Staat im römischen Italien*, p. 9) is refuted by many issues of Carteia, though it may apply to more recent foundations (cf. Sherwin-White, p. 110).

AUGUSTUS AS *CONSTITUTOR* OF LATIN CITIES 337

not, in this case, as *constitutor*. The single Latin city-issue of Lusitania occurs at *Liberalitas Iulia* Ebura,[1] with portraits of the 'Patricia' types: its unique legend PERMISSV CAESARIS AVGVSTI P. M. suggests commemoration of Augustus's election as *Pontifex Maximus*.[2] The record of Augustus's permission, found also at *colonia* Emerita in the same province (p. 221), confirms the probability that Latin cities, like Roman, usually only coined by special favour to celebrate a special occasion, and that they, too, were only exceptionally chosen to contribute to the economic scheme. Besides Carteia, the only Latin town selected for this purpose was Vienna in Narbonese Gaul.[3] The coinage of that city, with the ethnic C. I. V.—incorporating the honorary title *colonia* applied to Latin cities founded before the principate of Augustus[4]— consists of large bronze[5] pieces very similar in type to the issues of Lugdunum in c. 40–38 (p. 207). But its current attribution to the same date is decisively contradicted by the portrait of the *princeps*, which is certainly not earlier than the Eastern series of c. 21–19 B.C.[6] and probably as late as the 'Patricia' *denarii* (from c. 19).[7] It fulfilled the same purpose in the network of currency as had the Lugdunese series which it copies: finds occur in many parts of Gaul[8] and occasionally in free Germany.[9] It does not, however, bear any imperial countermarks, and is not sufficiently ambitious or extensive to warrant inclusion in the same category as the Nemausan official series which revived to supersede it in c. 15 (p. 114).[10] Cities of all categories were sometimes called upon to perform an active function in the currency of their region (p. 296). At Vienna, as at Roman cities, the portrait of the *princeps* is a manifestation of his *auctoritas*, as his juxtaposition to the divine Caesar emphasises. The same equation at Philippi is due to joint *patrocinium* of the city (p. 275), an explanation which may also be valid here.

---

[1] Pliny, *NH*. IV, 11; cf. van Nostrand, *UCPH*. IV, 2, 1916, p. 101. Sutherland, *RIS*. pl. III, 7.

[2] Laffranchi, *R.it.* 1916, p. 293, interprets some peregrine issues in the same way. See also p. 376.

[3] Jullian, *Histoire de la Gaule*, IV, p. 284 n. 3 (cf. Sherwin-White, p. 188), correcting Kornemann 191. The tribe Voltinia is found in no other Roman community in Narbonensis, but in at least two Latin towns—Antipolis and Cabellio. Kubitschek, *Imp.* 204, shows that the presence of Vienna in Pliny's list as *colonia* (*NH*. III, 36)—that is, by Pliny's usage, *colonia c. R.* (cf. Mommsen, *St.R.* III, p. 472) —causes no difficulty, since such later corrections to the list were not infrequent (cf. Jones, *CERP*. pp. 495 f.).

[4] Cf. Kornemann, pp. 519 f.; Sherwin-White, p. 177. [5] Spectrogram 7.

[6] E.g. *BMC. Imp. Aug.* 681.

[7] This is confirmed by H. Mattingly.

[8] Strack, *BJ*. CVIII, 1902, p. 10; also at S. Germain-en-Laye (Reinach, *Cat.* II, p. 319), Strasbourg (Forrer, *Strasbourg-Argentorate*, I, p. 273), Xanten, Neuss (Bonn mus.), Nijmegen (mus.), Narbonne (mus.), Toulouse (mus.), Nîmes (mus.), Nier coll., Vienne (mus.).

[9] E.g. at Deersheim (Hansen, *Sonderabzug aus Abhandlungen und Berichten aus dem Museum für Heimatkunde zu Magdeburg*, V, 1928): others at Utrecht (van Hoorn, *Gids*, p. 47).

[10] E.g. it bears no official countermarks.

C. AUGUSTUS AS *LIBERATOR* OF 'FREE' COMMUNITIES

It is not surprising that the custom of foundation-coinage, which has been shown to play so predominant a part in the numismatic history of the Roman and Latin cities, was adopted by the 'free' communities, whose privileges were likewise based on a charter from Rome.[1] Indeed, ἐλευθέριος was one of Augustus's most significant titles.[2] An example of such imitation is provided by **Leptis Minor**, known to Pliny as a *civitas libera*,[3] whose isolated first issue honours Caesar (DIVVS IVLIVS)[4] like foundation-pieces of Hadrumetum (c. 42 B.C.) and Achulla (c. 36–27) (pp. 227, 230). It is shown to be of the latter date by a second piece with Octavian's head ([IMP.] CAESAR DIVI F.),[5] as on inauguratory coinages of Achulla and Thapsus (p. 225). The portrait of Caesar indicates that, like them, Leptis Minor owed its privilege to a plan of Caesar's carried out by Octavian, and that this issue commemorates the plan and its confirmation. Such an interpretation is remarkably confirmed by the illustration of a kindred habit by the next mintage of Leptis Minor. This is represented by three issues, inscribed IMP. C(*aesar*) D(*ivi*) F. A(*ugustus*) P. M. P. P.,[6] TI. CAE. AVG. F. IMP. V.,[7] and [TI. CAE.] AVG[VST]. F. IMP. VII.[8] The second and third of these are dated to 8–10 and 12–14 respectively: the first, commemorating the *princeps* himself, is likely to be contemporary with, or a little earlier than, the second. Now coinage is found in precisely similar circumstances—date, interval and isolation are the same—at Carthage and Cirta: at both these cities (as also at Uselis, Lystra and Tarraco) the commemorative occasion is the half-centenary of Caesar's foundation (p. 295). At the other cities the privilege whose conferment is recalled was *libertas* of citizenry: here, too, is commemorated the fiftieth anniversary of a grant by the dictator of *libertas*—of the peregrine variety. At Carthage, where both the two earliest of these exceptional obverse-legends reappear—possibly on identical dies—the date of both alike must (owing to the same duoviral college) be A.D. 8. That year is suitable for the half-centenary of Carthage, but two years late for a conferment on Leptis Minor by Julius himself. It might, then, like Carthage, be commemorating the implementation of such a grant by Lepidus in 42. But the possible die-identity suggests that Carthage was required to supply obverse-dies to Leptis Minor—which, be it noted, invariably uses Greek, not Latin, for its ethnic[9]—and that, since Carthage did not begin to coin until A.D. 8,

---

[1] Cf. Jones, *Anatolian Studies to Buckler* (1939), p. 109.
[2] Cf. de Sanctis, *Rivista di filologia*, 1937, pp. 338 ff.
[3] *NH.* v, 25.
[4] Muller II, p. 49. 15, correcting *Rn.* 1841, p. 347.
[5] Muller, l.c. 16 (Paris). The IMP. appears on a BM specimen. Plates of all these African pieces will be hoped for in E. S. G. Robinson's *BMC*.
[6] Muller II, p. 49. 17 (Paris).
[7] Ibid. 18 (Paris).
[8] Ibid. 19 (Hague). A coin of Agrippina quoted by Muller (ibid. 20) from Séguin (cf. M. II, p. 317) is more than doubtful.
[9] ΛΕΠΤΙ[Σ]. With denomination-marks B or C.

Leptis also must needs delay its half-centenary issues until that date. In any case, the coincidence of their curious legends indicates that the two mintages were contemporary. The coins of Leptis Minor show in several respects the closest possible harmony with the practice of Roman cities, and bear witness to a careful imitation of *libertas et civitas* by mere *libertas* (p. 403).

A similar interpretation applies to the only two portrait-issues of Oea. Besides the ethnic,[1] these are inscribed with further neo-Punic words, *Maqr Biln*[2] and *Ththe Suq*.[3] Muller, searching for cities whose names these words could represent, unplausibly ascribes the series to 'alliances' of Oea with Macaraea and Bilan, and Zitha and Zuchis, respectively: but Hill[4] voices modern opinion by stating that such interpretations are quite discredited. These names must represent pairs of suffetes, such as appear, indeed, on other issues of Oea.[5] Now this city was clearly free in A.D. 69, when it attained the unenviable distinction of a war against the Roman government:[6] this would have been impossible for a stipendiary town.[7] On the other hand, its description without mention of *libertas* by Pliny[8]—who does not miss, though he misinterprets, Julian *oppida libera* in *Africa* (p. 226)—shows that Caesar did not confirm its freedom in his reorganisation of the province after Thapsus,[9] and that this had not been restored by c. 19–12 B.C. The conferment must, therefore, be placed between that date and A.D. 69. Numismatic and historical considerations alike indicate that this is the occasion celebrated by these coins. At the end of an autonomous series, they stand quite alone as portrait-issues; and Leptis Minor has demonstrated that peregrine towns adopted the habit of such inauguratory coinages. Moreover, the presence on these pieces of two colleges of suffetes, but no more, irresistibly recalls the large class of Roman cities whose foundation-fund permitted a single repetition of the inauguratory issue, and so, as here, the occurrence of a second pair of signatures (p. 291). Again Leptis Minor provides an analogy, by the duplication of its issue (honouring Tiberius). Here at Oea, the more careful of the two portraits, that with the names of *Maqr* and *Biln*, imitates a Lugdunese model of c. 12–11 B.C.:[10] and there is evidence of attention to Tripolitania by Augustus at about this date, since the *terminus post quem* of the foundation-coinage of *municipium* Zitha is c. 16–12 (p. 188). Since Oea certainly became free within the century, and every analogy points to the connection of these coins with some such

[1] Sometimes omitted—Muller II, p. 26. 46 f.; Hamburger sale (1925), 519; Hinglais, *Recueil de la Soc. arch. du dép. de Constantine*, XXXVIII, 1904, p. 186.
[2] Muller II, p. 23. 43 ff.; Madrid (Calvo y Sanchez, *Salón de Numismática*, p. 218).
[3] Muller II, p. 20. 38 ff.; cf. Gesenius, *Monumenta*, p. 326.
[4] *NC.* 1929, p. 78. Cf. above, pp. 121, 185 n. 6, 188 n. 12.
[5] Muller, *Suppl.* III, p. 35.

[6] Pliny, *NH.* v, 38; cf. Tac. *Hist.* IV, 50; Romanelli, *Africa italiana*, I, 1925, p. 18.
[7] Cf. Wilmanns, *CIL.* VIII, p. 5.
[8] *NH.* v, 27. His description of it as *civitas*, not in the usual way as *oppidum*, is merely a device to avoid monotony: elsewhere he describes many stipendiary cities as *civitates* (ibid., e.g. III, 18, IV, 22), and even calls Thespiae a *liberum oppidum* (ibid. IV, 25).
[9] As implied by Broughton, p. 51.
[10] *BMC. Imp. Aug.* 465.

inaugural occasion, we may conclude that they commemorated a grant of *libertas* soon after 12 B.C.

This conclusion is confirmed by the isolated portrait-issues of the two adjoining cities of the Tripolis. That of **Leptis Magna**[1] bears a marked resemblance in style, portrait and type to one of the inauguratory pieces of Oea. Leptis Magna, like Oea, cannot have been confirmed in its *libertas* by Caesar—although evidence for its punishment by him is confused[2]—since it also is not recorded as free by Pliny. But Oea's jealousy of it in A.D. 69[3] would have been strange if Leptis Magna had merely been stipendiary at that date; and not only does this coin strongly hint at a *raison d'être* like that of the analogous Oean issue, but it is accompanied by an 'autonomous' series remarkably including a silver piece.[4] Silver city currency (stipendiary) is only found at Laodicea ad Mare at this date, but occurs at free cities (p. 402); most significant, however, is the only African parallel,[5] which is a foundation-issue of *colonia* Hadrumetum (p. 227). There is, therefore, a strong presumption that Leptis Magna was freed, like its neighbour Oea, not long after 12 B.C. Corroboration is provided by evidence of remarkable progress in local institutions very soon after that date. In 8 B.C. we find, on a neo-Punic inscription, a *flamen divi Iuli*,[6] and shortly afterwards the name, in Latin, of a *patronus*.[7] But the city cannot yet have held Roman or Latin municipal rank (if it ever did),[8] since a suffete and *flamen* on a third inscription of c. A.D. 1, Annobal Rufus Himilchonis Tapapi f.,[9] is a *peregrinus*.[10] In view of the numismatic analogies from Zitha and Oea, it is necessary to assume that this sudden spate, at the turn of the century, of inscriptions recording advanced institutions is linked with the contemporary coinage, whose character is undoubtedly commemorative. The occasion which it celebrates is no doubt the reorganisation of Leptis Magna with a constitution on the Roman model, but with peregrine *libertas*: there is epigraphic record of the care with which the Semitic peoples made translations and adaptations of Roman officialdom.[11]

---

[1] Muller II, p. 5. 14; Paris.
[2] Cf. Romanelli, *Africa italiana*, I, 1925, p. 15, criticising Gsell, *Rivista della Tripolitania*, I, 1924, p. 42.
[3] Cf. Tac. *Hist.* IV, 50.
[4] Muller, II, p. 5. 13, wrongly dated by Cagnat, *Klio*, 1909, pp. 194 ff.
[5] Romanelli, l.c. p. 18 n. 2, wrongly states that there is no African parallel in this period.
[6] della Vida, *Africa italiana*, VI, 1935, p. 5.
[7] Caputo, ibid. p. 95; *L'année épigraphique*, 1938. 2.
[8] The assumption depends on highly dubious epigraphic evidence: vide *CIL*. VIII, 8*d*; Bartoccini, *Le terme di Leptis*, p. 92; Romanelli, l.c. p. 20, cf. n. 2; Caputo, l.c. p. 95. The occurrence of a few Roman citizens (della Vida, *Libya*, III, 1927, p. 99 nn. 1, 2) does not prove anything.
[9] Caputo, l.c. p. 98; *L'année épigraphique*, 1938, no. 3.
[10] Caputo, l.c. p. 99, suggests that the name Rufus is 'by adoption': but this is not necessary. For similar adoptions by *peregrini* of *cognomen* on the Roman model (but not the *nomen* implying citizenship) vide Milne, *NC*. 1924, pp. 316 ff.
[11] della Vida, *Africa italiana*, VI, 1935, pp. 4 f. But the restoration of [ME]TRO[POLIS] on a worn coin of autonomous type and ethnic (Muller, *Suppl.* p. 34; cf. Kenner, *NZ*. II, 1870, p. 251) cannot be accepted or rejected without further evidence (cf. Romanelli, l.c. p. 18 n. 2).

The exact date of the *liberatio* of Leptis Magna can be recovered with great probability from consideration of a second isolated portrait-issue. This occurs under Tiberius, who appears with the title IMP. TIB. CAESAR AVG. COS. III.[1] (A.D. 18–20), DIVOS AVGVSTVS being represented on a second piece.[2] Since this issue is bound, by every analogy, to be commemorative, it is highly probable that, by the analogy of Leptis Minor and Roman cities, it celebrates an important anniversary of the foundation: the coinage for Augustus recalls similar honours to DIVOS IVLIVS by cities in Africa which he had promoted.[3] At Dyrrhachium, Cnossus and perhaps Patrae the quarter-centenary is chosen for this purpose (p. 295): if the same assumption is made here, the *liberatio* can be ascribed to 7–5 B.C. This date is appropriate since it accords conveniently with the institution of new religious officials in 8 B.C. This was no doubt one of the elements in the new organisation, whose completion may, with the formal *liberatio*, be assigned to the following year. No doubt Oea was freed at the same date.

There is a general probability that the third city of the triad, **Sabrata**—likewise not mentioned as free in Pliny's list[4]—was promoted at the same date, just as their colonisation by Trajan is likely to have been contemporary.[5] This conjecture is remarkably confirmed by the fact that the only model whose use can be detected for its isolated group of portrait-pieces is derived from a *denarius* of c. 8 B.C.[6] Like Oea[7] and Leptis Magna,[8] Sabrata was a prosperous harbour and commercial *entrepôt*.[9] But there is a special reason for the promotion of all three at this date: their significance was enormously increased owing to the war raging against the Marmaridae far to the south (p. 141), and the supply of provisions to the Roman armies must have depended almost entirely upon these cities, which were at the roadhead.[10] Probably, in the absence of the proconsul of Africa, the liberation of all three cities can be attributed to his representative in Cyrenaica, in c. 7–6 B.C., P. Sextius Scaeva (p. 142). The *constitutio* of Zitha (p. 187) may have been a military measure at the same date. The demonstration by Leptis Magna that even peregrine *civitates liberae* had *patroni* clearly indicates that the presence of Augustus's head on the inauguratory issues of these cities is due, as at Roman communities, to the principle of *clientela*—that is, to motives coming under the heading of *auctoritas* rather than *imperium*.

In the province of Asia too there is a rich crop of coinages commemorating *liberatio* by Augustus. Immediately after Actium he conferred freedom upon **Mylasa**:[11] it is

---

[1] Vienna: incompletely read by Muller II, p. 6. 27 a.   [2] Ibid. 21.
[3] E.g. Achulla (p. 230).
[4] *NH.* v, 25.   [5] Broughton, p. 132.
[6] *BMC. Imp. Aug.* 500.
[7] Haywood, *ES.* IV, pp. 69, 75, 107 ff.
[8] Gsell, *Rivista della Tripolitania*, I, 1924, pp. 41 ff.; id. *Mémoires de l'Académie des Inscriptions*, XLIII,
1933, pp. 149 ff.; de Mathuisieulx, *Nouvelles archives des missions*, x, 1902, p. 270.
[9] Paribeni, *Dedalo*, v, 1925, pp. 665 ff.; Bartoccini, *Guida di Sabratha*.
[10] Cf. Romanelli, *Rivista delle colonie italiane*, III, 1929, p. 544; Guidi, *Africa romana*, p. 238.
[11] Dittenberger, *SIG.*³ 768 = Abbott and Johnson 30.

therefore not fortuitous that the only issues of that city which portray him in his lifetime imitate models of c. 31–29 (Pl. X, 52)[1] and c. 28 B.C.[2] Of these two coins the first was clearly struck at the time of the liberation, and the second recalls the custom of Roman cities to follow their inaugural issue by one other, after a very short interval and from the same fund (p. 291); a feature also met with at Leptis Minor and Oea (pp. 338 f.). A contemporary coin with the double ethnic of **Aphrodisias-Plarasa**[3] clearly celebrates Augustus's unification of the two communities,[4] previously a συμπολιτεία[5] —as a single *civitas libera*:[6] here, too, Augustus's portrait does not appear again during his lifetime. Since **Ilium** strikes an equally early piece,[7] this too may be supposed to refer to Augustus's confirmation, during his residence in Asia, of the *libertas* conferred on that city by Caesar;[8] this carried with it the headship of a Hexapolis worshipping Athena.[9] The privileges of these three cities are all recorded in Pliny's list.[10]

A later phase is introduced by an isolated issue of **Cyzicus**,[11] using a portrait-model of c. 20–18 B.C.[12] After the withdrawal of its *libertas* for five years,[13] Cyzicus obtained its return in c. 15 B.C.,[14] and this is probably the occasion which the coin commemorates. Equally significant is the single appearance of the living Augustus at **Cos** (Pl. XI, 32),[15] where his portrait is copied from a model of c. 2 B.C.–A.D. 11.[16] Cos does not figure as 'free' in the Agrippan statistics used by Pliny, but in A.D. 12 it was one of the few communities to retain its *ius exilii*[17]—a privilege peculiar to *civitates liberae*.[18] A suitable occasion for the conferment of *libertas* was the restoration of the city in c. 5 B.C. after its destruction by earthquake;[19] the single portrait-coinage is entirely appropriate to that date.

The post-Actian settlement to which Mylasa, Aphrodisias and Ilium refer is again recorded by coinages of the **Lycian League**. Both parts of this, Cragus and Massicytes,[20] produce large bronze issues with portraits imitated from *denarii* before 27 B.C.,[21] the former at **Tlos** (Pl. XII, 31),[22] and the latter at an unspecified mint,[23] probably its capital **Myra**. A commemorative character is clearly indicated by the exceptional

---

[1] *BMC.* 24: cf. *BMC. Imp. Aug.* 602.
[2] *BMC.* 19, Berlin: cf. *BMC. Imp. Aug.* 653.
[3] Berlin, *Wad.* 6526: cf. *BMC. Imp. Aug.* 647. Autonomous coin with the same style and ethnic: *KM.* 1, Gotha.
[4] Jones, *CERP.* pp. 77, 397 n. 80.
[5] Id. *GC.* p. 66.
[6] Henze, *De Civitatibus Liberis*, p. 52; Broughton, *ES.* IV, p. 707.
[7] In trade (types of *BMC.* 29); cf. *BMC. Imp. Aug.* 632.
[8] Strabo XIII, 1. 27 Henze, l.c. p. 39; see Jones, *GC.* p. 130, for earlier grant.
[9] *IGRR.* IV, 197; cf. Broughton, l.c. p. 716.
[10] *NH.* V, 108, 109, 124 respectively.
[11] BM, var. *BMC.* 210.
[12] *BMC. Imp. Aug.* 681 (?).
[13] Dio LIV, 7; cf. Jones, *CERP.* pp. 87, 401 n. 99.
[14] Dio LIV, 23; cf. Broughton, *ES.* IV, p. 706; Jones, *GC.* p. 130.
[15] *BMC.* 245. [16] *BMC. Imp. Aug.* 519.
[17] Dio LVI, 27. 2.
[18] Cf. Hartmann, *De Exilio apud Romanos*, Diss. Berlin, 1887, p. 24, and, for Cos, Broughton, l.c.
[19] Hieronymus, *Chronica Eusebii*, year 201 (Helm 168. 13); cf. Broughton, l.c. pp. 601, 721; Bürchner, *PW.* XI, 1480.
[20] Cf. Jones, *CERP.* p. 103; Head, *HN.* pp. 693 f.
[21] *BMC. Imp. Aug.* 633, etc.
[22] *Wad.* 3060. [23] *BMC.* 38; *Wad.* 3116.

AUGUSTUS AS *LIBERATOR* OF 'FREE' COMMUNITIES   343

occurrence of these large pieces amid the usual small 'autonomous' currency of the League.[1] The prototypes suggest the period of Octavian's presence in c. 30–29 when the *libertas* of the League was confirmed.[2] Myra and Tlos, never before first-grade cities,[3] probably owe their advancement to the same occasion, so that the coinage commemorates that also. This conclusion is confirmed by the only remaining portrait-pieces, which are equally large. One of these was struck by Cragus at **Telmessus**,[4] and the other, lacking mention of either federative half, was issued at **Cyaneae**.[5] Those, too, were not previously cities of the first class,[6] and the coins manifestly celebrate their elevation.[7]

The provinces of Eastern Europe bear witness to Octavian's sojourn after Actium by *liberatio* issues of three cities. Most important are coins whose legends ΑΥΓΟΥΣ-ΤΟΣ ΚΤΙΣΤΗΣ[8] and ΣΕΒΑΣΤΟΥ ΚΤΙΣΜΑ[9] explicitly (though not immediately) bear witness to the great συνοικισμός of **Nicopolis** in Epirus as a peregrine *civitas libera*,[10] perhaps carried out by C. Proculeius, who represented the *princeps* in these waters (p. 67). Here Octavian combines the *conditor* tradition of Romulus with the κτίστης tradition of the Diadochi. It is necessary also to refer a very early post-Actian coin of **Amphipolis**, with ΚΑΙΣΑΡ ΘΕΟΥ ΥΙΟΣ[11] and an appropriate portrait,[12] to his confirmation of the *libertas* of that city,[13] probably during a visit.[14] Since **Tanagra** likewise appears in the Augustan *formula provinciae* as a *civitas libera*,[15] it is tempting to ascribe its only contemporary portrait-issue[16] to a similar reconferment of privilege. The appearance at **Sparta** of a single portrait-coin soon after Actium[17] strongly suggests a kindred occasion;[18] the same, in the province of Crete and Cyrenaica, is true of **Cydonia**.[19]

[1] Cf. Head, *HN*. pp. 694 ff.
[2] Cf. Jones, *CERP*. p. 106.
[3] Cf. Broughton, *ES*. IV, p. 701.
[4] BM.   [5] *Wad.* 3064.
[6] Cf. Jones, *CERP*. p. 102; Broughton, l.c. p. 729.
[7] These pieces may be classified here since the League was 'free', but—since its cities were presumably already 'free' within its structure—are not true *liberatio* coinages in the same sense as the issues of Tlos and Myra.
[8] *BMC*. 9.   [9] *BMC*. 11.
[10] Larsen, *ES*. IV, p. 446; cf. Dorsch, *De civitatis romanae apud Graecos propagatione*, Diss. Breslau, 1886, p. 28, correcting Kornemann 109 and Mitteis, *Reichsrecht und Volksrecht in den östlichen Provinzen*, p. 147 n. 2. Cf. p. 404, n. 8.
[11] *BMC*. 76; Gaebler, *NG*. III, 2, pp. 38 ff.
[12] Of CAESAR DIVI F. class.
[13] Pliny, *NH*. IV, 38; cf. Larsen, *ES*. IV, p. 449.

[14] Mattingly, *BMC. Imp.* p. cxxi n. 4(c).
[15] Pliny, *NH*. IV, 26; cf. Larsen, l.c. p. 447.
[16] Athens (rev. tripod): of CAESAR DIVI F. class.
[17] *BMC*. 70; Weil, *Ath. Mitt.* VI, 1881, pp. 13, 16; Kjellberg, *Klio*, XVII, 1921, p. 49.
[18] West, *Corinth*, VIII, 2, 1931, pp. 46 ff., calls Sparta a 'kingdom like the Cottian Alps'; but Eurycles's part on the coinage is always strictly that of city-magistrate (client-kings regularly engrave their portraits), and it is preferable to accept the decision of Volkmann, *Münchener Beiträge zur Papyrusforschung*, XXI, 1935, p. 170, that it was a *civitas libera* within the province.
[19] Of the coins of this 'free' city (Henze, *De Civitatibus Liberis*, p. 78) only a single group can be considered certainly Augustan (Naples, var. *BMC*. 34, Christ Church [Oxford], Svoronos, *Crete* 94—perhaps these constitute the habitual double foundation-coinage).

Finally, the province of Syria-Cilicia adds three mintages to this category. The single Cilician coin with Augustus's head, at Aegeae,[1] is extremely likely to have some connection with the *liberatio*.[2] Gaza strikes an equally isolated piece dated to A.D. 5–6[3] to commemorate its detachment from the kingdom of Archelaus to live within the province as a *civitas libera*.[4] The remaining piece deserves a more detailed discussion.[5] Its types are imitated from the official issues with CA (p. 106): on the obverse is AVGVST. TR. POT., with a laureate[6] head to right, and on the reverse a wreath; but added to CA are the letters ΛΤ (Pl. IV, 15)—sometimes in very small letters[7]—or, on a variant,[8] ΤΛ. An explanation of CA. has been given above (p. 108). For the abbreviation ΛΤ or ΤΛ a number of interpretations have been hazarded, but all of them are far from satisfactory. Grueber's suggestion Λ(επτὰ) Τ(ρία)[9] is particularly unfortunate. The Greek numeral for 'three' is Γ, not Τ; in any case, the ambiguity between Τρία and Τέσσαρα is inconceivable. The Greeks would not have permitted such a confusion, in defiance of their numerical tradition, any more than we could write 'FS' for 'four shillings'. The interpretation of T. A. on another coin as Τ(ρία) Ἀ(σσάρια) is no better (p. 110). Nor can ΛΤ represent any known constitutional formula.

It only remains for it to be a date in some era.[10] There is, however, no possibility that Λ stands for Λ(υκάβας): the view that the ordinary year-symbol L is equivalent to Λυκάβας has been abundantly disproved,[11] so that even the remotest analogy for such a use of Λ has been eliminated. Accordingly, the date is not Τ (300), but ΛΤ (330). The era cannot, however, be that of the Seleucids (312 or 311),[12] since stylistic considerations render a date so late as c. A.D. 18 improbable, and Latin issues of the Julio-Claudian period do not imitate the Greek omission of ΘΕΟΣ by a corresponding neglect of DIVVS. For the same reason an era of 311–310 used by Ptolemy III and Ptolemy IV[13] is out of the question, while provenance and style also rule out the possibility of attribution to Citium, which reckoned from the same date.[14] There could, moreover, be no conceivable reason for the use of the short-lived era of Philip Arrhidaeus;[15] nor is de

---

[1] Berlin = M. S. VI, 2. 8, misattributed by Muensterberg, *Beamtennamen* s.v., to Aegae in Aeolis. The moneyer is Ari.

[2] Henze, *De Civitatibus Liberis*, p. 73.

[3] *BMC.* 10. Year 66 by era from 61 B.C. (cf. Gabae, founded by Marcius Philippus, Jones, *CERP.* p. 259).

[4] Josephus, *AJ*. XVII, 11. 4; cf. Momigliano, *CAH.* X, p. 338; Henze, l.c. p. 77; Mommsen, *St.R.* III, p. 707 n. 3.

[5] *BMC. Imp. Aug.* 742 ff., New York, Leningrad.

[6] Not bare, *pace BMC.* l.c.

[7] Leningrad.   [8] Berlin.

[9] *NC.* 1904, pp. 208 ff.

[10] Froehner's interpretation as the number of cities in the *Commune Asiae* (*Mélanges d'épigraphie et d'archéologie*, XXII, p. 78) is based on an unacceptable restoration of CA (p. 107).

[11] Cf. Foat, *JHS.* XXII, 1902, pp. 149 f.; Wilcken, *Griechische Ostraka*, p. 819. Regling, *WMK.* p. 121, s.v. *Datierung*.

[12] Abel, *Revue biblique*, 1938, p. 213.

[13] Bouché-Leclercq, *Histoire des Lagides*, I, p. 54 n. 3.

[14] Ibid. p. 48 n. 1.

[15] Ginzel, *Handbuch der mathematischen und technischen Chronologie*, I, p. 139; cf. *Babyloniaca*, XV, 1935, p. 11.

AUGUSTUS AS *LIBERATOR* OF 'FREE' COMMUNITIES 345

Saulcy[1] justified in inventing a local temple era to harmonise with his refuted theory that CA represents 'Caesarea Arca'. Eckhel[2] makes a similar attempt to confirm his equally false attribution to Caesarea Panias; but the era of 334–333 which he conjectured[3] has been eliminated successfully by Dussaud.[4] Now the last-named is also responsible for the discovery of an era (unknown to the exhaustive survey of Kubitschek),[5] whose existence and importance have since been shown by Abel.[6] This is the era of Alexander the Great (336)—not to be confused with the popular description of the Seleucid era as the 'era of Alexander'[7]—which was used by a number of Phoenician cities, including Tyre, Sidon, Ace and Aradus. The geographical and chronological relevance of this to the present coinage is clear: it assigns the issue to the only region appropriate to its style. The date, then, is 7–6 B.C.

A city-era recorded on a coin serves as its ethnic, and warrants the view that this is a local series, albeit of an unusual type. The formula C(*aesaris*) A(*uctoritate*) is no less relevant to a local than to an official issue, even if permission to coin was already at the disposal of the imperial *legatus*. The adaptation of the well-known Latin types is likely to be due to a special commemorative occasion. Since foundation-issues vastly predominate among coinages of this character, it is unlikely to be accidental that Sidon, deprived of its *libertas* since 20 B.C.,[8] first recommences its silver issues in 6–5[9]—a date very suitable for its recovery of 'freedom', which must have occurred during this period.[10] The conclusion that this exceptional *aes* piece, together with the renewed silver currency, celebrates the *liberatio* of Sidon in c. 6 B.C. is thus probable on historical and numismatic grounds; moreover, if, as has been suggested, Q. Articuleius (?) Regulus issued coinage for the newly 'enslaved' city (p. 126), there was particularly good reason for the local authorities to wish for monetary record of their subsequent liberation. Particularly appropriate to the category of *liberatio* coinages is the portrayal of Augustus in the role of Alexander, whose era is so exceptionally used: Alexander was the prince of κτίσται.[11]

[1] *Annuaire de la Société de Numismatique*, III, 1870, p. 259.
[2] *DN*. III, p. 339.
[3] Cf. Rouvier, *Revue des études grecques*, 1899, pp. 362 ff.; cf. *Rn*. 1903, pp. 239 ff.; cf. also Muller, Waddington, Pellerin, Droysen, and—doubtfully —Poole, *BMC. Ptolemies*, pp. lxxiv ff.
[4] *Rn*. 1908, pp. 445 ff., 453.
[5] *PW*. I, 632 ff.
[6] *Revue biblique*, 1938, p. 198.
[7] E.g. Michael Syrus (Chabot, *Chronique de Michel le Syrien*, I, p. 116); *Corpus Scriptor. Christian. Orient., Syri*, ser. III, t. IV, p. 130.
[8] Dio LIV, 7. 6; Suet. *Aug.* 47.
[9] *BMC*. 113.   [10] Honigmann, *PW*. II, 2226.
[11] Cf. Jones, *GC*. pp. 2 ff.

D. AUGUSTUS AS *CONSTITUTOR* OF 'STIPENDIARY' COMMUNITIES[1]

Since the 'free' communities issued inauguratory coinages, it would be very remarkable if the stipendiary cities—whose foundations played a large part in official policy[2]—did not do likewise. They, too, had constitutions of their own,[3] and constitutions whose legal basis was not inferior:[4] they were sometimes entitled even to levy their own customs-dues[5] and to conduct mutual agreements,[6] celebrated by types of Homonoia.[7] Many of their institutions, no less than those of 'free' communities such as Leptis Magna (p. 340), followed Roman models,[8] and they were allowed to retain many of their own traditional customs.[9] A more detailed analysis of the grades of privilege will be attempted elsewhere (pp. 401 ff.): here it is only desired to point out that the stipendiary cities wholly possessed the organism of government which was expressed and celebrated by foundation-coinage. Indeed, since even bare annexation by Rome was, by courtesy, considered an occasion for commemoration and a change of era[10]—even warranting the title ἐλευθέριος[11]—it is to be expected that interventions and reforms by the *princeps* will be recorded in this way.

It is therefore significant that **Thaena** issues bilingual coinage (the ethnic is *Tainat*[12] and the reverse-type a head of Astarte) with an early head of Octavian inscribed CAESAR DIVI F.[13] This legend and this portrait occur at four neighbouring cities—Hadrumetum, Achulla, Thapsus and Leptis Minor (p. 338). These commemorate the accomplishment by Octavian of a foundation-plan of Julius; Leptis Minor, moreover, is a peregrine city like Thaena. Two further considerations indicate that this coinage celebrates a similar occasion. First, Thaena must have had some such refoundation, since it passed from royal territory into the hands of Caesar and was destroyed in the process;[14] secondly, every other city in Africa which coins with the *princeps*' head does so for a special commemorative purpose of this kind. Thaena does

---

[1] I.e. *civitates iure stipendiario*.
[2] Cf. Jones, *GC*. p. 65.
[3] Ibid. pp. 117 f.; Last, *CAH*. XI, p. 436; Volkmann, *Neue Jahrbücher für Antike und deutsche Bildung*, I, 1938, pp. 16 ff.
[4] Jones, *Anatolian Studies to Buckler* (1939), p. 109, points out the only difference—that the charters of stipendiary cities were not formulated separately but incorporated in the *lex provinciae*.
[5] Cf. Dessau, *Hermes*, XIX, 1884, pp. 486 ff.; Heichelheim, *ES*. IV, p. 250.
[6] Cf. L. Weber, *JIAN*. XIV, 1911, pp. 109 ff.; Broughton, *ES*. IV, p. 872.
[7] E.g., in this period, Pergamum and Sardis (*BMC. Lydia*, p. 275. 213).
[8] Cf. Jones, *GC* pp. 123, 171, 180.
[9] Cf. Liebenam, *St.V.* III, p. 467; Stevenson, *RPA*. p. 165; Sherwin-White, p. 151.
[10] Cf. Jones, *GC*. p. 117.
[11] Cf. de Sanctis, *Riv. di filologia*, 1937, p. 342—the annexation of Egypt.
[12] Cf. Levy, *Phönizisches Wörterbuch*, p. 49.
[13] Glasgow (*Hu.* 1820), Copenhagen, Hague: Muller II, p. 40. 4.
[14] Strabo XVII, 831; cf. Broughton, p. 51 n. 33.

AUGUSTUS AND 'STIPENDIARY' COMMUNITIES 347

not appear as a *civitas libera* in the Augustan *formula provinciae*;[1] and it is not characteristic of Pliny to omit reference to that class of community. But it has been pointed out that this sort of inauguratory coinage is entirely appropriate to stipendiary cities. A charter of Thaena, as of Thapsus and Achulla, was no doubt drawn up by Caesar; but it was not incorporated in the *lex provinciae* until Octavian's government. Thaena's new status was not *libera*, but it was sufficiently high in the 'infinite gradation' of privilege[2] for commemoration to be desirable.[3] Indeed, a second piece (with an incompetent portrait), on which the Latin legend is omitted,[4] actually bears witness to the well-documented custom of making a supplementary issue from the balance of the foundation-fund (p. 291). The existence of this coin confirms our conclusion that the *civitas stipendiaria* of Thaena imitated its betters by celebrating with coinage its *constitutor* Octavian.

Another bilingual issue, with IMP. AVG. P. P. and a late portrait of Augustus, has, beside the head of Astarte, the neo-Punic ethnic *Sthdsr*.[5] The types recall the coins of Hadrumetum, and, when it is recollected that the initial letter, on coins of Carthage, means 'belonging to',[6] it is clear that the town named is **Thysdrus**.[7] This too was a Julian foundation, but in the form of a *colonia Iulia*.[8] The neo-Punic ethnic, however, is wholly incompatible with an enfranchised status. Nor can the colony have been Latin,[9] since Pliny describes the city as *libera*[10]—an epithet wholly applicable to possession of full citizenship, but not to *Latinitas*: moreover, only a single town of this rank is known in Africa at this time,[11] and Pliny could not have missed another. A double community is out of the question, since there would be no parallel or constitutional probability for coinage by the virtually subject peregrine half (only) of one of these (p. 404). At the only double community where the peregrine section possibly coins, Emporiae, the Roman settlement (p. 154) not only coins simultaneously but appears soon to exclude the peregrine mint:[12] moreover, that was not a colony but a *municipium*. It is necessary to conclude that, before this coin was struck, the colony at Thysdrus had failed like other Julian colonies at Heraclea Pontica and Dyme (pp. 254, 265). Now since, by every analogy, this issue was commemorative—here again there is the significant second issue (with AVGVSTVS, capricorn and Punic ethnic[13]), but no other—

[1] *NH*. v, 25.
[2] Jones, *Anatolian Studies to Buckler* (1939), p. 109.
[3] 'It kept whatever organisation it had' (Broughton, p. 51) is probably an understatement.
[4] Hague: Muller II, p. 40. 2; Judas, *Rn.* 1856, p. 110.
[5] Paris: Muller II, p. 58. 35, *Suppl.* p. 43. E. S. G. Robinson informs me that the letter supposed by Muller to be a P is a D.
[6] Muller II, p. 80. E. S. G. Robinson confirms this.
[7] Muller, II, p. 58, realised this in spite of his misreading. The metathesis of *sr* presents no difficulty. For other views vide Judas, *Rn.* 1856, p. 167; Levy, *Phönizisches Wörterbuch*, p. 45; Wilmanns, *CIL.* VIII, p. 12; Head, *HN.* p. 876—all missing the D.
[8] *CIL*. VI, 3884, XII, 686; Broughton, p. 49.
[9] As suggested by Kubitschek, *Imp.* p. 158.
[10] *NH*. v, 30.
[11] Uzalis: cf. Broughton, p. 51.   [12] Hill, p. 37.
[13] Hague, Stockholm, Constantine: Muller II, p. 58. 36; Hinglais, *Recueil de la Soc. arch. du dép. de Constantine*, XXXVIII, 1904, p. 186.

there is every probability that it celebrates the grant of a new constitution following the dissolution of the colony. During the existence of the latter, the peregrine community had no doubt been relegated to the inferior capacity of a *pagus*: by these coins it celebrated its return to full urban rank as a *civitas*. Since there is no evidence of 'freedom',[1] it may be assumed to have been stipendiary. The return of such Roman citizens as remained to the status of a *conventus* (p. 403), instead of a colony subordinating the peregrine community, was a good cause for commemorative coinage by the latter.

Manifestly in the same category of stipendiary foundation-issues are the mintages, with Augustus's head and name, of eight newly established communities in Asia. One of these (Pl. X, 70)[2] shows an interesting intermediate phase in the regular process of transition from tribe to city. The signature of Lycidas the son of Euxenus is accompanied by the ethnic ΕΥΚΑΡΠΙΤΙΚΟΥ. The tribe of the Corpeni in Phrygia, by a customary Hellenisation of their barbaric name, called their capital Eucarpia: but this was only one of the four cities into which the tribe later split.[3] At this stage—the portrait-model is of the 'Patricia' class[4]—the four are still combined; but they have substituted for their primitive tribal designation that of the Eucarpitic district, a provisional political unit. A similar process of evolution is illustrated by three coins, inseparable for stylistic reasons, of Nicaea Cilbianorum in Lydia:

(1) ΣΕΒΑΣΤΟΣ laureate head of Augustus r.—[ΝΙ]ΚΑΙΕΩΝ as last.[5]
(2) ΚΑΙΣΑΡ ΣΕΒ. ΝΙΚΑΙΕΩΝ head of Augustus r.—ΓΑΙΟΝ ΛΕΥΚΙΟΝ ΚΑΙΣΑΡΕΣ (*sic*) heads of Caius and Lucius to right (Pl. XI, 42).[6]
(3) ΓΑΙΟΣ ΛΕΥΚΙΟΣ[7] heads as on last—ΑΡΑΤΟΣ ΓΡΑΜΜΑΤΕΥΣ ΚΙΛΒΙΑΝΩΝ ΝΕΙΚΑΙΑΣ Demos standing l.[8]

(1) and (2) are both unpublished. A. H. M. Jones, who notes that the Lower Cilbiani inaugurate their coinage, presumably as a new unit,[9] as 'the Cilbiani about Nicaea'—other coins have ΠΕΡΙ ΝΕΙΚΑΙΑΝ[10]—attributes the fully developed urban ethnic Ν[Ε]ΙΚΑΙΕΩΝ to the second century.[11] Indeed, this advance under Augustus was evidently premature, since not long after this date the community reverts to the purely tribal style of Κιλβιανοὶ τῶν κάτω;[12] and subsequent coins adhere for many years, with minor variations, to the titulature of (3).[13] Whatever the cause of this retrogression, it is clear that (1) and (2) celebrate the ephemeral urbanisation. (3), whose portrait is later than that of (1), apparently commemorates the reconstitution

---

[1] The *libertas* of Pliny, l.c., refers to the colonial status which had now ceased.
[2] Winterthur, var. *BMC.* 13.
[3] Jones, *CERP.* p. 66; Broughton, *ES.* IV, p. 701.
[4] *BMC. Imp. Aug.* 376.
[5] Cast at Winterthur.
[6] Hague (misattributed to Nicaea in Bithynia).
[7] ΛΕΥΚΙΟΝ (*sic*) at Vienna.
[8] *Wad.* 4945, Vienna, Munich, Berlin, Copenhagen, Athens. Imhoof-Blumer, *NZ.* 1888, p. 9. 8. Misread by M. S. VII, 95.
[9] Cf. Broughton, l.c. p. 704.
[10] Cf. Head, *HN.* p. 649.
[11] *CERP.* pp. 78 f.; cf. *Denkschriften d. Ak. f. Wissenschaften in Wien*, LVII, no. 67.
[12] *Ath. Mitt.* 1894, pp. 102 ff.; cf. Jones, l.c. p. 398 n. 84.
[13] *BMC.* 1 ff.

on a semi-tribal basis. Pliny's record of the 'Cilbiani Inferiores'[1] indicates either that the urbanisation occurred too late for the Agrippan statistics, or that the retrograde step was early enough to be recorded in them. In view of the types, the former conclusion is perhaps preferable.

Less eventful was the evolution of two other tribes, the Caystriani and Epicteteis, whose conversion into cities was announced by portrait-issues (entirely isolated) at **Hypaepa** (Pl. X, 67)[2] and **Aezanis** (Pl. X, 62)[3] respectively. Such organisation as Hypaepa had possessed during the Republic[4] had not enabled it to supersede its tribe as a coining authority.[5] The change occurred in time for the Agrippan list,[6] and the 'Caesaraugusta' portrait-model[7] suggests attribution to the late twenties B.C.— perhaps to the time of Augustus's visit in c. 21–19. The same date is probable for the *constitutio* of Aezanis, whose coin—with the ethnic EZEANITωN found also on a few 'autonomous' pieces of the same issue[8]—uses an Eastern portrait-model of c. 20 B.C.[9] This city also, like others of the six into which the Epicteteis were converted,[10] is recorded by Pliny.[11] Another tribe too, the **Sibliani**, mark a political advance by issuing their first coin,[12] which is not repeated under Augustus; they may likewise have obtained a completely urban administration.[13] The ethnic ΣΙΒΛΙΑΝωΝ is accompanied by the name of a local dignitary (Callicles the son of Callistratus), as at the cities. The portrait is of an ideal type which is discussed elsewhere (p. 357). To Augustus's residence may also be ascribed the organisation of **Dioshieron** and **Heraclea Salbace**, and the celebration of each by a single portrait-issue (Pls. X, 64,[14] XI, 34[15]), whose models, of the 'Caesaraugusta'[16] and 'East II'[17] classes respectively, again accord with the literary *début* of the cities in Pliny's list.[18] A subsequent phase of κτίσμα, probably in the governorship of Agrippa, is illustrated by the single Augustan mintage—from a 'Patricia' model[19]—of **Trapezopolis** (Pl. XI, 46),[20] which likewise appears now in history for the first time.[21]

The isolated and commemorative character of these eight Asian mintages is obscured by the current attribution to the principate of Augustus of many coins whose real date is much later (p. 334). The present issues bear witness to an important aspect of the *princeps'* activity. He did not found Roman colonies in the East (p. 306); but he founded a number of peregrine stipendiary cities, by the synoecism and urbanisation of less developed communities.[22] His unwillingness to associate Romans with Greeks did not

[1] *NH.* v, 120. [2] Paris; cf. M. IV, 71. 386.
[3] *Wad.* 5541.
[4] Cf. Appian, *Mith.* 48; Cicero, *Ad Quintum fratrem*, I, 2. 14; Jones, *CERP.* p. 61.
[5] Cf. Broughton, *ES.* IV, p. 701.
[6] *NH.* v, 120. [7] *BMC. Imp. Aug.* 339.
[8] *BMC.* 1, 2, Munich, Vienna, *KM.* I. Not on subsequent coinage. [9] *BMC. Imp. Aug.* 700.
[10] Strabo XII, 8. 576; cf. Jones, *CERP.* p. 60; Broughton, *ES.* IV, p. 701.
[11] *NH.* v, 105.
[12] Berlin, *MG.* 411. 150.
[13] Broughton, p. 704; *pace* Jones, *CERP.* p. 71.
[14] *Wad.* 1960. [15] *BMC.* 18.
[16] *BMC. Imp. Aug.* 340. [17] Ibid. 664(?).
[18] *NH.* v, 120, 109: cf. Jones, *CERP.* pp. 77 f.; Broughton, *ES.* IV, p. 704.
[19] *BMC. Imp. Aug.* 387. [20] *BMC.* 9.
[21] Cf. Jones, *CERP.* p. 77.
[22] Id. *GC.* pp. 65 f.

lead him to deny the latter his beneficence as κτίστης. Further evidence of this policy will be obtained from a foundation-coinage, honouring P. Vedius Pollio, of Tralles— refounded as Caesarea after Actium (p. 383). This introduces a second category, of cities which were not founded by him for the first time, but given a new constitution and lease of life. The stipendiary foundation-issues in Africa (p. 346) belong to this class: so do single Augustan mintages at **Amorium** (Pl. X, 56)[1] and **Cibyra**[2]—known to have been re-established at this time[3]—whose portrait-models of c. 17 B.C.[4] again suggest ascription to the proconsulate of Agrippa. It is significant that all the ten cities of Asia, whose inauguratory portrait-issues of Augustus have been mentioned, belong to the comparatively undeveloped and un-Hellenised interior of the province. So do Sebaste and Metropolis, whose creation at the same time[5] is not recorded by foundation-coinage. This was a policy which Augustus took over from Antony, whose refoundation of **Eumenia** as *Fulvia*[6] is celebrated by an issue (signed by Smertorix the son of Philonides) with her portrait in the guise of Nike (Pl. XI, 52).[7] The analogy of this coin suggests that **Amorium** and **Philomelium**, whose issues with similar heads[8] have escaped notice, were likewise reconstituted by Antony. In this respect, then, he was heir to the Hellenistic founder-monarchs in these regions,[9] and Augustus followed his lead.

In the colonial and municipal series, the identification of a number of foundation-issues, often by fortuitous indications, made it necessary to ask how many other uninformative-looking pieces belonged to the same category. Here the same problem must be faced. Particularly suggestive of this character is a large group of pieces with portraits of Augustus, and apparently of his lifetime, whose nearest successors in the same class do not occur until later principates: all the ten stipendiary foundation-issues of Augustus that have been discussed are equally isolated. He repeated Antony's foundation at Amorium: why, then, should the single portrait-issue of another Phrygian city **Eumenia**[10] (from a Lugdunese model[11]) not represent another reform of an Antonian constitution? Augustus's marked activity in the same region makes it difficult to believe that lone coinages at **Hydrela**,[12] **Prymnessus**,[13] **Acmonia** (Pl. X, 61)[14] do not refer to similar occasions; and a similar mintage by **Apollonia Salbace**[15] recalls the foundation-piece of its neighbour Heraclea (p. 349).

[1] Naples, var. *BMC.* 23, Capitoline.
[2] Paris ('uncertain'). [ΚΙΒΥΡ]ΑΤΩΝ, Pallas r.
[3] Cf. Broughton, *ES.* IV, p. 714. *IGRR.* IV, 619, referring to an earlier *foedus*, does not justify its inclusion among the cities which were free at this time (as ibid. p. 706).
[4] *BMC. Imp. Aug.* 669, etc.
[5] Cf. Jones, *CERP.* pp. 71 f.; Broughton, l.c. p. 701.
[6] Cf. Waddington, *Voyage en Asie mineure*, p. 149; Broughton, l.c. On the importance of Fulvia, cf. Förtsch, *Würzburger Studien zur Altertumswissenschaft*, V, 1935, pp. 108 ff.
[7] Paris; cf. *BMC.* 20–21, Rome; *Gazette archéologique*, I, 1875, p. 123.
[8] Karlsruhe, Paris (de Ricci), respectively.
[9] Cf. Jones, *GC.* pp. 15, 17.   [10] *BMC.* 36.
[11] *BMC. Imp. Aug.* 536(?).
[12] Berlin, *KM.* 1: ideal style.
[13] *BMC.* 18–19; cf. *BMC. Imp. Aug.* 360(?).
[14] *BMC.* 31; cf. *BMC. Imp. Aug.* 700.
[15] Berlin, *KM.* 2: ideal style.

AUGUSTUS AND 'STIPENDIARY' COMMUNITIES

Equally exceptional portrait-issues in other parts of the province may well have the same purpose. Models suggesting Augustus's second visit are found at the stipendiary cities of **Adramyttium** (Pl. X, 66)[1] and **Magnesia ad Maeandrum** (Pl. X, 55);[2] the period of the *amici principis* is suited by those at **Colophon** (Pl. XI, 27)[3] and **Iasus**;[4] later are those of **Tabae** (Pl. XI, 31)[5] and **Scepsis**.[6] Of an ideal character (p. 357) are heads on the sole Augustan portrait-issues of **Assus** (Pl. XI, 21),[7] **Bargylia** (Pl. XI, 14),[8] **Miletus** (Pl. XI, 43),[9] and **Tenedus**.[10] Original or unidentifiable are the isolated portraits at **Alinda**,[11] **Myrina**,[12] **Phocaea**,[13] **Pitane**[14] and **Temnus**,[15] all likewise stipendiary communities.

How many of these are foundation-issues it is impossible to say; probably most of them.[16] A familiar topic adds with the strongest probability at least three names to the list. The 'free' cities of Leptis Minor and Oea (pp. 338, 339) demonstrated that the custom of issuing a second coinage from the foundation-fund was not limited to Roman cities; and stipendiary Thaena and Thysdrus (pp. 346, 347) have shown that it was not limited to the 'free'. It is therefore highly suggestive that **Antiochia ad Maeandrum**, **Apamea**, and **Euromus** issue two coinages under Augustus, and two alone: and that in each case the two portrait-models are very close in date—coincidences otherwise inexplicable. Thus Antiochia imitates two different types of head, both found on Lugdunese *denarii* with *C. L. Caesares*;[17] Apamea uses divergent models of the 'Patricia' class (Pl. X, 68,[18] 69[19]); and, most arrestingly of all, Euromus (Pl. X, 60) patronises two quite different models, of Eastern and 'Patricia' classes, which are, however, closely connected in date.[20] These curious pairs are, as one might expect, not restricted to cities whose sole coinage they constitute. **Sardes**, also (Pl. XI, 6), provides two different portraits of the 'Patricia' class,[21] and **Clazomenae** two slightly earlier ones of the 'East II' group.[22] In each case these are the first Augustan portrait-issues of the city, and at Clazomenae the *princeps* is actually called κτίστης. At **Hierapolis** a

---

[1] Oxford, *NC.* 1935, p. 199; cf. *BMC. Imp. Aug.* 330.
[2] Berlin, *KM.* 23; cf. *BMC. Imp. Aug.* 679(?).
[3] Berlin, *ZfN.* 1885, p. 315; cf. *BMC. Imp. Aug.* 519.
[4] Copenhagen, M. *S.* VII, 343. 506; cf. *BMC. Imp. Aug.* 472(?).
[5] BM, *KM.* 1; cf. *BMC. Imp. Aug.* 519.
[6] Copenhagen (capricorn)—wrongly attributed to Trajan! Cf. *BMC. Imp. Aug.* 508.
[7] Paris, M. II, 523. 58.
[8] *Wad.* 2284; *MG.* 28.
[9] Berlin, M. III, 167. 773.
[10] Cast at Winterthur, *MG.* p. 70.
[11] *BMC.* 11; *KM.* 4.
[12] Avignon (head of Zeus).
[13] *BMC.* 131.
[14] *Wad.* 991.
[15] *BMC.* 24, 27.
[16] But not necessarily all: e.g. Samos, Cos have isolated issues which do not commemorate foundations.
[17] *Kar. M.* 12, *KM.* 14: cf. *BMC. Imp. Aug.* 538; and *GM.* 40: cf. ibid. 543 (approx.).
[18] Cambridge, *KM.* 14, and *Wad.* 5700, *KM.* 13 a.
[19] *BMC.* 139.
[20] BM (ΑΥΓVΣΤΟΣ—*sic*): cf. *BMC. Imp. Aug.* 702; *BMC.* 7, clumsily copied from *BMC. Imp. Aug.* 408, etc.
[21] *BMC.* 97: cf. *BMC. Imp. Aug.* 413, etc.; *BMC.* 103: cf. *BMC. Imp. Aug.* 418, etc.
[22] BM: cf. *BMC. Imp. Aug.* 673; *BMC.* 118 (and *BMC.* 117, barbarous?): cf. *BMC. Imp. Aug.* 680(?).

'Caesaraugusta' portrait[1] is closely followed by a 'Patricia' type (Pl. XI, 7).[2] These six cities are very probably celebrating a *constitutio* by Augustus with a double coinage, of which so many examples have been met with elsewhere (p. 291). Perhaps in the same category is **Pergamum**[3] (Pl. XI, 29), which launches its portrait-coinage with no less than three different portraits from late Lugdunese *denarii*.[4]

Nor, of course, is there any reason why other stipendiary towns which strike more than one portrait-coin under Augustus should not (like many Roman cities equally well represented) have opened their series with a foundation issue. In particular, a group of pieces imitating the earliest post-Actian prototypes may well allude to the reforms of that time. These are provided by Abydus (Pl. X, 51),[5] **Dardanus** (Pl. X, 54),[6] **Laodicea**,[7] **Smyrna**[8] and **Teos**.[9] Laodicea may, like Cos, commemorate its reconstruction after an earthquake, which destroyed it in c. 20 B.C.[10] Somewhat later new portrait-coinages, and so perhaps new constitutions, are inaugurated at **Ephesus** (Pl. X, 63)[11] and **Erythrae**,[12] and then **Elaea**.[13]

But safer ground is reached in the provinces round Asia—Bithynia-Pontus, Macedonia-Moesia, Achaia, Galatia and the Cilician section of Syria. In spite of an infinity of attributions, only thirteen stipendiary mints in all these provinces together have contemporary portrait-coinage of Augustus; and, very significantly, this is in every case limited to a single issue. Again there is the strongest presumption of a uniform commemorative occasion, namely the presentation of a new status by the *princeps*. This conclusion is fortunately confirmed by the only two coinages of this type in Bithynia-Pontus[14]—

[1] *Wad.* 6153: cf. *BMC. Imp. Aug.* 315(?).
[2] *BMC.* 97 is a heroic version of *BMC. Imp. Aug.* 362, etc.
[3] The freedom of this city under Caesar (Robert, *Anatolian Studies to Buckler*, 1939, p. 228; cf. Segrè, *Athenaeum*, XXVI, 1938, p. 127; Passerini, ibid. XXV, 1937, pp. 252 ff.) does not seem to have continued under Augustus (cf. Broughton, *ES.* IV, p. 701).
[4] *BMC.* 239–241: cf. *BMC. Imp. Aug.* 510(?). *BMC.* 238: cf. *BMC. Imp. Aug.* 521. *BMC.* 236–237: cf. *BMC. Imp. Aug.* 519.
[5] *Wad.* 1065: cf. *BMC. Imp. Aug.* 599.
[6] BM, *Wad.* 1134, *NC.* 1920, p. 20: cf. *BMC. Imp. Aug.* 653(?).
[7] *BMC.* 151: cf. *BMC. Imp. Aug.* 650(?).
[8] *BMC.* 253: cf. *BMC. Imp. Aug.* 647(?).
[9] Paris = M. III, 1497, var. *BMC.* 68: cf. *BMC. Imp. Aug.* 647(?).
[10] Suet. *Ti.* 8; cf. Broughton, *ES.* IV, p. 601.
[11] Philon and Euthycrates (Rome, *KM.* 49) are the only magistrates to provide true 'Caesaraugusta' portraits.

[12] *BMC.* 255 ff.: cf. *BMC. Imp. Aug.* 342(??).
[13] Paris (ΕΠΙ ΝΑΡ.), apparently influenced by *BMC. Imp. Aug.* 660–4.
[14] Among those to be eliminated, in this province, are: Amasia (*Rec.* 6; cf. Berlin, attributed by Bosch [MS.] to Augustus), own collection shows ·····Υ ΣΕΒΑΣΤΟΥ—head is of Tiberius or Claudius; Neocaesarea (M. II, 352. 118, etc.) to Philadelphia; Prusias ad Hypium (M. *S.* V, 236. 1390). Jones (*CERP.* p. 164; cf. Broughton, *ES.* IV, p. 715) uses a coin—now lost—from the Stroganoff collection with ΣΕΒΑΣΤΟΣ (bare head to right) and ΚΑΙΣΑΡΕΩΝ ΤΩΝ ΕΝ ΒΕΙΘΥΝΙΑ Γ. (*caduceus*) (quoted by Boutkowski, *DN.* 1802 and repeated by Imhoof-Blumer, *GM.* 599. 115) to prove that the Caesarea-Germanica was a refoundation of a city already founded by Augustus; but even if the coin was not false, or misread in his usual way by Boutkowski, it is far more probably posthumous. Its denomination (27 mm.) is larger than any Asiatic city-issue of Augustus but equal to those of Claudius at Caesarea-Germanica (Moscow

at Nicaea[1] and Nicomedia;[2] here the occasion can be certainly identified. These isolated pieces[3] are ascribed to 29–28 B.C. by the name of Thorius Flaccus *pro cos.* (p. 384). Now it was at this very date that Nicaea and Nicomedia received new life and rights by their choice as the headquarters for the new κοινὸν Βειθυνίας.[4] Neither town coins again during the whole of Augustus's principate, and these are his only contemporary portraits in Bithynia. Such a geographical and chronological coincidence cannot be fortuitous. The coins are 'foundation'-issues of Nicaea and Nicomedia as capitals of the *Commune Bithyniae*, just as Myra(?) and Tlos had coined to celebrate their promotion in the newly established 'free' *Commune Lyciae* (p. 342).

A very close parallel is provided by two excessively rare, and almost unknown, portrait-coinages of the Euxine Hexapolis, in the Moesian section of *provincia* Macedonia. An apparently unique piece of **Odessus** has Augustus's head to right and a *cornucopiae* in wreath, with ΟΔΗΣΙΤ.[5] A second coin has identical types, but ΑΠΟΛΛΩΝΙΑΤWΝ; and the portrait is inscribed ΣΕΒΑΣΤΟΣ.[6] Exact similarity in style, as well as type, to the coin of Odessus disposes of Mionnet's attribution to Illyrian Apollonia,[7] and allows none of the other cities of that name to be preferred to the Euxine port **Apollonia Pontica**. The occasion of coinage is, therefore, happily identifiable. The κοινόν of Greek settlements on this coast was reorganised under a Pontarch by Augustus:[8] and a conspicuous feature of the reform was the inclusion, for the first time, of Apollonia, which made the original Pentapolis into a Hexapolis.[9] This, then, was, without a doubt, the occasion which inspired these exceptional issues. The coin of Odessus no doubt refers to the elevation of that city to the Presidency, already suggested by Blaramberg.[10] Here are two issues advertising the principate at the farthest fringes of Hellenism.

Four, then, of the thirteen stipendiary portrait-coinages now under discussion demonstrably celebrate a promotion of their city: and, since the others are equally isolated, the presumption that they belong to the same category is strengthened. In the same province as the Euxine Hexapolis was **Edessa** (ΚΑΙΣΑΡ ΣΕΒΑΣΤΟΣ).[11] The small procuratorial province of the Thracian Chersonese[12] is represented by **Sestus** (ΣΕΒΑΣΤΟΣ),[13] which is no doubt commemorating with this issue—unrepeated until Caligula—its establishment as the regional metropolis.[14] Elsewhere in the Balkans

= cast at Winterthur, cf. *Rec.* 1; variant at Christ Church with ΓΕΡΜΑΝΝΙΚΟΣ [*sic*] ΚΑΙΣΑΡΕWΝ).

[1] Moscow, Oxford, Hollschek coll., cast at Winterthur = *Rec.* 13.   [2] *BMC.* 5, *Wad.* 10.

[3] Additions to the Nicaean series, M. II, 80. 405 and *Rec.* 16, are due to total misreadings and misunderstandings.

[4] Dio LI, 20. 6; cf. Nock, *CAH.* x, p. 485.

[5] Sofia: Moushmov, *Rn.* 1929, p. 153 (illustrated).

[6] Glasgow, Paris, Vienna (2), Copenhagen; cf. von Schlosser, *Altgriechische Münzen*, p. 35.

[7] S. III, 321. 1736.

[8] Cf. Keil, *CAH.* XI, p. 574.

[9] Cf. Danoff, *Klio*, XXXI, 1938, pp. 436 ff.

[10] Cf. Boeckh, *CIG.* 2056c, p. 79. Tomis was later the President, but its portrait-coinage does not begin until Tiberius (Sofia, own collection).

[11] *BMC.* 16.

[12] Cf. Jones, *GC.* p. 84.

[13] Berlin, Istanbul; cf. Head, *HN.* p. 261.

[14] Jones, l.c.

peregrine portrait-coinage is strangely limited to three little island-towns,[1] all of which represent Augustus with the same legend—and never again portray a *princeps*. The status of two of these, **Imbrus**[2] and **Peparethus**,[3] was curiously anomalous. Both were still members of the 'free' Athenian Empire[4]—their coinage does not justify the supposition of a temporary 'autonomy'[5]—but presumably, wherever their taxes went, each was attached to the higher supervision of its nearest governor, the procurator of the Chersonese and the proconsul of Achaia[6] respectively. The coins may be supposed to commemorate a *constitutio* of these island-cities and a revision of the Athenian 'Empire' in general, undertaken by Augustus during his visit to Athens, in 20.[7] Similar to them in size and obverse type is an equally rare piece of **Myconus**[8]—the next is of Domitian—whose status in the province of Achaia was perhaps regulated by the *princeps* at the same date.

In *provincia* Galatia misattributions have multiplied so exceedingly that the nine cities, of which contemporary portrait-coinage of Augustus has been quoted, do not include two of the only three at which this is actually found.[9] Of these three, **Aspendus** —with no legend but ΑΣ[10]—is on the coast of Pamphylia; the remaining two, **Bubon**[11]

---

[1] In spite of many misattributions besides those based on iconography: e.g. Boutkowski (*DN*. 2082) quotes a coin of Delos from the Canino collection, adding that this passed to the Uffizi cabinet. A. Minto, the Director of this, has kindly searched the collection, and catalogues of all periods, and is (as he states in a letter of 25 Sept. 1937) still unable to trace the coin. Probably it was dismissed long ago as a mistaken attribution or a forgery: it is suspicious that the same type, a lyre, appears at Abydus. Rogers, *Ancient Coinage of Thessaly*, 361, misattributes to the Thessalian Magnetes a coin whose style, type and denomination all point to Magnesia ad Maeandrum (Pl. X, 55; cf. correctly Imhoof-Blumer, *KM*. 23). Wace, *JHS*. 1906, pp. 165 ff. 1, rightly queries the attribution to Augustus of a coin of the same Thessalian mint— the head is Caligulan and the inscription [ΓΑΙΟ]Σ ΣΕΒΑΣΤΟΣ. A piece at Dresden attributed to Melos is a badly preserved colonial coin of Corinth. Heads at Chalcis are not of Augustus but of governors (p. 385). I hope to show in a later work that an Aeginetan coin represents not Augustus, but a *legatus* of Tiberius.

[2] BM, Berlin, Athens (Postolacca, *Cat*. p. 163), Sofia: Chaix, *Choix des monnaies grecques*, p. 125.

[3] Glasgow = *Hu*. I, p. 460. 4.

[4] Cf. Last, *CAH*. XI, p. 559.

[5] As by Graindor, *Athènes sous Auguste*, pp. 4, 8.

[6] Including Thessaly; cf. (ending a long controversy) Keil, *CAH*. XI, p. 567; Larsen, *ES*. IV, pp. 437 f. Cf. p. 269 for Epirus.

[7] Cf. Graindor, l.c. pp. 39, 19 ff.

[8] Athens, Paris: Svoronos, *BCH*. XVII, 18, p. 455; M. II, 320.

[9] Besides purely iconographic errors, the wrongly attributed coinages fall into the following categories: (1) On coins of Sagalassus (*Wad.* 3821, ΓΑΙΟΣ ΚΑΙΣΑΡ and head of Caligula), and Side (own collection; cf. M. IV, 477. 184, reading [ΚΛΑ]ΥΔΙΟΣ ΚΑΙΣΑΡ) attributed to Augustus, the titles of later *principes* have escaped notice. (2) Mistaken readings of ethnics are responsible for attributions to Perga (M. IV, 461. 32: of Tanagra), Etenna (Muller, *Thorvaldsen Cat*. p. 274. 170; Boutkowski, *DN*. 2806: reads ETEI N., not ETEN., and is an official issue of Tiberius [cf. *GM*. 759]), and Pessinus (*Rb*. 1860, p. 21: of Adramyttium). (3) Official issues of T. Helvius Basila *leg*. under Tiberius have wrongly been considered city-coinages of Ancyra (M. *S*. VII, 633. 10) and Pessinus (*GM*. 759, *GR*. *Mzk*. 228. 1) under Augustus (see above, p. 328).

[10] Istanbul: *KM*. 48.

[11] *BMC*. 2.

and Termessus-Oenoanda (TEP.OI.)¹ are both in Cabalis, of which all but Cibyra was, like Pamphylia, allotted to the new province.² A change of province habitually brought a change of rights, and that is the reason for these isolated issues. In particular, the συμπολιτεία of Termessus minor and Oenoanda, first published by these coins, dates from this occasion.³ Termessus apparently predominated, and the issue bears its type of a horse, imitated from the mother-city in Pisidia.⁴ These three portrait-issues, like those of the Euxine towns, bear witness to a few outposts of Hellenism on the fringe of a province still generally tribal.⁵ They, like the rest, are evidence of the use of such coinages as vehicles for the popularisation of the new order. These large categories of peregrine foundation-issues—like their counterparts at Roman cities—are imposing evidence of the *princeps*' wish that *constitutiones* should be published by numismatic portrayal of his head. These portrayals played a vital part in the propaganda of his government.⁶

¹ Munich, Brussels, Berlin, Istanbul. Not a date Θl (as Boutkowski, *DN*. 2788—misread or tooled), since the same letters appear at later periods.
² Jones, *CERP*. pp. 106, 405 n. 15.
³ Ibid. pp. 108, 407 n. 20.
⁴ Cf. *BMC*. 3 ff. of Termessus major.
⁵ Cf. Jones, *CERP*. pp. 120, 146.

⁶ To this category may tentatively be attributed isolated portrait-issues at **Irippo** (Vives, pl. CX, 2) and **Laelia** (ibid. pl. CIII, 2). But since both imitate models of about 20–18 B.C. (*BMC. Imp. Aug.* 679, 681), they may merely commemorate Augustus's visit in c. 15–14, like issues of Roman cities in the province (p. 220).

E. AUGUSTUS AS ΚΤΙΣΤΗΣ AND ΘΕΟΣ ΕΠΙΦΑΝΗΣ

The analogy of the Roman communities is very close. He was not only *conditor* but κτίστης:[1] he is expressly so called on several coinages,[2] and this is his role at every peregrine city whose coinage has been discussed. Moreover, just as, by an easy transition, he became universal *conditor* (p. 318), so too he became κτίστης τῆς οἰκουμένης.[3] His title ἐλευθέριος[4] is particularly relevant to the *liberatio* coinages. To these roles his *imperium* does not contribute. But the conceptions of *clientela* and *patrocinium* were not at home in the Greek world,[5] where the implications of κτίσμα went farther. Here Augustus was the heir to Alexander, the Diadochi,[6] Pompey,[7] and Caesar; and it was his policy to allow the continuance of local tradition in such matters. A guide to the whole group of peregrine coinages hitherto discussed is the consideration that, as κτίστης, he was θεός: indeed, this was the foremost manifestation of ruler-worship.[8] Greek founders were the object of extensive cult-celebration,[9] and the Olympian gods themselves were often called κτίστης.[10]

In the light of this conclusion we may examine a remarkable group of portraits—many of them on foundation-issues—which are not imitated from any official model, but resemble most closely those of the 'candelabrum' class of *aurei* and *denarii*.[11] An investigation of some of these portraits, whose accompanying legends identify them with Caius, Lucius and Tiberius as Caesar (p. 471), reveals the paradox that many of them show not the least relation to the features of those princes, but have a singularly close relationship to each other. They also recall a long series of representations of Rome and the Senate[12]—apparently inaugurated in this principate at **Pergamum**.[13] Most arresting are heads of Caius at **Hierapolis** (e.g. Pl. XI, 12)[14] and **Tripolis** (Pl. XI, 20),[15] and of Tiberius at **Acmonia** (Pl. XI, 13)[16] and **Antiochia ad Maeandrum**.[17] To the

---

[1] For the correspondence of the two terms vide Nepos xx, 3. 2; Skard, *Festskrift til Koht*, p. 58 n. 2.
[2] Cf. Reinach, *Rev. arch.* 1916, p. 344.
[3] Cf. Charlesworth, *Harvard Theological Review*, xxviii, 1935, p. 26.
[4] *IG*. xii, 166; cf. de Sanctis, *Rivista di filologia*, 1937, p. 340.
[5] Cf. Hammond, *AJP*. 1938, p. 486.
[6] Cf. Jones, *GC*. pp. 6 ff.
[7] Cf. Wendland, *Zeitschrift für neutestamentliche Wissenschaft*, v, 1904, p. 341.
[8] Cf. Nock, *CAH*. x, p. 482. Signs of this have already been noted at the Roman cities (p. 318).
[9] Cf. Eitrem, *PW*. viii, 1136.
[10] Cf. Prehn, *PW*. ii, 2084.
[11] *BMC. Imp. Aug.* 683; cf. *CR*. 1944, pp. 46 ff.
[12] Cf. Dieudonné, *Mélanges numismatiques*, 2e sér., ii, p. 133 n. 2, Magie, *De Romanorum vocabulis*, i, pp. 4 f., correcting Eckhel, *DN*. iv, p. 190, de Witte, *Rn*. 1862, pp. 106 ff. Deification of Rome dates from the early part of the second century b.c.: cf. Stevenson, *RPA*. p. 122; Sherwin-White, p. 167.
[13] BM (Cephalion).
[14] *Wad*. 6144.
[15] Berlin, M. iv, 393. 521.
[16] Munich, Oxford, Nier coll.; M. iv, 198. 19 (var. Paris, different portrait).
[17] Copenhagen, M. iv, 316. 77.

AUGUSTUS AS ΚΤΙΣΤΗΣ AND ΘΕΟΣ ΕΠΙΦΑΝΗΣ   357

lean physiognomies of the two Caesars[1] this idealistic conception is entirely alien. But it is not restricted to the relatives of the *princeps*: most remarkable of all is its frequent reproduction with reference to Augustus himself, and accompanied by the legend ΣΕΒΑΣΤΟΣ. This occurs on the probable foundation-issues of Apollonia Salbace, Assus (Pl. XI, 21), Bargylia (Pl. XI, 14), Hydrela, Miletus (Pl. XI, 43), Siblia and Tenedus, and on coins not certainly to be included in this category at Abydus (Pl. XI, 22),[2] Cyzicus (Pl. XI, 15,[3] 25[4]), Ephesus,[5] Hierapolis (Pl. XI, 16,[6] 17,[7] 18[8]), Hypaepa,[9] Ilium,[10] Laodicea[11] and Mylasa.[12]

These issues—particularly those of Hierapolis—make it clear that not the least differentiation is attempted between portraits labelled 'Caius' and those labelled 'Augustus', and that not the least attention is paid to the actual features of either. Nor can the youthful heads described as Augustus be intended to recall his appearance as a boy, since this was quite different.[13] This portraiture is essentially impersonal, and completely neglects individual traits.[14] Similar examples of unrealistic youthful heads are provided, not only by the 'candelabrum' series with AVGVST.,[15] but by some Syro-Judaean portraits,[16] a garnet at New York,[17] a colossal head at Leptis Magna,[18] and some lead *tesserae*.[19] None of these is a portrait in the ordinary sense of the term.

Their explanation is suggested by a colossal Augustan statue in the Vatican,[20] whose boyish but impersonal features belong to precisely the same category. The veil and *cornucopiae* which there appear are symbols of the *Genius Augusti*;[21] and youthful

[1] E.g. statues from the Corinthian *Basilica Iulia* (Corinth mus.): Swift, *AJA*. 1921, p. 337, pls. X–XI; *Catalogo della Mostra Augustea di Romanità*, p. 96. 2.   [2] Own collection.
[3] Munich, BM, Karlsruhe, Copenhagen: *NC*. 1906, p. 27. 3, found in Mysia. Ethnic ΚΥΖΙ. often bungled and misread.
[4] Istanbul, Oxford (rev. two heads); cf. cast at Winterthur (rev. female head), BM (rev. second young male head).   [5] Athens.
[6] Gotha, *Wad*. 6136: cf. *BMC*. 99, Cambridge; and Paris (Acritas).
[7] *BMC*. 103: cf. *BMC*. 102.
[8] Berlin (Dryas); cf. *Wad*. 6137, own coll. = GR. M*ʒ*k. 152. 5.
[9] Paris (Charixenus). Cf. p. 349.
[10] Athens, var. *BMC*. 29.
[11] *BMC*. 145.   [12] In trade, Basle (axe).
[13] Cf. especially the head at the Musée Lavigerie at Carthage, *Catalogo della Mostra Augustea di Romanità*, p. 146. 6a. For further material vide Montini, *Civiltà Romana*, v, 1938, pp. 30 ff.
[14] But this group is to be distinguished from the other manifestations of idealism shown to be posthumous; cf. above, p. 334.
[15] Mattingly (*BMC. Imp.* pp. cxxvi f.) shows that the inscription AVGVST. is inconsistent with attribution to Caius Caesar; Drexel's suggestion AVGVST(*alia*) (*Phil. Woch.* XLVI, 1926, pp. 157 ff., cf. Rostovtzeff, *Klio*, Beih. III, 1905, p. 70) is unnecessary, since the parallels here enumerated indicate that such heads could be accompanied by the name of Augustus as well as Caius or Tiberius.
[16] E.g. Ascalon (Jerusalem mus.: Milne, *Quarterly of Dept. of Antiquities in Palestine*, I, 3, 1932, p. 130).
[17] Richter, *Catalogue of Engraved Gems in the Metropolitan Museum*, p. 129, pl. 57. 218; cf. exactly my Pl. XI. 11, 12.
[18] *Catalogo della Mostra Augustea di Romanità*, p. 115. 27.
[19] E.g. Rostovtzeff, *Festschrift zu Hirschfeld* (1905), p. 303. 2; id. *Rimskiya Svintsoveya Tessere* (1903), p. 263. 1.
[20] Montini, *Civiltà Romana*, v, 1938, pp. 72, 91 n. 95; *Catalogo della Mostra ecc.* p. 106. 1.
[21] *Catalogo della Mostra ecc.* p. 107.

features of this type are regularly employed to express the same idea.¹ The idealistic impersonality is explained by the idea of the *genius* or *numen*—'the more than normal will perceived in Augustus'²—whose comparative accessibility to the minds and household shrines of the masses³ secured it a leading part in the untiring and necessary propaganda of the new order. The *genius* itself was a purely Occidental concept:⁴ but there were Greek words which facilitated the translation of the idea for advertisement to the Hellenistic East. δαίμων is roughly the equivalent of *genius*,⁵ although far more extensive in range.⁶ In particular, δαίμων was θεός viewed as an efficient agent in daily life.⁷ Its relevance to the impersonality of the coins is best seen in connection with Nock's statement that Graeco-Roman belief in the early Empire was 'directed to divine power rather than to divine personalities'.⁸ Appeal was made to the emotions by emphasis on the universal and superhuman efficacy of the *Sebastos* rather than on his individual traits. It is in accordance with this interpretation that, on a local issue of Cyzicus (Pl. XI, 23), one of these youthful ideal heads is accompanied by the legend ΝΕΟΥ ΘΕΟΥ.⁹ The νέοι θεοί or θεοὶ ἐπιφανεῖς were 'young and approachable incarnations of the old gods':¹⁰ among them were Caesar,¹¹ Augustus, Caius,¹² and their kinsmen.¹³ This was the expression of *clientela*¹⁴—personal relationship—as it was adapted to the Greek world,¹⁵ in which Roman dignitaries like Pompey boasted of their vast *patrocinia*.¹⁶ As at the Roman cities, so in the Hellenic East the whole of Roman government was based on this principle—that is, on *auctoritas*.¹⁷ The conception of the νέος θεός accounts for the curious lack of individuality of this large group of ideal portraits. They are the product of a publicity policy which aimed at presenting to the religious emotions of the masses the power of the Sebastos¹⁸ (who monopolised such Romanophile affection as the Greeks possessed¹⁹) rather than his features to their eyes,

---

¹ Cf. Rink, *Die bildlichen Darstellungen des römischen Genius*, Diss. Giessen, 1933, pp. 25, 28. He neglects the evidence here quoted, however, when he claims as the earliest extant example of this motif a Neronian bronze in the Sambon coll. (Reinach, *Répertoire de la statuaire*, V, 20. 3).

² Nock, *CAH*. x, p. 485; cf. Sauter, *Tübinger Beiträge zur Altertumswissenschaft*, XXI, 1934, pp. 159 ff.

³ Volkmann, *Gnomon*, 1938, p. 191.

⁴ Pippidi, *Revue des études latines*, 1931, pp. 83 ff.

⁵ Cf. Waser, *PW*. IV, 2010.

⁶ Cf. Nock, *Gnomon*, 1932, p. 515.

⁷ Preller-Robert, *Griechische Mythologie*, p. 112.

⁸ *JHS*. 1925, p. 85.

⁹ Berlin: cf. Cahn sale, 60 (1928), 1377; Boutkowski, *DN*. 1861.

¹⁰ Nock, l.c. p. 93 n. 84.

¹¹ Pfister, *PW. Suppl.* IV, pp. 277 ff.; Christ, *Tübinger Beiträge zur Altertumswissenschaft*, XXXI, 1938, p. 124; cf. p. 93.

¹² *IGRR*. IV, 1064, 1094.

¹³ Ibid. 319, 74, 75, etc.

¹⁴ Cf. Skard, *Festskrift til Koht*, pp. 42 ff.

¹⁵ For the necessity of adaptation cf. Hammond, *AJP*. 1938, p. 486.

¹⁶ Cic. *Fam.* IX, 9. 2; cf. Syme, *RR*. pp. 15, 30; von Premerstein, pp. 16, 20; various cities, Romanising, call Augustus πάτρων (*Ath. Mitt.* XV, 1890, p. 217; cf. *CIG*. 3609; *SEG*. I, 1923. 383, IX, 1938. 56).

¹⁷ Cf. Sherwin-White, pp. 160 ff.

¹⁸ For the *suggestione spirituale* of Greek portraits of Augustus vide Montini, *Civiltà Romana*, V, 1938, p. 29; and for the blend of idealism and individualism, L'Orange, *Symbolae Osloenses*, VIII, 1929, p. 109.

¹⁹ Cf. Sherwin-White, pp. 168, 205.

AUGUSTUS AS ΚΤΙΣΤΗΣ AND ΘΕΟΣ ΕΠΙΦΑΝΗΣ 359

and which entirely neglected the dry constitutionality of *imperium* and the rest in favour of this psychological appeal. The imperial cult, no less than the *clientela* principle, is derived, not from *imperium*, but from *auctoritas* (p. 444).

In the entire series, therefore, the only reference to the constitution is a flowery record at Temnos of an event of no importance:[1] the twelfth consulship of Augustus is described as ΠΛΟΥΣΙΑ ΥΠΑΤΗΑ.[2] On the other hand the moral and religious ideas mirrored in the κτίστης-νέος θεός coinages, and issues of the κοινόν, are clearly perceptible on all sides. On a coin of Pergamum,[3] as on inscriptions,[4] Augustus is described as ΒΟΥΛΑΙΟΣ—hitherto the prerogative of deities.[5] At Mylasa he is equated with Zeus:[6] the coin is posthumous, but even in his lifetime the κοινόν identified him as Ζεὺς Πατρῷος,[7] and—more significantly in view of the *liberatio* and *constitutio* coinages—he sometimes appears as Ζεὺς Ἐλευθέριος.[8] Elsewhere he is deified as Ἀπόλλων Ἐλευθέριος,[9] and, by an easy transition, a coin of Tralles[10] names him Ἥλιος Σεβαστός.[11] But it is possible to show that this religious attitude was not confined to the few coinages with specific references, by word or portrait, to godhead.

Ignoring the numismatic evidence, McFayden[12] concludes that the title of αὐτοκράτωρ was particularly widespread in the Eastern provinces, and that its significance was peculiarly applicable to them. But, on all the multitudinous Asiatic local issues of Augustus after 27 B.C., there is not a single appearance of this title;[13] the few that are quoted by Muensterberg[14] have all been reattributed, on other grounds, to a later date. This omission has nothing to do with the 'senatorial' status of the province, since it is paralleled by a complete absence of the title from all Greek city-issues of the lifetime of Augustus throughout the Empire (p. 427). It is impossible then to think of it, or of *Imperator*, as the expression of the *princeps*' domination; the Punic equivalent *menokad*[15] is likewise absent from all African issues with that language. No less conspicuous is the absence of any mention of the tribunician power. The bases of the constitution appear to be utterly irrelevant to the Greek communities of Asia and elsewhere. The appeal of Augustus lay in another direction: it was based on his *auctoritas*.

ΚΑΙΣΑΡ, sometimes found, was a name which directly claimed heirship from a

---

[1] Cf. Stevenson, *RPA*. p. 104.
[2] *BMC*. 27; cf. *ZfN*. XII, 1885, pp. 360 f.
[3] *BMC*. 238.
[4] E.g. *CIG*. 1307; cf. *Ath. Mitt.* XIII, 1888, p. 20.
[5] Cf. Jessen, *PW*. III, 1019. For kindred titles borne by Augustus, vide Riccobono, *Annali del Seminario giuridico della R. Univ. di Palermo*, XV, 1936, p. 482; Christ, *Tübinger Beiträge zur Altertumswissenschaft*, XXXI, 1938, p. 93; Skard, l.c. pp. 61, 69; id. *Avhandlinger av Det Norske Videnskaps-Akademi i Oslo*, II (*h.-fil.*), 1931, 2; Schubart, *Archiv für Papyrusforschung*, 1937, pp. 13, 21.
[6] Cf. Robinson, *NC*. 1937, p. 247.
[7] *CIG*. 3187; cf. Brandis, *PW*. II, 479.
[8] Cf. de Sanctis, *Rivista di filologia*, 1937, pp. 338 f., 342.
[9] Ibid. p. 340; cf. *OGIS*. 457.
[10] *KM*. 2.
[11] Cf., for the principle, Riewald, *De Imperatorum Romanorum cum Certis Dis et Comparatione et Aequatione*, Diss. Halle, 1912.
[12] *CP*. XVI, 1921, pp. 34 ff., etc.
[13] Significantly there is one use in the triumvirate (p. 374).
[14] *Kaisernamen*, s.v.
[15] della Vida, *Africa italiana*, VI, 1935, p. 5.

360   THE COMMUNITIES AND THE *PRINCEPS*

god; far more frequent, however, on these coins is ΣΕΒΑΣΤΟΣ, usually standing alone. This rough equivalent of 'Augustus' ignores many of the implications of the Latin word,[1] and recalls associations which the Greeks could understand. Its close connection with the acts of 'worship'—ἰσόθεοι τιμαί—which were natural to them,[2] is indicated by its equivalence, as the translation of 'Augustus', to σεβάσμιος:[3] these words are clearly contrasted with ἀνθρώπινος,[4] and already actually imply apotheosis.[5] The Accusative case, ΣΕΒΑΣΤΟΝ, found on the coins of Pergamum, Hypaepa and Smyrna, is regularly employed for dedications to gods.[6] It must not, indeed, be thought that Augustus, or even his family, monopolised godhead: even benefactors of local origin were thus honoured, as at Mytilene.[7] Moreover, the implications of such divinity can be exaggerated: such deification did not much extend beyond an emotional recognition of power.[8] From this point of view, however, Augustus was far the most significant of νέοι θεοί: hence his predominance, though not to the exclusion of others, on the city-coinages of his principate.

Now too can be explained the posthumous issues (pp. 328 ff.). After his death[9] ΘΕΟΣ joins ΣΕΒΑΣΤΟΣ on the issues of the κοινά of Asia and Thessaly, which were officially and primarily devoted to his worship, but at only seven of all the cities of the Empire which coin in his honour.[10] The implications of Σεβαστός made the conjunction tautological, except as a strict and formal translation of DIVVS AVGVSTVS. On inscriptions and papyri it is noteworthy that Σεβαστός is omitted when the *princeps* bears any other divine epithet. It is, therefore, not surprising that Tiberius is described as ΣΕΒΑΣΤΟΣ ΣΕΒΑΣΤΟΥ at Lampsacus[11] and Byblus,[12] and ΣΕΒΑΣΤΟΣ ΣΕΒΑΣΤΟΥ ΚΑΙΣΑΡ at Olba,[13] Mopsus[14] and Seleucia.[15] Thus too the appearance of plain ΣΕΒΑΣΤΟΣ is warranted on coins struck in honour of Divus Augustus; and Dittenberger[16] is wrong in considering ΚΑΙΣΑΡΟΣ ΣΕΒΑΣΤΟΥ on a Tiberian inscription to be a mistake for ΘΕΟΥ ΣΕΒΑΣΤΟΥ. Equally justifiable is

[1] Cf. Muller, *Mededeelingen der Kon. Ak. van Wetenschappen, Afd. Lett.*, Deel 63, Ser. A, XI, 1927, p. 11; Koops, *Mnemosyne*, V, 1937, pp. 34 ff.; Heinze, *Hermes*, LX, 1925, p. 363. Cf. below, p. 444.
[2] Nock, *Gnomon*, VIII, 1932, p. 517; *Harvard Studies in Classical Philology*, XLI, 1930, p. 39.
[3] *Corpus Glossariorum Latinorum*, II, 21, 25, 26; cf. Herodian, 2. 3; Philo, *Leg. ad Gaium*, 143: αὐτὸς γενόμενος ἀρχὴ σεβασμοῦ καὶ τοῖς ἔπειτα.
[4] Reiter, *Phil. Woch.* 1930, 1199 f.
[5] Cf. Cichorius, *Römische Studien*, p. 376; Berlinger, *Zur inoffiziellen Titulatur*, Diss. Breslau, 1935, p. 76.
[6] Nock, *Harvard Studies in Classical Philology*, XLI, 1930, p. 20. Cf. below, p. 390.
[7] Charlesworth, *Harvard Theological Review*, XXVIII, 1935, p. 11.

[8] Cf. Nock, *Gnomon*, VIII, 1932, p. 518; Charlesworth, *CR.* XLVI, 1932, p. 225; vide especially Aristotle, *Rhetorica*, I, 5, p. 1361 a. 27. Syme (*RR*, pp. 54 f.) rightly describes the topic as 'fertile in misunderstandings'.
[9] During his lifetime the combination occurs once (p. 362).
[10] And three of these are caused by exceptional circumstances in Macedonia (p. 375): a fourth is due to a literal translation of Roman titulature.
[11] Paris; cf. M. S. V, 375. 595.
[12] Rouvier, *JIAN.* IV, 1901, p. 47. 679.
[13] *BMC.* 12.
[14] *KM.* p. 474. 4; *Wad.* 4378.
[15] *BMC.* 33; cf. *ZfN.* XIV, 1887, p. 311.
[16] *OGIS.* pp. 203 f. n. 14.

AUGUSTUS AS ΚΤΙΣΤΗΣ AND ΘΕΟΣ ΕΠΙΦΑΝΗΣ 361

the description of Augustus on a Neronian city-issue of Phrygia (p. 328) as ΑΥΤΟ. ΚΑΙ. ΣΕΒΑΣ.—again without ΘΕΟΣ, whose implications are sufficiently expressed by ΣΕΒΑΣΤΟΣ. Neronian inscriptions describe the reigning Emperor by the same titles.[1] It is also clear that, in the East, the Roman word 'Augustus' became impregnated with the significance of the Greek title. Euromus already writes on her coins ΑΥΓΥΣΤΟΣ,[2] and Cydonia ΑΥΓΟΥΣΤΟΣ[3]—found also on inscriptions;[4] Olbasa, a Roman colony but predominantly Greek in character, actually describes the first *princeps* as AVGVSTVS, without the addition of DIVVS, on a coin of Antoninus Pius;[5] and similar Graecisms occur elsewhere.[6] ΣΕΒΑΣΤΟΣ coinages continued throughout the first century, and later. Often the features of Augustus or other early *Sebastoi* are modified by the characteristics of the reigning *princeps*, just as artistic representations often mix the characteristics of two deities.[7] Such eclecticism was facilitated by the Greek concentration on the inner rather than the outer truth, on power rather than on personality,[8] and was encouraged by the reproduction and stylisation of only a small number of official portrait-busts.[9] Thus, at Laodicea, ΣΕΒΑΣΤΟΣ and ΚΛΑΥΔΙΟΣ ΚΑΙΣΑΡ are portrayed identically (p. 328). Except when care is taken to equate them with the reigning *princeps*, heads named ΣΕΒΑΣΤΟΣ may be supposed to refer to Augustus rather than his successors, since his cult remained so popular that he alone was worshipped in conjunction with Roma, to their exclusion.[10]

These conclusions make it possible to reconstruct the occasions of such portrait-coinages as are not of the 'foundation' category. These include the mintages of cities— Nicopolis,[11] Sidon,[12] Ascalon,[13] all 'free', and a group of 'free' and stipendiary in Asia (p. 469)—which, whether commencing with a foundation-coin or not, make more than one issue in the course of Augustus's principate. Some of these, like a number of Roman and Latin cities (pp. 296, 337), were selected as real contributors to the Imperial small change, and as points in the economic system constructed by the central bureau. Now the Roman cities taking part in this scheme generally coined at recurrent quinquennalian years: but the institution of the *lustrum* was alien to the custom of Greek communities. It is therefore necessary to search for the recurrent occasion which they invested with the same purpose.

---

[1] Dittenberger, *SIG.*³ 814; *IGRR.* III, 262; *JHS.* 1902, p. 119, no. 44; cf. de Sanctis, *Rendiconti della Pontificia Accademia romana di archeologia*, ser. III, XII, 1932, p. 14; Ramsay, *Anatolian Studies to Buckler* (1939), p. 222.
[2] BM.
[3] Cf. Muensterberg, *NZ.* LVIII, 1925, p. 43.
[4] At Cyrene it appears in the same sentence as Σεβαστός (*SEG.* VI, 1932. 2).
[5] Hill, *Anatolian Studies to Ramsay*, p. 221; BM.
[6] E.g. Abaecherli, *TAPA.* 1932, p. 266; cf. ibid. n. 38 (*Lex 'Narbonensis'*).
[7] Nock, *JHS.* 1925, p. 89. Cf. pp. 75, 463.
[8] Ibid. p. 85; cf. Ramsay, l.c.
[9] Cf. Brendel, *Ikonographie des Kaisers Augustus*, Diss. Heidelberg, 1931; Hinks, *JRS.* XXV, 1934, pp. 94 f.
[10] Brandis, *PW.* II, 479; cf. *BCH.* VI, 1882, p. 92.
[11] *BMC.* 9, 11, etc.
[12] Rouvier, *JIAN.* IV, 1901, p. 252. 1444–1452, etc.
[13] *BMC.* 75, BM = M. V, 525. 60, Oxford, Berlin = M. V, 525. 61, 63, etc.; de Saulcy, *Numismatique de la Terre Sainte*, p. 185. 5–8, 14, 17 are dated.

THE COMMUNITIES AND THE *PRINCEPS*

The principal feature of these issues is the portrait of Augustus. Kruse[1] has aptly pointed out that imperial portraiture, in its origins, was not only religious,[2] but was closely connected with the religious festivals in his honour, the Σεβαστά.[3] Not only did these fulfil a similar role to the *lustra* of Roman cities (recurring, however, at four years' interval, instead of five[4]), but they were expressly devoted to the worship of Augustus—which was the object of the entire group of coinages (p. 360). Indeed, later coins explicitly allude to these religious festivals as their occasion;[5] and at an earlier date many towns are known to have issued temple-coinages.[6] With the exception of a few surviving priest-kingships such as Olba,[7] these had, on the decrease of priestly power,[8] undergone a gradual *de facto* evolution to ordinary city-currency.[9] But the coins were still struck on religious occasions.[10] The festivals in honour of Augustus stood out as far the most important of these: they attracted vast crowds, on whose expenditure some cities largely depended.[11]

The conclusion that the mintages of this group of cities regularly coincided with the Σεβαστά is confirmed by four special considerations. First, the only relevant Phoenician city, Sidon, began its portrait-coinage with three issues made at precisely these quadriennial intervals[12]—a fact emphasised by the suspension of the mintages after the third.[13] Secondly, although many Asian cities portrayed Augustus, portrait-coinage of Antony, under whom a number of these communities coin, does not occur;[14] this may be explained by the fact that, although the honours of divinity were heaped on him with an extravagance avoided by Augustus,[15] the quadriennial festivals were not inaugurated until after Actium. Thirdly, an analogy is at hand from an unrecognised issue of the κοινὸν 'Ασίας:

ΣΕΒΑΣΤΟΥ ΘΕ. bare head of Augustus to right.
ΑΓΡΙΠΠΑΣ ΑΓΡΙΠΠΟΥ ΚΑΙ ΤΗΣ ΙΟΥΛΙΑΣ ΥΙΟΣ Agrippa Postumus standing, togate, to right (Pl. XII, 33).[16]

---

[1] *Studien zur Geschichte und Kultur des Altertums*, XIX, 3; cf. Toynbee, *CR*. 1936, p. 41.
[2] Bibliography, ibid. p. 9.
[3] *CIG*. 2810*b*. 13: Σεβαστῆα, ibid. 1186, 1586: Αὐγούστεια, *IG*. XIV, 738.
[4] Cf. Jones, *GC*. pp. 233 f.
[5] Cf. Eckhel, *DN*. IV, p. 436.
[6] E. Curtius, *Monatsbericht der königlichen Akademie der Wissenschaften zu Berlin*, 1869, pp. 472 f., 478.
[7] Cf. *ZfN*. XII, 1885, p. 369; *NC*. 1899, pp. 181 ff.
[8] Cf. Jones, *GC*. p. 227.
[9] Cf. Curtius, l.c. p. 479.
[10] This is suggested by McFayden, *CP*. XVI, 1921, p. 39. [11] Cf. Jones, *GC*. p. 229.
[12] *BMC*. 204, 205 ('102'), Paris = M. V, 380. 296 ('106'); *BMC*. 207 and Paris ('110').

[13] It is revived later in a different guise as yearly: Paris = Rouvier, *JIAN*. IV, 1901, 1440 ('117'); some doubtful, then: Berlin, Mabbott coll. ('120'); Rouvier, l.c. 1446 ('122'); Paris = M. V, 380. 301 ('123'); Vienna = ibid. 302 ('124').
[14] The rule-proving exception here is *BMC*. 191 (*et sim.*) at Ephesus, on which the heads of all three triumvirs appear, jugate.
[15] Cf. especially Immisch, *Aus Roms Zeitwende*, pp. 13 ff.
[16] The only specimen now accessible is at Paris ('uncertain'). Another belonged to Osman Nouri (sale, Sotheby's [July, 1905], 446). Morelli (*Familiarum Romanarum Numismata*, s.v. *Vipsania*) misread the obverse: the reverse-legend (unless likewise misread) varies on coins known to Harduin and Sestini (*Lettere* IV, p. 80; M. *S*. VI, 672, 409).

AUGUSTUS AS ΚΤΙΣΤΗΣ AND ΘΕΟΣ ΕΠΙΦΑΝΗΣ 363

Froehlich's attribution[1] to Agrippa II, son of Agrippa I and Cyprus, is invalidated by the Asian style.[2] Agrippa the son of Julia must be Agrippa Postumus. This is not a city-issue: considerations of type, legend and denomination combine to ascribe it to the provincial mint of the κοινόν.[3] The reverse inscription indicates a date between the birth of Agrippa Postumus in 12 B.C. and the disgrace of Julia in 2 B.C. There are reasons for concluding that the young prince is here honoured as eponymous 'Αρχιερεύς of the province, that is, President of the κοινόν.[4] Not only is communal coinage in honour of these 'Αρχιερεῖς known,[5] but there are parallels for its honorary conferment on Romans at this time: the proconsul L. Volcacius Tullus was one of them.[6] It was a natural step to extend this honour from proconsuls to members of the *domus principis*; and indeed, as an unknown coin demonstrates, an early high-priest had been Augustus himself (p. 378). Our present piece contributes a valuable analogy to the local coinages. The occasion for such an issue was clearly the central ceremony of the priesthood, namely the quadriennial 'Ρωμαῖα Σεβαστά at Pergamum,[7] whose celebration probably entitled the high-priest to the additional appellative 'Ασιάρχης.[8] There is no reason to suppose that Agrippa Postumus (whose public appearances in Rome were found embarrassing) did not preside at this festival in person, perhaps in 5 B.C.[9] Asian inscriptions[10] and some colonial coin-portraits may belong to the same occasion. It may be inferred from this issue that three portrait-issues of the Thessalian κοινόν[11] likewise were occasioned by the recurrent festival in honour of the *princeps*, whose worship was their principal *raison d'être*[12] and who favoured them politically.[13]

If the κοινὸν 'Ασίας issued money at its 'Ρωμαῖα Σεβαστά, it is, again, highly probable that the cities, in Asia at least, did likewise at their corresponding ceremonies. A fourth reason for believing that this was so can be deduced from a coin of Pergamum, with portraits of Caius and Lucius, and the name of the proconsul Q. Poppaeus Secundus(?).[14] Now Poppaeus was governor not before c. A.D. 19–20:[15] and the heads of the two princes are quite inexplicable except on the supposition that they, like Augustus,

[1] *Notitia Elementaris Numismatum*, p. 228.
[2] The portrait is a characteristically Asian, though unskilful, imitation of 'East II' *denarii* (*BMC. Imp. Aug.* 663, etc.).
[3] ΘΕ(οῦ) is a title not otherwise applied to Augustus in Asia during his lifetime. The coin is much larger than any Asian city-issue of the period.
[4] Cf. Buckler, *CR*. 1927, pp. 119 f.
[5] The next in date is a piece (of the same size) naming the 'Αρχιερεύς Alexander the son of Cleon, in c. A.D. 37: *ZfN*. XXIV, 1904, p. 256; cf. Fritze, *Münzen von Pergamon*, p. 80. 94; Paris. This involves many interesting questions relevant to its period.
[6] Buckler, l.c.
[7] Cf. Pfister, *PW*. (2R.), I, 1061.

[8] As, after centuries of controversy, Nock, *CAH*. X, p. 485 n. 4; Keil, *CAH*. XI, p. 581.
[9] Unless it is a fiction by which he is here represented as past infancy, the date cannot be much earlier. Cf. above, pp. 255, 268.
[10] E.g. *SEG*. I (1923), 385.
[11] By Megacles (Cambridge [*McLean* 4993]); Sosandrus (ibid. 4994, BM, Athens; Rogers, *Ancient Coinage of Thessaly*, 69), and Antigonus (*BMC*. 70).
[12] Their coins read ΘΕΣΣΑΛΩΝ ΣΕΒΑΣΤΩΝ.
[13] Cf. Arvanitopoulos, Πολέμων, I, 1929, p. 204.
[14] *BMC*. 250.
[15] *PIR*. III, 86. 628; Waddington, *Fastes des provinces asiatiques*, 68—cf. *BMC*. 251 with ΣΕΒΑΣΤΟΙ.

were the objects of worship and recurrent festival, which did not cease at their death. It should be noted that religious games were traditionally exempt from interference due to political changes;[1] also, that the worship of Caius and Lucius at Pergamum happens to be documented from other sources.[2] This conclusion also enables the explanation of a curious numismatic phenomenon at Tralles, where portraits of Caius in a pronounced Tiberian manner (Pl. XI, 45)[3] are in strong contrast to the contemporary version at the same city (Pl. XI, 50);[4] here, again, it must be supposed that their festivals continued, not only after their own deaths, but after the accession of their one-time rival, Tiberius.

The portrait-coins of Augustus, then, when not commemorating a foundation, were generally issued on the occasion of Σεβαστά, while those of members of his family were likewise struck for their appropriate festivals. Thus the new political order was skilfully displayed through the medium of coinage deriving its origin from ancient religious traditions. This interpretation of the purpose of Asian city-coinage is supported and amplified by an unpublished and apparently unique coin of Erythrae (Pl. XI, 66)[5] with a Tiberian head of ΣΕΒΑΣΤΟΣ: on the reverse, with the ethnic and a type of Cybele with two lions, is the word NOMH—undoubtedly referring to one of the official donatives[6] which played so large a part in municipal life.[7] A favourite occasion for one of these was the recurrent celebration of the local Σεβαστά,[8] in honour of the *princeps* who is posthumously commemorated on the obverse of this coin. Such religious festivals were often assisted from the Imperial purse, as well as by private munificence.[9] There is every probability that a large proportion of similar coinages of the first century—including no doubt many foundation-pieces—were issued for this charitable and propagandist purpose.[10] They only differ from the large groups of *tesserae*, issued by local authority with the same object,[11] in that the latter did not subsequently pass into currency. The volume of an issue can often determine whether it belongs to this category or to the mints which contributed materially to the Imperial small-change system (pp. 296, 337, 361).

The ceremonial and honorific occasion of the coinages is further illustrated by an investigation of the personages who sign them. These are usually not active local magistrates.[12] Thus it is not surprising that a number of personages are found at cities not their own.[13] The coinage was often the product of some eponymous

[1] Cf. Cary, *CP.* XXXIV, 1939, p. 160.
[2] *Inschriften von Pergamon*, p. 275, no. 384.
[3] *BMC.* 117. 114; cf. *BMC. Imp. Ti.* 47.
[4] Paris, *BMC.* 121. For an intermediate style vide *BMC.* 119–120, 123; Copenhagen (Pl. XI, 49).
[5] Own collection.
[6] For parallel uses of νομή, cf. Aeschines II, 76 (singular); Herodian VIII, 7. 19; *OGIS.* 566, line 50 (plural). Cf. Pliny, *Ep.* 116, *vereor ne...in speciem dianomes incidere videantur*.
[7] Cf. Hultsch, *PW.* IV, 875ff.

[8] Cf. Thédenat, *Daremberg and Saglio*, I, 2, pp. 1442 ff.
[9] Cf. Jones, *GC.* p. 230.
[10] Ibid., pp. 227 ff., for a general description.
[11] Cf. Muensterberg, *MBNGW.* 1913, pp. 159ff.
[12] *Rn.* 1896, pp. 466 ff.; 1898, pp. 77 ff., 127 ff., etc.
[13] E.g. Philinus at Orthosia (Paris = M. *S.* VI, 530. 462 misread) and Aninetus (*MG.* p. 470. 74), Opinas at Sardis (*BMC.* 102) and Amyzon (Copenhagen, *Wad.* 2138, misread), etc.

AUGUSTUS AS ΚΤΙΣΤΗΣ AND ΘΕΟΣ ΕΠΙΦΑΝΗΣ 365

sinecure.[1] Often no doubt these were the priesthoods—now involving worship of Augustus, and also gifts to the festivals in his honour.[2] Signed coinages may well have been the form taken by those gifts. An Augustan issue of Chios with ΒΑΣΙΛΕΩΣ ΑΝΤΙΟΧΟΥ ΔΩΡΟΝ[3] is one of a number[4] which explicitly describe their signatory as the benefactor responsible for the νομή.[5] Honorary, too, is the mention of not less than six Greeks on different coins of Hierapolis with the head of Paullus Fabius Maximus, in no more than a single year (p. 387); in the same way no less than four names had appeared on Republican tetradrachms of C. Claudius Pulcher.[6] It is therefore customary for these signatures to lack specific titles of office. But they are not infrequently accompanied by complimentary titles like φιλόκαισαρ[7]—the local imitation of *amicus principis*[8]—and φιλόπατρις.[9]

The privilege of this nominal or financial responsibility was, in fact, one accorded to loyal adherents of the Roman *régime*: prosopographical researches reveal, in Asia, a number of well-known pro-Caesarian names.[10] Besides Greeks who affected *cognomina*,[11] many of the men recorded were already enfranchised. Their coins, by portrayal of Augustus, provided publicity for the new government: and they themselves, by their names, provide us with an effective testimony to the spread of *civitas* as an advertisement of Rome. They could now make use of their Roman as well as their native citizenship;[12] if of local origin, they were bound by the laws of both.[13] C. Julius Dionysius, at Philadelphia,[14] had taught Augustus Greek and been a good friend to him.[15] Other men who testify by their Julian *gentilicium* to rewarded party-spirit are Julius Bito εὐεργέτης at Apollonia Salbace,[16] and Asclas, high-priest at Ephesus,[17] who is probably the Milesian financier C. Julius Asclas.[18] Demetrius at Ilium,[19] too, is probably identifiable with C. Julius Demetrius who appears at Thyatira[20]—no doubt a kinsman of the treacherous profiteer of that name who was Pompey's slave, Caesar's freedman, governor of Cyprus

---

[1] Cf. Gnädinger, *De Graecorum magistratibus eponymis*, Diss. Halle, 1892, pp. 22, 37; Liebenam, *St. V.* p. 283; Regling, *PW.* XVI, 455.
[2] Cf. Jones, l.c.
[3] Mavrogordato, *NC.* 1917, p. 227.
[4] E.g. Smyrna (*BMC.* 277), Side (Hill, *Anatolian Studies to Ramsay*, pp. 216 f.).
[5] Cf. *IGRR.* IV, 769; Broughton, *ES.* IV (1938), p. 887; Muensterberg, *MBNGW.* 1911, pp. 357 ff.
[6] Cf. *Rn.* 1852, p. 91.
[7] E.g. at Philadelphia, *KM.* 523; cf. *ILS.* 8958; Stevenson, *RPA.* p. 47.
[8] Cf. Muensterberg, *Jahreshefte des öst. arch. Instituts*, 1915, p. 317.
[9] Cf. Perizonius, ed. Aelian, *Vera Historia*, III, 26.
[10] E.g. Potamo (Laodicea, M. IV, 317. 712 = Istanbul; cf. Syme, *RR.* p. 262), Zeno (Laodicea,

BMC. 160; Syme, l.c. p. 259). Zeuxis φιλαληθής at the same town (*BMC.* 151) was the head of a great medical academy (Muensterberg, *NZ.* 1912, p. 112), and so of great importance (cf. Jones, *GC.* p. 219).
[11] For these cf. Milne, *NC.* 1924, pp. 316 ff., Muensterberg, *MBNGW.* 1912, l.c.: Dionysius Cilas, Cleon Agapetus, etc.
[12] Cf. Sherwin-White, p. 189; Jones, *GC.* p. 172.
[13] Sherwin-White, p. 213.
[14] *Wad.* 5137; *Weber* 3365.
[15] Cf. Stein, *PW.* V, 914 (78); Gardthausen II, 1, p. 21.
[16] *KM.* 1.
[17] *KM.* 60; *BMC.* 198, etc.
[18] *Revue des études grecques*, VI, p. 189; cf. Hatzfeld, p. 104 n. 2.
[19] *BMC.* 29.   [20] *IGRR.* IV, 1190.

for Antony, and murderer of Labienus.[1] It should be noted that dynastic names of this kind—and theophoric names like Dionysius—are often a sign of oriental origin.[2] C. Julius Callicles, who appears at Apamea under Tiberius[3] and at Siblia rather later,[4] was another *protégé* of Caesar or Augustus, and so perhaps was Julius Ponticus who is recorded at Prymnessus shortly after A.D. 14.[5] Another posthumous coiner, Philinus at Aninetus and Orthosia (p. 364 n. 13), is probably the Cn. Babbius Philinus who made his name under Augustus for his building operations at Corinth.[6] Likewise, Vipsanius Silvanus and Vipsanius Justus who appear at Amorium under Caligula[7] clearly owe their citizenship to Agrippa.[8] But A. Furius was lucky, or clever, to have enjoyed a full *cursus honorum* at Pergamum[9] if he was related by blood or *clientela* to A. Furius Tertius A. f. at Ephesus who supported the Republicans before Philippi.[10] Perhaps he was A. Furius Rufus, whose litigation was thought worthy of epigraphic record;[11] an A. Furius A. l. Seleucus was a leading figure in the goldsmiths' trade at about the time of Augustus.[12] Gessius Charidemus at Adramyttium,[13] who probably later attained the presidency of the κοινόν (p. 377), and Egnatius, on an autonomous issue of Elaea,[14] both belonged to the *patrocinium* of Caesarian families with large financial interests in the Near East, of senatorial[15] and equestrian rank respectively;[16] a Gessius Florus from Clazomenae later reached the procuratorship of Judaea.[17] Antistius Nicanor, at Aninetus,[18] also came of a family with Eastern business connections.[19] The social and commercial revolution is further illustrated by the presence at Apamea of C. Masonius Rufus[20] and (under Tiberius) M. Manneius,[21] members of bourgeois Etruscan families.[22] Manneii occur also at Tralles[23] and Delphi;[24] they became business-men in Rome before A.D. 51.[25] Valerius Smertorix at Eumenia under Tiberius[26] was enfranchised at

[1] Münzer, *PW*. IV, 2803; cf. Cic. *Phil*. XIII, 12; Dio XLVIII, 405 f. For a later personage of the same names at Metropolis, vide *KM*. 4, *Wad*. 1764.
[2] Cf. Jones, *GC*. p. 36.
[3] *BMC*. 142.   [4] *GM*. 737.
[5] Vienna = M. *S*. VII, 609; cf. *OGIS*. 533. This family became eminent again in the third century (*SEG*. VI [1932], 106; *BMC*. *Phrygia*, p. 174, Cotiaeum 78).
[6] Cf. Broneer, *Hesperia*, 1939, p. 190 n. 4.
[7] *BMC*. 25; *Rn*. 1851, p. 157.
[8] Cf. Broughton, *ES*. IV, p. 703.
[9] Munich = M. *S*. V, 426. 922, Berlin, Copenhagen, Oxford: cf. Milne, *NC*. 1936, p. 283.
[10] Josephus, *AJ*. XIV, 239; cf. Münzer, *PW*. VII, 316.
[11] *Ephemeris epigraphica*, IX, 1913, 892.
[12] *CIL*. VI, 9202; cf. Loane, *Johns Hopkins University Studies in History and Political Science*, LVI, 2, 1938, p. 88.

[13] Oxford; cf. Milne, *NC*. 1935, p. 199.
[14] *BMC*. 18.
[15] Cf. Münzer, *PW*. VII, 1324; Hatzfeld, *BCH*. XXXVI, 1912, p. 39.
[16] Cf. Cic. *Fam*. XIII, 73, 74, 45, 47; Münzer, *PW*. V, 1999.
[17] Josephus, *AJ*. XX, 11. 1; cf. *PIR*. II, 117. 103.
[18] Heberdey, *Forschungen in Ephesus*, III, p. 107 —not seen by me; perhaps posthumous. It reads Ἀνθέστιος: cf. Ἀνθέσθιος in *Amherst Pap*. II, 92.
[19] Cf. Hatzfeld, p. 177 n. 4.
[20] *BMC*. 139.   [21] *Wad*. 5703 = *KM*. 17.
[22] Schulze, pp. 189, 360. Cusinius at Ephesus (Munich = M. III, 93. 252; M. *S*. VI, 124. 319) is not of this date, as Ramsay (*Anatolian Studies to Buckler*, 1939, p. 209) thinks, but is manifestly Claudian.
[23] *IG*. XIV, 666; *ILS*. 7791.
[24] Wescher and Foucart, *Inscr. de Delphes*, 457.
[25] Herzog, *PW*. XVII, 1432.
[26] *BMC*. 34, *KM*. 5.

some date subsequent to his signature of Antonian coinage as Smertorix Philonidou.[1] The *nomen* of Caecilius Plocamus at Prymnessus[2]—possibly the Plocamus who managed the banking interests of the leading party-man L. Autronius Paetus[3]—may hark back to the pre-Caesarian oligarchy.[4] But even if, as is improbable, his thoughts did likewise, he would have been isolated among a crowd of men whose names and records bear witness to their adherence to the new order, and to their suitability for the privilege of signing (and paying for) these coinages, whose obverse and purpose were designed to popularise the *princeps* as κτίστης and νέος θεός.

[1] *BMC.* 20; *Rn.* 1898, pl. II, 11.
[2] *BMC.* 18, 19.
[3] Ritschl, *Opuscula Philologica*, IV, 29; Herzog, l.c. 1427.
[4] However, no Greek was enfranchised before c. 102 B.C.: cf. Box, *JRS.* XXII, 1932, p. 183; Sherwin-White, p. 188.

F. AUGUSTUS AS HEIR TO THE HELLENISTIC MONARCHS

It is not necessary to emphasise that, as κτίστης and θεός, Augustus was heir to Alexander and the Diadochi, who had viewed such roles as an integral part of their state-institutions.[1] His coin-portraiture in their dominions is bound to retain many of the associations of their rule. In *provincia* Syria, where Gaza and Sidon portray him on *liberatio*-coinages (p. 344), and there are extensive portrait-issues of Aradus (p. 333 n. 23), Antioch (p. 376) and Ascalon,[2] this aspect has particular interest, since here there is a vital link between Hellenistic and Roman Empires—the rule of Cleopatra, the last of the Ptolemies, in conjunction with Antony, who combined in the complex of his Imperial claims the heirship to the Seleucid Empire.

At Antioch Antony occupied this role,[3] with its implications of divinity:[4] it must be in this capacity that a local silver issue of that city[5] honours him. The same, too, must be the meaning of four bronze portrait-coinages of cities in Phoenicia, during the five years (42–c. 37) when this region was directly under his rule. These are **Tripolis** (with Fulvia, 41–40;[6] also Fulvia alone, 42–41[7]), **Aradus** (38–37),[8] **Ptolemais Ace** (38–37)[9] and **Balanea**.[10] The coins recall the municipal series inaugurated by Antiochus IV,[11] and show by their portraits, which had been a royal prerogative, that the Seleucid tradition was consciously maintained.

As regards subsequent coinages in honour of Antony, there are reasons for doubting Lederer's[12] arguments based on a marriage in 36 B.C. He ignores the uncertainty whether such a re-marriage (after the ἱερὸς γάμος at Tarsus) was necessary or took place,[13] and only mentions the further possibility that it occurred in 37.[14] It is at least certain that the initiation of a new and exceptional regnal era[15] accompanied the restoration to

---

[1] Cf. Ferguson, *CAH*. VII, p. 20; Rostovtzeff, ibid. pp. 114, 162; Jones, *GC*. pp. 2 ff. Cf. p. 356.
[2] *BMC*. 30 ff.; *Hu*. 72 ff., etc.
[3] Cf. Lederer, *NC*. 1938, p. 69.
[4] Cf. Ensslin, *Gnomon*, 1934, p. 215; Tarn, *CAH*. x, p. 33.   [5] *BMC*. 52.
[6] Paris, Hill, *BMC. Phoenicia*, p. cxviii, not Cleopatra, as Svoronos, *Ptolemies*, 1896: not Octavia, as Kahrstedt, *Klio*, 1910, p. 292. Date 23 (Pompeian era). Cf. Lederer, l.c. p. 72.
[7] Berlin, cf. Rouvier, *JIAN*. VI, 1903, 1640: date 22, confirming Kubitschek's view (*PW*. I. 649) that the Pompeian era commenced in 63 and not 64, since Antony's rule only began late in 42.
[8] *BMC*. 355, Berlin.
[9] *BMC*. 14: date 11 (Caesarian era) rightly attributed by Lederer, l.c. to this year, since although the era itself varies elsewhere from 49 to c. 45 (Lederer, *ZfN*. XXXIV, 1924, p. 179; Kubitschek, l.c. 650), the head of Antony is never likely to appear alone in the dominions of Cleopatra (ΣΚΕ error for ΣΚΒ in Rouvier, *JIAN*. III, 1900, 384), to whom the city passed in 37 (Tarn, *CAH*. x, p. 67).
[10] BM, Paris (Marquardt, *St.V*. I, p. 394 n. 5). There are four letters, not two, and they are a Phoenician magistrate's name, such as is found with a Greek ethnic under Augustus at Byblus (cast at Winterthur: *MG*. 26).
[11] Head, *HN*. p. 763.
[12] *NC*. 1938, p. 67; cf. n. 3.
[13] Levi II, p. 144.   [14] Tarn, l.c. p. 66.
[15] Ibid. p. 81, cf. n. 3; cf. Levi II, p. 143; Porphyrius, *Fragmenta Historicorum Graecorum*, III, 774. 9.

AUGUSTUS AS HEIR TO THE HELLENISTIC MONARCHS 369

Cleopatra, in 37, of the empire of Ptolemy Philadelphus, which had included most of Phoenicia.[1] Antony had already coined as a Seleucid at Ptolemais, Aradus and Tripolis; overlordship of the Ptolemaic realm is the cause of his portrait, with that of Cleopatra, at **Ptolemais Ace** (Pl. IX, 23)[2] and **Aradus**,[3] which were now in the Ptolemaic kingdom. The same conjunction of the two rulers appears on regal issues of uncertain mint.[4] Antony was never crowned King in the Lagid succession,[5] but in the new regnal era Egypt was one of the lands of which he was supreme ruler: he was honoured there as Osiris,[6] and the kingdom itself now, if not earlier,[7] formally assumed a client-status with regard to Rome.

For it was still Rome of which Antony was primarily the representative. On our first group of coins (42–37), indeed, he has appeared as a Seleucid, and on the second (after 37) as an overlord of Ptolemies; but on other issues, even in the last years of his rule, his titles are purely Roman. On official silver with Cleopatra—unfortunately of uncertain mint[8]—he is ΑΥΤΟΚΡΑΤωΡ ΤΡΙΤΟΝ ΤΡΙωΝ ΑΝΔΡωΝ; on a military *aes* issue at Patrae he is ΥΠΑΤΟΣ Γ΄ (p. 64). Moreover, outside Syria, even the cities significantly recognise the Roman character of his rule. At **Thessalonica**[9] he is ΑΥΤΟΚΡΑΤωΡ, and is named with Octavian, just as they appear in conjunction at Cnossus (p. 262). At **Ephesus**,[10] we find the heads of all three triumvirs (Pl. XI, 51 [p. 362 n. 14]). Such meticulousness is without parallel in the dominions of Octavian, whose cities completely ignore their ruler's colleagues. Elsewhere in the East, a coin of **Byzantium** with Antony's portrait[11] is equally Roman in allusion, since it imitates closely the types of a Roman *denarius*;[12] at **Alabanda** (Pl. XI, 54)[13] heads of him and Octavia—wrongly identified by Imhoof-Blumer as Augustus and Livia—likewise do not deserve the name of royal, since they merely appear as items in a considerable portrait-gallery (p. 373). Thus outside Phoenicia Antony appears only on issues which illustrate his Roman aspects or were struck by Roman officials;[14] and even on the Phoenician coinages of Seleucid character, the use of the Pompeian and Caesarian eras, at Tripolis and Ptolemais respectively, bear witness to the limitations of Hellenistic continuity. Although he unduly ignores the Hellenistic religious aspects of Antony's rule,[15]

---

[1] Tarn, l.c. p. 67; cf. Momigliano, *Athenaeum*, 1935, p. 144; *pace* Dobiáš, *Mélanges Bidez*, 1934, p. 287.
[2] Hannover; Lederer, *NC*. 1938, p. 371.
[3] Cast at Winterthur.
[4] Hill, *BMC. Phoenicia*, p. lv.
[5] Levi II, p. 144; Syme, *RR*. p. 273.
[6] Heinen, *Klio*, XI, 1911, p. 138.
[7] Tarn, l.c. p. 34 n. 3. Stevenson, *RPA*. p. 41, points out that this was practically the case at least from 168 B.C.; cf. Nicolaus Damasc., *De vita*, 5, of Caesar.
[8] Tarn, l.c. p. 82 n. 1.
[9] Gaebler, *NG*. II, 2, p. 97.
[10] *BMC*. 92, etc.
[11] *BMC*. 60.
[12] *BMCR*. II, p. 509. 147.
[13] *GM*. 406.
[14] Mionnet's coin of Corcyra with his head (*S*. III, p. 443) is a crude forgery; a bronze piece of Laodicea (Koehne, *Mémoires de la Société d'archéologie...de St Pétersbourg*, VI, p. 245) shows not Antony but Augustus (von Sallet, *De Asandro et Polemone*, Diss. Berlin, 1865, pp. 36 f.), and the same is true of a silver coin from the same mint (Friedländer, *BB*. II, 1865, p. 266, Uwaroff coll.).
[15] Levi II, p. 101.

Craven[1] is right in emphasising the Roman correctness of many of his arrangements. But the tradition which Antony followed was derived less from the Republic than from its greatest son. It is not by accident that the client-prince policy of Antony accorded with Caesar's views,[2] and that a coin commemorating Antony's Parthian expedition bore the *Sidus Iulium*.[3] Highly significant is the collection by Deutsch[4] of quotations which show that Antony considered himself the heir of Julius. He set up a monument *parenti optime merito*:[5] Cicero states that he even maintained that in a previous will he had held this place—*testamento, ut dicebas ipse, filius appellatus es*.[6] Octavianic propaganda has naturally left no trace of this state of affairs.[7] Granted Antony's predilection to Caesarism rather than Hellenism, there can be no doubt that, whatever Cleopatra might say, the purely Roman M. Antonius *jun*. (Antyllus), who alone of his father's sons and step-sons appears on the Roman coinage, was at the end considered the heir to the Caesarian-Antonian world-empire.[8] The little half-breed princes all had their niches in the fantastic structure of its ideology,[9] but even Ptolemy the son of Caesar,[10] King of Kings,[11] never emerges from the royal coinages to take an Imperial place with Antyllus on the official currency. Throughout the triumvirate, Antony is primarily a Roman magistrate, though one of the Caesarian rather than the Republican model. The Phoenician municipal coinages illustrate the change in the secondary aspects of his rule which took place in 37, when his Seleucid claims became merged in the project of a Roman world-empire, built on the ruins of Hellenistic monarchies and on a tenuous claim to the Caesarian succession. From the beginning most Romans must have seen with painful clarity two obstacles to these plans. It was dangerous that they excluded Octavian; that they, and Antony, embraced Cleopatra was disastrous. It is now necessary to follow the Lagid thread in the numismatic tangle of the triumvirate and early principate.

Antony was connected with the Ptolemaic kingdom in two ways. He was allied and perhaps married to its queen; and his Caesarian empire was linked to the Lagid realm

---

[1] *University of Missouri Studies (Social Science)*, III, 2, 1920, p. 22.

[2] Ibid. p. 55; cf. p. xi.

[3] Tarn, *JRS*. 1932, p. 135.

[4] *University of California Publications in Classical Philology*, IX, 6, 1928, pp. 186 f.; cf. especially Florus II, 15. 1. Cf. above, p. 64, below, p. 421.

[5] Cic. *Fam*. XII, 3. 1; cf. Syme, *RR*. p. 123.

[6] *II Phil*. 29.

[7] Cf. Scott, *Memoirs of the American Academy in Rome*, XI, 1933, pp. 8 ff.

[8] Cf. Tarn, *CAH*. x, p. 81. The readjustments of 34, involving the transference of Alexander Helios to an imaginary kingdom (Tarn, l.c. p. 80), mark a regression from the oriental point of view which had tempted Antony after the Parthian expedition (cf. Craven, l.c. p. xi). Coinage honours Antyllus, and Caesarion's paternity is proclaimed: only now is the first numismatic record of the new era. On the administrative ambiguity of the Donations see Syme, *RR*. p. 270, and above, p. 58.

[9] Tarn, l.c. p. 80 (Philadelphus), id. *JRS*. 1932, pp. 148 ff., and Meiklejohn, *JRS*. 1934, p. 192 (Helios).

[10] Charlesworth, *CQ*. XXVII, 1933, p. 176; *pace* Carcopino, *Points de vue*, pp. 141 ff., id. *Annuaire de l'École des Hautes Études de Gand*, 1937, pp. 37ff., Syme, *RR*. p. 273 n. 1. Cf. C. Oppius, who devoted a leaflet to this question in Octavian's interests: Scott, l.c. p. 49.

[11] Tarn, *CAH*. x, p. 80.

AUGUSTUS AS HEIR TO THE HELLENISTIC MONARCHS 371

by the person of its sovereign Ptolemy XIV, who was the son of Cleopatra by Julius.[1] He was not Antony's heir; but in 34 he succeeded Alexander Helios as the figurehead of Eastern propaganda,[2] and became overlord of the client-kings,[3] when the pan-Asian symbolism was abandoned owing to its hateful character in the eyes of Romans.[4] The colleague of Ptolemy XIV in the Egyptian kingdom was his mother Cleopatra. When the Empire of Philadelphus was restored in 37, the Graeco-Phoenician cities bear witness by their coinage to their position in the Ptolemaic realm.[5] At **Aradus**[6] and **Ptolemais Ace,**[7] the head of Cleopatra appears with that of her overlord Antony; on a second coin of Aradus, and at **Berytus,**[8] she is alone.[9] The last of these issues was made in 32–31 B.C.[10] It is dated to the twenty-first regnal year of Cleopatra and the sixth of the era of world-empire with Antony; but it bears also a third year-sign ΛΝ (50), which Brett[11] plausibly assigns to a newly invented era legitimising the accession of Ptolemy XI Auletes ('Nothos') in 81–80 B.C. and thus the Lagid dynasty. This is typical of the whole group of coinages, which is Ptolemaic in character.

Yet Cleopatra's position was more than Ptolemaic. A similar series was inaugurated inland, at **Damascus,** in the year 276 of the Seleucid era (36–5),[12] and the issue was repeated in 32–1.[13] But no head occurs of Ptolemy XIV Caesar, who was king of Syria until 34 and then overlord to the new king Ptolemy Philadelphus.[14] His only numis-

[1] See p. 370, n. 10.
[2] Meiklejohn, *JRS.* XXIV, 1934, p. 192.
[3] Tarn, *CAH.* X, p. 80.
[4] Id. *JRS.* XXII, 1932, p. 141.
[5] For the uncertainty of other evidence cf. Fink, *JRS.* XXII, 1932, p. 111.
[6] Cast at Winterthur.
[7] Hannover: Lederer, *NC.* 1938, p. 65.
[8] Athens: Svoronos, *Ptolemies*, 1886.
[9] An uncertain coin (Berlin), perhaps representing Cleopatra, is shown on Pl. XII, 19. Possibly some of these are foundation-issues.
[10] Tarn (*CAH.* X, p. 100 n.) is wrong in citing a regal coin of the same date, found at Berytus, to prove a change from regal to city coinage indicating a revolt from Cleopatra. In the first place, the local issue also bears her head (cf. Kahrstedt, *Klio*, X, 1910, p. 277), which could not appear after a revolt; secondly, the evidence of provenance is quite insufficient to demonstrate that the regal coin was struck at Berytus at all (Hill, *BMC. Phoenicia,* p. lv); and on grounds of fabric and style this is improbable.
[11] *AJA.* 1937, p. 460.
[12] Paris: Svoronos, l.c. 1890.
[13] Paris: ibid. 1892 f.

[14] Tarn, *CAH.* X, p. 80. The conjecture of Svoronos (l.c. 1891) that the head of Ptolemy XIV appears on a coin of this city with the date 277 (ZOC) must be disproved. Wroth, *BMC. Syria*, p. 282. 1, rightly ignores its possibility on iconographical grounds, and the piece is entirely out of keeping with autonomous Damascene issues of this period (e.g. *BMC.* p. 283). A better explanation is suggested by comparison with a coin of Caesarea Panias with ΚΑΙϹΑΡ ΠΑΝΙΑ ΔΟϹ ΡΟΒ (Paris, cf. de Saulcy, *Num. Terre Sainte*, 1) (Pl. XII, 23). The heads of the two coins are alike, and both have late styles and square 'sigmas'. Since Caesarea Panias was only founded in 3–2 B.C., there can be no possibility that its date 274 (ΔΟϹ) is of the Seleucid era; on the other hand the second date, 172 (POB), suits the foundation era. This will attribute the coin to A.D. 169–170 (a date entirely in accordance with the style), and establish the commencement of the earlier era at 105–4 B.C. The coin of Damascus is stylistically close, and ZOC is close to ΔΟϹ. The eras must have been related, if not identical. c. 105 is a particularly probable date for both cities to have obtained some form of recognition. The civil wars between Antiochus VIII Grypus and Antiochus IX Cyzicenus permitted

matic representation is in the inferior position of a babe (Eros) in the arms of Cleopatra (Aphrodite) on regal coinage of Cyprus (Pl. IX, 29).[1] The appearance of his name on another issue of that island[2] is very uncertain, since the coin has been badly tooled. Even in Egypt the head of Cleopatra appears alone.[3] Yet Ptolemy Caesar was first King, then King of Kings, in Egypt and in Cyprus as well as in Syria. The coinages recognise this fiction at its true worth.[4] Cleopatra, when not with Antony, appears alone, to the exclusion of her sons. In her new regnal era she was more than Queen of Egypt, more even than Queen of Kings. Thus her coins, like her position, impinged on the Roman state, and demand consideration in the present study. On *denarii*, struck perhaps at Alexandria,[5] not only is she REGINA REGVM FILIORVMQUE REGVM but her counterpart is Antony. A commentary on her status is provided by the three remaining local coinages in her honour.

The first of these includes silver tetradrachms of Ascalon issued in 49–8, 48–7 and 38–7 respectively.[6] Like the local bronze, they are noteworthy for their omission of Cleopatra's nominal colleagues, first Ptolemy XII and then Ptolemy XIV Caesar; it is clear that as early as 49–8 her seniority and predominance were recognised. Even an Alexandrian tetradrachm of 47–6 shows her alone:[7] the coins of Ascalon make it unnecessary to explain this by a period of rule without a colleague.[8] In view of her later rise to power, the issues of Ascalon are important by their demonstration that a Lagid could appear as protector outside his or her realm, and that the collegiate fiction was ignored in favour of Cleopatra from the very outset of her reign.

Her exceptional position, as an Empress in more than the Lagid sense, is even

Sidon and Tripolis to initiate eras in 111, Seleucia in 108 (Jones, *CERP*. p. 255), and Ascalon in 103 (Brett, *AJA*. 1937, p. 457; *pace* Jones, l.c.). Moreover, Damascus was the capital of Cyzicenus (cf. Tümpel, *PW*. IV, 2045), who is therefore especially likely to have granted the privileges to Damascus (not the same as Demetrias [p. 331]). Thus historical considerations support the numismatic evidence of a new era from 105–104. Benzinger (*PW*. III, 1290) shows that Caesarea Panias, as Panion, was already Hellenised in the time of Antiochus IV; the evidence of the coinage, and the analogies of Damascus, Ascalon, Seleucia, Tripolis and its near neighbour Sidon, indicate a commencement for its era in the same decade, perhaps also in 105–104.

[1] Poole, *BMC. Ptolemies*, p. 122. 1; cf. Curtius, *Röm. Mitt.* 1933, p. 182.
[2] Poole, l.c. p. 124.
[3] Ibid. p. 123. 4 ff.
[4] Cf. also the bronze issues of four governors, of whom one only (Crassus, p. 55) makes an oblique reference to his titular superior. It is not true that Antony deliberately excluded the Roman ruling class (Levi II, p. 153). Nor (as ibid. p. 146) did the domains of Ptolemy Philadelphus include Roman Syria, where Q. Oppius, unlike Crassus, coins as PR. (p. 61).

[5] Cf. Strong, *CAH*. Plates IV, 1, p. 198 f.
[6] Dates ΛNE (*BMC*. 3), ΛNΣ (Athens) and ΛΞΣ (Adda coll., Alexandria). Brett (*AJA*. 1937, pp. 452 ff.) suggests the right interpretation for these by her statement that Ascalon never belonged to the Lagid kingdom; she points out that others of its coins honour earlier Ptolemies in the same way, and that each issue coincides with a crisis in which the Egyptian monarchy intervened to protect Ascalon. She also shows the falsity of the era of 84 B.C. supposed by Svoronos, and the preferability of 103 to 104 for the beginning of the city era. Cf. also Curtius, *Röm. Mitt.* 1933, p. 183.
[7] Cf. Curtius, l.c. p. 182.
[8] As Poole, *BMC. Ptolemies*, p. lxxxiv.

better illustrated by a bronze coinage outside the Ptolemaic Empire, at **Alabanda**. The single extant example of this[1] has been completely misread and misinterpreted. Imhoof-Blumer describes it as follows:[2] ΑΛΑΒΑΝΔΕ.....ΓΙΤΟΥ ΤΗΛΕ. (?) head of Livia to right—[ΕΠΙ ΑΦ]ΡΟΔΙΤΟΥ Α[ΜΝ?]ΗΣΣΟ[Υ] head of Augustus to right. It has been pointed out that the same writer wrongly identified another Alabandean portrait as Augustus (p. 369, Pl. XI, 54); the features here are even less Augustan. The legend on the other side has been misread by Imhoof-Blumer owing to a misinterpretation of two badly executed 'K's as Y and H respectively. The true description is as follows:

ΑΛΑΒΑΝΔΕ[ΩΝ] ΕΠ. Τ. ΟΚΤ. ΚΛΕ. head of Cleopatra to right.
ΑΜ(?)Ν(?)ΗΣΣ[ΟΣ ΕΠΑΦ?]ΡΟΔΙΤΟΥ head of Amnessus (?) to right (Pl. XI, 55).

The distinctive head on the reverse is clearly that of a private citizen, like another in the same series—again mistakenly attributed to Augustus by Imhoof-Blumer—which is inscribed ΑΡΙΣΤΟΓΕΝΗΣ ΙΠΠΑΡΧΗΣ, whose features it presents (Pl. XI, 57).[3] The last three letters below the female bust on the present coin are distinguished by size from the rest of the inscription, and afford a clear identification with Cleopatra; the features, scantily executed as they are, accord well with known portraits of her.[4] The eponymous (?) magistrate named with her must be, after a custom already found earlier in Bithynia (p. 396), the governor. At this date there would be no parallel to the appearance of a local magistrate's name after ΕΠΙ: every supposed Augustan example has been shown to be posthumous. There is, moreover, a gap in the Asian *Fasti* in 32–31 (p. 395); T. Oct(avius?) may well have been a kinsman of the M. Octavius Cn. f. who commanded part of Antony's fleet at Actium.[5] In view of the rarity of the *praenomen* Titus in this clan, it may be permissible to refer the enfranchisement of T. Octavii at Sparta[6] to a governorship of Achaia by the present official; possibly also some of the numerous Octavii in Asia[7] owe him their names. Here is a deliberate conjunction of Cleopatra with a Roman proconsul. It suggests an attempt to bridge the gap between Rome and Cleopatra, and perhaps also a demonstration that Octavian was not supported even by members of his own family—just as Sextus had coined through another of his kinsmen, L. Appuleius Decianus (p. 24).[8] The portraits merely rank with others of Antony, Octavia, and even private citizens, who appear on the curious series at this mint.

A third issue in Cleopatra's honour was actually made on the opposite side of the

[1] Berlin. [2] *KM.* 107. 7.
[3] *GM.* 137. 407; Berlin, Milan, *Cat.* 418 (reverse misread to bear inscription of Livia).
[4] Cf. Curtius, *Röm. Mitt.* 1933, pp. 182 ff.
[5] Plutarch, *Antonius*, 65; cf. Syme, *RR.* pp. 269, 296.
[6] *IG.* v, 1. 115, 516, show their descendants; cf. Box, *JRS.* XXII, 1932, pp. 168, 179; cf. XXI, 1931, p. 205.
[7] e.g. Cyzicus (*Ath. Mitt.* VI, p. 42. 2), Thyatira (*Denkschr. d. Wien Ak.* 1911, II, p. 49. 101), Pergamum (Hatzfeld, p. 164).
[8] For the regular and often cynical schisms of noble families at this time, vide Syme, *RR.* p. 64.

Aegean. **Patrae** strikes a coin with ΒΑΣΙΛΙΣΣΑ ΚΛΕΟΠΑΤΡΑ (draped bust to right) (Pl. IX, 30) and ΑΓΙΑΣ ΛΥΣΩΝΟΣ ΠΑΤΡΕΩΝ (*sistrum*).[1] It is arresting to find that the Egyptian *sistrum* and the Ptolemaic title have come half the way to Rome; and the fears recalled by Horace seem justifiable. But Juba and his son are called REX at Carthago Nova, and Antiochus of Commagene ΒΑΣΙΛΕΥΣ on coins of Chios (pp. 216, 365). Nevertheless, Regling's explanation[2] that this piece is purely honorary (*Ehrung, nicht...Herrschaftsansprüche*) does not accord with the message to eye and mind conveyed by this piece to us, as to its ancient recipients. The coinage is as suggestive and allusive as the whole propaganda of which it formed a part—based on the syncretistic nightmare of the combined dreams of a Roman Emperor and a Graeco-oriental queen, whose ambitions were only alike in their magnitude and impracticability. It is certain that at the end Cleopatra stood by Antony's side, as ruler of all;[3] but a decade of unprofitable adjustments had been necessary to achieve this untenable result. Her contribution to the principate was a warning that, if Greek symbolism was necessary to rule the Greeks, the *princeps* must, without a Greek colleague, combine it in his own many-sided Imperial personality. For our numismatic study she and Antony illustrate the complexity of the Romano-Hellenistic tradition to which Augustus's portrait-coinage succeeded.

Yet another aspect of this is provided by three mints in the region which had been the core of royal Macedonia—*civitates liberae* **Amphipolis** and **Thessalonica**, and stipendiary **Edessa**. The two 'free' cities have series long enough to play an integral part in the currency of the Empire;[4] Edessa has a single foundation-issue, and Amphipolis probably inaugurates its coinage with a similar piece (p. 343).[5] Titulatures are ΚΑΙΣΑΡ ΘΕΟΥ ΥΙΟΣ, ΚΑΙΣΑΡ ΣΕΒΑΣΤΟΣ, ΚΑΙΣΑΡΟΣ ΣΕΒΑΣΤΟΥ, and ΣΕΒΑΣΤΟΥ.[6] Since, as triumvir, he has already had his title ΑΥΤΟΚΡΑΤωΡ placed upon several issues of the latter mint,[7] his invariable omission of it as *princeps* on all the numerous Greek issues of Macedonia, as elsewhere, confirms that there was a deliberate avoidance of emphasis on the *Imperator* title. On the other hand, not only is the coinage itself so large as to make an entirely religious character improbable, but there is evidence that the attitude of the Macedonians to the *princeps* differed from that of other Greek communities. The divergency is illustrated by the posthumous coinages in his honour. At Edessa,[8] Amphipolis,[9] Thessalonica,[10] and (a short distance within

---

[1] *BMC*. 15; cf. Curtius, *Röm. Mitt.* 1933, p. 183.
[2] *ZfN*. 1906, no. 1905.
[3] Tarn, *CAH*. x, p. 81; cf. n. 6; cf. Charlesworth, *Proceedings of the Cambridge Philological Society*, CLI, 1932, p. 6. Cf. above, pp. 64 f.
[4] *BMC*. 73 ff. of Amphipolis; *BMC*. 58 ff. of Thessalonica.
[5] Thessalonica, on the other hand, portrays Julius as ΘΕΟΣ. It has been pointed out that his posthumous heads only occur at cities 'founded' by him (p. 318); perhaps Augustus did not need to revise the constitution which he installed.
[6] A coin of Edessa with ΑΥΤΟΚ...., at Sofia (Imhoof-Blumer, *MG*. p. 62), is much later, and is rightly omitted by Gaebler.
[7] Gaebler, *NG*. II, 2, p. 97.
[8] BM = M. I, 475. 189.
[9] *BMC*. 74.
[10] *MG*. p. 94. 128.

AUGUSTUS AS HEIR TO THE HELLENISTIC MONARCHS 375

Thrace, but no doubt attached to the province rather than the kingdom) at **Abdera**,[1] he is invariably called, not plain ΣΕΒΑΣΤΟΣ as on other posthumous coinages, but ΘΕΟΣ [ΚΑΙΣΑΡ] [ΣΕΒΑΣΤΟΣ]. In all the rest of the Greek world only four cities out of hundreds translate *divus* in this way:[2] yet in Macedonia the practice is universal and invariable. It is reasonable to deduce that here alone the name of ΣΕΒΑΣΤΟΣ itself was not considered enough to imply posthumous divinity, and that in his lifetime—when that title is unaccompanied by ΘΕΟΣ—Augustus was not deified in the same way as by other Greek cities.

There is, moreover, a historical basis for this view. Augustus deliberately posed as the heir of the great Antigonids;[3] he was also, throughout the East, responsible for a revival of the spirit of Hellenistic monarchy.[4] Now the Antigonids, in their own country, had strongly and caustically discouraged their worship as deities, although cities had allowed their enthusiasm to overstep the bounds imposed by the official philosophic theory of the Macedonian kingdom.[5] The formula on which this was based was the duty of service: and this too was a no less vital element than religion in the *statio principis* evolved for and by Augustus.[6] It is therefore natural that in Macedonia, where the idea of living divinity was not traditional, it was subordinated to other and more suitable aspects of the manifold character of the principate. Exceptionally, Augustus, while alive, is treated as a man, and ΣΕΒΑΣΤΟΣ as a human title. After his death, when his deification is admitted, ΘΕΟΣ has to be added.[7]

---

[1] *NG.* 241.
[2] Ilium, Pergamum, Aphrodisias, Augusta. The last (*BMC.* 4) is rendering literally the Roman titulature of Tiberius. Cf. above, p. 360.
[3] Tarn, *CAH.* x, p. 113.
[4] Cf. Sherwin-White, p. 167.
[5] Tarn, *CAH.* vii, p. 202.
[6] Klostermann, *Philologus*, LXXXVII, 1932, pp. 358 ff.; cf. Gagé, *Rev. hist.* CLXXVII, 1936, p. 336.
[7] Nevertheless, it was probably not long before the Imperial cult established itself, as even under the Antigonids; Keil attributes the foundation of the κοινὸν Μακεδόνων at Beroea to the time of Augustus (*CAH.* xi, p. 567). But it may be significant that its earliest coin (at Sofia and Belgrade), attributed by M. S. III, 47 to his principate, is an imperfectly preserved example of a Claudian issue (cf. Gaebler, *ZfN.* XXIV, 1904, p. 245; id. XXXVI, 1926, p. 114). The error has lately been repeated by Newby (p. 77) and Elmer (*Belgrade Cat.* p. 4. 229).

G. AUGUSTUS AS 'ΑΡΧΙΕΡΕΥΣ

On two other coinages also Augustus is honoured as man rather than god. One of these is a series of **Antioch**, which played a larger part in the Imperial currency-system than that of any other peregrine mint.[1] It consists of *dupondii* and *asses* with the following types:

ΚΑΙΣΑΡΙ ΣΕΒΑΣΤΩ ΑΡΧΙΕΡΕΙ Laureate head to right.
ΑΡΧΙΕΡΑΤΙΚΟΝ ΑΝΤΙΟΧΕΙΣ in wreath.[2]

Dates, of the Actian era, range between 7–6 B.C.[3] and 1 B.C.–A.D. 1. Resemblances of style and module confirm that these were issued by the same mint as the main official group with SC (p. 100);[4] it will be seen elsewhere that Antioch issued several other kinds of currency at the same time (p. 396). The fact that a series of silver tetradrachms and another of 'pseudo-autonomous' small change began at the same date as the present category[5] suggests an extensive re-organisation during the *legatio* of Varus, whose financial acumen was conspicuous.[6] The double emphasis on the ἀρχιερεία is remarkable. Dieudonné[7] only remarks that the issue is dedicated to Augustus, and Bouchier[8] cannot decide whether the high-priesthood is Roman or Antiochene. But it is clear that the Antiochene people could not strike 'Archieratic' coinage—as the reverse legend asserts that they did—for a Roman high-priest: this would be quite different from merely honouring him in that capacity. Ramsay[9] must, therefore, be right in considering Augustus the high priest of Antioch. Eponymous priesthoods are a frequent phenomenon at Greek cities.[10] Many of them retained prerogatives of their previous dignity,[11] and at some, notably Olba, they still carry the rights of coinage; in Asia, too, the local issues are temple-currency in a modified form (p. 363). It may be added that the view that any of Augustus's priestly titles, even at Rome, gave him an *imperium*[12] has been exploded.[13] In general character, then, the Antiochene series is religious like those of the other cities. But the appearance of Augustus as high-priest rather than god is, as far as our evidence permits us to know, unique among city-coinages. Nor was the experiment continued under Tiberius, whose normal titulature

---

[1] E.g. found in Yugoslavia (Zagreb), Bulgaria (Sofia), Cilicia and Cappadocia (Milne, *Annals of Archaeology and Anthropology*, III, 1910, p. 91). For an Imperial countermark, vide above, p. 102 n. 4.
[2] *BMC*. 133 ff.
[3] Munich (EK), *pace* Macdonald, *NC*. 1904, pp. 105 ff. (ZK).   [4] Ibid. p. 109.
[5] Macdonald, l.c., corrected by Munich specimen.
[6] Velleius II, 117. Cf. above, p. 127.

[7] *Mélanges numismatiques*, II, 1919, p. 137.
[8] *A Short History of Antioch*, p. 307.
[9] *Cities and Bishoprics of Phrygia*, p. 56; pace Eckhel, *DN*. III, p. 274.
[10] Gnädinger, *De Graecorum magistratibus eponymis*, Diss. Halle, 1892, pp. 3 ff.
[11] Cf. Jones, *GC*. p. 227.
[12] Mommsen, *St.R.* II³, p. 20.
[13] Vide Rosenberg, *PW*. IX, 1207.

appears on coins of similar type and style in conjunction with the name of the *legatus*.[1] The Augustan issues at least may well have been provided from the temple-funds, since there is ample evidence in Syria of the existence of such treasuries[2] and of their use for public works.[3] How far this is true of other Syrian currencies as well cannot be said.

A curiously close parallel is provided by another coin, which is apparently unique:[4] it was very imperfectly read by Eckhel,[5] and has never since been published:

ΕΠΙ ΚΑΙΣΑΡΟΣ ΤΟ ΔΕΥΤΕΡΟΝ bare head of Augustus to right.

ΧΑΡΙΔΑΜΟΥ ΙΕΡΕΟΣ, ΑΥΤΟΜ. ΓΡΑΜ(Μ)ΑΤΕΟΣ[6] bearded head to right. Countermark ĪMP. (Pl. XII, 30).

The style of this piece requires attribution to *provincia* Asia; but there are various reasons for believing that it cannot be classed among city-issues. Those invariably have an ethnic, which is here lacking; indeed, the present inscriptions bear no relation whatever to such coinage. No use of ΕΠΙ in the local series can be attributed to the principate of Augustus (pp. 373, 396). The countermark is found elsewhere only on coins not issued by local authority (cf. p. 94).[7] Finally, the denomination is much larger than any employed at this date by the cities, whose mintage is restricted to very small pieces. But two issues of the κοινὸν 'Ασίας, under Augustus and Caligula (p. 363), are of precisely this module; and there can be little doubt that the present issue is of similar origin. In 29 B.C. the κοινόν was officially devoted to the cult, by the Asian Greeks—this coin cannot refer to the cult of resident Romans—of Rome and the *princeps* at Pergamum;[8] a temple was completed there ten years later.[9]

Now the portrait of Augustus is imitated from a model[10] which precludes a date earlier than 27. The retention of plain ΚΑΙΣΑΡ after that date is paralleled by many official and local issues (p. 359) and by the continuation of formulas such as ἔτος Καίσαρος (cf. p. 331). The unique obverse phrase with ΕΠΙ suggests that the *princeps* is here the holder of some honorary magistracy; and the omission to define this indicates that it was eponymous.[11] The eponymous magistrate of the κοινὸν 'Ασίας was the presiding 'Αρχιερεὺς 'Ασίας (p. 363); communal documents bear his name in conjunction with that of the γραμματεὺς ναῶν τῶν ἐν 'Ασία.[12] The γραμματεύς appears here also:

[1] *BMC.* 150 ff.
[2] Cf. Heichelheim, *ES.* IV, p. 248 nn. 10–14.
[3] Ibid. nn. 15–16. [4] Vienna. [5] *DN.* I, p. 77.
[6] Monogram 12. [7] E.g. *BMC. Imp.* p. xxxiii.
[8] Cf. Nock, *CAH.* X, p. 485; Hardy, *EHR.* V, 1890, p. 227. The provincial notables had already been occasionally convened by Caesar (Caesar, *BG.* IV, 6. 5, etc.; cf. Last, *CAH.* XI, p. 472) and Antony (Appian, *BC.* V, 4, etc.; cf. Monceaux, *De Communi Asiaé Provinciae*, Diss. Paris, 1885, p. 6).
[9] Tac. *Ann.* IV, 37; Dio LI, 20.
[10] *BMC. Imp. Aug.* 700.

[11] E.g. ΚΑΙΣΑΡ ΤΟ ΤΕΤΑΡΤΟΝ is the record of an eponymous local office as στεφανηφόρος (*BCH.* XXII, 1898, p. 368. 6). Moreover, ἐπί is regularly used to express eponymy (cf. Preisigke, *Wörterbuch der griechischen Papyrusurkunden*, s.v.; e.g. Turin Papyrus, I, v, 5, etc.) and, when two or more names occur together, that which is governed by ἐπί is eponymous (Gnädinger, *De Graecorum magistratibus eponymis*, Diss. Halle, 1892, p. 43).
[12] Cf. *OGIS.* 458, Μουσεῖον καὶ Βιβλιοθήκη τῆς Εὐαγγελικῆς Σχολῆς, V, 1884–5, 79; Brandis, *PW.* II, 1558; Schulthess, *PW.* VII, 1770.

he may be the Automedon who was a well-known poet of the period.¹ The high-priest must be Augustus himself. The same office is known to have been held by members of his family like Agrippa Postumus, and by proconsuls such as L. Volcacius Tullus (p. 363). Since the *terminus post quem* for the coins is 27 B.C., the visit of the *princeps* to Asia in c. 21–19² is indicated for his second high priesthood here recorded: a particularly probable occasion is that of the foundation of the temple at Pergamum in 19.³ His first tenure may well have coincided with the formal foundation of the κοινόν in 29.⁴

It did not seem anomalous to the ancients that the *princeps* should be high-priest of a cult which was largely devoted to his own worship⁵ (in combination with Rome⁶): he was in precisely the same situation as *Pontifex Maximus*.⁷ Moreover, like Julius and Antony, and later Hadrian,⁸ he is known to have presided in person over assemblies of provincial notables.⁹ But whether present in the province or not, he cannot have performed the arduous duties required of the provincial high-priest; nor could these have been delegated to the secular γραμματεύς. The priest who deputised for the Imperial high-priest could not himself have borne the title ἀρχιερεύς, but only that of ἱερεύς. This, then, is the situation of Charidamus, who thus naturally signs the issue in conjunction with his γραμματεύς Automedon. The unusual absence of the high-priestly title is thereby explained. Yet the prestige of the ἱερεύς representing the *princeps* may well have exceeded that of the ordinary presidents or ἀρχιερεῖς, in the same way as his *praefecti* at colonies were more respected than *duoviri*. It is clear that the bearded head on the reverse is not an idealistic conception, but a portrait:¹⁰ it must represent Charidamus, the senior member of the signatory pair. He is very likely to be the Gessius Charidemus whose name appears on a contemporary coin of Adramyttium (Pl. XI, 62).¹¹ An inscription from Smyrna recording the ἀρχιερεύς .....us Charidemus¹² may well refer to a year in which the same man held the high-priesthood himself—especially since many Gessii resided in Smyrna.¹³ Vowel-usage of the period permits the identification of Charidamus and Charidemus.¹⁴ Other bearded portraits on local coins—of Hypaepa and Dioshieron—likewise seem to represent religious officials, Attalus and Papion (Pl. XI, 64,¹⁵ 63¹⁶), or possibly Zeus 'in their image'.

---

¹ Hillscher, *Jahrbücher für classische Philologie*, Suppl. XVIII, 1892, p. 415.
² Suet. *Oct.* 17. 26; Dio LI, 18. 1, LIV, 7. 4.
³ Monceaux, l.c. p. 6; cf. Tac. *Ann.* IV, 37; Dio LI, 20.
⁴ Hardy, *EHR.* V, 1890, p. 226, calls it a 'modification and extension'.
⁵ Guiraud, *Les Assemblées Provinciales*, p. 82; Monceaux, l.c. p. 47.
⁶ Nock, *CAH.* X, p. 485.
⁷ Cf. van Buren, *QAS.* V, p. 14; Taylor, *Divinity of the Roman Emperor*, pp. 203 f.
⁸ Spartian, *Historia Augusta, Vita Hadriani*, 12.
⁹ Halgan, *Essai sur l'administration des provinces sénatoriales*, p. 201; Buckler, *Revue de philologie*, IX, 1935, p. 177; cf. Poland, *Festschr. zu 700 J. Feier der Kreuzschule zu Dresden* [1926], p. 54.
¹⁰ K. Pink has expressed his agreement with this view.   ¹¹ Oxford, cf. *NC.* 1935, p. 199.
¹² *IGRR.* IV, 1435; cf. *PIR*². II, 156. 712.
¹³ Cf. Hatzfeld, p. 110. The later procurator of Judaea, Gessius Florus, came from Clazomenae near by (Josephus, *AJ.* XX, 11. 1; *PIR.* II, 117. 103). For the interests of the family in this region, cf. Hatzfeld, *BCH.* XXXVI, 1912, p. 39.
¹⁴ Cf. Buck, *Greek Dialects*, pp. 154 ff.
¹⁵ *BMC.* 14.   ¹⁶ *Wad.* 1960.

Chapter 2
THE COMMUNITIES AND THE ROMAN OFFICIALS
A. HEADS OF OFFICIALS ON THE COINAGES

A CONSIDERABLE number of these can be discovered. Most of them escaped the notice of Muller, Waddington and Mommsen, whose conclusions regarding portraiture have been criticised elsewhere (p. 228). It may be said in recapitulation that any supposition of a *Bildnisrecht* is inaccurate: the procedure is entirely honorary. This view has been confirmed by the identification of numerous heads of private citizens—for example at Alabanda, Laodicea, Miletopolis, Dioshieron and Hypaepa—and by the attribution to Augustan portraits of a religious and social rather than a constitutional significance (p. 362). It is therefore not surprising to find governors honoured in the same way. On official coinage the barrier had been removed (though, as has been demonstrated, not by a formal decree) under the dictatorship, and the portrayal of living men was swiftly extended to two Roman groups. The colonies and *municipia* display the heads of their founders, and the 'imperatorial' silver soon produces portraits of living men—Octavian, Antony, the Pompeii (p. 22), Q. Labienus,[1] and possibly Cn. Domitius Ahenobarbus[2]—and even women, such as Octavia and perhaps Fulvia.[3] With these precedents it was natural for the peregrine communities to proceed to a similar practice in honour of their provincial authorities: it is possible to collect no less than a dozen that took advantage of the opportunity within this period.

The first two instances are provided by communities in Farther Spain. One of these is **Vesci** in Baetica. On the reverse is VESCI and a bull; on the obverse the name C. LIVIVS, accompanied by a bare head to right.[4] Vesci was stipendiary.[5] Given the stylistic probability of a late Republican date, the office of C. Livius can be recovered from a passage of Appian. He records the appointment of L. Antonius as proconsul of Spain in 40 B.C., and mentions that the previous *legati* of Nearer and Farther Spain[6] remained as his subordinates: ὑποστρατηγούντων αὐτῷ τῶν νῦν ἡγουμένων αὐτῆς Πεδουκαίου τε καὶ Λευκίου (*sic*).[7] Ganter's attribution of Peducaeus to the Farther province,[8] in opposition to Wilsdorf,[9] is based on erroneous numismatic information.

[1] *BMCR.* II, p. 500. 131.
[2] Von Sallet, *ZfN.* 1891, p. 203; cf. Syme, *RR.* p. 268; *pace* Grueber, *BMCR.* p. 487 f. 1.
[3] Grueber, l.c., p. 395. 40 ff. Maffii's addition of Calpurnia (*Storia*, 1939, *fasc.* 1) is very dubious; cf. Borelli, *Numismatica e scienze affini*, V, 1939, p. 25.
[4] Vives III, p. 46 (illustrated).
[5] Cf. Pliny, *NH.* III, 10.
[6] Cf. Ganter, p. 52; cf. Wilsdorf, *Fasti Hispaniarum provinciarum*, Diss. Leipzig, 1878, pp. 131 ff.
[7] *BC.* V, 54.
[8] P. 14.
[9] L.c. p. 140.

He cites coins of Carteia and Urso with Q. PEDECAI.[1] and Q. REDECAL. (*sic*)[2] respectively, and identifies the two (whom Eckhel[3] first considered to be the same) with the Peducaeus of Appian. The coin of Urso—even apart from the alteration necessitated—is only known from a very early authority, Como Rodrigo Caro,[4] and is rightly doubted by subsequent writers.[5] But even if it exists and can be dated to the forties B.C. its connection with the official at Carteia is out of the question. First, the Carteian coin seems pre-Caesarian; secondly, it is one of a homogeneous series—including many names accompanied by the titles of local magistrates.[6] Alone or in conjunction, the two issues fail to warrant Ganter's supposition that 'Q. Peducaeus' is Appian's *legatus*. There is therefore no reason to doubt Fischer's[7] identification of the latter with Sex. Peducaeus Sex. f. Sex. n., who had governed Sardinia in 48 B.C.[8] Since his attribution to Further Spain is baseless, the halves of the peninsula which he and 'Lucius' governed are still undetermined.

Fischer's[9] hypothesis that 'Lucius' is the *praenomen* of the distinguished soldier Carrinas is refuted by the demonstration by Münzer[10] that the latter was called Caius. Moreover, a Roman officer could not thus have been described by his *praenomen* alone. Appian's texts, weak on proper names,[11] are guilty of corruptions when, elsewhere, they describe an unknown consular as Μᾶρκος[12] and a victim of Antony's displeasure as Κούιντος.[13] Ganter[14] and Münzer[15] suggest rightly that the present word Λευκίου is corrupt also. In all three cases a common *praenomen* is substituted for what must have been a *cognomen* or *gentilicium*. Whatever the explanation for Μᾶρκος,[16] an examination of the present passage reveals that Λευκίου is the product of a particularly easy dittographical error. Appian has been speaking of L. Antonius as Λεύκιος, and continues to do so even in the very line following the sentence quoted: the passage reads: ... Πεδουκαίου τε καὶ [Λευκίου]. οὕτω μὲν δὴ καὶ Λεύκιον (sc. 'Αντώνιον) ὁ Καῖσαρ ἀπέπεμπε σὺν τιμῇ κ.τ.λ. The self-evident corruption is explained by these coins with the name of C. Livius. Appian wrote Λειουίου. Livius is a name notoriously often corrupted,[17] and this very same error may perhaps be found in Plutarch's

---

[1] Delgado I, p. 98; Madrid (del Rivero, *Cat.* p. 21).
[2] Cohen, *Description historique des monnaies frappées sous l'empire romain*, Aug. 630.
[3] *DN.* I, p. 18.
[4] *Chorografia del Convento jurídico de Sevilla*.
[5] E.g. Heiss, p. 333.   [6] Cf. Delgado I, pp. 86 ff.
[7] *Senatus Romanus qui fuerit Augusti temporibus*, Diss. Berlin, 1908, p. 32, no. 173.
[8] Klein, *Die römischen Verwaltungsbeamten*, I, II *Abt.*, p. 246, no. 59. For the family vide Syme, *RR.* pp. 285, 200.
[9] L.c.   [10] *PW.* III, 1612.
[11] E.g. Κάρκιος for Carisius (*BC.* v, 3; Syme, *RR.* p. 236 n. 1).

[12] *BC.* IV, 49. R. Syme points out the difficulties involved by this personage.
[13] *BC.* v, 4. 15; cf. Volkmann, *Münchener Beitr. z. Papyrusforschung*, XXI, 1935, p. 21.
[14] P. 14 n. 7.
[15] *PW.* XIII, 1652.
[16] It is possible to conjecture a haplography for Μᾶρκος Μάρκιος, and identification with the praetor of that name of uncertain date (cf. Holzapfel, *Rivista di storia antica*, IV, pp. 55 ff., 456 ff.). The *praenomen* was rare in the clan (Münzer, *PW.* XIV, 1545 [23]).
[17] Cf. Cichorius, *Römische Studien*, p. 255; Dio LIV, *init.*; Nepos, *Att.* XI, 2, etc.

HEADS OF OFFICIALS ON THE COINAGES 381

description of Livius Ocella as Λεύκιον Πέλλαν.[1] Attribution of C. Livius to the *legatio* of Farther Spain in c. 40 is entirely in accordance with the character of these pieces, whose style suggests such a date, and whose portrait is less likely to be that of a city official. Livius cannot be identified, but for political reasons is more likely to be a Drusus[2] than an Ocella.[3]

An ever rarer issue of another peregrine town in the same province, **Brutobriga**,[4] presents a close parallel:

T. MANLIVS[5] T. F. SERGIA., bare head to right
BRVTOBRIGA, galley and fish[6] (Pl. XII, 26).

An earlier *denarius* has displayed the name of a kinsman to the person here represented, namely A. Manlius Q. f. Ser.[7] Münzer[8] points out that a reference to the tribe Sergia[9] would have no numismatic parallel, and that the repetition of the name, on coins of widely different dates, indicates that it is rather a *cognomen* Sergia(nus). He shows also that the Manlii and Sergii were closely connected.[10] By analogy with C. Livius in the same province, T. Manlius T. f. is almost certainly another *legatus pro praetore* of about the same time. It is significant that the name of Lepidus's representative in Hispania Ulterior in c. 42 is unknown:[11] Manlius may well help to fill the gap. He is plausibly identifiable with T. Torquatus, described by Cicero in 45 B.C. as *optimus adulescens*.[12] The latter word is applicable to any age up to forty;[13] and there are many parallels for the addition of a second *cognomen* at this date, especially due to adoption.[14]

Thus Vesci and Brutobriga appear to provide for history the names and features of two provincial *legati*, C. Livius and T. Manlius T. f. Torquatus Sergianus. These coins are not comparable to the official issues of the quaestor L. Appuleius Decianus in the same province (p. 24): the present persons hold a rank high enough to be honoured by the cities, but not high enough to have flouted their superior *Imperator* by introducing their portraits, to his exclusion, on official coinage of their own. It may be added that both of the issues are likely to commemorate a grant of privilege—in this case Latin status—to their cities. Similar portraits occur to commemorate such promotions, not only at Roman cities (p. 206), but also at peregrine Tralles (p. 382); and a large number of foundation-issues of Latin communities have been identified (pp. 335 ff.).

---

[1] *Brutus*, 42. But here perhaps only Πέλλαν is corrupt.
[2] Cf. Fluss, *PW*. XIII, 884; Mommsen, *Ephemeris epigraphica*, I, 146.
[3] Cf. Cichorius, l.c.; Münzer, *PW*. XIII, 887.
[4] Not Segobriga: Kubitschek, *SB. Wien*, CLXVII, 6 *Abh.*, 1911, p. 73 n. 2, *pace* Grotefend, *Unedierte griechische und römische Münzen* (1864), pp. 28 ff.; Pais, *Ricerche sulla storia ecc.* ser. II, p. 302.
[5] Not MANIVS, *pace* Friedländer, *ZfN*. VIII, 1881, p. 11.
[6] Berlin, Madrid (del Rivero, *Cat.* p. 11); cf. Vives, III, p. 113. 1; Delgado I, p. 45.
[7] *BMCR*. II, p. 268.
[8] *PW*. XIV, 1191.
[9] Considered probable by Pais, del Rivero, ll.cc.
[10] *PW*. XIV, 1156 (18).
[11] Wilsdorf, l.c. p. 134. For Citerior, see above, p. 212. [12] *Pro Rege Deiotaro*, 32.
[13] Lewis and Short, p. 46, s.v.
[14] Cf. Doer, *Die römische Namengebung*, pp. 96 ff.

Latinity was common in Farther Spain,[1] but the names of its possessors have seldom survived.[2] Here, then, is a new aspect of triumviral policy.

The triumvirate provides one more example of a governor's portrait; this—like all that follow—comes from the Eastern half of the Empire. A coin of **Sparta**,[3] with ΛΑ. ΦΙΔΙ. and an eagle, has an expressive portrait labelled ΑΤΡΑΤΙΝΟΣ (Pl. XII, 3). An inscription from Hypata[4] proves that L. Sempronius Atratinus was Resident in Achaia with the rank of *legatus pro praetore*, probably as the titular subordinate of the governor of Macedonia (p. 37). Münzer[5] rightly assigns this governorship to the years before the activities of Atratinus in the Sicilian campaign: official coinages (p. 43) show that its outer limits are the autumn of 39 and the spring of 37.[6]

A rare Spartan piece of a smaller denomination has a similar head inscribed ATP.;[7] commoner are precisely similar pieces with AΓP.[8] These bear witness to a tactful numismatic change accompanying the revolt to Octavian in 32–31:[9] by a fine economy of effort and resources the same dies and same features did service for Atratinus and Agrippa.

Actium did not cause such coinages to cease. Issues of **Tralles** are relevant to the years immediately following the battle:

(1) ΠΩΛΛΙΩΝ ΚΑΙΣΑΡΕΩΝ, bare head to right, axe (Pl. IX, 31)—ΜΕΝΑΝΔΡΟΣ ΠΑΡΡΑΣΙΟΥ, octastyle temple, *caduceus*.[10]
(2) As last—Legend of last. Head of Zeus to right.[11]
(3) ΟΥΗΔΙΟΣ ΚΑΙΣΑΡΕΩΝ, same head—As last.[12]
(4) No legend; same head—ΚΑΙΣΑΡΕΩΝ ΜΕΝΑΝΔΡΟΣ ΠΑΡΡΑΣΙΟΥ. Type of (1).[13]
(5) As last—ΚΑΙΣΑΡΕΩΝ; monograms of ΜΕΝΑΝΔΡΟΣ ΠΑΡΡΑΣΙΟΥ. Hands clasped on *caduceus*.[14]
(6) ΚΑΙΣΑΡΕΩΝ, same head—Names in full; same type.[15]

Bernoulli[16] rightly points out that the heads are not those of Augustus, but must represent P. Vedius Pollio himself. This well-known knight died in 15 B.C.; since he was then out of favour,[17] it is unlikely that, as von Sallet[18] considers, the issues honour him posthumously. As so often, a remarkable light is thrown on his official career by

[1] E.g. Strabo III, 151, etc.
[2] Cf. Steinwenter, *PW*. x, 1269, etc.
[3] *BMC*. 69.   [4] *ILS*. 9461 = *IG*. IX, 2. 39.
[5] *PW*. (2R.), II, 1367.
[6] As on the Spanish pieces, the portraits suggest the character of an honorary city coinage rather than an official series. This interpretation is confirmed by the name of the local magistrate Phidi(ppides?).
[7] Berlin, Fox sale, 1334.
[8] Berlin, cf. Imhoof-Blumer, *MG*. p. 172. 87.
[9] Cf. Tarn, *CAH*. X, p. 100.
[10] *BMC*. 74; Milan, *Cat*. 413.
[11] Paris.
[12] *BMC*. 76; Milan, *Cat*. 412, wrongly described by M. S. VII, 466. 695. Coins with ΟΥΙΔΙΟΣ ΝΑΣΩΝ have, of course, been tooled (Pansa, *R.it*. 1912, p. 171).
[13] Berlin, cf. Imhoof-Blumer, *Lyd. S.* p. 173. 23.
[14] Ibid. 25.   [15] Ibid. 24.
[16] *Römische Ikonographie*, I, pp. 254 f., wrongly doubted by Waddington, *Rn*. 1867, p. 121.
[17] Cf. *PIR*. III, 390. 213.
[18] *ZfN*. III, 1876, p. 136; cf. IV, 1877, p. 198.

HEADS OF OFFICIALS ON THE COINAGES 383

inscriptions. One of these, which are both from Ephesus, consists of a pronouncement EX CONSTITVTIONE VEDI POLLIONIS;[1] a later edict describes Vedius's measure as a διάταξις.[2] *Constitutio* was not used as early as Augustus as a collective expression for Imperial legislation (p. 432),[3] but indicates a decisive ruling of some kind.[4] Such a decree by a knight is inconceivable, in the province of Asia, after the restoration of proconsular government in 29–28 (p. 385); the earlier Ephesian inscription must therefore be assigned to the years immediately following Actium, and with it no doubt the coinage. Both inscription and coins, and many later Vedii at Ephesus,[5] bear witness to Pollio's tenure of some exceptional post. He is also commemorated at Ilium.[6] C. Proculeius (p. 66) provides a parallel for Octavian's allotment of provinces, at this date, to distinguished equestrians in his confidence. Moreover, the *princeps* paid special attention to Asia during his residence in 30–29,[7] and important financial reforms were probably carried out.[8] These, and the province, were clearly in the hands of P. Vedius Pollio, as *procurator et praeses*.[9] His irregular position accounts for the use of the vague generality *constitutio*.

The occasion of the coinage can be clearly identified. Tralles was refounded as a stipendiary city, with a core of Roman residents (cf. p. 403) and the name of Caesarea, after the battle of Actium.[10] An army of parallels (pp. 349 ff.) makes it inevitable that this coinage commemorates the occasion.[11] Indeed, kindred pieces actually record the allotment, by the type of a plough.[12] The Roman cities have shown that portraits, outside the *domus principis* as within it, are peculiarly applicable to foundations (p. 184); this interpretation also provides the key to many coinages in the present category.

The seventh governor to be honoured in this way appears on two rare coins of **Nicaea**, which have both undergone drastic misreadings:

[1] *CIL*. III, 1724.
[2] Dörner, *Der Erlass des Statthalters von Asia Paullus Fabius Persicus*, Diss. Greifswald, 1935, pp. 38 f., 42.
[3] Jörs, *PW*. IV, 1106.
[4] Cf. Livy XXXIX, 53. 10; Cic. *Pro Quinctio*, 7. 4. 6, etc.
[5] E.g. *CIL*. III, 440 (early), 441, 442.
[6] Cf. Dörpfeld, *Troja und Ilion*, II, p. 471. 66.
[7] Cf. Waddington, *Fastes des provinces asiatiques*, 49.
[8] Syme, *RR*. p. 410.
[9] Chapot's suggestion (*La province romaine proconsulaire d'Asie*, p. 318) that he was proconsul cannot be accepted, since he never rose above equestrian rank (*PIR*. l.c. etc.). There is no evidence for the attribution of the proconsuls M. Herennius Picens and Norbanus Flaccus (Waddington, l.c. 50, 51) to this period rather than to the years before 31 and after 28 respectively. *PIR*[2]. 1, 186. 961 shows that the attribution by Broughton (*ES*. IV, p. 711) of Sex. Appuleius to 29 is equally unjustifiable.
[10] Cf. Broughton, *TAPA*. LXVI, 1935, p. 22; Jones, *CERP*. p. 78. Cf. Attaleia and Amisus, also with non-colonial *coloni*, Broughton, l.c., cf. Kornemann, *Berliner Studien für classische Philológie und Archäologie*, XIV, 1, 1892, pp. 13, 28, 45, *pace* Viale, *Atti del primo Congresso di Studi Romani*, I, p. 363. Marquardt's inclusion of Tralles among Roman colonies (*St.V.* I, p. 347) is rightly ignored by Kornemann, but followed by Miss Newby (p. 85).
[11] Recognised, without reference to analogies, by Hatzfeld, p. 171 n. 2.
[12] Berlin: Imhoof-Blumer, *KM*. 2.

384   THE COMMUNITIES AND THE ROMAN OFFICIALS

(1) NIKAIEωN head of Thorius Flaccus to right (Pl. XII, 9)—ΕΠΙ ΑΝΘΥΠΑΤΟΥ ΘωΡΙΟΥ ΦΛΑ., ΗΡΑ, two monograms of local magistrates' names. Head of Juno Lanuvina to right.[1]

(2) Same as last—ΕΠΙ ΑΝΘΥΠΑ[ΤΟΥ Θ]ωΡ[ΙΟΥ ΦΛΑ. or ΦΛΑΚΚΟΥ], monograms. *Sella curulis*.[2]

The reverse type of (1) is explained by the Lanuvian origin of the Thorii:[3] even in Rome Augustus's moneyers placed types connected with their families on their coins.[4] E. Babelon[5] recognises that neither portrait can represent Augustus. All specimens show features of an entirely distinctive character, whereas coins similarly inscribed, at Nicaea and at Nicomedia (p. 353), provide accurate and realistic portraits of the *princeps*. It is necessary, therefore, to assume that we have here the portrait of the proconsul Thorius Flaccus. His governorship can be dated with some certainty, owing to a striking similarity, noted by Cavedoni,[6] between the Nicomedian piece, and an official tetradrachm of 28 B.C.[7] Ap. Claudius Pulcher was proconsul of Bithynia-Pontus in 28–27 B.C. (p. 255): Thorius Flaccus may confidently be assigned to 29–28. It has been pointed out in connection with the Augustan heads on other coins of Thorius that the occasion for issue was the elevation of Nicaea and Nicomedia to the headship of the new κοινὸν Βειθυνίας (p. 353). Thorius, then, takes his place beside the *princeps* and Vedius as κτίστης. Mommsen[8] points out that the legend on the tetradrachm of 28—LIBERTATIS P. R. VINDEX—suggests that the province where they were struck had already been restored to normal government in the course of the *restitutio rei publicae* (p. 424): since the tetradrachm belongs to Bithynia rather than Asia where Mommsen used to attribute it, it is doubly relevant to the present local series. This, too, commemorates not only the promotion of Nicaea and Nicomedia, but also the end of the emergency period. It honours with portraiture the first governor under the new *régime*; the predecessor of Thorius was probably an equestrian procurator like C. Proculeius or P. Vedius.

An Asian city, **Magnesia ad Sipylum**, struck a coin which refers to the same constitutional occasion:[9]

---

[1] Vienna University, Paris; *Rec.* 19. Scholz, *NZ.* 1910, p. 14. 45 completely misreads the coins, and attributes them to Pythodoris of Pontus.

[2] Vienna; misread by *Rec.* 21, which gives the legend as ΕΠΙ ΑΝΘΥΠΑΤΟΥ only. A coin quoted as uncertain by M. S. IV, 669. 390 (*Mus. Sanclement. Num. Select.* II, p. 28) supplies vital letters which show that the proconsul is again Thorius; but the obverse of this is entirely misinterpreted. For ΕΠΙ see pp. 396 ff.

[3] Cf. *CIL.* XIV, p. 192; cf. Fluss, *PW.*(2R.), VI, 346; *PIR.* III, 313. 134.

[4] *BMC. Imp.* pp. cii ff.

[5] *Rec.* ll.cc.

[6] *Annali dell' Inst. di corr. arch.* 1850, p. 199; confirmed by Bosch, *KM.* p. 78; cf. Ganter, p. 34.

[7] *BMC. Imp. Aug.* 691.

[8] *RGDA*[2]. p. 147; cf. also Stuart Jones, *CAH.* X, pp. 123, 127; Weber, *Princeps*, I, p. 139 n. 557; Barwick, *Philologus*, XCI, 1936, p. 352.

[9] Munich, *BMC.* 13; illustrated by Mattingly, *RC.* Pl. LI, 4.

HEADS OF OFFICIALS ON THE COINAGES

ΜΑΡΚΟΣ ΤΥΛΛΙΟΣ ΚΙΚΕΡΩΝ bare-headed portrait to right (Pl. IX, 32)—ΜΑΓΝΗΤΩΝ ΤΩΝ ΑΠΟ ΣΙΠΥΛΟΥ ΘΕΟΔΩΡΟΣ hand holding vine-wreath and corn-ears.

Mommsen's[1] view that the portrait is that of the orator Cicero is refuted both by iconographical considerations[2] and by the political inadvisability of such a gesture under Augustus,[3] to whose principate the coin, for stylistic reasons, must belong.[4] Since Borghesi[5] is certainly wrong in seeing the features of the *princeps* himself, the head may be attributed, with Muller[6] and Bernoulli,[7] to the orator's son M. Tullius Cicero, whom we know from Seneca[8] to have held the proconsulate of Asia under Augustus. Since he was *consul suffectus* in 30 B.C.,[9] and already *legatus* of Syria before 23,[10] Waddington[11] rightly maintains that his proconsulate fell not long after Actium: infractions of the *Lex Pompeia*, requiring a five-year interval after consulships, were frequent during the civil wars,[12] and occurred also in the early principate.[13] Since the signal honour here paid to M. Cicero is only paralleled by the case of Thorius Flaccus, it is very probable that his appointment in Asia, like that of Thorius in Bithynia (p. 384), inaugurated the return to 'Republican' government after the dictatorial *régime* of Octavian's procurator Vedius Pollio; very probably too, he refounded Magnesia ad Sipylum in the stipendiary right.[14] The *restitutio* of senatorial *régimes* began earlier than 28: Thorius became governor in the previous year, and M. Licinius Crassus exceptionally received a Balkan command as proconsul in 30,[15] under Octavian's *maius imperium* (p. 421). In Asia, then, Cicero probably succeeded Vedius on Octavian's departure for the West in 29 (p. 422).

After an interval, another group of such coinages is provided by Chalcis in Euboea:

(1) Λ. ΡΟΥΦΙΝΟΣ ΑΝΘΥΠΑΤΟΣ bare head to right—ΧΑΛΚΙΣ female head to right (Pl. XII, 1).[16]

---

[1] *Hermes*, III, 1869, p. 269.
[2] Bernoulli, *Römische Ikonographie*, I, p. 134.
[3] Cf. Waddington, *Rn*. 1867; *Mélanges numismatiques*, 2 sér., II, p. 133.
[4] Under Antony it would be even less suitable.
[5] *Œuvres*, I, p. 171.
[6] *ZfN*. 1875, p. 298.   [7] L.c.
[8] *Suasoriae*, VII, 13; cf. *PIR*. III, 338. 272b.
[9] *CIL*. I², p. 61.
[10] Appian, *BC*. IV, 51; cf. Waddington, *Fastes des provinces asiatiques*, 53. Of Syme's suggestions, 29–27 and 27–25 (*RR*. p. 303 n. 1), the latter is the more probable.   [11] Ibid.
[12] Chapot, *La province romaine proconsulaire d'Asie*, p. 282.
[13] E.g. Renault, *Bulletin archéologique du Comité des travaux historiques et scientifiques*, 1897, pp. 250 ff.

[14] Cf. Jones, *GC*. p. 130; id. *Anatolian Studies to Buckler*, p. 116; *pace* Broughton, *ES*. IV, p. 708. It is noteworthy that Magnesia never portrays Augustus in his lifetime. Cf. above, p. 350.
[15] Cf. Charlesworth, *CAH*. X, p. 117.
[16] The true inscription is shown by Weber, 1611 (cf. Imhoof-Blumer, *MG*. p. 223. 56). The Paris specimen reading Α. Μ..ΙΙΝΟΣ has been tooled. A similar alteration on a coin at Milan (M. *S*. IV, 362. 74; *Milan Cat.* 334) has had wider consequences: the false reading Λ · ΛΙΟΥ.... has been accepted by Fischer (*Senatus Romanus qui fuerit Augusti temporibus*, Diss. Berlin, 1908, p. 62. 435), Box (*JRS*. XXII, 1932, p. 174), Dessau (*PIR*. II, 289. 198), Heiligenstädt (*Fasti aedilicii*, Diss. Halle, 1910, p. 39) and Groag, *SB*. IX, 1939, p. 18, but is refuted by Muensterberg (*Beamtennamen*, s.v.).

(2) ΜΕΣΚΙΝΙΟΣ ΣΤΡΑ. bare head to right—ΧΑΔΚΙΔΕШΝ same head. (Pl. XII, 2).[1]

These are the only issues of Chalcis in the principate of Augustus,[2] and are in most respects uniform:[3] only, Rufinus is called ἀνθύπατος and Mescinius στρατηγός. There are several reasons for believing that the latter is not a local official. In the first place, Rufinus *pro cos.* provides the only analogy for his issue. Secondly, the legends, and certain curiosities of portraiture, indicate that the heads can scarcely represent Augustus, as they have always been considered to. Similar mistakes have been noted at African colonies (p. 228); and partial adaptation of the features of lesser men to resemble the *princeps* is one of the commonest of iconographical phenomena (cf. p. 364). It seems likely therefore, from internal evidence, that Mescinius was a governor of Achaia like Rufinus.[4]

An explanation for the divergency of their titles, ΑΝΘΥΠΑΤΟΣ and ΣΤΡΑ(τηγός), is at hand. There is ample evidence for intervention by Agrippa in 'senatorial' provinces after 18 B.C. (p. 428), including two letters, reported by Josephus, sent by him to Silanus (?)[5] in Asia and Flavius (?)[6] in Cyrenaica. Now both of these are addressed as plain στρατηγοί. Waddington[7] has accordingly argued that they were technically subordinate to Agrippa, who must therefore have been governing the Eastern provinces through his *legati*.[8] Chapot[9] objected that the transcription by Josephus may have been inexact: but a coin of Q. Articuleius (?) Regulus (p. 125) shows that, at least in the 'imperial' province of Syria, Agrippa's agent at this time was actually called στρατηγός with official correctness. The terminology of Josephus need not, therefore, be inaccurate. Moreover, στρατηγός was a correct rendering of the title of a praetorian *legatus*, in a 'senatorial' as well as an 'imperial' province.[10] It is therefore highly probable that Mescinius, like Flavius and Silanus, held such a post. Not only is the evidence of the coinage strongly in favour of this view, but, as will be shown elsewhere, the theory that Agrippa possessed an *imperium maius* is entirely inadmissible (p. 429). Agrippa did not override proconsuls—a situation that would have recalled the past days of martial illegality—but merely possessed, with perfect constitutional correctness, a *provincia* of unusual size. This is not the first time that cities of Achaia had extended the privilege of portraiture to their governors: Sparta honoured L. Atratinus in this way, and the same issues add to the series by the discreet alteration, on some

---

[1] Berlin, Athens; Imhoof-Blumer, *MG.* p. 223. 57; cf. *Rn.* 1883, p. 66 n. 7.

[2] Another governor's portrait has been derived from a coin at Paris with ΑΦΡΙΚΑΝ., and a type of three nymphs. But it is clear that this has been drastically altered in modern times from *BMC.* 52ff. of Tanagra (p. 463).

[3] No importance can be attached to the variety of ethnic.

[4] Cf. Fluss, *PW.* xv, 1078; *pace* Dessau, *PIR.* II, 366. 361, Groag, *SB.* IX, 1939, p. 22.

[5] *AJ.* xvi, 6. 4; or Silvanus. The identification in *PIR.* II, 246. 549 is unlikely.

[6] *AJ.* xvi, 6. 5; *PIR.* II, 133; perhaps Fabius.

[7] *Fastes des provinces asiatiques*, p. 89.

[8] Cf. Zumpt, *Commenta epigraphica*, II, p. 80.

[9] L.c. p. 284.

[10] It emphasised his rank rather than his office.

HEADS OF OFFICIALS ON THE COINAGES 387

pieces, of ATP(ατῖνος) to ΑΓΡ(ίππας) (p. 382). The adapted issue may well have been produced during Agrippa's government of the East, in honour of that exceptionally important proconsul. Chalcis, however, prefers to flatter his subordinate who is on the spot, the acting-governor Mescinius.

Rufinus is probably to be identified with a curule aedile of the same name.[1] Renier[2] assigns him to the *gens* Cornelia, but he is much more likely to be a relative of C. Vibius Rufinus who was *consul suffectus* under Tiberius.[3] L. Rufinus must have governed Achaia either before or after Agrippa's tenure.[4] Since all preceding coinage in this Chapter may have been foundation-coinages, it is quite possible that the issues honouring Mescinius and Rufinus belong to the now familiar category of double mintages from a foundation-fund (p. 291). If so Rufinus will be very close in date to 18 or 13—probably the former, since the 'programme' ethnic ΧΑΛΚΙΣ suggests that his is the first of the two issues.

In c. 7 B.C. a new era began in which portraiture was limited to *amici principis* (p. 229). The three Asian coinages which inaugurated this custom are the following:

(1) **Temnus.** ΑΣΙΝΙΟΣ ΓΑΛΛΟΣ ΑΓΝΟΣ, head of C. Asinius Gallus to right (Pl. IX, 33)—ΑΠΟΛΛΑΣ ΦΑΙΝΙΟΥ ΤΑΜΝΙΤΑΝ, garlanded head of Dionysus to right.[5]

(2) **Pitane.** Π. ΣΚΙΠΙωΝΑ, head of P. Cornelius P. f. P. n. Scipio to right—ΣΕΒΑΣΤΟΝ ΠΙΤΑΝΑΙΟΙ head of Augustus to right; small head of Ammon, *pentalpha*.[6]

(3) A series of **Hierapolis** with ΦΑΒΙΟΣ ΜΑΞΙΜΟΣ, head of Paullus Fabius Q. f. Maximus to right (Pl. XI, 58). Names on the reverse include Tryphon,[7] Dryas,[8] Theocritus,[9] Bryon,[10] Zosimus Philopatris Charax,[11] and Cocus.[12]

C. Asinius Gallus was governor in 6–5 B.C.,[13] and the other two in the same period: perhaps Scipio was his predecessor[14] and Fabius his successor.[15] We have seen (p. 229) that all three were members of Augustus's circle, and that the coinage with their heads was intended as propaganda for the new *amicitia*. Asinius's title ἀγνός—applied else-

---

[1] *CIL.* XIV, 2866; cf. Heiligenstädt, *Fasti*, Diss. Halle, 1910, p. 39.
[2] *Rev. arch.* N.S. IX, 1864, p. 210.
[3] *PIR.* III, 424. 395. (I owe this suggestion to R. Syme.) This Rufinus is considered by Mommsen, *Korrespondenzblatt der Westdeutschen Zeitschrift*, VII, 1888, p. 58 n. 2, to be the son of a C. Vibius Rufus, but this is uncertain.
[4] Vide Fischer, Diss. c., p. 62.
[5] *BMC.* 24 (Temnus).
[6] *Wad.* 991, Vienna (Pitane).
[7] *BMC.* 95 (Hierapolis).
[8] *KM.* 14.
[9] *KM.* 15.
[10] *Wad.* 6142.
[11] *BMC.* 93.
[12] Berlin, cf. L. Weber, *Charites*, 486.
[13] *PIR*^{2}. I, 245. 1229; cf. *CIL.* III, 6070.
[14] Chapot, *La province romaine proconsulaire d'Asie*, p. 309; *pace* Muller, *ZfN.* 1875, p. 307, who preferred 11–10 B.C. Waddington, *Fastes des provinces asiatiques*, 56, and Groag, *PIR*^{2}. II, 354. 1438, are doubtful.
[15] As Muller, l.c. But Syme, *RR.* p. 395, ascribes him to 9–8 and Usener, *Bull. dell' Inst. di corr. arch.* 1874, p. 80 to 8–7.

where to a few Greeks,[1] but generally reserved for Roman governors[2]—lends him a measure of the superhumanity of the Σεβαστός himself,[3] and so gives his position a religious flavour, with which Imperial portraiture is likewise endowed. The Hellenistic συγγενεῖς too had possessed a measure of their master's divinity. It is by no means improbable that the three proconsuls were, like M. Cicero and Thorius Flaccus, responsible for reorganisations of the cities which honoured them in this way (pp. 384 f.).

Some years later another *amicus principis* is honoured at **Pergamum**:

ΣΕΒΑΣΤΟΝ ΔΗΜΟΦѠΝ Augustus standing in tetrastyle temple—ΠΕΡΓΑΜΗΝΟΙ ΣΙΛΒΑΝΟΝ M. Plautius Silvanus standing, being crowned by a god.[4]

In general, perhaps, such a full-length portrayal is less honorific than a portrait-bust; but in the present case the implied equation with the *princeps* removes any such disability. Various dates have been mentioned for the governorship of Silvanus, including A.D. 1–2,[5] 4–5, 5–6,[6] and 6–7;[7] Syme[8] has recently established the particular probability of 4–5. Like his three predecessors who are granted this numismatic distinction, Silvanus was connected to Augustus by marriage, being the son of Livia's friend Urgulania: he was therefore one of his *amici*.

The only remaining Augustan coinage honouring by its portrait an *amicus principis* is from **Priene**, in the same province. It celebrates one who is not a governor:

.......ΟΣ ΜΑΚΕΡ, portrait to right—ΠΡΙΗΝΕѠΝ Zeus standing to left by tripod-altar (Pl. IX, 34).[9]

The head is clearly not that of a *princeps* but of the personage described. E. Babelon's[10] interpretation of the name as that of C. Caesonius Macer Rufinianus, of the time of Severus Alexander, is entirely misplaced, since on grounds of style the issue could hardly be as late even as Tiberius, far less of the third century. A passage from Strabo can be cited to provide an identification. He speaks of a M. Pompeius who was procurator of Asia under Augustus;[11] Hillscher[12] rightly emends the passage to show that this was the son, not the grandson, of Theophanes. This M. Pompeius had a son called Macer,[13] and may therefore be identified with the Pompeius Macer who was the librarian of Augustus.[14] Since the latter served as procurator in Asia, there is every reason to accept Muensterberg's[15] identification of him with the Macer represented on

---

[1] Muensterberg, *Jahreshefte des öst. arch. Inst. in Wien*, XVIII, 1915, Beibl. p. 308; pace Imhoof-Blumer, *KM*. 287.

[2] Benndorf, *Festhefte der Wiener Studenten für Bormann*, p. 18.

[3] It is applied to gods—*CIG*. 5431, 5643, etc.

[4] *BMC*. 242 (Pergamum).

[5] Cf. *PIR*. III, 46. 361.   [6] Waddington, l.c.

[7] Groag, *Jahreshefte des öst. arch. Inst.* XXII, Beibl. 1924, pp. 467 f.

[8] *Klio*, XXVII, 1934, p. 139; cf. Waddington, *Fastes des provinces asiatiques*, 64 (correcting *Rn*. 1867).

[9] *Wad*. 1928.   [10] *Aréthuse*, I, 1923, p. 3.

[11] XIII, 618.

[12] *Jahrbücher für classische Philologie*, Suppl. XVIII, 1891, p. 427.

[13] Cf. Dessau, *PIR*. III, 67. 471; Syme, *RR*. p. 367.

[14] Suet. *Caes*. 56.   [15] *Beamtennamen*, s.v.

the coin.¹ The issues of Tralles with portraits of P. Vedius Pollio (p. 382) show that no objection was felt to honouring knights in this way. Moreover, Asia was a province in which Augustus's procurator was already of particular importance;² his power was quite sufficient to warrant cultivation by the city of Priene,³ which he may well, by analogy with the governors discussed, have 'refounded' in some way. It is less than half-a-century before coins of the neighbouring province of Bithynia even honour similar procurators with eponymy, by the side of their proconsuls.⁴ The passage of Strabo seems to indicate that it was this M. Pompeius Macer, rather than his son, who became one of the intimate circle of Tiberius;⁵ if that is so, his procuratorship of Asia is likely to fall late rather than early in the principate of Augustus.⁶ The coin in his honour provides an unusual piece of evidence regarding the prestige of these officials under the first *princeps*—when they were his *amici*.⁷ For portraiture had become a privilege restricted to the Imperial family and those whom its head honoured with the title of his Friends. Of *Bildnisrecht* however there can be no question: these personages do not usurp the authority for the coins which bear their heads.⁸

¹ But his citation of a Prienean inscription (*Inschriften von Priene* 247) to confirm this is irrelevant, since the Pompeius there is Cnaeus or Caius, and need not be Macer.
² Cf. Rostovtzeff, *Archiv für Papyrusforschung, Beih.* I, 1910, p. 287.
³ In addition, the Pompeii Macri were considerable landowners in Asia; cf. Broughton, *ES.* IV, p. 649; Strabo XIII.
⁴ Rostovtzeff, *Annals of the British School at Athens*, XXII, 1916–18; cf. Seltman, *NC.* 1928, p. 102.

⁵ Cf. Dessau, *PIR.* III, 67. 472, 473; pace Hillscher, l.c.
⁶ Cf. Klein, *Die römischen Verwaltungsbeamten*, I, pp. 180 ff.
⁷ Hirschfeld, *Die kaiserlichen Verwaltungsbeamten*, p. 449; Horovitz, *Revue belge de philologie et d'histoire*, XVII, 1938, p. 778, point out that knights often belonged to this class.
⁸ For some later examples, with which I hope to deal elsewhere, see pl. XII, 4, 10, 11, 16, 17.

B. NAMES OF OFFICIALS ON THE COINAGES

This subject presents considerable variety, since modes of expression were not yet stereotyped. In the last years of the Republic, in which most variations are encountered, the names appear in various Cases, and, as later, with the preposition ἐπί. Between each usage there are more or less subtle nuances of difference.[1] These are particularly difficult to define owing to two tendencies in the Greek spoken and written at this period: the slovenliness of the κοινή frequently caused confusion between Case-usages,[2] and the influence of Latin often perverted them.[3] Occasionally too it is hard to draw the line between peregrine city-coinages of this type and official currencies.[4] But the constitutional significance of this group of coins can generally be reached across such technical obstacles. The various Case-endings will be considered separately: besides those already met with in the last section,[5] fifteen names are represented, including some hitherto unidentified.

(1) The *Accusative Case* is used for the names of P. Cornelius Scipio and M. Plautius Silvanus (pp. 387f.) accompanying their portraits. It presents no ambiguity: it is clearly regarded as the Object of a verb, as on the reverses of Roman official pieces.[6] The titulature of the *princeps* is also occasionally couched in this form, both in Latin[7] and in Greek.[8] The usage is thus purely honorary and dedicative.[9] Only one instance without a portrait can be cited, and that depends on a new interpretation:

— —ΙΣ. ΔΗΜ.[10] head of Aphrodite (?) to right—ΑΝΤΙΠ. ΛΕΠ.[11] or ΑΝΤΙ. ΛΕΠΙ. (Pl. IX, 28)[12]; Nike crowning a trophy.

---

[1] Cf. Pansa, *R.it.* 1909, p. 377.

[2] Regard, *Des Prépositions dans la langue du Nouveau Testament*, p. 429.

[3] Muensterberg, *MBNGW.* IX (1913), p. 161.

[4] The following rules have been applied. When the Roman official and his needs are predominant, the issues have been described in Part I: the appearance of his name, written in Latin, on an otherwise Greek coin, has been considered to warrant definition as official (cf. Broughton, *AJA.* 1937, p. 249). But the final test is that of scope and circulation: inclusion in Part I is necessitated by a proof of military rather than of purely local needs, and an endeavour has been made to supply this for every coinage there described. A complete border-line case is provided by the co-operative issue of the naval commander L. Arruntanus Balbus and the city-mint of Melita (p. 59): both parties display their names, in their respective tongues and in full. In this case, however, the currency was clearly intended for Roman troops, as many contemporary analogies show. In the same way, the issues of L. Appuleius Decianus q. (p. 24) at various mints (without complete ethnics) were apparently official. The coinages that will here be discussed include every category where there is no reason to make the same deduction, including a number of co-operative series where the needs of the community were a primary consideration, and three where an indemnity had to be paid, but the mint was demonstrably not commandeered. Cf. above, p. 1 n. 1.

[5] These are recapitulated under their relevant headings here.

[6] Cf. Mattingly, *BMC. Imp.* pp. lxxiv, ccxxvi.

[7] E.g. at Corinth (Augustus) (Muensterberg, *Kaisernamen*).

[8] E.g. at Smyrna, Hypaepa, Pergamum (Augustus). Cf. above, p. 360.

[9] Cf. Stuart, *Portraiture of Claudius, Preliminary Studies*, p. 13.

[10] Variant readings given by M. S. 1, 130. 9 ff. are not authentic.   [11] BM.

[12] Berlin (unattributed). Unfortunately the obverse of this coin is almost obliterated.

The ethnic (confirmed by the style) indicates attribution to **Antipolis**, in Gallia Narbonensis. Only a single restoration has hitherto been attempted: Blanchet,[1] followed by Willers,[2] reads [E]ΙΣ ΔΗΜ(ον) ΑΝΤΙΠ(ολίτων) ΛΕΠ(ιδος), and observes that this may be considered a restrictive formula (*limitant la circulation de la pièce au seul territoire de cette cité*). But this interpretation is unparalleled and unplausible. The only analogy which Blanchet can find for his reading ΕΙΣ — ΕΙΣ ΘΑΝΑΤΟΥΣ(ια) ΚΥΡΙΟΥ on a coin of Severus[3]—is wholly irrelevant. No issue at a city by governor or triumvir is, or could be, described by the inscription which he suggests.

On the other hand, an alternative explanation can be supported by numerous analogies: [ΚΤ]ΙΣ(την) ΔΗΜ(ος) ΑΝΤΙΠ(ολίτων) ΛΕΠ(ιδον). In the first place, this is an orthodox and understandable mode of expression: elsewhere, at the same date, we find ΑΝΤΙΟΧΟΝ Ο ΔΗΜΟΣ ΜΙΛΗΤΟΠΟΛΙΤΩΝ[4] (Pl. XI, 60, obverse). Secondly, it has great historical plausibility. Antipolis gained the Latin right in time for inclusion in Pliny's list;[5] the date has not yet been ascertained—the Roman and Latin colonies in Gaul were founded at various times (p. 210)—but it is known that in the years 44–43, in which Lepidus first became governor of Narbonensis,[6] foundations were made in both the Transalpine provinces.[7] A third reason for this interpretation is its exceptional numismatic probability. The ramifications of Roman foundation series have been discussed, and a number celebrating the conferment of Latinity have been added to them (p. 335). The present issue displays all their characteristics, with the natural linguistic modification caused by the official survival of the Greek tongue at Latin cities in Gaul.[8] This issue at Antipolis is the only one of its city: other Latin towns, besides many of Roman rank, likewise have isolated issues, and nearly all are inauguratory (p. 473). Again, this coin bears the name of a governor such as appears on the currency of Roman cities also—but exclusively (when there is no portrait) to commemorate a foundation. This only differs from other Latin foundation-issues in that it curiously mingles the characteristics of peregrine and of Roman foundation coinage. But such a mixture is entirely appropriate to the Latin status (p. 335). As with Scipio and Silvanus, the Accusative Case is again honorary and dedicatory; but the dedication here is due to the special occasion of κτίσμα, like the commemoration of Vedius at Tralles (p. 382).

(2) *Uncertain Case*. Examples of usage that is no longer merely honorary may be introduced by the citation of two tribal issues of Gallia Comata. Several small coins have A.HIR.IMP. and a lion, together with the names and busts of local chiefs,

---

[1] *Traité*, p. 442.
[2] *NZ*. 1909, p. 80 n. 1.
[3] Cf. *ZfN*. xi, 1884, p. 52.
[4] *RS*. xiii, 1905, p. 208; Winterthur.
[5] Pliny, *NH*. iii, 35.
[6] Cf. *CAH*. x, p. 13, etc.
[7] Cf. Hirschfeld, *CIL*. xiii. 1, p. 250; Willers, *NZ*. 1902, p. 66, etc.
[8] E.g. also Avennio: Blanchet, *Traité*, pp. 440 f.; cf. Pliny, *NH*. iii, 35. Cf. below, p. 474.

Inecriturix, Athedias (Pl. IX, 24), and Coriarcos (?),[1] who have been rightly attributed to the **Remi**.[2] A. Hirtius was responsible for an official coinage in 50 B.C. (p. 3). But at that time he did not, as here, hold the title *imperator*, and indeed held no military command, but a private secretarial appointment. His salutation occurred during a later residence in Gaul, as *pro praetore*, in 45–44,[3] and it is to this occasion that the present coins must be referred. The names of the chieftains make it clear that the immediate responsibility for the issues was in tribal hands; thus the coinage cannot be called official. But the reference to Hirtius is unlikely to be entirely honorary, and some form of co-operation or control seems to be indicated.[4] The same is probably true of the tribal coins with L. MVNATI., the name of Hirtius's successor, Plancus (Pl. IX, 26): on the reverse, again, is the name of a local dignitary, ATTALV[S].[5] This issue too may have a connection with the governor's salutation as *imperator*, during his tenure of 44–43.[6] But the tribe is unidentifiable.[7]

The late Republic supplies three further Case-usages which can be interpreted with greater certainty as providing evidence for such co-operation.

(3) *The Nominative Case* is used in conjunction with most of the portraits described in the previous section. On those issues its significance is merely commemorative; but when no portrait appears, the character of the Case obviously leaves room for ambiguities. Clearly, its significance can be either honorary[8] or expressive of the source of issue.[9] That the latter of these meanings may well be expected on Greek coins is proved by its interchangeability with the Genitive after ΔΙΑ.[10] Again the late Republic provides but a single example of the use of this Case without a portrait, at **Agrigentum**: ΣΩΣΙΟΣ head of Demeter to right—ΑΚΡΑΓΑΝΤΙΝΩΝ Asclepius.[11] Hill[12] considers the personage here named to be a local magistrate: but two contemporary Sicilian coins, of similar style but with a different Case-ending, suggest a special usage due to the emergencies of the period:

(4) *Genitive Case*.

(1) **Entella**. ΑΤΡΑΤΙΝΟΥ radiate bust of Helios to right—ΕΝΤΕΛΛΙΝΩΝ Homonoia (?) standing to left with *patera* and *cornucopiae*.[13]

---

[1] Blanchet, *Traité*, pp. 382 f.
[2] Maxe-Werly, *État actuel de la numismatique rémoise*, p. 12.
[3] Münzer, *PW*. VIII, 1956 f.
[4] Cf. Willers, *NZ*. XXXIV, 1902, p. 79; Lenormant, *La monnaie dans l'Antiquité*, II, pp. 315, 342.
[5] BM, Paris; cf. Robert, *Rn.* 1859, p. 250; Blanchet, *Traité*, pp. 100, 426; De la Tour, *Atlas des monnaies gauloises*, pl. VII, 4794–5. In view of the analogy of Hirtius it is unlikely that L. Munatius is other than Plancus himself (p. 206).
[6] Cf. Hanslik, *PW*. XVI, 548.

[7] Cf. Willers, *NZ*. 1909, p. 79, correcting Hirschfeld, *CIL*. XIII, p. 251.
[8] Cf. Pansa, *R.it*. 1909, pp. 376; Stuart, l.c. p. 14. This category includes eponymous usages.
[9] Pick, *ZfN*. XIV, 1887, pp. 296 ff.; Mommsen, *St.R*[3]. II, 1, p. 261 n. 1. Mattingly (*BMC. Imp.* p. lxix) attributes the regular Imperial titulature to this category.
[10] E.g. at Apollonia Salbace (Trajan, *KM*. 120 f.).
[11] Holm 602; BΩΣΙΟΣ (*sic*) on *BMC*. p. 22. 153.
[12] *Coinage of Sicily*, p. 210.
[13] Holm 607, 607*a* = *BMC*. p. 61. 8.

(2) Lilybaeum. ATPATINO. ΠΥΘΙΩΝ serpent on altar—ΛΙΛΥΒΑΙΙΤΑΙΣ veiled head to right.[1]

The signatory of both these pieces must be L. Sempronius Atratinus, who brought an Antonian squadron to Octavian's assistance against Sextus Pompeius after the Treaty of Tarentum (p. 44). This must be the occasion of the Sicilian issues with his name. The similarity of these to the Agrigentine pieces signed by Sosius enable us to deduce that the Sicilian campaign attracted yet another naval officer of Antony, C. Sosius, who coined at Zacynthus (p. 39). It is on general grounds extremely probable that the Zacynthine fleet-station, which had easy access to Sicily, sent its quota of ships and men together with those of Atratinus and M. Oppius Capito (pp. 43, 52), and there is no reason why its commander should not have brought them in person; none of his coinage at Zacynthus is dated to 36.

Even if viewed apart from the issue of Sosius, the coinage in the name of Atratinus presents features of great interest. The delay in Octavian's capture of Lilybaeum until after the battle of Naulochus[2] provides an upper limit of September 36 for the coinage. This *terminus* may be applied also to the analogous issue of Entella. But Octavian had already dismissed the Antonian forces and ships to Tarentum[3] before he left for Rome —where he arrived on November 13th.[4] These chronological limits for the mintages naming Antony's officers are so narrow that it is possible to discern their *raison d'être*. After Naulochus, and the subsequent capitulation of Lepidus, Octavian imposed on some of the Sicilian towns an indemnity amounting to 1600 talents.[5] The present issues cannot have been intended for fleet-stations, since Entella is inland: nor can Atratinus —or Sosius—have held a governorship, since the first governor under the new administration was T. Statilius Taurus (p. 53). The names of the two commanders on these coinages strongly suggest that the indemnity was partially levied in bronze coin, and that, in autumn of 36, officers were sent round the unfortunate cities to collect it.

This view is confirmed by the legend of (2), as rightly interpreted by Muensterberg.[6] By way of precedent for a later custom, a private citizen defrays the cost of the issue. But here the gesture of Pythion is invested with a special significance. He is making a voluntary contribution to the indemnity. The appearance of his name indicates that this is not a true official issue: the name of Atratinus merely explains the special circumstances which prompted it. The analogy of Atratinus again applies to Sosius also. Thus neither the Genitive of the one nor the Nominative of the other are purely honorary: the former is rather Possessive, like a similar usage on Roman official coins.[7] It is also noteworthy that plain Genitive inflections are later interchangeable with uses not only of the eponymous ΕΠΙ,[8] which implies a general control (p. 397), but even of

[1] *BMC.* 5, Brussels.
[2] Cf. Levi II, p. 83.
[3] Appian, *BC.* v, 129.
[4] Cf. Charlesworth, *CAH.* x, p. 64.
[5] Appian, l.c.; Dio XLIX, 12. 5.
[6] *MBNGW.* VIII, 1911, pp. 357 ff.
[7] Cf. Mattingly, *BMC. Imp.* p. lxix.
[8] E.g. Synnada (Claudius Valerianus, *KM.* 9; cf. *BMC.* 34), etc.

ΔΙΑ,[1] which states actual control of the issue. The Nominative inflection of Sosius is likewise not otiose. These are instances not of co-operation, nor of control or expropriation of the local mints, but of their compulsion to produce coin by whatever methods they chose. The Greek rendering of the names of Atratinus and Sosius confirms that these exceptional issues may be considered local rather than official.

Plutarch and Appian enable us to reconstruct, from these coins, a lost Chapter of history. It is a curious coincidence that both the officers whose brutal task is thus commemorated were Antonian: Lepidus was not the only triumvir who coveted Sicily from Octavian (p. 51). In later years we hear that Antony's worst grievance was his exclusion from the island: μέγιστα ἦν ὧν ἐνεκάλει.....ὅτι Πομπηίου Σικελίαν ἀφελόμενος (sc. ὁ Καῖσαρ) οὐκ ἔνειμε μέρος αὐτῷ τῆς νήσου.[2] Sosius and Atratinus were employed among the cities of Sicily at the very time when such dispositions hung in the balance. Moreover, a coin of M. Oppius Capito at Lipara (p. 52) was only a little earlier. This numismatic record of Antonian officers is relevant to Octavian's prompt dismissal of the Antonian contingents to Tarentum. There they languished without employment for a few months; then, in Spring 35, he sent back to the East what remained of the ships, with replacements, without waiting for Antony to ask for them.[3] This ungracious behaviour is significant in view of Antony's claim to Sicily and the activity of his lieutenants there: Sosius was known for his hostility to Octavian. It is possible, then, to infer that he and Atratinus, who held at least three key-points of Western Sicily, were suspected of working to satisfy their master's claim. Thus it was that Octavian, whose relations with Antony were otherwise good enough at this time to warrant the promulgation of joint instructions,[4] hastily terminated their employment. Sosius was discreetly honoured with an overdue triumph,[5] Atratinus with the consulship to which he was destined;[6] M. Oppius Capito (whose Fleet coinage at Tarentum had explicitly described him as *praefectus classis* [p. 43]) was no doubt entrusted with the return of the ships to Antony. Thus ended a situation replete with danger to peace and to Octavian.

There is another isolated use of the Genitive in the same period:[7]

ΑΣΙΝΙΟΥ ΑΝΘΥΠΑΤΟΥ ΡΩΜΑΙΩΝ *Caduceus*—fore-part of horse to right, coiled serpent, and a monogram which has been interpreted as $\overline{\text{ATAP}}$(νείτων), but is far more probably $\overline{\text{ΑΔΡΑΜΥΤ}}$(ήνων).[8]

Adramyttium is the only city in Asia (to which this coin must be attributed on grounds of style) which is known to use a monogrammed ethnic in this period; there are a number of variations of this, all approximating closely to the present example but

---

[1] E.g. Apollonia Salbace (Faustina jun., *Wad.* 2244; cf. *BMC.* 55).
[2] Plutarch, *Ant.* 55.
[3] *CAH.* x, p. 92; Levi II, p. 134; cf. Dio XLIX, 14. 6.
[4] This is the latest and best interpretation of the second Edict of Rhosus (Levi, *Rivista di filologia*, 1938, p. 114).
[5] *CIL.* I², p. 76; cf. Fluss, *PW.*(2R.), III. 1178.
[6] Cf. Münzer, *PW.* II, 1367.
[7] *BMC. Mysia*, pl. 14, 7.
[8] Monogram 13.

apparently including only the first four letters.¹ Wroth,² Mommsen³ and Waddington⁴ identify Asinius with the father of Augustus's friend Pollio; but that would necessitate attribution of the coin to the seventies of the last century B.C., which is entirely incompatible with its style. This suggests a date not earlier than the thirties or forties—when Atarneus had virtually ceased to exist⁵—and shows particular kinship with early Augustan coins of Adramyttium.⁶ Furthermore, as R. Syme points out to the writer, the Asinii were in the seventies a distressed family who are unlikely yet to have attained a governorship.

Thus stylistic and social considerations confirm Groag's⁷ identification of the governor (ἀνθύπατος) with the elder brother of Vergil's patron, namely Asinius *Marrucinus*,⁸ whose table manners are rebuked by Catullus.⁹ Historical and numismatic considerations can be combined in support of this view. Ganter¹⁰ and Raillard¹¹ supply, for the *Fasti* of Asia during the triumvirate, only L. Munatius Plancus (39–37) and C. Furnius (36–35 or longer). The former of these should rather be dated c. 41–39/8 (p. 241), so that M. Cocceius Nerva, whom Syme¹² adds, will have governed between c. 39/8 and 36 (ibid.). Cuntz¹³ plausibly suggests the ascription of M. Herennius Picens to c. 33–32; coins of Lampsacus and Alabanda have added M. Turius *legatus* (42–41) and T. Octavius *pro cos.* (c. 32–31) (pp. 246, 373). There remain one or two gaps between 39 and 36, and others in 35–33.

It will here be argued that the year 35–34 should be assigned to Asinius *Marrucinus*. Syme¹⁴ considers that a dedication¹⁵ warrants the assumption that M. Titius held the post in this year: but his intervention to crush Sextus has been ascribed by Tarn¹⁶ to a Syrian governorship, and a Syrian proconsul was the obvious ally to a distressed governor of Asia. On the present coin Asinius's name is in the Genitive Case, and without a preposition. It is noteworthy that the only other known appearance of a Roman official's name in like circumstances (that of Atratinus at Entella) is to be dated only a single year earlier than the date here proposed. Moreover, that occurred in special circumstances: he was exerting pressure to extort an indemnity from the city whose name appears beside his. It is therefore important to note that extortions of a precisely similar character can be discovered in the history of North-Western Asia Minor in this very period 35–34. Early in 35 Sex. Pompeius, escaping from Sicily, endeavoured to secure a footing in this region. He occupied Lesbos,¹⁷ Nicaea, Nico-

---

¹ *GM.* 153; *M. Mys.* 101; *NC.* 1935, p. 199; *KM.* 1.
² *BMC.* l.c.   ³ *St. R.* 11³, p. 648.
⁴ *Fastes des provinces asiatiques*, p. 670. 17.
⁵ Pliny, *NH.* XXXVII, 156; Pausanias VII, 2. 11; cf. Jones, *CERP.* pp. 82, 399.
⁶ E.g. Oxford, *NC.* l.c.
⁷ *PIR².* I, 245. 1229.
⁸ For the relationship of the Asinii with their people the Marrucini vide Syme, *RR.* pp. 169, 193 n. 6.
⁹ XII, 1; cf. Klebs, *PW.* II, 1583 (2).   ¹⁰ P. 35.
¹¹ P. 12 (correcting Waddington).
¹² *RR.* p. 266 n. 3.
¹³ *Jahreshefte des öst. arch. Inst.* 1929, p. 72.
¹⁴ *RR.* l.c.   ¹⁵ *ILS.* 891.   ¹⁶ *CAH.* X, p. 77.
¹⁷ Dio XLIX, 17. 4; Appian, *BC.* V, 133; cf. Broughton, *ES.* IV, p. 586.

media¹ and Lampsacus (p. 246), and we are not told which of the smaller cities in the Troad, Mysia and Bithynia fell with them. The governor of Asia at this time was not Plancus, as Tarn² states, but C. Furnius:³ however, the proconsul of Syria, M. Titius, had to be called in to defeat and execute Sextus. We hear no more of Furnius. His failure may have caused his supersession, but there was in any case no reason why he should not leave in 35. Antony had already applied grievous extortions to the Asian cities,⁴ and the degradation of the colony at Lampsacus bears witness to his severity on this occasion also. His agent in this repression is likely to have been the successor to Furnius. Thus the coincidence in Case-usage of the present coin with the indemnity issues signed by Atratinus and Sosius is unlikely to be fortuitous: Adramyttium falls well within the triangle formed by the cities known to have been in Sextus's hands, and is very likely to have been among the towns which suffered for its voluntary or compulsory allegiance to him. It can, therefore, be maintained that the new governor of 35–34 was Asinius *Marrucinus*, and that he used at Adramyttium precisely the methods familiarised in Sicily during the previous year. There they are illustrated by a special numismatic Case-Usage which appears also on the present issue of Adramyttium but at no other date whatsoever.

Thus the peregrine coinage of the late Republic yields five names of Roman officials without the addition of their portraits. One, in the Accusative, owes its presence to a foundation, of one the Case is uncertain, and the rest—in Nominative and Genitive— are the product of special circumstances caused by the disturbance and brutality of the period. There remains a category which, unlike such testimonies to the use of *force majeure*, survived in the principate of Augustus.

(5) ΕΠΙ + *Genitive*. It has been customary to consider this usage eponymous:⁵ but the examples from the present period reveal that this view stands in need of correction. The governors whose names appear in this manner are the following:

(*a*) Proconsuls of Bithynia-Pontus under Caesar and Octavian: C. Vibius Pansa Caetronianus at **Apamea**,⁶ **Nicaea**⁷ and **Nicomedia**⁸ in 47–46 B.C. (pp. 12, 413), Thorius Flaccus (sometimes with his portrait) at Nicaea and Nicomedia in 29–28 B.C. (pp. 383 f.).

(*b*) Proconsul of Asia under Antony: T. Octavius (?) at **Alabanda** in 34–31 B.C. (p. 373).

(*c*) *Legati* of Syria under Augustus: P. Quinctilius Varus,⁹ L. Volusius Saturninus¹⁰ and Q. Caecilius Metellus Creticus Silanus¹¹ at **Antioch** in 7–3 B.C.,¹² A.D. 4–5,¹³ A.D. 12–15;¹⁴ the last also at **Seleucia**.¹⁵

¹ Appian, l.c. 139; cf. Levi II, p. 130; Hadas, *Sextus Pompey*, p. 155.
² *CAH*. x, p. 62.   ³ Cf. Raillard, p. 12.
⁴ Cf. Tarn, *CAH*. x, p. 33, etc.
⁵ E.g. Mommsen, *St. R.* II, 1, p. 261 n. 1; cf. Regling, *WMK*. p. 121.
⁶ *BMC*. p. 243; *Rec*. I, p. 250.
⁷ *BMC*. ibid.; *Rec*. I, p. 398.
⁸ Paris, *Rec*. I, p. 515.
⁹ *BMC. Syria*, etc. p. 158. 57 ff.; *Hu*. 55.
¹⁰ *BMC*. l.c. p. 159. 60; cf. *Hu*. 63.
¹¹ *BMC*. l.c. p. 159. 63 ff.
¹² *PIR*. III, 118. 27.
¹³ Liebenam, *Legaten*, p. 368. 9.
¹⁴ *PIR*². II, 10. 64.
¹⁵ *Wad*. 7268.

These usages bear witness, at the very least, to a general supremacy such as was enjoyed by governors and implied by eponymy. It is true that the use of ΕΠΙ with a name in the Genitive is, at a later date, merely eponymous and chronographical;[1] but its contexts in this period suggest strongly that, contrary to the general view, they imply, not only mere eponymy, but a practical control over the city-mint or some of its mintages. Nor is this historically improbable, since some kind of supervision of local finances is known to have been exercised as early as the Republic (p. 199), and various degrees of co-operation have already been noted. Now the proconsuls of Bithynia-Pontus in group (*a*) inherit the formula with ΕΠΙ from a predecessor, C. Papirius Carbo (61–59 B.C.), whose name appears on the issues of eight cities.[2] A. H. M. Jones[3] notes that the 'free' city of Prusias ad Mare[4] is not among these: he deduces from its absence that such formulas establish a distinction of some kind between subject and 'free' cities. But this view is invalidated by the appearance of ΕΠΙ with the names of Carbo[5] and a successor C. Caecilius Cornutus (56)[6] at Amisus, which was free at the time.[7] Thus no simple constitutional distinction between the rights of 'free' and subject cities can be applied to these formulas. This negative conclusion is confirmed, from a later date, by the 'freedom' of the cities on whose coins the governors of groups (*b*) and (*c*) are represented.[8] Yet there must be some distinction other than a purely arbitrary one: some cities omit these formulas, others display them, on coins otherwise uniform in style and arrangement. Since ΕΠΙ does not differentiate 'free' from stipendiary cities, it must indicate actual interference in the administrative processes which produced the coinages. Relevant to this supposition is the reputation of Pansa Caetronianus, the Perusian[9] nominee of Caesar, as a prominent financier:[10] other great magnates of the period, Hirtius and Balbus, also issued *aes* coinage at profit to themselves (pp. 3 ff., 19).

Confirmation is obtainable from group (*c*). Two contemporary varieties of *aes* from the mint of Antioch have already been discussed: one was official and the other Archieratic (pp. 100, 376). It is not therefore surprising to find yet another, the so-called 'pseudo-autonomous' class, consisting of smaller coins on which the name of the *legatus* is often predominant. Nor is it accidental that the first issue, with ΕΠΙ ΟΥΑΡΟΥ, coincides in date with the inauguration of the larger denomination of Archieratic

[1] Cf. Kühner, *Grammatik der griechischen Sprache*, sec. 438. 1; Blass, *Grammatik des neutestamentlichen Griechisch*, p. 134. 234 (8).
[2] *Rec.* I, p. 213 n. 5.
[3] *CERP.* p. 160.
[4] Strabo XII, 564.
[5] *Rec.* I, p. 224; cf. p. 58.
[6] *Rec.* I, p. 58; cf. Münzer, *PW.* III, 1200 (43).
[7] Both Lucullus (Plut. *Luc.* 19: cf. Hirschfeld, *PW.* I, 1839; Broughton, *ES.* IV, p. 533) and Pompey (Strabo XII, 547; cf. Cary, *CAH.* IX, p. 395) had respected the old-established freedom of the city. When Caesar later freed it (Dio XLII, 48; Strabo, l.c.; cf. Jones, *CERP.* p. 426 n. 38), he was freeing it not from a subject status received in Pompey's settlement, but from degradation resulting from the forcible occupation of Pharnaces (Strabo, l.c.; cf. Adcock, *CAH.* IX, p. 677).
[8] Henze, *De Civitatibus Liberis*, Diss. Berlin, 1892, pp. 49 (Alabanda), 75 (Antioch and Seleucia).
[9] Syme, *RR.* p. 90.
[10] Ibid. p. 95 n. 1.

bronze, and also with the silver tetradrachms.[1] But none of these contemporary groups need have proceeded from the same administrative source, since Malalas[2] specifically alludes to mints which included simultaneously active divisions under separate authority. Even within the narrow bounds of group (c), with the names of *legati*, there are inscriptional vicissitudes that can hardly be meaningless: these extend over a long period of years, but in the principate of Augustus alone there are three distinct phases. At first, under P. Varus and L. Volusius Saturninus, the formula introduced by ΕΠΙ follows the ethnic. Then, after a pause, coins of very similar appearance were struck in A.D. 5[3] and 11,[4] substituting for the governor's name the title ΜΗΤΡΟΠΟΛΕΩΣ with the monogram ΑΥΤ(ονόμου).[5] These issues present a significant divergence from their predecessors. But afterwards a retrograde step was taken. The name of the *legatus* returns under Silanus,[6] and appears also at another 'free' city, Seleucia;[7] moreover, it now precedes, instead of following, the ethnic.[8] Only the monogram ΑΥΤ(ονόμου) is retained at Antioch in consideration of the civic pride.[9]

There can be little doubt that these are *nuances appréciables*.[10] We have a series of fluctuations in the respective authorities of city and governor.[11] Since Antioch did not cease to be a *libera civitas*[12] these variations can be in no way connected with a political distinction between 'free' and stipendiary communities. As in the case of Amisus it seems necessary to infer that the point at issue is not theoretical but practical, namely the actual relationship of the governors to the local coining authorities. To the vicissitudes of this the Antiochene issues bear eloquent witness.

Other evidence also can be adduced in support of the view that these formulas are expressive, rather than a meaningless record of eponymy. Under Augustus local magistrates do not sign with ΕΠΙ,[13] with the exception of Eurycles at Sparta.[14] It is impossible to resist the conclusion that his usage bears witness to the special con-

---

[1] Wruck, *Die Syrische Provinzialprägung von Augustus bis Trajan*, no. 2.
[2] S.v. Μονῆτα.
[3] Paris, etc.; cf. Macdonald, *NC*. 1904, p. 110.
[4] Ibid. p. 111.
[5] Monograms 14a–c. It cannot represent the ethnic ANT. (as Macdonald, l.c.) since it appears elsewhere in conjunction with ΑΝΤΙΟΧΕΩΝ (*BMC*. 68). In any case it is difficult to decipher an N from it. For the contradictory character of this description see pp. 100, 402.
[6] *BMC*. 150, etc.
[7] *Wad*. 7268.
[8] Cf. Macdonald, l.c.
[9] Later, under Tiberius, the governor's name is extended to the larger denomination, consisting of adapted Archieratic issues (*BMC*. 161, etc.). A final change takes place during an interregnum between *legati* in 59–60 (cf. Tac. *Ann*. XIV, 26): after its omission on this occasion, the formula with ΕΠΙ never again returns to the 'pseudo-autonomous' small bronze, though it maintains for a few years its place on the larger pieces (cf. Macdonald, l.c.).
[10] Dieudonné, *Mélanges numismatiques*, 2 sér., p. 138.
[11] The 'victory' of the former under Nero is meaningless at so late a date but would have been significant under Augustus.
[12] Cf. Jones, *CERP*. p. 263.
[13] All apparent examples have been relegated to a later date: see above, pp. 328 ff.
[14] *BMC*. 62.

ditions of his semi-royal ἐπιστασία.[1] It is clear, too, that later generations regarded ΕΠΙ as significant: it is interchangeable with ΠΑΡΑ at Apamea,[2] and with ΕΠΙΜ (ελnθέντος) at Grimenothyrae;[3] it may sometimes even be an abbreviation for the latter word. But particularly relevant is a group of Cretan issues not later than the Julio-Claudian period. These have the names of governors, and of a procurator or Cretarch. The entirely indiscriminate appearance of the Genitive and Dative cases after ΕΠΙ,[4] in recording these officials' names, indicates that the former usage, as well as the latter, was held to imply a measure of control.[5] It was not merely eponymous and chronographic, but bore witness to the financial supervision of the proconsul, who was, indeed, as elsewhere, ultimately responsible for the κοινόν.[6] In the same way, on an issue of the κοινὸν 'Ασίας (p. 377), the legend ΕΠΙ ΚΑΙΣΑΡΟΣ ΤΟ ΔΕΥΤΕΡΟΝ suggests that the issue was actually sanctioned by Augustus, not merely made in his presidency. Two further considerations confirm that phrases with ΕΠΙ have this meaning. First, the *legatus* of Tiberius in Galatia, T. Helvius Basila, places his name after ΕΠΙ on coinage which has no ethnic and is official (p. 328). Here the idea of control clearly predominates over that of eponymy, since no other source of issue is recorded, or can be assumed. Secondly, the elimination from the Augustan period of the posthumous coinages has left not a single example of the name of a local dignitary with ΕΠΙ. Yet every city had its eponymous magistrate, and it is these who frequently appear (p. 364); so that the governors, whose names alone are found with ΕΠΙ, may be supposed not to appear in a merely eponymous capacity.

There are, therefore, various reasons for supposing that these formulas express the secondary and ultimate source of issue. Thus it is possible tentatively to compare ΕΠΙ

[1] Cf. Kjellberg, *Klio*, XVII, 1921, p. 50, for the distinctive intention. For different views regarding Eurycles's *régime*, see above, p. 343 n. 18.

[2] Commodus, *BMC*. 97; cf. *Wad*. 5717.

[3] Trajan, *Wad*. 6057; cf. Senate, *BMC*. 223.

[4] Augurinus: Genitive at Hierapytna (Vienna = Svoronos, *Crete* 50), Polyrhenium (Vienna = Svoronos, l.c. 53). Dative at Polyrhenium (*BMC*. 23, Cambridge [McLean 7196]), Latus (*NC*. 1891. p. 28), Gortyna (*BMC*. 80, Athens = Svoronos, l.c. 193). Lupus: Genitive at Polyrhenium (Paris = Svoronos, l.c. 52). Dative at Cydonia (BM = Svoronos, l.c. 110), Latus or Lappa (Copenhagen, unpublished). Laches: Dative at Cydonia, Paris = Svoronos, l.c. 109. The termination of Laches's name shows that the Datives are true ones, and not merely Cretan Genitives.

[5] Muensterberg (*MBNGW*. IX, 1913, p. 161) believes that the Dative usage with ΕΠΙ is due to a *Verquickung* of the normal eponymous Greek use with the Genitive and the Latin Ablative of Time. His similar view with regard to signatures in the plain Dative is, however, unsatisfactory. Imperial titulatures in Greek are regularly rendered in the Dative (e.g. of Augustus at Cydonia, Pergamum, Antioch, Smyrna, Mylasa, etc.), and such uses are, as in Latin, dedicatory: it is hard to consider ΚΑΙΣΑΡΙ ΣΕΒΑΣΤΩ fundamentally different from ΑΝΤΙΩ ΣΤΡΑΤΗΓΩ (*KM*. p. 257. 25). In this case too the simpler explanation is the more probable. ΕΠΙ with the Dative at all epochs carries a distinct connotation of control (cf. Kühner, *Grammatik der griechischen Sprache*, sec. 438, II, 3[*b*]): the laxity of contemporary usage (cf. Regard, *Des prépositions dans la langue du Nouveau Testament*, p. 429) does not in any way alter this fact, since confusions only occurred between inflections of similar meaning.

[6] Cf. in particular Strabo X, 483.

with PERM(*issu*).[1] But there is an important distinction between the two: the permission of *princeps* or governor was necessary for any Roman city to issue coin (p. 296), whereas the rarity of the occurrence of ΕΠΙ suggests that it indicates supervision of a stronger and more exceptional character. No doubt all the peregrine cities needed a general permission to coin,[2] but a few, even in the so-called privileged categories, were occasionally obliged to submit to special supervision by the governor. This supervision was expressed by the appearance of his name on their coinage after ΕΠΙ. This practice foreshadows the appointment of *correctores* and λογισταί, and is a very real encroachment on local *libertas*, comparable to, but distinct from, the several grades of 'co-operation' described in Part I (pp. 68, 390, etc.).

[1] Cf. Dieudonné, *Mélanges numismatiques*, 2 sér. II, p. 137.   [2] Cf. Bosch, *KM*. pp. 3 ff.

C. *LIBERTAS* AND *CIVITAS*

Recent research, especially by A. H. M. Jones[1] and A. N. Sherwin-White,[2] has established definitely that no fundamental distinction existed between 'free' and stipendiary cities. The rights of both depended on the unilateral declaration of Rome, being formulated in special charters and in the *lex provinciae* respectively. All cities had independent constitutions; all were subject to frequent intervention. There were many gradations of privilege which depended not so much on status as on the circumstances of transference to Rome (pp. 340f., 346).

The coins confirm these conclusions. *Civitates liberae*, like the others, frequently portray the living Augustus,[3] and record the active interference of their governors by formulas with ΕΠΙ.[4] Their mints are commonly requisitioned for official issues;[5] often too they do not coin at all.[6] Conversely, the stipendiary towns are under no obligation to refer on their coinage to the *princeps* or any Roman official or institution;[7] they produce foundation-issues and festival-issues as freely as the 'free'. Both classes alike contribute to the Imperial small-change system.[8] But just as the Roman *municipia*, in contrast to the colonies, occasionally give numismatic emphasis to their original independence (p. 325), so it is not surprising that a few *civitates liberae* record additional honours and privileges. On the whole, no doubt, they guarded their traditions more jealously than the stipendiary communities. The Romans connived at this by preferring the method of *auctoritas* for their government.[9] Thus the 'autonomous' currencies of 'free' Athens[10] and Chios,[11] for example, are, on the whole, more notice-

---

[1] *Anatolian Studies to Buckler* (1939), pp. 103 ff.; *GC.* III, pp. 117 ff.

[2] Pp. 151 ff. Cf. also (among a large literature) Henze, *De Civitatibus Liberis*, Diss. Berlin, 1892; Horn, *Foederati*, Diss. Frankfurt, 1930; Heuss, *Klio Beitr.* XXXI, 1933, pp. 78 f.; Zmigryder-Konopka, *Studi italiani di filologia classica*, XIV, 1937, pp. 93 ff.; Täubler, *Imperium Romanum*; Kloesel, *Libertas*, Diss. Breslau, 1935.

[3] E.g. Abydus, Alabanda, Aphrodisias, Cos, Ilium, Mylasa, Aegeae, Antioch, Ascalon, Gaza, Amisus, Cydonia, Amphipolis, Thessalonica, Nicopolis, Tanagra, Leptis minor, Sabrata, Oea, Leptis Magna, Lycian and Thessalian Leagues.

[4] Antioch, Seleucia; cf. Amisus under Caesar and Alabanda under Antony.

[5] Antioch, Cephallenia(?); cf. Panormus early in first century B.C., Amisus and Thessalonica under Caesar, Zacynthus under Antony (for its freedom, cf. Henze, l.c. p. 34; Larsen, *ES.* IV, p. 447).

[6] E.g. Astypalaea, Caunus, Cnidus, Prusias ad Mare, Aegina, Amphissa, Thespiae, Samothrace,

Apollonia in Illyricum, Cephallenia, Aenus, Lappa, Mopsus, Cercina, Massilia.

[7] E.g. at this period Bargasa (Paris), Thyatira (Paris), Samosata (*BMC.* 1 ff.), Rhosus (Brussels = M. V. 269. 836), Botrys (American College at Beyrouth = Rouvier, *JIAN.* XI, 1908, p. 9), Marathus (Rouvier, *JIAN.* IV, 1901, p. 146). Tyre does not stop her autonomous issues (*JIAN.* VI, 1903, 2089 ff.) when 'enslaved' in c. 20 B.C. (Dio LIV, 7. 6). Cf., probably a little later, Alia (Paris), Briula (*Wad.* 4929), Bagae (*Wad.* 4883) and Hyrcanis (*BMC.* 1).

[8] E.g. 'free' Chios, Rhodes, Antioch, Sidon, Ascalon, Athens, Amphipolis, Thessalonica, Nicopolis, Thessaly; stipendiary Ephesus, Smyrna, Philadelphia, Aradus.

[9] Cf. Sherwin-White, pp. 236 ff.

[10] The discovery by Mrs Shear (*Hesperia*, 1936, pp. 285 ff.) of coins reading ΣΕΒΑΣΤΟΣ cannot be accepted. E. S. G. Robinson confirms this.

[11] One of these does read ΣΕΒΑΣΤΟΣ (Mavrogordato, *NC.* 1917, p. 225).

402 THE COMMUNITIES AND THE ROMAN OFFICIALS

able than those of stipendiary Bargasa and Thyatira. Thus, too, a few 'free' communities are allowed to retain their mints for silver:[1] but this cannot be exalted into a general distinction, since they are so infrequent,[2] and silver is also minted at stipendiary Laodicea ad Mare.[3] Free cities are not required to portray *amici principis* or other governors under Augustus.[4] These minor dignities were in harmony with the Roman desire to maintain existing systems of government.[5]

Σύμμαχοι had been levelled down to ἐλεύθεροι,[6] and ἐλεύθεροι το αὐτόνομοι.[7] Το αὐτόνομοι even the stipendiary had been elevated:[8] they, as well as the 'free', could now be called *socii*.[9] In one sense, therefore, they possessed *libertas* no less than other classes of community. This was an ancient catchword which had been associated with the most anomalous imperialisms and annexations. It had never meant independence:[10] it postulated *mens bona, pudor, modus, fides, lex* (p. 324). Last aptly points out that the Greeks honestly thought that Rome had destroyed ἐλευθερία, but the Romans honestly thought that it preserved *libertas*[11]—the reward of the obedient (*qui maiestatem nostram comiter conservare debent*[12]). Cicero[13] echoes Epictetus' definition Ἐλεύθερός ἐστιν ὁ ζῶν ὡς βούλεται,[14] but sophistically adds that this involves a rigid obedience to the laws, since the people have created them.[15] The Empire was based on ubiquitous *libertas*,[16] and so, as Proculus explicitly states (p. 318), on ubiquitous *clientela* of Rome and the *princeps*—that is, on ubiquitous *auctoritas principis*. Even Caesar, who did not make *auctoritas* the basis of his government, united in his propa-

---

[1] Lycian League (in general, Berlin = M. S. VII, I. I with portrait, *BMC*. 1–4 'autonomous'; Cragus, *BMC*. 25, *Wad*. 3058; Massicytes, many varieties, *BMC*. 35 ff., *Wad*. 3108 ff., etc.; Tlos, BM, *Wad*. 3195 f.), Stratonicea (*KM*. p. 155, *GM*. 449: *BMC*. 33 and *GM*. 449 A are posthumous), Sidon (p. 345). The status of Tabae (*GM*. 456: *KM*. 1 is probably posthumous) is uncertain (vide Broughton, *ES*. IV, pp. 706 f.). See also p. 340.

[2] Cf. Mommsen, *M*ζ*w*. p. 331. But his alternative suggestion that this was a *Metropolenrecht* is rightly refuted by Bosch, *KM*. pp. 3 ff. [3] *BMC*. 30.

[4] But under Antony Sparta portrayed Atratinus (p. 382).

[5] Cf. Jones, *GC*. p. 52.

[6] For the unimportance of *foederati* at this time, vide Sherwin-White, p. 149; Stevenson, *RPA*. p. 164.

[7] For their identification vide Appian, *BC*. I, 102, αὐτόνομοί τε καὶ φόρων ἀτελεῖς = *liberae et immunes*; cf. Josephus, *AJ*. XVII, 9. 4; *BJ*. II, 2. 3; Strabo XII, 545, αὐτονομηθεῖσα δὲ πόλυν χρόνον οὐδὲ διὰ τέλους ἐφύλαξε τὴν ἐλευθερίαν. Thus Chersonesus, although attached to the Bosphoran kingdom (Strabo VII, 309), can now without inconsistency describe itself on its coins as ἐλεύθερα (Oreschnikov, *Numiςmaticheskago Svornika*, III, 1914, p. 44). Cf. the decay of peculiar features of ἐλεύθεροι: *postliminium* (Heuss, *Klio*, XXXI, 1933, pp. 10 f. n. 1), *asylum* (Barth, *De Graecorum Asylis*, Diss. Strassburg, 1888, pp. 5 f.) and *ius exilii* (Hartmann, *De Exilio apud Romanos*, Diss. Berlin, 1887, p. 24). The distinction of Mommsen (*St.R*. III, pp. 725 f.) is obsolete.

[8] Cf. Cic. *Att*. VI, 1. 15, *Graeci vero exsultant quod peregrinis iudicibus utuntur... se* αὐτονομίαν *adeptos putant*.

[9] Cf. Sherwin-White, pp. 159, 162.

[10] Cf. Jones, *Anatolian Studies to Buckler*, pp. 103 ff. [11] *CAH*. XI, p. 436.

[12] Proculus, *Dig*. XLIX, 15. 7.

[13] *De Officiis*, I, 70; cf. *De Republica*, II, 43; Syme, *RR*. p. 320.

[14] *Diss*. IV, 1. 1; cf. Zmigryder-Konopka, *Studi italiani di filologia classica*, XIV, 1937, p. 91 n. 1.

[15] Cf. Tellenbach, *Forschungen zur Kirchen- und Geistesgeschichte*, VII, 1936, p. 15.

[16] Cf. Mitteis, *Reichsrecht und Volksrecht in den östlichen Provinzen*, p. 146; Kornemann, *QAS*. IV, p. 14; id. *PW. Suppl*. I, p. 302.

ganda the slogans of *clientela* and *libertas*.¹ By the assistance of the κτίστης conception familiarised by the coinage, he, like Pompey, was able to boast of his peregrine *patrocinia* (p. 317). But it remained for Augustus to base his Empire on the institution. It is not surprising that his *Res Gestae* is schematically divided into two sections—comprehending *auctoritas* and *libertas* respectively (p. 324). The two were indissolubly linked (p. 443); *libertas* was very soon to become the keynote of official propaganda, universalised by the epithets *Publica*² and *Augusta*.³

There was, therefore, not much difference between the *libertas* of 'free' and stipendiary cities of peregrine rank. But there was, owing to Augustus's pro-Italian mentality, a fundamental distinction between peregrine and citizen *libertas*. It is not for nothing that Hippo Diarrhytus and Bilbilis adorn their coinages with LIBERA and ITALICA respectively (pp. 224, 170): these are the most distinctive descriptions of their *civitas* which they can find. It is significant that only the enfranchised communities were permitted the symbol of Liber Pater (p. 315). Further clues are provided by the small settlements of Romans who resided, without the rank of a city and without geographical separation, in the midst of a non-Roman community (p. 186).⁴ They were highly organised,⁵ granted official land-allotments (p. 383),⁶ and favoured in every possible way. Their privileged position, of which much evidence is extant,⁷ is best exemplified by inscriptions at Attaleia,⁸ Isaura,⁹ etc., where they appear in decrees, by the side of the peregrine community, as οἱ συμπολιτευόμενοι Ῥωμαῖοι.¹⁰ Particularly arresting is an inscription in which they actually precede οἱ Κυζικηνοί,¹¹ and another in

---

¹ Patron of *foederati*: *BG*. I, 31. 6, VI, 12. 2; cf. Horn, *Foederati*, Diss. Frankfurt, 1930, p. 57. *Libertas* of 'protected' states: *BC*. I, 9. 5, I, 22. 5; cf. Weickert, *Klio*, 1937, p. 247. Cf. Livy's phrase, of an earlier date, *patrocinium libertatis Graecorum* (XXXIV, 58. 11; cf. Skard, *Festskrift til Koht*, p. 65).

² From Galba (*BMC*. 68 ff.).

³ From Claudius (*BMC*. 145 ff.). Cf. Kloesel, l.c. p. 70 n. 29; Schöner, *Acta Seminarii Philologici Erlangensis*, II, 1881, p. 485; Charlesworth, *The Virtues of a Roman Emperor*, p. 12; Alföldi, *ZfN*. XL, 1930, p. 6.

⁴ Cf. Sherwin-White, p. 211, who compares the Roman core of the Latin city. These settlements were civil *conventus* or *pagi* (cf. *BCH*. X, 1886, p. 422 n. 87; Broughton, pp. 32, 210; id. *ES*. IV, pp. 546 ff.; Last, *CAH*. XI, p. 444; Haywood, *ES*. IV, pp. 103 ff.; Rostovtzeff, *SEH*. p. 580 n. 60) or semi-military *castella* (Rostovtzeff, l.c.; Jones, *GC*. p. 64).

⁵ With *patroni* (*CIL*. III, 455 n. 48), *curatores* (*CIG*. 2930; *CIL*. V, 5747), even *decuriones* (*Eph. epigr*. VII, p. 425 n. 5). Cf. Kornemann, *Berliner Studien für classische Philologie und Archäologie*, XIV, 1. 1892 *passim*; Hatzfeld, pp. 257 ff.

⁶ Cf. Broughton, *TAPA*. LXVI, 1935, pp. 18 ff.

⁷ Cf. especially Kornemann, l.c. p. 23; Hahn, *Rom und Romanismus*, p. 94; Volkmann, *Münchener Beiträge zur Papyrusforschung*, XXI, 1935, p. 205 n. 5; Box, *JRS*. XXI, 1931, p. 203 n. 2; Riccobono, *Annali del Seminario giuridico della R. Univ. di Palermo*, XV, 1936, p. 413 n. 2. The recent deduction from the Rhosus edicts by de Visscher (*Comptesrendus de l'Académie des Inscriptions*, 1938, pp. 24 ff.), that they were even allowed to hold local citizenship as well, is doubted by Levi, *Rivista di filologia*, 1938, pp. 126 f. n. 1.

⁸ Viale, *Atti del primo Congresso di Studi Romani*, I, p. 362, misinterprets this as a real colony; the evidence provided by Kornemann, l.c. pp. 11 ff., shows that this is not correct; cf. Broughton, *ES*. IV, 1938, p. 703.

⁹ *IGRR*. III, 292, 294; cf. Kornemann, l.c. p. 45; pace Viale, l.c. p. 363; Paribeni, *Augustus*, p. 413.

¹⁰ Cf. also *Ephemeris epigraphica*, V, p. 155 n. 57; *Papers of American School of Classical Studies at Athens*, I, 1882–3, p. 55, no. 28.

¹¹ Kornemann, l.c. p. 47.

which they not only precede the natives of Masculula, but appear in heavier type.¹ Unless they were aboriginal *liberti*, they were not subject to local law;² and the tralatician provincial edicts were still expressly designed for their protection.³ *Ubique vicit Romanus habitat*⁴—and ample provision was made for his habitation.⁵

It followed easily that such groups should be granted the colonial or municipal status to which their organisation and land-ownership had pointed.⁶ Then they became a geographically separate organism, and, except in the rare cases when all the *peregrini* were expropriated (p. 305 nn. 10, 11) or admitted to the franchise,⁷ we have a double community.⁸ The conclusion of Jones that, in accordance with Augustus's general policy, the natives were now placed in a state of subordination to the Roman minority⁹—whose boundaries were carved with the greatest lavishness¹⁰—is confirmed by the coinage. No peregrine mint survived the establishment of a colony. At a single *municipium*, Emporiae, there may have been a brief interlude of peregrine and municipal coinage at the same mint (p. 347); then the natives gave up the unequal struggle. It was even a promotion for *civitates foederatae* to achieve *Latinitas*,¹¹ and they are, by comparison, justifiably described as ὑποτασσόμενοι.¹²

There existed, in fact, a completely one-sided policy of exaltation of Roman citizens over even the most privileged *peregrini*. It is not therefore surprising that patriotism of *peregrini* to Rome had scarcely awakened at this period:¹³ that sharp local conflicts ensued,¹⁴ that the government had to intervene to check the citizens' arrogance,¹⁵ and that the condition of rural areas was particularly miserable.¹⁶ The Hellenistic sovereigns

---

¹ *ILS.* 6774; cf. Sherwin-White, p. 212.
² Sherwin-White, p. 213: cf. de Visscher, l.c. 1939, pp. 113 ff., who shows (p. 119) that even the *liberti* escaped many responsibilities.
³ Buckland, *Revue historique du droit français et étranger*, IV sér., XIII, 1934, p. 91.
⁴ Seneca, *Ad Helviam*, VII, 7.
⁵ Such facts are unduly minimised by Mommsen, *Ephemeris epigraphica*, VII, p. 441 n. 1.
⁶ Cf. Sherwin-White, pp. 171 f., 212.
⁷ For the unusualness of this, vide Jullian, *TP.* p. 30 n. 7; Jones, *GC.* p. 173; cf. Strabo XII, 546.
⁸ Proof of this natural phenomenon is forthcoming at individual communities, e.g. Thuburbo Maius (Merlin, *Cinquième Congrès international d'archéologie* [1930], pp. 208 ff.; Poinssot, *Comptes-rendus de l'Académie des Inscriptions*, 1915, pp. 328 f.; Rostovtzeff, *SEH.* p. 580 n. 59), Thysdrus (Gsell VIII, pp. 181 f.; Merlin, l.c. p. 210), Carthage (Haywood, *ES.* IV, p. 103; Barthel, *Zur Geschichte der römischen Städten in Africa*, p. 17; Broughton, p. 53; Sherwin-White, p. 172), Pisidian colonies (Kornemann, l.c. p. 45), perhaps Volubilis (Merlin,

l.c. p. 213; Gsell V, p. 132 n. 7; *pace* Kornemann, *PW.* XVI, 598); not Actium (cf. Jones, *GC.* p. 312 n. 80; Hierocles 651. 7; *pace* Kornemann [*coloniae*] 109; Mitteis, *Reichsrecht und Volksrecht in den östlichen Provinzen*, p. 147 n. 2), Isaura, or Attaleia (p. 383 n. 10). Sometimes two Roman communities are so joined (e.g. Frontinus, *De Controversiis Agrorum* [Feldm. p. 53, l. 1]; Jullian, *TP.* p. 30; Syme, *CQ.* 1938, p. 43).   ⁹ *GC.* p. 173.
¹⁰ Frontinus, l.c. (pp. 118 f.), Agennius Urbicus (ibid. 11. 27 ff.), Hyginus, *De Limitibus Constituendis* (ibid. p. 113, 11. 22 f.). But they too were discontented (p. 305).
¹¹ Cf. McElderry, *JRS.* VIII, 1918, p. 70; Hardy, *Roman Laws and Charters*, p. 64; Horn, *Foederati*, p. 52; Stevenson, *RPA.* p. 163.
¹² *Ed. Cyr.* 3 (*SEG.* IX, 1938, p. 14).
¹³ Cf. Sherwin-White, p. 205.   ¹⁴ Ibid. p. 213.
¹⁵ Cf. de Visscher, *Comptes-rendus de l'Ac. des Inscriptions*, 1939, p. 119.
¹⁶ Cf. Heitland, *Last words on the Roman municipalities*, p. 23. Vide also Rostovtzeff, *Mélanges Pirenne*, p. 430.

LIBERTAS AND CIVITAS

had provided a precedent by their favour to their own compatriots,[1] and Rome followed their lead wholeheartedly.[2] The *Lex Iulia de maiestate*, probably adapted by Octavian,[3] was ready for dissenters. The sentiments of the *princeps* were peculiarly suited for the intensification of such a policy. But even Caesar's watchword at Pharsalus had been *parce civibus*.[4] In one sense, *libertas* was indeed now universal; but in this period too Pliny the younger could have spoken of *residuum libertatis nomen*.[5] To gain potency it needed the addition of *civitas*.[6] At the bottom of the scale, in this *concordia discors* of *libertas*,[7] were the rural populations, over which even the peregrine communities lorded it:[8] at the top were the ubiquitous *cives Romani*. (Yet even on *civitas*, as has been shown, a great many obligations were imposed by the central government, which claimed the paramount rights of the Roman *res publica* over municipal allegiances and over the individual *res privata*.[9]) It is often suspected that the periodical exertions of paternalistic administrations were not enough to invalidate the conclusion of Heitland[10] and Reinhold: 'Judged by ... the greatest good of the greatest number, the Augustan reconstruction must be found wanting'.[11] The new *libertas*—which was good for nothing but futile expenditure of civic income[12]—was responsible for the decline from the healthy municipal pride of Cicero[13] to the sneering abuse of *Kleinstädterei* by Martial[14] and Juvenal.[15] It is linked in the strongest way to the *régime* of Augustus: its compatibility with monarchy depended on the degree of the ruler's *auctoritas*.[16] The fourth Part of this book will discuss the evolution of this characteristic as the basis of government, in substitution for the franker, but no more decisive, *imperium*.

---

[1] Cf. Rostovtzeff, *CAH*. VII, p. 164; Jones, *GC*. p. 161. But vide Westermann, *Actes du Ve Congrès int. de Papyrologie*, 1937, p. 566, for interpretation of this as plutocratic rather than racial.

[2] It is very doubtful whether, as suggested by Schönbauer, *Sav. Z.* 1929, p. 398, cf. Haarhoff, *The Stranger at the Gate*, p. 257, the Greeks were treated much better than other *peregrini*: vide de Visscher, l.c. p. 115; von Premerstein, *Sav. Z.* 1931, p. 436.

[3] Cf. Ciaceri, *Studi storici per l'Antichità classica*, II, 1909, p. 380 n. 1, III, 1910, p. 2 (Octavianic); pace Arango-Ruiz, *Augustus*, p. 137 (Caesarian). Vide also Last, *JRS*. XXVIII, 1938, p. 213.

[4] Suet. *Caes.* 75. 2; cf. Syme, *RR*. p. 159. Attributed by Orosius, VI, 15. 26, to Pompey.

[5] *Ep.* VIII, 24; cf. Koehne, *Description du musée de feu le Prince Kotschoubey*, p. 171.

[6] The conclusion also of Riccobono, *Annali del Seminario giuridico della R. Univ. di Palermo*, XV, 1936, p. 453; Sutherland, *RIS.* p. 186.

[7] For the new *Concordia*, vide Skard, *Avhandlinger av Det Norske Videnskaps-Akademi i Oslo*, II

(*h.-fil.*), 1931, 2; for the Republican conception, vide Strasburger, *Concordia Ordinum*, Diss. Frankfurt, 1929.

[8] Cf. Rostovtzeff, *Mélanges Pirenne*, p. 430; Cary, *History*, XXII, 1938, p. 60.

[9] Cf. Kloesel, *Libertas*, Diss. Breslau, 1935, pp. 18, 25; Burck, *Auf dem Wege zum nationalpolitischen Gymnasium*, VI, 1938, pp. 54 ff. The 'totalitarian' aspects of the government have also been discussed by Stark, *Respublica*, Diss. Göttingen, 1937 and Biondi, *Annuario della R. Univ. di Catania*, 1928–9, p. 19. Cf. above, pp. 317 ff.

[10] *Repetita*, pp. 5 ff.

[11] *CJ*. 1938, p. 369.

[12] Jones, *GC*. pp. 135 f., 243 f.

[13] *De Legibus*, II, 2. 5; *De Rep.* I, 26; *Pro Sulla*, 7. 23, 8. 24; *Pro Plancio*, 6. 9; cf. Sherwin-White, p. 14.

[14] 4. 66, etc.; cf. Jullian, *TP*. p. 35.

[15] 3. 34, 4. 43, 10. 100–4.

[16] Cf. Tellenbach, *Forschungen zur Kirchen- und Geistesgeschichte*, VII, 1936, p. 16.

Part IV
IMPERIUM AND AUCTORITAS

―‹‹›―

INTRODUCTION

NUMEROUS coins have been shown to allude to contemporary constitutional problems. In the present Part, these are reviewed, and related to other ancient material and modern theories. The coins provide evidence which seems to justify and necessitate several divergencies from current views. Of late years, chiefly owing to the impetus given by the *Cambridge Ancient History*, research on the Augustan constitution has continued with redoubled vigour. All but the numismatic material has been employed frequently and exhaustively—often to produce directly opposed results. The present study does not aim at yet another survey of this vast and inconclusive bulk of literary and epigraphic evidence. Consideration will rather be given to such parts of it as are relevant to the neglected coins and to the problems which they illuminate; and an attempt will be made to check by these numismatic contributions the latest theories which the rapid development of the subject has yielded. Owing to the large number of these and their voluminous character, recapitulations of them, and indeed all references, must be of the briefest. An attempt has rather been made to reconstruct the constitutional edifice with care that, for once, the coins shall play their fair share as bricks.

Chapter 1
RULE BY *IMPERIUM MAIUS*, 49—28 B.C.

THE two decades which are here discussed were a period in which the Roman constitution was modified in favour of a military autocracy. This Chapter is concerned with the two predominant features of this *régime*, the new title of *Imperator* and the *imperium maius*. It will be shown that, throughout the period, the former continued to be the deliberate expression, and the latter the legal basis, of the successive governments. This is important to the principal argument, which will maintain that both these phenomena disappeared in 27 B.C., and did not return under Augustus: so far from being earlier adumbrations of the principate, they are directly opposed to its theory and practice. Owing to their existence, the years 49–28—the subject of this Chapter—were an isolated period of constitutional experiment, from which the principate was developed only by reaction, not in continuity.

A. THE REVOLUTIONARY TITLE OF *IMPERATOR*: EARLIEST OFFICIAL DOCUMENTS

The origins of the new title of supremacy have been buried under a vast controversy. The failure of this to achieve a solution is hardly surprising in view of the disastrous lack of official, contemporary documentation. It has at least, with reason, been generally believed that the later statements of Dio[1] and Suetonius[2] concerning Caesar's title have a germ of truth in them: the dictator must have used the appellation in a peculiar and unconstitutional way.[3] McFayden,[4] however, has rightly realised that the literary and epigraphic evidence is entirely inconclusive.

The coinages discussed in this book bring to bear upon this problem official documents of an earlier date than any usually quoted. First come the following legends on coins of the two Pompeian leaders:[5]

(1) CN. MAGNVS IMP. and IMP. F. (46 B.C.).
(2) MAGNVS PIVS IMP. and IMP. F. (c. 45).
(3) IMP. SEX. MAGNVS (44).

[1] XLIII, 44. 2–5. [2] *Caes.* 76.
[3] E.g. most recently Radin, *Studi Riccobono*, II, pp. 21 ff.; de Labriolle, *Revue des études latines*, 1933, p. 263; Carcopino, *Histoire romaine*, II, pp. 1000 f.; von Premerstein, pp. 235 ff.; Kahrstedt, *GGA*. 1938, p. 21; Gagé, *Revue historique*, 1936, p. 339; Volkmann, *Forschungen und Fortschritte*,
13, XXX, 1938, pp. 349 f.; Andersen, *Neue Deutsche Forschungen*, CXCVI, 1938, p. 34. De Sanctis, *Studi Riccobono*, II, pp. 57 ff. shows that this may, to some extent, have been true of Sulla; cf. Momigliano, *Augustus* (1938), p. 197.
[4] Pp. 11, 28 ff.
[5] See above, p. 22.

THE REVOLUTIONARY TITLE OF *IMPERATOR*   409

These illuminate somewhat the early history of the title. It has been shown that, by the analogy of REGVLVS F. etc., the correct interpretation of (1) and (2) should be IMP(*erator*) F(*ilius*). Cn. Magnus, *Imperator filius*, is quite different from Cn. Magnus *filius, imperator*:[1] the sons of Pompey must, retrospectively, have been considering their father as *Imperator* in some special and inheritable sense.[2] No attempt must be made to apply this significance to the lifetime of Pompey himself, since that would risk an anachronism: but tendencious reinterpretations of dead personages are frequent in this period.[3] The coins show distinctly that a title far removed from the traditional *cognomen* of salutations had found its way into political thought as early as 46. This is confirmed by the strange appellation of the Pompeian headquarters in South Spain: *Vrbs Imperatoria* Salacia.[4] IMP. F. alternatives with IMP.; and *Magnus Imp.*, where the title does not refer specifically to salutation, is only at a short remove from *Imp. Magnus*.[5] (3) indicates in a decisive manner that this transition was accepted in the Pompeian camp before the end of 44. It is not an accident that this coin also breaks with precedent by the substitution of Sextus's own head for that of his father: its use of *Imperator* recalls that the only title borne as a prefix during the Republic was *Rex*.[6] Nor is it a chance coincidence that this coinage was made during a brief period of reconciliation with the senate late in 44.[7] Sextus was profiting by the death of the dictator, and by his agreement with the Roman authorities, to claim for himself Caesar's position.

The retention of SEX. in his titulature indicates that the adoption of *Imperator* as a personal *praenomen* had not been considered after March 44,[8] any more than before it. Yet its use by Sextus, as a prefix, at least implies a similar use by the dictator, or an informal one by his supporters. These conclusions accord with the often maligned and rejected[9] statement of Suetonius that Julius received the *praenomen Imperatoris, cognomen patris patriae*.[10] The latter of these phrases shows that only 'prefix' and 'suffix' are meant,[11] and supplies no evidence for the view that the title was a proper name, rather than a definition of competence.[12] Sextus's emphasis on *Imperator* does not suit Kahrstedt's suggestion[13] that, since this title was only granted him by the senate as a deliberate substitute for his real desire, the name of *rex*, Caesar neglected it. On the other hand, Radin's[14] reasons for believing *rex* to be etymologically the less autocratic

---

[1] In the present Chapters the word in this new sense is spelt with a capital letter.
[2] Cf. recent interpretation of a *denarius* by Liegle, *Transactions of International Numismatic Congress of 1936*, p. 212.
[3] Cf. below, p. 418. For Pompey himself see pp. 411 ff., 438 n.
[4] See above, p. 23 n. 1.
[5] Cf. Carcopino, *Histoire romaine*, II, p. 1001.
[6] Cf. McFayden, p. 3 n. 12.
[7] Cf. Ulrich, *Pietas (pius) als politischer Begriff*, Diss. Breslau, 1930, p. 12.
[8] Cf. von Premerstein, p. 246, cf. n. 6; McFayden, pp. 10 f.; *pace* Mommsen, *St. R.* II^3, p. 767.
[9] As by Mommsen, l.c.
[10] *Caes.* 76.
[11] Cf. McFayden, p. 13 n. 25.
[12] See below, p. 415.
[13] *GGA.* 1938, p. 21.
[14] *Studi Riccobono*, II, pp. 24, 28.

of the two titles are equally tenuous;[1] the royal implications of *Imperator* arose, not from antiquarianism, but from the authoritarian conduct of those who bore it during the present period. Our three first coins have demonstrated that two transitions at least, from title of salutation to title of competence, and from title of competence to prefix, were accepted even at the Republican headquarters before the end of 44.

[1] Cf. de Labriolle, *Revue des études latines*, 1933, p. 263. Alternative origins for the word are suggested by Basanoff, *Rev. arch.* x, 1937, pp. 43 ff; Rudolph, *Neue Jahrbücher für Antike und deutsche Bildung*, 1, 1939, p. 145; vide also Sherwin-White, pp. 121 f.

B. THE *IMPERIUM MAIUS* ON WHICH THE TITLE OF *IMPERATOR* WAS BASED

It is now necessary to define the implications of the novel title of competence to which these coinages have borne witness.

In the first place, the literary authorities confirm the numismatic evidence to the effect that the curious convention by which holders of *imperium* could only bear the title *imperator* after salutation[1] was relaxed in the last years of the Republic, when it was abundantly clear that the old order had gone.[2] The title now came to be the appellation of commanders with *imperium*,[3] as even Dio at a much later date realised.[4] Sulla had already been characterised vaguely and informally as 'the' *Imperator*,[5] and a municipality described Pompey in the same way[6] at a time when his last salutation title had been obliterated from his style by a triumph.[7] Thus Cicero can now say, in general terms: *universus populus Romanus..unum sibi ad...bellum Cn. Pompeium Imperatorem depoposcit*.[8] The Table of Heraclea likewise uses the word as the equivalent of 'commander'.[9] The dying Scipio's *mot* was *Imperator bene se habet*,[10] and Labienus even inscribes on his coins the shocking title *Parthicus Imperator*—the Parthian Marshal.[11] Significant too is Cicero's sneer at the grandiose new title illustrated by the coins, when he thanks the dictator for allowing him a salutation *cum ipse Imperator in toto imperio populi Romani* unus esset.[12] In none of these instances has the title any connection with salutation by the troops: in all of them it refers to high commands, and to the *imperium* by which they were undertaken. In the last passage Cicero permits himself a *jeu de mots* on the two conceptions, now allied, of the *imperium populi Romani*[13] and the *imperium Caesaris*. In Rome, the new use of *Imperator* may still have been of an unofficial character, as its neglect by Caesar's own coins suggests. But at the Pompeian headquarters the *de facto* arrogations of the dictator were applied openly to his deceased rival, and published on the coinage of that rival's sons.

[1] Cf. Nesselhauf, *Klio*, 1937, p. 315; McFayden, p. 2; Appian, *BC*. II, 44.
[2] Cf. Syme, *RR*. p. 8.
[3] Cf. Levi, *Rivista di filologia*, 1932, p. 207; Strack, *Auf dem Wege zum nationalpolitischen Gymnasium*, VI, 1938, p. 10 n. 12.
[4] This is the point of his distinction in XLIII, 44. 2, as seen by McFayden, p. 8, cf. n. 6. Zmigryder-Konopka, *VIIIe Congr. int. des sciences historiques*, 1938, I, p. 24, interprets a definition in LII, 41. 3 (τὴν τὸ κράτος διασημαίνουσαν) in the same way: but it is more probable that Dio is there referring to the *Herrscheramt* (cf. von Premerstein, p. 260) as he knew it.
[5] de Sanctis, *Studi Riccobono*, II, p. 60.
[6] *ILS*. 877 (Auximum dedication). F. E. Adcock has pointed out to me the dangers of utilising this for more exact constitutional deductions. Cf. also Hammond, p. 225 n. 8. The usage of this earlier period needs a thorough reconsideration.
[7] McFayden, p. 5 n. 17.
[8] *De Imperio Cn. Pompei*, 15. 44.
[9] I, 121. [10] Val. Max. III, 2. 13.
[11] *BMCR*. II, p. 500. 131; cf. Tarn, *CAH*. X, p. 47.
[12] *Pro Ligario*, 3.
[13] For this vide Levi, *Rivista di filologia*, 1932, p. 207; von Premerstein, p. 127; Sherwin-White, p. 156 n. 4.

RULE BY *IMPERIUM MAIUS*, 49–28 B.C.

So the title *Imperator*, in its new sense, meant, in the realistic years of the late Republic, what it said. Irrespective of salutations, it signified the Commander, that is, the holder of a particularly important *imperium*.[1] Used as a suffix, then, it bore the connotation of 'a' war-lord, and, as a prefix, of 'the' War-lord.[2] These were new ideas. But the Republican *imperium* was a familiar and finite conception which did not warrant such novelties: the title could not have been derived from ordinary proconsular or consular *imperia*. It is, therefore, necessary to ask what change the *imperium* underwent in the 'forties to create the new use of *Imperator*.

It is not difficult to find the answer. Caesar's dictatorial *imperium* which began in 49 B.C. was an *imperium maius*. This had not been the case with the informal *conspiratio* which has invited false comparisons by its posthumous title 'First Triumvirate'.[3] Again, when Pompey had governed an unusually large *provincia* by his *legati*,[4] it had indeed been a step forward, and perhaps even an 'anomalous and arbitrary' one;[5] but, after due allowance for Caesar's propaganda,[6] it was not actually unconstitutional, since *provinciae* of any size could be voted.[7] Although it was clear enough that the Republic was breaking down,[8] Pompey did not claim to represent the entire Roman State.[9] An *imperium maius*, however, was of a new quality, since it controlled the *provinciae* of others, and subordinated *imperia* to an *imperium*.[10] This was certainly the character of Caesar's *imperium*, by which—*cum ipse Imperator in toto imperio populi Romani unus esset*[11]—he could nevertheless permit men like Cicero and Q. Fabius Maximus[12] to triumph, since their *imperium* was not abolished by his, but overridden. Caesar inaugurated the new constitutional era of δυναστεῖαι[13] by concentrating in himself the ultimate responsibilities of the whole government.[14] (The same principle is illustrated by coinages. M. Acilius(?) in Macedonia, although a holder of *imperium*, strikes

[1] This evidence disposes of the view of Andersen, *Neue Deutsche Forschungen*, CXCVI, 1938, p. 34, that the title of the *Herrscheramt*—lacking *rechtliche Befugnisse*—was already fully established before the Ides of March. Such anachronisms as applied to the *régimes* of 49–28 are particularly misleading—as is the statement, true only of a later period, that the title was unconnected with the *imperium* (cf. Momigliano, *Augustus* [1938], p. 197, etc., etc.).
[2] On this conception, cf. Syme, *RR*. p. 310.
[3] Cf. Sanders, *Memoirs of the American Academy in Rome*, X, 1932, p. 55.
[4] Cf. Hammond, p. 10.
[5] Syme, *RR*. p. 42.   [6] E.g. *BC*. I, 85.
[7] See below, pp. 419 f. On Pompey as forerunner of Augustus see (among a vast literature) Gagé, *Rev. historique*, CLXXVII, 1936, pp. 324, 336; Syme, *Papers of the British School at Rome*, XIV (N.S. I), 1938, p. 3.

[8] Cf. Syme, l.c. p. 8.
[9] Id. *RR*. p. 190.
[10] For a definition of *imperium maius* vide Cic. *Att.* IV, 1. 7; cf. Mommsen, *St. R.* I³, pp. 25 f.; Lauria, *Studi Bonfante*, II, pp. 488, 491; de Francisci, *Augustus* (1938), p. 83.
[11] See above, p. 411 n. 12.
[12] Cf. Brassloff, *PW*. VI, 1791.
[13] Dio LII, 1. 1; cf. Syme, *RR*. p. 324 n. 6. It cannot be determined whether Tacitus (*Ann.* III, 28) reckons the era of military anarchy—*continua... discordia, non mos non ius*—from 52 or 49 B.C.; cf. Syme, *Papers of the British School at Rome*, XIV (N.S. I), 1938, p. 8.
[14] Cf. Syme, *RR*. l.c. It will be shown below (p. 420) that the authority of consuls does not warrant the definition by Boak (*Amer. Hist. Rev.* 1918, p. 23) as *imperium maius*.

THE *IMPERIUM MAIUS*

orichalcum with the head, not of his governor, but of Caesar,[1] whose name, too, regularly appears on the silver of lesser *imperatores*.[2] Earlier Caesar had qualified, by the loyal initiative of Pansa Caetronianus at Apamea, Nicaea and Nicomedia,[3] for the first portrait of a living Roman on coins signed by a governor.[4]) Now even apart from the startling fact that Caesar's *imperium* was *in perpetuum*, such a command practically disposed of the accepted Republican view that an *imperium* was responsible solely to the sovereign people.[5] Caesar's complete cynicism in choosing it is revealed by a *mot* in which he dismissed the *res publica*, from which his *imperium* was constitutionally derived, as *appellatio modo sine corpore ac specie*;[6] and by his sarcastic advice to the academic L. Pontius Aquila[7] to ask him, Caesar, for the *res publica* when he wanted it back.[8] Furthermore, the *Lex de maiestate*, of which Julius was probably the author,[9] safeguarded not the *res publica* but himself. Nevertheless, a façade of adequate respectability usually concealed the state of mind which these sneers reveal, and it was Caesar's claim that the senate had refused his offer to take a share in the administration.[10] Moreover, his choice of the dictatorship had the advantage that its *imperium maius* was actually recognised by the constitution.[11] Thus he could accept it without difficulty only a few months after sneering at Pompey's clumsier but less dangerous expedients as *novi generis imperia*.[12] Levi[13] goes farther, and claims that it was defined by the traditional formula *rei gerendae causa*;[14] even if this should be corrected to *rei publicae constituendae*,[15] a precedent was probably supplied by Sulla.[16] At all events, the constitution was mobilised for its own destruction by the weapon of the *imperium maius*. It may be added that since Sex. Pompeius endeavoured to step into the dictator's shoes,[17] he too must have claimed (and as far as possible exercised) an *imperium maius* of the same order.

This, then, was the exceptional feature which converted the *imperium* of a proconsul into the autocratic command of a war-lord, and these were the war-lords to define whose position the new title of *Imperator* was invented. It was by virtue of the *imperium*

---

[1] See above, p. 13.
[2] E.g. *BMCR*. II, p. 559. 5.
[3] See above, p. 396.
For Flamininus, whose head had appeared without a signature, vide Babelon, *Monnaies de la République romaine*, II, p. 391. Cf. above, pp. 151, 241.
[4] Cf. McFayden, p. 26.
[5] Festus 43 L; cf. Zmigryder-Konopka, *VIIIe Congr. int. des sciences historiques*, 1938, I, p. 25.
[6] Suet. *Caes*. 77; cf. Wickert, *Klio*, 1937, pp. 249f.
[7] On whom vide Pais, *Studi storici per l'Antichità classica*, V, 1912, pp. 129 ff.
[8] Suet. l.c. 78; cf. Zmigryder-Konopka, l.c. p. 23.
[9] See above, p. 405.
[10] See above, p. 6.

[11] Livy IV, 31; cf. Greenidge, *Roman Public Life*, p. 191; L. Lange, *Kleine Schriften*, II, pp. 302, 304.
[12] *BC*. I, 85; cf. Wickert, l.c. p. 247.
[13] *Atti del primo Congresso Nazionale di Studi romani*, I, 1929, pp. 353 ff.; cf. *La constituzione romana dai Gracchi a Giulio Cesare*, pp. 207 ff.; *Athenaeum*, 1936, p. 210.
[14] For this formula, vide Last, *CAH*. IX, pp. 283f.
[15] Cf. Adcock, *CAH*. IX, p. 900 n. 6; Homo, *Roman Political Institutions*, p. 191; Syme, *RR*. p. 52.
[16] Cf. Last, l.c.; *pace* McFayden, *Washington Univ. Studies in Language and Literature*, III, 1930, p. 65. For the pretensions of the title vide Syme, *RR*. pp. 52, 160.
[17] See above, p. 409.

maius that the entire administration of the Empires of Caesar and Sex. Pompeius was carried out—without reference to the senate, as the coinage of Balbus at Corduba shows.[1] But the lesson of its danger was ignored. Little more than a year after the Ides, powers of similar character—though not of universal scope—were conferred on Brutus and Cassius.[2] No doubt, in view of their scruples,[3] only a tenure for the duration of the emergency was envisaged; but it was by just this *imperium* that Brutus overrode the proconsul Q. Hortensius, who coined for him at Thessalonica.[4] Whether or not these Republicans used the *Imperator* title in its new sense, its close connection with the *imperium maius*, demonstrated for Caesar, becomes clearer still in the ten years[5] of the second Triumvirate. Then too the existence of power and title alike is amply documented. That a true *imperium maius* was granted to the *tresviri rei publicae constituendae* is shown by the vote of a triumph in 38 both to Antony and to Ventidius[6] for the victories of the latter. The lack of precedents created a preliminary uncertainty as to his status;[7] the final recognition that both could triumph signalises the formalisation of *imperium maius*.[8] Subsequently Antony allows his commanders many salutations,[9] but, for their most distinguished victories, continues to share with them the titles.[10] Octavian also showed his acceptance of this principle by allowing salutations to certain of his subordinates.[11] It is scarcely necessary to add that, as long as they were at large, Lepidus and Sex. Pompeius were in no way behindhand with their claims. But L. Antonius Pietas, according to the sources of Appian,[12] deliberately contrasted the revolutionary *imperium maius* with his own consular *imperium*.[13] This gesture is the exception which proves the rule of *imperium maius* by all other governments of the period. Until 33 B.C. at least, it was the basis of every executive activity. The dictatorship was abolished in 44,[14] but its vicious characteristic remained—and indeed so increased that, in retrospect, even the rule of Caesar seemed a Golden Age.[15]

It is therefore not an accident that we have, from all sides, evidence that the new title of *Imperator* persisted simultaneously. The earliest document of the period is, like those of the previous decade, a neglected coin. ANTONIVS IMP., on an Italian *aes* piece struck in 40–39 by L. Sempronius Atratinus,[16] is half-way between *M. Antonius Imp.* and *Imp. Antonius*. The exceptional omission of Antony's personal *praenomen* on an

---

[1] See above, p. 6.
[2] Cf. Charlesworth, *CAH*. x, p. 15; Syme, *Anatolian Studies to Buckler*, p. 323.
[3] Cf. Syme, *RR*. p. 320.
[4] See above, p. 33.
[5] For its renewal in 37, see above, p. 46.
[6] Dio XLIX, 21.   [7] Id. XLVIII, 41.
[8] *Konsulgleich*—Siber, *Sav. Z.* 1935, p. 131—is not enough. Gomme, *European Civilisation*, p. 153 n. 1, wrongly implies that the lesser commanders lacked *imperium*, i.e. that the triumvirs merely possessed large *provinciae*.
[9] Cf. Ganter, p. 45; McFayden, p. 36 n. 44.
[10] Sources in Charlesworth, *CAH*. x, p. 50 n. 1: also Caland, *De nummis M. Antonii IIIviri*, pp. 10 f.; von Sallet, *ZfN*. 1884, p. 169; Bahrfeldt, *BMB*. 1905, pp. 332 f.
[11] See below, p. 424.   [12] *BC*. v, 19. 74, etc.
[13] Syme, *RR*. p. 208 n. 1. For a later weakening of the contrast see below, pp. 419, 437 f. n. 2.
[14] Cf. Syme, *RR*. p. 188.
[15] Dio XLVII, 15. 4; cf. Syme, *Papers of the British School at Rome*, XIV (N.S. I), 1938, p. 11.
[16] See above, p. 37.

THE *IMPERIUM MAIUS*

official issue is only explicable by the assumption that he, too, was imbued with the new constitutional idea: *Imperator* is a title of competence, and that competence is the *imperium maius*. Not more than a year later, as we might expect, Octavian also openly took the new title. After certain preparatory steps,[1] it first appears on his *denarii* of the year 38;[2] in the following year, it helped to tide him over the delay in the renewal of the triumvirate.[3] But the appellation, as it now is, marks a further advance. It is no longer a suffix, like Antony's title, and it is no longer merely a prefix, like that of Sextus: IMP. CAESAR differs from IMP. SEX. MAGNVS in that the personal *praenomen* is abandoned, never officially to return.[4] *Imperator* took its place. This change is emphasised by an entry in the official *Fasti Capitolini*, dating from c. 36 B.C.,[5] in which Octavian, for his consulship in 43, is retrospectively described, with accuracy, as C. IVLIVS C. F. [*C. n. Caesar qui*] POSTEA IMP. [*Caesar appellatus*] EST. His successful assumption of the new *praenomen* is emphasised by its avoidance, from now on, by his colleagues and enemies. Antony lost interest in Roman constitutional affairs, and fell back on ordinary titles of salutation;[6] Sextus, his own thunder as *Imperator* stolen, tried a novel experiment of his own by the adoption of Magnus as a *praenomen*.[7] Octavian was thus secure in the possession of the name *Imperator* as his peculiar and personal attribute.[8] After him, Tiberius never ventured to accept it,[9] and when it reappeared under Nero it was not a proper *praenomen*, since the personal

---

[1] Cf. Gagé, *Mél. d'arch. et d'hist.* XLVII, 1930, p. 172; Syme, *RR.* pp. 113 n. 1, 202 (DIVI F., etc.).

[2] Cf. von Premerstein, p. 249, etc. That supposed earlier examples are anachronistic is shown by Volkmann, *ap.* von Premerstein, l.c. n. 2, McFayden, p. 33. For the experimental title IMP. DIVI IVLI F. ITER. see Hohl, *GGA.* 1936, p. 136; Berve, *Hermes*, LXI, 1936, p. 251 n. 3; Wilcken, *Aegyptus*, Suppl. V, p. 108, correcting Schulz, *ZfN.* 1935, p. 103, who reads TER. It is inconceivable that both ITER. and TER. occur on precisely similar coins (as Newby, pp. 6 f.; cf. Mattingly, *CR.* 1938, p. 237). A similar order is found on a colonial coin; see above, p. 218. It seems probable that Octavian at first maintained the characteristic fiction that salutations were the immediate *raison d'être* of his title, especially as Agrippa refused these (Dio XLVIII, 49. 4; cf. Hammond, p. 50) as though they were responsible for the new title. It has been shown, however, that the real basis was different. Pre-Actian manifestations of the title were surprisingly unknown to Schöner, *Acta seminarii philologici Erlangensis*, II, 1881, p. 452.

[3] Cf. von Premerstein, pp. 258, 260; *pace* Levi, *Rivista di filologia*, 1938, p. 115.

[4] A probable exception in the second Edict to Rhosus (Roussel, *Syria*, XV, 1934, p. 34), apparently of 36–5 B.C. (Levi, *Riv. di filologia*, 1938, p. 114; cf. below, p. 433), is cleverly explained by Levi (l.c.) as due to the collegiate character of the Edict, in which the titulatures of the two triumvirs are made as uniform as possible.

[5] *CIL.* I, p. 28.

[6] *BMCR.* II, pp. 520 ff.

[7] Chief material is *BMCR.* II, p. 560. 7 ff. and *ILS.* III, 8891. Exact date uncertain: cf. Hadas, *Sextus Pompey*, p. 40; von Premerstein, p. 250 (4); Liegle, *Transactions of Int. Numismatic Congress of 1936*, p. 213; Mras, *Wiener Studien*, XXV, pp. 288 ff.; Rosenberg, *PW.* IX, 1145, for divergent opinions.

[8] This seems to qualify the otherwise salutary observation of Kornemann, *Gercke-Nordens Einleitung in die Altertumswissenschaft*, III, 2, 1933, pp. 71 ff., that Octavian was, during the triumvirate, as openly a Hellenistic βασιλεύς as Antony.

[9] See also below, p. 440.

praenomen was not superseded.[1] The same is true of the uses by Galba,[2] Otho[3] and Titus[4]—so closely connected with the first *princeps* was the distinctive name. Nevertheless, Octavian enhanced its glory by an obvious manœuvre, when he attributed it retrospectively in the same autocratic sense to the divine Julius,[5] just as Cn. and Sex. Pompeius, *Imperatores filii*, had applied the title to their own dead father. Octavian, then, was *the* Marshal both by hereditary and by personal right. His new name was a direct and conscious derivative of the active *imperium maius*, which had supplied also the titles of Caesar, Antony and their rivals. By its assumption, Octavian made himself inseparable from the *imperium maius*, just as Sulla's offspring had consciously associated themselves with their father's renowned Fortuna[6] by the adoption of the *praenomina* Faustus[7] and Felix.[8] Thus he revived the ancient connection of *praenomina* with a feeling of power.[9] This was a remarkable piece of statesmanship:[10] *provinciae* might be voted and lapse, but it was difficult to see how a man whose very name signified the special *imperium* could ever lack it.[11] Nor was this a rash renewal of the dictator's mistake: the *Lex Titia*, by its temporal limits and collegiality, had avoided the odium of dictatorship,[12] and the popular vote was emphasised.[13]

Sextus's counterblast to Octavian, the *praenomen* Magnus, duly stressed his inheritance, and conveniently avoided the question of a *provincia*. Thus if the fundamental quality of Octavian was to be *imperium*—'rule', that of Sextus was to be *magnitudo*—'greatness'. Comparable is the slogan *Pietas* which L. Antonius had incorporated into his name (though only as a cognomen) at Perusia.[14] That Sextus's *praenomen*, like Octavian's, was intended to have royal implications is shown by its retention by descendants[15] and its removal from one of them by Caligula,[16] although in his time its significance was merely antiquarian. By the fortunes of war in 36 B.C., it left the future to Octavian's *praenomen Imperatoris*,[17] which was based directly on military *imperium maius*.

When the second *quinquennium* elapsed at the end of 33, Antony had recourse to an

---

[1] 'Nero' is the formal *praenomen* (cf. Mommsen, *Neues Rheinisches Museum für Philologie*, 1860, Bd. 15, p. 169).

[2] *BMC. Imp.* 2 ff.   [3] Ibid. 1 ff.

[4] M. and S. II, pp. 116 ff.

[5] E.g. *Fasti Vallenses* (*CIL*. I², p. 140); cf. von Premerstein, p. 246.

[6] Cf. Berlinger, *Zur inoffiziellen Titulatur*, Diss. Breslau, 1935, p. 9; Carcopino, *Sylla*, pp. 107 ff.

[7] Cf. Mommsen, *Römische Forschungen*, I, 1864, p. 34 n. 50.

[8] Cf. Levi, *Rivista di filologia*, 1932, p. 218.

[9] Mommsen, l.c. p. 43.

[10] It is traditionally associated with Agrippa, whose name appears on the reverse of the *denarii*.

[11] This was a kind of safeguard against the temporary character of his successive powers—emphasised by Sprey, *Mnemosyne*, III, 1935, pp. 291 ff.

[12] Cf. Levi, *Athenaeum*, XXVI, 1939, p. 88; id. *Rivista di filologia*, 1939, p. 123.

[13] Appian, *BC*. IV, 8.

[14] Cf. Syme, *RR*. p. 208; Charlesworth, *CAH*. X, p. 28.

[15] Cf. Marini, *Fasti Arvalium*, p. 75.

[16] Suet. *Cal*. 35; cf. Mommsen, *Neues Rheinisches Museum*, 1860, Bd. 15, p. 169.

[17] Octavian appropriated another of Sextus's titles too, *custos terrae marisque*: *IGRR*. IV, 309, 315; cf. Syme, *RR*. p. 473.

illegal prolongation of his triumviral powers,[1] but with apology and a promise to abandon them at the earliest possible opportunity. Octavian must be taken at his word, as far as the letter of the law went,[2] when he denies such a prolongation.[3] In 32, then, he possessed no triumviral *imperium maius*: L. Cornificius and Ap. Claudius Pulcher triumphed in their own right.[4] Furthermore, the *coniuratio* of that year[5] was in no way connected with this *imperium* and did not at once take its place,[6] but was an oath of personal fealty, as of clients to a *patronus*, against a private *inimicitia* with Antony.[7] Nor can any trace of an *imperium* be detected in Octavian's actions during the year, which reveal a considerable embarrassment, not appreciably lessened by the alleged spontaneity of the *coniuratio*[8] and by the fact that his very name expressed rule.[9] The year 32 witnessed an exceptional break in the *imperium*, whose renewals in various forms carried it without a second gap to its fifty-seventh year. Attention was diverted from its momentary absence by an unusually vicious outburst of propaganda.[10]

In the following year the threads can be gathered again. It is possible to demonstrate that, from 31 to 28, the *régime* of *imperium maius*, expressed by the special appellative of *Imperator*, continued in the same constitutional forms as had prevailed since its inauguration during the dictatorship. The need for this appellative to be confirmed by the senate in 29[11]—after the triumph of that year[12]—and its subsequent publication on an extensive coinage[13] entirely accord with its close connection with the *imperium* and clearly recall the latter's old meaning. By immemorial tradition a triumph implied the abandonment of the *imperium* by which it had been earned,[14] and such an abandonment is known to have taken place in 29.[15] Thus the senatorial decree was in no sense a tautological repeti-

---

[1] Dio L, 7. 1; cf. Berve, *Hermes*, LXXI, 1936, p. 251; Syme, *RR*. p. 279.

[2] For the discrepancy between this and the real position vide Syme, *RR*. p. 277 n. 6.

[3] *RG.* 7—*per continuos annos decem*—cf. Tarn and Charlesworth, *CAH.* x, p. 94, etc.; *pace* Wilcken, *Berlin SB.* 1925, p. 83. Kolbe, *Hermes*, XLIX, 1914, pp. 274 f.; Rice Holmes, *Architect*, I, pp. 231 ff.; van Groningen, *Mnemosyne*, 1926, pp. 1 ff.; Roos, *Tijdschr. voor Geschiedenis*, XLIX, 1929, pp. 350 ff. [4] Cf. Syme, l.c. p. 292.

[5] On the question of its exact date see (most recently) Last, *JRS.* XXVIII, 1938, p. 213.

[6] Cf. Glauning, *Die Anhängerschaft des M. Antonius und des Oktavian*, p. 44 n. 1; *pace* Caspari, *CQ.* v, 1911, pp. 234 f.

[7] First apparently seen by Markowski, *Eos*, XXXIV, 1933, pp. 477 ff.; cf. von Premerstein, p. 40; id. *Phil. Woch.* 1935, p. 316; Piganiol, *Journal des Savants*, 1937, pp. 163 f.; Stone, *CR.* 1938, p. 35;

Kahrstedt, *GGA.* 1938, p. 8; Volkmann, *Forschungen und Fortschritte*, 13, XXX, 1938, p. 349.

[8] Salutary remarks on the real character of these familiar plebiscites are made by Syme, *RR*. pp. 284 ff.

[9] A municipality does not omit the *praenomen Imperatoris* in an inscription of this year (*ILS.* 77; cf. von Premerstein, p. 249), but Octavian himself had for some years been anticipating this emergency by giving publicity to the alternative title CAESAR DIVI F. (see above, p. 49).

[10] Cf. Scott, *Memoirs of the American Academy in Rome*, 1933, pp. 37 ff.

[11] Dio LII, 41. 3; cf. von Premerstein, p. 252, etc.

[12] Cf. Kornemann, *Gnomon*, 1938, p. 563.

[13] Cf. Mattingly, *JRS.* 1919, p. 218.

[14] Cf. McFayden, p. 5 n. 17, etc.

[15] Cf. Berve, *Hermes*, LXI, 1936, p. 250; Barwick, *Philologus*, XCI, 1936, p. 352; Kornemann, *Klio*, 1938, pp. 84 f.

tion of the assumption of the name in c. 38. The same close connection with *imperium*, which existed in 38 and 29, explains another phenomenon which has sometimes been noted with surprise:[1] all the other elements of the titulature of Augustus are recorded in the *Res Gestae*, but there is no mention whatever of the *praenomen Imperatoris*. The scheme of the *Res Gestae* is complete, but economical: the *praenomen* is merely an expression of *imperium*, and thus the *princeps* merely says (of Jan. 1, 43 B.C.[2]) *senatus.... imperium mihi dedit*.[3] There is no need to mention the *praenomen*, since it was constitutionally dependent upon *imperium*. Nor can it reasonably be objected that, since Octavian did not already in 43 deduce the title from this *imperium*, the latter does not explain the absence of the *praenomen* from the *Res Gestae*: he, like his contemporaries,[4] indulged frequently in tendencious misinterpretations of the near past. His propaganda is full of them,[5] but particularly relevant is his application of this very title to Caesar on official documents,[6] though the dictator's own coinage had invariably avoided the prefix. In the present case the starting point of his campaigns in 43 *in libertatem*[7] is highly suitable for such a perversion of accuracy; indeed, its anniversary remained for centuries an occasion for celebration.[8] Furthermore, not only does the *princeps*, in his *Res Gestae*, refrain from mentioning the *praenomen*, but he does not allude to any of the subsequent renewals and readjustments of the *imperium*:[9] these, and the title which had accompanied them, were, for purposes of propaganda, entirely subordinated to the heroic investment in 43.[10] Both title and *imperium* are correctly and characteristically comprehended in the single statement concerning that. Augustus's evident desire to avoid emphasis on the *praenomen* is to be explained by the eclipse of the powers for which it stood: it will be shown that, when the *Res Gestae* were compiled, the appellation no longer played any role except to recall the victories won in the past epoch of military rule—namely, the period initiated by the campaigns *in libertatem*, continued under the *Lex Titia* and by its renewal, and concluded in the period 31–28.[11]

From 31 to 28, then, the special name of *Imperator* still played the same important part in official publicity as it had during the preceding period. It is only to be expected that the *imperium maius* will be found also as before. There is, indeed,

[1] E.g. von Premerstein, p. 255; McFayden, p. 43.
[2] Cf. Weber, *Princeps*, 1, p. 145; Syme, *RR*. p. 167, etc.
[3] *RG*. 1.
[4] E.g. Cn. and Sex. Pompeius (p. 409).
[5] Best appreciated by Syme, *RR*.
[6] E.g. Fasti Vallenses, *CIL*. 1², p. 140, etc.
[7] *RG*. 1—*eo nomine*.
[8] Cf. Andersen, *Neue Deutsche Forschungen*, CXCVI, 1938, p. 51.
[9] Strack, *Auf dem Wege zum nationalpolitischen Gymnasium*, VI, 1938, p. 11, says that these are omitted as being pro- (un-) magisterial. But the grant of 43, which is included, was no less so. Syme, *RR*. p. 337, suggests that the *imperium* of 23 was so dominant that it was studiously omitted: but its powers were really very limited (see below, pp. 427 ff.).
[10] E.g. *ILS*. 108, *eo die Caesar primum fasces sumpsit*, and, with a play on the meanings of *imperium*, id. 112, *qua die primum imperium orbis terrarum auspicatus est* (cf. above, p. 411).
[11] See below, p. 424.

THE *IMPERIUM MAIUS* 419

conclusive evidence that the campaigns of 31 and 30 were undertaken with an *imperium maius*, though this is generally neglected, especially by those who have recently established the informality of the *coniuratio*. Without the *imperium* Octavian could neither have received his salutation in 31,¹ nor have triumphed for Actium and Egypt.² Again, if there was a private *inimicitia* against Antony, there was also a public *bellum* against Cleopatra,³ and a war needed a commander. In the light of these considerations it is necessary to reinterpret a passage in the Res Gestae: *Iuravit in mea verba tota Italia sponte sua et me belli, quo vici ad Actium, ducem depoposcit. Iuravit in eadem verba provinciae Galliae Hispaniae Africa Sicilia Sardinia. Qui sub signis meis tum militaverunt*, etc.⁴ *Belli ducem depoposcit* is a familiar phrase, and often a technical one. We find elsewhere *universus populus Romanus....unum sibi ad...bellum Cn. Pompeium Imperatorem depoposcit*,⁵ and *respublica ab Augusto ducem in bellum poposcit Tiberium*.⁶ In those cases it naturally refers to an *imperium*;⁷ it must also in the Res Gestae. The style of Augustus is not tautological, and neither of the co-ordinate clauses separated by *et* can be otiose: they express different actions, the *coniuratio* and the grant of a *provincia* respectively. This distinction is emphasised by the repetition of the first clause, but not the second, in connection with the provinces—which had no say in grants of *imperium*. Augustus can speak of *signa mea* only because he still had *imperium*.

Furthermore, his command was still in the form of an *imperium maius*. C. Carrinas became governor of Gallia Comata in 30 or more probably 31,⁸ and for his victories had to share a triumph with Octavian.⁹ If even Farther Gaul was within the scope of an *imperium maius* intended for Eastern campaigns, it is clear that this was universal: since Antony had been legally deprived of all his powers,¹⁰ it comprised his provinces also.

A prerequisite for the further definition of this *imperium maius* is the abolition of theories of several 'cumulative' *imperia*.¹¹ The *princeps* commanded in 31 and subsequent years by virtue of his consulship and that alone. Cicero twice makes it quite clear that consuls possessed authority in any province which they visited: *nam..cum imperio sunt...ipsi consules, quibus more maiorum concessum est vel omnes adire provincias*;¹² and again, *omnes enim in consulis iure et imperio debent esse provinciae*.¹³ These were his rulings as regards the consuls of 49 and 43 respectively;¹⁴ both pairs left Italy, and, between those years, Dolabella did likewise in 44.¹⁵ Nor can Cicero's words be dis-

¹ Cf. Mattingly, *BMC. Imp*. p. xcii.
² Cf. Charlesworth, *CAH*. x, p. 119.
³ This is admitted by von Premerstein, p. 41. For the *iustum bellum* vide Baviera, *Archivio giuridico Filippo Serafini*, N.S. 1, 1898.
⁴ *RG*. 25.
⁵ Cicero, *De Imperio Cn. Pompeii*, 15. 44: see also above, p. 411.   ⁶ Velleius, II, 112. 2.
⁷ Von Premerstein, p. 43 n. 1, admits a *Kommando*.
⁸ Ganter, p. 10; *PIR*². II, 105. 447; McFayden, p. 36 n. 44; cf. Syme, *RR*. p. 302 n. 5.

⁹ Dio LI, 21. 6.   ¹⁰ Dio L, 4. 3.
¹¹ Cf. below, pp. 425, 437.
¹² *Att*. VIII, 15. 3; cf. de Francisci, *Augustus* (1938), p. 75.
¹³ *IV Phil*. 9.
¹⁴ The latter commanded in the campaign of Mutina, in Cisalpine Gaul, which was still *militiae* (cf. Hardy, *EHR*. XXXI, 1916, p. 357). Cf. the comment of P. Lentulus (Cic. *Fam*. XII, 14. 5; cf. Syme, *RR*. p. 162 n. 1).
¹⁵ Appian, *BC*. III, 24. 57; Dio XLV, 12. 2, XLVII, 29. 1.

missed as partisan antiquarianism,[1] since, as Balsdon has convincingly shown,[2] at least ten consuls acted in accordance with them between 79 and 53 B.C. Sulla's dyarchic distinction between *domi* and *militiae* is a fiction of Mommsen's.[3] A consul was entitled to command in any province[4] if his departure from Italy was permitted by a *lex curiata*.[5] It was not, therefore, anomalous for Caius Caesar to hold a provincial command during his consulship of A.D. 1.[6] There is no reason or need to postulate cumulations of *imperia*;[7] it is very doubtful whether any Roman of this date would have understood such a concept,[8] since the *imperium* of proconsuls and consuls alike was described as *consulare*.[9] It was natural for a consul to command the troops.[10] For precisely the same reason it is not accurate to say that salutations as *imperator* were limited to proconsuls:[11] C. Pansa Caetronianus was saluted when consul,[12] and, two years earlier, Q. Fabius Maximus was consul for a fortnight before he triumphed and so abandoned his title of salutation.[13] The late Republican version of the title was also not inconsistent with the consulship.[14]

[1] Cf. Syme, *RR*. p. 162 n. 1.

[2] *JRS*. xxix, 1939, pp. 58 f., 63 n. 50.

[3] *St. R.* II, pp. 94 f.; *Gesammelte Schriften*, IV, p. 130, followed (most recently) by Strack, l.c. p. 13; Hammond, p. 9; Lombardi, *Civiltà Romana*, x, 1939, p. 113. Those who fine down Mommsen's 'law' to a 'convention' are listed by Balsdon, l.c., p. 58 n. 11.

[4] It is not, however, true to say with Boak (*American Historical Review*, xxiv, 1918, p. 23) that consuls automatically possessed universal *imperium maius*, since (1) Cicero only says that they commanded where they were (i.e. not *in absentia*, like holders of *i. m.*); (2) a specific *provincia militiae* had to be voted, as to Augustus in 27 (see below, p. 426). Cicero's statements therefore, although naturally opportunistic, do not quite warrant condemnation as 'the most impudent sophistries' (Syme, *RR*. p. 162). The distinction between the *imperium* of consuls and the *imperium maius* of triumvirs was underlined for publicity purposes by L. Antonius (cf. Syme, l.c. p. 208 n. 1). Thus it is hardly true to say that Augustus could control, by his *imperium consulare* of 27, the governors of provinces not in his *provincia* (as Syme, l.c. p. 315: see below, p. 426).

[5] For this stipulation vide Syme, *RR*. p. 279 n. 2, who points out that in this respect the consuls of 49 (like those of 32) were not in order.

[6] Stuart Jones, *CAH*. x, p. 156.

[7] Last, *JRS*. xxviii, 1938, p. 213, accepts this view when he says that the common view of *imp. procos.* +*cos.* after 19 B.C. 'approaches the incredible'.

[8] Cf. Sunden, *De romerska antikviteterna*[2], p. 215, for the *naïveté* of most contemporary constitutional thought. In the case of Pompey in 52 such a cumulation might seem to have occurred because Pompey, already *pro consule*, became consul. But *de jure* it was now as consul, not *pro consule*, that he continued to govern Spain.

[9] Cf. Mommsen, *St. R.* II[3], p. 647 n. 1. See also below, p. 426.

[10] Cf. Stroux, *Die Antike*, 1937, p. 203. This principle is rightly applied to Augustus by Kromayer, *Die Rechtliche Begrundung des Principats*, pp. 33 f.; Pelham, *Essays*, pp. 60 ff.; Betti, *Il carattere giuridico del principato di Augusto*, p. 11; de Francisci, *Studi Bonfante*, p. 24; Siber, *Abh. Leipzig*, 42, III, 1934, p. 1 n. 7; it is perhaps implied by Charlesworth and Tarn, *CAH*. x, p. 99 (the consulship of 31 'greatly strengthened Octavian's position') and by Stevenson, *JRS*. xxvi, 1936 (referring to 27). For earlier consular *provinciae*, id. *RPA*. p. 53.

[11] Cf. Hammond, pp. 13, 39, etc.; McFayden, p. 2 n. 8.   [12] Cf. Cic. *XIV Phil.* 9. 25.

[13] Cf. Brassloff, *PW*. vi, 1791.

[14] E.g. perhaps Pompey (p. 412). Cf. also Dio XLIII, 44. 2, who points out that either *imperium militiae* or *domi* (τινὰ αὐτοτέλη ἡγεμονίαν ἢ καὶ ἄλλην τινὰ ἐξουσίαν—cf. McFayden, p. 8) warranted this title. McFayden, ibid., arbitrarily denies the truth of this.

THE *IMPERIUM MAIUS*

Consuls, then, could be called *imperator*, and could hold an *imperium militiae* as well as *domi*. Thus the consulship alone was the basis of Octavian's *imperium maius* and appellative of *Imperator* in 31. It is significant indeed that Antony's last official *aes* coin, struck at Patrae (?) early in 31,[1] omits all his usual titles, and describes him merely as ΥΠΑ(τος) Γ. He thus lays claim, as his highest distinction, to the consulship of which the government at Rome had deprived him;[2] for this was the foundation of his adversary's supremacy, as it had been and remained his own most effective constitutional justification.[3] *Coniurationes* on both sides[4] were gestures of psychological value; but Actium was fought, and Egypt occupied, by virtue of consulships, to which were assigned, *maiore cum imperio*, a *provincia* including the whole Empire: its holder was distinguished from lesser governors by the name of *Imperator*. The last man to have held such a *provincia*, Julius, had held it as dictator; Octavian preferred to justify his equally revolutionary appointment as *dux belli*.[5] In this way he was, as always, careful to avoid the odium that had assailed the dictator.[6] The earlier definition was vague, and had even lent itself to extension *in perpetuum*: but it was clear enough that the end of the war terminated Octavian's commission. On the other hand, his elections to the consulship did not cease, so that the abandonment of the universal *provincia* really depended upon his own definition of the end of the war. Since no move was made until the summer of 29, he presumably regarded the Eastern reorganisation of 30–29 as part of his commission assumed in 31. Thus, since he still held the universal *imperium maius*, a triumph was voted to him as well as to M. Crassus for the latter's first victories in 29.[7] (The coins of P. Vedius at Tralles[8] and C. Proculeius at Ithaca[9] show that his agents in some provinces did not even possess an *imperium*.)

Then at last, in August 29, his triumph signalised the abandonment of the extraordinary commission, and, with it, of the *praenomen Imperatoris*. He was still consul; but he needed a fresh grant of *provincia militiae*.[10] The grant is revealed by a passage in the Res Gestae: *postquam bella civilia extinxeram, per consensum universorum potitus rerum omnium*.[11] The two phrases are closely connected[12] and indicate this date.[13] *Potitus* must refer, not to an informal oath,[14] but to a formal *potestas* or *imperium*.[15] That, as the *princeps* explicitly states, still comprised the whole Empire; it continued, whether by

---

[1] See above, p. 64. Cf. p. 370. [2] Dio L, 4. 3.
[3] Syme, RR. p. 291, cf. p. 271.
[4] Cf. von Premerstein, p. 41, for Antony.
[5] RG. 25.
[6] Cf. Kornemann, QAS. IV, 1937, p. 5.
[7] Dio LI, 25. 2: Syme, RR. p. 303, prefers this date to 30.
[8] See above, p. 382.   [9] See above, p. 66.
[10] Abbott, *Roman Political Institutions*³, p. 267, points out that a new definition was attempted in this year, but says that its character is unknown.
[11] RG. 34.

[12] As seen by Helmchen, *Dissertationen-Jahrbuch der philosophischen Fakultät zu Marburg*, 1923, p. 22; pace van Groningen, *Mnemosyne*, 1926, pp. 1 ff., etc.
[13] Cf. Berve, *Hermes*, 1936, p. 250; Barwick, *Philologus*, 1936, p. 352, confirmed by Kornemann, *Klio*, 1938, p. 82, etc.
[14] As Gelzer, *Meister der Politik*, I, p. 179.
[15] Wilcken, *SB. Berlin*, 1925, p. 84 n. 2, Berve, l.c.; this seems more satisfactory than the view of Syme, RR. p. 307, that it is a bombastic allusion to victory and conquest.

one or two grants, during the remainder of 29 and throughout 28,[1] and the *praenomen* was re-established by senatorial decree.[2] Thus Octavian still claims an *imperium maius* over M. Licinius Crassus.[3] Furthermore, coins of Apamea[4] show—by their epithet *Iulia*—that his refoundation of its colony was already legalised in 28; the fact that, in the same year or a little earlier,[5] C. Calvisius Sabinus personally constituted a Spanish *municipium*[6] indicates that his own *auctoritas* was not yet, as later, employed by the *princeps* for such activities, so that it must have been as consul and *Imperator* that he acted at Apamea. His *imperium maius*, therefore, still subordinated Thorius Flaccus and (at first) Ap. Claudius Pulcher in Bithynia, and no doubt also M. Tullius Cicero in Asia.[7] (It has been pointed out that he exercised this check by the appointment of confidential city-governors for extended tenures, such as Cn. Stati. Libo, A. Ambatus, and L. Aclutius Gallus at Saguntum, Zama Regia and Venafrum respectively.[8]

It is now clear that the great commands of 49–28 B.C. were, as far as their titles were concerned, of the most diverse character, including dictatorships, proconsulates, triumvirates, and finally consulships. They were connected, however, in one vital respect: each was based on an *imperium maius*, the revolutionary element which permitted the un-Republican subordination of *imperia* to an *imperium*. The clause in the constitution which permitted dictatorships in emergencies was perverted to apply its principal administrative peculiarity to a prolonged period. It is not surprising that the consciences, or propaganda departments, of each successive Leader demanded a fresh and unfamiliar formula to adorn the unvarying basis of military tyranny.[9] Yet these expressions of autocracy were united by a single comprehensive word which threads its way throughout the two decades—*Imperator* in its new sense. This began by being an informal description of holders of *imperium maius*, but already by 44 had crept into the official parlance of one of the rival factions; soon, by the degrees which have been noted, it became the public appellation of the war-lords who held the revolutionary power.

This name of *Imperator*, and this power of *imperium maius*, are therefore inseparable manifestations of the same phenomenon. But their connection, and the isolated character of the period which has been discussed, can only be seen in their true colours by demonstration of the following independently attested but interdependent facts: first, that Augustus exercised no *imperium maius* over the 'senatorial' proconsuls from 27 B.C., from 23 B.C., or at any time during his entire principate; secondly, that the appellation of *Imperator*—although since it is an honourable part of his personal name it still

---

[1] Cf. de Francisci, *Augustus* (1938), p. 65. For a suggested distinction between his powers in these years, see below, p. 424 n. 5.
[2] Cf. von Premerstein, p. 252.
[3] Dio LI, 24. 4, 25. 2.
[4] See above, p. 257.   [5] See above, p. 163.
[6] See above, pp. 158, 292.
[7] See above, pp. 384, 255, 385.
[8] See above, pp. 158, 182, 285, 293 f.
[9] On the misuse of the formula *rei publicae constituendae* vide Syme, *RR*. p. 160. On the abolition of the dictatorship after Caesar's death, ibid. p. 188.

THE *IMPERIUM MAIUS*

appears in the *princeps*' full titulatures—entirely faded, from now on, from the constitutional and propagandist prominence to which the dominant *imperium maius* had alone entitled it (and was not restored until several reigns had quite altered the theory of the principate). It is the task of the next Chapter to show that these changes took place in 27 B.C., and that a new basis of power was developed in 23 B.C. to cover every contingency.

Chapter 2

RULE BY *AUCTORITAS PRINCIPIS*, 27 B.C.–A.D. 14

A. ABOLITION OF GOVERNMENT BY *IMPERIUM* IN 27 B.C.

SOME have said that the 'senatorial' provinces instituted in 27 B.C. were from the outset under the supreme control of Augustus's *imperium maius*; others, that this control was waived in 27 but reassumed in 23. With the aid of the coins both these assertions will be contested in turn. As a preliminary we may point to certain indications that this form of military government was becoming unattractive to the *princeps* in the years before 27.[1] It is particularly significant that the official propaganda in these years compares him with Romulus rather than Caesar:[2] he is honoured as father and founder rather than *Imperator*, and he ceased henceforward to address his soldiers as comrades.[3] Moreover, the title LIBERTATIS P. R. VINDEX on coins of 28[4] seems to indicate that the control by *imperium maius* of the proconsuls restored in 30/28 was only a preliminary and temporary precaution; and a *senatus consultum*, not the *imperium*, is already used for the restoration of Apamea, which was completed in 27 but whose epithet *Iulia* indicates that the decree was passed as early as 28. The reduction of his lictors from twenty-four to twelve[5] can also be cited as evidence for the diminution of his powers. Finally, as occasionally during the triumvirate, commanders are now regularly allowed the sole possession of their salutations: these are accorded in 29–28 to T. Statilius Taurus,[6] C. Calvisius Sabinus, L. Autronius Paetus[7] and M. Nonius Gallus.[8] The first three are also permitted triumphs. The new Romulus thought he need not be jealous of military glory, until the victories and claims of M. Crassus made him change his mind: then a new formula had to be sought, in which the revolutionary *imperium maius* could be abandoned rather than ignored, and yet control could be maintained.

A recent theory has argued that the subsequent reforms of 27 left intact an *imperium*

---

[1] Andersen, *Neue Deutsche Forschungen*, CXCVI, 1938, p. 50 n. 139 goes further, and cites Suet. *Aug.* 28 to prove that a change was mooted in c. 30. But the passage in question refers to 27 (cf. Shuckburgh, ed., p. 61) and to a *complete* abandonment of responsibilities, as the sequel shows: *De reddenda republica bis cogitavit...in retinenda perseveravit.*

[2] Cf. Kornemann, *Klio*, 1938, p. 82, and material in Gagé, *Mél. d'arch. et d'hist.* XLVII, 1930, pp. 167 ff.

[3] Suet. *Aug.* 24; cf. Syme, *JRS.* XXIII, 1933, p. 5; id. *RR.* p. 353.

[4] *BMC. Imp. Aug.* 691. See above, p. 384.

[5] F. E. Adcock has suggested to me that the change consisted of a restriction of his powers to the level of his colleague in the consulship, and that this equality had not existed in 31–29. Cf. pp. 293 f., 384 ff. for events of this period.

[6] *PIR.* III, 264. 615.

[7] *PIR*[2]. I, 32. 1680. For Sabinus, see pp. 160 ff.

[8] *PIR.* II, 412. 105; cf. McFayden, p. 36 n. 45.

ABOLITION OF GOVERNMENT BY *IMPERIUM* IN 27 B.C. 425

maius over the 'senatorial' provinces.[1] The positive grounds for this view consist merely of the record of so-called *mandata*.[2] Those, however—if they are indeed to be ascribed to this and not a later date[3]—were still entirely informal like all the other executive pronouncements of the *princeps*. It is quite erroneous to read into any of them the formalisation of Ulpian's day.[4] Control was not, indeed, lost, as the head and name of Augustus on official coins of the proconsul M. Acilius Glabrio[5] show: but the foundation coinages of colonies have given decisive indications that it was, from 27 B.C., exercised in a different manner.[6] In c. 29–28 C. Calvisius Sabinus is still able, by virtue of his *imperium*, to be called *conditor municipi* at Saguntum;[7] but in 27 Augustus himself is the refounder of Apamea.[8] This is the first of a series of foundations in 'senatorial' provinces undertaken, as coins of Pella[9] suggest, by the *auctoritas* of the *princeps*, the proconsul being merely his *adsignator* or *curator*.[10] Moreover, that *auctoritas* is the γνώμη which Primus must invoke, since he cannot claim to have acted at the behest of a superior *imperium*;[11] it is owing to lack of the latter that Augustus takes no official credit for the triumph of Sex. Appuleius in 26 from 'senatorial' Spain.[12] Furthermore, the sentence *post id tempus auctoritate omnibus praestiti*, following the description of events of 28–27 (*in consulatu sexto et septimo*), implies a strong contrast between the later reign of *auctoritas* and the previous domination by definite powers.[13] This is another indication that *imperium maius* came to an abrupt end in 27. Finally, it was in that very year that the *princeps* took the name of *Augustus*, which is linked in the closest possible way to the conception of *auctoritas*.[14] Henceforward the *praenomen Imperatoris* is no longer stressed.[15] *Augustus* was the symbol of the new *régime* of *auctoritas*, just as *Imperator* had been the symbol and direct outcome of the old *imperium maius*.

Augustus replaces *Imperator* as the catchword of the new order; *auctoritas* replaces *imperium* as its substance. This is precisely what Velleius means when he speaks of *imperium magistratuum ad pristinum redactum modum*:[16] this is how the sovereign people obtained its due.[17] The *imperium* of Augustus from 27 to 23—not 'proconsular'[18] or

---

[1] Siber, *Sav. Z.* LVII, 1937, p. 10; von Premerstein, p. 231, cf. n. 6; Strack, *Auf dem Wege zum nationalpolitischen Gymnasium*, VI, 1938, pp. 6, 9. Riccobono, *Annali del Seminario giuridico della R. Univ. di Palermo*, XV, 1936, can scarcely be cited with confidence in favour of this view, since on p. 374 he speaks of an *imperium militiae infinitum* in 27 B.C., but on p. 487 says that this same grant was *non più* infinitum *ma sempre illimitato*.
[2] E.g. Dio LIII, 15. 4; cf. Kreller, *PW.* XIV, 1023; cf. below, p. 431.
[3] This is questioned by Andersen, l.c. p. 62.
[4] These are all discussed in connection with the year 23 (see below, pp. 430 ff.).
[5] See above, p. 81.   [6] See above, p. 292.
[7] See above, p. 158.   [8] See above, p. 257.

[9] See above, p. 281.   [10] See above, p. 294.
[11] See above, p. 84.   [12] *PIR*². I, 961. 187.
[13] I owe this point to F. E. Adcock.
[14] Muller, *Mededeelingen van de Kon. Akademie van Wetenschappen, Afd. Lett., Deel* 63, *Ser. A*, XI, 1927, p. 8; Levi, *Rivista di filologia*, 1938, p. 198; cf. Gagé, *Mél. d'arch. et d'hist.* XLVII, 1930, pp. 161 ff., etc. The alternative derivation of Augustus from *ug- vigere* (Vaniček, *Etymologisches Wörterbuch*, II, 1877, p. 865; cf. Schöner, *Acta seminarii philologici Erlangensis*, II, 1881, p. 459) cannot be accepted.
[15] See below, p. 440.   [16] II, 89. 3.
[17] Cf. Zmigryder-Konopka, *VIIIe Congrès international des sciences historiques*, 1938, I, p. 24.
[18] Proconsular +consular—Kolbe, *Das Erbe der Alten* (2R.), XX, pp. 45 ff.; Schulz, *Wochenschrift*

'nameless'[1] or 'exceptional'[2] but based on his consulship[3]—was *aequum*, and did not subordinate the proconsuls. To these he was, as far as his office was concerned, only superior by reason of the traditionally greater *auctoritas* of the consuls:[4] thus even at Apamea, in a 'senatorial' province, his titulature stresses the consulship.[5] He was, indeed, superior to proconsuls and fellow consuls alike by reason of his superior *auctoritas* (of which a larger *provincia* was a visible sign[6]). It was clear enough to everyone that a consul had a better right to govern by *auctoritas* than anyone else, and a better one still if he was Augustus.

Government by military force had given way to government by personality and by advice. Thus the vital element in this revived Republic was the elimination of the revolutionary *imperium maius*.[7] Only in its absence could the Republic breathe; whereas the 'restoration' as defined by Siber and von Premerstein lacks even a formal meaning. It stands to reason, however, that a decree recognising as legally valid the workings of the new *auctoritas*, such as has lately been postulated,[8] would have been the very negation of Augustus' aim, since it would have caused merely a purposeless substitution of one autocratic constitution for another.[9] A special argument against any such formalisation will be suggested in the next section.[10]

für Philologie, 1916, p. 1196; Gelzer, *Historisches Zeitschrift*, CXVIII, 1917, p. 279; Cary, *A History of Rome*, p. 492; Miller, *European Civilisation*, II, p. 289; Nesselhauf, *Klio*, 1937, p. 308; Anderson, *JRS*. XXIX, 1939, p. 97. For the impossibility of such 'cumulation', cf. above, pp. 419 f.

[1] Siber, *Abh. Leipzig*, XLII, 3, 1934, pp. 1 ff.; Ensslin, *Gnomon*, XI, 1935, p. 532; Kornemann, ibid. 1938, p. 562. This description is rightly censured by Riccobono, l.c. p. 374.

[2] *Ausnahmeerscheinung*—Strack, l.c. p. 8 n. 8.

[3] Recognised (most recently) by Taeger, *Nachrichten der Giessener Hochschulgesellschaft*, X, 1934, pp. 1 ff.; van Groningen, *Mnemosyne*, LIV, 1926, p. 8; Boak, *American Historical Review*, XXIV, 1919, p. 23; Vaubel, *Untersuchungen zu Augustus' Politik*, Diss. Giessen, 1934, p. 60; Betti, *Il carattere giuridico del principato di Augusto*, p. 11. Stevenson, *JRS*. XXVI, 1936, p. 95, says this is a 'tenable view'.

[4] Cf. Fürst, *Die Bedeutung der Auctoritas*, Diss. Marburg, 1934, pp. 13 ff.; Lauria, *Studi Bonfante*, II, p. 483; also above, p. 420 n. 4, where it is pointed out that a consular *imperium* in Rome could not influence proconsuls abroad (*pace* Syme, *RR*. p. 315). But his *auctoritas* almost warrants the statement of Cardinali, *Augustus* (1938), p. 163, that Augustus still intervenes in 'senatorial' provinces by virtue of his consulship. Cf. above, pp. 80 f. (Cyprus).

[5] Levi, *Rendiconti del R. Ist. Lombardo*, LXII, III, 2, 1938, pp. 102 ff. has alluded to the part played by *auctoritas* in magistracies, by means of the *auspicia*. The close connection between *imperator* and *augur* has been noted by Gagé, l.c. p. 161.

[6] Cf. de Francisci, *Augustus* (1938), p. 76.

[7] Cf. Greenidge, *Roman Public Life*, p. 386; McFayden, *CP*. XVI, 1921, p. 34; Piganiol, *Journal des Savants*, 1937, p. 154; Syme, *RR*. p. 313 n. 1; Anderson, *JRS*. XXIX, 1939, p. 97.

[8] By von Premerstein, pp. 188, 192; De Martino, *Lo stato di Augusto*, p. 41; Volkmann, *Münchener Beiträge zur Papyrusforschung*, XXI, 1935, pp. 218 f.; id. *Forschungen und Fortschritte*, 13, XXX, 1938, pp. 349 f.; de Francisci, *Augustus*, p. 97; Ensslin, *CAH*. XII, p. 352.

[9] Realised by Siber, *Sav. Z.* LVII, 1937, pp. 443, 454; Kahrstedt, *GGA*. 1938, pp. 5 ff.; Anderson, *JRS*. XXIX, 1939, p. 97; Kübler, *Gnomon*, 1939, p. 325; and Levi, *Athenaeum*, XXVI, 1938, p. 93, who shows that the substitution of a legal for a moral power was a Flavian development. Kornemann, *Gnomon*, 1938, p. 560, reserves his judgment.

[10] See below, pp. 452 f. n. 5. Cf. p. 445 n. 5.

ABOLITION OF GOVERNMENT BY *IMPERIUM* IN 27 B.C.

Far wider acceptance has been won by the view that the *imperium maius*, though abolished in 27 B.C., was restored to control the 'senatorial' provinces in 23.[1] McFayden's[2] arresting arguments to the contrary have been passed over without disproof. His opponents can certainly prove control; but they fail utterly to prove that this was exercised by an *imperium*, rather than by *auctoritas*. The controversy was well reviewed by Hammond.[3] But his conclusion is only this: 'though this oversight might be attributed to his *auctoritas*, it is certainly simpler to accept the *imperium maius* attested by Dio and Ulpian'. If no more than this can be said, the conclusion is indeed uncertain. Ulpian is demonstrably speaking of a later date,[4] and Dio's statement ἐν τῷ ὑπηκόῳ τὸ πλεῖον τῶν ἑκασταχόθι ἰσχύειν is perfectly true of the control Augustus derived from *auctoritas*.[5] But it is not intended to discuss yet again the evidence which has filled so many books: extensive and significant new material is provided by the coins. In the first place, official *aes* is issued in the 'senatorial' provinces, not by virtue of an *imperium*, but *Caesaris auctoritate*;[6] *senatus consulto* appears too, but is found no less in the 'imperial' provinces,[7] since the official authority of the senate, as of the *auctoritas principis*, was universal. Secondly, peregrine coinages in the 'senatorial' provinces, as elsewhere,[8] fail to provide a single example of the title *Imperator*— αὐτοκράτωρ. The relationship to the central government of this class of community, stipendiary and 'free' alike, was totally unconnected with the *imperium*, being based on an adaptation of the conceptions of *clientela* and *auctoritas* to current religious customs.[9] It is again *Caesaris auctoritate* that foundations and restorations of Roman cities in these provinces are undertaken, as a number of coins explicitly state.[10] Nor is the *imperium* utilised for subsequent supervision of their government, since this was ensured by a complexity of special interventions, and formalised by the emphasis on *patrocinium* and *clientela*—which have no connection whatever with the *imperium*.[11] Thus Roman and

---

[1] E.g. (most recently) Kornemann, *Gercke-Nordens Einleitung in die Altertumswissenschaft*, III, 2, 1933, pp. 71–3; Rollo, *Archivium Historicum Romanum*, p. 62; Rice Holmes, *Architect*, p. 29; Lengle, *Neue Wege zur Antike*, XI, 1934, p. 74; Ensslin, *Gnomon*, XI, 1935, p. 532; Stuart Jones, *CAH*. x, p. 137; von Premerstein, pp. 241 ff.; De Martino, *Lo stato di Augusto*, pp. 23 ff.; Siber, *Sav. Z*. LVII, 1937, p. 450; Piganiol, l.c. p. 156; Nesselhauf, *Klio*, 1937, p. 310; Kahrstedt, l.c. pp. 21 ff.; Andersen, l.c. p. 29 n. 74, p. 42; Arangio-Ruiz, *Augustus* (1938), p. 127; de Francisci, ibid. p. 82; Syme, *RR*. p. 336 n. 2. See p. 434 (renewals).

[2] *CP*. XVI, 1921, pp. 34 ff.; ibid. XXIII, 1928, pp. 388 ff.; id. *Washingion University Studies*, X, 1923, pp. 249 ff.; cf. also for general principle, Greenidge, *Roman Public Life*, p. 386. Levi,

Athenaeum, XXVI, 1938, p. 87, now cautiously says *le originarie norme giuridiche augustee...non prevedevano esattamente un* imperium *illimitato*.

[3] P. 58.

[4] Cf. McFayden, *CP*. XVI, 1921, pp. 34 ff.

[5] Cf. below, pp. 429, 445.

[6] See above, p. 109 etc. [7] See above, p. 101.

[8] See above, p. 359.

[9] See above, pp. 318 ff., 358 ff.

[10] But Miss Newby 'can cite no coins which relate to' *auctoritas* (p. 34) in the course of an erroneous description of the concept. Fraccaro's comment *Era quindi inutile occuparsene* (*Athenaeum*, 1938, p. 326) is as relevant here as to certain other parts of her book, e.g. the colonial section.

[11] See above, p. 317 n. 6.

Latin coinage in Baetica is *permissu Augusti*. Even a direct sanction to a 'senatorial' province is represented by that formula, whose lack of connection with the *imperium*, implicit in its wording, is confirmed by inscriptions combining the formula with *auctoritas*[1]—and by a great variety of evidence which shows that quite other executive methods were used, after 23 B.C. as after 27.[2]

Indeed, in his control of the senatorial provinces by *auctoritas*, Augustus started at the very top of the administration. In the last decade B.C., at a time when his own family was failing to provide him with suitable helpers, he filled the consular governorships of Asia and Africa for several successive years with his personal *amici*, and a series of coin-portraits shows the significance to which their informal bond with the *princeps* was suddenly elevated.[3] This bond was not based on any *imperium maius*. *Auctoritas* also accounts perfectly for the authority exercised by Augustus during his travels in 'senatorial' provinces in 21–19 B.C.: McFayden[4] deserts *auctoritate omnibus praestiti* when he weakens so far as to suppose, like Gardthausen,[5] that there was a temporary grant of *imperium maius*[6] for this occasion. Moreover, the proconsular title of his *adsignator* for colonial foundations in Sicily at this time, L. Mussidius, named on coins of Tyndaris,[7] shows that the *princeps* did not, as Chapot[8] assumed, become proconsul in the provinces which he visited.

Finally, the view that Agrippa possessed a 'vicegerent' *imperium maius* during his residence in the East from 18 to 13 B.C.[9] is definitely disproved by two hitherto uninterpreted coinages naming Q. Articuleius (?) Regulus and Mescinius, at Sidon (?) and Chalcis respectively.[10] It has been pointed out that these, in combination with the literary evidence, indicate that Agrippa was merely a proconsul with an exceptionally large *provincia*, comprising the whole East.[11] He could not have possessed an *imperium maius* over proconsuls, since his governors were *legati*; nor was he in a position to possess one, since—as his refusal to accept a triumph or communicate his actions to the senate[12] shows—he considered himself to be a *legatus* under the auspices of Augustus.[13]

---

[1] E.g. *CIL*. x, 5393: *ex auctoritate Ti. Caesaris Augusti et permissu eius.* Cf. Mommsen, *St. R.* II³, p. 1081.

[2] Even in Italy, *Iussu Augusti*(?) at Paestum is merely a bald alternative for *Caesaris auctoritate*: see above, p. 289. [3] See above, pp. 229, 387.

[4] L.c. pp. 36 f. [5] I, pp. 806–33.

[6] The inconsistency is recognised by Anderson, *JRS*. XVII, 1927, p. 43; Cardinali, *Augustus* (1938), p. 165. [7] See above, p. 237.

[8] *La province romaine proconsulaire d'Asie*, p. 311.

[9] Reinhold, *Marcus Agrippa*, pp. 167 ff.; Taylor, *JRS*. XXVI, 1936, p. 163 n. 12. Stuart Jones, *CAH*. X, pp. 142, 146 hesitates to pronounce an opinion. Agrippa is shown to have held no Eastern *imperium maius* from 23 to 18 by Taylor, l.c.; Hammond, p. 69; Reinhold, l.c.; cf. Chapot, Mommsen; *pace* Magie, *CP*. III, 1908, pp. 145 ff.; Daniel, *M. Vipsanius Agrippa* (1933); Richardson, *JRS*. XXV, 1935, p. 102; von Premerstein, p. 134.

[10] See above, pp. 125, 386.

[11] On the *transmarinae provinciae* which this included vide Stuart Jones, l.c. p. 142.

[12] Dio LIV, 24. 7.

[13] Even possessors of an *imperium minus* had been permitted to triumph (cf. above, pp. 419, 421). Probably Agrippa possessed such a power, like the other most important *legati Augusti* (p. 435 n. 1), but carefully avoided using any of its more independent-looking prerogatives.

ABOLITION OF GOVERNMENT BY *IMPERIUM* IN 27 B.C. 429

In answer to a petition he stated μηδὲν αὐτῷ καινίζειν ἐξεῖναι.[1] The inclusion in his command of a number of provinces previously 'senatorial' is immaterial (at a time when changes from either status to the other were frequent[2]): the conversion of a 'senatorial' province to 'imperial' administration, as then occurred, is quite different from its domination, while still 'senatorial', by *imperium maius*. Thus Agrippa was merely a *legatus Augusti* with an exceptionally important military commission. Indeed, when this was renewed with a different *provincia* in 13 B.C.,[3] Dio attributes to him the authority μεῖζον...τῶν ἑκασταχόθι...ἀρχόντων ἰσχῦσαι,[4] a phrase used elsewhere of Augustus.[5] In both cases this should refer, not to an *imperium maius*, but to superior *auctoritas* to which proconsuls deferred.[6] Agrippa's *auctoritas* was already proved;[7] it was enhanced in potency by his *tribunicia potestas*.[8] But his *imperium* was a military commission, delegated by the *princeps*. It is entirely irrelevant to the government of 'senatorial' provinces and provides no evidence for their control by *imperium maius*. The refusal of salutations to Tiberius and Drusus in 12-11[9] shows that their formal relation to the *princeps* was the same as Agrippa's had been. The recognition of their *imperium* (*minus*) by salutations and triumphs in 9 B.C.[10] (a precedent followed with Caius in A.D. 3,[11] and later with Tiberius and Germanicus[12]) is again irrelevant to the 'senatorial' sphere, since Augustus's *imperium maius* in those cases only applied to his own *provincia* and family. There were many precedents for the endowment of his *legati* with *imperium*;[13] and it was absurd that the most important of them, on whom his military command entirely devolved owing to his age and weak health[14] and whom he recog-

---

[1] Josephus, *AJ*. XII, 3.
[2] E.g. (likewise from 'senatorial' to 'imperial') Illyricum, Sardinia, Macedonia, Africa and Cyrenaica (as interpreted above, p. 143).
[3] Probably Macedonia-Moesia and Illyricum-Pannonia (cf. Stuart Jones, l.c. p. 152). That his subordinates were still *legati* is indicated by the fact that L. Piso Frugi could not triumph (Dio LIV, 34; Tac. *Ann*. VI, 10). It has, for other reasons also, been suggested that this officer was a *legatus* and not a proconsul (Zippel, *Römische Herrschertum in Illyrien*, pp. 245 f.; cf. Groag, *PW.* III, 1937; *PIR*[2]. II, 64. 289).
[4] LIV, 28. 1.   [5] See pp. 427, 445.
[6] Possibly the grant of a new *provincia* coincided with special advice to 'senatorial' governors to respect Agrippa's *auctoritas*, of which the coinage suggests an enhancement: e.g. issues of Scato in Cyrenaica, portrait on Roman coinage (*BMC. Imp. Aug.* 110 ff.) and exceptional election as Augustus's colleague as II*vir* at Saguntum. See pp. 138, 159.
[7] E.g. coin-portraits at Apamea and Parium (soon after Actium), government of Rome without office in 21 (Stuart Jones, l.c. p. 144 n. 1), coin-portrait at Gades in 19 for *adsignatio*. See pp. 255, 249, 171.
[8] Stuart Jones, l.c. p. 146. Cf. above, p. 164.
[9] Cf. Rosenberg, *PW*. IX, 1147.
[10] Cf. Stuart Jones, l.c. p. 154.
[11] Cf. Mommsen, *St. R.* II[3], p. 1155 n. 4. This warrants the definition of his command by Zonaras (X, 36) as ἀνθύπατος ἐξουσία. His *provincia* was composite like that of his predecessors from the *domus principis*; but the words of Orosius (VII, 3), *ad ordinandas Aegypti Syriaeque provincias*, suggest that, no doubt on account of his extreme youth, no 'senatorial' provinces were, at least at first, transferred to him.
[12] Dio LVI, 25. 2; Hammond, p. 241 n. 62. Cf. also later under Tiberius, Tac. *Ann*. I, 14 ff.; Gelzer, *PW*. XIX, 438.   [13] See below, p. 435 n. 1.
[14] The influence of this upon his plans is emphasised by Nilsson, *Svenska Dagbladet*, 6 and 8 Oct. 1925; Piganiol, *Revue historique*, 1936, p. 152; Kornemann, *QAS*. IV, 1937, p. 4.

nised as an essential element in his government,[1] should not have *de jure* what they possessed *de facto*. Furthermore, the *princeps* tactfully implied his equality to the senior proconsuls, his *amici*, by permitting them also to control officials who possessed *imperium*.[2] These adjustments relate entirely to the 'imperial' provinces and to military problems. They fail wholly to demonstrate an *imperium maius* of Augustus's vicegerents over the proconsuls. The same is true of the final equation, in A.D. 13,[3] of Tiberius's *imperium* to that of the aged Augustus.[4] There were now *collegae imperii*[5] and their *provincia* was coterminous;[6] the 'senatorial' proconsuls were not affected.

Thus an investigation of the vicegerency is equally uncompromising in its failure to provide examples of an *imperium maius* over the 'senatorial' provinces. This evidence can be supported by information of another kind which shows that, contrary to the frequently expressed belief, the 'legislative' activities of this period had no inherent connection with an *imperium maius* of Augustus, or, for that matter, with his *imperium*. In the first place, various scholars have shown conclusively that imperial *decreta*,[7] *edicta*,[8]

---

[1] Vide Dio LVI, 33. 4 as interpreted by Cornelius, *Phil. Woch.* 1939, p. 735. Cf. also Brogan, *History*, 1936, p. 356.

[2] See above, pp. 139, 135, for C. Livineius Gallus and Capito, *quaestores pro praetore* under the proconsuls of Africa and Cyrenaica respectively. Note also L. Passienus *Imp.* (p. 140).

[3] Siber, *Sav. Z.* 1935, p. 138, attributes the change to A.D. 11, but this view is not otherwise supported.

[4] Velleius, II, 121. 1; Suet. *Ti.* 21. 1; Ovid, *Tristia*, II, 174; cf. Weber, *Princeps*, p. 34 n. 156; von Premerstein, p. 57; Kornemann, *Phil. Woch.* LII, 1932, p. 1174; id. *Doppelprinzipat und Reichseinteilung*, pp. 26 ff.; Gelzer, *Meister der Politik*, I, p. 184; Siber, *Sav. Z.* 1935, p. 138. This is important owing to the monopoly of glory by the *Victoria Augusti*, Gagé, *Rev. Arch.* XXXII, 1930, p. 30; Momigliano, *Augustus* (1938), p. 199.

[5] Tac. *Ann.* I, 3.

[6] Von Premerstein, p. 189 n. 2: neither was 'limited' by the other, *pace* Dieckmann, *Klio*, XV, 1918, p. 375.

[7] Connected neither with *imperium* (Jobbé-Duval, *Studi Bonfante*, III, p. 197; *pace* Leifer, *Die Einheit des Gewaltgedankens im römischen Staatsrecht*, pp. 124 f., Pernice, *Festgabe Beseler*, pp. 51 ff., etc.) nor with *iurisdictio* (Jobbé-Duval, l.c. p. 201; *pace* Wenger, *Institutionen der römischen Zivilprozessrechts*, pp. 28 f., 232 f.). Decrees from *imperium* are the product of a later period (cf. next note).

[8] The characteristic formulas *dico*, *arbitror*, *existimo*, *censeo*, etc. (Kipp, *PW*. V, 1947; Orestano, *Bullettino dell' Istituto di diritto romano*, 1937, p. 234 n. 57; von Premerstein, *Sav. Z.* XLVIII, 1928, p. 434) are quite incompatible with *imperium* (cf. Arangio-Ruiz, *Augustus* [1938], p. 144, querying his decision on p. 127). Edicts from *imperium* (except, of course, purely military ones relating to troop-movements, etc.) are the product of a later period (cf. Buckland, *CAH.* XI, p. 815). This is partially but incompletely seen by Savigny, *System des heutigen römischen Rechts*, I, p. 122, who realises that many edicts cannot be ascribed to *imperium* (cf. the distinction of Pacchioni, *Corso di diritto romano*, I, p. 247); by Pernice, *Sav. Z.* VI, 1885, pp. 297 f., who classes *edicta* with *mandata*; by Mommsen, *St. R.* I[3], p. 204; and by Orestano, l.c. pp. 230, 233, 330, who distinguishes sharply between Imperial *edicta* and those of magistrates, but does not elucidate the vagueness of their origins. Such considerations as these have led to the assumption of a new statutory *ius edicendi* separate from the *imperium* (Herzog, *Geschichte und System der römischen Staatsverfassung*, II, p. 151 n. 1; Jörs, *PW*. 1107; Abbott and Johnson, p. 236; Orestano, l.c.; Piganiol, *Journal des Savants*, 1937)—wrongly, see pp. 432 f., 438 n. 1, 446. Biondi, *CA*. pp. 159 f., sees that many so-called *edicta Augusti* are really *leges*.

ABOLITION OF GOVERNMENT BY *IMPERIUM* IN 27 B.C.   431

epistulae[1] and *mandata*[2]—like administrative *commendationes*,[3] and juridical *cognitiones*[4] and *responsa prudentium*[5]—are totally unconnected in origin with any *imperium* whatsoever. The fact that *decreta* or *edicta* or both[6] were attached to the competence of *imperium* is irrelevant, since many persons besides holders of *imperium* promulgated them.[7] They were not the exclusive prerogative of the *imperium* in practice, and existed independently from it even in theory. It must again be emphasised that no one doubts that Augustus, after 27, exercised administrative control by instructions to proconsuls;[8] there is, however, the strongest reason to disbelieve the hypothesis which has been so often assumed, namely that he did this by virtue of an *imperium*.[9]

The origins then of these specialised forms of Imperial 'legislation' were quite unconnected with *imperium*. But, in order to avoid anachronism, it is necessary to

---

[1] Finkelstein, *Tijdschrift voor Rechtsgeschiedenis*, XIII, 1934, p. 152 n. 1, distinguishes two uses. Of these one (coming under the heading of *rescripta*, Ulp. *Dig.* 1. 4. 1; cf. Wilcken, *Hermes*, LV, 1920, p. 1) must date from the second century (cf. Cuq, *Rev. hist. de droit français et étranger*, IV, sér. XI, 1932, p. 117 n. 1; Buckland, *CAH.* XI, p. 816): the other comprises replies, mostly by *libelli*, to *appellatio* (Stevenson, *CAH.* X, p. 166), which was received in various forms (Brassloff, *PW.* VI, 207) by virtue of the *ius auxilii* (Greenidge, *Roman Public Life*, p. 346), which was part of the *tribunicia potestas* (cf. Charlesworth, *CAH.* X, p. 121; Hammond, p. 15) (cf. below, p. 448). For executive measures arising from the *tribunicia potestas*, vide Savigny, l.c., and below, pp. 446 f.

[2] See above, p. 425, for the unplausibility of the views which attach them to the *imperium maius*. The omission of these by the jurists from the legalised *constituones principum* of their own day (as by Gaius, *Inst.* 1, 5, and Ulp. *Dig.* I, 4. 1. 1; cf. Kreller, *PW.* XIV, 1023) suggests that their informality even outlived that of the other Imperial sources of law. This is shown by Finkelstein, l.c. pp. 150, 162 ff., 167 f., correcting Kuntze, *Excurse über römisches Recht*[2], p. 135. Finkelstein, l.c. pp. 155, 164, points out that the only relevant use is that referring to instructions delivered to governors *before* they set out for their provinces, and shows (p. 169 n. 5) that the 'Edicts' of Cyrene (*Suppl. epigr. gr.* IX, 1938, p. 11) were not *mandata* (*pace* Wenger, *SB. München*, XXXIV, 2, 1928, p. 69).

[3] Cf. von Premerstein, pp. 215 ff., Syme, *RR*. pp. 395 n. 3, 406 n. 3.

[4] Von Premerstein, pp. 198 ff. (developing McFayden, *CP.* XVI, 1921, p. 43; id. *Washington University Studies in Language and Literature*, X, 1932, pp. 249 ff., and criticising Stevenson, *CAH.* X, p. 169) shows conclusively that these were informal products of *auctoritas*. Cf. also Riccobono, *Mélanges Cornil*, II, p. 375.

[5] The character of these is revealed by a description in Gaius (*Inst.* 1, 7) as *sententiae et opiniones* (cf. von Premerstein, pp. 202 ff.; Buckland, *CAH.* XI, pp. 816 f.; Wenger, *Deutsche Literaturzeitung*, 1939, p. 876). P. W. Duff informs me that the phrase in Gaius may be a gloss: but even if so it was clearly intended to emphasise the informal origin of the *responsa*. The *sententia* of the senate is its *auctoritas* (see above, p. 288).

[6] For the confusion between these, see below, p. 432.

[7] Cf. McFayden, *CP.* XXIII, 1928, p. 393 (*pace* von Premerstein [letter quoted]); and for *edicta*, Lauria, *Studi Bonfante*, II, pp. 508, 510; for *decreta*, Jobbé-Duval, ibid. III, pp. 197. This conclusion is confirmed by P. W. Duff.

[8] Cf. especially, Syme, *RR*. p. 3.

[9] McFayden, *CP.* XXIII, l.c., rightly emphasises this in connection with the 'Edicts' of Cyrene, and his view is tentatively accepted by Arangio-Ruiz, *Augustus* (1938), p. 127. Cardinali, ibid. p. 163, is doubtful, but decides for *imperium* on p. 164. Augustus's instructions to his troops are not, of course, relevant to the present discussion: even in 'imperial' provinces, it will be shown that his *imperium* was only utilised for military purposes (see below, p. 435).

examine these origins more closely, and to simplify a subject which has been needlessly complicated. There is not the least reason to believe that the terms discussed were ever consistently applied to Augustus's executive measures, or that the latter can be divided among the various categories, any more than that they can be collectively termed *constitutiones*.[1] Imperial *decreta*, like *rescripta*, are only known as products of the second century:[2] moreover, their origins[3] are inextricably confused with those of *edicta*.[4] *Mandata*, too, were as yet so little defined that they have been ascribed to Augustus in widely divergent connections. Of *epistula*[5] and *rescriptum*[6] there are several different meanings. There is no reason to consider the Augustan (?) διάταγμα found at Nazareth as one of these rather than another,[7] and an Egyptian manifesto of Germanicus is demonstrably informal.[8] The Venafran 'edict'[9] is the only Augustan document which appears to describe itself as such;[10] but even there *edictum* means little more than *dictum*, and *dico* is one of the characteristic expressions (all informal[11]) of these measures.[12] Indeed, *dicta principis* are all that they can be called. The complete elasticity of terminology makes it highly improbable that any classification was yet attempted, and Flavian or later definitions are useless.[13] Controversies as to whether individual Augustan measures were *edicta* or *decreta*,[14] *edicta* or *rescripta*,[15] are beside the

[1] See above, pp. 312, 383.
[2] Cf. Buckland, *CAH*. XI, p. 816. Syme, *RR*. p. 468, rightly sees that a *decretum* cited by Ovid (*Tristia*, II, 131) is informal.
[3] Lauria, l.c. pp. 512 f.; cf. Orestano, l.c.
[4] For the obscurity of the beginnings of these vide Karlowa, *Römische Rechtsgeschichte*, I, pp. 646 ff.; Orestano, l.c. p. 223.
[5] Finkelstein, l.c. p. 152 n. 1; cf. Cuq, *Rev. hist. du droit français et étranger*, IV, sér. XI, 1932, p. 117 n. 1; Wilcken, *Hermes*, LV, 1920, p. 2.
[6] I.e. *epistulae* and *subscriptiones*: Ulp. *Dig.* 1. 4. 1; cf. Cuq, Wilcken, ll.cc.
[7] Markowski, *Poznańskie Towarzystwo Przyjaciól Nauk, Prace Kom. Fil.* VIII, 1937, calls it an 'edict', and Wenger, *Sav. Z.* LI, 1931, pp. 378 ff. a 'rescript' (i.e. presumably an *epistula* or *subscriptio*). But it has been shown that the extensive controversy centring round this choice of terms is largely irrelevant, since the διάταγμα cannot have been legislative (unless it was a product of the military *imperium principis* in Palestine, which is unlikely, since this was not used even in 'imperial' provinces for civilian tasks: see below, p. 435). Furthermore, the attribution by Markowski, l.c., and Arangio-Ruiz, *Augustus*, pp. 129 f., to Augustus is quite unproven; cf. Nock, *AJP.* 1939, p. 121. It is, however, at least improbable that the document is false, as Zancan maintains (*Atti del R. Ist. Veneto di scienze, lettere e belle arti*, XCI, 1931, pp. 51 ff.).

[8] Cf. Rollo, *Archivium Historicum Romanum*, p. 68 (principate of Tiberius). It implements instructions to a private secretary.
[9] *CIL.* 4842.
[10] Even here only ··ICT. survives. The only other contemporary uses of *edictum* are from the unofficial sources of the *Laudatio Turiae* (*ILS.* 8393) and Ovid (*Trist.* V, 2. 58): cf. Orestano, l.c. pp. 244 ff.
[11] Cf. Orestano, l.c. p. 234 n. 57.
[12] Kipp, *PW*. V, 1947, etc.
[13] No argument can be based on the *Lex de imperio Vespasiani* (*CIL.* VI, 930); cf. Levi, *Athenaeum*, XVI, 1938, pp. 85 ff.; Hammond, p. 28; *pace* Stuart Jones, *CAH*. X, p. 140. For example, the phrase *acta gesta decreta imperata ab Imp. Caes. Vesp.* provides a generalising use of *decretum* for the already crystallised Imperial sources of law. Nor are Suetonius, etc., any more reliable: naturally, in speaking of Augustus's measures, use was made of terms current in the writer's own day.
[14] E.g. Lauria, l.c. pp. 512 f.; Finkelstein, l.c. p. 151 n. 3; Wlassak, *Kritische Studien zur Theorie der Rechtsquellen*, p. 135.
[15] E.g. Markowski, Wenger, ll.cc.

ABOLITION OF GOVERNMENT BY *IMPERIUM* IN 27 B.C. 433

point. Many of them are likely to have been merely informal annotations: for an *acceptor a subscriptionibus* is found as early as Tiberius,[1] whereas secretaries for other departments do not appear until Claudius.[2]

The *dicta principis* which emerge from this discussion were, like the *cognitiones extra ordinem* of Augustus and the *responsa* given by his influence, products of his novel advisory *auctoritas*. His use of this for executive as for so many other purposes had already been foreshadowed during the triumvirate by his so-called 'edicts' to Rhosus,[3] which was at that time outside the sphere of his *imperium* but within the scope of his *auctoritas*.[4] The *dicta principis* 'are explanation rather than legislation'[5]—rulings and answers *Caesaris auctoritate*. It is therefore far from surprising that instructions to which such *religio* was attached remained in force after the death of their author[6]—a fact which causes difficulty to those who postulate *imperium* as their source.[7] Augustus possessed no means of legislation by his own fiat:[8] for that he was obliged to utilise the *ius edicendi* of someone else or to proceed through the *comitia tributa* or *concilium plebis*.[9] This interpretation of the *princeps*' independent executive measures as informal is given particular plausibility by the analogy of the *senatus consultum*, which was itself at this time only an advisory *sententia* or *auctoritas*.[10] Indeed, a favourite executive method combined the *auctoritas* of *princeps* and senate in the formula *senatus consulto Caesaris auctoritate*.[11] Moreover, even when he neither used this executive method nor acted through the *comitia* or *concilium*, he avoided a semblance of autocracy by incorporating *senatus consulta* in his instructions.[12] Sometimes too the converse occurred, his *dicta* being cited in senatorial decrees.[13]

It is impossible to avoid the conclusion that Augustus's so-called legislation, like his other activities,[14] was based on *auctoritas*,[15] whether exercised in the 'senatorial'

---

[1] *CIL*. VI, 5181; cf. Cuq, l.c. p. 117.

[2] Cf. Charlesworth, *CAH*. x, p. 687; Stevenson, *RPA*. p. 114.

[3] Roussel, *Syria*, XV, 1934, pp. 34 ff.

[4] Levi, *Rivista di filologia*, 1938, p. 122, points out that this is the basis of 'edicts' I and II (cf. above, p. 415). In his own provinces, of course, he had issued edicts at that time by *imperium*, under the provisions of the *Lex Titia* (ibid. p. 114).

[5] Buckland, l.c. p. 815.

[6] Proved by Orestano, l.c. p. 330.

[7] Material collected by Orestano, l.c. pp. 220 ff.

[8] Except *domi* for recruiting etc. (cf. pp. 436 f.), and for equally military purposes *militiae* (cf. below, p. 435). This resembles the conclusion of Arangio-Ruiz, *Augustus* (1938), p. 101.

[9] Cf. Stevenson, *CAH*. x, p. 168 n. 3. His grants of *civitas* were confirmed by the people (Orestano, l.c. p. 224); even Caesar had admitted this (cf. Rice Holmes, *The Roman Republic*, III, p. 77 n. 1), and it is unlikely that Augustus behaved less 'democratically' (*pace* Mommsen, *St. R.* II³, p. 889).

[10] See above, pp. 98, 288.   [11] See pp. 108, 445.

[12] *Ed. Cyr.* 5 (*SEG*. IX, 1938, p. 15); cf. Stevenson, *CAH*. x, p. 167.

[13] Orestano, l.c. p. 283.

[14] For *pontifex* see p. 376.

[15] P. W. Duff agrees with this conclusion. It may be added that *leges rogatae* by Augustus (cf. Manilius, *Astronomicon*, IV, 550) are no exception, since although Aelius Gallus (Fest. 266) can say *rogatio est genus legis*, Festus (282) shows that the act of *rogatio* was merely consultatory: '*rogat*' est *consulit populum vel petit ab eo ut id sciscat quod ferat*. McFayden, *Washington University Studies*, III, 1930, p. 71, shows that he did not possess the right of making *leges datae*; *pace* Mommsen, *St. R.* II³, p. 888.

provinces or elsewhere. He limited his powers to the necessary minimum: it would therefore have been alien to his method to 'possess the *imperium maius*, but prefer to act by *auctoritas*'.[1] Moreover, it is now possible to say that an important category of evidence which has commonly led to exaggeration of Augustus's *imperium* as the basis of government must be used as an argument to the contrary. Dio links the renewals of Augustus's *provincia* with *vota quinquennalia* and *decennalia*:[2] but the quinquennial and decennial festivals[3] which he anachronistically calls by those names fell, not in 18, 13, 8, 3 B.C., etc., but in 17, 12, 7, 2, etc., and celebrated not the renewals of *imperium* in the former set of years, but anniversaries of the *régime* (of *auctoritas*) established in 27,[4] which was formally inaugurated by the *clipeus virtutis* of that year.[5] Coincidences of the *vota* with appearances of the *Imperator* title in the second century[6] are no less irrelevant than Dio's material, since by that time the title was synonymous with that of *princeps*.[7] Nor does the anniversary of the *tribunicia potestas*, by whose years, from 23 B.C., the principate was dated,[8] coincide with the *dies imperii*.[9]

There are, then, no signs whatever of any emphasis accorded to Augustus's military powers outside their limited 'imperial' province. The whole substance of the *restituta res publica* in 27 was the abandonment of the revolutionary *imperium*: it was indeed far from the *princeps'* intentions that the new Golden Age should last only four years. So distant was von Premerstein from the truth when he considered a permanent *imperium maius* to have been the corner-stone of the principate.[10] It did not even exist. Until the end of Augustus's principate the only provinces in which his *imperium* was valid were those which he was theoretically engaged in pacifying,[11] and which, when peaceful, were to be—and to some extent were[12]—restored to the senate.

It can however be proved, by reference to the coinage, that even in these 'imperial' provinces the regular non-military administration was based on Augustus's *auctoritas*

---

[1] Giles, *CR.* XLIX, 1935, p. 198. This would have involved quite a different principle from his only partial application of the *tribunicia potestas* after 36 (see below, p. 449), since the content of that novel power was undefined, whereas the various aspects of the *imperium* were well-known and frequently utilised. It will, however, be shown that his presence in Italy necessitated certain military functions (see below, p. 438). [2] LVII, 24. 1, etc.

[3] For the existence of these vide Aymard, *Mél. d'arch. et d'hist.* LV, 1938, p. 54. One of them (12 B.C.) celebrated the conferment of the chief-priesthood, which Homo (*Mélanges Glotz*, p. 443) interestingly calls one of the three bases of rule; cf. Kornemann, *QAS.* IV, 1938, p. 11, 'the first plebiscite of the dawning monarchy'.

[4] This is shown in detail by Strack, *Gnomon*, 1937, p. 678; id. *Auf dem Wege zum national-politischen Gymnasium*, VI, 1938, p. 17; Andersen, *Neue Deutsche Forschungen*, CXCVI, 1938, pp. 47 f.; pace Wissowa, *PW.* IV, 2265; Piganiol, *Journal des Savants*, 1937, p. 153.

[5] Cf. Sutherland, *JRS.* XXVIII, 1938, p. 137.

[6] M. and S. III, p. 288, no. 945, p. 232, nos. 243 ff., p. 292, nos. 987 ff. provide these, as H. Mattingly points out to me.

[7] Cf. von Premerstein, p. 260.

[8] See below, p. 449.

[9] Hammond, *Memoirs of the American Academy in Rome*, XV, 1938, p. 60.

[10] Pp. 234 ff.

[11] Strabo XVII, 840; Dio LIII, 2; Suet. *Aug.* 47; cf. Stevenson, *CAH.* X, p. 211; Andersen, l.c. p. 58, cf. p. 102.

[12] E.g. Cyprus, Narbonensis, Baetica (Broughton, *ES.* IV, p. 594; Cardinali, *Augustus*, p. 161, etc.).

ABOLITION OF GOVERNMENT BY *IMPERIUM* IN 27 B.C. 435

rather than his *imperium*.¹ It is, in the first place, suggestive that the Roman SC currency circulated unchecked in 'imperial' just as in 'senatorial' provinces.² *Senatus consulta* did not originate from *imperium*. Moreover, not only were SC issues minted in 'imperial' provinces in East and West alike,³ but one of them was actually struck at a Syrian mint producing, practically simultaneously, currency with C(*aesaris*) A(*uctoritate*).⁴ Here are the characteristic formulas on which administration of the 'senatorial' provinces was based. Most striking of all is the deliberate opposition by P. Carisius *legatus*⁵ of TR. P. on his *aes* and IMP. on his silver. It will be shown that the *tribunicia potestas* was, in the finished system, employed as the vehicle of *Caesaris auctoritas* for the administration of the 'imperial' provinces as of the rest.⁶ Finally, it should be noted that Q. Metellus Creticus Silanus *legatus*⁷ uses the formula *permissu Augusti*, which is elsewhere used by Baetican towns coining by the *auctoritas principis*⁸ and is quite incompatible with coinage by *imperium*. In his case it is substituted for the process TR. P.–C. A.–S. C. since the vehicle of permission is the *consilium* of Augustus, from c. A.D. 13 endowed with the executive *auctoritas* of the senate.

But this was a temporary adjustment of *auctoritas*, to suit the convenience of the aged *princeps*. Until c. A.D. 13 the administrative machinery in the 'imperial' provinces was precisely similar to that elsewhere, and based on the civilian executive for which the coins have provided so much evidence. Even in these provinces, then, the *imperium* was not utilised for administration. Civilians, wherever they might be, were governed by Augustus's *auctoritas*: his *imperium* was only exercised to control the troops under his command, namely those in the 'imperial' provinces.⁹ He was not Commander-in-Chief, and the disposition of his troops along the frontiers¹⁰ emphasised the total dis-

---

¹ The writer is inclined to think that this was often a simple *imperium* and not an *imperium maius*, i.e. that the *legati Augusti* were frequently not in possession of a propraetorian *imperium*, and that assumptions to the contrary (e.g. by Cardinali, l.c. p. 162) are anachronistic deductions from the practice of the developed principate (see von Premerstein, *PW*. XII, 1143): (1) Augustus restored Republican forms, and the possession of *imperium* by *legati* was a late development (from 67 B.C.), which remained exceptional and carried autocratic associations (cf. von Premerstein, ibid.). (2) Agrippa, as *legatus Augusti*, carefully denied himself the prerogatives of *imperium* (see p. 428). (3) The conferment of these on Tiberius and Drusus in 9 B.C. was considered a novelty (see p. 429). (4) Such multiplications of *imperium* were a later feature: it has been shown that certain attributions of it to the quaestors and *legati* of 'senatorial' provinces at this date are false (see pp. 141, 136).

Those officials were only entitled to it in exceptional circumstances (double provinces, wars, etc.): the same is probably true of *legati Augusti*. Examples of their promotion for special purposes are provided by P. Carisius, fighting in Spain (p. 119), and M. Lollius, entrusted with the conversion of Galatia to a province in 20 B.C. Probably there are many others, since the 'imperial' provinces were theoretically in a continuous state of emergency (see above, p. 434). In any case, the problem is purely a military one, since, as will be shown, the civilian administration of these provinces was not conducted by *imperium*. See also above, pp. 129, 430.

² See above, pp. 92, etc.
³ See above, pp. 101, etc.   ⁴ See above, p. 106.
⁵ See above, p. 120.   ⁶ See below, p. 446.
⁷ See pp. 128, 453.   ⁸ See above, p. 174.
⁹ E.g. not those in Africa, Macedonia-Moesia. Cf. below, p. 441.
¹⁰ Cf. Syme, *RR*. p. 314.

connection of his *imperium* from the normal administrative functions. This *imperium* therefore was limited, since 27, not only geographically but in the means of its application. It was relegated to the military sphere and removed from the normal executive: furthermore, it was the express intention of the *princeps* only to exercise even this limited command as long as the emergency warranted it. His interpretation of the power as military is illustrated by the frequent delegation of all or part of it to eminent soldiers from his own house. The limitation of Agrippa and succeeding vicegerents to the 'imperial' provinces has already been emphasised: but even in those their powers were purely military. Their *imperium* completely fails to warrant interpretation as a dual sovereignty,[1] and they were no more heirs of Augustus than the Viceroy of India is heir to the British Crown: the cases of Sinope and Berytus demonstrate that, already from c. 15 B.C., a special place of honour was reserved for Caius.[2] His adoption as Augustus's son gave him a superior claim to a measure of that *auctoritas* on which the *statio principis* was based: the *clientela* conception was hereditary.[3] Even when Tiberius was equal *collega imperii*, he was not *princeps*, as the embarrassment after Augustus's death was to show.[4] The reason why this distinction was possible remained undiscovered[5] until recent researches revealed the scope of *auctoritas*.[6] The latest coins before A.D. 14 lay emphasis exclusively on this aspect of the *princeps*,[7] and explicitly subordinate Tiberius by the words AVG(*usti*) F(*ilius*).[8] Great commands in the 'imperial' provinces bore no relation to the essential character of the principate; in those as in the 'senatorial' provinces the regular business of government was based, not on Augustus's *imperium*, whether delegated or not, but on his *auctoritas*.

It remains to determine whether the same can be said of Rome and Italy. In a sense, these were parts of the 'imperial' sphere, since Augustus possessed *imperium domi*, first as consul from 27 to 23, and then for the rest of his principate[9]—without the

---

[1] As by Kornemann, *Doppelprinzipat und Reichseinteilung*, pp. 6 ff.; Piganiol, l.c. p. 164 (*la curieuse formule du double principat, un prince de la paix, un prince de la guerre*). This view has been frequently attacked, most recently by Syme, *RR*. p. 345.

[2] These coinages, and many others in honour of Caius, are ignored by those who minimise the dynastic element, e.g. Sprey, *De grondslagen van het principaat van Augustus*, Diss. Amsterdam, 1933, p. 11. See above, pp. 140, 145, 253, 259, 429, 471.

[3] See below, p. 443 n. 3.

[4] Cf. Kornemann, l.c. [*Doppelpr*.], pp. 8 ff.; Hohl, *Hermes*, LXVIII, 1933, pp. 106 ff.; id. *GGA*. 1936, p. 137.

[5] E.g. by Dieckmann, *Klio*, XV, 1918, p. 375.

[6] It may be noted also that the validity of *imperium* depended strictly upon the auspices (cf. Levi, *Rendiconti del R. Ist. Lombardo*, LXII, 111, 2, 1938, pp. 102 ff.): thus the stronger the *auctoritas* (which was closely connected with augury—cf. F. Muller, *Mededeelingen der K. Ak. van Wetenschappen, Afd. Lett., Deel* 63, Ser. *A*, XI, 1927, pp. 7 ff.), the more impressive the *imperium*. Even in the consulship of 31–29 B.C. the *princeps* had not been considered strictly equal to his colleagues (see above, p. 424).

[7] *Caesar Augustus, Divi f., Pater Patriae*: *BMC. Imp. Aug.* 506 ff.

[8] Ibid. Cf. above, pp. 136, 166.

[9] For his reasons for abandoning the consulship, vide Velleius, II, 89. 5; Pelham, *Essays*, pp. 79 f.; Rice Holmes, *Architect*, II, p. 29; Marsh, *The Founding of the Roman Empire*, pp. 226 f.; Abbott, *Roman Political Institutions*[3], p. 270.

ABOLITION OF GOVERNMENT BY *IMPERIUM* IN 27 B.C. 437

intermission sometimes assumed for the years 23–19[1]—by a *consulare imperium* separated from office, a not unknown phenomenon both in the peninsula and the capital.[2] And yet Rome and Italy were the regions where such a military power was

[1] Dio LIII, 32. 5 (23 B.C.): τήν τε ἀρχὴν τὴν ἀνθύπατον ἐσαεὶ καθάπαξ ἔχειν ὥστε μήτε ἐν τῇ ἐσόδῳ τῇ εἴσω τοῦ πωμηρίου κατατίθεσθαι κτλ. But much confusion has been caused by Dio LIV, 10. 5 (of 19, not 23, B.C.): καὶ τὴν ἐξουσίαν...τὴν...τῶν ὑπάτων διὰ βίου ἔλαβεν. This has been accepted by Abele, *Der Senat unter Augustus*, Dessau, *Geschichte der römischen Kaiser*, II, p. 832, Siber, *Sav. Z.* LVII, 1937, p. 453, Kornemann, *QAS.* IV, 1937, p. 11, Piganiol, l.c. p. 156, de Francisci, *Augustus*, p. 93. The two statements are not only inconsistent (cf. Last, *JRS*. XXVIII, 1938, p. 213), but wholly irreconcilable, for the reason that the grants which they record are identical. It has been pointed out that to speak of a cumulation of proconsular and consular *imperium* is an absurdity (pp. 419, 425). Augustus was no longer consul: his *imperium* was therefore proconsular. However, just as, not a tribune, he possessed the *tribunicia potestas*, so, *pro consule*, he held the *consulare imperium*. Mommsen defines a pro-magistrate as one who, though not a magistrate, acts with equal authority and validity. Thus the *imperium* of the *princeps* can be described in either way: there is not the least contradiction between his own description of censuses undertaken *consulari cum imperio* (*RG*. 8) and a statement of Dio that these were performed by his ἀνθύπατος ἐξουσία (LV, 13. 5).

It is therefore clear that of Dio's two statements, referring to 23 and 19 respectively, one at least must be rejected. The acceptance of the latter involves the admission that during the period 23–19 the *princeps* possessed no *imperium* within the city. But the praetorian cohorts, which had been established since (Mommsen, *St. R.* II,[3] p. 864), and did not cease to exist after 27 (cf. von Premerstein, p. 137), were partly stationed in Rome (ibid.). They were the bodyguard of Augustus in his military capacity (Suet. *Aug.* 49; cf. Stevenson, *CAH.* X, p. 233) and by virtue of his *imperium* he was their titular commander (Mommsen, l.c. p. 865; cf. Shuckburgh, ed. Tac. *Ann.* I, 7; Anderson, *JRS.* XXIX, 1939, p. 97). At this time he had not even intermediary *praefecti* (cf. Mommsen, l.c. p. 864). Augustus was in Rome for nearly half the four years in question; praetorian cohorts must have been with him (Festus, *Ep.* p. 233; Mommsen, *Hermes*, XIV, pp. 25f.): therefore he cannot have lacked an *imperium* to command them within the city—and in Italy, where they were also stationed (Patsch, *Arch.-ep. Mitt.* XIV, 1891, pp. 100 ff.; Momigliano, *Augustus*, p. 20). Von Premerstein's belief to the contrary (p. 148) marches with his theory (see below, p. 452) of the *cura et tutela*. Furthermore, the *cohortes urbanae*, which were supplementary to the praetorians and like them part of the regular army (Stevenson, l.c. p. 201; cf. Mommsen, *St. R.* II[3], p. 865 n. 1), were likewise without a special *praefectus* (*urbi*) during the period 23–19 (Dio LIV, 6; cf. Mommsen, l.c. pp. 1059 ff.)—it is probable they already existed (von Domaszewski, *BJ*. CXVII, 1908, p. 16; Durry, *Les cohortes prétoriennes*, p. 12, ascribes their inauguration to 27 B.C. Von Premerstein, pp. 135 f., is obliged to prefer c. 19 B.C. to accord with his *custodia urbis* [*cura et tutela*], which is here rejected). These *praefecti*, when they existed, possessed the *imperium* (Dio II, 4. 2; Tac. *Ann.* VI, 11; cf. Mommsen, l.c. p. 1061 n. 5; *pace* von Premerstein, l.c.), but when they were not appointed—as in the greater part of Augustus's principate (Tac. *Ann.* I, 7; cf. Mommsen, l.c. p. 1060 n. 3)—the commander was again Augustus (Mommsen, l.c. p. 1060; von Premerstein, p. 13). Here are further signs that he possessed an *imperium* within the city in the years immediately following 23, and that the duplicate information concerning 19 is false. Indeed, for other reasons, most scholars have concurred in the latter of these conclusions. It may be confidently explained as a characteristic misunderstanding of a grant of consular insignia. Cf. Stuart Jones, *CAH.* X, pp. 138, 143; Schulz, *Das Wesen des römischen Kaisertums*, pp. 24, 45; Kromayer, *Die rechtliche Begründung des Prinzipats*, p. 12; id. *GGA*. 1919, pp. 421 f.; von Premerstein, pp. 237 f.; de Martino, *Lo stato di Augusto*, p. 19, etc. etc.

[2] Devious attempts to explain this away (*e.g.* Kromayer, *GGA*. 1919, p. 431; Hardy, *Studies in*

RULE BY *AUCTORITAS PRINCIPIS*, 27 B.C.—A.D. 14

least likely to be emphasised, and where 'senatorial' authority survived most nearly intact.[1] Here, too, was centred the coinage which bears witness by its formula SC to the exercise, not of the *imperium* of Augustus, but of his *auctoritas*. I(*ussu*) A(*ugusti*) (?) at Paestum[2] may bear witness to the same methods, which we have seen to be the mainspring of administration throughout the Empire. In Italy, then, even more than elsewhere, the *imperium* may be expected to have had a purely military purpose. It is not surprising that this can be identified. *Imperium* was necessary for the control of the urban and praetorian cohorts[3]—*corps d'élite* intended (like similar bodies in certain modern countries) for sudden emergencies,[4] but especially for the defence of their fatherland,[5] whose sons were, with few exceptions,[6] recruited for their exclusive use.[7] Augustus had reason to know what an enormous part Italian stock played in a crisis. This was the object of his *imperium domi*, which supplied not only the command of these picked troops but their recruiting also[8]—equally impossible by *auctoritas*. It is now possible to explain the military significance of Augustus's statement[9] that the accomplishment

---

Roman History, p. 293; von Premerstein, p. 238) ignore abundant precedents. Just as the consuls were not necessarily limited to Italy (p. 419), so conversely, in the post-Sullan period—(a supposed earlier example is eliminated by Sack, *Hannibals Marsch auf Rom in 216 v. Chr.*, Diss. Frankfurt, 1937, pp. 36 f., 66 f.)—those who were not consuls (or dictators) could be voted an *imperium domi*: e.g. Pompey under the Lex Gabinia (cf. von Premerstein, p. 242: F. E. Adcock prefers to attribute his command in 49 [*CAH*. IX, p. 635] to an extension of the *senatus consultum ultimum*: for Pompey's whole position, see above, pp. 411 f.), Caesar's *silvae callesque* in 59 (Suet. *Caes.* 19; Cary, *CAH.* IX, p. 513: cf. Furneaux, ed. Tac. *Ann.* IV, 27), Octavian himself in 43 (cf. Weber, *Princeps*, I, p. 145, etc.), C. Clodius Vestalis between 37 and 16 (*ILS.* 904; cf. Groag, *PW.* IV, 104 f. [62]; Mommsen, *ZfN.* XV, 1887, pp. 202 ff.), in the Transpadane area L. Piso (Suet. *De viris illustribus claris rhet. et gram.* 6; cf. von Domaszewski, *Eranos Vindobonensis*, pp. 63 f.; Jullian, *TP.* p. 88), and *legati* (*ILS.* 86; cf. Syme, *RR.* p. 329 n. 4), etc., etc. Hammond (*pace* de Sanctis, *Studi Riccobono*, II, p. 57) must admit that the retention of the *imperium* within the *pomoerium* on the day of a triumph indicated that no formal limitation *militiae* existed. Nor does the *Res Gestae* omit reference to this power of Augustus—*consulari cum imperio* (for census, *RG.* 8). For the principle of separation of power from office, cf. Charlesworth,

CAH. X, p. 123; Strack, *Auf dem Wege zum nationalpolitischen Gymnasium*, VI, 1938, p. 13.

[1] Stevenson, *CAH.* X, p. 204. Piganiol, l.c. p. 156, connects the *consulare imperium* with the *ius edicendi*: but the so-called *edicta* of the *princeps* were informal products of *auctoritas* (see above, p. 430). Siber's contention (*Sav. Z.* LVII, 1937, p. 453) that the grant—which he too places in 19—was intended to enable prosecutions to be introduced in the consular-senatorial court, is equally to be rejected: the new 'Imperial' court, which was already in existence (Dio LV, 7. 2), and was likewise based on *auctoritas* (von Premerstein, pp. 198 ff.), served that purpose.

[2] See above, p. 289.   [3] See above, p. 437 n. 1.

[4] Tac. *Ann.* VI, 11, *qui subitis mederetur*; vide Stevenson, *CAH.* X, p. 233, for their pay and prestige.

[5] Cf. Jullian, *TP.* p. 55.

[6] Seeck, *Rheinisches Museum*, XLVIII, 1893, pp. 616 ff.; Stevenson, *RPA.* p. 125. These exceptions mostly occur before the new system is definitely established, or in emergencies.

[7] *TP.* pp. 54 ff.; Syme, *RR.* pp. 456 f.; Momigliano, *Augustus*, p. 17; Durry, *Les cohortes prétoriennes*, p. 240, gives the origins of the first Augustan recruits—Etruria, Umbria and the old colonies.

[8] Levies in Italy did not cease in 23: vide Piganiol, l.c.   [9] *RG.* 8.

ABOLITION OF GOVERNMENT BY *IMPERIUM* IN 27 B.C.

of censuses (*lustra*) also was within the sphere of this *consulare imperium*. Not only were these ceremonies an indispensable preliminary to any recruiting, but in the early years of the Republic they had been entirely devoted to the drawing up of lists for this specific purpose.[1] Furthermore, in those days before the advent of the censorship, they had been in the hands of the consuls: it is not fortuitous that Augustus, by an otherwise inexplicable archaism, carried out the *lustra*, during his finished principate, not by means of a *censoria potestas* but *consulari cum imperio*, and that the censors whom he appointed in 22 B.C. were not entrusted with a *lustrum*.[2] In a similar census of A.D. 13 Tiberius, as *collega imperii*, is associated:[3] it is only in Augustus's extreme old age that the vicegerency is extended to include the vital military area of Italy.[4]

Thus the *princeps* was consistent in his interpretation of the *imperium*. At home as in all provinces, it was restricted to military necessities. Emphasis on the reform of the *imperium* in 23[5] is therefore entirely misplaced, since it was merely a minor episode in military history. Not only did Augustus possess no *imperium maius* in the 'senatorial' provinces, but elsewhere too throughout the Empire his *imperium* did not influence in the slightest the administration of the civilian populations.

[1] Greenidge, l.c. p. 115; cf. p. 75.
[2] Cf. de Boor, *Fasti Censorii*, Diss. Berlin, 1873, p. 30.
[3] *RG*. 8.
[4] It is significant of the importance of the Italian element in the army that the section of Augustus's *imperium* which was within the *pomoerium* (and therefore, probably, his command within Italy) was held, as Dio explicitly states (LIII, 32. 5), without limitations in time. Parallels could, however, be cited for all features of the new situation: a *provincia imperio infinito* had precedent (cf. Hammond, p. 15) no less than a non-consular *provincia domi*, and dissociations in tenure of two parts of the same *provincia* had been familiarised in 27–23.
[5] E.g. by Kolbe, *Das Erbe der Alten* (2R.), xx, pp. 47, 59; von Premerstein, pp. 234 ff.; Kornemann, *Revue des études latines*, 1933, p. 264.

B. ECLIPSE OF THE TITLE *IMPERATOR* FROM 27 B.C.

It is on general grounds in the highest degree probable that the special appellation of *Imperator*, which had vividly and compendiously expressed to the public the circumstances of the *imperium maius*, should have shared in the eclipse of that power and the removal of the *imperium* from administration. Since, indeed, *Imperator* was part of the *princeps'* own name, and a part which reflected past military glories, it was naturally not entirely suppressed. It still served as a convenient description for the limited *imperium* that remained.[1] But decisive evidence from both numismatic and literary sources can be cited to show its irrelevance to the principles and propaganda of the new government. After its prominent appearances in the last years of the old *régime*, the *praenomen* is conspicuously absent from the official gold and silver currency after 27 B.C. It does not occur at all in seven of the nine subdivisions.[2] On two it makes single and ephemeral appearances, whose rarity is emphasised by the exceptional circumstances which required them. At Emerita under P. Carisius, the *praenomen* still described the *imperium* by which Augustus continued to coin silver in 'imperial' provinces such as this, just as TR. P. explains the origin of the same commander's *aes*.[3] At Rome the title only appears on transcriptions of official dedications where the full titulature survived;[4] it is not used as a coin-titulature. That is all. On the Roman *aes*, which was the product of powers totally unconnected with the *imperium*, the *praenomen Imperatoris* is equally neglected. It is only found on a very special occasion in order to differentiate Augustus from Tiberius, the mention of whose own extensive *imperium* is, on contemporary issues, significantly limited to a *cognomen* with salutation number.[5] Particularly noteworthy is the entire absence of the title on the currencies of the Greek cities, which refutes McFayden's supposition that it played a part in the administration of these.[6] Nor are the Roman cities much more concerned with it:[7] a single appearance at Caesaraugusta shows its irrelevance to present conditions by the inaccurate formula IMP. AVGVSTVS XIV.[8] Thus the negative evidence of Augustan coinage is, as a whole, very strong: the *praenomen Imperatoris* is the least favoured of all titles.

A second and equally valuable category of numismatic evidence concerns the immediate successors of Augustus in the principate, before this had yet reverted to

---

[1] See above, p. 439.
[2] For these see below, p. 468; the seven are 'Patricia I', 'Patricia II', 'East II', 'Caesaraugusta', 'Lugdunum I', 'Lugdunum II', and the 'candelabrum mint' (p. 357).
[3] See above, p. 120.
[4] *BMC. Imp. Aug.* 77, 79, 82, 89.

[5] *BMC. Imp. Aug.* 271. In the 'senatorial' provinces its appearance on official issues (with a single exception in Cyrenaica) is limited to 'programme' pieces (Africa, Bithynia, pp. 139, 145).
[6] See above, p. 359.
[7] Cf. above, pp. 320, 323.
[8] See above, pp. 218, 415.

ECLIPSE OF THE TITLE *IMPERATOR* FROM 27 B.C. 441

formal autocracy. For half a century there is not a single occurrence of the *praenomen* on official coinage. It is approached by slow stages, as the divine memory of the great Augustus who alone had held it—and the unwelcome memory of the autocratic period in which he had gained it and to which he had put an end—grew ever weaker. Tiberius[1] and Caligula[2] avoid the title altogether; it appears as a suffix under Claudius,[3] and as a prefix—but not a *praenomen*[4]—from the last years of Nero[5] to the first half of Otho's reign.[6] These are not the manifestations of a regular 'programme' title, but of one which was hard to dissociate from the exceptional period 49–28 B.C. From 27 B.C. until A.D. 66 such limited concrete significance of the title as had survived—namely, its application to the soldiers in the 'imperial' provinces[7]—was unable to find stereotyped expression and was subordinated to more important aspects of the new system. Nero's reform heralded the birth of the *Herrscheramt*,[8] as Vitellius, who was careful to avoid the prefix, saw. This evidence is corroborated extensively by the literary authorities. Several references explicitly distinguish between the ruler's military command of the troops—but not, be it noted, of the civilians[9]—in the 'imperial' provinces, and his administration of all other elements of the Empire. This is the point of the words of Tiberius: δεσπότης μὲν τῶν δούλων,[10] αὐτοκράτωρ δὲ τῶν στρατιωτῶν, τῶν δὲ δὴ λοιπῶν πρόκριτός εἰμι[11]—echoed by the younger Pliny's phrase: *cum cernerent, cui principi cives, cui Imperatori milites peperissent.*[12] This, too, supplies the sting to Tacitus' sneer at a timid proconsul of Africa—whose troops were exceptionally still under his own *imperium* and not that of Tiberius[13]—*iussa principis magis quam incerta belli metuens.*[14]

This antithesis was the conscious intention of Augustus. The evidence of his coins is corroborated from elsewhere. For example, the name *Imperator* is never once applied to him in the official propaganda in verse and prose of the period. Even those poets whose metre permitted its use totally ignore it,[15] and its verb is not attributed to the ruler until

---

[1] Cf. Suet. *Ti.* 26. 1; Dio LVII, 2. 1; von Premerstein, p. 255.

[2] A coin from the Gréau coll. (*BMC. Imp.* p. 154 n.) is misdescribed.

[3] *BMC. Imp.* 61 ff.

[4] Cf. for Nero, Mommsen, *Neues Rheinisches Museum für Philologie*, XV, 1860, p. 169.

[5] Mattingly, *BMC. Imp.* p. clxv; Sydenham, *The Coinage of Nero*, p. 29.

[6] Cf. Mattingly, *BMC. Imp.* pp. ccxix f.: then the personal *praenomen* drops out.

[7] This would be the popular connotation of the title as applied to rulers lacking the associations of Augustus.

[8] Von Premerstein, p. 260. [9] See above, p. 435.

[10] Hence his and Augustus's avoidance of the title

dominus: cf. Pallu de Lessert, *Bulletin de la Soc. des antiquaires de France*, LXI, 1900, p. 66; de Francisci, *Bullettino dell' Istituto di diritto Romano*, XXXIV, 1925, p. 334 n.; cf. Fincke, *De appellationibus Caesarum*, Diss. Königsberg, 1867, p. 22. This is the point of Lucan's gibe (I, 670) *cum domino pax ista venit* (cf. Syme, *RR*. p. 9 n. 7). Greeks naturally neglected this scruple (e.g. *CIG.* IIIa, 4923).

[11] Dio LVII, 8.

[12] *Panegyr.* 22. 3; cf. Schöner, *Acta Seminarii Philologici Erlangensis*, II, 1881, p. 449.

[13] Cf. McFayden, *CP.* XVI, 1921, p. 39; Syme, *RR.* p. 314; Last, *JRS.* XXVIII, 1938, p. 214.

[14] *Ann.* IV, 23. 2.

[15] Schöner, l.c. p. 454; Christ, *Tübinger Beiträge zur Altertumswissenschaft*, XXXI, 1938, p. 118.

the Flavian period.[1] An exact parallel to the eclipse of the *praenomen Imperatoris* is provided by the title *dux*,[2] which was also relegated to the background[3] and, more important still, demilitarised.[4] It is noteworthy that when African communities needed an equivalent for the *praenomen* in Augustus's titulature, the usual translation was avoided owing to its old military associations;[5] and an important group of Greek inscriptions from Egypt exchange the prefix for the suffix to which Augustus was entitled as provincial governor.[6] Popular slogans and official terminology bore no relation to the title,[7] and were mostly connected with peace, not war.[8] It was Augustus's desire to draw every possible contrast between the years before 27 and those which followed it:[9] the Imperial propagandists (especially Livy[10]) were hard put to it to know how to deal with Julius,[11] who was the divine father of the *princeps* but had inaugurated the ill-starred age of *imperium maius* and the title of *Imperator*, both abolished in 27.

Thus any attempt to assimilate the *Imperator* titles of the military autocracy and the earlier principate,[12] or to judge either from evidence of a later period, is foredoomed to failure. Dio's remarks on this subject frequently suffer from the latter defect.[13] The title did not yet express the *Herrscheramt*. Before 27, indeed, it had directly expressed the *imperium maius* that was the basis of rule: thereafter, until A.D. 10 at least, it remained in the background, as a reminder of past glories (and, incidentally, of the surviving *imperium* which directed the military defence of the frontier)—but of no other aspect of the new government. It was now indeed for the most part an expression of the *auctoritas* of Augustus[14] (his successors were chary of the title owing to their consciousness of their comparative lack of this *charisma*[15]). Augustus possessed this quality to such a degree that, from 27 B.C., it became the sole basis of his government.

---

[1] Cf. Christ, l.c. Nor do uses by Vitruvius (I. *praef.* 1, IV. *praef.* 1) provide any exception to this rule (as Schöner, l.c.), since—apart from the fact that he was employed in a military capacity (I. *praef.* 2)—his invariable avoidance of the name 'Augustus' in favour of 'Caesar' suggests that his work was completed before 27 B.C. (cf. Granger, Loeb ed. p. xiv).

[2] For bibliography, see below, p. 444.

[3] Cf. Syme, *RR*. p. 311.

[4] Ibid. p. 312.

[5] I.e. *amenonkal. Menokad*—a new word—was selected; cf. della Vida, *Africa italiana*, VI, 1935, p. 5.

[6] *OGIS*. 655; *IGRR*. I, 1206; *BGU*. II, 543; cf. de Sanctis, *Rivista di filologia*, 1937, p. 337.

[7] See below, p. 444.

[8] *Pax* (p. 281) is emphasised most strongly; cf. Christ, l.c. pp. 105 ff.; Syme, *RR*. p. 156.

[9] Cf. Syme, *RR*. p. 2.

[10] Seneca, *Naturales Quaestiones*, V, 18. 4. Augustus jokingly called Livy *Pompeianus* because of such difficulties: Tac. *Ann*. IV, 34, cf. Syme, *JRS*. XXVIII, 1938, p. 125 n. 82.

[11] Syme, *RR*. pp. 317 f.; ibid. *JRS*. XXVIII, 1938, p. 125.

[12] As de Francisci, *Augustus* (1938), p. 77, who says that the title was 'stabilised' in 27.

[13] E.g. his connection both of *vota* and of administration by *auctoritas* (pp. 434, 429) with the *imperium*. For a 'doublet' concerning the *imperium domi* see above, p. 437 n. 1: cf., for Dio's method, Riccobono, *Annali del Seminario giuridico della R. Univ. di Palermo*, XV, 1936, p. 460 n. 2; Andersen, *Neue Deutsche Forschungen*, CXCVI, 1938 *passim*; Rice Holmes, *Architect*, II, p. 199; McFayden, *CP*. XVI, 1921, p. 35 n. 4.

[14] Cf. Nesselhauf, *Klio*, 1937, p. 317; Levi, *Rendiconti del R. Ist. Lombardo*, LXII, III, 2, 1928, pp. 102 ff.; Momigliano, *Augustus* (1938), p. 198: cf. also Gagé, *Mél. d'arch. et d'hist*. XLVII, 1930, p. 161.

[15] Cf. Ensslin, *CAH*. XII, p. 354. This made an institution of it—not an Augustan phenomenon.

C. AUCTORITAS

On the subject of this magic property, which has rightly been called the strongest moral force in Roman public life,[1] the last few years have produced a vast literature which has gone far, but not far enough, towards the recognition of its extraordinary activity. Every office, every power, and every success—the constituents of *dignitas*[2] —enhanced the inherited[3] *auctoritas* of Augustus until it became his unique and personal attribute or characteristic, enabling him to act (in a way not permitted to mere men) without *potestas* or *imperium*.[4] It was, in current political theory, the natural complement of *libertas*—it was the people's return to him for what he gave to them.

In other words, such was the force of his record and character (and, in the background, his armaments[5]) that his hints and words of advice, unlike those of anyone else, only needed to be offered to be accepted. This informal process may be at least partly comprehensible to a generation which has witnessed, or experienced, personal leadership in modern Europe; but it still presents to our understanding certain difficulties, which the Romans did not feel owing to the concrete and clearly graduated significance attached by them to such matters of prestige.[6] That range of ideas is defined by the word *auctoritas*, which accordingly, when referred to Augustus, comprises all the elements in his power which were apart from *potestas* or *imperium*.

---

[1] Tellenbach, *Forschungen zur Kirchen- und Geistesgeschichte*, VII, 1936, p. 16; cf., from another point of view, Weiss, *Grundzüge der römischen Rechtsgeschichte* (1936), p. 83.

[2] Cf. Syme, *RR*. pp. 13 n. 2, 48: cf. also Wegehaupt, *Die Bedeutung und Anwendung von dignitas* (Diss. Breslau, 1932), and Riccobono, l.c. p. 382 n. 3.

[3] Cf. Stone, *CR*. LI, 1937, p. 29; Weber, *Princeps*, p. 221; von Premerstein, p. 17; Anderson, *JRS*. 1939, p. 94; *pace* Kübler, *Gnomon*, 1939, p. 325.

[4] This is the sum of the views of Heinze, *Hermes*, LX, 1925, pp. 348 ff.; M. Weber, *Grundriss der Sozialökonomik*, III, pp. 140, 753 f.; Adcock, *CAH*. X (1934), pp. 589, 596; Fürst, *Die Bedeutung der Auctoritas usw.*, Diss. Marburg, 1934, pp. 12 ff.; Vaubel, *Untersuchungen zu Augustus' Politik usw.*, Diss. Giessen, 1934, pp. 59 ff.; Alföldi, *Röm. Mitt.* L, 1935, pp. 74 ff.; Gagé, *Revue historique*, CLXXVII, 1936, pp. 289, 335 ff.; Schulz, *Principles of Roman Law* (1936), pp. 180 ff.; Klotz, *Phil. Woch.* LVI, 1936, p. 1395; Siber, *Sav. Z.* LVII, 1937, pp. 443 ff., 450 ff.; W. Weber, *Princeps*, p. 221; Stone, *CR.* LI, 1937, p. 29; Gmelin, *Forschungen zur Kirchen- und Geistesgeschichte*, XI, 1937, pp. 58 ff.; Kahrstedt, *GGA*. 1938, pp. 5 ff.; Stein, *VIIIe Congrès int. des sciences historiques*, 1938, I, p. 47; Levi, *Rivista di filologia*, 1938, pp. 196 ff.; id. *Rendiconti del R. Ist. Lombardo*, LXXI, III, 2, 1938, pp. 101 ff.; Zancan, *Atene e Roma*, XL, 1938, p. 98; Weickert, *Die Antike*, 1938, pp. 209 f.; Riccobono, l.c. p. 382 n. 3; de Francisci, *Augustus* (1938), p. 72; Pettazoni, ibid. p. 231; *Classical Bulletin*, 1938, p. 42; Anderson, *JRS.* XXIX, 1939, p. 96; Syme, *RR.* pp. 322, 388, 447; Wenger, *Deutsche Literaturzeitung*, 1939, pp. 873 f.

[5] Cf. Todd, *The Ancient World*, p. 328, Biondi, *CA.* p. 182.

[6] Zancan, *Atene e Roma*, XL, 1938, p. 98, points out this subjective psychological element. The same aspect is emphasised by Arangio-Ruiz, *Storia del diritto romano*, II, p. 175.

444 RULE BY *AUCTORITAS PRINCIPIS*, 27 B.C.—A.D. 14

Among its outward manifestations are the exceptional titles of *princeps*,[1] *dux-ductor*,[2] *conditor*-κτίστης,[3] ἡγεμών,[4] Augustus,[5] *pater patriae*,[6] and (to a certain extent) *Imperator*,[7] which can, in the briefest possible generalisation, be said to crystallise the civilian, national, reconstructive, Hellenistic, religious, Romulean (or cliental) and victorious aspects of his rule respectively.[8] It is not fortuitous that the first and last of these titles were derived from Julius:[9] the title *Divi filius* itself was a further manifestation of *auctoritas*.

The *princeps* and *pater patriae* had great moral responsibilities.[10] But their basis, the *auctoritas*, was actually the chief executive organ of the principate.[11] This vital consideration has hitherto been entirely obscured by the current belief that the *imperium maius* survived in the 'senatorial' provinces after 28 B.C. It did not, in fact, so survive, and elsewhere too the *imperium* was abolished from the executive. The *auctoritas principis* stepped into its place as an active administrative organ. The gigantic scope of its

[1] Cf. Grimm, *Zapiski S. Peterburgskago Univ.* LV, 1900, pp. 156 ff.; Wittrock, *Historisk Tidskrift*, 1908, pp. 220 ff.; Gwosdz, *Der Begriff des römischen 'Princeps'*, Diss. Breslau, 1933; Wagenvoort, *Philologus*, XCI, 1936, pp. 206 ff.; Piganiol, *Journal des Savants*, 1937, pp. 159 ff.; Kornemann, *QAS.* IV, 1937, p. 15 n. 1; Riccobono, l.c. p. 427; Christ, *Tübinger Beiträge zur Altertumswissenschaft*, XXXI, 1938, pp. 91, 117.

[2] Emphasised, e.g., by Levi, *Rendiconti del R. Ist. Lombardo*, LXXI, III. 2, 1938, pp. 114 ff.; Kornemann, *Gnomon*, 1938, p. 564. Cf. also Syme, *RR*. pp. 311 f.; Sauter, *Tübinger Beiträge zur Altertumswissenschaft*, XXI, 1934, p. 28 n. 1; Christ, ibid. XXXI, 1938, p. 118.

[3] See above, pp. 318, 356.

[4] Kornemann, *Breslauer Historische Forschungen*, IV, 1937, p. 7; id. *Klio*, 1938, p. 85; Syme, *RR*. p. 312 n. 5.

[5] Cf. Haverfield, *JRS*. 1915, pp. 249 ff.; F. Muller, *Mededeelingen der Koninklijke Akademie van Wetenschappen, Afd. Lett.*, Deel 63, Ser. A, XI, 1927, pp. 7 ff.; Reiter, *Phil. Woch.* 1930, pp. 1199 f.; Gagé, *Mél. d'arch. et d'hist.* XLVII, 1930, pp. 161 ff.; Manni, *Il mondo classico*, 1934, pp. 106 f.; Berlinger, *Beiträge zur inoffiziellen Titulatur der römischen Kaiser*, Diss. Breslau, 1935, pp. 75 f.; Cichorius, *Römische Studien*, p. 376; A. E. Glauning, *Festgabe für O. Glauning*, 1936, pp. 54 ff.; Koops, *Mnemosyne*, V, 1937, pp. 34 ff.; Ribezzo, *Rivista indo-greco-italica*, XXI, 1937, p. 19; Solari, *Philologus*, XCII, 1937, pp. 430 f.; Altheim, *History of Roman Religion*, p. 363; Zancan, *Atene e Roma*, 1938, p. 98; Levi, *Rivista di filologia*, 1938, p. 198; Scott, *Archiv für Religionswissenschaft*, XXXV, 1938, p. 128; Ensslin, *CAH*. XII, p. 355.

[6] Cf. Skard, *Festskrift til Koht*, pp. 42 ff.; id. *QAS*. III, 1937, pp. 28 f.; Manni, l.c.; Gagé, *Revue historique*, CLXXVII, 1936, pp. 332 ff.; Kornemann, *QAS*. IV, 1937, p. 11; *Klio*, 1938, p. 91; Berlinger, l.c. p. 77; von Premerstein, pp. 168 ff.; Sauter, *Tübinger Beiträge zur Altertumswissenschaft*, XXI, 1934, pp. 28 ff.; Christ, ibid. 1938, p. 121.

[7] I.e. in so far as this now largely eclipsed title was thought of as applying to past victories rather than to the limited *imperium* which survived (see above, p. 442, and Nesselhauf, Momigliano, Levi, ll.cc.).

[8] Each, of course, contained additional implications also.

[9] *Princeps*: coin of Troas (p. 244). *Pater (parens) patriae*: *denarii* and Dio, see above, p. 15; inscriptions, cf. Volkmann, *Gnomon*, XIII, 1937, p. 313.

[10] Cf. Piganiol, l.c. p. 161; Klostermann, *Philologus*, LXXXVII, 1932, pp. 358 ff., etc. But not legal ones, as Kornemann, l.c. p. 11; Volkmann, l.c. p. 312; Weber, *Princeps*, I, pp. 264, 692: cf. below, p. 452 n. 5. See also p. 426.

[11] Already suggested by Alföldi, Vaubel, Schulz, Gmelin, ll.cc., Levi, *Rivista di filologia*, 1935, p. 404 (criticising Stuart Jones, *CAH*. x); Giles, *CR*. XLIX, 1935, p. 198; Kornemann, *QAS*. IV, 1937, p. 12, etc.

provincial activities has been amply demonstrated by the coins.¹ Moreover, not only could Augustus delegate to his personal *amici* and representatives—to Agrippa for example, both in Rome² and elsewhere³—his own authority, but he was competent, by reason of the immeasurable superiority of his *auctoritas* to theirs, to give cogent advice to the proconsuls—or, in the words of Dio, ἐν τῷ ὑπηκόῳ τὸ πλεῖον τῶν ἑκασταχόθι ἀρχόντων ἰσχύειν.⁴ It was by means of this capacity, not an *imperium maius*, that without any reference to the senate he could give instructions which had, in practice, the force of laws.⁵ Thus *iussu Augusti* is the formula for the enfranchisement of Philippi, where *iussu populi* would have stood before.⁶

But he preferred, when convenient, to act through the senate. The collaboration of the *auctoritas* of Augustus and that of the senate for the administration of 'senatorial' provinces is proved for the very outset of the new *régime* by an issue of Apamea in 27 B.C.⁷ The two forms of *auctoritas* are often recorded in unmistakably deliberate combination.⁸ SC and CA alternate regularly and indiscriminately on the official currency, even appearing on otherwise identical issues from the same mint. Instances, too, have been given of their combination, for various executive functions, in the common formulas *ex senatusconsulto auctore Caesare, ex auctoritate Caesaris et senatusconsulto*,⁹ κατὰ...δόγμα συνκλήτου...τῷ ἐμῶι ἐπικρίματι,¹⁰ etc. The existence and prevalence of this executive co-operation is therefore demonstrated. Indeed, it was the keystone of the civilian administrative system which Augustus had substituted for the military *régime*.¹¹ It will now be demonstrated that, four years after the inauguration of the new system, a constitutional link was invented to provide for the permanent collaboration of the *auctoritas* of *princeps* and of senate, and that this element was therefore justly—though otherwise inexplicably—emphasised beyond all other elements in the titulature of Augustus.

---

¹ See above, pp. 427 f., 434 f.
² Cf. Syme, *RR*. p. 388: and the admission of Stuart Jones, *CAH*. x, p. 144 n. 1. Frontinus (*De Aq. Urb. Rom.* 98) describes Agrippa as *velut perpetuus curator* of the water-supply: cf. Homo, *Mélanges Glotz*, p. 443; cf. also *responsa prudentium* (Stevenson, ibid. p. 165).
³ Cf. the development sketched by von Premerstein, pp. 223 ff.
⁴ LIII, 32. 5. Cf. above, pp. 427, 429.
⁵ Since, however, even the *auctoritas* of *senatusconsulta* was not yet in theory legally binding (p. 108), it is, as has been pointed out, unreasonable to suppose that the *auctoritas principis* was already formulated as an official source of law (pp. 426, 452).

⁶ Sisenna, *frag.* 17. 119; cf. Sherwin-White, p. 132. See above, p. 275.
⁷ See above, p. 257.
⁸ See above, p. 108.
⁹ Cf. von Premerstein, pp. 222 f.
¹⁰ *Ed. Cyr.* 3; cf. de Visscher, *Comptes-rendus de l'Académie des Inscriptions*, 1939, p. 112.
¹¹ Syme, *RR*. p. 412 n. 2, points out that the 'rights of war and peace' attributed to the *princeps* by the *Lex de imperio Vespasiani* have no bearing on the Augustan period—*pace* Stuart Jones, *CAH*. x, p. 141; Stevenson, ibid. p. 174. That decision, like others of equal importance, would naturally be made SC–CA. The system of Augustus is easy to interpret anachronistically (cf. p. 442).

D. THE VEHICLE OF *AUCTORITAS*: *TRIBUNICIA POTESTAS*

This constitutional link was the tribunician power. The incidence of TR. P[OT.], without number,[1] in the titulatures of Augustus's coinage enables conclusions to be drawn with confidence: it is found on the official *aes* of Italy and no less than seven provinces,[2] whereas the many hundreds of local coinages provide only two examples— and those both at Romanised provincial centres, Pisidian Antioch and Tarraco.[3] It must be concluded that the title is chiefly relevant to the official series, but not to city currency. Now in three of the territories on whose coinage the title appears, it is *vis-à-vis* with the formula S(*enatus*) C(*onsulto*).[4] Issues of Caracalla and his successors,[5] in the tradition of the Eastern SC mints and recently shown to originate from Cyprus,[6] prove that this coincidence is not fortuitous. On them appear within a wreath, in juxtaposition and without additional legend, the two formulas SC and Δ(ημαρχικῆς) Ε(ξουσίας).[7] Their deliberate conjunction confirms the indications of the Augustan statistics. So does the coinage of P. Carisius, who invariably places on his *denarii* Augustus's *praenomen Imperatoris* but invariably also omits it on his *aes*: in its place is TRIBVNICIA POTESTATE.[8] Carisius's silver was imperatorial, whereas official *aes* was issued by *senatus consulta*:[9] here, then, is yet another indication that these were connected with the tribunician power.

The clue to this connection is provided by the currencies revealing that the senatorial decrees which sanction *aes* coinage were, in many or all cases, passed on the motion of Augustus—C(*aesaris*) A(*uctoritate*).[10] This formula actually appears at two mints which issue similar and contemporary coinage with S. C. and TR. P.[11] The power which gave him authority to bring forward such motions was the *ius senatus consulendi*,[12] facilitated by a *ius primae relationis*[13] and *ius senatus conferendi*.[14] These powers were now, like the *ius*

[1] Its rare occurrences with a number cannot be taken into consideration, since they are merely chronographic.

[2] Syria, Cyprus, Asia, Hispania Ulterior, Cyrenaica, Bithynia, Africa. See above, pp. 99 f., 106, 119, 135, 145, 139.

[3] See above, pp. 251, 219.

[4] Italy, Syria, Cyprus, pp. 91 ff., 100, 99.

[5] *BMC. Galatia*, etc. pp. 194. 357, 198. 383 ff., etc. On some ΔΕ occurs alone (ibid. p. 205. 447).

[6] Westholm, *Temples of Soli*, p. 135 (confirmed by C. Bosch).

[7] Cf. Regling, *WMK*. p. 123, s.v. Δ.Ε. Titulatures of many Emperors combine to make this interpretation supersede Mommsen's conjecture Δόγματι 'Εκκλησίας (*Berichte über die Verhandlungen der k. sächs. Ges. der Wissenschaften zu Leipzig, ph.-h. Kl.* III, 1851, p. 209 n.).

[8] See above, p. 120. [9] See above, p. 97.

[10] See above, p. 108. [11] See above, pp. 99 f., 106.

[12] Cf. Hammond, p. 82; Heitland, *Roman Republic*, III, p. 510: this aspect emphasised by Greenidge, *Roman Public Life*, p. 346.

[13] Dio LIII, 32. 5, mentioned with *tribunicia potestas*. This is the logical outcome of the *ius senatus consulendi*, and was therefore thought of as connected with the *potestas*, cf. Homo, *Roman Political Institutions*, p. 222 n. 1; Hellems, *Lex de Imperio Vespasiani*, Diss. Chicago, 1902; O'Brien Moore, *PW. Suppl.* VI, 772; Greenidge, l.c. p. 342; Riccobono, *Annali del Sem. giuridico della R. Univ. di Palermo*, XV, 1936, p. 378; Strack,

VEHICLE OF *AUCTORITAS*: *TRIBUNICIA POTESTAS* 447

agendi cum populo[1]—which, also by his *auctoritas*,[2] introduced similar executive measures into the *comitia*—thought of as a part of his *tribunicia potestas*.[3] This explains perfectly the emphasis laid upon this power by official *aes*: the immediate cause of such coinage was a *senatus consultum* on a motion of the *princeps*, and its ultimate basis his tribunician power which enabled this motion to be made.

The existence of this executive machinery is relevant to a difficult numismatic problem from the principate of Tiberius. With the exception of small groups at the beginning[4] and end[5] of his principate, his only Roman *aes* with tribunician dates is that with TR. P. XXIIII. (A.D. 22–23).[6] This last category includes a multiplicity of types.[7] It may or may not be considered curious that there should have been 'a period of intense coinage, followed by a complete lull of twelve years',[8] but suspicions are justly aroused when the individual types are examined: Mattingly and Sydenham are agreed that a number of them refer to events later than A.D. 22–23. Sutherland[9] has summarised their arguments, by which certain types should be reassigned to A.D. 29 and 31.[10] His only valid reason for rejecting these reattributions is the apparently inexplicable persistence, on new issues and new dies, of the date TR. P. XXIIII., which refers to 22–23 alone.[11] But the present interpretation of the tribunician power suggests

---

Footnotes continued from previous page.
Auf dem Wege zum nationalpolitischen Gymnasium, VI, 1938, p. 8. Mommsen, *St. R.* II³, p. 898, Andersen, *Neue Deutsche Forschungen*, CXCVI, 1938, p. 29 n. 72 do not differentiate between this *ius* and a *Schriftliche Antragstellung*, but the title of the former indicates that verbal motions need not be excluded from its competence (*orationes principis*, Biondi, *CA.* p. 160).

[14] Apparently in the next year, Dio LIV, 3. 3.

---

[1] Cf. Arangio-Ruiz, *Augustus* (1938), p. 127; Hammond, *Memoirs of the American Academy in Rome*, xv, 1938, p. 24; and below, p. 452 n. 4.

[2] E.g. *Ed. Cyr.* III (*SEG.* IX, 1938, p. 13) κατὰ νόμον τῶι ἐμῶι ἐπικρίματι.

[3] Cf. von Premerstein, p. 184; de Francisci, *Augustus* (1938), p. 82 n. 3. The *princeps*' activity in this respect was given retrospective validity also by the right to exercise *intercessio* against *senatus consulta*: von Premerstein, pp. 221, 280; Greenidge, l.c. p. 346. For earlier mediums of these powers, see pp. 450, 452.

[4] *BMC. Ti.* 65 ff.   [5] Ibid. 210 ff.

[6] Ibid. 70 ff. Mattingly (ibid. p. 129 f.) rightly rejects an alleged reading TR. P. XXIII. from the Viry and Thomsen collections.

[7] The present writer hopes to make a study of this period, which stands in need of a drastic reconsideration.

[8] *BMC. Ti.* p. cxxxii.

[9] *JRS.* XXVIII, 1938, pp. 131 f.

[10] I.e. the *S.P.Q.R. Iuliae Augustae* (*Carpentum*) and *Salus Augusta* types respectively. A third argument based on the *Clementia* type is shown to be inapplicable by Sutherland in his very satisfactory reinterpretation of that type (l.c. pp. 136ff.). But it is noteworthy that the *Pietas* type is copied by *aes* of Caesaraugusta in the *praefectura i.d.* of C. Caesar (Caligula) (Hill, p. 92; BM), which can scarcely have occurred before 29 and so suggests a prototype later than 23.

[11] Ibid. p. 132. He adds that the *carpentum* need not be posthumous, since it was permitted to Messalina (Dio LX, 22; Suet. *Claud.* 17) and Agrippina jun. (Dio LX, 33; Tac. *Ann.* XII, 42) in their lifetimes: but the usage of the Claudian *divina domus* (cf. Charlesworth, *CAH.* X, p. 498) cannot be compared with that of Tiberius, who was very careful in these matters. Indeed, apart from the honour to Livia here recorded, even posthumous awards of a *carpentum* are not attested until Caligula (to Agrippina sen., Suet. *Cal.* 15; cf. Abaecherli, *Bollettino dell' Associazione Inter-*

a complete explanation of this phenomenon on new lines. The invariable presence of the formula S. C. on these issues indicates that their ultimate source was a *senatus consultum*. This confirmed a motion *auctoritate principis*, which the *princeps* was enabled to propose by virtue of his tribunician power. All the groups with TR. P. XXIIII. were derived from a single *senatus consultum*, which was moved by the *princeps* and passed in A.D. 22–23: only that tribunician year, therefore, is relevant to the various types, including those as late as 29 and 31—since all were issued, in the last resort, by virtue of the *princeps*' tribunician power during its twenty-fourth year. Thus an obstacle is overcome, and further evidence is obtained for the close connection of the formulae *Senatus Consulto—Caesaris Auctoritate—Tribunicia Potestate*.

Thus too the significance attached to *tribunicia potestas* is no longer surprising. The *auctoritas* of the *princeps* was the executive basis of rule, and it was habitually applied through the medium of a *senatus consultum*.[1] So that the *potestas*, which made this application possible, was the power on which depended practically the entire machinery of the Imperial administration. Scholars have endeavoured to explain away the importance which was attached to this power;[2] but its importance was not only real, but paramount. Only its executive application can account for its bestowal as the principal sign of vicegerency,[3] its supersession of the consulship in 'regnal' chronometry[4] as the primary title of the principate,[5] and its exceptional twofold mention in the *Res Gestae*.[6] Without the *tribunicia potestas* the Imperial organism, depending upon the interplay of *princeps* and senate, would have been static. Descriptive phrases of Tacitus and Vopiscus, *summi fastigii vocabulum*[7] and *pars maxima regalis imperii*,[8] can only be explained by this administrative competence. The same words throw light on a neglected but characteristic piece of constitutional hypocrisy. It must have been clear that this competence supplied a control over the senate and Empire which was practically monarchic. But the *tribunicia potestas* possessed other elements of less practical significance, including the *ius auxilii*.[9] Another Tacitean sneer reveals that this popular function

nazionale degli Studi Mediterranei, VI, 1935–6, p. 5). Nor is it possible to base arguments on the frequency of breaks in the coinage at other times or on the correct dating of other issues: it has never been asserted that Roman *aes* appeared at regular intervals or followed an unbroken line of development.

[1] See above, p. 445.
[2] E.g. Hammond, p. 79 'sentimental associations rather than...practical usefulness'; id. *Memoirs of the American Academy in Rome*, XV, 1938, p. 24 'how much this power enlarged the emperor's competence is open to dispute'; cf. Ferrero, *The Greatness and Decline of Rome*, IV, p. 242; Greenidge, *Roman Public Life*, p. 346 'an artificial prominence'. Syme, *RR*. p. 337, calls it 'elusive'.

[3] Velleius, IX, 99; cf. Hammond (*Principate*), l.c.; Andersen, l.c. p. 39.
[4] Stobbe, *Philologus*, XXXII, 1873, pp. 1 ff.; cf. Mattingly, *JRS*. 1930, pp. 78 ff.; Hammond, *Memoirs of the American Academy in Rome*, XV, 1938, p. 24; Salmon, *History of the Roman World* (1944), p. 16.
[5] *RG*. 15, Tac. *Ann*. I, 9, etc.; cf. Hammond (*Principate*), p. 246 n. 14, etc.
[6] Weber, *Princeps*, I, p. 163; Kolbe, *GGA*. 1939, p. 157.
[7] *Ann*. III, 56.
[8] *Historia Augusta, Vita Taciti*, I, 5.
[9] Cf. Charlesworth, *CAH*. X, p. 121; Hammond, p. 15; Sherwin-White, p. 215.

VEHICLE OF *AUCTORITAS*: *TRIBUNICIA POTESTAS* 449

was given publicity as the *raison d'être* of the tribunician power:[1] the *princeps* is represented as *se ferens..ad tuendam plebem tribunicio iure contentum*.[2] The *summi fastigii vocabulum* really owed its pre-eminence, as Tacitus knew perfectly well, not to humanitarian benevolence, but to the means which it provided for influencing the senate.[3] A motion before this body supported by the *auctoritas principis* could not fail to be passed, as Cn. Piso unkindly hinted to Tiberius.[4]

So the tribunician power was the link which permitted the administrative collaboration of the *auctoritas* of *princeps* and senate.[5] This view of its substance and pretext enables the vexed problem of its chronological development to be attacked from a new angle. Since it was only in its thirty-seventh year at the death of Augustus,[6] it must date in its final form from 23 B.C.;[7] on the other hand, the apparently independent testimony of no less than three authors[8] who record its conferment in 36 B.C. is hardly controvertible.[9] It is therefore unhelpful to ascribe to yet a third date, 30 B.C., to which Dio assigns a minor adjustment, the final vote of the full *potestas*.[10] To escape from the *impasse* created by the evidence of 36 and 23, a hypothetical abandonment in c. 28–27 has been suggested.[11] Kahrstedt has since pointed out the improbability of this theory.[12] The scheme which he substitutes for it is as follows. There was a complete and lifelong grant in 36 for Rome; in 30, as Dio says, its validity was widened to the radius of one mile beyond the *pomoerium*; in 23 it was extended to the whole Empire. Unfortunately this

---

[1] Cf. Levi, *Rivista di filologia*, 1935, p. 404.

[2] *Ann.* I, 2; cf. Grimm, *Zapiski S. Peterburgskago Univ.* LV, 1900, p. 103; Zmigryder-Konopka, *VIIIe Congrès international des sciences historiques*, 1938, I, p. 27.

[3] This is substantially the view taken—without the evidence of the coins—by Strack, l.c. p. 8. There is now no reason to reject the theory—albeit unproved—of Andersen (l.c. p. 39) that *lectiones senatus* were also authorised by this *potestas*, since Augustus expressly ascribes (*RG.* 6) to the *tr. p.* measures which might have been carried out by a *cura legum morumque* (cf. Strack, l.c. p. 20; *pace* von Premerstein, pp. 149 f.). It was characteristic of Augustus to employ a decree of the senate (*Caesaris auctoritate*) for the reform of that body itself.

[4] Tac. *Ann.* I. 74.

[5] Arangio-Ruiz (*Storia del diritto romano*, 1937, pp. 208 f.) sees that there was no 'dyarchy', but a 'dualism of régimes': there is much truth in his comparison of the relationship of *princeps* to *respublica* with that of Rome to *civitates foederatae*, or of Philip of Macedon to the Greek city-states. Kornemann (*Einleitung in die Altertumwissenschaft*, III, 2, 1933, pp. 71–73) thus rightly points out that Augustus and the senate were not 'co-rulers' but 'co-administrators'.

[6] Tac. *Ann.* I, 9; *RG.* 4.

[7] Cf. Lengle, *Neue Wege zur Antike*, XI, 1934, p. 75, etc.

[8] Dio XLIX, 15. 5; Appian, V, 132; Orosius IV, 18. 34.

[9] Kahrstedt, *GGA.* 1938, p. 22; cf. Mommsen, *RGDA.* pp. 44 f.; Pelham, *Essays*, p. 73; Gardthausen, pp. 468, 727; Fitzler-Seeck, *PW*. X, pp. 230, 337; von Premerstein, pp. 262 ff., etc.

[10] As Kornemann, *Mausoleum und Tatenbericht des Augustus*, pp. 48 ff.; Stobart, *CQ.* II, pp. 302 f.; Haverfield, *JRS.* II, 1912, p. 197; Malcovati, *Atti del IV Congresso di Studi Romani*, I (1938), p. 562, corrected e.g. by von Premerstein, Kahrstedt, ll.cc.; Hammond, *Memoirs of the American Academy in Rome*, XV, 1938, p. 24.

[11] As Fitzler-Seeck, *PW*. X, 342; Gelzer, ibid. XIX, 348; von Premerstein, l.c.; Piganiol, *Journal des Savants*, 1937, p. 157; Anderson, *JRS.* 1939, p. 97.

[12] *GGA.* 1938, pp. 22 ff.; cf. Hohl, *Klio*, 1939, p. 68 n. 1.

P

solution raises greater difficulties than it solves:—(1) Dio's statement concerning 36[1] emphasises sacrosanctity, and his addition καὶ γὰρ ἐπὶ τῶν αὐτῶν βάθρων συγκαθέζεσθαί σφισιν ἔλαβε is, as Adcock sees,[2] only 'the obvious way of marking this' in public; there can, then, be no reason for dissociating this reform from the closely following grant to Octavia and Livia (35 B.C.), where sacrosanctity alone is mentioned by Dio[3] and alone is possible.[4] Moreover, for what it is worth, Octavian's first assumption of tribunician power is likely to have been on the lines of Caesar's, which (if he had one[5]) cannot have included more than sacrosanctity[6] and perhaps a few honorary privileges.[7] (2) The interpretation of the adjustment of 30 as a geographical enlargement (but nothing more), by way of an *unentbehrlicher Präzedenzfall*,[8] is unparalleled and unplausible. (3) 'Extension to the whole Empire' is a strongly suspect idea as applied to the tribunician power, whose direct validity could never have extended beyond the citizenry[9] and whose principal application, as has been shown, was limited to the senate-house. Thus peregrine city-coinages ignore the power completely, and other numismatic references from the provinces refer almost exclusively to its connection with *senatus consulta*. (4) The 'extension' fails to explain the commencement of official tribunician dating in 23.[10] There is, indeed, ample evidence that 23, not 36, was the decisive year. The principal exercise of the *potestas* in the principate was to permit consultation of the senate, and it was this which caused the administrative combination TR. P.–C. A.–S. C. But until 23 this *ius senatus consulendi* was held by the *princeps* from quite other sources—the *Lex Titia* at first,[11] and then the consulship, by which for example he rose (or wrote) to propose the refoundation of Apamea in 28–27.[12]

[1] XLIX, 15. 5. [2] *CAH*. IX, p. 901.
[3] XLIX, 38. 1.
[4] Cf. Adcock, l.c.; Andersen, l.c. p. 28; Hohl, *Klio*, 1939, p. 70. It is shown by Messina-Vitrano, *Studi Brugi*, that other honours to Imperial ladies (e.g. Ulp. *Dig.* 1, 3. 31) are of much later date.
[5] It is rejected by Hohl, *Klio*, 1939, pp. 72 f. as a retrospective misunderstanding by Dio of *sacrosanctitas* derived from an oath of 44 (cf. von Premerstein, pp. 39 f.).
[6] Adcock, l.c. p. 900; *pace* Wiegand, *Jahresbericht des Königlichen Gymnasiums zu Dresden-Neustadt*, 1898; Levi, *Atti del primo Congresso di Studi romani*, I, 1929, pp. 353 ff. For sacrosanctity see Groh, *Mémoires de la Société Royale des Sciences de Bohème*, 1922–3, p. 5; Lange, *Kleine Schriften*, II, pp. 545 ff.; Rouyard, *Revue des études latines*, IV, 1926, pp. 218 ff.
[7] Vide Andersen, l.c. pp. 26 f., who points out that interpretations must vary according as ἔλαβε (Dio XLIV, 4. 2) is translated as an Aorist or a Pluperfect. For further discussion Rice Holmes, *The Roman Republic*, III, pp. 514 ff. It may be noted that this power circumvented the ineligibility of patricians for the tribunate; cf. Hammond, *Memoirs of the American Academy in Rome*, XV, 1938, p. 23.
[8] Kahrstedt, l.c. p. 23.
[9] Even the provincial citizens were only concerned directly in so far as they could benefit by the *ius provocationis*: cf. Sherwin-White, p. 215. The *de facto* extension of this right to *peregrini* was juristically nothing to do with this *potestas*; such appeals were merely made to Augustus's supreme *auctoritas*.
[10] Tac. *Ann.* I, 9.
[11] In the same way Caesar, as dictator, had possessed the right of *prima relatio* (Dio XLIII, 14. 5).
[12] See p. 257. As consul he had also possessed the kindred *ius senatus conferendi* (Varro, *ap.* Gell. *NA*. XIV, 7)—another power reconferred (in 22) (Dio LIV, 3. 3), probably also as part of the *tribunicia potestas*. But see also pp. 446 n. 14, 452 n. 1.

Until those had expired, therefore, he did not need this pre-eminent manifestation of the tribunician power. Finally, it can hardly be accidental that a highly important product of the nexus TR. P.–C. A.–S. C., the *aes* coinage, obtained its principal expression by the reopening of the long dormant Roman mint in the very same year of 23.[1] Every indication points to the institution of *tribunicia potestas*, in its vital administrative sense, in that year: its chronological use from then onwards marks the definite establishment of the new era.[2]

This must not however be taken to imply rejection of Dio's statements that Octavian received the 'tribunician power' in 36 and 30, as Julius had before him. The dissociation of power from office was a new principle,[3] and the *tribunicia potestas* a new thing: it is not to be supposed that its possessor at once performed all the functions of a tribune any more than the holders of the *censoria potestas* in 28 performed all the functions of a censor. The tribunician power was, to use an athletic metaphor, a useful store of 'bisques', which could be claimed when necessary. Each new function it adopted gave it a new meaning.[4] The *raison d'être* of its conferments in 44 (?), 36 and 35 was its inherent *sacrosanctitas*: Augustus himself distinguishes between such conferments and the power in its final form in 23.[5] As the cause of the adjustment in 30 Dio emphasises the recognition, within a specified radius, of *ius auxilii*.[6] This was no doubt dormant in the undefined grant of 36; but—especially since it was a popular function—it was tactful before its exercise to have the senate confirm it (together with the earlier measure). Thus Dio is not completely wrong when he describes the contents of the vote of 30 as τὴν τε ἐξουσίαν τὴν τῶν δημάρχων διὰ βίου ἔχειν.[7] Only, this was not understood in the same way as after the inauguration of the collaborative *régime* in 23; and until then the potentialities of the tribunician power were still comparatively little utilised.[8] But the abandonment of the consulship by the *princeps* was part of a long-cherished plan,[9] and equally this final system, based on the *ius senatus consulendi*, had long been in his mind. Both the grant of 36 and the first confirmation of 30 occurred at times when the loss of a constitutional means of influencing the senate was envisaged as a possibility. In 36, the title *Imperator* ceases temporarily to be emphasised, since the triumviral *imperium*, renewed with dubious justification, had been still further illegalised by the elimination of one of the partners, Lepidus;[10] in 30, the *imperium maius* was limited to the duration of the war and was to be abandoned at the forthcoming triumph.[11] These coincidences with the initial grants of *tribunicia*

---

[1] See p. 91.
[2] Its successful inauguration was fatal to the hopes of those who wanted a real as opposed to a 'collaborative' Republic: there is therefore much interest in the suggestion of McDermott (*CW*. 1938, p. 43) that the new *tribunicia potestas* provoked the conspiracy of A. Terentius Varro Murena.
[3] See pp. 437f. n. 2.
[4] Cf. Hohl, *Klio*, 1939, pp. 72 f., for the misunderstandings which this caused in retrospect.
[5] Ibid. p. 74 (*RG*. 10).
[6] LI, 19; cf. Andersen, l.c. p. 28; de Francisci, *Augustus* (1938), p. 68.   [7] Ibid.
[8] Cf. Syme, *RR*. p. 308 n. 1.
[9] Velleius II, 89—*cum saepe obnitens repugnasset*.
[10] See pp. 46, 417 n. 9.   [11] See p. 421.

potestas are indications that its administrative use was never far from the thoughts of the *princeps*. Again, the final abandonment of *imperium maius* was very shortly preceded by the conferment of an office which could include the *ius senatus consulendi*, namely the *principatus senatus* (28 B.C.).[1] This conferment was a precaution against a later abandonment of the consulship, and against the consequent hiatus before the necessary adjustment of the tribunician power could be made:[2] thus it bridged the transition between the military and civil administrations, the new era and the old. The long postponement of the final *tribunicia potestas* was necessitated by wars, crises, illnesses, preparations; meanwhile, the preliminary grants of 36 and 30, which envisaged it, could easily be justified, the first by inheritance from Julius, and the second by the popular appeal of the *ius auxilii*.

Thus whereas the chief constitutional change of the epoch, the abolition of control based on *imperium*, took place in 27, it was the year 23 which after a series of tentative enactments witnessed the inauguration of the civilian executive machinery of the principate,[3] whose most important manifestation is summed up in the triple formula *tribunicia potestate—Caesaris auctoritate—senatus consulto*.[4] Without recourse to the martial law of an *imperium* or to the '*princeps*-magistracy' implied by von Premerstein's conception of the legalised *cura et tutela universa*,[5] the interaction of these three elements

[1] *RG.* 7; cf. Piganiol, *Journal des Savants*, 1937, p. 161; for lack of connection with title *princeps*, cf. Charlesworth, *CAH.* x, p. 612 n. 1; Stuart Jones, ibid. p. 132; Gwosdz, *Der Begriff des römischen 'Princeps'*, Diss. Breslau, 1933, p. 49; von Premerstein, p. 22 n. 1; *pace* Sihler, *Studies in Honor of Gildersleeve*, pp. 77 ff. For the *prima relatio* of the *princeps senatus*, cf. Greenidge, *Roman Public Life*, p. 269; cf. von Premerstein, p. 220 n. 4. But in 23 such rights were thought of as part of the *tribunicia potestas* (p. 446).

[2] The length of the interval which actually occurred in 23 is thought to be short by Hammond, *Memoirs of the American Academy in Rome*, xv, 1938, p. 24.

[3] Hohl, *Klio*, 1939, p. 74, for other reasons, recognises the grant of *tribunicia potestas* in this year as the vital moment of the principate.

[4] This year also, presumably, initiated the second element by which *tribunicia potestas* was the vehicle of *auctoritas principis*, namely the *ius agendi cum populo* (e.g. *ILS.* 4966, *e lege Iulia ex auctoritate Aug.*, cf. von Premerstein, p. 223; Arangio-Ruiz, *Augustus*, p. 127; de Francisci, ibid. p. 82; *Ed. Cyr.* 3). Its inclusion in the *potestas* is no less likely than that of the *ius senatus consulendi*. It is possible to make a general distinction between the functions of the two *iura* as interpreted by Augustus: *senatus consulta* comprehended such day-by-day administrative processes as the coinage, and *leges* were devoted to more fundamental and infrequent measures of reform. Cf. Buckland, *CAH.* xi, p. 814.

[5] Pp. 117 ff.; cf. Volkmann, *Forschungen und Fortschritte*, 13, xxx, 1938, pp. 349 f.; id. *Jahrbücher für Antike und deutsche Bildung*, I, 1938, pp. 16 ff. The same idea was suggested in part by Grimm, *Zapiski S. Peterburgskago Univ.* LV, 1900, p. 165; Petri, *Jahrbücher für Wissenschaft und Jugendbildung*, 1927, pp. 268 ff., and has been modified farther south to provide a *dux*—e.g. by Levi, *Rendiconti del R. Ist. Lombardo*, LXXI, III, 2, 1938, p. 114. Von Premerstein postulates the senate's confirmation for this general commission: he is not content with a permanent *imperium maius* and a legalised *auctoritas* (p. 126). Moreover, he implies and states, on different pages, that each of these three formalisations was the chief basis of the principate. They are, in this rôle, hopelessly incompatible, since approximately the same administrative tasks are allotted to each. It has been shown that an

VEHICLE OF *AUCTORITAS*: *TRIBUNICIA POTESTAS*

solved in an unobtrusive manner the administrative problems of the ruler, by permitting the exercise of his unique *auctoritas* (informal still) within the Republican constitution. Its necessity was only diminished by the reform in A.D. 13 of the *consilium principis*, which now could authorise Q. Silanus to coin *permissu Augusti* without reference to the senate[1] and so without mention of the tribunician power: *auctoritas* had devolved from its aged possessor to a committee. But until then, the efficacy of the *princeps* as head of the government depended upon the triple process, whose existence and predominance in the executive have been revealed by the *aes* coinage.

imperium maius did not exist, and that the *auctoritas* which took its place was not legalised (pp. 426, 445): the general *cura et tutela* has even less plausibility. Its inventor failed to explain its absence from the *Res Gestae* and the other ancient sources (cf. Kahrstedt, *GGA*. 1938, p. 17), and, even if his work had not been left unfinished (Volkmann, *ap.* von Premerstein, p. iii), he could never have reconciled it with *auctoritas*: the consecutive position of the chapters on the two topics shows only too clearly the utter anomaly of their joint existence (cf.—independently—Syme, *RR*. p. 313 n. 1). They must be considered alternative solutions, between which von Premerstein did not live to choose (similar contradictions are pointed out by Kornemann, *Gnomon*, 1938, p. 563; Kolbe, *GGA*. 1939, p. 153). We have seen that *auctoritas*, though not yet a legal institution, possessed, indeed, no less importance than is allotted to it by von Premerstein. In fact, its importance was such that there is no room whatever left for an officially recognised *cura et tutela*. It is true that Augustus viewed his task, the *statio principis*, in the moral light of an universal protectorship (cf. Klostermann, *Philologus*, LXXXVII, 1932, pp. 358 ff.; Kahrstedt, l.c. p. 13): but he exercised this by virtue of his supreme *auctoritas*, and through the intermediacy of the sovereign senate. The assumption of a legalised *cura et tutela* is completely alien to the spirit of this *auctoritas*—cf. McFayden, *CW*. 1938, p. 240; Kahrstedt, Kolbe, ll.cc.; Kornemann, l.c. p. 566; Strack, *Auf dem Wege zum nationalpolitischen Gymnasium*, VI, 1938, p. 6. For the non-existence of a *cura legum morumque* see Andersen, l.c. pp. 39 f., and for protests against a similar legalisation of *auctoritas*, see above, p. 426. The whole idea of the *cura et tutela* is too subjective: it is based on an anachronistic application of specialised modern phenomena to ancient and different conditions (cf. Machkin, *Vestnik Drevnei Istorii*, I, 1938, p. 120). It does not deserve to be called 'an attractive view' (Anderson, *JRS*. XXIX, 1939, p. 95).

[1] Decisions of the *consilium* now had the validity of *senatus consulta*: cf. above, pp 128, 435.

Appendices

Appendix 1

SUMMARY OF THE OFFICIAL *AES* COINAGES, 49–28 B.C.

(* signifies that it has been necessary to alter the current attribution, or to suggest a new one)

Mint-Authority	Probable Mint	Date	Average Weight (to nearest grain or ½ grain)
A. Pomp. M. f. Vic. *q. ad aerarium*	Utica*	48–46*	c. 350 (Berlin, Copenhagen)
Cn. Julius L. f. *q.*	Corduba	c. 47–46*	*quadrans* c. 75
C. Clovius, *praef. a. d. a. et c. d.**	Mediolanum (?)*	45	232 (Willers)
P. Sulpicius Rufus *pro pr.**	Amisus*	45*	218 (Istanbul)
Cn. Magnus *Imp.*	Corduba	46–45	as c. 333 (*BMC.*)
Magnus Pius *Imp.*	Corduba	45–44	as c. 333 (*BMC.*)
M. Eppius *Leg.*	Corduba	45–44	as c. 267 (*BMC.*)
quaestor	Thessalonica (?)	45–44*	347–319, 136·5–103·5, c. 58 (Gaebler)
L. Ap. Dec. *q. ad aerarium**	Urso	c. 44*	c. 512, 303, 200 (BM)
L. Ap. Dec. *q. ad aerarium**	Myrtilis	c. 44*	c. 240 (Copenhagen), 105 (BM)
L. Ap. Dec. *q. ad aerarium**	Baelo	c. 44*	c. 83 (BM)
L. Ap. Dec. *q. ad aerarium**	Lilybaeum	c. 44–42*	c. 100·5
Q. Hortensi. *pro cos. praef. c. d.**	Thessalonica	43–42	231 (Berlin), 221·5 (BM)
P. Lepidus *pro q. pro pr.,** P. Licinius *pro q.*	Cnossus	43–42	56·41 (*BMC.*)
L. Juni. *Leg.*, Hispanorum	Panormus	c. 43–42	c. 116 (Berlin)
[L. Juni *Leg.*], Hispanorum	Syracuse	c. 43–42	c. 95 (Berlin etc.)
L. Scribonius Libo	Agrigentum*	c. 43–36	c. 22·5
C. Allius Bala	Agrigentum*	c. 43–36	c. 31
L. Cnorius (?)*	Agrigentum*	c. 43–36	c. 42
L. Q.	Agrigentum*	c. 43–36	c. 45
Q. Annius	Lilybaeum*	c. 43–36	c. 80·5
L. Atratinus *augur*	Brundusium (?)*	39	c. 209
C. Sosius *q.*	Zacynthus	39–38	c. 99 (*BMC.*)
C. Sosius *cos.*	Zacynthus	32	31·5 (*BMC.*)
Caesar	Arelate (?)*	39–38*	c. 250
Crassipes	Lilybaeum*	c. 38–37*	c. 96
Crassipes	Agrigentum*	c. 38–37*	c. 65 (?)
L. Bibulus *pr. desig.*	Tarentum (?)*	37*	as c. 91·5 (Bahrfeldt)
L. Atratinus *cos. desig.*	Tarentum (?)*	37–36*	c. 68

APPENDIX 1

Mint-Authority	Probable Mint	Date	Average Weight (to nearest grain or ½ grain)
M. Oppius Capito *pro pr. praef. cl.*	Tarentum (?)*	37–36*	c. 68
M. Agrippa *cos. praef. cl.*	Puteoli (?)*	37*	424·5 (BM)
Divi f.	Puteoli (?)*	37*	c. 282 (Sydenham)
Caesar divi f.	Puteoli (?)*	37*	c. 278 (Sydenham)
[Lepidus],* Divos Julius	Carthage (?)*	37–36*	143 (Copenhagen)
C. Sosius *imp.*	Zacynthus	37–36	70 (*BMC.*)
Cn. Piso Frugi	Sicilian port*	37–36*	357 (Pesaro)
Q. B.	Lilybaeum*	37–36	c. 115·5
Q. B.	Agrigentum*	37–36	c. 109·5
M. Oppius Capito	Lipara*	37–36	c. 79·5
L. Caecina (?)*	Lipara*	37–35*	c. 47
P. Cornelius [Dolabella (?)]*	Lipara*	37–35*	c. 85
[Carsidius (?)] Sacerdos*	Lipara*	37–35*	c. 52
P. Calpurnius	Lipara*	37–35*	—
M. Aufidius Scaeva	Lipara*	37–35*	—
Sex. Annius	Lipara*	37–35*	c. 104
L. Annius	Lipara*	37–35*	*quadrans* c. 18
P. Annius	Lipara*	37–35*	*quadrans* (?) c. 29·5
Dec. Porcius	Lipara*	37–35*	c. 55
P. Al[fenus Varus?]*	Lipara*	37–35	—
T. Statilius [Taurus *pro cos.*]*, Trebonius *q.*	Lipara*	c. 36–35*	—
[T. Statilius Taurus] *imp.*	Lipara*	c. 36–35	—
Cap.	Lipara*	c. 36–35	—
[Caesar], Victoria	Agrigentum (?)*	c. 36	—
C. Arruntanus Balbus *pro pr.*	Melita*	c. 36–31*	—
C. Sosius *cos. desig.*	Zacynthus	36–34	159, 86·5 (*BMC.*)
[M. Licinius] Crassus*	Cnossus (?)	c. 36*	—
[M. Licinius] Crassus*	Ptolemais	c. 36*	204·5 (Vienna)
[M. Licinius] Crassus*	Cyrene	c. 36*	c. 45 (*BMC.*)
L. Lollius	Cyrene	c. 35*⎫	355–293, 185–139, 77–69·5
L. Lollius	Cnossus (?)	c. 35*⎭	(*BMC.*)
Imp. Caesar divi f. [*praef. c. d.*]*	Iol (?)*	c. 33*	373, c. 112 (Copenhagen)
C. Sosius *cos.*	Zacynthus	32	31·5 (*BMC.*)
Q. Oppius *pro cos.**	Antioch (?)*	c. 32–31*	202·5 (Willers)
Q. Oppius *pro cos.**	Laodicea (?)*	c. 32–31*	c. 182 (Laffranchi)
ΑΝΤΩ. ΥΠΑ. Γ.	Patrae (?)*	32–31	238–138, 85–62 (Svoronos)
C. Proculeius [*procurator**]	Cephallenia (?)	c. 30–28*	43·5 (Munich)
C. Proculeius [*procurator**]	Ithaca*	c. 30–28*	ç. 91·5, 30·1 (BM)
[C. Cornelius Gallus, *praef. Alexandriae et Aegypti*]	Alexandria	30–27	265·5, 128 (Milne)
A. Pupius Rufus *q. propr.*	Cyrene	c. 30–27	202, 95 (BM)
quaestors	Melita (?)	c. 30–27*	93–32, 31–20 (Bahrfeldt)
Divo Iulio [Thorius Balbus *pro cos.*] (? genuine)	Apamea*	c. 28–27*	—
Imp. Divi f. (I. 1)	Nemausus	c. 28–27	c. 270 (Willers)

Appendix 2

SUMMARY OF THE OFFICIAL *AES* COINAGES, 27 B.C.–A.D. 14

Mint-Authority	Probable Mint	Date
Imp. Caesar divi f. Augustus	Paphos	B.C. 27
M. Acilius Glabrio *pro cos.*	Byzacenian mint*	25
[M. Primus *pro cos.* (?)]*	Thessalonica (?)*	24–23
tresviri a. a. f. f., SC	Italian mints*	23–c. 6
P. Carisius *leg. Aug.*	Emerita	23–22
[Lollius (?)] Palikanus *pro cos.*	Cyrene	c. 23–15
praefecti Alexandriae et Aegypti	Alexandria	c. B.C. 23–A.D. 14
A. Plautius *pro cos.*	Paphos, Salamis (?)	c. 22
Imp. Aug. divi f.	Lusitania (?)	c. 22–19
SC	Ionia (?)	c. 21–19
Regulus *leg. Agrippae*	Sidon (?)*	c. 19
Imp. Aug. divi f.	Baetica	c. 19–16
SC	Antioch	c. B.C. 17–A.D. 14
CA, Augustus, Imp. August. *tr. pot.*	Ephesus, Pergamum 3 Syrian & 3 Balkan mints (?)* }	c. B.C. 17–
Aug. (colonist)	Parium, Syria, Bithynia, Paphlagonia (?)* }	c. 17–
Augustus (capricorn)	Parium	c. 17
SC, August.	Paphos	c. 15
Capito *q. pro pr.*	Cyrene	c. 15
Augustus...*Imp. X.*	Gallic tribe	c. 15–13
Imp. Divi f. (IB)	Nemausus	c. 15–8*
Scato *pro cos.*	Cyrene, Cnossus (?)	c. 13–12
Imp. Caesar Augustus divi f.	Lugdunum (?)	c. 10
SC	Damascus (?)*	c. 10 (?)
Q. Am. Quinti. *pro cos.*	Paphos	c. 2 (?)
Caesar *Pont. Max.*	Lugdunum	c. 8–6
Augustus *tr. pot. XVII. im...*	Hadrumetum	7–6
P. Quinctilius Varus *leg. Aug.*	Berytus	c. B.C. 7–4
Africanus Fabius Maximus *pro cos.* L. Livinejus Gallus *q. pro pr.* }	Hadrumetum	c. 6–5
quattuorviri a. a. f. f., SC	Rome	c. 6–4
SC, SC	Castulo mine	?
August. *Trib. Pot. Pont. Max.*	Paphos	c. B.C. 5–A.D. 4
Caesar August. *Pat. Patr.*	Paphos	c. B.C. 2–A.D. 4
Imp. Caesar Augustus	Lugdunum (?)	c. A.D. 2–14
L. Passienus Rufus *imp.*	Africa	c. A.D. 3
procuratores Aug.	Caesarea Samariae	6–12
SC	Italian mints	c. 10–14
Caesar Augustus divi f. *Pater Patriae*	Lugdunum	c. 10–14
Imp. Caesar divi f. Augustus *P. P.*	Africa	c. 10–14
Caesar	Laodicea in Syria (?)	c. 10–14 (?)
Q. Creticus Silanus *leg. Aug., p. Aug.*	Berytus	c. 13–14
M. Granius Marcellus *pro cos.*	Apamea in Bithynia	14

Appendix 3

PROPOSED ADDITIONS AND ALTERATIONS TO LISTS OF PROVINCIAL GOVERNORS

Hispania Ulterior
T. Manlius T. f. Torquatus Sergianus *leg.* c. 45–41 B.C.
C. Livius *leg.* 40 B.C.

Hispania Citerior
M. Sempronius Rutilus *leg.* (?)
Sex. Peducaeus *leg.* 40 B.C.

Sardinia
M. Atius Balbus *jun.* c. 38 B.C.

Sicily
L. Junius *leg.* c. 43–40 B.C.
L. Scribonius Libo *leg.* c. 43–40.
C. Caninius Rebilus *leg.* c. 42–37.
Cn. Calpurnius Piso Frugi *leg.* c. 37–36.
L. Mussidius *pro cos.* 21–20.
Cornelius(?) Sisenna *pro cos.* c. 20–12 B.C.
Q. Terentius Culleo *pro cos.* c. 12 B.C.–A.D. 14.
L. Clodius Rufus *pro cos.* c. 2 B.C.–A.D. 14.
L. Seius *pro cos.* c. 12–14.
[P. F. Silva *pro cos.* c. 14–19.]

Macedonia-Achaia
Q. Paquius Rufus *leg.* 42–41 B.C.
L. Sempronius Atratinus *leg.* 38–37.
T. Octavius *leg.* (?) c. 33–32.
Agrippa *leg.* (*legati*) 18–13.

Achaia
C. Proculeius *procurator et praeses* c. 30–28.
Agrippa *leg.* (Mescinius *leg.*) 18–13.

Creta
Q. Caepio Brutus *pro cos.* (P. Lepidus P. f. *pro q.*) 43–42.

Cyrenaica
Q. Caepio Brutus *pro cos.* (P. Licinius *pro q.*) 43–42.

Creta et Cyrenaica
L. Lollius c. 36–34.

M. Licinius Crassus c. 36–34.
Palikanus *pro cos.* c. 23–17.
P. Sulpicius Quirinius *pro cos.* (Capito *q. pro pr.*) c. 15.
Scato *pro cos.* c. 13–12.
Q. Lucanius Proculus *pro cos.* c. 12–9.
— *pro cos.* Africae (M. Tillius Sex. f. *q. pro pr.*) c. 9–8.
P. Quinctilius Varus(?) *pro cos.* Africae (—*q. pro pr.*) c. 8–7.
L. Volusius Saturninus *pro cos.* Africae (P. Sextius Scaeva *q. pro pr.*) c. 7–6.
Africanus Fabius Maximus *pro cos.* Africae (Q. Livineius Gallus *q. pro pr.*) c. 6–5.

Asia
M. Sempronius Rutilus *pro cos.* early 43.
M. Turius *leg.* 42–41/0 B.C.
Asinius Marrucinus *pro cos.* c. 35–34.
M. Herennius Picens *pro cos.* c. 33–32.
T. Octavius *pro cos.* c. 32–31.
P. Vedius Pollio *procurator et praeses* 31–29.
M. Tullius Cicero *pro cos.* 29–28.
Agrippa *leg.* (Silanus(?) *leg.*) 18–13.

Pontus et Bithynia
P. Sulpicius Rufus *pro pr.*, then *pro cos.* 46–45 B.C.
M. Licinius Crassus *pro cos.* after 35.
Thorius Flaccus *pro cos.* 29–28.
Ap. Claudius Pulcher *pro cos.* 28–27.
Agrippa *leg.* 18–13.

Galatia
Agrippa *leg.* 18–13.

Syria
Q. Oppius *pro cos.* c. 33/2–31/0 B.C.
Agrippa *leg.* (Q. Articuleius (?) Regulus *leg.*) 18–13.

Cyprus
A. Plautius *pro cos.* 22–21 B.C.
Agrippa *leg.* 18–13.
Q. Am. Quinti. *pro cos.* c. 2 B.C.–A.D. 14.

Appendix 4

SUMMARY OF FOUNDATION COINAGES

(An asterisk denotes that the reference is explicit)

I. *Praefecti coloniis deducendis et agris dandis adsignandis* (official coinage)

C. Clovius *praef.*, in Cisalpine Gaul, c. 45 B.C.
*Q. Hortensius *pr[o Q. Caepione Bruto?] praef. colon. dedu.* [*pro cos.*], in Macedonia and Achaia, 43–42.
L. Junius *leg. Siciliae*, at Panormus and Syracusae, 'Hispanorum', c. 43–42.
M. Licinius Crassus, at Cnossus, c. 36–34.
A representative of Octavian, in Mauretania, c. 33.

II. *Municipia*

a. Constitutores without adsignatores.
*P. Sittius, at Simitthu (?), 44 B.C.
M. Atius Balbus *patronus reipublicae*, at Uselis, c. 38.
Octavian, at Osca, c. 28.
*Caesar [Augustus], at Zitha, after c. 19.
Augustus, at Bilbilis, Ilerda and Italica, c. 15–14.

b. Adsignatores without constitutores.
A. Ambatus, at Zama Regia, c. 29–28 B.C.
M. Agrippa *cos. III. municipi patronus parens*, at Gades, c. 19.

c. Constitutores with adsignatores.
C. Caninius Rebilus and C. L.,[1] at Cephaloedium, c. 42–40 B.C.
L.M. and L.Q.,[1] at Messana (?), c. 42–40.
Rex Bocchus and Sosius L. f., at Tingis, c. 38.
*C. Calvisius Sabinus *imp.* and Cn. Statius Libo,[1] at Saguntum, c. 29.
Octavian and T. Statilius Taurus *pro cos.*(?),[2] at Calagurris, c. 28.
Augustus and Cornelius(?) Sisenna *pro cos.*, at Messana(?), c. 20–12.
Augustus and Q. Terentius Culleo *pro cos.*, at Lilybaeum, after c. 12 B.C.
Augustus and L. Clodius Rufus *pro cos.*, at Agrigentum, c. 2 B.C.–A.D. 14.

[1] On separate coins.
[2] Represented by a bull, as a pun on his name (?).

d. First magistrates called Augusti.
Virres *IIIIvir Aug.*, at Thuburnica(?), c. 27–12 B.C.
M. Paccius Maximus *Flamen Aug. IIvir Aug. des.*, at Halaesa, after c. 12 B.C.

e. First colleges of magistrates.
Sex. Antonius Athenio and C. Julius Dionysius *IIviri*, at Panormus, c. 44–43 B.C.
L. Munatius and L. Cestius *IIviri*, at Henna, c. 44–43.
M. Cassius and M. Antonius, at Halaesa, c. 44–43.
Aristo and Mutumbal ben Ricoce *suffetes*, at Caralis, after c. 38.
C. Marcius and L. Ausonius(?) *IIviri*, at Lipara, c. 36.
Helvius Pollio and Albinus *quinq.* at Saguntum,[3] c. 29.
C. Valerius and C. Sextius *aed.*, at Calagurris,[4] c. 28.

f. Unsigned foundation-issues.
Emporiae, c. 40–39 B.C.
Assorus, c. 44–42.
Cossura, c. 44–42.
Agrigentum, c. 44–42.
Tyndaris(?), c. 43–42.
Lix, c. 38–25.
Dertosa, c. 30–28.
Turiaso, c. 28.

g. Second issues from foundation fund.
C. Julius f. Longus *IIviri*, at Panormus, c. 43–42 B.C.
Caecilius Rufus *IIvir*, at Halaesa, c. 43–42.
Cossura, c. 43–42.
Gades, after c. 19.
Lilybaeum, after c. 11.

[3] With C. Calvisius Sabinus *imp. constitutor* (see above).
[4] With Octavian and T. Statilius Taurus (?) (see above).

III. Colonies

a. Deductores without adsignatores.
*P. Sulpicius Q. f. Rufus *pro cos.*, at Sinope, c. 45.
*Q. Hortensius *pro cos.*, at Cassandrea, c. 44–42.
*M. Sempronius Rutilus *pro cos.*, at Lystra, 43.
P. Cosconius, at Cyrene, 42.
*M. Lurius, at Turris Libisonis, c. 42–40.
*Q. Paquius Rufus *leg.*, at Philippi and Dyrrhachium, c. 42–40.
M. Turius *leg.*, at Lampsacus, c. 42–40.
T. Statilius Taurus *pro cos.* (?),[1] at Carthago Nova, c. 29.
Augustus at Emerita, c. 25–23.
Augustus at Caesaraugusta, c. 19.

b. Adsignatores without deductores.
T. Statilius Taurus *leg. pro pr.* (?),[1] at Celsa, c. 44–42.

c. Deductores and adsignatores (duoviri col. ded.).
C. Car. and C. Cos., at Rhodes, 42 B.C.
Tadius and Marius, at Melita, 42.
*L. Vene. and D. Fadius *Epul.*, at Paestum, c. 36–25.
Augustus and L. Mussidius *pro cos.*, at Tyndaris and Syracuse, c. 21.

d. First magistrates called 'Augusti'.
L. Junius and L. Acilius *IIviri quin. Aug.*, at Thermae Himeraeae(?), c. 27–12 B.C.

e. Other first magistrates.
L. Nep. and L. Sura *praef. pro IIviris* at Celsa, 44–43 B.C.[2]
Mucius and Pic., T. Anicius and C. Matuinus *IIIIviri*, at Parium, c. 42–41.
*Q. Lucretius and L. Pontius *IIviri*, at Lampsacus, c. 42–41.[3]
Pe. or Ep. *IIvir*, at Alexandria Troas, c. 42–41.
C. Fabius Catulus and D (?). Sextilius Cornutus *IIviri*, at Hadrumetum, c. 42–40.

[1] Represented by a bull, as a pun on his name (?).
[2] With T. Statilius Taurus *pro cos.* (?) (see above).
[3] With M. Turius *leg. deductor* (see above).
[4] With M. Lurius *deductor* (see above).

Q. Am. and P. C. *IIviri*, at Turris Libisonis, c. 42–40.[4]
C. Julius Tang. and C. Arri. A. f. *IIviri*, at Dyme, c. 42–36 B.C.
Cn. Octavius and M. Antonius Aristarchus *IIviri*, at Dyme, c. 36–31.
Nonius and Sulpicius *quinq.*, at Pella, 30.[5]
P. Vibius *sacerdos Caesaris* and Q. Barbatius *praef.*, M. Barbatius and M (?). Acilius *IIviri*, at Parium, 29.[5]
Conductor and Malleolus *quinq.*[1], at Carthago Nova, c. 29–28.
L. Maecius and L. Appuleius *quinq.*, at Ilici, c. 28.
C. Cassius C. f. *IIvir*, at Apamea, 27.[5]
L. Manlius and T. Petronius *IIviri*, at Ilici, c. 15–14.[5]
C. Vibius and L. Pontius *IIviri*, at Berytus, c. 16–13.
M. Ius. and M. Herenn. *IIviri quinq.*, at Dyrrhachium, c. 12–11.[5]

f. Unsigned foundation-issues.
Corinth, c. 45–44 B.C.[6]
Lugdunum, 43.
Dium, 43–42.
Arausio (?), c. 33.

g. Second issues from foundation fund.
Q. Am. and L. C. Ve. *IIviri*, at Turris Libisonis, c. 41–40 B.C.
Q. Papirius Carbo and Q. Terentius Montanus *IIviri quinq.*, at Ilici, c. 14–13.
Antioch in Pisidia, c. 20–10.

h. Augustus as restitutor.
*Pella, 30 B.C.
Parium, 29.
*Apamea, 28–27.
Ilici, c. 15–14.
*Dyrrhachium, c. 12–11 B.C.
*Philippi, c. 2 B.C.–A.D. 6.

[5] With Augustus *restitutor* (see below).
[6] This bears the head of Caesar, who was, however, not the *deductor*.

Appendix 5

PROPOSED ADDITIONS AND ALTERATIONS TO LISTS OF ROMAN FOUNDATIONS[1]

Corduba, ded. 46–45 B.C.
Buthrotum, ded. 45 B.C., rest. 10 B.C.–A.D. 13.
Sinope, ded. 45 B.C.
Cisalpine Gaul communities, const. 45 B.C.
Corinth, ded. 45–44 B.C.
Emporiae, const. 45–44 B.C.
Gades, oppidum c. R. 45–44 B.C.
Hippo Diarrhytus, ded. c. 47 B.C.
Urso, ded. 44 B.C.
Myrtilis, const. or ded. 44–27 B.C.
Simitthu, const. 44 B.C., ded. c. 5–4 B.C. (?)
Celsa, ded. 44–43 B.C.
Panormus, const. 44–43 B.C., rest. c. 43–42 B.C., stip. from 36 B.C., ded. c. A.D. 14–19.
Syracuse, const. 44–43 B.C., rest. c. 43–42 B.C., stip. from 36 B.C.
Messana, const. 44–43 B.C., rest. c. 43–36 B.C., stip. from 36 B.C.
Melita, const. 44–43 B.C., ded. 42 B.C., stip. from 36 B.C.
Cephaloedium, const. 44–43 B.C., rest. c. 42–36 B.C., stip. from 36 B.C.
Haluntium, const. 44–43 B.C., stip. from 36 B.C., const. c. A.D. 12–14.
Lystra, ded. 43 B.C., stip. from 43–42 B.C., ded. c. 42–41 B.C.
Dium, ded. 43–42 B.C. [rest. after c. A.D. 80.]
Cyrene, ded. 42 B.C., stip. from 42 B.C.
Rhodes, ded. 42 B.C., peregrine from 42 B.C.
Alexandria Troas, ded. c. 42–41 B.C., rest. c. 20 B.C.
Parium, ded. 42–41 B.C., rest. 29 B.C. [rest. A.D. 117–138.]
Lampsacus, ded. 42–41 B.C., stip. from 35 B.C.

Dyrrhachium, ded. 42–41 B.C., rest. c. 16 B.C.–A.D. 6.
Philippi, ded. 42–41 B.C., rest. c. 2 B.C.–A.D. 6.
Turris Libisonis, ded. 42–40 B.C.
Hadrumetum, ded. 42–40 B.C.
Apamea, ded. c. 42–40 B.C., rest. 28–27 B.C.
Dyme, ded. c. 42–36 B.C., rest. c. 36–31 B.C., rest. c. 27–16 B.C., stip. from c. 16 B.C.
Tauromenium, const. c. 41 B.C., ded. 36 B.C.
Pella, ded. 40 B.C., rest. 30 B.C. [rest. after A.D. 14.]
Tingis, const. 38 B.C.
Uselis, const. c. 38 B.C.
Cnossus, ded. c. 36 B.C.
Paestum, [const. 90 B.C.], ded. c. 36–28 B.C.
Achulla, ded. c. 36–27 B.C.
Thapsus, ded. c. 36–27 B.C.
Colonies in Eastern Mauretania, ded. c. 32 B.C.
Babba, ded. 33–32 B.C.
Carthago Nova, ded. c. 29 B.C.
Zama Regia, const. c. 45–44 B.C.
Saguntum, const. c. 29 B.C.
Zama Regia, const. c. 29 B.C. [ded. A.D. 117–138.]
Ilici, ded. c. 28 B.C., rest. 15–14 B.C.
Calagurris, const. c. 28 B.C.
Osca, const. c. 28 B.C.
Turiaso, const. c. 28 B.C.
Thuburnica, const. c. 27–12 B.C.
Caesaraugusta, ded. c. 19 B.C.
Berytus, ded. 16–13 B.C.
Bilbilis, const. 15–14 B.C.
Ilerda, const. 15–14 B.C.
Italica, const. 15–14 B.C.
Zitha, const. 7 B.C.

[1] ded.=*deducta* (*colonia civium Romanorum*), const.=*constituta* (*municipium c. R.*), rest.=*restituta* (*colonia* or *municipium c. R.*), stip.=*iure stipendiario*.

Appendix 6

PROPOSED ADDITIONS AND ALTERATIONS TO LISTS OF PEREGRINE FOUNDATIONS[1]

[Damascus, 311 B.C.]
[Epiphaneia, 85.]
Ilici, Latin c. 48.
Orthòsia (Phoenicia), stip. 47.
Balanea, stip. 46.
Leptis minor, lib. 45–44.
Myrtilis, Urso, Baelo, Latin 45–44.
Carthago Nova, Latin c. 44.
Antipolis, Latin 44–43.
Brutobriga, Latin c. 42–41.
Eumenia, stip. c. 42–40, stip. c. 2 B.C.–A.D. 14.
Amorium, Philomelium, stip. c. 42–40.
Vesci, Latin c. 40–39.
Thaena, stip. c. 36.
Demetrias, [87], stip. 31.
Gabala, Gadara, stip. 31.
Amphipolis, lib. c. 30.
Antioch, lib. 30.
Ace, [156–5], stip. 30.
Ilium, lib. c. 30–29.
Abydus, Dardanus, Laodicea (Phrygia), Smyrna, Teos, stip. c. 30–29(??).
Nicaea, Nicomedia, stip. c. 29–28.
Segovia, Latin c. 29–28(?)
Segesta, Latin c. 27–15.
Sidon, [336], stip. 20, lib. c. 6.

Aezanis, Heraclea Salbace, Dioshieron, Siblia, urb. c. 20–19.
Adramyttium, Magnesia ad Maeandrum, Clazomenae, Ephesus(?), Erythrae(?), Hierapolis, Apollonia Pontica, Odessus, stip. c. 20–19.
Acmonia, stip. c. 20–15.
Hydrela, Apollonia Salbace, Assus, Bargylia, Miletus, Tenedus, stip. c. 20–5.
Apamea in Syria, stip. 15.
Trapezopolis, urb. c. 15.
Eucarpiticum, semi.-urb. c. 15.
Prymnessus, Apamea in Phrygia, Euromus, Sardes, Elaea(?), stip. c. 15.
Ercavica, Latin c. 15–14.
Termessus and Oenoanda, synoecism, c. 15–5.
Segobriga, Latin c. 14–9.
Cilbiani inferiores, urb. c. 14–2, tribe c. 2 B.C.–A.D. 14.
Oea, Leptis Magna, Sabrata, lib. c. 7–5 B.C.
Colophon, Iasus, stip. c. 7 B.C.–A.D. 3.
Cos, lib. c. 5 B.C.
Thysdrus, [col. Jul.], stip. c. 2 B.C.–A.D. 14.
Antiochia ad Maeandrum, Tabae, c. 2 B.C.–A.D. 14.
Abdera in Baetica, Latin c. A.D. 4–14(?).
Pergamum, stip. c. A.D. 10–14.
Scepsis, stip. c. A.D. 13–14.

[1] Including reconstitutions and promotions (stip.=*stipendiaria*, lib.=*libera*, urb.=urbanization).

Appendix 7

POSTHUMOUS LOCAL ISSUES WITH HEADS OF AUGUSTUS

Shortly after Augustus' death, Pl. X, 5, 9 of Aezanis bear witness to a Tiberian prototype; a cameo in the Cathedral Treasure at Aachen[1] and the Torlonia Augustus[2]—recognised as Tiberian by Montini[3]—reveal the origin of the conception. Pl. X, 34 of Aphrodisias is of a style recalling the head of 'young Caligula(?)' on the Paris cameo.[4] An iconographic investigation of this kind adds the following to the posthumous issues (whose existence is revealed by other arguments on pp. 328 ff.):

(1) TIBERIUS. *Asia:* Abydus (Pl. X, 1),[5] Alabanda (Pl. X, 12),[6] Assus,[7] Clazomenae,[8] Dioshieron (Pl. X, 10),[9] Ephesus,[10] Heraclea Salbace,[11] Hypaepa,[12] Lampsacus (Pl. X, 3),[13] Magnesia ad Sipylum(?) (Pl. X, 7),[14] Methymna,[15] Miletus (Pl. X, 2),[16] Philadelphia,[17] Philomelium(?),[18] Prymnessus (Pl. X, 11),[19] Samos.[20] *Galatia:* Aspendus,[21] Sagalassus,[22] Termessus minor.[23] *Crete:* Cydonia (Pl. XII, 7).[24] *Epirus:* Nicopolis (Pl. XII, 5).[25] *Achaia:* Tanagra(?).[26]

On the whole the portraiture of the reign is undistinguished, and even the ideal heads do not attain the standard reached during the last years of Augustus. It is, indeed, necessary to point out that some of the present coins may be even later than the principate of Tiberius: the series of Aezanis shows that the choice of portraits was to some extent eclectic, since for its coins with the name of Claudius models are taken from heads of Tiberius[27] and Caligula,[28] besides Claudius himself.[29] But the specimens illustrated show the ugly general characteristics of the Tiberian epoch.[30]

---

[1] Bock, *Reliquienschatz zu Aachen*, pp. 67 f., cf. Montini, *Catalogo della Mostra Augustea di Romanità*, p. 111, 22 a, pl. XXXI.
[2] Visconti, *Les monuments de sculpture antique du musée Torlonia*, p. 121. 164.   [3] L.c. pp. 76, 78.
[4] As named by Curtius, *Röm. Mitt.* 1934, p. 130, cf. Abb. 4.
[5] Own collection with ΣΕΒΑΣΤΟΥ; cf. portrait on Vienna onyx (Eichler-Kris, *Die Kameen im Kunsthistorischen Mus.* Pl. 7. 14).
[6] *BMC.* 26.   [7] Munich, Istanbul.
[8] *BMC.* 115; cf. Divus Augustus, *BMC. Imp.* (Ti.) 158.
[9] Paris, cf. M. IV, 36. 184 (Zeus standing): perhaps bad copy of Bernoulli, *Römische Ikonographie*, II, 1, p. 178 n. 2, gem in BM. Also of this mint: own coll., Paris, Berlin, head of Zeus.
[10] Munich, Aristeas and Nicolaus [cf. *GM.* 282], has Tiberian head and is attributed to him; BM cast, Aristeas and Teisam. [cf. *BMC.* 197, *Numismatic Circular*, 1915, p. 512], has similar features; *Wad.* 1611 = Pl. XI, 9, Aristeas and Agreus, may well be post-Augustan. If this supposition is correct, the following, also signed by Aristeas, must be removed to a similar date: *BMC.* 198 with Nicostratus, Oxford = M. and S. VI, 124. 307 with Asclepiades, Vienna = *GM.* 282a with Metrobeis [sic].
[11] *BMC.* 18; cf. Divus Augustus, *BMC. Imp.* (Ti.) 141.
[12] *Lyd. S.* 78. 4.
[13] *Wad.* 892; cf. Berlin. Cf., for technique, Florence cameo (Bernoulli, l.c. II, 1, p. 95, pl. XXVII, 8).
[14] Paris, cf. Berlin, Munich.
[15] Paris = M. III, 39. 55.
[16] Paris = M. III, 167. 773, var. Berlin, Istanbul. Cf. Paris sardonyx (Babelon, *Catalogue des camées antiques et modernes de la Bibliothèque Nationale*, p. 117. 252, pl. XXVI).
[17] Paris ΔΗΜΟΣ, misdescribed by M. IV, 101. 553.
[18] *BMC.* 8; cf. Berlin.
[19] Vienna = M. and S. VII, 609. 551. Also *BMC.* 20. MG. 410. 141, Copenhagen; cf. *BMC.* 23. Cf. *BMC. Imp.* (Ti.) 46 for head.
[20] *Wad.* 2073; cf. Weber 6325.
[21] Cast in Winterthur = *KM.* 319. 39.
[22] Wrongly attributed by Muller, *Thorvaldsen cat.* p. 268, not only to Augustus but to Gargara: it reads CAΓ. Γ. like a coin of Ariassus (BM) with ΑΡΙΑΣ.Β., which it closely resembles in style.
[23] Gotha, Munich (rightly attr. by *BMC.* 15).
[24] Naples, var. Berlin, Munich, etc.
[25] ΣΕΒΑΣΤΟΥ ΚΤΙΣΜΑ: Zagreb.
[26] *BMC.* 52 ff. (cf. p. 386 n. 2).   [27] *BMC.* 87, 90.
[28] *BMC.* 76–7, 89.   [29] *BMC.* 75, 84–6.
[30] On a curious coin of Perga (Paris = Pl. XII, 14) the legend ΤΙΒΕΡΙΟΣ ΣΕΒΑΣΤΟΣ is accompanied by a portrait not in the least resembling Tiberius. It may however, be of Claudius.

APPENDIX 7

(2) CALIGULA. Provedly post-Augustan coins[1] of Aphrodisias (p. 329) indicate the influence of Caligula's features on the portraiture of ΣΕΒΑΣΤΟΣ coins—a subject also illustrated by the coinage of Nemausus[2] (e.g. Pl. II, 24), where the identification of the head was no less ambiguous. A number of other Asian coins with ΣΕΒΑΣΤΟΣ etc. likewise bear witness to the iconographic tendencies which began in this reign, to which, perhaps, a posthumous[3] seated figure of Augustus at the Hermitage[4] is to be referred. *Asia:* Aphrodisias (Pl. X, 17),[5] Apollonia Salbace (Pl. X, 13),[6] Attaea,[7] Cidramus (Pl. X, 14),[8] Dardanus(?),[9] Lampsacus,[10] Laodicea (Pl. X, 18),[11] Midaeum (Pl. X, 15),[12] Pergamum,[13] Trapezopolis(?).[14] *Galatia:* Aspendus,[15] Sagalassus (Pl. XII, 12).[16] *Epirus:* Nicopolis (Pl. XII, 6).[17] *Syria-Cilicia:* Ascalon,[18] Gaza,[19] Mallus (Pl. XII, 18).[20]

(3) CLAUDIUS. Coins with idealized portraits, proved on non-iconographic grounds to be of Claudian date,[21] are all paralleled in other mediums, and lead us to conclude that some of the finest and most popular conceptions of Augustus are those of Claudian engravers and sculptors.[22] Other styles, demonstrably of similar date,[23] are more grotesque.[24] Nemausan issues afford good analogies,[25] and some are closely akin to a posthumous[26] statue of Augustus at Aquileia.[27] On many of these the unheroic features of Claudius are more or less adapted; on others they are adapted little or not at all. But strong

[1] Compare a head at Copenhagen (Poulsen, *Kongelige Danske Videnskabernes Selskab, Archaeologisk-Kunsthistorisk Meddelelser*, II, I. 1–37, pl. LXI fig. 73).
[2] See above, p. 75.
[3] Montini, l.c. pp. 77f.
[4] Kieseritzky, *Eremitage*, p. 95. 193.
[5] *BMC.* 85; cf. Vienna onyx (Bernoulli, l.c. p. 310, pl. XXVI, 13).
[6] Rome, cf. *GM.* 428; cf. idealistic conception of terracotta at Amsterdam (Allard Pierson, *Allgemeene Gids*, p. 186, 1716). Rightly attributed by *GM.* 428.
[7] Karlsruhe, with ΚΑΙΣΑΡ.
[8] Cambridge, cf. *KM.* 139, Hirsch sale, XIII, 3881.
[9] BM = *NC.* 1920, p. 20.
[10] Own coll., cf. Baldwin, *Coins of Lampsacus*, 2 f.: cf. *BMC. Imp.* (Cal.) 14.
[11] *BMC.* 151; cf. glass cameo at Berlin (Furtwängler, cat. p. 349. 11210, pl. 68).
[12] Vienna: Germanicus not C. Caesar, *pace MG.* 409. 137; cf. New York head (Curtius, l.c. p. 131, Abb. 10), and *BMC. Imp.* (Cal.) 10, 11.
[13] BM = M. and S. v, 92 (with ΑΥ[τοκράτωρ]).
[14] Munich = M. III, 388. 494.
[15] Istanbul = M. S. VII. 28. 11.
[16] Munich, *Wad.* 3820, *Ant. GM.* 255.
[17] ΣΕΒΑΣΤΟΥ ΚΤΙΣΜΑ: Rome, var. Thorvaldsen coll. (rev. ΜΥΡΙΩΝΥΜΟΣ). ΑΥΓΟΥΣΤΟΣ (rev. tetrastyle temple): Christ Church (Oxford).
[18] Boutkowski, *DN.* 1745 etc.
[19] Morelli = M. and V. 536. 115.
[20] Milan = M. and S. VII, 226. 286.
[21] E.g. Laodicea ad Lycum (Pl. X, 20, 21, 22), Apollonia (ibid. 27), Tripolis (ibid. 30), Dionysopolis (ibid. 28), Pergamum (ibid. 46), Synnada (ibid. 25, 26), Siblia (ibid. 71), Metropolis (ibid. 72), Prymnessus (Pl. XI, 1), etc. See pp. 328 ff. above.
[22] The principal group (Laodicea etc.) recalls a Paris sardonyx (Babelon, l.c. p. 109. 237, Pl. XXIV) and probably explains its non-Augustan style, viewed with suspicion by Babelon. Cf. Marlborough sardonyces (Sale [1899] 390, 422), Uffizi sardonyx (Mustilli, *QA.*

VI, pl. IV, 19). The finest example is perhaps a cameo belonging to E. J. Hope-Masham, of which a photograph was given to the writer by R. P. Hinks. Possibly a prototype is the Vatican statue (Bernoulli, l.c. p. 29). In all cases the Asian coin-engravers take liberties in the direction of idealisation.
Other portraits in this undoubtedly Claudian category recall the following: Prima Porta Augustus (Strong, *CAH.* pl. VI, p. 148 is not invalidated but supplemented by Alföldi, *Röm. Mitt.* 1937, pp. 48 ff.—*pace* Frank, *AJP.* LVI, 1936, p. 405); Vatican bust (Fuchs, *Röm. Mitt.* 1936, pl. 30. 1); Louvre statue attributed to Caligula(?) (Bernoulli, l.c. p. 314, pl. XVI); or represent refined versions of *BMC. Imp.* (Claudius) 229, cf. Beverley cameo (Lippold, *Gemmen und Kameen*, p. 179, pl. 72. 3), and perhaps Athens head (Stuart, *The Portraiture of Claudius, Preliminary Studies*, p. 77. 38, not Claudius, *pace* Curtius, l.c. p. 135, Abb. 13).
[23] E.g. Dionysopolis (Pl. X, 32), Sebaste (ibid. 33), Philomelium (ibid. 40), Hierapolis (ibid. 35), etc. See above l.c.
[24] Such curious types strengthen the conclusion of Stuart, l.c. p. 50; cf. n. 257, that equally incompetent portrait-statues were not intended as burlesques. Cf. also Cervetri Claudius in Lateran, ibid. p. 70. 7; Bernoulli, l.c. pl. XIIIa. The peculiarities of these styles resemble those of a Paris sardonyx (Babelon, l.c. p. 110. 240, pl. XXIV) and the Vatican Claudius as Jupiter. For the Hierapolis coin cf. Berlin glass cameo (Furtwängler, l.c. p. 349. 11211), and sardonyx in BM (Walters, p. 339. 3596).
[25] Pl. III, 6, 7 (r), cf. Paris chalcedony 'Drusus jun.' (Babelon, pl. XXVI, 258). Pl. III, 7 (l), cf. Lateran statue of Nero Drusus (Bernoulli, l.c. p. 204, pl. XIII). Pl. III, 1 (l), cf. Gabii 'Germanicus' (Babelon, l.c. pl. X, cf. p. 237). Pl. III, 1. 4—elongated types of Caligulan coins, cf. Paris sardonyx as early as Tiberius (Babelon, l.c. pl. XXVI, 249).
[26] Cf. Montini, l.c. p. 81.
[27] Brusin, *Il Regio Museo Archeologico di Aquileia*, p. 9.

APPENDIX 7

iconographic probabilities have always been ignored in favour of a false deduction from the word ΣΕΒΑΣΤΟΣ, or a conventional attribution when this is absent.[1] Among coins whose portrait, rather than internal evidence, bears witness to a Claudian date are the following: Aninetus,[2] Antiochia ad Maeandrum (Pl. X, 36),[3] Cibyra (Pl. X, 41),[4] Clazomenae,[5] Cos (Pl. X, 37),[6] Dionysopolis(?),[7] Lampsacus (Pl. X, 43),[8] Magnesia ad Maeandrum (Pl. X, 39,[9] Pl. X, 42),[10] Miletus,[11] Mylasa (Pl. X, 38),[12] Nysa,[13] Orthosia,[14] Priene,[15] Thyatira,[16] Tiberiopolis.[17] *Galatia:* Sillyum (Pl. XII, 15),[18] Termessus minor (Pl. XII, 13).[19] *Thessaly:* Magnetes.[20] *Epirus:* Nicopolis.[21] *Macedonia* (Thrace): Abdera.[22]

(4) NERO. Group (4) (Pergamum) shows Neronian idealism, of which Nemausus records a more powerful variety.[23] The ideal Augustus of the period is conveniently dated by Aezanis (p. 328).[24] Iconographic considerations necessitate the addition of the following to the period: *Asia:* Alabanda,[25] Apollonia Salbace (Pl. X, 44),[26] Clazomenae (Pl. XI, 44),[27] Elaea,[28] Ephesus,[29] Euromus,[30] Germe,[31] Lampsacus,[32] Miletus(?),[33] Pergamum,[34] Tabae (Pl. X, 45),[35] Teos,[36] Thyatira.[37] *Galatia:* Attaleia.[38] *Thessaly:* Magnetes.[39] *Syria Cilicia:* Anazarbus.[40]

(5) GALBA. *Asia:* Cibyra (Pl. X, 48),[41] Clazomenae,[42] Cotiaeum.[43]

(6) FLAVIANS. *Asia:* Ephesus,[44] Euromus,[45] Priene,[46] Scepsis,[47] Tabae,[48] uncertain.[49] *Galatia:* Attaleia.[50] *Epirus:* Nicopolis.[51] *Moesia:* Istrus,[52] Tomis.[53] *Syria-Cilicia:* Augusta.[54] Now that the style becomes

[1] With very few exceptions, e.g. Ephesus, *BMC*. 203 ff.
[2] Cast at Winterthur = *MG*. 470. 74.
[3] Cambridge, cf. *BMC*. 28.
[4] *Wad*. 5819. For curious skull cf. Braccio Nuovo bust (Fuchs, *Röm. Mitt.* 1936, pl. 30. 1).
[5] *BMC*. 115 (probably).
[6] *BMC*. 224; cf. *BMC*. 229. *BMC*. 226 may or may not belong to the same generation. For nasal exaggeration of *BMC*. 224 cf. Paris sardonyx (Babelon, l.c. p. 142. 269, pl. XXVI).
[7] *BMC*. 16; *Wad*. 593. 6.
[8] Gotha (ΔΗΜΟΣ ΡѠΜΑΙѠΝ).
[9] Hague, cf. *KM*. 19; cf. *BMC. Imp.* (Cl.) 5, Berlin carnelian (Furtwängler, l.c. p. 110. 2331), Paris sardonyx (Babelon, l.c. p. 143. 272, pl. XXX), Evans cameo (Mustilli, *QA*. VI, p. 10, pl. III, 14).
[10] Berlin, cf. Thorvaldsen paste (Fossing, *Cat*. p. 266. 1967).
[11] Glasgow (*Hu*. 17), Cambridge (Grose 8242).
[12] Paris 20; cf. *BMC*. 22.
[13] Winterthur = *RS*. XIV, p. 11. 3.
[14] Paris (Philinus) wrongly described by M. III, 374. 462.
[15] Munich, cf. *KM*. 6 (attr. Vespasian).
[16] Copenhagen, cf. M. IV, 156. 889; a Paris specimen is more Neronian.
[17] *NZ*. XXXVIII, 1906, p. 248 (ΔΙΔΥΜΟΙ).
[18] Berlin, *Wad*. 3522; cf. *BMC. Imp.* (Cl.) 61.
[19] Athens, cf. Pl. X, 30 etc.
[20] Copenhagen.
[21] Munich, cf. M. II, 56. 80. Other Julio-Claudian of about this time are *BMC*. 7 ff., Paris (Naumachia), Thorvaldsen, and M. and S. III, 374. 101, Vienna var. *BMC*. 1, Hollschek coll. (rider).
[22] Gotha (ΑΥΤΟΚΡΑΤ. ΚΑΙΣΑΡ ΣΕΒΑΣ.).
[23] Pl. III, 9, 10; cf. above, p. 76 n. 4.
[24] Mabbott, *Rassegna Monetaria*, XXXIII, 1936, p. 548. Cf. posthumous sardonyx of Augustus and Agrippa at Paris (Babelon, l.c. pl. XXV, 245), Berlin carnelian (Furtwängler, l.c. p. 229. 9209), and Blacas agatonyx (Walters, *BMC*. pl. XXXVIII, 3577).
[25] *BMC*. 25; cf. 27—or Flavian.
[26] Berlin, cf. *KM*. 1; cf. Vienna onyx (Bernoulli, l.c. p. 158, pl. XXVIII. 1).
[27] Rome, cf. *NC*.1895, p. 283; also Paris, cf. Weber 5801.
[28] Munich, cf. *KM*. 1; Athens, *Wad*. 1326.
[29] Paris (ΣΕΒΑΡΤ. [sic]). [30] *BMC*. 8 (ΣΕΒΑΣΤΟΙ).
[31] BM (ΑΥΤΟΚ. ΚΑΙ. ΣΕΒΑΣ.).
[32] Own coll.; cf. *BMC*. 77, Baldwin 1.
[33] Muensterberg, s.v.; cf. M. III, 1240.
[34] Munich (ΑΥΤΟ. ΚΑΙΣ. ΣΕΒΑΣ.).
[35] Gotha, cf. M. and S. VI, 529; cf. (?) Rossie Priory head (Poúlsen, *Greek and Roman portraits in English country houses*, p. 63. 42). Perhaps Flavian: but Stratonicea (p. 330) shows that Nero's features could produce similar effects.
[36] Gotha, cf. *BMC*. 69 (ΣΕΒΑΣΤΟΣ ΚΤΙΣΤΗΣ).
[37] Paris, cf. M. IV, 156. 889.
[38] Berlin, cf. M. IV, 450. 27 f.
[39] Athens, cf. Wace, *JHS*. 1906, pp. 165 ff., 2.
[40] Istanbul, Oxford (ΚΑΙΣΑΡΕѠΝ ΤѠΝ ΠΡΟΣ ΑΝΑΖΑΡ[Βω]).
[41] Berlin, cf. *KM*. 24. [42] Paris, cf. M. and S. VI, 79.
[43] Winterthur, Gotha (ΣΥΝΚΛΗΤΟΣ).
[44] Own coll. For style of these cf. Berlin carnelian (Furtwängler, l.c. 8937).
[45] Vienna, 28236 (ΕΠΙ ΚΛΑΡΟΥ); *pace* Muensterberg.
[46] *KM*. 6 (ΑΥΤΟΚΡΑΤωΡ ΚΑΙΣΑΡ ΣΕΒΑΣΤΟΣ).
[47] *KM*. 6, correcting *MG*. s.v. [48] Vienna (ΚΑΙΣΑΡ).
[49] Hollschek (ΑΥΤΟ. ΚΑΙ. ΣΕΒΑΣΤΟΣ).
[50] Own collection.
[51] Athens (ΑΥΓΟΥΣΤΟΣ ΚΤΙΣΤΗΣ, Victory), *BMC*. 12 (ΣΕΒΑΣΤΟΥ ΚΤΙΣΜΑ), Paris (galley).
[52] Sofia, *NG*. I, 1, p. 171. 484 (ΑΥΤΟΚΡΑΤ. ΣΕΒΑΣ.).
[53] *NG*. l.c. p. 673. 2576, correcting Soutzo.
[54] Vienna (M. III, 43).

distinctively post-Augustan, efforts have occasionally been made to detach coins from the Augustan series.

(7) NERVA. *Asia:* Apollonis (Pl. X, 49).[1]

(8) TRAJAN. *Asia:* Attaea,[2] Ephesus.[3] *Galatia:* Attaleia.[4] *Syria-Cilicia:* Augusta.[5]

(9) ANTONINES. *Epirus:* Nicopolis.[6]

[1] Munich.
[2] *BMC.* 3, 4 (ΑΥΤ. ΚΑΙΣΑΡ ΣΕΒ.).
[3] Berlin (ΚΑΙΣΑΡ ΑΥΓΟΥΣΤΟΣ).
[4] Gotha.
[5] Vienna (galley).
[6] Athens (ΑΥΓΟΥΣΤΟΣ ΚΤΙΣΤΗΣ, Tyche), BM (ΣΕΒΑΣΤΟΥ ΚΤΙΣΜΑ, Naumachia), Copenhagen, cf. M. and S. III, 372. 88.

Appendix 8

ASIAN LOCAL ISSUES WITH CONTEMPORARY HEADS OF AUGUSTUS

The coins will be classified according to the following official categories of *denarius* of which they imitate the portraits:[1]
(1) c. 36 B.C. or earlier (pp. 49 f. n. 14).[2] (2) 'East I', c. 36–27 B.C. (ibid.). (3) 'Emerita', c. 25–22. (4) 'Caesaraugusta', c. 25–19. (5) 'East II', c. 20(?)–17.[3] (6) Rome, c. 19–12. (7) 'Patricia I', c. 19–15.[4] (8) 'Patricia II', c. 19–15.[5] (9) 'Lugdunum I', c. 15–6 B.C.[6] (10) 'Lugdunum II', c. 2 B.C.–A.D. 14.
The titles (except (6)) are intended as generic appellations—not as indications of mint, for which they are meaningless (pp. 122, 468 n. 11). The following table comprises the most frequent imitations by cities.[7]

A proviso must be added that many coins in Groups (8) and (10) may well be post-Augustan. The 'heroic' types which became so popular in Julio-Claudian times (p. 464) were strongly influenced by (8), as their juxtaposition in the Plates suggests.[8] Chief among the models for (10) were the famous 'CL Caesares' issues, which may well have continued after the *princeps*' death:[9] a hybrid[10] has this reverse with an obverse of Tiberius. The time-lags observed elsewhere (p. 463) make it particularly probable that a number of Asian coins imitating this category are posthumous. Two unpublished coins show particularly clearly the likelihood of this: a portrait at Apollonia Salbace inscribed ΤΙΒΕΡΙΟΣ ΣΕΒΑΣΤΟΣ (Pl. XI, 37)[11] is based on coins of this class,[12] and one at Siblia with · · · · ΟΣ ΣΕΒΑΣΤΟΣ (reverse ΔΗΜΟΣ ΣΙΒΛΙΑΝΩΝ;

---

[1] There are some whose barbaric or original execution make it impossible to discover what, if any, prototype was used. Among these are the following, most of which may be posthumous: Alinda (*KM*. 107. 4, *BMC*. 11), Cibyra (Paris), Cilbiani (Hague: Pl. X, 42 NIKAIEΩN, misattributed to Bithynian Nicaea), Cos ([Berlin] Perdicus, cf. M. III, 409. 86), Cyzicus (Ball 39. 1128 etc.), Dardanus (*Wad*. 1134), Elaea (*Wad*. 1324, cf. Oxford), Erythrae (*BMC*. 246, *KM*. 5), Ilium (*BMC*. 28, 31, *Wad*. 1154), Magnesia ad Maeandrum (Gotha, Euphemus Euphem., var. *KM*. 20), Myrina (Avignon: r. head of Zeus), Pergamum (*BMC*. 242), Phocaea (*BMC*. 131), Pitane (*Wad*. 991), Smyrna (*BMC*. 248), Temnus (*BMC*. 24, 27), Teos (*BMC*. 67, 68), Tralles (*BMC*. 114). The issues of Chios include a coin with Augustus's name but without his head (Mavrogordato, *NC*. 1917, p. 225).

[2] Including the *denarii* with a shield (*BMC*. 309 etc.).

[3] H. Mattingly agrees that the *denarii* with cow and IOVI OLV. as types (*BMC*. 659–69) are to be transferred from c. 27 to c. 17 B.C. (cf. above p. 103): these are here combined with the Armenian types (671 ff.) and later tetradrachms (694 ff.) to form 'East II'.

[4] E. A. Sydenham has pointed out to the writer a radical distinction between a class with thin features, a pointed skull, and a small muscular neck (*BMC*. 427 etc. = 'Patricia I') and the remainder, which are of idealised 'fine' style.

[5] Within this group with idealised portraits it is not possible to follow a differentiation of mint between coins with CAESARI AVGVSTO and a laureate head, and CAESAR AVGVSTVS and a bare head. They may represent successive varieties, but they are never far apart and sometimes merge completely, e.g. BM (in tray between 375 and 376) with legend of former and portrait of latter type (cf. 375).

[6] Differences of style, if not of mint, warrant a partition between *BMC*. 503 and 504: the groups are entitled 'Lugdunum I' and 'Lugdunum II' respectively. For the interval between them see Frank, *AJP*. LVI, 1935, pp. 336 ff.

[7] The numbers within the brackets refer to the Plates: those outside the brackets are from the Imperial Catalogue (Augustus): they are intended to give a general indication of the portrait-group to which the present pieces belong, rather than to point out an exact resemblance. The former is nearly always possible, since, as Brendel shows (*Ikonographie des Kaisers Augustus*, Diss. Heidelberg, 1931), the number of official prototypes was comparatively small.

[8] Montini, *Civiltà Romana*, v, 1938, p. 29, explains this fact by the contemporaneity of (8) with Augustus' last visit to the East: thereafter it was modified in accordance, not with the *princeps*' features, which were not again seen in the East, but with the imagination of successive artists. For the probable Eastern origin of (8) see below, p. 468 n. 11.

[9] For similar survivals see above, p. 75 (Nemausus), and Pick, *Die Münzkunde in der Altertumswissenschaft*, pp. 30 ff., Rostovtzeff, *SEH*. p. 513 n. 17.

[10] Own collection.

[11] Copenhagen = Rhousopoulos cat. 3873.

[12] *BMC. Imp.* 544 etc.

APPENDIX 8

Pl. XI, 38)[1] is clearly imitated from another.[2] Furthermore, a precisely similar head of Augustus occurs on a sheath decorated with types concerning the principate of Tiberius.[3] A head of Bacchus at Rhodes (Pl. XI, 47)[4] and the portrait on a chalcedony at Vienna[5] show the transition to a Tiberian type.

(1) has been omitted from this table since it is only represented at Nysa (Pl. XI, 40,[6] 41[7]) and Philadelphia (Pl. X, 50),[8] whose issues, being post-Actian, show a considerable time-lag. More surprising is the great scarcity of (3) 'Emerita', (6) Rome, and (7) 'Patricia I'. These groups are almost totally neglected by the Asian engravers. The first is entirely excluded in favour of the contemporary 'Celsa' type. The others may conceivably have influenced one issue each—at Magnesia ad Maeandrum (Pl. XI, 10)[9] and Laodicea (Pl. XI, 8)[10] respectively—but no more: they are ignored in favour of the abundantly copied 'East II' and 'Patricia II'. This fact may open the way to a new orientation of the official *aurei* and *denarii*, against whose accepted arrangement, as has been shown, much criticism can be levelled (pp. 83, 122, 269 nn.).[11]

---

[1] Own collection.

[2] *BMC.* 538. However, Cesano, *QA.* III, p. 26 illustrates a variety of this portrait as early as c. A.D. 3.

[3] BM, cf. *Proceedings of the Society of Antiquaries, NS.* II, 1866, p. 358.

[4] BM.   [5] Eichler-Kris, l.c. Pl. 6. 3.

[6] Istanbul, var. *BMC.* 24: cf. *BMCR.* pl. V, 3, attributed to 39 B.C.

[7] Cambridge (McLean 8684): severe style recalls head at Lansdowne House (Poulsen, *Greek and Roman portraits in English country houses*, p. 57. 34), attributed to the very beginning of the Empire. Montini's attribution (l.c. pp. 44 ff.) of numerous Hellenising busts to the first years after Actium is very dubious.

[8] *Wad.* 5135 = *Lyd. S.* 20 (Attalicos): closely imitated from *denarii* with shield (*BMC. Imp.* 309). So also are *Wad.* 5134 (Antiochus Apollodotou), Weber 3365 (C. Julius Dionysus), Cephale (Berlin = *RS.* VI, 269), Cleandrus (*Lyd. S.* 116. 18), Macedon (Vienna), Moschion Moschionos (*BMC.* 54). A curious feature of these is the legend ΓΑΙΟΣ ΚΑΙΣΑΡ, which has almost invariably led to attribution to Caligula: but these issues differ entirely in style and execution, as well as iconographically, from others that are certainly Caligula's (e.g. *BMC.* 51, 52, 53 etc.). Although this epigraphic standard is usually unhelpful (cf. below, Appendix 11, p. 479), the fact that the present group invariably have C, and Caligula's coins Σ, is in accordance with the other distinctions. ΓΑΙΟΣ ΚΑΙΣΑΡ might refer to the grandson of Augustus, but the early date of the portraits makes it much more probable that it belatedly applies to the *princeps* himself a title superseded at Rome a few years earlier (p. 415).

[9] Rome = *KM.* 23; cf. *BMC. Imp. Aug.* 100 etc.(?)

[10] *BMC.* 153; cf. *BMC. Imp. Aug.* 353 etc.(?)

[11] Between the termination of 'East I' and the establishment of 'Lugdunum I', two main stages have been noted: in the first of these Emerita and 'Celsa' are active, and in the second—from c. 19 B.C.—'Patricia I', 'Patricia II', 'East II' and Rome. It is highly significant that, in Asia, Emerita is first totally ignored (in favour of 'Celsa'), and then Rome and 'Patricia I' (in favour of 'East II' and 'Patricia II'). Since at least two of the three ignored mints are demonstrably Western, there is a strong presumption that emphasis or neglect by the engravers of the Asian local issues was, in general, determined by the extent to which the products of the various official mints circulated in their midst—and therefore, in all probability, by the geographical situation of those mints. (Although the *aurei* and *denarii* were universally accepted, their mints were presumably placed in such a way as to provide for neighbouring groups of provinces.) It is, in this connection, highly significant that the types on the official series can be divided into two principal lines of succession, (1) Emerita—'Patricia I'—'Lugdunum I' and (2) 'Celsa'—'Patricia II'. This main division corroborates the evidence of the Asian local issues: the two groups of official gold and silver are likely to be Western and Eastern respectively. In c. 15 B.C. all these provincial groups are merged in 'Lugdunum I', where portraits recalling all previous models are found. This rearrangement seems to be warranted by internal and external evidence.

APPENDIX 8

Group	(2)	(4)	(5)	(8)	(9)	(10)
Abydus	599 (X, 51)[1]	—	672[9]	—	—	—
Acmonia	—	—	700[10]	—	—	—
Adramyttium	—	330 (X, 66)[4]	—	—	—	—
Aezanis	—	—	700 (X, 62)[11]	—	—	—
Alabanda	—	322 (X, 65)[5]	—	—	—	—
Amorium	—	—	669 (X, 56)[12]	—	—	—
Antiochia ad Mae.	—	—	—	—	—	538,[30] 543[31]
Apamea	—	—	—	385 (X, 68),[22] 395 (X, 69)[23]	—	—
Aphrodisias	647(?)[2]	—	—	—	—	—
Clazomenae	—	—	680(?),[13] 673[14]	—	492[26]	—
Colophon	—	—	—	—	482 (XI, 27)[27]	—
Cos	—	—	—	—	—	519 (XI, 35)[32]
Cyzicus	—	—	681(?)[15]	—	—	—
Dardanus	653? (X, 54)[3]	—	—	—	—	—
Dioshieron	—	340 (X, 64)[6]	—	—	—	—
Elaea	—	—	660–4(?)[16]	—	—	—
Ephesus	—	(X, 63)[7]	678,[17] 702 (X, 59),[18] 697 (X, 58)[19]	—	490 (XI, 33)[28]	—
Erythrae	—	342(??)[8]	678(?)[20]	—	457 (XI, 26)[29]	534 (XI, 32)[33]
Eucarpitic district	—	—	—	376 (X, 70)[24]	—	—
Eumenia	—	—	—	—	—	536(?)[34]
Euromus	—	—	702 (X, 60)[21]	408[25]	—	—

[1] *Wad.* 1065.
[2] Berlin = *Wad.* 2526.
[3] BM, cf. *NC.* 1920, p. 20; *Wad.* 1134.
[4] Oxford, cf. *NC.* 1935. 199.
[5] Istanbul, ΚΑΙΣΑΡ ΣΕΒΑΣΤΟΣ.
[6] *Wad.* 1960 = Pl. VI, 64.
[7] Rome, cf. *KM.* 49, Philon and Euthycrates, shows the influence of this group, but most signed by Philon are later: vide 'East II', column (5).
[8] *BMC.* 255 ff.
[9] Paris = *Nomisma* VIII, 1913, 2. 1.
[10] *BMC.* 31.
[11] *Wad.* 5541.
[12] Naples, variants *BMC.* 23, Capitoline.
[13] *BMC.* 118; cf. *BMC.* 117, barbarous of same class (?).
[14] BM, ΚΤΙΣΤΗΣ.
[15] BM, cf. *BMC.* 210.
[16] Paris, ΕΠΙ ΝΑΡ., or posthumous ideal type.
[17] *KM.* pl. II, 17, Philon and Tryphonas; cf. Philon, with other names, *BMC.* 202, Paris = *RS.* XIII, 224.
[18] Paris, cf. *BMC.* 196, Asclas and Pammenes; others of Asclas vary more or less from this type, e.g. *BMC.*

195, 196 and 198; Karlsruhe = *Wad.* 1613, *KM.* 61, *GM.* 284 = 702.
[19] Gotha, cf. M. and S. VI, 309, Memnon and Nicolaus; cf. others of Memnon, Munich, cf. *NC.* 1841, p. 82; *Wad.* 1619, cf. *KM.* 57; *Wad.* 1618, cf. *KM.* 58, *KM.* 59.
[20] *BMC.* 248f., 251f.
[21] BM, ΑVΓVΣΤΟΣ [*sic*].
[22] Cambridge = *KM.* 14; cf. *Wad.* 5700, *KM.* 13a.
[23] *BMC.* 139 = 395 etc.
[24] Winterthur, cf. *BMC.* 13.
[25] *BMC.* 7, clumsily copied.
[26] *BMC.* 119.
[27] Berlin, cf. *ZfN.* XII, 1885, p. 315.
[28] Paris, Artemas = 490 etc., idealised; cf. others, perhaps posthumous.
[29] Copenhagen, cf. *BMC.* 250.
[30] *Kar. M.* 12; cf. *KM.* 110. 14(?).
[31] *GM.* 40.
[32] *BMC.* 220; cf. *BMC.* 223.
[33] *BMC.* 245.
[34] *BMC.* 36.

APPENDIX 8

Group	(2)	(4)	(5)	(8)	(9)	(10)
Heraclea Salbace	—	—	664(?) (XI, 34)[11]	—	—	536 (XI, 34)[11]
Hierapolis	—	315(?)[7]	—	362 (XI, 7)[16]	—	—
Hypaepa	—	339 (X, 67)[8]	—	412[17]	—	534[27]
Iasus	—	—	—	—	472(?)[25]	—
Ilium	632[1]	—	681[12]	—	→	—
Laodicea	650(?)[2]	—	—	414 (XI, 5)[18]	—	—
Magnesia ad Mae.	—	—	679 (X, 55)[13]	—	—	—
Mylasa	653,[3] 602 (X, 52)[4]	(?)[9]	—	—	—	—
Nysa	—	—	—	—	482[26]	526 (XI, 28)[28]
Pergamum	—	—	—	—	—	510(?),[29] 521,[30] 519 (XI, 29)[31]
Prymnessus	—	—	—	360(?)[19]	—	—
Samos	—	—	—	—	—	528[32]
Sardes	—	—	—	413,[20] 418 (XI, 6)[21]	—	508,[33] 510(?)[34]
Scepsis	—	—	—	—	—	508[35]
Smyrna	647(?)[5]	—	—	?407 (XI, 3),[22] ?418 (XI, 4)[23]	—	—
Tabae	—	—	—	—	—	539 (XI, 31)[36]
Teos	647(?)[6]	342[10]	670,[14] 713[15]	—	—	—
Tralles	—	—	—	—	—	526[37]
Trapezopolis	—	—	—	387 (XI, 46)[24]	—	—

[1] In trade, London: cf. *BMC.* 29 but head r.
[2] *BMC.* 151.
[3] *BMC.* 19; cf. Berlin = M. III, 355. 304.
[4] *BMC.* 24.
[5] *BMC.* 253.
[6] Paris = M. III, 1497; cf. *BMC.* 68.
[7] *Wad.* 6135.
[8] Paris, cf. M. IV, 71. 386.
[9] *BMC.* 24, of coarse execution, perhaps of this class.
[10] Ball 39. 1132; cf. *BMC.* 67.
[11] *BMC.* 18.
[12] Own collection = Schotten coll. 3110; Copenhagen = *GM.* 222.
[13] Berlin, cf. *KM.* 23.
[14] *BMC.* 70 = 670.
[15] *BMC.* 69 = 713.
[16] *BMC.* 97 is a heroic version of 362 etc.
[17] Berlin, Artemidorus.
[18] Istanbul, cf. M. IV, 317. 712.
[19] *BMC.* 18 f.
[20] *BMC.* 97 = 413 etc.
[21] *BMC.* 103.
[22] Glasgow = *Hu.* 182; cf. *BMC.* 248.
[23] BM, cf. *BMC.* 251.
[24] *BMC.* 9.
[25] Copenhagen, cf. M. and S. VII, 343. 506.
[26] Glasgow (*Hu.* 8684), Oxford (*NC.* 1939, p. 192 n. 2).
[27] Paris = Hirsch sale, XIII, 4052.
[28] *BMC.* 23.
[29] *BMC.* 239–41.
[30] *BMC.* 238.
[31] *BMC.* 236; cf. *BMC.* 237.
[32] BM = Weber 6324.
[33] *BMC.* 103.
[34] *BMC.* 213 (Homonoia).
[35] Copenhagen (capricorn)—attr. to Trajan !
[36] BM, cf. *KM.* 517. 1.
[37] *BMC.* 81 (Sun).

Appendix 9

ASIAN LOCAL ISSUES OF THE PRINCIPATE OF AUGUSTUS PORTRAYING MEMBERS OF HIS FAMILY

(1) LIVIA. Reason has been given for believing that many of her commemorations were post-Augustan (p. 329): many others are hard to date, since heads of the 'Livian type' may or may not be intended to represent deities invested with her attributes.[1] In this category (among others) are coins of Alinda,[2] Antiochia ad Maeandrum,[3] Astypalaea,[4] Germe,[5] Orthosia(?).[6] Some of these may be of the principate of Tiberius or even later. The only certainly Augustan issues that remain are of Pergamum:[7] possibly too she may be represented at Cyzicus.[8]

(2) JULIA. Cyzicus(?),[9] Pergamum.[10]

(3) CAIUS CAESAR. It has been pointed out that even his portraits cannot be certainly called Augustan, since some at Pergamum and Tralles are demonstrably later (p. 363). There are also heads[11] at: Alabanda,[12] Antiochia ad Maeandrum,[13] Aphrodisias,[14] Cilbiani,[15] Clazomenae,[16] Cyzicus,[17] Hierapolis,[18] Ilium,[19] Magnesia ad Maeandrum,[20] Magnesia ad Sipylum,[21] Nysa,[22] Pergamum,[23] Pitane,[24] Scepsis,[25] Sibliani,[26] Temnus(?),[27] Tralles,[28] Tripolis,[29] and issue without ethnic.[30] Apart from the possibility that many of these are post-Augustan, a further caution is imposed by the use of ΓΑΙΟΣ ΚΑΙΣΑΡ as a titulature not only by Caligula but by Augustus also (e.g. at Philadelphia [p. 468 n. 8]). Caius appears riding in a quadriga at Apamea.[31]

(4) LUCIUS CAESAR. Aegae,[32] Alabanda,[33] Cilbiani,[34] Clazomenae,[35] Cyzicus,[36] Elaea,[37] Ilium,[38] Magnesia ad Maeandrum,[39] Magnesia ad Sipylum,[40] Pergamum,[41] Pitane,[42] Scepsis,[43] Temnus(?),[44] Tralles:[45] also certain title issues without ethnic.[46] The name of Lucius—unless it is a magistrate's—appears without his head at Prymnessus.[47]

(5) TIBERIUS. It is impossible to determine when issues with ΤΙΒΕΡΙΟΣ ΚΑΙΣΑΡ belong to his principate and when to that of Augustus: but the portraits on issues of Acmonia[48] and Antiochia ad Maeandrum[49] make it very probable that a number are to be allotted to the earlier period.[50]

[1] As at Rome: Mattingly, *BMC. Imp.* p. cxxxv.
[2] Munich (club in wreath). [3] Munich (Apollo).
[4] Berlin, Munich = M. IV, 400. 2 (head of Dionysus).
[5] Berlin. [6] *BMC.* 2, Paris, Zagreb: or earlier(?).
[7] *BMC.* 248 (Charinus) (with Julia). Perhaps Tabae (Hirsch sale, XIII, 3940) is of similar date.
[8] Oxford (two female heads).
[9] As last. [10] *BMC.* 248 (with Livia).
[11] With name unless otherwise stated.
[12] Istanbul (with Augustus and Lucius).
[13] Cast at Winterthur = *Kar. M.* 12.
[14] *BMC.* 97, Gotha, Athens.
[15] *Wad.* 4945, Vienna etc. = M. IV, 29. 148.
[16] *BMC.* 120: posthumous(?).
[17] BM, Oxford, Munich, Gotha = Cahn sale, 60 (1928), 1378, M. II, 536. 161 (no name: with Lucius).
[18] *Wad.* 6145 (Cocus), 6144 (Heras), 6146 (Diphilus), Berlin (Papias, Acritas).
[19] Gotha, Athens (with Lucius).
[20] Berlin, *Wad.* 1742.
[21] Munich, correcting *Lyd. S.* 87. 2, M. IV, 71. 387 (no name: with Lucius).
[22] Gotha, correcting Boutkowski, *DN.* 2924.
[23] *BMC.* 246, 247.
[24] *Wad.* 990, Mabbott coll. = *GM.* 186.
[25] Berlin (with Lucius).
[26] *BMC.* 5 = *NC.* 1861, p. 200: posthumous(?).
[27] Turin (jugate heads).
[28] Copenhagen = M. IV, 183. 1060.
[29] *Wad.* 2680, Berlin = Egger sale, XLVI, 1589, M. IV, 593. 521 (incomplete).
[30] BM, Munich (different). Both insignificant and probably local. [31] *BMC.* 139: posthumous(?).
[32] Hollschek coll., correcting *MG.* 211 (Diphilus).
[33] Istanbul.
[34] *Wad.* 4945, Vienna etc. = M. IV, 29. 148.
[35] *BMC.* 120: posthumous(?).
[36] BM, Oxford, Munich, Gotha = Cahn sale, 60 (1928), 1378, M. II, 536. 161 (no name: with Caius).
[37] Gotha = M. and S. VI, 29. 194.
[38] Gotha, Athens. [39] Berlin, *Wad.* 1742.
[40] Munich, correcting *Lyd. S.* 87. 2, M. IV, 71. 387 (no name: with Caius).
[41] *BMC.* 246, 247.
[42] *Wad.* 990, Mabbott coll. = *GM.* 186.
[43] Berlin. [44] Turin (see n. 27).
[45] Berlin, Paris = M. and S. VII, 467. 698.
[46] BM, Munich (different). [47] Berlin = *GM.* 725.
[48] Munich, Nier coll., correcting M. IV, 198. 19.
[49] Copenhagen = M. IV, 316. 77.
[50] But Claudius also may possibly use this titulature (p. 463 n. 30).

Appendix 10

THE 'AUTONOMOUS' SERIES

This book has been planned to deal with such currencies of the period as are relevant, directly or indirectly, to the Roman State. For the sake of completeness, allusion will briefly here be made to the peregrine series which ignore Rome and its institutions, and may loosely be described as 'autonomous'. Mints whose output was partially of this type, but partially also of the types discussed in Part III, will not again be mentioned here unless their 'autonomous' issues are distinguished from their others in date. The following review does not claim to be critical or exhaustive, since the difficulties raised by the 'autonomous' groups are vast, and irrelevant to the historical purposes of this work. It is hoped, however, that even a general summary may facilitate reference and provide a slight assistance to research in this obscure subject.

(1) HISPANIA CITERIOR. In this region no peregrine city strikes purely autonomous Latin coinage under Augustus: but at an earlier date such series are provided by four Latin cities—Valentia,[1] Castulo,[2] Saetabis,[3] Osicerda[4]—and four probably stipendiary—Clunia,[5] Toletum,[6] Gili,[7] Tamusia.[8] A bilingual Osicerdan issue[9] is imitated from a *denarius* of Caesar:[10] otherwise chronological indications are lacking. Some of the series, e.g. those of Valentia, Clunia and Toletum, are likely to have ceased before our period. The chronology of Zobel etc.[11] has been entirely upset by Hill's demonstration that issues with Iberian legends continued until late in the first century B.C. (cf. p. 347).[12] It may be added that Iberian coins of the Ilergetes,[13] Tarraco,[14] Seθiscen[15] and perhaps Eustivaicola[16] appear to be influenced by Augustan portraiture, and those of Castulo bear the same countermark as Latin issues by Obulco.[17] It must, then, be supposed that these issues still flourished in the 'thirties B.C. and probably even later. The coins of Valentia[18] are signed by *quinquennales*[19] including members of some rare Italian *gentes*—C. Lucienus,[20] L. Coranius,[21] T. Ahius T. f.,[22] L. Trinius L. f.[23] The magistrates of Castulo are partly Iberian and partly Romanised. Toletum provides a C. Viccius,[24] the mysterious name CELTAMB[25] and the formula EX SC, probably referring to the local authority (cf. p. 473).[26] The numerous problems relating to these issues deserve a thorough study, which is beyond the scope of this work.

[1] Vives IV, p. 15; Hübner, *MLI*. p. 90; for status vide Kornemann, pp. 516, 528, Kubitschek, *Imp*. p. 200; cf. Pliny, *NH*. III, 20, Livy, *Epit*. 55, Sall. *Hist*. II, frg. 96. 6, Plut. *Pomp*. 18.
[2] Delgado III, 83, Hübner, l.c. p. 103 etc.; for status vide Pliny, *NH*. III, 25, Kubitschek, *Imp*. p. 191.
[3] Hill, p. 129; Pliny, *NH*. III, 25.
[4] Hill, l.c.; Pliny, *NH*. III, 24.
[5] Vives IV, pl. CLXXIII; Hübner, l.c. p. 77.
[6] Delgado III, p. 403; Hübner, l.c. pp. 8, 97; for status cf. Schulten, *PW*. (2R.), VI.
[7] Hübner, l.c. p. 47.
[8] Vives III, p. 113; Hübner, l.c. p. 96; Schulten, *PW*. (2R.) IV, 2151.
[9] Hübner, l.c. p. 42.
[10] Cf. Sutherland, *RIS*. pl. II, 7; Hill, l.c.
[11] *Commentationes philologicae in honorem Th. Mommsen* (1877), p. 820.
[12] P. 139; cf. Delgado III, p. 130.
[13] Hill, p. 73 (pl. X. 7).
[14] Ibid. p. 45 (pl. IV. 16).
[15] Ibid. p. 105 (pl. XIX. 8); cf. Caesaraugusta, pl. XIV. 2!
[16] Ibid. p. 62 (pl. VIII. 6).
[17] Lenormant, *La monnaie dans l'antiquité*, II, p. 20.
[18] Not a Roman colony as supposed by Sutherland, *RIS*. p. 79. For coins see his pl. II. 2.
[19] Cf. Kubitschek, *Imp*. p. 200.
[20] Vives, l.c. 1; cf. Schulze, p. 105. A certain Q. Lucienus was a senator in c. 67 B.C. (Münzer, *PW*. XIII, 1615).
[21] Vives, l.c. 2, cf. Schulze, pp. 355, 532.
[22] Vives, l.c. 3, cf. Schulze, p. 163.
[23] Vives, l.c. 3, cf. Schulze, p. 550.
[24] Cast in *BMC*.; for Vicius, Vicceius, vide Schulze, p. 261. The *gens* appears in Asia in the early Empire (*Eph. ep.* VII, p. 442. 1, and Hatzfeld, p. 167).
[25] BM cast. Misread by *Hu*. 109, Heiss, p. 263. 2, etc. Inadequate conjectural interpretation by Hübner, p. 97, Delgado III, p. 403, Vives etc.
[26] Schulten, *PW*. (2R.) VI, rightly discredits the reconstruction of other jumbled legends as the name of a quaestor Coelius Caldus.

APPENDIX 10

(2) HISPANIA ULTERIOR. The pre-Augustan period witnessed an unparalleled development of local currency in this region: coins have survived of more than sixty peregrine cities, mostly in Baetica. Resemblances to the dateable official and local mintages at Salacia, Vesci, Myrtilis, Baelo and Urso (pp. 23 f., 379) make it necessary to attribute the most productive period of coinage to the 'forties. The system was perhaps inaugurated by Caesar,[1] in whose monetary policy it clearly played an important part; it did not long survive the administration of Sextus. Every grade of peregrine community contributed (cf. p. 296):[2] the composition of an accurate list, although highly desirable, cannot be attempted here owing to the large number of unsolved problems which have no relevance to the historical themes of this book.

During the triumvirate the responsibility for local currency was transferred from the *peregrini* to the Roman cities, whose issues have been discussed. The only non-Roman community whose coinage may have survived for a time in entirely autonomous form was the *civitas foederata* Malaca,[3] which uses Punic legends: the Latin city of Carteia (p. 336) also continued to coin, but honoured the *princeps* on one occasion and later elected Germanicus and Drusus as its duoviri,[4] so that Malaca remains an isolated exception in the strictly autonomous category. Other Latin towns which still issued a few pieces include Sexi,[5] Osset,[6] and Nabrissa[7] (Pl. VII, 26); the coinage of the last three suggests inclusion in the foundation-category.[8]

The peregrine coinage of the earlier period is signed by the holders of various magistracies.[9] Roman names predominate, especially in Latin communities. Unusual are formulas such as *M. An. Ant. et Conl(egae)* at Baesuris,[10] the names of Q. Opsilius and L. Raius at Carteia[11], and the initials (?) CONIPP. at Obulco.[12] *Colp.* at Onuba[13] may be the transliterated version of a native title of office, and likewise *Bodo* at Lascuta.[14] The bilingual coin on which the latter designation is applied to L. Terentius and L. Numitorius[15] bears a remarkable type of boar and serpent which has been referred to the war of the Turdetani with Bogud II:[16] but many points remain obscure. Another issue of Lascuta[17] may or may not bear the formula SC; if it occurs, it is likely, as at Toletum, to refer to the local authority. Celtic and Iberian names occur at several cities which are mostly unidentifiable;[18] even at Carteia P. Mion.,[19] if this exists, recalls the

---

[1] Cf. Hübner, l.c. p. 8.
[2] E.g. Epora (Aipora) (Hübner, p. 111) (*foederata*, Pliny, *NH.* III, 10); Ceretani (Hübner, l.c. p. 132, id. *PW.* III, 1979, cf. Vives III, p. 78) (Latin, Pliny, *NH.* III, 23, cf. 'most of Turdetani' Strabo III, 151) and Myrtilis, Salacia, see above, ll. cc.; Callet (Vives III, p. 84) (*stipendiaria*, Pliny, *NH.* III, 12); etc.
[3] Hübner, l.c. p. 118; for status cf. McElderry, *JRS.* VIII, 1918, p. 70 etc.
[4] Hübner, l.c. p. 120.
[5] Vives V, p. 21. 14, cf. Heiss, p. 315. Neo-Punic word for *civitas* (p. 174 n. 8). Epithets F(*irmum* I(*ulium*) (Pliny, *NH.* III, 8) indicate Roman or Latin status (cf. van Nostrand, *UCPH.* IV, 2, 1916, p. 114). Owing to Pliny's frequent neglect of *Latinitas* in this region (ibid.) the latter is more likely here; it is also more in accordance with the character of the coin.
[6] Vives V, p. 95: L. Luc. P. Vet. (Madrid). Not likely to be Roman, as Hübner, *La Arqueología de España*, p. 178.
[7] Heiss p. 405: head of Minerva—CVIN statue on column. Suggestions that this can be attributed to Carthago Nova or Norba (ibid.) are absurd, since the ethnic at the former was [C]VINC(or K), and Norba was not *Iulia* but *Caesarina* (Pliny, *NH.* IV, 117, *CIL.* II, p. 81. 694). Since Heiss bears witness to S. Spanish provenance (the present writer has seen several in trade from Spanish sources), Nabrissa—of which earlier peregrine issues are known (Hübner, *MLI.* p. 127)—is entirely suitable. Pliny, l.c., describes it as *oppidum*,

and Detlefsen (*Philologus*, XXX, 1870, p. 296) mentions the probability of Latin status.
[8] See above pp. 335 ff. They are also not unlike the coins of Pax (p. 221), of which the model is of the 'Patricia' class, but the coins differ totally from contemporary issues of Roman colonies: perhaps Pax *Julia* (Kornemann 180) was Latin (it is omitted by Pliny) and the later *Augusta* Roman (Strabo III, 151).
[9] For *censores* and *quinquennales* at Carteia cf. above, p. 156.
[10] *Rn.* 1899, p. 244.
[11] Vives IV, p. 21.
[12] Ibid. III, p. 56.
[13] Ibid. III, p. 73.
[14] Delgado I, p. clxvii; cf. Zobel de Zangroniz, *Zeitschrift der deutschen morgenländischen Gesellsch.* 1863, p. 8, etc. Probably of Punic origin; cf. Vogüé, *Cyprische Inschriften*, Levy, *Phönizische Studien*, III, p. 10.
[15] An Antonian family: cf. Scott, *Memoirs of the American Academy*, XI, 1933, p. 13; Cic. *Phil.* III, 6, 15–17.
[16] Heiss, p. 358, Delgado, l.c. cf. p. 169, Hübner, *Mémoires numismatiques*, I, p. 18.
[17] Heiss, p. 357.
[18] Particularly mysterious is a group ascribed by Zobel de Zangroniz, *Rn.* VIII, 1863, p. 369 (cf. Hübner, *MLI.* p. 136) to Salacia, by Delgado II, p. 371 to Vama; for a signature *Odacis. A*, cf. Holder, *Altceltischer Sprachschatz*, II, p. 834. For other obscure issues vide Vives III, pp. 63, 92, 101, 114, Hübner, l.c. pp. 119, 128 etc., etc.
[19] Attribution not accepted by Delgado I, p. 92.

Iberian language,[1] and Obulco, which may also be Latin,[2] provides several further examples.[3] Other languages also occur.[4]

(3) AFRICA, Africa nova, Mauretania. The 'autonomous' issues of the African communities present problems of quite extraordinary difficulty. They are conspicuously lacking in any historical indication that would have warranted discussion in the text of this book or served to assist chronology. General stylistic considerations indicate that the issues did not commence until the triumvirate at the earliest, and that they continued until late in the principate of Augustus, to whose monetary scheme they brought considerable variety, but, as their extreme rarity suggests, no great material contributions. The neo-Punic ethnics are often obscure enough to have warranted the most varying interpretations: these need not be cited here (British Museum catalogues are hoped for and expected to supersede all previous literature). A Latin ethnic appears at Iol-Caesarea,[5] whose 'autonomous' coinage resembles those of Agrippias-Caesarea, Eusebeia-Caesarea and Perinthus, in that these cities were not free but royal property.[6]

(4) GAUL. Gallic tribal coinage continued to be current throughout the principate of Augustus (p. 124). With the exception of a few already quoted, references to Roman authorities are absent. The signatures of tribal officials are often inadequate for identification of their tribe, which must therefore depend largely on provenance: since inter-circulation was wide, attributions are seldom decisive. The latest general study, that of Blanchet,[7] leaves many questions unanswered and many answers disputed. Still obscure, for example, are the interesting issues of T. Pom. Sex. f. (p. 124 n. 10),[8] Cemiso *Ex s. c.*,[9] and Germanus Indutilli l. (ibid. n. 9). Spectrographic tests reveal that the last of these coins is composed of *orichalcum*;[10] further metrological researches could be based on the legend of the Lixovii, *Publicos simissos* (*sic*).[11] Gallic legends occur;[12] Greek is found in the south at the Latin city of Avennio[13] and in the tribe of the Samnagetes.[14]

(5) SICILY. There is much difference of opinion concerning the *terminus ante quem* of the 'autonomous' issues of Catana with Greek legends. As Hill[15] points out, it is improbable that Holm[16] is right in supposing that the coinage long survived the change from stipendiary[17] to colonial status (probably in 21 B.C.):[18] all other Sicilian colonies use Latin legends (p. 237). On the other hand, the belief of Head[19] and Scramuzza[20] that the series ceased as early as c. 100 B.C. does not do justice to the late style of some of the coins.[21] It cannot, however, be determined whether the mint still continued to function after the brief period of general franchise after 44 (p. 189). The same must be said of the Greek coinage of the stipendiary town

---

[1] Cf. Miono(?) at Mirebeau (*CIL.* XIII, 5617) and Limoges (Holder, l.c. s.v.).
[2] Pliny, *NH.* III, 10, epithet *Pontificense*. The general uncertainty as to statuses is suggested by McElderry, *JRS.* VIII, 1918, pp. 70, 77; cf. Steinwenter, *PW.* X, 1269 ff.
[3] Hübner, l.c. pp. 107ff.; Vives III, p. 57.
[4] Cf. Zobel de Zangroniz, *Z. d. deutschen morgenländ. Ges.* 1863, pp. 8 ff.
[5] Cherchell, Vienna, Copenhagen: Muller III, p. 138. 209 f.
[6] For Caesarea see Strabo XVII, 831. Some (but not all) coins bear the king's head and name (e.g. Muller III, p. 105. 50, p. 107. 72).
[7] *Traité*.
[8] *Traité*, p. 255; differing opinions of Barthélemy, *Étude des Monnaies gauloises frappées en Poitou* (1874), p. 14 (official), la Saussaye, *Numismatique de la Gaule Narbonnaise*, p. 181 (Sextantio), Longpérier, *Rn.* 1860, p. 178 (Petrocorii), Chaugarnier-Moissenet, *Numismatique gauloise* (1874), p. 3 (Arverni), Galy *pace* Senckler, *BJ.* XXI, 1854, p. 84 (Pompeians in 'Midi'), de la Tour, *Atlas des monnaies gauloises*, 4353 (Atectorix). For the *clientela* of Pompey in the Narbonese province cf. Syme, *Papers of the British School at Rome*, XIV, 1938, p. 15 n. 75.
[9] *Traité*, p. 86; cf. *Rb.* 1875, p. 304. As at Toletum and Lascuta, the formula is likely to refer to a local senate.
[10] Spectrogram 25.   [11] *Traité*, p. 321.
[12] E.g. Remi, ibid. p. 379.
[13] *Traité*, p. 440 f.; ibid. Pl. III, 35. Cf. above, p. 391 n. 8.
[14] *Traité*, p. 240.
[15] *Coins of Sicily*, p. 207.
[16] III, 709; *Das alte Catania*, pp. 44 ff.
[17] Orosius V, 13; cf. Kubitschek, *Imp.* p. 130.
[18] Pliny, *NH.* III, 89; cf. Kornemann 166, Mommsen, *CIL.* X, p. 720. Cf. above, p. 199.
[19] *HN.* p. 135.   [20] *ES.* p. 308.
[21] Recognised by Mattingly, *BMC. Imp.* p. xxiii n. 4.

APPENDIX 10

Amestratus,[1] some of whose issues[2] resemble the latest of Catana. Under Augustus no Sicilian peregrine city strikes 'autonomous' coins, with the possible exception of Panormus;[3] indeed, only one peregrine other mint survived, namely Segesta, which places the head of the *princeps* on its coins (p. 335).

(6) ACHAIA. Mrs Shear[4] has recently shown that, contrary to the general view, the free city of Athens coined regularly throughout the principate of Augustus; her discovery of ΣΕΒΑΣΤΟΣ on certain specimens, however, is unauthenticated (p. 401 n. 10). The coinage of Sparta[5] is mainly, but not entirely, autonomous (pp. 343, 382). It is very hard to decide which other currencies fall in this period, owing to the uninformative character of types and feeble eclecticism of style. On the mainland Aegium[6] and Pheneus[7] are likely to have coined in the triumvirate or a little later; Lemnos[8] (in the Athenian Empire),[9] Andros[10] and Paros[11] perhaps swelled the exiguous island-coinage under Augustus of which the part with Imperial portraits has been described (p. 354).[4] The Epirote mints of Cassope[12] and Corcyra[13] (*civitas libera*)[14] may also not have been entirely inactive, and the Thessalian league, before coining under Augustus (p. 363), may have issued an autonomous piece to celebrate its liberation by Caesar.[15] But the criteria are inadequate for the compilation of a complete list.

(7) MACEDONIA-MOESIA. The main body of the double province adds only Tomi[16] to the list of cities with an exclusively 'autonomous' coinage in this period. But the principle may be established that independent urban enclaves in the territory of client-kingdoms were attributed to the general supervision of the nearest governor: thus Abdera (*civitas libera*) (p. 375),[17] which coined perhaps under the triumvirate,[18] must be mentioned here. Chersonesus[19] also issued pieces at this time, the word EΛEY. indicating that the change from royal dominion (Strabo[20]) to *libertas* (Pliny's source)[21] had already occurred. However, as in Numidia at Iol-Caesarea, royal rule was here no obstacle to local coinage, since issues of Augustan date occur at Panticapaeum[22] and Agrippias-Caesarea[23] (Phanagoria), both of which belonged to the Bosporan dynasty.[24] Olbiopolis produced an extensive series,[25] whose imitation of Roman and Bosporan portraiture does not warrant identifications with Caesar,[26] Antony,[27] Augustus[28] or kings.[29]

(8) ASIA. This province provides a large bulk of 'autonomous' *aes* coinages during this period. They may—by a very rough approximation—be classed in two groups, with Actium as the point of division:

(a) c. 49–31 B.C. (cities sometimes referring to Antony or his wives, or to governors of the period, are here omitted).[30] Alinda,[31] Aphrodisias-Plarasa,[32] Blaundus(?),[33] Caunus,[34] Chios,[35] Dionysopolis,[36] Elaea,[37]

---

[1] Hülsen, *PW*. I, 1828, Mommsen, *CIL*. X, p. 769.
[2] Vatican: variety of *BMC*. p. 31.
[3] *BMC. Sicily*, p. 58 etc. Cf. above, pp. 197 f. n. 6.
[4] *Hesperia*, 1936, pp. 285 ff.
[5] *BMC.* 62 ff. etc.
[6] *BMC.* 6–9 (Theoxius).
[7] *BMC.* 25 (Hermaxous).
[8] Gotha, Athens.
[9] Cf. Fredrich, *PW*. XII, 1930.
[10] Hague.
[11] Oxford, cf. *BMC.* 28 etc.
[12] *BMC.* 16.
[13] *BMC.* 604 ff.(?), cf. Glasgow (*Hu.* II, p. 21. 52).
[14] Pliny, *NH.* IV, 12. 19.
[15] Glasgow (*Hu.* I, p. 459. 27, cf. Macdonald, l.c., *pace BMC.* 43 f. attr. to Thessalonica). See Rogers, *Ancient Coinage of Thessaly*.
[16] Sofia, Gotha, Paris, *BMC.* 4 f.; several varieties.
[17] Pliny, *NH.* IV, 42; cf. Jones, *CERP*. p. 14.
[18] Paris.
[19] Colls. Prowe, Bertier Delagarde; Koehne, *Description du Musée de feu le prince Kotschoubey*, pp. 186 ff.; Oreshnikov, *Numizmaticheskago Svornika*, III, 1914, p. 44; cf. von Sallet, *ZfN.* I, 1874, p. 27, IV, 1877, p. 273.
[20] VII, 308; cf. Brandis, *PW*. III, 2268.
[21] *NH.* IV, 85.
[22] Giel, *Zapiski Imp. Russk. Arch. Obschch.* V, p. 349. 34.
[23] *BMC.* 1 ff.; cf. *NZ.* 1870, p. 250, *NC.* XVI, p. 98.
[24] Cf. Tomaschek, *PW*. I, 899.
[25] Burachkov, Koehne (l.c. p. 80), catalogues of Odessa and Kotschoubey collections, are the completest studies.
[26] Couris coll., cf. Boutkowski, *DN. s.v.*
[27] Specimens at Paris show a resemblance.
[28] Specimens at Paris show a resemblance; cf. attributions by Boutkowski, *DN.* 1604 f.; Head, *HN.* p. 273.
[29] Specimens at Paris recall the style of royal coinage.
[30] References will be given to single coins rather than to books since types often persisted through a long period.
[31] Gotha.
[32] Athens.
[33] BM (or earlier?).
[34] Berlin (*KM.* 1).
[35] Cf. Mavrogordato, *NC.* 1917, p. 207.
[36] Munich.
[37] *BMC.* 16 ff., 28, 29.

Epicteteis(?),[1] Eriza,[2] Erythrae,[3] Heraclea ad Latmum(?),[4] Hydisus(?)[5] Ilium,[6] Laodicea,[7] Neapolis ad Harpasum,[8] Orthosia,[9] Pergamum,[10] Samos,[11] Tabae.[12] The lack of chronological indications is so serious, and stylistic criteria so uncertain, that this list makes no claim to completeness or accuracy; the coins cited could not, however, be much earlier than Caesar or later than Antony.

(b) c. 31 B.C.–A.D. 14 (cities sometimes referring to Augustus or his family, or to the senate and its governors, are here omitted). Amyzon,[13] Bargasa,[14] Lebedus,[15] Rhodes,[16] Samos,[17] Thyatira.[18] Many more coinages appear to fall to the first three decades after the death of Augustus. The present lists are, as far as they go, entirely in harmony with the conclusion concerning *libertas* reached elsewhere (p. 401), but it is difficult to see how they could be anything but fragmentary.

(9) GALATIA. The cities Aspendus, Bubon and Termessus, and the Lycian League, which place the head of Augustus on their coins (pp. 354 f., 342 f.), appear to have monopolised the peregrine currency of this province from Actium until A.D. 14. To the rule of Caesar or Antony may tentatively be ascribed issues of the following communities: Balbura,[19] Cremna[20] (Pl. XII, 11), Etenna,[21] Iconium,[22] Perga,[23] Pessinus,[24] Tavium;[25] the coinage of Termessus major[26] ceased soon after Zela.

(10) BITHYNIA-PONTUS. Byzantium, which was a free city attached to this province, issued a single coin with Antony's head (p. 369), but during the principate of Augustus only struck pieces of 'autonomous' type.[27] Many of its issues have a curious style suggesting the use of the chisel, which adds to the usual difficulties of chronological attribution.

(11) SYRIA-CILICIA. In Syria etc. Tyre[28] and Samosata[29] coin regularly, and Botrys,[30] Marathus[31] and Rhosus[32] occasionally, without reference of any kind to the Roman state. In Cilicia purely 'autonomous' series are more plentiful than those with the *princeps*' head, being found, at various dates within this period, at Adana,[33] Celenderis,[34] Corycus,[35] Elaeussa,[36] Seleucia ad Calycadnum[37] and Tarsus.[38]

[1] Vienna (or earlier?).
[2] BMC. 1.
[3] Berlin (KM. p. 65).
[4] Copenhagen, Athens.
[5] BM (or earlier?).
[6] BMC. 18 f.
[7] Brussels.
[8] BM.
[9] BM.
[10] BMC. 163, 183 etc.
[11] Milan.
[12] Wad. 2614.
[13] Berlin, in trade (Paris).
[14] Paris.
[15] BMC. 13, 15.
[16] Oxford.
[17] BMC. 210 ff.
[18] Paris.
[19] BM.
[20] BM.
[21] Paris.
[22] BM.
[23] Wad. 3333.
[24] Wad. 6653.
[25] BMC. 1 f.
[26] BMC. 12 ff.
[27] Christ Church, Paris, Istanbul, Glasgow (?) (Hu. I, p. 395).
[28] Rouvier, JIAN. VI, 1903, pp. 308 ff.
[29] BMC. 1 ff., Paris. For Sidon see above, pp. 126, 345.
[30] Beyrouth (American College), Hoffmann coll.; cf. Rouvier, JIAN. II, 1899, p. 9, IV, 1901, p. 35.
[31] Rouvier, JIAN. IV, 1901, p. 146.
[32] Brussels; cf. M. v, p. 269. 836.
[33] BMC. 12, Oxford, Istanbul.
[34] BMC. 40.
[35] BMC. 9; Wad. 4251 is tooled.
[36] BMC. 10 etc. (before 20 B.C.).
[37] BMC. 15, Oxford; perhaps also Wad. 4454.
[38] BMC. 122 etc.

Appendix 11

ART

The *aes* coinage throughout the Empire provides an extraordinary wealth of material for the study of provincial art. It includes a series of documents which outdoes all other contemporary evidence in extent and probably also in value: this value is enhanced by the unselfconscious carelessness with which many of the types are executed. Yet this unique source is entirely ignored. The individuality of the native traits which were to contribute so much to the evolution of medieval art is indicated by the fact that not much experience is needed to determine at first sight, with fair certainty, the region in which an *aes* coin of this period was struck.[1]

It is only to be expected that the general level of accomplishment is low. As on the official gold and silver,[2] very little care is devoted to reverse-types. The portraiture too sometimes sinks to depths untouched by those series, often in attempts to imitate them: but it also records some astonishing successes which, for their brilliant use of a small field, are worthy of inclusion among the most interesting artistic productions of the Roman world. Good and bad alike bear the stamp of regional influences, which are sometimes (though not usually) as perceptible on official as on local *aes*. This is not the place for an attempt to assess the numerous artistic influences that were at work, or to institute comparisons with other arts: but such tasks, whose importance would be very great, may be assisted by a rapid review of the principal tendencies and most remarkable achievements. Before this is attempted, however, it must be pointed out that many of the criteria for regional attribution are based on considerations too intangible for description.

The earliest Italian issue, of Clovius, is in the best Hellenistic tradition, and Antony's 'Fleet' coinage, at the other end of the peninsula (?), attains some notable compositions under Greek influence. The finest products of Octavian's official mint at Puteoli(?) (Pl. I, 14) are expressive Italic portraits in low relief, better than those later attained on the Roman *aes*. The latter varies widely, but remains undistinguished, though never so poorly executed as the output of Paestum (Pl. VII, 9–15). An interesting Italian style of portraiture is that of the CA mint at Aquileia(?) (Pl. IV, 10). Until the first enfranchisement of Sicily its numismatic art under the Romans is colourless; thereafter it is abominable (Pl. VI, 1, 2, 3, 18). The contrast to its heyday is hardly credible. Occasionally a certain unpleasing individuality is attained by its portraiture (Pl. VI, 17, XII, 28). The military mint at Lipara, however, has more competent craftsmen whose native origin is revealed by pronounced Libyo-Punic traits; if more could be seen of it, a portrait of Statilius Taurus(?) (Pl. II, 13) might have merit. The coinage of other islands in the neighbourhood of Sicily, Melita and Cossura, has an unmistakable style in which the Semitic element is even stronger. The technique of **Sardinian** engravers is rudimentary (e.g. the eye is rendered most primitively—Pl. VI, 4), but there is much character in the portrait of M. Lurius(?) (Pl. VI, 19). Here too Punic influences are strong.

Spanish mints provide examples of native influences (Pl. V, 18–22). The style at Malaca is predominantly Punic, and there is not much difference between the issues of South Baetica and the Mauretanian coast. Celtiberian traits are frequent: they persist in exaggerated form—perhaps for political reasons (p. 325)—at *municipium* Emporiae (Pl. V, 15–17). Elsewhere they diminish gradually. But the colonies soon achieve the 'academic and banal'[3] semi-Romanised style characteristic of Spain, with a Greek tinge in the South. The portraits are mostly slavish imitations of Roman official coinage; but a head of Cn. Statius Libo at Saguntum (Pl. VI, 9) is an original application of late Republican methods.

The official mints in **Gaul** show very strong native influences. Of the Augustan issues at Nemausus very few rise above a semi-barbarous technique, whose persistence makes it impossible to consider every coin which manifests it an 'imitation' (Pl. II, 17, 18, 21, 22, 23). The only successful aesthetic achievement

---

[1] For the strength of provincialism in the Empire, vide Stevenson, *RPA*. p. 132.
[2] Cf. Mattingly, *BMC. Imp.* p. lxii.
[3] Albertini, *CAH*. XI, p. 498.

is a portrait of Agrippa (Pl. II, 20). The earlier products of Lugdunum as an official mint are equally variegated, and often very poor; but a few heads show traces of Greek idealism. Towards the end of the reign a more sober and consistent Roman style was initiated. Official issues from Northern Gaul (e.g. Hirtius, Pl. IX, 24–25, and Pl. IV, 19) are wholly Gallic in appearance.

In Africa the issues of Byzacene, Zeugitana and Numidia show an unmistakable and persistent individuality which bears witness to a firm fusion of the three principal racial elements (Roman, Libyan, Punic[1]) to form a homogeneous graphic art. Of Greek influences the signs are few. Characteristic of the area is a virile *gaucherie* to which Roman Republican art contributes much. But the portraits, which are the most curious manifestations of the African spirit, owe their measure of success not a little to native originality. The ill-preserved coins still bear witness to fine impressions of Julius (Pl. II, 12), Sittius (Pl. VI, 15, 16) and Augustus (Pl. VIII, 3), and the sketch of Ambatus (Pl. VI, 13) is expressive and vigorous. But even here the treatment of the eye is lateral and rudimentary; the technique of other coins is frankly barbarous (Pl. II, 4, 5) or incompetent (Pl. VI, 24). The official foundation coinage issued at Iol-Caesarea provides interesting animal-studies (Pl. II, 16); Tingis, after several native efforts, produces a competent full-faced head of Baal (Pl. VI, 11). In Tripolitana the Punic element predominates. The official currency of Cyrenaica is mostly very crude, but the head of a divinity on the issues of Lollius is an accomplished Hellenistic performance. The Alexandrian mint under Augustus shows various interesting types but dull execution.

Characteristic of the **Balkan provinces** is a mild, neat, uninspired style, of which both Greek and Roman constituents can be noted, the former usually predominating, e.g. on CA portraits of the region (Pl. IV, 11, 13, 14). Hellenistic heads of Augustus in the Euxine Pentapolis and of Zeus at Buthrotum (Pl. VIII, 20) are in good taste; more interesting is a bust of Atratinus in the same manner at Sparta (Pl. XII, 3). A head of Hortensius (Pl. II, 7), to which the condition of the two surviving specimens does not do justice, was probably not much inferior. A Greek conception of Julius Caesar from his shortlived official mint at Thessalonica (Pl. II, 3) is of quite exceptional merit and must rank very high among extant iconographic records of the dictator. A severer version of him, also of merit, is provided by the foundation-issue of Corinth (Pl. VIII, 19), which later portrays the *domus Augusta* (Pl. IX, 13–16). Roman influences, and flattering adaptations to the physical type of Augustus, can be noted at Chalcis (Pl. XII, 1, 2). Other portraits show the incompetence of native work (Pl. VIII, 26 etc.). This region is one of the few to make some attempt at reverse composition. Among the Greek cities Tanagra provides the three Graces, and Nicopolis a sea-fight. Hortensius uses the Roman devices of plough, yoke and vexillum with streamers flying in the wind (Pl. II, 8), and, by faulty co-ordination, his foundation-issue at Dium shows just such a vexillum being trampled on by Diana Baphyra (Pl. IX, 18). At Pella appears a sketch of the town-walls (Pl. IX, 19).

Asia is sufficiently extensive and variegated for its several regions to have characteristics that enable a fairly close attribution of uncertain coins within the province. In **Mysia-Troas** the Greek issues are generally very small and feeble: heads of Antiochus at Miletopolis (Pl. XI, 60) and Augustus at Cyzicus are interesting but not competent. Characteristic of local technique is the portrait of the 'capricorn' coinage (Pl. IV, 32); the 'colonist' issues in this region include nothing of note. The colonial coinages soon after Philippi provide some curiosities, such as a less refined adaptation of the Macedonian head of Julius (Pl. II, 3) at Alexandria Troas (Pl. VIII, 5), another version of the dictator at Lampsacus (Pl. VIII, 6), and a ploughing scene in perspective at the same mint. Some portraits of Octavian and Agrippa at Parium show a mixture of Greek and Roman motifs. **Ionian** art achieves some portraits on the CA coinage which are among the best products of the time (Pl. III, 29, Pl. IV, 1), and include numerous spirited variations on the theme of the 'cow' *denarii* portraits (Pl. III, 28). Elaea (Pl. X, 57) and Clazomenae (Pl. XI, 44) strike an even more idealistic note, and Erythrae improves on the heroic Augustan type (Pl. XI, 32), perhaps after the *princeps'* death. Other portraits are not very skilful, except one of Cicero *pro cos.* at Magnesia (Pl. IX, 32). In **Caria** barbaric tendencies are noticeable, and Greek work is usually undistinguished; a series of portraits at Alabanda, however, includes some of considerable merit (Pl. XI, 54, 55, 56, 57, 65), and a high standard is maintained at Rhodes. **Lydian** work is generally confined to inferior Graecised

[1] Cf. Albertini, l.c. p. 487.

copies of Roman models, but Nysa provides two unusual renderings of Octavian (Pl. XI, 40, 41). In **Phrygia** reverse-types are as usual stiff and characterless, but the portraits show a better average of taste than those of any other district. An original creation of Hierapolis is the 'Young god' version of Augustus (Pl. XI, 11, 12, 13, 16, 17, 18). Fabius Maximus at the same mint (Pl. XI, 58) and Pythes at Laodicea (Pl. XI, 61) have personality. Characteristic of the region is a mature Hellenistic idealism, best seen in the numerous adaptations of the 'Patricia' type of head (e.g. Pl. X, 69-72, Pl. XI, 1, 7). Roman influence is lacking; the Phrygian issues of the Commune Asiae (Pl. XII, 33) may show barbarian tendencies.

The remaining parts of Asia Minor mostly have styles which are distinguishable at least within certain broad limits. The modified Hellenism of the north coast is best expressed by the 'colonist' pieces which can be attributed to **Bithynia-Pontus**. The colony of Sinope uses a coarse and primitive style without Greek elements (e.g. Pl. VIII, 13); at Apamea there is a neat and sober Romanism (Pl. VIII, 15, 16, 17) with certain traits shared by other Bithynian cities. The heads of Pulcher at that city (Pl. VIII, 14) and Thorius at Nicaea (Pl. XII, 9) are unsuccessful; but the coinage of an earlier proconsul, Pansa, provides an admirable portrait of Caesar (Pl. XII, 8). In the province of **Galatia** barbaric traits predominate, even on the official currency of Basila (Pl. IV, 22, 23). Lycian art is imitative (e.g. Pl. XII, 31), Pamphylian non-existent (Pl. XII, 12, 15). Stranger is the mixture of elements at the Roman colonies—as at Antioch in Pisidia (Pl. VIII, 12) and Lystra (Pl. VIII, 10, 11). The foundation-issue of the latter colony in the 'forties B.C. is remarkable for an extraordinary feat of realistic portraiture—the head of Rutilus (Pl. VIII, 8). A contrast in styles is provided by a fine portrait at Mallus in Cilicia (Pl. XII, 18). One of the aesthetic curiosities of the period is the strong individuality maintained by the official mint in **Cyprus** (Pl. III, 17, IV, 8, 24, 25). The output of the two cities in **Crete**, Cnossus (Pl. VIII, 18) and Cydonia (Pl. XII, 7), is of execrable quality, with the exception of a few Hellenised portraits at the former.

Research would be most rewarded in the **Syrian** region, where numismatic styles are as unusual, mixed and obscure as those in other mediums. Antioch is the centre at which Hellenism is most competent and from which it radiates: Antiochene local and official issues (Pl. III, 21, 22) have characteristic Graeco-Roman versions of Augustus. A more original and sympathetic study of the *princeps*, however, is afforded by the official mint of Regulus at Sidon(?) (Pl. IV, 21) and its imitator at Balanea (Pl. XII, 20). The earliest issues of Berytus, however, are strangely devoid of Greek influence. Strzygowski might also discern native and oriental influences of various kinds at Orthosia (Pl. XII, 21), Damascus (ibid. 22), Ascalon (ibid. 24) and Petra (ibid. 25). No less striking and diverse are the techniques of various unidentifiable SC mints (Pl. III, 16, 18, 20, cf. 24, 25), the SC-CA mint (Pl. III, 19, IV, 6), an AVGVSTVS mint (Pl. IV, 7), and Sidon(?) its copier (Pl. IV, 15, 17). See also Pl. I, 19 (Victory) and Pl. IX, 23 (Antony).

Epigraphy is virtually useless as a guide. It is true that African inscriptions are generally large and coarse, Bithynian cramped and meagre, etc., but there is no uniformity. Nor are individual letters more helpful, except in rare cases. A certain evolution in the letter P can be noted at Emporiae, but retrogressions are frequently found. G appears in a curious form in Mysia (Pl. IV, 32) and Syria (Pl. III, 19, IV, 6); it is often indistinguishable from C. Early forms of L may occur at Paestum and Turris Libisonis. As an aid to chronology, *Sigma* is disappointing: taken all in all, there is a general tendency to the square form, but variations occur from city to city and even from coin to coin. Punctuation is very unreliable, but only at Emporiae are dots inserted, as a decorative motif, in the middle of words. Monograms and ligatures are ingenious and arbitrary often to the point of insolubility (p. 494).

ABBREVIATIONS

AA.	Archäologischer Anzeiger.	CIL.	Corpus Inscriptionum Latinarum.
Abbott and Johnson.	Municipal Administration in the Roman Empire.	CJ.	Classical Journal.
		CP.	Classical Philology.
Abh.	Abhandlungen.	CQ.	Classical Quarterly.
AJA.	American Journal of Archaeology.	CR.	Classical Review.
AJP.	American Journal of Philology.	CW.	Classical Weekly.
Ann. dell' Inst.	Annali dell' Instituto di Corrispondenza archeologica.	Delgado.	Nuevo Metodo de Clasificación de las medallas autónomas de España.
Ant. GM.	Imhoof-Blumer, Antike Griechische Münzen.		
Ath. Mitt.	Mitteilungen des deutschen archäologischen Instituts, Athen. Abt.	Diz. ep.	Ruggiero, Dizionario epigrafico.
		Eckhel, DN.	Doctrina Numorum.
BB.	Berliner Blätter für Münz-, Siegel-, und Wappenkunde.	EHR.	English Historical Review.
		ES.	Economic Survey of Ancient Rome.
BCH.	Bulletin de correspondance hellénique.	Feldm.	Blume, Lachmann und Rudorff, Schriften der römischen Feldmesser.
BGU.	Ägyptische Urkunden aus den Museen zu Berlin, Griechische Urkunden.		
BJ.	Bonner Jahrbücher.	Gabrici.	Atti della reale accademia di scienze, lettere e belle arti di Palermo 1926.
Blanchet, Traité.	Traité des monnaies gauloises.		
BMB.	Berliner Münzblätter.		
BMC.	British Museum Catalogues (Greek).	Ganter.	Die Provinzialverwaltung der Triumvirn, Diss. Strassburg, 1912.
BMC. Imp.	Ditto (Imperial, Augustus unless stated).	Gardthausen.	Augustus und seine Zeit.
		GGA.	Göttingische Gelehrte Anzeigen.
BMCR.	Ditto (Republic).	GM.	Imhoof-Blumer, Griechische Münzen.
Bolin, Fynden.	Fynden af Romerska Mynt i det fria Germanien.		
		GRMzk.	Imhoof-Blumer, Zur griechischen und römischen Münzkunde.
Bosch, KM.	Die Kleinasiatische Münzen der römischen Kaiserzeit.	Gsell.	Histoire ancienne de l'Afrique du Nord.
Boutkowski, DN.	Dictionnaire numismatique.		
Broughton.	'The Romanisation of Africa Proconsularis' (Johns Hopkins Univ. Studies, NS. V, 1929).	Hammond.	The Augustan Principate.
		Hatzfeld.	Les trafiquants italiens dans l'Orient hellénique.
		Head, HN.	Historia Numorum.
CA.	Conferenze Augustee (Pubblicazioni dell' Università Cattolica del S. Cuore, Sc. stor. Ser. V, XVII, 1939).	Heiss.	Monnaies antiques de l'Espagne.
		Hill.	'The coinage of Hispania Tarraconensis', Numismatic Notes and Monographs (NNM), L, 1933.
CAH.	Cambridge Ancient History.	Holm.	Geschichte Siciliens in Alterthum.
Cat.	Catalogue.	Hu.	Macdonald, Catalogue of the Hunterian Collection (Glasgow).
CIG.	Corpus Inscriptionum Graecarum.		

ABBREVIATIONS

Hübner, MLI.	Monumenta Linguae Ibericae.	MJSEA.	Memorias de la Junta Superior de Excavaciones y Antiguedades.
HZ.	Historische Zeitung.	M. Mys.	Imhoof-Blumer, Die Antiken Münzen Mysiens.
IG.	Inscriptiones Graecae.		
IGRR.	Inscriptiones Graecae ad Res Romanas Pertinentes.	MNE.	Memorial Numismático Español.
		Mommsen, Mzw.	Das römische Münzwesen.
ILS.	Dessau, Inscriptiones Latinae Selectae.	Mommsen, RGDA.	Res Gestae Divi Augusti.
JEA.	Journal of Egyptian Archaeology.	Mommsen, St. R.	Das römische Staatsrecht.
JHS.	Journal of Hellenic Studies.		
Jones, CERP.	Cities of the Eastern Roman Provinces.	Muensterberg, Beamtennamen.	Numismatische Zeitschrift.
Jones, GC.	The Greek City from Alexander to Justinian.	Muensterberg, Kaisernamen.	Numismatische Zeitschrift.
JRS.	Journal of Roman Studies.	Muller.	Numismatique de l'ancienne Afrique.
Jullian, TP.	Les transformations politiques de l'Italie sous les Empereurs romains.	NC.	Numismatic Chronicle.
		Nestle, Funde.	Funde antiker Münzen im Königreich Württemberg.
KM.	Imhoof-Blumer, Kleinasiatische Münzen.	Newby.	A Numismatic Commentary on the Res Gestae of Augustus.
Kar. M.	Imhoof-Blumer, Karische Münzen.	NG.	Die Münzen Nordgriechenlands.
Kornemann.	Pauly-Wissowa-Kroll, Realencyclopädie, II, 511 ff., s.v. colonia.	NNM.	Numismatic Notes and Monographs.
Kubitschek, Imp.	Imperium Romanum tributim discriptum.	NZ.	Numismatische Zeitschrift.
		Phil. Woch.	Philologische Wochenschrift.
Lenormant.	La monnaie dans l'antiquité.	PIR.	Prosopographia Imperii Romani.
Levi.	Ottaviano Capoparte.	von Premerstein.	Vom Werden und Wesen des Prinzipats (Abh. München, ph.-hist. Abt., N.F. xv, 1937).
Liebenam, Legaten.	Forschungen zur Verwaltungsgeschichte des römischen Kaiserreichs: Die Legaten.		
		PW.	Pauly-Wissowa-Kroll, Realencyclopädie.
Lyd. S.	Imhoof-Blumer, Lydische Stadtmünzen.		
		QA.	Quaderni Augustei.
M.	Mionnet, Descriptions de médailles antiques grecques et romaines.	QAS.	Quaderni Augustei (studi stranieri).
McFayden.	The title Imperator.	Raillard.	Die Anordnungen des M. Antonius im Orient, Diss. Zürich, 1894.
M. and S.	Mattingly and Sydenham, Roman Imperial Coinage.		
MAPS.	Memoirs of the American Philosophical Society.	Rb.	Revue belge de numismatique.
		Rec.	Waddington, Babelon and Reinach, Recueil général des monnaies grecques d'Asie Mineure.
Marquardt, St. V.	Die römische Staatsverwaltung.		
Mattingly, RC.	Roman Coins.	RG.	Res Gestae Divi Augusti.
MBNGW.	Monatsblätter der numismatischen Gesellschaft in Wien.	Rice Holmes, Architect.	The Architect of the Roman Empire.
MG.	Imhoof-Blumer, Monnaies grecques.	R. it.	Rivista italiana di numismatica.
Mitt.	Mitteilungen.	Rn.	Revue numismatique.

ABBREVIATIONS

Röm. Mitt.	Mitteilungen des deutschen archäologischen Instituts, Römische Abt.	Svoronos, Crete.	Numismatique de la Crète ancienne.
Rostovtzeff, SEH.	Social and Economic History of the Roman Empire.	Svoronos, Ptolemies.	Νομίσματα τοῦ κράτους τῶν Πτολεμαίων.
RS.	Revue suisse de numismatique (Schweizerische Numismatische Rundschau).	Syme, RR.	The Roman Revolution.
		TAPA.	Transactions of the American Philological Association.
S.	Supplement.		
Sav.Z.	Zeitschrift der Savigny Stiftung für Rechtsgeschichte.	UCPH.	University of California Publications in History.
SB.	Sitzungsberichte.		
SBK.	Schriften der Balkankommission.	Vives.	Vives y Escudero, La moneda hispánica.
Schulze.	Die römischen Eigennamen (Abh. Göttingen, N.F. v, 5, 1904).		
Sestini, Fontana.	Descrizione d'alcune medaglie greche del museo del Sig. C. d' O. Fontana.	Wad.	Babelon, Inventaire de la Collection Waddington.
		Weber.	Forrer, Catalogue of the Weber Collection.
Sestini, Hedervar.	Ditto, del museo Hedervariano.		
Sherwin-White.	The Roman Citizenship.	Willers, Geschichte	Geschichte der römischen Küpferprägung.
Smith, DA.	Dictionary of Antiquities.	WMK.	von Schrötter, Wörterbuch der Münzkunde.
Stevenson, RPA.	Roman Provincial Administràtion.		
Sutherland, RIS.	The Romans in Spain.	ZfN.	Zeitschrift für Numismatik.

SOURCES[1]

A. ANCIENT

1. LATIN WRITERS

pseudo-Acro *ap.* Hor. *Carmina.*
Aelius Gallus (Fest.).
Agennius Urbicus *ap.* Frontin. *de controv. agr.*
Albertus Magnus (*ed.* Ven.).
Albucius (Suet.).
Asconius on Cic.
pseudo-Asconius on Cic.
Augustus, *Res Gestae* (*RG.*).
Ausonius, *Ordo nobilium urbium.*
Bithynicus, A. Pompeius (Cic. Fam.).
pseudo-Boethius, *Demonstratio artis geometricae.*
Brutus, Dec. Junius (Cic. *Fam.*).
Brutus, M. Junius (Cic.).
Caesar, *Bellum Civile, Pro Bithynis* (Gell.).
[Caesar], *Bellum Africanum.*
Capitolinus, *Vita Antonini Pii.*
Cassiodorus, *Chronica; variae.*
Cassius (Cic. *Fam.*).
Catullus.
Cedrenius, *Historia.*
Cicero, *Ad Atticum, Pro Balbo, Brutus, Pro Cluentio, Pro Rege Deiotaro, De Domo sua, Ad Familiares, Pro Flacco, De Imperio Cn. Pompei, De Lege Agraria, De Legibus, Pro Ligario, De Officiis, Philippica, In Pisonem, Pro Plancio, Pro Quintio, De Republica, Pro Scauro, Pro Sestio, Pro Sulla, Pro Vatinio, In Verrem.*
Claudius (Dessau, *ILS.*).
Columella, *De re rustica.*
Diculius, *De mensura orbis terrae.*
Digesta.
Donatus (Aelius), *ap.* Ter. *Adelph.*
Donatus (Claudius), *Vita Vergilii.*
Felix Malleolus, *De nobilitate et rusticitate.*
Festus, *De verborum significatu.*
Florus, *Bella omnia.*
Frontinus, *De condicionibus agrorum, De controversiis, De aquaeductibus, Urbis Romae.*
Fronto, *Ad amicos.*
Gaius, *Institutiones.*

Gellius, *Noctes Atticae.*
Geographus Ravennas.
Hadrian (Gellius).
Hieronymus, *Chronica Eusebii.* (*Helm*).
Hirtius [Caesar], *Bellum Alexandrinum, Bellum Gallicum* VIII.
Historia Augusta, see: Capitolinus, Lampridius, Spartian.
Hyginus, *De condicionibus agrorum; De limitibus constituendis.*
Isidorus, *Origines.*
itinerarium Antonini (Parthey-Pinder).
Jerome.
Julius Honorius, *Cosmographia* (Gronov.).
Justin, *Epitome Trogi.*
[Justinian], *Institutiones.*
Lampridius, *Vita Antonini Diadumeni.*
Latinus and Mysrontius, *De locis suburbanis.*
laus Pisonis.
Lentulus Spinther, P. Cornelius (Cic. *Fam.*).
liber coloniarum.
anon. *ap. libr. coloniarum* (MS. Arcerian.).
Livy.
[Livy], *Periochae.*
Lucan, *Pharsalia.*
Macrobius, *Saturnalia.*
Martial, *Epigrams.*
Martianus Capella, *Encyclopaedia.*
Mela, *De chronographia.*
Nepos, *Atticus.*
Orosius, *Historia.*
Ovid, *Amores, Fasti, ex Ponto, Tristia.*
Papinian (*Dig.*).
passio S. Theodoti Ancyrani.
Paulus, *Sententiae* (and *Dig.*).
Pliny jun., *Epistulae, Panegyricus.*
Pliny sen., *Historia Naturalis.*
Proculus (*Dig.*).
Quintilian, *Institutio oratoria.*
Rufus, Sex., *Breviarium.*

[1] For collections of coins, see Preface.

SOURCES

Seneca jun., *Ad Helviam, De ira, Naturales Quaestiones*.
Seneca sen., *Suasoriae, Controversiae*.
Servius *ap.* Verg. *Aen., Ecl.*
Siculus Flaccus, *De condicionibus agrorum*.
Silius Italicus, *Punica*.
Sisenna.
Solinus Polyhistor, *Collectanea*.
Spartian, *Vita Hadriani; Vita Aelii*.
Statius, *Silvae*.
Suetonius, *De Vita Caesarum, De viris illustribus*.

Symmachus, *Epistulae*.
tabula *Peutingeriana* (Miller).
Tacitus, *Annales, Historiae*.
Ulpian (*Dig.*), *De censibus*.
Valerius Maximus.
Varro, *De lingua latina* (Gell.).
Velleius Paterculus.
vita *Vergilii* (Reifferscheid).
Vitruvius, *De architectura*.
Vopiscus, *Vita Taciti*.

2. GREEK WRITERS

Acts of the Apostles.
Aeschines.
Anecdota (Bekker).
Appian, *Bellum Civile, Historia Romana, Mith.*
Aristotle, *Rhetorica*.
Artemidorus of Ephesus (*Onirocritae*).
Corpus scriptorum Christianorum orientalium.
Demosthenes.
Dio Cassius, *Historia Romana*.
Dio Chrysostom.
Diodorus, *Historia*.
Dioscorides, *De materia medica*.
Epictetus, *Dissertationes*.
Eusebius, *Chronicon*.
Herodian, *Historia*.
Herodotus.
Hierocles.
Josephus, *Antiquitates Judaicae, Bellum Judaicum*.
Lucian, *Alexander*.
Luke, St.

Lydus, Laurentius, *De magistratibus reipublicae Romanae*.
Malalas, *Lexicon Chronicon* (Dindorf).
Menander Rhetor (Heeren).
Michael Syrus, *Chronicon* (Chabot).
Nicolaus Damascenus, *De vita Caesaris; De vita sua; fragmenta*.
Pausanias.
Perizonius.
Philo, *Legatio ad Gaium*.
Plutarch, *Reipublicae gerendae praecepta; Vitae*.
Pollux, *Onomasticon*.
Polybius.
Porphyrius (*fragm. Hist. Graec.*).
Procopius, *De Aedificiis, De Bello Vandalico*.
Ptolemy.
Strabo.
Suidas, *Lexicon*.
Syncellus (Georgius) (Dindorf).
Synesius.
Zonaras, *Lexicon*.

3. HEBREW WRITERS

Bab. Kiddush (quoted by Heichelheim).

M. Maaser Scheni (quoted by Heichelheim).

4. ARAB WRITERS

Al-Jaqubi, *Kitab-el-Boldân* (quoted by Muller).

SOURCES

5. Iconographic Sources

a. Public Collections.

Aachen Cathedral, Amsterdam (Allard Pierson), Aquileia, Athens, Berlin, Carthage (Lavigerie), Copenhagen, Copenhagen (Thorvaldsen), Corinth, Florence, Hague, Leningrad, Lepcis, London (British Museum), Naples, New York (Metropolitan), Paris, Parma, Pesto, Rome (Lateran), Rome (Torlonia), Vatican, Vienna.

b. Private Collections.

Beverley, Evans, Hope-Masham, Lansdowne, Rossie Priory, Sambon.

6. Epigraphic Sources

Abhandlungen des archäologisch-epigraphischen Seminares der Universität Wien.
Africa italiana.
Αθηνᾶ.
Annales du Service des Antiquités de l'Égypte.
L'Année épigraphique.
Le antichità pestane (Bamonte).
Archäologisch-epigraphische Mitteilungen.
Atti della Società Italiana per il Progresso delle Scienze (Marzullo).
Bulletin de correspondance hellénique (*BCH.*).
Bulletin épigraphique.
Corpus Inscriptionum Graecarum (*CIG.*).
Corpus Inscriptionum Latinarum (*CIL.*).
Corpus Inscriptionum Rhenanarum.
Corpus Inscriptionum Semiticarum (*CIS.*).
Cyprische Inschriften (Vogüé).
Denkschrift der Wiener Akademie (1911).
Documenti antichi dell' Africa italiana.
Edicts of Cyrene, Rhosus etc. (and literature).
Ephemeris epigraphica.
Fontes Iuris Romani (Bruns).
Inschriften von Pergamon.
Inschriften von Priene.
Inscriptiones Confoederationis Helveticae Latinae (Zürich Mitt., Bd. 9).
Inscriptiones Graecae (*IG.*).
Inscriptiones Graecae ad Res Romanas pertinentes (*IGRR.*).
Inscriptiones Latinae selectae (Orelli).
Inscriptiones Latinae selectae (Dessau) (*ILS.*).
Inscriptiones regni Neapolitani Latinae.
Inscriptiones antiques de Lyon (Boissieu).
Inscriptions de Delphes (Wescher and Foucart).
Journal of Roman Studies (Hill and Sandars) (*JRS.*).
Latin Historical Inscriptions (Rushforth).
Mélanges d'épigraphie et d'archéologie.
Monumenta Linguae Ibericae (Hübner, *MLI.*).
Orientalistische Literaturzeitung.
Orientis Graecae Inscriptiones Selectae (*OGIS.*).
Phönizische Studien (Levy).
Recueil d'inscriptions égyptiennes.
Répertoire d'épigraphie grecque.
Répertoire d'épigraphie sémitique.
Res Gestae Divi Augusti (*RG.*).
Revue épigraphique.
Storia della Lucania (l'Antonini).
Supplementum Epigraphicum Graecum (*SEG.*).
Sylloge Inscriptionum Graecarum (Dittenberger) (*SIG.*).
Voyages archéologiques (Waddington and Lebas).
Wolfe Expedition (Sterrett).
Zeitschrift für Ägyptische Sprache und Altertumskunde.
Ägyptische Urkunden aus den Museen zu Berlin, Griechische Urkunden (*BGU.*).
Amherst Papyri.
Oxyrhynchus Papyri.
Turin Papyri.
Tabula Peutingeriana.

SOURCES

B. MODERN

1. Works on Local History

(*Note.* Works on the Roman constitution are listed in the relevant footnotes in Part IV, q.v.)

PW. ss. vv. cities etc.

Abbott and Johnson, *Municipal Administration in the Roman Empire.*
Abel, *Revue biblique*, 1938 (eras).
Adcock, *CAH.* IX (Julius).
Alföldi, *ZfN.* XL, 1930 (*libertas*).
Babelon (E.), *Carthage.*
Barth, *De Asylis Graecis* (Diss. Strassburg, 1888).
Barthel, *Zur Geschichte der römischen Städten in Africa.*
Beaudouin, *Revue générale du droit, de la législation, et de la jurisprudence*, 1896 (colonies and *municipia*).
Beloch, *Die Bevölkerung der griechisch-römischen Welt.*
Bernardi, *Athenaeum*, 1938 (*suffragium*).
Bersanetti, *Bollettino di filologia classica*, 1936 (*Latinitas*).
Biondi, *Annuario della reale Università di Catania*, 1928–9 (*libertas*).
Bosch, *Kleinasiatische Münzen*, I, 2.
Bouchier (E.S.), *A short history of Antioch*; *Sardinia in Ancient Times.*
Box, *JRS.* 1932 (prosopographical).
Brett, *AJA.* 1937 (eras).
Broughton, *CJ.* 1935 (Caesarea); *ES.* IV (Asia); *Johns Hopkins University Studies in Historical and Political Science* (Africa); *TAPA.* 1935 (*consistentes*).
Brusin, *Aquileia nostra.*
Buckland, *Revue historique de droit français et étranger*, 1934 (*cives* and *peregrini*).
Busolt, *Jahrbücher für classische Philologie, Suppl.* VII (*autonomia*).
Cagnat, *Revue épigraphique*, 1913 (*coloniae Concordiae*).
Calder, *JRS.* 1913 (*colonia Antiochia in Pisidia*).
Calderini, *Rendiconti del Reale Istituto Lombardo di scienze e lettere* (*sc.-mor. e stor.*), 1931 (census).
Cantor, *Die römischen Agrimensoren.*
Carcopino, *Revue historique*, 1929 (colonies in Africa).
Cary, *JRS.* 1929, 1937 (legislation of Julius).
Chapot, *La province romaine proconsulaire d'Asie.*
Charlesworth, *Trade Routes and Commerce of the Roman Empire*; *Harvard Theological Review*, 1935 (emperor-worship).

Chatelain, *Bibliothèque de l'école des hautes études*, 1908 (*colonia Arausio*).
Christ (F.), *Tübinger Beiträge zur Altertumswissenschaft*, 1938 (*pater urbium*).
Collart, *Philippes, Ville de Macédoine.*
Cuntz, *Jahrbücher für classische Philologie, Suppl.* XVII, 1890 (sources); *Jahreshefte des österreichischen archäologischen Institutes in Wien*, 1929 (prosopographical); *Klio*, VI, 1906 (Sicily).
Degrassi, *Rivista di filologia*, 1938 (magistrates).
Dessau, *Hermes*, 1884 (eras, dues); *Klio*, VIII, 1912 (double communities).
Detlefsen, *Philologus*, 1870 (*colonia Nabrissa*).
Digonnet, *Orange antique.*
Dorsch, *De civitatis Romanae apud Graecos propagatione* (Diss. Breslau, 1886).
Dussaud, *Revue numismatique*, 1908 (eras).
Ensslin, *Gnomon*, 1934 (worship of Antony).
Espérandieu, *Gaule romaine.*
Fluss, *PW.* (2 Reihe), II, 952 (*Sebasteia*).
Fraccaro, *Geografia*, XVIII, 1930 (censuses).
Fuchs, *Der geistige Widerstand gegen Rom.*
Fürst, *Die Bedeutung der Auctoritas* (Diss. Marburg, 1934).
Gagé, *Byzantion*, 1936 (*restitutor*).
Gauckler, *Bulletin de la société nationale des antiquaires de France*, 1898 (*conditor*).
Gelzer, *Frankfürter Universitätsreden*, 1924 (*municipes*); *PW.* XII, 940 (Latium).
Ginzer, *Handbuch der mathematischen und technischen Chronologie.*
Gnädinger, *De Graecorum magistratibus eponymis* (Diss. Halle, 1892).
Goodfellow, *Roman Citizenship* (Diss. Bryn Mawr, 1930).
Graindor, *Athènes sous Auguste.*
Grenier, *ES.* III (Gaul).
Gsell, *Revue historique*, CLVI (Carthage).
Hahn, *Rom und Romanismus im griechisch-römischen Osten.*
Halgan, *Essai sur l'administration des provinces sénatoriales.*

Hardy, *Six Roman Laws*; *Some Problems in Roman History*; *Roman Laws and Charters*; *Three Spanish Charters*; *Journal of Philology*, 1920 (Julius).
Hartmann, *De Exilio apud Romanos* (Diss. Berlin, 1887).
Hatzfeld, *Les trafiquants italiens dans l'Orient hellénique*.
Haywood, *ES*. IV (Africa).
Head, *HN*. p. 755 (Seleucids and cities).
Heichelheim, *ES*. IV (Syria).
Heinen, *Klio*, 1911 (Emperor-worship).
Heiss, *Monnaies antiques de l' Espagne*.
Heitland, *Last words*, etc.; *Repetita*.
Henze, *De Civitatibus Liberis* (Diss. Berlin, 1892).
Herzog, *Gallia Narbonensis*.
Heuss, *Klio, Beih*. XXXI, 1933 (*libertas, postliminium*).
Hill (Sir G. F.), *NNM*. L, 1933 (*Hispania Tarraconensis*).
Hoeppfner, *Bulletin de la Faculté de Lettres de l'Université de Strasbourg*, 1931-2 (*Liber pater*).
Holm (A.), *Geschichte Siciliens in Alterthum*; *Das alte Catania*.
Horn (H.), *Foederati* (Diss. Frankfurt, 1930).
Hübner, *MLI*.; *La Arqueología de España*.
Hülsen, *PW*. IV, 1815 (*curia*).
Hultsch, *PW*. IV, 875 (*congiaria*).
Jenison, *The History of the Province of Sicily* (Diss. Columbia, 1919).
Jessen, *PW*. IV, 244 (*eponymos*).
Jones (A. H. M.), *CERP*.; *GC*.; *Anatolian Studies to Buckler* (1939).
Jordan, *Marsyas auf dem Forum in Rom*.
Jullian, *Histoire de la Gaule*; *Les transformations politiques de l'Italie sous les Empereurs romains*; *Revue des études anciennes*, 1913 (Marsyas).
Keil, *CAH*. XI (Greek cities).
Kjellberg, *Klio*, 1921 (magistrates).
Kloesel, *Libertas* (Diss. Breslau, 1935).
Klotz, *Phil. Woch.* 1936 (*libertas*).
Kornemann, *PW*. II, 511 (*colonia*); *PW*. XVI, 570 (*municipium*); *PW*. XVIII, 708 (*oppidum*); *PW*. Suppl. I, 300 (*civitas*); in Gercke-Norden, *Einleitung in die Altertumswissenschaft*, III, 2 (*libertas*); *QAS*. IV, 1937 (*libertas*); *Berliner Studien für classische Philologie und Archäologie*, XIV, 1892 (*consistentes*).
Kromayer, *Hermes*, 1896 (*colonia Arausio*).
Kubitschek, *Imperium Romanum tributim discriptum*; *Abhandlungen des archäologischen-epigraphischen Seminares der Universität Wien*.

(tribes); *Sitzungsberichte der Akademie der Wissenschaften in Wien* (*philos.-hist. Kl.*), CLXXVII, *Abh*. 4, 1916 (*libertas*); *Gnomon*, 1937 (Macedonian colonies); *PW*. IX, 2308 (*Itinerarien*).
Kübler, *PW*. IV, 2319 (*decurio*); *PW*. XIX, 639 (*peregrinus*).
Larsen, *ES*. IV (Greece and Macedonia); *CP*. 1931 (*quinquennales perpetui*).
Last, *CAH*. XI (*libertas*); *JRS*. 1932 (races).
Lécrivain, *Revue historique*, 1927 (military colonies).
Lenormant, *La monnaie dans l'antiquité*.
Liebenam, *Städteverwaltung im römischen Kaiserreiche*; *Forschungen zur Verwaltungsgeschichte des römischen Kaiserreichs*; *PW*. V, 1798 (*duoviri*).
McElderry, *JRS*. 1918 (magistrates, *Latinitas*).
Mantey, *De gradu et statu quaestorum in municipiis coloniisque* (Diss. Halle, 1882).
Marquart, *Die römische Staatsverwaltung*.
Marzullo, *Atti della Società Italiana per il Progresso delle Scienze*, 1932 (*Marsyas, colonia Paestum*).
Merlin, *Cinquième Congrès international d'archéologie*, 1930 (double communities).
Mitteis, *Reichsrecht und Volksrecht in den östlichen Provinzen*.
Momigliano, *Athenaeum*, 1935 (Phoenician cities).
Mommsen, *Provinces of the Roman Empire*; *Res Gestae divi Augusti*; *Gesammelte Schriften*; *Römisches Staatsrecht*; *Die römischen Feldmesser*; *Die Stadtrechte*; *Hermes*, 1873 (*consistentes*), 1883 (*coloniae Juliae*), 1885 (*colonia Zama*), 1892 (colonies and *municipia*), 1904 (autonomy); *ZfN*. 1875 (governors and cities).
Monceaux, *De Communi Asiae Provinciae* (Diss. Paris, 1885).
Mowat, *Rn*. 1902 (eponymy).
Muensterberg, *MBNGW*. 1911, 1913; *NZ*.; *Jahreshefte des österreichischen archäologischen Institutes in Wien, Beibl*. XVIII, 1915 (magistrates).
Muller, *Numismatique de l'ancienne Afrique*.
Muttelsee, *Untersuchungen über die Lex Julia municipalis* (Diss. Freiburg, 1913).
Neumann (J.), *De quinquennalibus coloniarum et municipiorum* (Diss. Leipzig, 1892); *PW*. VI, 2818 (*foederati*); *HZ*. 1917 (*postliminium*).
Nissen, *Pompeianische studien*.
Nock, *Harvard Studies in Classical Philology*, 1930; *Gnomon*, 1932; *JHS*. 1925 (Emperor-worship).
van Nostrand, *ES*. III; *UCPH*. IV, 2, 1916 (Spain).
Pais, *Storia della Sardegna e della Corsica*; *Memorie della Reale Accademia Nazionale dei Lincei* (*Cl. sc.-mor., stor., fil.*), VI, 1, 1925 (colonies).

Pansa, *R. it.* 1909 (eponymy).
Paoli, *Mélanges d'archéologie et d'histoire*, 1938 (Marsyas).
Parker, *CR.* 1938 (magistrates).
Partsch, *Africae veteris itineraria* (Diss. Breslau, 1874).
Petersen, *Rheinisches Museum für Philologie*, 1853 (*mensio*).
Pfister, *PW.* (2 Reihe), I, 1061 (*Rhomaia*).
Pisani, *Annali della Reale Scuola Normale Superiore di Pisa*, 1938 (*municipia*).
Poinssot, *Comptes-rendus de l'Académie des Inscriptions et Belles Lettres*, 1915 (double communities); *Bulletin de la Société Nationale des Antiquaires de France*, 1928 (*municipium Caralis*).
Prehn, *PW.* XI, 2083 (*Ktistes*).
von Premerstein, *PW.* X, 1238 (*ius Italicum*); *Sav. Z.* 1922 (*coloniae Juliae* of Antony); *Sav. Z.* 1931 (no pro-Greek policy).
Ramsay, *Cities and Bishoprics of Phrygia*; *JRS.* 1914, 1916 (*colonia Antiochia in Pisidia*); *Anatolian Studies to Buckler* (1939).
Reid, *Municipalities of the Roman Empire*; *JRS.* 1915 (Julius).
Reinach and Babelon (E.), *Bull. du com.* 1886 (*municipium Zitha*).
Reinhold, *CJ.* 1938 (bureaucracy).
Riccobono, *Annali del Seminario giuridico della Reale Università di Palermo*, 1936 (*libertas*).
Ritschl, *Rheinisches Museum für Philologie*, 1842 (*mensio*).
Ritterling, *PW.* XII, 1186 (*legio*).
Robinson (D. M.), *AJP.* 1926 (*deductio*).
Romanelli, *Africa italiana*, 1925; *Rivista delle colonie italiane*, 1929 (Tripolitana).
Ronzevalle, *Mélanges de l'Université S. Joseph de Beyrouth*, 1934 (Heliopolis).
Rostovtzeff, *Archiv für Papyrusforschung*, Beih. I, 1910 (taxation); *CAH.* VII (Seleucids, Ptolemies).
Rouvier, *Revue biblique*, 1899 (eras).
Rudolph, *Stadt und Staat im römischen Italien*.
Rudorff, *Gromatische Institutionen*.
Ruggiero, *Le colonie dei romani*.
Säflund, *Skrifter utgivna av Svenska Institutet i Rom*, IV, 1934 (Italian colonies).
Savigny, *Vermischte Schriften*.
Scharf, *Neue Deutsche Forschungen*, CLXXXV, 1938 (prosopographical).
Scheffer-Boichorst, *Mitteilungen des Instituts für österreichischen Geschichtsforschung*, 1885 (Graecisation of colonies).

Schürer, *Geschichte des jüdischen Volkes*.
Schulz, *Mnemosyne*, 1937 (censuses).
Schulze, *Abh. Göttingen*, N.F. V, 5, 1904 (prosopographical).
Scramuzza, *ES.* III (Sicily).
Sebastian (A.), *De patronis coloniarum atque municipiorum Romanorum* (Diss. Halle, 1884).
Seston, *Mélanges de l'École Française de Rome*, 1926–7 (Marsyas).
Sherwin-White, *The Roman Citizenship*.
Spehr, *De summis magistratibus coloniarum atque municipiorum* (Diss. Halle, 1881).
Stevenson (G. H.), *CAH.* X (colonisation); *Roman Provincial Administration*.
Strasburger, *Gnomon*, 1937 (Julius).
Stuart Jones, *EHR.* 1931 (bureaucracy).
Sutherland, *JRS.* 1934 (Roman cities in Spain).
Syme, *CQ.* 1938 (double communities); *CR.* 1938 (*colonia Philippi*).
Taylor (L. R.), *TAPA.* 45 (*Augustales*); *Divinity of the Roman Emperor*.
Tellenbach, *Forschungen zur Kirchen- und Geistesgeschichte*, VII, 1936 (*libertas*).
Tenney Frank, *JRS.* 1927 (Sicily); *ES.* I (Italy).
Tissot, *Géographie de la province romaine d'Afrique*.
Toutain, *Mélanges d'archéologie et d'histoire*, 1896, 1898 (colonies and *municipia*).
Viale, *Atti del primo Congresso di Studi Romani*, I, 1930 (double communities).
della Vida, *Africa italiana*, 1935 (Tripolitana).
de Visscher, *Comptes-rendus de l'Ac. des Inscriptions et Belles Lettres*, 1938, 1939 (double citizenship).
Volkmann, *Münchener Beiträge zur Papyrusforschung*, XXI, 1935 (jurisdiction); *Neue Jahrbücher für Antike und deutsche Bildung*, 1938 (self-government).
Wachsmuth, *Die Stadt Athen*.
Waddington, *Rn.* 1867 (governors and cities).
Walltafen, *Die Einrichtung und kommunale Entwicklung der römischen Provinz Lusitanien*.
Walton, *JRS.* 1929 (prosopographical).
Waser, *PW.* V, 2346 (*eleutheria*); *PW.* IV, 2010 (*daimon*).
Weber (M.), *Römische Agrargeschichte*; *Wirtschaft und Gesellschaft im römischen Reich*.
Weickert, *Klio*, 1937 (Julius and *libertas*).
Weiss, *PW.* X, 1231 (*ius honorum*).
West, *AJA.* 1926 (*colonia Corinthus*).
Zumpt, *Commenta epigraphica*.

SOURCES

2. Reports of Coin-finds[1]

Records on labels of collections; information from numismatists. Also:

A. Periodicals.

Abhandlungen und Berichte aus dem Museum für Natur- und Heimatkunde in Magdeburg.
Acta et commentationes Universitatis Dorpatensis (human:).
Annalen des Vereins für Nassauische Altertumskunde.
Annali dell' Istituto di Correspondenza Archeologica, p. 74 (Liria).
Annals of Archaeology and Anthropology, 1910 (Derek Maden).
Annuaire de la Société de Numismatique, III, 1868, pp. 259, 279.
Annual of the Palestine Exploration Fund.
Antiquaries' Journal.
Anzeiger für Schweizerische Altertumskunde.
Archaeological Report of the Egypt Exploration Fund.
Archaeologisch-historische Bijdragen.
Archäologische Zeitung, 1871, p. 180 (Aegina).
Archeologo Portugues.
Archivio storico per la Sicilia orientale.
Arquivos da Universidade de Lisboa.
Atti della Società Italiana per il progresso delle Scienze.
Bayerische Vorgeschichtsblätter.
Bericht der römisch-germanischen Kommission des archäologischen Instituts.
BB. IV, p. 27 (Smyrna).
Blätter für Münzfreunde, 1900, pp. 156f. (Sardinia)
Bonner Jahrbücher.
Bulletin de la Commission Archéologique de la Seine Inférieure.
Bulletin hispanique.
Bullettino archeologico sardo.
Bullettino della Commissione Archeologica Comunale di Roma.
Bullettino dell' Istituto di Correspondenza Archeologica.
Corriere numismatico, 1911, p. 102 (Pompeii).
Fundberichte aus Österreich.
Fundberichte aus Schwaben.
Glasnik Skopskog Naučnog Društva.
Jahrbuch der Gesellschaft für lothringische Geschichte und Altertumskunde.
Jahrbuch des Bernischen historischen Museums.
Jahrbuch für Landeskunde von Niederösterreich.
Jahresbericht über das Realgymnasium in Magdeburg, 1902–3, p. 19 (Sicily).
Jahresberichte an die Mitglieder der Sinsheimer Gesellschaft.
JEA.
JHS. 1914, p. 46 (S.W. Asia minor).
JIAN. 1911, p. 222 (Cephallenia).
JRS. 1911, p. 103 (el Centenillo).
Klio, 1914, pp. 200 ff. (Africa).
Mémoires de la Société Archéologique du Midi de la France.
Mémoires de la Société d'Histoire de Genève.
Mitteilungen der antiquarischen Gesellschaft in Zürich.
MJSEA.
Neue Zeitschrift des Ferdinandeums in Salzburg.
Notizie degli Scavi di Antichità.
NC. 1914, pp. 312ff. (Pisidia); 1924, p. 14 (Cyprus); 1927, p. 381 (Magnesia ad Maeandrum).
Numismatic Circular, 1902, 5216 (M. Jouer à S. Goussano).
NNM. LXXXI, 1938, p. 22 (Gerasa).
NZ. 1905, p. 37 (Asia minor); 1913 (Gaul); 1933, p. 56 (Carnuntum).
Numismatisches Literaturblatt, 1934, p. 2781.
Numizmaticheskago Svornika.
Numizmatikai Közlöny.
Oudheidkundige Mededeelingen uit's Rijksmuseum van Oudheden te Leiden.
Prähistorische Zeitschrift.
Programm des grossherzoglichen Gymnasiums zu Mainz.
Programm des königlichen kaiserlichen Gymnasiums zu Bozen.
Publications de la Section des Sciences Historiques de l'Institut Grand-Ducal de Luxembourg.
Recueil des notices et mémoires de la Société archéologique du département de Constantine.
Revue africaine.
Revue archéologique, 1903, p. 283 (Apt); 1904, p. 286 (M. S. Michel).
Rn. 1898, p. 629 (Cilicia).
Rivista archeologica della provincia di Como.
Römisch-germanische Forschungen.
Saalburg Jahrbuch.

[1] Particulars are added to the titles when these do not indicate the geographical origin of the finds.

A. *Periodicals* (contd)

Schriften der Balkankommission (ant. *Abt.*).
Scoperte archeologiche fattesi nell' isola di Sardegna.
SB. München, 1897, pp. 530, 533 (Cappadocia).
Skrifter utgivna av det Kongl. Humanistiska Vetenskapssamfundet i Uppsala, XXIX, 2, p. 49 (Viminacium).
Sonderschriften des österreichischen archäologischen Instituts in Wien.
Verhandlungen der Berliner Gesellschaft für Anthropologie.
Verhandlungen des historischen Vereins für Niederbayern.
Verhandlungen des historischen Vereins von Oberpfalz.
Viestnik Hrvatskoga Arheologickoga Društva.
Vjestnik Kr. Hrvatsk-slav.-dalm. Arkiva.
Westfalen.
Zapiski Imp. Russk. Arch. Obschch.
Zeitschrift des historischen Vereins für Schwaben und Neuburg.
ZfN. 1884, p. 187 (Syria); 1900, pp. 40ff. (Vindonissa); 1901, p. 186 (Asia minor); 1904 *Jahresb.* p. 1 (Preignan).

B. *Books.*

Abramic, *Führer durch Poetovio.*
Archäologische Karte von Jugoslavien, Blätter Kavadarci, Zagreb, Prilep-Bitolj.
Bayer, *Diario das primeiras viagens que fez pelas terras de Portugal.*
Bell, *Sardis* (XI).
Bellinger, *Dura.*
Bissinger, *Funde römischer Münzen im Grossherzogtum Baden.*
Blanchet, *Traité des monnaies gauloises; Les trésors des monnaies romaines en Gaule.*
Bolin, *Fynden av Romerska Mynt i det fria Germanien.*
Bouchier (E. S.), *Sardinia in Ancient Times.*
Boutkowski-Glinka, *Dictionnaire numismatique*, p. 75 (Sillingy); p. 684 (Syria, Palestine).
BMC. Cyrenaica, Cyprus, Peloponnese; Imp. p. 115 (Black Sea), etc.
Brusin, *Gli scavi di Aquileia.*
Clerc and d'Agnel, *Découvertes archéologiques à Marseille.*
Courby and Picard, *Recherches archéologiques à Stratos d'Acarnanie.*
Coutil, *Inventaire des monnaies gauloises de la Seine-Inférieure.*
Eckhel, *Doctrina Numorum* (Gaul).

Edwards (K. M.), *Corinth* (VI).
Elmer, *Catalogue of the Belgrade collection* (MS.).
Evelein, *Gids van het Rijksmuseum G.M. Kam te Nijmegen.*
Forrer, *Strasbourg-Argentorate; Die keltische Numismatik.*
Gjerstad, *The Swedish Cyprus Expedition.*
Goudard, *Monographie des monnaies frappées à Nîmes.*
Head, *Historia Numorum*, p. 786 (Smyrna, Hayling Island).
Heiss, *Monnaies antiques de l' Espagne.*
van Hoorn, *Gids van het Centraal Museum te Utrecht.*
Kataloge West- und Süddeutscher Altertumssammlungen.
Kunkel, *Oberhessens vorgeschichtliche Altertümer.*
McDowell, *Preliminary Report upon the Excavations at Tell Umar (Iraq).*
Maiuri and Jacopich, *Clara Rhodos.*
della Marmora, *Voyage en Sardaigne.*
Maxe-Werly, *État actuel de la numismatique rémoise.*
Mommsen, *Die nordetruskischen Alphabete auf Inschriften und Münzen*, p. 235 (Alps).
Nestle (W.), *Funde antiker Münzen im Königreich Württemberg.*
Noe, *NNM.*
Oberhummer, *Die Insel Cypern.*
Oberhummer and Zimmerer, *Durch Syrien und Kappadokien.*
Otschetof *Archaeological Commission.*
Pallmann, *Die Pfahlbauten und ihre Bewohner.*
Parura, *La Sicilia antica.*
Pichler, *Repertorium der steierischen Münzkunde.*
Regling, *Münzfunde aus Pergamon.*
Reinach, *Catalogue illustré du Musée des antiquités nationales au château de S. Germain-en-Laye.*
Ritterling, *Das frührömische Lager in Hofheim bei Taunus.*
Ruggiero, *Degli scavi di antichità nelle provinze di terraferma dell' antico regno di Napoli.*
Schulten, *Numantia.*
Sestini, *Descrizione d'alcune medaglie greche del museo del Sig. C. d'O. Fontana*, I, p. 126 (Cyrenaica).
Sterrett, *The Wolfe Expedition.*
Sutherland, *Coinage and Currency in Roman Britain.*
Teixeira de Aragão, *Descripção Historica das moedas romanas (coll. Rey Luiz I).*
Toulmouche, *Histoire archéologique de la ville de Rennes.*
Ugolini, *Albania antica.*
Westholm, *Temples of Soli.*

SOURCES

3. OTHER NUMISMATIC WORKS

A. Periodicals.

American Journal of Numismatics.
Amtliche Berichte aus den königlichen Kunstsammlungen zu Berlin.
Annuaire de la Société française de numismatique.
Archäologischer Anzeiger.
Archivio storico per la Sicilia orientale.
Aréthuse.
Atti della Reale Accademia di scienze, lettere e belle arti di Palermo.
BB., BMB.
Blätter für Münzfreunde.
Bollettino del Circolo Numismatico Napolitano.
Bollettino di numismatica.
Bulletin mensuel de numismatique et d'archéologie.
Corriere numismatico.
Documenti inediti per servire alla storia dei musei d'Italia.
Hesperia.
Historia.
Jahrbücher des Vereins von Alterthumsfreunden im Rheinlande.
JEA., JHS., JIAN., JRS.
Klio.
Mémoires de la Société d'archéologie et de numismatique de S. Pétersbourg.
Mémoires de la société française de numismatique et d'archéologie.
MAPS.
MNE.
Mitteilungen der numismatischen Gesellschaft in Berlin.
MBNGW.
Münzstudien.
Nomisma.
NC.
NNM.
Numismática.
Numismatica e scienze affini.
Numismatickar.
NZ.
Numismatisches Literaturblatt.
Numizmaticheskago Svornika.
Numizmatikai Közlöny.
Quaderni Augustei.
Quarterly of the Department of Antiquities in Palestine.
Rassegna monetaria.
Rassegna numismatica.
Rb., Rn., RS., R. it.
Studi e materiali di archeologia e numismatica.
Transactions of the International Numismatic Congress.
Transactions of the Yorkshire Numismatic Society.
Zapiski imp. russk. arch. Obschch.
ZfN.

B. Books.

Akerman, *Ancient coins of cities and princes* (Hispania, Gallia, Britannia).
Antiken Münzen Nordgriechenlands, Die.
Babelon (E.), *Monnaies de la République romaine*; *Recueil etc.*, see Waddington.
Baldwin (A.), *The coinage of Lampsacus.*
Barthélemy, *Étude des monnaies gauloises frappées en Poitou.*
Bernhart, *Handbuch zur Münzkunde der römischen Kaiserzeit.*
Blanchet, *Traité des monnaies gauloises*; *Manuel de numismatique française.*
Borghesi, *Œuvres*; *Memorie numismatiche*².
Bosch, *KM.*; *Kaiserdaten auf Kleinasiatischen Münzen.*
Botet y Siso, *Noticia historica y arqueologica de la antiga ciudad de Emporion.*
Boutkowski-Glinka, *DN.*
BMC. Imp., BMCR., BMCs.
Caetano de Bem, *Memorias historicas.*
Caland, *De nummis M. Antonii IIIviri res gestas illustrantibus commentatio* (Diss. Leyden, 1883).
Campaner y Fuertes, *Numismática Balear.*
Caro, *Chorografia del convento giuridico de Sevilla.*
Cavedoni, *Appendice al Saggio*; *Numismatica Biblica.*
Charrier, *Description des monnaies de la Numidie et de la Maurétanie.*
Chaugarnier-Moissenet, *Numismatique gauloise.*
Cohen, *Description historique des monnaies frappées sous l'empire romain.*
Delgado, *Nuevo metodo de clasificación de las medallas autónomas de España.*
Dieudonné, *Mélanges numismatiques.*
Eckhel, *DN.*

B. Books (contd)

Florez, *Medallas de las colonias, municipios y pueblos antigos de España*.
Fraccia, *Antiche monete siciliane*.
Fritze, *Münzen von Pergamon*.
Froehlich, *Notitia Elementaris Numismatum Antiquorum*.
Gaebler, v. *Antiken Münzen Nordgriechenlands*.
Garrucci, *Le monete dell' Italia antica*.
Goudard, *Monographie des monnaies frappées à Nîmes*.
Grotefend, *Unedierte griechische und römische Münzen*.
Harduin, *Opera varia*.
Haym, *Trésor britannique*.
Head, *HN*.
Hill (Sir G. F.), *Coins of Ancient Sicily*; *Historical Roman Coins*; *Handbook of Greek and Roman Coins*; *Anatolian Studies to W. M. Ramsay*.
Holm (A.), *Geschichte Siciliens in Alterthum*.
Hübner, *Monumenta Linguae Ibericae*.
Imhoof-Blumer, *Ant. GM.*; *M. Mys.*; *MG.*; *GM.*; *KM.*; *Kar. M.*; *Lyd.S.*; *GRMzk.*; see also *Antiken Münzen Nordgriechenlands*; and Keller, *Tier- und Pflanzenbilder auf Münzen*.
Lambros, 'Αναγραφὴ τῶν νομισμάτων τῆς κυρίας Ἑλλάδος.
Landolina-Paterno, *Ricerche numismatiche sull' antica Sicilia*.
Lenormant, *La monnaie dans l'antiquité*.
Lorichs, *Recherches numismatiques*.
Mattingly, *RC.*; and Sydenham (M. and S.).
Maxe-Werly, *L'état actuel de la numismatique rémoise*.
Mayr, *Die antiken Münzen der Inseln Malta*.
Milne, *The Development of Roman Coinage*.
Mionnet, *Description de médailles antiques grecques et romaines*.
Mommsen, *Mzw*.
Morelli, *Familiarum Romanarum numismata*.
Muensterberg, *Kaisernamen, Beamtennamen*, vide *NZ*.

Muller, *Numismatique de l'ancienne Afrique*.
Newby, *A Numismatic Commentary on the Res Gestae of Augustus*.
Palosy, *Discertacion sobra el theatro y circo di Sagunto*.
Pellerin, *Recueil de médailles de peuples et de villes*.
Pick, *Die Münzkunde in der Altertumswissenschaft*.
Riccio, *Monete di famiglie romane*.
Robert (C.), *Histoire générale de la province de Languedoc*.
Rogers (E. E.), *Ancient Coinage of Thessaly*.
Rostovtzeff, *Svintsoveya Tessere*.
Sambon, *Recherches sur les monnaies de la presqu'île italique*.
de Saulcy, *Numismatique de la Terre Sainte*; *Mélanges de numismatique*.
de Saussaye, *Numismatique de la Gaule narbonnaise*.
Segrè, *Metrologia e circolazione degli antichi*.
Sestini, *Descrizione di molte medaglie*; *Lettere e dissertazioni numismatiche*; *Descrizione d'alcune medaglie greche del museo del Sig. C. d'O. Fontana*, ditto, *del museo Hedervariano*.
Stevenson, *Dictionary of Roman Coins*.
Sutherland, *Coinage and Currency in Roman Britain*.
Svoronos, *Numismatique de la Crète ancienne* (I); Νομίσματα τοῦ κράτους τῶν Πτολεμαίων.
Sydenham, *The Spanish Mints of Augustus* (M. and S.).
Torremuzza (Castelli), *Siciliae populorum et urbium, regum quoque et tyrannorum veteres nummi*.
Vives y Escudero, *La moneda hispánica*.
Vogt, *Alexandrinische Münzen*.
Waddington, Babelon and Reinach, *Rec.*; and Lebas, *Voyages archéologiques et Fastes des provinces asiatiques*.
Weber (L.), *Charites*.
Werlhof, *Handbuch der griechischen Numismatik*.
Willers, *Geschichte der römischen Küpferprägung*.
WMK.
Wruck, *Die Syrische Provinzialprägung von Augustus bis Trajan*.
Zobel de Zangroniz, *Commentationes philologicae in honorem Th. Mommsen*.

KEY TO SPECTROGRAMS

The spectrographic analyses undertaken for me by the British Non-Ferrous Metals Research Association were carried out as follows:

The spectrum of the spark between a pointed upper electrode of pure copper and the edge of the coin as lower electrode was photographed on an Ilford Zenith Plate, with a Hilger medium-size quartz spectrograph (E. 34). No condensing lens was used, the spark being placed at a distance of 20 cms. from the spectrograph slit. With a slit width of 0.01 mm. an exposure time of 90 seconds was given. The standard Hilger equipment was used for the production of the spark, the capacity being 0.006 μF, the self-inductance 0.06 mH. and the spark gap 3 mm.

The quantities of zinc, tin and lead revealed by the spectrograph are graded in the following list from 'A' to 'G'. Smaller constituents, such as iron, silver, nickel, etc., which are shown by the spectrograph, are here omitted since they are irrelevant to metrology. 'A' represents a quantity of c. 23–15%; 'G' signifies the presence of traces only. *Orichalcum* coins contain 'A'–'C' of zinc.

	Mint	Zinc	Tin	Lead		Mint	Zinc	Tin	Lead
1	Nemausus (I. 1)	—	B	F	36	SC (3)	—	B	F
2	Nemausus (I. 2)	—	C	D	37	SC (7)	—	B	G
3	Nemausus (II)	—	C	D	38	SC (*as*)	—	C	F
4	Nemausus (III)	—	A	F	39	Colonist	G	B	B
5	Puteoli (?)	—	C	A	40	Colonist	—	B	C
5A	Puteoli (?)	E	C	A	41	Colonist	—	C	D
6	Arausio (?)	—	A	G	42	Colonist	—	C	C
7	Vienna	—	A	C	43	Panormus (Ti.)	C/D	B	C
8	Ancyra (Basila) (Ti.)	—	C	C	44	Panormus (Ti.)	—	C	C
9	Macedonia (Primus?)	—	D	A	45	Agrigentum	—	B	C
10	Arelate (?)	G	D	A	46	Agrigentum	—	B	B
11	Cyprus	—	B	A	47	Haluntium (Seius)	E/F	B	C
12	Macedonia (?) (Q)	C	G	F	48	Panormus (Silva) (Ti.)	—	B	C
13	Urso	—	B	B	49	Celsa	G	C	B
14	Celsa	—	A	A	50	Ilici	G	C	B
15	Amphipolis	—	B	F	51	Saguntum	—	D	D
16	SC (1)	G	C	C	52	Saguntum (Libo)	—	D	D
17	Pergamum (Augustus)	B	E	F	53	Saguntum (Ti.)	—	B	C
18	AVGVSTVS	—	D	E	54	Corduba (Cn. Juli.)	—	B	C
19	AVGVSTVS	—	—	G	55	Utica (Ti.)	—	D	D
20	AVGVSTVS	—	C	G	56	DDPP (Ti.)	—	E	D
21	Amisus	G	A	E	57	Aezanis (Cl.)	B	E	G
22	SC (3A)	—	C	G	58	Hierapolis (Cl.-Aug.)	—	C	F
23	Caralis	—	B	A	59	Hierapolis (young)	—	B	D
24	Gaul (eagle)	B	G	F	60	Ilium (Aug.)	—	C	D
25	Gaul (bull)	A	E	D	61	Lampsacus (Ner.-Aug.)	E/F	B	B
26	Cyprus (A. Plautius)	E	A	B	62	Smyrna (Aug.)	—	B	C
27	Cyprus (A. Plautius)	G	B	A	63	Smyrna (Cal.)	A	D	F
28	Rome (Celer)	A	D	F	64	Philippi	—	E	F
30	Spain (shield)	E	B	A	65	Pella (C. Aquinus P. Baebius)	—	B	B
31	AVGVSTVS	E	A	B	66	'Hispanorum'	—	B	C
32	CA.	A	E	F	67	Paestum (Q. Tre.)	—	B	F
33	Smyrna	G	B	E	68	Paestum (M. I. Ne.)	—	B	D
34	Cyprus (27 B.C.)	—	A	A	69	Paestum (Q. Egn. M. Oct.)	—	C	G
35	Emerita (Carisius)	—	E	D					

KEY TO MONOGRAMS AND LIGATURES

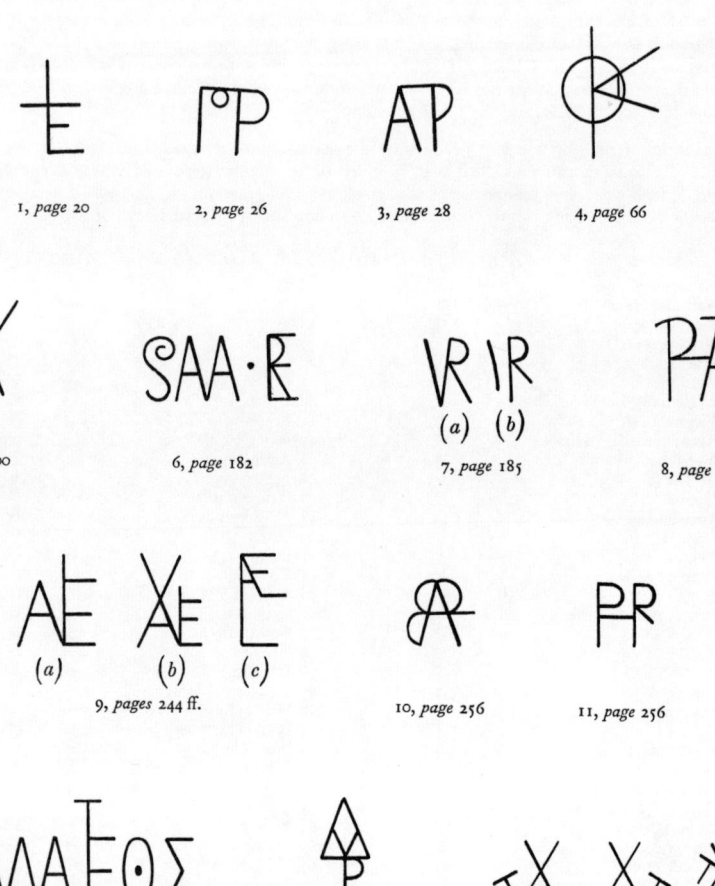

1, *page* 20

2, *page* 26

3, *page* 28

4, *page* 66

5, *page* 100

6, *page* 182

7, *page* 185
(a) (b)

8, *page* 225

9, *pages* 244 ff.
(a) (b) (c)

10, *page* 256

11, *page* 256

12, *page* 377

13, *page* 394

14, *page* 398
(a) (b) (c)

INDICES

I. FINDS

*Acireale 46
Adalia 101 n. 16, 105 n. 12
Agram, see Zagreb
Agrigento 29 n. 13, 299 n. 8
Ain el Hout 298 n. 1
Ajia Irini (Cyprus) 80 n. 4
Albania, uncertain site 116 n. 13
Alcacer do Sal 23
Algeria, uncertain site 60, 71 n. 13, 93–4 n. 11
Amman 99 n. 12
Anatolia, uncertain site 11, 63, 92 n. 14, 101 n. 14, n. 15, 102 n. 8, 105 n. 11, n. 22, 111 n. 17, 238, 244 n. 16, 251, 298 n. 12, 376 n. 1 (see also Dardanelles)
Andeer 71 n. 4
Andernach 71 n. 2, 116 n. 4
Antakya (Antioch) 100
Antas 205
Apt 70 n. 7
Aquae Calidae 105 n. 6
Aquileia 71 n. 9, 92 n. 6, 107 n. 16
Aquitaine, uncertain site 7
Arbus 92 n. 8
Argos 298
Arles 70 n. 7, 116 n. 5, 299 n. 5
Austria, uncertain site 105 n. 7
Autun 71 n. 1
*Avignon 70 n. 7, 72 n. 1, 107 n. 7, 116 n. 5

Baden (Aargau) 71 n. 2
Baden (Baden) 116 n. 7
Badenweiler 116 n. 7
Bandirma 101 n. 4
Banostor 105 n. 5
Basel-Kaiseraugst 7, 71 n. 2, 93 n. 3, 101 n. 22, 116 n. 4
Beirut 106 n. 14, 111 n. 20
*Belgrade 93 n. 1, 105 n. 5, 116 n. 12, 298 f. n. 22
Bergama 105 n. 4
Berne 71 n. 2
Besançon 71 n. 1, 93 n. 3, 116 n. 4, 297 n. 11
Beyrouth, see Beirut
Bingen 71 n. 2, 93 n. 3, 116 n. 4
Bir Bou Rekba 225
Bithynia, see Anatolia
Bohemia, uncertain site 105 n. 15
Bonn 49 n. 8, 93 n. 3, 117 n. 1, 297 n. 11
Bordeaux 71 n. 1
Bourges 298 n. 6
Breteuil 71 n. 1
Brusa, see Bursa

Bucharest 101 n. 19, 105 n. 16
*Budapest 71 n. 7
Bulgaria, uncertain site 93 n. 2, 101 n. 18, 105 n. 6, 106 n. 2, 111 n. 14, 282, 376 n. 1
Bursa 111 n. 17, 113 n. 8, 256

Cadiz 172, 298 n. 2, 299 n. 4
Cagliari 92 n. 8, 93–4 n. 11, 116 n. 11, 149, 299 n. 7
Cahaignes 71 n. 1
Calcar 71 n. 2
Campania, uncertain site 47
Cannstatt 132 n. 11
Cappadocia, see Anatolia
Capua 7
Carthage 92 n. 10, 299 n. 9
Castagnet 71 n. 1
Catania 29 n. 13
Caudebec-lès-Elbeuf 71 n. 1
Cavder Hissar 105 n. 4
el Centenillo 134
Cephalonia 66
Chantenay 49 n. 14
Châtillon 116 n. 4
Chester 71 n. 12, 77 n. 1
Chur 92 n. 15
Cilicia, see Anatolia
Cirenaica, uncertain site 57, 138 n. 8
Citania de Troña 123 n. 4
Coblenz 71 n. 2
Colmar 132 n. 11
Cologne, see Köln
Como 299 n. 1
Constance, see Konstanz
Constantine 47 n. 13, 71 n. 13, 93–4 n. 11, 298 n. 7
Corinth 92 n. 12, 298 n. 22, 299 n. 9
Courroux 71 n. 2, 116 n. 4
Crefeld 71 n. 2
Crete, uncertain site 55, 57
Cyprus, uncertain site 99, 106, 143 n. 16
Cyrenaica, see Cirenaica

Dalmatia, uncertain site 116 n. 12
Dardanelles, uncertain site 246, 248 n. 1
Darmstadt 71 n. 3
Daxlanden 116 n. 7
Deersheim 337 n. 9
Delos 92 n. 12, 105 n. 10
Derek Maden 105 n. 14
Despeña Perros 297 n. 4

---

* Denotes that the place mentioned is the repository, but not necessarily the actual place of discovery of the coins.

496   INDICES

Diarbekr 111 n. 21
Dijon 116 n. 4
Donaueschingen 93 n. 6
Dreimannsdorf bei Salis 132 n. 11
Dura 102 n. 2

Egridir 111 n. 19
Ehl 116 n. 4
Eisenstadt 298 f. n. 22
Elbeuf 71 n. 1
Elche 297 n. 4
Enge 71 n. 2
England, uncertain site 77, 132 n. 11
Enns 92 n. 16
Ereğli 111 n. 17
Eski Hisarlik 111 n. 15
Este 7

Feniki 131 n. 12, 298 n. 5
France, uncertain site 131 n. 12, 132, 157 n. 8, 297 n. 11
Franche-Comté, see France
Frankfurt-am-Main 71 n. 3

Geneva 70 n. 7
Girgenti, see Agrigento
Giubiasco 92 n. 15, 101 n. 17, 116 n. 6
Gotha 74 n. 9
Graubünden (Grisons) 7
Greece, uncertain site 93–4 n. 11, 105 n. 10, 107 n. 8, n. 14
Grimlinghausen 93 n. 3
Grisons, see Graubünden
Gschiess (Sércz) 93 n. 6
Guerbaville-la-Mailleraye 71 n. 1

*Hague 74 n. 9
Haltern 298 n. 6
Hammeran 71 n. 3
Hanau 93 n. 6
Hayling Island 105 n. 17
Hazzen 92 n. 15
Heerewaarden 116 n. 4
Hees 71 n. 2, 93 n. 3, 116 n. 4
Hegau 92 n. 15, 116 n. 6
Helden 116 n. 4
Hofheim bei Taunus 71 n. 3, 93 n. 6, n. 11, 297 n. 13
Hungary, uncertain site 71 n. 7, 93 n. 1

*Istanbul 82, 105 n. 22, 111 n. 16, 298 n. 12, n. 16
Italy, uncertain mint 47, 49 n. 9, 71 n. 9
Izmir 105 n. 4, 244 n. 16

Jagsthausen 116 n. 7
Jerash 298 n. 15, 298 f. n. 22
Jerusalem 106 n. 14, 298 f. n. 22
Jerwen 93 n. 6

Kaiseraugst, see Basel
Karlsruhe 116 n. 7

Kašina 93 n. 1
Kef 298 n. 4
Kephallenia, see Cephalonia
Köln 93 n. 3, 101 n. 21, 298 f. n. 22, 299 n. 11
Konstanz 92 n. 15, 116 n. 6

Lampsak 105 n. 4
Lausanne 71 n. 2
Lebanon 101 n. 12, 105 n. 13
Leibnitz 93 n. 1
Leiden (Leyden) 74 n. 9
Lenzburg 71 n. 2
Lewes 105 n. 17
*Lisbon 23, 92 n. 13, 132 n. 11, 297 n. 8
Lorch 116 n. 7
Lorraine 3 n. 5, 124 n. 9
*Luxembourg 3 n. 5, 124 n. 5
Lyon 116 n. 4

*Madrid 71 n. 10
Magdeburg 116 n. 10
Mahlberg 93 n. 6
Mainz 93 n. 3
Manisa 105 n. 4
Mannheim 71 n. 2, n. 3
Maresfield 298 f. n. 22
*Marseille 70 n. 7, 72 n. 1, n. 3, 74 n. 9, 116 n. 5, 297 n. 10, 298 n. 13
Masala 205
Mayenne 118
Melendugno 298 n. 14, 299 n. 1
Metz 71 n. 1
Migliadino S. Vitale 92 n. 6
Milan 47 n. 15
Minas de S. Domingos 297 n. 8
Mitrovica 105 n. 5
Mönchsberg 92 n. 16
Mologno 92 n. 6
Montans 92 n. 11, 116 n. 5, 297 n. 10
Montivilliers 71 n. 1
Mont Jouer à S. Goussand 93 n. 3
Mont S. Michel 71 n. 1
Mook 94 n. 6
Mulhouse 71 n. 2, 93 n. 3, 116 n. 4, 132 n. 11
Mysia-Troad, see Anatolia

Nabeul 225
Naples 48 n. 1, 116 n. 9
Narbonne 41 n. 10, 70 n. 7, 72 n. 1, 92 n. 11, 105 n. 8, 116 n. 5, 297 n. 10, 298 n. 6, 337 n. 8
Nauheim 71 n. 3
Neidenstein 93 n. 6
Nemi 299 n. 1
Nettersheim 93 n. 3
Neuss 42, 47 n. 9, 71 n. 2, 77, 93 n. 3, 105 n. 19, 116 n. 4, 118 n. 11, 297 n. 11, 298 n. 6, 337 n. 8
Neustadt am Donau 116 n. 6
Nijmegen 22 n. 5, 71 n. 2, 93 n. 3, 116 n. 4, 298 n. 6, 337 n. 8

INDICES

Nîmes 22 n. 5, 41 n. 10, 47 n. 8, 70 n. 7, 72 n. 1, n. 3, 111 n. 23, 116 n. 5, 298 n. 6, 337 n. 8
Nová Ves 93 n. 6
Novi Banovci 93 n. 1, 105 n. 5, 116 n. 12, 117 n. 1, 298 n. 20
Numantia 71 n. 10, 93 n. 4, 297 n. 4

Oberhausen 71 n. 4, 92 n. 15, 105 n. 9, 297 n. 12
Obernau 116 n. 7
Öhringen 49 n. 8, 71 n. 3, 93 n. 6
*Oporto 92 n. 13, 297 n. 8
Orange 70 n. 7, 72 n. 1, 92 n. 11, 116 n. 5
Orival 71 n. 1
Osijek 71 n. 8, 105 n. 5

Padria 205
Painten 7
*Palermo 30
Paris 42 n. 9, 71 n. 1, 298 n. 6
Pavia 92 n. 6
Pergamum, see Bergama
Perušić 93 n. 1
Petronel 71 n. 7, 93 n. 1, n. 11, 116 n. 12
Pettau, see Ptuj
Pforzheim 116 n. 7
Phrygia, see Anatolia
Pisidia, see Anatolia
Pitres 71 n. 1
Ploaghe 205
Poitiers 71 n. 1
Pommern 71 n. 2, 93 n. 3, 116 n. 4
Pompeii 22 n. 5, 298 f. n. 22
Pontevedra 123 n. 4
Porto, see Oporto
Portugal, uncertain site 116 n. 8, 132 n. 11
*Prague 105 n. 5, 116 n. 7
Preignan 71 n. 1, 297 n. 11
Priene 105 n. 4
Propontis, see Dardanelles
Prozor 93 n. 1
Ptuj (Pettau) 71 n. 7, 93 n. 1, n. 11, 299 n. 11
Pujol 157 n. 8

Remagen 93 n. 3
Rennes 71 n. 1, 93 n. 3, 116 n. 4, 297 n. 11
Rheims 3 n. 5, 71 n. 1
Rhodes 298 f. n. 22
Riedlingen 71 n. 4, 298 n. 3
Riegel 71 n. 3
Risstissen 116 n. 6, 143 n. 11
Rixdorf 298 f. n. 22
Rodi, see Rhodes
Rokytzan 7
Rome 47 n. 15, 63
Rossum 93 n. 6
Rottenburg 7
Rottweil 71 n. 3, 116 n. 7

Saalburg 71 n. 3, 93 n. 6, 116 n. 7
Sagunto 71 n. 10, 297 n. 4, 299 n. 3

S. André sur Cailly 93 n. 3
S. Antioco 146 n. 5
S. Bernard 71 n. 6
S. Bertrand de Comminges 70 n. 7, 297 n. 10
S. Blaise 71 n. 1, 298 n. 6
S. Gall 71 n. 3
S. Germain-en-Laye 71 n. 1, 116 n. 4, 337 n. 8
S. Polo di Piave 92 n. 6
S. Saens 71 n. 1
Salerno 48 n. 1
Samos 105 n. 4
Sardinia, uncertain site 47, 92 n. 8, 93 f. n. 11, 116 n. 11, 149 f., 152, 205
Sart 105 n. 4
Sassari 205
Selče 93 n. 1
Serbia, uncertain site 111 n. 13, 116 n. 12
Sércz, see Gschiess
Serravalle Scrivia 92 n. 6
Serrazeda 71 n. 11
Sicily, uncertain site 92 n. 9, 197
Sillingy 47 n. 8
Sinalungo 7
Sišak 71 n. 8, 93 n. 1, 111 n. 12, 116 n. 12, 298 n. 20
Smyrna, see Izmir
*Sofia 101 n. 18, 106 n. 2, 111 n. 14, 298
Sotin 116 n. 12
Soukh-Aras 92 n. 10, 298 n. 22
Sousse 92 n. 10
Spain, uncertain site 47, 74 n. 9, 93 n. 4, 93–4 n. 11, 157 n. 8, 159, 216, 298 f. n. 22, 473 n. 7
Stankamen 93 n. 1
Strasbourg 93 n. 3, 116 n. 4, 337 n. 8
Stratos 298, 298 f. n. 22
Syracuse 92 n. 9, 93–4 n. 11
Syria, uncertain site 100

Tangermunde 71 n. 3
Tarragona 297 n. 4, 299 n. 2
Tebtunis 102 n. 3
Tell Umar 102
Teutre 71 n. 1
Tewkesbury 71 n. 12, 77 n. 1
Thrace, uncertain site 15, 82 f., 107
Toulouse 70 n. 7, 72 n. 1, 105 n. 18, 298 n. 6
Transjordan, uncertain site 99 n. 12
Trier 3 n. 5, 93 n. 3
Trieste 71 n. 9
Truvine 205
Tübingen 71 n. 3
Tulca 298 n. 20
Tulle 298 f. n. 22
Tunis, uncertain site 140 n. 3
Turkey, see Anatolia, Thrace

Ubbergen 71 n. 2, 93 n. 3, 116 n. 4
Unterkirchberg 111 n. 26
Urmitz 71 n. 2, 93 n. 3, 116 n. 4
Utrecht 71 n. 3, 337 n. 9

498 INDICES

Valkenburg 116 n. 4
Vechten 93 n. 6, 116 n. 7
Verneuil 71 n. 1
Vetera 297 n. 11
Vienna 71 n. 7, 74 n. 9, 105 n. 7
Vienne 41 n. 10, 70 n. 7, 72 n. 1, 92 n. 11, 116 n. 5, 298 n. 6, 337 n. 8

Walldorf 116 n. 7
Wangen 116 n. 6
Wels 92 n. 16
Widin 299 n. 11
Wiesbaden 71 n. 2
Wiesloch 116 n. 7

Winchester 71 n. 12, 77 n. 1
Windisch 71 n. 2, 93 n. 3, n. 11, 116 n. 4, 297 n. 11, 298 n. 6
Winterthur 71 n. 2, 116 n. 6
Woodeaton 93 n. 7

Xanten 7, 71 n. 2, 93 n. 3, 116 n. 4, 337 n. 8

Yalvaç (Pisidian Antioch) 101 n. 16,

Zagreb 102 n. 4, 376 n. 1
Zillis 132 n. 11
Zollfeld 71 n. 5

II. MINTS[1]

Abdera A 10 (7)
Abydus 351f., 357, A 8
Acci 220
Ace, see Ptolemais
Achulla 230
Acmonia 350, 356, A 8, A 9
Adana A 10 (11)
Adramyttium 351, 366, 394, A 8
Aegae A 9
Aegeae 344
Aegium A 10 (6)
Aezanis 349, A 8
Agrigentum 28, 191, 196, 392
Agrippias A 10 (7)
Alabanda 369, 373, 396, A 8, A 9
Alexandria 68, 131
Alexandria Troas 244
Alinda 351, A 9, A 10 (8)
Amisus 11
Amorium 350, A 8
Amphipolis 343, 374
Amyzon A 10 (8)
Andros A 10 (6)
Aninetus 366
Antioch (Caria) 113, 351, 356, A 8, A 9
Antioch (Pisidia) 250
Antioch (Syria) 61, 100, 113, 376, 396
Antipolis 390
Apamea (Bithynia) 69, 145, 255, 396
Apamea (Phrygia) 351, 366, A 8
Aphrodisias-Plarasa 342, A 8, A 9, A 10 (8)
Apollonia Salbace (Caria) 350, 357, 365
Apollonia (Pontus) 353
Aradus 330, 368f., 371
Arausio 208
Arelate 41
Ascalon 361
Asia, *commune* 362, 377
Asia, uncertain mint 99

Aspendus 354
Assus 351, 357
Astypalaea A 9
Athens 401
Avennio 391 n. 8, A 10 (4)

Babba 222
Baelo 24
Baesuris A 10 (2)
Balanea 368
Balbura A 10 (9)
Bargasa 402, A 10 (8)
Bargylia 351, 357
Berytus 127, 258, 371
Bilbilis 170
Bithynia, uncertain mint 113
Blaundus A 10 (8)
Botrys A 10 (11)
Brundusium 37
Brutobriga 381
Bubon 354
Buthrotum 269
Byzacene, uncertain mint 81
Byzantium 369, A 10 (10)

Cabellio 336
Caesaraugusta 217
Caesarea, see Agrippias
Caesarea, see Iol
Caesarea (Samaria) 131
Calagurris 165
Caralis 149
Carteia 336, A 10 (2)
Carthage 50, 231
Carthago Nova 215
Cassandrea 272
Cassope A 10 (6)
Castulo 134, A 10 (1)
Caunus A 10 (8)

[1] Only mints believed to have issued *aes* coinage in the period 49 B.C.–A.D. 14 are included, and references only apply to the pages on which this coinage is actually described. 'A 1, 2' etc. indicates 'Appendices 1, 2' etc. (not pages).

INDICES 499

Celenderis A 10 (11)
Celsa 211
Cephallenia 66
Cephaloedium 192
Chalcis (Euboea) 385
Chersonesus A 10 (7)
Chios 365, 401, A 10 (8)
Cibyra 350
Cilbiani, see Nicaea
Cirta 232
Clazomenae 351, A 8, A 9
Clunia A 10 (1)
Cnossus 35, 55, 138, 261
Colophon 351, A 8
Corcyra A 10 (6)
Corduba 4, 22, 220
Corinth 265
Corycus A 10 (11)
Cos 113, 351 n. 16, A 8
Cossura 191
Cragus district 342
Cremna A 10 (9)
Cyaneae 343
Cydonia 343
Cyprus 80, 99, 106, 143
Cyrene 57, 69, 135, 260
Cyzicus 342, 357, A 8, A 9

Damascus 99, 371
Dardanus 352, A 8
Dertosa 158
Dionysopolis A 10 (8)
Dioshieron 349, A 8
Dium 272
Dyme 264
Dyrrhachium 275

Ebura 337
Edessa (Macedonia) 353, 374
Elaea 352, A 8, A 9, A 10 (8)
Elaeussa A 10 (11)
Emerita 119, 221
Emporiae 154
Entella 392
Ephesus 104, 352, 357, 365, 369, A 8
Epicteteis A 10 (8)
Ercavica 336
Eriza A 10 (8)
Erythrae 352, A 8, A 10 (8)
Etenna A 10 (9)
Eucarpitic district 348, A 8
Eumenia 350, A 8
Euromus 351, A 8
Eustivaicola A 10 (1)

Fulvia, see Eumenia

Gades 171
Gaul, uncertain tribe 123, 392

Gaza 344
Germe A 9
Gili A 10 (1)

Hadrumetum 139, 226
Halaesa 191, 195
Haluntium 199
Henna 190
Heraclea ad Latmum A 10 (8)
Heraclea Salbace (Caria) 349, A 8
Heraclea (Pontus) 254
Hierapolis 351, 356f., 387, A 8, A 9
Hippo Diarrhytus 224
Hydisus A 10 (8)
Hydrela 350, 357
Hypaepa 349, 357, A 8

Iasus 351, A 8
Iconium A 10 (9)
Ilerda 170
Ilergetes A 10 (1)
Ilici 213
Ilium 357, 365, A 8, A 9, A 10 (8)
Imbros 354
Iol 59, A 10 (3)
Ionia, uncertain mint 145
Irippo 355 n. 6
Italica 173
Italy, uncertain mint 91
Ithaca 66

Laelia 355 n. 6
Lampsacus 246
Laodicea (Phrygia) 352, 357, A 8, A 10 (8)
Laodicea (Syria) 61, 129
Lascuta A 10 (2)
Lebedus A 10 (8)
Lemnos A 10 (6)
Leptis Magna 340
Leptis Minor 338
Lilybaeum 26, 196, 393
Lipara 52, 195
Lix 174
Lugdunum 115, 206
Lycia, *commune* 342
Lystra 238, 249

Macedonia, uncertain mint 82
Magnesia ad Maeandrum (Ionia) 351, A 8, A 9
Magnesia ad Sipylum (Lydia) 384, A 9
Malaca A 10 (2)
Marathus A 10 (11)
Massicytes district 342
Mauretania, uncertain mint 59
Mediolanum 7
Melita 59, 68, 191, 234
Messana 194, 199
Miletopolis 391
Miletus 351, 357

Myconus 354
Mylasa 341, 357, A 8
Myra 342
Myrina 351
Myrtilis 24

Nabrissa A 10 (2)
Neapolis ad Harpasum A 10 (8)
Nemausus 70, 114
Nicaea (Bithynia) 353, 383, 396
Nicaea Cilbianorum (Lydia) 348, A 9
Nicomedia 353, 396
Nicopolis 343, 361
Nysa A 8, A 9

Obulco A 10 (2)
Odessus 353
Oea 339
Olbiopolis A 10 (7)
Onuba A 10 (2)
Orthosia A 9, A 10 (8)
Osca 167
Osicerda A 10 (1)
Osset A 10 (2)

Paestum 200, 284
Panormus 29, 189
Panticapaeum A 10 (7)
Paphos 80, 99, 106, 143
Parium 111, 248
Paros A 10 (6)
Patrae 64, 265, 374
Patricia, see Corduba
Pax 221
Pella 279
Peparethus 354
Perga A 10 (9)
Pessinus A 10 (9)
Phanagoria, see Agrippias
Pheneus A 10 (6)
Philadelphia 365, A (8)
Philippi 274
Philomelium 350
Phocaea 351
Pitane 351, 387, A 9
Pontus, uncertain mint 113
Priene 388
Prymnessus 350, 367, A 8, A 9
Ptolemais Ace 368f., 371
Puteoli 46

Remi 392
Rhodes 243, A 10 (8)
Rhosus A 10 (11)
Rome 91
Romula 220

Sabrata 341
Saetabis A 10 (1)
Saguntum 158

Salamis (Cyprus) 143
Saldubia, see Caesaraugusta
Samnagetes A 10 (4)
Samos 351 n. 16, A 8, A 10 (8)
Samosata A 10 (11)
Sardes 351, A 8
Scepsis 351, A 8, A 9
Segesta 335
Segobriga 335
Segovia 336
Seleucia ad Calycadnum (Cilicia) ʿA 10 (11)
Seleucia (Syria) 396
Sestus 353
Seθiscen A 10 (1)
Sexi 473 n. 5
Sibliani 349, 357, A 9
Sidon 125, 344f., 361
Simitthu 178, 232
Sinope 251
Smyrna 352, A 8
Spain, uncertain mint 123
Sparta 343, 382, A 10 (6)
Syracuse 30

Tabae 351, A 8, A 10 (8)
Tamusia A 10 (1)
Tanagra 343
Tarentum 43
Tarraco 218
Tarsus A 10 (11)
[Tauromenium 236, see corrigenda]
Tavium A 10 (9)
Telmessus 343
Temnus 351, 387, A 9
Tenedus 351, 357
Teos 352, A 8
Termessus Major A 10 (9)
Termessus Minor-Oenoanda 355
Thaena 346
Thapsus 225
Thermae Himeraeae 238
Thessalia 475
Thessalonica 33, 369, 374
Thessaly 475
Thuburnica 185
Thyatira 402, A 10 (8)
Thysdrus 347
Tingis 175
Tlos 342
Toletum A 10 (2)
Tomi A 10 (7)
Traducta 220
Tralles 382, A 8, A 9
Trapezopolis 349, A 8
Tripolis (Lydia) 356, A 9
Tripolis (Phoenicia) 368
Turiaso 168
Turris Libisonis 205
Tyndaris 194, 237
Tyre A 10 (11)

INDICES 501

Urso 24
Uselis 151
Utica 20

Valentia A 10 (1)

Vesci 379
Vienna 337

Zacynthus 39
Zama Regia 182
Zitha 187

III. PERSONS[1]

M.A.B. 157
L. Acilius 237; Man. 81; A. 249; Q.A. 213; M.A. Aviola(?) 17; Man.A. Caninus(?) 26; M.A. Glabrio 81
D. Acu(?tilius) Tam. 262; M.A. 262
P. Aebutius 266; P.A. Sp.f. 268 n. 4
L. Aeficius Certus 266
C. Aelius 167; L.A.(?); Lamia 91 n. 2; Q.A. Lamia 91 n. 2
L. Aemilius 177; M.A. 262; Q.A. 166 n. 1; M.A. Labeo 262; M.A. Lepidus (IIIvir) 50, 390; P.A. Lepidus 35; A. Pollio 177
Agrippa, see L. Vipsanius
Agrippa Postumus 255, 268, 362
T. Ahius A 10 (1)
Albius 177
C. Alliarius 218 n. 2
A. Allienus 177
P. Allius 52; C.A. Bala 28
C. Alsanus 218 n. 1
Q. Am. 205
Q. Am. Quinti. 144
A. Ambatus 182
M. Ambibulus 131
M. An. Ant. A 10 (2)
T. Anicius 248
C. Annius 91 n. 2; L.A. 52; Q.A. 26; Sex. A. 52
Antiochus *rex* 365
Antistius Nicanor 366
M. Antonius (*IIIvir*) 37, 39, 43, 64, 253, 274, 368 ff.; M.A. 191; M.A. 262; Q.A. 166 n. 1; M.A. Arista(rchus?) 264; Sex. A. Athenio 190; M.A. Hipparchus 268 n. 3; M.A. Orestes 268 n. 5; M.A. Primus 82; M.A. Theophilus 267
L. Appuleius 213; L.A. Decianus 24
L. Apronius 91 n. 3
C. Aquinus Mela 283
Aristo ben Ricoce 149
C. Arrius 264
C. Arruntanus Balbus 59
L. Art. Ve. 202
(Q. Articuleius?) Regulus 125
C. Asinius Gallus 91 n. 2, 387; A. *Marrucinus* 394
M. Atius Balbus 150
L. Aufidius Pansa 213 n. 2; A. Rufus 336
M. Aufi(dius?) Scaeva 52
L. Ausonius(?) 195
C. Axius 202

Q.B. 26
P. Baebius Pollio 282 f.; L.B. Priscus 166
L. Baggius 213 n. 1
Balbus 197; C.B. 212
M. Barbatius 249; Q.B. 249
L. Bennius 159
P. Betilienus Bassus 91 n. 3
Bocchus *rex* 175

P.C. 205
C.C. At. 156 n. 14
Q.C.C. 157 n. 14
L.C.F. 156 n. 14
L. Cae. 52
M. Caec. 212 n. 4
Q. Caecilius Metellus Creticus Silanus 127, 396; Q.C. Niger 266; C. Plocamus 367; C. Rufus 191; M.C. Severus 169 n. 4
C. Caesar Aug. n. 139, 143 ff., 172, 221, 224, 227, 230, 253 n. 3, 348, 356, A 9 (3)
L. Caesar Aug. n., ditto
L. Cal. 211
P. Calpurnius 52; L.C. Bibulus 43; Cn. C. Piso 91 n. 2; Cn. C. Piso Frugi 31
C. Calvisius Sabinus 158
Man. Caninius 218 n. 1; C.C. Rebilus 192
Cap. 52
Capito 135
C. Car. 243
P. Carisius 119
C. Cassius 255; L.C. 218 n. 1; L.C. 266; M.C. 191
Celt. Amb. A 10 (1)
Cerdonius(?) A.f. 236 (see also corrigenda); L.C.(?) Ve(ratus?) 205
T. Cervius 218 n. 1
L. Cestius 190
Sex. Cethegus 213
Ti. Claudius Nero, see Tiberius; C. Pulcher 91 n. 2; Ap. C. Pulcher 255; Cn. C. Pulcher 157; P.C. Pulcher 156 n. 14
Ti. Clodius Flavus 218; L.C. Rufus 196
C. Clovius 7
L. Cnorius(?) 28
A. Cocceius 269
C. Cominius 202
Conduc. 216
Conipp.(?) 473
Coponius 131

[1] Only persons directly concerned with *aes* coinage during the period are included. *Peregrini* are generally omitted. See also p. 498 n. 1.

L. Cor. Calidus 170 n. 11
L. Cor. Terrenus 213 n. 1
L. Coranius A 10 (1)
L. Cornelius 269; P.C. 52; L.C. Balbus *major* 6; L.C. Balbus *minor* 172; C.C. Gallus 68; P.C. Scipio 387; C (?). Sisenna 91 n. 2
C. Cos. 243
P. Cosconius 260
P. Cotta Balbus 196

P. Dastidius 269
Cn. Domitius 213 n. 1; Cn. D. Ampianus 218
Drusus *jun.* 268

Egnatius 366
Ep. (or Pe.) 244
M. Eppius 22
Q. Eq. 202

M.F.M. 157
L. Fabius 166 n. 1; M.F. 217; Q.F. 26; C.F. Catulus 226; Q.F. Fabullus 177; Africanus F. Maximus 139, 224, 228; Paullus F. Maximus 387
M. Fabricius 218 n. 1
Cn. Fadius 218 n. 3; Dec. F. 284; L.F. 202
L. Feneste. 169
A. Feridius 238
M. Fictorius 281
Man. Flaminius(?) 254; L.F. Capito 227
Man. Flavius Festus 213 n. 1; P.F. 156
T. Fufius 262
M. Fulvius 212 n. 3; C.F. Rutilus 166 n. 9; Fulvia 350, 368
A. Furius 366; F. Crassipes 26

C. Gallius Lupercus 91 n. 2
Num. Gavius 202
Germanicus 268
Gessius Charidemus 366, 377
L. Granius 166 n. 2; C.G. Brocchus 166 n. 8; M.G. Marcellus 145

C. Heius Pamphilus sen. 266; C.H. Pamphilus jun. 268 n. 3; C.H. Pollio 268 n. 3
Helvius Pollio 159
C. Herennius 282; M.H. 277
Hiberus 159
Hinsteius, see Insteius
A. Hirtius 391
A. Hirtuleius 269
Q. Hortensius 33, 272

M.I. Ne. 284
Insteius 266
Iuba *rex* 216
Cn. Iulius 4; L.I. 222; L.I. 266; C.I. Aeschinus 262; C.I. Antonius 263; C.I. Asclas 365; C.I. Atticus 177; I. Bito 365; Q.I. Caesar (*dictator*) = Divus I. 13, 47, 50, 207, 230, 253 n. 3, 255 f., 258 n. 3, 275, 374 n. 5; C.I. Caesar Aug. n., see Caesar, C.; L.I. Caesar Aug. n., see Caesar, C.I .Demetrius 365 ;C.I. Dionysius 190;C.I. Dionysius 365; C.I. Heraclanus 268 n. 5; C.I. Longus 190; C.I. Nicephorus 266; C.I. Nicom. 156; Sex. I. Pollio 212; C.I. Tang. 264; Iulia Aug. f. A 9(2); Iulia, see Livia. See also Germanicus, Drusus
L. Iunius 30; L.I. 166 n. 1; L.I. 237; M.I. Hisp. 213 n. 1
M. Ius. 277
L. Iuventius Lupercus 218

Kaninius, see Caninius

C.L. 192
L.L. 156 n. 13
P.L. 156 n. 13
C. Laetilius Apalus 216
Leiv., see Liv.
P. Licinius 35; M.L. Capella 166 n. 9; M.L. Crassus 55, 57; A.L. Nerva Silianus 91 n. 2; P.L. Stolo 91 n. 2; L.L. Varus 170 n. 11
Liv. Pertinax 227
C. Livineius Gallus 139
C. Livius 379; Livia 132, 145, 169, A 9 (1)
L. Lollius 56; L.(?) Palikanus 135
C. Lucienus A 10 (1)
Q. Lucretius 246
M. L(urius?) 205; P.L. Agrippa 91 n. 2
Q. Lutatius 217

M.M.A. 232
L.M. Ruf. 156 n. 14
M. Maecilius Tullus 91 n. 2
C. Maecius (Celer) 213
Maior. 177
Malleolus, see Poblicius
L. Manlius 215; T.M. Sergia(nus) 381
C. Mar. Cap. 166 n. 2
C. Marcius 195; M.M. 202; C.M. Censorinus 91 n. 2
Marius 234; L.M. 169 n. 4
Marullus 167
C. Masonius Rufus 366 n. 20
C. Matuinus 248
Man. Memmius 166 n. 4
Mescinius 386
P. Mion. A 10 (2)
Mucius 248
L. Munatius 190; L.M. (Plancus) 392
L. Mussidius 237
C. Mussius Priscus 268 n. 3
Mutumbal 149

C. Naevius Capella 91 n. 3; Q.N. Sura 269; L.N. Surdinus 91
P(?). Naso 26
L. Nep. 211
Nonius 279; Sex. N. Quinctilianus 91 n. 2
Novius(?) 266; L.N. 169 n. 4; M.N. Bassus 268 n. 3
L. Novus 166 n. 9
M.Nun. 284

C.O.Car. 156 n. 14
M.O.H. 157

INDICES

Cn. Octavius 264; M.O. 200; T.O. 373, 396; Octavia 44, 369
Q. Oppius 61; M.O. Capito 43, 52
Q. Opsilius A 10 (2)
C. Otacilius 212 n. 5

M. Paccius Maximus 195
Q. Papirius Carbo 215
Q. Paquius Rufus 274f.
L. Passienus Rufus 139
Pe. (or Ep.) 244
Q. Peducaeus 380
C. Petronius 262; M.P. 263; T.P. 215
Pic. 248
L. Pinnius 266
M. Plaetorius Tranquillus 166 n. 2
A. Plautius 143; M.P. Silvanus 388
L. Plotius Plebeius 262; C.P. Rufus 91 n. 2
Poblicius(?) Malleolus 216; Cn.P. Regulus 268 n. 5
Pollio 262
T. Pom. A 10 (3)
Q. Pomp. Secundinus 213 n. 1
C. Pompeius 213 n. 1; Cn.P. (Magni f.) 22; Sex.P. (= Magnus P.) 22; L.P. Bucco 213 n. 1; M.P. Macer 388; Sex.P. Niger *sen.* 211; Sex.P. Niger *jun.* 213 n. 2
L. Pomponius 222; P.P. Graecinus Milesius 269; A.P. Victor 21
L. Pontius 246; L.P. 258
Porcius(?) 26; Dec.P. 52; L.P. 212; M.P. 218 n. 3; L.P. Capito 215
M. Postumius Albinus 215; C.P. Mil. 166 n. 1
C. Proculeius 66
Publicius, see Poblicius
M. Pullienus 269
A. Pupius Rufus 69

L.Q. 194
P. Quinctilius Varus 127, 228, 230, 396
T. Quinctius Crispinus Sulpicianus 91 n. 2

Raius(?) 67; L.R. A 10 (2)
Regulus 91 n. 2
C. Rubellius Blandus 91 n. 3
Rufinus, see Vibius
Sex. Rufus 196

C. Sabinus 218 n. 1
Sacer. 52
P. Sal. Pa. 212 n. 3
Salassus 196
M. Salvius Otho 91 n. 2
M. Sanquinius 91 n. 2
M. Sat. 202
Scato 137
L. Scribonius Libo 29
L. Seius 197; L.S(?). 202
L. Sempronius Atratinus 37, 43, 382, 393; C.S. Barb. 166 n. 9; Ti. S. Gracchus 91 n. 2; L.S. Maximus 212 n. 4; L.S. Rutilus 170 n. 11; M.S. Rutilus 238; M.S. Tiberi. 170 n. 11

L....ius Seneca 177
Sept. 197
M. Septimius 281
L. Seranus 169 n. 4
C. Servilius Primus 268 n. 3
C. Sex. 165
Dec(?). Sextilius Cornutus 226
P(?). Silius 91 n. 2
Simint. 177
P. Sittius 178, 232
Sosius *filius* 175; C.S. 39, 392
Sparsus 167f.
L. Sta. 202
L. Staius Murcus 234
Cn. Stati. Libo 158
T. Statilius Taurus 52, 91 n. 2, 212
Q. Statius 218 n. 1; L.S. Flaccus 196
L. Suillius 284
Sulpicius 279; S(?). Galus 91 n. 3; P.S. Rufus 11, 251
L. Sura 211

C.T.C. 157
C.T.C. 255
M.T.F. 232
Tadius 234; P.T. Chilo 266
Ti. Tarius 276
Q. Terentius Culleo 196; Q. T. Montanus 215; A.T. Tiro 182
Thorius Flaccus 384, 396
Tiberius (later Emperor) 91 n. 8, 139, 224, 230, 253 n. 3, 268, 356, A 9 (5)
L. Titius 218 n. 1
L. Titucius 282
Trebonius 52; Q.T. 284
L. Trinius A 10 (1)
M. Tullius Cicero 385
M. Turius 246
Turpilius Priscus 152
P. Turullius 215

Q. Ursus 166 n. 2

C. Valentinus 218 n. 1; L.V. 166 n. 9
C. Valerius 166 n. 2; C.V. 165; L.V. 177; M.V. 166 n. 8; C.V. Aquinus 169 n. 4; L.V. Catullus 91 n. 3; C.V. Fen(estella?) 218 n. 1; L.V. Flavus 166 n. 10; T.V. Merula 166 n. 10; V. Messalla 91 n. 3; Volusus V. Messalla 91
Q. Varius 159; C.V. Rufus 212
L. Ve. Ne. 284
P. Vedius Pollio 382
M. Vehilius Tuscus 152
T. Verrius 218 n. 2
C. Vet. Lancia 218 n. 4
C. Vibius 258; P.V. 249; C.V. Pansa Caetronianus 396; L.V(?). Rufinus 385
C. Viccius A 10 (1)
L. Vipsanius Agrippa 46, 171, 249, 255, 387
Virres 185
L. Volusius Saturninus 228, 230, 232, 396
T. Vomanius 254

IV. TYPES[1]

acrostolium 42, 43, 171
Aesculapius 392
Africa 60
Ammon 57, 60, 69, 272, 387
anchor 158
apex, see pontifical emblems
Aphrodite, see Venus
Apollo 25, 55, 57, 67, 191, 196 (see also Bacchus)
aquila, see eagle
Artemis, see Creta, Diana
Asclepius, see Aesculapius
aspergillum, see pontifical emblems
Astarte 224, 347
Athena, see Minerva
axe 66

Baal 177
Bacax 182
Bacchus 52 n. 16
Bacchus-Apollo 40
bee 3 n. 2
'bird's eye' view of town, see walls
boar 52 n. 16, 179, 202, 473
bridge 222
bull 60, 118, 124, 165, 191, 206, 208, 211, 216, 238, 379 (see also oxen, plough)

caduceus 57, 382, 394
capricorn 61, 96, 112, 118 n. 3, 132, 143, 174, 187, 347
centaur 52 n. 16
Ceres 146, 224, 250, 258, 392
cippus, figures on 275
city-goddess 11, 57, 187, 206, 253 n. 3, 336
club 28, 54, 56
cock 42
colonists, see plough
column 66
Concordia 271, 392
corn-ear 57, 175, 177, 182, 221, 272
cornucopiae 174, 187, 220, 253 n. 3, 353
corona navalis 73 f., 102 f., 107, 110
cow 103
crescent 61, 63, 91, 102, 102 n. 8
Creta-Diana 35
crocodile 55, 57, 69, 70
Crysas 191
cultus-statues 144
Cupid 4, 52 n. 16

Demeter, see Ceres
Diana 56, 62, 154, 272 (see also Creta)
Diogenes 253
Dionysus, see Bacchus

Dioscuri 189, 194
dolphin 41, 128, 158, 161, 162 n. 5
dromedary 57

eagle 40, 68, 124, 127, 214, 220, 237, 251 (see also standards)
elephant 52 n. 16, 53, 60, 139, 175
Eros, see Cupid
Euthenia 132
eye 207

fasces 55, 236, 264
Felicitas 62
fiscus 13

galley 31, 43, 50, 158, 214 (see also prow)
gate of city 221
Genius Populi Romani 173
globe 174, 187, 220, 253 n. 3
Gorgon, see Medusa
gorgoneion 46
grapes 221
grapnels 42

hammer 216
hands clasped 382
hasta donatica 13, 69
Health, see Salus
Helios, see Sol
Hephaestus, see Vulcan
Hercules 52 n. 16, 171, 173, 185, 192, 254
Hermes, see Mercury
hippocamp 43, 336
Homonoia, see Concordia
Honos 178
Hope, see Spes
horse 123, 134, 355
horseman 29, 106, 168, 282

Janus 31, 37, 52 n. 16, 86, 175
Juno 146, 224, 384
Jupiter 26, 52 n. 16, 66, 143, 178, 388 (see also Ammon)

knife 122

labyrinth 262
laurel-branches 56, 139, 145
Libya 35, 57, 137
lighthouse, see Pharos
lion 60, 391
lituus 50, 72, 128, 134, 139 (see also pontifical emblems)
locust 258
lyre 25

[1] Only types possessing special interest and only those on *aes* coinage 49 B.C.–A.D. 14 are included.

INDICES

Medusa 52 n. 16
Melkart 185
Mercury 49 n. 14, 52 n. 16, 225, 254
Minerva (Roma) 3 n. 2, 7, 29, 132, 154, 185, 202, 211, 236, 244, 263, 264, 277, 356
modius 274

Neptune 41, 49 n. 14, 226
Nike, see Victory

Odysseus, see Ulysses
owl 11, 112
oxen, humped 238, 250

palm-branch 54
panther 52 n. 16
Pax 50 n. 14, 281
Pegasus 154
pentalpha 387
pertica 34
Pharos 194
pig, see boar
plough, ploughing scene 34, 102, 111, 152 f., 221, 238, 244, 246, 249, 250, 253 n. 3, 258, 264, 272, 274, 277
pontifical emblems 128, 172, 212, 220, 237, 251, 253 n. 3, 281 (see also *lituus*)
poppy 57
Poseidon, see Neptune
prow 37, 42, 55, 82, 112, 146 n. 5, 207 f., 246 (see also galley)

quadriga 50 n. 14

ram 69, 137, 208
rider, see hippocamp, horseman
river-deity 162 n. 5, 221
Roma, see Minerva
rose 243
rostral crown, see *corona navalis*
rudder 187

sacculus 69
Salus 271
Sardus 150, 205
scorpion 143
sella castrensis 69, 135, 138
    curulis 56 f., 59, 236, 279, 384
    quaestoria 13, 69, 234

Senate 356
serpent 69, 137, 159 n. 6, 392, 473
shield 121, 178, 216, 281
ship, see galley, prow
sidus Iulium, see star
silphium 57, 260
simpulum, see pontifical emblems
sistrum 374
skate 66
snake, see serpent
Sol 226, 258, 392
spear, spearhead 122, 150
Spes 281
staff, see *hasta*
stag 56
standards 42, 127, 220 (see also eagle, *vexillum*)
star 50, 61, 112, 125, 143, 207, 253 n. 3
strigiles 282
subsellium 264

temple 149, 205, 215, 266, 382, 388
throne 144
thunderbolt 61, 63
Thuso-Chusartis 224
trident 41, 128
tripod 40, 275
triskeles (triquetra) 43, 46 f., 96, 196
trophy 40, 160
tunny-fish 221
Tyche, see city-goddess

Ulysses 52 n. 16

Vagax, see Bacax
Venus 49 f. n. 14, 62, 143, 211, 275, 390
vexillum 34, 215, 272, 273 n. 7 (see also standards)
Victory 54 etc.
Virtus 178
Vulcan 52, 195

walls 119, 221, 281
warrior 26, 173, 224
wheel 112
wolf 170
wolf and twins 174, 255

yoke 34

Zeus, see Jupiter

V. GENERAL

Ablative Case 5, 25, 28, 69, 159, 189f., 196f., 224, 246, 262
Accusative Case 100, 390
aediles 162, 166, 177
aerarium 20f., 25, 79, 95, 97, 129f., 133, 136, 292f., 296, 311; *militare* 197 n. 6
aes Cordubense (Marianum) 7, 24, 87; *Corinthium* 107 n. 9
ἀγορανόμοι 300
Aion 63
ala equestris 117
'alliance' coinages 121, 185 n. 6, 188 n. 12, 339, 346
amenonkal, see *menokad*
amicus principis 136 n. 3, 140, 229f., 257, 295, 365, 387ff., 402, 430
Antigonids 374f.
apposition 158
arca 118, 129
archieratic coinage, ἀρχιερεύς, see priesthood
art 477 ff.
ascriptio 265 n. 1
Asiarches 363
asylum 402 n. 7
auctoritas 1, 82, 84, 97, 108ff., 114f., 117, 120f., 128ff., 132, 134, 146f., 198, 220, 280f., 289, 292ff., 312, 314, 319ff., 324f., 337, 341, 345, 358, 401ff., 422, 424ff.
aurei, see silver and gold coinage, official
auspicia 426 n. 5
αὐτοκράτωρ, see *imperator*, *imperium*
αὐτονομία 398, 402

bellum 419
bilingual coinage 26, 28, 30 n. 6, 35, 40, 59, 66, 155, 162 n. 5, 192, 338, 347
bimetallism 3
birth certificates 312
Βουλαῖος 359
British coinage 124

cadmea 11, 87
caesa ruta, see *ruta caesa*
calamine 87
castellum civium Romanorum 306
castrensis moneta 50 n. 14, 120 n. 5
censores 154 n. 5, 156, 439
censuit 233
censuses 129, 164 n. 4, 310f., 439
centenary issues, see jubilee coinage
city-badges, see *types parlants*
Cleopatra 62, 64, 371ff.
clientela 151, 157, 176, 223 n. 3, 249, 259, 265f., 317ff., 341, 356, 358, 366, 402f., 417, 427, 436, 444, 474 n. 8
cohortes urbanae 437 n. 1
coiffure 35, 50 n. 14, 62, 143, 284 n. 5, 288 n. 12
comitia 433
comitialis 196 n. 13, 248
commune, see League

concilium, see League; *plebis* 433
Concordia 227, 232, 256, 346
confusion of portraits 74f., 228, 334, 361, 463f., 467
consilium principis 128, 130, 146, 435, 453
conventus 315; *civium Romanorum*, see *castellum*, *pagus*
copper 77, 87, 89ff., 96, 104, 107, 110, 300 n. 2
Cosmocrator 13
Cosmographia 310
countermarks 22 n. 6, 41 n. 10, 42, 66, 70, 72, 92ff., 102, 105f., 111ff., 117f., 122, 155, 230, 246, 256, 299 n. 11, n. 12, 300, 377, 472
creator 266
Cretarch 55f.
cura, see *tutela*

δαίμων, see *genius*
Dative Case 69, 103, 187, 215, 224f., 228, 399
decemvirate 41
decennial coinage, see jubilee coinage
decreta 430ff.
denarii, see silver and gold coinage, official
διά 392
διάταγμα 131, 432
dicta principis 432f.
dictatorship 413
Dioscuri 145
divus, see θεός
dominus 143, 441
δῶρον 365
double communities 155, 158 n. 4, 383 n. 10, 403f.
dupondius 13, 31, 86, 91, 96, 99ff., 104, 106f., 119, 138, 145, 172, 217
dux 421, 442, 444, 452 n. 5

edicta 313, 430ff., 438 n. 1
elasticity of administration 143
ἐλευθερία, see *libertas*
ἐπί 373, 377, 390, 393, 396ff., 401
ἐπιμεληθέντος 399
ἐπιφανής 358
epistulae 431f.
epulones 287
era 253, 331ff., 344f., 368f., 371f. n. 14, 372 n. 6
exercitus 20

felix 14
festival coinage 362ff.
financiers as moneyers 6, 11, 18f., 24, 41, 64, 89, 127, 397
fiscus 18, 95, 97, 118, 129, 296
foederati 161, 350 n. 3, 402 n. 6, 404, 473
fora 147 n. 1, 171
forgeries, see imitations, modern
fragmentum Atestinum 9

gallus 42, 67 n. 12
Garamantes 137

INDICES

gemina, gemella 248
Genitive Case 29 f., 68, 98, 131, 153 n. 2, 157, 190, 207, 225, 228 n. 13, 230, 250 n. 2, 392 ff.
genius 173, 320, 357 ff.
gens Augusta 146, 471
γνώμη 84, 425
gold coinage, see silver and gold coinage, official
γραμματεύς 378

ἁγνός 387
hairdressing, see coiffure
half-coins, 71–77, 111, 124
haplography 380 n. 16
ἡγεμών 444
ἱερὸς γάμος 368
Homonoia, see Concordia
hybrids 49 n. 2, n. 5, 74 f. n. 9, 99, 467
ὑποστρατηγός 126

ἰδιόλογος 131
imitations, barbarous 20 n. 5, 72, 76, 85 n. 8, 93, 101 f., 105; modern 7 f., 41 n. 9, 49 n. 3, 61, 223 f. n. 4, 369 n. 14 (see also tooling)
immunitas 35, 55, 315, 324, 402 n. 7
imperator, imperium 1, 4 f., 10, 16 ff., 22, 32 f., 35 ff., 39, 53, 57 ff., 65, 67 ff., 79 ff., 84, 117, 120 f., 126, 130, 133, 135 ff., 140 ff., 151 n. 16, 181 n. 1, 203, 234 ff., 242, 247, 287, 293, 321, 323, 341, 359, 374, 376, 386, 405, 408 ff.
incision 76 n. 7
indemnity coinage 393, 395
indulgentia 295
inimicitia 417
intercessio 447 n. 3

Jews 129 f. n. 14, 131
jubilee coinage 147, 153, 158 n. 3, 222, 254, 277, 295, 331 ff., 338 ff.
iurisdictio 324
ius: agendi cum populo 447, 452 n. 4; *auxilii* 431 n. 1, 448 f., 451 f.; *edicendi*, see *edicta*; *exilii* 342, 402 n. 7; *honorum* 324 n. 11; *Italicum* 315 f.; *Latinum*, see *Latinitas*; *primae relationis* 446; *provocationis* 450 n. 9; *senatus conferendi* 446; *senatus consulendi* 120, 293, 446, 450 f., 452 n. 4
iussu 12, 252, 289, 321, 438, 445

κατοικία 158 n. 5
kingship 17, 368 ff., 409 f., 475
knights as moneyers 4 n. 1, 6, 67 ff., 131 ff., 138, 382 f., 388 f., 392 (see also *procurator*)
κοινόν, see League

Lagids, see Ptolemies
Latinitas 25, 155 n. 3, 161, 201, 214, 318, 335 ff., 404, 473
Laurium 107 n. 9
League coinage (*commune*, κοινόν) 107, 115, 144 f., 342 ff., 353, 362 ff., 377, 384

lectio senatus 449 n. 3
legionary coinage 60 n. 7, 102 n. 4, 117, 209, 217 n. 10, 220, 250
lex 452 n. 4; *curiata* 242; *data* 433 n. 14; *dicta* 205 n. 18; *rogata* 433 n. 14; *Agraria* 160; *Antonia* 180; *coloniae Genetivae Iuliae* 34, 151, 172, 214, 322; *de imperio Vespasiani* 445; *Fundana* 309; *Iulia* (colonies) 30, 154 n. 5, 236; *Iulia maiestatis* 83, 405, 413; *Iulia peculatus* 101; *Iulia vicesimaria* 325; *Mamilia* 34; *Patavina* 309; *Plautia Papiria* 199 f.; *Pompeia* 140, 385; *Roscia* 9; *Rubria* 9; *Titia* 46, 48, 416, 433 n. 4, 450
libelli 431 n. 1
libertas 13, 35, 55 f., 100, 126, 183, 224 ff., 315 f., 318, 324 f., 338 ff., 397 f., 401 ff., 418, 424, 443, 475 f.
libertus 262, 404
lictors 424

Magnus 22 f., 415
mandata 425, 431 n. 2
Marmaridae 137, 141, 341
menokad 359, 442 n. 5
mens bona 324
mensores 312 n. 6
metropolis 100, 340 n. 11, 353, 398
militias, local 303
mine coinage 134 f.
mint-marks 1, 5, 25 f., 28, 35, 40, 57, 66, 72, 192, 394
municipal reforms 308 ff., 335 ff., 338 ff., 346 ff.
munita 285
Myron 103

νέος θεός 358
νομή 364
Nominative Case 392
numen, see *genius*

oratio 312, 446 f. n. 13
orichalcum 11, 13 f., 18 f., 61 f., 64, 77, 85 ff., 91, 104, 107 n. 9, 124 f., 300, 474, 493
orthography 8, 155, 182, 187 f., 215 n. 11, 216 n. 18, 347 n. 7, 378 n. 14, 474, 479
overstriking 47, 53, 55

pagus civium Romanorum 186, 239 n. 1, 348, 383, 403 f.
παρά 399
parens, pater 15 f., 152, 166 f., 170, 251, 265, 319, 444
patrimonium Augusti 97, 130
patrocinium, see *clientela*
Pax 271, 281, 442
pecunia publica 78 n. 11, 231
permissu 128, 130, 232, 260, 295, 321, 337, 400, 428, 435, 453
Pharaonic succession 132 f., 370 f.
φιλόκαισαρ, φιλόπατρις 365
Pietas 23 n. 2, 153, 416
plena legis actio 324
pontifex, see priesthood
portrait-rights 15, 33 ff., 133, 152, 224, 228 ff., 258, 317, 373 f., 379 ff., 389

posthumous coinages 73 ff., 222, 328 ff., 463 ff.
postliminium 402 n. 7
praefecti 4, 7 ff., 11, 25, 33 ff., 39, 46, 62, 65, 69, 97, 161, 163 f., 169, 183 f., 212, 247, 263, 268, 273, 285, 323, 437 n. 1
praefecturae 147 n. 1, 171
Praetorian Guard 437 n. 1
praetorium 135 n. 13
priesthood 100, 158, 163, 249, 252, 287, 363, 376 ff., 434 n.
princeps 14, 244, 441, 444, 452
privy-marks 31, 57
procurator 4 n. 1, 66 f., 118, 129, 131, 135, 136 n. 3, 322, 382 f., 388 f. (see also knights)
προστασία 142
protome 42
Ptolemies 132 f., 369 ff.

quadrans 4 ff., 28 ff., 35, 52 ff., 68, 86, 93, 114, 116, 125, 138, 162 n. 5, 211, 217
quaestorium 135 n. 13
quaestors 5, 16, 21 ff., 25, 69, 135 ff., 140, 270, 276 n. 10
quinquennales 154 n. 5, 156, 159, 161 ff., 202 n. 9, 212, 222 f., 236 f., 267 f., 270, 279 f., 282 f., 310 f.

recruiting 438 f.
religious coinage, see temple coinage
rependatur 117
rescripta 431 f.
res privata, see *patrimonium*
responsa prudentium 431, 433, 445 n. 2
retouched coins, see tooling
rex, see kingship
'Ρωμαῖα 363
Romulus 424, 444
ruta caesa 280

sacerdos 158, 163, 249
sacrosanctitas 451
Σεβαστά 362
Σεβαστός 359 ff.
Seleucids 368 ff.
semuncial coinage 154 n. 5
sententia 98, 203, 288, 431 n. 5
sextans 45
silver and gold coinage, official 5 ff., 14, 17 n. 3, 23 n. 1, 29, 32, 38, 41, 43 ff., 48, 49 n. 14, 58, 60 n. 7, 62, 73 f., 82, 83 n. 1, 90, 95 f., 99 f., 103 f., 114 f., 121 ff., 125, 132, 139, 144, 146, 155, 164, 167, 173, 207 ff., 221,
222 n. 3, 234, 243, 248, 264, 269 n. 4, 273, 337, 339, 341 f., 349 ff., 356 f., 363 n. 2, 369, 372, 377, 379, 384, 408 f., 416 n. 10, 467 f.
silver in bronze 132 n. 10
silver coinage, local 56, 64, 99 f., 145, 191 n. 14, 227, 340, 368, 372, 398, 401
spectatio 86 f., 89
spodium 87 n. 5
stipendiariae civitates 346, 401 ff., 462
στρατηγός 126, 386
subscriptio 432 f.
suffectio 160 n. 1
suffetes 149
συγγενής 388
σύμμαχοι 402
συμπολιτεία, see synoecism
synoecism 342, 349, 355, 403 f.

taxes 203, 315
temple coinage 362, 376
termini 313
tesserae nummulariae 86
θεὰ νεωτέρα 63 f.
θεός 318, 358, 375, 444
Thurinus 124
token coinage 3, 19, 45, 86 ff., 96, 131 f., 300
tooling 42 n. 4, 81 n. 2, 277 f. n. 8, 382 n. 12, 385 n. 16, 386 n. 2
'travelling' mint, see *castrensis moneta*
tressis, tripondius 31, 44, 88, 208
tribes 1, 123 f., 348 f., 391 f., 474
tribunicia potestas 120, 128, 219, 359, 429, 434 f., 446 ff.
trilingual issue 155 n. 5
Troy 245
tutela et cura 318, 437 n. 1, 452 f.
types parlants 1, 42, 67, 162 n. 5, 165, 188 n. 3, 194, 216 f., 259, 271

urban cohorts, see *cohortes urbanae*
urbanization 147, 348 f.
urbs 215

vectigalia, see taxes
vicus civium Romanorum 5, 173
vigintiviri 117
vota 434, 442 n. 13

zodiac, signs of 209

KEY TO PLATES[1]

Plate I

1 BM, 2 BM, 3 BM, 4 BM (R), 5 Berlin, 6 Berlin, 7 BM (R), 8 BM (R), 9 BM (O), 10 Berlin (O), 11 Paris, 12 Berlin, 13 BM, 14 BM (R), 15 Berlin, 16 Berlin, 17 Copenhagen, 18 BM (R), 19 Cambridge (R), 20 BM, 21 BM (R), 22 BM, 23 Paris, 24 BM, 25 BM, 26 Berlin (R), 27 Berlin, 28 BM.

Plate II

1 Istanbul, 2 Istanbul, 3 Berlin, 4 Berlin, 5 Berlin (R), 6 BM (R), 7 Berlin (O), 8 BM (R), 9 Capitoline, 10 Copenhagen (O), 11 Cambridge (R), 12 Copenhagen, 13 Turin (O), 14 Glasgow, 15 Berlin, 16 Copenhagen, 17 Paris (O), 18 Paris (O), 19 Berlin (O), 20 BM (O), 21 Paris (O), 22 Cambridge (O), 23 Cambridge (O), 24 Grant (O).

Plate III

1 Grant (O), 2 Berlin (O), 3 Berlin (O), 4 Paris (O), 5 Grant (O), 6 Paris (O), 7 Copenhagen (O), 8 Berlin (O), 9 Berlin (O), 10 Paris (O), 11 Grant (O), 12 Copenhagen (O), 13 Berlin (O), 14 Paris (R), 15 Grant (O), 16 Milan (O), 17 Vienna (O), 18 Vatican (O), 19 Glasgow (O), 20 Paris (O), 21 Vienna (O), 22 Paris (O), 23 Cambridge (O), 24 BM (O), 25 Paris (O), 26 Vienna (O), 27 Prague (O), 28 Cambridge (O), 29 Naples, 30 Oxford (O).

Plate IV

1 Prague (O), 2 Gotha (O), 3 Grant (O), 4 Grant (O), 5 Sofia (R), 6 BM (O), 7 Gotha (O), 8 BM (O), 9 BM (O), 10 Zagreb (O), 11 Rome (O), 12 Leningrad (O), 13 Paris (O), 14 Berlin (O), 15 Berlin (O), 16 Hague (R), 17 Berlin (R), 18 BM (O), 19 Paris, 20 Paris, 21 Paris, 22 Grant (O), 23 Paris (R), 24 BM (O), 25 Berlin (R), 26 Paris (O), 27 Milan, 28 Hague, 29 BM (O), 30 Turin (O), 31 Oxford (O), 32 Paris, 33 Cambridge (O), 34 Paris (R).

Plate V

1 Paris (O), 2 Paris (O), 3 Vienna, 4 BM (O), 5 BM (O), 6 BM (R), 7 BM, 8 BM (O), 9 BM (O), 10 BM (R), 11 New York, 12 BM (O), 13 Paris, 14 BM, 15 BM (O), 16 BM (O), 17 BM (O), 18 BM, 19 BM, 20 BM (O), 21 BM (R), 22 BM, 23 BM (R), 24 BM, 25 BM (O), 26 BM (R), 27 BM (O), 28 BM (O), 29 BM (O).

Plate VI

1 Berlin (O), 2 Berlin, 3 Berlin (O), 4 Rome, 5 Berlin, 6 BM, 7 Berlin (O), 8 Berlin (O), 9 BM, 10 Vatican, 11 Copenhagen, 12 Paris (O), 13 BM (R), 14 Paris, 15 Paris, 16 Paris, 17 Athens (O), 18 Cambridge, 19 Rome, 20 Gotha (O), 21 Paris, 22 Paris, 23 Berlin, 24 Paris, 25 Grant.

Plate VII

1 BM, 2 Paris, 3 BM, 4 BM, 5 BM, 6 Paris, 7 Berlin, 8 BM, 9 BM, 10 Berlin (R), 11 Berlin, 12 Berlin, 13 Berlin, 14 Berlin, 15 Berlin, 16 Berlin (R), 17 BM, 18 BM (O), 19 BM (O), 20 BM (O), 21 BM (O), 22 Berlin (O), 23 Cambridge (R), 24 Paris, 25 BM, 26 BM (R), 27 Paris, 28 Paris (O), 29 Milan (O), 30 Paris (O), 31 Paris (R), 32 Glasgow.

Plate VIII

1 Copenhagen, 2 BM, 3 Paris, 4 Paris, 5 Berlin, 6 Berlin, 7 Paris (R), 8 BM (O), 9 Berlin (R), 10 Cambridge (R), 11 Berlin, 12 Berlin, 13 Paris, 14 Paris, 15 Paris, 16 Berlin, 17 BM, 18 Berlin, 19 Vienna, 20 Naples, 21 Berlin, 22 BM (O), 23 Gotha, 24 Vatican, 25 Gotha (R), 26 Paris (R), 27 Berlin, 28 BM.

Plate IX

1 BM (O), 2 BM (R), 3 Paris, 4 Paris, 5 Vienna (R), 6 Paris, 7 BM, 8 BM (R), 9 Berlin, 10 BM, 11 BM, 12 BM, 13 BM (O), 14 BM (O), 15 BM (O),

[1] O = Obverse only; R = Reverse only.

16 BM (O), 17 Paris, 18 BM, 19 BM, 20 Copenhagen, 21 Paris, 22 BM, 23 Hannover (O), 24 Paris, 25 Paris (O), 26 BM (O), 27 Berlin, 28 Berlin (O), 29 BM (O), 30 BM (O), 31 BM (O), 32 BM (O), 33 BM (O), 34 Paris.

Plate X

All O or R only: 1 Grant (Abydus), 2 Paris (Miletus), 3 Paris (Lampsacus), 4 Paris (Lebedus), 5 BM (Aezanis), 6 Grant (Erythrae), 7 Paris (Magnesia ad Sipylum), 8 BM (Alabanda), 9 Berlin (Aezanis), 10 Paris (Dioshieron), 11 Vienna (Prymnessus), 12 BM (Alabanda), 13 Rome (Apollonia Salbace), 14 Cambridge (Cidramus), 15 Vienna (Midaeum), 16 Paris (Eumenia), 17 BM (Aphrodisias), 18 BM (Laodicea), 19 BM (Laodicea), 20 BM (Laodicea), 21 BM (Laodicea), 22 Cambridge (Laodicea), 23 R. of 20, 24 R. of 21, 25 BM (Synnada), 26 Paris (Synnada), 27 BM (Apollonia Salbace), 28 Paris (Dionysopolis), 29 BM (Heraclea Salbace), 30 BM (Tripolis), 31 BM (Eumenia), 32 BM (Dionysopolis), 33 Rome (Sebaste), 34 BM (Aphrodisias), 35 Gotha (Hierapolis), 36 Cambridge (Antiochia ad Maeandrum), 37 BM (Cos), 38 BM (Mylasa), 39 Hague (Magnesia ad Maeandrum), 40 Vienna (Philomelium), 41 Paris (Cibyra), 42 Berlin (Magnesia ad Maeandrum), 43 Gotha (Lampsacus), 44 Berlin (Apollonia Salbace), 45 Gotha (Tabae), 46 Cambridge (Pergamum), 47 BM (Stratonicea), 48 Berlin (Cibyra), 49 Munich (Apollonis), 50 Paris (Philadelphia), 51 Paris (Abydus), 52 BM (Mylasa), 53 BM (Mylasa), 54 BM (Dardanus), 55 Berlin (Magnesia ad Maeandrum), 56 Naples (Amorium), 57 Paris (Elaea), 58 Gotha (Ephesus), 59 Paris (Ephesus), 60 BM (Euromus), 61 BM (Acmonia), 62 Paris (Aezanis), 63 Rome (Ephesus), 64 Paris (Dioshieron), 65 Istanbul (Alabanda), 66 Oxford (Adramyttium), 67 Paris (Hypaepa), 68 Paris (Apamea), 69 BM (Apamea), 70 Winterthur (Eucarpia), 71 BM (Siblia), 72 Paris (Metropolis).

Plate XI

All O unless stated: 1 Berlin (Prymnessus), 2 BM (Prymnessus), 3 Glasgow (Smyrna), 4 BM (Smyrna), 5 Istanbul (Laodicea), 6 BM (Sardes), 7 BM (Hierapolis), 8 BM (Laodicea), 9 Paris (Ephesus), 10 Rome (Magnesia ad Maeandrum), 11 BM (Hierapolis), 12 Paris (Hierapolis), 13 Munich (Acmonia), 14 Paris (Bargylia), 15 Munich (Cyzicus), 16 Gotha (Hierapolis), 17 BM (Hierapolis), 18 Berlin (Hierapolis), 19 BM (Laodicea), 20 Berlin (Tripolis), 21 Paris (Assus), 22 Grant (Abydus), 23 Berlin (Cyzicus), 24 Paris (dub. Mysia), 25 Istanbul (Ilium), 26 Copenhagen (Erythrae), 27 Berlin (Colophon), 28 BM (Nysa), 29 Berlin (Pergamum), 30 BM (uncertain), 31 BM (Tabae), 32 BM (Erythrae), 33 Paris (Ephesus), 34 BM (Heraclea Salbace), 35 BM (Cos), 36 BM (Samos), 37 Copenhagen (Apollonia Salbace), 38 Grant (Siblia), 39 BM (Tripolis), 40 Istanbul (Nysa), 41 Cambridge (Nysa), 42 Hague (Cilbiani inferiores), 43 Berlin (Miletus), 44 Rome (Clazomenae), 45 BM (Tralles), 46 BM (Trapezopolis), 47 BM (Rhodes), 48 Berlin (uncertain) (O and R), 49 Copenhagen (Tralles), 50 Paris (Tralles), 51 Naples (Ephesus), 52 Paris (Eumenia), 53 R. of 41, 54 Berlin (Alabanda), 55 Berlin (Alabanda) (O and R), 56 Vatican (Alabanda), 57 Milan (Alabanda), 58 BM (Hierapolis), 59 R. of 37, 60 Winterthur (Miletopolis), 61 Paris (Laodicea), 62 Oxford (Adramyttium), 63 R. of X 64, 64 BM (Hypaepa), 65 Naples (Alabanda) (O and R), 66 R. of X. 6.

Plate XII

1 Paris, 2 BM (O), 3 BM (O), 4 Berlin, 5 Vienna, 6 Rome, 7 Naples, 8 Vienna (O), 9 Vienna University, 10 Paris (O), 11 BM, 12 Munich, 13 BM (O), 14 Paris, 15 Paris, 16 Berlin (O), 17 Berlin (O), 18 Berlin, 19 Berlin, 20 Berlin (O), 21 Munich, 22 Paris, 23 Paris, 24 Rome, 25 BM, 26 Berlin (O), 27 BM (O), 28 Berlin (O), 29 Berlin, 30 Vienna, 31 Paris, 32 Winterthur, 33 Paris.

PAGE REFERENCES FOR THE PLATES

The following list of page-references for the Plates was compiled by the late Dr Karl Pink and published in the *Numismatische Zeitschrift*, 1946–7, pp. 138 f. I am very grateful to the Austrian Numismatic Society for permission to reproduce it.

Plate I

1 p. 4, 2–3 p. 26, 4 p. 29, 5–6 p. 28, 7 p. 40, 8 p. 41, 9 p. 40, 10 p. 29, 11 p. 30, 12 p. 52, 13 p. 46, 14 p. 49, 15 p. 52, 16 p. 53, 17 p. 52, 18 p. 62, 19 p. 61, 20 p. 64, 21–22 p. 66, 23 p. 81, 24–28 p. 91.

Plate II

1 p. 11, 2–3 p. 13, 4–5 p. 20, 6 p. 24, 7–8 p. 33, 9 p. 37, 10–11 p. 42, 12 p. 50, 13 p. 52, 14 p. 54, 15 p. 35, 16 p. 60, 17–18 p. 73, 19–23 p. 74, 24 p. 75.

Plate III

1–5 p. 76, 6–12 p. 78, 13–14 p. 82, 15 p. 98, 16 p. 100, 17–20 p. 99, 21–25 p. 100, 26–27 p. 102, 28–30 p. 103.

Plate IV

1 p. 478, 2 p. 103, 3–4 p. 104, 5 p. 105, 6–8 p. 106, 9 [p. 106], 10 p. 107, 11 p. 106, 12–13 p. 107, 14 p. 478, 15 p. 344, 16 p. 107, 17 p. 479, 18 p. 122, 19 p. 123, 20–21 p. 105, 22–23 p. 328, 24–25 p. 143, 26 p. 139, 27 p. 146, 28 p. 139, 29–31 p. 111, 32 p. 113, 33–34 p. 145.

Plate V

1–2 p. 111, 3 p. 113, 4–5 p. 115, 6 p. 121, 7 p. 134, 8–9 p. 124, 10 p. 120, 11 p. 145, 12 p. 132, 13 p. 128, 14 p. 149, 15–16 p. 154, 17 p. 477, 18 p. 154, 19 p. 170, 20 p. 165, 21 p. 170, 22 p. 168, 23 p. 195, 24 p. 194, 25 p. 167, 26 p. 173, 27 p. 175, 28 p. 175, 29 p. 171.

Plate VI

1–3 p. 190, 4 p. 150, 5 p. 152, 6 p. 158, 7 p. 162 n., 8 p. 159, 9 p. 158, 10 p. 177, 11 p. 177, 12–14 p. 182, 15–16 p. 178, 17 p. 477, 18 p. 237, 19–20 p. 205, 21 p. 208, 22 p. 222, 23 [p. 227], 24 p. 224, 25 p. 231.

Plate VII

1 p. 177, 2–3 p. 185, 4 p. 190, 5 p. 196, 6 p. 195, 7 p. 194, 8 p. 197, 9–10 p. 200, 11 p. 284, 12 p. 202, 13–15 p. 284, 16 p. 203, 17 p. 159 n., 18 p. 216, 19 p. 219, 20–21 p. 211, 22–23 p. 207, 24 p. 206, 25 p. 234, 26 p. 473, 27 p. 236, 28–30 p. 228, 31 p. 230, 32 p. 243.

Plate VIII

1 p. 225, 2–4 p. 232, 5 p. 244, 6–7 p. 246, 8–9 p. 238, 10–11 p. 250, 12–13 p. 251, 14–17 p. 255, 18 p. 262, 19 p. 266, 20 p. 269, 21 p. 272, 22 p. 274, 23 p. 276, 24–25 p. 277, 26 p. 278, 27 p. 279, 28 p. 283.

Plate IX

1–2 p. 249, 3 p. 254, 4 p. 253, 5 p. 251, 6 p. 260, 7–8 p. 262, 9–10 p. 260, 11 p. 265, 12 p. 266, 13 p. 268 n., 14–16 p. 268, 17 p. 283, 18 p. 272, 19 p. 281, 20 p. 282, 21–22 p. 275, 23 p. 369, 24 p. 392, 25 p. 478, 26 p. 392, 27 p. 336, 28 p. 390, 29 p. 372, 30 p. 374, 31 p. 382, 32 p. 385, 33 p. 387, 34 p. 388.

Plate X

1 p. 334 n., 2–3 p. 334, 4–5 p. 329, 6 p. 364, 7 p. 334, 8—, 9 p. 329, 10 p. 334, 11 p. 463, 12–15 p. 334, 16 p. 329, 17–18 p. 334, 19 p. 329, 20–21 p. 328, 22 p. 329, 23–24 p. 328, 25 p. 330, 26 p. 330, 27–30 p. 329, 31–33 p. 330, 34 p. 329, 35 p. 330, 36–39 p. 334, 40 p. 329, 41 p. 468, 42 p. 334, 43 p. 465, 44–45 p. 334, 46–47 p. 330, 48–49 p. 334, 50 p. 468, 51 p. 352, 52 p. 342, 53 [p. 342], 54 p. 352, 55 p. 351, 56 p. 350, 57 p. 478, 58–59 p. 469, 60 p. 351, 61 p. 350, 62 p. 349, 63 p. 352, 64 p. 349, 65 p. 478, 66 p. 351, 67 p. 349, 68–69 p. 351, 70 p. 348, 71 p. 329, 72 p. 330.

Plate XI

1 p. 330, 2–5 p. 470, 6 p. 351, 7 p. 352, 8 p. 468, 9—, 10 p. 468, 11 p. 479, 12–13 p. 356, 14 p. 351, 15–18 p. 357, 19 [p. 357], 20 p. 356, 21 p. 351, 22 p. 357, 23 p. 358, 24 [cf. p. 357], 25 p. 357, 26 p. 469, 27 p. 351, 28 p. 470, 29 p. 352, 30—, 31 p. 351, 32 p. 342, 33 p. 479, 34 p. 349, 35 p. 334 n., 36 [cf. p. 463 n. 7], 37–38 p. 467, 39 [p. 329], 40–41 p. 468, 42 p. 348, 43 p. 351, 44 p. 334 n., 45 p. 364, 46 p. 349, 47 p. 468, 48—, 49 p. 364, 50 p. 364, 51 p. 369, 52 p. 350, 53 p. 468, 54 p. 369, 55 p. 373, 56 [cf. p. 373], 57 p. 373, 58 p. 387, 59 [cf. p. 389 n. 8], 60 p. 391, 61 p. 228, 62–64 p. 378, 65 [cf. p. 373], 66 p. 364.

Plate XII

1–2 pp. 385–6, 3 p. 382, 4 p. 389, 5 p. 463, 6 p. 464, 7–8 p. 479, 9 p. 384, 10—, 11 p. 476, 12 p. 479, 13 [p. 463 n. 23], 14 p. 463 n. 30, 15 p. 479, 16–17 p. 389, 18 p. 479, 19 p. 371 n. 9, 20–21 p. 331, 22 [p. 332 n. 6], 23 p. 371 n. 14, 24 [cf. p. 361 n. 13], 25—, 26 p. 381, 27 p. 336, 28 p. 192, 29 p. 187, 30 p. 377, 31 p. 342, 32 p. 333, 33 p. 362.

For the CUPLE reprint the coins have been reproduced 85 per cent of actual size.

PLATE I

PLATE II

PLATE III

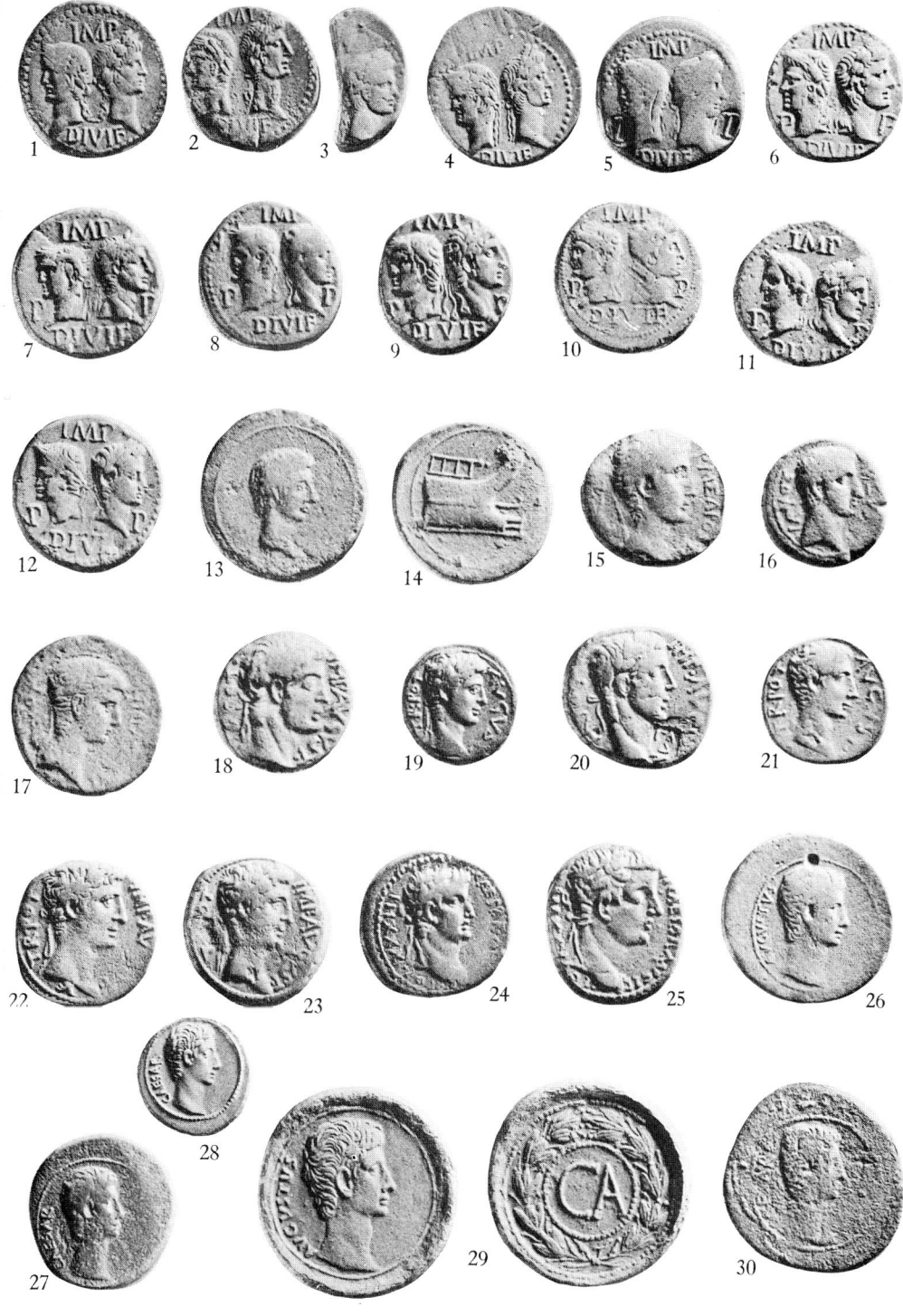

PLATE IV

PLATE V

PLATE VI

PLATE VII

PLATE VIII

PLATE IX

PLATE X

PLATE XI

PLATE XII

LIBRARY